Advance Praise for the Fourth Edition of *Mergers, Acquisitions, and Other Restructuring Activities*

"Professor DePamphilis' book is among the most comprehensive and best-written books on the topic of mergers and acquisitions I have ever read. In a world where private equity and hedge funds are supplanting traditional commercial and investment banking, a book like this comes in handy when traditional valuations fail to keep up with financial innovation. It marries the theory and practice. It is practical and complete. It is comprehensive and well-structured. And its attention to the world of cross-border transactions is timely and valuable."

—**Paul Schulte**, Lecturer, Hilton School of Business, Loyola Marymount University; Chief Investment Strategist, Asia Pacific, Lehman Brothers

*"**Mergers, Acquisitions, and Other Restructuring Activities** provides a comprehensive overview of all types of corporate restructurings. The book clearly shows which valuation technique is ideally suited for each type of restructuring. Not only is the validity of the motives of takeovers scrutinized, but this book also deals with corporate (governance) regulation. The book comprises an exhaustive treatment of all issues that arise in the restructuring processes, be it for takeovers, joint ventures, leverage buyouts, equity carve-outs, etc. This book is a superb handbook, a must-read for scholars, practitioners, and policy makers concerned with corporate acquisitions."*

—**Luc Renneboog**, Professor of Corporate Finance, Tilburg University, The Netherlands; Research Fellow at the Center for Economic Research and the European Corporate Governance Institute, Brussels

"Anyone interested in mergers, acquisitions, and restructuring can profit greatly by reading this very fine treatise by Dr. DePamphilis. It is comprehensive, insightful, and well-written. There are many case studies that show how the analyses discussed in the book may be applied. I wish this text had been available for my students at the Tuck School when I was teaching the mergers and acquisitions course there. I have no hesitation in recommending this book to students and practitioners, as well."

—**Dennis E. Logue**, Emeritus Professor of Management at the Amos Tuck School, Dartmouth College and Chair, Board of Directors Ledyard National Bank; former Dean of the Michael B. Price College of Business at the University of Oklahoma

*"This edition of **Mergers, Acquisitions, and Other Restructuring Activities** provides an excellent framework for mergers and acquisitions analysis. By combining theories, practical aspects, cases, and discussion questions, Professor DePamphilis creates an invaluable book not only for the professionals who work on these deals, but also for the business students learning the insights about the mergers and acquisitions business. This book is a complete and well-structured guide on the important aspects in mergers and acquisitions, covering the process in phase-by-phase details, and the essential background information on regulatory issues and corporate takeover market. What I find most useful and effective in this book as a graduate text is the integration of valuation models, financing strategies, alternative strategies (such as strategic alliances, joint ventures, spin-offs), and a specific focus on the cross-border deals. This book should be a must-read for anyone interested in mergers and acquisitions."*

—**Tao-Hsien Dolly King**, Associate Professor, Department of Finance and Business Law, The Belk College of Business, University of North Carolina at Charlotte

*"**Mergers, Acquisitions, and Other Restructuring Activities, Fourth Edition** is no ordinary M&A text. It is simply the most comprehensive text I have ever read. While most texts, including M&A texts,*

focus on the technical "nuts and bolts," this book goes far beyond the core M&A issues, to deal with everything that could possibly impact on mergers and acquisitions, from strategic planning and strategic evaluation, to valuation and modeling, substitutes (e.g., strategic alliances, licensing), due diligence, accounting, tax and legal implications, hedge funds, LBOs, integration and post-integration issues surrounding M&As, divestitures, bankruptcy, and liquidations.

This text is a tour de force, the go-to text, the magnum opus of mergers and acquisitions. In addition to finance and accounting faculty, I recommend it to commercial bankers, venture capitalists, and the larger financial community, as well as government regulators such as the SEC and anti-trust folks."

—**Ian Lee**, PhD, Professor of Strategic Management, Sprott School of Business, Carleton University, Ottawa, Canada

*"**Mergers, Acquisitions, and Other Restructuring Activities** is an interesting and comprehensive look at every aspect of M&A and corporate restructuring—from strategic and regulatory considerations and M&A deal process, through several chapters on M&A valuation and deal structuring, to other types of restructuring activities. It not only provides a road map for the M&A and other corporate restructuring process, but also highlights the key things to watch for. The book is clearly written, with extensive but easy-to-follow case examples and empirical findings to illustrate the points in the text. It is a book by an expert, and for M&A instructors and students as well as practitioners."*

—**Qiao Liu**, PhD, Professor of Business and Economics, University of Hong Kong, China

*"**Mergers, Acquisitions, and Other Restructuring Activities, Fourth Edition** is no ordinary M&A text. It is simply the most comprehensive text I have ever read. Exceptionally well-organized and engagingly written, Dr. DePamphilis' excellent Fourth Edition provides a comprehensive and in-depth treatment of mergers and acquisitions for anyone, from the seasoned practitioner to the student novice. The book's expansive scope and up-to-date cases and examples provide practical, useful guidance for every phase of the restructuring process, derived from the author's considerable experience, and anchored in solid academic research."*

—**Wesley B. Truitt**, PhD, Adjunct Professor, Anderson Graduate School of Management, UCLA and former Vice President of Northrop Grumman Corporation

"Whether one is a new student or an experienced M&A professional, Don DePamphilis' latest book is an invaluable resource. For students and faculty, Don's book provides a well-structured, comprehensive framework for understanding this important business process; the chapters are enriched with useful real-life examples, case studies, and discussion questions. For experienced business executives engaged in M&A or about to embark on this increasingly demanding process, Dr. DePamphilis draws on his extensive experience to offer practical tools and insights for avoiding the pitfalls—and maximizing the opportunities for success—throughout all phases of the M&A process."

—**Richard M. Stafford**, Principal, Human Capital Management LLC and former Senior Vice President of Human Resources, Montgomery Watson, Inc

"I found Dr. DePamphilis' book to be a comprehensive explanation of all aspects of mergers, acquisitions, and restructuring activities, including the business motivations for using these strategies, the tools of analysis to determine a go or no-go decision and the issues related to implementation. He provides a useful balance of theory, examples, exhibits, spreadsheets, and cases. Given the importance of the financial calculations, he has an appropriate level of emphasis in this area. Dr. DePamphilis explains the financial calculations used in these activities and walks the reader through them with examples and exercises for the reader. He also explains why these analytical tools are used or not used, known issues or limitations with each analytical tool, and he suggests practical solutions to resolve the issue or limitation. He also goes beyond the financial issues including the legal, tax, accounting, and implementation issues such as deal structuring, common implementation mistakes, and organizational issues.

Because of the broad scope of the book, I appreciated the many references to additional sources of information for the reader. In this way, if the reader has a particular area of interest on a specific subject or issue, they can easily go deeper into this area. I recommend Dr. DePamphilis' book to anyone wanting a complete understanding of the theory and practical application of mergers, acquisitions, and restructuring activities."

Brant Kline, CEO B/Kline Consulting and former VP General Manager, Latin America, Avery Dennison Office Products

*"Seldom do you discover a finance book that is crisp, direct, content-rich, and lucid with easy-to-read formulae, like Dr. DePamphilis' latest book, **Mergers, Acquisitions, and Other Restructuring Activities**. All aspects of mergers and acquisitions are thoughtfully brought into the limelight. The cases are enlightening, the discussion questions are instructive and the references enhance each chapter masterfully. Completing the book leaves you with a gripping understanding of mergers and acquisitions, including its international facets. DePamphilis has given the business world a classic."*

Dr. Anthony F. Laviano, Executive Director at Nanotechnology Center, Loyola Marymount University Los Angeles, College of Business Administration

*"There are very few books on my read and re-read list. The Fourth Edition of **Mergers, Acquisitions, and Other Restructuring Activities** is one of them. Dr. DePamphilis presents the reader with a rich treatment from the perspective of a market participant. He shows a deep appreciation for the broad scope of business, understands the fundamental role of mergers and acquisitions, and is gifted with the talent to share his insights.*

Dr. DePamphilis presents the critical nature of analysis (and how to do it) within the context of the psychological drama that plays out every day in almost every company. The result is a compelling, integrated look at the one of the most interesting aspects of running or investing in a company. The balanced treatment of the macro influences of M&A on economic growth and equity valuations and the micro decision-making process has earned this book a place on the reference shelf. Highly recommended!"

—Michael Lovelady, Portfolio Manager, Oceans 4 Capital Group, LLC

"The text provides a well-balanced discussion of mergers, acquisitions, and restructuring processes, the regulatory environment, valuation methods, the conclusions of decades of academic research, as well as the latest trends and developments in the field. As a result, the book represents a comprehensive resource for anyone interested in studying or carrying out M&A and restructuring activities."

—Randall Heron, Associate Professor of Finance, Kelley School of Business, Indiana University

"I read the book and I think it does a good job covering the Mergers and Acquisitions field. The structure, divided into five parts, is logical and easy to follow, with a nice blend of theory, empirical research findings, and practical issues. The case studies are up-to-date, covering a wide range of topics. I especially like the chapter on private equity and hedge funds, since acquisitions by these players are becoming increasingly important these days. Overall, I believe that MBA students would find the book useful both as a textbook in class and as a reference book for later use."

—P. Raghavendra Rau, Associate Professor of Finance, Krannert Graduate School of Management, Purdue University, West Lafayette

"This book contains a very informative and thorough treatment of critical business issues regarding mergers and acquisitions. Professor DePamphilis integrates a wide range of relevant material in his discussion, including the regulatory, financial, planning, and implementation aspects of these transactions. The book also usefully describes alternative mechanisms for restructuring the firm,

including joint ventures, strategic alliances, and divestitures. I am impressed with the breadth and depth of the discussion."

—**Anju Seth**, Professor of Strategy, University of Illinois at Urbana-Champaign

"The book is organized by restructuring type and gives the history as well as the present trends and techniques. Each section contains a detailed account of the restructuring, including key details such as landmark cases, regulations, tax issues, etc. The author is also careful to present both the academic evidence as well as the view from a practitioner perspective. This is the most thorough text I have seen on restructuring and should give students a more complete picture than traditional texts. The exercises, examples, and case studies also enable students to implement the quantitative techniques necessary to evaluate the restructurings. Overall, this is an excellent book on restructurings."

—**Matthew T. Billett**, Associate Professor of Finance, Henry B. Tippie Research Fellow, Henry B. Tippie College of Business, University of Iowa

"Dr. DePamphilis' Fourth Edition is extremely thorough and the cases presented are clear illustrations of the M&A principles. This is a text that most will retain as a personal bookshelf reference in their professional life."

—**Jeffrey D. Covert**, Vice President North America Solution Sales, Dassault Systemes

MERGERS, ACQUISITIONS, AND OTHER RESTRUCTURING ACTIVITIES

Fourth Edition

Donald M. DePamphilis, Ph.D.

College of Business Administration
Loyola Marymount University
Los Angeles, California

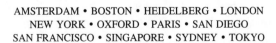

AMSTERDAM • BOSTON • HEIDELBERG • LONDON
NEW YORK • OXFORD • PARIS • SAN DIEGO
SAN FRANCISCO • SINGAPORE • SYDNEY • TOKYO

Academic Press is an imprint of Elsevier

Academic Press is an imprint of Elsevier
30 Corporate Drive, Suite 400, Burlington, MA 01803, USA
525 B Street, Suite 1900, San Diego, California 92101-4495, USA
84 Theobald's Road, London WC1X 8RR, UK

This book is printed on acid-free paper. ∞

Library of Congress Cataloging-in-Publication Data
Application submitted

British Library Cataloguing-in-Publication Data
A catalogue record for this book is available from the British Library

ISBN: 978-0-12-374012-0

For information on all Academic Press publications,
visit our Web site at www.books.elsevier.com

Printed in the United States of America
07 08 09 10 11   9 8 7 6 5 4 3 2 1

Working together to grow
libraries in developing countries

www.elsevier.com | www.bookaid.org | www.sabre.org

ELSEVIER   BOOK AID
             International   Sabre Foundation

*I extend my heartfelt gratitude to my wife, Cheryl,
and my daughter, Cara, without whose patience and understanding
this book could not have been completed, and to
my brother, Mel, without whose encouragement this book
would never have been undertaken.*

Contents

PART V   Alternative Business and Restructuring Strategies   565

CHAPTER 14   Joint Ventures, Partnerships, Strategic Alliances, and Licensing   567

CHAPTER 15   Alternative Exit and Restructuring Strategies   607

CHAPTER 16   Cross-Border Mergers and Acquisitions: Analysis and Valuation   657

Contents of CDROM Accompanying Textbook

Acquirer Due Diligence Question List
Acquisition Process: The Gee Whiz Media Case Study (Including discussion
  questions and solutions)
Applying Experience Curves to M&A (New)
Examples of Agreements of Purchase and Sale for Asset and Stock Purchases
  and Related Documents (New)
Excel Based Mergers and Acquisitions Valuation and Structuring Model
Excel Based LBO Valuation and Structuring Model
Excel Based Decision Tree Valuation Model
Guidelines for Organizing ESOPs (New)
MCI/Verizon-MCI 2005 Merger Agreement (New)
Student Chapter PowerPoint Presentations (Updated and Revised)
Student Study Guide, Practice Questions, and Answers (Updated and Revised)
Supernormal Growth Model Valuation Example (New)

Preface to the Fourth Edition

A brief review of the financial pages of a major newspaper or magazine offers a bewildering array of headlines.

"HCA Goes Private"
"HP Spins Out Agilent"
"Mittal Overwhelms Arcelor in a Hostile Cross-Border Takeover"
"SBC Swallows AT&T"
"Anthem–WellPoint Merger Hits Regulatory Snag"
"Pepsi Buys Quaker Oats in a Highly Publicized Food Fight"
"Investors Force USX Breakup"

Designed to entice us to read further, such headlines are sometimes amusing but more often confusing to the casual reader. Welcome to the wonderful world of mergers, acquisitions, and other forms of corporate restructuring. The overarching objective of this book is to bring clarity to what can be both an exciting and frustrating subject.

Mergers and acquisitions (M&As) are a critical part of the fabric of doing business in a free market economy. Business combinations are an integral part of the global business community. Such combinations include mergers, acquisitions, and business alliances both within a country and across political boundaries. As a testimony to the vitality of the global economy, the dollar volume of announced M&As set a new worldwide record in 2006, significantly above the torrid pace of the late 1990s, despite the recession of 2001, the tragedy of 9/11, and lingering concerns about terrorism. As of mid-year, 2007 is on track to set new records.

Because business combinations often entail a common set of activities, the manager or analyst is able to view mergers, acquisitions, or business alliances in the context of a process or logical sequence of activities. A properly defined process disciplines the manager or analyst to consider all relevant activities in an orderly manner, to understand how the various activities interact, to review the range of reasonable options, and to select the option that best satisfies the primary needs of all parties involved. This book is intended to help the reader think of all the activities that contribute to the success or failure of mergers, acquisitions, and business alliances in an integrated way. Ultimately, the importance of understanding a time- and transaction-tested M&A process is that, while it does not guarantee success, it heightens the potential for meeting or exceeding expectations.

Integration is addressed in this book mainly by viewing M&A as a process. The M&A process outlined in this book consists of 10 interrelated phases and is sufficiently flexible to be applicable to businesses of various sizes, in different industries, and in different countries. The first two phases make up the planning stage and comprise the development of a business plan, defining where and how a firm chooses to compete, and an acquisition plan—if management believes that an acquisition is the most desirable option for implementing the business plan. The remaining eight phases make up the implementation stage, comprising such activities as search, screen, first contact, negotiation, integration planning, and closing, as well as postmerger integration and evaluation.

Exciting New Content in the Current Edition

- *Three New or Completely Revised Chapters:* One new chapter (Chapter 16) is entirely devoted to how to structure, analyze, and value cross-border (i.e., international) transactions. A second chapter (Chapter 8) includes an expanded discussion of relative valuation methods and real options analysis. The third chapter (Chapter 12) includes a more detailed discussion of the impact of tax strategies and financial accounting considerations in the deal-structuring process.

- *Up-to-Date Information:* Each chapter, including many business case studies, has been updated to reflect current developments and trends, as well as the latest academic and empirical research.

    —Chapter 1: The overview discussion of M&A now includes a detailed discussion of the growing role of hedge and private equity funds as participants in the M&A process.
    —Chapter 2: The discussion of regulatory considerations has been expanded to include merger and antitrust law in developed (the EU example) and in emerging (the China example) nations. The chapter also addresses the M&A implications of recent changes in U.S. pension law, the impact of the growth in private credit markets on securities' regulators, and how increasing concerns about national security affect M&As.

—Chapter 5: The discussion of how to contact target firms has been expanded to include an increased emphasis on relationship-building strategies.

—Chapter 7: This chapter on cash-flow valuation methods now contains a detailed discussion of how to select the appropriate tax rate, how to account for deferred taxes, how to estimate "excess" cash balances and alternative ways to project cash flows for both target and acquirer firms.

—Chapter 9: The section on applying financial modeling to M&A now includes more discussion of how to modify valuation models to include the effects of synergy such as cost savings due to staff reduction and increases in productivity.

—Chapter 10: The discussion of privately owned firms now includes the challenges of negotiating with family-owned businesses, the increasing role of private investment in public equity financing, alternative measures of value and valuation, and how to use historical data to recast target firm financial statements.

—Chapter 11: This chapter's focus on payment and legal considerations associated with the deal-structuring process provides new examples of earnout structures, including those commonly used by private equity investors.

—Chapter 12: The discussion of tax strategies has been updated to include recent changes that expand the flexibility of Type A tax-free reorganizations, tax-free transactions that arise from "like-kind" exchanges, the valuation of net operating loss carry forwards and carry backs, and Morris Trust transactions.

—Chapter 13: The discussion of leveraged buyouts and transaction financing methods now addresses the proliferation of credit-default swaps to manage risk in highly leveraged transactions, private investment in public equity, and the growing role of the leveraged loan market in financing such transactions.

—Chapter 15: The discussion of alternative restructuring strategies now includes a more detailed analysis of how the divestiture process works and how spin-offs are structured.

- *Thirty-eight New Business Cases:* In addition to the new cases, all 99 case studies, whether contained within or at the end of the chapter, include discussion questions. Ninety-eight percent of the new case studies and more than 90% of all case studies in the book involve transactions that have taken place since 2003. Sixteen of the case studies involve cross-border transactions. One-fourth of the case studies from prior editions have been updated to include recent information. See the "Business Case Study" listing the titles of all business cases included in this book. The phrase in parentheses next to the title suggests the primary focus of the case study. A single asterisk indicates that the case is new from the last edition, while a double asterisk indicates the case study has been updated.

- *Expanded Valuation and Forecasting Discussion*: Approximately one-quarter of the text is now devoted to the latest valuation and modeling methodologies as applied to both public and private companies subject to mergers, acquisitions, and leveraged buyouts. In addition to new information on relative valuation methods as applied to both public and private firms, the discussion of real options methods has been expanded significantly to include numerous detailed examples. The text also addresses how to use statistical techniques to facilitate cash-flow forecasting.

- *Student Study Guide Expanded:* PowerPoint presentations and chapter summaries have been included to reflect new content. The "Student Study Guide" now includes examples of business and acquisition plans. Students have access to the Learning Interactions Library (LIL), a software package that enables the management and delivery of electronic content to learners. The LIL is a Flash-based product specifically created to facilitate "anytime, any place, any pace" access to learning content and administration. Easy to access by simply clicking a link where indicated on the CD, the LIL provides the students with a dynamic way of testing their knowledge through multiple choices and true-false exercises."

- *Online Instructor's Manual Expanded:* The online manual has been revised and expanded to reflect the book's new content and contains more short essays, case studies, true/false, multiple-choice questions, and quantitative problems than ever before, with the test bank now including more than 1,500 questions and answers.

- **Expanded CD-ROM contents:**
  —Acquirer Due Diligence Question List
  —Acquisition Process: The Gee Whiz Media Integrative Case
   Study (including discussion questions and solutions). Formerly the final chapter in previous editions
   of this book, this case study has been moved to the CD-ROM to provide space for new content.
  —Applying Experience Curves to M&A (new)
  —Examples of Merger and Acquisition Agreements of Purchase and Sale (new)
  —Excel-Based Mergers and Acquisitions Valuation and Structuring Software
  —Excel-Based Leveraged Buyout Valuation and Structuring Software
  —Excel-Based Decision Tree M&A Valuation Software
  —Guidelines for Organizing ESOPs (new)
  —MCI/Verizon 2005 Merger Agreement (new)
  —Student Chapter PowerPoint Presentations (updated)
  —Chapter Summaries (expanded and updated)
  —Supernormal Growth Model Valuation Example (new)

Who Might Be Interested in This Book

The text is intended for students of M&As, corporate restructuring, business strategy, management, industrial organization, and entrepreneurship courses at both the undergraduate and the MBA level. Moreover, the material has worked effectively in Executive MBA, development, and training programs. The book also should interest those actively pursuing careers as financial analysts, chief financial officers, corporate treasurers, operating managers, hedge fund managers, private equity investors, investment bankers, business brokers, portfolio managers, or investors, as well as corporate development and strategic planning managers. Others who may have an interest include bank lending officers, venture capitalists, business appraisers, actuaries, government regulators and policymakers, human resource managers, and entrepreneurs. Hence, from the classroom to the boardroom, this text offers something for anyone with an interest in M&As, business alliances, and other forms of corporate restructuring.

To the Instructor

This text is an attempt to provide organization to a topic that is inherently complex due to the diversity of applicable subject matter and the breadth of disciplines that must be applied to complete most transactions. Consequently, the discussion of M&A is not easily divisible into highly focused chapters. Efforts to compartmentalize the topic often result in the reader not understanding how the various seemingly independent topics are integrated. Understanding M&A involves an understanding of a full range of topics including management, finance, economics, business law, financial and tax accounting, organizational dynamics, and the role of leadership.

With this in mind, this book attempts to provide a new organizational paradigm for discussing the complex and dynamically changing world of M&A. The book is organized according to the context in which topics normally occur in the M&A process. As such, the book is divided into five parts: M&A environment, M&A process, M&A valuation and modeling, deal structuring and financing, and alternative business and restructuring strategies. Topics that are highly integrated are discussed within these five groupings. See the figure on p. xx for the organizational layout of the book.

Finally, this book equips the instructor with the information and tools needed to communicate effectively with students having differing levels of preparation. The generous use of examples and contemporary business cases makes the text suitable for distance learning and self-study programs, as well as large, lecture-focused courses. Prerequisites for this text include familiarity with basic accounting, finance, economics, and general management concepts.

Online Instructors' Manual

The manual contains PowerPoint presentations for each chapter (completely consistent with those found on the CD-ROM), suggested learning objectives, recommended ways for teaching the materials, detailed syllabi

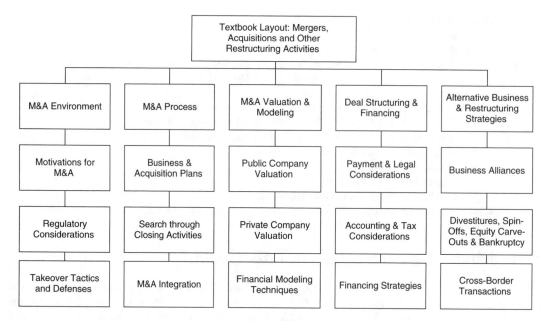

Textbook Layout: Mergers, Acquisitions, and Other Restructuring Activities.

for both undergraduate- and graduate-level classes, examples of excellent papers submitted by the author's students, and an exhaustive test bank. The test bank contains more than 1500 test questions and answers (including true/false, multiple-choice, short essay questions, case studies, and computational problems) and solutions to end-of-chapter discussion questions and chapter business case studies in the book. The online manual also contains, in a file folder named "Preface to the Online Instructors' Manual and Table of Contents," suggestions as to how to teach the course to both undergraduate and graduate classes.

Please e-mail the publisher at textbook@elsevier.com (within North America) and emea.textbook@ elsevier.com (outside of North America) for access to the online manual. Please include your contact information (name, department, college, address, e-mail, and phone number) along with your course information: course name and number, annual enrollment, ISBN, book title, and author. All requests are subject to approval by the company's representatives. For authors who have already adopted this book, please go to *textbooks.elsevier.com* (Elsevier's new instructors' Web site) and click on the button in the upper left-hand corner entitled "Instructors' Manual." You will find detailed instructions on how to gain access to the online manual for this book.

Learning Made Easier Through the Learning Interactions Library

The Fourth Edition of *Mergers, Acquisitions, and Other Restructuring Activities* introduces readers to the Learning Interactions Library (LIL), offering students a dynamic way of testing their knowledge through multiple choice quizzes, true-false exercises, case studies (including discussion questions and answers), and practice problems and solutions. Other than being online, the exercises are identical to any other type of exam given to the student. However, in this case the student can see the answer and evaluate instantaneously their mastery of the material. Because it is "flash-based," it runs on the student's browser and works as easily on a Mac as a PC. The LIL can be accessed by launching CD-ROM the accompanying this book.

Many Practical, Timely, and Diverse Examples and Current Business Cases

Each chapter begins with a vignette intended to illustrate a key point or points that will be described in more detail as the chapter unfolds. Hundreds of examples, business cases, tables, and figures illustrate the application of key concepts. Many exhibits and diagrams summarize otherwise diffuse information and the results of numerous empirical studies substantiating key points made in each chapter. Each chapter concludes with a series of 10 discussion questions and integrative chapter business cases intended to stimulate critical thinking and test the reader's understanding of the material. Other chapters include a series of practice problems to facilitate learning of the chapter's content.

Comprehensive, Yet Flexible Organization

Although the text is sequential, each chapter was developed as a self-contained unit to enable adaptation of the text to various teaching strategies and to students with diverse backgrounds. The flexibility of the organization also makes the material suitable for courses of various lengths, from one quarter to two full semesters. The amount of time required depends on the students' level of sophistication and the desired focus of the instructor. Undergraduates have consistently demonstrated the ability to master 8 or 9 chapters of the book during a typical semester, whereas graduate-level students are able to effectively cover 12 to 14 chapters during the same period.

Acknowledgments

I would like to express my sincere appreciation for the many helpful suggestions received from a number of anonymous reviewers and the many resources of Academic Press/Elsevier. I would like to thank Jon Saxon, John Mellen, Jim Healy, David Offenberg, Alan Cherry, Michael Lovelady, Ross Bengal, Pat Douglas, and Chris Manning for their many constructive comments. Finally, I would like to thank Karen Maloney (Publisher-Finance Books), Roxana Boboc (Assistant Editor), Jay Donahue (Project Manager), and Joe Selby (ITS Director) of Elsevier Publishing.

About the Author

Donald M. DePamphilis, Ph.D., has managed through closing more than 30 transactions including acquisitions, divestitures, joint ventures, minority investments, licensing, and supply agreements in a variety of different industries. These industries included financial services, software, metals manufacturing, business consulting, health care, automotive, and real estate. He earned a Masters and Ph.D. in economics from Harvard University and a B.A. in economics from the University of Pittsburgh. He is currently a Clinical Professor of Finance at Loyola Marymount University in Los Angeles, where he teaches undergraduate, MBA, and Executive MBA students mergers and acquisitions, corporate restructuring, finance, micro- and macroeconomics, business strategy, and corporate governance. He also has been a lecturer on M&A and corporate restructuring, finance, and economics at the University of California, at Irvine, Chapman University, and Concordia University. He has also taught mergers and acquisitions as a visiting professor at the Antai School of Management, Shanghai Jiao Tong University in Shanghai, China.

Donald M. DePamphilis, Ph.D., has more than 25 years of experience in business in various industries and with varying degrees of responsibility. Previously, he served as Vice President of Electronic Commerce for Experian Corporation, Vice President of Business Development at TRW Information Systems and Services, Senior Vice President of Planning and Marketing at PUH Health Systems, Director of Corporate Business Planning at TRW, and Chief Economist for National Steel Corporation. He also served as Director of Banking and Insurance Economics for Chase Econometric Associates and as an Economic Analyst for United California Bank. He also is a graduate of the TRW and National Steel Corporation Executive Management programs. Donald M. DePamphilis, Ph.D., also has authored numerous articles on M&A, business planning and development, and economics in academic, business, and trade journals. Please forward any comments you may have about this book to the author at ddepamph@lmu.edu.

Business Case Studies

Chapter 1: Introduction to Mergers and Acquisitions

Inside M&A: Andarko Petroleum Acquires Smaller Competitors (Horizontal merger example)*

1-1. Procter & Gamble Acquires Competitor (Horizontal merger example)*
1-2. Illustrating the Free Market Process of Creative Destruction: Consolidation in the Telecommunications Industry (Realizing economies of scale and scope)*

Chapter 2: Regulatory Considerations

Inside M&A: Justice Department Approves Maytag–Whirlpool Combination Despite Resulting Increase in Concentration (The importance of defining market share)*

2-1. Justice Department Requires AlliedSignal and Honeywell to Divest Overlapping Businesses (Illustrates consent decrees)
2-2. FTC Prevents Staples from Acquiring Office Depot (Illustrates challenges of defining markets)
2-3. JDS Uniphase (JDSU) Acquires SDL—What a Difference Seven Months Makes! (Vertical merger example)**
2-4. FCC Uses Its Power to Stimulate Competition in the Telecommunications Market (Using penalties to stimulate competition)
2-5. FCC Blocks EchoStar, Hughes Merger (Horizontal merger example)
2-6. Exelon Abandons the Acquisition of PSEG Due to State Regulatory Hurdles (Challenges of overcoming multiple regulatory layers)*
2-7. Global Financial Exchanges Pose Regulatory Challenges (Challenges of regulating global markets)*
2-8. GE's Aborted Attempt to Merge with Honeywell (EU antitrust case)**

Chapter 3: The Corporate Takeover Market: Common Takeover Tactics, Antitakeover Defenses, and Corporate Governance

Inside M&A: Hewlett-Packard Family Members Oppose Proposal to Acquire Compaq (Proxy Contest)**

3-1. Mittal Acquires Arcelor—A Battle of Global Titans in the European Market for Corporate Control (Successful hostile cross-border takeover)*
3-2. Verizon Acquires MCI: The Anatomy of Alternative Bidding Strategies (Bidding strategy analysis.)*

Chapter 4: Planning: Developing Business and Acquisition Plans—Phases 1 and 2 of the Acquisition Process

Inside M&A: eBay Struggles to Reinvigorate Growth (Strategy realignment)*

4-1. Dell Computer's Drive to Eliminate the Middleman (Gaining strategic advantage)**
4-2. Maturing Businesses Strive to "Remake" Themselves—UPS, Boise Cascade, and Microsoft (Developing a new vision)
4-3. The Market Share Game: Anheuser-Busch Battles SABMiller to Acquire China's Harbin Brewery (Global strategy execution)
4-4. Disney Buys Pixar—A Deal Based Largely on Intangible Value (Leveraging intellectual property)*
4-5. Pepsi Buys Quaker Oats in a Highly Publicized Food Fight (Achieving market leadership)
4-6. Oracle Continues Its Efforts to Consolidate the Software Industry (Industry consolidation.)*

Chapter 5: Implementation: Search through Closing—Phases 3–10
Inside M&A: Mattel Overpays for The Learning Company (Illustrates impact of overpaying)

5-1. The Cash Impact of Product Warranties (Illustrates destroyers of value)
5-2. When "Reps and Warranties" Do Not Provide Adequate Protection (Contract issues)
5-3. Vodafone Finances the Acquisition of AirTouch (Financing transactions)
5-4. The Downside of Earnouts (Earnout risks)
5-5. Sleepless in Philadelphia: A Dramatic Closing (The closing process)
5-6. The Anatomy of a Transaction: K2 Incorporated Acquires Fotoball USA (Abbreviated example of business and acquisition plans)
5-7. Cingular Acquires AT&T Wireless in a Record-Setting Cash Transaction (Financing transactions)

Chapter 6: Integration Mergers, Acquisitions, and Business Alliances
Inside M&A: GE's Water Business Fails to Meet Expectations (Culture clash)*

6-1. HP Acquires Compaq—The Importance of Preplanning Integration (Plan before executing)
6-2. M&A Gets Out of Hand at Cisco (Employee turnover)**
6-3. Case Corporation Loses Sight of Customer Needs in Integrating New Holland Corporation (Postmerger customer attrition)
6-4. Promises to PeopleSoft's Customers Complicate Oracle's Integration Efforts (Factors affecting synergy realization)
6-5. Lenovo Adopts a Highly Decentralized Organization Following Its Acquisition of IBM's Personal Computer Business (Role of organization in postacquisition implementation)*
6-6. Exxon-Mobil: A Study in Cost Cutting (Postmerger integration)
6-7. Albertson's Acquires American Stores—Underestimating the Costs of Integration (Implementation expenses)
6-8. Integrating Supply Chains: Coty Cosmetics Integrates Unilever Cosmetics International (IT integration challenges)*
6-9. Overcoming Culture Clash: Allianz AG Buys Pimco Advisors LP (Cross-border integration)
6-10. Culture Clash Exacerbates Efforts of the Tribune Corporation to Integrate the Times Mirror Corporation (Challenges of incompatible cultures)*
6-11. Avoiding the Merger Blues: American Airlines Integrates TWA (Postclosing integration)
6-12. Alcatel Merges with Lucent Highlighting Cross-Cultural Issues (International culture clash)*
6-13. The Travelers and Citicorp Integration Experience (Postmerger integration challenges)

Chapter 7: A Primer on Merger and Acquisition Cash-Flow Valuation
Inside M&A: The Importance of Distinguishing between Operating and Nonoperating Assets (The value of nonoperating assets)*

7-1. The Hunt for Elusive Synergy—@ Home Acquires Excite (The importance of understanding valuation assumptions)
7-2. Creating a Global Luxury Hotel Chain (Misunderstanding value)*

Chapter 8: Applying Relative, Asset-Oriented, and Real Option Valuation Methods to Mergers and Acquisitions
Inside M&A: A CBS "Decision Tree" (Defining real options)*

8-1. Google Buys YouTube—Brilliant or Misguided?*
8-2. Merrill Lynch and BlackRock Agree to Swap Assets (Determining ownership percentages)*
8-3. Valuation Methods Employed in Investment Banking Fairness Opinion Letters (Applying alternative valuation methods)*

Chapter 14: Joint Ventures, Partnerships, Strategic Alliances, and Licensing

Inside M&A: Getting Wired: Wal-Mart–America Online and Other Internet Marketing Alliances (Cross-marketing agreements)

Chapter 15: Alternative Exit and Restructuring Strategies: Divestitures, Spin-Offs, Carve-Outs, Split-Ups, Split-Offs, Bankruptcy, and Liquidation

Inside M&A: Financial Services Firms Streamline Their Operations (Divestitures and spin-offs of noncore businesses)*

Chapter 16: Cross-Border Mergers and Acquisitions: Analysis and Valuation

Inside M&A: Arcelor Outbids ThyssenKrupp for Canada's Dofasco Steelmaking Operations (Auction)*

*A single asterisk indicates that the case study is new since the third edition of this book.
**A double asterisk indicates that the case study has been updated since the third edition.

PART · I

The Mergers and Acquisitions Environment

CHAPTER ◆ 1

Introduction to Mergers and Acquisitions

If you give a man a fish, you feed him for a day. If you teach a man to fish, you feed him for a lifetime.

—Lao Tze

Inside M&A: Andarko Petroleum Acquires Smaller Competitors

At a time when natural gas and oil prices are high by historical standards, oil and natural gas producer, Andarko Petroleum, announced in June 23, 2006, the acquisition of two competitors, Kerr-McGee Corp. and Western Gas Resources, for $16.4 billion and $4.7 billion in cash, respectively. These purchase prices represent a substantial 40% premium for Kerr-McGee and a 49% premium for Western Gas. Andarko will also assume $560 million in Western Gas debt. The acquisitions would more than double Andarko's annual sales, improving its position in the Gulf of Mexico and in the western United States.

The acquired assets strongly complement Andarko's existing operations, providing the scale and focus necessary to cut overlapping expenses and to concentrate resources in adjacent properties. The acquisitions enable Andarko to utilize its existing finance, human resource, engineering, etc. departments to support exploration and development activities in the other companies. The acquisitions also give Andarko access to necessary skilled labor. With the cost of exploration rising and companies' access to new properties limited by environmental restrictions, the acquisitions represented a faster and cheaper way to acquire energy assets.

Chapter Overview

The first decade of the new millennium heralded a new era of global megamergers. As was true of the frenetic levels of mergers and acquisitions (M&As) in the 1980s and

3

1990s, the current level of activity is being fueled by readily available credit, historically low interest rates, rising equity markets, technological change, global competition, and industry consolidation. In terms of dollar volume, M&A transactions reached a record level worldwide in 2006.

While impacted by many of the factors just mentioned, the current buoyant M&A market is different from the past. Structural changes in financial markets since the 1980s enable banks to spread the risk to a more diverse pool of investors worldwide. These changes include bundling loans in ways that make them more attractive to a wider variety of investors. Hedge funds and private equity investors are playing an increasingly important role in the M&A process. This is not only true in the United States but also in Europe. The ongoing juggernaut of globalization is motivating more businesses to engage in cross-border transactions, as it becomes increasingly clear that the economies of most countries today do not stop at their political boundaries.

The intent of this chapter is to provide the reader with the information necessary to understand the underlying dynamics of M&As in the context of an increasingly interconnected world. This includes a working knowledge of the relevant vocabulary, the role of the various participants in the M&A process, and the wide range of factors influencing M&A activity historically. The dynamics of the six (including the current one) major merger waves that have taken place since the close of the nineteenth century are also described. Moreover, the chapter addresses the question of whether mergers pay off for target and acquiring company shareholders as well as for society. The most frequently cited reasons for many M&A's failure to meet expectations also are discussed. The chapter concludes with several stimulating case studies. These include consumer powerhouse Procter & Gamble's recent acquisition of Gillette and a discussion of how the free market forces of "creative destruction" promoted consolidation in the U.S. telecommunications industry. A review of this chapter is available on the CD ROM accompanying this book.

Building a Common Vocabulary

Any field of endeavor tends to have its own jargon. The study of buying and selling entire businesses or parts of businesses is no exception. Understanding the field requires a familiarity with the vocabulary. This section defines terms that will be used frequently throughout the book.

Corporate Restructuring

Actions taken to expand or contract a firm's basic operations or fundamentally change its asset or financial structure are referred to as *corporate restructuring* activities. Corporate restructuring is a catchall term that refers to a broad array of activities from reorganizing business units from product lines to divisions to takeovers and joint ventures to divestitures and spin-offs and equity carve-outs. In the literature, corporate restructuring activities often are broken into two specific categories: operational and financial restructuring. *Operational restructuring* usually refers to the outright or partial sale of companies or product lines or to downsizing by closing unprofitable or nonstrategic facilities. *Financial restructuring* describes actions by the firm to change its total debt and equity structure.

Examples of financial restructuring include share repurchases or adding debt to either lower the corporation's overall cost of capital or as part of an antitakeover defense (see Chapter 3).

Acquisitions, Divestitures, Spin-Offs, Carve-Outs, and Buyouts

Generally speaking, an *acquisition* occurs when one company takes a controlling ownership interest in another firm, a legal subsidiary of another firm, or selected assets of another firm such as a manufacturing facility. An acquisition may involve the purchase of another firm's assets or stock, with the acquired firm continuing to exist as a legally owned subsidiary of the acquirer. In contrast, a *divestiture* is the sale of all or substantially all of a company or product line to another party for cash or securities. A *spin-off* is a transaction in which a parent creates a new legal subsidiary and distributes shares it owns in the subsidiary to its current shareholders as a stock dividend. An *equity carve-out* describes a transaction in which the parent firm issues a portion of its stock or that of a subsidiary to the public. See Chapter 15 for more about divestitures, spin-offs, and carve-outs.

A *leveraged buyout* (LBO) or *highly leveraged transaction* involves the purchase of a company financed primarily by debt. The term LBO often is applied to a firm which buys back its stock using primarily borrowed funds to convert from a publicly owned to a privately owned company (see Chapter 11). A *management buyout* is a leveraged buyout in which managers of a publicly held firm or division of a publicly held company want to take the firm or division private. A firm that attempts to acquire or merge with another company is called an *acquiring company* or *acquirer*. The *target company* or the *target* is the firm that is being solicited by the acquiring company. *Takeovers* or *buyouts* are generic terms referring to a change in the controlling ownership interest of a corporation.

Mergers and Consolidations

Mergers can be described from a legal perspective and an economic perspective. This distinction is relevant to later discussions in this book concerning deal structuring, regulatory issues, and strategic planning.

A Legal Perspective

This perspective refers to the legal structure used to consummate the transaction. Such structures may take on many forms depending on the nature of the transaction. A *merger* is a combination of two or more firms in which all but one legally cease to exist, and the combined organization continues under the original name of the surviving firm. In a typical merger, shareholders of the target firm exchange their shares for those of the acquiring firm, after a shareholder vote approving the merger. Minority shareholders, those not voting in favor of the merger, are required to accept the merger and exchange their shares for those of the acquirer. Mergers requiring a shareholder vote are sometimes called *long form mergers*. If the parent firm is the primary shareholder in the subsidiary, the merger does not require approval of the parent's shareholders in the majority of states. Such a merger is called a *short form merger*. The principal requirement is that the parent's ownership exceeds the minimum threshold set by the state. For example, Delaware allows a parent corporation to merge without a shareholder vote with a subsidiary if the parent owns at least 90% of the outstanding voting shares. A *statutory merger* is one in which the acquiring company assumes the assets and liabilities of the target in accordance with the statutes of the state in which the combined companies will be incorporated. A *subsidiary merger* of two companies occurs when the target becomes a subsidiary of the parent.

Although the terms *mergers* and *consolidations* often are used interchangeably, a *statutory consolidation*, which involves two or more companies joining to form a new company, is technically not a merger. All legal entities that are consolidated are dissolved during the formation of the new company, which usually has a new name. In a merger, either the acquirer or the target survives. The 1999 combination of Daimler-Benz and Chrysler to form DaimlerChrysler is an example of a consolidation. The new corporate entity created as a result of consolidation or the surviving entity following a merger usually assumes ownership of the assets and liabilities of the merged or consolidated organizations. Stockholders in merged companies typically exchange their shares for shares in the new company.

A *merger of equals* is a merger framework usually applied whenever the merger participants are comparable in size, competitive position, profitability, and market capitalization. Under such circumstances, it is unclear if either party is ceding control to the other and which party is providing the greatest synergy. Consequently, target firm shareholders rarely receive any significant premium for their shares. It is common for the new firm to be managed by the former CEOs of the merged firms who will be coequal and for the composition of the new firm's board to have equal representation from the boards of the merged firms. The 1998 formation of Citigroup from Citibank and Travelers is an example of a merger of equals. Research suggests that the CEOs of target firms often negotiate to retain a significant degree of control in the merged firm for both their board and management in exchange for a lower premium for their shareholders (Wulf, 2001, p. 28).

An Economic Perspective

Business combinations also may be classified as horizontal, vertical, and conglomerate mergers. How a merger is classified depends on whether the merging firms are in the same or different industries and on their positions in the corporate value chain (Porter, 1985). Defining business combinations in this manner is particularly important from the standpoint of antitrust analysis (see Chapter 2). Horizontal and conglomerate mergers are best understood in the context of whether the merging firms are in the same or different industries. A *horizontal merger* occurs between two firms within the same industry. Examples of horizontal acquisitions include Procter & Gamble and Gillette (2006) in household products, Oracle and PeopleSoft in business application software (2004), oil giants Exxon and Mobil (1999), SBC Communications and Ameritech (1998) in telecommunications, and NationsBank and BankAmerica (1998) in commercial banking. *Conglomerate mergers* are those in which the acquiring company purchases firms in largely unrelated industries. An example would be U.S. Steel's acquisition of Marathon Oil to form USX in the mid-1980s.

Vertical mergers are best understood operationally in the context of the corporate value chain (see Figure 1-1). Vertical mergers are those in which the two firms participate at different stages of the production or value chain. A simple value chain in the basic steel industry may distinguish between raw materials, such as coal or iron ore; steel making, such as "hot metal" and rolling operations; and metals distribution. Similarly,

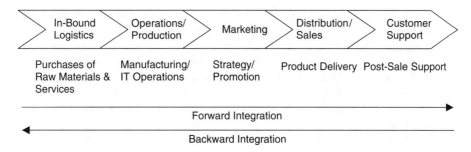

FIGURE 1-1 Corporate value chain

Note: IT refers to information technology.

a value chain in the oil and gas industry would separate exploration activities from production, refining, and marketing. An Internet value chain might distinguish between infrastructure providers, such as Cisco; content providers, such as Dow Jones; and portals, such as Yahoo and Google. In the context of the value chain, a ***vertical merger*** is one in which companies that do not own operations in each major segment of the value chain choose to "backward integrate" by acquiring a supplier or to "forward integrate" by acquiring a distributor. An example of forward integration includes paper manufacturer Boise Cascade's acquisition of office products distributor, Office Max, for $1.1 billion in 2003. An example of backward integration in the technology industry is America Online's purchase of media and content provider Time Warner in 2000. According to Gugler, Mueller, Yurtoglu, and Zulehner (2003), horizontal, conglomerate, and vertical mergers accounted for 42, 54, and 4% of the 45,000 transactions analyzed between 1981 and 1998.

Friendly versus Hostile Takeovers

In a ***friendly takeover*** of control, the target's board and management are receptive to the idea and recommend shareholder approval. To gain control, the acquiring company generally must offer a premium to the current stock price. The excess of the offer price over the target's premerger share price is called a ***purchase premium***. U.S. merger premiums averaged about 38% between 1973 and 1998 (Andrade, Mitchell, and Stafford, 2001). Rossi and Volpin (2004) document an average premium of 44% during the 1990s for U.S. mergers. The authors also find merger premiums in 49 countries ranging from 10% for Brazil and Switzerland to 120% for Israel and Indonesia. M&A premiums in many of the other countries are close to the U.S. average.

The purchase premium reflects both the perceived value of obtaining a controlling interest in the target and the value of expected synergies (e.g., cost savings) resulting from combining the two firms. Analysts often attempt to identify the amount of premium paid for a controlling interest (i.e., ***control premium***) and the amount of incremental value created the acquirer is willing to share with the target's shareholders (see Chapter 9). An example of a pure control premium would be a conglomerate willing to pay a price significantly above the prevailing market price for a target firm to gain a controlling interest even though potential operating synergies are limited. In this instance, the acquirer often believes it will be able to recover the value of the control premium by providing better management for the target firm.

Dyck and Zingales (2004) have estimated that the average control premium differs dramatically across the 39 countries they studied. While the premium paid for a controlling interest in the target averaged about 14% (almost one-third of the average purchase premium), the range varied widely from a low of 4% to a high of 65%. The wide range of estimates may reflect the value attached to the special privileges associated with control in various countries. For example, insiders in Russian oil companies have been able to divert a large fraction of profits by selling some of their oil to their own companies at below market prices.

The offer to buy shares in another firm, usually for cash, securities, or both, is called a *tender offer*. While tender offers are used in a number of circumstances, they most often result from friendly negotiations (i.e., negotiated tender offers) between the acquirer's and the target firm's boards. *Self-tender offers* are used when a firm seeks to repurchase its stock. Finally, those that are unwanted by the target's board are referred to as *hostile tender offers*.

An *unfriendly* or *hostile takeover* occurs when the initial approach was unsolicited, the target was not seeking a merger at that time, the approach was contested by the target's management, and control changed hands (i.e., more than half of the target's common stock was acquired). The acquirer may attempt to circumvent management by offering to buy shares directly from the target's shareholders (i.e., a hostile tender offer) and by buying shares in a public stock exchange (i.e., an *open market purchase*).

Bidders usually find friendly takeovers preferable to hostile transactions, because they often can be consummated at a lower purchase price. A hostile takeover attempt may attract new bidders, who otherwise may not have been interested in the target. Such an outcome is often referred to as putting the target *in play*. In the ensuing auction, the final purchase price may be bid up to a point well above the initial offer price. Acquirers also prefer friendly takeovers, because the postmerger integration process usually is accomplished more expeditiously when both parties are cooperating fully. For these reasons, most transactions tend to be friendly. See Figure 1-2 for a summary of the various elements of the corporate restructuring process.

The Role of Holding Companies in Mergers and Acquisitions

A *holding company* is a legal entity having a controlling interest in one or more companies. The primary function of a holding company is to own stock in other corporations. In general, the parent firm has no wholly owned operating units of its own. The segments owned by the holding company are separate legal entities, which in practice are controlled by the holding company. This differs from firms having multiple divisions or profit centers reporting to a single corporate headquarters.

The key advantage of the holding company structure is the leverage achieved by gaining effective control of other companies' assets at a lower overall cost than if the firm were to acquire 100% of the target's outstanding shares. Effective control sometimes can be achieved by owning as little as 20% of the voting stock of another company. This is possible when the target company's ownership is highly fragmented, with few shareholders owning large blocks of stock. Effective control generally is achieved by acquiring less than 100% but usually more than 50% of another firm's equity. One firm is said to have *effective control* when control has been achieved by buying voting stock, it is not likely to be temporary, there are no legal restrictions on control (such as from a bankruptcy court), and there are no powerful minority shareholders.

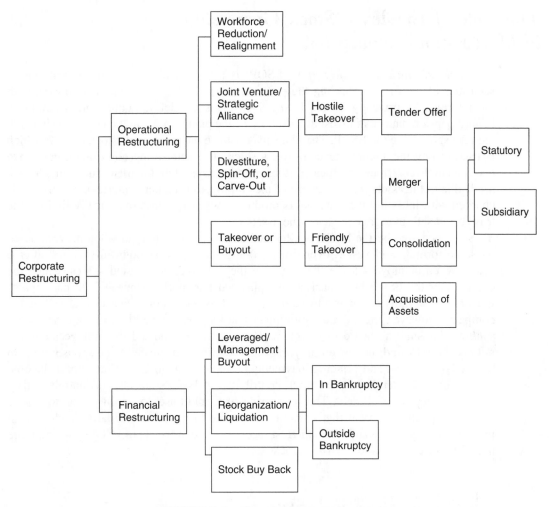

FIGURE 1-2   Corporate restructuring process

The holding company structure can create significant management challenges. Because the holding company can gain effective control with less than 100% ownership, the holding company is left with a significant number of minority shareholders. Such shareholders may not always agree with the strategic direction of the company. Consequently, implementing holding company strategies may become very contentious. Furthermore, in highly diversified holding companies, managers also may have difficulty making optimal investment decisions because of their limited understanding of the different competitive dynamics of each business. The holding company structure also can create significant tax problems for its shareholders. Subsidiaries of holding companies pay taxes on their operating profits. The holding company then pays taxes on dividends they receive from their subsidiaries. Finally, holding company shareholders pay taxes on dividends they receive from the holding company. This is equivalent to triple taxation of the subsidiary's operating earnings.

The Role of Employee Stock Ownership in Mergers and Acquisitions

An *employee stock ownership plan* (ESOP) is a trust fund or plan that invests in the securities of the firm sponsoring the plan. About 12,000 ESOPs exist nationwide, with most formed by privately owned firms. Such plans are defined contribution employee benefit pension plans that invest at least 50% of the plan's assets in the common shares of the firm sponsoring the ESOP. The plans may receive the employer's stock or cash, which is used to buy the sponsoring employer's stock. The sponsoring corporation can make tax-deductible contributions of cash, stock, or other assets into the trust. The plan's trustee holds title to the assets for the benefit of the employees (i.e., beneficiaries). The trustee is charged with investing the trust assets productively; and, unless specifically limited, the trustee can sell, mortgage, or lease the assets.

Stock acquired by the ESOP is allocated to accounts for individual employees based on some formula and vested over time. Often participants become fully vested after 6 years. When employees leave the company they receive their vested shares, which the company or the ESOP buys back at an appraised fair market value. ESOP participants must be allowed to vote their allocated shares at least on major issues such as selling the company. However, there is no requirement that they be allowed to vote on other issues such as choosing the board of directors. The assets are allocated to employees and are not taxed until withdrawn by employees. Cash contributions made by the sponsoring firm to pay both interest and principal payments on bank loans to ESOPs are tax deductible by the firm. Dividends paid on stock contributed to ESOPs are also deductible if they are used to repay ESOP debt. The sponsoring firm could use tax credits equal to .5% of payroll, if contributions in that amount were made to the ESOP. Finally, lenders must pay taxes on only one-half of the interest received on loans made to ESOPs owning more than 50% of the sponsoring firm's stock.

ESOPs as an Alternative to Divestiture

If a subsidiary cannot be sold at what the parent firm believes to be a reasonable price and liquidating the subsidiary would be disruptive to customers, the parent may sell directly to employees through a shell corporation. A *shell corporation* is one that is incorporated but has no significant assets or operations. The shell sets up the ESOP, which borrows the money to buy the subsidiary. The parent guarantees the loan. The shell operates the subsidiary, whereas the ESOP holds the stock. As income is generated from the subsidiary, tax-deductible contributions are made by the shell to the ESOP to service the debt. As the loan is repaid, the shares are allocated to employees who eventually own the firm.

ESOPs and Management Buyouts

ESOPs may be used by employees in leveraged or management buyouts to purchase the shares of owners of privately held firms. This is particularly common where the owners have most of their net worth tied up in their firms. The mechanism is similar to owner-initiated sales to employees.

ESOPs as an Antitakeover Defense

A firm concerned about the potential for a hostile takeover creates an ESOP. The ESOP borrows with the aid of the sponsoring firm's guarantee and uses the loan proceeds to buy stock issued by the sponsoring firm. While the loan is outstanding, the ESOP's trustees retain voting rights on the stock. Once the loan is repaid, it generally is assumed that employees will tend to vote against bidders who they perceive as jeopardizing their jobs.

Business Alliances as Alternatives to Mergers and Acquisitions

In addition to mergers and acquisitions, businesses also may combine through joint ventures (JVs), strategic alliances, minority investments, franchises, and licenses. These alternative forms of combining businesses are addressed in more detail in Chapter 14. The term *business alliance* will be used to refer to all forms of business combinations other than mergers and acquisitions.

Joint ventures are cooperative business relationships formed by two or more separate parties to achieve common strategic objectives. While the JV is often an independent legal entity in the form of a corporation or partnership formed for a specific time period and for a specific purpose, they may take any organizational form deemed appropriate by the parties involved. JV corporations have their own management reporting to a board of directors consisting of representatives of those companies participating in the JV. The JV generally is established for a limited time. Each of the JV partners continues to exist as separate entities. In contrast, *strategic alliances* generally fall short of creating a separate legal entity. They can be an agreement to sell each firm's products to the other's customers or to codevelop a technology, product, or process. Such agreements often are cancelable without significant penalties. The terms of such an agreement may be legally binding or largely informal. *Minority investments* represent less than controlling interests in other firms and require little commitment of management time and may be highly liquid if the investment is in a publicly traded company. Investing companies may choose to assist small or start-up companies in the development of products or technologies useful to the investing company. The investing company often receives representation on the board of the firm in which the investor has made the investment.

A *franchise* is a privilege given to a dealer by a manufacturer or franchise service organization to sell the franchiser's products or services in a given area. Such arrangements can be exclusive or nonexclusive. Under a franchise agreement, the franchiser may offer the franchisee consultation, promotional assistance, financing, and other benefits in exchange for a share of the franchise's revenue. Franchises represent a low-cost way for the franchisor to expand, because the capital usually is provided by the franchisee. However, the success of franchising has been limited largely to such industries as fast-food services and retailing in which a successful business model can be more easily replicated. *Licenses* represent the granting of specific rights to others to use proprietary assets and require no initial capital and represent a convenient way for a company to extend its brand to new products and new markets by licensing their brand name to others. Alternatively, a company may gain access to a proprietary technology through the licensing process. A franchise is a specialized form of a license agreement.

The major attraction of these alternatives to outright acquisition is the opportunity for each partner to gain access to the other's skills, products, and markets at a lower overall cost in terms of management time and money. Major disadvantages include limited control, the need to share profits, and the potential loss of trade secrets and skills.

Participants in the Mergers and Acquisitions Process

Investment Bankers

Investment bankers provide strategic and tactical advice and acquisition opportunities; screen potential buyers and sellers; make initial contact with a seller or buyer; and provide negotiation support, valuation, and deal-structuring guidance. The major investment banking firms usually have groups within their corporate finance departments that offer advice on M&A strategies. Leading U.S. investment banks include Goldman Sachs, Merrill Lynch, Morgan Stanley Dean Witter, Credit Suisse First Boston, and Citigroup/Salomon Smith Barney. Increasingly, acquirers in large, complex transactions are using multiple investment bankers. For example, an average of 7 investment banks was hired in each of the 10 largest M&A transactions during the first half of 2006 (Bloomberg.com, August 14, 2006). This trend reflects the demands of financing ever-larger transactions, the growing complexity of many deals, and a desire to deprive other potential suitors and the target firm from having access to good investment banking advice.

Investment bankers derive significant income from writing so-called fairness opinion letters. A *fairness opinion letter* is a written and signed third-party assertion certifying the appropriateness of the price of a proposed deal involving a tender offer, merger, asset sale, or leveraged buyout. It discusses the price and terms of the deal in the context of comparable transactions. A typical fairness opinion provides a range of fair prices, with the presumption that the actual deal price should fall within that range. Although such opinions are intended to inform investors, they actually are developed as legal protection for members of the boards of directors against possible shareholder challenges of their decisions.

The size of an investment banking advisory fee is often contingent on the completion of the deal and may run about 1–2% of the value of the transaction. Such fees generally vary with the size of the transaction. The size of the fee paid may exceed 1–2%, if the advisors achieve certain incentive goals. Fairness opinion fees often amount to about one-fourth of the total advisory fee paid on a transaction (Sweeney, 1999). Although the size of the fee may vary with the size of the transaction, the fairness opinion fee usually is paid whether or not the deal is consummated. Problems associated with fairness opinions include the potential conflicts of interest with investment banks that generate large fees. In many cases, the investment bank that brought the deal to a potential acquirer is also the same one that writes the fairness opinion. Also, they are often out of date by the time shareholders vote on the deal, they do not address whether the firm could have gotten a better deal, and the overly broad ranges of value given in such letters reduces their relevance. Courts agree that, because the opinions are written for boards of directors, the investment bankers have no obligation to the shareholders (Henry, November 24, 2003).

The size of the transaction often will determine the size of the investment bank that can be used as an advisor. The largest investment banks are unlikely to consider any transaction valued at less than $100 million. So-called investment boutiques can be very helpful in providing specialized industry knowledge and contacts. Investment banks often provide large databases of recent transactions, which are critical in valuing potential target companies. For highly specialized transactions, the investment boutiques are apt to have more relevant data. Finally, the large investment banks are more likely to be able to assist in funding large transactions because of their current relationships with institutional lenders and broker distribution networks.

In large transactions, a group of investment banks, also referred to as a *syndicate*, agrees to purchase a new issue of securities (e.g., debt, preferred, or common stock) from the acquiring company for sale to the investing public. Within the syndicate, the banks underwriting or purchasing the issue are often different from the group selling the issue. The selling group often consists of those firms with the best broker distribution networks. After registering with the Securities and Exchange Commission (SEC), such securities may be offered to the investing public as an *initial public offering* (IPO), at a price agreed on by the issuer and the investment banking group. Alternatively, they may be *privately placed* with institutional investors, such as pension funds and insurance companies. Unlike public offerings, private placements do not have to be registered with the SEC if the securities are purchased for investment rather than for resale.

Lawyers

The legal framework surrounding a typical transaction has become so complex that no one individual can have sufficient expertise to address all the issues. On large, complicated transactions, legal teams can consist of more than a dozen attorneys, each of whom represents a specialized aspect of the law. Areas of expertise include the following: M&As, corporate, tax, employee benefits, real estate, antitrust, securities, and intellectual property. In a hostile transaction, the team may grow to include litigation experts. Leading law firms in terms of their share of the dollar value of transactions include Wachtell Lipton Rosen & Katz, Simpson Thatcher & Bartlett, Skadden Arps Slate Meagher & Flom, Sullivan & Cromwell, and Davis Polk & Wardwell.

Accountants

Services provided by accountants include advice on the optimal tax structure, financial structuring, and on performing financial due diligence. A transaction can be structured in many different ways, with each having different tax implications for the parties involved (see Chapter 12). In conducting due diligence, accountants also perform the role of auditors by reviewing the target's financial statements and operations through a series of onsite visits and interviews with senior and middle-level managers. The accounting industry is dominated by the group of firms called the "big four." These include the following: Ernst & Young, PricewaterhouseCooper, KPMG, and Deloitte & Touche. Regional firms are those likely to have some national service lines and possibly some international clients, but they are largely tied to specific regional practices. Examples of large regional firms include Grant Thornton and BDO Seidman. Local accounting firms operate in a small number of cities and tend to focus on small businesses and individuals.

Proxy Solicitors

Proxy contests are attempts to change management control of a company by gaining the right to cast votes on behalf of other shareholders. In contests for the control of the board of directors of a target company, it is often difficult to compile mailing lists of stockholders' addresses. Proxy solicitors often are hired to obtain such addresses by the acquiring firm or dissident shareholders. The target's management may also hire proxy solicitors to design strategies to educate shareholders and communicate why shareholders should follow the board's recommendations. Major proxy-solicitation companies include Georgeson & Company and D. F. King & Company.

Public Relations

Communicating a consistent position during a takeover attempt is vital. Inconsistent messages reduce the credibility of the parties involved. From the viewpoint of the acquiring company in a hostile takeover attempt, the message to the shareholders must be that their plans for the company will increase shareholder value more than the plans of incumbent management. The target company's management frequently will hire private investigators, such as Kroll Associates, to develop detailed financial data on the company and to do background checks on key personnel. The target firm may use such information to discredit publicly the management of the acquiring firm. Major public relations firms with significant experience in the M&A arena include Kekst & Company, Hill & Knowlton, and Robinson Lerer & Montgomery.

Institutional Investors

Institutional investors include public and private pension funds, insurance companies, investment companies, bank trust departments, and mutual funds. Although a single institution generally cannot influence a company's actions, a collection of institutions can. Federal regulations require institutional shareholders who are seeking actual proxies or who hold a large percentage of a company's stock to file a proxy statement with the SEC (see Chapter 3). Shareholders may announce how they intend to vote on a matter and advertise their position to seek support.

Institutional investors also influence M&A activity by providing an important source of financing. While commercial banks have always played an important role in providing both short- and long-term financing, often backed by the assets of the target firm, institutional investors have become increasingly important as sources of financing for corporate takeovers. For example, institutional investors in the United States bought two-thirds of all leveraged loans (e.g., second mortgage loans often resulting from leveraged buyouts) in 2006, up by almost 50% from its level in 2000. In Europe, the growth is even stronger. In 1999, there were only three institutions active in the loan syndication market, with only a tiny fraction of a very small market. In 2006, the number of institutions grew to 76, capturing almost one-half of a rapidly growing market (*The Economist*, September 28, 2006). Since this growth is outside of the regulated banking system, securities regulators in both the United States and the European Union are becoming increasingly concerned about the growth in markets that are not transparent to investors or regulators.

Hedge and Private Equity Funds

Private equity funds are usually private investment limited partnerships (for U.S. investors) or offshore investment corporations (for non-U.S. or tax exempt investors) in which the general partner has made a substantial personal investment. Once a partnership has reached its target size, the partnership is closed to further investment from new investors or even existing investors. Companies in which the hedge or private equity fund has made investments are called *portfolio companies*. Institutional investors such as pension funds, endowments, insurance companies, and private banks, as well as high net worth individuals, commonly invest in these types of funds. According to KPMG (2006), there are about 9000 hedge funds worldwide with about $1.2 trillion under management. This compares to about 3000 private equity funds with about $500 billion under management.

An important difference between hedge funds and private equity funds is the length of time investors are required to commit funds. Investors in hedge funds are usually given more frequent access to their money than are those who invest in private equity funds. The need to maintain liquidity to satisfy investor withdrawals causes hedge funds to focus on investments that can be converted to cash relatively easily, such as comparatively small investments in companies. Hedge funds often sell or exit their investments after 6 to 18 months in order to keep sufficient liquidity to satisfy investor withdrawals. In contrast, private equity funds often attempt to buy all of the stock of a company and typically exit their investments only after 5 to 7 years. Hedge funds manage risk through a broad array of alternative hedging (i.e., risk reduction) strategies. These may include the buying and selling of put and call options and short-selling. Put options represent the right to sell securities at a particular price during a specific time period, while call options grant the right to buy securities at a particular price during a specific time period. Short-selling involves selling borrowed securities with the expectation of buying them at a future date at a lower price. Private equity funds attempt to control risk by getting more actively involved in managing the firm in which they have invested.

In the past, one could generalize by saying that hedge funds are traders, while private equity funds are more likely to be long-term investors. However, in recent years, this distinction has blurred, as hedge funds have taken more active roles in acquiring entire companies. For example, Highfields Capital Management, a hedge fund, which owned 7% of Circuit City, made a bid to buy the entire company in 2005. That same year hedge fund manager Edward Lampert, after buying a large stake in Kmart, engineered an $11 billion takeover of Sears. The Blackstone Group (a private equity firm) and Lio Capital (a hedge fund) banded together to purchase the European beverage division of Cadbury Schweppes in early 2006. Blackstone also acted like a hedge fund that same year with its purchase of a 4.5% stake in Deutsche Telekom. According to Dealogic, hedge funds accounted for at least 50 leveraged buyouts in 2006.

Unlike mutual funds, hedge funds generally do not have to register with the Securities and Exchange Commission. Consequently, a hedge fund is allowed to use aggressive strategies that are unavailable to mutual funds. Hedge funds are exempt from many of the rules and regulations governing mutual funds. Effective February 2006, the Securities and Exchange Commission passed regulations requiring hedge funds managing over $30 million to register as investment advisors and make their financial statements available to the SEC. However, hedge funds do not have to register if their investors agree to commit their funds for a minimum of 2 years, during which investors cannot withdraw their funds.

Like mutual funds, hedge and private equity funds receive a management fee from participating investors. Such fees usually average about 2% of the assets under management. In addition, hedge fund managers also receive 20% of any profits realized from the sale of portfolio companies before any monies are distributed to investors. Furthermore, hedge funds and private equity investors usually receive fees from their portfolio companies for completing transactions, arranging financing, performing due diligence, and for monitoring business performance while the company is in the fund's portfolio. Kaplan and Schoar (2005) found little evidence that private equity funds on average outperform the overall stock market, once their fees are taken into account. In contrast, hedge funds have tended to outperform the overall market by 1–2 percentage points, even after fees are considered, although the difference varies with the time period selected (*The Deal*, 2006). Moreover, hedge fund returns appeared to be less risky than the overall market as measured by the standard deviation of their returns. However, these data may be problematic, since hedge fund financial returns are self-reported and not subject to public audit. Furthermore, such returns could be upward biased due to the failure to report poorly performing funds. Private equity and hedge fund investment strategies are discussed in more detail in Chapter 13. For excellent discussion of hedge fund investing, see Stefanini (2006).

M&A Arbitrageurs

When a bid is made for a target company, the target company's stock price often trades at a small discount to the actual bid. This reflects the risk that the offer may not be accepted. *Merger arbitrage* refers to an investment strategy that attempts to profit from this spread. *Arbitrageurs* ("arbs") buy the stock and make a profit on the difference between the bid price and the current stock price if the deal is consummated. Hedge fund managers often play the role of arbs.

Arbs may accumulate a substantial percentage of the stock held outside of institutions to be in a position to influence the outcome of the takeover attempt. For example, if other offers for the target firm appear, arbs promote their positions directly to managers and institutional investors with phone calls and through leaks to the financial press. Their intention is to sell their shares to the highest bidder. Acquirers involved in a hostile takeover attempt often encourage hedge funds to buy as much target stock as possible with the objective of gaining control of the target by buying the stock from the hedge funds. In 2006, hedge funds, acting as arbitrageurs, were the deciding factor in the battle over Swedish insurance company Skandia AB. Skandia opposed a takeover bid by Old Mutual PLC, but Old Mutual eventually gained control of Skandia because enough hedge funds purchased Skandia shares and sold their stock to Old Mutual.

Arbs monitor rumors and stock price movements to determine if investors are accumulating a particular stock. Their objective is to identify the target before the potential acquirer is required by law to announce its intentions. Reflecting arb activity and possibly insider trading, empirical studies show that the price of a target company's stock often starts to rise in advance of the announcement of a takeover attempt (Ascioglu, McInish, and Wood, 2002). Also, if one firm in an industry is acquired, it is commonplace for the share prices of other firms in the same industry to also increase, because they are viewed as potential takeover targets.

Arbs also provide market liquidity (i.e., the ease with which a security can be bought or sold without affecting its current market price) during transactions. In a cash-financed merger, the merger arbitrageur provides liquidity to the target shareholders that want to sell on the announcement day or shortly thereafter. While arbitrageurs may provide some liquidity in the target firm's stock, they may reduce liquidity for the acquirer's stock in a stock-for-stock merger, because they immediately "short" the acquirer shares. The downward pressure on the acquirer's share price at the time the transaction is announced from widespread arb short-selling makes it difficult for others to sell without incurring a loss from the premerger announcement price. Merger arbitrage short-selling may account for about one-half of the downward pressure on acquirer share prices around the announcement of a stock-financed merger (Mitchell, Pulvino, and Stafford, 2004).

Merger arbitrage has the potential to be highly profitable. A number of studies find that such arbitrage generates financial returns ranging from 4.5% to more than 100% in excess of what would be considered normal in a highly competitive market (Dukes, Frohlich, and Ma, 1992; Jindra and Walkling, 1999; Karolyi and Shannon, 1998; Mitchell and Pulvino, 2001). Exhibit 1-1 illustrates the implementation of a typical merger arbitrage strategy.

Exhibit 1-1
Merger Arbitrage in Practice

Assume an acquirer offers to exchange one share of its stock for each share of the target's stock. Furthermore, assume the acquirer's and target's stocks currently are trading at $90 and $70 per share, respectively; and an arb buys the target's stock at $85. This is the price the target's share reached immediately after the announcement. The arb hedges his or her position by selling the acquirer's stock short at $90. As the merger date approaches, this $5 spread between the arb's purchase price for the target's stock and the acquirer's share price will diminish as the prices of the target's and acquirer's share price converge. Once the merger is consummated and the target's stock is converted to the acquirer's stock, the arb locks in the $5 gain regardless of the current price of the acquirer's stock. The arb covers the short sale with the acquirer's stock valued at $90. If during the interim the market has declined, sending the acquirer's stock down to $70, the investor makes $20 on the short sale of the acquirer's stock at $90, less the loss of $15 on the target's shares for which the investor paid $85.

Arbitrage Strategy: Buy one share of target at $85/sell short one share of acquirer stock at $90.

Scenarios After Merger	Gain (Loss) on Long Position of $85	Gain (Loss) on Short Position of $90	Total Gain (Loss)
Rise in Acquirer's Stock to $110:	$25	($20)	$5
Fall in Acquirer's Stock to $70:	($15)	$20	$5

If the merger takes 6 months to complete from the announcement date, the 5% profit realized in this example equates to a compound annualized gain of 10.25% [i.e., (1.05) × (1.05)]. If the arb had borrowed half of the total investment in the arbitrage transaction, the annualized return would double. The risk is that the merger will not be completed. The target's stock price should return to its original price of $70. The result would be a loss of $15 on the purchase of the target's stock at $85. Similarly, even if the acquirer's share price had fallen after the merger announcement, the acquirer's share price should return to its previous price of $90 after the transaction is called off. This occurs as short sellers cover their positions by buying the acquirer's stock. Any investor who sold the acquirer's stock short at less than $90 would incur a loss on their short position in addition to the loss incurred on the target's shares.

Common Motivations for Mergers and Acquisitions

There are numerous theories of why mergers and acquisitions take place. In reality, most M&As are a result of a number of different motives. Table 1-1 lists some of the more prominent theories about why mergers happen. Each of these theories is discussed in greater detail in the remainder of this section.

Synergy

Synergy is the rather simplistic notion that the combination of two businesses can create greater shareholder value than if they are operated separately. There are two basic types of synergy: operating and financial.

Operating Synergy (Economies of Scale and Scope)

Operating synergy consists of both economies of scale and economies of scope. Gains in efficiency can come from either factor and from improved managerial practices. Empirical

TABLE 1-1   Common Theories of What Causes Mergers and Acquisitions

Theory	Motivation

Operating Synergy
  Economies of Scale
  Economies of Scope
	Improve operating efficiency through economies of scale or scope by acquiring a customer, supplier, or competitor

Financial Synergy	Lower cost of capital

Diversification
  New Products/Current Markets
  New Products/New Markets
  Current Products/New Markets
	Position the firm in higher growth products or markets

Market Power	Increase market share to improve ability to set prices above competitive levels

Strategic Realignment
  Technological Change
  Regulatory and Political Change
	Acquire capabilities to adapt more rapidly to environmental changes than could be achieved if they were developed internally

Hubris (Managerial Pride)	Acquirers believe their valuation of target more accurate than the market's, causing them to overpay by overestimating synergy
Buying Undervalued Assets (Q-Ratio)	Acquire assets more cheaply when the stock of existing companies is less than the cost of buying or building the assets
Mismanagement (Agency Problems)	Replace managers not acting in the best interests of the owners
Managerialism	Increase the size of a company to increase the power and pay of managers
Tax Considerations	Obtain unused net operating losses and tax credits, asset write-ups, and substitute capital gains for ordinary income
Misevaluation	Investor overvaluation of acquirer's stock encourages M&As

studies suggest that such synergies are important determinants of shareholder wealth creation (Houston, James, and Ryngaert, 2001; DeLong, 2003).

Economies of scale refer to the spreading of fixed costs over increasing production levels. Scale is defined by such fixed costs as depreciation of equipment and amortization of capitalized software; normal maintenance spending; obligations such as interest expense, lease payments, and union, customer, and vendor contracts; and taxes. Such costs are fixed in the sense that they cannot be altered in the short run. Consequently, for a given scale or amount of fixed expenses, the dollar value of fixed expenses per dollar of revenue decreases as output and sales increase. For example, if a firm leases a print shop for $1 million a year and prints one million documents in the first year, the lease payment (i.e., fixed expense) per document is $1. If the number of documents printed in the second year increases to two million, the lease payment per document is $.50 and so on.

Economies of scope refer to using a specific set of skills or an asset currently employed in producing a specific product or service to produce related products or services. They are most often found when it is cheaper to combine two or more product lines in one firm than to produce them in separate firms. For example, Procter & Gamble, the consumer products giant, uses its highly regarded consumer marketing skills to sell a full range of personal care as well as pharmaceutical products. Honda utilizes its skills in enhancing internal combustion engines to develop motorcycles, lawn mowers, and snowblowers, as well as automobiles. Sequent Technology lets customers run applications on UNIX and NT operating systems on a single computer system. Citigroup uses the same computer center to process loan applications, deposits, trust services, and mutual fund accounts for its bank's customers. In each example, a specific set of skills or assets are used to generate more revenue by applying those skills or assets to producing or selling multiple products.

Financial Synergy (Lowering the Cost of Capital)

Financial synergy refers to the impact of mergers and acquisitions on the cost of capital (i.e., the minimum return required by investors and lenders) of the acquiring firm or the newly formed firm resulting from the merger or acquisition. Theoretically, the cost of capital could be reduced if the merged firms have uncorrelated cash flows (i.e., so-called co-insurance), realize financial economies of scale from lower securities and transactions costs, or result in a better matching of investment opportunities with internally generated funds. Combining a firm with excess cash flows with one whose internally generated cash flow is insufficient to fund its investment opportunities may result in a lower cost of borrowing. A firm in a mature industry whose growth is slowing may produce cash flows well in excess of available investment opportunities. Another firm in a high-growth industry may have more investment opportunities than the cash to fund them. Reflecting their different growth rates and risk levels, the firm in the mature industry may have a lower cost of capital than the one in the high-growth industry. Combining the two firms might result in a lower cost of capital for the merged firms.

Diversification

Diversification refers to a strategy of buying firms outside of a company's current primary line of business. There are two commonly used justifications for diversification. The first relates to the creation of financial synergy resulting in a reduced cost of capital.

TABLE 1-2   Product–Market Matrix

Products \ Markets	Current	New
Current	Lower Growth/Lower Risk	Higher Growth/Higher Risk (Related Diversification)
New	Higher Growth/Higher Risk (Related Diversification)	Highest Growth/Highest Risk (Unrelated Diversification)

The second common argument for diversification is for firms to shift from their core product lines or markets into product lines or markets that have higher growth prospects. Such diversification can be either related or unrelated to the firm's current products or markets.

The product–market matrix illustrated in Table 1-2 identifies a firm's primary diversification options. If a firm is facing slower growth in its current markets, it may be able to accelerate growth by selling its current products in new markets that are somewhat unfamiliar and, therefore, more risky. For example, pharmaceutical giant Johnson and Johnson's announced unsuccessful takeover attempt of Guidant Corporation in late 2004 reflected its attempt to give its medical devices business an entrée into the fast growing market for implantable devices, a market in which it does not currently participate. Similarly, a firm may attempt to achieve higher growth rates by developing or acquiring new products, with which it is relatively unfamiliar, and selling them into familiar and less risky current markets. Examples of this strategy include retailer J. C. Penney's acquisition of the Eckerd Drugstore chain or J&J's $16 billion acquisition of Pfizer's consumer health care products line in 2006. In each instance, the firm is assuming additional risk. However, each of these related diversification strategies are generally less risky than an unrelated diversification strategy of developing new products for sale in new markets.

Empirical studies have supported the conclusion that investors do not benefit from unrelated diversification. The share prices of conglomerates often trade at a discount from shares of focused firms or from their value if they were broken up and sold in pieces by as much as 10 to 15% (Berger and Ofek, 1995; Lins and Servaes, 1999). This discount is called the ***conglomerate or diversification discount***. Investors often perceive companies diversified in unrelated areas (i.e., those in different standard industrial classifications) as riskier, because they are difficult for management to understand and management often fails to fully fund the most attractive investment opportunities (Morck, Shleifer, and Vishny, 1990). Moreover, outside investors may have a difficult time understanding how to value the various parts of highly diversified businesses (Best and Hodges, 2004). Harding and Rovit (2004) and Megginson, Morgan, and Nail (2003) argue that the most successful mergers are those that focus on deals that promote the acquirer's core business.

Other studies argue that the magnitude of the conglomerate discount is overstated. The discount is more related to the fact that diversifying firms are often poor performers before becoming conglomerates than to the simple act of diversification (Campa and Simi, 2002; Hyland, 2001). Still others conclude that the conglomerate discount is a result of how the sample studied is constructed (Villalonga, 2004; Graham, Lemmon, and Wolf, 2002).

Numerous studies suggest that the conglomerate discount is reduced when firms either divest or spin-off businesses in an effort to achieve greater focus in the core business portfolio (Comment and Jarrell, 1993; Daley, Mehrotra, and Sivakumar, 1996; Lamont, 1997; Shin and Stulz, 1998; Scharfstein, 1998; Gertner, Powers, and Scharfstein, 2002; Dittmar and Shivdasani, 2003). Although the empirical evidence suggests that corporate performance is likely to be greatest for firms that tend to pursue a more focused corporate strategy, there are always exceptions. Among the most famous are the legendary CEO of Berkshire Hathaway, Warren Buffet, and Jack Welch of General Electric (see Case Study 2-8, Chapter 2 of this book). Fauver, Houston, and Narango (2003) argue that diversified firms in developing countries where access to capital markets is limited may sell at a premium to more focused firms. Under these circumstances, corporate diversification may enable more efficient investment as diversified firms may use cash generated by mature subsidiaries to fund those with higher growth potential.

Strategic Realignment

The strategic realignment theory suggests that firms use M&As as ways of rapidly adjusting to changes in their external environments. Although change can come from many different sources, only changes in the regulatory environment and technological innovation are considered. During the last 20 years these two factors have been major forces in creating new opportunities for growth or threats to a firm's primary line of business. This process of "creative destruction" is illustrated in Case Study 1-2.

Regulatory Change

M&A activity in recent years has centered in industries that have been subject to significant deregulation. These industries include financial services, health care, utilities, media, telecommunications, and defense. There is significant empirical evidence that takeover activity is higher in deregulated industries than in regulated ones (Jensen, 1993; Mitchell and Mulherin, 1996; Mulherin and Boone, 2000). The advent of deregulation broke down artificial barriers in these industries and stimulated competition. In some states, utilities now are required to sell power to competitors, which can resell the power in the utility's own marketplace. Some utilities are responding to this increased competition by attempting to achieve greater operating efficiency through mergers and acquisitions. In financial services, commercial banks are moving well beyond their historical role of accepting deposits and granting loans and into investment banking, insurance, and mutual funds. The Financial Services Modernization Act of 1999 repealed legislation dating back to the Great Depression that prevented banks, securities firms, and insurance companies from merging. The legislation accelerated the trend toward huge financial services companies typified by the 1998 Citicorp–Travelers merger.

Historically, local and long-distance phone companies were not allowed to compete against each other. Cable companies were essentially monopolies. Following the Telecommunications Reform Act of 1996, local and long-distance companies are actively encouraged to compete in each other's markets. Cable companies are offering both Internet access and local telephone service. During the first half of the 1990s, the U.S. Department of Defense actively encouraged consolidation of the nation's major defense contractors to improve their overall operating efficiency. In early 2002, a Federal Appeals Court rejected a Federal Communications Commission regulation that prohibited a company from owning a cable television system and a TV station in the same city. Moreover, it also overturned a rule that barred a company from owning TV stations that reach more than 35% of U.S. households. These rulings encourage combinations among the largest media companies or purchases of smaller broadcasters.

Technological Change

Technological advances create new products and industries. The development of the airplane created the passenger airline, avionics, and satellite industries. The vacuum tube, transistor, and microchip provided the basis for the television, radio, and personal computer. The emergence of satellite delivery of cable network to local systems ignited explosive growth in the cable industry. Today, with the expansion of broadband technology, we are witnessing the convergence of voice, data, and video technologies on the Internet. The emergence of the digital camera technology has dramatically reduced the demand for analog cameras and film, causing such household names in photography as Kodak and Polaroid to shift their focus to the newer digital technology. The advent of satellite radio is increasing its share of the radio advertising market at the expense of traditional radio stations.

As the pace of technological change accelerates, M&A often is viewed as a way of rapidly exploiting new products and industries made possible by the emergence of new technologies. Large, more bureaucratic firms often are unable to exhibit the creativity and speed smaller, more nimble, niche players display. With engineering talent often in short supply and product life cycles shortening, firms often do not have the luxury of time or the resources to innovate. Consequently large companies often look to mergers and acquisitions as a fast and sometimes less expensive way to acquire new technologies and proprietary know-how to fill gaps in their current product offering or to enter entirely new businesses. Acquiring technologies also can be used as a defensive weapon to keep important new technologies out of the hands of competitors. In 2006, eBay acquired Skype Technologies, the Internet phone provider, for $2.6 billion in cash and stock. eBay hopes that the move will boost trading on its online auction site and prevent competitors from gaining access to the technology. Skype offers downloadable software that enables users to talk to one another over the Internet through their computers. Skype's voice communications technology is expected to make online trading easier for eBay's 157 million users, particularly with transactions involving real estate, big-ticket items, and services that require detailed conversations (see Chapter 4).

Hubris and the "Winners Curse"

As a result of hubris, managers sometimes believe that their own valuation of a target firm is superior to the market's valuation. Thus, the acquiring company tends to overpay for the target because of overoptimism in evaluating synergies. Competition among bidders also is likely to result in the winner overpaying because of hubris, even if significant synergies are present (Roll, 1986). Senior managers tend to be very competitive and sometimes self-important. The desire not to lose can result in a bidding war that can drive the purchase price of an acquisition well in excess of the actual economic value (i.e., cash generating capability) of that company.

Hubris or ego-driven decision making is a factor contributing to the so-called "winner's curse." In an auction environment where there are many bidders, there is likely to be a wide range of bids for a target company. The winning bid is often substantially in excess of the expected value of the target company. This is attributable to the difficulty all participants have in estimating the actual value of the target and the competitive nature of the process. The winner is cursed in that he paid more than the company is worth and ultimately may feel remorse in having done so.

Buying Undervalued Assets (The Q-Ratio)

The *Q-ratio* is the ratio of the market value of the acquiring firm's stock to the replacement cost of its assets. Firms interested in expansion have a choice of investing in new plant and equipment or obtaining the assets by acquiring a company whose market value is less than the replacement cost of its assets (i.e., Q-ratio <1). This theory was very useful in explaining M&A activity during the 1970s when high inflation and interest rates depressed stock prices well below the book value of many firms. High inflation also caused the replacement cost of assets to be much higher than the book value of assets. More recently, gasoline refiner Valero Energy Corp. acquired Premcor Inc. in an $8 billion transaction that created the largest refiner in North America. The estimated cost of building a new refinery with capacity equivalent to Premcor would have cost 40% more than the acquisition price (Zellner, May 9, 2005). Similarly, the flurry of mergers among steel and copper companies in 2006 reflected the belief that the stock price of the target firms did not fully reflect the true market value of their assets.

Mismanagement (Agency Problems)

Agency problems arise when there is a difference between the interest of incumbent managers (i.e., those currently managing the firm) and the firm's shareholders. This happens when management owns a small fraction of the outstanding shares of the firm. These managers may be more inclined to focus on maintaining job security and a lavish lifestyle than on maximizing shareholder value. When the shares of a company are widely held, the cost of mismanagement is spread across a large number of shareholders. Each shareholder bears only a small portion of the cost. This allows for such mismanagement to be tolerated for long periods. According to this theory, mergers take place to correct situations where there is a separation between what the managers want and what the owners want. Low stock prices put pressure on managers to take actions to raise the share price or become the target of acquirers, who perceive the stock to be undervalued (Fama and Jensen, 1983). Mehran and Peristiani (2006) found that agency problems also are an important factor contributing to management-initiated buyouts, particularly when managers and shareholders disagree over how excess cash flow should be used.

Tax Considerations

There are two important issues in discussing the role of taxes as a motive for M&As. First, tax benefits, such as loss carry forwards and investment tax credits, can be used to offset the combined firms' taxable income. Additional tax shelter is created if the acquisition is recorded under the purchase method of accounting, which requires the book value of the acquired assets to be revalued to their current market value. The resulting depreciation of these generally higher asset values also reduces the amount of future taxable income generated by the combined companies. Second, the taxable nature of the transaction frequently will play a more important role in determining if the merger takes place than any tax benefits that accrue to the acquiring company. The tax-free status of the transaction may be viewed by the seller as a prerequisite for the deal to take place. A properly structured transaction can allow the target shareholders to defer any capital gain resulting from the transaction. If the transaction is not tax free, the seller normally will want a higher purchase price to compensate for the tax liability resulting from the transaction (Ayers, Lefanowicz, and Robinson, 2003). These issues will be discussed in more detail in Chapter 12.

Market Power

This theory suggests that firms merge to improve their monopoly power to set product prices at levels not sustainable in a more competitive market. There is very little empirical support for this theory. Many recent studies conclude that increased merger activity is much more likely to contribute to improved operating efficiency of the combined firms than to increased market power (see the section of this chapter entitled "Do Mergers and Acquisitions Pay Off for Society?").

Misevaluation

The misevaluation approach to takeovers has traditionally been overshadowed by the presumption that markets are efficient. Efficiency implies that a target's share price will reflect accurately its true economic value (i.e., cash generation potential). While the empirical evidence that over time asset values reflect their true economic value is substantial, the evidence that assets may temporarily not reflect their underlying economic value is growing. The Internet bubble in the late 1990s is the most recent example of market inefficiencies. Just as these market inefficiencies impact investor decisions in buying individual stocks, they also impact the M&A market. Shleifer and Vishny (2003) suggest that irrational changes in investors' sentiment will sometimes affect takeover decisions. While evident in earlier periods, empirical support for the misevaluation hypothesis was stronger in the 1990s than during earlier periods (Dong, Hirshleifer, Richardson, and Teoh, 2006). The authors suggest that acquirers can periodically profit by buying undervalued targets for cash at a price below its actual value or by using equity (even if the target is overvalued) as long as the target is less overvalued than the bidding firm's stock. The tendency of overvalued acquirers to use stock as long as it is more overvalued than the target's stock (including premium) also is supported by Ang and Cheng (2006).

Historical Merger and Acquisition Waves

M&A activity in the United States came in five multiyear waves in the last century, each of which was characterized by identifiable underlying trends. Mergers tended to occur during periods of sustained high rates of economic growth, low or declining interest rates, and a rising stock market. Historically, each merger wave differed in terms of a specific development such as the emergence of a new technology; industry focus such as rail, oil, or financial services; degree of regulation; and type of transaction such as horizontal, vertical, conglomerate, strategic, or financial.

Why M&A Waves Occur

There are two competing theories as to why M&As tend to cluster in waves. The first, sometimes referred to as the neoclassical hypothesis, argues that merger waves occur when firms in industries react to "shocks" in their operating environments (Brealey and Myers, 2003; Mitchell and Mulherin, 1996). Shocks could reflect such events as deregulation or the emergence of new technologies, distribution channels, or substitute products. The size and length of the M&A wave depends largely on the number of industries impacted by and the extent to which they are affected by such shocks. Some shocks, such as the emergence of the Internet, are pervasive in their impact, while others are more specific such as deregulation of financial services and utilities or rapidly escalating commodity prices. In response to shocks, firms within the industry often acquire either all or parts of other firms.

The second theory (sometimes referred to as the behavioral hypothesis) is based on the misevaluation hypothesis discussed earlier and suggests that managers use overvalued stock to buy the assets of lower-valued firms. For M&As to cluster in waves, this theory requires that valuations of many firms measured by their price-to-earnings or market-to-book ratios compared to other firms must increase at the same time. Managers, whose stocks are believed to be overvalued, move concurrently to acquire companies whose stock prices are lesser valued (Rhodes-Kropf and Viswanathan, 2004; Shleifer and Vishny, 2003). Reflecting the influence of overvaluation, the method of payment according to this theory would normally be stock. Numerous studies confirm that long-term fluctuations in market valuations and the number of takeovers are correlated (Dong *et al.*, 2006; Ang and Cheng, 2006; Andrade *et al.*, 2001; Holmstrom and Kaplan, 2001; Daniel, Hirshleifer, and Subrahmanyam, 1998). However, whether high valuations contribute to greater takeover activity or increased M&A activity boosts market valuations is less clear.

In an effort to compare each of the these two theories, Harford (2005) finds greater support for the neoclassical or "shock" model modified to include the effects of the availability of capital in causing and sustaining merger waves. Harford underscores the critical role played by capital availability in determining merger waves. He points out that shocks alone, without sufficient liquidity to finance the transactions, will not initiate a wave of merger activity. Moreover, readily available, low-cost capital (often cited as a major determinant in the current M&A wave) may cause a surge in M&A activity even if industry shocks are absent.

Trends in Recent M&A Activity

Table 1-3 illustrates the trend in both global and U.S. merger and acquisition activity in recent years. M&A activity worldwide reached an historical peak in 2000 in terms of both the number and dollar value of transactions, following surging economic growth and the Internet bubble of the late 1990s. During 2000, the dollar value of transactions in the United States accounted for almost one-half of the global total. The ensuing recession in 2001, escalating concerns about terrorism, and the subsequent decline in the world's stock markets caused both the number and dollar value of global and U.S. transactions to decline through 2002. However, by this time, conditions were in place for a resurgence in M&A activity. Partially reflecting catch-up to the frenetic pace of U.S. M&A activity in the late 1990s, the dollar value of announced global M&A transactions reached a new high in 2006. Fifty-five of the more than 37,000 transactions worldwide in 2006 were valued at more than $10 billion, according to Thompson Financial. In contrast, the 2006 level in the United States fell short of its previous 2000 peak.

The sixth and current takeover wave began in 2003. This wave is different from that of the 1980s and 1990s in that mergers tend to be larger in size, horizontal, cross-border, and heavily concentrated in banking, telecommunications, health care, utilities,

TABLE 1-3   Trends in Announced Mergers and Acquisitions[1]

Year	Global M&As		U.S. M&As		U.S. as % of Global M&As	
	Number	$Value (Billions)	Number	$Value (Billions)	Number	$Value (Billions)
1995	22,027	980	3,510	356	15.9	36.3
1996	23,166	1,146	5,848	495	25.2	43.2
1997	22.642	1,676	7,800	657	34.5	39.2
1998	27,256	2,581	7,809	1,192	28.7	46.2
1999	31,701	3,439	9,278	1,426	29.3	41.5
2000	37.204	3,497	9,566	1,706	25.7	48.8
2001	28,828	1,745	8,290	759	28.8	43.5
2002	26.270	1,207	7,303	441	27.7	36.5
2003	27,753	1,333	8,131	559	29.3	41.9
2004	31,467	1,949	9,783	812	31.1	41.7
2005	33,574	2,775	10,644	1,045	31.7	37.7
2006	37,032	3,794	10,977	1,563	29.6	41.2

Note:
[1] All Valuations include the value of debt assumed by the acquirer.
Source: Thompson Financial Securities Data Corporation and Dealogic.

and in such commodity industries as oil, gas, and metals. Ongoing deregulation in the banking, telecommunications, and utilities industries has promoted M&A activity in these sectors. Expectations of continued high commodity prices have encouraged consolidation in natural resource industries as a less costly and more rapid means of getting raw materials to market than by developing new mines and engaging in new exploration. Finally, increasing interdependence of economies across the globe has accelerated the frequency of cross-border transactions to achieve the scale necessary to compete with larger global competitors. In a world awash in liquidity, the current wave also differs from previous cycles in that private equity investors are major participants, accounting for about one in five transactions globally and 27% in the United States during 2006. In the United States, private equity investors were responsible for five of the ten largest transactions in 2006. Table 1-4 summarizes key attributes of the various U.S. merger waves.

Do Mergers and Acquisitions Pay Off for Shareholders?

The answer seems to depend on for whom and over what period of time. Around the announcement date of the transaction, average returns to target firm shareholders, including both friendly and hostile takeovers, are about 30%. In contrast, the shareholders of acquiring firms generally show returns that range from slightly negative to modestly positive around the announcement date. Over longer periods, many M&As either underperform their industry peers or destroy shareholder value. Two approaches have been used to measure the impact of takeovers on shareholder value. The first approach, premerger returns, involves the examination of abnormal stock returns to the shareholders of both bidders and targets around the announcement of an offer and includes both successful and unsuccessful takeovers. Such analyses are referred to as "event" studies, with the event

TABLE 1-4 U.S. Historical Merger Waves

Time Period	Driving Force(s)	Type of M&A Activity	Key Impact	Key Transactions	Factors Contributing to End of Wave
1897–1904	Drive for efficiency Lax antitrust law enforcement Westward migration Technological change	Horizontal consolidation	Increasing concentration: Primary metals Transportation Mining	U.S. Steel Standard Oil Eastman Kodak American Tobacco General Electric	Fraudulent financing 1904 stock market crash
1916–1929	Entry into WWI Post-WWI boom	Largely horizontal consolidation	Increased industry concentration	Samuel Insull builds utility empire in 39 states called Middle West Utilities	1929 stock market crash Clayton Antitrust Act
1965–1969	Rising stock market Sustained economic boom	Growth of conglomerates	Financial engineering and conglomeration	LTV ITT Litton Industries Gulf and Western Northwest Industries	Escalating purchase prices Excessive leverage
1981–1989	Rising stock market Economic boom Underperformance of conglomerates Relative weakness of U.S. dollar Favorable regulatory environment Favorable foreign accounting practices	Retrenchment era Rise of hostile takeovers Corporate raiders Proliferation of financial buyers using LBOs and MBOs Increased takeover of U.S. firms by foreign buyers	Break-up of conglomerates Increased use of junk (unrated) bonds to finance transactions	RJR Nabisco MBO Beecham Group (U.K.) buys SmithKline Campeau of Canada buys Federated Stores	Widely publicized bankruptcies 1990 recession
1992–2000	Economic recovery Booming stock market Internet revolution Lower trade barriers Globalization	Age of strategic megamerger	Record levels of transactions in terms of numbers and prices	AOI acquires Time Warner Vodafone AirTouch acquires Mannesmann Exxon buys Mobil	Slumping economy and stock market in 2001–2002
2003–?	Low interest rates Rising stock market Booming global economy Globalization High commodity prices	Age of cross-border transactions, horizontal megamergers, and growing influence of private equity investors	Increasing synchronization among world's economies	Mittal acquires Arcelor P&G buys Gillette Verizon acquires MCI Blackstone buys Equity Office Properties	Rising interest rates? Geopolitical risk? Falling commodity prices? LBO leverage? Weaker equity markets?

being the takeover announcement. The second approach, postmerger returns, measures the impact on shareholder value after the merger has been completed.

Premerger Returns to Shareholders

Positive abnormal returns represent gains for shareholders, which could be explained by such factors as improved efficiency, pricing power, or tax benefits. They are abnormal in the sense that they exceed what an investor would normally expect to earn for accepting a certain level of risk. For example, if an investor can reasonably expect to earn a 10% return on a stock but actually earns 25% due to a takeover, the abnormal or excess return to the shareholder would be 15%. Abnormal returns are calculated by subtracting the actual return from a benchmark indicating investors' required returns, which often are approximated by the capital asset pricing model (see Chapter 7) or the return on the S&P 500 stock index. Abnormal returns are forward looking in that share prices usually represent the present value of expected future cash flows.

Abnormal or excess returns to target shareholders are not necessarily the same as the purchase price premium they receive for their shares. While the purchase price premium is calculated with respect to the premerger share price, abnormal or excess returns reflect the difference between the premium shareholders receive for their stock and what is considered a normal return for the risk they are assuming. The abnormal/excess return would be the same as the purchase price premium only if the premerger share price reflected accurately the normal rate of return for the level of risk assumed by investors in the target stock.

The average results of numerous so-called event studies of returns to shareholders of both bidding and target firms are summarized in Table 1-5. These returns are generally computed over a period starting immediately before and ending shortly after the announcement date. These studies often associate tender offers and mergers with hostile and friendly takeovers, respectively. An acquisition often is classified as a hostile takeover in empirical studies if the bidder purchases the majority of the target's stock through a hostile tender offer. Moreover, these studies usually assume that share prices fully adjust to reflect anticipated synergies; therefore, they reflect both the short- and long-term effects of the acquisition.

Target Shareholders Realize High Returns in Both Successful and Unsuccessful Bids

These studies suggest that average excess or abnormal returns to target company shareholders for successful tender offers (i.e., hostile takeovers) have risen from 22% during the 1960s to the mid-to-high 30s during the 1970s and 1980s, and in some studies to more than 50% in the early 1990s. While averaging 30% between 1962 and 2001, Bhagat, Dong, Hirshleifer, and Noah (2005) also document that abnormal returns for tender offers have risen steadily over time. These substantial returns reflect the frequent bidder strategy of offering a substantial premium to preempt other potential bidders and the potential for revising the initial offer because of competing bids. Other contributing factors include the increasing sophistication of takeover defenses, as well as federal and state laws requiring bidders to notify target shareholders of their intentions before completing the transaction (see Chapters 2 and 3 for more details). Moreover, the abnormal gains tend to be higher for shareholders of target firms, whose financial performance is expected to deteriorate

TABLE 1-5 Empirical Evidence on Returns to U.S. Bidders and U.S. Targets around Announcement Dates

Outcome of Takeover Attempt	Impact on Shareholder Value	
	Target	Bidder
Average Return on Mergers		
1960s[1]	20%	0%
1970s[1,3]	20%	0.5%
980s[3,9]	20%	1%
1990s[10,11]	20%	0.7%
1980s and 1990s[11,12]	20%	0.2%
Average Return on Tender Offers		
1960s[1,2,4,5]	22%	4%
1970s[1,4,5,6]	35%	2.4%
1980s[4,5,6,7]	38%	(1.3)%
1990s[8]	52%	Not applicable
1962–2001[13]	30%	0%
Average Return on All M&As		
1980s and 1990s[14]	24%	(0.7)%
Jensen and Ruback (1983)[1]	30% (Tender offers only)	4% (Tender offers only)
(Review of 13 studies during 1960s and 1970s)	20% (Mergers only)	0% (Mergers only)
Asquith (1983)[2]	20% (1962–1976)	2% (1962–1976)
(Sample = 211 successful tender offers)		
You, Caves, Smith, and Henry (1986)[3]	20% (1975–1984)	1% (1975–1984)
(Sample = 133 mergers)		
Jarrell, Brickley, and Netter (1988)[4]	19% (1962–1965)	4% (1962–1965)
(Sample = 663 successful tender	30% (1970–1979)	2% (1970–1979)
offers)	35% (1980–1985)	(1)% (1980–1985)
Bradley, Desai, and Kim (1988)[5]	19% (1963–1969)	4% (1963–1969)
(Sample = 236 successful tender	35% (1968–1980)	1.3% (1968–1980)
offers)	35% (1981–1984)	(3)% (1981–1984)
Bhagat and Hirshleifer (1996)[6]	45% (1958–1984)	1.3% (1958–1984)
(Sample = 290 successful tender offers)		
Lang, Stulz, and Walkling (1989)[6]	40% (1968–1986)	Not applicable
(Sample = 87 tender offers)		
Jarrell and Poulsen (1989)[6]	29% (1963–1986)	Not applicable
(Sample = 526 tender offers)		
Schwert (1996)[7]	35% (1975–1991)	0% (1975–1991)
(Sample size = 1814 tender offers)		
Cotter, Shivdasani, and Zenner (1997)[8]	62% (1989–1992) Highly independent board	Not applicable
(Sample = 169 successful tender offers)	41% (1989–1992) Less independent board	
Ghosh and Lee (2000)[9]	20.3% (1981–1990)	Not applicable
(Sample = 1587 mergers)	28% (1981–1990) Underperforming firms	

continued

TABLE 1-5   continued

Outcome of Takeover Attempt	Impact on Shareholder Value	
	Target	Bidder
Mulherin and Boone (2000)[10] (Sample = 376 mergers)	21.2% (1990–1999)	0.7% (1990–1999)
Boone and Mulherin (2006)[10] (Sample = 400 mergers)	21.6% (1990–1999)	Not applicable
Akhigbe, Borde, and Whyte (2000)[11] (Sample = 135 mergers)	18.4% (1987–1996)	Not applicable
Billett, King, and Mauer (2004)[12] (Sample = 3083 mergers)	21.4% (1979–1997)	0.3% (1979–1997)
Fee and Thomas (2004)[12] (Sample = 554 mergers)	18.8% (1980–1997)	(0.6)% (1980–1997)
Bhagat, Dong, Hirshleifer, and Noah (2005)[13] (Sample = 1018 tender offers)	30.1% (1962–2001)	0% (1962–2001)
Andrade et al. (2001)[14] (Sample = 4256 mergers and tender offers)	23.8% (1979–1998)	(0.7)% (1979–1998

over the long term (Ghosh and Lee, 2000). This may suggest that the bidding firms see the highest potential for gain among those target firms whose management is viewed as ineffective.

These returns compare to about 20% for presumed friendly mergers since the 1960s. The magnitude of such returns has been remarkably stable over time. Leeth and Borg (2000) found evidence that abnormal returns to target shareholders in friendly transactions typically exceeded 15% as far back as the 1920s. Returns from hostile tender offers typically exceed those from friendly mergers, which are characterized by less contentious negotiated settlements between the boards and management of the bidder and the target firm. Moreover, mergers often do not receive competing bids.

Unsuccessful takeovers also may result in significant returns for target company share-holders around the announcement date, but much of the gain dissipates if another bidder does not appear. Studies show that the immediate gain in target share prices following a merger announcement disappears within 1 year if the takeover attempt fails (Akhigbe, Borde, and Whyte, 2000; Asquith, 1983; Bradley, Desai, and Kim, 1988; Sullivan, Jensen, and Hudson, 1994). Consequently, target firm shareholders, in an unsuccessful bid, must sell their shares shortly after the announcement of a failed takeover attempt to realize abnormal returns.

Bidder's Shareholders Often Disappointed in Both Successful and Unsuccessful Bids

For successful takeovers, returns are modest to slightly negative for both tender offers and mergers. Bidder returns generally have declined slightly over time, as the premiums paid for targets have increased. Finally, even if the excess returns are zero or slightly neg-ative, these returns are consistent with returns in competitive markets in which financial returns are proportional to risk assumed by the average competitor in the industry. For unsuccessful takeovers, bidder shareholders have experienced negative returns in the 5 to 8% range (Bradley, Desai, and Kim, 1988). Such returns may reflect investors' reassessment of the firm's business plan more than it does about the acquisition (Grinblatt and Titman, 2002).

Fuller, Netter, and Stegemoller (2002) note that it is important to distinguish publicly traded targets and targets which are private firms or subsidiaries of publicly traded firms. Their findings show that bidders have significantly negative returns when buying public targets and significantly positive returns when buying private or subsidiaries of public companies. Closer monitoring of management and the acquired firm's performance may partially explain why acquirers of private firms and public firms' subsidiaries experience abnormal positive returns. This result is discussed further in Chapter 10.

Interestingly, acquirer returns may not be as disappointing as they often appear. The results simply reflect averages which can be distorted by a relatively few large transactions. Acquirer returns around transaction dates were positive during the 1990s, particularly during the 1990 to 1997 period (Moeller, Schlingemann, and Stulz, 2005). However, losses incurred by a relatively few megatransactions between 1998 and 2001 offset much of the gains during the earlier period. Moreover, the acquirer's stock return cannot be completely attributed to the anticipated impact of the acquisition on the firm's cash flow.

Luo (2005), using a sample of 1576 transactions between 1995 and 2001, found evidence that the magnitude of abnormal returns to acquirers around the announcement date is a good predictor of whether the initial offer price will either be renegotiated or that the deal will be canceled. The acquirer's management will react to a significant negative decline in their stock immediately following a merger announcement as investors display their displeasure with the deal. Cancellation is much less likely if an agreement of purchase and sale had been signed before the announcement. Reneging on a signed agreement can be prohibitively expensive. Getty Oil in the early 1980s reneged on a merger agreement with Pennzoil in favor of merging with Texaco. A federal court later ruled that Texaco would have to pay Pennzoil $10 billion in compensatory damages.

Cross-Border Returns Comparable to U.S. Empirical Results

Event studies involving U.S. buyers of foreign firms or foreign firms' acquisitions of U.S. firms give results that are remarkably similar to those involving completely domestic transactions. Target company shareholders experience large, abnormal positive returns, whereas buyer shareholders experience little or no positive abnormal returns (Doukas and Travlos, 1988; Eun, Kolodny, and Scheraga, 1996; Harris and Ravenscraft, 1991; Klaus, Mueller, Yurtoglu, and Zulehner, 2003; Kuipers, Miller, and Patel, 2003; Seth, Song, and Petit, 2000).

Postmerger Returns to Shareholders

The second approach to measuring the performance of M&As has been to examine accounting or other performance measures, such as cash flow and operating profit, during the 3- to 5-year period following completed transactions. The objective is to assess how performance changed following closing. Unfortunately, these studies, as shown in Table 1-6, provide conflicting evidence about the long-term impact of M&A activity. Some studies find a better than average chance that M&As create shareholder value.

TABLE 1-6   Postmerger Performance Studies: Returns to Merged Companies versus Industry Average Returns

Underperform Industry Average	Approximate Industry Average	Overperform Industry Average
(3–5 Years Following Announcement Date)		
McKinsey & Company (1990)	Mueller (1985)	Healy, Palepu, and Ruback (1992)
Mangenheim and Mueller (1988)	Ravenscraft and Sherer (1987 and 1988)	Kaplan and Weisbach (1992)
Franks, Harris, and Titman (1991)	Bradley and Jarrell (1988)	Rau and Vermaelen (1998)[2]
Agrawal, Jaffe, and Mandelker (1992)	Ghosh (2001)	Carline, Linn, and Yadav (2001)
Sirower (1997)		
Gregory (1997)		
Loughran and Vijh (1997)		
Rau and Vermaelen (1998)[1]		
Agrawal and Jaffe (1999)[1]		
Black, Carnes, and Jandik (2000)		
Deogun and Lipin (2000)		
Sanford Bernstein & Company (2000)		

Notes:
[1] Pertains to business combinations involving mergers.
[2] Pertains to business combinations involving tender offers.

However, others have found that as many as 50–80% underperform their industry peers or fail to earn their cost of capital. The diversity of conclusions about postmerger returns may be the result of sample and time period selections, methodology employed in the studies, or factors unrelated to the merger such as a slowing economy (Barber and Lyon, 1997; Fama, 1998; Lyon, Barber, and Tsai, 1999). Presumably, the longer the postmerger time period analyzed the greater the likelihood that other factors, wholly unrelated to the merger, will affect financial returns.

Long-Term Performance Similar for M&As, Business Alliances, and Solo Ventures

Even if a substantial percentage of M&As underperform their peers or fail to earn appropriate financial returns, it is important to note that there is no compelling evidence that growth strategies undertaken as an alternative to M&As fare any better. Such alternatives include solo ventures in which firms reinvest excess cash flows and business alliances including joint ventures, licensing, franchising, and minority investments. Failure rates among alternative strategies tend to be remarkably similar to those documented for M&As. The estimated failure rate for new product introductions is well over 70% (ACNielsen, 2002), while failure rates for alliances of all types exceed 60% (Ellis, 1996; Klein, 2004). See Chapters 4 and 14 of this book for a more detailed discussion of these issues.

Key Findings

Acquirers Tend to Overpay for Growth Firms In an exhaustive study of 22 different papers examining long-run postmerger returns, Agrawal and Jaffe (1999) separate financial performance following mergers and hostile tender offers. Although the authors review a number of arguments purporting to explain postmerger performance, they find the argument that acquirers tend to overpay for so-called high-growth glamour companies based on their past performance to be most convincing. Consequently, the postmerger share price for high growth companies should underperform broader industry averages as their future growth slows to more normal levels.

Shareholders Profit by Selling around Merger Announcement Dates Loughran and Vijh (1997) found that, in the case of stock mergers, the gains experienced around the announcement date tend to dissipate within 5 years even if the acquisition succeeds. These findings imply that shareholders, selling around the announcement dates, may realize the largest gains from either tender offers or mergers. Those who hold onto the acquirer's stock received as payment for their shares may see their gains diminish over time.

Acquirer Experience Improves Long-Term Performance of Combined Companies The importance of experience was documented in a 1995 joint study by Mercer Management Consulting and *BusinessWeek* of 248 acquirers, which purchased 1045 companies from January 1990 through July 1995. Experienced acquirers tended to substantially outperform less experienced acquirers in terms of returns to shareholders during the 3 years following the transaction when they were compared with their industry peers (Lajoux, 1998). Experienced acquirers were defined as those that had completed six or more transactions annually; less experienced buyers were those that completed less than five transactions per year. Experienced buyers constituted 24% of the entire sample. Of the firms in this group, 72% generated returns in excess of their industry average. In contrast, only 55% of those firms in the less experienced group earned financial returns above their industry average. In a study of 21 corporate acquirers and financial buyers during the 10-year period ending in 1994, Anslinger and Copeland (1996) found that 80% of the 839 acquisitions made by these companies earned their cost of capital. The cumulative experience of this sample was substantial, with each firm averaging 40 acquisitions during this period.

The role of experience in successful deal making has been particularly noticeable for high-tech firms. For the 10-year period ending in 2000, high-tech companies, averaging 39% annual total return to shareholders, undertook twice as many acquisitions and as many as 10 times as many alliances as less profitable firms. Although experience seems to be a factor contributing to long-term profitability, the size of the average transaction also may play an important role. Deals for these high-tech acquirers tended to be small, with an average transaction value of less than $400 million, about 1% of the market value of the acquiring firms (Frick and Torres, 2002).

Method of Payment May Affect Longer-Term Returns Bidding firms using cash to purchase the target seem to exhibit better long-term performance than do those using stock (Heron and Lie, 2002; Linn and Switzer, 2001; Loughran and Vijh, 1997; Megginson, Morgan, and Nail, 2003; Sanford Bernstein & Company, 2000; Sirower, 1997). The use of stock to acquire a firm seems to negatively impact the return to the bidders' shareholders during the 3–5 years following the transaction. Stock is more likely to be used to finance larger transactions than smaller ones. Acquirers may not be able to borrow enough to finance the major portion of the purchase price of large transactions with cash. To induce the target to accept its stock, the bidder may have to offer a higher price than would have been necessary using some other form of payment. This results in more frequent overpayment for target firms and to longer-term underperformance for acquirers. In particular, the Sanford Bernstein & Company study found that large stock-for-stock transactions tended to underperform the S&P 500 the most because the degree of overpayment tends to be the greatest.

The use of stock may also reflect the acquirer's belief that its stock is overvalued. Jensen (2005) argues that a firm's stock is overvalued when a firm's management cannot expect to make investments that will sustain the current share price except by pure luck. Consequently, management will be enticed to pursue larger, more risky investments such as unrelated acquisitions in a vain attempt to support the overvalued share price. These actions destroy shareholder value as the firm is unable to earn its cost of capital. Consequently, the longer-term performance of the combined firms suffers as the stock price declines to its industry average performance.

Do Mergers and Acquisitions Pay Off for Bondholders?

Recent evidence suggests that below investment grade bonds issued by target firms earn average excess returns of 4.3% around the merger announcement date. Moreover, excess returns to target bonds are even larger when the target firm's credit rating is less than the acquirer's and when the merger is expected to decrease the target's risk or leverage (Billett, King, and Mauer, 2004). The evidence for excess returns to acquirer bondholders is contradictory (Asquith and Kim, 1982; Dennis and McConnell, 1986; Eger, 1983; Kim and McConnell, 1977; and Maquierira, Megginson, and Nail, 1998).

Do Mergers and Acquisitions Pay Off for Society?

Although postmerger performance study results are ambiguous, event studies show generally consistent results. Such studies suggest that M&A activity tends to improve aggregate shareholder value (i.e., the sum of the shareholder value of both the target and acquiring firms). If financial markets are indeed efficient, the large increase in the combined shareholder values of the two firms will reflect future efficiencies that are expected to result from the merger. However, the target firm's shareholders often capture the bulk of this increase in combined shareholder value.

Moreover, there is no evidence that M&A activity results in increasing industry concentration. Mergers and acquisitions have continued to increase in number and average size during the last 30 years. Despite this trend, M&A activity has not increased industry concentration in terms of the share of output or value produced by the largest firms in the industry, either in manufacturing or in the overall economy, since 1970 (Carlton and Perloff, 1999).

Finally, recent research suggests that gains in aggregate shareholder value are attributable more to the improved operating efficiency of the combined firms than to increased market or pricing power (Akhigbe, Borde, and Whyte, 2000; Benerjee and Eckard, 1998; Fee and Thomas, 2004; Ghosh, 2004; Shahrur, 2005; Song and Walking, 2000). In an exhaustive study of 10,079 transactions between 1974 and 1992, Maksimovic and Phillips (2001) conclude that corporate transactions result in an overall improvement in efficiency by transferring assets from those who are not using them effectively to those who can.

Why Do Mergers and Acquisitions Often Fail to Meet Expectations?

Overpaying, Slow Integration, and Poor Business Strategy

There are many reasons given for the failure of takeovers to meet expectations. Table 1-7 identifies seven of the most commonly cited reasons ranked by the number of studies in which they are mentioned. The top three include overestimation of synergy or overpaying,

TABLE 1-7   Most Commonly Cited Reasons for M&A Failure[1]

Overestimating synergy/overpaying[2]	Harper and Schneider (2004)
	Boston Consulting Group (2003)
	Henry (2002)
	Bekier, Bogardus, and Oldham (2001)
	Chapman, Dempsey, Ramsdell, and Bell (1998)
	Agrawal and Jaffe (1999)
	Rau and Vermaelen (1998)
	Sirower (1997)
	Mercer Management Consulting (1998)
	Hillyer and Smolowitz (1996)
	Bradley, Desai, and Kim (1988)
	McKinsey & Company (1990)
Slow pace of integration	Adolph (2006)
	Carey and Ogden (2004)
	Mitchell (1998)
	Coopers & Lybrand (1996)
	Anslinger and Copeland (1996)
	Business Week (1995)
	McKinsey & Company (1990)
Poor strategy	Mercer Management Consulting (1998)
	Bogler (1996)
	McKinsey & Company (1990)
	Salter & Weinhold (1979)
Form of payment[3]	Sanford Bernstein & Company (2000)
	Loughran and Vijh (1997)
	Sirower (1997)
Poor postmerger communication	Mitchell (1998)
	Chakrabarti (1990)
Conflicting corporate cultures	Mercer Management Consulting (1998)
	Hillyer and Smolowitz (1996)
Weak core business	Anslinger and Copeland (1996)
	McKinsey & Company (1990)

Notes:
[1] Factors are ranked by the number of times they have been mentioned in studies.
[2] Some studies conclude that postmerger underperformance is a result of overpayment. However, it is difficult to determine if overpayment is a cause of merger failure or a result of other factors such as overestimating synergy, the slow pace of integration, a poor strategy, or simply the bidder overextrapolating past performance.
[3] These studies find that firms that pay for an acquisition using stock generally are overvalued and their performance subsequent to the merger is simply a reversion to their industry's average performance.

the slow pace of postmerger integration, and a flawed strategy. Conversely, acquiring firms that tend not to overpay, focus on rapid integration of the target firm, and have a well-thought-out strategy tend to meet or exceed expectations.

Things to Remember

There are many theories of why M&As take place. Operating and financial synergies are commonly used rationales for takeovers. Operating synergy consists of both economies of scale—the spreading of fixed costs over increasing production levels—and economies of scope—the use of a specific set of skills or an asset currently used to produce a specific product to produce related products. Financial synergy is the reduction in the cost of capital as a result of more stable cash flows, financial economies of scale, or a better matching of investment opportunities with available funds. Diversification is a strategy of buying firms outside of the company's primary line of business. There is little evidence that shareholders benefit from a company's efforts to diversify on their behalf, because investors can more efficiently spread their investments and risk among industries on their own. Recent studies suggest that corporate strategies emphasizing focus deliver more benefit to shareholders.

Strategic realignment suggests that firms use takeovers as a means of rapidly adjusting to changes in their external environment such as deregulation and technological innovation. Hubris is an explanation for takeovers that attributes a tendency to overpay to excessive optimism about the value of a deal's potential synergy or excessive confidence in management's ability to manage the acquisition. The undervaluation of assets theory states that takeovers occur when the market value of a target is less than the replacement value of its assets. The mismanagement or agency theory postulates that mergers take place when there are differences between what managers and shareholders want. Low share prices of such firms pressure managers to take action to either raise the share price or become the target of an acquirer.

Tax considerations are generally not the driving factor behind acquisitions. The value of tax benefits may represent a significant but relatively small percentage of the target's total value. A more important factor is the tax status of the deal. The seller may make a tax-free transaction a prerequisite for the deal to take place. The market power hypothesis suggests that firms merge to gain greater control over pricing, but the empirical support for this notion is extremely weak. According to the managerialism theory, managers acquire companies to increase the acquirer's size and their own remuneration. Finally, the misevaluation theory suggests that firms are periodically improperly valued making it possible for an acquirer to buy another firm at a discount from its true economic value.

Most acquisitions require a broad array of different skills to complete a corporate takeover. Few firms have all of the needed skills in-house. Investment bankers offer strategic and tactical advice, acquisition opportunities, screening of potential buyers and sellers, making contact with a buyer or seller, negotiation support, valuation, and deal structuring. Legal expertise often is required in such specialized areas as mergers and acquisitions, corporate, tax, employee benefits, real estate, antitrust, securities, and intellectual property law. Accountants provide advice on financial structuring, on tax issues, and on performing due diligence. Proxy solicitation companies often are hired to compile lists of stockholder mailing addresses. Public relations advisors ensure that both the target and acquiring companies present a compelling and consistent message to their respective constituencies. Hedge funds and private equity investors are playing an increasingly important role in affecting takeover strategies.

Although there is substantial evidence that mergers pay off for target company shareholders around the time the takeover is announced, shareholder wealth creation in the 3–5 years following closing is problematic. Abnormal returns to target shareholders around takeover tender offer announcement dates have risen from an average of 20% in the 1960s to the mid-to-high 30s in the 1970s and 1980s. Recent studies suggest that such returns in the early 1990s could have averaged more than 50%. Returns to shareholders around the date of merger announcements have remained remarkably stable at about 20% since the 1960s. In contrast, excess or abnormal returns to acquirer shareholders have declined from slightly positive to slightly negative levels.

Studies suggest that as many as 50% to almost 80% of M&As fail to outperform their peers or to earn their cost of capital. Not surprisingly, the performance for more experienced acquirers is much better. The most commonly cited reasons for failure is the overestimation of synergies and subsequent overpayment, the slow pace of postmerger integration, and the lack of a coherent business strategy. Empirical studies also suggest that M&As tend to pay off for society because on average the summation of bidder and target shareholder value tends to increase. More often than not, this increase seems to be related to improved operating efficiency of the combined firms rather than an increase in pricing power.

Despite the somewhat disappointing success rate for many mergers and acquisitions, the experience for M&As is very similar to alternative growth strategies that may be undertaken. Such strategies may include reinvesting excess cash flow in the firm, business alliances, licensing, franchising, and minority investments. Corporations, holding companies, ESOPs, and JVs represent alternative vehicles for engaging in various types of business combinations intended to enhance shareholder value.

Chapter Discussion Questions

1-1. Discuss why mergers and acquisitions occur.

1-2. What are the advantages and disadvantages of a holding company structure in making acquisitions?

1-3. How might a leveraged ESOP be used as an alternative to a divestiture, to take a company private, or as a defense against an unwanted takeover?

1-4. What is the role of the investment banker in the M&A process?

1-5. Describe how arbitrage typically takes place in a takeover of a publicly traded company.

1-6. In your judgment, why is potential synergy often overestimated by acquirers in evaluating a target company?

1-7. What are the major differences between the merger waves of the 1980s and 1990s?

1-8. In your opinion, what are the motivations for two mergers or acquisitions currently in the news?

1-9. What are the arguments for and against corporate diversification through acquisition? Which do you support and why?

1-10. What are the primary differences between operating and financial synergy? Give examples to illustrate your statements.

Answers to these Chapter Discussion Questions are available in the Online Instructor's Manual for instructors using this book.

Chapter Business Case

Case Study 1-1
Procter & Gamble Acquires Competitor

Procter & Gamble Company ("P&G") announced on January 28, 2005, an agreement to buy Gillette Company ("Gillette") in a share for share exchange valued at $55.6 billion. This represented an 18% premium over Gillette's preannouncement share price. P&G also announced a stock buyback of $18 to $22 billion, funded largely by issuing new debt. The combined companies will retain the P&G name and have annual 2005 revenue of more than $60 billion. Half of the new firm's product portfolio will consist of personal care, health care, and beauty products, with the remainder consisting of razors and blades and batteries. The deal is expected to dilute P&G's 2006 earnings by about 15 cents per share. To gain regulatory approval, the two firms may have to divest some overlapping operations such as deodorants and oral care.

P&G is often viewed as a premier marketing and product innovator. The firm prides itself on being able to transfer knowledge from one brand to another. Consequently, some of P&G's R&D and marketing skills in developing and promoting women's personal care products could be used to enhance and promote Gillette's women's razors. Gillette is best known for its ability to sell an inexpensive product (e.g., razors) and hook customers to a lifetime of refills (e.g., razor blades). Although Gillette is the number one and number two supplier in the lucrative toothbrush and men's deodorant markets, respectively, it has been much less successful in improving the profitability of its Duracell battery brand. Despite its number one market share position, it has been beset by intense price competition from Energizer and Rayovac Corp., which generally sell for less than Duracell batteries.

Suppliers such as P&G and Gillette have been under considerable pressure from the continuing consolidation in the retail industry due to the ongoing growth of Wal-Mart and industry mergers such as Sears and Kmart. About 17% of P&G's $51 billion in 2005 revenues and 13% of Gillette's $9 billion annual revenue come from sales to Wal-Mart. Moreover, the sales of both Gillette and P&G to Wal-Mart have grown much faster than sales to other retailers. The new company will have more negotiating leverage with retailers for shelf space and in determining selling prices, as well as with its own suppliers such as advertisers and media companies. The broad geographic presence of P&G will facilitate the marketing of such products as razors and batteries in huge developing markets such as China and India. Cumulative cost cutting is expected to reach $16 billion, including layoffs of about 4% of the new company's workforce of 140,000. Such cost cuts are likely to be realized by integrating Gillette's deodorant products into P&G's structure as quickly as possible. Other Gillette product lines such as the razor and battery businesses are expected to remain intact.

P&G's corporate culture is often described as conservative, with a "promote-from-within" philosophy. While Gillette's CEO will become vice chairman of the new company, it is unclear what will happen to other Gillette senior managers in view of the perception that P&G is laden with highly talented top management.

Case Study Discussion Questions

1. Is this deal a merger or a consolidation from a legal standpoint? Explain your answer.
2. Is this a horizontal or vertical merger? What is the significance of this distinction? Explain your answer.

3. What are the motives for the deal? Discuss the logic underlying each motive you identify.

4. Immediately following the announcement, P&G's share price dropped by 2% and Gillette's share price rose by 13%. Explain why this may have happened?

5. P&G announced that it would be buying back $18 to $22 billion of its stock over the 18 months following the closing of the transaction. Much of the cash required to repurchase these shares requires significant new borrowing by the new companies. Explain what P&G is trying to achieve in buying back its own stock. Explain how the incremental borrowing may help or hurt P&G in the long run?

6. Explain how actions required by antitrust regulators may hurt P&G's ability to realize anticipated synergy.

7. Identify some of the obstacles that P&G and Gillette are likely to face in integrating the two businesses. Be specific. How would you overcome these obstacles?

Answers to these Case Study Discussion Questions are available in the Online Instructor's Manual for instructors using this book.

Chapter Business Case

Case Study 1-2
Illustrating the Free Market Process of Creative Destruction: Consolidation in the Telecommunications Industry

Background: The Role of Technological Change and Deregulation
Economic historians, such as Joseph Schumpeter, described the free market process by which new technologies and deregulation create new industries, often at the expense of existing ones, as "creative destruction." As discussed elsewhere in this chapter, examples of this process abound.

In the short run, this process of "creative destruction" can have a highly disruptive impact on current employees whose skills are made obsolete, investors and business owners whose businesses are no longer competitive, and communities which are ravaged by increasing unemployment and diminished tax revenues. However, in the long run, the process tends to raise living standards by boosting worker productivity and increasing real income and leisure time, stimulating innovation, and expanding the range of products and services offered, often at a lower price, to consumers. Much of the change spurred by the process of "creative destruction" takes the form of mergers and acquisitions.

Consolidation in the Telecommunications Industry
The blur of consolidation in the U.S. telecommunications industry in recent years is a dramatic illustration of how free market forces can radically restructure the competitive landscape spurring improved efficiency and innovation. Verizon's and SBC's acquisition of MCI and AT&T, respectively, in 2005 and SBC's merger with BellSouth in 2006 pushed these two firms to the top of the U.S. telecommunications industry. In 2006, SBC was renamed AT&T to take advantage of the globally recognized brand name. In all, Verizon and SBC spent about $170 billion in acquisitions during this 2-year period.

By buying BellSouth, AT&T wins full control of the two firms' wireless joint venture, Cingular (later renamed AT&T Wireless), which is the biggest mobile operator in the

United States. Following this acquisition, one-third of the firm's combined revenues will come from cellular, up from 28% prior to the acquisition. Unlike Europe, where markets are saturated, there is still room for growth, with only 70% of the U.S. population having cell phones. This exposure to cell phones will help to offset the decline in the number of fixed lines as some subscribers go to wireless only or utilize Internet telephony.

Both Verizon and SBC bought their long-distance rivals to obtain access to corporate customers to whom they can sell discounted packages of telecom services. SBC and Verizon had the ability to buy AT&T and MCI's networks and business customers at a price that was less than the cost of obtaining these customers and replicating their networks. The combination of these companies created numerous opportunities for cost savings by eliminating redundant or overlapping functions.

A 2004 ruling by the FCC to roll back the requirement that local phone companies offer their networks at regulated rates to long-distance carriers has made it prohibitively expensive for MCI and AT&T to offer price-competitive local phone service. This factor increased the inevitability of their eventual sale, as the viability of basically standalone long-distance phone businesses became problematic.

The Emergence of Nontraditional Telecom Competitors

Many cable companies have been racing to add phone service to the TV and Internet packages they already offer. Phone companies are responding with offers of combined cell phone, Internet and landline phone service. The pace at which TV services are being offered will accelerate once the new fiber-optic networks are completed. Besides cable and telephone companies, consumers also have the option of such new technologies as Vonage, which has signed up more than 500,000 customers for its Internet calling services. Local phone companies are also expected to face increasing competition from wireless calling. In December 2004, Sprint and Nextel Communications merged to form a wireless giant in a $35 billion transaction. The new company is exploring innovative technologies such as Wi-Fi connections to compete directly with traditional phone lines.

Changes in technology mean that there will likely be many more companies competing against the phone companies than just cable companies. The integration of voice and data on digital networks and the arrival of Internet calling have attracted many new competitors for phone companies. These include Microsoft, Sony, Time Warner's AOL subsidiary, Google, and Earthlink.

Implications of Telecom Industry Consolidation for Businesses and Consumers

Some analysts say that fewer providers will leave business customers with less leverage in their negotiations with the telecommunications companies. While others believe that pricing for consumers is going to continue to be very competitive. In the business market, cable is not an effective alternative to phone service since the nation's cable infrastructure was built to offer television service to homes. Consequently, existing cable networks do not reach all commercial areas. Cable companies are often unwilling to invest the capital required, because it is unclear if they will be able to acquire the customer density to achieve the financial returns they require. In the consumer market, telecom companies are rushing to sell consumers bundles of services including local and long-distance service, cellular service, and Internet access for one monthly fee. These competitive forces are likely to prevent higher prices for local phone service, which is already eroding at a rapid rate due to emerging technologies like Internet calling.

Concluding Comments

The free market forces of "creative destruction" have resulted in a dramatic transformation of the competitive landscape in the U.S. telecommunications industry. Historically, the U.S. telecom industry was clearly defined, with the former monopolist AT&T providing the bulk of local and long-distance services in the United States. However, "Ma Bell" was required by the government to spin-off its local telephone operating companies in the mid-1980s in an attempt to stimulate competition for both local and long-distance services. The telecommunications industry changed from a single provider of both local and long-distance services to many aggressive competitors.

In the wake of far reaching deregulation in the 1990s, various competitors began to combine, increasing industry concentration. However, incursions by the cable industry into the traditional market for telephone services and the proliferation of new technologies such as Wi Fi and Internet telephony changed the competitive landscape once again. Today, software, entertainment, media, and consumer electronics firms now compete with the more traditional phone companies. When adjusted for inflation, prices paid by consumers and businesses are a fraction of what they were a generation ago. While the effects of these changes may impact the business and consumer telecom markets differently, the unmistakable imprint of the free market's "creative destruction" process is highly visible.

Case Study Discussion Questions

1. How has technological and regulatory change affected competition in the telecommunications industry?
2. How has technological and regulatory change affected the rate of innovation and customer choice in the telecom industry?
3. The process of "creative destruction" has stimulated substantial consolidation in the U.S. telecom industry. Is bigger always better? Why?/Why not? (Hint: Consider the impact on a firm's operating efficiency, speed of decision making, creativity, ability to affect product and service pricing, etc.)
4. Comment on the following statement: To determine the extent to which industry consolidation is likely to lead to higher, lower, or unchanged product selling prices, it is necessary to consider current competitors, potential competitors, the availability of substitutes, and customer pricing sensitivity.
5. What factors motivated Verizon and SBC to acquire MCI and AT& T, respectively? Discuss these in terms of the motives for mergers and acquisitions described in Chapter 1 of this textbook.

Answers to these Case Study Discussion Questions are available in the Online Instructor's Manual for instructors using this book.

References

ACNielsen, "Retailer Support Is Essential for New Product Success," *Bases*, http://www.bases.com/news/news112002.html.

Adolph, Gerald, "Mergers: Back to Happily Ever After," *Strategy and Business*, Booz Allen Hamilton, New York, February 16, 2006.

Agrawal, Anup, and Jeffrey F. Jaffe, "The PostMerger Performance Puzzle," Working Paper Series, Social Science Research Network, December 1999.

Agrawal, Anup, Jeffrey F. Jaffe, and Gershon N. Mandelker, "The PostMerger Performance of Acquiring Firms: A Reexamination of an Anomaly," *Journal of Finance*, Vol. 47, September 1992, pp. 1605–1621.

Akhigbe, Aigbe, Stephen F. Borde, and Anne Marie Whyte, "The Source of Gains to Targets and Their Industry Rivals: Evidence Based on Terminated Merger Proposals," *Financial Management*, Vol. 29, Winter 2000, pp. 101–118.

Andrade, Gregor, Mark L. Mitchell, and Erik Stafford, "New Evidence and Perspectives on Mergers," *Journal of Economic Perspectives*, Vol. 15, 2001, pp. 103–120.

Ang, James S., and Yingmei Cheng, "Direct Evidence on the Market-Driven Acquisition Theory," *Journal of Financial Research*, Vol. 29, 2006, pp. 199–216.

Anslinger, P., and T. Copeland, "Growth Through Acquisitions: A Fresh Look," *Harvard Business Review*, Vol. 79, January/February, 1996, pp. 101–107.

Ascioglu, N. Asli, Thomas H. McInish, and Robert A. Wood, "Merger Announcements and Trading," *Journal of Financial Research*, Vol. 25, No. 2, Summer 2002, pp. 263–278.

Asquith, Paul, "Merger Bids and Stock Returns," *Journal of Financial Economics*, Vol. 11, 1983, pp. 51–83.

Asquith, Paul, and E. Han Kim, "The Impact of Merger Bids on the Participating Firms' Security Holders," *Journal of Finance*, Vol. 37, pp. 1209–1228.

Ayers, Benjamin C., Craig E. Lefanowicz, and John R. Robinson, "Shareholder Taxes and Acquisition Premiums: The Effects of Capital Gains Taxation," *Journal of Finance*, Vol. 68, December 2003, pp. 2783–2804.

Barber, Brad M., and John D. Lyon, "Detecting Long-Run Abnormal Stock Returns: The Empirical Power and Specification of Test Statistics," *Journal of Financial Economics*, Vol. 43, 1997, pp. 341–372.

Bekier, Matthias M., Anna J. Bogardus, and Tim Oldham, "Why Mergers Fail," *McKinsey Quarterly*, 4, 2001, p. 3.

Benerjee, Ajeyo, and E. Woodrow Eckard, "Are Mega-Mergers Anti-Competitive? Evidence from the First Great Merger Wave," *Rand Journal of Economics*, Vol. 29, Winter 1998, pp. 803–827.

Berger, Phillip G., and Eli Ofek, "Diversification's Effect on Firm Value," *Journal of Financial Economics*, Vol. 37, January 1995, pp. 39–65.

Berger, Phillip G., and Eli Ofek, "Bustup Takeovers of Value Destroying Diversified Firms," *Journal of Finance,* Vol. 51, September 1996, pp. 1175–1200.

Best, Ronald, and Charles W. Hodges, "Does Information Asymmetry Explain the Diversification Discount?," *Journal of Financial Research*, Vol. 27, Summer 2004, pp. 235–249.

Bhagat, Sanfai, and David Hirshleifer, "Do Takeovers Create Value?: An Intervention Approach," University of Michigan Business School, Working Paper 9505-03-R, http://eres.bus.umich.edu/docs/workpap/wp9505-03-R.pdf, December 1996, p. 35.

Bhagat, Sanfai, Ming Dong, David Hirshleifer, and Robert Noah, "Do Takeovers Create Value? New Methods and Evidence," *Journal of Financial Economics*, Vol. 76, 2005, pp. 3–60.

Billett, Matthew T., Tao-Hsien Dolly King, and David C. Mauer, "Bondholder Wealth Effects in Mergers and Acquisitions: New Evidence from the 1980s and 1990s," *Journal of Finance*, February 2004, pp. 107–135.

Black, Ervin L., Thomas A. Carnes, and Tomas Jandik, "The Long-Term Success of Cross-Border Mergers and Acquisitions," Social Science Research Network Electronic Paper Collection, December 2000, http://papers.ssrn.com/5013/delivery.cfn/ssrn_id272782_010705100.pdf.

Bloomberg.com, "Goldman Loses Cachet in M&A as Companies Seek Multiple Advisors," August 14, 2006, www.bloomberg.com/apps/news?pid=2067000&refer=top_world_news& sid=aKM.

Bogler, Daniel, "Post-Takeover Stress Disorder," Summary of a PA Consulting Study in *Financial Times*, May 22, 1996, p. 11.

Boone, Audra L., and J. Harold Mulherin, "How Are Firms Sold?," *Journal of Finance*, December 2006.

Boston Consulting Group, "Weak Economy Is Ideal Time for Mergers and Acquisitions," July 10, 2003, http://www.srimedia.com/artman/ppublish/printer_657.shtml.

Bradley, Michael, Anand Desai, and E. Han Kim, "Synergistic Gains from Corporate Acquisitions and Their Division Between the Stockholders of Target and Acquiring Firms," *Journal of Financial Economics*, Vol. 21, 1988, p. 3.

Bradley, Michael, and Gregg Jarrell, "Comment on Mergers and Acquisitions," Chapter 15 in John Coffee, Jr., Louis Lowenstein, and Susan Rose-Ackerman, eds., *Knights, Raiders, and Targets*, Oxford University Press, Oxford, 1988, pp. 253–259.

Brealey, R., and S. Myers, *Principles of Corporate Finance*, McGraw-Hill, New York, 2003.

Campa, Jose, and Kedia Simi, "Explaining the Diversification Discount," *Journal of Finance*, Vol. 57, December 2002, pp. 135–160.

Carey, Dennis C., and Dayton Ogden, *The Human Side of M&A*, Oxford University Press, Oxford, 2004, p. 164.

Carline, N., S. Linn, and P. Yadav, "The Impact of Firm-Specific and Deal-Specific Factors on the Real Gains in Corporate Mergers and Acquisitions," University of Oklahoma Working Paper, 2002.

Carlton, Dennis, and Jeffrey Perloff, *Modern Industrial Organization*, 3rd Ed., Addison Wesley Longmans, New York, 1999, p. 27.

Chakrabarti, Alok K., "Organizational Factors in Post-Acquisition Performance," *IEEE Transactions on Engineering Management*, Vol. 37, November 1990, p. 135.

Chapman, Timothy L., Jack J. Dempsey, Glenn Ramsdell, and Trudy J. Bell, "Purchasing's Big Moment—After a Merger," *The McKinsey Quarterly*, 1, 1998, pp. 56–65.

Comment, Robert, and Gregg A. Jarrell, "Corporate Focus and Stock Returns," *Journal of Financial Economics*, Vol. 37, 1993, pp. 67–87.

Coopers & Lybrand, "Most Acquisitions Fail, C&L Study Says," *Mergers & Acquisitions*, Report 7, Vol. 47, November 1996, p. 2.

Cotter, James F., Anil Shivdasani, and Marc Zenner, "Do Independent Directors Enhance Target Shareholder Wealth during Tender Offers?," *Journal of Financial Economics*, Vol. 43, February 1997, pp. 237–266.

Daley, Lane, Vikas Mehrotra, and Ranjini Sivakumar, "Corporate Focus and Value Creation: Evidence from Spin-Offs," *Journal of Financial Economics*, Vol. 45, 1996, pp. 257–281.

Daniel, Kent D., David Hirshleifer, and Avanidhar Subrahmanyam, "Investor Psychology and Security Market Under and Over-Reactions," *Journal of Finance*, Vol. 53, 1998, pp. 1839–1886.

DeLong, G., "Does Long-Term Performance of Mergers Match Market Expectations?," *Financial Management*, Summer 2003, pp. 5–25.

Deogun, Nikhil, and Steven Lipin, "Big Mergers in '90s Prove Disappointing to Shareholders," Salomon Smith Barney study quoted in *The Wall Street Journal*, October 30, 2000, p. C12.

Dennis, Debra K., and John J. McConnell, "Corporate Mergers and Security Returns," *Journal of Financial Economics*, Vol. 16, 1986, pp. 143–187.

Dittmar, Amy, and Anil Shivdasani, "Divestitures and Divisional Investment Policies," *Journal of Finance*, December 2003, pp. 36–62.

Dong, Ming, David Hirshleifer, Scott Richardson, and Siew Hong Teoh, "Does Investor Misvaluation Drive the Takeover Market?," *Journal of Finance*, Vol. 61, April 2006, pp. 725–762.

Doukas, John, and Nickolaso G. Travlos, "The Effect of Corporate Multinationalism on Shareholders' Wealth: Evidence from International Acquisitions," *Journal of Finance*, Vol. 43, December 1988, pp. 1161–1175.

Dukes, William, Cheryl Frohlich, and Christopher Ma, "Risk Arbitrage in Tender Offers: Handsome Rewards—and Not for Insiders Only," *Journal of Portfolio Management*, Vol. 18, 1992, pp. 47–55.

Dyck, Alexander, and Luigi Zingales, "Control Premiums and the Effectiveness of Corporate Governance Systems," *Journal of Applied Finance*, Vol. 16, Spring/Summer, 2004, pp. 51–72.

Eger, Carol E., "An Empirical Test of the Redistribution Effect in Pure Exchange Mergers," *Journal of Financial and Quantitative Analysis*, Vol. 4, 1983, pp. 547–542.

Ellis, Caroline, "Briefings from the Editors," *Harvard Business Review*, Vol. 74 (1), July/August 1996, p. 8.

Eun, C., R. Kolodny, and C. Scheraga, "Cross-Border Acquisitions and Shareholder Wealth: Tests of the Synergy and Internationalization Hypothesis," *Journal of Banking and Finance*, 20, 1996, pp. 1559–1582.

Fama, E. F., and M. C. Jensen, "Separation of Ownership and Control," *Journal of Law and Economics*, 26, 1983, pp. 301–325.

Fama, Eugene F., "Market Efficiency, Long-Term Returns, and Behavioral Finance," *Journal of Financial Economics*, 47, 1998, pp. 427–465.

Fauver, Larry, Joel Houston, and Andres Narango, "Capital Market Development, International Integration, and the Value of Corporate Diversification: A Cross-Country Analysis," *Journal of Financial and Quantitative Analysis*, Vol. 38, March 2003, pp. 138–155.

Fee, C. Edward, and Shawn Thomas, "Sources of Gains in Horizontal Mergers: Evidence from Customer, Supplier, and Rival Firms," *Journal of Financial Economics*, Vol. 74, December 2004, pp. 423–460.

Franks, Julian R., Robert S. Harris, and Sheridan Titman, "The Post-Merger Share-Price Performance of Acquiring Firms," *Journal of Financial Economics*, Vol. 29, 1991, pp. 81–96.

Frick, Kevin A., and Alberto Torres, "Learning from High Tech Deals," *McKinsey Quarterly*, 1, 2002, p. 2.

Fuller, Kathleen, Jeffrey Netter, and Mike Stegemoller, "What Do Returns to Acquiring Firms Tell Us? Evidence from Firms That Make Many Acquisitions," *Journal of Finance*, August 2002, pp. 1763–1793.

Gertner, Robert, Eric Powers, and David Scharfstein, "Learning about Internal Capital Markets from Corporate Spin-Offs," *Journal of Finance*, Vol. 57, 2002, pp. 2479–2506.

Ghosh, A., "Does Operating Performance Really Improve Following Corporate Acquisitions?," *Journal of Corporate Finance*, Vol. 7, 2001, pp. 151–178.

Ghosh, Aloke, "Increasing Market Share as a Rationale for Corporate Acquisitions," *Journal of Business, Finance, and Accounting*, Vol. 31, March 2004, pp. 78–91.

Ghosh, Aloke, and Chi-Wen Jevons Lee, "Abnormal Returns and Expected Managerial Performance of Target Firms," *Financial Management*, Vol. 29, Spring 2000, pp. 40–52.

Graham, J., M. Lemmon, and J. Wolf, "Does Diversification Destroy Firm Value?," *Journal of Finance*, Vol. 57, 2002, pp. 695–720.

Grinblatt, Mark, and Sheridan Titman, *Financial Markets and Corporate Strategy*, 2nd Ed., McGraw-Hill, New York, 2002.

Gugler, Klaus, Dennis C. Mueller, B. Burcin Yurtoglu, and Christine Zulehner, "The Effects of Mergers: An International Comparison," *International Journal of Industrial Organization*, Vol. 21, Issue 5, May 2003, pp. 625–653.

Harding, David, and Sam Rovit, *Mastering the Merger: Four Critical Decisions That Make or Break the Deal*, Harvard Business School Press, Cambridge, MA, 2004.

Harford, Jarrad, "What Drives Merger Waves," *Journal of Financial Economics*, Vol. 77, September 2005, pp. 529–560.

Harper, Neil W., and Antoon Schneider, "Where Mergers Go Wrong," *The McKinsey Quarterly*, Number 2, 2004.

Harris, Robert S., and David Ravenscraft, "The Role of Acquisitions in Foreign Direct Investment: Evidence from the U.S. Stock Market," *Journal of Finance*, Vol. 46, 1991, pp. 825–844.

Healy, Paul M., Krishna G. Palepu, and Richard S. Ruback, "Does Corporate Performance Improve After Mergers?," *Journal of Financial Economics*, 31, 1992, pp. 135–175.

Henry, David, "Mergers: Why Most Big Deals Don't Pay Off," *BusinessWeek*, October 14, 2002, pp. 60–64.

Henry, David, "A Fair Deal—But for Whom," *BusinessWeek*, November 24, 2003, pp. 108–109.

Heron, R., and E. Lie, "Operating Performance and the Method of Payment in Takeovers," *Journal of Financial and Quantitative Analysis*, 2002, pp. 137–155.

Hillyer, Clayton, and Ira Smolowitz, "Why Do Mergers Fail to Achieve Synergy?" *Director's Monthly*, January 1996, p. 13.

Holmstrom, Bengt R., and Steven N. Kaplan, "Corporate Governance and Merger Activity in the U.S.: Making Sense of the 1980s and 1990s," MIT Department of Economics Working Paper, No. 01-11, 2001.

Houston, J., C. James, and M. Ryngaert, "Where Do Merger Gains Come From?," *Journal of Financial Economics*, May/June 2001, pp. 285–331.

Hyland, David, "Why Firms Diversify: An Empirical Examination," Working Paper, University of Texas, Arlington, 2001.

Jarrell, G., and A. Poulsen, "The Returns to Acquiring Firms in Tender Offers: Evidence from Three Decades," *Financial Management*, Vol. 18, 1989, pp. 12–19.

Jarrell, Gregg A., James A. Brickley, and Jeffry M. Netter, "The Market for Corporate Control: The Empirical Evidence Since 1980," *Journal of Economic Perspectives*, Vol. 2, 1988, pp. 49–68.

Jensen, M. C., "The Modern Industrial Revolution: Exit, and the Failure of Internal Control Systems," *Journal of Finance*, Vol. 48, 1993, pp. 831–880.

Jensen, Michael C., "Agency Costs of Overvalued Equity," *Financial Management*, Vol. 34, Spring 2005, pp. 5–19.

Jensen, Michael C., and Robert S. Ruback, "The Market for Corporate Control: The Scientific Evidence," *Journal of Financial Economics*, 11, 1983, pp. 5–53.

Jindra, Jan, and Ralph Walkling, "Arbitrage Spreads and the Market Pricing of Proposed Acquisitions," Working Paper, Ohio State University, Columbus, 1999.

Kaplan, Steven N., and Antoinette Schoar, "Returns, Persistence and Capital Flows," *Journal of Finance*, Vol. 60, August 2005, pp. 1791–1823.

Karolyi, G. Andrew, and John Shannon, "Where's the Risk in Risk Arbitrage?," Working Paper, Richard Ivey School of Business, The University of Western Ontario, London, Ontario, 1998.

Kim, E. Han, and John J. McConnell, "Corporate Mergers and the Co-Insurance of Corporate Debt," *Journal of Finance*, Vol. 32, 1977, pp. 349–365.

Klaus, Gugler, Dennis C. Mueller, B. Burein Yurtoglu, and Chrisine Zulehner, "The Effects of Mergers: An International Comparison," *International Journal of Industrial Organization*, Vol. 21, Issue 5, May 2003, pp. 625–653.

Klein, Karen E., "Urge to Merge? Take Care to Beware," *BusinessWeek*, July 1, 2004, p. 68.

KPMG, "When Hedge Funds Start to Look Like Private Equity Firms," *Global M&A Spotlight*, Spring 2006.

KPMG, "Mergers and Acquisitions," *2006 M&A Outlook Survey*, April 11, 2006.

Kuipers, D., D. Miller, and A. Pate, "The Legal Environment and Corporate Valuation: Evidence from Cross-Border Mergers." Univ. Texas Tech Working Paper, Lubbock, January 2003.

Lajoux, Alexandra Reed, *The Art of M&A Integration*, McGraw-Hill, New York 1998, p. 8.

Lamont, Owen, and Christopher Polk, "The Diversification Discount: Cash Flows versus Returns," *Journal of Finance*, Vol. 56, 1997, 1693–1721.

Lang, L. R. M. Stulz, and R. A. Walkling, "Managerial Performance, Tobin's Q, and the Gains from Successful Tender Offers," *Journal of Financial Economics*, Vol. 24, 1989, pp. 137–154.

Leeth, John D., and J. Rody Borg, "The Impact of Takeovers on Shareholders' Wealth During the 1920's Merger Wave," *Journal of Financial and Quantitative Analysis*, Vol. 35, June 2000, pp. 29–38.

Linn, Scott C., and Jeannette A. Switzer, "Are Cash Acquisitions Associated with Better Post Combination Operating Performance Than Stock Acquisitions," *Journal of Banking and Finance*, Vol. 25, June 2001, pp. 1113–1138.

Lins, Karl, and Henri Servaes, "International Evidence on the Value of Corporate Diversification," *Journal of Finance*, Vol. 54, 1999, pp. 2215–2239.

Loughran, Tim, and Anand M. Vijh, "Do Long-Term Shareholders Benefit from Corporate Acquisitions?," *Journal of Finance*, Vol. 22, April 1997, pp. 321–340.

Luo, Yuanzhi, "Do Insiders Learn from Outsiders? Evidence from Mergers and Acquisitions," *Journal of Finance*, Vol. 60, August 2005, pp. 1951–1982.

Lyon, John D., Brad M. Barber, and Chih-Ling Tsai, "Improved Methods for Tests of Long-Run Abnormal Stock Returns," *Journal of Finance*, Vol. 54, 1999, pp. 165–201.

McKinsey & Company, "Creating Shareholder Value through Merger and/or Acquisition: A McKinsey & Company Perspective," an internal 1987 memorandum cited in Copeland, Tom, Tim Koller, and Jack Murrin, *Valuation: Measuring and Managing the Value of Companies*, John Wiley & Sons, New York, 1990, p. 321.

Maier, Angela, and Elisabeth Atzler, "Hedge Funds Seek Private Equity," *Financial Times Deutschland*, May 10, 2006.

Maksimovic, Vojislav, and Gordon M. Phillips, "The Market for Corporate Assets: Who Engages in Mergers and Asset Sales and Are There Efficiency Gains," *Journal of Finance*, December 2001, pp. 332–355.

Mangenheim, Ellen B., and Dennis C. Mueller, "Are Acquiring Firm Shareholders Better Off After an Acquisition," Chapter 11 in John Coffee, Jr., Louis Lowenstein, and Susan Rose-Ackerman, eds., *Knight, Raiders, and Targets*, Oxford University Press, Oxford, 1988, pp. 171–193.

Maquierira, Carlos P., William L. Megginson, and Lance A. Nail, "Wealth Creation versus Wealth Redistributions in Pure Stock-for-Stock Mergers," *Journal of Financial Economics*, Vol. 48, 1998, pp. 3–33.

Megginson, William L., Angela Morgan, and Lance Nail, "The Determinants of Positive Long-term Performance in Strategic Mergers: Corporate Focus and Cash," *Journal of Banking and Finance*, 2003.

Mehran, Hamid, and Stavros Peristiani, "Financial Visibility and the Decision to Go Private," Working Paper, Federal Reserve Bank of New York, April 2006.

Melicher, Ronald W., and Edgar A. Norton, *Finance: Introduction to Institutions, Investments, and Management*, Cincinnati: Southwestern College Publishing, 1999, p. 320.

Mercer Management Consulting, 1995 and 1997 surveys cited in Alexandra Reed Lajoux, *The Art of Integration*, McGraw-Hill, New York, 1998, pp. 19–21.

Mergerstat LP, "Dealmakers Hope for Better Days Ahead in 2002," Press Release, January 2, 2002, www.mergerstat.com.

Mitchell, David, survey conducted by Economist Intelligence Unit, cited in Alexandra Reed Lajoux, *The Art of M&A Integration*, McGraw-Hill, New York, 1998, p. 19.

Mitchell, M. L., and Mulherin, J. H., "The Impact of Industry Shocks on Takeover and Restructuring Activity," *Journal of Financial Economics*, 41, 1996, pp. 193–229.

Mitchell, Mark L., and Todd C. Pulvino, "Characteristics of Risk and Return in Arbitrage," *Journal of Finance*, Vol. 56, December 2001, pp. 2135–2175.

Mitchell, Mark, Todd Pulvino, and Erik Stafford, "Price Pressure around Mergers," *Journal of Finance*, February 2004, pp. 31–63.

Moeller, Sara B., Frederik P. Schlingemann, and Rene M. Stulz, "Wealth Destruction on a Massive Scale? A Study of the Acquiring Firm Returns in the Recent Merger Wave," *Journal of Finance*, Vol. 60, April 2005, pp. 757–782.

Morck, Randall, Andrei Shleifer, and Robert W. Vishny, "Do Managerial Objectives Drive Bad Acquisitions?" *Journal of Finance*, Vol. 45, March 1990, pp. 31–48.

Mueller, Dennis, "Mergers and Market Share," *Review of Economics and Statistics*, Vol. 47, 1985, pp. 259–267.

Mulherin, J. Harold, and Audra L. Boone, "Comparing Acquisitions and Divestitures," Working Paper Series, Social Sciences Research Network, April 19, 2000, p. 17.

Porter, Michael, *Competitive Advantage*, The Free Press, New York, 1985.

Rau, P. Raghavendra, and Theo Vermaelen, "Glamour, Value, and the Post-Acquisition Performance of Acquiring Firms," *Journal of Financial Economics*, Vol. 49, August, 1998, pp. 223–253.

Ravenscraft, David, and Frederick Scherer, "Life after Takeovers," *Journal of Industrial Economics*, Vol. 36, 1987, pp. 147–156.

Ravenscraft, David, and Frederick Scherer, "Mergers and Managerial Performance," in John Coffee, Louis Lowenstein, and Susan Rose Ackerman, eds., *Knights and Targets*, Oxford University Press, New York, 1988, pp. 194 –210.

Rhodes-Kropf, M., and S. Viswanathan, "Market Valuation and Merger Waves," *Journal of Finance*, Vol. 59, 2004.

Roll, Richard, "The Hubris Hypothesis of Corporate Takeovers," *Journal of Business*, Vol. 59, April 1986, pp. 197–216.

Rossi, Stefano, and Paolo F. Volpin, "Cross-Country Determinants of Mergers and Acquisitions," ECGI–Finance Working Paper No. 25/2003, AFA 2004 San Diego Meetings, September 2004.

Salter, Malcolm S., and Wolf A. Weinhold, *Diversification Through Acquisition: Strategies for Creating Economic Value*, The Free Press, New York, 1979, pp. 30–31.

Sanford Bernstein & Company, "Net Equation," *BusinessWeek*, January 31, 2000, pp. 39–41.

Scharfstein, David, and Jeremy Stein, "The Dark Side of Internal Capital Markets: Divisional Rent-Seeking and Inefficient Investment," *Journal of Finance*, Vol. 55, 2000, pp. 2537–2564.

Schwert, William, "Markup Pricing in Mergers and Acquisitions," *Journal of Financial Economics*, Vol. 41, 1996, pp. 153–192.

Seth, Anju, Kean P. Song, and Richard Petit, "Synergy, Managerialism or Hubris: An Empirical Examination of Motives for Foreign Acquisitions of U.S. Firms," *Journal of International Business Studies*, Vol. 31, 2000, pp. 387–405.

Shahrur, Husan, "Industry Structure and Horizontal Takeovers: Analysis of Wealth Effects on Rivals, Suppliers, and Corporate Customers," *Journal of Financial Economics*, Vol. 76, April 2005, pp. 61–98.

Shin, Hyun-Han, and Rene Stulz, "Are Internal Capital Markets Efficient?," *Quarterly Journal of Economics*, Vol. 113, 1998, pp. 531–552.

Shleifer, Andrei, and Robert W. Vishny, "Stock Market Driven Acquisitions," *Journal of Financial Economics*, Vol. 70, 2003, pp. 295–311.

Sirower, Mark, *The Synergy Trap*, New York: The Free Press, 1997.

Song, H. H., and R. A. Walking, "Abnormal Returns to Rivals of Acquisitions Targets: A Test of the Acquisition Probability Hypothesis," *Journal of Financial Economics*, Vol. 55, 2000, pp. 439–457.

Stefanini, Filippo, *Investment Strategies of Hedge Funds*, John Wiley & Sons, New York, 2006.

Sullivan, M. J., M. R. H. Jensen, and C. D. Hudson, "The Role of Medium of Exchange in Merger Offers: Examination of Terminated Merger Proposals," *Financial Management*, Vol. 23, 1994, pp. 51–62.

Sweeney, Paul, "Who Says It's A Fair Deal?," *Journal of Accountancy*, Vol. 188, August 6, 1999, p. 6.

The Deal, February 6–10, 2006.

The Economist, "In the Shadows of Debt," September 23, 2006, pp. 80–83.

Villalonga, Belen, "Diversification Discount or Premium? New Evidence from the Business Information Tracking Series," *Journal of Finance*, Vol. 59, April 2004, pp. 479–506.

Wulf, J., "Do CEOs in Mergers Trade Power for Premium?: Evidence from Mergers of Equals," Working Paper, Wharton School, University of Pennsylvania, Philadelphia, June 2001.

You, Victor, Richard Caves, Michael Smith, and James Henry, "Mergers and Bidders' Wealth: Managerial and Strategic Factors," Chapter 9 in Lacy Glenn Thomas III, ed., *The Economics of Strategic Planning*, Lexington Books, Lexington, MA, 1986, pp. 201–220.

Zellner, Wendy, "This Big Oil Deal Shouldn't Hurt a Bit," *BusinessWeek*, May 9, 2005, p. 42.

CHAPTER ◆ 2

Regulatory Considerations

Character is doing the right thing when no one is looking.

—J. C. Watts

Inside M&A: Justice Department Approves Maytag–Whirlpool Combination Despite Resulting Increase in Concentration

When announced in late 2005, many analysts believed that the $1.7 billion transaction would face heated regulatory opposition. The proposed bid was approved despite the combined firms' dominant market share of the U.S. major appliance market. The combined companies would control an estimated 72% of the washer market, 81% of the gas dryer market, 74% of the electric dryers, and 31% of refrigerators. Analysts believed that the combined firms would be required to divest certain Maytag product lines to receive approval. Recognizing the potential difficulty in getting regulatory approval, the Whirlpool–Maytag contract allowed for Whirlpool to withdraw from the contract by paying a "reverse break-up" fee of $120 million to Maytag. Break-up fees are normally paid by targets to acquirers if they choose to withdraw from the contract.

U.S. regulators tended to view the market as global in nature. When the appliance market is defined in a global sense, the combined firms' share drops to about one-fourth of the previously mentioned levels. The number and diversity of foreign manufacturers offered a wide array of alternatives for consumers. Moreover, there are few barriers to entry for these manufacturers wishing to do business in the United States. Many of Whirlpool's independent retail outlets wrote letters supporting the proposal to acquire Maytag as a means of sustaining financially weakened companies. Regulators also viewed the preservation of jobs as an important consideration in its favorable ruling.

Chapter Overview

Regulations that affect merger and acquisition (M&A) activity exist at all levels of government. Regulatory considerations can be classified as either general or industry specific. General considerations are those that affect all firms, whereas industry-specific considerations affect only certain types of transactions in particular industries. General considerations include federal security, antitrust, environmental, racketeering, and employee benefits laws. Examples of industries that are subject to substantial regulation include public utilities, insurance, banking, broadcasting, telecommunications, defense contracting, and transportation. M&A activities in these industries may require government approvals to transfer government-granted licenses, permits, and franchises. State antitakeover statutes place limitations on how and when a hostile takeover may be implemented. Moreover, approval may have to be received to make deals in certain industries at both the state and federal levels. Cross-border transactions may be even more complicated, because it may be necessary to get approval from regulatory authorities in all countries in which the acquirer and target companies do business.

This chapter will focus on the key elements of selected federal and state regulations and their implications for M&As. Considerable time is devoted to discussing the prenotification and disclosure requirements of current legislation and how decisions are made within the key securities law and antitrust enforcement agencies. This chapter provides only an overview of the labyrinth of environmental, labor, and benefit laws affecting M&As. Because a detailed discussion is well beyond the scope of this book, the intent of this overview is simply to make the reader aware of the challenges of complying with all of the applicable laws. See Table 2-1 for a summary of applicable legislation. A review of this chapter is available on the CD-ROM accompanying this book.

Federal Securities Laws

Whenever either the acquiring or the target company is publicly traded, the firms are subject to the substantial reporting requirements of the current federal securities laws. Passed in the early 1930s, these laws were a direct result of the loss of confidence in the securities markets following the crash of the stock market in 1929. See the Securities and Exchange Commission Web site (www.sec.gov), Loss and Seligman (1995), and Gilson and Black (1995) for a comprehensive discussion of federal securities laws.

Securities Act of 1933

Originally administered by the FTC, the Securities Act of 1933 requires that all securities offered to the public must be registered with the government. Registration requires, but does not guarantee, that the facts represented in the registration statement and prospectus are accurate. However, the law makes providing inaccurate or misleading statements in the sale of securities to the public punishable with a fine, imprisonment, or both. The registration process requires the description of the company's properties and business, a description of the securities, information about management, and financial statements certified by public accountants. Section 8 of the law permits the registration statement to automatically become effective 20 days after it is filed with the SEC. However, the SEC may delay or stop the process by requesting additional information.

TABLE 2-1 Laws Affecting M&A

Law	Intent
Federal Securities Laws	
Securities Act (1933)	Prevents the public offering of securities without a registration statement; defines minimum data requirements and noncompliance penalties
Securities Exchange Act (1934)	Established the Securities and Exchange Commission (SEC) to regulate securities trading. Empowers Securities and Exchange Commission (SEC) to revoke registration of a security if issuer is in violation of any provision of the 1934 Act
Section 13	Defines content and frequency of, as well as events triggering, SEC filings
Section 14	Defines disclosure requirements for proxy solicitation
Section 16(a)	Defines what insider trading is and who is an insider
Section 16(b)	Defines investor rights with respect to insider trading
Williams Act (1968)	Regulates tender offers
Section 13D	Defines disclosure requirements
Sarbanes–Oxley Act (2002)	Initiates extensive reform of regulations governing financial disclosure, governance, auditing standards, analyst reports, and insider trading
Federal Antitrust Laws	
Sherman Act (1890)	Made "restraint of trade" illegal. Establishes criminal penalties for behaviors that unreasonably limit competition
Section 1	Makes mergers creating monopolies or "unreasonable" market control illegal
Section 2	Applies to firms already dominant in their served markets to prevent them from "unfairly" restraining trade
Clayton Act (1914)	Outlawed certain practices not prohibited by the Sherman Act such as price discrimination, exclusive contracts, and tie-in contracts and created civil penalties for illegally restraining trade Also established law governing mergers.
Celler–Kefauver Act of 1950	Amended Clayton Act to cover asset as well as stock purchases
Federal Trade Commission Act (1914)	Established a federal antitrust enforcement agency; made it illegal to engage in deceptive business practices
Hart–Scott–Rodino Antitrust Improvement Act (1976)	Requires waiting period before a transaction can be completed and sets regulatory data submission requirements
Title I	Defines what must be filed
Title II	Defines who must file and when
Title III	Enables state attorneys general to file triple damage suits on behalf of injured parties
Other Legislation Affecting M&As	
State Antitakeover Laws	Define conditions under which a change in corporate ownership can take place; may differ by state
State Antitrust Laws	Similar to federal antitrust laws; states may sue to block mergers, even if the mergers are not challenged by federal regulators

continued

TABLE 2-1   continued

Law	Intent
Exon–Florio Amendment to the Defense Protection Act of 1950	Establishes authority of the Committee on Foreign Investment in the United States (CFIUS) to review the impact of foreign direct investment (including M&As) on national security
Industry Specific Regulations	Banking, communications, railroads, defense, insurance, and public utilities
Environmental Laws (federal and state)	Define disclosure requirements
Labor and Benefit Laws (federal and state)	Define disclosure requirements
Applicable Foreign Laws	Cross-border transactions subject to jurisdictions of countries in which the bidder and target firms have operations

Securities Exchange Act of 1934

The Securities Exchange Act of 1934 extends disclosure requirements stipulated under the Securities Act of 1933 covering new issues to include securities already trading on the national exchanges. In 1964, coverage was expanded to include securities traded on the Over-the-Counter (OTC) Market. Moreover, the act prohibits brokerage firms working with a company and others related to the securities transaction from engaging in fraudulent and unfair behavior such as insider trading. The act also covers proxy solicitations (i.e., mailings to shareholders requesting their vote on a particular issue) by a company or shareholders. For a more detailed discussion of proxy statements, see Chapter 3.

Registration Requirements

Companies that are required to register are those with assets of more than $1 million and with more than 500 shareholders. Even if both parties are privately owned, an M&A transaction is subject to federal securities laws if a portion of the purchase price is going to be financed by an initial public offering of stock or a public offering of debt by the acquiring firm.

Section 13: Periodic Reports

The Form 10K or annual report summarizes and documents the firm's financial activities during the preceding year. The four key financial statements that must be included are the income statement, balance sheet, statement of retained earnings, and the statement of cash flows. The statements must be well documented with information on accounting policies and procedures, calculations, and transactions underlying the financial statements. The Form 10K also includes a relatively detailed description of the business, the markets served, major events and their impact on the business, key competitors, and competitive market conditions. The Form 10Q is a highly succinct quarterly update of such information.

If an acquisition or divestiture is deemed significant, the Form 8K must be submitted to the SEC within 15 days of the event. The Form 8K describes the assets acquired or disposed, the type and amount of consideration (i.e., payment) given or received, and the identity of the person (or persons) for whom the assets were acquired. In an acquisition, the Form 8K also must identify who is providing the funds used to finance the purchase and the financial statements of the acquired business. Acquisitions and divestitures are deemed significant if the equity interest in the acquired assets or the amount paid or received exceeds 10% of the total book value of the assets of the registrant and its subsidiaries.

Section 14: Proxy Solicitations

Where proxy contests for control of corporate management are involved, the act requires the names and interests of all participants in the proxy contest. Proxy materials must be filed in advance of their distribution to ensure that they are in compliance with disclosure requirements. If the transaction involves the shareholder approval of either the acquirer or target firm, any materials distributed to shareholders must conform to the SEC's rules for proxy materials.

Insider Trading Regulations

Insider trading involves individuals buying or selling securities based on knowledge not available to the general public. Historically, insider trading has been covered under the Securities and Exchange Act of 1934. Section 16(a) of the act defines insiders as corporate officers, directors, and any person owning 10% or more of any class of securities of a company. The Sarbanes–Oxley Act of 2002 (SOA) amended Section 16(a) of the 1934 Act by requiring that insiders disclose any changes in ownership within 2 business days of the transaction. This compares to the previous requirement that it be done on a monthly basis. Furthermore, the SOA requires that changes in ownership be filed electronically, rather than on paper. The SEC is required to post the filing on the Internet within 1 business day after the filing is received.

The SEC is responsible for investigating insider trading. Regulation 10b-5 issued by the SEC under powers granted by the 1934 Securities and Exchange Act prohibits the commission of fraud in relation to securities transactions. In addition, regulation 14e-3 prohibits trading securities in connection to a tender offer based on information not available to the general public. According to the Insider Trading Sanctions Act of 1984, those convicted of engaging in insider trading are required to give back their illegal profits. They also are required to pay a penalty three times the magnitude of such profits. A 1988 U.S. Supreme Court ruling gives investors the right to claim damages from a firm that falsely denied it was involved in negotiations that subsequently resulted in a merger.

Williams Act: Regulation of Tender Offers

Passed in 1968, the Williams Act consists of a series of amendments to the Securities Act of 1934. The Williams Act was intended to protect target firm shareholders from lightning-fast takeovers in which they would not have enough information or time to assess adequately the value of an acquirer's offer. This protection was achieved by requiring more disclosure by the bidding company, establishing a minimum period during which a tender offer must remain open, and authorizing targets to sue bidding firms. The disclosure requirements of the Williams Act apply to anyone, including the target, asking shareholders to accept or reject a takeover bid. The major sections of the Williams Act as they affect M&As are in Sections 13D and 14D. Note that the procedures outlined in the Williams Act for prenotification must be followed diligently. The Williams Act requirements apply to all types of tender offers including those negotiated with the target firm (i.e., negotiated or friendly tender offers), those undertaken by a firm to repurchase its own stock (i.e., self-tender offers), and those that are unwanted by the target firm (i.e., hostile tender offers).

Sections 13D and 13G Provides for Ownership Disclosure Requirements

Section 13D of the Williams Act is intended to regulate "substantial share" or large acquisitions and serves to provide an early warning for a target company's shareholders and management of a pending bid. Any person or firm acquiring 5% or more of the stock of a public corporation must file a Schedule 13D with the SEC within 10 days of reaching that percentage ownership threshold. The disclosure is necessary even if the accumulation of the stock is not followed by a tender offer.

Under Section 13G, any stock accumulated by related parties such as affiliates, brokers, or investment bankers working on behalf of the person or firm are counted toward the 5% threshold. This prevents an acquirer from avoiding filing by accumulating more than 5% of the target's stock through a series of related parties. Institutional investors, such as registered brokers and dealers, banks, and insurance companies, can file a Schedule 13G, a shortened version of the Schedule 13D, if the securities were acquired in the normal course of business.

The information required by the Schedule 13D includes the identities of the acquirer, their occupation and associations, sources of financing, and the purpose of the acquisition. If the purpose of the acquisition of the stock is to take control of the target firm, the acquirer must reveal its business plan for the target firm. The plans could include the breakup of the firm, the suspension of dividends, a recapitalization of the firm, or the intention to merge it with another firm. Otherwise, the purchaser of the stock could indicate that the accumulation was for investment purposes only. Whenever a material change in the information on the Schedule 13D occurs, a new filing must be made with the SEC and the public securities exchanges. The Williams Act is vague when it comes to defining what constitutes a material change. It is generally acceptable to file within 10 days of the material change.

Section 14D Created Rules for the Tender Offer Process

Although Section 14D of the Williams Act relates to public tender offers only, it applies to acquisitions of any size. The 5% notification threshold also applies.

Obligations of the Acquirer An acquiring firm must disclose its intentions, business plans, and any agreements between the acquirer and the target firm in a Schedule 14D-1. The schedule is called a **tender offer statement**. The commencement date of the tender offer is defined as the date on which the tender offer is published, advertised, or submitted to the target. Schedule 14D-1 must contain the identity of the target company and the type of securities involved; the identity of the person, partnership, syndicate, or corporation that is filing; and any past contracts between the bidder and the target company. The schedule also must include the source of the funds used to finance the tender offer, its purpose, and any other information material to the transaction.

Obligations of the Target Firm The management of the target company cannot advise its shareholders how to respond to a tender offer until it has filed a Schedule 14D-9 with the SEC within 10 days after the tender offer's commencement date. This schedule is called a tender offer solicitation/recommendation statement. Target management is limited to telling its shareholders to defer responding to the tender offer until it has completed its consideration of the offer. The target also must send copies of the Schedule 14D-9 to each of the public exchanges on which its stock is traded.

Shareholder Rights: 14(D) (4)–(7) The tender offer must be left open for a minimum of 20 trading days. The acquiring firm must accept all shares that are tendered during this period. The firm making the tender offer may get an extension of the 20-day period if it believes that there is a better chance of getting the shares it needs. The firm must purchase the shares tendered at the offer price, at least on a pro rata basis, unless the firm does not receive the total number of shares it requested under the tender offer. The tender offer also may be contingent on attaining the approval of such regulatory agencies as the Department of Justice (DoJ) and the FTC. Shareholders have the right to withdraw shares that they may have tendered previously. They may withdraw their shares at any time during which the tender offer remains open. The law also requires that when a new bid for the target is made from another party, the target firm's shareholders must have an additional 10 days to consider the bid.

Best Price Rule: 14(D)-10 The "best price" rule requires that all shareholders are paid the same price in a tender offer. As a result of SEC rule changes on October 18, 2006, the best price rule was clarified to underscore that compensation for services that might be paid to a shareholder should not be included as part of the price paid for their shares. The rule changes also protect special compensation arrangements that are approved by independent members of a firm's board and specifically exclude compensation in the form of severance and other employee benefits. The rule changes make it clear that the best price rule only applies to the consideration (i.e., cash, securities, or both) offered and paid for securities tendered by shareholders.

The best price rule need not apply in tender offers in which a controlling shareholder, a management group, or a third party makes a tender offer for all of the outstanding publicly held shares of a firm with the goal of obtaining at least a certain threshold percentage of the total outstanding shares. Once this threshold has been reached, the acquirer can implement a short form merger and buy out the remaining shareholders (see Chapter 1). This threshold may be as high as 90% in states such as Delaware. Under such circumstances, the courts have ruled that the controlling shareholder is not legally compelled to purchase the remaining shares at any particular price, unless there is evidence that material information concerning its tender offer has been withheld or misrepresented (Siliconix Inc. Shareholders, 2001).

Sarbanes–Oxley Act of 2002

The Sarbanes–Oxley Act (SOA) was signed in the wake of the egregious scandals at such corporate giants as Enron, MCI WorldCom, ImClone, Qwest, Adelphia, and Tyco. The Act has implications ranging from financial disclosure to auditing practices to corporate governance. Key elements of the Act are provided in Table 2-2. Section 302 of the Act requires quarterly certification of financial statements and disclosure controls and procedures for CEOs and CFOs. This section became effective in September 2002.

Section 404 requires most public companies to certify annually that their internal control system is designed and operating successfully. It became effective November 15, 2004. The legislation, in concert with new listing requirements at public stock exchanges, requires a greater number of directors on the board who do not work for the company.

TABLE 2-2 Sarbanes–Oxley Bill (7/31/02)

Key Elements of Legislation	Key Actions

• Creates Public Company Accounting Oversight Board (PCAOB)	• Private, nonprofit corporate entity separate from SEC, but subject to SEC oversight
	• 5 members appointed by SEC for a 5-year term
	• Duties include
	  —Register public accounting firms
	  —Establish audit report standards
	  —Inspect registered public accounting firms
	  —Suspend registrations or impose fines on public accounting firms for violations
	  —Promote a professional standard of conduct

• Promotes auditor independence	• Prohibits a registered public accounting firm from providing certain nonaudit services (e.g., information technology) to clients contemporaneously with the audit

• Promotes corporate responsibility reform	• Directs stock markets to require that audit committees of listed firms:
	  —Be responsible for appointment, compensation, and oversight of auditors
	  —Be composed of independent members of the board of directors
	  —Have the authority to engage independent counsel to carry out duties
	• Requires CEOs and CFOs to certify that financial statements do not violate antifraud and disclosure standards

• Provides for financial disclosure reform	• Requires detailed disclosure of all material off-balance sheet transactions • Pro-forma financial statements must be consistent with GAAP • Generally prohibits personal loans to executives • Reduces period for principal stockholders, officers, and directors to disclose stock sales to 2 business days after the transaction is executed.
• Expands corporate and criminal fraud accountability	• Increases criminal penalties to include a prison sentence of up to 20 years for destroying records with intent to impede a criminal investigation

In addition, the Act requires board audit committees to have at least one financial expert while the full committee must review financial statements every quarter after the CEO and CFO certify them. Independent directors are encouraged to meet separately from management on a regular basis.

As noted in a number of studies cited in Chapter 13, there is growing evidence that monitoring costs imposed by Sarbanes–Oxley have been a factor in many small firms going private since the introduction of the legislation. Furthermore, many companies have been raising money through private placements rather than public offerings. For the first time, funds raised through private placements ($154 billion) exceeded initial public offerings ($147 billion) in 2006 (Gangahar, 2007). However, a recent study illustrates the positive impact this legislation can have for the shareholders of firms that were required to overhaul their existing governance systems because of Sarbanes–Oxley. Chhaochharia and Grinstein (2007) conclude that large firms that are the least compliant with the rules around the announcement dates of certain rule implementations are more likely to display significantly positive abnormal financial returns. In contrast, small firms that are less compliant earn negative abnormal returns.

In an effort to reduce some of the negative effects of Sarbanes–Oxley, the U.S. Securities and Exchange Commission allowed foreign firms to avoid having to comply with the reporting requirements of the Act. Effective June 15, 2007, foreign firms, whose shares traded on U.S. exchanges comprise less than 5% of the global trading volume during the last 12 months, are not subject to the Sarbanes–Oxley Act. This action was taken to enhance the attractiveness of U.S. exchanges as a place for foreign firms to list their stock. This regulatory change affects about 360 of the 1200 foreign firms listed on U.S. stock exchanges (Grant, March 23, 2007).

Sarbanes–Oxley versus European Union's 8th Directive

While both focus on the relationship between the auditing firm and top company management, transparency, and accountability, the European Union's (EU's) 8th Directive is widely viewed as less onerous than the U.S.'s Sarbanes–Oxley legislation. In contrast to rapid action taken in the United States following the wave of corporate scandals in 2001 and 2002, the EU took longer to overhaul European company law, having started the process in the mid-1990s. While the U.S. law mandates only independent (i.e., non-executive) directors can serve on audit committees, the 8th Directive allows the audit committee to consist of both independent and inside directors as long as the committee contains at least one independent member with substantial accounting and auditing experience. Furthermore, the 8th Directive contains far fewer reporting requirements, but it does require auditing firms to report on key issues arising from the audit such as weak internal controls for financial reporting. Unlike Sarbanes–Oxley, the 8th Directive requires firms to rotate auditing companies as well as senior audit partners.

Sarbanes–Oxley versus Public Stock Exchange Regulations

New York Stock Exchange listing requirements far exceed the auditor independence requirements of the Sarbanes–Oxley Act. Companies must have board audit committees consisting of at least three independent directors and a written charter describing its responsibilities in detail. Moreover, the majority of all board members must be independent and non-management directors must meet periodically without management. Board compensation and nominating committees must consist entirely of independent directors.

Shareholders must be able to vote on all stock option plans. Listed firms must also adopt a set of governance guidelines and a code of business ethics.

Impact of Sarbanes–Oxley on Mergers and Acquisitions

While the Act does not specifically address M&As, its implications are likely to be far reaching. Acquirers will do more intensive due diligence on target firms which are viewed as having weak internal controls. Due diligence will become more complex and take longer to complete. This will be especially true when the target firm is highly significant to the buyer. The timing of Sections 302 and 404 certification reporting requirements could increasingly cause delays in deal closings. Failure to properly coordinate a firm's responses to Sections 302 and 404 could undermine management's credibility and lead to SEC investigations.

The Regulators' Conundrum: The Growth of Private Markets

Credit markets during the last decade have been undergoing dynamic structural changes. While the regulatory authorities focus on the public markets, so-called private markets, not subject to domestic or international regulatory bodies, have exploded in size. Firms are raising more capital through privately issued loan instruments rather than through the public debt or equity markets. Such private transactions are not transparent to ordinary investors or regulators. This lending takes place largely outside of the regulated banking industry by hedge funds, pension funds, and insurance companies. Such institutions often are subject to relatively light regulation. Moreover, private market loans are used increasingly by hedge funds to buy out public companies, thereby removing them from the public markets (see Chapter 13 for a more detailed discussion of these developments). Current securities laws generally do not have any significant impact on these rapidly growing private markets.

Antitrust Laws

Federal antitrust laws exist to prevent individual corporations from assuming too much market power such that they can limit their output and raise prices without concern for any significant competitor reaction. The DoJ and the FTC have the primary responsibility for enforcing federal antitrust laws. The FTC was established in the Federal Trade Commission Act of 1914 with the specific purpose of enforcing antitrust laws such as the Sherman, Clayton, and Federal Trade Commission Acts. For excellent discussions of antitrust law, see the DoJ (www.usdoj.gov) and FTC (www.ftc.gov) Web sites, and the American Bar Association (2005).

Generally speaking, national laws do not impact firms outside their domestic political boundaries. There are two important exceptions. These include antitrust laws and laws applying to the bribery of foreign government officials (Truitt, 2006). Outside the United States, antitrust regulation laws are described as competitiveness laws intended to minimize or eliminate anticompetitive behavior. As illustrated in Case Study 2-8, the European Union antitrust regulators were able to thwart the attempted takeover of Honeywell by General Electric, two U.S. corporations with operations in the EU. Remarkably, this occurred following the approval of the proposed takeover by U.S. antitrust authorities. The other exception, the Foreign Corrupt Practices Act, will be discussed later in this chapter.

Sherman Act

Passed in 1890, the Sherman Act makes illegal all contracts, combinations, and conspiracies that "unreasonably" restrain trade (U.S. Department of Justice, 1999). Examples include agreements to fix prices, rig bids, allocate customers among competitors, or monopolize any part of interstate commerce. Section I of the Sherman Act prohibits new business combinations that result in monopolies or in a significant concentration of pricing power in a single firm. Section II applies to firms that already are dominant in their targeted markets.

The Sherman Act remains the most important source of antitrust law today. The Act defines broad conditions and remedies for such firms that are deemed to be in violation of current antitrust laws. The Act applies to all transactions and businesses involved in interstate commerce or, if the activities are local, all transactions and business "affecting" interstate commerce. The latter phrase has been interpreted to allow broad application of the Sherman Act. Most states have comparable statutes prohibiting monopolistic conduct, price-fixing agreements, and other acts in restraint of trade having strictly local impact.

Clayton Act

Passed in 1914 to strengthen the Sherman Act, the Clayton Act was created to outlaw certain practices not prohibited by the Sherman Act and to help government stop a monopoly before it developed. Section 5 of the Act made price discrimination between customers illegal, unless it could be justified by cost savings associated with bulk purchases. Tying of contracts—in which a firm refused to sell certain important products to a customer unless the customer agreed to buy other products from the firm—also was prohibited. Section 7 prohibits mergers and acquisitions that may substantially lessen competition or tend to create a monopoly. Under Section 7 of the Act, it is illegal for one company to purchase the stock of another company if their combination results in reduced competition within the industry. Interlocking directorates also were made illegal when the directors were on the boards of competing firms.

Unlike the Sherman Act, which contains criminal penalties, the Clayton Act is a civil statute. The Clayton Act allows private parties injured by the antitrust violation to sue in federal court for three times their actual damages. State attorneys general also may bring civil suits. If the plaintiff wins, costs must be borne by the party violating prevailing antitrust law, in addition to the criminal penalties imposed under the Sherman Act.

Acquirers soon learned how to circumvent the original statutes of the Clayton Act of 1914, which applied to the purchase of stock. They simply would acquire the assets, rather than the stock, of a target firm. In the Celler–Kefauver Act of 1950, the Clayton Act was amended to give the FTC the power to prohibit asset as well as stock purchases. The FTC also may block mergers if it believes that the combination will result in increased market concentration (i.e., fewer firms having increased market shares) as measured by the sales of the largest firms.

Federal Trade Commission Act of 1914

The Federal Trade Commission Act of 1914 created the FTC consisting of five full-time commissioners appointed by the president for a 7-year term. The commissioners are supported by a staff of economists, lawyers, and accountants to assist in the enforcement of antitrust laws.

Hart–Scott–Rodino Antitrust Improvements Act (HSR) of 1976

Acquisitions involving companies of a certain size cannot be completed until certain information is supplied to the federal government and until a specified waiting period has elapsed. The pre-merger notification allows the FTC and the DoJ sufficient time to challenge acquisitions believed to be anticompetitive before they are completed. Once the merger has taken place, it is often exceedingly difficult to break it up. See Table 2-3 for a summary of prenotification filing requirements.

Title I: What Must Be Filed?

Title I of the Act gives the DoJ the power to request internal corporate records if it suspects potential antitrust violations. In some cases, the requests for information result in truckloads of information being delivered to the regulatory authorities because of the extensive nature of the prenotification form. The information requirements include background information on the "ultimate parent" of the acquiring and target parents, a description of the transaction, and all background studies relating to the transaction. The ultimate parent will be the corporation that is at the top of the chain of ownership if the actual buyer is a subsidiary. In addition, the reporting firm must supply detailed product line breakdowns, a listing of competitors, and an analysis of sales trends.

Title II: Who Must File and When?

Title II addresses the conditions under which filings must take place. Effective February 17, 2006, to comply with the "size-of-transaction" test, transactions in which the buyer purchases voting securities or assets valued in excess of $57.6 million must be reported under the HSR Act. However, according to the "size-of-person" test, transactions valued at less than $57.6 million may still require filing if the acquirer or the target firm has annual net sales or total assets of at least $113.4 million and the other party has annual net sales or total assets of at least $11.3 million. These thresholds will be adjusted upward by the annual rate of increase in gross domestic product.

Bidding firms must execute a HSR filing at the same time as they make an offer to a target firm. The target firm also is required to file within 15 days following the bidder's filing. Filings consist of information on the operations of the two companies and their financial statements. The required forms also request any information on internal documents, such as the estimated market share of the combined companies, before extending the offer. Consequently, any such analyses should be undertaken with the understanding that the information ultimately will be shared with the antitrust regulatory authorities. The waiting period begins when both the acquirer and target have filed. Either the FTC or the DoJ may request a 20-day extension of the waiting period for transactions involving

TABLE 2-3   Summary of Regulatory Prenotification Filing Requirements

	Williams Act	Hart–Scott–Rodino (HSR) Act
Required filing	1. Schedule 13D within 10 days of acquiring 5% stock ownership in another firm 2. Ownership includes stock held by affiliates or agents of bidder 3. Schedule 14D-1 for tender offers 4. Disclosure required even if 5% accumulation not followed by a tender offer	HSR filing is necessary when:[1] 1. The buyer purchases assets or securities >$57.6 million or 2. Buyer or seller has annual sales or assets ≥ $113.4 million and other party has sales or assets ≥ $11.3 million Thresholds in (1) and (2) are adjusted annually by the increase in gross domestic product
File with whom	Schedule 13D 1. 6 copies to SEC 2. 1 copy via registered mail to target's executive office 3. 1 copy via registered mail to each public exchange on which target stock traded Schedule 14D-1 1. 10 copies to SEC 2. 1 copy hand delivered to target's executive offices 3. 1 copy hand delivered to other bidders 4. 1 copy mailed to each public exchange on which target stock traded (each exchange also must be phoned)	1. Pre-Merger Notification Office of the Federal Trade Commission 2. Director of Operations of the DoJ Antitrust Division
Time period	1. Tender offers must stay open a minimum of 20 business days 2. Begins on date of publication, advertisement, or submission of materials to target 3. Unless the tender offer has been closed, shareholders may withdraw tendered shares up to 60 days after the initial offer	1. Review/waiting period: 30 days 2. Target must file within 15 days of bidder's filing 3. Period begins for all cash offer when bidder files; for cash/stock bids, period begins when both bidder and target have filed 4. Regulators can request 20-day extension

Note:
[1] These are the thresholds as of 2006.

securities and 10 days for cash tender offers. If the acquiring firm believes that there is little likelihood of anticompetitive effects, it can request early termination. However, the decision is entirely at the discretion of the regulatory agencies.

In 2005, the FTC reviewed only about 4% of all M&As and challenged about 2%. Of the firms that had to file with the agency, only 25 received "second requests" for information (Lindell, 2006). If the regulatory authorities suspect anticompetitive effects, they will file a lawsuit to obtain a court injunction to prevent completion of the proposed transaction. Although it is rare for either the bidder or the target to contest the lawsuit because of the expense involved and even rarer for the government to lose, it does happen.

Regulators filed a suit on February 27, 2004, to block Oracle's $26 per share hostile bid for PeopleSoft on antitrust grounds. On September 9, 2004, a U.S. District Court Judge denied a request by U.S. antitrust authorities that he issue an injunction against the deal arguing that the government failed to prove that large businesses can turn to only three suppliers (i.e., Oracle, PeopleSoft, and SAP) for business applications software. Government antitrust authorities indicated that, given the strong findings on behalf of the plaintiff by the judge, they would not attempt to appeal the ruling.

If fully litigated, a government lawsuit can result in substantial legal expenses as well as a significant use of management time. The acquiring firm may be required to operate the target firm as a wholly independent subsidiary until the litigation has been resolved. Even if the FTC's lawsuit is ultimately overturned, the perceived benefits of the merger often have disappeared by the time the lawsuit has been decided. Potential customers and suppliers will be less likely to sign lengthy contracts with the target firm during the period of trial. Moreover, new investment in the target is likely to be limited, and employees and communities, where the target's operations are located, will be subject to substantial uncertainty. For these reasons, both regulators and acquirers often seek to avoid litigation.

How Does HSR Affect State Antitrust Regulators?

Title III expands the powers of state attorneys general to initiate triple damage suits on behalf of individuals in their states injured by violations of the antitrust laws. This additional authority gives states the incentive to file such suits to increase state revenues.

Procedural Rules

When the DoJ files an antitrust suit, it is adjudicated in the federal court system. When the FTC initiates the action, it is heard before an administrative law judge at the FTC. The results of the hearing are subject to review by the commissioners of the FTC. Criminal actions are reserved for the DoJ, which may seek fines or imprisonment for violators. Individuals and companies also may file antitrust lawsuits. The FTC reviews complaints that have been recommended by its staff and approved by the Commission. Each complaint is reviewed by one of the FTC's hearing examiners. The Commission as a whole then votes whether to accept or reject the hearing examiner's findings. The decision of the Commission then can be appealed in the federal circuit courts. In 1999, the FTC implemented new "fast-track" guidelines that commit the FTC to making a final decision on a complaint within 13 months.

As an alternative to litigation, a company may seek to negotiate a voluntary settlement of its differences with the FTC. Such settlements usually are negotiated during the review process and are called *consent decrees*. The FTC then files a complaint in the federal court along with the proposed consent decree. The federal court judge routinely approves the consent decree.

The Consent Decree

A typical consent decree requires the merging parties to divest overlapping businesses or to restrict anticompetitive practices. If a potential acquisition is likely to be challenged by the regulatory authorities, an acquirer may seek to negotiate a consent decree in advance of consummating the deal. In the absence of a consent decree, a buyer often requires that an agreement of purchase and sale includes a provision that allows the acquirer to back out of the transaction if it is challenged by the FTC or the DoJ on antitrust grounds. In a report evaluating the results of 35 divestiture orders entered between 1990 and 1994, the FTC concluded that the use of consent decrees to limit market power resulting from a business combination has proven to be successful by creating viable competitors (Federal Trade Commission, 1999). The study found that the divestiture is likely to be more successful if it is made to a firm in a related business rather than a new entrant into the business (see Case Study 2-1).

Case Study 2-1
Justice Department Requires AlliedSignal and Honeywell to Divest
Overlapping Businesses

AlliedSignal Inc. and Honeywell Inc. were ordered to divest significant portions of their avionics—airplane electronics systems—businesses in 1999 to resolve the Justice Department's competitive concerns involving their proposed $16 billion merger. Both companies are major providers of avionics and other advanced technology products to a broad range of commercial, space, and U.S defense customers. The DoJ concluded that the transaction as originally proposed would have been anticompetitive, resulting in higher prices and lower quality for these products.

The department's Antitrust Division filed a lawsuit and proposed a consent decree in U.S. District Court in Washington, D.C., which if approved by the Court, would resolve the issue. According to the complaint, the proposed merger would have substantially lessened competition in four product areas. In each of these product areas, the merger would leave at most two or three major competitors. Consequently, the DoJ alleged that these competitors would have been able to coordinate their pricing and more easily increase prices for customers. Both AlliedSignal and Honeywell agreed to divest specific product lines to comply with the consent decree.

Case Study Discussion Questions

1. Do you believe consent decrees involving the acquiring firm to dispose of certain target company assets is an abuse of government power? Why or why not?
2. What alternative actions could the government take to limit market power resulting from a business combination?
3. Should the government be concerned about such factors as job loss and disruption to communities that may result from the merger if the merger is expected to result in improved overall efficiency for the combined firms? Why or why not?

Antitrust Guidelines for Horizontal Mergers

Understanding an industry begins with understanding its market structure. Market structure may be defined in terms of the number of firms in an industry; their concentration, cost, demand, and technological conditions; and ease of entry and exit. The size of individual competitors does not tell one much about the competitive dynamics of an industry. Some industries give rise to larger firms than do other industries because of the importance of economies of scale or huge capital and research and development requirements. For example, although Boeing and Airbus dominate the commercial airframe industry, industry rivalry is intense.

Beginning in 1968, the DoJ issued guidelines indicating the types of M&As the government would oppose. Intended to clarify the provisions of the Sherman and Clayton Acts, the largely quantitative guidelines were presented in terms of specific market share percentages and concentration ratios. Concentration ratios were defined in terms of the market shares of the industry's top four or eight firms. Because of their rigidity, the guidelines have been revised to reflect the role of both quantitative and qualitative data. Qualitative data include factors such as the enhanced efficiency that might result from a combination of firms, the financial viability of potential merger candidates, and the ability of U.S. firms to compete globally.

In 1992, both the FTC and the DoJ announced a new set of guidelines indicating that they would challenge mergers creating or enhancing market power, even if there are measurable efficiency benefits. Market power is defined as a situation in which the combined firms will be able to profitably maintain prices above competitive levels for a significant period. M&As that do not increase market power are acceptable. The 1992 guidelines were revised in 1997 to reflect the regulatory authorities' willingness to recognize that improvements in efficiency over the long term could more than offset the effects of increases in market power. Consequently, a combination of firms, which enhances market power, would be acceptable to the regulatory authorities if it could be shown that the increase in efficiency resulting from the combination more than offsets the increase in market power. Numerous recent empirical studies support this conclusion (see Chapter 1).

In the 1980s and 1990s, a merger in an industry with five major competitors would face scrutiny from either the Federal Trade Commission or the Department of Justice and might face significant regulatory opposition. Today, mergers reducing the number of competitors from three to two are the only ones regulators are likely to block due to the supposition that the efficiencies the merger partners might realize would be offset by the potential harm to consumers of reduced competition. Indeed, even under this scenario, unusually high market concentration may be overlooked if the market is broadly defined to include foreign competitors. For example, Whirlpool Corporation's acquisition of Maytag Corporation resulted in a combined postmerger market share of about 70% of the U.S. home appliance market. (See the section entitled "Inside M&A" at the beginning of this chapter.)

In general, horizontal mergers, those between current or potential competitors, are most likely to be challenged by regulators. Vertical mergers, those involving customer–supplier relationships, are considered much less likely to result in anticompetitive effects, unless they deprive other market participants of access to an important resource. The antitrust regulators seldom contest conglomerate mergers involving the combination of dissimilar products into a single firm.

The 1992 guidelines describe the process the antitrust authorities go through to make their decisions. This process falls into five discrete steps.

Step 1: Market Definition, Measurement, and Concentration

A substantial number of factors are examined to determine if a proposed transaction will result in a violation of law. However, calculating the respective market shares of the combining companies and the degree of industry concentration in terms of the number of competitors is the starting point for any investigation.

Defining the Market Regulators define a market as a product or group of products offered in a specific geographic area. Market participants are those currently producing and selling these products in this geographic area as well as potential entrants. Regulators calculate market shares for all firms or plants identified as market participants based on total sales or capacity currently devoted to the relevant markets. In certain cases, the regulatory agencies have chosen to segment a market more narrowly by size or type of competitor. This is the approach adopted in the FTC's investigation of Staples' attempted acquisition of Office Depot (Case Study 2-2).

Case Study 2-2
FTC Prevents Staples from Acquiring Office Depot

As the leading competitor in the office supplies superstore market, Staples' proposed $3.3 billion acquisition of Office Depot received close scrutiny from the FTC immediately after its announcement in September 1996. The acquisition would create a huge company with annual sales of $10.7 billion. Following the acquisition, only one competitor, OfficeMax with sales of $3.3 billion, would remain. Staples pointed out that the combined companies would comprise only about 5% of the total office supply market. However, the FTC considered the superstore market as a separate segment within the total office supply market. Using the narrow definition of "market," the FTC concluded that the combination of Staples and Office Depot would control more than three-quarters of the market and would substantially increase the pricing power of the combined firms. Despite Staples' willingness to divest 63 stores to Office Max in markets in which its concentration would be the greatest following the merger, the FTC could not be persuaded to approve the merger.

Both Staples and Office Depot had a history of lowering prices for their customers because of the efficiencies associated with their "superstores." The companies argued that the merger would result in more than $4 billion in cost savings over 5 years that would be passed on to their customers. However, the FTC argued and the federal court concurred that the product prices offered by the combined firms still would be higher, as a result of reduced competition, than they would have been had the merger not taken place. The FTC relied on a study showing that Staples tended to charge higher prices in markets in which it did not have another superstore as a competitor. In early 1997, Staples withdrew its offer for Office Depot.

Case Study Discussion Questions

1. How important is defining properly the market segment in which the acquirer and target companies compete to determine the potential increased market power if the two are permitted to combine? Explain your answer.
2. Do you believe the FTC was being reasonable in not approving the merger even though Staples agreed to divest 63 stores in markets where market concentration would be the greatest following the merger? Explain your answer.

Determining Market Concentration The number of firms in the market and their respective market shares determine market concentration (i.e., the extent to which a single or a few firms control a disproportionate share of the total market). Concentration ratios are an incomplete measure of industry concentration. Such ratios measure how much of the total output of an industry is produced by the "*n*" largest firms in the industry. The shortcomings of this approach include the frequent inability to define accurately what constitutes an industry, the failure to reflect ease of entry or exit, foreign competition, regional competition, and the distribution of firm size.

In an effort to account for the distribution of firm size in an industry, the FTC measures concentration by using the ***Herfindahl–Hirschman Index*** (HHI), which is calculated by summing the squares of the market shares for each firm competing in the market. For example, a market consisting of five firms with market shares of 30, 25, 20, 15, and 10% would have an HHI of 2250 ($30^2 + 25^2 + 20^2 + 15^2 + 10^2$). Note that an industry consisting of five competitors with market shares of 70, 10, 10, 5, and 5% will have a much higher HHI score of 5150, because the process of squaring the market shares gives the greatest weight to the firm with the largest market share.

Likely FTC Actions Based on the Herfindahl–Hirschman Index. The HHI ranges from 10,000 for an almost pure monopoly to approximately zero in the case of a highly competitive market. The index gives proportionately more weight to the market shares of larger firms to reflect their relatively greater pricing power. The FTC has developed a scoring system, described in Figure 2-1, which is used as one factor in determining whether the FTC will challenge a proposed merger or acquisition.

Step 2: Potential Adverse Competitive Effects of Mergers

Market concentration and market share data are based on historical data. Consequently, changing market conditions may distort the significance of market share. Suppose a new technology that is important to the long-term competitive viability of the firms within a market has been licensed to other firms within the market but not to the firm with the largest market share. Regulators may conclude that market share information overstates the potential for an increase in the market power of the firm with the largest market share. Therefore, before deciding to challenge a proposed transaction, regulators will consider factors other than simply market share and concentration to determine if a proposed merger will have "adverse competitive effects." These other factors include evidence of coordination among firms, differentiated products, and similarity of substitute products.

Coordinated Interaction Regulators consider the extent to which a small group of firms may exercise market power collectively by cooperating in restricting output or setting prices. Collusion may take the form of firms agreeing to follow simple guidelines

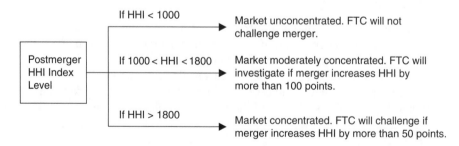

FIGURE 2-1   Federal Trade Commission (FTC) actions at various market share concentration levels. HHI, Herfinahl–Hirschman Index. (From FTC Merger Guidelines, www.ftc.gov.)

such as maintaining common prices, fixed price differentials, stable market shares, or customer or territorial restrictions.

Differentiated Products In some markets the products are differentiated in the eyes of the consumer. Consequently, products sold by different firms in the market are not good substitutes for one another. A merger between firms in a market for differentiated products may diminish competition by enabling the merged firms to profit by raising the price of one or both products above premerger levels.

Similarity of Substitutes Market concentration may be increased if two firms whose products are viewed by customers as equally desirable merge. In this instance, market share may understate the anticompetitive impact of the merger if the products of the merging firms are more similar in their various attributes to one another than to other products in the relevant market. In contrast, market share may overstate the perceived undesirable competitive effects when the relevant products are less similar in their attributes to one another than to other products in the relevant market.

Step 3: Entry Analysis

The ease of entry into the market by new competitors is considered a very important factor in determining if a proposed business combination is anticompetitive. Ease of entry is defined as entry that would be timely, likely to occur, and sufficient to counter the competitive effects of a combination of firms that temporarily increases market concentration. Barriers to entry—such as proprietary technology or knowledge, patents, government regulations, exclusive ownership of natural resources, or huge investment requirements—can serve to limit the number of new competitors and the pace at which they enter a market. In such instances, a regulatory agency may rule that a proposed transaction will reduce competitiveness. Ease of entry appears to have been a factor in the DoJ's assessment of Maytag's proposal to acquire Whirlpool (see "Inside M&A" at the beginning of this chapter).

Step 4: Efficiencies

Increases in efficiency that result from a merger or acquisition can enhance the combined firms' ability to compete and result in lower prices, improved quality, better service, or new products. However, efficiencies are difficult to measure and to verify, because they will be realized only after the merger has taken place. Efficiencies are most likely to make a difference in the FTC's decision to challenge when the likely effects of market concentration are not considered significant. An example of verifiable efficiency improvements would be a reduction in the average fixed cost of production due to economies of scale.

Step 5: Alternative to Imminent Failure

Regulators also take into account the likelihood that a firm would fail and exit a market if it is not allowed to merge with another firm. The regulators must weigh the potential cost of the failing firm, such as a loss of jobs, against any potential increase in market power that might result from the merger of the two firms. The failing firm must be able to demonstrate that it is unable to meet its financial obligations, that it would be unable to successfully reorganize under the protection of the U.S. bankruptcy court, and that it has been unsuccessful in its good-faith efforts to find other potential merger partners.

Antitrust Guidelines for Vertical Mergers

The guidelines described for horizontal mergers also apply to vertical mergers between customers and suppliers. Vertical mergers may become a concern if an acquisition by a supplier of a customer prevents the supplier's competitors from having access to the customer. Regulators are not likely to challenge this type of merger unless the relevant market has few customers and as such is highly concentrated (i.e., an HHI score in excess of 1800). Alternatively, the acquisition by a customer of a supplier could become a concern if it prevents the customer's competitors from having access to the supplier. The concern is greatest if the supplier's products or services are critical to the competitor's operations (see Case Study 2-3).

Case Study 2-3

JDS Uniphase (JDSU) Acquires SDL: What a Difference Seven Months Makes!

What started out as the biggest technology merger in history at that time saw its value plummet in line with the declining stock market, a weakening economy, and concerns about the cash-flow impact of actions the acquirer would have to take to gain regulatory approval. The challenge facing JDSU was to get Department of Justice approval of a merger that could result in a supplier (i.e., JDS Uniphase/SDL) that could exercise pricing power over products ranging from components to packaged products purchased by equipment manufacturers. The regulatory review lengthened the period between the signing of the merger agreement and the closing to 7 months.

JDSU manufactures and distributes fiber-optic components and modules to telecommunication and cable systems providers worldwide. The company is the dominant supplier in its market for fiber-optic components. JDSU's strategy is to package entire systems into a single integrated unit, thereby reducing the number of vendors that fiber network firms must deal with when purchasing systems that produce the light that is transmitted over fiber. SDL's products, including pump lasers, support the transmission of data, voice, video, and Internet information over fiber-optic networks by expanding their fiber-optic communications networks much more quickly and efficiently than conventional technologies. Consequently, SDL fit the JDSU strategy perfectly.

Regulators expressed concern that the combined entities could control the market for a specific type of laser (i.e., 980-nanometer wavelength pump lasers) used in a wide range of optical equipment. SDL is one of the largest suppliers of this type of laser, and JDS is one of the largest suppliers of the chips used to build them. Other manufacturers of pumped lasers, such as Nortel Networks, Lucent Technologies, and Corning, complained to regulators that they would have to buy some of the chips necessary to manufacture pump lasers from a supplier (i.e., JDSU), which in combination with SDL also would be a competitor.

On February 6, 2001, JDSU agreed as part of a consent decree to sell a Swiss subsidiary, which manufactures pump laser chips, to Nortel Networks Corporation, a JDSU customer, to satisfy DoJ concerns about the proposed merger. The divestiture of this operation set up an alternative supplier of such chips. The deal finally closed on February 12, 2001. JDSU shares had fallen from their 12-month high of $153.42 to $53.19. The deal that originally had been valued at $41 billion when first announced more than 7 months earlier had fallen to $13.5 billion on the day of closing, a staggering loss of more than two-thirds of its value.

Case Study Discussion Questions

1. The JDS Uniphase/SDL merger proposal was somewhat unusual in that it represented a vertical rather than horizontal merger. Why does the FTC tend to focus primarily on horizontal rather than vertical mergers?
2. How can an extended regulatory approval process change the value of a proposed acquisition to the acquiring company? Explain your answer.
3. Do you think that JDS Uniphase's competitors had legitimate concerns, or were they simply trying to use the antitrust regulatory process to prevent the firm from gaining a competitive advantage? Explain your answer.

Antitrust Guidelines for Collaborative Efforts

On April 7, 2000, the FTC and DoJ jointly issued new guidelines entitled "Antitrust Guidelines for Collaborations Among Competitors" intended to explain how the agencies analyze antitrust issues with respect to collaborative efforts. A collaborative effort is the term used by the regulatory agencies to describe a range of horizontal agreements among competitors such as joint ventures, strategic alliances, and other competitor agreements. Note that competitors include both actual and potential. Collaborative efforts that might be examined include production, marketing or distribution, and R&D activities.

The analytical framework for determining if the proposed collaborative effort is pro- or-anticompetitive is similar to that described earlier in this chapter for horizontal mergers. The agencies evaluate the impact on market share and the potential increase in market power. The agencies may be willing to overlook any temporary increase in market power if the participants can demonstrate that future increases in efficiency and innovation will result in lower overall selling prices or increased product quality in the long term. In general, the agencies are less likely to find a collaborative effort to be anticompetitive under the following conditions: (1) the participants have continued to compete through separate, independent operations or through participation in other collaborative efforts; (2) the financial interest in the effort by each participant is relatively small; (3) each participant's ability to control the effort is limited; (4) there are effective safeguards to prevent information sharing; and (5) the duration of the collaborative effort is short.

The regulatory agencies have established two "safety zones" which provide participants in collaboration with a degree of certainty that the agencies will not challenge them. First, the market shares of the collaborative effort and of the participants collectively accounts for no more than 20% of the served market. Second, for R&D activities, there must be at least three or more independently controlled research efforts, in addition to those of the collaborative effort. These independent efforts must possess the required specialized assets and the incentive to engage in R&D that is a close substitute for the R&D activity of the collaborative effort.

The Limitations of Antitrust Laws

Antitrust laws have faced serious challenges in recent years in terms of accurately defining market share, accommodating rapidly changing technologies, and promoting competition without discouraging innovation. Efforts to measure market share or concentration inevitably must take into account the explosion of international trade during the last

20 years. Actions by a single domestic firm to restrict its output to raise its selling price may be thwarted by a surge in imports of similar products. Moreover, the pace of technological change is creating many new substitute products and services, which may make a firm's dominant position in a rapidly changing market indefensible almost overnight. The rapid growth of electronic commerce, as a marketplace without geographic boundaries, has tended to reduce the usefulness of conventional measures of market share and market concentration. What constitutes a market on the Internet often is difficult to define.

Is Current U.S. Antitrust Policy Effective?

Empirical evidence strongly suggests that current policy is successful, on average, in discouraging anticompetitive practices. Consequently, there is virtually no case for a more aggressive policy. In fact, there is a compelling case for a more lax policy. The substantial majority of empirical studies (see the section in Chapter 1 entitled "Do Mergers and Acquisitions Pay Off for Society?") indicate that mergers, on average, create economic value by increasing operating efficiency. The implication is that a more lenient antitrust policy would contribute to greater efficiency of U.S. businesses. The case for a more relaxed policy may even be stronger today due to the increase in global competition and its effect on restraining the pricing practices of U.S. businesses (Kaplan, February 2006).

State Regulations Affecting Mergers and Acquisitions

Numerous regulations affecting takeovers exist at the state level. The regulations often differ from one state to another, making compliance with all applicable regulations a challenge. State regulations often are a result of special interests that appeal to state legislators to establish a particular type of antitakeover statute to make it more difficult to complete unfriendly takeover attempts. Such appeals usually are made in the context of an attempt to save jobs in the state.

State Antitakeover Laws

States regulate corporate charters. **Corporate charters** define the powers of the firm and the rights and responsibilities of its shareholders, boards of directors, and managers. However, states are not allowed to pass any laws that impose restrictions on interstate commerce or that conflict in any way with federal laws regulating interstate commerce. State laws affecting M&As tend to apply only to corporations that are incorporated in the state or that conduct a substantial amount of their business within the state. These laws typically contain **fair price provisions** requiring that all target shareholders of a successful tender offer receive the same price as those tendering their shares. In a specific attempt to prevent highly leveraged transactions such as leveraged buyouts, some state laws include **business combination provisions**, which may specifically rule out the sale of the target's assets for a specific period. By precluding such actions, these provisions limit LBOs from using the proceeds of asset sales to reduce indebtedness.

Other common characteristics of state antitakeover laws include cash-out and control share provisions. **Cash-out provisions** require a bidder, whose purchases of stock exceed a stipulated amount, to buy the remainder of the target stock on the same terms granted to those shareholders whose stock was purchased at an earlier date. By forcing the acquiring firm to purchase 100% of the stock, potential bidders lacking substantial financial resources effectively are eliminated from bidding on the target. *Share control provisions* require that a bidder obtain prior approval from stockholders holding large blocks of target stock once the bidder's purchases of stock exceed some threshold level. The latter provision can be particularly troublesome to an acquiring company when the holders of the large blocks of stock tend to support target management.

Such state measures may be set aside if sufficient target firm votes can be obtained at a special meeting of shareholders called for that purpose. Ohio's share control law forced Northrop Grumman to increase its offer price from its original bid of $47 in March 2002 to $53 in mid-April 2002 to encourage those holding large blocks of TRW shares to tender their shares. Such shareholders had balked at the lower price, expressing support for a counter proposal made by TRW to spin off its automotive business and divest certain other assets. TRW had valued its proposal at more than $60 per share. The Ohio law, among the toughest in the nation, prevented Northrop from acquiring more than 20% of TRW's stock without getting the support of other large shareholders.

State Antitrust Laws

As part of the Hart–Scott–Rodino Act of 1976, the states were granted increased antitrust power. The state laws are often similar to federal laws. Under federal law, states have the right to sue to block mergers they believe are anticompetitive, even if the DoJ or FTC does not challenge them.

State Securities Laws

State blue sky laws are designed to protect individuals from investing in fraudulent security offerings. State restrictions can be more onerous than federal ones. An issuer seeking exemption from federal registration will not be exempt from all relevant registration requirements until a state-by-state exemption has been received from all states in which the issuer and offerees reside.

National Security-Related Restrictions on Direct Foreign Investment in the United States

While in existence for more than 50 years, the Committee on Foreign Investment in the United States (CFIUS) made the headlines in early 2006 when Dubai Ports (DP) Worldwide proposed to acquire control of certain U.S. port terminal operations. The subsequent political firestorm catapulted what had previously been a relatively obscure committee into the public limelight. CFIUS operates under the authority granted by Congress in the Exon–Florio amendment (Section 721 of the Defense Production Act of 1950). CFIUS includes representatives from an amalgam of government departments and agencies with diverse expertise to ensure that all national security issues are identified and considered in the review of foreign acquisitions of U.S. businesses. Member agencies include the Departments of Treasury (which chairs the committee), State, Defense, Justice, Commerce, and Homeland Security. In addition, the National Security Council, National

Economic Council, the U.S. Trade Representative, Office of Management and Budget, Council of Economic Advisors, and the Office of Science and Technology are represented. The Departments of Energy and Transportation, and other U.S. agencies are invited to participate in the consideration of transactions that have an impact on the industries under their respective jurisdictions.

The president can under the authority granted under Section 721 (also known as the Exon–Florio provision) block an acquisition of a U.S. corporation under certain conditions. These conditions include the existence of credible evidence that the foreign entity exercising control might take action that threatens national security and that existing laws do not adequately protect national security if the transaction is permitted. To assist in making this determination, Section 721 provides for the president to receive written notice of an acquisition, merger, or takeover of a U.S. corporation by a foreign entity. Once CFIUS has received a complete notification, it begins a thorough investigation. Section 721 provides for a 30-day review process which can be extended an additional 45 days. After the review is completed, the findings are submitted to the president, whose decision must by law be announced within 15 days. The total process is not to exceed 90 days.

Section 721 requires that the impact of the proposed transaction on the following factors be considered during the review process:

1. Domestic production needed for projected national defense requirements;
2. The capability and capacity of domestic industries to meet national defense requirements;
3. The control of domestic industries and commercial activity by foreign citizens as it affects the capability and capacity to meet the requirements of national security;
4. The effects of the transaction on the sales of military equipment and technology to a country that supports terrorism or the proliferation of missile technology, chemical, or biological technology; and
5. The potential effects of the transaction on U.S. technological leadership areas affecting U.S. national security.

U.S. Foreign Corrupt Practices Act

Originally passed in 1976 and later amended in 1988, this Act prohibits individuals, firms, and foreign subsidiaries of U.S. firms from paying anything of value to foreign government officials in exchange for obtaining new business or retaining existing contracts. This type of law is unique to the United States. Even though many nations have laws prohibiting bribery of public officials, enforcement often tends to be lax. The Act permits so-called "facilitation" payments to foreign government officials if relatively small amounts of money are required to expedite goods through foreign custom inspections, gain approvals for exports, obtain speedy passport approvals, and related considerations. Such payments are considered legal according to U.S. law and the laws of countries in which such payments are considered routine (Truitt, 2006).

In 2004, while performing due diligence on Titan Corporation, Lockheed Corporation uncovered a series of bribes that Titan had paid to certain West African government officials to win a telecommunications contract. After Lockheed reported the infraction, Titan was required to pay $28.5 million to resolve the case. In 1996, Lockheed was required to pay $24.8 million for similar violations of the Act.

Regulated Industries

In addition to the DoJ and the FTC, a variety of other agencies monitor activities in certain industries, such as commercial banking, railroads, defense, and cable TV. In each industry, the agency is typically responsible for both the approval of M&As and subsequent oversight. Mergers in these industries often take much longer to complete because of the additional filing requirements.

Banking

According to the Bank Merger Act of 1966, any bank merger not challenged by the attorney general within 30 days of its approval by the pertinent regulatory agency could not be challenged under the Clayton Antitrust Act. Moreover, the Bank Merger Act stated that anticompetitive effects could be offset by a finding that the deal meets the "convenience and needs" of the communities served by the bank. Currently, three different agencies review banking mergers. Which agency has authority depends on the parties involved in the transaction. The Comptroller of the Currency has responsibility for transactions in which the acquirer is a national bank. The Federal Deposit Insurance Corporation oversees mergers where the acquiring or resulting bank will be a federally insured state-chartered bank that operates outside of the Federal Reserve System. The third agency is the Board of Governors of the Federal Reserve System. It has the authority to regulate mergers in which the acquirer or the resulting bank will be a state bank, which is also a member of the Federal Reserve System. Although all three agencies conduct their own review, they consider reviews undertaken by the DoJ in their decision-making process.

Communications

The federal agency charged with oversight, the Federal Communications Commission (FCC), has deferred to the DoJ and the FTC for antitrust enforcement. The FCC is an independent U.S. government agency directly responsible to Congress. Established by the 1934 Communications Act, the FCC is charged with regulating interstate and international communication by radio, television, wire, satellite, and cable. The FCC is responsible for the enforcement of such legislation as the Telecommunications Act of 1996. This Act is intended to promote competition and reduce regulation while promoting lower prices and higher quality services. (See the Federal Communications Commission Web site at www.fcc.gov.)

The FCC has moved aggressively in recent years to promote competition. The FCC used an innovative solution to perceived competitive issues in the 1999 merger of Ameritech and SBC Communications (see Case Study 2-4). A tight timetable coupled with substantial fines, if certain conditions are not satisfied, was intended to accelerate the achievement of the objectives of the Telecommunications Act of 1996. In Case Study 2-5, the FCC blocked the proposed combination of EchoStar and Hughes' DirecTV satellite TV operations in late 2002, because it believed the merger would inhibit competition in the market for cable services.

Case Study 2-4
FCC Uses Its Power to Stimulate Competition in the Telecommunications Market

Having received approval from the Justice Department and the Federal Trade Commission, Ameritech and SBC Communications received permission from the Federal Communications Commission to combine to form the nation's largest local telephone company. The FCC gave its approval of the $74 billion transaction, subject to conditions requiring that the companies open their markets to rivals and enter new markets to compete with local phone companies.

The combined business would control 57 million, or one-third, of the nation's local phone lines in 13 states. The FCC adopted 30 conditions to ensure that the deal would serve the public interest. The new SBC must enter 30 new markets within 30 months to compete with established local phone companies. In the new markets, it would face fierce competition from Bell Atlantic, BellSouth, and U.S. West. The company is required to provide deep discounts on key pieces of their networks to rivals who want to lease them. The merged companies also must establish a separate subsidiary to provide advanced telecommunications services such as high-speed Internet access. At least 10% of its upgraded services would go toward low-income groups. Failure to satisfy these conditions would result in stiff fines. The companies could face up to $1.2 billion in penalties for failing to meet the new market deadline and could pay another $1.1 billion for not meeting performance standards related to opening up their markets.

SBC has had considerable difficulty in complying with its agreement with the FCC. Between December 2000 and July 2002, SBC paid the U.S. government more than $50 million for failing to provide adequately rivals with access to its network. The government noted that SBC failed repeatedly to make available its network in a timely manner, to meet installation deadlines, and to notify competitors when their orders were filled.

Case Study Discussion Questions

1. Comment on the fairness and effectiveness of using the imposition of heavy fines to promote social policy.
2. Under what circumstances, if any, do you believe the government should relax the imposition of such fines in the SBC case?

Case Study 2-5
FCC Blocks EchoStar, Hughes Merger

On October 10, 2002, the FCC voted, 4-0, to block a proposed $18.8 billion merger of the two largest satellite TV companies in the United States. The Commission stated that the merger would create a virtual monopoly that would be particularly harmful to millions of Americans without access to cable television. Living largely in rural areas, such Americans would have no viable alternative to subscribing to a satellite TV hookup. This was the first time the Commission had blocked a major media merger since 1967. The companies were also facing opposition from the Justice Department and 23 states that were seeking to block the merger.

EchoStar manages the DISH Network, while Hughes operates DirecTV. Together they serve about 18 million subscribers and, if allowed, would have been the largest pay-television service. The two companies had argued that the merger is needed to offset competition from cable TV. In presenting the proposal to the Commission, the companies offered to maintain uniform pricing nationwide to ease fears they would gouge consumers where no alternative is available.

While expressing disappointment, the two firms pledged to work with the Commission to achieve approval. On November 30, 2002, EchoStar and Hughes offered to sell more assets to help create a viable satellite-television rival to overcome the regulators' opposition. The companies proposed selling 62 frequencies to Cablevision Systems Corporation. Continued opposition from the FCC, Justice Department, and numerous states caused Hughes and EchoStar to terminate the merger on December 14, 2002.

Case Study Discussion Questions

1. Why do you believe the regulators continued to oppose the merger after EchoStar and Hughes agreed to help establish a competitor?
2. What alternatives could the regulators have proposed that might have made the merger acceptable?
3. Compare and contrast the different outcomes in Case Studies 2-4 and 2-5. Why do you think the FCC came to different conclusions in the two cases? Explain your answer.

Railroads

The Surface Transportation Board (STB), the successor to the Interstate Commerce Commission (ICC), governs mergers of railroads. Under the ICC Termination Act of 1995, the STB employs five criteria to determine if a merger should be approved. These criteria include the impact of the proposed transaction on the adequacy of public transportation, the impact on the areas currently served by the carriers involved in the proposed transaction, and the burden of the total fixed charges resulting from completing the transaction. In addition, the interest of railroad employees is considered, as well as whether the transaction would have an adverse impact on competition among rail carriers in regions affected by the merger.

Defense

During the 1990s, the defense industry in the United States underwent substantial consolidation. The consolidation that has swept the defense industry is consistent with the Department of Defense's (DoD) philosophy that it is preferable to have three or four highly viable defense contractors that could more effectively compete than to have a dozen weaker contractors. Examples of transactions include the merger of Lockheed and Martin Marietta, Boeing's acquisition of Rockwell's defense and aerospace business, Raytheon's acquisition of the assets of defense-related product lines of Hughes Electronics, Boeing's acquisition of Hughes space and communication business, and Northrop Grumman's takeover of TRW's defense business. However, regulators did prevent the proposed acquisition by Lockheed Martin of Northrop Grumman. Although defense industry mergers are technically subject to current antitrust regulations, the DoJ and FTC have assumed a secondary role to the DoD. As noted previously, efforts by a foreign entity to acquire national security-related assets must be reviewed by the Council on Foreign Investment in the United States.

Other Regulated Industries

The insurance industry is regulated largely at the state level. Acquiring an insurance company normally requires the approval of state government and is subject to substantial financial disclosure by the acquiring company. The acquisition of more than 10% of a U.S. airline's shares outstanding is subject to approval of the Federal Aviation Administration. Effective March 8, 2008, the 27-nation European Union and the United States agreed to reduce substantially restrictions on cross-border flights under the Open Skies Act. While the act permits foreign investors to acquire more than 50% of the total shares of a U.S. airline, they cannot purchase more than 25% of the voting shares. In contrast, U.S. investors are permitted to own as much as 49% of the voting shares of EU nation airlines. The accord allows the EU to suspend air traffic rights of U.S. airlines if the United States fails to open its domestic market further by the end of 2010.

Public utilities are highly regulated at the state level. Like insurance companies, their acquisition requires state government approval. In 2006, the federal government eliminated the 1935 Public Utility Holding Company Act (PUHCA), which limited consolidation among electric utilities unless they are in geographically contiguous areas. Proponents of the repeal argue that mergers will produce economies of scale, improve financial strength, and increase investment in the nation's aging electricity transmission grid. With more than 3000 utilities nationwide, the relaxation of regulation has the potential to stimulate future industry consolidation. However, state regulators will continue to have the final say in such matters. Case Study 2-6 illustrates the challenges of satisfying a multiplicity of regulatory bodies.

Case Study 2-6

Exelon Abandons the Acquisition of PSEG Due to State Regulatory Hurdles

On September 14, 2006, Exelon, owner of utilities in Chicago and Philadelphia, announced that it was discontinuing its effort to acquire New Jersey's Public Service Enterprise Group (PSEG) due to an impasse with New Jersey state regulators. If completed, the transaction would have created the nation's largest utility. Exelon had reached an agreement to buy PSEG in December 2004. Exelon's management argued that they could manage PSEG's facilities, especially its nuclear power plants, more efficiently because of their more extensive experience. Exelon's management also argued that improved efficiency would increase the supply of electricity available in New Jersey's competitive wholesale electricity market and ultimately lower prices. The combined companies would have created an energy giant serving 7.1 million electricity customers and 2.2 million natural gas customers in three states. It would also have controlled 25% of the capacity of the power grid between the Mid-Atlantic states and the Midwest.

Exelon offered $600 million in cash, with additional future rate concessions, if New Jersey would agree to approve the acquisition. Both Exelon and PSEG had agreed previously to sell six power plants in New Jersey and Pennsylvania and place 2600 megawatts of nuclear power capacity under contract for as long as 15 years to win approval from the U.S. Department of Justice and the Federal Energy Regulatory Commission. However, New Jersey regulators felt that even with these concessions the combined companies would exert too much pricing power.

The demise of this transaction marked the fourth such utility takeover blocked by state regulatory officials in recent years. In 2003, Exelon was also forced to drop its offer for Dynergy Inc.'s Illinois Power Co. after the Illinois legislature rejected the proposal. Kohlberg Kravis Roberts & Co., JPMorgan Chase & Co., and Wachovia Corp. abandoned an $800 million bid in 2004 for Tucson's UniSource Energy Corp. after the Arizona Corporation Commission required buyers to put in more equity to reduce the amount of debt the utility would have had to carry. Oregon's public utility commission prevented the $1.4 billion sale of Portland General Electric Company in mid-2005, deciding the proposed takeover by Texas Pacific Group would hurt customers.

Case Study Discussion Questions

1. Why do you believe that federal regulators accepted the proposed transaction while it was rejected at the state level?
2. Many other nonutility transactions have been approved both at the federal and the state level on the basis of the anticipated improved efficiency of the combined firms. Why does the efficiency argument seem to be less convincing to regulators when it is applied to proposed utility mergers?

Environmental Laws

Environmental laws create numerous reporting requirements for both acquirers and target firms. Failure to comply adequately with these laws can result in enormous potential liabilities to all parties involved in a transaction. These laws require full disclosure of the existence of hazardous materials and the extent to which they are being released into the environment, as well as any new occurrences. Such laws include the Clean Water Act (1974), the Toxic Substances Control Act (TSCA) of 1978, the Resource Conservation and Recovery Act (1976), and the Comprehensive Environmental Response, Compensation, and Liability Act (CERCLA or Super-fund) of 1980. Additional reporting requirements were imposed in 1986 with the passage of the Emergency Planning and Community Right to Know Act (EPCRA). In addition to EPCRA, several states also have passed "right-to-know" laws, such as California's Proposition 65. The importance of state reporting laws has diminished because EPCRA is implemented by the states.

Labor and Benefit Laws

A diligent buyer also must ensure that the target is in compliance with the labyrinth of labor and benefit laws. These laws govern such areas as employment discrimination, immigration law, sexual harassment, age discrimination, drug testing, and wage and hour laws. Labor and benefit laws include the Family Medical Leave Act, the Americans with Disabilities Act, and the Worker Adjustment and Retraining Notification Act (WARN). WARN governs notification before plant closings and requirements to retrain workers.

Benefit Plan Liabilities

Employee benefit plans frequently represent one of the biggest areas of liability to a buyer. The greatest potential liabilities often are found in defined pension benefit plans, postretirement medical plans, life insurance benefits, and deferred compensation plans. Such liabilities arise when the reserve shown on the seller's balance sheet does not accurately indicate the true extent of the liability. The potential liability from improperly structured benefit plans grows with each new round of legislation starting with the passage of the Employee Retirement Income and Security Act of 1974. Laws affecting employee retirement and pensions were strengthened by additional legislation including the following: the Multi-Employer Pension Plan Amendments Act of 1980, the Retirement Equity Act of 1984, the Single Employer Pension Plan Amendments Act of 1986, the Tax Reform Act of 1986, and the Omnibus Budget Reconciliation Acts of 1987, 1989, 1990, and 1993. Buyers and sellers also must be aware of the Unemployment Compensation Act of 1992; the Retirement Protection Act of 1994; and Statements 87, 88, and 106 of the Financial Accounting Standards Board (Sherman, 1998).

The Pension Protection Act of 2006 places a potentially increasing burden on acquirers of targets with underfunded pension plans. The new legislation requires employers with defined benefit plans to make sufficient contributions to meet a 100% funding target and erase funding shortfalls over 7 years. Furthermore, the legislation requires employers with so-called "at risk" plans to accelerate contributions. "At risk" plans are those whose pension fund assets cover less than 70% of future pension obligations.

Cross-Border Transactions

Transactions involving firms in different countries are complicated by having to deal with multiple regulatory jurisdictions in specific countries or regions. Antitrust regulators tend to follow different standards and impose different fee structures from one country to another. The number of antitrust regulatory authorities globally has grown to 100 from 6 in the early 1990s (*New York Times,* January 28, 2001).

Reflecting the effects of this mishmash of regulations and fee structures, Coca-Cola's 1999 acquisition of Cadbury Schweppes involved obtaining antitrust approval in 40 jurisdictions globally. Fees paid to regulators ranged from $77 in Austria to $2.5 million in Argentina. In contrast, the fee in the United States is limited to $280,000 for transactions whose value exceeds $500 million. Following the failed merger attempt of Alcan Aluminum, Pechiney, and Alusuisse, Jacques Bougie, CEO of Alcan Aluminum, complained that his company had to file for antitrust approval in 16 countries and in eight languages. In addition, his firm had to submit more than 400 boxes of documents and send more than 1 million pages of e-mail (Garten, 2000). Several reports advocate the use of regional antitrust authorities created through multilateral rather than bilateral agreements to streamline the antitrust process and reduce administrative and financial burdens on businesses (Brookings Institute, 2000; U.S. Attorney General, 2000). However, recent developments suggest that even such agreements may not easily resolve fundamental philosophical differences.

The recent collapse of the General Electric and Honeywell transaction underscores how much philosophical differences can jeopardize major deals (see Case Study 2-8). Mario Monti, then head of the EU Competition Office, had taken a highly aggressive posture in this transaction. The GE–Honeywell deal was under attack almost from the day it was announced in October 2000. Rival aerospace companies including United Technologies, Rockwell, Lufthansa, Thales, and Rolls Royce considered it inimical to their ability to compete. Philosophically, U.S. antitrust regulators focus on the impact of a proposed deal on customers. In contrast, EU antitrust regulators are more concerned about the impact on rivals. Reflecting this disparate thinking, U.S. antitrust regulators approved the transaction rapidly, concluding that it would have a salutary impact on customers. However, EU regulators refused to approve the transaction without GE making major concessions, which it was unwilling to make.

The following sections illustrate the disparate regulatory challenges faced by firms interested in cross-border transactions. Such challenges often differ considerably between developed and emerging economies. Since a detailed discussion of regulatory practices in many countries is beyond the scope of this book, the European Union (EU) and China have been selected to illustrate certain types of challenges commonly faced in cross-border transactions.

M&A Regulations in Developed Countries—The European Union Example

In response to the increasing frequency of cross-border transactions in 2006, European governments instituted a variety of actions to block foreign takeovers. The French government declared 11 industrial sectors as off-limits to takeovers due to their strategic value. The French government also arranged a merger of two utilities, publicly traded Suez and state-controlled Gaz de France, to fend off a potential takeover bid by Enel of Italy. Following a takeover attempt of Spanish electric utility, Edessa, by a major German utility, EOn, Spain promptly declared utilities strategic assets and passed a law giving regulators veto power over foreign takeovers of utilities. Finally, Poland demanded that Italian bank, UniCredito, divest itself of the Polish holdings of its recently acquired subsidiary, HVB Group of Germany. Such moves reflect a collision between greater economic integration within the EU and protectionism. Nevertheless, despite these developments, 2006 represented the highest level of cross-border deals in Europe since 2000.

Growing protectionist sentiment is not unique to the EU. Political opposition in the United States prevented CNOOC, a Chinese oil company, from acquiring Unocal in 2005 (see Case Study 16-3). More recently, Congressional intervention blocked a state-owned Dubai company, DP Worldwide, from acquiring the rights to manage terminal operations at six U.S. ports.

U.S. and EU Antitrust Laws

As in the United States, EU antitrust law addresses the level of competition within an industry and mergers. Article 81 of the European Community Treaty prohibiting cartels and other anticompetitive practices is similar to Section I of the Sherman Act, which outlaws actions to restrain trade. Under the EU's Article 82, companies found to be in violation of antitrust laws are subject to financial penalties equal to as much as 10% of a company's worldwide annual revenue. However, unlike the United States, the EU provides no criminal penalties for individuals violating antitrust laws (Bumgardner, 2005). Despite the similarity of EU Articles 81 and 82 to U.S. law, their applications have been quite different. U.S. antitrust law is aimed more at promoting competition, while EU law is more concerned with protecting competitors.

New EU Regulations

Effective May 1, 2004, new regulations allow EU officials to engage in highly intrusive surprise inspections of business offices as well as personal homes and cars of directors or employees of a company under investigation. The most complicated aspects of the new competition regulations deal with the division of power between the Competition Commission at the EU central office in Brussels and the competition authorities in the 27 member nations. The new rules enable the competition authorities and courts to enforce EU competition law within each member nation, thereby permitting the Brussels' central office to focus on larger and more significant cases. Since the member nations and courts are expected to apply EU-wide law in most circumstances, this further centralizes antitrust law in the EU. Nevertheless, having 27 different competing authorities and courts applying EU law could result in inconsistent application from one nation to another, thereby creating greater regulatory uncertainty for business.

Merger Regulations

Also as of May 1, 2004, the EU has authority over any proposed merger regardless of the nationality of the companies involved, if the worldwide revenue of the combined firms exceeds €5 billion (about $6 billion) and at least two of the merging companies would have annual revenue exceeding €250 million (about $300 million). This new standard is intended to enable the EU to block more mergers. The new regulation also includes new guidelines for evaluating horizontal mergers between current or potential competitors. These guidelines are very close to those used by U.S. antitrust authorities. However, an important difference remains in that U.S. antitrust authorities must go to the federal court to request an injunction to block a proposed merger. In contrast, the EU's Competition Commissioner can block a merger without involving a court.

The new rules have resulted in some convergence between EU and U.S. law, especially with regard to mergers. Furthermore, the EU and the United States have taken steps to coordinate merger reviews in an effort to avoid disagreements such as the GE–Honeywell case. Despite this convergence, it is still possible for a company unhappy with U.S. antitrust regulators' unwillingness to block a proposed merger to appeal to EU regulators for a different outcome. For a detailed discussion of EU M&A regulatory issues, see Navarro (2005).

M&A Regulations in Emerging Countries— The China Example

In 2006, M&A activity exploded. According to Dealogic, 2263 acquisitions of Chinese companies were announced, up from 1786 in 2005. The total value of such transactions exceeded $100 billion, 68% higher than the previous year (Batson, January 12, 2007). The motivation for the upsurge in activity reflected a variety of factors including firms seeking to take advantage of economies of scale, horizontal or vertical integration, improving the quality of management, and of increasing market power by eliminating competitors. Moreover, the central government has been actively seeking to reduce its ownership of companies. Since 2005, the number of countries owned by the central government fell to

161 from 196, mostly as a result of mergers. However, as explained later in this chapter, the upsurge in M&A activity reflected a sharp increase in mergers between Chinese firms. While foreign firms continue to make inroads into China, the longer-term outlook is unclear.

M&A Regulatory Agencies

In China, the government takes a higher profile in regulating such transactions than is typical of more developed countries. Despite some recent relaxation of regulations, approval requirements are very stringent. Agencies in the Peoples Republic of China (PRC) play an important role in reviewing and approving deals.

The Ministry of Commerce (MOC) and the State Development and Reform Commission (SDRC) have primary responsibility for supervising foreign-related transactions. As the principal regulator of foreign investment, the MOC has general oversight, supervisory, and approval authority over M&A transactions. The SDRC is an administrative agency responsible for both approving the foreign investment project application and supervising restructuring of state-owned enterprises. In practice, both agencies are involved in most M&A transactions.

The State-Owned Assets Supervision and Administration Commission (SASAC), which has supervisory authority over state-owned assets, plays a significant role in transactions involving state-owned enterprises. It will participate in approving the transaction and may also act as the seller through one of its designated agencies or companies. The China Securities Regulatory Commission (CSRC), which is responsible for monitoring and regulating China's capital markets, also reviews transactions involving publicly traded companies. Depending on the nature of the transaction and the industrial sector, other agencies may be involved. For example, the approval of the Ministry of Information Industry may be required for certain acquisitions targeting the consumer electronics sector.

M&A Regulations

Over the past 5 years, China has enacted a preliminary regulatory framework for M&A transactions. The framework provides greater guidance for foreign investors engaging in M&A transactions. It also has standardized procedures, which had previously been largely determined on a case-by-case basis. Under China's civil law system, even basic types of business transactions are subject to detailed regulations. A foreign firm is not permitted to directly operate a business in China. It must do so through a foreign investment enterprise (FIE). Majority Chinese equity is required in some restricted sectors, while in other restricted sectors, wholly owned foreign enterprises are prohibited. Regulations now permit foreign investors to engage in asset or equity acquisitions of FIEs, domestic enterprises, state-owned enterprises, and publicly traded companies. Moreover, the range of permissible targets has been expanded.

M&A Approvals

The specific approvals required for an M&A transaction depend on the deal structure (i.e., asset or stock purchase), the type of target, and the value of the transaction. In general, transactions involving permitted projects with a total investment value equal to or greater than $100 million require the approval of MOC and SDRC. Permitted projects with a total investment value less than $100 million can generally be approved by the Ministries' provincial or lower level branches. Restricted projects with a total investment amount of $50 million or more require a national level approval from the MOC and SDRC, while smaller restricted projects may be approved by provincial level offices of the Ministries. Depending on the industry, the approval of specialized administrative agencies may also be required. If the target is a state-owned enterprise, the transaction will generally require the approval of the MOC, SDRC, and SASAC.

Antitrust Review

China is beginning to examine market concentration issues. Drafts of proposed antitrust laws are circulating, and it is anticipated that such a law will be adopted soon. The new proposals will establish a special antitrust enforcement agency. This agency will address market concentration issues and administer the antitrust review in certain circumstances. For example, a review may be required if a foreign acquirer has current annual sales or market share in China that exceeds certain thresholds as a consequence of the transaction. Antitrust reviews are not expected to become common until detailed implementing regulations are adopted.

China has made considerable progress in developing a regulatory framework for M&A and other business transactions. As the "rules of the game" are clarified, it is easier for foreign investors to make prudent business decisions. For example, the Enterprise Bankruptcy Law of 2006, which covers both state and privately owned businesses, requires insolvent firms to pay off obligations guaranteed by the firm's assets first, with employees salaries and other commitments paid out of what remains. Moreover, China has increased the number of industries in which acquisitions are allowed and in the types of permissible takeovers (i.e., asset or equity purchases or statutory mergers). However, the number of regulatory agencies is still large and each has its own agenda and constituency. Gaining acceptance by one does not guarantee acceptance by others. Moreover, the lack of a history of M&A law and transactions means that foreign entrants early in the market are likely to be the victims of emerging policies for which few precedents exist. Consequently, businesses will be subject to considerable uncertainty about the outcome of the approval process.

Recent events also suggest that progress in China opening up its economy to global M&A will come in fits and starts. Early in 2006, Chinese officials blocked Citigroup's proposal to acquire 85% of Guangdong Development Bank, an insolvent state-owned lender. However, later that same year, a Citigroup-led consortium was able to purchase 85% of the bank for $3.1 billion; however, the stake held by foreign investors was limited to 24.7% (i.e., Citigroup with 20% and IBM with 4.7%). Private U.S. equity investor, the Carlyle Group, was rebuffed in its effort to acquire 85% of Xugong Construction Machinery, a state-owned heavy equipment manufacturer. In late 2006, Arcelor Mittal, the world's largest steelmaker, failed in its bid to purchase a minority position in Laiwu Steel Corporation because of the failure to get support from certain government regulatory agencies. Beijing also introduced new rules requiring foreign investors to register with the Ministry of Commerce any transactions resulting in foreign control of any companies in "key industries," without clearly defining which industries fell into this category. If continued, these gestures may suggest a subtle shift in Chinese policy toward welcoming direct foreign investments in new operations, while discouraging foreign takeovers of existing firms.

Things to Remember

The Securities Acts of 1933 and 1934 established the SEC and require that all securities offered to the public must be registered with the government. The registration process requires the description of the company's properties and business, a description of the securities, information about management, and financial statements certified by public accountants. Passed in 1968, the Williams Act consists of a series of amendments to the 1934 Securities Exchange Act, which were intended to provide target firm shareholders with sufficient information and time to adequately assess the value of an acquirer's offer. Any person or firm acquiring 5% or more of the stock of a public corporation must file a Schedule 13D disclosing their intentions and business plans with the SEC within 10 days of reaching that percentage ownership threshold.

Federal antitrust laws exist to prevent individual corporations from assuming too much market power. Passed in 1890, the Sherman Act makes illegal such practices as agreements to fix prices and allocate customers among competitors, as well as attempts to monopolize any part of interstate commerce. In an attempt to strengthen the Sherman Act, the Clayton Act was passed in 1914 to make illegal the purchase of stock of another company if their combination results in reduced competition within the industry. Current antitrust law requires prenotification of mergers or acquisitions involving companies of a certain size to allow the FTC and the DoJ to have sufficient time to challenge business combinations believed to be anticompetitive before they are completed.

There are numerous state regulations affecting M&As such as state antitakeover and antitrust laws. A number of industries also are subject to regulatory approval at the federal and state level. Considerable effort also must be made to ensure that a transaction is in full compliance with applicable environmental and employee benefit laws. Failure to do so can result in litigation and fines that could erode the profitability of the combined firms or even result in bankruptcy.

Chapter Discussion Questions

2-1. What was the motivation for the Federal Securities Acts of 1933 and 1934?

2-2. What was the rationale for the Williams Act?

2-3. What factors do U.S. antitrust regulators consider before challenging a transaction?

2-4. What are the obligations of the acquirer and target firms according to the Williams Act?

2-5. Discuss the pros and cons of federal antitrust laws.

2-6. Why is premerger notification (HSR filing) required by U.S. antitrust regulatory authorities?

2-7. When is a person or firm required to submit a Schedule 13D to the SEC? What is the purpose of such a filing?

2-8. What is the rationale behind state antitakeover legislation?

2-9. Give examples of the types of actions that may be required by the parties to a proposed merger subject to an FTC consent decree?

2-10. How might the growth of the Internet affect the application of current antitrust laws?

Answers to these Chapter Discussion Questions are available in the Online Instructor's Manual for instructors using this book.

Chapter Business Case

Case Study 2-7
Global Financial Exchanges Pose Regulatory Challenges

Background

In mid-2006, the NYSE Group, the operator of the New York Stock Exchange, and Euronext NV, the European exchange operator, announced plans to merge. This merger created the first transatlantic stock and derivatives market. The transaction is valued at $20 billion. Organizationally, NYSE-Euronext will be operated as a holding company and will be the world's largest publicly traded exchange company. The combined firms would trade stocks and derivatives through the New York Stock Exchange, on the electronic Euronext Liffe exchange in London, and on the stock exchanges in Paris, Lisbon, Brussels, and Amsterdam.

In recent years, most of the world's major exchanges have gone public and pursued acquisitions. Before this latest deal, the NYSE merged with electronic trading firm Archipelago Holdings, while Nasdaq Stock Market Inc. acquired the electronic trading unit of rival Instinet. This consolidation of exchanges within countries and between countries is being driven by declining trading fees, improving trading information technology, and relaxed cross-border restrictions on capital flows, and in part increased regulation in the United States. U.S. regulation, driven by Sarbanes–Oxley, has contributed to the transfer of new listings (IPOs) overseas. The best strategy U.S. exchanges have for recapturing lost business is to follow these new listings overseas.

Larger companies that operate across multiple continents also promise to attract more investors to trading in specific stocks and derivatives contracts, which could lead to cheaper, faster, and easier trading. As exchange operators become larger, they can more easily cut operating and processing costs by eliminating redundant or overlapping staff and facilities and, in theory, pass the savings along to investors. Moreover, by attracting more buyers and sellers the gap between prices at which investors are willing to buy and sell any given stock (i.e., the bid and ask prices) should narrow. The presence of more traders means there are more people bidding to buy and sell any given stock. This saves investors money and results in prices that more accurately reflect the true underlying value of the security because of more competition. Furthermore, the cross-border mergers also should make it easier and cheaper for individual investors to buy and sell foreign shares. Currently, the cost and complexity of buying an overseas stock typically limits most U.S. investors to buying mutual funds that invest in foreign stocks. Finally, corporations will now be able to sell their shares on several continents through a single exchange.

Regulatory Challenges

Before these benefits are realized numerous regulatory hurdles have to be overcome. Even if exchanges merge, they must still abide by local government rules when trading in the shares of a particular company, depending on where the company is listed. Generally, companies are not eager to list on multiple exchanges worldwide because that subjects them to many countries' securities regulations and a bookkeeping nightmare.

At the local level, little will change in how markets are regulated under the new holding company. European companies will list their shares on exchanges that are owned by the combined companies. These exchanges will still be overseen by individual national regulators, which cooperate but are still technically separate. In the United States, the SEC will still oversee the NYSE but will not have a direct say over Europe, except in that it will oversee the parent company since it will be headquartered in New York.

Whether this will work in practice is another question. EU member states continue to set their own rules for clearing and settlement of trades. If the NYSE and Euronext truly want a more unified and seamless trading system, the process could spark a regulatory war over which rules prevail. Consequently, it may be years before much of the anticipated synergies are realized.

Case Study Discussion Questions

1. What are the key challenges facing regulators resulting from the merger of financial exchanges in different countries? How do you see these challenges being resolved?
2. In what way are these regulatory issues similar or different from those confronting the SEC and state regulators and the European Union and individual country regulators?
3. Who should or could regulate global financial markets? Explain your answer.
4. In your opinion, will the merging of financial exchanges increase or decrease international financial stability?

Answers to these Case Study Discussion Questions are available in the Online Instructor's Manual for instructors using this book.

Chapter Business Case

Case Study 2-8
GE's Aborted Attempt to Merge with Honeywell

Many observers anticipated significant regulatory review because of the size of the transaction and the increase in concentration it would create in the markets served by the two firms. Nonetheless, most believed that after making some concessions to regulatory authorities, the transaction would be approved due to its widely perceived benefits. Although the pundits were indeed correct in noting that it would receive close scrutiny, they were completely caught off guard by divergent approaches taken by the U.S. and EU antitrust authorities. U.S. regulators ruled that the merger should be approved because of its potential benefits to customers. In marked contrast, EU regulators ruled against the transaction based on its perceived negative impact on competitors.

Background
Honeywell's avionics and engines unit would add significant strength to GE's jet engine business. The deal would add about 10 cents to GE's 2001 earnings and could eventually result in $1.5 billion in annual cost savings. The purchase also would enable GE to continue its shift away from manufacturing and into services, which already comprised 70% of its revenues in 2000 (*BusinessWeek*, November 6, 2000). The best fit is clearly in the combination of the two firms' aerospace businesses. Revenues from these two businesses alone would total $22 billion, combining Honeywell's strength in jet engines and cockpit avionics with GE's substantial business in larger jet engines. As the largest supplier in the aerospace industry, GE could offer airplane manufacturers "one-stop shopping" for

everything from engines to complex software systems by cross-selling each other's products to their biggest customers.

Honeywell had been on the block for a number of months before the deal was consummated with GE. Its merger with Allied Signal had not been going well, and it had contributed to deteriorating earnings and a much lower stock price. Honeywell's shares declined in price by more than 40% since its acquisition of Allied Signal. While the euphoria surrounding the deal in late 2000 lingered into the early months of 2001, rumblings from the European regulators began to create an uneasy feeling among GE's and Honeywell's management.

Regulatory Hurdles Slow the Process

Mario Monti, the European Competition Commissioner at that time, expressed concern about possible "conglomerate effects" or the total influence a combined GE and Honeywell would wield in the aircraft industry. He was referring to GE's perceived ability to expand its influence in the aerospace industry through service initiatives. GE's service offerings help differentiate it from others at a time when prices of many industrial parts are being pressured by increased competition, including low-cost manufacturers overseas. In a world in which manufactured products are becoming increasingly commodity-like, the true winners are those able to differentiate their product offering. GE and Honeywell's European competitors complained to the EU regulatory commission that GE's extensive service offering would give it entrée into many more points of contact among airplane manufacturers—from communications systems to the expanded line of spare parts GE would be able to supply. This so-called "range effect" or "portfolio power" is a relatively new legal doctrine that has not been tested in transactions the size of this one (Murray, April 5, 2001).

U.S. Regulators Approve the Deal

On May 3, 2001, the U.S. Department of Justice approved the buyout after the companies agreed to sell Honeywell's helicopter engine unit and to take other steps to protect competition. The U.S. regulatory authorities believed that the combined companies could sell more products to more customers and therefore could realize improved efficiencies, although it would not hold a dominant market share in any particular market. Thus, customers would benefit from GE's greater range of products and possibly lower prices, but they still could shop elsewhere if they chose. The U.S. regulators expressed little concern that bundling of products and services could hurt customers, since buyers can choose from among a relative handful of viable suppliers.

Understanding the European Union Position

To understand the European position, it is necessary to comprehend the nature of competition in the EU. France, Germany, and Spain have spent billions subsidizing their aerospace industry over the years. The GE–Honeywell deal has been attacked by their European rivals from Rolls-Royce and Lufthansa to French avionics manufacturer, Thales. Although the EU imported much of its antitrust law from the United States, the antitrust law doctrine has evolved in fundamentally different ways. In Europe, the main goal of antitrust law is to guarantee that all companies should be able to compete on an equal playing field. The implication is that the EU is just as concerned about how a transaction affects rivals as it is consumers. Complaints from competitors are taken more seriously in Europe, whereas in the United States it is the impact on consumers that constitutes the litmus test. Europeans have accepted the legal concept of "portfolio power," which argues that a firm may achieve an unfair advantage over its competitors by bundling goods and services. Also, in Europe, the European Commission's Merger Task Force can prevent a merger without taking a company to court. By removing this judicial remedy, the EU makes it possible for the regulators, who are political appointees, to be biased.

GE Walks Away from the Deal

The EU authorities continued to balk at approving the transaction without major concessions from the participants, concessions that GE believed would render the deal unattractive. On June 15, 2001, GE submitted its final offer to the EU regulators in a last-ditch attempt to breathe life into the moribund deal. GE knew that, if it walked away, it could continue as it had before the deal was struck, secure in the knowledge that its current portfolio of businesses offered substantial revenue growth or profit potential. Honeywell clearly would fuel such growth, but it made sense to GE's management and shareholders only if it would be allowed to realize potential synergies between the GE and Honeywell businesses.

GE said it was willing to divest Honeywell units with annual revenue of $2.2 billion, including regional jet engines, air-turbine starters, and other aerospace products. Anything more would jeopardize the rationale for the deal. Specifically, GE was unwilling to agree not to bundle (i.e., sell a package of components and services at a single price) its products and services when selling to customers. Another stumbling block was GE Capital Aviation Services unit, the airplane-financing arm of GE Capital. The EU Antitrust Commission argued that this unit would use its clout as one of the world's largest purchasers of airplanes to pressure airplane manufacturers into using GE products. The Commission seemed to ignore that GE had only an 8% share of the global airplane-leasing market and would therefore seemingly lack the market power the Commission believed it could exert.

On July 4, 2001, the EU vetoed the GE purchase of Honeywell, marking it the first time a proposed merger between two U.S. companies has been blocked solely by European regulators. Having received U.S. regulatory approval, GE could ignore the EU decision and proceed with the merger as long as it would be willing to forego sales in Europe. GE decided not to appeal the decision to the EU Court of First Instance (the second highest court in the EU), knowing that it could take years to resolve the decision, and withdrew its offer to merge with Honeywell.

The GE–Honeywell Legacy

On December 15, 2005, a European court upheld the European regulator's decision to block the transaction, although the ruling partly vindicated GE's position. The European Court of First Instance said regulators were in error in assuming without sufficient evidence that a combined GE–Honeywell could crush competition in several markets. However, the Court demonstrated that regulators would have to provide data to support either their approval of or rejection of mergers by ruling on July 18, 2006, that regulators erred in approving the combination of Sony BMG in 2004. In this instance, regulators failed to provide sufficient data to document their decision. These decisions affirm that the EU needs strong economic justification to overrule cross-border deals. GE and Honeywell in filing the suit said that their appeal had been made to clarify European rules with an eye toward future deals as they had no desire to resurrect the deal.

Case Study Discussion Questions

1. What are the important philosophical differences between U.S. and EU antitrust regulators? Explain the logic underlying these differences. To what extent are these differences influenced by political rather than economic considerations? Explain your answer.

2. This is the first time that a foreign regulatory body has prevented a deal involving U.S. firms only from occurring. What are the long-term implications, if any, of this precedent?

3. What were the major stumbling blocks between GE and the EU regulators? Why do you think these were stumbling blocks? Do you think the EU regulators were justified in their position?

4. Do you think that competitors are using antitrust to their advantage? Explain your answer.

5. Do you think the EU regulators would have taken a different position if the deal had involved a less visible firm than General Electric? Explain your answer.

References

American Bar Association, *Mergers and Acquisitions: Understanding Antitrust Issues*, 2nd Ed., 2006.

Batson, Andrew, "China's Merger Boom Continues," *The Wall Street Journal*, January 12, 2007, p. C2.

Brookings Institute, "Antitrust Goes Global," November 2000.

Bumgardner, Larry, "Antitrust Law in the European Union: The Law Is Changing—But to What Effect?," *Journal of Relevant Business Information and Analysis*, Vol. 8, 2005.

BusinessWeek, "Jack's Risky Last Act," November 6, 2000, pp. 40–45.

Chhaochharia, Vidhi, and Yaniv Grinstein, "Corporate Governance and Firm Value: The Impact of the 2002 Governance Rules," *Journal of Finance*, Forthcoming 2007.

Federal Trade Commission, Bureau of Competition, "A Study of the Commission's Divestiture Process," 1999.

Federal Trade Commission, *Merger Guidelines*, 1999, www.ftc.com.

Ganghar, Anuj, "Private Placement Exceed IPOs," *Financial Times*, May 18, 2007, p. 13.

Garten, Jeffery E., "As Business Goes Global, Antitrust Should Too," *BusinessWeek*, November 13, 2000, p. 38.

Gilson, Ronald J., and Bernard S. Black, *The Law and Finance of Corporate Acquisitions*, 2nd Ed., The Foundation Press, Inc., Westbury, NY, 1995.

Grant, Jeremy, "SEC Hopes Sarbox Fix Will Revive Foreign Listings in U.S.," *Financial Times*, March 23, 2007, p. 2.

Kaplan, Steven N., "Mergers and Acquisitions: A Financial Economics Perspective," paper prepared for the Antitrust Modernization Commission Economist's Roundtable on Merger Enforcement, February 19, 2006.

Lindell, Cecile Kohrs, "More Merger Reviews, Fewer Hurdles," *Law and Regulation*, September 8, 2006.

Loss, Louis, and Joel Seligman, *Fundamentals of Securities Regulation*, 3rd Ed., Little, Brown, Boston, 1995.

Murray, Matthew, "GE's Honeywell Deal Is More Than the Sum of Airplane Parts," *The Wall Street Journal*, April 5, 2001, p. B6.

Navarro, Edward, *Merger Control in the EU: Law, Economics, and Practice*, 2nd Ed., Oxford University Press, Oxford, 2005.

New York Times, "The Spread of Antitrust Authorities," January 28, 2001, Section 3, p. 4.

"Sale of Zurich Subsidiary to Nortel Networks Completed," SDL Press Release, February 14, 2001, www.sdli.com/about/release/pr_021301.html.

Sherman, Andrew J., *Mergers and Acquisitions from A to Z, Strategic and Practical Guidance for Small and Middle Market Buyers and Sellers,* AMACOM, 1998, pp. 78–94.

Siliconix Inc. Shareholders Litigation, Delaware Court, C.A. No. 18700, July 19, 2001.

Truitt, Wesley B., *The Corporation*, Greenwood Press: Westport, Connecticut, 2006, pp. 140–143.

United States Attorney General, "Global Antitrust Regulation: Issues and Solutions," *Final Report of the International Competition Policy Advisory Committee*, February 2000.

United States Department of Justice, Antitrust Division, www.usdoj.gov, 1999.

United States v. Primestar, L.P., 58 Fed. Reg., 33944, June 22, 1993 (Proposed Final Judgment and Competitive Impact Study).

CHAPTER ◆ 3

The Corporate Takeover Market

Common Takeover Tactics, Antitakeover Defenses, and Corporate Governance

Treat a person as he is, and he will remain as he is. Treat him as he could be, and he will become what he should be.

—Jimmy Johnson

Inside M&A: Hewlett-Packard Family Members Oppose Proposal to Acquire Compaq

On September 4, 2001, Hewlett-Packard (HP) announced its proposal to acquire Compaq Computer Corporation for $25 billion in stock. Almost immediately, investors began to doubt the wisdom of the proposal. The new company would face the mind-numbing task of integrating overlapping product lines and 150,000 employees in 160 countries. Reflecting these concerns, the value of the proposed merger had sunk to $16.9 billion within 30 days following the announcement, in line with the decline in the value of HP's stock.

In November 2001, Walter Hewlett and David Packard, sons of the cofounders, and both the Hewlett and Packard family foundations, came out against the transaction. These individuals and entities controlled about 18% of HP's total shares outstanding. Both Carly Fiorina, HP's CEO, and Michael Capellas, Compaq's CEO, moved aggressively to counter this opposition by taking their case directly to the remaining HP shareholders. HP management's efforts included a 49-page report written by HP's advisor Goldman Sachs to rebut one presented by Walter Hewlett's advisors. HP also began advertising in national newspapers and magazines, trying to convey the idea that this deal is not about PCs but about giving corporate customers everything from storage and services to printing and imaging.

After winning a hotly contested 8-month long proxy fight by a narrow 2.8 percentage point margin, HP finally was able to purchase Compaq on May 7, 2002, for approximately

$19 billion. However, the contentious proxy fight had lingering effects. The delay in integrating the two firms resulted in the defection of key employees, the loss of customers and suppliers, the expenditure of millions of dollars, and widespread angst among shareholders.

Chapter Overview

The corporate takeover has been dramatized in Hollywood as motivated by excessive greed, reviled in the press as a job destroyer, hailed as a means of dislodging incompetent management, and often heralded by shareholders as a source of windfall gains. The reality is that corporate takeovers may be a little of all of these things. The purpose of this chapter is to discuss the effectiveness of commonly used tactics to acquire a company in a hostile takeover attempt and to evaluate the effectiveness of various takeover defenses. The market in which such takeover tactics and defenses are employed is called the "corporate takeover market," which serves two important functions in a free market economy. First, it facilitates the allocation of resources to sectors in which they can be used most efficiently. Second, it serves as a mechanism for disciplining underperforming corporate managers. By replacing such managers through hostile takeover attempts or through proxy fights, the corporate takeover market can help to promote good corporate governance practices. Traditionally, the goal of corporate governance has been viewed as the protection of shareholder rights. More recently, the goal has expanded to include

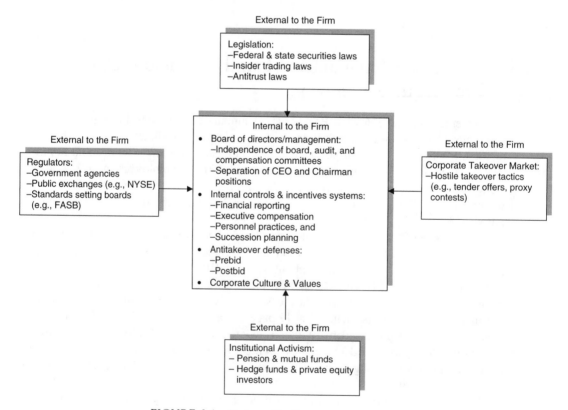

FIGURE 3-1   Factors affecting corporate governance.

more corporate stakeholders including customers, employees, the government, lenders, communities, regulators, and suppliers. For our purposes, corporate governance is defined as factors internal and external to the firm that interact to protect the rights of corporate stakeholders.

While this chapter will discuss corporate governance practices primarily in the United States, it is clear that no country seems to have yet developed a highly effective governance system. The visible breakdown in the system of corporate governance in the United States early in 2002 brings to mind such names as Enron, WorldCom, and Tyco. However, this malaise is not unique to the United States. In 2002, French conglomerate Vivendi, German telecom giant Deutsche Telekom, and British mobile phone behemoth Vodafone experienced precipitous declines in shareholder value and the ouster of CEOs. Major scandals rocked Italy's Parmalat in 2003 and Royal Dutch Shell in 2004. Parmalat's management team went to jail and Shell's CEO was fired.

Figure 3-1 illustrates the factors impacting corporate governance, including the corporate takeover market. Following a discussion of these factors, the corporate takeover market is discussed in more detail in terms of commonly used takeover tactics and defenses. Finally, case studies at the end of the chapter provide an excellent illustration of how takeover tactics are used in a hostile takeover to penetrate a firm's defenses. A chapter review is available on the CD ROM accompanying this book.

Factors Affecting Corporate Governance

Alternative Models of Corporate Governance

The ultimate goal of a successful corporate governance system should be to hold those in power accountable for their actions. Where capital markets are liquid (i.e., investors can easily sell their shares), investors discipline bad managers by selling their shares. Where capital markets are illiquid, bad managers are disciplined by those owning large blocks of stock in the firm or those whose degree of control is disproportionate to their ownership position. The latter situation may develop through the concentration of shares having multiple voting rights in the hands of a few investors. Table 3-1 describes two alternative approaches to governance described as the market model and the control model. The former is prevalent in the United States and the United Kingdom, while the latter is more common in Europe, Asia, and Latin America. For a more detailed discussion of the market model, see Atkinson and Salterio (2002) and Robinson (2002). Shleifer and Vishny (1997) and LaPorta and Shleifer (1999) provide an excellent discussion of the control model.

TABLE 3-1   Alternative Models of Corporate Governance

Market Model Applicable When:	Control Model Applicable When:
Capital markets are highly liquid	Capital markets are illiquid
Equity ownership is widely dispersed	Ownership is heavily concentrated
Board members are largely independent	Board members largely "insiders"
Ownership and control are separate	Ownership and control overlap
Financial disclosure is high	Financial disclosure is limited
Shareholder focus more on short-term gains	Shareholder focus more on long-term gains

This chapter focuses on governance under the market model, while the control model is discussed in more detail in Chapter 10, which deals with analyzing privately – family owned firms.

The market model relies on two basic principles. First, the incentives of managers should be aligned with the goals of the shareholders and other primary stakeholders. Second, the firm's financial condition should be sufficiently transparent to enable shareholders and other stakeholders to evaluate the performance of managers based on public information. Accountability is achieved through market forces, regulation, or some combination of the two. What follows is a discussion of those factors internal and external to the firm that impact corporate governance.

Factors Internal to the Firm

Corporate governance is impacted by the integrity and professionalism of the firm's board of directors, as well as the effectiveness of the firm's internal controls and incentive systems, takeover defenses, and corporate culture and values.

Board of Directors/Management

Boards serve as advisors to the CEO and review the quality of recommendations received by the CEO from corporate management. Boards also hire, fire, and set compensation for a company's chief executive, who runs the daily operations of the firm. Moreover, boards are expected to oversee management, corporate strategy, and the company's financial reports to shareholders. Board members, who are also employees or family members, may be subject to conflicts of interest, which may cause them to act in ways not necessarily in the stakeholders' interest. Some observers often argue that boards should be dominated by independent directors and that the CEO and Chairman of the Board should be separate positions. Hermalin (2005); Huson, Parrino, and Starks (2001); and Dahya and McConnell (2001) have documented the following trends with respect to board composition and compensation. First, the proportion of independent directors has steadily increased in the United States and in other countries. The average percentage of outside directors increased from 35% in 1989 to 61% in 1999. Second, the use of incentive compensation for outside directors has increased significantly. Eighty-four percent of firms reporting to a Conference Board Survey used stock-based compensation for outside directors in 1997 versus 6% in 1989. Unfortunately, empirical studies have not consistently demonstrated that such proposals improve shareholder wealth (*Economic Report to the President*, 2003, p. 90).

In the United States, the standard of review for a director's conduct in an acquisition begins with the ***business judgment rule***. Directors are expected to conduct themselves in a manner that could reasonably be seen as being in the best interests of the shareholders. This "rule" is a presumption that the courts will not interfere with, or second-guess, business decisions made by directors. However, when a party to the transaction is seen as having a conflict of interest, the business judgment rule does not apply. In such circumstances, the director's actions are subject to the so-called fairness test consisting of fair dealing (i.e., a fair process) and a fair price. An example of a fair process would be when a seller does not favor one bidder over another. An example of a fair price would be when the seller accepts the highest price offered for the business. However, the determination of what constitutes the highest price may be ambiguous when the purchase price consists of stock (whose value will fluctuate) rather than cash.

So-called "bright line" standards have been enacted by the Securities and Exchange Commission (SEC) and the New York Stock Exchange (NYSE) requiring that a majority of directors and board members sitting on key board committees, such as compensation and audit, be considered independent. According to the NYSE, directors having received more than $100,000 over the prior 3 years from a company cannot be considered to be independent. For the SEC, the amount is $60,000. The NYSE also requires that firms explain even nonfinancial relationships to shareholders so that they may determine if such relationships should be viewed as material and, if so, whether they should disqualify the director from being considered independent.

Internal Controls and Incentive Systems

Tax rules and accounting standards in the United States send mixed signals. On the one hand, the U.S. tax code requires compensation above $1 million to be "performance based" to be tax deductible. This encourages firms to pay executives with stock options rather than with cash. In contrast, firms are now required to charge the cost of options against current earnings, as opposed to their ability to defer such costs in the past. This has a dampening effect on the widespread use of options. Moreover, the current practice of fixed strike or exercise prices (i.e., prices at which option-holders can buy company stock) for options led to enormous profits simply because the overall stock market rose even though the firm's performance lagged the overall market.

By eliminating such tax rules, boards would be encouraged to design compensation plans that reward exceptional performance rather than the exploitation of tax rules. Furthermore, linking option strike prices to the performance of the company's stock price relative to the stock market would ensure that increases in the stock market do not benefit managers whose companies are underperforming. Indexing option strike prices will also reduce the incentive to reset the strike price of existing options when a stock price declines and renders current options worthless.

Another way to align corporate managers' interests with those of other stakeholders is for managers to own a significant portion of the firm's outstanding stock or for the manger's ownership of the firm's stock to comprise a substantial share of their personal wealth. The proportion of shares owned by managers of public firms grew from 1935, from an average of 12.9% to an average of 21.1% in 1998 (*Economic Report to the President*, 2003, p. 86). There appears to have been little change in this ownership percentage in recent years. An alternative to concentrating ownership in management is for one or more managers, who are not managers, to accumulate a significant block of voting shares. Corporations having outside shareholders with large blocks of stock may be easier to acquire, thereby increasing management's risk of being ousted due to poor performance.

There is some evidence that the composition of a manager's compensation may affect what they are willing to pay for an acquisition. The share prices of acquirers whose managers' total compensation includes a large amount of equity tend to exhibit positive responses to the announcement of an acquisition. In contrast, the share price of those firms whose managers' compensation is largely cash based display negative responses (Dutta, Dutta, and Raman, 2001). The authors found that the premium paid by managers whose compensation was heavily based on equity tended to be smaller than that paid by acquirers whose management's compensation was mostly cash. Investors apparently believe that smaller premiums would increase the likelihood the acquirer would realize appropriate financial returns.

Antitakeover Defenses

Takeover defenses may be employed by a firm's management and board to gain leverage in negotiating with a potential suitor. Alternatively, such practices may be used to solidify current management's position within the firm. The range of such defenses available to a target's management is discussed in some detail later in this chapter.

Corporate Culture and Values

Regulations, monitoring systems, and incentive plans are only part of the answer to improved corporate governance. While internal systems and controls are important, good governance is also a result of instilling the employee culture with appropriate core values and behaviors. Setting the right tone and direction comes from the board of directors and senior management and their willingness to behave in a manner consistent with what they demand from other employees. One can only speculate as to the degree to which the scandal that rocked Hewlett-Packard in late 2006 undermined the firm's internal culture. The scandal made it clear that some members of top management sanctioned internal spying on the firm's board members and gaining access illegally to their private information. Such missteps understandably drastically reduce employee confidence in senior management's pronouncements about desired corporate values and behaviors. See Chapter 6 for a more detailed discussion of corporate culture.

Factors External to the Firm

Federal and state legislation, the court system, regulators, institutional activists, and the corporate takeover market all play an important role in maintaining good corporate governance practices.

Legislation and the Legal System

As noted in Chapter 2, the basis of modern securities legislation can be found with the Securities Acts of 1933 and 1934, which created the SEC and delegated to it the task of writing and enforcing securities regulations. The U.S. Congress has also transferred some the enforcement task to public stock exchanges, such as the New York Stock Exchange. Such exchanges operate under SEC oversight as self-regulatory organizations. Furthermore, the SEC has delegated certain responsibilities for setting and maintaining accounting standards to the Financial Accounting Standards Board. Under the Sarbanes–Oxley Act, the SEC is overseeing the new Public Company Accounting Oversight Board, whose primary task is to develop, maintain, and enforce the standards that guide auditors in monitoring and certifying corporate financial reports. State legislation also has a significant impact on governance practices by requiring corporate charters to define the responsibilities of boards and managers with respect to shareholders.

Regulators

Regulators such as the FTC, SEC, and DoJ can discipline firms with inappropriate governance practices through formal and informal investigations, lawsuits filed, and settlements. Data suggest that the announcement of a regulatory investigation punishes firms, with firms subject to investigations suffering an average decline in share prices of 6% around the announcement date (Hirschey, 2003). In mid-2003, The SEC approved new listing standards for the NYSE that would require that many lucrative, stock-based pay plans be subject to a vote by shareholders. This means that investors in more than 6200 companies listed on the NYSE, Nasdaq, and other major markets can exercise significant control over CEO pay packages. Effective January 1, 2007, the SEC implemented additional disclosure requirements concerning CEO pay and perks. The new rules require companies to disclose perks whose value exceeds $10,000. In contrast, the old rules required disclosure of perks valued at more than $50,000 (White and Lublin, 2007).

Institutional Activists

Even if shareholders vote overwhelmingly in favor of specific resolutions, boards need not implement these resolutions as most are simply advisory only. Managers often need to be able to go about managing the business without significant outside interference from single-agenda dissident shareholders. Shareholder proposals tend to be nonbinding because in many states, including Delaware, board classification must appear in the charter, and a charter amendment must be initiated by board, not shareholder, action.

During the 1970s and 1980s, institutional ownership of public firms increased substantially, with the percentage of equity held by institutions at 49.1% in 2001 versus 31% in 1970 (*Federal Reserve Bulletin*, December 2003, p. 33). In the 1980s, pension funds, mutual funds, and insurance firms were often passive investors, showing little interest in matters of corporate governance. While pension funds became more aggressive in the 1990s, the Investment Company Act of 1940 restricts the ability of institutions to discipline corporate management. For example, mutual funds in order to achieve diversification are limited in the amount they can invest in any one firm's outstanding stock. State regulations often restrict the share of a life insurance or property casualty company's assets that can be invested in stock to as little as 2%. Nevertheless, institutional investors that have huge portfolios can be very effective in demanding governance changes. Despite some limitations, there is evidence that institutions are taking increasingly aggressive stands against management.

TIAA-CREF, the New York-based investment company that manages pension plans for teachers, colleges, universities, and research institutions, believes it has a responsibility to push for better corporate governance as well as stock performance. The Louisiana Teachers Retirement System brought legal pressure to bear on Siebel Systems Inc., resulting in a settlement in mid-2003 in which the software company agreed to make changes in its board and to disclose how it sets executive compensation, which has been criticized as excessive. In a case brought against some officers and directors of Sprint Corp. in 2003 by labor unions and pension funds, Sprint settled by agreeing to governance changes that require at least two-thirds of its board members to be independent.

Following the SEC requirement in late 2004 to make their proxy votes public, mutual funds are increasingly challenging management on such hot-button issues as antitakeover defenses, lavish severance benefits for CEOs, and employee stock option accounting. A study of the 24 largest mutual funds in the United States indicated that the American Funds, T. Rowe Price, and Vanguard voted against management and for key shareholder proposals in 2004 70, 61, and 51% of the time, respectively, sharply higher than in 2003. However, industry leader Fidelity voted against management only 33% of the time. Voting against management could become more problematic as some mutual funds manage both retirement plans and increasingly a host of outsourcing services from payroll to health benefits for their business clients (Farzad, October 16, 2006).

Kini, Kracaw, and Mian (2004) document a decline in the number of executives serving as both Chairman of the Board and Chief Executive Officer from about 91% during the 1980s to 58% during the 1990s. This general decline may be attributable to increased pressure from shareholder activists (Brickley, Coles, and Jarrell, 1997; Goyal and Park, 2002). In some instances, CEOs are willing to negotiate with activists rather than face a showdown in an annual shareholders meeting. Activists are finding that they may avoid the expense of a full-blown proxy fight by simply threatening to withhold their votes in support of a CEO or management proposal. Institutional investors may choose to express their dissatisfaction by abstaining rather than casting a "no" vote, although in some instances they may only have the choice of abstaining or voting affirmatively. By abstaining, institutional investors can indicate their dissatisfaction with a CEO or a firm's policy without jeopardizing future underwriting or M&A business for the institution. In early 2004, in an unprecedented expression of no confidence, 43% of the votes cast were in opposition to the continuation of Disney Chairman of the Board and Chief Executive Officer Michael Eisner as Chairman of the Board. While he had still received a majority of the votes, the Disney board voted to strip Eisner of his role as Chairman of the Board. Michael Eisner retired at the end of his contract in 2006.

Activist strategies in which votes are withheld are likely to have a greater impact on removing board members in the future as more firms adopt majority voting policies, which require directors to be reelected by a majority of the votes cast. Under the traditional voting system, votes withheld were not counted and such activity was largely a symbolic gesture. With 53% of all S&P 500 firms having adopted majority voting as of early 2007, withheld votes are counted making it possible that a director could not get majority approval (Whitehouse, February 18, 2007).

The importance of institutional ownership in maintaining good governance practices is evident in the highly concentrated ownership of firms in Europe. Ownership in U.S. companies tends to be dispersed, which makes close monitoring of board and management practices difficult. European companies are characterized by concentrated ownership. While this ownership structure facilitates closer operational monitoring and removal of key managers, it also enables the controlling shareholder to extract certain benefits at the expense of other shareholders (Coffee, 2005). Controlling shareholders may have their company purchase products and services at above-market prices directly from another firm they own. Parmalat and Hollinger are examples of firms whose principal shareholders exploited their firms in this manner.

In recent years, hedge funds and private equity investors have assumed increasing roles as activist investors. In 2006, a shareholder revolt led by New York-based Knight Vinke Asset Management prompted the $9.6 billion sale of the underperforming Dutch conglomerate VNU to a group of private equity investors. In 2007, U.S. hedge fund, Trian, prompted soft drink and candy giant Cadbury Schweppes to split the firm in two after taking a 3% ownership position and threatening a proxy contest.

Corporate Takeover Market

Changes in corporate control can occur because of a hostile (i.e., bids contested by the target's board and management) or a friendly takeover of a target firm or because of a proxy contest initiated by dissident shareholders. When mechanisms internal to the firm governing management control are relatively weak, there is significant empirical evidence that the corporate takeover market acts as a "court of last resort" to discipline inappropriate management behavior (Kini et al., 2004). In contrast, when a firm's internal governance mechanisms are strong, the role of the takeover threat as a disciplinary factor is lessened. Moreover, disciplining effect of a takeover threat on a firm's management can be reinforced when it is paired with a large shareholding by an institutional investor (Cremers and Nair, 2005).

Several theories have evolved as to why managers may resist a takeover attempt. The *management entrenchment theory* suggests that managers use a variety of takeover defenses to ensure their longevity with the firm. Hostile takeovers or the threat of such takeovers have historically played a useful role in maintaining good corporate governance by removing bad managers and installing better ones (Morck, Shleifer, and Vishny, 1988). Indeed, there is evidence of frequent management turnover even if a takeover attempt is defeated, as takeover targets are often poor financial performers (*Economic Report to the President*, 2003, p. 81). An alternative viewpoint is the *shareholder interest's theory*, which suggests that management resistance to proposed takeovers is a good bargaining strategy to increase the purchase price to the benefit of the target firm's shareholders (Franks and Mayer, 1996; Schwert, 2000).

Proxy contests are attempts by a dissident group of shareholders to gain representation on a firm's board of directors or to change management proposals. Proxy contests addressing issues other than board representation do not bind a firm's board of directors. While their success rate is relatively low (i.e., 20–30%), even unsuccessful contests often lead to an eventual change in management, a tendency for management to restructure the firm, or investor expectations that the firm will be acquired ultimately.

While hostile takeovers continue to constitute a comparatively small percentage of total M&A activity, corporate and private equity investors initiated 110 such bids in 2006 valued at $351 billion according to Thomson Financial. This figure is the highest since 2000 when 129 offers worth $117 billion were undertaken. With potential bidders awash in cash and interest rates low, many potential targets are looking increasingly vulnerable. Many firms have stripped away their takeover defenses to satisfy shareholder demands for better governance practices. In 2006, Thomson Financial data indicates that only 118 companies adopted poison pills (i.e., plans giving shareholders the right to buy stock below the current market price) compared to an average of 234 annually throughout the 1990s. To explain these developments in more detail, the remainder of this chapter describes the common takeover tactics and antitakeover defenses that characterize the corporate takeover market.

Alternative Takeover Tactics in the Corporate Takeover Market

Takeovers may be classified as friendly or hostile. Friendly takeovers are negotiated settlements that often are characterized by bargaining, which remains undisclosed until an agreement has been signed. An example of a friendly takeover is a company desirous of being acquired soliciting another firm to assess its interest in combining the two firms. A hostile takeover generally is considered an unsolicited offer made by a potential acquirer that is resisted by the target firm's management and board. Hostile transactions normally are disclosed in the press.

Friendly takeovers may be viewed as ones in which a negotiated settlement is possible without the acquirer resorting to such aggressive tactics as the bear hug, proxy contest, or tender offer. A *bear hug* involves the mailing of a letter containing an acquisition proposal to the board of directors of a target company without prior warning and demanding a rapid decision. A *proxy contest* is an attempt by dissident shareholders to obtain representation on the board of directors or to change a firm's bylaws by obtaining the right to vote on behalf of other shareholders. A *hostile tender offer* is a takeover tactic in which the acquirer bypasses the target's board and management and goes directly to the target's shareholders with an offer to purchase their shares. Unlike a merger in which the traditional legal doctrine holds that the minority must agree to the terms of the agreement negotiated by the board and management once the majority of the firms' shareholders (i.e., 51% or more) approve the proposal, the tender offer specifically allows for minority shareholders. In a traditional merger, minority shareholders are said to be frozen out of their positions. This majority approval requirement is intended to prevent minority shareholders from stopping a merger until they are paid a premium over the purchase price agreed to by the majority.

Following the tender offer, the target firm becomes a partially owned subsidiary of the acquiring company. In some instances, the terms of the transaction may be *crammed down* or imposed on the minority. This is achieved by the parent firm merging the partially owned subsidiary that resulted from the failure of the tender offer to get substantially all of the target firm's shares into a new wholly owned subsidiary. Alternatively, the acquirer may decide not to acquire 100% of the target's stock. In this case, the minority is subject to a *freeze-out or squeeze-out,* in which the remaining shareholders are dependent on the decisions made by the majority shareholders; as such, minority shareholders often feel pressure to sell their shares to the acquirer. See Chapter 11 for a more detailed discussion of these terms.

The Friendly Approach: "Sweet-Talking the Target"

Friendly takeovers involve the initiation by the potential acquirer of an informal dialogue with the target's top management. In a friendly takeover, the acquirer and target reach agreement on key issues early in the process. These key issues usually include the combined businesses' long-term strategy, how the combined businesses will be operated in the short term, and who will be in key management positions. A *standstill agreement* often is negotiated, in which the acquirer agrees not to make any further investments in the target's stock for a stipulated period. This compels the acquirer to pursue the acquisition only on friendly terms, at least for the time period covered by the agreement. It also permits negotiations to proceed without the threat of more aggressive tactics, such as a tender offer or proxy contest.

According to Thompson Financial Securities Data Corporation (2000), the vast majority of transactions were classified as friendly during the 1990s. However, this was not always the case. The 1970s and early 1980s were characterized by blitzkrieg-style takeovers. Hostile takeovers of U.S. firms peaked at about 14% of total transactions in the 1980s before dropping to a low of about 4% in the 1990s. The federal prenotification regulations have slowed the process dramatically (see Chapter 2). A number of states and public stock exchanges also require shareholder approval for certain types of offers. Moreover, most large companies have antitakeover defenses in place, such as poison pills. Hostile takeover battles are now more likely to last for months.

Although hostile takeovers today are certainly more challenging than in the past, they have certain advantages over the friendly approach. In taking the friendly approach, the acquirer is surrendering the element of surprise. Even a warning of a few days gives the target's management time to take defensive action to impede the actions of the suitor. Negotiation also raises the likelihood of a leak and a spike in the price of the target's stock as arbitrageurs ("arbs") seek to profit from the spread between the offer price and the target's current stock price. The speculative increase in the target's share price can add dramatically to the cost of the transaction, because the initial offer by the bidder generally includes a premium over the target's current share price. Because a premium usually is expressed as a percentage of the target's share price, a speculative increase in the target firm's current share price will add to the overall purchase price paid by the acquiring firm. For these reasons, a bidder may opt for a more hostile approach.

The Aggressive Approach

Successful hostile takeovers depend on the premium offered to target shareholders, the board's composition, and the composition, sentiment, and investment horizon of the target's current shareholders. Other factors include the provisions of the target's bylaws and the potential for the target to implement additional takeover defenses.

The target's board will find it more difficult to reject offers exhibiting substantial premiums to the target's current stock price. Concern about their fiduciary responsibility and about stockholder lawsuits puts pressure on the target's board to accept the offer. Despite the pressure of an attractive premium, the composition of the target's board also greatly influences what the board does and the timing of its decisions. A board dominated by independent directors, nonemployees, or family members is more likely to resist offers in an effort to induce the bidder to raise the offer price or to gain time to solicit competing bids than to protect itself and current management. Shivdasani (1993) concluded that the shareholder gain from the inception of the offer to its resolution is 62.3% for targets with an independent board, as compared with 40.9% for targets without an independent board.

Furthermore, the final outcome of a hostile takeover is also heavily dependent on the composition of the target's stock ownership, how stockholders feel about management's performance, and how long they intend to hold the stock. Gaspara and Massa (2005) found that firms held predominately by short-term investors (i.e., less than 4 months) show a greater likelihood of receiving a bid and exhibit a lower average premium of as much as 3% when acquired. The authors speculate that firms held by short-term investors have a weaker bargaining position with the bidder. To assess these factors, an acquirer compiles to the extent possible lists of stock ownership by category: management, officers, employees, and institutions such as pension and mutual funds. Such information can be used to estimate the target's *float*, the number of shares that are outstanding and available for trading by the public. The larger the share of stock held by corporate officers, family members, and employees the smaller the float, as these types of shareholders are less likely to sell their shares. Float is likely to be largest for those companies in which shareholders are disappointed with the financial performance of the firm.

Finally, an astute bidder will always analyze the target firm's bylaws for provisions potentially adding to the cost of a takeover. Such provisions could include a staggered board, the inability to remove directors without cause, or supermajority voting requirements for approval of mergers. These and other measures also will be discussed in more detail later in this chapter.

The Bear Hug: Limiting the Target's Options

If the friendly approach is considered inappropriate or is unsuccessful, the acquiring company may attempt to limit the options of the target's senior management by making a formal acquisition proposal, usually involving a public announcement, to the board of directors of the target. The intent is to move the board to a negotiated settlement. The board may be motivated to do so because of its fiduciary responsibility to the target's shareholders. Directors who vote against the proposal may be subject to lawsuits from target stockholders. This is especially true if the offer is at a substantial premium to the target's current stock price. Once the bid is made public, the company is effectively "put into play" (i.e., likely to attract additional bidders). Institutional investors and arbitrageurs add to the pressure by lobbying the board to accept the offer. Arbs are likely to acquire the target's stock and to sell the bidder's stock short (see Chapter 1). The accumulation of stock by arbs makes purchases of blocks of stock by the bidder easier.

Proxy Contests in Support of a Takeover

The primary forms of proxy contests are those for seats on the board of directors, those concerning management proposals (e.g., an acquisition), and those seeking to force management to take some particular action (e.g., dividend payments and share repurchases). The most common reasons for dissidents to initiate a proxy fight are to remove management due to poor corporate performance, a desire to promote a specific type of restructuring of the firm (e.g., sell or spin off a business), the outright sale of the business, and to force a distribution of excess cash to shareholders (Faleye, 2004). Proxy fights enable dissident shareholders to replace specific board members or management with those more willing to support their positions. By replacing board members, proxy contests can be an effective means of gaining control without owning 51% of the voting stock, or they can be used to eliminate takeover defenses, such as poison pills, as a precursor of a tender offer. In 2001, Weyerhauser Co. placed three directors on rival Willamette Industries nine-member board. The prospect of losing an additional three seats the following year ultimately brought Willamette to the bargaining table and ended Weyerhauser's 13-month attempt to take over Willamette. In mid-2005, billionaire Carl Icahn and his two dissident nominees won seats on the board of Blockbuster, successfully ousting Chairman John Antioco.

The cost of initiating a proxy contest to replace a board explains why there are so few contested board elections. Between 1996 and 2004, an average of 12 firms annually faced contested board elections (*Economist*, March 11, 2006). For the official slates of directors nominated by the board, campaigns can be paid out of corporate funds. For the shareholder promoting their own slate of candidates, substantial fees must be paid to hire proxy solicitors, investment bankers, and attorneys. Other expenses include those related to printing and mailing the proxy statement, as well as advertising. Litigation expenses also may be substantial. The cost of litigation easily can become the largest single expense item in highly contentious proxy contests. Nonetheless, a successful proxy fight represents a far less expensive means of gaining control over a target than a tender offer, which may require purchasing at a substantial premium a controlling interest in the target.

Implementing a Proxy Contest

When the bidder is also a shareholder in the target firm, the proxy process may begin with the bidder attempting to call a special stockholders' meeting. Alternatively, the bidder may put a proposal to replace the board or management at a regularly scheduled stockholders' meeting. Before the meeting, the bidder may undertake an aggressive public relations campaign consisting of direct solicitations sent to shareholders and full-page advertisements in the press in an attempt to convince shareholders to support their proposals. The target will undertake a similar campaign, but it will have a distinct advantage in being able to deal directly with its own shareholders. The bidder may have to sue the target corporation to get a list of its shareholders' names and addresses. Often such shares are held in the name of banks or brokerage houses under a "street name," and these depositories generally do not have the authority to vote such shares.

Once the proxies are received by shareholders, they may then sign and send their proxies directly to a designated collection point such as a brokerage house or bank. Shareholders my change their votes until the votes are counted. The votes are counted, often under the strict supervision of voting inspectors to ensure accuracy. Both the target firm and the bidder generally have their own proxy solicitors present during the tabulation process.

Legal Filings in Undertaking Proxy Contests

Securities Exchange Commission (SEC) regulations cover the solicitation of the target's shareholders for their proxy or right to vote their shares on an issue that is being contested. All materials distributed to shareholders must be submitted to the SEC for review at least 10 days before they are distributed. Proxy solicitations are regulated by Section 14(A) of the Securities Exchange Act of 1934. The party attempting to solicit proxies from the target's shareholders must file a ***proxy statement*** and Schedule 14(A) with the SEC and mail it to the target's shareholders. Proxy statements include the date of the future shareholders' meeting at which approval of the transaction is to be solicited, details of the merger agreement, company backgrounds, reasons for the proposed merger, and opinions of legal and financial advisors. Proxy statements may be obtained from the companies involved, as well as on the Internet at the SEC site (www.sec.gov).

The Impact of Proxy Contests on Shareholder Value

Despite a low success rate, there is some empirical evidence that proxy fights result in abnormal returns to shareholders of the target company regardless of the outcome. The gain in share prices occurs despite only one-fifth to one-third of all proxy fights actually resulting in a change in board control. In studies covering proxy battles during the 1980s through the mid-1990s, abnormal returns ranged from 6 to 19%, even if the dissident shareholders were unsuccessful in the proxy contest (DeAngelo and DeAngelo, 1989; Dodd and Warner, 1983; Faleye, 2004; Mulherin and Poulsen, 1998). Reasons for the gains of this magnitude may include the eventual change in management at firms embroiled in proxy fights, the tendency for new management to restructure the firm, investor expectations of a future change in control due to M&A activity, and possible special cash payouts for firms with excess cash holdings.

Pre-Tender Offer Tactics: Purchasing Target Stock in the Open Market

Potential bidders often purchase stock in a target before a formal bid to accumulate stock at a price lower than the eventual offer price. Such purchases are normally kept secret to avoid driving up the price and increasing the average price paid for such shares.

The primary advantage accruing to the bidder of accumulating target stock before an offer is the potential leverage achieved with the voting rights associated with the stock it has purchased. This voting power is important in a proxy contest to remove takeover defenses, to win shareholder approval under state antitakeover statutes, or for the election of members of the target's board. In addition, the target stock accumulated before the acquisition can be later sold, possibly at a gain, by the bidder in the event the bidder is unsuccessful in acquiring the target firm.

Once the bidder has established a toehold ownership position in the voting stock of the target through open market purchases, the bidder may attempt to call a special stockholders' meeting. The purpose of such a meeting may be to call for a replacement of the board of directors or for the removal of takeover defenses. The conditions under which such a meeting can be called are determined by the firm's articles of incorporation governed by the laws of the state in which the firm is incorporated.

Using a Hostile Tender Offer to Circumvent the Target's Board

The hostile tender offer is a deliberate effort to go around the target's board and management. The early successes of the hostile tender offer generated new, more effective defenses (discussed later in this chapter). Takeover tactics had to adapt to the proliferation of more formidable defenses. For example, during the 1990s, hostile tender offers were used in combination with proxy contests to coerce the target's board into rescinding takeover defenses.

While target boards often discourage unwanted bids initially, they are more likely to relent when a hostile tender offer is initiated. In a study of 1018 tender offers between 1962 and 2001, target boards resisted tender offers about one-fifth of the time (Bhagat *et al.*, 2005). While they have become more common in recent years, hostile takeovers are also rare outside the United States. Rossi and Volpin (2004) found in a study of 49 countries that only about 1% of 45,686 M&A transactions considered between 1990 and 2002 were opposed by target firm boards.

Implementing a Tender Offer

Tender offers can be for cash, stock, debt, or some combination. Unlike mergers, tender offers frequently use cash as the form of payment. Securities transactions involve a longer period for the takeover to be completed, because new security issues must be registered with and approved by the SEC, as well as with states having security registration requirements. During the approval period, target firms are able to prepare defenses and to solicit other bids, resulting in a potentially higher purchase price for the target. If the tender offer involves a share-for-share exchange, it is referred to as an *exchange offer*. Whether cash or securities, the offer is made directly to target shareholders. The offer is extended for a specific period and may be unrestricted (any-or-all offer) or restricted to a certain percentage or number of the target's share.

Tender offers restricted to purchasing less than 100% of the target's outstanding shares may be oversubscribed. Because the Williams Act of 1968 requires that all shareholders tendering shares must be treated equally, the bidder may either purchase all of the target stock that is tendered or purchase only a portion of the tendered stock. For example, if the bidder has extended a tender offer for 70% of the target's outstanding shares and 90% of the target's stock actually is offered, the bidder may choose to prorate the purchase of stock by buying only 63% (i.e., 0.7×0.9) of the tendered stock from each shareholder.

If the bidder chooses to revise the tender offer, the waiting period automatically is extended. If another bid is made to the target shareholders, the waiting period also must be extended by another 10 days to give them adequate time to consider the new bid. Once initiated, tender offers for publicly traded firms are usually successful, although the success rate is lower if it is contested. Between 1980 and 2000, the success rate of total attempted tender offers was more than 80%, with the success rate for uncontested offers more than 90% and for contested (i.e., by the target's board) offers slightly more than 50% (Mergerstat, 2001).

Multitiered Offers

The form of the bid for the target firm can be presented to target shareholders as either a one-tier or a two-tiered offer. In a *one-tier offer*, the acquirer announces the same offer to all target shareholders. This strategy provides the acquirer with the potential for quickly purchasing control of the target, thereby discouraging other potential bidders from attempting to disrupt the transaction. A *two-tiered offer* occurs when the acquirer offers to buy a certain number of shares at one price and more shares at a lower price at a later date. The form of payment in the second tier may also be less attractive, consisting of securities rather than cash. The intent of the two-tiered approach is to give target shareholders an incentive to tender their shares early in the process in order to receive the higher price. Once the bidding firm accumulates enough shares to gain control of the target (usually 51%), the bidder may initiate a so-called *back-end merger* by calling a special shareholders' meeting seeking approval for a merger in which minority shareholders accede to the majority vote. Alternatively, the bidder may operate the target firm as a partially owned subsidiary, later merging it into a newly created wholly owned subsidiary.

While two-tier tender offers are not illegal per se, many state statutes have been amended requiring equal treatment for all tendering shareholders. Many states also give target shareholders *appraisal rights* such that those not tendering shares in the first or second tier may seek to have the state court determine a "fair value" for the shares. The appraised value for the shares may be more or less than the offer made by the bidding firm.

Legal Filings in Undertaking Tender Offers

Federal securities laws impose a number of reporting, disclosure, and antifraud requirements on acquirers initiating tender offers. Once the tender offer has been made, the acquirer cannot purchase any target shares other than the number specified in the tender offer. As noted in Chapter 2, Section 14D of the Williams Act covers tender offers. It requires that any individual or entity making a tender offer resulting in owning more than 5% of any class of equity must file a Schedule 14D-1 and all solicitation material with the SEC. For additional detail, see Chapter 2.

Other Potential Takeover Strategies

With the average length of time between signing the initial agreement and completion or termination of the agreement about 6 months, both the buyer and seller have an incentive to hold up the deal to renegotiate the terms of the agreement based on new information. A number of strategies have been designed to minimize the so-called "holdup problem."

To heighten the chance of a successful takeover, the bidder will include a variety of provisions in a letter of intent designed to discourage the target firm from backing out of any preliminary agreements. The *letter of intent* (LOI) is a preliminary agreement between two companies intending to merge that stipulates major areas of agreement between the parties, as well as their rights and limitations. The LOI may contain a number of features protecting the buyer. The *no-shop agreement* is among the most common. This agreement prohibits the takeover target from seeking other bids or making public information that is not currently readily available. Related agreements commit the target firm's management to use its best efforts to secure shareholder approval of the bidder's offer.

Contracts often grant the target the right to forego the merger and pursue an alternative instead and the acquirer to withdraw from the agreement. However, the right to break the agreement is usually not free. *Break-up (or termination) fees* are sums paid to the initial bidder or target if the transaction is not completed. This fee reflects legal and advisory expenses, executive management time, and the costs associated with opportunities that may have been lost to the bidder who was involved in trying to close this deal. Hotchkiss, Qian, and Song (2004) found for a sample of 1100 stock mergers between 1994 and 1999 that in 55% of all deals a target termination or break-up fee is included in the initial agreement, while in 21% of the deals both target and acquirer termination fees are included. Termination fees are used more frequently on the target side than on the acquirer because targets have greater incentives to break contracts and seek other bidders. Such fees tend to average about 3% of the purchase price. Officer (2003) finds that the use of such fees increases the probability of a deal being completed.

Another form of protection for the bidder is the *stock lockup*. This is an option granted to the bidder to buy the target firm's stock at the first bidder's initial offer that is triggered whenever a competing bid is accepted by the target firm. Because the target may choose to sell to a higher bidder, the stock lockup arrangement usually ensures that the initial bidder will make a profit on its purchase of the target's stock. The initial bidder also may require that the seller agree to a *crown jewels lockup*, in which the initial bidder has an option to buy important strategic assets of the seller, if the seller chooses to sell to another party.

Developing a Bidding or Takeover Strategy Decision Tree

The tactics that may be used in developing a bidding strategy should be viewed as a series of decision points, with objectives and options usually well defined and understood before a takeover attempt is initiated. Prebid planning should involve a review of the target's current defenses, an assessment of the defenses that could be put in place by the target after an offer is made, and the size of the float associated with the target's stock. Poor planning can result in poor bidding, which can be costly to CEOs. Lehn and Zhao (2006) found that between 1990 and 1998, for a sample of 714 acquisitions, 47% of acquiring firm CEOs were replaced within 5 years. Moreover, top executives are more likely to be replaced at firms that had made poor acquisitions sometime during the prior 5 years.

Common bidding strategy objectives include winning control of the target, minimizing the control premium, minimizing transaction costs, and facilitating postacquisition integration. If minimizing the cost of the purchase and transaction costs, while maximizing cooperation between the two parties is considered critical, the bidder may choose the "friendly" approach. The friendly approach has the advantage of generally being less costly than more aggressive tactics and minimizes the loss of key personnel, customers, and suppliers during the fight for control of the target. Friendly takeovers avoid an auction environment, which may raise the target's purchase price. Moreover, as noted in Chapter 6, friendly acquisitions facilitate pre-merger integration planning and increase the likelihood that the combined businesses will be quickly integrated following closing. The primary risk of this approach is the loss of surprise. If the target is unwilling to reach a negotiated settlement, the acquirer is faced with the choice of abandoning the effort or resorting to more aggressive tactics. Such tactics are likely to be less effective because of the extra time afforded the target's management to put additional takeover defenses in place. In reality, the risk of loss of surprise may not be very great because of the prenotification requirements of the Williams and the Hart–Scott–Rodino Acts.

Reading Figure 3-2 from left to right, the bidder initiates contact casually through an intermediary or through a more formal inquiry. The bidder's options under the friendly approach are to either walk away or to adopt more aggressive tactics if the target's management and board spurn the bidder's initial offer. If the choice is to become more aggressive, the bidder may undertake a simple bear hug to nudge the target toward a negotiated settlement due to pressure from large institutional shareholders and arbs.

If the bear hug fails to convince the target's management to negotiate, the bidder may choose to buy stock in the open market. This tactic is most effective when ownership in the target is concentrated among relatively few shareholders. The bidder may accumulate a sufficient number of voting rights to call a special stockholders' meeting if a proxy fight is deemed necessary to change board members or to dismember the target's defenses.

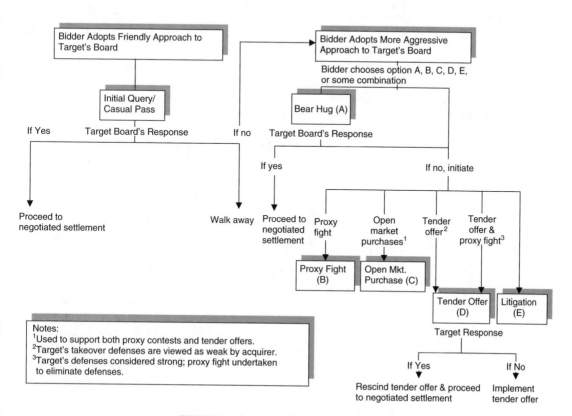

FIGURE 3-2   Alternative takeover tactics.

If the target's defenses are viewed as relatively weak, the bidder may forego a proxy contest and initiate a tender offer for the target's stock. In contrast, if the target's defenses appear formidable, the bidder may implement concurrently a proxy contest and a tender offer. However, implementing both simultaneously is a very expensive strategy. Tender offers are costly, because they are offers to buy up to 100% of the target's outstanding stock at a significant premium. While a proxy fight is cheaper, they are still costly, involving professional fees paid to such advisors as proxy solicitors, investment bankers, and attorneys. Printing, mailing, and advertising costs can also be substantial. Finally, both proxy fights and tender offers involve significant legal fees due to the likelihood of extensive litigation. Litigation is a common tactic used to put pressure on the target board to relent to the bidder's proposal or to remove defenses. Litigation is most effective if the firm's defenses appear to be especially onerous. The board may be accused of not giving the bidder's offer sufficient review or it may be told that the target's defenses are intended only to entrench senior management. As such, the acquirer will allege that the board is violating its fiduciary responsibility to the target shareholders. Table 3-2 relates takeover tactics to specific bidder objectives and strategies.

TABLE 3-2   Advantages and Disadvantages of Alternative Takeover Tactics

Common Bidder Strategy Objectives:
- Gain control of target firm
- Minimize the size of the control premium
- Minimize transactions costs
- Facilitate postacquisition integration

Tactics	Advantages	Disadvantages
Casual Pass (i.e., informal inquiry)	• May learn target is receptive to offer	• Gives advance warning
Bear Hug	• Raises pressure on target to negotiate a deal	• Gives advance warning
Open Market Purchases	• May lower cost of transaction • Creates profit if target agrees to buy back bidder's toehold position (i.e., greenmail) • May discourage other bidders	• Can result in a less than controlling interest • Limits on amount can purchase without disclosure • Some shareholders could hold out for higher price • Could suffer losses if takeover attempt fails
Proxy Contest	• Less expensive than tender offer • May obviate need for tender offer	• Relatively low probability of success if target stock widely held • Adds to transactions costs
Tender Offer	• Pressures target shareholders to sell stock • Bidder not bound to purchase tendered shares unless desired number of shares tendered	• Tends to be most expensive tactic • Disruptive to post closing integration due to potential loss of key target management, customers, and suppliers.
Litigation	• Puts pressure on target board	• Expense

Alternative Takeover Defenses in the Corporate Takeover Market: Prebid and Postbid

Alternative takeover defenses can be grouped into two categories: those put in place before receiving a bid and those implemented after receipt of a bid. Prebid defenses are used to prevent a sudden, unexpected hostile bid from gaining control of the company before management has time to assess their options properly. If the prebid defenses are sufficient to delay a change in control, the target firm has time to erect additional defenses after an unsolicited bid is received. Table 3-3 identifies the most commonly used defenses. Public companies make use on average of about three of the various pre- and postbid defenses listed in this table (Field and Karpoff, 2000). These defenses are discussed in more detail later in this chapter.

TABLE 3-3   Alternative Prebid and Postbid Takeover Defenses

Prebid Defenses	Postbid Defenses
Poison Pills:	Greenmail (Bidder's investment purchased at a premium to what they paid as inducement to refrain from any further activity)
First Generation (Preferred Stock Plans)	
Second Generation (Flip-Over Rights Plans)	
Third Generation (Flip-In Rights Plans)	
Back-End Plans	
Poison Puts	
Shark Repellants (Implemented by Changing Bylaws or Charter):	Standstill Agreements (Often used in conjunction with an agreement to buy bidder's investment)
Strengthening the Board's Defenses	
Staggered or Classified Board Elections	
Cumulative Voting Rights	
"For Cause" Provisions	
Limiting Shareholder Actions	
Calling Special Meetings	
Consent Solicitations	
Advance Notice Provisions	
Super Majority Rules	
Other Shark Repellants	
Antigreenmail Provisions (Discourages target's use of greenmail as a takeover tactic)	
Fair Price Provisions	
Super Voting Stock	
Reincorporation	
Golden Parachutes	Pac-Man Defense
	White Knights
	Employee Stock Ownership Plans
	Leveraged Recapitalization
	Share Repurchase or Buyback Plans
	Corporate Restructuring
	Litigation

The Role of Planning

The best defense against unwanted suitors may be advance planning and a strong financial performance. Large public companies routinely review their takeover defenses. Many companies have "stock watch" programs in place that are intended to identify stock accumulations or stock price movements that reflect an impending takeover attempt. Such a program tracks trading patterns in a company's stock. Companies require their stock transfer agent to provide up-to-date and accurate stock transfer sheets and to report any unusual movements in stock transfer activity. Stock watch programs routinely review SEC records for any Schedule 13D filings.

The rapidity of events once a takeover is under way may make an effective defense impossible unless certain defenses are already in place. A prebid strategy involves building defenses that are adequate to the task of slowing down a bidder to give the target company's management and board time to assess the situation and to decide on an appropriate response to an offer. A company's strategy should never be to try to build insurmountable defenses. Courts will disallow defenses, which appear to be designed only to entrench the firm's management.

Once a bid has been received, most companies choose never to comment on merger discussions until an agreement has been signed. When such an event must be disclosed depends on how far along discussions are with the bidder. The U.S. Supreme Court has said that a company has an obligation to make accurate and nonmisleading statements once it has commented on a situation (Wasserstein, 1998, p. 689). The Supreme Court also has said that a company's statement of "no comment" will be taken as silence and therefore will not be considered as misleading.

Prebid Defenses

Prebid defenses generally fall into three categories: poison pills, shark repellants, and golden parachutes. The sophistication of such measures has increased dramatically since 1980 in lockstep with the effectiveness of takeover tactics. The objective of these defensive measures is to slow the pace and raise the cost of the takeover attempt.

Poison Pills

In the popular press, poison pills are a generic name that refers to a range of protections against unsolicited tender offers. In practice, they represent a very specific type of antitakeover defense. Sometimes referred to as shareholder rights plans, *poison pills* represent a new class of securities issued by a company to its shareholders. Because pills are issued as a dividend and the board has the exclusive authority to issue dividends, a pill can often be adopted without a shareholder vote. Consequently, poison pills can be adopted not only before but also after the onset of a hostile bid. Thus, even a company that does not have a poison pill in place can be regarded as having a "shadow poison pill" that could be used in the event of a hostile bid (Coates, 2000). These securities have no value unless an investor acquires a specific percentage (often as low as 10%) of the target firm's voting stock. If this threshold percentage is exceeded and the pill is a so-called *flip-in pill*, the poison pill securities are activated and typically allow existing target shareholders to purchase additional shares of the target firm's common stock at a discount from the current market price. Alternatively, if the pill is a **_flip-over pill_**, existing shareholders may purchase additional shares of the acquirer or surviving firm's common shares (i.e., the shares of the combined companies), also at a discount.

Triggering the flip-in pill has the effect of increasing the cost of the transaction for the acquirer by increasing the number of target shares that need to be purchased for cash in a cash-for-share exchange or the number of new shares that must be issued by the acquirer in a share-for-share exchange. In a cash-for-share exchange, the change in the acquirer's cash outlay will depend on the number of target shareholders exercising their right to buy additional target shares. For example, if the number of target shares outstanding doubled and the price per share offered by the acquirer remained unchanged, the amount of cash required to buy all or a specific portion of the target's shares would double. In share-for-share exchange, the increased number of acquirer shares issued imposes a cost on acquirer shareholders by diluting their ownership position. News Corp's November 8, 2004 announcement that it would give its shareholders the right to buy one News Corp share at half price for each share they own, if any party buys a 15% stake in the firm, is a recent example of a flip-in poison pill. The flip-in rights plan would exclude the purchaser of the 15% stake.

Table 3-4 illustrates the dilution of the acquirer's shareholders ownership position resulting from a poison pill in a share-for-share exchange offer. Assume the acquirer has one million shares currently outstanding and has agreed to acquire the one million shares of target stock outstanding by exchanging one share of acquirer stock for each share of target stock. To complete the transaction, the acquirer must issue one million shares of

TABLE 3-4   Acquirer Shareholder Dilution Due to Poison Pill

	New Company Shares Outstanding[1]		Ownership Distribution in New Company (%)	
Flip-In Pill Defenses[2]	Without Pill	With Pill	Without Pill	With Pill
Target Firm Shareholders				
Shares Currently Outstanding	1,000,000	2,000,000	50	67[3]
Total Shares Outstanding	1,000,000	2,000,000		
Acquiring Firm Shareholders				
Shares Currently Outstanding	1,000,000	1,000,000	50	33
New Shares Issued	1,000,000	2,000,000		
Total Shares Outstanding	2,000,000	3,000,000		
Flip-Over Pill Defense[4]	Without Pill	With Pill	Without Pill	With Pill
Target Firm Shareholders				
Shares Currently Outstanding	1,000,000	1,000,000	50	67
Total Shares Outstanding	1,000,000	1,000,000		
Acquiring Firm Shareholders				
Shares Currently Outstanding	1,000,000	1,000,000	50	33
New Shares Issued	1,000,000	2,000,000		
Total Shares Outstanding	2,000,000	3,000,000		

Notes:
[1] Acquirer agrees to exchange one share of acquirer for each share of target stock. The target shares outstanding are cancelled.
[2] Poison pill provisions enable each target shareholder to buy one share of target stock for each share they own at a nominal price.
[3] 2,000,000/3,000,000
[4] One million new shares must be issued to target shareholders exercising their right to buy shares in the surviving or new company at a nominal price.

new stock, with the target's stock being canceled. The total number of shares outstanding for the new company would be two million shares (i.e., one million of existing acquirer stock plus one million in newly issued shares). Target company and acquirer shareholders would each own one-half of the new company. However, if target company shareholders are able to buy at a nominal price one million new shares of target stock because of a flip-in pill, the number of shares that now must be acquired would total two million. The total number of shares of the new company would be three million, of which target company shareholders would own two-thirds and acquirer shareholders one-third. Note that a flip-in or flip-over pill has the same dilutive effect on acquirer shareholders. With the flip-in pill, target shareholders purchased one million new shares of target stock, while for a flip-over pill, they bought one million new shares of the acquirer or surviving firm's shares. In either case, the acquirer had to issue one million new shares.

Poison pills have evolved through three generations, as new versions were introduced to solve problems existing with earlier versions (see Table 3-5). The *first-generation poison pill* was developed in 1982 and involved issuing preferred stock, which had to be registered with the SEC, in the form of a dividend to shareholders convertible into the common stock but only after the takeover was completed. To implement this type of plan, companies customarily use *blank check preferred stock*, which is stock that has been authorized but not yet issued. The board normally has broad discretion to establish voting, dividend, conversion, and other rights for this stock. The *second-generation poison pill* (also known as a flip-over pill) included a rights plan, which did not require the expense of registration that could be exercised before the takeover but only if 100% of the stock had been acquired. The third-generation poison pill (also referred to as a flip-in pill) could be exercised with less than 100% change in ownership.

Other types of poison pills include back-end plans and poison puts. With *back-end plans*, shareholders receive a dividend of rights, giving them the option of exchanging the rights for cash or senior debt securities at a specific price set by the target's board. With *poison puts*, the target issues bonds containing put options exercisable if and only if an unfriendly takeover occurs. This enables holders of these puts to cash in their bonds, thereby placing substantial cash demands on the acquiring company. A *chewable poison pill* is one which becomes void in the face of a fully financed offer at a substantial premium to the target's current share price.

Proponents of the pill defense argue that it prevents a raider from acquiring a substantial portion of the firm's stock without board permission. Since the board generally has the power to rescind the pill, bidders are compelled to negotiate with the target's board, potentially resulting in a higher offer price. Pill defenses may be most effective when used with staggered board defenses in which a raider would be unable to remove the pill without winning two successive elections. With such a combination of defenses, the likelihood of remaining independent rose from 34 to 61%, and the probability that the first bidder would be successful dropped from 34 to 14% (Bebchuk, Coates, and Subramanian, 2002). Detractors argue that pill defenses simply serve to entrench management and encourage disaffected shareholders to litigate. In recent years, boards have been under pressure to require a shareholder approval of all rights plans and to rescind existing pill defenses.

The poison pill has proven to be an effective means of delaying a takeover and of increasing the overall expense to the acquiring company. Most pills are put in place with an *escape clause* where the board of the issuing company can redeem the pill through a nominal payment to the shareholders. This is necessary to avoid dilution of the bidder's ownership position in the event the acquiring company is considered friendly. However, the existence of this redemption feature has made pill defenses vulnerable. For example,

TABLE 3-5 Advantages and Disadvantages of Prebid Takeover Defenses—Poison Pills

Type of Poison Pill	Advantages for Target Firm	Disadvantages for Target Firm
First Generation (Preferred Stock Plans convertible into stock of the acquirer) Activated following completion of takeover	1. Dilutes ownership position of the acquirer and raises cost of acquisition 2. May result in positive abnormal returns to target shareholders if investors view that a takeover is imminent	1. Activated following completion of merger 2. Issuer may redeem only after an extended time period (sometimes 10 years); limits target's flexibility if it is later decided to pursue a merger. 3. Increases leverage because preferred stock is counted as debt by credit rating agencies
Second Generation (Flip-Over Rights to buy stock in the acquirer) Countdown to expiration begins with a specific event occurring such as a hostile tender for 20% of a firm's stock Exercisable after buyer purchases 100% of target's stock	1. No impact on leverage 2. Simpler to implement because does not require issuance of preferred stock with attendant SEC filing requirements 3. Rights redeemable by buying them back from shareholders at nominal price	1. Ineffective in preventing acquisition of less than 100% of target. Hostile bidders could buy controlling interest only and buy the remainder after rights expire. 2. Subject to hostile tender contingent on target board's redemption of the pill 3. Makes issuer less attractive to white knights
Third Generation (Flip-In Rights to buy stock in target) Activated by an event such as a less than 100% change in ownership	1. Effective in dealing with bidders buying less than 100% of target. Dilutes target stock regardless of amount purchased by acquirer. 2. Flip in rights are discriminatory (i.e., not given to investor who activated the rights) 3. Rights are redeemable at any point before the triggering event	1. May not be permissible in certain states due to their discriminatory nature 2. No poison pill provides any protection against proxy contests
Back-End Plans	1. Back-end price set above market price, effectively setting a minimum price for a takeover. Deals effectively with two-tiered tender offer.	1. Target's board put in position of effectively setting a sale price, while saying publicly that the company is not for sale
Poison Puts	1. Places large cash demands on the combined firms	1. Rendered ineffective if acquirer can convince put holders not to exercise their options. Particularly true if bond's coupon rate exceeds market rates of interest.

a tender offer may be made conditional on the board's redemption of the pill. The target's board will be under substantial pressure from institutions and arbs to redeem the pill if the bidder has offered a significant premium over the current price of the target's stock. Alternatively, such takeover defenses could be dismantled through a proxy fight. One strategy that has sometimes been used to mitigate this redemption feature is the **dead hand poison pill**. This security is issued with special characteristics, which prevent the board of directors from taking action to redeem or rescind the pill unless the directors were the same directors who adopted the pill.

Shark Repellants

Shark repellants are specific types of takeover defenses that can be adopted by amending either a corporate charter or its bylaws. The charter gives the corporation its legal existence. The **corporate charter** consists of the **articles of incorporation**, a document filed with a state government by the founders of a corporation, and a **certificate of incorporation**, a document received from the state once the articles have been approved. The charter contains the corporation's name, purpose, amount of authorized shares, and number and identity of directors. The corporation's powers thus derive from the laws of the state and from the provisions of the charter. Rules governing the internal management of the corporation are described in the **corporation's bylaws**, which are determined by the corporation's founders.

Shark repellants are put in place largely to reinforce the ability of a firm's board of directors to retain control. Although shark repellants predate poison pills, their success in slowing down and making takeovers more expensive has been mixed. These developments have given rise to more creative defenses such as the poison pill. Today, shark repellants are intended largely as supplements to the poison pill defenses. Their role is primarily to make gaining control of the board through a proxy fight at an annual or special meeting more difficult. In practice, most shark repellants require amendments to the firm's charter, which necessitate a shareholder vote. Although there are many variations of shark repellants, the most typical include staggered board elections, restrictions on shareholder actions, antigreenmail provisions, supervoting, and debt-based defenses. Table 3-6 summarizes the primary advantages and disadvantages of each type of shark repellant defense divided into three categories: those which strengthen the board's defenses, those limiting shareholder actions, and all other. Note that golden parachutes are generally not considered shark repellants as they are designed more to raise the cost of the buyout to the bidder and to retain management rather than to gain time for the target board. They are discussed here as they are generally put in place prior to a takeover bid.

Strengthening the Board's Defenses A **staggered (or classified) board election** involves dividing the firm's directors into a number of different classes. Only one class is up for reelection each year. For example, for a board consisting of 12 members, the directors may be divided into four classes with each director elected for a 4-year period. In the first year, the three directors designated as class 1 directors are up for election, in the second year class 2 directors are up for election, and so on. Consequently, an insurgent stockholder, who may hold the majority of the stock, still would have to wait for three elections to gain control of the board. Moreover, the size of the board is limited to preclude the insurgent stockholder from adding board seats to take control of the board. The target may have to accede to the majority stockholder's demands because of litigation initiated by dissident shareholder groups. The likelihood of litigation is highest and pressure on the board is greatest whenever the offer price for the target is substantially above the target firm's

TABLE 3-6 Advantages and Disadvantages of Prebid Takeover Defenses—Shark Repellants and Golden Parachutes

Type of Defense	Advantages for Target Firm	Disadvantages for Target Firm
Shark Repellants: Strengthening the Board's Defenses		
Staggered or Classified Boards	Delays assumption of control by a majority shareholder	May be circumvented by increasing size of board, unless prevented by charter or bylaws
Cumulative Voting	Delays assumption of control by a majority shareholder	Gives dissident shareholder a board seat and access to confidential information
Limitations on When Can Remove Directors	"For cause" provisions narrow range of reasons for removal	Can be circumvented unless supported by a supermajority requirement for repeal
Shark Repellants: Limiting Shareholder Actions		
Limitations on Calling Special Meetings	Limits ability to use special meetings to add board seats, remove or elect new members	States may require a special meeting if a certain percentage of shareholders request a meeting.
Limiting Consent Solicitations	Limits ability of dissident shareholders to expedite a proxy contest process	May be subject to court challenge
Advance Notice Provisions	Gives board time to select its own slate of candidates and to decide an appropriate response	May be subject to court challenge
Supermajority Provisions	May be applied selectively to events such as hostile takeovers	Can be circumvented unless a supermajority of shareholders are required to change the provision
Other Shark Repellants		
Antigreenmail Provision	Eliminates profit opportunity for raiders	Eliminates greenmail as a takeover defense
Fair Price Provisions	Increases the cost of a two-tiered tender offer	Raises the cost to a white knight, unless waived by typically 95% of shareholders
Super Voting Stock	Concentrates control by giving "friendly" shareholders more voting power than others.	Difficult to implement because requires shareholder approval; only useful when voting power can be given to pro-management shareholders.
Reincorporation	Takes advantage of most favorable state anti-takeover statutes	Requires shareholder approval; time consuming to implement unless subsidiary established before takeover solicitation
Golden Parachutes[1]	Emboldens target management to negotiate for a higher premium and raises the cost of a takeover to the hostile bidder	Negative public perception; makes termination of top management expensive; cost not tax deductible.

Note:
[1] Generally not considered a shark repellant but included in this table as they are usually put in place before a bid is made for the firm.

current share price. Bebchuk, Coates, and Subramanian (2002, 2003) find that staggered boards can be effective in helping a target to ward off a hostile takeover attempt.

Some firms have common stock carrying **cumulative voting rights** to maximize minority representation. Cumulative voting in the election of directors means each shareholder is entitled to as many votes as shall equal the number of shares the shareholder owns multiplied by the number of directors to be elected. Furthermore, the shareholder may cast all of these votes for a single candidate, or for any two or more of them. Using the preceding example of a 12-member board, a shareholder, who has 100 shares of stock, has 300 votes for three open seats for class 1 directors. The shareholder may cumulate her votes and cast them for a specific candidate. A dissident stockholder may choose this approach to obtain a single seat on the board to gain access to useful information that is not otherwise readily available. However, cumulative voting rights also may backfire against the dissident shareholder. Cumulative voting may be used to counter the ability of insurgents to gain control of the board by cumulating the votes of opposing shareholders and casting them for candidates who would vigorously represent the board's positions. **For cause provisions** specify the conditions for removing a member of the board of directors. This narrows the range of reasons for removal and limits the flexibility of dissident shareholders in contesting board seats.

Limiting Shareholder Actions Other means of reinforcing the board's ability to retain control include limiting the ability of shareholders to gain control of the firm by bypassing the board altogether. These include limiting their ability to call special meetings and to engage in consent solicitations and limiting the use of supermajority rules.

Many states require a firm to call a special shareholders' meeting if it is requested by a certain percentage of its shareholders. Special meetings may be used as a forum for insurgent shareholders to take control by replacing current directors with those who are likely to be more cooperative or by increasing the number of board seats. To limit this type of action, firms frequently rely on the conditions under which directors can be removed (i.e., the for cause provision discussed earlier) and a limitation on the number of board seats as defined in the firm's bylaws or charter. Furthermore, special meetings may be used by shareholders to engage in a nonbinding vote to remove certain types of defenses such as a poison pill. The board then must decide to ignore the will of the shareholders or to remove the defenses.

In some states, shareholders may take action to add to the number of seats on the board, to remove specific board members, or to elect new members without a special shareholders' meeting. These states allow dissident shareholders to obtain shareholder support for their proposals by simply obtaining the written consent of shareholders by mailing proxy cards to them under what is known as **consent solicitation**. Shareholders willing to authorize a proxy to vote their shares sign and return these cards to the dissident shareholders. Although the consent solicitation must abide by the disclosure requirements applicable to proxy contests, dissident stockholders may use this process to expedite their efforts to seize control of the board or to remove defenses without waiting for a shareholders meeting to gain approval of their proposals as is required in a proxy contest. This process circumvents delays inherent in setting up a meeting to conduct a stockholder vote. An important difference between a consent solicitation and a proxy contest is that the winning vote in a consent solicitation is determined as a percentage of the number of shares outstanding. In a proxy fight, the winner is determined as a percentage of the number of votes actually cast. Therefore, it may be easier for a dissident shareholder to win by initiating a proxy contest rather than a consent solicitation, because many shareholders simply do not vote. Companies have attempted to limit shareholders' ability to use this procedure by amending charters or bylaws. Bylaw amendments may not require shareholder approval. However, the courts frequently have frowned upon actions restricting shareholder rights without shareholder approval.

Advance notice provisions in corporate bylaws require the announcement of shareholder proposals and board nominations well in advance of an actual vote. Some bylaws require advance notice of as long as 2 months, buying time for the target's management. *Supermajority rules* require that a higher level of approval is required for amending the charter or for certain types of transactions such as a merger or acquisition. Such rules are triggered if an "interested party" acquires a specific percentage of the ownership shares (e.g., 5–10%). Supermajority rules may require that as much as 80% of the shareholders must approve a proposed merger or a simple majority of all shareholders except the "interested party." Supermajority rules often include escape clauses, which allow the board to waive the requirement. For example, supermajority rules may not apply to mergers approved by the board.

Other Shark Repellants The final category of prebid defenses includes antigreenmail and fair price provisions, as well as supervoting stock, and reincorporation.

During the 1980s, many raiders profited by taking an equity position in a target firm, threatening takeover, and subsequently selling their ownership position back to the target firm at a premium over what they paid for the target's shares. Many corporations adopted charter amendments called *antigreenmail provisions* restricting the firm's ability to repurchase shares at a premium. By removing the incentive for greenmail, companies believed they were making themselves less attractive as potential takeover targets. As such, antigreenmail provisions may be viewed as an antitakeover tactic.

Fair price provisions require that any acquirer pay minority shareholders at least a fair market price for their stock. The fair market price may be expressed as some historical multiple of the company's earnings or as a specific price equal to the maximum price paid when the buyer acquired shares in the company. Fair price provisions are most effective when the target firm is subject to a two-tiered tender offer. The fair price provision forces the bidder to pay target shareholders, who tender their stock in the second tier, the same terms offered to those tendering their stock in the first tier. Most such provisions do not apply if the proposed takeover is approved by the target firm's board of directors or if the bidder obtains a specified supermajority level of approval from the target's shareholders.

A firm may create more than one class of stock for many reasons, including separating the performance of individual operating subsidiaries, compensating subsidiary operating management, maintaining control with the founders, and preventing hostile takeovers. As a takeover defense, a firm may undertake a *dual class recapitalization* in which the objective is to concentrate stock with the greatest voting rights in the hands of those who are most likely to support management. One class of stock may have 10 to 100 times the voting rights of another class of stock. Such stock is called *supervoting stock*. Supervoting stock is issued to all shareholders along with the right to exchange it for ordinary stock. Most shareholders are likely to exchange it for ordinary stock, because the stock with the multiple voting rights usually has a limited resale market and pays a lower dividend than other types of voting stock issued by the corporation. Management usually will retain the special stock. This effectively increases the voting control of the corporation in the hands of management. For example, Ford's dual class or supervoting shares enable the Ford family to control 40% of the voting power while owning only 4% of the total equity of the company.

Under the voting rights policies of the SEC and the major public exchanges, U.S. firms are allowed to list dual class shares. However, once such shares are listed, firms cannot reduce the voting rights of existing shares or issue a new class of superior voting shares. Several hundred U.S. companies issue dual class shares including the *New York Times*, Dow Jones, the *Washington Post*, Coors, Tyson Foods, Adelphia, Comcast, Viacom, and Google. While relatively limited among U.S. firms, dual class firms are very common in other countries. Recent research suggests that firms with dual class shares often underperform the overall stock market. This may result from efforts to entrench controlling shareholders by erecting excessive takeover defenses and policies that are not in the best interests of noncontrolling shareholders (such as excessive compensation for key managers and board members). Moreover, such firms often have excessive leverage due to an unwillingness to raise additional funds by selling shares that could dilute the controlling shareholders (Gompers, Ishii, and Metrick, 2003).

Reincorporation involves a potential target firm changing its state of incorporation to one in which the laws are more favorable for implementing takeover defenses. Several factors need to be considered in selecting a state for possible reincorporation. These include how the state's courts have ruled in lawsuits alleging breach of corporate director fiduciary responsibility in takeover situations and the state's laws pertaining to poison pills, staggered boards, and hostile tender offers. Reincorporation involves the creation of a subsidiary in the new state into which the parent is merged at a later date. Reincorporation requires shareholder approval.

Golden Parachutes

Golden parachutes are employee severance arrangements, which are triggered whenever a change in control takes place. Such a plan usually covers only a few dozen employees and obligates the company to make a lump-sum payment to employees covered under the plan who are terminated following a change in control. A change in control usually is defined to occur whenever an investor accumulates more than a fixed percentage of the corporation's voting stock. Such severance packages may serve the interests of shareholders by making senior management more willing to accept an acquisition. The 1986 Tax Act imposed stiff penalties on these types of plans if they create what is deemed an excessive payment. Excessive payments are those exceeding three times the employee's average pay over the last 5 years and are not tax deductible by the paying corporation. The employee receiving the parachute payment also must pay a 20% surcharge in addition to the normal tax due on the parachute payment.

Postbid Defenses

Once an unwanted suitor has approached a firm, there are a variety of additional defenses that can be introduced. These include greenmail to dissuade the bidder from continuing the pursuit; defenses designed to make the target less attractive, such as restructuring and recapitalization strategies; and efforts to place an increasing share of the company's ownership in friendly hands by establishing ESOPs and seeking white knights. Table 3-7 summarizes the primary advantages and disadvantages of such postbid defenses.

Greenmail

Greenmail is the practice of paying a potential acquirer to leave you alone. It consists of a payment to buy back shares at a premium price in exchange for the acquirer's agreement to not undertake a hostile takeover. In exchange for the payment, the potential

TABLE 3-7 Advantages and Disadvantages of Postbid Takeover Defenses

Type of Defense	Advantages for Target Firm	Disadvantages for Target Firm
Greenmail	Encourages raider to go away (usually accompanied by a standstill agreement)	Reduces risk to raider of losing money on a takeover attempt; unfairly discriminates against nonparticipating shareholders; often generates litigation; and triggers unfavorable tax consequences and negative public image
Standstill Agreement	Prevents raider from returning for a specific time period	Increases amount of greenmail paid to get raider to sign standstill; provides only temporary reprieve
White knights	May be a preferable to the hostile bidder	Involves loss of target's independence
ESOPs	Alternative to white knight and highly effective if used in conjunction with certain states' antitakeover laws	Employee support not guaranteed. ESOP cannot overpay for stock because transaction could be disallowed by federal law.
Recapitalizations	Makes target less attractive to bidder and may increase target shareholder value if incumbent management motivated to improve performance	Increased leverage reduces target's borrowing capacity.
Share Buyback Plans	Reduces number of target shares available for purchase by bidder, arbs, and others who may sell to bidder	Securities laws limit ability to self-tender without SEC filing once hostile tender under way. A reduction in the shares outstanding may facilitate bidder's gaining control.
Corporate Restructuring	Going private may be attractive alternative to bidder's offer for target shareholders and for incumbent management	Going private, sale of attractive assets, making defensive acquisitions, or liquidation may reduce target's shareholder value versus bidder's offer
Litigation	May buy time for target to build defenses and increases takeover cost to the bidder	May have negative impact on target shareholder returns

acquirer is required to sign a ***standstill agreement***, which typically specifies the amount of stock, if any, that the investor can own, the circumstances under which the raider can sell stock currently owned, and the term of the agreement. Despite their discriminatory nature, courts in certain states, such as Delaware, have found greenmail an appropriate response as long as it is made for valid business reasons. However, courts in other states, such as California, have favored shareholder lawsuits, contending that greenmail breaches fiduciary responsibility (Wasserstein, 1998, pp. 719–720).

White Knights

A target company seeking to avoid being taken over by a specific bidder may try to be acquired by another firm, a ***white knight***, which is viewed as a more appropriate suitor. To complete such a transaction, the white knight must be willing to acquire the target on more favorable terms than those of other bidders. More favorable terms need not involve an offer price higher than the current bidder's proposal. The presumed white knight may be viewed as more favorable in terms of their willingness to allow the target firm's management to stay in place and to continue to pursue their current strategy.

Fearing that a bidding war might ensue, the white knight often demands some protection in the form of a lockup. The lockup may involve giving the white knight options to buy stock in the target that has not yet been issued at a fixed price or to acquire at a fair price specific target assets. Such lockups usually have the effect of making the target less attractive to other bidders. In the event a bidding war ensues, the knight may exercise the stock options and sell the shares at a profit to the acquiring company. German drug and chemical firm Bayer AG's white knight bid for Schering AG in 2006 (which was recommended by the Schering board) was designed to trump a hostile offer from a German rival, Merck KGaS.

Employee Stock Ownership Plans

ESOPs are trusts that hold a firm's stock as an investment for their employees' retirement program. ESOPs may be viewed as an alternative to a white knight. They can be established quickly, with the company either issuing shares directly to the ESOP or having an ESOP purchase shares on the open market. The stock held by ESOPs is likely to be voted in support of management in the event of a hostile takeover attempt.

Leveraged Recapitalization

Recapitalization may require shareholder approval, depending on the company's charter and the laws of the state in which it is incorporated. A company may recapitalize by assuming substantial amounts of new debt, which is used to either buy back stock or finance a dividend to shareholders. In doing so, the target becomes less attractive to a bidder, because the additional debt reduces its borrowing capacity, which may have been used by the bidder to help finance the takeover of the target. Moreover, the payment of a dividend or a stock buyback may persuade shareholders to support the target's management in a proxy contest or hostile tender offer. The target firm is left in a highly leveraged position. Whether the recapitalization actually weakens the target firm in the long term depends on its impact on the target firm's shareholder value. Shareholders will benefit from the receipt of a dividend or from capital gains resulting from a stock repurchase. Furthermore, the increased debt service requirements of the additional debt will shelter a substantial amount of the firm's taxable income and may encourage management to be more conscientious about improving the firm's performance. Thus, the combination of these factors may result in current shareholders benefiting more from this takeover defense than from a hostile takeover of the firm. The primary differences between a leveraged recapitalization and a leveraged buyout are that the firm remains a public company and that management does not take a significant equity stake in the firm.

Share Repurchase or Buyback Plans

Firms may repurchase shares in one of two ways: through a tender offer or by direct purchases of shares in public markets. Firms engage in such activities for a variety of reasons including rewarding shareholders, signaling undervaluation, funding employee stock option plans, adjusting capital structure, and defending against unwanted takeovers. Firms frequently increase their share repurchase activities when confronted with an imminent takeover threat (Billett and Xue, 2007). When used as an antitakeover tactic, share repurchase or buyback plans are intended to reduce the number of shares that could be purchased by the potential acquirer or by those such as arbitrageurs who will sell to the highest bidder. This tactic reflects the belief that, when a firm initiates a tender offer (i.e., a self-tender) for a portion of its own shares, the shareholders who offer their shares for sale are those most susceptible to a tender offer by a hostile bidder. This leaves the target firm's shares concentrated in the hands of shareholders who are less likely to sell, thereby reducing so-called "float." Therefore, for a hostile tender offer to succeed in purchasing the remaining shares, the premium offered would have to be higher. The resulting higher premium might discourage some prospective bidders. A share buyback may work well in combination with a self-tender by allowing the firm to buy shares (perhaps at a somewhat higher price) in addition to those tendered to the firm. The deterrent effect of buyback strategies has been supported in a number of studies. Potential acquirers are less likely to pursue firms with substantial excess cash, which could be used to adopt highly aggressive share repurchase programs (Faleye, 2004; Harford, 1999; Pinkowitz, 2002).

The repurchase tactic may in fact be subject to the "law of unintended consequences." By reducing the number of shares on the open market, it is easier for the buyer to gain control because fewer shares have to be purchased to achieve 51% of the target's voting shares. Moreover, self-tenders actually may attract potential bidders if they are seen as a harbinger of improving target company cash flows. Federal securities law prohibits purchase by an issuer of its own shares during a tender offer for its shares. However, an exception is made if the firm files a statement with the SEC disclosing the identity of the purchaser, stock exchanges that will be used for the purchase, the intent of the purchase, and the intended disposition of the shares.

Corporate Restructuring

Restructuring may involve taking the company private, the sale of attractive assets, undertaking a major acquisition, or even liquidating the company. "Going private" typically involves the management team's purchase of the bulk of a firm's shares. This may create a win–win situation for shareholders who receive a premium for their stock and management who retain control. To avoid lawsuits, the price paid for the stock must represent a substantial premium to the current market price. Alternatively, the target may make itself less attractive by divesting assets the bidder wants. The cash proceeds of the sale could fund other defenses such as share buybacks or payment of a special stockholder dividend. A target company also may undertake a so-called *defensive acquisition* to draw down any excess cash balances and to exhaust its current borrowing capacity. A firm may choose to liquidate the company, pay off outstanding obligations to creditors, and distribute the remaining proceeds to shareholders as a *liquidating dividend*. This makes sense only if the liquidating dividend exceeds what the shareholders would have received from the bidder (see Chapter 15).

Litigation

Takeover litigation often includes antitrust concerns, alleged violations of federal securities laws, inadequate disclosure by the bidder as required by the Williams Act, and alleged fraudulent behavior. Targets often try to get a court injunction temporarily stopping the takeover attempt until the court has decided that the target's allegations are groundless. By preventing the potential acquirer from buying more stock, the target firm is buying time to erect additional takeover defenses. Table 3-8 lists the most commonly employed defensive strategies.

Impact on Shareholder and Bondholder Value of Takeover Defenses

As noted in Chapter 1 of this book, average abnormal returns to target shareholders about the time of a hostile tender offer announcement have increased dramatically since the 1960s to significantly more than 35%, whereas abnormal returns to acquirer shareholders have deteriorated from marginally positive to slightly negative. In contrast, the abnormal return to shareholders following merger announcements (i.e., those presumed to be "friendly") has remained remarkably stable at about 20%. The increase in target company shareholder returns may be attributable to potential improvements in efficiency, tax savings, or market power. However, if this were true, one would have expected abnormal returns for mergers to also show a correspondingly large increase over time. Consequently, other factors must be at work.

It is probably more than coincidental that the increase in abnormal returns began with the introduction of the 1967 Wallace Act prenotification period. This provided a respite for target firms to erect takeover defenses and to search for other potential bidders. Takeover defenses such as poison pills, although unlikely to prevent a takeover, could add significantly to the overall purchase price. The purchase price could be further boosted by any auction that might take place as the initial bidder lost precious time in trying to overcome myriad defenses the target may have in place. Thus, the increasing sophistication of takeover defenses since 1980 would seem to be a highly plausible factor explaining the sustained increase in abnormal returns to target shareholders following the announcement of a hostile tender offer.

TABLE 3-8   Proportion of S&P 500 with Defense Provisions in Place

Defense Provision	S&P 500 (2003)	S&P 500 (2002)
Classified Boards with Staggered Terms	57.2%	61.2%
Supermajority Vote for Mergers	29.3%	31.1%
Poison Pills in Force	57.6%	60.6%

Source: TrueCourse, Inc., www.SharkRepellent.net.

Early Empirical Studies Show Mixed Results

Unfortunately, it is difficult to substantiate this intuitive argument empirically. Those studies showing a negative return to shareholders support the argument that incumbent management acts in its own self-interest—the management entrenchment hypothesis. Studies showing a positive shareholder return support the argument that incumbent management acts in the best interests of shareholders—the shareholder interests' hypothesis. For many takeover defenses, empirical results cannot be confirmed by multiple studies, the available evidence is largely contradictory, or the findings are statistically insignificant. The empirical evidence seems to suggest that takeover defenses in general have virtually no statistically significant impact on shareholder returns or, as in the case of poison pills, have a positive impact.

In a comprehensive review of previous studies, Comment and Schwert (1995) found that most takeover defensives such as staggered boards, supermajority provisions, fair price provisions, reincorporation, and dual capitalization resulted in a slightly negative decline in shareholder returns of about 0.5%. These studies included the following: Jarrell and Poulsen, 1987; Karpoff and Malatesta, 1989; Malatesta and Walkling, 1988; Romano, 1993; Ryngaert, 1988. Other studies found no statistically significant negative results (DeAngelo and Rice, 1983; Linn and McConnell, 1983). Another study found that shareholder efforts to remove takeover defenses had no significant impact on shareholder returns, suggesting that such efforts were viewed by investors as largely inconsequential (Karpoff and Walkling, 1996). Field and Karpoff (2002) concluded in a study of 1019 initial public offerings between 1988 and 1992 that the presence of takeover defenses had no impact on the takeover premiums of those firms acquired after the IPO.

The Comment and Schwert (1995) study also found that poison pills would have a positive impact on shareholder returns if their addition by the potential target were viewed by investors as a signal that a takeover was imminent or that the firm's management would use such a defense to improve the purchase price during negotiation. The existence of poison pills often requires the bidder to raise its bid or to change the composition of its bid to an all-cash offer to put the target's board under pressure to dismantle its pill defenses. Timing also is important. For example, whenever a merger announcement or a rumor of an impending merger coincided with the announcement of a poison pill, abnormal returns to target shareholders increased by 3–4%. A number of studies suggest that investors will react positively to the announcement of the adoption of takeover defenses if the firm's management interests are viewed as aligned with those of the shareholders and negatively if management is viewed as seeking to entrench itself (Bhaghat and Jefferis, 1991; Boyle, Carer, and Stover, 1998; McWilliams, 1991).

More Recent Empirical Studies

Despite the largely mixed results of earlier studies, more recent studies suggest that takeover defenses may destroy shareholder value. In an effort to assess which of 24 governance provisions tracked by the Investor Responsibility Research Center (IRRC) had the greatest impact on shareholder value, Bebchuk, Cohen, and Ferrell (2005) created a "management entrenchment index" that is negatively correlated with firm value between 1990 and 2003. The index consists of staggered boards, limits to shareholder bylaw amendments, supermajority requirements for mergers, supermajority requirements for charter amendments, poison pills, and golden parachutes. The study's major finding is that firms with a low entrenchment index (i.e., management's interests are more aligned with those of the shareholders) have larger abnormal returns than firms with a high entrenchment index. The authors do not find any correlation between firm value and the other 18 IRRC provisions during the sample period. The authors note that the mere existence of correlation does not necessarily mean that these takeover defenses cause a reduction in the value of the firm. The correlation could reflect the tendency of underperforming firms that are likely to be takeover targets to adopt takeover defenses.

Masulis, Wang, and Xie (2007) provide additional support for the destructive effect of takeover defenses on shareholder value. In a study of 3333 completed acquisitions between 1990 and 2003, they conclude that managers at firms protected by takeover defenses are less subject to the disciplinary power of the market for corporate control. Moreover, such managers are more likely to engage in "empire building" acquisitions that destroy shareholder value.

Takeover Defenses May Benefit Initial Public Offerings

Event studies examine only how takeover defenses affect shareholder wealth after the corporation has been formed, shareholders have purchased its stock, and after employees and managers have been hired. Takeover defenses may in fact create significant firm value at the point when the firm is formed. Consequently, to fully evaluate the impact of takeover defenses on firm value, the analyst must consider both the potentially beneficial effects before the event of a takeover attempt and the potentially destructive effect on firm value after the announcement.

Takeover defenses may add to firm value before a takeover attempt if they help the firm to attract, retain, and motivate effective managers and employees. Furthermore, such defenses give the new firm time to fully implement its business plan and to invest in upgrading the skills of employees (Stout, 2002). Coates (2001) found that the percentage of IPO firms with staggered boards in their charters at the time of the initial public offering rose from 34% in the early 1990s to 82% in 1999. This finding suggests that investors may prefer the adoption of takeover defenses during the early stages of a firm's development.

Things to Remember

The market in which takeover tactics and defenses are employed is called the "corporate takeover market," which in a free market economy facilitates the allocation of resources and disciplines underperforming managers. By replacing such managers through hostile takeover attempts or through proxy fights, the corporate takeover market can help to promote good corporate governance practices that protect stakeholder interests. In addition to the corporate takeover market, other factors external to the firm such as federal and state legislation, the court system, regulators, and institutional activism serve important roles in maintaining good corporate governance practices. Corporate governance is also impacted by the integrity and professionalism of the firm's board of directors, as well as the effectiveness of the firm's internal controls and incentive systems, takeover defenses, and corporate culture.

Takeovers often are divided into friendly and hostile categories. A hostile takeover generally is considered an unsolicited offer made by a potential acquirer that is resisted by the target's management. If the friendly approach is considered inappropriate or is unsuccessful, the acquiring company may attempt to limit the options of the target's senior management by making a formal acquisition proposal, usually involving a public announcement, to the target's board of directors. This tactic is called a bear hug and is an attempt to pressure the target's board into making a rapid decision. Alternatively, the bidder may undertake a proxy contest. By replacing board members, proxy contests can be an effective means of gaining control without owning 51% of the voting stock, or they can be used to eliminate takeover defenses as a precursor to a tender offer. In a tender offer, the bidding company goes directly to the target shareholders with an offer to buy their stock.

Takeover defenses are designed to raise the overall cost of the takeover attempt and to provide the target firm with more time to install additional takeover defenses. Prebid defenses usually require shareholder approval and fall into three categories: poison pills, shark repellants, and golden parachutes. Poison pills represent a new class of securities issued by a company to its shareholders, which have no value unless an investor acquires a specific percentage of the firm's voting stock. Takeover defenses that can be included in either a corporate charter or bylaws often are referred to as shark repellants. These defenses are put in place largely to reinforce the ability of a firm's board of directors to retain control. Golden parachutes are large severance packages granted senior management, which are activated if an individual or a single entity purchases a specific percentage of the target's outstanding voting stock. Postbid defenses are those undertaken in response to a bid. One example is greenmail, which is the practice of paying a potential acquirer to leave you alone. A target company seeking to avoid being taken over by a specific bidder may try to be acquired by another firm, a white knight, which is viewed as a more appropriate suitor. Takeover litigation often is initiated under the guise of antitrust concerns, alleged violations of federal securities laws, inadequate disclosure by the bidder as required by the Williams Act, and alleged fraudulent behavior.

In general, takeover defenses benefit the shareholders of firms that are performing well and whose managers' interests are aligned with those of their shareholders. In contrast, shareholders of underperforming firms are often penalized by significant takeover defenses as they may tend to entrench incompetent management. The results of earlier studies are mixed, while more recent studies suggest that takeover defenses have a small negative impact on abnormal shareholder returns. However, takeover defenses put in place prior to an IPO can benefit shareholders.

Chapter Discussion Questions

3-1. What are the management entrenchment and shareholder interests hypotheses? Which seems more realistic in your judgment? Explain your answer.

3-2. What are the advantages and disadvantages of the friendly versus hostile approaches to a corporate takeover? Be specific.

3-3. What are proxy contests and how are they used?

3-4. What is a tender offer? How do they differ from open market purchases of stock?

3-5. How are target shareholders affected by a hostile takeover attempt?

3-6. How are the bidder's shareholders affected by a hostile takeover attempt?

3-7. What are the primary advantages and disadvantages of commonly used takeover defenses?

3-8. Of the most commonly used takeover defenses, which seem to have the most favorable impact on target shareholders? Explain your answer.

3-9. How may golden parachutes for senior management help a target firm's shareholders? Are such severance packages justified in your judgment? Explain your answer.

3-10. How might recapitalization as a takeover defense help or hurt a target firm's shareholders?

Answers to these Chapter Discussion Questions are available in the Online Instructor's Manual for instructors using this book.

Chapter Business Case

Case Study 3-1
Mittal Acquires Arcelor—A Battle of Global Titans in the European Market for Corporate Control

Ending 5 months of maneuvering, Arcelor agreed on June 26, 2006, to be acquired by larger rival Mittal Steel Co. for $33.8 billion in cash and stock. The takeover battle was one of the most acrimonious in recent European Union history. After decades in which hostile transactions were rare, the battle between the two steel titans illustrates Europe's move toward less regulated markets. Hostile takeovers are now increasingly common in Europe. The battle is widely viewed as a test case as to how far a firm can go in attempting to prevent an unwanted takeover.

Arcelor was created in 2001 by melding steel companies in Spain, France, and Luxembourg. Most of its 90 plants are in Europe. In contrast, most of Mittal's plants are outside of Europe in areas with lower labor costs. Mr. Lakshmi Mittal, Mittal's CEO and a member of an important industrial family in India, started the firm and built it into a powerhouse through two decades of acquisitions in emerging nations. The company is headquartered in the Netherlands for tax reasons. Prior to the Arcelor acquisition, Mr. Mittal owned 88% of the firm's stock.

Mittal acquired Arcelor to accelerate steel industry consolidation to reduce industry overcapacity. The combined firms' could have more leverage in setting prices and negotiating contracts with major customers such as auto and appliance manufacturers, suppliers such as iron ore and coal vendors, and eventually realize $1 billion annually in pretax cost savings.

The War of Words
After having been rebuffed by Mr. Guy Dolle, Arcelor's President, in an effort to consummate a friendly merger, Mittal launched a tender offer in January 2006 consisting of mostly stock and cash for all of Arcelor's outstanding equity. The offer constituted a 27% premium over Arcelor's share price at that time. The reaction from Arcelor's management, European unions, and government officials was swift and furious. Guy Dolle stated flatly that the offer was "inadequate and strategically unsound." European politicians supported Mr. Dolle. Luxembourg's Prime Minister Jean Claude Juncker said a hostile bid "calls for a hostile response." French Finance Minister Thierry Breton said that Mittal's logic ran contrary to what he called "the grammar of business." Trade unions expressed concern about potential job loss.

The Chess Match Begins

Mr. Dolle engaged in one of the most aggressive takeover defenses in recent corporate history. In early February, Arcelor doubled its dividend and announced plans to buy back about $8.75 billion in stock at a price well above the then current market price for Arcelor stock. These actions were taken to motivate Arcelor shareholders not to tender their shares to Mittal. Arcelor also backed a move to change the law so that Mittal would be required to pay in cash. However, the Luxembourg parliament rejected that effort.

To counter these moves, Mittal Steel said in mid-February that, if it received more than one-half of the Arcelor shares submitted in the initial tender offer, it would hold a second tender offer for the remaining shares at a slightly lower price. Mittal pointed out that it could acquire the remaining shares through any available compulsory buyback procedure, merger, or corporate reorganization. Such rhetoric was designed to encourage Arcelor shareholders to tender their shares during the first offer.

In late 2005, Arcelor outbid German steelmaker Metallsheshcft to buy Canadian steelmaker Dofasco for $5 billion. Mittal was proposing to sell Dofasco to raise money and avoid North American antitrust concerns. Following completion of the Dofasco deal in April 2006, Arcelor set up a special Dutch trust to prevent Mittal from getting access to the asset. The trust is run by a board of three Arcelor appointees. The trio has the power to determine if Dofasco can be sold during the next 5 years. Mittal immediately sued to test the legality of this tactic.

In a deal with Russian steelmaker OAO Severstahl, Arcelor agreed to issue shares to buy Mr. Alexei Mordashov's 90% stake in Severstahl. The transaction would give Mr. Mordashov a 32% stake in Arcelor. Arcelor also scheduled an unusual vote that created very tough conditions for Arcelor shareholders to prevent the deal with Severstahl from being completed. Arcelor's board stated that the Severstahl deal could be blocked only if at least 50% of all Arcelor shareholders would vote against it. However, Arcelor knew that only about one-third of shareholders actually attend meetings. This is a tactic permissible under Luxembourg law, where Arcelor is incorporated.

Arcelor Shareholders Revolt

Investors holding more than 30% of Arcelor shares signed a petition to force the company to make the deal with Severstahl subject to a traditional 50.1% or more of actual votes cast. After major shareholders pressured the Arcelor board to at least talk to Mr. Mittal, Arcelor demanded an intricate business plan from Mittal as a condition that had to be met. Despite Mittal's submission of such a plan, Arcelor still refused to talk. In late May, Mittal raised its bid by 34% and said that if the bid succeeded, Mittal would eliminate his firm's two-tiered share structure giving the Mittal family shares 10 times the voting rights of other shareholders.

A week after receiving the shareholder petition, the Arcelor board rejected Mittal's sweetened bid and repeated its support of the Severstahl deal. Shareholder anger continued as many investors said they would reject the share buyback. Some investors opposed the buyback because it would increase Mr. Mordashov's ultimate stake in Arcelor to 38% by reducing the number of Arcelor shares outstanding. Under the laws of most European nations, any entity owning more than a third of a company is said to have effective control. Arcelor canceled a scheduled June 21 shareholder vote on the buyback. Despite Mr. Mordashov's efforts to enhance his bid, the Arcelor board asked both Mordashov and Mittal to submit their final bids by June 25.

Arcelor finally agreed to Mittal's final bid, which had been increased by 14%. The new offer consisted of $15.70 in cash and 1.0833 Mittal shares for each Arcelor share. The new bid is valued at $50.54 per Arcelor share, up from Mittal's initial bid in January 2006 of

$35.26. The final offer represented an unprecedented 93% premium over Arcelor's share price of $26.25 immediately before Mittal's initial bid. Lakshmi Mittal will control 43.5% of the combined firm's stock. Mr. Mordashov would receive a $175 million break-up fee due to Arcelor's failure to complete its agreement with him. Finally, Mittal agreed not to make any layoffs beyond what Arcelor already has planned.

Case Study Discussion Questions

1. Identify the takeover tactics employed by Mittal. Explain why each was used.
2. Identify the takeover defenses employed by Arcelor? Explain why each was used.
3. Using the information in this case study, discuss the arguments for and against encouraging hostile corporate takeovers.
4. Was Arcelor's board and management acting to protect their own positions (i.e., the management entrenchment hypothesis) or in the best interests of the shareholders (i.e., the shareholder interests hypothesis)? Explain your answer.

Answers to these Case Study Discussion Questions are available in the Online Instructor's Manual for instructors using this book.

Chapter Business Case

Case Study 3-2
Verizon Acquires MCI: The Anatomy of Alternative Bidding Strategies

While there were many parties interested in acquiring MCI, the major players included Verizon and Qwest. U.S.-based Qwest is an integrated communications company that provides data, multimedia, and Internet-based communication services on a national and global basis. The acquisition would ease the firm's huge debt burden of $17.3 billion (more than twice its stock market value), because the debt would be supported by the combined company with a much larger revenue and asset base. The deal would also give the firm access to new business customers and opportunities to cut costs.

Verizon Communications, created through the merger of Bell Atlantic and GTE in 2000, is the largest telecommunications provider in the United States. The company provides local exchange, long-distance, Internet, and other related services to residential, business, and government customers. In addition, the company provides wireless services to over 42 million customers in the United States, through its 55%-owned joint venture with Vodafone Group plc.

Interest Grows in MCI
By mid-2004, MCI had received several expressions of interest from Verizon and Qwest regarding potential strategic relationships. By July, Qwest and MCI entered into a confidentiality agreement and proceeded to perform a more detailed due diligence. Others also expressed interest in acquiring or converting MCI to a private company through a leveraged buyout. However, they were rebuffed by the MCI board. Mr. Ivan Seidenberg, Verizon's Chairman and CEO, inquired about a potential takeover and was rebuffed by MCI's board, which was evaluating its strategic options. These included Qwest's proposal regarding a share-for-share merger, following a one-time cash dividend to MCI shareholders from MCI's cash in excess of its required operating balances (i.e., excess cash). In view of Verizon's

interest, MCI's board of directors directed management to advise Mr. Richard Notebaert, the Chairman and CEO of Qwest, that MCI was not prepared to move forward with a potential transaction.

The stage was set for what would become Qwest's laboriously long and ultimately unsuccessful pursuit of MCI in which the firm would be rejected by MCI four times. The key events of this 11-week period are summarized in Table 3-9.

TABLE 3-9   Transaction Timeline

Key Date	Bidder	Price per MCI Share	Comment
4/20/04			MCI emerged from bankruptcy after a multibillion accounting scandal nearly destroyed the company.
2/2/05	Qwest	$19.45	At $6.32 billion, the offer consisted of $17.85 per share in cash and provided for the payment of $0.40 per share in quarterly dividends for the four quarters anticipated between signing and closing.
2/7/05	Verizon	$20.00	At $6.5 billion, the proposal consisted of $5.99 per share payable in cash plus the conversion of each MCI share into 0.3802 shares of Verizon stock.
2/10/05	Qwest	$19.87	Valued at $6.46 billion, the all cash offer included four quarterly dividends between signing and closing dates.
2/11/05	Qwest	$24.60	The revised offer was valued at $7.5 billion, consisting of $7.50 in cash and 3.735 shares of Qwest stock for each share of MCI stock. It continued to include the dividend payouts of its previous offers.
2/14/05	Verizon	$20.75	MCI agreed to a $6.75 billion deal in which Verizon would convert each MCI share into 0.4062 shares of Verizon stock and pay cash in the amount of $1.50 per MCI share. MCI stockholders would also receive a special cash dividend of $4.50 per share. (1st rejection of Qwest)
2/24/05	Qwest	$24.60	Valued at $8.1 billion, the revised proposal provided for $6.00 in cash in quarterly and special dividends; $3.10 in cash at closing; and 3.735 shares of Qwest common stock for each share of MCI common stock.
3/29/05	Verizon	$23.50	Verizon increases its bid to $8.45 billion, consisting of $8.75 per share in cash and the higher of 0.4032 shares of Verizon or $14.75 in stock. (2nd rejection of Qwest)
3/31/05	Qwest	$27.50	Qwest raised bid to $8.9 billion consisting of 3.733 shares of Qwest stock and $13.50 in cash.
4/6/05			MCI's board votes to reject Qwest's $8.9 billion offer. (3rd rejection of Qwest)
4/8/05			Qwest said a survey of investors indicated that investors controlling more than 50% of MCI's stock favor the higher Qwest bid.

continued

TABLE 3-9   continued

Key Date	Bidder	Price per MCI Share	Comment
4/9/05			Verizon bought out MCI's largest shareholder, Mexican millionaire Carlos Slim, for $1.1 billion. Mr. Slim had invested $700 million in MCI.
4/12/05			MCI announces that it will not amend its rights plan allowing shareholders to buy more shares if a single investor acquires 15% or more of MCI's stock.
4/21/05	Qwest	$30.00	Qwest raised its bid to $9.9 billion, saying this was its final offer, after having been rejected 3 times. Qwest added $2.50 in cash per share to the previous bid.
4/25/05			MCI declared the Qwest offer superior to the accepted merger with Verizon.
5/2/05	Verizon	$26.00	Verizon raised its bid to $8.45 billion or $26 per share, consisting of $5.60 per share in cash payable upon approval by MCI shareholders plus the greater of 0.5743 Verizon shares for every MCI common share or the equivalent number of Verizon shares equal to $20.40, whichever is higher. This collar enabled MCI shareholders to benefit from a floor of $20.40 and would benefit from the upside potential of an increase in Verizon's share price. MCI's board votes to accept the Verizon offer. (4th and final rejection of Qwest)

Verizon's Reasons for the Merger

Verizon stated that the merger would enable it to more efficiently provide a broader range of services, give the firm access to MCI's business customer base, accelerate new product development using MCI's fiber-optic network infrastructure, and create substantial cost savings opportunities.

MCI's Reasons for the Merger

After assessing its strategic alternatives, including the option to remain a standalone company, MCI's board of directors concluded that the merger with Verizon was in the best interests of the MCI stockholders. MCI's board of directors noted that Verizon's bid of $26 per share represented a 41.5% premium over the closing price of MCI's common stock on January 26, 2005. Furthermore, the offer included "price protection" in the form of a collar.

The merger agreement also provided for the MCI board to declare a special dividend of $5.60 once the firm's shareholders approved the deal. MCI's board of directors also considered the additional value that its stockholders would realize since the merger is expected to be a tax-free reorganization. Consequently, only the cash portion of the purchase price would be taxable, with the payment of taxes on any gains from the receipt of Verizon stock deferred until the MCI shareholders chose to sell their shares. MCI's board of directors also noted that a large number of MCI's most important business customers had indicated that they preferred a transaction between MCI and Verizon rather than a transaction between MCI and Qwest.

Analysis of Verizon's Bidding Strategies

While it is clearly impossible to know for sure, the sequence of events reveals a great deal about Verizon's possible bidding strategy. Any bidding strategy must begin with a series of management assumptions about how to approach the target firm. It was certainly in Verizon's interest to attempt a friendly rather than hostile takeover of MCI, due to the challenges of integrating these two complex businesses. Verizon also employed an increasingly popular technique in which the merger agreement includes a special dividend payable by the target firm to its shareholders contingent upon their approval of the transaction. This special dividend is to serve as an inducement to gain shareholder approval.

Given the modest 3% premium over the first Qwest bid, Verizon's initial bidding strategy appears to have been based on the low end of the purchase price range it was willing to offer MCI. Verizon was initially prepared to share relatively little of the potential synergy with MCI shareholders, believing that a bidding war for MCI would be unlikely in view of the recent spate of mergers in the telecommunications industry and the weak financial position of other competitors. SBC and Nextel were busy integrating AT&T and Sprint, respectively. Moreover, Qwest appeared to be unable to finance a substantial all-cash offer due to its current excessive debt burden, and its stock appeared to have little appreciation potential because of ongoing operating losses. Perhaps stunned by the persistence with which Qwest pursued MCI, Verizon believed that its combination of cash and stock would ultimately be more attractive to MCI investors than Qwest's primarily all cash offer, due to the partial tax-free nature of the bid.

Throughout the bidding process, many hedge funds criticized MCI's board publicly for accepting the initial Verizon bid. Since its emergence from Chapter 11, hedge funds had acquired significant positions in MCI's stock, with the expectation that MCI constituted an attractive merger candidate. In particular, Carlos Slim Helu, the Mexican telecommunications magnate and largest MCI shareholder, complained loudly and publicly about the failure of MCI's board to get full value for the firm's shares. Pressure from hedge funds and other dissident MCI shareholders may have triggered a shareholder lawsuit to void the February 14, 2005, signed merger agreement with Verizon.

In preparation for a possible proxy fight, Verizon entered into negotiations with Carlos Slim Helu to acquire his shares. Verizon acquired Mr. Slim's 13.7% stake in MCI in April 2005. Despite this purchase, Verizon's total stake in MCI remained below the 15% ownership level that would trigger the MCI rights plan.

About 70% (i.e., $1.4 billion) of the cash portion of Verizon's proposed purchase price consisted of a special MCI dividend payable by MCI when the firm's shareholders approved the merger agreement. Verizon's management argued that the deal would cost their shareholders only $7.05 billion (i.e., the $8.45 billion purchase price less the MCI special dividend). The promise of the special dividend served as an inducement for the MCI shareholders to approve the deal. The $1.4 billion special dividend reduces MCI's cash in excess of what is required to meet its normal operating cash requirements.

Analysis of Qwest's Bidding Strategy

Qwest consistently attempted to outmaneuver Verizon by establishing a significant premium between its bid and Verizon's, often as much as 25%. Qwest realized that its current level of indebtedness would preclude it from significantly increasing the cash portion of the bid. Consequently, it had to rely on the premium to attract enough investor interest, particularly among hedge funds, to pressure the MCI board to accept the higher bid. However, Qwest was unable to satisfy enough investors that its stock would not simply lose value once more shares were issued to consummate the stock and cash transaction.

Qwest could have initiated a tender or exchange offer directly to MCI shareholders proposing to purchase or exchange their shares without going through the merger process. The tender process requires lengthy regulatory approval. However, if Qwest initiated a tender offer, it could trigger MCI's poison pill. Alternatively, a proxy contest might have been preferable because Qwest already had a bid on the table and the contest would enable Qwest to lobby MCI shareholders to vote against the Verizon bid. This strategy would have avoided triggering the poison pill.

Ultimately, Qwest was forced to capitulate simply because it did not have the financial wherewithal to increase the $9.9 billion bid. It could not borrow any more because of its excessive leverage. Additional stock would have contributed to earnings dilution and caused the firm's share price to fall.

Governance Issues

It is unusual for a board to turn down a higher bid, especially when the competing bid was 17% higher. In accepting the Verizon bid, MCI stated that a number of its large business customers had expressed a preference for the company to be bought by Verizon rather than Qwest. MCI noted that these customer concerns posed a significant risk in being acquired by Qwest. The MCI board's acceptance of the lower Verizon bid could serve as a test case of how well MCI directors are conducting their fiduciary responsibilities. The central issue is how far boards can go in rejecting a higher offer in favor of one they believe offers more long-term stability for the firm's stakeholders.

The bidding war illustrated how forces outside of the company can force management and boards to modify their decisions. The bidding war featured an almost daily exchange between the bidders and the powerful role of hedge funds and arbitrageurs who owned a majority of MCI shares and pushed the company to extract two higher bids from Verizon.

Ron Perlman, the 1980s' takeover mogul, saw his higher all-cash bid rejected by the board of directors of Revlon Corporation, which accepted a lower offer from another bidder. In a subsequent lawsuit, a court overruled the decision by the Revlon board in favor of the Perlman bid. Consequently, from a governance perspective, legal precedent compels boards to accept higher bids from bona fide bidders where the value of the bid is unambiguous as in the case of an all-cash offer. However, for transactions in which the purchase price is composed largely of acquirer stock, the value is less certain. Consequently, the target's board may rule that the lower bidder's shares have higher appreciation potential or at least are less likely to decline than those shares of other bidders. This is a particularly important consideration when the time between the signing of a merger agreement and the actual closing is expected to be lengthy.

MCI's president and CEO Michael Capellas and other executives could collect $107 million in severance, payouts of restricted stock, and monies to compensate them for taxes owed on the payouts. In particular, Capellas stands to receive $39.2 million if his job is terminated "without cause" or if he leaves the company for "good reason."

Case Study Discussion Questions

1. Discuss how changing industry conditions have encouraged consolidation within the telecommunications industry.
2. What alternative strategies could Verizon, Qwest, and MCI have pursued? Was the decision to acquire MCI the best alternative for Verizon? Explain your answer.
3. Who are the winners and losers in the Verizon–MCI merger? Be specific.

4. What takeover tactics were employed or threatened to be employed by Verizon? By Qwest? Be specific.
5. What specific takeover defenses did MCI employ? Be specific.
6. How did the actions of certain shareholders affect the bidding process? Be specific.
7. In your opinion, did the MCI board act in the best interests of their shareholders? Of all their stakeholders? Be specific.
8. Do you believe that the potential severance payments that could be paid to Capellas were excessive? Explain your answer. What are the arguments for and against such severance plans for senior executives?
9. Should the antitrust regulators approve the Verizon–MCI merger? Explain your answer.
10. Verizon's management argued that the final purchase price from the perspective of Verizon shareholders was not $8.45 billion but rather $7.05 billion. This was so, they argued, because MCI was paying the difference of $1.4 billion from their excess cash balances as a special dividend to MCI shareholders. Why is this misleading?

Answers to these Case Study Discussion Questions are available in the Online Instructor's Manual for instructors using this book.

References

Atkinson, A., and Salterio, S., "Shaping Good Conduct," *Management*, Vol. 49, 2002, pp. 18–34.

Bebchuk, L. J. Coates, and G. Subramanian, "The Powerful Anti-Takeover Force of Staggered Boards: Theory, Evidence, and Policy," *Stanford Law Review*, Vol. 54, 2002, pp. 887–951.

Bebchuk, L. J., John C. Coates IV, and Guhan Subramanian, "The Powerful Antitakeover Force of Staggered Boards," Working paper, Harvard Law School, and NBER, 2003.

Bebchuk, Lucian, Alma Cohen, and Allen Ferrell, "What Matters in Corporate Governance," Harvard University Law School Discussion Paper, No. 49, 2005.

Bhagat, Sanjai, Ming Dong, David Hirshleifer, and Robert Noah, "Do Tender Offers Create Value? New Methods and Evidence," *Journal of Financial Economics*, Vol. 76, April 2005, pp. 3–60.

Billett, Matthew T., and Hui Xue, "The Takeover Deterrent Effect of Open Market Share Repurchases," *Journal of Finance*, Forthcoming 2007.

Boyle, G. W., R. B. Carer, and R. D. Stover, "Extraordinary Anti-Takeover Provisions and Insider Ownership Structure" The Case of Converting Savings and Loans," *Journal of Financial and Quantitative Analysis*, Vol. 33, 1998, pp. 291–304.

Brickley, James A., Jeffrey L. Coles, and Gregg Jarrell, "Leadership Structure: Separating the CEO and Chairman of the Board," *Journal of Corporate Finance*, Vol. 3, 1997, pp. 189–220.

Coates, John C., "Takeover Defenses in the Shadow of the Pill: A Critque of the Scientific Evidence," *Texas Law Review*, Vol. 79, 2000, pp. 271–282.

Coates, John C. "Explaining Variation in Takeover Defenses: Blame the Lawyers," *California Law Review*, Vol. 89, 2001, p. 1376.

Comment, Robert, and G. William Schwert, "Poison or Placebo: Evidence on the Deterrence and Wealth Effects of Modern Anti-Takeover Measures," *Journal of Financial Economics,* 39, 1995, pp. 3–43.

Cremers, Martijn, and Vinay Nair, "Governance Mechanisms and Equity Prices," *Journal of Finance*, Vol. 60, 2005, pp. 2859–2894.

Dahya, Jay, and John J. McConnell, "Outside Directors and Corporate Board Decisions: A Natural Experiment," Working Paper Purdue University, Lafayette, IN, 2001.

DeAngelo, Harry, and Eugene Rice, "Anti-Takeover Charter Amendments and Stockholder Wealth," *Journal of Financial Economics,* 11, 1983, pp. 329–360.

DeAngelo, Harry, and Linda DeAngelo, "Proxy Contests and the Governance of Publicly Held Corporations," *Journal of Financial Economics,* 23, 1989, pp. 29–60.

Dodd, Peter, and Jerrold Warner, "On Corporate Government: A Study of Proxy Contests," *Journal of Financial Economics*, 11, 1–4, April 1983, pp. 401–438.

Dutta, Sanip, Mai Iskandar-Dutta, and Kartik Raman, "Executive Compensation and Corporate Acquisition Decisions," *Journal of Finance*, Vol. 56, December 2001, pp. 2299–2396.

Economic Report to the President, U.S. Government Printing Office, Washington, D.C., February 2003.

Economist, "Battling for Corporate America," March 11, 2006, pp. 69–71.

Faleye, Olubunmi, "Cash and Corporate Control," *Journal of Finance*, October, 2004.

Farzad, Roben, "Fidelity's Divided Loyalties," *BusinessWeek*, October 16, 2006.

Field, Laura Casares, and Jonathan M. Karpoff, "Takeover Defenses of IPO Firms," *Journal of Finance*, 57 (5), 2002, pp. 1629–1666.

Federal Reserve Bulletin, Board of Governors, U.S. Federal Reserve System, December 2003, p. 33.

Franks, Julian, and Colin Mayer, "Hostile Takeovers and the Correction of Managerial Failure," *Journal of Financial Economics*, Vol. 40, 1996, pp. 163–181.

Gaspara, Jose-Miguel, and Pedro Matos, "Shareholder Investment Horizons and the Market for Corporate Control," *Journal of Financial Economics*, Vol. 76, 2005, pp. 135–165.

Gompers, Paul A., Joy Ishii, and Andrew Metrick, "An Analysis of U.S. Dual Class Companies," Harvard and NBER Working Paper, December 1, 2003.

Goyal, Vidhan K., and Chul W. Park, "Board Leadership Structure and CEO Turnover," *Journal of Corporate Finance*, Vol. 8, pp. 49–66.

Harford, Jarrad, "Corporate Cash Reserves and Acquisitions," *Journal of Finance*, Vol. 54, 1999, pp. 1969–1997.

Hermalin, Bejamin E., "Trends in Corporate Governance," *Journal of Finance*, Vol. 60, October 2005, pp. 2351–2384.

Hirschey, Mark, *Tech Stock Valuation*, Academic Press, New York, 2003, pp. 245–252.

Hotchkiss, Edith, Jun Qian, and Weihong Song, "Holdup, Renegotiation, and Deal Protection in Mergers," Working Paper, Boston College, Chestnut Hill, MA, 2005.

Huson, Mark R., Robert Parrino, and Laura T. Starks, "Internal Monitoring Mechanism and CEO Turnover: A Long-Term Perspective," *Journal of Finance*, Vol. 55, 2001, pp. 2265–2297.

Jarrell, Gregg, "Wealth Effects of Litigating by Targets: Do Interests Diverge in a Merger?," *Journal of Law and Economics,* Vol. 28, April 1985, pp. 151–177.

Jarrell, Gregg, and Annette B. Poulsen, "Shark Repellents and Stock Prices: The Effects of Antitakeover Amendments Since 1980," *Journal of Financial Economics,* Vol. 19, September 1987, pp. 127–168.

Karpoff, Jonathan M., and Paul H. Malatesta, "The Wealth Effects of Second Generation State Takeover Legislation," *Journal of Financial Economics*, Vol. 25, 1989, pp. 291–322.

Karpoff, Jonathan M., and Ralph A. Walkling, "Corporate Governance and Shareholder Initiatives: Empirical Evidence," *Journal of Financial Economics*, Vol. 42, 1996, pp. 365–395.

Kini, Imesh, William Kracaw, and Shehzad Mian, "The Nature of Discipline by Corporate Takeovers," *Journal of Finance*, August 2004.

La Porta, R. F., and A. Shleifer, "Corporate Ownership Around the Word," *Journal of Finance*, Vol. 54, 1999, pp. 471–518.

Lehn, Kenneth M., and Mengxin Zhao, "CEO Turnover after Acquisitions: Are Bad Bidders Fired?," *Journal of Finance*, Vol. 61, August 2006, pp. 1383–1412.

Linn, Scott C., and John J. McConnell, "An Empirical Investigation of the Impact of Anti-Takeover Amendments on Common Stock Prices," *Journal of Financial Economics*, Vol. 11, April 1983, pp. 361–399.

Malatesta, Paul H., and Ralph A. Walkling, "Poison Pills Securities: Stockholder Wealth, Profitability and Ownership Structure," *Journal of Financial Economics*, Vol. 20, January/March 1988, pp. 347–376.

Masulis, Ronald W., Cong Wang, and Fei Xie, "Corporate Governance and Acquirer Returns," *Journal of Finance*, Forthcoming 2007.

Mergerstat Review, 1988, p. 85 and 2001, p. 38.

McWilliams, V. B., "Tobin's Q and the Stock Price Effects of Anti-Takeover Amendment Proposals," *Financial Management*, Vol. 22, 1993, pp. 16–18.

Morck, Randall, Andrei Shleifer, and Robert W. Vishny, "Characteristics of Targets of Hostile and Friendly Takeovers," in A. J. Auerbach, ed., *Corporate Takeovers: Causes and Consequences*, University of Chicago Press, Chicago, 1988.

Mulherin, J. Harold, and Annette B. Poulsen, "Proxy Contests and Corporate Change: Implications for Shareholder Wealth," *Journal of Financial Economics*, Vol. 47, 1998, pp. 279–313.

Officer, Micah S., "Termination Fees in Mergers and Acquisitions," *Journal of Financial Economics*, Vol. 69, 2003, pp. 431–467.

Pinkowitz, Lee, "The Market for Corporate Control and Corporate Cash Holdings," Working Paper, Georgetown University, Washington, DC, 2002.

Reuters, "HP Board Belittles Merger Foe Hewlett," *Orange County Register*, Business Section, January 18, 2002, p. 7.

Robinson, A., "Is Corporate Governance the Solution or the Problem?," *Corporate Board*, Vol. 23, 2002, pp. 12–16.

Romano, Roberta, "Competition for Corporate Charters and the Lesson of Takeover Statutes," *Fordham Law Review*, Vol. 61, 1993, pp. 843–864.

Rossi, Stefano, and Paolo F. Volpin, "Cross-Country Determinants of Mergers and Acquisitions," ECGI-Finance Working Paper No. 25/2003, AFA 2004 San Diego Meetings, September 2003.

Ryngaert, Michael, "The Effects of Poison Pill Securities on Stockholder Wealth," *Journal of Financial Economics*, Vol. 20, January/March 1988, pp. 377–417.

Schwert, G. William, "Hostility in Takeovers: In the Eyes of the Bidder?," *Journal of Finance*, Vol. 55, 2000, pp. 2599–2640.

Shivdasani, Anil, "Board Composition, Ownership Structure, and Hostile Takeovers," *Journal of Accounting and Economics*, Vol. 16, 1993, pp. 167–198.

Shleifer, A., and R. Vishny, "A Survey of Corporate Governance," *The Journal of Finance*, Vol. 52, 1997, pp. 737–784.

Stout, Lynn A., "Do Antitakeover Defenses Decrease Shareholder Wealth? The Ex Post/Ex Ante Valuation Problem," *Stanford Law Review*, December 2002, pp. 845–861.

Stromfeld v. Great Atlantic & Pacific Tea Company, 484 F. Supplement, 1264 (S.D.N.Y. 1980), aff'd 6464 F. 2d 563 (2nd Circuit 1980).

Thompson Financial Securities Data Corporation, "The World Is Not Enough...To Merge," Press release, January 5, 2000.

Unocal v. Mesa, 493 A.2d 949 (Del. 1985).

Wasserstein, Bruce, *Big Deal: The Battle for Control of America's Leading Corporations,* Warner Books, New York, 1998, pp. 601–644, 689, 719–720.

White, Erin, and Joann S. Lublin, "Companies Trim Executive Perks to Avoid Glare," *The Wall Street Journal*, January 13, 2007, p. A1.

Whitehouse, Kaia, "Your Vote Can Count in Company Elections," *The Wall Street Journal*, February 18, 2007, p. 5.

CHAPTER ✦ 4

Planning

Developing Business and Acquisition Plans—Phases 1 and 2 of the Acquisition Process

If you don't know where you are going, any road will get you there.

—Alice in Wonderland

Inside M&A: eBay Struggles to Reinvigorate Growth

Founded in September 1995, eBay views itself as the world's online market place for the sale of goods and services to a diverse community of individuals and small businesses. Currently, eBay has sites in 24 different countries, and it offers a wide variety of tools, features, and services enabling members to buy and sell on its sites quickly, safely, and conveniently. The firm's primary business is marketplaces consisting of eBay, Shopping.com, and classified Web sites. In 2006, this business accounted for 90% of eBay's sales and profits. Historically, acquisitions made by eBay have always been related to e-commerce. For example, concern about slowing growth in its core U.S. market caused eBay to acquire online payments provider, PayPal, in 2002. The firm has achieved significant synergy between eBay and PayPal by facilitating the payments process between buyers and sellers.

In late 2005, eBay announced that it had acquired Skype International SA for $2.6 billion. Skype was a firm whose software enabled PC users to make calls over the Internet. Skype had revenue of $60 million in 2005, a tiny fraction of eBay's $4.4 billion in 2005 sales, and it was unprofitable. Skype's existing businesses include services that give people the ability to call landline phones for about 3 cents a minute, voicemail, and providing a traditional phone number for Skype accounts. Skype is facing new competition from Google, Yahoo, and many start-ups.

eBay expects Skype to facilitate trade on their sites by increasing the ability of buyers and sellers to negotiate. In addition to paying eBay listing and completed-auction fees, sellers also could pay eBay a fee for getting an Internet call, or lead, via Skype. eBay will also use Skype to facilitate entering new markets, such as new cars, travel, real estate, and personal and business services. Sellers in these markets are already accustomed to paying for leads and talking directly to customers throughout the purchase process. Skype software may also give eBay an advantage in certain international markets such as China, Eastern Europe, and Brazil, where online trust is not well established and where haggling may be more a part of the culture.

The acquisition of a communications company represented a marked departure for eBay, which had previously acquired companies directly related to e-commerce. Meg Whitman, eBay's CEO, denied that the firm is attempting to become a broader Internet portal like Yahoo and Google. eBay is venturing into new territory without any overt request from or support of its buyers and sellers. Historically, buyers and sellers guided eBay into new markets through their activities, such as embracing PayPal years before eBay acquired it, or by requesting new features. In the past when eBay has gone off on its own, such as partnering with Christy's for live auctions, its efforts have fallen flat. Only time will tell how well this acquisition will work.

Chapter Overview

A poorly designed or inappropriate business strategy is among the most frequently cited reasons for the failure of mergers and acquisitions (M&As) to satisfy expectations. Surprisingly, many textbooks on the subject of M&As fail to address adequately the overarching role that planning should take in conceptualizing and implementing business combinations. The purpose of this chapter is to introduce a planning-based approach to mergers and acquisitions, which discusses M&A activity in the context of an integrated process consisting of 10 interrelated phases. This chapter focuses on the first two phases of the process—building the business and acquisition plans—and on tools commonly used to evaluate, display, and communicate information to key constituencies both inside (e.g., board of directors and management) and outside (e.g., lenders and stockholders) of the corporation. Phases 3–10 are discussed in Chapter 5.

Many companies view M&A as a business growth strategy. In this book, mergers and acquisitions are not considered a business strategy but rather as a means of implementing a business strategy. While firms may accelerate overall growth in the short run through acquisition, the higher growth rate often is not sustainable without a business plan enabling the firm to fully integrate the acquired firms and realize significant synergy. Furthermore, growth will also slow as the number of potential target firms that create value declines.

The planning concepts described in this chapter are largely prescriptive in nature in that they recommend certain strategies based on the results generated by applying specific tools (e.g., experience curves) and answering checklists of relevant questions. Although these tools introduce some degree of rigor to strategic planning, their application should not be viewed as a completion of the planning process. Business plans must be updated frequently to account for changes in the firm's operating environment and its competitive position within that environment. Indeed, business planning is not an event—it is an evolving process. A review of this chapter is available on the CD ROM accompanying this book. For a more detailed discussion of business planning, see Hunger and Wheeler (2007), Thompson (2007), and Deusen, Williamson, and Babson (2007).

A Planning-Based Approach to Mergers and Acquisitions

The acquisition process envisioned in this chapter can be separated into a planning and an implementation stage. The planning stage consists of the development of the business and the acquisition plans. The implementation stage includes the search, screening, contacting the target, negotiation, integration planning, closing, integration, and evaluation activities. To understand the role of planning in the M&A process, it is necessary to understand the purpose of the acquiring firm's mission and strategy.

Key Business Planning Concepts

A planning-based acquisition process consists of both a business plan and a merger/acquisition plan, which drive all subsequent phases of the acquisition process. The *business plan* articulates a mission or vision for the firm and a *business strategy* for realizing that mission for all of the firm's stakeholders. *Stakeholders* include such constituent groups as customers, shareholders, employees, suppliers, regulators, and communities. The business strategy is long-term oriented and usually cuts across organizational lines to affect many different functional areas. It is often broadly defined and provides relatively little detail.

With respect to business strategy, it is often appropriate to distinguish between corporate level strategy, where decisions are made by the management of a diversified or multiproduct firm, and business level strategy, where decisions are made by the management of the operating unit within the corporate organizational structure. *Corporate-level strategies* generally cross business unit organizational lines and entail such decisions as financing the growth of certain businesses, operating others to generate cash, divesting some units, or pursuing diversification. *Business-level strategies* pertain to a specific operating unit and may involve the business unit attempting to achieve a low-cost position in its served markets, differentiating its product offering, or narrowing its operational focus to a specific market niche.

The *implementation strategy* refers to the way in which the firm chooses to execute the business strategy. It is usually far more detailed than the business strategy. The *merger/acquisition plan* is a specific type of implementation strategy and describes in detail the motivation for the acquisition and how and when it will be achieved. *Functional strategies* describe in detail how each major function (e.g., manufacturing, marketing, and human resources) within the firm will support the business strategy. *Contingency plans* are actions that are taken as an alternative to the firm's current business strategy. The selection of which alternative action to pursue is often contingent on certain events occurring (e.g., failure to realize revenue targets or cost savings). Such events are called *trigger points*. At such points, a firm is faced with a number of alternatives that are sometimes referred to as *real options*, alternatives to continuing the same strategy. These options include abandoning, delaying, or accelerating the base strategy. Real options are not the same as strategic options discussed later in this chapter, as they represent decisions that can be made after a business strategy has been implemented. See Chapter 8 for a more detailed discussion of how real options may be applied to M&As.

The Acquisition Process

It is sometimes convenient to think of an acquisition process as a series of largely independent events culminating in the transfer of ownership from the seller to the buyer. In theory, thinking of the process as discrete events facilitates the communication and understanding of the numerous activities that are required to complete the transaction. In practice, the steps involved in the process are frequently highly interrelated; do not necessarily follow a logical order; and involve, as new information becomes available, reiteration of steps in the process thought to have been completed. Thinking of M&As in the context of a transaction-tested process, while not ensuring success, increases the likelihood of meeting or exceeding expectations.

Good Planning Expedites Sound Decision Making

Some individuals tend to shudder at the thought of following a structured process because of perceived delays in responding to both anticipated and unanticipated opportunities. Anticipated opportunities are those identified as a result of the business planning process. This process consists of understanding the firm's external operating environment, assessing internal resources, reviewing a range of reasonable options, and articulating a clear vision of the future of the business and a realistic strategy for achieving that vision (Hill and Jones, 2001). Unanticipated or unforeseen opportunities result from new information becoming available. Rather than delaying the pursuit of an opportunity, the presence of a well-designed business plan provides for a rapid yet substantive evaluation of the perceived opportunity based on work completed while having developed the business plan. Decisions made in the context of a business plan are made with the confidence that comes from already having asked and answered the difficult questions.

Mergers and Acquisitions Are a Process Not an Event

Figure 4-1 illustrates the 10 phases of the acquisition process described in this chapter and in Chapter 5. These phases fall into two distinct sets of activities (i.e., pre- and post-purchase decision activities). The crucial phase of the acquisition process is the negotiation phase. Negotiation consists of four largely concurrent and interrelated activities. The decision to purchase or walk away is determined as a result of continuous iteration through the four activities comprising the negotiation phase. Assuming the transaction ultimately is completed, the price paid for the target is actually determined during the negotiation phase. The phases of the acquisition process are summarized as follows:

Phase 1: Develop a strategic plan for the entire business (Business Plan).
Phase 2: Develop the acquisition plan supporting the business plan (Acquisition Plan).
Phase 3: Actively search for acquisition candidates (Search).
Phase 4: Screen and prioritize potential candidates (Screen).
Phase 5: Initiate contact with the target (First Contact).
Phase 6: Refine valuation, structure deal, perform due diligence, and develop financing plan (Negotiation).
Phase 7: Develop a plan for integrating the acquired business (Integration Plan).
Phase 8: Obtain all necessary approvals, resolve postclosing issues, and implement closing (Closing).
Phase 9: Implement postclosing integration (Integration).
Phase 10: Conduct postclosing evaluation of acquisition (Evaluation)

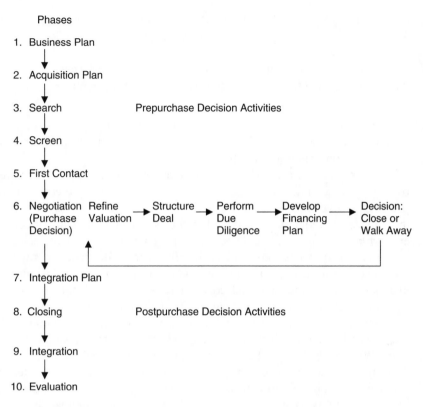

FIGURE 4-1   The acquisition process flow diagram.

Phase 1: Building the Business Plan

Key Activities

A well-designed business plan is a result of the following activities:

1. External analysis involves determining where to compete (i.e., the industry or market in which the firm has chosen to compete) and how to compete [i.e., conducting an external industry or market evaluation to determine how the firm can most effectively compete in its chosen market(s)]
2. Internal analysis or self-assessment (i.e., conducting an internal analysis of the firm's strengths and weaknesses relative to its competition)
3. Defining a mission statement (i.e., summarizing where and how the firm has chosen to compete and the basic operating beliefs and values of management)
4. Setting objectives (i.e., developing quantitative measures of financial and non-financial performance)
5. Business strategy selection (i.e., selecting the strategy most likely to achieve the objectives in an acceptable time period, subject to constraints identified in the self-assessment)
6. Implementation strategy selection (i.e., selecting the best means of implementing the business strategy from a range of reasonable options)

7. Functional strategy development (i.e., defines the roles, responsibilities, and resource requirements of each major functional area within the firm needed to implement the firm's business strategy)
8. Establishing strategic controls (i.e., monitoring actual performance to plan, implementing incentive systems, and taking corrective actions as necessary)

The first two activities, the external and internal analyses, often are referred to in the planning literature as a *SWOT analysis* (i.e., the determination of a business' strengths, weaknesses, opportunities, and threats).

In practice, the process of actually developing a business plan can be greatly facilitated by addressing a number of detailed questions corresponding to each activity listed previously. Extensive checklists can be found in Porter (1985) and Stryker (1986). Answering these questions requires the accumulation of substantial amounts of economic, industry, and market information. See Appendix A for common sources of such data.

Figure 4-2 provides a convenient framework for understanding how the various activities involved in developing the business plan interact. This illustration is intended to underscore that planning is indeed an iterative process. Following an exhaustive and objective analysis of the external environment and introspective internal assessment of the firm, management has a clearer understanding of emerging opportunities and threats to the firm and of the firm's primary internal strengths and weaknesses. Table 4-1 illustrates how SWOT analysis could be used to identify opportunities and threats for Amazon.com. This hypothetical example suggests that Amazon.com sees its greatest opportunity as becoming an "online department store" and the growing Internet presence of sophisticated competitors as its greatest threat. The table then summarizes how Amazon.com sees its major strengths and weaknesses compared to the primary perceived opportunity and threat. This information enables management to set an overall direction for the firm in terms of where and how the firm intends to compete, which is communicated to the firm's stakeholders in the form of a mission/vision statement and a set of quantifiable financial and nonfinancial objectives.

Information gleaned from the external and internal analyses drives the development of business, implementation, and functional strategies. Each level of strategy involves an increased level of detail. The business strategy defines in general terms how the business intends to compete (i.e., through cost leadership, differentiation, or increased focus). The implementation strategy identifies how the business strategy will be realized (i.e., the firm acts on its own, partners with others, or acquires/merges with another firm). Finally, functional strategies define in considerable detail how each functional department (e.g., legal, finance, and human resources) in the firm will support the implementation strategy. Functional strategies often entail setting objectives and performance milestones for each employee supporting the implementation strategy. Strategic controls are put in place to heighten the prospect that vision, objectives, and strategies will be realized on schedule. Such controls involve establishing bonus plans and other incentive mechanisms to motivate all employees to achieve their individual objectives on or ahead of schedule. Systems are also put in place to track the firm's actual performance to plan. Significant deviations from the implementation plan may require switching to contingency plans.

The eight key activities involved in developing an appropriate business plan are discussed in more detail during the remainder of this chapter. Of the various implementation strategy alternatives, the merger/acquisition implementation plan is discussed

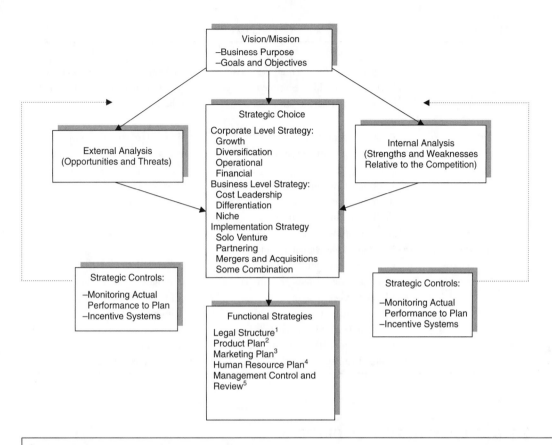

[1]Includes legal/accounting/tax structures required to implement chosen strategy.

[2]Product plan includes management of supply chain from new product development, supplier/customer channel relationships, manufacturing & IT operations, customer service and postsale support.

[3]Includes product/brand positioning, promotion, and pricing.

[4]Includes organizational design and effectiveness, identifying staffing requirements, and plans for satisfying those requirements.

[5]Includes systems for monitoring performance to objectives, reward mechanisms, and contingency plans.

[6]Timeline for achieving business objectives, including milestones.

[7]Projected income, cash flow, and balance sheet statements, including how the chosen strategy will be financed.

FIGURE 4-2   Framework for developing the business.

in considerable detail. Shared growth/shared control or partnering strategies are discussed in detail in Chapter 14. Implementing solo ventures are beyond the scope of this book.

External Analysis

This analysis involves the development of an in-depth understanding of the business' customers and their needs, underlying market dynamics or factors determining profitability, and emerging trends that affect customer needs and market dynamics. This analysis starts with answering two basic questions, which involve determining where the firm should compete and how the firm should compete. The primary output of the external analysis is the identification of important growth opportunities and competitive threats.

TABLE 4-1   Hypothetical Amazon.com SWOT Matrix

	Opportunity	Threat
	To be perceived by Internet users as the preferred online "department store" to exploit accelerating online retail sales	Wal-Mart, Best Buy, Costco, etc., are increasing their presence on the Internet
Strengths	• Brand recognition • Convenient online order entry system • Information technology infrastructure • Fulfillment infrastructure for selected products (e.g., books)	• Extensive experience in online marketing, advertising, and fulfillment (i.e., satisfying customer orders)
Weaknesses	• Inadequate warehousing and inventory management systems to support rapid sales growth • Limited experience in merchandising non-core retail products (e.g., pharmaceuticals, sport equipment) • Limited financial resources	• Substantially smaller retail sales volume limits ability to exploit purchase economies • Limited financial resources • Limited name recognition in selected markets (e.g., consumer electronics) • Retail management depth

Determining Where to Compete

Deciding where a firm should compete starts with identifying the firm's current and potential customers and their primary needs. This is the single most important activity in building a business plan and is based on the process of market segmentation.

Market Segmentation

Market segmentation involves identifying customers with common characteristics and needs. Whether individual consumers or other firms, collections of customers comprise *markets*. A collection of markets is said to comprise an *industry*. In manufacturing, examples include the automotive industry, which could be defined to consist of the new and used car markets as well as the aftermarket for replacement parts. Markets may be further subdivided by examining cars by makes and model years. The automotive market also could be defined regionally (e.g., North America) or by country. Each subdivision, whether by product or geographic area, defines a new market within the automotive industry.

The process for identifying a target market involves a three-step procedure. The first step entails establishing evaluation criteria used to distinguish the market to be targeted by the firm from other potential target markets. This requires the management of the firm conducting the market segmentation to determine the factors likely to affect a firm's overall attractiveness. The evaluation criteria may include market size and growth rate, profitability, cyclicality, the price sensitivity of customers, amount of regulation, degree of unionization, and entry and exit barriers. The second step entails continuously subdividing industries and the markets within these industries and analyzing the overall attractiveness of these markets in terms of the evaluation criteria. For each market, the evaluation criteria are given a numerical weight reflecting the firm's perception of the relative importance of each criterion applied to that market to determine overall attractiveness. Higher numbers imply greater perceived significance. Note that some criteria may be given a zero weight. The evaluation criteria then are ranked from 1 to 5, with 5 indicating that the firm finds a market to be highly favorable in terms of a specific evaluation criterion. In the third step, a weighted average score is calculated for each market and the markets are ranked according to their respective scores. The market with the highest score is considered to be the most attractive. This three-step procedure is illustrated in Table 4-2. Such a matrix is constructed for each market evaluated.

TABLE 4-2   Industry/Market Attractiveness Matrix

Industry or Market Evaluation Criteria[1]	Weight: (Relative Importance of Criteria)	Ranking: (5 = Highly Favorable; 1 = Highly Unfavorable)[2]	Weighted Score: (Weight × Ranking)
Market size: Is it large or small? Global, national, or regional?	0.10	4	0.40
Growth rate: Is it slowing, declining, or accelerating?	0.20	5	1.00
Profitability: Is it currently profitable? Is it expected to remain so?	0.20	4	0.80
Cyclicality: Is profitability volatile?	0.05	2	0.10
Seasonality: Is profitability seasonal?	0.00	3	0.00
Customers: Are the number, average size, and needs changing?	0.05	4	0.20
Competitors: Is it currently highly competitive? Will competition intensify?	0.10	4	0.40
Suppliers: Are they reliable?	0.00	3	0.00
Culture: What are the emerging trends?	0.00	4	0.00
Regulation: Is the industry heavily regulated?	0.06	4	0.24
Politics: Is the political climate stable?	0.05	3	0.15
Labor unions: Is it heavily unionized? Are unions cooperative or militant?	0.05	4	0.20
Technology: What are the emerging technological trends?	0.10	5	0.50
Entry and exit barriers: Is it difficult to enter or leave?	0.04	3	0.12
Total	1.00		4.11

Notes:
[1] Some of the criteria are viewed as insignificant when applied to this industry or market and are given a zero weight.
[2] The ranking is the extent to which each criterion is viewed as favorable by the firm.

Determining How to Compete

Determining how to compete involves a clear understanding of the factors critical for successfully competing in the targeted market. This outward-looking analysis applies to the primary factors governing the environment external to the firm. Understanding market dynamics and knowing in what areas the firm must excel when compared with the competition is crucial if the firm is to compete effectively in its chosen market.

Profiling the Targeted Markets

Market profiling entails collecting sufficient data to accurately assess and characterize a firm's competitive environment within its chosen markets. Using Michael Porter's (1985) Five Forces framework, the market or industry environment can be described in terms of such competitive dynamics as the firm's customers, suppliers, current competitors, potential competitors, and product or service substitutes. The three potential determinants of the intensity of competition in an industry include competition among existing firms, the threat of entry of new firms, and the threat of substitute products or services. While the degree of competition determines whether there is potential to earn abnormal profits (i.e., those in excess of what would be expected for the degree of assumed risk), the actual profits or cash flow are influenced by the relative bargaining power of the industry's customers and suppliers.

This framework may be modified to include other factors that determine actual industry profitability and cash flow such as the severity of government regulation and the impact of global influences (e.g., fluctuations in exchange rates). While labor costs often represent a relatively small percentage of total expenses in many areas of manufacturing, they frequently constitute the largest portion of the nonmanufacturing sector. With the manufacturing sector in most industrialized nations continuing its long-term decline as a percentage of the total economy, the analyst should also include the factors affecting the bargaining power of labor (Figure 4-3). The analyst may also choose to identify the capital markets as a key determinant of industry profitability for those industries relying heavily on external sources of financing such as the electric utility industry.

The data required to analyze industry competitive dynamics include the following: (1) types of products and services, (2) market share in terms of dollars and units, (3) pricing metrics, (4) selling and distribution channels and associated costs, (5) type, location, and age of production facilities, (6) product quality metrics, (7) customer service metrics, (8) compensation by major labor category, (9) research and development (R&D) expenditures, (10) supplier performance metrics, and (11) financial performance in terms of growth and profitability. These data must be collected on all significant competitors in the firm's chosen markets.

Determinants of the Intensity of Industry Competition

How intense industry competition becomes is affected by competition among existing firms, the potential for new entrants, and the potential for substitute products and services.

The intensity of competition among current industry competitors is affected by industry growth rate, industry concentration, degree of differentiation and switching costs, scale and scope economies, excess capacity, and exit barriers. If an industry is growing rapidly, existing firms have less need to compete for market share. If an industry is highly concentrated, firms can more easily coordinate their pricing activities in contrast to a highly fragmented industry in which price competition is likely to be very intense. If the cost of

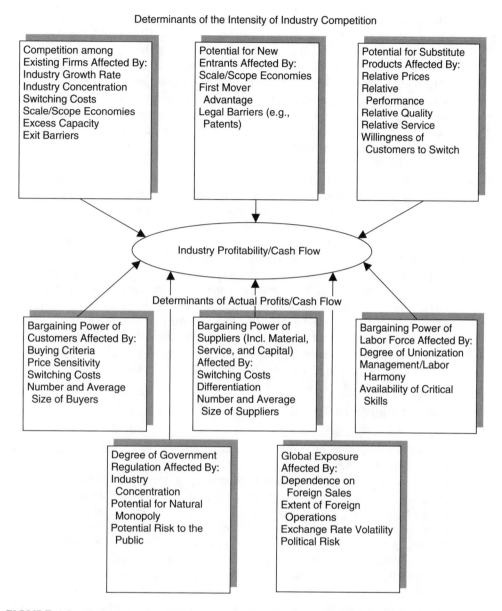

FIGURE 4-3   Defining market/industry competitive dynamics (adapted from Palepu, Healy, and Bernard, 2004, p. 2-2).

switching from one supplier to another is minimal because of low perceived differentiation, customers are likely to switch based on relatively small differences in price. Furthermore, in industries in which production volume is important, companies may compete aggressively for market share to realize economies of scale. Moreover, firms in industries exhibiting substantial excess capacity often reduce prices to fill unused capacity. Finally, competition may be intensified in industries in which it is difficult for firms to exit due to high exit barriers such as large unfunded pension liabilities and single purpose assets.

Current competitors within an industry characterized by low barriers to entry have limited pricing power. Attempts to raise prices resulting in abnormally large profits will attract new competitors, thereby adding to the industry's productive capacity. In contrast, high entry barriers may give existing competitors significant pricing power. Barriers to new entrants include situations in which the large-scale operations of existing competitors give them a potential cost advantage due to economies of scale. New entrants may enter only if they are willing to invest in substantial additional new capacity. "First mover advantage" (i.e., being an early competitor in an industry) may also create entry barriers as such firms achieve widespread brand recognition, establish industry standards, or develop exclusive relationships with key suppliers and distributors. Finally, legal constraints such as copyrights and patents may inhibit the entry of new firms. Examples of new entrants abound. Internet-based technologies loom as an enormous threat to cable. Phone giants AT&T and Verizon are planning to use such technologies to offer consumers a variety of movies and TV shows that could be watched at any time. Furthermore, program owners such as ESPN are working with consumer electronics manufacturers to develop a set-top box that would provide access to college football games not available on cable or satellite. Users of Apple Computer's iPod will be able to watch shows from Disney's ABC unit.

The relative price (i.e., the selling price of one product compared to a close substitute) or performance of competing products, perceived quality, and the willingness of the customer to switch products determine the threat of substitution. Potential substitutes include those that are substantially similar to existing products and those performing the same function. Examples include the shift of many products formerly ordered through traditional brick-and-mortar retail outlets to the Internet such as books, compact discs, and airline tickets. Other examples include e-mail and faxes as substitutes for letters, and the replacement of the electric typewriter by the word processor.

Determinants of Actual Profits and Cash Flow

The bargaining power of customers, suppliers, and the labor force are important factors impacting profits and cash flow. Other factors include the degree of government regulation and global exposure.

The relative bargaining power of buyers depends on their primary buying criteria (i.e., price, quality/reliability, service, convenience, or some combination), price sensitivity or elasticity, switching costs, and their number and size compared to the number and size of suppliers. For example, if a customer's primary criterion for making a purchase is product quality and reliability, they may be willing to pay a premium for a Toyota due to their perceived higher relative quality. Customers are more likely to be highly price sensitive in industries whose products are largely undifferentiated and when the cost of switching is relatively low. For example, companies lending to consumers and businesses rely heavily on information supplied by the major credit reporting companies, such as Experian, Equifax, Trans-Union, and Dun & Bradstreet, for information to make credit-granting decisions. Although lenders require accurate, complete, and timely data, small differences in price will cause lenders to switch suppliers or renegotiate contracts with existing suppliers as soon as the current contracts expire. Finally, buyers are likely to have considerable bargaining leverage when there are relatively few large buyers relative to the number of suppliers such as automotive manufacturers as compared to automotive component suppliers.

The relative leverage of suppliers reflects the ease with which customers can switch suppliers, perceived differentiation, their number, and how critical they are to the customer. Switching costs are highest when customers must pay penalties to exit long-term supply contracts or when new suppliers would have to undergo an intensive learning process to meet the customers' requirements. Moreover, reliance on a single or a small number of suppliers shifts pricing power from the buyer to the seller. Examples include Intel's global dominance of the microchip market and Microsoft's worldwide supremacy in the market for personal computer operating systems.

Work stoppages create opportunities for competitors to gain market share. Customers are forced to satisfy their product and service needs elsewhere. Although the loss of customers may be temporary, it may become permanent if the customer finds that another firm's product or service is superior to what it had been purchasing. Frequent work stoppages also may have long-term impacts on productivity and production costs as a result of a less motivated labor force and increased labor turnover. High turnover can contribute to escalating operating expenses as firms incur substantial search and retraining expenses to fill positions.

Governments may choose to regulate industries that are heavily concentrated, are natural monopolies (e.g., electric utilities), or provide a potential risk to the public. Regulatory compliance adds significantly to an industry's operating costs. Regulations also create barriers to both entering and exiting an industry. The government may choose to regulate industries that are heavily concentrated to minimize anticompetitive practices or those such as utilities whose economics justifies relatively few competitors. Companies wishing to enter the pharmaceutical industry must have the capabilities to produce and test new drugs to the satisfaction of the Food and Drug Administration. Companies with large unfunded or underfunded pension liabilities may find exiting an industry impossible until they have met their pension obligations to the satisfaction of the U.S. regulatory agencies.

Global exposure refers to the extent to which participation in an industry necessitates having a multinational presence. For example, the automotive industry is widely viewed as a global industry in which participation requires having assembly plants and distribution networks in major markets throughout the world. As the major auto assemblers move abroad, they also are requiring their parts suppliers to build nearby facilities to ensure "just-in-time" delivery of parts. Global exposure introduces the firm to significant currency risk as well as political risk that could result in the confiscation of the firm's properties.

Internal Analysis

The primary output of internal analysis is the determination of the firm's strengths and weaknesses. What are the firm's critical strengths and weaknesses as compared with the competition? Can the firm's critical strengths be easily duplicated and surpassed by the competition? Can these critical strengths be used to gain strategic advantage in the firm's chosen market? Can the firm's key weaknesses be exploited by competitors? These questions must be answered as objectively as possible for the information to be useful in formulating a viable business strategy.

Business Attractiveness Matrix

Competing successfully ultimately means satisfying the firm's targeted customers' needs better than competitors can. Conducting a self-assessment consists of identifying those strengths or competencies necessary to compete successfully in the firm's chosen market. These strengths often are referred to as *success factors*. Examples of success factors could include the following: high market share compared to the competition, product line breadth, cost-effective sales distribution channels, age and geographic location of production facilities, relative product quality, price competitiveness, R&D effectiveness, customer service effectiveness, corporate culture, and profitability.

Once identified for the firm's target market, success factors are weighted to reflect their relative importance in determining the firm's probable degree of success in its target market. When success factors do not apply or are relatively insignificant in a specific market, they should be given a zero weight. The firm's competitive position with respect to each success factor is ranked relative to its primary competitors. A 5 ranking means that the firm is highly competitive with respect to a specific success factor when compared with the competition. A ranking of 1 indicates a very poor competitive position. The Business Attractiveness Matrix, shown in Table 4-3, illustrates how the firm's overall attractiveness in its chosen market is determined.

TABLE 4-3   Business Attractiveness Matrix

Success Factor	Weight	Compared to Primary Competitor	
		Ranking (5 = highly favorable; 1 = highly unfavorable)	Weighted Score
Market share: Firm's current market share?	0.20	3	0.60
Product line breadth: Does firm offer a broad or limited product line?	0.0	3	0.00
Sales distribution: Are firm's distribution channels cost effective?	0.15	4	0.60
Price competitiveness: Are firm's prices high or low compared to the competition?	0.10	2	0.20
Age and location of facilities: Are firm's facilities properly located and new?	0.05	2	0.10
Production capacity: Can customer demand be served?	0.05	3	0.15
Relative product quality: How does the firm's product quality compare with the competition?	0.15	4	0.60
R&D: Is the firm a product innovator or follower?	0.10	3	0.30
Customer service: How does it compare with the competition?	0.03	3	0.09
Corporate culture: Is the firm's culture suitable for the industry?	0.02	3	0.06
Profitability: Can the firm attract capital and funds needed for investments?	0.15	2	0.30
Total	1.00		3.00

The weighted average score of 3.00 out of a possible score of 5.00 suggests that the firm's overall competitive position is somewhat favorable when compared with its primary competitor. This same matrix can be constructed for other competitors to compile a subjectively determined assessment of the firm's competitive position against other major competitors.

Case Study 4-1 illustrates how Michael Dell's insight into how PCs were sold changed the basis of competition in the PC industry. In doing so, he rendered the competitive models of other firms obsolete. However, the case study also illustrates that a firm's competitive advantage is not easily sustainable and must be continuously reviewed due to changes in the firm's competitive environment.

Case Study 4-1
Dell Computer's Drive to Eliminate the Middleman

Historically, personal computers were sold either through a direct sales force to businesses (e.g., the IBM model), through company-owned stores (e.g., the Gateway model), or through independent retail outlets and distributors to both businesses and consumers (e.g., the Comp-USA model). Retail chains and distributors constituted a large percentage of the customer base of other PC manufacturers such as Compaq and Gateway. Consequently, most PC manufacturers were saddled with the large overhead expense associated with a direct sales force, a chain of company-owned stores, a demanding and complex distribution chain contributing a substantial percentage of revenue, or some combination of all three.

Michael Dell, the founder of Dell Computer, saw an opportunity to take cost out of the distribution of PCs by circumventing the distributors and selling directly to the end user. Dell Computer introduced a dramatically new business model for selling personal computers directly to consumers. By starting with this model when the firm was formed, Dell did not have to worry about being in direct competition with its distribution chain.

Dell changed the basis of competition in the PC industry not only by shifting much of its direct order business to the Internet but also by introducing made-to-order personal computers. Businesses and consumers can specify online the features and functions of a PC and pay by credit card. Dell assembles the PC only after the order is processed and the customer's credit card has been validated. This has the effect of increasing customer choice and convenience as well as dramatically reducing Dell's costs of carrying inventory.

While Dell's logistical efficiency is often admired, its business model is showing signs of tarnish. Selling direct to the customer instead of through retailers and resellers no longer distinguishes it from the competition. Hewlett-Packard and Lenovo are currently Dell's most formidable global competitors, and Dell's vaunted advantage in efficiency is diminishing. Moreover, Dell in an effort to cut costs by outsourcing large portions of its customer service function to India and the Philippines has experienced a substantial customer backlash. Dell in mid-2006 announced that it was hiring thousands of people (most from North America) and has dramatically reduced its reliance on temporary employees. Dell has also been slow to change its product mix, with its core offering continuing to be centered on Windows-based personal computers. In contrast, Apple has demonstrated extraordinary success with the iMac, the MacBook models, the iPod, and the iTunes Music Store. Similarly, HP has introduced MediaSmart TV, which can function as a conventional TV or as a wireless monitor for a PC.

Despite these missteps, it is far too early to write Dell's epitaph. Survey results indicate that 50% of those planning to buy a PC in the United States during the second half of 2006 were planning to buy a Dell and that its market share among large businesses is a stunning 45%. Dell's direct to consumer sales approach is also continuing to prosper, with its U.S. consumer market share rising from 6% in 2000 to 30% in 2005. In 2006, unit sales of Dell products rose by 37% in China, 77% in Brazil, and 82% in India (see Kirkpatrick, September 18, 2006). The Dell business model is by no means dead; however, it clearly needs to be reinvigorated.

Case Study Discussion Questions

1. Who are Dell's primary customers? Current and potential competitors? Suppliers?
2. In your opinion, what market need(s) was Dell able to satisfy better than his competition?
3. Describe the key "success factors" in Dell's strategy. Be specific.
4. How did the way Dell sold its computers make it more profitable initially than its competitors? Why were competitors relying on "brick-and-mortar" retailers slow to catch up?
5. If you were running Dell, what would you do differently? Be specific.

Core Competencies

Gary Hamel and C. K. Prahalad (1994) argue that a firm's strategy should be based on core competencies, which represent bundles of skills that can be applied to extend a firm's product offering in new areas. For example, Honda Motor Corporation traditionally has had a reputation for being able to manufacture highly efficient internal combustion engines. In addition to cars, these skills have been applied to lawn mowers and snowblowers. Similarly, Hewlett-Packard was able to utilize its skills in producing highly precise measurement instruments to move successfully into calculators and later into PCs.

Defining the Mission Statement

At a minimum, a corporate mission statement seeks to describe the corporation's purpose for being and where the corporation hopes to go. The mission statement should not be so general as to provide little practical direction. A good mission statement should include references to such areas as the firm's targeted markets, product or service offering, distribution channels, and management beliefs with respect to the firm's primary stakeholders. Ultimately, the market targeted by the firm should reflect the fit between the corporation's primary strengths and competencies and its ability to satisfy customer needs better than the competition. The product and service offering should be relatively broadly defined so as to allow for the introduction of new products, which can be derived from the firm's core competencies. Distribution channels address how the firm chooses to distribute its products (e.g., through a direct sales force, agents, distributors, resellers, the Internet, or some combination). Customers are those targeted by the firm's products and services. Management beliefs establish the underpinnings of how the firm intends to behave with

---

Case Study 4-2
Maturing Businesses Strive to "Remake" Themselves:
UPS, Boise Cascade, and Microsoft

UPS, Boise Cascade, and Microsoft are examples of firms that are seeking to redefine their business models due to a maturing of their core businesses. With its U.S. delivery business maturing, UPS has been feverishly trying to transform itself into a logistics expert. By the end of 2003, logistics services supplied to its customers accounted for $2.1 billion in revenue, about 6% of the firm's total sales. UPS is trying to leverage decades of experience managing its own global delivery network to manage its customer's distribution centers and warehouses. After having acquired the Office Max superstore chain in 2003, Boise Cascade announced the sale of its core paper and timber products operations in late 2004 to reduce its dependence on this highly cyclical business. Reflecting its new emphasis on distribution, the company changed its name to Office Max, Inc. Microsoft, after meteoric growth in its share price throughout the 1980s and 1990s, experienced little appreciation during the 6-year period ending in 2006, despite a sizeable special dividend and periodic share buybacks during this period. Microsoft is seeking a vision of itself that motivates employees and excites shareholders. Steve Ballmer, Microsoft's CEO, sees innovation as the key. However, in spite of spending more than $4 billion annually on research and development, Microsoft seems to be more a product follower than a leader.

Case Study Discussion Questions

1. In your opinion, what are the primary challenges for each of these firms with respect to their employees, customers, suppliers, and shareholders? Be specific.
2. Comment on the likely success of each of their intended transformation?

---

respect to its stakeholders. See Case Study 4-2 to understand how some firms are dealing with these issues.

Setting Strategic or Long-Term Business Objectives

Business objectives are defined as what is to be accomplished within a specific time period. A good objective is measurable and has a time frame in which it is to be realized. Typical corporate objectives include revenue growth rates, minimum acceptable financial returns, and market share. A good objective might state that the firm seeks to increase revenue from $1 billion currently to $5 billion by the year 20??. A poorly written objective would be that the firm seeks to increase revenue substantially.

Common Business Objectives

Return: The firm seeks to achieve a rate of return that will equal or exceed the return required by its shareholders (cost of equity), lenders (cost of debt), or the combination of the two (cost of capital).

Size: The firm seeks to achieve the critical mass defined in terms of sales volume to realize economies of scale.

Growth:
— Accounting objectives: The firm seeks to grow earnings per share (EPS), revenue, or assets at a specific rate of growth per year.
— Valuation objectives: Such objectives may be expressed in terms of the firm's common stock price per share divided by earnings, book value, cash flow, or revenue per share.

Diversification: The firm desires to sell current products in new markets, new products in current markets, or new products in new markets. For example, the firm intends to derive 25% of its revenue from new products by 20??.

Flexibility: The firm desires to possess production facilities and distribution capabilities that can be shifted rapidly to exploit new opportunities as they arise. For example, the major automotive companies have moved toward standardizing parts across car and truck platforms to reduce the time required to introduce new products and to facilitate the companies' ability to shift production from one region to another.

Technology: The firm desires to possess capabilities in core or rapidly advancing technologies. Microchip and software manufacturers, as well as defense contractors, are good examples of industries in which staying abreast of new technologies is a prerequisite for survival.

Selecting the Appropriate Corporate-Level Strategy

Corporate-level strategies are adopted at the corporate or holding company level and may include all or some of the business units, either wholly or partially, owned by the corporation. A ***growth strategy*** entails a focus on accelerating the firm's consolidated revenue, profit, and cash-flow growth. This strategy may be implemented in many different ways. This will be described in more detail later in this chapter in the discussion of implementation strategies. A ***diversification strategy*** involves a decision at the corporate level to enter new businesses. These businesses may be either related or totally unrelated to the corporation's existing business portfolio. An ***operational restructuring strategy***, sometimes referred to as a turnaround or defensive strategy, usually refers to the outright or partial sale of companies or product lines, downsizing by closing unprofitable or non-strategic facilities, obtaining protection from creditors in bankruptcy court, or liquidation. A ***financial restructuring strategy*** describes actions by the firm to change its total debt and equity structure. The motivation for this strategy may entail better utilization of corporate cash balances in excess of the level required for financing normal operations through share-repurchase programs, reducing the firm's cost of capital by increasing leverage, or increasing management's control by acquiring publicly traded company shares through a management buyout. The later strategy is discussed in more detail in Chapter 13.

Selecting the Appropriate Business-Level Strategy

A firm should choose that business strategy from among the range of reasonable alternatives that enables it to achieve its stated objectives in an acceptable time period subject to resource constraints. Resource constraints include limitations on the availability of management talent and funds. Gaining access to highly competent management talent is frequently the more difficult of the two to overcome. Strategies can be reduced to one of four basic categories: (1) price or cost leadership, (2) product differentiation, (3) focus or niche strategies, and (4) hybrid strategies.

Price or Cost Leadership

The price or cost leadership strategy reflects the influence of a series of tools introduced and popularized by the Boston Consulting Group (BCG). These tools include the experience curve, the product life cycle, and portfolio balancing techniques (Boston Consulting Group, 1985). Cost leadership is designed to make a firm the cost leader in its market by constructing efficient production facilities, tightly controlling overhead expense, and eliminating marginally profitable customer accounts. The *experience curve* postulates that as the cumulative historical volume of a firm's output increases, cost per unit of output decreases geometrically as the firm becomes more efficient in producing that product. Therefore, the firm with the largest historical output also should be the lowest cost producer. The implied strategy for this firm should be to enter markets as early as possible and to reduce product prices aggressively to maximize market share. See the CD-ROM accompanying this book for an example of how to calculate an experience curve.

The applicability of the experience curve varies across industries. It seems to work best for largely commodity-type industries in which scale economies can lead to substantial reductions in per unit production costs. Examples include the manufacturing of PCs or cell phone handsets. The strategy of continuously driving down production costs may make most sense for the existing industry market share leader. If the leader already has a cost advantage over its competitors because of its significantly larger market share compared with its competitors, it may be able to improve its cost advantage by more aggressively pursuing market share through price-cutting. This strategy may be highly destructive if pursued concurrently by a number of firms with approximately the same market share in an industry whose customers do not see measurable differences in the products or services offered by the various competitors. Under such circumstances, repetitive price-cutting by firms within the industry is likely to drive down profitability for all firms in the industry. Case Study 4-3 illustrates how Anheuser-Busch is attempting to reduce its per unit production costs in the rapidly consolidating Chinese beer market.

Case Study 4-3

The Market Share Game: Anheuser-Busch Battles SABMiller to Acquire China's Harbin Brewery

China's beer industry is the world's fastest growing and second largest, after the United States. It is highly fragmented and offers many potential acquisition targets. At the end of 2000, there were about 470 independent brewers; however, industry consolidation reduced the number from almost 800 in 1992. The level of concentration is still relatively low, with the top 10 brewers producing about 30% of the country's total annual production. This compares to the United States where Anheuser-Busch alone controls about one-half of the American beer market.

Foreign brewers found it nearly impossible to achieve profitability in the highly price competitive Chinese market and scaled back their operations in the late 1990s. However, China's brewing industry has entered a new round of acquisitions ever since Anheuser-Busch, the world's largest brewery, announced in October 2002 plans to increase its share in Tsingtao Beer, China's largest brewery, from 4.5 to 27% by 2006. The difference this time from the merger boom in the early 1990s is that foreign breweries are concentrating on building market share in local beer markets rather than trying to roll out their international brands.

On July 12, 2004, Anheuser-Busch acquired 99.7% of the issued shares of Harbin Brewery Group Ltd. for $720 million, by offering to pay a 30% premium over the next highest bid. The takeover of Harbin began with the May 2, 2004, announcement by Anheuser-Busch that it completed its purchase of approximately 29% of Harbin for $139 million. This announcement triggered a hostile takeover bid for Harbin by its largest shareholder, SABMiller, the world's second largest brewer, which had a 29.6% stake in Harbin. The SABMiller bid was the first hostile takeover attempt of a publicly traded Chinese company by a foreign firm. With the Harbin takeover, Anheuser-Busch's market share would be more than twice that of any other competitor in northeastern China.

Conceding to Anheuser-Busch, SABMiller agreed to sell its share of Harbin to Anheuser-Busch. SABMiller indicated that it would receive $211 million from Anheuser Busch for its stake in Harbin, which it had acquired in July 2003 for $87 million. SABMiller said publicly that Anheuser-Busch placed a greater value on Harbin's growth potential than they did and that Harbin was not of great value to their growth strategy in China. Reflecting the extent to which existing Chinese brewery assets have increased in value in recent years compared to the cost of starting up a new brewery, SABMiller announced in late 2004 its intention to invest $82.2 million in 2005 to build a new brewery in affluent Guangdong in southeast China.

Case Study Discussion Questions

1. In your judgment, why was Anheuser-Busch willing to pay more than SABMiller for Harbin? Be specific.
2. In what way did SABMiller gain from their failure to acquire Harbin in the short run? How might they lose in the long run? Explain your answer.

BCG's second major contribution is the ***product life cycle***, which characterizes a product's evolution in four stages: embryonic, growth, maturity, and decline. Strong sales growth and low barriers to entry characterize the first two stages. However, over time entry becomes more costly as early entrants into the market accumulate market share and experience lower per unit production costs as a result of the effects of the experience curve. New entrants have substantially poorer cost positions as a result of their small market shares when compared with earlier entrants and cannot catch up to the market leaders as overall market growth slows. During the later phases characterized by slow market growth, falling product prices force marginal firms and unprofitable firms out of the market or to consolidate with other firms.

Management can obtain insight into the firm's probable future cash requirements and in turn its value by determining its position in its industry's product life cycle. During the high-growth phase, firms in the industry normally have high investment requirements associated with capacity expansion and increasing working capital needs. Operating cash flow is normally negative. During the mature and declining growth phases, investment requirements are lower and cash flow becomes positive. Although the phase of the product life cycle provides insights into current and future cash requirements for both the acquiring and target companies, determining the approximate length of each phase can be challenging. The introduction of significant product innovation can reinvigorate industry growth and extend the length of the current growth phase. This is particularly true in such industries as microchip, PC, and cellular.

In addition to its applicability to valuing the firm, the product life cycle also can be useful in selecting the appropriate business strategy for the firm. In the early stages of the product life cycle, the industry tends to be highly fragmented, with many participants having very small market shares. Often firms in the early stages adopt a niche strategy in which they focus their marketing efforts on a relatively small and homogeneous customer group. If economies of scale are possible, the industry will begin to consolidate as firms aggressively pursue cost leadership strategies.

In 2005, Mittal Steel announced a $4.5 billion deal to buy International Steel Group, a collection of five once-bankrupt steel companies consolidated by U.S. workout specialist, Wilbur Ross. With the transaction, Mittal became the largest steel producer in the world. In a creative application of a cost leadership strategy, Mittal wants to integrate its eight U.S. mills (ISG and three others it already owned)—clustered around the Great Lakes—to achieve "regional" economies of scale. By running the facilities as a single unit, the firm hopes to extract better terms from iron ore, coal, and electricity suppliers. Moreover, Mittal hopes to gain better pricing power with the individual plants no longer competing with each other.

The final BCG innovation, ***portfolio balance theory***, reflects the movements of products and firms through the product life cycle. Portfolio balance theory suggests that companies should fund high-growth, cash-poor businesses or product lines with cash provided by the more mature cash-generating businesses. Businesses in the growth phase of the product life cycle have low market share but substantial cash needs, and those in the mature or declining growth phase have higher market share. Note that this tool can be used to develop strategy at the corporate level, where the portfolio consists of operating units, or at the business level, where the portfolio may consist only of specific product lines.

Businesses in a firm's portfolio having high market share and high growth rates relative to the industry's growth rate and excellent profit potential are referred to as ***stars***. The high-growth potential of the stars means they also have high reinvestment requirements. As the industry moves through its product life cycle and reaches the maturity stage, the stars begin to generate cash flow well in excess of their reinvestment requirements. As their potential growth rate slows, management may reclassify such businesses as cash cows. This excess cash flow generated by these ***cash cows*** can be used by the firm to fund other stars within the firm's portfolio or to acquire new or related businesses that appear to have the potential to become stars. Businesses that have low growth and market share are deemed to be either ***question marks*** or ***dogs*** and frequently are candidates for divestiture. High-growth, low-market-share question marks may be the next stars or dogs. Question marks use up more cash than they generate and may become liabilities if they cannot be transformed into market leaders. Most companies cannot afford to fund all of their stars and question marks; consequently, some are likely to be divested, spun off to shareholders, or combined with other businesses in a joint venture operation.

Product Differentiation

Differentiation represents a range of strategies in which the product or service offered is perceived to be slightly different by customers from other product or service offerings in the marketplace. Differentiation can be accomplished through brand image, technology features, or through alternative distribution channels, such as the ability to download products via the Internet. For example, firms may compete by offering customers a range of features or functions. For example, many banks issue credit cards such as MasterCard or Visa. Each bank tries to differentiate its card by offering a higher credit line, a lower interest rate, or annual fee or by providing prizes. Software companies justify charging for upgrades based on additional features to word-processing or spreadsheet programs, which are not found on competing software packages. Other firms compete on the basis of consistent product quality by providing excellent service. Today, Dell Computer is perceived to be a strong competitor by providing both excellent quality and service (although its service has suffered in recent years), which in certain cases allows the firm to charge a slightly higher price for its PCs. Other firms attempt to compete by offering their customers excellent convenience. Amazon.com falls in this category by offering consumers the opportunity to buy books and other products whenever and from wherever they choose. Apple Computer has used catchy TV ads and innovative technology to stay ahead of competitors selling MPS devices, most recently with video capabilities of its newer iPods. Starbucks is staying ahead of the competition by creating new drinks aimed at baby boomers. All these things give customers new reasons to keep coming back.

Focus or Niche Strategies

Firms adopting these types of strategies tend to concentrate their efforts by selling a few products or services to a single market and compete primarily on the basis of understanding their customers' needs better than the competition does. In this strategy, the firm seeks to carve a specific niche with respect to a certain group of customers, a narrow geographic area, or a particular use of a product. Examples include the major airlines, airplane manufacturers (e.g., Boeing), and major defense contractors (e.g., Lockheed-Martin).

Hybrid Strategies

Hybrid strategies involve some combination of the previously mentioned strategies (see Table 4-4). For example, Coca-Cola pursues both a differentiated and highly market-focused strategy. Coca-Cola derives the bulk of its revenues by focusing on the worldwide soft drink market. Its product is differentiated in that consumers perceive it to have a distinctly refreshing taste. Moreover, consumers can expect the taste to be consistently the same. Other companies that pursue focused yet differentiated strategies include fast-food industry giant McDonald's, which competes on the basis of providing fast food of a consistent quality in a clean, comfortable environment.

Business–Market Attractiveness Matrix

The Business–Market Attractiveness Matrix matches the attractiveness of markets with a firm's capabilities (see Table 4-5). McKinsey & Company and General Electric Corporation introduced this analytical tool, which incorporates the results of internal and external analyses, as a means of summarizing the competitive position of all of a firm's lines of business. This matrix can be constructed from information obtained from the Industry/Market Attractiveness Matrix (Table 4-2) and the Business Attractiveness Matrix (Table 4-3) for each line of business (LOB) in the firm's business portfolio. Each LOB

TABLE 4-4   Hybrid Strategies

	Cost Leadership	Product Differentiation
Niche focus approach	Cisco Systems WD-40	Coca-Cola McDonald's
Multimarket approach	Wal-Mart Oracle	America Online Microsoft

TABLE 4-5   Business–Market Attractiveness Matrix

Business	Industry/Market Attractiveness Scores				
Attractiveness Scores by Line of Business (LOBs)	5	4	3	2	1
5					
4					
3		*			
2					
1					

is positioned in the Business–Market Attractiveness Matrix by using as coordinates the weighted average numerical scores from its Industry/Market Attractiveness and Business Attractiveness Matrices. For example, the Industry/Market and Business Attractiveness scores for a particular LOB from Tables 4-2 and 4-3 are 4.11 and 3.00, respectively. Their position in the matrix is denoted by an asterisk. The position of the asterisk in the matrix suggests that the firm finds this particular LOB of average attractiveness in a market that is above average in attractiveness. Note that a score of 5 indicates highest attractiveness, while a score of 1 suggests lowest attractiveness.

The Business–Market Attractiveness Matrix displays what the firm believes to be those LOBs that are most attractive in terms of the firm's strengths and in terms of the characteristics of the marketplace. The strategic implications of this planning tool are that a firm should invest or acquire in that market which has favorable growth and profit potential and in which the firm is likely to satisfy customer needs better than other competitors in the market. The firm should divest those LOBs in those markets that are viewed as unattractive and in which the firm has a weak overall competitive position. Those LOBs with the highest scores fall in the upper left-hand cell (high market attractiveness and business strengths) and those with the lowest fall in the lower right-hand cell of the matrix.

Selecting the Appropriate Implementation Strategy

Once a firm has determined the appropriate business strategy, attention must be turned to deciding the best means of implementing the desired strategy. Implementation involves selecting the right option from the range of reasonable options. Generally, a firm has five choices: (1) solo venture, go it alone, or build (i.e., implement the strategy based solely on internal resources), (2) partner, (3) invest, (4) acquire, or (5) swap assets. Each option has significantly different implications. Table 4-6 provides a comparison of the different options in terms of their advantages and disadvantages. In theory, the decision to choose among alternative options should be made based on the discounting of the projected cash-flow stream to the firm resulting from each option. In practice, there are many other considerations at work.

The Role of Intangible Factors

Although financial analyses are conducted to evaluate the various options, the option chosen ultimately may depend on such nonquantifiable factors as the senior manager's risk profile, patience, and ego. The degree of control offered by the various alternatives displayed in Table 4-6 is often the central issue confronted by senior management in

TABLE 4-6   Strategy Implementation—Solo Venture, Partner, Invest, Acquire, or Asset Swap

Basic Options	Advantages	Disadvantages
Solo venture or build (organic growth)	—Control	—Capital/expense requirements —Speed
Partner (Shared growth/shared control) —Marketing/distribution alliance —Joint venture —License —Franchise	—Limits capital and expense investment requirements —May be precursor to acquisition	—Lack of or limited control —Potential for diverging objectives —Potential for creating a competitor
Invest (e.g., minority investments in other firms)	—Limits initial capital/expense requirements	—High risk of failure —Lack of control —Time
Acquire or merge	—Speed —Control	—Capital/expense requirements —Potential earnings dilution
Swap assets	—Limits use of cash —No earnings dilution —Limits tax liability if basis in assets swapped remains unchanged	—Finding willing parties —Reaching agreement on assets to be exchanged

choosing among the various options. Although the solo venture and acquisition options offer the highest degree of control, they are often among the most expensive but for very different reasons. Typically a build strategy will take considerably longer to realize key strategic objectives; and it may, depending on the magnitude and timing of cash flows generated from the investments, have a significantly lower current value than the alternatives. In contrast, gaining control through acquisition also can be very expensive because of the substantial premium the acquirer normally has to pay to gain a controlling interest in another company.

The joint venture may represent a practical alternative to either a build or acquire strategy by giving a firm access to such factors as skills, product distribution channels, proprietary processes, and patents at a lower initial expense than might be involved otherwise. The joint venture is frequently a precursor to an acquisition, because it gives both parties time to determine if their respective corporate cultures and strategic objectives are compatible (see Chapter 14).

Asset swaps may represent an attractive alternative to the other options, but they are generally very difficult to establish in most industries unless the assets involved are substantially similar in terms of physical characteristics and use. The best example of an industry in which this practice is relatively common is in commercial and industrial real estate. The cable industry is another example of how asset swaps can be used to achieve strategic objectives. In recent years, the cable industry has been swapping customers in different geographic areas to allow a single company to dominate a specific geographic area and to realize the full benefits of economies of scale. In 2005, Citigroup exchanged its fund management business for Legg Mason's brokerage and capital markets businesses, with difference in the valuation of the businesses being paid in cash and stock. Similarly,

Royal Dutch Shell and Russia's Gazprom reached a deal to swap major natural gas producing properties in late 2005.

Accounting Considerations

Table 4-6 distinguishes between capital investment and expense investment. Although both types of investment have an immediate impact on actual cash flow, they have substantially different effects on accounting or reported profits. The impact of capital spending affects reported profits by adding to depreciation expense. This effect is spread over the accounting life of the investment. In contrast, *expense investment* refers to expenditures made on such things as application software development, database construction, research and development, training, and advertising to build brand recognition. Although it may be possible to capitalize and to amortize some portion of these investments over several years, they usually are expensed in the year in which the monies are spent. Publicly traded firms may base strategic investment decisions on accounting considerations (e.g., the preservation of earnings per share) rather than on purely economic considerations. Consequently, a publicly traded company may be inclined to purchase a very expensive piece of depreciable equipment rather than develop a potentially superior piece of equipment internally through R&D expenditures, which may have to be expensed.

Analyzing Assumptions

With the assumptions displayed, the reasonableness of the various options can be compared more readily. The option with the highest net present value is not necessarily the preferred strategy if the assumptions underlying the analysis strain credulity. Understanding clearly stated assumptions underlying the chosen strategy and those underlying alternative strategies forces senior management to make choices based on a discussion of the reasonableness of the assumptions associated with each option. This is generally preferable to placing a disproportionately high level of confidence in the numerical output of computer models. Case Study 4-4 illustrates some of the complexities of selecting the appropriate implementation strategy.

Case Study 4-4
Disney Buys Pixar—A Deal Based Largely on Intangible Value

In the wake of a stagnating share price, Walt Disney Corporation (Disney) sought to revive its animation capabilities as investors flocked to more successful animation studios such as Pixar Animation Studios (Pixar) and DreamWorks Inc. Disney's efforts in animated films in recent years have been disappointing. In an industry in which creative talent rules, Disney had simply not been able to assemble the right combination of talent in an environment conducive to creating blockbuster animation films.

Disney and Pixar had been in a joint venture involving three pictures since 1991, in which Disney shared the production costs and profits and distributed the films. Disney has benefited from Pixar's success by cofinancing and distributing Pixar films. Talks to extend this arrangement disintegrated in 2004 due to the failure of Pixar CEO Steve Jobs and Disney CEO Michael Eisner to reach agreement on allowing Pixar to own films it produces in the future.

With the current distribution agreement set to expire in June 2006, Robert Iger, Eisner's replacement, moved to repair the relationship with Pixar. Consequently, a deal that was unthinkable a few years ago was now possible. Disney announced the acquisition of Pixar, one of the most successful moviemakers in Hollywood history, on January 25, 2006. The move reflected Disney's desire to infuse the firm's internal animation resources with those from a proven animation company. A key Disney strategy is to use popular Disney movie characters across different venues (i.e., theme parks, merchandise, and television). Disney agreed to exchange 2.6 shares of its stock for each share of Pixar stock. The total deal is valued at $7.4 billion for the Pixar stock or $6.4 billion including $1 billion of Pixar cash that Disney will receive. The $1 billion in cash and marketable securities represents the equivalent of $1 billion in Disney stock; as such, it enables Disney to recover a portion of the purchase price. The deal represents a 4% premium to the price of Pixar stock on the day of the announcement price and a 15% premium since the beginning of 2006.

Despite near-term dilution of Disney EPS of as much as 10%, investors seem focused on the long-term impact to growth in Disney's shares. Disney's shares rose 1% on news of the announcement. Nevertheless, the risk associated with the transaction can be measured in terms of what Disney could have done with cash raised by issuing the same number of new shares to the public. At $6.4 billion, Disney could make 64 sequels at $100 million each. Moreover, Disney is probably paying top dollar for Pixar as the filmmaker is coming off a string of six consecutive movie blockbusters. Moreover, revenue from DVD sales may be maturing. Finally, the companies face a daunting cultural challenge.

The long-term success of the combination hinges on the ability of the two firms to meld their corporate cultures without losing Pixar's creative capabilities. Pixar President, Ed Catmull will become president of the combined Pixar/Disney animation business. Mr. John Lasseter, Pixar's creative director, will assume the role of Chief Creative Officer of the combined firms, helping to design attractions for the theme parks and advising Disney's Imagineering division. In an effort to insulate the Pixar culture from the Disney culture, Pixar will remain based in Emeryville, California, far from Disney's Burbank, California headquarters. As a condition of closing, all key Pixar employees must sign long-term employment contracts.

As part of the deal, Pixar Chairman and Chief Executive Steve Jobs, holder of 50.6% of Pixar stock, will become Disney's largest individual shareholder at about 6.5% of Disney stock and a member of Disney's board of directors. Jobs' advice may serve to rejuvenate the Disney board at a time when the entertainment industry is scrambling to reinvent itself in the digital age. Jobs, who is also the Chairman and CEO of Apple Computer Inc. (Apple), is in a position to apply Apple's substantial technical skills to Disney's animation efforts.

It is unclear if Disney could not have achieved many of these benefits at a much lower cost by partnering with Pixar and by offering Steve Jobs a seat on the Disney board. Ultimately, the opportunity to prevent Pixar's acquisition by a competitor may be the primary reason why Disney moved so aggressively to acquire the animation powerhouse.

Case Study Discussion Questions

1. Discuss the advantages and disadvantages of an acquisition of Pixar versus a partnership. What would you have recommended and why? Be specific.
2. Pixar's key creative employees have long-term contracts and have assumed key roles in the combined firms. Does such an arrangement heighten the prospects for Disney producing successful animated films? What challenges is Disney likely to face?
3. If you were the CEO of Disney, what might you have done differently? Be specific.

Functional Strategies

Functional strategies are focused on short-term results and generally are developed by functional areas; they also tend to be very detailed and highly structured. Such strategies will result in a series of concrete actions for each function or business group, depending on the company's organization. It is common to see separate plans containing specific goals and actions for such functions as marketing, manufacturing, R&D, engineering, and financial and human resources. Functional strategies should include clearly defined objectives, actions, timetables for achieving those actions, resources required, and the individual responsible for ensuring that the actions are completed on time and within budget.

Specific functional strategies could read as follows:

- Set up a product distribution network in the northeastern United States capable of handling a minimum of 1 million units of product annually by 12/31/20??. (Individual responsible: Oliver Tran; estimated budget: $2 million.)
- Develop and execute an advertising campaign to support the sales effort in the northeastern United States by 10/31/20??. (Individual responsible: Maria Gomez; estimated budget: $.5 million.)
- Hire a logistics manager to administer the distribution network by 9/15/20??. (Individual responsible: Patrick Petty; estimated budget: $100,000.)
- Acquire a manufacturing company with sufficient capacity to meet the projected demand for the next 3 years by 6/30/20?? at a purchase price not to exceed $100 million. (Individual responsible: Chang Lee.)

The relationship between the business mission, business strategy, implementation strategy, and functional strategies can be illustrated for an application software company, which is targeting the credit card industry.

- Mission: To be recognized by its customers as the leader in providing accurate high-speed, high-volume transactional software for processing credit card remittances by 20??.
- Business Strategy: Upgrade the firm's current software by adding the necessary features and functions to differentiate the firm's product and service offering from its primary competitors and to satisfy projected customer requirements through 20??.
- Implementation Strategy: Purchase a software company at a price not to exceed $400 million capable of developing "state-of-the-art" remittance processing software by 12/21/20??. (Individual responsible: Donald Stuckee.) Note that this assumes that the firm has completed an analysis of available options including internal development, partnering, licensing, or acquisition.
- Functional Strategies to Support Implementation Strategy:

  —Research & Development: Identify and develop new applications for remittance processing software.
  —Marketing & Sales: Assess impact of new product offering on revenue generated from current and new customers.

—Human Resources: Determine appropriate staffing requirements to support the combined firms (i.e., the acquirer and target firms).

—Finance: Identify and quantify potential cost savings generated from improved productivity as a result of replacing existing software with the newly acquired software and from the elimination of duplicate personnel in acquirer and target companies. Evaluate the impact of the acquisition of on the combined companies' financial statements.

—Legal: Ensure that all target company customers have valid contracts and that such contracts are transferable to the acquirer without penalty. Also, ensure that the acquirer will have exclusive and unlimited rights to use the remittance processing software.

—Tax: Assess the tax impact of the acquisition on the acquiring firm's cash flow.

Strategic Controls

Strategic controls consist of both incentive and monitoring systems. *Incentive systems* include bonus, profit sharing, or other performance-based payments made to motivate both acquirer and target company employees to work to implement the business strategy for the combined firms. Such a strategy normally would have been agreed to during negotiation. Incentives often include *retention bonuses* made to key employees of the target firm, if they remain with the combined companies for a specific period following completion of the transaction. *Monitoring systems* are implemented to track the actual performance of the combined firms against the business plan. Such systems can be accounting based (i.e., monitoring such financial measures as revenue, profits, and cash flow) or activity based. Activity-based systems monitor variables, which drive financial performance. Such variables include customer retention, average revenue per customer, employee turnover, and revenue per employee.

The Business Plan as a Communication Document

The necessary output of the planning process is a document designed to communicate effectively with key decision makers and stakeholders. Although there are many ways to develop such documents, Exhibit 4-1 outlines the key features that should be addressed in a good business plan (i.e., one that is so well reasoned and compelling to cause decision makers to accept its recommendations). A good business plan should be short, focused, and well documented. Supporting documentation should be referred to in the text but placed primarily in appendices to the business plan. The executive summary may be the most important and difficult piece of the business plan to write. It must communicate succinctly and compellingly what is being proposed, why it is being proposed, how it is to be achieved, and by when. It also must identify the major resource requirements and risks associated with the critical assumptions underlying the plan. The executive summary is often the first and only portion of the business plan that is read by the time-constrained Chief Executive Officer (CEO), lender, or venture capitalist. As such, it may represent the first and last chance to catch the attention of the key decision maker.

Exhibit 4-1
Typical Business Unit Level Business Plan Format

1. Executive summary: In 1–2 pages, describe what you are proposing to do, why, how it will be accomplished, by what date, critical assumptions, risks, and major resource requirements.
2. Industry/market definition: Define the industry/market in which the firm competes in terms of size, growth rate, product offering, and other pertinent characteristics.
3. External analysis: Describe industry/market competitive dynamics in terms of the factors affecting customers, competitors, potential entrants, product/service substitutes, and suppliers and how they interact to determine profitability and cash flow (e.g., Porter or Modified Porter Framework). Discuss major opportunities and threats that exist because of the industry's competitive dynamics. Information accumulated in this section should be used to develop the assumptions underlying revenue and cost projections in building financial statements for the business.
4. Internal analysis: Describe the company's strengths and weaknesses and how they compare with the competition. Identify which of these strengths and weaknesses are important to the firm's targeted customers, and explain why. Similarly, information obtained in this section can be used to develop key cost and revenue assumptions underlying the business's projected financial statements.
5. Business mission/vision statement: Describe the purpose of the corporation, what it intends to achieve, and how it wishes to be perceived by its stakeholders. For example, an automotive parts manufacturer may envision itself as being perceived by the end of the decade as the leading supplier of high-quality automotive components worldwide by its customers and as fair and honest by its employees, the communities in which it operates, and its suppliers.
6. Quantified strategic objectives (including completion dates): Indicate both financial (e.g., rates of return, sales, cash flow, share price) and nonfinancial goals (e.g., market share; being perceived by customers or investors as number one in the targeted market in terms of market share, product quality, price, innovation).
7. Business strategy: Identify how the mission and objectives will be achieved (e.g., become a cost leader, adopt a differentiation strategy, focus on a specific market segment, or some combination of these strategies). Show how the chosen business strategy satisfies a key customer need or builds on a major strength possessed by the firm. For example, a firm whose targeted customers are highly price sensitive may pursue a cost leadership strategy to enable it to lower selling prices and to increase market share and profitability. Alternatively, a firm with a well-established brand name may choose to pursue a differentiation strategy by adding features to its product that are perceived by its customers as valuable.
8. Implementation strategy: From a range of reasonable options (solo venture or "go it alone" strategy, partner via a joint venture or less formal business alliance, license, minority investment, and acquisition/merger), indicate which option would enable the firm to best implement its chosen business strategy. Indicate why the chosen implementation strategy is superior to alternative options. For example, an acquisition strategy may be appropriate if the perceived "window of opportunity" is believed to be brief. Alternatively, a solo venture may be preferable if there are few

attractive acquisition opportunities or if the firm believes that it has the necessary resources to develop the needed processes or technologies.

9. Functional tactical strategies: Identify plans and resources required by each major functional area including manufacturing, engineering, sales and marketing, research and development, finance, legal, and human resources.

10. Business plan financials and valuation: Provide projected 5-year income, balance sheet, and cash-flow statements for the company and estimate the firm's value based on the projected cash flows. State key forecast assumptions underlying the projected financials and the valuation.

11. Risk assessment: Evaluate the potential impact on valuation by changing selected key assumptions one at a time. Briefly identify contingency plans (i.e., alternative ways of achieving the firm's mission and objectives) that would be undertaken if critical assumptions prove to be inaccurate. Identify specific events that, if they occur, would cause the firm to pursue a contingency plan. Such "trigger points" could include deviations in revenue growth of more than x% or the failure to acquire or develop a needed technology within a specific time period.

Phase 2: Building the Merger/Acquisition Implementation Plan

If it is determined following an analysis of available options that an acquisition or merger is necessary to implement the business strategy, a merger/acquisition plan is required. (The merger/acquisition implementation plan subsequently will be referred to as the "acquisition plan.") The acquisition plan is a specific type of implementation strategy. The acquisition plan focuses on tactical or short-term rather than strategic or longer-term issues. It consists of management objectives, a resource assessment, a market analysis, senior management's preferences about how the acquisition process should be managed, a timetable for completing the acquisition, and the name of the individual responsible for making it all happen. The acquisition plan communicates to those charged with acquiring a company senior management's intentions. These are expressed in terms of management objectives and preferences. The objectives specify management's expectations for the acquisition and how it supports business plan objectives, and management preferences provide guidance on how the acquisition process should be managed. This guidance could include the specification of the criteria for selecting potential acquisition targets and willingness to engage in a hostile takeover. Moreover, preferences also could indicate management's choice of the form of payment (stock, cash, or debt), willingness to accept temporary earnings per share dilution, preference for a stock or asset purchase, and limitations on contacting competitors.

Management Objectives

The acquisition plan's stated objectives should be completely consistent with the firm's strategic objectives. Objectives include both financial and nonfinancial considerations.

Financial objectives in the acquisition plan could include a minimum rate of return or operating profit, revenue, and cash-flow targets to be achieved within a specified time period. Minimum or required rates of return targets may be substantially higher than those specified in the business plan, which relate to the required return to shareholders or to total capital. The required return for the acquisition may reflect a substantially higher level of risk as a result of the perceived variability of the amount and timing of the expected cash flows resulting from the acquisition.

Nonfinancial objectives address the motivations for making the acquisition that support the achievement of the financial returns stipulated in the business plan. In many instances, such objectives provide substantially more guidance for those responsible for managing the acquisition process than financial targets. Nonfinancial objectives in the acquisition plan could include the following:

1. Obtain rights to products, patents, copyrights, or brand names.
2. Provide growth opportunities in the same or related markets.
3. Develop new distribution channels in the same or related markets.
4. Obtain additional production capacity in strategically located facilities.
5. Add R&D capabilities.
6. Obtain access to proprietary technologies, processes, and skills.

Market Analysis

Assuming the proposed acquisition is in the firm's target market, there is no need to conduct a separate external or internal assessment, which was completed as part of the business plan. If the market to be entered is new to the firm, a complete market assessment is required. Market assessments were discussed earlier in this chapter under the modified Porter Competitive Framework (see Figure 4-3).

Resource Availability

Early in the acquisition process it is important to determine the maximum amount of the firm's available resources that senior management will commit to a merger or acquisition. This information is used when the firm develops target selection criteria before undertaking a search for potential target firms. Financial resources that are potentially available to the acquirer include those provided by internally generated cash flow in excess of normal operating requirements plus funds from the equity and debt markets. If the target firm is known, the potential financing pool includes funds provided by the internal cash flow of the combined companies in excess of normal operating requirements, as well as the capacity of the combined firms to issue equity or increase leverage.

Financial theory suggests that a firm always will be able to attract sufficient funding for an acquisition if the acquiring firm can demonstrate that it can earn its cost of capital. In practice, senior management's risk tolerance plays an important role in determining what the acquirer believes it can afford to spend on a merger or acquisition. Consequently, risk-adverse management may be inclined to commit only a small portion of the total financial resources potentially available to the firm.

Three basic types of risk confront senior management considering making an acquisition. These risks affect how they feel about the affordability of an acquisition opportunity.

These include operating risk, financial risk, and overpayment risk. How managers perceive these risks will determine how much of their potential available resources they will be willing to commit to making an acquisition.

Operating risk addresses the ability of the buyer to manage the acquired company. It generally is perceived to be higher for M&As in markets that are unrelated to the acquirer's core business. The limited understanding of managers in the acquiring company of the competitive dynamics of the new market and the inner workings of the target firm may negatively affect the postmerger integration effort as well as the ongoing management of the combined companies.

Financial risk refers to the buyer's willingness and ability to leverage a transaction as well as the willingness of shareholders to accept near-term earnings per share dilution. To retain a specific credit rating, the acquiring company must maintain certain levels of financial ratios such as debt to equity and interest coverage (i.e., earnings before interest expense divided by interest expense). A firm's incremental debt capacity can be approximated by comparing the relevant financial ratios to those of comparable firms in the same industry that are rated by the credit rating agencies. The difference represents the amount they theoretically could borrow without jeopardizing their current credit rating. Senior management could also gain insight into how much EPS dilution equity investors may be willing to tolerate through informal discussions with Wall Street analysts and an examination of recent comparable transactions financed by issuing stock.

Overpayment risk involves the dilution of EPS or a reduction in its growth rate resulting from paying significantly more than the economic value of the acquired company. The effects of overpayment on earnings dilution can last for years. To illustrate the effects of overpayment risk, assume the acquiring company's shareholders are satisfied with the company's projected annual average increase in EPS of 20% annually for the next 5 years. The company announces that it will be acquiring another company and that a series of "restructuring" expenses will slow EPS growth in the coming year to 10%. However, management argues that the savings resulting from combining the two companies will raise the combined companies' EPS growth rate to 30% in the second through fifth year of the forecast. The risk is that the savings cannot be realized in the time frame assumed by management and the slowdown in earnings extends well beyond the first year.

Management Preferences

Senior management's preferences for conducting the acquisition process are usually expressed in terms of boundaries or limits management chooses to impose on the process. To ensure that the process is managed in a manner consistent with management's risk tolerance and biases, management must provide guidance to those responsible for finding and valuing the target, as well as negotiating the transaction, in the following areas:

1. Determining the criteria used to evaluate prospective candidates (e.g., size, price range, current profitability, growth rate, or geographic location)
2. Specifying acceptable methods for finding candidates (e.g., soliciting board members; analyzing competitors; and contacting brokers, investment bankers, lenders, law firms, and the trade press)

3. Establishing roles and responsibilities of the acquisition team, including the use of outside consultants and defining the team's budget
4. Identifying acceptable sources of financing (e.g., equity issues, bank loans, unsecured bonds, seller financing, or asset sales)
5. Preferences for an asset or stock purchase and form of payment (cash, stock, or debt)
6. Tolerance for goodwill
7. Openness to partial rather than full ownership
8. Willingness to launch an unfriendly takeover
9. Setting affordability limits (such limits can be expressed as a maximum price to earnings, book earnings before interest and taxes, or cash-flow multiple or a maximum dollar figure)
10. Desire for related or unrelated acquisitions

Substantial up-front participation by management will help dramatically in the successful implementation of the acquisition process. Unfortunately, senior management frequently avoids providing significant input early in the process, despite recognizing the value of communication. Limited participation by management inevitably leads to miscommunication, confusion, and poor execution later in the process by those charged with making it happen.

Schedule

The final component of a properly constructed acquisition plan is a schedule that recognizes all of the key events that must take place throughout the acquisition process. Each event should be characterized by beginning and ending milestones or dates as well as the name of the individual responsible for ensuring that each milestone is achieved. The timetable of events should be aggressive but realistic. The timetable should be sufficiently aggressive to motivate all participants in the process to work as expeditiously as possible to meet the management objectives established in the acquisition plan. However, an overly optimistic timetable may prove to be demotivating to those involved because uncontrollable or unforeseen circumstances may delay reaching certain milestones.

Exhibit 4-2 outlines the contents of a typical acquisition plan as discussed in this chapter. The linkage between the acquisition plan and business plan is that the former describes how the firm will realize the business strategy, whose execution is believed to require an acquisition or merger. Note the same logic would apply if the implementation of the firm's business strategy required some other business combination such as a joint venture or business alliance (see Chapter 14). Exhibit 4-3 provides a number of examples of how carefully crafted acquisition plan objectives can be linked directly to specific business plan objectives.

Exhibit 4-2
Acquisition Plan for the Acquiring Firm

1. Plan objectives: Identify the specific purpose of the acquisition. This should include what specific goals are to be achieved (e.g., cost reduction, access to new customers, distribution channels or proprietary technology, expanded production capacity) and how the achievement of these goals will better enable the acquiring firm to implement its business strategy (see Exhibit 4-1).

2. Timetable: Establish a timetable for completing the acquisition, including integration if the target firm is to be merged with the acquiring firm's operations.

3. Resource/capability evaluation: Evaluate the acquirer's financial and managerial capability to complete an acquisition. Identify affordability limits in terms of the maximum amount the acquirer should pay for an acquisition. Explain how this figure is determined.

4. Management preferences: Indicate the acquirer's preferences for a "friendly" acquisition; controlling interest; using stock, debt, cash, or some combination; etc.

5. Search plan: Develop screening criteria for identifying potential target firms and explain plans for conducting the search, why the target ultimately selected was chosen, and how you will make initial contact with the target firm. This activity will be explained in more detail in Chapter 5.

6. Negotiation strategy: Identify key buyer/seller issues. Recommend a deal structure that addresses the primary needs of all parties involved. Comment on the characteristics of the deal structure. Such characteristics include the proposed acquisition vehicle (i.e., the legal structure used in acquiring the target firm), the postclosing organization (i.e., the legal framework used to manage the combined businesses following closing), and form of payment (i.e., cash, stock, or some combination). Other characteristics include the form of acquisition (i.e., whether assets or stock are being acquired) and tax structure (i.e., whether it is a taxable or a nontaxable transaction). Indicate how you might "close the gap" between the seller's price expectations and the offer price. These considerations will be discussed in more detail in Chapter 5.

7. Determine initial offer price: Provide projected 5-year income, balance sheet, and cash-flow statements for the acquiring and target firms individually and for the consolidated acquirer and target firms with and without the effects of synergy. (Note that the projected forecast period can be longer than 5 years if deemed appropriate.) Develop a preliminary minimum and maximum purchase price range for the target. List key forecast assumptions. Identify an initial offer price, the composition (i.e., cash, stock, debt, or some combination) of the offer price, and why you believe this price is appropriate in terms of meeting the primary needs of both target and acquirer shareholders. The appropriateness of the offer price should reflect your preliminary thinking about the deal structure. See Chapters 11 and 12 for a detailed discussion of the deal structuring process.

8. Financing plan: Using the combined/consolidated financial statements, determine if the proposed offer price can be financed without endangering the combined firm's credit worthiness or seriously eroding near-term profitability and cash flow. For publicly traded firms, pay particular attention to the near-term impact of the acquisition on the earnings per share of the combined firms. For a more detailed explanation of M&A financial modeling, see Chapter 9.

9. Integration plan: Identify potential integration challenges and possible solutions. (See Chapter 6 for a detailed discussion of how to develop integration strategies.) For financial buyers, identify an "exit strategy." Highly leveraged transactions are discussed in detail in Chapter 13.

Exhibit 4-3

Examples of Linkages between Business and Acquisition Plan Objectives

Business Plan Objective	Acquisition Plan Objective
Financial: The firm will Achieve rates of return that will equal or exceed its cost of equity or capital by 20?? Maintain a debt/total capital ratio of $x\%$	Financial returns: The target firm should have A minimum return on assets of $x\%$ A debt/total capital ratio $\leq y\%$ Unencumbered assets of $\$z$ million Cash flow in excess of operating requirements of $\$x$ million
Size: The firm will Be the number one or two market share leader by 20?? Achieve revenue of $\$x$ million by 20??	Size: The target firm should be at least $\$x$ million in revenue
Growth: The firm will achieve through 20?? annual average Revenue growth of $x\%$ Earnings per share growth of $y\%$ Operating cash-flow growth of $z\%$	Growth: The target firm should Have annual revenue, earnings, and operating cash-flow growth of at least $x\%$, $y\%$, and $z\%$ Provide new products and markets Possess excess annual production capacity of x million units
Diversification: The firm will reduce earnings variability by $x\%$.	Diversification: The target firm's earnings should be largely uncorrelated with the acquirer's earnings.
Flexibility: The firm will achieve flexibility in manufacturing and design.	Flexibility: The target firm should use flexible manufacturing techniques.
Technology: The firm will be recognized by its customers as the industry's technology leader.	Technology: The target firm should possess important patents, copyrights, and other forms of intellectual property.
Quality: The firm will be recognized by its customers as the industry's quality leader.	Quality: The target firm's product defects must be $<x$ per million units manufactured.
Service: The firm will be recognized by its customers as the industry's service leader.	Warranty record: The target firm's customer claims per million units sold should be not greater than x.
Cost: The firm will be recognized by its customers as the industry's low-cost provider.	Labor costs: The target firm should be nonunion and not subject to significant government regulation.
Innovation: The firm will be recognized by its customers as the industry's innovation leader.	R&D capabilities: The target firm should have introduced at least x new products in the past 12 months.

Things to Remember

The success of an acquisition is frequently dependent on the focus, understanding, and discipline inherent in a thorough business plan. There are four overarching questions that must be addressed in developing a viable business plan. These include the following:

1. Where should the firm compete?
2. How should the firm compete?
3. How can the firm satisfy customer needs better than the competition?
4. Why is the chosen strategy preferable to other reasonable options?

To answer these questions, the business planning process should consist of a thorough analysis of customers and their needs and an intensive analysis of the firm's strengths and weaknesses compared with the competition. In addition, the planning process should result in a clearly articulated mission and set of quantified objectives with associated time frames and individuals responsible for meeting these objectives by the targeted dates. Using this information, a strategy is selected from a range of reasonable options. The assumptions underlying the strategy and supporting financial statements should be identified clearly. Information obtained from the external and internal analyses provides the basis for developing the key revenue and cost assumptions underlying the business' projected financial statements.

An acquisition is only one of many options available for implementing a business strategy. The decision to pursue an acquisition often rests on the desire to achieve control and a perception that the acquisition will result in achieving the desired objectives more rapidly than other options. Firms all too often pay far too much for control. Alternative options may prove to be less risky. A firm may choose to implement what amounts to a phased acquisition by first entering into a joint venture with another company before acquiring it at a later date.

Once a firm has decided that an acquisition is critical to realizing the strategic direction defined in the business plan, a merger/acquisition plan should be developed. The acquisition plan provides the detail needed to implement effectively the firm's business strategy. The acquisition plan defines the specific objectives management hopes to achieve by completing an acquisition, addresses issues of resource availability, and identifies the specific boundaries management chooses to use to complete a transaction. The acquisition plan also establishes a schedule of milestones to keep the process on track and clearly defines the authority and responsibilities of the individual charged with managing the acquisition process.

Chapter Discussion Questions

4-1. Why is it important to think of an acquisition or merger in the context of a process rather than as a series of semirelated, discrete events?
4-2. How does planning facilitate the acquisition process?
4-3. What are the major activities that should be undertaken in building a business plan?
4-4. What is market segmentation and why is it important?
4-5. What are the basic types of strategies that companies commonly pursue and how are they different?

4-6. What is the difference between a business plan and an acquisition plan?

4-7. What are the advantages and disadvantages of using an acquisition to implement a business strategy as compared with a joint venture?

4-8. Why is it important to understand the assumptions underlying a business plan or an acquisition plan?

4-9. Why is it important to get senior management heavily involved early in the acquisition process?

4-10. In your judgment, which of the acquisition plan tactical limits discussed in this chapter are the most important and why?

Answers to these Chapter Discussion Questions are available in the Online Instructor's Manual for instructors using this book.

Chapter Business Case

Case Study 4-5
Pepsi Buys Quaker Oats in a Highly Publicized Food Fight

Food Fight

On June 26, 2000, Phillip Morris, which owned Kraft Foods, announced its planned $15.9 billion purchase of Nabisco, ranked seventh in the United States in terms of sales at that time. By combining Nabisco with its Kraft operations, ranked number one in the United States, Phillip Morris created an industry behemoth. Not to be outdone, Unilever, the jointly owned British–Dutch giant, which ranked fourth in sales, purchased Bestfoods in a $20.3 billion deal. Midsized companies such as Campbell's could no longer compete with the likes of Nestle, which ranked number three; Procter & Gamble, which ranked number two; or Phillip Morris. Consequently, these midsized firms started looking for partners. Other companies were cutting back. The U.K.'s Diageo, one of Europe's largest food and beverage companies, announced the restructuring of its Pillsbury unit by cutting 750 jobs—10% of its workforce. PepsiCo, ranked sixth in U.S. sales, spun off in 1997 its Pizza Hut, KFC, and Taco Bell restaurant holdings. Also, eighth-ranked General Mills spun off its Red Lobster, Olive Garden, and other brand name stores in 1995. In 2001, Coca-Cola announced a reduction of 6000 in its worldwide workforce.

As one of the smaller firms in the industry, Quaker Oats faced a serious problem: it was too small to acquire other firms in the industry. As a result, they were unable to realize the cost reductions through economies of scale in production and purchasing that their competitors enjoyed. Moreover, they did not have the wherewithal to introduce rapidly new products and to compete for supermarket shelf space. Consequently, their revenue and profit growth prospects appeared to be limited.

The Quaker Quandary

Despite its modest position in the mature and slow-growing food and cereal business, Quaker Oats had a dominant position in the sports drink marketplace. As the owner of Gatorade, it controlled 85% of the U.S. market for sports drinks. However, its penetration abroad was minimal. Gatorade was the company's cash cow. Gatorade's sales in 1999 totaled $1.83 billion, about 40% of Quaker's total revenue. Cash flow generated from this product line was being used to fund its food and cereal operations. Gatorade's management recognized that it was too small to buy other food companies and therefore could not realize the benefits of consolidation.

After a review of its options, Quaker's board decided that the sale of the company would be the best way to maximize shareholder value. This alternative presented a serious challenge for management. Most of Quaker's value was in its Gatorade product line. It quickly found that most firms wanted to buy only this product line and leave the food and cereal businesses behind. Quaker's management reasoned that it would be in the best interests of its shareholders if it sold the total company rather than to split it into pieces. That way they could extract the greatest value and then let the buyer decide what to do with the non-Gatorade businesses. In addition, if the business remained intact, management would not have to find some way to make up for the loss of Gatorade's substantial cash flow. Therefore, Quaker announced that it was for sale for $15 billion. Potential suitors viewed the price as very steep for a firm whose businesses, with the exception of Gatorade, had very weak competitive positions. Pepsi was the first to make a formal bid for the firm, quickly followed by Coca-Cola and Danone.

The Beverage Wars Begin
By November 21, 2000, Coca-Cola and PepsiCo were battling to acquire Quaker. Their interest stemmed from the slowing sales of carbonated beverages. They could not help noticing the explosive growth in sports drinks. Not only would either benefit from the addition of this rapidly growing product, but they also could prevent the other from improving its position in the sports drink market. Both Coke and PepsiCo could boost Gatorade sales by putting the sports drink in vending machines across the country and selling it through their worldwide distribution network.

PepsiCo's $14.3 billion fixed exchange stock bid consisting of 2.3 shares of its stock for each Quaker share in early November was the first formal bid Quaker received. However, Robert Morrison, Quaker's CEO, dismissed the offer as inadequate. Quaker wanted to wait, since it was expecting to get a higher bid from Coke. At that time, Coke seemed to be in a better financial position than PepsiCo to pay a higher purchase price. Investors were expressing concerns about rumors that Coke would pay more than $15 billion for Quaker and seemed to be relieved that PepsiCo's offer had been rejected. Coke's share price was falling and PepsiCo's was rising as the drama unfolded. In the days that followed, talks between Coke and Quaker broke off, with Coke's board unwilling to support a $15.75 billion offer price.

Could the Third Time Be a Charm?
After failing to strike deals with the world's two largest soft drink makers, Quaker turned to Danone, the manufacturer of Evian water and Dannon yogurt. Much smaller than Coca-Cola or PepsiCo, Danone was hoping to hype growth in its healthy nutrition and beverage business. Gatorade would complement Danone's bottled-water brands. Moreover, Quaker's cereals would fit into Danone's increasing focus on breakfast cereals. However, few investors believed that the diminutive firm could finance a purchase of Quaker. Danone proposed using its stock to pay for the acquisition, but the firm noted that the purchase would sharply reduce earnings per share through 2003. Danone backed out of the talks only 24 hours after expressing interest, when its stock got pummeled on the news.

PepsiCo Shows Renewed Interest
Nearly 1 month after breaking off talks to acquire Quaker Oats because of disagreements over price, PepsiCo once again approached Quaker's management. Its second proposal was

the same as its first. PepsiCo was now in a much stronger position this time, especially because Quaker had run out of suitors. Under the terms of the agreement, Quaker Oats would be liable for a $420 million break-up fee if the deal was terminated, either because its shareholders did not approve the deal or the company entered into a definitive merger agreement with an alternative bidder. Quaker also granted PepsiCo an option to purchase 19.9% of Quaker's stock, exercisable only if Quaker is sold to another bidder. Such a tactic sometimes is used in conjunction with a break-up fee to discourage other suitors from making a bid for the target firm.

With the purchase of Quaker Oats, PepsiCo became the leader of the sports drink market by gaining the market's dominant share. With more than four-fifths of the market, PepsiCo dwarfs Coke's 11% market penetration. This leadership position is widely viewed as giving PepsiCo, whose share of the U.S. carbonated soft drink market is 31.4% as compared with Coke's 44.1%, a psychological boost in its quest to accumulate a portfolio of leading brands.

Case Study Discussion Questions

1. What factors were driving consolidation within the food manufacturing industry? Name other industries that are currently undergoing consolidation. What is driving consolidation in these industries?
2. Why did food industry consolidation prompt Quaker to announce that it was for sale?
3. Why do you think Quaker wanted to sell its consolidated operations rather than to divide the company into the food/cereal and Gatorade businesses?
4. Under what circumstances might the Quaker shareholder have benefited more if Quaker had sold itself in pieces (i.e., food/cereal and Gatorade) rather than in total?
5. Do you think PepsiCo may have been willing to pay such a high price for Quaker for reasons other than economics? Do you think these reasons make sense? Explain your answer.

Answers to these Case Study Discussion Questions are available in the Online Instructor's Manual for instructors using this book.

Chapter Business Case

Case Study 4-6
Oracle Continues Its Efforts to Consolidate the Software Industry

Background
Oracle CEO Larry Ellison continued his effort to implement his software industry strategy when he announced the acquisition of Siebel Systems Inc. for $5.85 billion in stock and cash on September 13, 2005. The global software industry includes hundreds of firms.

During the first 9 months of 2005, Oracle had closed seven acquisitions, including its recently completed $10.6 billion hostile takeover of PeopleSoft. In each case, Oracle realized substantial cost savings by terminating duplicate employees and related overhead expenses. The Siebel acquisition accelerates the drive by Oracle to overtake SAP as the world's largest maker of business applications software, which automates a wide range of administrative tasks. The consolidation strategy seeks to add the existing business of a competitor, while broadening the customer base for Oracle's existing product offering.

Siebel, founded by Ellison's one-time protégé turned bitter rival, Tom Siebel, gained prominence in Silicon Valley in the late 1990s as a leader in customer relationship management (CRM) software. CRM software helps firms track sales, customer service, and marketing functions. Siebel's dominance of this market has since eroded amidst complaints that the software was complicated and expensive to install. Moreover, Siebel ignored customer requests to deliver the software via the Internet. Also, aggressive rivals, like SAP and online upstart Salesforce.com have cut into Siebel's business in recent years with simpler offerings. Siebel's annual revenue has plunged from about $2.1 billion in 2001 to $1.3 billion in 2004.

In the past, Mr. Ellison has attempted to hasten Siebel's demise, declaring in 2003 that Siebel would vanish and putting pressure on the smaller company by revealing he had held takeover talks with the firm's CEO, Thomas Siebel. Ellison's public announcement of these talks heightened the personal enmity between the two CEOs, making Siebel an unwilling seller.

Why Siebel?

Oracle's intensifying focus on business applications software largely reflects the slowing growth of its database product line, which accounts for more than three-fourths of the company's sales.

Siebel's technology, and deep customer relationships give Oracle a competitive software bundle that includes a database, middleware (i.e., software that helps a variety of applications work together as if they were a single system), and high-quality customer relationship management software. The acquisition also deprives Oracle competitors, such as IBM, of customers for their services business.

Customers, who once bought the so-called "best of breed" products, now seek a single supplier to provide programs that work well together. Oracle has pledged to deliver an integrated suite of applications by 2007. What brought Oracle and Siebel together in the past was a shift in market dynamics. The customer and the partner community is communicating quite clearly that they are looking for an integrated set of products.

Competitor Reaction

Germany's SAP, Oracle's major competitor in the business applications software market, played down the impact of the merger, saying they had no reason to react and described any deals SAP is likely to make as "targeted, fill-in acquisitions." For IBM, the Siebel deal raised concerns about the computer giant's partners falling under the control of a competitor. IBM and Oracle compete fiercely in the database software market. Siebel has worked closely with IBM, as did PeopleSoft and J.D. Edwards, which had been purchased by PeopleSoft shortly before its acquisition by Oracle. Retek, another major partner of IBM, had also been recently acquired by Oracle. IBM had declared its strategy to be a key partner to thousands of software vendors and that it would continue to provide customers with IBM hardware, middleware, and other applications.

Case Study Discussion Questions

1. How would you characterize the Oracle business strategy (i.e., cost leadership, differentiation, niche, or some combination of all three)? Explain your answer.
2. What other benefits for Oracle, and for the remaining competitors such as SAP, do you see from further industry consolidation? Be specific.

3. Conduct an external and internal analysis of Oracle. Briefly describe those factors that influenced the development of Oracle's business strategy. Be specific.
4. In what way do you think the Oracle strategy was targeting key competitors? Be specific.

Answers to these Case Study Discussion Questions are available in the Online Instructor's Manual available for instructors using this book.

Appendix A

Common Sources of Economic, Industry, and Market Data

Economic Information

Business Cycle Development (U.S. Department of Commerce)
U.S. Census Bureau publications on population, transportation, and housing
Current Business Reports (U.S. Department of Commerce)
Economic Indicators (U.S. Joint Economic Indicators)
Economic Report of the President to the Congress (United States)
Long-Term Economic Growth (U.S. Department of Commerce)
Regional statistics and forecasts from large commercial banks
Monthly Labor Review (U.S. Department of Labor)
Monthly Bulletin of Statistics (United Nations)
Overseas Business Reports (By country, published by U.S. Department of Commerce)
World Trade Annual (United Nations)
U.S. Industrial Outlook (U.S. Department of Commerce)
Survey of Current Business (U.S. Department of Commerce)
Statistical Yearbook (United Nations)
Statistical Abstract of the United States (U.S. Department of Commerce)

Industry Information

Forbes (Mid-January issues provide performance data on firms in various industries)
BusinessWeek (provides weekly economic and business information, and quarterly profit and sales rankings of corporations)
Fortune (each April issue includes listings of financial information on corporations within selected industries)
Industry Survey (published quarterly by Standard and Poor's Corporation)
Industry Week (March/April issue provides information on 14 industry groups)
Inc. (May and December issues give information on Entrepreneurial firms)
Directory of National Trade Associations
Encyclopedia of Associations
Funk and Scott's Index of Corporations and Industries
Thomas' Register of American Manufacturers
Wall Street Journal Index

References

Bloomberg.com, "Glaxo, SmithKline Agree to Merge," January 18, 2000.

Boston Consulting Group, *The Strategy Development Process*, The Boston Consulting Group, Boston, 1985.

BusinessWeek, "Burying the Hatchet Buys a Lot of Drug Research," January 31, 2000, p. 43.

Deogun, Nikhil, and Betsy McKay, "PepsiCo Revives Discussions on Takeover of Quaker Oats," Dow Jones News Service, *Wall Street Journal*, November 30, 2000, p. C6.

Deusen, Cheryl, Steven Williamson, and Harold C. Babson, *Business Policy and Strategy: The Art of Competition*, 7th Ed., Auerbach, 2007.

Hamel, Gary C., and C. K. Prahalad, *Competing for the Future*, Harvard Business School Press, Cambridge, MA, 1994.

Hill, Charles W. L., and Gareth R. Jones, *Strategic Management: An Integrated Approach*, 5th Ed., Houghton-Mifflin, Boston, 2001, pp. 158–233.

Hunger, David, and Thomas L. Wheeler, *Concepts: Strategic Management and Business Policy*, 11th Ed., Prentice-Hall, Chicago, 2007.

Kirkpatrick, David, "Dell in the Penalty Box," *Fortune*, September 18, 2006, pp. 69–77.

Palepu, Krishna G., Paul M. Healy, and Victor L. Bernard, *Business Analysis and Valuation*, 3rd Ed., Thomson, 2004.

Porter, Michael E., *Competitive Advantage*, The Free Press, New York, 1985.

Pursche, William A., "Pharmaceuticals—The Consolidation Isn't Over," *The McKinsey Quarterly*, 2, 1996, pp. 110–119.

Stryker, Steven C., *Plan to Succeed: A Guide to Strategic Planning*, Petrocelli Books, Princeton, NJ, 1986.

Thompson, Samuel C., *Business Planning for Mergers and Acquisitions*, Academic Press, Durham, North Carolina, 2007.

CHAPTER ◆ 5

Implementation

Search through Closing—Phases 3–10

> *A man that is very good at making excuses is probably good at nothing else.*
>
> —Ben Franklin

Inside M&A: Mattel Overpays for The Learning Company

Despite disturbing discoveries during due diligence, Mattel acquired The Learning Company (TLC), a leading developer of software for toys, in a stock-for-stock transaction valued at $3.5 billion on May 13, 1999. Mattel had determined that TLC's receivables were overstated because product returns from distributors were not deducted from receivables and its allowance for bad debt was inadequate. A $50 million licensing deal also had been prematurely put on the balance sheet. Finally, TLC's brands were becoming outdated. TLC had substantially exaggerated the amount of money put into research and development for new software products. Nevertheless, driven by the appeal of rapidly becoming a big player in the children's software market, Mattel closed on the transaction aware that TLC's cash flows were overstated.

For all of 1999, TLC represented a pretax loss of $206 million. After restructuring charges, Mattel's consolidated 1999 net loss was $82.4 million on sales of $5.5 billion. TLC's top executives left Mattel and sold their Mattel shares in August, just before the third quarter's financial performance was released. Mattel's stock fell by more than 35% during 1999 to end the year at about $14 per share. On February 3, 2000, Mattel announced that its Chief Executive Officer (CEO), Jill Barrad, was leaving the company.

On September 30, 2000, Mattel virtually gave away The Learning Company to rid itself of what had become a seemingly intractable problem. This ended what had become a disastrous foray into software publishing that had cost the firm literally hundreds of millions of dollars. Mattel, which had paid $3.5 billion for the firm in 1999, sold the unit to an affiliate of Gores Technology Group (GTG) for rights to a share of future profits. Essentially, the deal consisted of no cash up front and only a share of potential future revenues. In lieu of cash, GTG agreed to give Mattel 50% of any profits and part of any future sale of TLC. In a matter of weeks, GTG was able to do what Mattel could not do in

181

a year. GTG restructured TLC's seven units into three, put strong controls on spending, sifted through 467 software titles to focus on the key brands, and repaired relationships with distributors. GTG also sold the entertainment division.

Chapter Overview

The firm's business plan sets the overall direction for the business. It defines where the firm has chosen to compete (i.e., target market) and how the firm has chosen to compete (i.e., through price–cost leadership, differentiation, or a focused strategy). A merger/acquisition implementation plan (subsequently referred to as the "acquisition plan") is required if the firm decides that an acquisition is needed to execute the firm's business strategy. The acquisition plan communicates to those charged with acquiring a company the preferences of senior management about the key objectives to be achieved and how the process should be managed. It ensures that the acquisition team conducts itself in a manner consistent with management's risk tolerance.

The acquisition plan defines the criteria, such as size, profitability, industry, and growth rate, used to select potential acquisition candidates. It may specify the degree of relatedness to the acquiring firm's current businesses and define the types of firms that should not be considered (e.g., current competitors). The plan also stipulates the roles and responsibilities of team members, including outside consultants, and sets the team's budget. Moreover, the plan indicates management's preference for such things as the form of payment (stock, cash, or debt), for acquiring stock or assets, and for partial or full ownership. It may preclude any hostile takeover attempts or indicate a desire to limit goodwill. It also may specify management's desire to minimize the impact of the acquisition on the earnings per share of the combined companies immediately following closing. Finally, the acquisition plan may establish limits as determined by management on what the acquiring firm is willing to pay for any acquisition by setting a ceiling on the purchase price in terms of a maximum price-to-earnings multiple or multiple of some other measure of value.

This chapter starts with the presumption that a firm has developed a viable business plan that requires an acquisition to realize the firm's strategic direction. Whereas Chapter 4 addressed the creation of business and acquisition plans (Phases 1 and 2), this chapter focuses on Phases 3–10 of the acquisition process, including search, screen, first contact, negotiation, integration planning, closing, integration implementation, and evaluation. The negotiation phase is the most complex aspect of the acquisition process, involving refining the preliminary valuation, deal structuring, due diligence, and developing a financing plan. It is in the negotiation phase that all elements of the purchase price are determined. A review of this chapter is contained on the CD-ROM accompanying this book. The CD-ROM also contains a comprehensive acquirer due diligence question list and redacted agreements of purchase and sale for stock and asset purchases.

Phase 3: The Search Process

Initiating the Search

Initiating the search for potential acquisition candidates involves a two-step procedure. The first step is to establish the primary screening or selection criteria. At this stage of the search process, it is best to use a relatively small number of criteria. The primary criteria should include the industry and size of the transaction. It also may be appropriate to add a geographic restriction. The size of the transaction is best defined in terms of the maximum purchase price a firm is willing to pay. This can be expressed as a maximum price-to-earnings, book, cash flow, or revenue ratio or a maximum purchase price stated in terms of dollars.

For example, an acute-care private hospital holding company wants to buy a skilled nursing facility within a range of 50 miles of its largest acute-care hospital in Allegheny County, Pennsylvania. Management believes that it cannot afford to pay more than $25 million for the facility. Its primary selection criteria could include the following: an industry (skilled nursing), location (Allegheny County), and maximum price (five times cash flow not to exceed $25 million). Similarly, a Texas-based manufacturer of patio furniture with manufacturing operations in the southwestern United States is seeking to expand its sales in California by purchasing a patio furniture manufacturer in the far western United States for an amount not to exceed $100 million. Its primary selection criteria could include an industry (outdoor furniture), a location (California, Arizona, and Nevada), and a maximum purchase price (15 times after-tax earnings not to exceed $100 million).

The second step is to develop a search strategy. Such strategies normally entail using computerized databases and directory services such as Disclosure, Dun & Bradstreet, Standard & Poor's *Corporate Register,* or Thomas' *Register* and *Million Dollar Directories* to identify qualified candidates. Firms also may query their law, banking, and accounting firms to identify other candidates. Investment banks, brokers, and leveraged buyout firms are also fertile sources of candidates, although they are likely to require an advisory or finder's fee. The Internet makes research much easier than in the past. Today the analyst has much more information at their fingertips. Such services as Yahoo! Finance, Hoover's, or EDGAR Online enable researchers to gather quickly data about competitors and customers. These sites provide easy access to a variety of public documents filed with the Securities and Exchange Commission (SEC). Exhibit 5-1 provides a listing of commonly used sources of information that can be highly useful in conducting a search for prospective acquisition candidates.

Exhibit 5-1

Information Sources on Individual Companies

SEC Filings (Public Companies Only)

10-K: Provides detailed information on a company's annual operations, business conditions, competitors, market conditions, legal proceedings, risk factors in holding the stock, and other related information.

10-Q: Updates investors about the company's operations each quarter.

S-1: Filed when a company wants to register new stock. Can contain information about the company's operating history and business risks.

S-2: Filed when a company is completing a material transaction such as a merger or acquisition. Provides substantial detail underlying the terms and conditions of the transaction, the events leading up to completing the transaction, and justification for the merger or acquisition.

8-K: Filed when a company faces a "material event" such as a merger.

Schedule 14A: A proxy statement. Gives details about the annual meeting and biographies of company officials and directors including stock ownership and pay.

Web sites

www.sec.gov
www.edgar-online.com
www.freeedgar.com
www.quicken.com
www.hooversonline.com
www.aol.com
http://finance.yahoo.com
www.bizbuysell.com
www.dialog.com

www.lexisnexis.com
www.mergernetwork.com
www.mergers.net
www.washingtonresearchers.com
www.twst.com
www.worldm-anetwork.com
www.onesource.com
http://edgarscan.pwcglobal.com/serviets.edgarscan

Organizations

Value Line Investment Survey: Information on public companies
Directory of Corporate Affiliations: Corporate affiliations
Lexis/Nexis: Database of general business and legal information
Thomas Register: Organizes firms by products and services
Frost & Sullivan: Industry research
Findex.com: Financial information
Competitive Intelligence Professionals: Information about industries
Dialog Corporation: Industry databases
Wards Business Directory of U.S. and Public Companies
Predicasts: Provides databases through libraries
Business Periodicals Index: Business and technical article index
Dun & Bradstreet Directories: Information about private and public companies
Experian: Information about private and public companies
Nelson's Directory of Investment Research: Wall Street Research Reports
Standard & Poor's Publications: Industry surveys and corporate records
Harris Infosource: Information about manufacturing companies
Hoover's Handbook of Private Companies: Information on large private firms
Washington Researchers: Information on public and private firms, markets, and industries
The Wall Street Journal Transcripts: Wall Street research reports
Directory of Corporate Affiliations (Published by Lexis-Nexus Group)

If confidentiality is not an issue, a firm may seek to advertise its interest in acquiring a particular type of firm in *The Wall Street Journal* or the trade press. Although this is likely to generate substantial interest, it is less likely to generate high-quality prospects. Considerable time is wasted sorting through responses from those interested in getting a free valuation of their own company to those responses from brokers claiming their clients fit the buyer's criteria as a ruse to convince the buyer that they need the broker's services.

Finding reliable information about privately owned firms is a major problem. Often by using sources such as Dun & Bradstreet or Experian, an analyst is able to accumulate fragmentary data. Nonetheless, it is possible to use publicly available information to obtain additional detail. For example, industry surveys provided by trade associations or the U.S. Census Bureau often provide such data as average sales per employee for specific industries. A private firm's sales can be estimated by multiplying an estimate of its workforce by the industry average ratio of sales per employee. An estimate of the private firm's workforce may be obtained by searching the firm's product literature, Web site, or trade show speeches or even by counting the number of cars in the firm's parking lot. For additional detail on how to develop information on private firms, see Chapter 10.

Brokers and Finders: Do You Really Need to Hire An Outside Investment Banker?

In 2003, the number of M&As handled without an outside investment banker helping either the buyer or the seller accounted for 83% of all U.S. transactions, up from 73% in 2002 (Thornton, June 2, 2004). This reflects a trend of more and more companies moving investment banking "in-house." Such companies are identifying potential targets on their own and are during their own valuation as well as due diligence. While large companies such as General Electric, PepsiCo, and Johnson and Johnson have long handled many deals themselves, even mid-size firms such as funeral services chain Hillenbrand Industries Inc. and diet empire Weight Watchers International Inc. are doing their own work. The trend toward in-house banking reflects efforts to save on investment banking fees that could easily be more than $5 million plus expenses on a $500 million transaction.

Employing Brokers and Finders in the Search Process

Brokers or so-called finders may be used to supplement your search process. A broker has a fiduciary responsibility to either the potential buyer or seller. The broker is not permitted to represent both parties. The broker is compensated by his or her client. In some states, the government licenses brokers. In contrast, a finder is someone who introduces both parties, without representing either one. The finder does not have a fiduciary responsibility to either party and is compensated by either party or both. Generally, finders are not regulated; consequently, they do not require a license. The line between whether the agent is a broker or a finder is often fuzzy. Courts often determine a finder to be a broker if the finder discusses price or any significant terms of the transaction. Brokers and finders are regulated at the state or local level—not by the federal government.

Fees Paid to Brokers and Finders

As a note of caution, it is important to always respond in writing if you receive a solicitation from a broker or finder. This is particularly important if you reject their services. If you at a later date acquire the firm they claim to have represented, the broker or finder may sue your firm for compensation. If you choose to use the broker or finder, make sure that the fees and terms are clearly stipulated in writing. It also is advisable to keep a written record of all telephone conversations and meetings with the finder or broker. These may at a later date be used in court if the broker or finder sues for fees that may be in dispute.

Actual fee formulas are most often based on the purchase price. The so-called *Lehman formula* was at one time a commonly used fee structure in which broker or finder fees would be equal to 5% of the first million dollars of the purchase price, 4% of the second, 3% of the third, 2% of the fourth, and 1% of the remainder. Today, this formula often is ignored in favor of a negotiated fee structure. A common fee structure consists of a basic fee, a closing fee, and an "extraordinary" fee. A basic fee or retainer is paid regardless of whether the deal is consummated. The closing fee is an additional amount paid on closing. Finally, the "extraordinary" fee is paid under unusual circumstances, which may delay eventual closing, such as gaining antitrust approval or achieving a hostile takeover. Fees vary widely, but 1% of the total purchase price plus reimbursement of expenses is often considered reasonable. For small deals, investment bankers often insist on the Lehman formula.

Phase 4: The Screening Process

The screening process is a refinement of the search process. It starts with a pruning of the initial list of potential candidates created by applying such primary criteria as the type of industry and the maximum size of the transaction. Because relatively few primary criteria are used, the initial list of potential acquisition candidates may be lengthy. Additional or secondary selection criteria may be used to shorten the list.

Care should be taken to limit the number of secondary criteria used. An excessively long list of selection criteria will severely limit the number of candidates that will pass the screening process. Whenever possible, the selection criteria should be quantified. In addition to the maximum purchase price, industry, or geographic location criteria used to develop the initial list, secondary selection criteria may include a specific market segment within the industry or a specific product line within a market segment. Other measures often include the firm's profitability, degree of leverage, and market share.

Market Segment

The search process involved the specification of the target industry. It is now necessary to identify the target segment in the industry. For example, a steel fabrication company may decide to diversify by acquiring a manufacturer of aluminum flat-rolled products. A primary search criterion would include only firms in the aluminum flat-rolled products industry. Subsequent searches may involve a further segmenting of the market to identify only those companies that manufacture aluminum tubular products.

Product Line

The product line criterion identifies a specific product line within the target market segment. The steel fabrication company in the previous example may decide to focus its search on companies manufacturing aluminum tubular products used in the manufacturing of lawn and patio furniture.

Profitability

The profitability criterion should be defined in terms of the percentage return on sales, assets, or total investment. This enables a more accurate comparison among candidates of different sizes. A firm with after-tax earnings of $5 million on sales of $100 million may be less attractive than a firm earning $3 million on sales of $50 million because the latter firm may be more efficient.

Degree of Leverage

Debt-to-equity or debt-to-total capital ratios often are used to measure the level of leverage or indebtedness. The acquiring company may not want to purchase a company whose heavy debt burden may cause the acquiring company's leverage ratios to exceed targeted levels and jeopardize the acquirer's credit rating. A firm's credit rating is an evaluation by such companies as Standard & Poor's or Moody's of the likelihood that a firm will repay its debt and interest on a timely basis.

Market Share

The acquiring firm may be interested only in firms that are number one or number two in market share in the targeted industry or in firms whose market share is some multiple (e.g., 2 × the next largest competitor). Firms having substantially greater market share than their competitors often are able to achieve lower cost positions than their competitors because of economies of scale and experience curve effects.

Phase 5: First Contact

Alternative Approach Strategies

The approach suggested for initiating contact with a target company depends on the size of the company, if the target is publicly or privately held, and on the acquirer's time frame for completing a transaction. The later factor can be extremely important. If time permits, there is no substitute for developing a personal relationship with the sellers. Often, if a rapport is developed, companies can be acquired that are not perceived to be for sale. Such relationships can only be formed at the highest level within the target firm. In large and small privately owned firms, founders or their heirs often have a strong paternalistic view of their businesses. Such firms often have great flexibility in negotiating a deal that "feels right" rather than simply holding out for the highest possible price. Relationship building is often a critical factor in cross-border transactions (see Chapter 16). However, personal relationships can only go so far in negotiating with a public company that has a fiduciary responsibility to get the best price.

If time is a critical factor, acquirers often do not have the luxury of developing close personal relationships with the seller. Under these circumstances, a more expeditious approach may be taken. However, the approach taken may well differ depending on the size or public/private status of the potential target firm.

Small Companies

For small companies (<$25 million in sales) in which the buyer has no direct contacts, a vaguely worded letter expressing interest in a joint venture or marketing alliance and indicating that you will follow up with a telephone call is often all that is necessary. During the follow-up call, be prepared to discuss a range of options with the seller.

Preparation before the first telephone contact is essential. If possible, script your comments. Get to the point quickly but indirectly. Identify yourself, your company, and its strengths. Demonstrate your understanding of the contact's business and how an informal partnership could make sense. Be able to quickly and succinctly explain the benefits of your proposal to the contact. If the opportunity arises, propose a range of options, including an acquisition. Listen carefully to the contact's reaction. Request a face-to-face meeting, if the contact is willing to entertain the notion of an acquisition. Choose a meeting place that provides sufficient privacy so that each party can be assured of confidentiality. Create a written agenda for the meeting after soliciting input from all prospective participants. The meeting should start with a review of your company and your perspective on the outlook for the industry. Encourage the potential target firm to provide information on its own operations and its outlook for the industry. Look for areas of consensus. Request information from the potential target firm to fill in any gaps in your knowledge of the firm.

Medium-Sized Companies

For medium-sized companies (between $25 and $100 million), make contact at the highest level possible in the potential target firm's organization through an intermediary. Intermediaries can be less intimidating than a direct approach. Intermediaries include members of the acquirer's board of directors or the firm's outside legal counsel, accounting firm, lender, broker/finder, or investment banker.

Large Companies

For large, publicly traded companies, contact also should be made through an intermediary at the highest level possible. Discretion is extremely important because of the target's concern about being "put into play." A company is said to be in play if circumstances suggest that it may be an attractive investment opportunity for other firms.

Even rumors of an acquisition can have substantial, adverse consequences for the target. Current or potential customers may express concern about the uncertainty associated with a change of ownership. Such a change could imply variation in product or service quality, reliability, and the level of service provided under product warranty or maintenance contracts. Suppliers worry about possible disruptions in their production schedules as the transition to the new owner takes place. Employees worry about possible layoffs or changes in compensation. Competitors will do what they can to fan these concerns to persuade current customers to switch and potential customers to defer buying decisions; key employees will be encouraged to defect to the competition. Shareholders may experience a dizzying ride as arbitrageurs buying on the rumor bid up the price of the stock only to bail out if denial of the rumor appears credible.

Discussing Value

Neither the buyer nor seller has an incentive to be the first to provide an estimate of value. Getting a range may be the best you can do. This may be accomplished by discussing values for recent acquisitions of similar businesses. Listen carefully to the contact's reasons for wanting to sell so that any proposal made can be structured to satisfy as many of the seller's primary needs as possible. With the seller's consent, establish a timeline consisting of next steps and stick to it.

Preliminary Legal Documents

A common first step in many transactions is to negotiate a confidentiality agreement, term sheet, and letter of intent (LOI). Usually all parties to the deal desire to have a confidentiality agreement. This may not be true for an LOI. The LOI is useful in that it generally stipulates the initial areas of agreement, the rights of all parties to the transaction, and certain provisions protecting the interests of both the buyer and seller. However, the LOI could result in some legal risk to either the buyer or seller if the deal is not consummated. The LOI may create legal liabilities if one of the parties is later accused of not negotiating in "good faith." This is often the basis for many lawsuits that are filed when transactions are undertaken but not completed as a result of disagreements emerging during lengthy and often heated negotiations. For illustrations of legal documents associated with M&As, see Oesterle (2006) and the CD-ROM accompanying this book.

Confidentiality Agreement

A confidentiality agreement (also called a nondisclosure agreement) is generally mutually binding in that it covers all parties to the transaction. In negotiating the confidentiality agreement, the buyer requests as much audited historical data and supplemental information as the seller is willing to provide. The prudent seller requests similar information about the buyer to assess the buyer's financial credibility. It is important for the seller to determine the buyer's credibility early in the process so as not to waste time with a potential buyer incapable of raising the financing to complete the transaction. The agreement should cover only information that is not publicly available and should have a reasonable expiration date. Note that the confidentiality agreement can be negotiated independently or as part of the term sheet or letter of intent.

Term Sheet

A term sheet is a discussion document outlining the primary terms with the seller and is often used as the basis for a more detailed letter of intent. The involvement of lawyers and accountants is often unnecessary at this stage. It is the last stage in the negotiation before the parties to the potential transaction start incurring significant legal, accounting, and consulting expenses. A standard term sheet may be two to four pages in length. It stipulates the total consideration or purchase price (often as a range), what is being acquired (i.e., assets or stock), limitations on the use of proprietary data, a **_no-shop provision_** preventing the seller from sharing the terms of the buyer's proposal with other potential buyers with the hope of instigating an auction environment, and a termination date. Many transactions skip the term sheet and go straight to the negotiating of a letter of intent.

Letter of Intent

The LOI often is useful in identifying early in the process areas of agreement and disagreement. However, it may delay the signing of a definitive agreement of purchase and sale. In the case of a public company, it may necessitate a public announcement to be in compliance with securities laws if the agreement is likely to have a "material" impact on the buyer or seller. Depending on how it is written, it may or may not be legally binding. The LOI formally stipulates the reason for the agreement and major terms and conditions. It also indicates the responsibilities of both parties while the agreement is in force, a reasonable expiration date, and how all fees associated with the transaction will be paid. Major terms and conditions include a brief outline of the structure of the transaction, which may entail the payment of cash or stock for certain assets and the assumption of certain target company liabilities. The letter also may specify certain conditions such as an agreement that selected personnel of the target will not compete with the combined companies for some time period if they should leave. Another condition may indicate that a certain portion of the purchase price will be allocated to the noncompete agreement. Such an allocation of the purchase price is in the interests of the buyer, because the amount of the allocation can be amortized over the life of the agreement. As such, it can be taken as a tax-deductible expense. However, it may constitute taxable income for the seller. The agreement also may place a portion of the purchase price in escrow.

The proposed purchase price may be expressed as a specific dollar figure, as a range, or as a multiple of some measure of value such as operating earnings or cash flow. The LOI also specifies the types of data to be exchanged and the duration and extent of the initial due diligence. The LOI usually will terminate if the buyer and the seller do not reach agreement by a certain date. Legal, consulting, and deed transfer fees (i.e., payments made to governmental entities when ownership changes hands) may be paid for by the buyer or seller, or they may be shared. As discussed in Chapter 3, buyers are sometimes able to negotiate break-up fees and options to purchase target stock or selected assets if the deal is not completed. These features may be part of the LOI or the agreement of purchase and sale.

A well-written LOI usually contains language that limits the extent to which the agreement binds the two parties. Price or other provisions are generally subject to *closing conditions*. Such conditions could include the buyer having full access to all of the seller's books and records; having completed due diligence; obtaining financing; and having received approval from both boards of directors, stockholders, and regulatory bodies. Other standard conditions include the requirement for signed employment contracts for key executives of the selling company and the completion of all necessary merger and acquisition documents. Failure to satisfy any of these conditions will invalidate the agreement. A well-written LOI also should describe the due diligence process in some detail. It should stipulate how the potential buyer should access the potential seller's premises, the frequency and duration of such access, and how intrusive such activities should be. The LOI also should indicate how the buyer should meet and discuss the deal with the seller's employees, customers, and suppliers. Sometimes the provisions of a standard confidentiality agreement are negotiated as part of the LOI. The letter of intent becomes the governing document for the deal that the potential acquirer can show to prospective financing sources.

In recent years, letters of intent sometimes include *go-shop provisions*, which allow the seller to continue to solicit higher bids for several months. However, if the seller accepts another bid, the seller would have to pay the bidder with whom they have a signed agreement a break-up fee. In early 2007, auto parts manufacturer Lear Corp. announced that it had signed a deal to be bought by financier Carl Icahn's American Real Estate Partners. Under the terms of the deal, Lear had 45 days to find another suitor.

Phase 6: Negotiation

Phases 1–5 of the acquisition process could be viewed as discrete activities or events. Unlike the previous phases, the negotiation phase is an interactive, iterative process. Many activities are conducted concurrently by various members of the acquisition team. The actual purchase price paid for the acquired business is determined during this phase and frequently will be considerably different from the initial valuation of the target company made before due diligence and based on sketchy publicly available information.

Developing a Negotiating Strategy

Negotiating is essentially a process in which two or more parties, representing different interests, attempt to achieve a consensus on a particular issue. A useful starting point in any negotiation is to determine the areas of disagreement as soon as possible. This may be achieved by having the parties review and agree on the facts pertaining to the deal. In general, parties will be able to reach agreement on most facts relatively easily. Once a list of areas of agreement has been compiled, it is easy to identify areas in dispute. Each party then determines if the list of disputed subjects contains any "deal breakers." **Deal breakers** refer to issues that a party to the negotiation cannot concede without making the deal unacceptable. Good negotiators make concessions on issues not considered deal breakers, but only if they receive something in return. The easiest areas of disagreement should be resolved first until only a few remain on the list. By this point, all parties to the negotiation have invested a great deal of money, time, and emotional commitment to the process. All parties generally will be looking forward to a near-term resolution of the remaining issues. All arguments should be explained in as logical and disciplined a manner as possible. Unreasonable demands at this point in the negotiation are likely to evoke frustration by the other party and encourage them to end discussions. If the parties can reach a point where one side or the other is willing to state at least a price range, reaching the final agreement is within striking distance.

Defining the Purchase Price

There are three commonly used definitions of purchase price. These include the total consideration, the total purchase price or enterprise value, and the net purchase price. Each definition serves a different purpose.

Total Consideration

In the agreement of purchase and sale, the ***total consideration*** consists of cash (C), stock (S), new debt issues (D), or some combination of all three. It is a term commonly used in legal documents to reflect the different types of remuneration received by target company shareholders. Note that the remuneration can include both financial and nonfinancial assets such as real estate. Nonfinancial compensation sometimes is referred to as ***payment-in-kind*** (PIK). The debt counted in the total consideration is what the target company shareholders receive as payment for their stock, along with any cash or acquiring company stock.

Each component of the total consideration may be viewed in present value terms; therefore, the total consideration is itself expressed in present value terms (PV_{TC}). The present value of cash is its face value. The stock component of the total consideration would be the present value (PV_S) of future dividends or net cash flows or the acquiring firm's stock price per share times the number of shares to be exchanged for each outstanding share of the seller's stock. New debt issued by the acquiring company as part of the compensation paid to shareholders can be expressed as the present value (PV_{ND}) of the cumulative interest payments plus principal discounted at some appropriate market rate of interest (see Chapter 7).

Total Purchase Price (Enterprise Value)

The **total purchase price** or **enterprise value** (PV_{TPP}) of the target firm consists of the total consideration (PV_{TC}) plus the market value of the target firm's debt (PV_{AD}) assumed by the acquiring company. The enterprise value is sometimes expressed as the total purchase price plus net debt. **Net debt** includes the market value of debt assumed by the acquirer less cash and marketable securities on the books of the target firm. The enterprise value of the firm often is quoted in the financial press and other media as the purchase price, because it is most visible to those not familiar with the details to the transaction. It is important to analysts and shareholders alike, because it approximates the total investment made by the acquiring firm to purchase the target firm. It is an approximation because it does not necessarily measure liabilities the acquirer is assuming that are not visible on the target firm's balance sheet. Nor does it reflect the potential for recovering a portion of the total consideration paid to target company shareholders by selling undervalued or redundant assets.

Net Purchase Price

The **net purchase price** (PV_{NPP}) is the total purchase price plus other assumed liabilities (PV_{OAL}) less the proceeds from the sale of discretionary or redundant target assets (PV_{DA}) on or off the balance sheet. PV_{OAL} are those assumed liabilities not fully reflected on the target firm's balance sheet or in the estimation of the economic value of the target firm. Other assumed liabilities and discretionary assets will be explained in more detail later.

The net purchase price is the most comprehensive measure of the actual price paid for the target firm. It includes all known cash obligations assumed by the acquirer as well as any portion of the purchase price that is recovered through the sale of assets. It may be larger or smaller than the total purchase price. The various definitions of price can be summarized as follows:

$$\text{Total Consideration:}\ PV_{TC} = C + PV_S + PV_{ND}$$

$$\text{Total Purchase Price/Enterprise Value:}\ PV_{TPP} = PV_{TC} + PV_{AD}$$

$$\text{Net Purchase Price:}\ PV_{NPP} = PV_{TPP} + PV_{OAL} - PV_{DA}$$

$$= (C + PV_S + PV_{ND} + PV_{AD}) + PV_{OAL} - PV_{DA}$$

Although the total consideration is most important to the target company's shareholders as a measure of what they receive in exchange for their stock, the acquirer's shareholders tend to focus on the total purchase price or enterprise value as the actual amount paid for the target firm. However, the total purchase price tends to ignore other adjustments that should be made to determine actual or pending "out-of-pocket" cash spent by the acquirer. The net purchase price reflects the relevant adjustments to the total purchase price and is a much better indicator of whether the acquirer overpaid (i.e., paid more than its economic value including synergy) for the target firm. *Economic value* is the present value of a firm's projected cash flows. The application of the various definitions of the purchase price is addressed in more detail in Chapter 9.

Other Assumed Liabilities

The adjustment to the total purchase price referred to as other assumed liabilities consists of items that are not adequately accounted for on the target's balance sheet. If all of the target firm's balance sheet reserves reflected accurately all known future obligations, and if there were no significant potential off–balance sheet liabilities, there would be no need to adjust the purchase price for assumed liabilities other than for short- and long-term debt assumed by the acquiring company. Earnings and book value per share would accurately reflect the expected impact of known liabilities. Operating cash flows, which reflect both earnings and changes in items on the balance sheet, would also accurately reflect future liabilities. Therefore, valuations based on a multiple of earnings, book value, or discounted cash flow would accurately reflect the economic value of the business.

In practice, this is rarely the case. Reserves are often inadequate to satisfy pending claims. This is particularly true if the selling company attempts to improve current earnings performance by understating reserves. Common examples include underfunded or underreserved employee pension and health care obligations and uncollectable receivables, as well as underaccrued vacation and holidays, bonuses, and deferred compensation, such as employee stock options. Other examples include product warranties, environmental liabilities, pending lawsuits, severance expenses, maintenance and service agreements, and any other obligations of the selling company accepted by the buyer at closing. To the extent that such factors represent a future use of cash, the present value of their future impact, to the extent possible, should be estimated. Case Study 5-1 illustrates how these liabilities can add to the actual out-of-pocket cost of an acquisition.

Case Study 5-1
The Cash Impact of Product Warranties

Reliable Appliances, a leading manufacturer of washing machines and dryers, acquired a marginal competitor, Quality-Built, which had been losing money during the last several years. To help minimize losses, Quality-Built reduced its quality-control expenditures and began to purchase cheaper parts. Quality-Built knew that this would hurt business in the long run, but it was more focused on improving its current financial performance to increase the firm's prospects for eventual sale. Reliable Appliances saw an acquisition of the competitor as a way of obtaining market share quickly at a time when Quality-Built's market value was the lowest in 3 years. The sale was completed quickly at a very small premium to the current market price.

Quality-Built had been selling its appliances with a standard industry 3-year warranty. Claims for the types of appliances sold tended to increase gradually as the appliance aged. Quality-Built's warranty claims' history was in line with the industry experience and did not appear to be a cause for alarm. Not surprisingly, in view of Quality-Built's cutback in quality-control practices and downgrading of purchased parts, warranty claims began to escalate sharply within 12 months of Reliable Appliances's acquisition of Quality-Built. Over the next several years, Reliable Appliances paid out $15 million in warranty claims. The intangible damage may have been much higher because Reliable Appliances's reputation had been damaged in the marketplace.

Case Study Discussion Questions

1. Should Reliable Appliances have been able to anticipate this problem from its due diligence of Quality-Built? Explain how this might have been accomplished.
2. How could Reliable have protected itself from the outstanding warranty claims in the definitive agreement of purchase and sale?

Discretionary Assets

Discretionary assets are undervalued or redundant assets not required to run the acquired business and that can be used by the buyer to recover some portion of the purchase price. Such assets include land valued at its historical cost on the balance sheet or inventory and equipment whose resale value exceeds its fully depreciated value. Other examples include cash balances in excess of normal working capital needs and product lines or operating units considered nonstrategic by the buyer. The sale of discretionary assets are not considered in the calculation of the economic value of the target firm because economic value is determined by future operating cash flows before consideration is given to how the transaction will be financed.

Concurrent Activities

The negotiation phase consists of four concurrent activities: (1) refining valuation, (2) deal structuring, (3) due diligence, and (4) developing a financing plan. Refining the preliminary valuation based on new information uncovered during due diligence provides the starting point for negotiating the agreement of purchase and sale. Deal structuring involves meeting the needs of both parties by addressing issues of risk and reward by constructing an appropriate set of compensation, legal, tax, and accounting structures. Due diligence provides additional information enabling the buyer to better understand the nature of the liabilities the buyer is being asked to assume and to confirm perceived sources of value. Finally, the financing plan provides a reality check on the buyer, because it defines the maximum amount the buyer can reasonably expect to finance and in turn pay for the target company.

Refining Valuation

The first activity within the negotiation phase of the acquisition process deals with updating the preliminary target company valuation based on new information. At this stage, the buyer requests and reviews at least 3 to 5 years of historical financial data. Although it is highly desirable to examine data that have been audited in accordance with Generally Accepted Accounting Principals (GAAP), such data may not be available for small, privately owned companies. In fact, small companies rarely hire outside accounting firms to conduct expensive audits unless they are required to do so as part of a loan agreement.

The 3 to 5 years of historical data should be normalized or adjusted for nonrecurring gains, losses, or expenses. Nonrecurring gains or losses can result from the sale of land, equipment, product lines, patents, software, or copyrights. Nonrecurring expenses include severance, employee signing bonuses, and settlement of litigation. These adjustments are necessary to allow the buyer to smooth out irregularities in the historical information and to better understand the underlying dynamics of the business. Once the data have been normalized, each major expense category should be expressed as a percentage of revenue. By observing year-to-year changes in these ratios, sustainable trends in the data are more discernable. The process of refining valuations using standard financial modeling techniques is described in more detail in Chapter 9.

Deal Structuring

In purely financial terms, deal structuring involves the allocation of cash-flow streams (with respect to amount and timing); the allocation of risk; and, therefore, the allocation of value between different parties to the transaction. In terms of the personalities of the parties involved, it is the process of identifying and satisfying as many of the highest priority objectives of the parties involved in the transaction subject to their tolerance for risk.

In practice, deal structuring is about understanding the potential sources of disagreement from a simple argument over basic facts to substantially more complex issues, such as the form of payment, legal, accounting, and tax structures. It also requires understanding the potential conflicts of interest that can influence the outcome of the discussions. For example, when a portion of the purchase price depends on the long-term performance of the acquired business, the management of the business, often the former owner, may not behave in a manner that is in the best interests of the acquirer. The deal-structuring process also embodies feedback effects in which one element of the process such as the nature of payment, including amount, timing, and risk, may affect tax strategies.

Moreover, decisions made throughout the deal-structuring process influence various attributes of the deal. These attributes include, but are not limited to, how ownership is determined, how assets are transferred, how ownership is protected (i.e., governance), and how risk is apportioned among parties to the transaction. Other attributes include the type, number, and complexity of the documents required for closing; the types of approvals required; and the time needed to complete the transaction. These decisions also will influence how the combined companies will be managed, the amount and timing of resources committed, and the magnitude and timing of current and future tax liabilities (McCarthy, 1998; Tillinghast, 1998).

Reflecting this complexity, the deal-structuring process should be viewed as consisting of a number of interdependent components. At a minimum, these include the acquisition vehicle, the postclosing organization, the legal form of the selling entity, the form of payment, the form of acquisition, and tax considerations. The process starts with the determination by each party of their initial negotiating positions, potential risks, options for managing risk, levels of tolerance for risk, and conditions under which either party will "walk away" from the negotiations. The ***acquisition vehicle*** refers to the legal structure (e.g., corporation or partnership) used to acquire the target company. The ***postclosing organization*** is the organizational and legal framework (e.g., corporation or partnership) used to manage the combined businesses following the completion of the transaction.

The *legal form of the selling entity* refers to whether the seller is a C or Subchapter S Corporation, a limited liability company, or a partnership. These considerations will affect both the tax structure of the deal and form of payment. The *form of payment* may consist of cash, common stock, debt, or some combination. Some portion of the payment may be deferred or be dependent on the future performance of the acquired entity. The *form of acquisition* reflects both what is being acquired (e.g., stock or assets) and the form of payment. Consequently, the form of acquisition largely determines the tax structures. As a general rule, a transaction is taxable if remuneration paid to the target company's shareholders is primarily something other than the acquirer's stock, and it is nontaxable (i.e., tax deferred) if what they receive is largely acquirer stock. How and why these things happen are discussed in substantial detail in Chapters 11 and 12.

Conducting Due Diligence

The parties to any transaction always should conduct their own due diligence to accurately assess potential risks and rewards. Although some degree of protection is achieved through a well-written contract, legal agreements should never be viewed as a substitute for conducting formal due diligence. Exhibit 5-2 lists convenient online sources of information helpful in conducting due diligence on the principals to the transaction. A detailed preliminary acquirer due diligence question list is provided on the CD-ROM included with this book. For a detailed discussion of the due diligence process and best practices, see Selim (2003).

Buyer Due Diligence

Buyer due diligence is the process of validating assumptions underlying valuation. The primary objectives are to identify and confirm "sources of value" and to mitigate real or potential liability by looking for fatal flaws that reduce value. Due diligence involves three primary reviews: (1) a strategic/operational/marketing review conducted by senior operations and marketing management; (2) a financial review directed by financial and accounting personnel; and (3) a legal review conducted by the buyer's legal counsel. A rigorous due diligence requires the creation of comprehensive checklists. The strategic and operational review questions focus on the seller's management team, operations, and sales and marketing strategies. The financial review questions focus on the accuracy, timeliness, and completeness of the seller's financial statements. Finally, legal questions deal with corporate records, financial matters, management and employee issues, tangible and intangible assets of the seller, and material contracts and obligations of the seller such as litigation and claims. The interview process provides invaluable sources of information. By asking the same questions of a number of key managers, the acquirer is able to validate the accuracy of their conclusions. See Appendix A of this chapter for a further discussion of buyer due diligence question lists and the CD-ROM accompanying this book for an example of a detailed buyer due diligence question list.

McKesson Corporation, the nation's largest drug wholesaler, acquired medical software provider HBO & Co. in a $14.1 billion stock deal in early 1999. In its haste, McKesson closed the deal even before an in-depth audit of HBO's books had been completed. In fact, the audit did not begin until after the close of the 1999 fiscal year. Within days, fraudulent accounting practices were uncovered. Shareholders quickly abandoned the company. McKesson's senior management had to contend with rebuilding

---

Exhibit 5-2
Convenient Information Sources for Conducting Due Diligence

Web Address	Content
Securities and Exchange Commission:	Financial Information/Security Law Violations:
www.sec.gov	Public filings for almost 10 years available through the Edgar database
http://www.sec.gov/litigation.shtml	Enforcement actions
U.S. Patent Office:	Intellectual Property Rights Information:
www.uspto.gov	Search patent database
www.uspto.gov/patft/index.html	Database if you have patent number
Federal Communications Commission:	Regulates Various Commercial Practices:
www.fcc.gov	General information
http://www.fcc.gov/searchtools.html	Access to database of individuals sanctioned for illegal marketing practices
U.S. and States Attorneys General Offices:	Information on Criminal Activities:
http://www.naag.org/ag/full_ag_table.php	Listing of states attorneys general
National Association of Securities Dealers:	Regulates Securities Industry:
www.nasdr.com	Information on investment bankers
http://www.nasdr.com	Database
Better Business Bureau (BBB):	Compiles Consumer Complaints:
http://search.bbb.org/search.html	Database
Paid Services:	Information on:
U.S. Search (www.ussearch.com)	–Criminal Violations
KnowX (www.knowx.com)	–Liens/bankruptcies
	–Credit history
	–Litigation

McKesson's reputation, resolving more than 50 lawsuits, and attempting to recover $9.5 billion in market value lost since the need to restate earnings was first announced.

Limiting Due Diligence

Due diligence is an expensive and exhausting process. The buyer frequently will want as much time as necessary to complete due diligence. In contrast, the seller often will want to limit the length and scope as much as possible. By its nature, due diligence is highly intrusive and places substantial demands on managers' time and attention. Due diligence rarely works to the advantage of the seller, because a long and detailed due diligence is likely to uncover items that the buyer will use as an excuse to lower the purchase price. Consequently, sellers may seek to terminate due diligence before the buyer feels it is appropriate.

In some instances, buyers and sellers may agree to an abbreviated due diligence period. The theory is that the buyer can be protected in a well-written agreement of purchase and sale. In the agreement, the seller is required to make certain representations and warrant that they are true. Such "reps and warranties" could include the seller's acknowledgment that they own all assets listed in the agreement "free and clear" of any liens or attachments. If the representation is breached (i.e., found not to be true), the agreement generally will include a mechanism for compensating the buyer for any material loss. What constitutes material loss is defined in the contract. Relying on reps and warranties as a substitute for a thorough due diligence is rarely a good idea (Case Study 5-2).

Case Study 5-2
When "Reps and Warranties" Do Not Provide Adequate Protection

A large financial services firm in the mid-1990s acquired a small database company that provided data supporting the lending process. The seller signed a contract with all the necessary reps and warranties that all their computer systems were fully operational and in compliance with prevailing laws. The buyer also withheld about 20% of the purchase price in the event that the operational effectiveness of the systems was not at the level specified in the contract. It became apparent almost immediately after closing that the seller had misstated dramatically the viability of his business. The buyer had to eventually shut down the business and write off the full purchase price. The buyer also had to submit to binding arbitration to recover that portion of the purchase price that had been placed in escrow. The buyer had virtually no recourse to the seller who had few assets in his own name and who may have moved the bulk of the cash received for his stock to banks that were beyond the jurisdiction of the U.S. legal system.

Case Study Discussion Questions

1. Comment on the statement that there is no substitute for thorough due diligence.
2. How might the acquirer have been better able to protect itself in this situation?

A *data room* is another method commonly used by sellers to limit due diligence. This amounts to the seller sequestering the acquirer's team in a single room to complete due diligence. Typically, the data room consists of a conference room filled with file cabinets and boxes of documents requested by the buyer's due diligence team. Formal presentations by the seller's key managers are given in the often cramped conditions of the data room. Not surprisingly, the data room is a poor substitute for a tour of the seller's facilities.

Seller's Due Diligence

Although the bulk of due diligence is performed by the buyer on the seller, the prudent seller also should perform due diligence on the buyer and on themselves. In doing so, the seller can determine if the buyer has the financial wherewithal to finance the purchase price. In addition, a seller, as part of its own due diligence process, frequently will require all of its managers to sign documents (i.e., affidavits) stating that to the "best of their knowledge" what is being represented in the contract that pertains to their area of responsibility is indeed true. By conducting an internal investigation of their own operations, the seller hopes to mitigate liability stemming from inaccuracies in the seller's representations and warranties made in the definitive agreement of purchase and sale.

Lender's Due Diligence

If the acquirer is borrowing to buy a target firm, the lender(s) will want to perform their own due diligence independent of the buyer's. It is easy to see how burdensome multiple lender due diligences, often performed concurrently, can be on the target firm's management and employees. The seller should not agree to such intrusive and disruptive activities unless confident that the transaction will be consummated within a reasonable period.

Developing the Financing Plan: The Reality Check

The final activity of the negotiation phase is to develop balance sheet, income, and cash-flow statements for the combined firms, in accordance with GAAP. Unlike the financial projections of cash flow made to value the target, these statements should include the expected cost of financing the transaction. This activity is a key input into the determination of the purchase price, because it places a limitation on the amount of the purchase price the buyer can offer the seller.

According to capital budgeting theory, an investment should be funded as long as its net present value (NPV) is greater than or equal to zero. The same concept could be applied to an acquisition. The buyer should be able to finance a purchase price (P_{TPP}) up to the present value of the target company as an independent or standalone entity (PV_I) plus synergy (PV_{SYN}) created by combining the acquiring and target companies discounted at the appropriate cost of capital.

$$NPV = (PV_I + PV_{SYN}) - P_{TPP} \geq 0$$

The financing plan is appended to the acquirer's business and acquisition plans and is used to obtain financing for the transaction. No matter what size the transaction, lenders and investors will want to see a coherent analysis explaining why the proposed transaction is a good investment opportunity for them. Regardless of the intended audience, the financing plan largely is used as a marketing or sales document to negotiate the best possible terms for financing the proposed transaction. See Chapters 9 and 13 for more detail on developing the financing plan.

Obtaining Bridge or Interim Financing

For an all-cash transaction, the buyer will go to the traditional sources of financing. These include banks, insurance companies, investment bankers and underwriters, venture capitalists and leveraged buyout funds, and the seller. Banks commonly are used to provide temporary or *bridge financing* to pay all or a portion of the purchase price and to meet possible working capital requirements until permanent or long-term financing is found. Buyers usually seek more long-term sources of financing to replace bank debt because of the onerous covenants that restrict how the buyer may operate the combined firms. *Covenants* are promises made by the borrower that certain acts will be performed and others will be avoided. Covenants are designed to protect the lender's interests and may require the borrower to maintain a certain ratio of working capital to sales, debt-to-equity ratio, and credit rating. Covenants also may limit the amount of dividends the borrower can pay and future acquisitions or divestitures.

Case Study 5-3 describes how acquiring companies arrange interim financing to meet immediate cash requirements at closing. These cash requirements consist of the need to pay target company shareholders the cash portion of the total consideration as well as the payment of cash for fractional shares. For large transactions, banking syndicates will include many banks to spread the risk of the transaction. These bank loans are usually short term in nature and are either "rolled over" (i.e., continued) at the prevailing rate of interest or refinanced using long-term debt.

Case Study 5-3
Vodafone Finances the Acquisition of AirTouch

In April 1999, Vodafone Group plc reached an agreement with 11 banks to underwrite and arrange the "facility" or line of credit for financing the merger with AirTouch Communications, Inc. Under the terms of the transaction, AirTouch common shareholders would receive five Vodafone AirTouch ADSs (equivalent to five Vodafone AirTouch ordinary shares) plus $9 in cash. The transaction closed in July 1999 and was valued at $55 billion. The banking syndicate consisted of Bank of America, Barclay's, Banque Nationale de Paris, Citibank, Deutsche Bank, Goldman Sachs, HSBC, ING Barings, National Australia Bank, NatWest, and WestLB. The total facility, or amount that could be borrowed, was set at between $10 billion and $13 billion. The actual amount required could not be determined until the closing, when a more precise estimate of cash requirements could be determined. The term of the major part of the facility was for 364 days, with the remaining balance multiyear. The initial borrowing rate was to be 60 basis points (six-tenths of 1%) above the London Interbank Overnight Rate. This rate is similar to the U.S. federal funds rate. The actual spread would vary with the tranche (term) selected, utilization level (amount borrowed), and guarantee structure (the creditworthiness of those banks issuing letters of credit). Following completion of the merger, much of the facility was to be refinanced in the bond and commercial paper markets through the banks, which had arranged the facility.

Case Study Discussion Questions

1. Why is short-term bank financing often used to finance an acquisition?
2. Why did Vodafone seek to convert the short-term bank financing to longer-term debt?

Mezzanine and Permanent Financing

Mezzanine financing refers to capital that in liquidation has a repayment priority between senior debt and common stock. Although mezzanine financing may take the form of redeemable preferred stock, it generally is subordinated debt, with warrants convertible into common stock. It generally is unsecured, with a fixed coupon rate and a maturity of 5–10 years. Mezzanine investors usually look for firms with revenues in excess of $10 million. *Permanent financing* usually consists of long-term unsecured debt. Such debt is generally not rated by the major credit-rating agencies, such as Standard & Poor's and Moody's services, and may be referred to as junk bond financing. Such financing may be obtained by investment bankers or underwriters raising funds by a "private placement" of all or a portion of the bond issue with investors willing to hold the bonds for long periods. Private placements avoid going through the public securities markets. Investors in private transactions often include insurance companies and pension funds, which are interested in matching their investment income stream with their obligations to policyholders and pensioners. Such debt is usually subordinate to bank debt if the firm is forced into bankruptcy. In addition, junk bonds may be sold to mutual funds or directly to the public. If a significant percentage of the debt is to be sold to the public, raising permanent financing will require many months to satisfy SEC requirements for full disclosure of risks.

Venture Capital Firms

Venture capitalists (VCs) are also a significant source of funds for financing both start-ups and acquisitions. VC firms identify and screen opportunities, transact and close deals, monitor and add value, and raise additional capital. General partners receive a 2–3% fee and 15–25% of any capital gains from initial public offerings and mergers. The remaining 75–85% of capital gains plus a return of principal goes back to investors in the VC fund (Bygrave and Timmons, 1992). Only 2–4% of the firms contacting VC firms actually receive funding (Vachon, 1993). VCs sometimes are willing to lend when the more traditional sources, such as banks, insurance companies, and pension funds, are not. VCs usually demand a large equity position in the firm in exchange for their paying the firm a relatively low price per share. VC firms often require a 40–60% return on their investments.

Seller Financing

Seller financing represents a highly important source of financing for buyers and involves the seller deferring the receipt of a portion of the purchase price until some future date. The advantages to the buyer include a lower overall risk of the transaction because of the need to provide less capital at the time of closing and the shifting of operational risk to the seller if the buyer ultimately defaults on the loan to the seller.

The "Road Show"

To arrange both bridge and permanent financing, the buyer will develop elaborate presentations to take on a "road show" to convince potential lenders of the attractiveness of the debt. It is referred to as a "road show" for good reason—immaculately dressed borrowers passionately display confidence in their business plan through carefully rehearsed and choreographed multimedia presentations in stuffy conference rooms throughout the country. It represents an opportunity for potential lenders to see management and to ask the "tough questions." If the "road show" is successful, at least several lenders will compete for all or a portion of the bond issue. Lender competition will result in lower interest rates and less onerous loan covenants.

Selecting Alternative Financial Structures

The various methods of financing the transaction include cash, cash and notes, stock, and all debt. The latter option usually requires the presence of substantial amounts of unencumbered assets and a consistently strong operating cash flow. In practice, the total consideration paid to the seller often is financed using some of these alternative sources of funds. Table 5-1 summarizes the various types and sources of financing.

TABLE 5-1   Financing Mergers and Acquisitions

	Debt	Equity
Alternative Types		
Asset-Based Lending collateralized by fixed assets, accounts receivable, and inventories	Revolving credit lines Term loans Sale/Lease-back	
Cash-Flow Based	Projected cash flow	
Seller Financing	Deferred payments Earnouts Installment sales	Common stock Preferred stock
Public Offering and Private Placements	Senior Convertible Subordinated	Common stock Preferred stock
Alternative Sources	Commercial banks Insurance companies Pension funds Investment/Merchant banks	Hedge or buyout funds Venture capital Strategic investors Individual investors ("angels")

Computer models, which simulate the financial impact of various financial structures on the combined firms, are excellent tools for determining the appropriate capital structure (see Chapter 9). Although leverage raises the potential rate of return to equity investors, it also adds to risk. Increasing credit obligations to lenders implies increasing fixed interest expense, which raises the point at which the firm's revenue covers its costs (i.e., its break-even point). An unanticipated downturn in the economy or aggressive pricing actions by competitors can erode cash flow and the firm's ability to meet its interest expense. This ultimately could lead to bankruptcy. This risk can be measured by creating various scenarios, each representing a different capital structure and determining the impact of lower-than-expected sales growth.

Financing Contingencies

Most well written agreements of purchase and sale contain a financing contingency. The buyer is not subject to the terms of the contract if the buyer cannot obtain adequate funding to complete the transaction. As previously discussed, break-up fees can be particularly useful to ensure that the buyer will attempt to obtain financing as aggressively as possible. In some instances, the seller may require the buyer to put a nonrefundable deposit in escrow to be forfeited if the buyer is unable to obtain financing to complete the transaction.

Phase 7: Developing the Integration Plan

The euphoria that surrounds the successful completion of a transaction erodes quickly once the challenges of making the combined firms perform in line with the predictions laid out in the business and acquisition plans become apparent. Once the documents are signed the buyer has lost most, if not all, leverage over the seller.

Earning Trust

Decisions made before closing affect postclosing integration activity. Benefits packages, employment contracts, and bonuses to retain key employees (i.e., retention bonuses) normally are negotiated before closing. Contractual covenants and conditions also affect integration. *Earnouts*, payments to the seller based on the acquired business achieving certain profit or revenue targets, and ***deferred purchase price payments***, involving the placement of some portion of the purchase price in escrow until certain contractual conditions have been realized, can limit the buyer's ability to effectively integrate the target into the acquirer's operations. Successfully integrating firms requires getting employees in both firms to work toward achieving common objectives. This comes about through building credibility and trust, not through superficial slogans, pep talks, and empty promises. Trust comes from cooperation and experiencing success.

Earnouts

Earnouts are generally very poor ways to create trust and often represent major impediments to the integration process. The two firms generally are kept physically separate. Accounting and management reporting systems are not merged immediately, data centers remain separate, and sales forces remain largely independent. The buyer's concern is that the effort to integrate the firms as soon as possible after closing will make tracking the financial progress of the acquired company toward meeting its earnout goals difficult. Moreover, the merging of facilities and sales forces could create a highly contentious situation once the earnout period has elapsed if the acquired company did not meet the earnout goals. Employees covered by the earnout could plead in court that they were prevented from doing so by not being allowed by the buyer to implement the business plan on which the earnout was based. The hazards of earnouts are illustrated in Case Study 5-4. See Chapter 11 for a discussion of how to calculate earnout payments.

Case Study 5-4
The Downside of Earnouts

In the mid-1980s, a well-known aerospace conglomerate acquired a high-growth systems integration company by paying a huge multiple of earnings. The purchase price ultimately could become much larger if certain earnout objectives, including both sales and earnings targets, were achieved during the 4 years following closing. However, the buyer's business plan assumed close cooperation between the two firms, despite holding the system integrator as a wholly owned but largely autonomous subsidiary. The dramatic difference in the cultures of the two firms was a major impediment to building trust and achieving the cooperation necessary to make the acquisition successful. Years of squabbling over policies and practices tended to delay the development and implementation of new systems. The absence of new systems made it difficult to gain market share. Moreover, because the earnout objectives were partially defined in terms of revenue growth, many of the new customer contracts added substantial amounts of revenue but could not be completed profitably under the terms of these contracts. The buyer was slow to introduce new management into its wholly owned subsidiary for fear of violating the earnout agreement. Finally, market conditions changed, and what had been the acquired company's unique set of skills became commonplace. Eventually, the aerospace company wrote off most of the purchase price and merged the remaining assets of the acquired company into one of its other product lines after the earnout agreement expired.

Case Study Discussion Questions

1. Describe conditions under which an earnout might be most appropriate.
2. In your opinion, are earnouts more appropriate for firms in certain types of industries than for others? If so, give examples. Explain your answer.

Choosing the Integration Manager and Other Critical Decisions

The integration manager should have excellent interpersonal and project management skills. During the integration phase, the skills of being able to get along with others are frequently more important than professional and technical skills. The buyer must determine what is critical for continuation of the acquired company's success during the first 12–24 months following closing. Critical activities include the identification of key managers, vendors, and customers and what is needed to retain these valued assets. The preclosing integration planning activity also should include the determination of operating norms or standards required for continued operation of the businesses. These include executive compensation, labor contracts, billing procedures, product delivery times, and quality metrics. Finally, a communication plan must be designed for all stakeholders to be implemented immediately following closing (Porter and Wood, 1998). Preclosing planning and postclosing integration are discussed in considerable detail in Chapter 6.

Phase 8: Closing

The closing phase of the acquisition process consists of obtaining all necessary shareholder, regulatory, and third-party consents (e.g., customer and vendor contracts), as well as completing the definitive agreement of purchase and sale. Like all other phases, this activity requires significant planning at the outset if it is to go smoothly. Unfortunately, this is frequently impractical in view of all the activities that are under way during the acquisition process. All such activities tend to converge on the closing date.

Assigning Customer and Vendor Contracts

In a purchase of assets, many customer and vendor contracts cannot be assigned to the buyer without receiving written approval from the other parties. Although this may be a largely mechanical process, both vendors and customers may view this as an opportunity to attempt to negotiate more favorable terms. Licenses also must receive approval from the licensor, and they also can be a major impediment to a timely closing if not properly planned for well in advance. For example, a major software vendor demanded a substantial increase in royalty payments before they would transfer the license to the buyer. The vendor knew that the software was critical for the ongoing operation of the business's data center. The exorbitant increase in the fee had an adverse impact on the economics of the transaction from the buyer's viewpoint and almost caused the deal to collapse.

A number of transitional issues also must be addressed before closing. These include continued payroll processing support by the seller on behalf of the buyer until the buyer is able to assume this function and the return of checks received by the seller from customers continuing to send checks to the seller's bank accounts after closing. Similarly, the buyer will want to be reimbursed by the seller for payments made by the buyer to vendors for materials supplied or services provided before closing but not paid until after closing.

Gaining the Necessary Approvals

The buyer's legal counsel is responsible for ensuring that the transaction is in full compliance with securities, antitrust, and state corporation laws. Significant planning before closing is again crucial to minimizing roadblocks that a target company may place before the buyer. Great care must be exercised to ensure that all of the filings required by law have been made with the Federal Trade Commission and the Department of Justice. Noncompliance can delay or prevent a merger or acquisition (see Chapter 2). Finally, many transactions require approval by the acquirer and target company shareholders.

Completing the Definitive Agreement

The cornerstone of the closing documents is the definitive agreement of purchase and sale, which indicates all of the rights and obligations of the parties both before and after closing. The length of the definitive agreement depends on the complexity of the transaction. The major segments of an asset purchase agreement are outlined in the following sections (Sherman, 1998). See Chapters 11 and 12 for additional detail on definitive agreements.

Purpose of Acquisition

In an asset purchase, the purpose of the acquisition section of the agreement specifies the assets or the shares to be acquired. It also stipulates the assets to be excluded from the transaction.

Price

The purchase price or total consideration may be fixed at the time of closing, subject to future adjustment, or it may be contingent on future performance. The purchase price may be initially fixed based on the seller's representations of the firm's total assets, total book value, tangible book value, or some other measure of value. However, the agreed-upon price may be adjusted following a postclosing audit. An independent auditing firm typically does such audits. In asset transactions, cash on the target's balance sheet frequently is excluded from the transaction; the price paid for noncurrent assets such as plant and intangible assets will be fixed, but the price for current assets will depend on their levels at closing. Chapter 11 discusses how the postclosing adjustment to current assets is calculated.

Allocation of Price

The buyer typically has an incentive to allocate as much of the purchase price as possible to depreciable assets such as fixed assets, customer lists, and noncompete agreements, which will enable the buyer to depreciate or amortize these upwardly revised assets and reduce future taxable income. However, such an allocation may constitute taxable income to the seller. Both parties should agree on how the purchase price should be allocated to the various assets acquired in an asset transaction before closing. This eliminates the chance that the parties involved will take different positions for tax purposes. Nonetheless, the IRS may still challenge the transaction.

Payment Mechanism

Payment may be made at closing by wire transfer or cashier's check. The buyer may defer the payment of a portion of the purchase price by issuing a promissory note to the seller. The buyer and seller also may agree to put the unpaid portion of the purchase price in escrow or through a holdback allowance, thereby facilitating the settlement of claims that might be made in the future. The escrow account involves the buyer putting a portion of the purchase price in an account held by a third party, while the holdback allowance generally does not.

Assumption of Liabilities

The seller retains those liabilities not assumed by the buyer. In instances such as environmental liabilities, unpaid taxes, and inadequately funded pension obligations, the courts may go after the buyer and seller. In contrast, the buyer assumes all known and unknown liabilities in a merger or purchase of shares.

Representations and Warranties

"Reps and warranties" are intended to provide for full disclosure of all information germane to the transaction. They typically cover the areas of greatest concern to both parties.

Covenants

Covenants cover the obligations of both parties between the signing of the definitive agreement and closing. An example is the requirement that the seller continues to conduct business in the usual and customary manner. The seller often will be required to seek approval for all expenditures that may be considered out of the ordinary, such as one-time dividend payments or sizeable increases in management compensation.

Conditions for Closing

Closing cannot take place until certain conditions have been satisfied. These conditions could include the continued accuracy of the seller's representations and warranties and extent to which the seller is living up to their obligations under the covenants. Other examples include obtaining all necessary legal opinions, the execution of other agreements such as promissory notes, and the absence of any "material adverse change" in the condition of the target company.

Indemnification

The definitive agreement requires the seller to indemnify or absolve the buyer of liability in the event of misrepresentations or breaches of warranties or covenants. Similarly, the buyer usually agrees to indemnify the seller. Both parties generally want to limit the period during which the indemnity clauses remain in force. At least 1 full year of operation and a full audit is necessary to identify claims. Some claims such as environmental claims extend beyond the survival period of the indemnity clause. Usually, neither party can submit claims to the other until some minimum threshold, expressed in terms of the number or dollar size of claims, has been exceeded.

Merger Agreements

A merger is structurally simpler than an asset agreement, because it does not require the stipulation of assets being transferred to the buyer and liabilities assumed by the buyer. Although it may take less time to negotiate and draft than an asset agreement, it may take longer to complete. A merger with a public company generally requires approval of the target companies' shareholders and must comply with the full public disclosure and filing requirements of both federal and state securities laws (see Chapter 2).

Other Closing Documents

In addition to resolving the issues outlined above, closing may be complicated by the number of and complexity of the documents required to complete the transaction. In addition to the agreement of purchase and sale, the more important documents often include the following (Sherman, 1998):

a. Patents, licenses, royalty agreements, trade names, and trademarks
b. Labor and employment agreements
c. Leases
d. Mortgages, loan agreements, and lines of credit
e. Stock and bond commitments and details
f. Supplier and customer contracts
g. Distributor and sales representative agreements
h. Stock option and employee incentive programs
i. Health and social benefit plans (must be in place at closing to eliminate lapsed coverage)
j. Complete description of all foreign patents, facilities, and investments
k. Intermediary fee arrangements
l. Insurance policies, coverage, and claims pending
m. Litigation pending for and against each party
n. Environmental compliance issues resolved or on track to be resolved
o. Seller's corporate minutes of the board of directors and any other significant committee information
p. Articles of incorporation, bylaws, stock certificates, and corporate seals

See the folder entitled "Example M&A Legal Documents" found on the CD-ROM accompanying this book for examples of agreement of purchase and sale and associated legal documents. These documents were reproduced with permission of Eric Steinmann, Director of Development and Glenn Ishihara, President of NTCH Inc.

Is Closing Ever Simple?

The closing experience runs the gamut from mind-numbing routine to bombastic confrontation. How smoothly the process goes depends on its overall complexity and the level of trust among the parties involved. The size of the transaction is not a good indicator of complexity. Small transactions in terms of revenue or purchase price can be horrifically complicated where multiple parties are involved, significant off–balance sheet liabilities exist, or multiple levels of regulatory approval are required. Even when it appears that both parties have reached agreement on the major issues, what were previously minor issues seem to resurface on a grander, more challenging scale. Sometimes this happens because the parties did not realize the significance of an item until the last minute. Other times, one party intentionally takes a hard line on an issue as the closing date approaches in the hope of gaining a negotiating advantage. In one instance, a buyer of a computer maintenance business sat in the seller's mahogany-filled boardroom just minutes before the closing documents were to be signed and began to enumerate concerns he had with the deal. Tempers began to flare. Only after the seller threatened to walk away from the transaction did the buyer relent and the transaction closed. This strategy is ill advised.

Although closing normally involves one central location, off-site locations may be needed if documents for transferring deeds and titles to assets must be signed and filed from remote locations. Remote signings may be completed by having power of attorney for the buyer and seller transferred to local attorneys at each remote site. It is also a good idea to have separate conference rooms for the buyer and seller to ensure privacy and another room in which the parties meet to execute the documents. Finally, lenders should be kept separate from each other to minimize any exchange of information during closing that might cause them to reopen discussions between the buyer and the lender about the terms and conditions of loans.

For small, uncomplicated transactions, the closing can consist of a simple faxing back and forth of documents between the buyer and seller to ensure that there is complete agreement on the closing documents. Signature pages then are signed by one party and sent via overnight mail to the other party for their signature. However, other situations are far less mechanical. Case Study 5-5 illustrates the circus-like atmosphere that characterizes some closings.

Case Study 5-5

Sleepless in Philadelphia: A Dramatic Closing

Closings can take on a somewhat surreal atmosphere. In one transaction valued at $20 million, the buyer intended to finance the transaction with $10 million in secured bank loans, a $5 million loan from the seller, and $5 million in equity. However, the equity was to be provided by wealthy individual investors (i.e., "angel" investors) in amounts of $100,000 each. The closing took place in Philadelphia around a long conference room table in the law offices of the firm hired by the buyer, with lawyers and business people representing the buyer, the seller, and several banks reviewing the final documents. Throughout the day and late into the evening, wealthy investors (some in chauffeur-driven limousines) and their attorneys would stop by to provide cashiers' checks, mostly in $100,000 amounts, and to sign the appropriate legal documents. The sheer number of people involved created an almost circus-like environment. Because of the lateness of the hour, it was not possible to deposit the checks on the same day. The next morning a briefcase full of cashiers' checks was taken to the local bank.

Case Study Discussion Question

1. What do you think are the major challenges faced by the buyer in financing a transaction in this manner?

Phase 9: Implementing Postclosing Integration

The postclosing integration activity is widely viewed as among the most important phase of the acquisition process. Postclosing integration will be discussed in considerable detail in Chapter 6. What follows is a discussion of those activities required immediately following closing. Such activities generally fall into five categories: (1) implementing an effective communication plan, (2) retaining key managers, (3) identifying immediate operating cash-flow requirements, (4) employing the best practices of both companies, and (5) addressing cultural issues.

Communication Plans

Implementing an effective communication plan immediately following closing is crucial for purposes of retaining employees of the acquired firm and maintaining or boosting morale and productivity. The plan should address employee, customer, and vendor concerns. The message always should be honest and consistent. Employees need to understand how their compensation, including benefits, might change under new ownership. Employees may find a loss of specific benefits palatable if they are perceived as offset by improvements in other benefits or working conditions. Customers will want reassurance that there will not be any deterioration in product or service quality or delivery time during the transition from old to new ownership. Vendors also will be very interested in understanding how the change in ownership will affect their sales to the new firm. Whenever possible, communication is best done on a face-to-face basis. Senior officers of the acquiring company can be sent to address employee groups (on site, if possible). Senior officers also should contact key customers preferably in person or at least by telephone to provide the needed reassurances. Meeting these reasonable requests for information from employees, customers, and vendors immediately following closing with complete candor will contribute greatly to the sense of trust among stakeholders that is necessary for the ultimate success of the acquisition.

Employee Retention

Retaining middle-level managers should be a top priority during this phase of the acquisition process. Frequently, senior managers of the target company that the buyer chooses to retain are asked to sign employment agreements as a condition of closing. Without these signed agreements, the buyer would not have completed the transaction. Although senior managers provide overall direction for the firm, middle-level managers execute the day-to-day operations of the firm. Plans should be in place to minimize the loss of such people. Bonuses, stock options, and enhanced sales commission schedules are commonly put in place to keep such managers.

Satisfying Cash-Flow Requirements

Invariably, operating cash-flow requirements are higher than expected. Conversations with middle-level managers following closing often reveal areas in which maintenance expenditures have been deferred. Receivables, previously thought to be collectable, may have to be written off. Production may be disrupted as employees of the acquired firm find it difficult to adapt to new practices introduced by the acquiring company's management or if inventory levels are inadequate to maintain desired customer delivery times. Finally, more customers than had been anticipated may be lost to competitors, which use the change in ownership as an opportunity to woo them away with various types of incentives.

Employing Best Practices

An important motivation for takeovers is to realize specific operating synergies, which result in improved operating efficiency, product quality, customer service, and on-time delivery. Both parties in a transaction are likely to excel in different areas. An excellent way for the combined companies to take advantage of the strengths of both companies is to use the "best practices" of both. However, in some areas, neither company may be employing what its customers believe to be the best practices in the industry. In these circumstances, management should look beyond its own operations to accept the practices of other companies.

Cultural Issues

Corporate cultures reflect the set of beliefs and behaviors of the management and employees of a corporation. Some corporations are very paternalistic, and others are very "bottom-line" oriented. Some empower employees, whereas others believe in highly centralized control. Some promote problem solving within a team environment; others encourage individual performance. Inevitably different corporate cultures will impede postacquisition integration efforts. The key to success is to be sensitive to these differences and to take the time to explain to all employees of the new firm what is expected and why these behaviors are desired in the new company.

Phase 10: Conducting Postclosing Evaluation

The primary reasons for conducting a postclosing evaluation of all acquisitions are to determine if the acquisition is meeting expectations, to determine corrective actions if necessary, and to identify what was done well and what should be done better in future acquisitions.

Do Not Change Performance Benchmarks

Once the acquisition appears to be operating normally, evaluate the actual performance to that projected in the acquisition plan. Success should be defined in terms of actual to planned performance. Too often, management simply ignores the performance targets in the acquisition plan and accepts less than plan performance to justify the acquisition. This may be appropriate if circumstances beyond the firm's control cause a change in the operating environment. Examples include a recession, which slows the growth in revenue, or changing regulations, which preclude the introduction of a new product.

Ask the Difficult Questions

The types of questions asked should vary depending on the elapsed time since closing. After 6 months, what has the buyer learned about the business? Were the original valuation assumptions reasonable? If not, what did the buyer not understand about the target company and why? What did the buyer do well? What should have been done differently? What can be done to ensure that the same mistakes are not made in future acquisitions? After 12 months, is the business meeting expectations? If not, what can be done to put the business back on track? Is the cost of fixing the business offset by expected returns? Are the right people in place to manage the business for the long term? After 24 months, does the acquired business still appear attractive? If not, should it be divested? If yes, when and to whom?

Learn from Mistakes

It always pays to take the time to identify lessons learned from each transaction. This is often a neglected exercise and results in firms repeating the same mistakes. This occurs even in the most highly acquisitive firms, because those involved in the acquisition process may change from one acquisition to another. Lessons learned in an acquisition completed by the management of one of the firm's product lines may not be readily communicated to those about to undertake acquisitions in other parts of the company. Highly acquisitive companies can benefit greatly by dedicating certain legal, human resource, marketing, financial, and business development resources to support acquisitions made throughout the company.

Things to Remember

The acquisition process consists of 10 identifiable phases. During the first phase, the business plan defines the overall direction of the business. If an acquisition is believed necessary to implement the firm's business strategy, an acquisition plan is developed during the second phase and defines the key objectives, available resources, and boundaries for completing an acquisition. The next phase consists of the search for appropriate acquisition candidates. To initiate this phase, selection criteria need to be developed. At this stage, selection criteria should be relatively few in number and, whenever possible, should be quantified. The screening phase is a refinement of the search phase and entails applying more criteria to reduce the list of candidates surfaced during the search process.

How the potential acquirer initiates first contact depends on the size of the target and the availability of intermediaries with highly placed contacts within the target firm. If the target is interested in proceeding, an LOI formally defining the reasons for the agreement, responsibilities of the two parties while the agreement is in force, and the expiration date is negotiated. Confidentiality agreements covering both parties also should be negotiated. The negotiation phase consists of the following activities: refining valuation, structuring the deal, conducting due diligence, and developing a financing plan. The actual amount and composition of the purchase price is determined during this phase.

There is no substitute for performing a complete due diligence on the target company. Refining a valuation based on new information uncovered during due diligence affects the determination of the total consideration to be paid to the seller. The financing plan may be affected by the discovery during due diligence of assets that can be sold to pay off debt accumulated to finance the transaction. Due diligence is not limited to the buyer. The seller should perform due diligence on the buyer to ensure that it will be able to finance the purchase price. Moreover, the seller also should perform due diligence on its own operations to ensure that its representations and warranties in the definitive agreement are accurate.

Integration planning is a highly important aspect of the acquisition process that must be done before closing. Without adequate planning, integration is unlikely to provide the synergies anticipated by, at the cost included in, and on the timetable provided in the acquisition plan. The closing phase goes well beyond organizing, finalizing, and signing all the necessary legal documents. It includes wading through the logistical quagmire of getting all the necessary third-party consents and regulatory and shareholder approvals. The postclosing integration phase consists of communicating effectively with all stakeholders, retaining key employees, and identifying and resolving immediate cash-flow needs. The postclosing evaluation phase is the most commonly overlooked phase. Although many acquiring companies do closely monitor the performance of the acquisition to plan, many stop short of formally questioning how effective they were in managing the acquisition process.

Chapter Discussion Questions

5-1. What resources are commonly used to conduct a search for potential acquisition targets?

5-2. Identify at least three criteria that might be used to select a manufacturing firm as a potential acquisition candidate. A financial services firm? A high-tech firm?

5-3. Identify alternative ways to make "first contact" with a potential acquisition target. Why is confidentiality important? Under what circumstances might a potential acquirer make its intentions public?

5-4. What are the advantages and disadvantages of a letter of intent?

5-5. How do the various activities that are undertaken concurrently as part of the negotiation phase affect the determination of the purchase price?

5-6. What are the differences between total consideration, total purchase price – enterprise value, and net purchase price? How are these different concepts used?

5-7. What is the purpose of the buyer and seller performing due diligence?

5-8. What is the purpose of a financing plan? In what sense is it a "reality check."

5-9. Why is preclosing integration planning important?

5-10. What are the key activities that comprise a typical closing?

Answers to these Chapter Discussion Questions are available in the Online Instructor's Manual for instructors using this book.

Chapter Business Case

Case Study 5-6
The Anatomy of a Transaction: K2 Incorporated Acquires Fotoball USA

On January 26, 2004, K2 Inc. completed the purchase of Fotoball USA in an all-stock transaction. What follows is an attempt to reconstruct the preclosing events to illustrate how the acquisition process discussed in Chapters 4 and 5 may have been applied in this transaction. Note that this is a highly condensed version of an actual business and acquisition plan.

Industry/Market Definition

K2 is a sporting goods equipment and accessories manufacturer. K2's portfolio of brands includes Rawlings, Worth, Shakespeare, Pflueger, Stearns, K2, Ride, Olin, Morrow, Tubbs, and Atlas. The company's diversified mix of products is used primarily in team and individual sports activities such as baseball, softball, fishing, water sports activities, alpine skiing, snowboarding, snowshoeing, in-line skating, and mountain biking.

External Analysis

The firm's current top competitors include Adidas-Salomon, Rollerblade, Inc., and Skis Rossignol S.A. While other sporting goods suppliers such as Amer Group Plc, Head N.V., NIKE, Inc., Fila USA, and Reebok International Ltd. do not currently compete in K2's served markets, they could easily enter due to their substantial brand recognition and financial resources. Not only must K2 be concerned about existing and potential competitors, a variety of substitute popular or "cool" sports such as horseback riding, ice hockey, sky diving, surfing, and cross-country skiing could erode growth in their targeted markets.

   The firm's primary customers are sporting goods retailers. Many of K2's smaller retailers and some larger retailers are not strongly capitalized. Adverse conditions in the sporting goods retail industry can adversely impact the ability of retailers to purchase K2 products or could force retailers to insist upon credit terms that involve significant risks of nonpayment. Secondary customers include individuals, both hobbyists as well as professionals. K2's success is dependent on its ability to keep abreast of changes in taste and style, and its ability to provide high-quality products at competitive prices.

   The majority of K2 products are manufactured in China, which helps to ensure cost competitiveness. However, disruptions of international trade or shipping could adversely affect the availability or cost of K2 products. K2's revenue from international operations was approximately 32% of total revenue for fiscal 2002, and approximately 26% of K2's sales denominated in foreign currencies. K2's international operations are subject to a variety of risks, including: recessions in foreign economies; currency conversion risks and currency fluctuations; limitations on repatriation of earnings; and reduced protection of intellectual property rights in some countries. Other factors include social, political, and economic instability; the adoption and expansion of government trade restrictions; unfavorable political developments affecting international trade; and unexpected changes in regulatory requirements.

K2 believes that the most successful sporting goods suppliers will be those with greater resources. In addition to financial capabilities, such resources include the ability to produce or source high-quality, low-cost products and deliver these products on a timely basis and the ability to access distribution channels with a broad array of products and brands. In addition, as the influence of large sporting goods retailers grows, management believes these retailers will prefer to rely on fewer and larger sporting goods suppliers to help them manage the supply of products and the allocation of shelf space.

Internal Analysis

K2 has a number of leading brands in major sporting goods markets. K2 is also involved in the sports apparel business and faces stiff competition in this industry from Nike and Reebok. Wal-Mart accounted for over 10% and 5% of K2's consolidated annual net sales and operating income, respectively, in 2003. No one customer of K2 accounted for 10% or more of its consolidated annual net sales or 5% of its operating income in 2002.

Despite its strong brand names, K2 is susceptible to being duplicated. The sporting goods markets and recreational products markets are generally highly competitive, with competition centering on product innovation, performance and styling, price, marketing, and delivery. Competition in these products consists of a relatively small number of large producers, some of whom have substantially greater financial resources than K2. K2's relationships with the many collegiate and professional leagues and teams cannot be easily usurped by smaller competitors that may want to enter into these markets. It takes time for the necessary trust to build up in these relationships. Larger competitors may have the capacity to take away some of these relationships, but K2 has so many that the loss of one or two will not seriously hinder their overall revenue growth.

Its relatively small size in comparison to major competitors is the firm's primary weakness. Historically, the firm has been able to achieve profitable growth by introducing new products into fast growing markets. The firm has historically applied its core competencies of producing fiberglass and assembling structures for manufacturing skis to new markets such as snowboarding and in-line skating.

Mission Statement and Strategic Objectives

"K2 will accept nothing less than the best…. We will create ever better products that raise the bar of performance and celebrate the human spirit…. We will build value by growing and succeeding where others have failed." The firm's long-term objective is to achieve the number one market share position in its served markets. Toward that end, K2 seeks to meet or exceed its corporate cost of capital of 15%. In addition, K2 intends to achieve sustained double-digit revenue growth, gross profit margins above 35%, and net profit margins in excess of 5% within the next 5 years. The firm also seeks to reduce its debt to equity ratio to the industry average of 25% in the next 5 years.

Business Strategy

K2 intends to achieve its mission and objectives by becoming the low-cost supplier in each of its niche markets. The firm intends to achieve a low-cost position by using its existing administrative and logistical infrastructure to support entry into new niche segments within the sporting goods and recreational markets, new distribution channels, and new product launches through existing distribution channels. Furthermore, the firm intends to pursue continued aggressive cost cutting and to expand its global sourcing to include other low-cost countries in addition to Mainland China.

Implementation Strategy

In view of its great success in acquiring and integrating a series of small acquisitions in recent years, K2 has decided to avoid product or market extension through partnering because of the potential for loss of control and for creating competitors once such agreements lapse. Consequently, K2 believes that it can accelerate its growth strategy by seeking strategic acquisitions of other sporting goods companies with well-established brands and with complementary distribution channels.

M&A-Related Functional Strategies

Functional strategies have been developed based on an acquisition-oriented implementation strategy. A potential target for acquisition is a company that holds many licenses with professional sports teams. Through their relationship with these sports teams K2 can further promote its long line of sporting gear and equipment. The different business functions within K2 all have roles to play in supporting the implementation strategy.

Research & Development

K2's R&D activities are focused on developing only the highest quality sports equipment and apparel. The NBA, NFL, and Major League Baseball are all potential licensing partners. To support these critical activities, the research and development budget will be increased by 10% annually during the next 5 years. High-quality and innovative new products can be sold into the customer bases of firms acquired during this period.

Marketing and Sales

The licensing agreements in existence between the target firm and its partners can be enhanced to include the many products that K2 now offers. It must be determined whether one sales force can sell both the products sold by K2 currently and those obtained through an acquisition. If so, the two sales forces can be merged, resulting in significant cost savings.

Other Functional Departments

The HR department is charged with the responsibility to determine appropriate staffing requirements and how those can be best satisfied immediately following a merger. Potential job overlaps are expected to contribute to significant cost savings. The finance department is charged with quantifying the potential increase in revenue from cross selling K2 and the target's products into each firm's existing customer bases and to determine the feasibility of realizing anticipated cost synergies. The legal department is responsible for determining the validity of customer and supplier contracts; and, in conjunction with the finance department, their overall profitability. Finally, the tax department is responsible for assessing the tax impact an acquisition would have on K2's after-tax cash flow and shareholders.

Strategic Controls

Incentives Systems

K2 has incentive systems in place to motivate employees to work toward implementing its business strategy. Employees are awarded yearly bonuses based on their performance throughout the year. At the end of the year, employees working in sales are given up to 5% of the sales revenues, for which they were personally responsible. Management is given a bonus based on how well their department has performed. They are given a bonus made up of 10% of the operating income achieved by their department. This way they are motivated not only to increase sales but to minimize costs as well.

Monitoring Systems

Monitoring systems are in place to monitor the actual performance of the firm against the business plan. Activity-based systems monitor variables, which drive financial performance. Such variables include customer retention, average revenue per customer, and average revenue per dealer.

Business Plan Financials and Valuation

K2's net revenue is projected to grow from $790 million in 2004 to $988 million in 2008 on a standalone basis. After-tax income is expected to increase from $17.6 million to $41.2 million during the same period. Reflecting a sharp improvement in free cash flow from ($7.6) million in 2004 to $46 million in 2008, K2's current valuation based on discounted cash flow (without any new acquisitions) is $812 million or $23.79 per share.

Acquisition Plan

K2's overarching financial objective for any acquisition is to at least earn its cost of capital, and its primary nonfinancial objectives are to acquire a firm with well-established brands and complementary distribution channels. More specifically, K2 is seeking a firm with a successful franchise in the marketing and manufacturing of souvenir and promotional products that could be easily integrated into K2's current operations.

Timetable

February 28, 2003	Acquisition plan completed
March 30, 2003	Search for potential target companies should be completed
May 30, 2003	Screening for potential target companies completed
June 30, 2003	First contact completed
October 30, 2003	Negotiations completed
November 30, 2003	Develop integration plan
December 30, 2003	Closing completed
June 30, 2004	Integration completed
September 30, 2004	Acquisition process evaluation completed

Resource/Capability Evaluation

Operating Risk After completion of a merger, K2 must successfully integrate the target's sourcing and manufacturing capabilities into K2's sourcing and manufacturing operations. In addition, the firm must sell K2's portfolio of products and brands through the target's distribution channels, increase the target's sales to team sports and sporting goods retailers, and develop a licensing and cobranding program. K2 will need to retain the management, key employees, customers, distributors, vendors, and other business partners of both companies. It is possible that these integration efforts will not be completed as planned, which could have an adverse impact on the operations of the combined company. K2 believes that given its successful track record in acquiring and integrating businesses, its management team can deal with these challenges.

Financial Risk Borrowing under K2's existing $205 million revolving credit facility and under its $20 million term loan, as well as potential future financings, may substantially increase K2's current leverage. Among other things, such increased indebtedness could adversely affect K2's ability to expand its business, to market its products, to make needed infrastructure investments, and adversely affect the cost and availability of funds from commercial lenders.

Overpayment Risk If new shares of K2 stock are issued to pay for the target firm, K2's earnings per share may be diluted for an extended time period if anticipated synergies are not realized in a timely fashion. Moreover, overpaying for any firm could result in K2 failing to earn its cost of capital.

Management Preferences
- The target should be smaller than $100 million in market capitalization and should have positive cash flows. Also, it should be focused on the sports or outdoor activities market.
- The search should be conducted initially by analyzing current competitors.
- The company has an experienced acquisition team in place, which will be utilized to complete this acquisition.
- The form of payment would be new K2 nonvoting common stock.
- The form of acquisition would be a purchase of stock.
- K2 will not consider purchases involving less than 100% of the target's stock.
- Only friendly takeovers will be considered.
- The target firm's current year P/E (price-to-earnings ratio) should not exceed 20.

Search Plan
Potential target firms will be identified using a series of search criteria. Potential candidates' main line of business must be the sports equipment market in which they are generating positive cash flows, have a market capitalization no greater than $100 million, and possess a complementary product offering.

   After an exhaustive search, K2 identified Fotoball USA as its most attractive target due to its size, predictable cash flows, complementary product offering, and many licenses with most of the major sports leagues and college teams. Fotoball USA represents a premier platform for expansion of K2's marketing capabilities because of its expertise in the industry and place as an industry leader in many sports and entertainment souvenir and promotional product categories.

Negotiation Strategy
K2 has positioned itself as a holding company and does not take an active management role in the businesses they acquire. The firm generally allows acquired companies to function independently. In 2003, Fotoball lost $3.2 million so it is anticipated that they will be receptive to an acquisition proposal. A stock-for-stock exchange offer would be very attractive to the shareholders of Fotoball due to the combined firms' anticipated high earnings growth rate. The transaction is expected to qualify as a "tax-free" reorganization for federal income tax purposes. Additionally, management and most employees would be retained.

Fotoball is a very young company and many of its investors are looking to make their profits through the growth of the stock. The stock-for-stock offer contains a significant premium, which would be well received considering that the company has been in the red, and it would allow Fotoball shareholders to defer taxes until they decide to sell their stocks and be taxed at the capital gains rate. Earnouts would also be included in the deal to give management incentives to run the company effectively and meet deadlines in a timely order.

The acquisition vehicle used in the deal would be a C-type corporation. Postclosing, Fotoball would be run as a wholly owned subsidiary of K2. This form would work best because K2 is in the process of acquiring many companies, and they cannot actively manage all of them. In addition, such an organizational structure would be most conducive to a possible earnout and the preservation of the unique culture at Fotoball.

Determining the Initial Offer Price

Valuations for both K2 Inc. and Fotoball were done using discounted cash-free flow methods. The valuations reflect the following anticipated synergies due to economies of scale and scope; a reduction in selling expenses of approximately $1 million per year; a reduction in distribution expenses of approximately $500,000 per year; and an annual reduction in general and administrative expenses of approximately $470,000. The standalone value of K2 was $23.79 per share or $812 million. The standalone value of Fotoball was $3.97 per share or $14.3 million. Including the effects of anticipated synergy, the estimated combined market value of the two firms is $909 million. This represents an increase in the shareholder value of the combined firms of $82.7 million over the sum of the standalone values of the two firms.

Based on Fotoball's outstanding common stock of 3.6 million shares and the current stock price of $4.02 at that time, a minimum offer price was determined by multiplying the current stock price by the number of shares outstanding. The minimum offer price was $14.5 million. If K2 were to concede 100% of the value of synergy to Fotoball, the value of the firm would be $97.2 million. However, sharing more than 45% of synergy with Fotoball would cause a serious dilution of earnings and significantly raise the required rate of return on this deal. To determine the amount of synergy to share with Fotoball's shareholders, K2 looked at what portion of the combined firms revenues would be contributed by each of the players and then applied that proportion to the synergy. Since 96% of the projected combined firms revenues in fiscal year 2004 were expected to come from K2, only 4% of the synergy value was added to the minimum offer price to come up with an initial offer price of $17.8 million or $4.94 per share. This represented a premium of 23% over the then current market value of Fotoball's stock.

Financing Plan

Due to the synergies involved in this transaction as well as the relatively small size of the target (Fotoball) as compared to the acquirer (K2), it is unlikely that this merger would endanger K2's creditworthiness or near-term profitability.

Integration Plan

Organizationally, the integration of Fotoball into K2 would be achieved by operating Fotoball as a wholly owned subsidiary of K2, with current Fotoball management remaining in place. All key employees would receive retention bonuses as a condition of closing. Integration teams consisting of employees from both firms will move expeditiously according to a schedule put in place prior to closing to implement the best practices of both firms. Immediately following closing, senior K2 managers will communicate on site, if possible, with Fotoball customers, suppliers, and employees to allay their immediate concerns.

(This case study is adapted from a paper written by Curt Charles, Tuukka Luolamo, Jeffrey Rathel, Ryan Komagome, and Julius Kumar, Loyola Marymount University, April 28, 2004.)

Case Study Discussion Questions

1. How did K2's acquisition plan objective support the realization of its corporate mission and business plan objectives?
2. What alternatives to M&As could K2 have employed to pursue its growth strategy? Why were the alternatives rejected?
3. What was the role of "strategic controls" in implementing the K2 business plan?
4. How did the K2 negotiating strategy seek to meet the primary needs of the Fotoball shareholders and employees?

Answers to these Case Study Discussion Questions are available in the Online Instructor's Manual for instructors using this book.

Chapter Business Case

Case Study 5-7
Cingular Acquires AT&T Wireless in a Record-Setting Cash Transaction

Cingular outbid Vodafone to acquire AT&T Wireless, the nation's third largest cellular telephone company, for $41 billion in cash plus $6 billion in assumed debt in February 2004. This represented the largest all-cash transaction in history. The combined companies, which surpass Verizon Wireless as the largest U.S. provider, have a network that covers the top 100 U.S. markets and span 49 of the 50 U.S. states. While Cingular's management seemed elated with their victory, investors soon began questioning the wisdom of the acquisition.

By entering the bidding at the last moment, Vodafone, an investor in Verizon Wireless, forced Cingular's parents, SBC Communications and BellSouth, to pay a 37% premium over their initial bid. By possibly paying too much, Cingular put itself at a major disadvantage in the U.S. cellular phone market. The merger did not close until October 26, 2004, due to the need to get regulatory and shareholder approvals. This gave Verizon, the industry leader in terms of operating margins, time to woo away customers from AT&T Wireless, which was already hemorrhaging a loss of subscribers because of poor customer service. By paying $11 billion more than their initial bid, Cingular will have to execute the integration, expected to take at least 18 months, flawlessly to make the merger pay for their shareholders.

With AT&T Wireless, Cingular will have a combined subscriber base of 46 million, as compared to Verizon Wireless' 37.5 million subscribers. Together, Cingular and Verizon control almost one-half of the nation's 170 million wireless customers. The transaction gives SBC and BellSouth the opportunity to have a greater stake in the rapidly expanding wireless industry. Cingular is assuming that they will be able to achieve substantial operational synergies and a reduction in capital outlays by melding AT&T Wireless' network into its own. Cingular expects to trim combined capital costs by $600 million to $900 million in 2005 and $800 million to $1.2 billion annually thereafter. However, Cingular may feel pressure from Verizon Wireless, which is investing heavily in new mobile wireless services. If Cingular is forced to offer such services quickly, it may not be able to realize the reduction in projected capital outlays. Operational savings may be even more difficult to realize. Cingular expects to save $100 million to $400 million in 2005 and $500 million to $800 million in 2006 and $1.2 billion in each successive year. However, in view of AT&T Wireless' continued loss of customers, Cingular may have to increase spending to improve customer service. To gain regulatory approval, Cingular agreed to sell assets in 13 markets in 11 states. The firm will have 6 months to sell the assets before a trustee appointed by the FCC will become responsible for disposing of the assets.

SBC and BellSouth, Cingular's parents, will have limited flexibility in financing new spending if it is required by Cingular. Both SBC and BellSouth each borrowed $10 billion to finance the transaction. With the added debt, S&P put SBC, BellSouth, and Cingular on credit watch, which is often a prelude in a downgrade of a firm's credit rating.

Case Study Discussion Questions

1. What is the total purchase price of the merger?
2. What are some of the reasons Cingular used cash rather than stock or some combination to acquire AT&T Wireless? Explain your answer.
3. How might the amount and composition of the purchase price affect Cingular's, SBC's, and BellSouth's cost of capital?
4. With substantially higher operating margins than Cingular, what strategies would you expect Verizon Wireless to pursue? Explain your answer.

Answers to these Case Study Discussion Questions are available in the Online Instructor's Manual for instructors using this book.

Appendix A

Legal Due Diligence Preliminary Information Request

The due diligence question list, which is found in a file folder entitled "Due Diligence Question List" contained on the CD-ROM accompanying this book, applies mainly to transactions involving large public companies. For smaller, privately owned target firms, the list may be substantially more focused. Normally the length and complexity of a "due diligence question list," submitted by the acquiring firm to the target firm's management, is determined through negotiation. The management of the target firm normally would view a lengthy list as both intrusive and costly to complete. Consequently, the target firm's management often will try to narrow both the number and breadth of the questions included in the initial request for information. The request for such a list often is included as part of the letter of intent signed by the acquirer and target firms.

The acquirer typically attempts to protect itself either through an exhaustive review of the target's records and facilities (i.e., due diligence), extensive representations and warranties (i.e., claims and promises made by the seller), or some combination of the two. If the target firm is successful in reducing the amount of information disclosed to the acquirer firm, it can expect to be required to make more representations and warranties as to the accuracy of its claims and promises in the agreement of purchase and sale. This will no doubt add to the time required to negotiate such a document. Notwithstanding the intrusiveness of the due diligence question list contained on the CD-ROM accompanying this book, the buyer is well advised to rely more on an on-site review of facilities and records and personnel interviews than it would be to rely on the seller's contract obligations. If the seller declares bankruptcy, cannot be found, or moves assets to offshore accounts, receiving remuneration for breach of contract may be impossible. Note that all references to the Company in the due diligence question list refer to the target.

References

Bygrave, William D., and Jeffrey A. Timmons, *Venture Capital at the Crossroads,* Harvard Business School Press, Boston, 1992.

Creswell, Julie, "Would You Give This Man Your Company?," *Fortune,* May 28, 2001, pp. 127–129.

McCarthy, Paul, "Legal Aspects of Acquiring U.S. Enterprises," in David J. BenDaniel and Arthur H. Rosenbloom, eds., *International M&A, Joint Ventures & Beyond: Doing the Deal,* Wiley & Sons, New York, 1998, pp. 27–57.

Oesterle, Dale A., *Mergers and Acquisitions in a Nutshell,* 2nd Ed., Thomson West Publishers, New York, 2006.

Porter, Richard, and Cynthia N. Wood, "Post-merger Integration," in David J. BenDaniel and Arthur H. Rosenbloom, eds., *International M&A, Joint Ventures & Beyond: Doing the Deal,* Wiley & Sons, New York, 1998, pp. 457–459.

Selim, Georges, *Mergers, Acquisitions and Divestitures: Control and Audit Best Practices,* The Institute of Internal Auditing Research Foundation, 2003.

Sherman, Andrew, *Mergers and Acquisitions from A to Z: Strategic and Practical Guidance for Small- and Middle-Market Buyers and Sellers,* AMACOM, New York, 1998, pp. 171–218.

Thornton, Emily, "Bypassing the Street," *BusinessWeek,* June 2, 2004, pp. 78–79.

Tillinghast, David R., "Tax Aspects of Inbound Merger and Acquisition and Joint Venture Transactions," in David J. BenDaniel and Arthur H. Rosenbloom, eds., *International M&A, Joint Ventures & Beyond: Doing the Deal,* Wiley & Sons, New York, 1998, pp. 151–172.

Vachon, Michael, "Venture Capital Reborn," *Venture Capital Journal,* January 1993, p. 32.

CHAPTER • 6

Integration Mergers, Acquisitions, and Business Alliances

What could be worse than being without sight? Being born with sight and no vision.

—Helen Keller

Inside M&A: GE's Water Business Fails to Meet Expectations

When Jeffrey Immelt, GE's CEO, assumed his position in September 2001, he identified water as one of five industries that would fuel future growth for the firm. Since 2001, General Electric (GE) has invested more than $4 billion in acquiring four companies to grow its water treatment business. In an unusual strategy for GE, the firm's intention was to build a business from scratch through acquisition to enter the $400 billion global water treatment business. In doing so, GE would be competing against a number of global competitors. GE had historically entered many new markets by growing a small portion of a larger existing business unit through a series of relatively small, but highly complementary, acquisitions.

GE's experience in integrating these so-called "bolt-on" acquisitions emboldened the firm to pursue this more aggressive strategy. However, the challenge has proved to be more daunting than originally assumed. The largest of the units, which sells chemicals, has faced aggressive price competition in what has become a commodity business. Furthermore, expectations of huge contracts to build water treatment plants have not yet materialized.

Amid the unit's failure to spur revenue growth, GE has been struggling to meld thousands of employees from competing corporate cultures into its own highly disciplined culture with its focus on excellent financial performance. As the cornerstone to accelerating revenue growth, GE has attempted to restructure radically the diverse sales forces of the four acquired companies. The new sales and marketing structure divides the combined sales forces into teams that are geographically focused. Within each region, one sales team is responsible for pursuing new business opportunities. More than 1500 engineers have been retrained to sell the unit's entire portfolio from chemicals to equipment that removes salt and debris from water. Another group is focused on servicing customers in "vertical markets" or industries such as dairy products, electronics, and health care. However, the task of retraining even highly educated engineers to do substantially different things has required much more time and expense than originally anticipated. For example, in an effort to rapidly redirect the business, GE retrained a group of 2000 engineers who had previously sold chemicals to sell sophisticated equipment. The latter sales effort required a much different set of skills than what the engineers had been originally trained to do.

Reflecting these problems, Immelt in mid-2006 reduced the water business unit's operating profit forecast for the year from $400 million to $200 million. Immelt also replaced George Oliver, the executive he put in charge of the water business in 2002. "We probably moved quicker than we should have in some areas," Immelt conceded, adding that "training has taken longer than expected (Kranhold, August 22, 2006)."

Chapter Overview

As noted in Chapter 1, motives for purchasing a company vary widely. Acquirers tend to fall into two broad categories: strategic buyers and financial buyers. Financial buyers are typically those who buy a business for eventual resale. In general, they do not intend to integrate the acquired business into another entity. Moreover, instead of managing the business, they are inclined to monitor the effectiveness of current management, intervening only if there is a significant and sustained deviation between actual and projected performance. In contrast, strategic buyers are interested in making a profit by managing a business for an extended period. The strategic buyer may choose to manage the acquisition as a separate subsidiary in a holding company or merge it into another business. These choices influence greatly the extent of and speed with which integration takes place.

This chapter assumes that integration is the goal of the acquirer immediately after the transaction closes. The chapter begins by stressing the importance of the integration phase of the acquisition process in contributing to the eventual success of the merger or acquisition. As noted in Chapter 1, ineffective integration is the second most commonly cited factor contributing to the failure of mergers and acquisitions (M&As) to meet or exceed expectations. The factors critical to the success of any integration activity are addressed in this chapter. These include careful premerger planning, candid and continuous communication, the pace at which the businesses are combined, the appointment of an integration manager and team with clearly defined goals and lines of authority, and making the difficult decisions early in the process. This chapter views integration as a process consisting of six activities: planning, developing communication plans, creating a new organization, developing staffing plans, implementing functional integration, and integrating corporate cultures. This chapter concludes with a discussion of how to overcome some of the unique obstacles encountered in integrating business alliances. A chapter review is available on the CD-ROM accompanying this book.

The Role of Integration in Successful Mergers and Acquisitions

While overpayment and poor strategy are among the most common explanations for the failure of M&As, numerous studies support the conclusion that rapid integration efforts are more likely to result in mergers that achieve the acquirer's expectations (*Business-Week*, 1995; Coopers & Lybrand, 1996; Marks, 1996; McKinsey Company, 1987). In a global study of 100 acquisitions, each of which is valued at more than $500 million, Andersen Consulting (1999) concluded that most postmerger activities are completed within 6 months to 1 year. Moreover, the study suggested that integration must be done quickly to generate the financial returns expected by shareholders and to minimize employee turnover and customer attrition.

Realizing Projected Financial Returns

The importance of rapid integration can be demonstrated using a simple numerical example. Suppose a firm has a current market value of $100 million and this value accurately reflects the firm's future cash flows discounted at its cost of capital. Assume an acquirer is willing to pay a $25 million premium for this firm, believing that it can recover the premium by realizing cost savings resulting from integrating the two firms. The amount of cash the acquirer will have to generate to recover the premium will increase the longer it takes to integrate the target company. If the cost of capital is 10% and integration is completed by the end of the first year, the acquirer will have to earn $27.5 million by the end of the first year to recover the control premium plus its cost of capital (i.e., $25 + $25 × .10). If integration is not completed until the end of the second year, the acquirer will have to earn an incremental cash flow of $30.25 million (i.e., $27.5 + $27.5 × .10).

The Impact of Employee Turnover

Although there is little evidence that firms necessarily experience an actual reduction in their total workforce following an acquisition, studies do show that turnover among management and key employees does increase after a corporate takeover (Hayes, 1979; Shivdasani, 1993; Walsh, 1989; Walsh and Ellwood, 1991). Some loss of managers is intentional as part of an effort to eliminate redundancies and overlapping positions, whereas others quit during the turmoil of integration. Flanagan and O'Shaughnessy (1998) found that layoffs were announced about the same time as mergers about 50% of the time. What is difficult to measure in any of these studies is whether the employees that leave represent a significant "brain drain" or loss of key managers. For many acquisitions, talent and management skills represent the primary value of the target company to the acquirer. This is especially true in high technology and service companies for which assets are largely the embodied knowledge of their employees (Lord and Ranft, 2000). Consequently, the loss of key employees rapidly degrades the value of the target company, making the recovery of any premium paid to target shareholders difficult for the buyer. The cost of employee turnover does not stop with the loss of key employees. The loss of any significant number of employees can be very costly. Current employees already have been recruited and trained. Firms will incur both recruitment and training costs again when equally qualified employees are hired to replace those lost. Moreover, the loss of employees is likely to reduce the morale and productivity of those who remain.

Acquisition-Related Customer Attrition

During normal operations, businesses can expect a certain level of churn in their customer list. Depending on the industry, normal churn as a result of competitive conditions can be anywhere from 20–40%. A newly merged company will experience a loss of another 5–10% of its existing customers as a direct result of the merger (Down, 1995). The loss of customers may reflect uncertainty about on-time delivery and product quality, as well as more aggressive pricing by competitors following the merger. Moreover, many companies lose revenue momentum as they concentrate on realizing expected cost synergies. The loss of customers may continue well after closing. A McKinsey study of 160 acquisitions by 157 publicly traded firms in 11 different industries in 1995 and 1996 found that on average these firms grew 4 percentage points less than their peers during the 3 years following closing. Moreover, 42% of the sample actually lost ground. Only 12% of the sample showed revenue growth significantly ahead of their peers (Bekier, Bogardus, and Oldham, 2001).

Rapid Integration Does Not Mean Doing Everything at the Same Pace

Rapid integration may result in more immediate realization of synergies, but it also contributes to employee and customer attrition. Therefore, intelligent integration involves managing these trade-offs by quickly identifying and implementing those projects offering the most immediate payoff while deferring those whose disruption would result in the greatest loss in revenue. Consequently, acquirers will frequently postpone integrating data processing and customer service call centers until much later in the integration process, if such activities are viewed as pivotal to maintaining on-time delivery and high-quality customer service. Moreover, sometimes significant differences in the corporate cultures of the acquirer and target firms will require a more measured pace of integration. This was certainly the situation in GE's effort to integrate the four acquisitions comprising its water treatment business illustrated in the opening case study to this chapter.

Viewing Integration as a Process

The activities involved in integrating an acquired business into the acquirer's operations do not fall neatly into a well-defined process. Some activities fall into a logical sequence, whereas others are continuous and in some respects unending. The major activities fall loosely into the following sequence: premerger planning, resolving communication issues, defining the new organization, developing staffing plans, integrating functions and departments, and building a new corporate culture. In practice, communicating with all major stakeholder groups and developing a new corporate culture are largely continuous activities, running through the integration period and beyond. Each of these six activities will be discussed in the coming sections of this chapter in the sequence outlined in Figure 6-1.

Integration Planning	Developing Communication Plans	Creating a New Organization	Developing Staffing Plans	Functional Integration	Building a New Corporate Culture
Premerger Planning: – Refine valuation – Resolve transition issues – Negotiate contract assurances	Stakeholders: – Employees – Customers – Suppliers – Investors – Lenders – Communities (including regulators)	Learn from the past	Determine personnel requirements for the new organization	Revalidate due diligence data	Identify cultural issues through corporate profiling
		Business needs drive organizational structure	Determine resource availability	Conduct performance bench-marking	Integrate through shared: – Goals – Standards – Services – Space
			Establish staffing plans & timetables	Integrate functions: – Operations – Information technology – Finance – Sales – Marketing – Purchasing – R&D – Human resources	
			Develop compensation strategy		
			Create supporting information systems		

FIGURE 6-1   Viewing merger integration as a process

Integration Planning

Carey and Ogden (2004) argue that integration planning should begin as soon as the merger is announced. However, assumptions made before the closing based on information accumulated during due diligence must be reexamined once the transaction is consummated to ensure their validity. For an excellent discussion of the challenges of integration, see Reed-Lajoux (1998), Schweiger (2002), and Galpin and Herndon (2007).

Premerger Integration Planning: Begin Planning before Closing

The planning process enables the acquiring company to refine further its original estimate of the value of the target company and to deal with transition issues in the context of the definitive agreement of purchase and sale. Furthermore, the buyer has an opportunity to insert into the agreement the appropriate representations (claims) and warranties (promises), as well as conditions of closing that facilitate the postmerger integration process. Finally, the planning process creates a postmerger integration organization to expedite the integration process following closing. It is important to include representatives from the negotiating team on the postmerger integration organization. As negotiators hand off to those responsible for postmerger integration, there is often a lack of shared understanding as to why certain items were included and others excluded from the agreement and what certain contract terms mean. The 2002 acquisition of Compaq Computer by Hewlett-Packard offers some interesting insights into the benefits of preclosing planning (see Case Study 6-1).

Case Study 6-1

Hewlett-Packard Acquires Compaq: The Importance of Preplanning Integration

The proposed marriage between Hewlett-Packard (HP) and Compaq Computer got off to a rocky start, when the sons of the founders came out against the transaction. The resulting long and drawn out proxy battle threatened to divert management's attention from planning for the postclosing integration effort. The complexity of the pending integration effort appeared daunting. The two companies would need to meld employees in 160 countries and assimilate a large roster of products from personal computers to consulting services. When the transaction closed on May 7, 2002, critics predicted that the combined businesses would become stalled like so many tech mergers over the years in a mess of technical and personal entanglements.

Instead, HP's then CEO Carly Fiorina methodically began to plan for integration prior to the deal closing. She formed an elite team that studied past tech mergers, mapped out the merger's most important tasks, and then checked regularly whether key projects were on schedule. A month before the deal was even announced on September 4, 2001, Carly Fiorina and Compaq CEO Michael Capellas each tapped a top manager to tackle the integration effort. The integration managers immediately moved to form a 30-person integration team. The team learned, for example, that during Compaq's merger with Digital, some server computers slated for elimination were never killed off. In contrast, HP executives quickly decided what to jettison. Every week they pored over progress charts to review how each product exit was proceeding. By early 2003, HP had eliminated 33 business-computer product lines it had inherited from the two companies reducing the remaining number to 27. Another six were phased out in 2004.

The team also scoured literature describing other recent transactions. As a result, the team recommended that the firms offer rich retention bonuses as Citigroup had done to employees they wanted to keep and that moves be taken to create a unified culture to avoid the kind of divisions that plagued AOL Time Warner. HP executives also learned that they had to move quickly making tough decisions early with respect to departments, products, and executives. By studying the 1984 merger between Chevron and Gulf Oil, where it had taken months to name new managers, integration was delayed and employee morale suffered. In contrast, after Chevron merged with Texaco in 2001, new managers were appointed in days. The subsequent merger proved to be relatively smooth.

Disputes between HP and former Compaq staff sometimes emerged over issues such as the different approaches to compensating sales people. These issues were resolved by setting up a panel of up to six sales managers drawn from both firms to referee the disagreements. HP also created a team to deal with melding the corporate cultures and hired consultants to document the differences. For examples, HP staff typically used voicemail while Compaq employees used e-mail. Compaq managers were viewed by HP managers as "shooting from the hip," whereas HP managers were viewed as bureaucrats. A series of workshops involving employees from both organizations were established to find ways to bridge actual or perceived differences. Teams of sales personnel from both firms were set up to standardize ways to market to common customers. Schedules were set up to ensure that agreed-upon tactics were actually implemented in a timely manner. The integration managers met with Ms. Fiorina weekly.

The results of this intense preplanning effort were evident by the end of the first year following closing. HP has eliminated numerous duplicate product lines and closed dozens of facilities. The firm had cut 12,000 jobs, 2000 more than had been planned at that point in time, from its combined 150,000 employees. HP had achieved $3 billion in savings from layoffs, office closures, and consolidation of its supply chain. Its original target was for savings of $2.4 billion after the first 18 months.

Despite realizing greater than anticipated cost savings, operating margins by 2004 in the PC business fell far short of expectations. This shortfall was due largely to declining selling prices and a slower than assumed recovery in PC unit sales. The failure to achieve the level of profitability forecast at this time of the acquisition contributed to the termination of Ms. Fiorina in early 2005.

Case Study Discussion Questions

1. Explain how premerger planning aided in the integration of HP and Compaq?
2. What did HP learn by studying other mergers? Give examples.
3. Cite key cultural differences between the two organizations. How were they resolved?

Part of the integration planning process involves the preclosing due diligence activity. One responsibility of the due diligence team is to identify ways in which assets, processes, and other resources can be combined to realize cost savings, productivity improvements, or other perceived synergies. This information is also essential for refining the valuation process by enabling planners to better understand the necessary sequencing of events and the resulting pace at which the expected synergies may be realized. Consequently, understanding how and over what time period the integration will be implemented is important in determining the magnitude and timing of the cash flows of the combined companies used in making the final assessment of value.

Integration planning also involves addressing human resource, customer, and supplier issues that overlap the change of ownership. These issues should be resolved as part of the agreement of purchase and sale. For example, the agreement may stipulate how target company employees will be paid and how their benefit claims will be processed. Payroll systems must be in place to ensure that employees of the acquired company continue to be paid without disruption. For a small number of employees, this may be accommodated easily by loading the acquirer's payroll computer system with a computer tape containing the necessary salary and personal information before closing or by having a third-party payroll processor perform these services. For larger operations or where employees are dispersed geographically, the target's employees may continue to be paid for a specific time period using the target's existing payroll system.

Employee health care or disability claims tend to escalate just before a transaction closes. Studies by the American Management Association and CIGNA Corporation show that employees, whether they leave or stay with the new firm, file more disability claims for longer periods after downsizing (*The Wall Street Journal,* November 21, 1996). The sharp increase in such expenses can pose an unexpected financial burden for the acquirer if the responsibility for payment of such claims has not been addressed in the merger agreement. For example, the agreement may read that all claims incurred within a specific number of days before closing, but not submitted by employees for processing until after closing, will be reimbursed by the seller after the closing. Alternatively, such claims may be paid from an escrow account containing a portion of the purchase price set aside to cover these types of expenses.

Similar timing issues exist for target company customers and suppliers. For example, the merger agreement should specify how the seller should be reimbursed for products shipped or services provided by the seller before closing but not paid for by the customer until after closing. A prudent buyer typically would be the recipient of such payments because the seller's previous lockboxes (i.e., checking accounts) would have been closed and replaced by the buyer's. Likewise, the buyer will want to be reimbursed by the seller for monies owed to suppliers for products or services provided to the seller before closing but not billed until after closing. The merger agreement may indicate that both parties will keep track of customer and supplier invoices paid during the 60–90 days following closing and will submit them for reimbursement to the other party at the end of that period.

At a minimum, the agreement of purchase and sale will contain basic assurances that the seller is what it claims to be and that the seller has a right to sell the business. Similar assurances will apply to the acquiring company. For example, the buyer must assert that it has the right and the financial capacity to buy the target firm. A comprehensive set of "reps and warranties" may be viewed as a due diligence checklist for the buyer. The reps and warranties provide the buyer with recourse to the seller if any of these claims or promises is untrue.

A prudent buyer will want to include certain assurances in the agreement of purchase and sale to limit its postclosing risk. Most seller representations and warranties made to the buyer refer to the past and present condition of the seller's business. Such reps and warranties usually pertain to such items as the ownership of securities; real and intellectual property; current levels of receivables, inventory, and debt; and pending lawsuits, worker disability, customer warranty claims, and that the target's accounting practices are in accordance with Generally Accepted Accounting Principles. Although reps and warranties apply primarily to the past and current state of the seller's business, they do have ramifications for the future. For example, if a seller claims that there are no lawsuits pending and a lawsuit is filed shortly after closing, the buyer may seek to recover damages from the seller.

The buyer also may insist that certain conditions be satisfied before closing can take place. Common conditions include employment contracts, agreements not to compete, financing, and regulatory and shareholder approval. The buyer usually will insist that key target company employees sign contracts obligating them to remain with the newly formed company for a specific period. The former owners, managers, and other key employees also are asked to sign agreements precluding them from going into any business that would directly compete with the new company during the duration of the noncompete agreement. Finally, the buyer will want to make the final closing contingent on receiving approval from the appropriate regulatory agencies and shareholders of both companies before any money changes hands.

Postmerger Integration Organization: Put in Place before Closing

A postmerger integration organization with clearly defined goals and responsibilities should be in place before closing. For friendly mergers, the organization, including supporting work teams, should consist of individuals from both the acquiring and target companies who have a vested interest in the newly formed company. The extent to which such an organization can be assembled during a hostile takeover is problematic given the lack of trust that may exist between the parties to the transaction. In such circumstances, the acquiring company is likely to find it difficult to gain access to the necessary information and to get the involvement of the target company's management in the planning process before the transaction actually closes.

In those instances where the target firm is going to be integrated into one of the acquirer's business units, it is critical to place responsibility for integration in that business unit. Personnel from the business unit should be well represented on the due diligence team to ensure they understand how best to integrate the target to expeditiously realize synergies.

Postmerger Integration Organization: Composition and Responsibilities

The postmerger integration organization should consist of a management integration team (MIT) and a series of integration work teams. Each work team is focused on implementing a specific portion of the integration plan. The MIT consists of senior managers from the two merged organizations and is charged with implementing synergies identified during the preclosing due diligence. The composition of the work teams also should reflect employees from both the acquiring and target companies. Other team members might include outside advisors, such as investment bankers, accountants, attorneys, and consultants. The MIT's emphasis during the integration period should be on those activities creating the greatest value for shareholders. The MIT's primary responsibility is to focus on key concerns such as long-term revenue, cost, and cash-flow performance targets, as well as product and customer strategies. Exhibit 6-1 summarizes the key tasks that should be performed by the MIT to realize anticipated synergies.

Exhibit 6-1
Key Management Integration Team Responsibilities

1. Build a master schedule of what should be done by whom and by what date.
2. Determine the required economic performance for the combined entity.
3. Establish work teams to determine how each function and business unit will be combined (e.g., structure, job design, and staffing levels).
4. Focus the organization on meeting ongoing business commitments and operational performance targets during the integration process.

---

5. Create an early warning system consisting of performance indicators to ensure that both integration activities and business performance stay on plan.
6. Monitor and expedite key decisions.
7. Establish a rigorous communication campaign to aggressively support the integration plan. Address both internal (e.g., employees) and external (e.g., customers, suppliers, and regulatory authorities) constituencies.

Dedicated integration work teams perform the detailed integration work. In addition to driving the integration effort, the MIT ensures that the managers not involved in the integration effort remain focused on running the business. The MIT allocates dedicated resources to the integration effort and clarifies nonteam membership roles and enables day-to-day operations to continue at premerger levels. The MIT should be careful to give the work teams not only the responsibility to do certain tasks but also the authority to get the job done. The teams should be encouraged to inject ideas into the process to foster creativity by encouraging solutions rather than by dictating processes and procedures. To be effective, the work teams must have access to accurate, timely information and should receive candid, timely feedback. The teams also should be given adequate resources to execute their responsibilities and be kept informed of the broader perspective of the overall integration effort so that they will not become too narrowly focused.

Institutionalizing the Integration Process

In recognition of the importance of integration, firms that frequently acquire companies in the same industry often have staffs fully dedicated to managing the integration process. The presumption is that integration is likely to proceed more smoothly and rapidly if those guiding the process have substantial experience in integrating certain types of businesses. It is ironic that some firms can have such discipline when it comes to postacquisition integration but display such poor judgment by consistently overpaying for acquisitions. By overpaying for the target, the acquirer is implicitly assuming that all anticipated synergies used to justify the exorbitant purchase price can be realized in a reasonable time period following closing (see Case Study 6-2). Thus, overpayment leaves little room for errors during the integration process.

Case Study 6-2
M&A Gets Out of Hand at Cisco

Cisco Systems, the Internet infrastructure behemoth, provides the hardware and software to support efficient traffic flow over the Internet. Between 1993 and 2000, Cisco completed 70 acquisitions using its high-flying stock as its acquisition currency (Frank and Sidel, 2002). With engineering talent in short supply and a dramatic compression in product life cycles, Cisco turned to acquisitions to expand existing product lines and to enter new businesses. The firm's track record during this period in acquiring and absorbing these acquisitions was impressive. In fiscal year 1999, Cisco acquired 10 companies. During the same period, its sales and operating profits soared by 44% and 55%, respectively. In view of its pledge not to layoff any employees of the target companies, its turnover rate among employees acquired through acquisition was 2.1%, versus an average of 20% for other software and hardware companies.

Cisco's strategy for acquiring companies was to evaluate its targets' technologies, financial performance, and management talent with a focus on ease of integrating the target into Cisco's operations. Cisco's strategy was sometimes referred to as an R&D strategy in that it sought to acquire firms with leading edge technologies that could be easily adapted to Cisco's current product lines or used to expand its product offering. In this manner, its acquisition strategy augmented internal R&D spending. Cisco attempted to use its operating cash flow to fund development of current technologies and its lofty stock price to acquire future technologies. Cisco targeted small companies having a viable commercial product or technology. Cisco believed that larger, more mature companies tended to be difficult to integrate, due to their entrenched beliefs about technologies, hardware, and software solutions.

The frequency with which Cisco was making acquisitions during the last half of the 1990s caused the firm to "institutionalize" the way in which it integrated acquired companies. The integration process was tailored for each acquired company and was implemented by an integration team of 12 professionals. Newly acquired employees received an information packet including descriptions of Cisco's business strategy, organizational structure, benefits, a contact sheet if further information was required, and an explanation of the strategic importance of the acquired firm to Cisco. On the day the acquisition was announced, teams of Cisco human resources people would travel to the acquired firm's headquarters and meet with small groups of employees to answer questions.

Working with the acquired firm's management, integration team members would help place new employees within Cisco's workforce. Generally, product, engineering, and marketing groups were kept independent, whereas sales and manufacturing functions were merged into existing Cisco departments. Cisco payroll and benefits systems were updated to reflect information about the new employees, who were quickly given access to Cisco's online employee information systems. Cisco also offered customized orientation programs intended to educate managers about Cisco's hiring practices, salespeople about Cisco's products, and engineers about the firm's development process. The entire integration process generally was completed in 4–6 weeks. This lightning-fast pace was largely the result of Cisco's tendency to purchase small, highly complementary companies; to leave much of the acquired firm's infrastructure in place; and to dedicate a staff of human resource and business development people to facilitate the process (Cisco Systems, 1999; Goldblatt, 1999).

Cisco was unable to avoid the devastating effects of the explosion of the dot-com bubble and the 2001–2002 recession in the United States. Corporate technology buyers, who used Cisco's high-end equipment, stopped making purchases because of economic uncertainty. Consequently, Cisco was forced to repudiate its no-layoff pledge and announced a workforce reduction of 8500, about 20% of its total employees, in early 2001. Despite its concerted effort to retain key employees from previous acquisitions, Cisco's turnover began to soar. Companies that had been acquired at highly inflated premiums during the late 1990s lost much of their value as the loss of key talent delayed new product launches.

By mid-2001, the firm had announced inventory and acquisition-related write-downs of more than $2.5 billion. A precipitous drop in its share price made growth through acquisition much less attractive than during the late 1990s, when its stock traded at lofty price-to-earnings ratios. Thus, Cisco was forced to abandon its previous strategy of growth through acquisition to one emphasizing improvement in its internal operations. Acquisitions tumbled from 23 in 2000 to 2 in 2001. Whereas in the past, Cisco's acquisitions appeared to have been haphazard, in mid-2003 Cisco set up an investment review board that analyzes investment proposals, including acquisitions, before they can be implemented. Besides making sure the proposed deal makes sense for the overall company and determining the ease with which it can be integrated, the board creates detailed financial projections and the deal's sponsor must be willing to commit to sales and earnings targets.

Case Study Discussion Questions

1. Describe how Cisco "institutionalized" the integration process. What are the advantages and disadvantages to the approach adopted by Cisco?
2. Why did Cisco have a "no-layoff" policy? How did this contribute to maintaining or increasing the value of the companies it acquired?
3. What evidence do you have that the high price-to-earnings ratio associated with Cisco's stock during the late 1990s may have caused the firm to overpay for many of its acquisitions? How might overpayment have complicated the integration process at Cisco?

Developing Communication Plans: Talking to Key Stakeholders

Before publicly announcing an acquisition, the acquirer should have prepared a communication plan. The plan should be developed jointly by the MIT and the public relations (PR) department or outside PR consultant. It should contain key messages and specify target stakeholders and appropriate media for conveying the messages to each group. The major stakeholder groups should include employees, customers, suppliers, investors, communities, and regulators.

Employees: Address the "Me Issues" Immediately

As noted earlier, target company employees typically represent a substantial portion of the value of the acquired business. This is particularly true for technology and service-related businesses having few tangible assets. Therefore, preserving the value of an acquisition requires that companies must be sensitive to when and how something is communicated to employees and to the accuracy of its content. Communication, particularly during crisis periods, should be as frequent as possible. A report of "nothing to report" can be comforting. It is better to report that there is no change than to remain silent. Silence breeds uncertainty, which adds to stress associated with the integration effort. Deteriorating job performance, absences from work, fatigue, anxiety, and depression are clear signs of workforce anxiety.

The CEO should lead the effort to communicate to employees at all levels through employee meetings on site or via teleconferencing. Many companies find it useful to create a single source of information accessible to all employees. This may be an individual whose job it is to answer questions or a menu-driven automated phone system programmed to respond to commonly asked questions. The best forum for communication in a crisis is through regularly scheduled employee meetings. All external communication in the form of press releases should be coordinated with the PR department to ensure that the same information is released concurrently to employees. This minimizes the likelihood that employees will learn about important developments second hand. Internal e-mail systems, voicemail, or intranets may be used to facilitate employee communications. In addition, personal letters, question-and-answer sessions, newsletters, or videotapes are highly effective ways of delivering the desired messages.

Employees are highly interested in any information pertaining to the merger and, more importantly, how it will affect them. They will want to know how changes will affect the overall strategy, business operations, job security, working conditions, and total compensation. The human resources (HR) staff plays an important role in communicating to employees. HR representatives must learn what employees know and want to know, what the prevailing rumors are, and what employees find most disconcerting. This can be achieved through surveys, interviews, focus groups, or employee meetings.

Customers: Undercommit and Overdeliver

To minimize customer attrition, the newly merged firm must commit to customers that it will maintain or improve product quality, on-time delivery, and customer service. The commitments should be realistic in terms of what needs to be accomplished during the integration phase. Despite these efforts some attrition related to the acquisition is inevitable. The firm continuously must communicate to customers realistic benefits associated with the merger. From the customer's perspective, the merger can increase the range of products or services offered or provide lower selling prices as a result of economies of scale and new applications of technology. However, the firm's actions must support its talk.

Case Study 6-3 illustrates the negative effects of failure to meet customer commitments in a timely manner. History shows that companies are vulnerable to market share loss immediately following mergers. Competitors use these periods to sow doubt among the firm's customers about its ability to achieve and sustain acceptable product quality and customer service as well as on-time delivery. In this case study, the protracted integration clearly is eroding the value of the deal, as the overall competitive position of CNH Corporation continued to deteriorate.

Case Study 6-3
Case Corporation Loses Sight of Customer Needs
in Integrating New Holland Corporation

Farm implement manufacturer Case Corporation acquired New Holland Corporation in a $4.6 billion transaction in 1999. Overnight, its CEO, Jean-Pierre Rosso, had engineered a deal that put the combined firms, with $11 billion in annual revenue, in second place in the agricultural equipment industry just behind industry leader John Deere. The new firm was named CNH Global (CNH). Although Rosso proved adept at negotiating and closing a substantial deal for his firm, he was less agile in meeting customer needs during the protracted integration period. CNH has become a poster child of what can happen when managers become so preoccupied with the details of combining two big operations that they neglect external issues such as the economy and competition. Since the merger in November 1999, CNH began losing market share to John Deere and other rivals across virtually all of its product lines.

Rosso remained focused on negotiating with antitrust officials about what it would take to get regulatory approval. Once achieved, CNH was slow to complete the last of its asset sales

---

as required under the consent decree with the FTC. The last divestiture was not completed until late January 2001, more than 20 months after the deal had been announced. This delay forced Rosso to postpone cost cutting and to slow their new product entries. This spooked farmers and dealers who could not get the firm to commit to telling them which products would be discontinued and which the firm would continue to support with parts and service. Fearful that CNH would discontinue duplicate Case and New Holland products, farmers and equipment dealers switched brands. The result was that John Deere became more dominant than ever. CNH was slow to reassure customers with tangible actions and to introduce new products competitive with Deere. This gave Deere the opportunity to fill the vacuum in the marketplace.

The integration was deemed to have been completed a full 4 years after closing. As a sign of how painful the integration had been, CNH was laying workers off as Deere was hiring to keep up with the strong demand for its products. Deere also appeared to be ahead in moving toward common global platforms and parts to take fuller advantage of economies of scale.

Case Study Discussion Questions

1. Why is rapid integration important? Illustrate with examples from the case study.
2. What could CNH have done differently to slow or reverse its loss of market share?

When rival PeopleSoft agreed to be acquired in a $10.3 billion cash deal on December 14, 2004, after a protracted 18-month struggle for control, Larry Ellison, Oracle's CEO, immediately took steps to reduce customer attrition. The final purchase price of $26.30 per share represented a 75% premium over its original offer made on June 5, 2003, and Ellison believed he had to move quickly to earn back this outsized premium (see Case Study 6-4).

Case Study 6-4
Promises to PeopleSoft's Customers: Complicate Oracle's Integration Efforts

When Oracle first announced its bid for PeopleSoft in mid-2003, the firm indicated that it planned to stop selling PeopleSoft's existing software programs and halt any additions to its product lines. This would result in the termination of much of PeopleSoft's engineering, sales, and support staff. Oracle indicated that it was more interested in PeopleSoft's customer list than its technology. PeopleSoft earned sizeable profit margins on its software maintenance contracts, under which customers pay for product updates, fixing software errors, and other forms of product support. Maintenance fees represented an annuity stream that could improve profitability even when new product sales are listless. However, PeopleSoft's customers worried that they would have to go through the costly and time-consuming process of switching software. To win customer support for the merger and to avoid triggering $2 billion in guarantees PeopleSoft had offered its customers in the event Oracle failed to support its products, Oracle had to change dramatically its position over the next 18 months.

One day after reaching agreement with the PeopleSoft board, Oracle announced it would release a new version of PeopleSoft's products and would develop another version of J. D. Edwards' software, which PeopleSoft had acquired in 2003. Oracle has committed to support the acquired products even longer than PeopleSoft's guarantees would have. Consequently, Oracle had to maintain programs that run with database software sold by rivals such as IBM. Oracle also had to retain the bulk of PeopleSoft's engineering staff and sales and customer support teams.

Among the biggest beneficiaries of the protracted takeover battle has been German software giant SAP. SAP has been successful in winning customers uncomfortable about dealing with either Oracle or PeopleSoft. SAP claimed that its worldwide market share has grown from 51% in mid-2003 to 56% by late 2004. SAP had taken advantage of the highly public hostile takeover by using sales representatives, e-mail, and an international print advertising campaign to target PeopleSoft customers. The firm touted its reputation for maintaining the highest quality of support and service for its products.

Case Study Discussion Questions

1. How might the commitments Oracle made to PeopleSoft's customers affect its ability to realize anticipated synergies? Be specific.
2. Explain why Oracle's willingness to pay such a high premium for PeopleSoft and its willingness to change its position on supporting PeopleSoft products and retaining the firm's employees may have negatively impacted Oracle shareholders? Be specific.

Suppliers: Develop Long-Term Vendor Relationships

Just as a current customer is often worth more than a new one, a current supplier with a proven track record also may be worth more than a new one. It is a buyer's market following an acquisition, so the new company should approach its suppliers carefully. Although substantial cost savings are possible by "managing" suppliers, the new company should be seeking a long-term relationship rather than simply a way to reduce costs. Aggressive negotiation can get high-quality products and services at lower prices in the short run, but it may be transitory if the new company is a large customer of the supplier and if the supplier's margins are squeezed continuously. The supplier's product or service quality will suffer, and the supplier eventually may exit the business. Ways to effectively manage suppliers following an acquisition will be discussed later in this chapter.

Investors: Maintain Shareholder Loyalty

The new firm must be able to present a compelling vision of the future to investors. In a share-for-share exchange, there are compelling reasons for appealing to current investors of both the acquirer and target companies. Target shareholders will become shareholders in the newly formed company. Loyal shareholders tend to provide a more stable ownership base, and they may contribute to lower share price volatility. All firms attract particular types of investors—some with a preference for high dividends and others for capital gains. The acquisition of Time Warner by America Online in January 2000 illustrated the potential clash between investor preferences. The combined market value of the two firms lost 11% in the 4 days following the announcement, as investors puzzled over what had been created. The selling frenzy following the announcement may have involved different groups of investors who bought Time Warner for its stable growth and America Online for its meteoric growth rate of 70% per annum. The new company may not have met the expectations of either group.

Communities: Build Strong, Credible Relationships

Companies should communicate plans to build or keep plants, stores, or office buildings in a community as soon as they can be confident that these actions will be implemented. These pronouncements translate readily into new jobs and increased taxes for the community. Good working relations with surrounding communities are simply good public relations.

Creating a New Organization

The combined firms' new leaders must appoint the best possible top management team for achieving the goals of the new company. In turn, the management team must be highly supportive of achieving these goals. Individual senior manager's roles must be clearly defined to achieve effective collaboration. While easy to articulate, the appointment of the new team at the top is highly challenging in the frenetic period immediately before or after closing. The process can become time consuming in that it can involve the appointment of anywhere from 10 to 40 executives, including key functional, group, and often divisional heads. Nonetheless, it must be done adroitly and expeditiously. McKinsey & Company in a study of 161 mergers found that the early appointment of the top management team was a strong predictor of the long-term success of the combined firms (Fubini, Price, and Zollo, 2006).

Business Needs Drive Structure

Organization or structure traditionally is defined in terms of titles and reporting relationships. For the purpose of this chapter, we will follow this definition. A properly structured organization should support, not retard, the acceptance of a culture in the new company that is desired by top management. An effective starting point in setting up a structure is to learn from the past and to recognize that the needs of the business drive structure and not the other way around.

Learn from the Past

Building new reporting structures for combining companies requires knowledge of the target company's prior organization, some sense as to the effectiveness of this organization in the decision-making process, and the future business needs of the newly combined companies. Therefore, in creating the new organization, it is necessary to start with previous organization charts. They provide insights into how individuals from both the target and acquiring companies will interact within the new company, because they reveal the past experience and future expectations of individuals with regard to reporting relationships.

Structure Facilitates Decision Making, Provides Internal Controls, and Promotes Desired Behaviors

The next step is to move from the past into the future by creating a structure that focuses on meeting the business needs of the combined companies rather than attempting to please everyone. Often, acquiring companies simply impose their reporting structures on the target company. This is particularly true if the acquirer is much larger than the target.

By ignoring the target's existing organizational structure, the acquiring company is in effect ignoring the expectations of the target's employees. Unfulfilled expectations will demotivate target company employees (Lajoux, 1998, pp. 175–214).

There are three basic types of structures: functional, product or service, and divisional. The functional tends to be the most centralized, and the divisional tends to be the most decentralized.

In a *functional organization*, people are assigned to specific groups or departments such as accounting, engineering, marketing, sales, distribution, customer service, manufacturing, or maintenance. This type of structure tends to be highly centralized and is becoming less common. In a *product or service organization*, functional specialists are grouped by product line or service offering. Each product line or service offering has its own accounting, human resources, sales, marketing, customer service, and product development staffs. These types of organizations tend to be somewhat decentralized. Individuals in these types of organizations often have multiple reporting relationships, such as a finance manager reporting to a product line manager and the firm's CFO. *Divisional organizations* continue to be the dominant form of organizational structure, in which groups of products are combined into independent divisions or "strategic business units." Such organizations have their own management teams and tend to be highly decentralized.

The popularity of decentralized versus centralized management structures varies with the state of the economy. During recessions when top management is under great pressure to cut costs, companies often tend to move toward centralized management structures, only to decentralize when the economy recovers. Highly decentralized authority can retard the pace of integration, because there is no single authority to resolve issues or determine policies. In contrast, a centralized structure may make postmerger integration much easier. Senior management can dictate policies governing all aspects of the combined companies, centralize all types of functions providing support to operating units, and resolve issues among the operating units.

Although centralized control does provide significant advantages during postmerger integration, it also can be highly detrimental if the policies imposed by the central headquarters are simply not appropriate for the operating units. Highly centralized parent company management may destroy value by imposing too many rigid controls, by focusing on the wrong issues, by hiring or promoting the wrong managers, or by monitoring the wrong performance measures. Moreover, highly centralized parent companies often have multiple layers of management to link multiple operating units and centralized functions providing services to the operating units. The parent companies pass the costs of centralized management and support services on to the operating units. Studies suggest that the costs of this type of structure often outweigh the benefits (Alexander, Campbell, and Gould, 1995; Campbell, Sadler, and Koch, 1997; Chakrabarti, 1990).

The right structure may be an evolving one. The substantial benefits of a well-managed, rapid integration of the two businesses suggest a centralized management structure initially with relatively few layers of management. In general, flatter organizations are becoming common among large companies. The distance between the CEO and division heads, measured in terms of intermediate positions, decreased by 25% between 1986 and 1999. Moreover, the span of a CEO's authority has widened, with about 50% more positions reporting directly to the CEO (Wulf and Rajan, 2003). This does not mean that all integration activities should be driven from the top without any input from middle managers and supervisors of both companies. It does mean taking decisive and timely action based on the best information available.

Once the integration is viewed as relatively complete, the new company should move to a more decentralized structure in view of the well-documented costs of centralized corporate organizations. Case Study 6-5 shows how Lenovo reacted to organizational issues following its acquisition of IBM's personal computer operations in mid-2005.

Case Study 6-5

Lenovo Adopts a Highly Decentralized Organization Following Its Acquisition of IBM's Personal Computer Business

China's largest computer manufacturer completed its acquisition of IBM's PC business in mid-2005. Before closing, Lenovo announced that former IBM PC executive, Steve Ward, would be appointed as chief executive officer of Lenovo's worldwide operations. Lenovo's management will be scattered around the globe. Mr. Ward and several dozen other top executives and operations staff will work from a new corporate headquarters in Pennsylvania. Asian-based executives will reside in Beijing and in Hong Kong. Many of the company's sales, marketing, and engineering employees will be Raleigh, North Carolina and the ThinkPad design group will remain in Japan.

One-half of Lenovo's top 30 executives are from Lenovo and the remainder is from IBM's former PC group. The management team intends to develop a culture that exhibits respect for one another, candor, integrity, and a willingness to compromise. Lenovo made a decision before the acquisition to run the company in English.

Case Study Discussion Questions

1. What do you believe are some of the benefits and challenges of Lenovo's decision to disperse the management, design, and marketing functions? Be specific.
2. Why do you believe Lenovo selected an American to run the global operations and adopted English as the language in which business would be conducted inside the firm?

Developing Staffing Plans

Staffing plans should be formulated as soon as possible in the integration process. In friendly acquisitions, the process should begin before closing. The early development of such plans provides an opportunity to include the key personnel from both firms in the integration effort. Other benefits from early planning include the increased likelihood of retaining those with key skills and talents, maintaining corporate continuity, and team building. Figure 6-2 describes the logical sequencing of staffing plans and the major issues addressed in each segment.

Personnel Requirements

The appropriate organizational structure is one able to meet the current functional requirements or needs of the business and flexible enough to be expanded to satisfy future business requirements. The process for creating such a structure should involve input from all levels of management, should be consistent with the combined firm's business

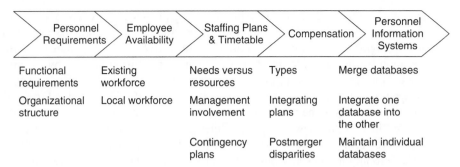

Personnel Requirements	Employee Availability	Staffing Plans & Timetable	Compensation	Personnel Information Systems
Functional requirements	Existing workforce	Needs versus resources	Types	Merge databases
Organizational structure	Local workforce	Management involvement	Integrating plans	Integrate one database into the other
		Contingency plans	Postmerger disparities	Maintain individual databases

FIGURE 6-2   Staffing strategy sequencing

strategy, and should reflect expected sales growth. Before establishing the organizational structure, the integration team should agree on what specific functions are needed to run the combined businesses. These discussions should reflect a clear understanding of the specific roles and responsibilities of each function. Once the necessary functions have been identified, the effort to project personnel requirements by function should start with each functional department describing the ideal structure to meet the roles and responsibilities assigned by senior management. By asking for their input, department personnel are involved in the process, can communicate useful insights, and can contribute to the creation of a consensus for changing the organization.

Employee Availability

Employee availability refers to the number of each type of employee required by the new organization that can be identified in the new company's existing workforce and in the local communities in which the new company has operations. The skills of the existing workforce should be documented and compared with the current and future functional requirements of the new company. The local labor pool can be used to augment the existing workforce. These workers represent potential new hires for the combined firms. Data should be collected on the educational levels, skills, and demographic composition of the local workforce, as well as prevailing wage rates by skill category.

Staffing Plans and Timetable

Following the determination of the organizational structure and the pool of current and potential employees available to staff the new organization, a detailed staffing plan can be developed.

By matching the number of workers and skills required to support current and future business requirements with the current workforce, gaps in the firm's workforce needing to be filled from recruiting outside the company can be readily identified. The effort to recruit externally should be tempered by its potentially adverse impact on current employee morale. The filling of gaps should be prioritized and phased in over time in recognition of the time required to fill certain types of positions and the impact of major hiring programs on local wage rates in communities with relatively small labor pools.

Once management positions have been filled, the managers should be enlisted to interview, evaluate, and select new employees to fill job openings in their departments and operations. Senior management should stress that filling job openings should be given top priority, particularly when the skills required are crucial to successfully completing the integration of the acquired business. During the integration period, managers are under the enormous stress of having to continue to conduct normal business operations as well as to integrate portions of the acquired business. In view of the increased workload, it is common for managers to defer the time-consuming hiring process by assuming multiple responsibilities. This hurts the manager's morale and health and the completion of the integration process, because managers often are insufficiently trained to handle many of the responsibilities they have assumed. As noted previously, key employees inevitably will be lost by the new company. Other employees should be trained to fill positions considered critical to the long-term viability of the organization. This can be accomplished by developing job descriptions that clearly identify the skills required to fill the position and then by cross-training other workers in the position.

Compensation

Merging compensation plans can be one of the most challenging activities of the integration process. Such activities must be conducted in compliance with prevailing regulations and with a high degree of sensitivity. Total compensation consists of base pay, bonuses or incentive plans, benefits, and special contractual agreements. Bonuses may take the form of a lump sum of cash or stock paid to an employee for meeting or exceeding these targets. Special contractual agreements may consist of noncompete agreements in which key employees, in exchange for an agreed on amount of compensation, sign agreements not to compete against the newly formed company if they should leave. Special agreements also may take the form of golden parachutes (i.e., lucrative severance packages) for senior management. Finally, retention bonuses often are given to employees if they agree to stay with the new company for a specific time period. For a more detailed discussion of these issues, see Page (2006) and Ferenczy (2005).

Personnel Information Systems

The extent to which compensation plans are integrated depends on whether the two companies are going to be managed separately or integrated. Financial acquirers may be intent on reselling the acquired business in a few years; as such, they may choose to keep compensation plans separate. The strategic acquirer also may keep the plans separate especially if it is moving into an industry in which compensation differs from that prevailing in its current industry. In instances in which the parent chooses to combine plans, the design of the new plan generally is done in consultation with the acquired unit's management. The parent will set guidelines, such as how much stock senior executives should own (e.g., a percentage of base pay) and how managers will receive the stock (e.g., whether they will be awarded stock or will have to buy it at a discount from its current market price). The parent also will set guidelines for base pay. For example, the parent may decide that base pay will be at market, below market, or above market adjusted for regional differences in the cost of living. Moreover, the parent may also decide how bonuses will be paid, with the operating unit determining who receives them. Finally, the parent will determine the benefits policy and plans.

The acquiring company may choose to merge all personnel data into a new database, to merge one corporate database into another, or to maintain the personnel databases of each business. A single database enables authorized users to more readily access employee data, to more efficiently plan for future staffing requirements, and to conduct analyses and print reports. Maintenance expense associated with a single database also may be lower. The decision to keep personnel databases separate may reflect plans to divest the unit at some time in the future.

Functional Integration

Previous activities within the integration process dealt primarily with planning for the actual integration of the acquired business into the acquirer's business. Functional integration refers to the actual execution of the plans. The first consideration of the MIT is to determine the extent to which the two companies' operations and support staffs are to be centralized or decentralized. The main areas of focus should be information technology (IT), manufacturing operations, sales, marketing, finance, purchasing, R&D, and the requirements to staff these functions. However, before any actual integration takes place, it is crucial to revalidate data collected during due diligence and to benchmark all operations by comparing them to industry standards.

Due Diligence Data Revalidation: Verify Assumptions

Data collected during due diligence should be revalidated immediately after closing. The pressure exerted by both the buyer and the seller to complete the transaction often results in a haphazard preclosing due diligence review. For example, in an effort to compress the time devoted to due diligence, sellers often allow buyers' access to senior managers only. Middle-level managers, supervisory personnel, and equipment operators often are excluded from the interview process. For similar reasons, site visits by the buyer often are limited to only those with the largest concentrations of employees, thus ignoring the risks and opportunities that might exist at sites not visited. The buyer's legal and financial reviews normally are conducted only on the largest customer and supplier contracts, promissory notes, and operating and capital leases. Receivables are evaluated and physical inventory is counted using sampling techniques. The effort to determine if intellectual property has been properly protected, with key trademarks or service marks properly registered and copyrights and patents filed, is often spotty. Exxon's merger with Mobil demonstrates how revalidation of earlier due diligence findings resulted in an approximate 26% upward revision in expected pretax cost savings as a result of personnel reductions (Case Study 6-6). In contrast, Albertson's acquisition of American Stores shows the downside of inadequate due diligence, which resulted in seriously underestimating actual integration costs (Case Study 6-7).

Case Study 6-6
Exxon-Mobil: A Study in Cost Cutting

Having obtained access to more detailed information following consummation of the merger, Exxon-Mobil announced dramatic revisions in its estimates of cost savings. The world's largest publicly owned oil company would cut almost 16,000 jobs by the end of 2002. This was an increase from the 9000 cuts estimated when the merger was first announced in December 1998. Of the total, 6000 would come from early retirement. Estimated annual savings reached $3.8 billion by 2003, up by more than $1 billion from when the merger originally was announced. As time passed, the companies seemed to have become a highly focused, smooth-running machine remarkably efficient at discovering, refining, and marketing oil and gas. An indication of this is the fact that the firm spent less per barrel to find oil and gas in 2003 than at almost any time in history. With revenues of $210 billion, Exxon-Mobil surged to the top of the Fortune 500 in 2004.

Case Study Discussion Question

1. In your judgment, are acquirers more likely to under- or overestimate anticipated cost savings? Explain your answer.

Case Study 6-7
Albertson's Acquires American Stores: Underestimating the Costs of Integration

In 1999, Albertson's acquired American Stores for $12.5 billion, making it the nation's second largest supermarket chain, with more than 1000 stores. The corporate marriage stumbled almost immediately. Escalating integration costs resulted in a sharp downward revision of its fiscal year 2000 profits. In the quarter ended October 28, 1999, operating profits fell 15% to $185 million, despite an increase in sales of 1.6% to $8.98 billion. Albertson's proceeded to update the Lucky supermarket stores that it had acquired in California and to combine the distribution operations of the two supermarket chains. It appears that Albertson's substantially underestimated the complexity of integrating an acquisition of this magnitude. Albertson's spent about $90 million before taxes to convert more than 400 stores to its information and distribution systems as well as to change the name to Albertson's. By the end of 1999, Albertson's stock had lost more than one-half of its value (Bloomberg.com, November 1, 1999).

Case Study Discussion Questions

1. In your judgment, do you think acquirers' commonly (albeit not deliberately) understate integration costs? Why or why not?
2. Cite examples of expenses you believe are commonly incurred in integrating target companies.

Performance Benchmarking

Benchmarking important functions such as the acquirer's and the target's manufacturing and IT operations and processes is a useful starting point for determining how to integrate these activities. Standard benchmarks include the International Standards Organization's (ISO) 9000 Quality Systems-Model for Quality Assurance in Design, Development, Production, Installation, and Servicing. Other benchmarks that can be used include the U.S. Food and Drug Administration's Good Manufacturing Practices and the Department of Commerce's Malcolm Baldrige Award. Sanderson and Uzumeri (1997, p. 135) provide a comprehensive list of standards-setting organizations.

Integrating Manufacturing Operations

The data revalidation process for integrating and rationalizing facilities and operations requires in-depth discussions with key target company personnel and on-site visits to all facilities. The objective should be to reevaluate overall capacity, the potential for future cost reductions, the age and condition of facilities, adequacy of maintenance budgets, and compliance with environmental laws. Careful consideration should be given to manufacturing capabilities that duplicate those of the acquirer. The integration team also needs to determine if the duplicate facilities are potentially more efficient than those of the buyer. As part of the benchmarking process, the operations of both the acquirer and the target company should be compared with industry standards to properly evaluate their efficiency.

Process effectiveness is an accurate indicator of overall operational efficiency (Porter and Wood, 1998). The four processes that should be examined include planning, materials ordering, order entry, and quality control. For example, production planning is often very inaccurate, particularly when the operations are not easily changed and require long-term forecasts of sales. The production planning and materials ordering functions need to work closely together, because the quantity and composition of the materials ordered depends on the accuracy of sales projections. Inaccurate projections result in shortages or costly excess inventory accumulation.

The order entry activity may offer significant opportunities for cost savings. Companies that produce in anticipation of sales, subsequently satisfying orders from finished product inventories, frequently have huge working capital requirements. For this reason, companies such as personal computer manufacturers are building inventory according to orders received to minimize finished product inventories. A key indicator of the effectiveness of quality control is the percentage of products that go through the manufacturing process without being inspected. Companies whose "first-run yield" (i.e., the percentage of finished products that do not have to be reworked due to quality problems) is in the 70–80% range may have serious quality problems.

Plant consolidation starts with the adoption of a common set of systems and standards for all manufacturing activities. Such standards include cycle time between production runs, cost per unit of output, first-run yield, and scrap rates. Links between the different facilities then are created by sharing information management and processing systems, inventory control, supplier relationships, and transportation links. Vertical integration can be achieved by focusing on different stages of production. Different facilities specialize in the production of selected components, which then are shipped to other facilities to assemble the finished product. Finally, a company may close certain facilities whenever there is excess capacity.

Integrating Information Technology

IT spending constitutes an ever-increasing share of most businesses' budgets. In view of this trend, it is crucial that IT operations be monitored not only by technical people but also by general managers. Studies have shown that about 80% of software projects have failed to meet their performance expectations or deadlines (*Financial Times,* 1996). Almost one-half are scrapped before they are completed, and about one-half cost two or three times their original budgets and take three times as long as expected to complete (*The Wall Street Journal,* November 18, 1996). Studies conclude that managers tend to focus too much on technology and not enough on the people and processes that will use it. If the buyer intends to operate the target company independently, the information systems of the two companies may be kept separate as long as communications links between the two companies' systems can be established. However, if the buyer intends to integrate the target, the process can be daunting. Studies show that nearly 70% of buyers choose to combine their information systems immediately after closing. Almost 90% of acquirers eventually combine these operations (Cossey, 1991). Case Study 6-8 illustrates how Dutch fragrance maker Coty overcame successfully many of the challenges of integrating its supply chain with that of Unilever Cosmetics International.

Case Study 6-8
Integrating Supply Chains: Coty Cosmetics Integrates
Unilever Cosmetics International

In mid-August 2005, Coty, one of the world's largest cosmetic and fragrance manufacturers, acquired Unilever Cosmetics International (UCI), a subsidiary of the Unilever global conglomerate for $800 million. Coty viewed the transaction as one in which it could become a larger player in the prestigious fragrance market of expensive perfumes. Coty believed it could reap economies of scale from having just one sales force, marketing group, etc., selling and managing the two sets of products. It hoped to retain the best people from both organizations. However, Coty's management understood that if it were not done quickly enough they may not realize the potential cost savings and would risk losing key personnel.

By mid-December, Coty's IT team had just completed moving UCI's employees from Unilever's infrastructure and onto Coty's. This involved such tedious work as switching employees from Microsoft's Outlook to Lotus Notes. Coty's information technology (IT) team was faced with the challenge of combining and standardizing the two firms' supply chains including order entry, purchasing, processing, financial, warehouse and shipping systems. At the end of 2006, Coty's management announced that it anticipated that the two firms would be fully integrated by June 30, 2006. From an IT perspective, the challenges were daunting. The new company's supply chain spanned 10 countries and employed four different enterprise resource planning (ERP) systems that had three warehouse systems running five major distribution facilities on two continents. ERP is an information system or process that integrates all production and related applications across an entire corporation.

On January 11–12, 2006, 25 process or function "owners," including the heads of finance, customer service, distribution, and IT, met to create the integration plan for the firm's disparate supply chains. In addition to the multiple distribution centers and ERP systems, operations in each country had unique processes that had to be included in the integration planning effort. For example, Italy was already using the SAP system on which Coty would eventually standardize. The largest customers there usually placed orders at the individual store level and expected products to be delivered to these stores. In contrast, the United Kingdom used a legacy (i.e., a highly customized, nonstandard system) ERP system and Coty's largest customer in the United Kingdom, the Boots pharmacy chain, placed orders electronically and had them delivered to central warehouses. Smaller, but important, differences among the various operations included such things as label reformatting.

Coty's IT team, facing a very demanding schedule, knew they could not accomplish all that needed to be done in the time frame required. Therefore, they started with any system that touched the customer, such as sending an order to the warehouse, shipment notification, or billing. The decision to focus on "customer-facing" systems came at the expense of internal systems, such as daily management reports tracking sales and inventory levels. These systems were to be completed after the June 30, 2006, deadline imposed by senior management.

To minimize confusion, Coty created small project teams consisting of project managers, IT directors, and external consultants. Smaller teams did not require costly overhead like dedicated office space and eliminated chains of command that might have prevented senior IT management from receiving timely and candid feedback on actual progress against the integration plan. The use of such teams is credited with allowing Coty's IT department to combine sales and marketing forces as planned at the beginning of the 2007 fiscal year in July 2006. While much of the customer-facing work was done, many tasks remained. The IT department now had to go back and work out the details it had neglected during the previous integration effort, such as those daily reports its senior mangers wanted and the real-time monitoring of transactions. By setting priorities early in the process and employing small project-focused teams, Coty was able to integrate successfully the complex supply chains of the different firms in a timely manner.

Case Study Discussion Questions

1. Do you agree with Coty management's decision to focus on integrating customer-facing systems first? Explain your answer.
2. How might this emphasis on integrating customer-facing systems have affected the new firm's ability to realize anticipated synergies? Be specific.
3. Discuss the advantages and disadvantages of using small project teams? Be specific.

Integrating Finance

Some target companies will be operated as stand-alone operations, whereas others will be completely merged with the acquirer's existing business. Many international acquisitions involve companies in areas that are geographically remote from the parent company and operate largely independently from the parent. Such situations require a great deal of effort to ensure that the buyer can monitor the financial results of the new business's operations from a distance, even if the parent has its representative permanently on site. The acquirer also should establish a budgeting process and signature approval levels to control spending. Signing authority levels refer to levels of expenditures that must be approved in writing by a designated manager. The magnitude of approval levels will vary by the size of the firm. At a minimum, the budget should require projections of monthly cash inflows and outflows for the coming year.

Integrating Sales: It Is Often Hard to Teach an Old Dog New Tricks

The extent to which the sales forces of the two firms are combined depends on their relative size, the nature of their products and markets, and their geographic location. Based on these considerations, the sales forces may be wholly integrated or operated separately. A relatively small sales force may be readily combined with the larger sales force if the products they sell and the markets they serve are sufficiently similar. In contrast, the sales forces may be kept separate if the products they sell require in-depth understanding of the customers' needs and a detailed knowledge of the product. For example, firms using the "consultative selling" approach employ highly trained specialists to advise current or potential customers on how the firm's product and service offering can be used to solve particular customer problems. Consequently, a firm may have a separate sales force for each product or service sold to specific markets. Sales forces in globally dispersed businesses often are kept separate to reflect the uniqueness of their markets. However, support activities such as sales training or technical support often are centralized and used to support sales forces in several different countries.

The benefits of integrating sales forces include significant cost savings by eliminating duplicate sales representatives and related support expenses such as travel and entertainment expenses, training, and management. A single sales force also may minimize potential confusion by enabling customers to deal with a single sales representative in the purchase of multiple products and services. Moreover, an integrated sales force may facilitate product cross-selling (i.e., the sale of one firm's products to the other firm's customers).

Integrating Marketing: Avoid Brand Confusion

Enabling the customer to see a consistent image in advertising and promotional campaigns is often the greatest challenge facing the integration of the marketing function. For example, the acquired company may be offering an explicit or implied warranty that the acquirer finds unacceptable. However, ensuring consistency should not result in confusing the customer by radically changing a product's image or how it is sold. The location and degree of integration of the marketing function depends on the global nature of the business, the diversity or uniqueness of product lines, and the pace of change in the marketplace. A business with operations worldwide often is inclined to decentralize marketing to the local countries to increase awareness of local laws and cultural patterns. Companies with a large number of product lines, which can be grouped into logical categories or which require extensive product knowledge, may opt to disperse the marketing function to the various operating units. Finally, if the market for a product or set of products is changing rapidly, it is crucial that the marketing function be kept as close to the customer as possible. This expedites the inclusion of changing customer requirements into product development cycles and changes in the advertising and promotional campaigns needed to support the sale of these products.

Integrating Purchasing

According to an analysis of 50 M&As, managing the merged firm's purchasing function efficiently can reduce the total cost of goods and services purchased by merged companies by 10–15%. Companies in this sample were able to recover at least half of the premium paid for the target company by moving aggressively to manage their purchasing activities (Chapman, Dempsey, Ramsdell, and Bell, 1998). For firms in this sample, purchased goods and services, including office furniture, raw materials, and outside contractors, constituted up to 75% of the firms' total spending. The opportunity to reap these substantial savings from suppliers comes immediately following closing of the transaction. A merger creates uncertainty among both companies' suppliers, particularly if they might have to compete against each other for business with the combined firms. Many will offer cost savings and new partnership arrangements, given the merged organization's greater bargaining power to renegotiate contracts. The new company may choose to realize savings by reducing the number of suppliers. As part of the premerger due diligence, both the acquirer and the acquired company should identify their critical suppliers. The list should be kept relatively short. The focus should be on those accounting for the largest share of purchased materials expenses.

Integrating Research and Development

The role of R&D is an extremely important source of value in many M&As. Often the buyer's and seller's organizations are either working on duplicate projects or projects not germane to the buyer's long-term strategy. The integration team responsible for managing the integration of R&D activities needs to define future areas of R&D collaboration and set priorities for future R&D research subject to senior management approval. Barriers to R&D integration include the differing research time frames of different projects and of the personnel involved in conducting research. For example, some scientists and engineers may feel that their current projects require at least 10 years of continuing research, whereas others are looking for results in a much shorter time frame. Another obstacle is that some personnel stand to lose in terms of titles, prestige, and power if they collaborate. Finally, the acquirer's and the target's R&D financial return expectations may be different. The acquirer may wish to give R&D a higher or lower priority in the combined operation of the two companies. A starting point for integrating R&D is to have researchers from both companies make presentations of their work to each other, meet with each other, and colocate. Work teams also can follow a balanced scorecard approach for obtaining funding for their projects. In this process, R&D projects are scored according to their impact on key stakeholders, such as shareholders and customers. Those projects receiving the highest scores are fully funded.

Integrating Human Resources

Traditionally, HR departments have been highly centralized and have been responsible for conducting opinion surveys, assessing managerial effectiveness, developing hiring and staffing plans, and providing training. HR departments are often instrumental in conducting strategic reviews of the strengths and weaknesses of potential target companies, integrating the acquirer's and target's management teams, recommending and implementing pay and benefit plans, and disseminating information about acquisitions. More recently, the trend has been to disperse the HR function to the operating unit. Highly centralized HR functions have been found to be very expensive and not responsive to the local needs of the operating units. Hiring and training often can be more effectively done at the operating unit level. Most of the traditional HR activities are conducted at the operating units with the exception of the administration of benefit plans, management of HR information systems, and in some cases organizational development (Porter and Wood, 1998).

Building a New Corporate Culture

Culture refers to a common set of values, traditions, and beliefs that influence behavior. Large, diverse businesses have an overarching culture and a series of subcultures that reflect local conditions. When two companies with different cultures merge, the newly formed company often will take on a new culture that may be quite different from either the acquirer's or the target's culture. Cultural differences are not inherently bad or good. They can instill creativity in the new company or create a contentious environment.

A firm's culture takes both tangible and intangible forms. Tangible symbols of culture include statements hung on walls containing the firm's mission and principles, as well as the trappings of power and status such as the executive office floor and designated parking spaces. Intangible forms of corporate culture include the behavioral norms communicated through implicit messages about how people are expected to act. Since they represent the extent to which employees and managers actually "walk the talk," these behavioral messages are often far more influential in forming and sustaining corporate culture than the tangible trappings of corporate culture. Kennedy and Moore (2004) argue that the most important source of communication of cultural biases in an organization is the individual behavior of others, especially those with the power to reward appropriate and to punish inappropriate behavior. Since speed in integrating the acquirer and target firms is critical to realizing anticipated synergies, dealing with potentially contentious cultural issues early in the integration process is crucial. For an excellent discussion of how to analyze cultural issues during preintegration planning, see Carleton and Lineberry (2004).

Identifying Cultural Issues through Cultural Profiling

The first step in building corporate cultures is to develop a cultural profile of both the acquirer and the acquired companies. The information may be obtained from employee surveys and interviews and by observing management styles and practices in both companies. The information then is used to show how the two cultures are alike or different and what are the comparative strengths and weaknesses of each culture. Common differences may include having one culture value individualism and the other value teamwork. Cultural issues can be categorized in terms of company size, maturity, and industry, as well as geographic and international considerations. For our purposes, maturity is defined by the number of years in business.

The relative size and maturity of the acquirer and target firms can have major implications for cultural integration. Start-up companies are usually highly unstructured and informal in terms of dress and decision making. Compensation may consist largely of stock options and other forms of deferred income. Benefits, beyond those required by state and federal law, and other "perks," such as company cars, are largely nonexistent. Company policies are frequently either nonexistent, not in writing, or drawn up as needed. Internal controls covering items such as employee expense accounts are often minimal. In contrast, larger, mature companies are frequently more highly structured with well-defined internal controls, compensation structures, benefits packages, and employment policies. Such firms have grown too large and complex to function in an orderly manner without some structure in the form of internal policies and controls. Employees usually have clearly defined job descriptions and career paths. Decision making can be either decentralized at the operating unit level or centralized within a corporate office. In either case, the process for decision making often is well defined. Decision making may be ponderous, requiring consensus within a large management bureaucracy. Cultural differences may be exacerbated in cross-industry or even across segments within the same industry. For example, when Travelers merged with Citicorp, resentment arose as a result of the huge differences between investment banking salaries and those elsewhere in the combined companies (see Case Study 6-9).

Geographic and international considerations also represent important challenges in integrating corporate cultures. Language barriers and different customs, working conditions, work ethics, and legal structures create an entirely new set of challenges in integrating cross-border transactions. If cultures are extremely different, integration may be inappropriate. For this reason, acquiring and acquired companies in international transactions frequently maintain separate corporate headquarters, stock listings, and CEOs for an extended period (*The Wall Street Journal,* September 26, 1996). Moreover, in choosing how to manage an acquisition in a new country, a manager with an in-depth knowledge of the acquirer's priorities, decision-making processes, and operations is appropriate, especially when the acquirer expects to make very large new investments. However, when the acquirer already has existing operations within the country, a manager with substantial industry experience in the country is generally preferable because of their cultural sensitivity and knowledge of local laws and regulations. Local managers are especially helpful when foreign customer requirements are substantially different from domestic customers or when all production is done within the foreign country.

Case Study 6-9 illustrates how the acquirer's sensitivity to potential cultural conflicts before the merger helped maintain the value of the target company. Note how Allianz AG attempted to minimize cultural conflict by keeping Pimco's operations largely intact and allowing a high level of local autonomy. Allianz recognized that the real value in this acquisition is in the expertise and reputation of Pimco's money managers. To retain key personnel, Allianz offered operational independence, employment contracts, and very lucrative deferred compensation packages. Allianz also recognized that the highly successful portfolio management techniques used by Pimco's money managers could best be applied to managing customer accounts in Europe by transferring selected Pimco personnel to their European operations.

Case Study 6-9
Overcoming Culture Clash: Allianz AG Buys Pimco Advisors LP

On November 7, 1999, Allianz AG, the leading German insurance conglomerate, acquired Pimco Advisors LP for $3.3 billion. The Pimco acquisition boosts assets under management at Allianz from $400 billion to $650 billion, making it the sixth largest money manager in the world.

The cultural divide separating the two firms represented a potentially daunting challenge. Allianz's management was well aware that firms distracted by culture clashes and the morale problems and mistrust they breed are less likely to realize the synergies and savings that caused them to acquire the company in the first place. Allianz was acutely aware of the potential problems as a result of difficulties they had experienced following the acquisition of Firemen's Fund, a large U.S.-based property–casualty company.

A major motivation for the acquisition was to obtain the well-known skills of the elite Pimco money managers to broaden Allianz's financial services product offering. Although retention bonuses can buy loyalty in the short run, employees of the acquired firm generally need much more than money in the long term. Pimco's money managers stated publicly that they wanted Allianz to let them operate independently, the way Pimco existed under their former parent, Pacific Mutual Life Insurance Company. Allianz had decided not only to run Pimco as an independent subsidiary but also to move $100 billion of Allianz's assets to Pimco. Bill Gross, Pimco's legendary bond trader, and other top Pimco money managers, now collect about one-fourth of their compensation in the form of Allianz stock. Moreover, most of the top managers have been asked to sign long-term employment contracts and have received retention bonuses.

Joachim Faber, chief of money management at Allianz, played an essential role in smoothing over cultural differences. Led by Faber, top Allianz executives had been visiting

Pimco for months and having quiet dinners with top Pimco fixed income investment officials and their families. The intent of these intimate meetings was to reassure these officials that their operation would remain independent under Allianz's ownership.

Case Study Discussion Questions

1. How did Allianz attempt to retain key employees? In the short run? In the long run?
2. How did the potential for culture clash affect the way Alliance acquired Pimco?
3. What else could Allianz have done to minimize potential culture clash? Be specific.

Following a review of the information obtained from the corporate profile, senior management must decide those characteristics of both cultures that should be emphasized in the new business' culture. As noted previously, when two separate corporate cultures combine, it is crucial to realize from the outset that the combined companies often will create a new culture that in some respects may be distinctly different from the two previous cultures. Because a company's culture is something that evolves over a long time, it often is wishful thinking that changing the culture can be managed carefully or quickly. A more realistic expectation is that employees in the new company can be encouraged to take on a shared vision, set of core values, and behaviors deemed important by senior management. However, getting to the point at which employees wholly embrace management's desired culture may take years and may be unachievable in practice. Case Study 6-10 illustrates how the Tribune Corporation's seeming inattention to the profound cultural differences between itself and the Times Mirror Corporation may have contributed to the failure of this merger to meet expectations.

Case Study 6-10
Culture Clash Exacerbates Efforts of the Tribune Corporation
to Integrate the Times Mirror Corporation

Chicago-based Tribune Corporation (Tribune) owns 11 newspapers, including such flagship publications as the *Chicago Tribune*, the *Los Angeles Times*, and *Newsday*, as well as 25 television stations. Attempting to offset the long-term decline in newspaper readership and advertising revenue, Tribune acquired the Times Mirror (owner of the *Los Angeles Times* newspaper) for $8 billion in 2000. The merger combined two firms that historically had been intensely competitive and which had dramatically different corporate cultures. The Tribune was famous for its emphasis on local coverage, with even its international stories having a connection to Chicago. In contrast, the *L.A. Times* had always maintained a strong overseas and Washington, D.C., presence, with local coverage often ceded to local suburban newspapers. To some Tribune executives, the *L.A. Times* was arrogant and overstaffed. To *L.A. Times* executives, Tribune executives seemed too focused on the "bottom line" to be considered good newspaper people (Ellison, November 11, 2006).

The overarching strategy for the new company was to sell packages of newspaper and local TV advertising in the big urban markets. It soon became apparent that the strategy would be unsuccessful. Consequently, the Tribune's management turned to aggressive cost cutting to improve profitability. The Tribune wanted to encourage centralization and cooperation among its newspapers to cut overlapping coverage and redundant jobs.

Coverage of the same stories by different newspapers owned by the Tribune added substantially to costs. After months of planning, the Tribune moved five bureaus belonging to Times Mirror papers (including the *L.A. Times*) to the same location as its four other bureaus in Washington, D.C., *L.A. Times* staffers objected strenuously to the move saying that their stories needed to be tailored to individual markets and that they did not want to share reporters with local newspapers. As a result of the consolidation, the Tribune's newspapers shared as much as 40% of the content from Washington, D.C., among the papers in 2006, compared to as little as 8% in 2000. Such changes allowed for significant staffing reductions.

In trying to achieve cost savings the firm ran aground in a culture war. Historically, the Times Mirror, unlike the Tribune, had operated its newspapers more as a loose confederation of separate newspapers. Moreover, the Tribune wanted more local focus, while the *L.A. Times* wanted to retain its national and international presence. The controversy came to a head when the *L.A. Times'* editor was forced out in late 2006.

Many newspaper stocks, including the Tribune, had lost more than half of their value between 2004 and 2006. The long-term decline in readership within the Tribune appears to have been exacerbated by the internal culture clash. As a result, the Chandler Trusts, Tribune's largest shareholder, put pressure on the firm to boost shareholder value. In September, the Tribune announced that it wanted to sell the entire newspaper and that it was willing to sell the entire firm. Finally, after months of searching for a suitable buyer, the Tribune corporation announced on April 2, 2007 that it would be acquired by renounced real estate tycoon, Sam Zell, in a transaction valued at $8.2 billion.

Case Study Discussion Questions

1. Why do you believe the Tribune thought it could overcome the substantial cultural differences between itself and the Times Mirror Corporation? Be specific.
2. What would you have done differently following closing in order to overcome the cultural challenges faced by the Tribune? Be specific.

Integrating Corporate Cultures

Sharing common goals, standards, services, and space can be a highly effective and practical way to integrate disparate cultures (Lajoux, 1998, pp. 187–191; Malekzadeh and Nahavandi, 1990). Common goals serve to drive different units to cooperate. For example, at the functional level, setting exact timetables and processes for new product development can drive different operating units to collaborate as project teams to introduce the product by the target date. At the corporate level, incentive plans spanning many years can focus all operating units to pursue the same goals. Although it is helpful in the integration process to have shared or common goals, individuals still must have specific goals to minimize the tendency of some to underperform while benefiting from the collective performance of others. Shared standards or practices enable the adoption of the "best practices" found in one unit or function by another entity. Standards include operating procedures, technological specifications, ethical values, internal controls, employee performance measures, and comparable reward systems throughout the combined companies. Finally, some functional services can be centralized and shared by multiple departments or operating units. The centralized functions then provide services to the operating units. Commonly centralized services include accounting, legal, public relations, internal audit, and information technology. The most common way to share services is to use a common staff. Alternatively, a firm can create a support services unit and allow operating units to purchase services from it or to buy similar services outside the company.

Isolating target company employees in a separate building or even a floor of the same building will impair the integration process. Mixing offices or even locating acquired company employees in space adjacent to the parent's offices is a highly desirable way to improve communication and idea sharing. Sharing laboratories, computer rooms, or libraries also can facilitate communication and cooperation. Case Study 6-11 illustrates the many gut-wrenching challenges that must be overcome in integrating two highly similar yet complex businesses.

Case Study 6-11
Avoiding the Merger Blues: American Airlines Integrates TWA

Trans World Airlines (TWA) had been tottering on the brink of bankruptcy for several years, jeopardizing a number of jobs and the communities in which they are located. Despite concerns about increased concentration, regulators approved American's proposed buyout of TWA in 2000 largely on the basis of the "failing company doctrine." This doctrine suggested that two companies should be allowed to merge despite an increase in market concentration if one of the firms can be saved from liquidation.

American, now the world's largest airline, has struggled to assimilate such smaller acquisitions as AirCal in 1987 and Reno Air in 1998. Now, in trying to meld together two major carriers with very different and deeply ingrained cultures, a combined workforce of 113,000 and 900 jets serving 300 cities, American faced even bigger challenges. For example, because switches and circuit breakers are in different locations in TWA's cockpits than in American's, the combined airlines must spend millions of dollars to rearrange cockpit gear and to train pilots how to adjust to the differences. TWA's planes also are on different maintenance schedules than American's jets. For American to see any savings from combining maintenance operations, it gradually had to synchronize those schedules. Moreover, TWA's workers had to be educated in American's business methods, and the carrier's reservations had to be transferred to American's computer systems. Planes had to be repainted, and seats had to be rearranged (McCartney, 2001).

Combining airline operations always has proved to be a huge task. American has studied the problems that plagued other airline mergers, such as Northwest, which moved too quickly to integrate Republic Airlines in 1986. This integration proved to be one of the most turbulent in history. The computers failed on the first day of merged operations. Angry workers vandalized ground equipment. For 6 months, flights were delayed and crews did not know where to find their planes. Passenger suitcases were misrouted. Former Republic pilots complained that they were being demoted in favor of Northwest pilots. Friction between the two groups of pilots continued for years. In contrast, American adopted a more moderately paced approach as a result of the enormity and complexity of the tasks involved in putting the two airlines together. The model they followed was Delta Airline's acquisition of Western Airlines in 1986. Delta succeeded by methodically addressing every issue, although the mergers were far less complex because they involved merging far fewer computerized systems.

Even Delta had its problems, however. In 1991, Delta purchased Pan American World Airways' European operations. Pan Am's international staff had little in common with

Delta's largely domestic-minded workforce, creating a tremendous cultural divide in terms of how the combined operations should be managed. In response to the 1991–1992 recession, Delta scaled back some routes, cut thousands of jobs, and reduced pay and benefits for workers who remained.

Before closing, American had set up an integration management team of 12 managers, 6 each from American and TWA. An operations czar, who was to become the vice chair of the board of the new company, directed the team. The group met daily by phone for as long as 2 hours, coordinating all merger-related initiatives. American set aside a special server to log the team's decisions. The team concluded that the two lynchpins to a successful integration process were successfully resolving labor problems and meshing the different computer systems. To ease the transition, William Compton, TWA's CEO, agreed to stay on with the new company through the transition period as president of the TWA operations.

The day after closing the team empowered 40 department managers at each airline to get involved. Their tasks included replacing TWA's long-term airport leases with short-term ones, combining some cargo operations, changing over the automatic deposits of TWA employees' paychecks, and implementing American's environmental response program at TWA in case of fuel spills. Work teams, consisting of both American and TWA managers, identified more than 10,000 projects that must be undertaken before the two airlines can be fully integrated.

Some immediate cost savings were realized as American was able to negotiate new lease rates on TWA jets that are $200 million a year less than what TWA was paying. These savings were a result of the increased credit rating of the combined companies. However, other cost savings were expected to be modest during the 12 months following closing as the two airlines were operated separately. TWA's union workers, who would have lost their jobs had TWA shut down, have been largely supportive of the merger. American has won an agreement from its own pilots' union on a plan to integrate the carriers' cockpit crews. Seniority issues proved to be a major hurdle. Getting the mechanics' and flight attendants' unions on board required substantial effort. All of TWA's licenses had to be switched to American. These ranged from the Federal Aviation Administration operating certificate to TWA's liquor license in all the states.

Case Study Discussion Questions

1. In your opinion, what are the advantages and disadvantages of moving to integrate operations quickly? What are the advantages and disadvantages of moving more slowly and deliberately?
2. Why did American choose to use managers from both airlines to direct the integration of the two companies? What are the specific benefits in doing so?
3. How did the interests of the various stakeholders to the merger affect the complexity of the integration process?

Despite the various approaches taken to achieve cooperation in corporations with significantly disparate cultures, the challenges are enormous. In early 2006, Time Warner president, Jeffre Bewkes stopped requiring its corporate units to cooperate. This was a complete philosophical turnabout from what the firm espoused following its 2001 merger with AOL. At that time, executives promised to create a well-oiled vertically integrated profit generator. Books and magazines and other forms of content would feed the television, movie, and Internet operations. Now managers are encouraged to cooperate only if they cannot make more money on the outside. Other media companies such as Viacom and Liberty Media have already broken themselves up because their efforts to achieve corporate-wide synergies with disparate media businesses proved unsuccessful.

Integrating Business Alliances

Business alliances, particularly those created to consolidate resources such as manufacturing facilities or sales forces, also must pay close attention to integration activities. Unlike M&As, alliances usually involve shared control. Successful implementation requires maintaining a good working relationship between venture partners. When partners cannot maintain a good working relationship, the alliance is destined to fail. The breakdown in the working relationship is often a result of an inadequate integration (Lynch, 1993, pp. 189–205).

Integrating Mechanisms

Robert Porter Lynch suggests six integration mechanisms to apply to business alliances: (1) leadership, (2) teamwork and role clarification, (3) control by coordination, (4) policies and values, (5) consensus decision making, and (6) resource commitments.

Leadership

Although the terms leadership and management often are used interchangeably, there are critical differences. A leader sets direction and makes things happen, whereas a manager follows through and ensures that things continue to happen. Leadership involves vision, drive, enthusiasm, and strong selling skills; management involves communication, planning, delegating, coordinating, problem solving, making choices, and clarifying lines of responsibility. Successful alliances require the proper mix of both sets of skills. The leader must provide clear direction, values, and behaviors to create a culture that focuses on the alliance's strategic objectives as its top priority. Managers foster teamwork and promote long-term stability in the shared control environment of the business alliance.

Teamwork and Role Clarification

Teamwork is the underpinning that makes alliances work. Teamwork comes from trust, fairness, and discipline. Teams reach across functional lines and often consist of diverse experts or lower-level managers with critical problem-solving skills. The team provides functional managers with the broader, flexible staffing to augment their own specialized staff. Teams tend to create better coordination and communication at lower levels of the alliance, as well as between partners in the venture. Because teams represent individuals with varied backgrounds and possibly conflicting agendas, they may foster rather than resolve conflict. The alliance manager must be diligent in clarifying what behaviors will not be tolerated.

Coordination

In contrast to an acquisition, no one company is in charge. Alliances do not lend themselves to control through mandate; rather, in the alliance, control is best exerted through coordination. The best alliance managers are those who coordinate activities through effective communication. When problems arise, the manager's role is to manage the decision-making process, not necessarily to make the decision.

Policies and Values

Alliance employees need to understand how decisions are made, what the priorities are, who will be held accountable, and how rewards will be determined. When people know where they stand and what to expect, they are better able to deal with ambiguity and uncertainty. This level of clarity can be communicated through a distinct set of policies and procedures that are well understood by joint venture or partnership employees.

Consensus Decision Making

Consensus decision making does not mean that decisions are based on unanimity. Rather, decisions are based on the premise that all participants have had an opportunity to express their opinions and that they are willing to accept the final decision even though they may not be in complete agreement. Like any other business, operating decisions must be made within a reasonable time frame. The formal decision-making structure will vary with the type of legal structure. Joint ventures often have a board of directors and a management committee, which meet quarterly and monthly, respectively. Projects normally are governed by steering committees.

Resource Commitments

Many alliances are started to take advantage of complementary skills or resources available from alliance participants. The alliance can achieve its strategic objective only if all parties to the alliance live up to the resources they agreed to commit. The failure of one party to meet its commitments will erode trust and limit the alliance's ability to meet its objectives.

Things to Remember

Postclosing integration is a critical phase of the M&A process. Integration itself can be viewed in terms of a process consisting of six activities: integration planning, developing communication plans, creating a new organization, developing staffing plans, functional integration, and integrating corporate cultures. Both communication and cultural integration extend beyond what normally is considered the conclusion of the integration period. Combining companies must be done quickly (i.e., 6–12 months) to achieve proper staffing levels, eliminate redundant assets, and generate the financial returns expected by shareholders. Delay contributes to employee anxiety and accelerates the loss of key talent and managers; delay also contributes to the deterioration of employee morale among those that remain. The loss of key talent and managers often is viewed as the greatest risk associated with the integration phase. Nevertheless, although speed is important to realize cost savings and retain key employees, highly complex operations must be integrated in a more deliberate and systematic fashion to minimize long-term problems.

Successfully integrated M&As are those that demonstrate leadership by candidly and continuously communicating a clear vision, a set of values, and clear priorities to all employees. Successful integration efforts are those that are well planned, that appoint an integration manager and a team with clearly defined lines of authority, and that make the tough decisions early in the process. These decisions include organizational structure, reporting relationships, spans of control, people selection, roles and responsibilities, and workforce reduction. During integration, the focus should be on those issues having the greatest near-term impact.

Unlike M&As, the integration of business alliances tends to be phased. Resources are contributed at the outset to enable the formation of the alliance. Subsequent resource contributions are subject to a lengthy negotiation process in which the partners are trying to get the most favorable terms. Because alliances involve shared control, the integration process requires good working relationships with the other participants. Successful integration also requires leadership capable of defining a clear sense of direction and well-defined priorities, and managers who accomplish their objectives as much by coordinating activities through effective communication as by unilateral decision making. Like M&As, cross-functional teams are used widely to achieve integration. Finally, the successful integration of business alliances, as well as M&As, demands that the necessary resources, in terms of the best people, the appropriate skills, and sufficient capital, be committed to the process.

Chapter Discussion Questions

6-1. Why is the integration phase of the acquisition process considered so important?

6-2. Why should acquired companies be integrated quickly?

6-3. Why might the time required to integrate acquisitions vary by industry?

6-4. What are the costs of employee turnover?

6-5. Why is candid and continuous communication so important during the integration phase?

6-6. What are the messages that might be communicated to the various audiences or stakeholders of the new company?

6-7. Cite examples of difficult decisions that should be made early in the integration process.

6-8. Cite the contract-related "transition issues" that should be resolved before closing.

6-9. How does the process for integrating business alliances differ from that of integrating an acquisition?

6-10. How are the processes for integrating business alliances and M&As similar?

Answers to these Chapter Discussion Questions are available in the Online Instructor's Manual for instructors using this book.

Chapter Business Case

Case Study 6-12
Alcatel Merges with Lucent Highlighting Cross-Cultural Issues

Alcatel SA and Lucent Technologies signed a merger pact on April 3, 2006, to form a Paris-based telecommunications equipment giant. The combined firms will be led by Lucent's Chief Executive Officer Patricia Russo. Her charge will be to meld two cultures during a period of dynamic industry change. Lucent and Alcatel have been considered natural merger partners because they have overlapping product lines and different strengths. More than two-thirds of Alcatel's business comes from Europe, Latin America, the Middle East, and Africa. The French firm is particularly strong in equipment that enables regular telephone lines to carry high-speed Internet and digital television traffic. Nearly two-thirds of Lucent's business is in the United States. The new company is expected to eliminate 10% of its workforce of 88,000 and to save $1.7 billion annually within 3 years by eliminating overlapping functions.

While billed as a merger of equals, Alcatel of France, the larger of the two, will take the lead in shaping the future of the new firm, whose shares will be listed in Paris, not in the United States. The board will have six members from the current Alcatel board and six from the current Lucent board, as well as two independent directors that must be European nationals. Alcatel CEO, Serge Tehuruk, will serve as the Chairman of the Board. Much of Ms. Russo's senior management team, including the chief operating officer, chief financial officer, the head of the key emerging markets unit, and the director of human resources will come from Alcatel. To allay U.S. national security concerns, the new company will form an independent U.S. subsidiary to administer American government contracts. This subsidiary would be separately managed by a board composed of three U.S. citizens acceptable to the U.S. government.

International combinations involving U.S. companies have had a spotty history in the telecommunications industry. For example, British Telecommunications PLC and AT&T Corp. saw their joint venture, Concert, formed in the late 1990s collapse after only a few years. Even outside of the telecom industry, trans-Atlantic mergers have been fraught with problems. For example, Daimler-Benz's 1998 deal with Chrysler, which was also billed as a merger of equals, was heavily weighted toward the German company from the outset.

In integrating Lucent and Alcatel, Ms. Russo faces a number of practical obstacles including who will work out of Alcatel's Paris headquarters. Ms Russo, who became Lucent's chief executive in 2000 and does not speak French, will have to navigate the challenges of doing business in France. The French government has a big influence on French companies and remains a large shareholder in the telecom and defense sectors. Ms. Russo's first big fight might come over job cuts anticipated in the merger plan. French unions tend to be strong and employees enjoy more legal protections than elsewhere. Hundreds of thousands took to the streets in mid-2006 to protest a new law that would make it easier for firms to hire and fire younger workers. Ms Russo has had extensive experience with big layoffs. At Lucent, she helped orchestrate spin-offs, layoffs, and buyouts involving nearly four-fifths of the firm's workforce.

Making choices about cuts in a combined company will likely be even more difficult, with Ms. Russo facing a level of resistance in France unheard of in the United States, where it is generally accepted that most workers are subject to layoffs and dismissals. Alcatel has been able to make many of its job cuts in recent years outside of France, thereby avoiding the greater difficulty of shedding French workers. Lucent workers may fear that they will be dismissed first simply because it is easier than dismissing their French counterparts. The election of reform-minded Nicolas Barkozy in May 2007 in France may make decisions of where to lay off workers easier for Alcatel management.

Ms. Russo will have to avoid paralysis. The merger of Daimler-Benz and Chrysler has been a major disappointment, partly because of initial management confusion over whether it was a merger of equals or a takeover by Daimler. In 2004, the merged company paid $300 million to settle a class-action lawsuit charging that former Daimler CEO Jurgen Schrempp misled investors with his description of the transaction as a merger of equals. Finally, on May 14, 2007, Daimler sold Chrysler to Cerberus Capital Management for what amounted to Cerberus' willingness to accept responsibility for Chrysler's future retirement and health liabilities.

Case Study Discussion Questions

1. Explain the logic behind combining the two companies. Be specific.
2. What are the major challenges the management of the combined companies are likely to face? How would you recommend resolving these issues?
3. Most corporate mergers are beset by differences in corporate cultures. How do cross-border transactions compound these differences?
4. Why do you think mergers, both domestic and cross-border, are often communicated by the acquirer and target firms' management as mergers of equals?
5. In what way would you characterize this transaction as a merger of equals? In what ways should it not be considered a merger of equals?

Answers to these Case Study Discussion Questions are available in the Online Instructor's Manual for instructors using this book.

Chapter Business Case

Case Study 6-13
The Travelers and Citicorp Integration Experience

Promoted as a merger of equals, the merger of Travelers and Citicorp to form Citigroup illustrates many of the problems encountered during postmerger integration. At $73 billion, the merger between Travelers and Citicorp was the second largest merger in 1998 and is an excellent example of how integrating two businesses can be far more daunting than consummating the transaction. Their experience demonstrates how everything can be going smoothly in most of the businesses being integrated, except for one, and how this single business can sop up all of management's time and attention to correct its problems. In some respects, it highlights the ultimate challenge of every major integration effort: getting people to work together. It also spotlights the complexity of managing large, intricate businesses when authority at the top is divided among several managers.

The strategic rationale for the merger relied heavily on cross-selling the financial services products of both corporations to the other's customers. The combination would create a financial services giant capable of making loans, accepting deposits, selling mutual funds, underwriting securities, selling insurance, and dispensing financial planning advice. Citicorp had relationships with thousands of companies around the world. In contrast, Travelers' Salomon Smith Barney unit dealt with relatively few companies. It was believed that Salomon could expand its underwriting and investment banking business dramatically by having access to the much larger Citicorp commercial customer base. Moreover, Citicorp lending officers, who frequently had access only to mid-level corporate executives at companies within their customer base, would have access to more senior executives as a result of Salomon's investment banking relationships.

Although the characteristics of the two businesses seemed to be complementary, motivating all parties to cooperate proved a major challenge. Because of the combined firm's co-CEO arrangement, the lack of clearly delineated authority exhausted management time and attention without resolving major integration issues. Some decisions proved to be relatively easy. Others were not. Citicorp, in stark contrast to Travelers, was known for being highly bureaucratic with marketing, credit, and finance departments at the global, North American, and business unit levels. North American departments were eliminated quickly. Salomon was highly regarded in the fixed income security area, so Citicorp's fixed income operations were folded into Salomon. Citicorp received Salomon's foreign exchange trading operations because of their premerger reputation in this business. However, both the Salomon and Citicorp derivatives business tended to overlap and compete for the same customers. Each business unit within Travelers and Citicorp had a tendency to believe they "owned" the relationship with their customers and were hesitant to introduce others that might assume control over this relationship. Pay was also an issue, as investment banker salaries in Salomon Smith Barney tended to dwarf those of Citicorp middle-level managers. When it came time to cut costs, issues arose around who would be terminated.

Citicorp was organized along three major product areas: global corporate business, global consumer business, and asset management. The merged companies' management structure consisted of three executives in the global corporate business area and two in each of the other major product areas. Each area contained senior managers from both companies. Moreover, each area reported to the cochairs and CEOs John Reed and Sanford Weill, former CEOs of Citicorp and Travelers, respectively. Of the three major product areas, the integration of two was progressing well, reflecting the collegial atmosphere of the top managers in both areas. However, the global business area was well behind schedule, beset by major riffs among the three top managers. Travelers' corporate culture was characterized as strongly focused on the bottom line, with a lean corporate overhead structure and a strong predisposition to impose its style on the Citicorp culture. In contrast, Citicorp, under John Reed, tended to be more focused on the strategic vision of the new company rather than on day-to-day operations.

The organizational structure coupled with personal differences among certain key managers ultimately resulted in the termination of James Dimon, who had been a star as president of Travelers before the merger. On July 28, 1999, the cochair arrangement was dissolved. Sanford Weill assumed responsibility for the firm's operating businesses and financial function, and John Reed became the focal point for the company's Internet, advanced development, technology, human resources, and legal functions. This change in organizational structure was intended to help clarify lines of authority and to overcome some of the obstacles in managing a large and complex set of businesses that result from split decision-making authority. On February 28, 2000, John Reed formally retired.

Although the power-sharing arrangement may have been necessary to get the deal done, Reed's leaving made it easier for Weill to manage the business. The co-CEO arrangement had contributed to an extended period of indecision, resulting in part to their widely divergent views. Reed wanted to support Citibank's Internet efforts with substantial and sustained investment, whereas the more bottom-line–oriented Weill wanted to contain costs.

With its $112 billion in annual revenue in 2000, Citigroup ranked sixth on the Fortune 500 list. Its $13.5 billion in profit was second only to Exxon-Mobil's $17.7 billion. The combination of Salomon Smith Barney's investment bankers and Citibank's commercial bankers is working very effectively. In a year-end 2000 poll by *Fortune* magazine of the Most Admired U.S. companies, Citigroup was the clear winner. Among the 600 companies judged by a poll of executives, directors, and securities analysts, it ranked first for using its assets wisely and for long-term investment value (Loomis, 2001). However, this early success has taken its toll on management. Of the 15 people initially on the management committee, only 5 remain in addition to Weill. Among those that have left are all those that were with Citibank when the merger was consummated. Ironically, in 2004, James Dimon emerged as the head of the JP Morgan Chase powerhouse in direct competition with his former boss Sandy Weill of Citigroup.

Case Study Discussion Questions

1. Why did Citibank and Travelers resort to a co-CEO arrangement? What are the advantages and disadvantages of such an arrangement?
2. Describe the management challenges you think may face Citigroup's management team as a result of the increasing global complexity of Citigroup?
3. Identify the key differences between Travelers' and Citibank's corporate cultures. Discuss ways you would resolve such differences.
4. One justification for the merger was the cross-selling opportunities it would provide. Comment on the challenges involved in making such a marketing strategy work.

Answers to these Case Study Discussion Questions are available in the Online Instructor's Manual for instructors using this book.

References

Alexander, Marcus, Andrew Campbell, and Michael Gould, "Parenting Advantage," *Prism,* Arthur D. Little, Inc. 2nd Quarter 1995, pp. 23–33.

Bekier, Matthias M., Anna J. Bogardus, and Tim Oldham, "Why Mergers Fail," *The McKinsey Quarterly,* 4, 2001, p. 3.

Bloomberg.com, "Albertson's and American Stores: A Marriage in Trouble," November 1, 1999.

BusinessWeek, "The Case against Mergers," October 31, 1995, pp. 122–125.

BusinessWeek, "A Merger's Bitter Harvest," February 5, 2001, p. 112.

Campbell, Andrew, David Sadler, and Richard Koch, *Breakup! When Companies Are Worth More Dead than Alive,* Capstone, Oxford, 1997.

Carey, Dennis C., and Dayton Ogden, *The Human Side of M&A,* Oxford University Press, Oxford, 2004, p. 162.

Carleton, J. Robert, and Claude S. Lineberry, *Achieving Post-Merger Success*, Wiley & Sons, New York, 2004.

Chakrabarti, Alok, "Organizational Factors in Post-Acquisition Performance," *IEEE Transactions in Engineering Management,* Vol. 37, November 1990, pp. 259–266.

Chapman, Timothy L., Jack J. Dempsey, Glenn Ramsdell, and Trudy E. Bell, "Purchasing's Big Moment—After a Merger," *The McKinsey Quarterly,* 1, 1998, pp. 56–65.

Cisco Systems, "Annual Report, 1999," www.reportgallery.com.

Cossey, Bernard, "Systems Assessment in Acquired Subsidiaries," *Accountancy,* January 1991, pp. 98–99.

Down, James W., "The M&A Game Is Often Won or Lost after the Deal," *Management Review Executive Forum,* November 1995, p. 10.

Ellison, Sarah, "Clash of Cultures Exacerbates Woes for Tribune Co.," *The Wall Street Journal,* November 11, 2006, p. 1.

Ferenczy, Ilene, *Employee Benefits in Mergers and Acquisitions*, Aspen Publishers, New York, 2005.

Financial Times, "Bugged by Failures," November 29, 1996, p. 8.

Flanagan, David J., and K. C. O'Shaughnessy, "Determinants of Layoff Announcements Following Mergers and Acquisitions: An Empirical Investigation," *Strategic Management Journal,* 19 (10), October 1998, pp. 989–999.

Frank, Robert, and Robin Sidel, "Firms that Lived by the Deal in the 1990s Now Sink by the Dozens," *The Wall Street Journal,* June 6, 2002, p. A1.

Fubini, David G., Colin Price, and Maurizio Zollo, "Successful Mergers Start at the Top," *McKinsey Quarterly*, November 8, 2006.

Galpin, Timothy, and Mark Herndon, *The Complete Guide to Mergers and Acquisitions: Process Tools to Support Integration at Every Level*, 2nd Ed., Jossey Bass, San Francisco, 2007.

Goldblatt, Henry, "Merging at Internet Speed," *Fortune,* November 8, 1999, pp. 164–165.

Hayes, Robert H., "The Human Side of Acquisitions," *Management Review,* November 1979, p. 41.

Kennedy, Kevin, and Mary Moore, *Going the Distance: Why Some Companies Dominate and Others Fail*, Prentice-Hall, Upper Saddle River, NJ, 2003, p. 155.

Kranhold, Kathryn, "GE's Water Unit Remains Stagnant As It Struggles to Integrate Acquisitions," *The Wall Street Journal*, August 22, 2006, p. C2.

Lajoux, Alexandra Reed, *The Art of M&A Integration,* McGraw-Hill, New York, 1998.

Loomis, Carol J., "Sandy Weill's Monster," *Fortune*, April 16, 2001, pp. 107–110.

Lord, Michael D., and Annette L. Ranft, "Acquiring New Knowledge: The Role of Retaining Human Capital in Acquisitions of High Tech Firms," *Journal of High Technology Management Research,* 11 (2), Autumn 2000, pp. 295–320.

Lynch, Robert P., *Business Alliances Guide: The Hidden Competitive Weapon,* Wiley & Sons, New York, 1993.

Malekzadeh, Ali R., and Nahavandi, Afsaneh, "Making Mergers Work by Managing Cultures," *Journal of Business Strategy,* 11 (3), May/June 1990, pp. 55–57.

Marks, Mitchell L., *From Turmoil to Triumph: New Life after Mergers, Acquisitions, and Downsizing*, Lexington Books, Lexington, MA, 1996.

McCartney, Scott, "Flying Lessons," *The Wall Street Journal*, April 20, 2001, p. 1.

McKinsey & Company, "Creating Shareholder Value through Merger and/or Acquisition: A McKinsey & Company Perspective," April 1987, cited in Tom Copeland, Tim Koller, and Jack Murrin, eds., *Valuation: Measuring and Managing the Value of Companies,* Wiley & Sons, New York, 1990, p. 321.

McNatt, Robert, "Chrysler Not Quite So Equal," *BusinessWeek*, November 13, 2000.

Page, M. Beth, "Done Deal," *Your Guide to Mergers and Acquisitions Due Diligence*, Authenticity Press, Lanham, Maryland, 2006.

Porter, Richard, and Cynthia N. Wood, "Post-Merger Integration," in David J. Ben Daniel and Arthur H. Rosenbloom, eds., *International M&A: Joint Ventures and Beyond*, Wiley & Sons, New York, 1998, pp. 459–497.

Sanderson, Susan, and Mustafa Uzumeri, *The Innovative Imperative: Strategies for Managing Products, Models, and Families*, Irwin Professional, Publishing, Burr Ridge, IL, 1997.

Schweiger, David M., *M&A Integration: Framework for Executives and Managers*, McGraw-Hill, New York, 2002.

Shivdasani, Anil, "Board Composition, Ownership Structure, and Hostile Takeovers," *Journal of Accounting and Economics*, 16, 1993, pp. 167–198.

Tam, Pui-Wing, "An Elaborate Plan Forces HHP Union to Stay on Target," *The Wall Street Journal*, April 28, 2003, p. 1.

The Wall Street Journal, "When Things Go Wrong," November 18, 1996, p. R-25.

The Wall Street Journal, "Disability Claims Mirror Rising Job Cuts," November 21, 1996, p. A-2.

The Wall Street Journal, "Together but Equal," September 26, 1996, p. R-20.

Tierney, Christine, "Can Schrempp Stop the Careening at Chrysler?," *BusinessWeek*, December 4, 2000, p. 40.

Walsh, James P., "Doing a Deal: Merger and Acquisition Negotiations and Their Impact Upon Target Company Top Management Turnover," *Strategic Management Journal*, Vol. 10, July/August 1989, pp. 307–322.

Walsh, James P., and John W. Ellwood, "Mergers, Acquisitions, and the Pruning of Managerial Deadwood," *Strategic Management Journal*, 12 (3), March 1991, pp. 201–217.

Wulf, Julie, and Raghuram Rajan, "The Flattening Firm: Evidence from Panel Data on the Changing Nature of Corporate Hierarchies," Working Paper, University of Chicago, Chicago, 2003.

Merger and Acquisition Valuation and Modeling

CHAPTER ◆ 7

A Primer on Merger and Acquisition Cash-Flow Valuation

The greater danger for most of us is not that our aim is too high and we might miss it, but that it is too low and we reach it.

—Michelangelo

Inside M&A: The Importance of Distinguishing between Operating and Nonoperating Assets

On February 14, 2005, Verizon Communications and MCI Inc. executives announced that they had agreed to a deal in which MCI shareholders would receive $6.7 billion for 100% of MCI stock. Verizon's management argued that the deal would cost their shareholders only $5.3 billion in Verizon stock, with MCI agreeing to pay its shareholders a special dividend of $1.4 billion contingent upon their approval of the transaction. The $1.4 billion special dividend reduces MCI's cash in excess of what is required to meet its normal operating cash requirements.

To understand the actual purchase price, it is necessary to distinguish between operating and nonoperating assets. Without the special dividend, the $1.4 billion in cash would transfer automatically to Verizon as a result of the purchase of MCI's stock. Verizon would have to increase its purchase price by an equivalent amount to reflect the face value of this nonoperating cash asset. Consequently, the purchase price would be $6.7 billion. With the special dividend, the excess cash transferred to Verizon is reduced by $1.4 billion, and the purchase price is $5.3 billion. In fact, the alleged price reduction is no price reduction at all. It simply reflects Verizon's shareholders receiving $1.4 billion less in acquired assets. Moreover, since the $1.4 billion represents excess cash that would have been reinvested in MCI or paid out to shareholders anyway, the MCI shareholders are simply getting the cash earlier than they may have otherwise.

Chapter Overview

There are five basic methods of valuation. These include the following: income or discounted cash flow (DCF), market-based, asset-oriented, replacement cost, and the contingent claims or real options approach. The purpose of this chapter is to provide an overview of the basics of valuing mergers and acquisitions (M&As) using discounted cash-flow methods. The remaining valuation methods will be discussed in Chapter 8.

This chapter begins with a brief review of rudimentary finance concepts including measuring risk and return, the capital asset pricing model (CAPM), and the effects of leverage on risk and return. The cash-flow definitions, free cash flow to equity or to the firm, discussed in this chapter will be used in valuation problems in subsequent chapters. The distinction between these cash-flow definitions will be particularly relevant for the discussion of leveraged buyouts in Chapter 13. This chapter concludes with a discussion of the valuation of a firm's debt and other obligations and nonoperating assets such as excess cash and marketable securities, investments in other firms, unutilized and pension fund assets, and intangible assets. For more exhaustive analyses of valuation, see Damodaran (2001) and Copeland, Koller, and Murrin (2005). For those seeking a more rigorous quantitative approach to valuation, see Abrams (2001) and Levy (2004). A review of this chapter is available on the CD-ROM accompanying this book. The appendix to this chapter addresses alternative ways to project cash flows.

Required Returns

Investors require a minimum rate of return on an investment to compensate them for the level of perceived risk associated with that investment. The required rate of return must be at least equal to what the investor can receive on alternative investments exhibiting a comparable level of perceived risk. For an excellent discussion of basic concepts of finance, see Gitman (2000), Lasher (2000), and Moyer, McGuigan, and Kretlow (1998).

Cost of Equity and the Capital Asset Pricing Model

The cost of equity (k_e) is the rate of return required to induce investors to purchase a firm's equity. The cost of equity also can be viewed as an ***opportunity cost*** (i.e., a foregone opportunity) because it represents the rate of return investors could earn by investing in equities of comparable risk. The cost of equity can be estimated by using the capital asset pricing model (CAPM), which measures the relationship between expected risk and expected return. It postulates that investors require higher rates of return for accepting higher levels of risk. Specifically, the CAPM states that the expected return on an asset or security is equal to a risk-free rate of return plus a risk premium.

Selecting the Appropriate Risk-Free Rate of Return

A ***risk-free rate of return*** is one for which the expected return is certain. For a return to be considered risk-free over some future time period, it must be free of default risk and there must not be any uncertainty about the reinvestment rate (i.e., the rate of return that can be earned at the end of the investor's holding period). While there is widespread agreement on the use of U.S. Treasury securities as assets that are free of default risk, there is some controversy over whether a short- or long-term Treasury rate should be used in applying the CAPM. Whether you should use a short- or long-term rate depends on how long the investor intends to hold the investment. Consequently, if the investor anticipates holding an investment for 5 or 10 years, she needs to use either a 5- or 10-year Treasury bond rate. A 3-month Treasury bill rate is not free of risk for a 5- or 10-year period, since interest and principal received at maturity must be reinvested at 3-month intervals, resulting in considerable reinvestment risk. In this book, a 10-year Treasury bond rate will be used to represent the risk-free rate of return. This would be most appropriate for a strategic acquirer interested in valuing a target firm with the intent of operating the firm over an extended time period.

Estimating Market Risk Premiums

The *market risk or equity premium* refers to the additional rate of return in excess of the risk-free rate that investors require to purchase a firm's equity. While the risk premium represents the perceived risk of the stock and should therefore be forward looking, obtaining precise estimates of future market returns often is exceedingly difficult. The objectivity of Wall Street analysts' projections is problematic and efforts to develop sophisticated models show results that vary widely with their underlying assumptions. Consequently, analysts often look to historical data, despite results that vary based on time periods selected and whether returns are calculated as arithmetic or geometric averages. CAPM relates the cost of equity to the risk-free rate of return and market risk premium as follows:

$$\text{CAPM: } k_e = R_f + \beta(R_m - R_f), \tag{7-1}$$

where
R_f = risk-free rate of return
β = beta (See the section of this chapter entitled "Analyzing Risk.")
R_m = the expected rate of return on equities
$R_m - R_f$ = 5.5% [i.e., the simple average of the arithmetic and geometric average equity premium between 1900 and 2002: Arzac (2005), p. 39.]

Despite its intuitive appeal, the CAPM has limitations. Betas tend to vary over time and are quite sensitive to the time period and methodology employed in their estimation. For a detailed discussion of these issues, see Fama and French (1992, 1993, 2006). Other studies show that the market risk premium is unstable, lower during periods of prosperity and higher during periods of economic slowdowns (Claus and Thomas, 2001; Easton, Taylor, Shroff, and Sougiannis, 2001).

While there is controversy around the measurement of the market risk or equity premium derived from arithmetic or geometric averages of historic returns, the author has chosen to calculate the simple average of the historical rates estimated by using both approaches. Also, some may argue that the "risk premium" should be changed to reflect fluctuations in the stock market. However, history shows that such fluctuations are relatively short term in nature. Consequently, the risk premium should reflect more long-term considerations such as the expected holding period of the investor or acquiring company. Therefore, for the strategic or long-term investor or acquirer, the risk premium should approximate the 5.5% long-term historical average. Escherich (1998) found in a survey of 200 companies that most firms estimate the cost of equity using CAPM and use an equity risk premium of between 5 and 7%.

Since CAPM measures a stock's risk only relative to the overall market and ignores returns on assets other than stocks, some analysts have begun using multifactor models. Such models adjust the CAPM by adding other risk factors that determine asset returns such as firm size, bond default premiums, the bond term structure (i.e., difference between short- and long-term interest rates on securities which differ only by maturity), and inflation.

Adjusting CAPM for Firm Size

Studies show that of these factors firm size appears to be among the most important (Bernard, Healy, and Palepu, 2000; Pastor and Stambaugh, 2001). The size factor serves as a proxy for factors such as smaller firms being subject to higher default risk and generally being less liquid than large capitalization firms (Berk, 1995). Table 7-1 provides estimates of the amount of the adjustment to the cost of equity to adjust for firm size, as measured by market value, based on actual data since 1926. This is explored in more detail in Chapter 9 in the discussion of adjusting CAPM for firm-specific risk.

Equation (7-1) can be rewritten to reflect an adjustment for firm size as follows:

$$\text{CAPM}: k_e = R_f + \beta(R_m - R_f) + \text{FSP} \qquad (7\text{-}2)$$

where FSP = firm size premium.

Assume a firm has a market value of less than $50 million and a β of 1.75. Also, assume the risk-free rates of return and equity premium are 5.0 and 5.5%, respectively. The firm's cost of equity using the CAPM method adjusted for firm size can be estimated as follows:

$$k_e = .05 + 1.75(.055) + .092 \text{ (see Table 7-1)} = .238 = 23.8\%$$

TABLE 7-1   Estimates of the Size Premium

Market Value (000,000)	Percentage Points Added to CAPM Estimate
>$12,400	0.0
$5,250 to $12,400	0.3
$2,600 to $5,250	0.6
$1,650 to $2,600	0.8
$700 to $1,650	1.2
$450 to $700	1.3
$250 to $450	1.9
$100 to $250	2.4
$50 to $100	3.5
<$50 million	9.2

Source: Adapted from estimates provided by Ibbotson Associates.

Pretax Cost of Debt

The cost of debt represents the cost to the firm of borrowed funds. It reflects the current level of interest rates and the level of default risk as perceived by investors. Interest paid on debt is tax deductible by the firm. In bankruptcy, bondholders are paid before shareholders as the firm's assets are liquidated. Default risk can be measured by the firm's credit rating. Default rates vary from an average of .52% of AAA-rated firms for the 15-year period ending in 2001 to 54.38% for those rated CCC by Standard & Poor's Corporation (Burrus and McNamee, April 8, 2002).

For nonrated firms, the analyst may estimate the pretax cost of debt for an individual firm by comparing debt-to-equity ratios, interest coverage ratios, and operating margins with those of similar rated firms. Alternatively, the analyst may use the firm's actual interest expense as a percent of total debt outstanding. Some analysts prefer to use the average yield to maturity of the firm's outstanding bonds. Much of this information can be found in local libraries in such publications as Moody's *Company Data*; Standard & Poor's *Descriptions, The Outlook*, and *Bond Guide*; and Value Line's *Investment Survey*.

Cost of Preferred Stock

Preferred stock exhibits some of the characteristics of long-term debt in that its dividend is generally constant and preferred stockholders are paid before common shareholders in the event the firm is liquidated. Unlike interest payments on debt, preferred dividends are not tax deductible. Because preferred stock is riskier than debt but less risky than common stock in bankruptcy, the cost to the company to issue preferred stock should be less than the cost of equity but greater than the cost of debt. Viewing preferred dividends as paid in perpetuity, the cost of preferred stock (k_{pr}) can be calculated as dividends per share of preferred stock (d_{pr}) divided by the market value of the preferred stock (PR). (See section of this chapter entitled "Zero-Growth Valuation Model.") Consequently, if a firm pays a $2 dividend on its preferred stock whose current market value is $50, the firm's cost of preferred stock is 4% (i.e., $2/$50). The cost of preferred stock can be generalized as follows:

$$k_{pr} = \frac{d_{pr}}{PR} \qquad (7\text{-}3)$$

Cost of Capital

The weighted average cost of capital (WACC) is the broadest measure of the firm's cost of funds and represents the return that a firm must earn to induce investors to buy its common stock, preferred stock, and bonds. The WACC is calculated using a weighted average of the firm's cost of equity (k_e), cost of preferred stock (k_{pr}), and pretax cost of debt (i).

$$WACC = k_e \times \frac{E}{(D+E+PR)} + i \times (1-t) \times \frac{D}{(D+E+PR)} + k_{pr} \times \frac{PR}{(D+E+PR)} \qquad (7\text{-}4)$$

where   E = the market value of common equity
      D = the market value of debt
   PR = the market value of preferred stock
      t = the firm's marginal tax rate.

A portion of interest paid on borrowed funds is recoverable by the firm because of the tax deductibility of interest. For every dollar of taxable income, the tax owed is equal to $1 multiplied by t. Since each dollar of interest expense reduces taxable income by an equivalent amount, the actual cost of borrowing is reduced by $(1 - t)$. Therefore, the after-tax cost of borrowed funds to the firm is estimated by multiplying the pretax interest rate, i, by $(1 - t)$.

Note that the weights (i.e., $[E/(D+E+PR)]$, $[D/(D+E+PR)]$, and $[PR/(D+E+PR)]$) associated with the cost of equity, preferred stock, and debt, respectively, reflect the firm's target capital structure or capitalization. These are targets in the sense that they represent the capital structure the firm hopes to achieve and sustain in the future. The actual market value of debt, equity, and preferred stock as a percentage of total capital (i.e., $D+E+PR$) may differ from the targets. Market values rather than book values are used because the WACC measures the cost of issuing debt, preferred stock, and equity securities. Such securities are issued at market and not book value. The use of the target capital structure avoids the circular reasoning associated with using the current market value of equity to construct the weighted average cost of capital, which is subsequently used to estimate the firm's current market value.

Noninterest-bearing liabilities such as accounts payable are excluded from the estimation of the cost of capital for the firm to simplify the calculation of WACC. Although such liabilities do have an associated cost of capital, it is assumed to have been included in the price paid for the products and services whose purchase generated the accounts payable. Consequently, the cost of capital associated with these types of liabilities affects free cash flow through its inclusion in operating expenses (e.g., the price paid for raw materials). Estimates of industry betas, cost of equity, and WACC are provided by firms such as Ibbotson Associates, Value Line, Standard & Poor's, and Bloomberg. Such estimates provide a "reality check" since they serve as a benchmark against which the analyst's estimate of a firm's WACC can be compared.

Analyzing Risk

Risk is the degree of uncertainty associated with the outcome of an investment. It takes into consideration the probability of a loss as well as a gain on an investment. Risk consists of a *diversifiable* component—such as strikes, defaulting on debt repayments, and lawsuits—and a *nondiversifiable* component—such as inflation and war—that affects all firms. *Beta* (β) is a measure of nondiversifiable risk or the extent to which a firm's (or asset's) return changes because of a change in the market's return. It is a measure of the risk of a stock's financial returns, as compared with the risk of the financial returns to the general stock market. $\beta = 1$ means that the stock is as risky as the general market; $\beta < 1$ means the stock is less risky, whereas $\beta > 1$ means that the stock is more risky than the overall stock market.

β may be estimated by applying linear regression analysis to explain the relationship between the dependent variable, stock returns (R_j), and the independent variable, market returns (R_m). The intercept or constant term (also referred to as "alpha") of the regression equation provides a measure of R_j's performance as compared with the general market during the regression period. In Wall Street parlance, alpha is the premium (or discount) an investment earns above (below) some performance benchmark, such as the S&P 500 index.

The following equations express R_j as defined by the linear regression model and R_j as defined by the CAPM.

$R_j = \alpha + \beta R_m$ (regression equation formulation)

$R_j = R_f + \beta(R_m - R_f)$

$\quad = R_f + \beta R_m - \beta R_f$

$\quad = R_f(1 - \beta) + \beta R_m$ (CAPM formulation)

If α is greater than $R_f(1 - \beta)$, this particular stock's rate of return, R_j, performed better than would have been expected using the CAPM during the same time period. The cumulative daily difference between α (i.e., actual returns) and $R_f(1 - \beta)$ (i.e., expected returns) is a measure of "abnormal or excess return" for a specified number of days around the announcement of a transaction. Abnormal returns are often calculated in empirical "event" studies to assess the impact of acquisitions on the shareholder value of both acquiring and target firms (Exhibit 7-1).

Exhibit 7-1

Estimating β for Publicly Traded Companies

Calculate the return to the jth company's shareholders as capital gains (or losses) plus dividends paid during the period adjusted for stock splits that take place in the current period. This adjusted return should then be regressed against a similarly defined return for a broadly defined market index.

$$\frac{SP \times (P_{jt} - P_{jt-1}) + SP \times Dividends}{P_{jt-1}} = \alpha + \beta \frac{(S\&P500_t - S\&P500_{t-1}) + Dividends}{S\&P500_{t-1}}$$

Notes:

1. SP is equal to 2 for a two-for-one stock split, 1.5 for a three-for-two split, and 1.33 for a four-for-three split, etc. If we do not adjust for stock splits that may take place in the current period, the stock price will drop, resulting in a negative return.
2. Betas for public companies can be obtained from estimation services such as Value Line, Standard & Poor's, Ibbotson, and Bloomberg. Betas for private companies can be obtained by substituting a beta for comparable publicly traded companies. (See Chapter 10.)

In practice, betas are frequently estimated using the most recent 3 to 5 years of data. Consequently, betas are sensitive to the time period selected. The relationship between the overall market and a specific firm's beta may change significantly if a large sector of stocks that make up the overall index increase or decrease substantially. While over longer periods of time the impact on beta is problematic, it may be quite substantial over relatively short time periods. For example, the telecommunications, media, and technology sectors of the S&P 500 rose dramatically in the late 1990s and fell precipitously after 2000. Other sectors were relatively unaffected by the wild fluctuations in the overall market, resulting in a reduction in their betas. To illustrate, the beta for electric utilities fell to .1 in 2001 from .6 in 1998, falsely suggesting that the sector's risk and in turn cost of equity had declined (Annema and Goedhart, 2006).

Effects of Leverage on Beta

The presence of debt magnifies financial returns to shareholders. A firm whose total capital consists of $1 million in equity generates a return to shareholders of 10% if its after-tax profits are $100,000. A firm whose total capital is $1 million, consisting of $500,000 in equity and $500,000 in debt, will achieve a 20% return ($100,000/$500,000) to shareholders given the same level of after-tax profits.

In the absence of debt, β measures the volatility of a firm's financial return to changes in the general market's overall financial return. Such a measure of volatility or risk is called an unlevered β and is denoted as β_u. Risk to shareholders may also be viewed as the likelihood that they are going to receive a sufficiently large enough share of the firm's cash flow to meet or exceed their minimum required returns. Increasing leverage will raise the level of risk or uncertainty and increase the value of β, because interest payments represent fixed expenses that must be paid before any payments can be made to shareholders. However, this will be offset somewhat by the tax deductibility of interest, which reduces shareholder risk by increasing after-tax cash flow available for shareholders. The reduction in the firm's tax liability due to the tax deductibility of interest is often referred as a ***tax shield***. A beta reflecting the effects of both the increased volatility of earnings and the tax-shield or shelter effects of leverage is called a leveraged or levered β and is denoted as β_l (Exhibit 7-2). Note that this discussion is implicitly static in that it ignores the potential for increasing future cash flows as a result of investing the borrowed funds at or above the firm's weighted average cost of capital.

These relationships can be expressed as follows:

$$\beta_l = \beta_u[1 + (1-t)(D/E)] \text{ and} \tag{7-5}$$

$$\beta_u = \beta_l/[1 + (1-t)(D/E)] \tag{7-6}$$

Exhibit 7-2

Calculating a Levered β

Company X has no debt (D), a marginal tax rate (t) of .4, and an unlevered beta of 1.2. It is considering borrowing up to 50% of its equity value (E) in 2000 and up to 75% in 2003. What would be the impact of this decision on its unlevered beta (see Equation 7-5)?

$$\beta_{l,2000} = \beta_u[1 + (1-t)(D/E)_{2000}] = 1.2[1 + (1 - .4)(.5)] = 1.2(1.30) = 1.56$$

$$\beta_{l,2003} = \beta_u[1 + (1-t)(D/E)_{2003}] = 1.2[1 + (1 - .4)(.75)] = 1.2(1.45) = 1.74$$

Note:

1. Corporate income is generally taxed by the federal government at rates that begin at 15% and go up to 35% on taxable income of $10 million or more. A typical state tax rate is 5%. Because larger firms generally pay approximately 40% of their pretax income in taxes, this is the marginal rate used in examples in this textbook.

Note that Equations 7-5 and 7-6 apply only when the level of net debt is constant and the tax shield is risk free. *Net debt* is defined as all of the firm's interest bearing debt less the value of cash and marketable securities. However, when the firm increases its debt in direct proportion to the market value of its equity, the level of the debt is perfectly correlated with the firm's market value. Consequently, the risk associated with the tax shield (resulting from interest paid on outstanding debt) is the same as that associated with the firm. Therefore, the beta associated with the tax shield and with the firm's equity are the same. When firms increase net debt in direct proportion to the market value of their equity (as is often the case), the use of Equations 7-5 and 7-6 will result in an overstatement of the unlevered beta by an amount equal to the beta associated with the firm's debt times the firm's debt-to-equity ratio. Therefore, in this instance, levered and unlevered betas should be estimated using the following equations:

$$\beta_l = (1 + (D/E)\beta_U \text{ and} \qquad (7\text{-}7)$$

$$\beta_u = \beta_l/(1 + D/E) \qquad (7\text{-}8)$$

For a derivation of Equations 7-5 to 7-8, see Arzac (2006, pp. 47–50).

Calculating Free Cash Flows

Generally speaking, a firm's operating, investment, and financing activities generate its cash flow. The difference between cash inflows and cash outflows often is referred to as *free cash flow*. Such cash flow is free or discretionary in that it can be either reinvested in the firm or distributed to shareholders as dividends or share repurchases. Note that this difference can be positive or negative, resulting in an increase or decrease in the firm's cash balances between the beginning and end of the accounting period. Cash-flow statements based on Generally Accepted Accounting Principles (GAAP) are very useful for explaining changes in a firm's beginning- and ending-year cash balances. However, for purposes of valuation, cash-flow statements based on GAAP, need to be restated. The resulting restatement produces what are commonly referred to as *valuation cash flows*. Several different definitions of valuation cash flows are discussed in this chapter. These include free cash flow to the firm (FCFF), often referred to as *enterprise cash flow*, and free cash flow to equity investors (FCFE), also known as *equity cash flow*. By redefining cash flows in this manner, it is possible to relate those having claims against a firm's cash flows with their minimum required rates of return.

Free cash flow to the firm is more frequently used for valuation than free cash flow to equity investors or equity cash flow for several reasons. First, it is simpler to apply because it does not require estimation of principal repayments and preferred dividends. FCFF is most helpful when a firm's level of future borrowing is expected to change substantially during the forecast period, thereby making the estimation of debt repayment schedules difficult. However, the estimation starting with earnings before interest and taxes (EBIT) does require assumptions about the acquiring firm's target debt-to-equity ratio to calculate the firm's weighted average cost of capital. Second, it can be applied to the valuation of the total firm or individual operations. Free cash flow to equity investors is best suited for special situations such as for valuing financial institutions and leveraged buyouts. For an excellent discussion of cash-flow concepts, see Damodaran (2002).

Free Cash Flow to the Firm (Enterprise Cash Flow)

Free cash flow to the firm represents cash available to satisfy all investors holding claims against the firm's resources. These claim holders include common stockholders, lenders, and preferred stockholders. This definition assumes implicitly that a firm can always get financing, if it can generate sufficient future cash flows to meet or exceed minimum returns required by investors and lenders. Consequently, enterprise cash flow is calculated before the sources of financing are determined and, as such, is not affected by the firm's financial structure. However, the financial structure may affect the firm's cost of capital and therefore its value.

FCFF can be calculated by adjusting operating EBIT as follows

$$FCFF = EBIT(1 - Tax\ Rate) + Depreciation\ and\ Amortization$$

$$- Gross\ Capital\ Expenditures - \Delta Net\ Working\ Capital \qquad (7\text{-}9)$$

Under this definition, only cash flow from operating and investment activities, but not financing activities, is included. The tax rate refers to the firm's marginal tax rate. Net working capital is defined as current operating assets less cash balances in excess of the amount required to meet normal operating requirements less current operating liabilities.

Selecting the Right Tax Rate

The calculation of after-tax operating income requires multiplying EBIT by either a firm's marginal tax rate (i.e., the rate paid on each additional dollar of earnings) or effective tax rate (i.e., taxes due divided by taxable income). The effective tax rate is calculated from actual taxes paid based on accounting statements prepared for tax-reporting purposes. The marginal tax rate in the United States is usually 40%, 35% for federal taxes and 5% for most state and local taxes, and it is typically used to calculate after-tax income on the firm's accounting statements prepared for financial reporting purposes (e.g., to the public). The effective rate is usually less than the marginal tax rate and will vary among firms due to the use of tax credits to reduce actual taxes paid or accelerated depreciation to defer the payment of taxes. While favorable tax rules may temporarily reduce the effective tax rate, it is unlikely to be permanently reduced. Once tax credits have been used and the ability to further defer taxes exhausted, the effective rate can exceed the marginal rate at some point in the future. For example, if future capital expenditures are expected to diminish, projected depreciation will also decline and the difference between taxable income reported on financial statements and that recorded for tax purposes will shrink requiring firms to eventually pay deferred taxes. How deferred taxes can be treated for valuation purposes will be discussed later in this chapter.

Because favorable tax treatment cannot be extended indefinitely, the marginal tax rate should be used if taxable income is going to be multiplied by the same tax rate during each future period. However, an effective tax rate lower than the marginal rate may be used in the early years of cash-flow projections and eventually increased to the firm's marginal tax rate, if the analyst has reason to believe that the current favorable tax treatment is likely to continue into the foreseeable future. However, whatever the analyst chooses to do with respect to the selection of a tax rate, it is critical to use the marginal rate in calculating after-tax operating income in perpetuity. Otherwise, the implicit assumption is that some portion of taxes can be deferred indefinitely.

Adjusting EBIT for Operating Lease Expense

For many firms, future operating lease commitments are substantial. As noted later in this chapter, future lease commitments should be discounted to the present at the firm's pretax cost of debt (i) and included in the firm's total debt outstanding. Once operating leases are converted to debt, operating lease expense (OLE_{EXP}) must be added to EBIT, because it is a financial expense. Depreciation expense associated with the leased asset (DEP_{OL}) then must be deducted from EBIT, as is depreciation expense associated with other fixed assets owned by the firm, to calculate an "adjusted" EBIT ($EBIT_{ADJ}$). $EBIT_{ADJ}$ then is used to calculate free cash flow to the firm. EBIT may be adjusted as follows:

$$EBIT_{ADJ} = EBIT + OLE_{EXP} - DEP_{OL} \qquad (7\text{-}10)$$

Alternatively, if the depreciation on the leased asset is assumed to approximate the principal portion of the debt being repaid, adjusted EBIT may be calculated by adding back the imputed interest, i, on the debt value of the operating lease (PV_{OL}). Depreciation expenses associated with the leased assets need not be deducted from EBIT, because free cash flow to the firm is calculated before how the expenditure will be financed is considered. Consequently, adjusted EBIT ($EBIT_{adj}$) also may be shown as follows:

$$EBIT_{ADJ} = EBIT + PV_{OL} \times i \qquad (7\text{-}11)$$

Free Cash Flow to Equity Investors (Equity Cash Flow)

Free cash flow to equity investors is the cash flow remaining for returning cash through dividends or share repurchases to current common equity investors or for reinvesting in the firm after the firm satisfies all obligations (Damodaran, 2002). These obligations include debt payments, capital expenditures, changes in net working capital, and preferred dividend payments. Income and cash-flow statements differ in terms of how they treat depreciation. The income statement amortizes the cost of equipment over its depreciable accounting life and deducts depreciation expense from revenue. Depreciation is an expense item that does not actually involve an outlay of cash by the firm. Although depreciation reduces income, it does not reduce cash flow. In calculating FCFE, depreciation is added back to net income. FCFE can be defined as follows:

FCFE = Net Income + Depreciation and Amortization − Gross Capital Expenditures

     − ΔNet Working Capital + New Debt and Equity Issues

     − Principal Repayments − Preferred Dividends   (7-12)

Other expense items that do not involve an actual expenditure of cash that should be added back to net income in the calculation of free cash flow include the amortization expense associated with such items as capitalized software and changes in deferred taxes.

Deferred taxes may arise if a company uses accelerated depreciation for tax purposes but straight-line depreciation for reporting its financial statements to investors.

Exhibit 7-3 summarizes the key elements of enterprise (Equation 7-9) and equity cash flow (Equation 7-12). The example delineates the difference between equity and enterprise cash flow. The former reflects operating, investment, and financing activities, whereas the latter excludes cash flow from financing activities. Using actual data on Intel Corporation, Exhibit 7-4 reconciles the differences between conventional cash-flow statements based on GAAP and valuation cash flow. Note that in calculating enterprise cash flow, the analyst adds after-tax interest expense to net income in order to get cash available for both equity investors and lenders. While total interest expense was deducted from operating profits in calculating net income, the actual cash outlay was only the after-tax portion of interest expense, since interest expense is deductible for tax purposes. In contrast, in calculating equity cash flow or cash flow available for common shareholders, we must subtract after-tax interest expense from enterprise cash flow since this is paid to lenders and therefore is not available to common shareholders.

Exhibit 7-3
Defining Valuation Cash Flows: Equity and Enterprise Cash Flows

Free Cash Flow to Common Equity Investors (Equity Cash Flow: FCFE)

$$FCFE = \{\text{Net Income} + \text{Depreciation and Amortization} - \Delta\text{Working Capital}\}^1$$
$$- \text{Gross Capital Expenditures}^2 + \{\text{New Preferred Equity Issues}$$
$$- \text{Preferred Dividends} + \text{New Debt Issues} - \text{Principal Repayments}\}^3$$

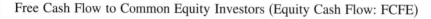 Cash flow (after taxes, debt repayments and new issues, preferred dividends, preferred equity issues, and all reinvestment requirements) available for paying dividends on or repurchasing common equity.

Free Cash Flow to the Firm (Enterprise Cash Flow: FCFF)

$$FCFF = \{\text{Earnings Before Interest \& Taxes } (1 - \text{Tax Rate})$$
$$+ \text{Depreciation and Amortization} - \Delta\text{Working Capital}\}^1$$
$$- \text{Gross Capital Expenditures}^2$$

Cash flow (after taxes and reinvestment requirements) available to repay lenders and/or pay common and preferred dividends and repurchase equity.

[1] Cash from operating activities.
[2] Cash from investing activities.
[3] Cash from financing activities.

Exhibit 7-4
Reconciling GAAP-Based and Valuation Cash Flows

Standardized Intel Corporation GAAP Consolidated Statement of Cash Flows

Year Ended December 31 ($Millions)	2003
Cash and Cash Equivalents, Beginning of Year	$7,970
Cash Flows Provided by (used for) Operating Activities:	
Net Income	3,117
Adjustments Reconciling Net Income to Net Cash from Operating Activities:	
Nonoperating Losses (Gains) (e.g., net gain on sales of equity investments)	372
Depreciation and Amortization Expense	5,344
Long-Term Operating Accruals (e.g., net gain on retirements of plant & equip.; deferred taxes)	681
Net Change in Operating Working Capital	(405)
Net Cash Provided by Operating Activities	9,109
Cash Flows Provided by (used for) Investing Activities:	
Net (Investment) Liquidation in Long-Term Operating Assets (e.g., additions to plant & equip.)	(5,765)
Net Cash Used for Investing Activities	(5,765)
Cash Flows Provided by (used for) Financing Activities:	
Net Debt (Repayments) or Issuance	(64)
Net Stock (Repurchase) or Issuance	(3,333)
Dividends Paid on Common Stock	(533)
Net Cash Used for Financing Activities	(3,930)
Net Increase (Decrease) in Cash and Cash Equivalents	($586)
Cash and Cash Equivalents, End of Year	$7,384

Intel Corporation Consolidated Valuation Cash Flows

Year Ended December 31 ($Millions)	2003
Net Income	$3,117
After-Tax Net Interest Expense (Income)	144
Nonoperating Losses (Gains)	372
Depreciation and Amortization Expense	5,344
Long-Term Operating Accruals	681
Operating Cash Flow Before Operating Working Capital	9,658
Net Change in Operating Working Capital	(405)
Operating Cash Flow Before Investment in Long-Term Operating Assets	9,253
Net (Investment in) or Liquidation of Operating Long-Term Assets	(5,765)
Free Cash Flow to the Firm (Enterprise Cash Flow)	3,488
After-Tax Net Interest Expense (Income)[1]	144
Net Debt (Repayment) or Issuance	(64)
Dividends on Preferred Stock	0
Free Cash Flow Available to Equity (Equity Cash Flow)	3,280
Net Stock (Repurchase) or Issuance	(3,333)
Dividends on Common Stock	(533)
Net Increase (Decrease) in Cash & Cash Equivalents	($586)

[1] Subtracted from free cash flow to the firm in calculating free cash flow available to equity investor.

Applying Income or Discounted Cash-Flow Methods

DCF methods provide estimates of the economic value of a company (i.e., the firm's ability to generate future cash flows), which do not need to be adjusted if the intent is to acquire a small portion of the company. However, if the intention is to obtain a controlling interest in the firm, a control premium must be added to the estimated economic value of the firm to determine the purchase price. A controlling interest generally is considered more valuable to an investor than a minority interest, because the investor has the right to final approval of important decisions affecting the business.

The various DCF models used to value acquisitions are special cases of the conventional capital budgeting process. Capital budgeting is the process for evaluating and comparing alternative investment opportunities to ensure the best long-term financial return for the firm. In the capital budgeting process, cash flows are projected over the expected life of the project and discounted to the present at the firm's cost of capital. M&As can be viewed as one of the alternative investment opportunities available to the firm.

Enterprise Discounted Cash-Flow Model (Enterprise or FCFF Method)

The enterprise valuation or FFCF approach discounts the after-tax free cash flow available to the firm from operations at the weighted average cost of capital to obtain the estimated enterprise value. The firm's estimated common equity value then is determined by subtracting the market value of the firm's debt and other investor claims on cash flow such as preferred stock from the enterprise value. The estimate of equity derived in this manner will equal the value of equity determined by discounting the cash flow available to the firm's shareholders at the cost of equity. This assumes that the discount rates used to calculate the present values of the firm's debt and other investor claims on cash flow reflect accurately the risk associated with each cash-flow stream.

The enterprise approach is consistent with the capital budgeting process in that value is determined independently of how the business is financed. Moreover, it can be applied to individual business units or the parent firm in precisely the same manner. For example, for multiunit businesses, the value of equity using this method is equal to the sum of the value of each individual business unit owned by the parent firm plus excess cash balances less the present value of corporate overhead, debt, and preferred stock.

Equity Discounted Cash-Flow Model (Equity or FCFE Method)

The equity valuation or FCFE approach discounts the after-tax cash flows available to the firm's shareholders at the cost of equity. This approach is used primarily in special situations such as for valuing highly leveraged transactions in which the capital structure is changing frequently and for financial services firms in which the cost of capital for various operations within the firm may be very difficult to estimate. For example, a retail commercial banking operation typically finances its operations using non-interest-bearing checking accounts. Determining the actual cost of acquiring such accounts is often quite arbitrary. By focusing on FCFE, the analyst only needs to estimate the financial services firm's cost of equity. The enterprise or FCFF method and the equity or FCFE method are illustrated in the following sections of this chapter using three different cash-flow growth scenarios: zero-growth, constant-growth, and variable growth rates.

Zero-Growth Valuation Model

This model assumes that free cash flow is constant in perpetuity. The value of the firm at time zero (P_0) is the discounted or capitalized value of its annual cash flow. In this instance (Exhibit 7-5), the discount rate and the capitalization rate are the same. (See Chapter 10 for a more detailed discussion of the difference between discount and capitalization rates.) The present value of a constant payment in perpetuity is a diminishing series, because it represents the sum of the PVs for each future period. Each PV is smaller than the preceding one; therefore, the perpetuity is a diminishing series that converges to one divided by the discount rate. The subscript FCFF or FCFE refers to the definition of cash flow used in the valuation.

$$P_{0,\text{FCFF}} = \text{FCFF}_0/\text{WACC}, \qquad (7\text{-}13)$$

where FCFF_0 is free cash flow to the firm at time zero and WACC is the cost of capital.

$$P_{0,\text{FCFE}} = \text{FCFE}_0/k_e, \qquad (7\text{-}14)$$

where FCFE_0 is free cash flow to common equity investors at time zero and k_e is the cost of equity.

While seemingly overly simplistic, the zero growth method has the advantage of being easily understood by all parties involved in a negotiation. Moreover, there is little evidence that more complex methods provide consistently better valuation estimates due to their greater requirement for more inputs/assumptions. This method is commonly used to value commercial real estate transactions.

Exhibit 7-5
Zero-Growth Valuation Model

1. What is the enterprise value of a firm whose annual FCFF_0 of \$1 million is expected to remain constant in perpetuity and whose cost of capital is 12% (see Equation 7-13)?

$$P_{0,\text{FCFF}} = \$1/.12 = \$8.3 \text{ million}$$

2. Calculate the weighted average cost of capital (see Equation 7-4) and the enterprise value of a firm whose capital structure consists only of common equity and debt. The firm desires to limit its leverage to 30% of total capital.[1] The firm's marginal tax rate is .4 and its beta is 1.5. The corporate bond rate is 8% and the 10-year U.S.

Treasury bond rate is 5%. The expected annual return on stocks is 10%. Annual FCFF is expected to remain at $4 million indefinitely.

$$k_e = .05 + 1.5(.10 - .05) = .125 = 12.5\%$$

$$WACC = .125 \times .7 + .08 \times (1 - .4) \times .3 = .088 + .014 = .102 = 10.2\%$$

$$P_{0,FCFF} = \$4/.102 = \$39.2 \text{ million}$$

[1] If you only know a firm's debt-to-equity ratio (D/E), it is possible to calculate the firm's debt-to-total capital ratio (D/D + E) by dividing (D/E) by (1 + D/E), since D/(D + E) = (D/E)/(1 + D/E) = [(D/E)/(D + E)/E] = (D/E) × (E/D + E) = D/(D + E).

Constant-Growth Valuation Model

The constant growth model (also known as the Gordon growth model) is applicable for firms in mature markets, characterized by a moderate and somewhat predictable rate of growth. Examples of such industries include beverages, cosmetics, prepared foods, and cleaning products. To project growth rates, extrapolate the industry's growth rate over the past 5–10 years. The constant-growth model assumes that cash flow grows at a constant rate, g, which is less than the required return, k_e. The assumption that k_e is greater than g is a necessary mathematical condition for deriving the model (Gitman, 2000). In this model, next year's cash flow to the firm ($FCFF_1$), or the first year of the forecast period, is expected to grow at the constant rate of growth g. Therefore, $FCFF_1 = FCFF_0 (1 + g)$.

$$P_{0,FCFF} = FCFF_1/(WACC - g), \tag{7-15}$$

$$P_{0,FCFE} = FCFE_1/(k_e - g), \quad \text{where } FCFE_1 = FCFE_0(1 + g) \tag{7-16}$$

Note that the zero growth model is a special case of the constant growth model for which g is equal to zero.

This simple valuation model also provides a means of estimating the risk premium component of the cost of equity as an alternative to relying on historical information as is done in the capital asset pricing model. This model was developed originally to estimate the value of stocks in the current period (P_0) using the level of expected dividends (d_1) in the next period. This formulation provides an estimate of the present value of dividends growing at a constant rate forever. Assuming the stock market values stocks correctly and we know P_0, d_1, and g, we can estimate k_e. Therefore:

$$P_0 = d_1/(k_e - g) \quad \text{and} \quad k_e = (d_1/P_0) + g \tag{7-17}$$

This expression suggests that increases in a firm's share price relative to earnings (i.e., increases in its P/E ratio) lowers the firm's required return on acquisitions financed by issuing stock. This explains why high levels of M&A activity frequently coincide with booming stock markets. For example, if d_1 is $1, g is 10%, and $P_0 = \$10$, k_e is 20%. However, if P_0 increases to $20 and g and d_1 remain the same, k_e declines to 15%. Note that an increase in P_0 without an increase in earnings growth, g, implies a higher P/E ratio for the firm. Exhibit 7-6 illustrates how to apply the constant growth model.

Exhibit 7-6
Constant Growth Model

1. Determine the enterprise value of a firm whose projected free cash flow to the firm next year is $1 million, WACC is 12%, and expected annual cash-flow growth rate is 6% (see Equation 7-15).

$$P_{0,FCFF} = \$1/(.12 - .06) = \$16.7 \text{ million}$$

2. Estimate the equity value of a firm whose cost of equity is 15% and whose free cash flow to equity holders in the prior year is projected to grow 20% this year and then at a constant 10% annual rate thereafter. The prior year's free cash flow to equity holders is $2 million (see Equation 7-16).

$$P_{0,FCFE} = (2.0 \times 1.2)(1.1)/(.15 - .10) = \$52.8 \text{ million}$$

Variable-Growth Valuation Model

Many firms experience periods of high growth followed by a period of slower, more stable growth. Examples of such industries include cellular phones, personal computers, and cable TV. Firms within such industries routinely experience double-digit growth rates for periods of 5–10 years because of low penetration of these markets in the early years of the product's life cycle. As the market becomes saturated, growth inevitably slows to a rate more in line with the overall growth of the economy or the general population. The PV of such firms is equal to the sum of the PV of the discounted cash flows during the high-growth period plus the discounted value of the cash flows generated during the stable growth period. In capital budgeting terms, the discounted value of the cash flows generated during the stable growth period is called the *terminal, sustainable, horizon, or continuing growth value*.

The terminal value may be estimated using the constant growth model. Free cash flow during the first year beyond the nth or final year of the forecast period, $FFCF_{n+1}$, is divided by the difference between the assumed cost of capital and the expected cash-flow growth rate beyond the nth year forecast period. The terminal value is the value in the nth year of all future cash flows beyond the nth year. Consequently, to convert the terminal value to its value in the current year, it is necessary to discount the terminal value applying the discount rate used to convert the nth year value to a present value.

Although there are other ways to calculate the terminal value, the use of the constant growth model provides consistency in estimating the value of the firm created beyond the end of the forecast period. It enables the application of discounted cash-flow methodology in estimating value during both the variable and stable growth periods. However, the selection of the earnings growth rate and cost of capital must be done very carefully. Small changes in assumptions can result in dramatic swings in the terminal value and, therefore, in the valuation of the firm. Table 7-2 illustrates the sensitivity of a terminal value of $1 million to different spreads between the cost of capital and the stable growth rate. Note that using the constant-growth model formula, the terminal value declines

TABLE 7-2   Impact of Changes in Assumptions on a
Terminal Value of $1 Million

Difference between Cost of Capital and Cash-Flow Growth Rate	Terminal Value ($ Millions)
3%	33.3[1]
4%	25.0
5%	20.0
6%	16.7
7%	14.3

Note:
  [1] $1.0/.03

dramatically as the spread between the cost of capital and expected stable growth for cash flow increases by one percentage point.

Note that the expected stable growth rate in cash flow can be either positive or negative. The use of a positive growth rate suggests that the firm is expected to continue forever. This assumption is not as bizarre as it may seem, because companies frequently are acquired or liquidated, thereby enabling the investor to earn a premium on their investment or to recover at least some portion of their original investment. In contrast, the use of a negative growth rate implies that the firm will shrink each year until it eventually disappears. Therefore, we may use the constant growth model to estimate the terminal value of a firm that we do not expect to last forever.

There are numerous other ways terminal values can be estimated. The price-to-earnings, price-to-cash flow, or price-to-book techniques value the target as if it is sold at the end of a specific number of years. At the end of the forecast period, the terminal year's earnings, cash flow, or book value is projected and multiplied by a P/E, cash-flow, or book value multiple believed to be appropriate for that year. The terminal value also may be estimated by assuming the firm's cash flow or earnings in the last year of the forecast period will continue in perpetuity. This is equivalent to the zero-growth valuation model discussed previously.

Using the definition of free cash flow to the firm, $P_{0,FCFF}$ can be estimated using the variable growth model as follows:

$$P_{0,FCFF} = \sum_{t=1}^{n} \frac{FCFF_0 \times (1+g_t)^t}{(1+WACC)^t} + \frac{P_n}{(1+WACC)^n} \qquad (7\text{-}18)$$

where
$$P_n = \frac{FCFF_n \times (1+g_m)}{(WACC_m - g_m)}$$

$FCFF_0$ = FCFF in year 0
$WACC$ = weighted average cost of capital through year n
$WACC_m$ = cost of capital assumed beyond year n (Note: $WACC > WACC_m$)
p_n = value of the firm at the end of year n (terminal value)
g_t = growth rate through year n
g_m = stabilized or long-term growth rate beyond year n (Note: $g_t > g_m$)

Similarly, the value of the firm to equity investors can be estimated using Equation 7-18. However, projected cash flows are discounted using the firm's cost of equity. See Exhibit 7-7 for an illustration of when and how to apply the variable growth model.

Exhibit 7-7
Variable-Growth Valuation Model

Estimate the enterprise value of a firm (P_0) whose free cash flow is projected to grow at a compound annual average rate of 35% for the next 5 years. Growth then is expected to slow to a more normal 5% annual growth rate. The current year's cash flow to the firm is $4 million. The firm's weighted average cost of capital during the high-growth period is 18% and 12% beyond the fifth year, as growth stabilizes. The firm's cash in excess of normal operating balances is assumed to be zero. Therefore, the present value of cash flows during the high-growth forecast period are as follows:

$$PV_{t-5} = \frac{4.00 \times 1.35}{1.18} + \frac{4.00 \times 1.35^2}{1.18^2} + \frac{4.00 \times 1.35^3}{1.18^3} + \frac{4.00 \times 1.35^4}{1.18^4} + \frac{4.00 \times 1.35^5}{1.18^5}$$

$$= 5.40/1.18 + 7.29/1.18^2 + 9.84/1.18^3 + 13.29/1.18^4 + 17.93/1.18^5$$

$$= 4.58 + 5.24 + 5.99 + 6.85 + 7.84 = 30.50$$

Calculation of the terminal value is as follows:

$$PV_5 = \frac{[(4.00 \times 1.35^5 \times 1.05)]/(.12 - .05)}{1.18^5}$$

$$= \frac{18.83/.07}{2.29} = 117.60$$

$$P_{0,FCFF} = PV_{t-5} + PV_5 = 30.50 + 117.60 = 148.10$$

Supernormal "High-Flyer"–Growth Valuation Model

Some companies display initial periods of what could be described as hypergrowth, followed by an extended period of rapid growth, before stabilizing at a more normal and sustainable growth rate. Initial public offerings and start-up companies may follow this model. This pattern reflects growth over their initially small revenue base, the introduction of a new product, or the sale of an existing product to a new or underserved customer group. Calculating the discounted cash flows is computationally more difficult for firms expected to grow for multiple periods, each of whose growth rates differ, before assuming a more normal long-term growth rate. Because each period's growth rate differs, the cost of capital in each period will differ. Consequently, each year's cash flows must be discounted by the "cumulative cost of capital" from prior years. A more detailed discussion of this method is provided on the CD-ROM accompanying this book in a file folder entitled "Supernormal Valuation Model."

Determining Growth Rates

Projected growth rates for sales, profit, cash flow, or other financial variables can be readily calculated based on the historical experience of the firm or of the industry. See

Appendix A to this chapter for a more detailed discussion of using regression methods for forecasting purposes.

Duration of High-Growth Period

Intuition suggests that the length of the high-growth period should be longer when the current growth rate of a firm's cash flow is much higher than the stable growth rate. This is particularly true when the high-growth firm has a relatively small market share and there is little reason to believe that its growth rate will slow in the foreseeable future. For example, if the industry is expected to grow at 5% annually and the target firm, which has only a negligible market share, is growing at three times that rate, it may be appropriate to assume a high-growth period of 5–10 years. Moreover, if the terminal value comprises a substantial percentage (e.g., three-fourths) of total PV, the forecast period should be extended beyond the customary 5 years to at least 10 years. The extension of the time period reduces the impact of the terminal value in determining the market value of the firm. High-growth rates usually are associated with increased levels of uncertainty. In applying discounted cash-flow methodology, risk is incorporated into the discount rate. Consequently, the discount rate during the high-growth (i.e., less predictable) period or periods should generally be higher than during the stable growth period.

According to Palepu, Healy, and Bernard (2000, pp. 10-2 and 10-3), historical evidence shows that sales and profitability tend to revert to normal levels within 5 to 10 years. Between 1979 and 1998 sales growth for the average U.S. firm reverted to an average of 7–9% within 5 years. Firms with initial growth rates in excess of 50% experience a decline to about 6% growth within 3 years; those with the lowest initial growth rate tend to increase to about 8% by year 5. This suggests that the conventional use of a 5-year to 10-year annual forecast before calculating a terminal value makes sense.

More sophisticated forecasts of growth rates involve an analysis of the firm's customer base. Annual revenue projections are made for each customer or product and summed to provide an estimate of aggregate revenue. A product or service's life cycle (see Chapter 4) is a useful tool for making such projections. In some industries, a product's life cycle may be a matter of months (e.g., software) or years (e.g., an automobile). This information is readily available by examining the launch dates of new products and services in an industry in publications provided by the industry's trade associations. By determining where the firm's products are in their life cycle, the analyst can project annual unit volume by product.

Stable or Sustainable Growth Rate

The stable growth rate generally is going to be less than or equal to the overall growth rate of the industry in which the firm competes or the general economy. Stable growth rates in excess of these levels implicitly assume that the firm's cash flow eventually will exceed that of its industry or the general economy. Similarly, for multinational firms, the stable growth rate should not exceed the projected growth rate for the world economy or for a particular region of the world.

Determining the Appropriate Discount Rate

The question of whether to use the acquirer's or the target's cost of capital to value the target's cash flows often arises in valuations. The appropriate discount rate is generally the target's cost of capital if the acquirer is merging with a higher risk business resulting in an increase in the cost of capital of the combined firms. However, either the acquirer's or the target's cost of capital may be used if the two firms have substantially similar risk profiles and are based in the same country.

DCF versus Earnings/Dividend Valuation Controversy

Considerable attention has been paid to whether cash flow, earnings, or dividends are better estimates of firm valuation. In valuation, differences in earnings, cash flows, and dividends are largely attributable to timing differences (i.e., differences between when a cash outlay is recorded and when it is actually incurred). For example, when a firm buys a piece of equipment, it generally pays for the equipment in the period in which it is received. However, for financial reporting purposes, the purchase price of the equipment is spread or amortized over its estimated useful life. Over the life of the firm, the present values of future earnings, cash flows, and dividends will be equal if based on internally consistent assumptions. Studies suggest that cash flows and earnings are highly positively correlated with stock returns over long periods such as 5-year intervals. However, for shorter time periods, earnings show a stronger association with stock returns than cash flows (Cheng, Liu, and Schaefer, 1996; Dechow, 1994; Sloan, 1996). As a practical matter, cash flow is more often used for valuation than earnings or dividends simply because firms often do not pay out dividends or generate profits for a significant time period. This is particularly true for start-ups or firms that are experiencing temporary or "special situations."

Valuing Firms under Special Situations

Firms with Temporary Problems

When cash flow is temporarily depressed due to strikes, litigation, warranty claims, employee severance, or other one-time events, it is generally safe to assume that cash flow will recover in the near term. One solution is to base projections on cash flow prior to the one-time event. Alternatively, actual cash flow could be adjusted for the one-time event by adding back the pretax reduction in operating profits of the one-time event and then recalculating after-tax profits. If the cost of the one-time event is not displayed on the firm's financial statements, it is necessary to compare each expense item as a percent of sales in the current year with the prior year. Any expense items that look abnormally high should be "normalized" by applying an average ratio from prior years to the current year's sales. Alternatively, the analyst could use the prior year's operating margin to estimate the current year's operating income.

Firms with Longer-Term Problems

Deteriorating cash flow may be symptomatic of a longer-term deterioration in the firm's competitive position due to poor strategic decisions having been made by management. Under such circumstances, the analyst must decide whether the firm is likely to recover and how long will it take to restore the firm's former competitive position. The answer to such questions requires the identification of the cause of the firm's competitive problems. Firms with competitive problems often are less profitable than key competitors or the average firm in the industry. Therefore, the firm's recovery can be included in the forecast of cash flows by allowing its operating profit margin to increase gradually to the industry average or to the level of the industry's most competitive firm. The speed of the adjustment will depend on the firm's problems. For example, replacing outmoded equipment or back-office processing systems may be done more quickly than workforce reductions when the labor force is unionized or when the firm's products are obsolete.

Cyclical Firms

The projected cash flows of firms in highly cyclical industries can be distorted depending on where the firm is in its business cycle (i.e., the up and down movement of the economy). The most straightforward solution is to project cash flows based on an average historical growth rate during a prior full business cycle for the firm.

Valuing a Firm's Debt and Other Obligations

In the previous sections, we estimated the equity value of the firm by discounting the projected free cash flows to equity investors by the firm's cost of equity. Alternatively, the equity value may be estimated by subtracting the market or present value of the firm's debt and other obligations from the firm's estimated enterprise value. This section discusses how to value long-term debt, operating leases, and deferred tax liabilities to illustrate this alternative means of estimating the equity value of the firm.

Determining the Market Value of Long-Term Debt

In some instances, the analyst may not know the exact principal repayment schedule for the target firm's debt. To determine the market value of debt, treat the book value of all of the firm's debt as a conventional coupon bond in which interest is paid annually or semiannually and the principal is repaid at maturity. The coupon is the interest on all of the firm's debt, and the principal at maturity is a weighted average of the maturity of all of the debt outstanding. The weighted average principal at maturity is the sum of the amount of debt outstanding for each maturity date multiplied by its share of total debt outstanding. The estimated current market value of the debt then is calculated as the sum of the annuity value of the interest expense per period plus the present value of the principal. The only debt that must be valued is the debt outstanding on the valuation date. Future borrowing is irrelevant if we assume that cash inflows generated from investments financed with future borrowings are sufficient to satisfy interest and principal payments associated with these borrowings.

Determining the Market Value of Operating Leases

Both capital and operating leases also should be counted as outstanding debt of the firm. When a lease is classified as a capital lease, the present value of the lease expenses is treated as debt. Interest is imputed on this amount that corresponds to debt of comparable risk and maturity. This imputed interest is shown on the income statement. Although operating lease expenses are treated as operating expenses on the income statement, they are not counted as part of debt on the balance sheet for financial reporting purposes. For valuation purposes, operating leases should be included in debt because failure to meet lease payments will result in the loss of the leased asset, which is contributing to the generation of operating cash flows. Future operating lease expenses are shown in financial statement footnotes. These future expenses should be discounted at an interest rate comparable to current bank lending rates for unsecured assets. The discount rate may be approximated using the firm's current pretax cost of debt. The pretax cost of debt is used to reflect the market rate of interest lessors would charge the firm. If future operating lease expenses are not available, the analyst can approximate the principal amount of the operating leases by discounting the current year's operating lease payment as a perpetuity using the firm's cost of debt (see Exhibit 7-8).

Exhibit 7-8
Estimating the Market Value of a Firm's Debt

According to its 10K report, Gromax, Inc. has two debt issues outstanding, with a total book value of $220 million. Annual interest expense on the two issues totals $20 million. The first issue, whose current book value is $120 million, matures at the end of 5 years; the second issue, whose book value is $100 million, matures in 10 years. The weighted average maturity of the two issues is 7.27 years [i.e., $5 \times (120/220) + 10 \times (100/220)$]. The current cost of debt maturing in 7–10 years is 8.5%. The firm's 10K also shows that the firm has annual operating lease expenses of $2.1, $2.2, $2.3, and $5.0 million in the fourth year and beyond (the 10K indicated the firm's cumulative value in the fourth year and beyond to be $5.0). (For our purposes, we may assume that the $5.0 million is paid in the fourth year.) What is the total market value of the firm's total long-term debt, including conventional debt and operating leases?

$$PV_D \text{ (Long-Term Debt)}^1 = \$20 \times \frac{[1 - (1/(1.085)^{7.27})]}{.085} + \frac{\$220}{(1.085)^{7.27}}$$

$$= \$105.27 + \$121.55$$

$$= \$226.82$$

$$PV_{OL} \text{ (Operating Leases)} = \frac{\$2.1}{(1.085)} + \frac{\$2.2}{(1.085)^2} + \frac{\$2.3}{(1.085)^3} + \frac{\$5.0}{(1.085)^4}$$

$$= \$1.94 + \$1.87 + \$1.80 + \$3.61$$

$$= \$9.22$$

$$PV_{TD} \text{ (Total Debt)} = \$226.82 + \$9.22 = \$236.04$$

[1] The present value of debt is calculated using the PV of an annuity formula for 7.27 years and an 8.5% interest rate plus the PV of the principal repayment at the end of 7.27 years. Alternatively, rather than using the actual formulas, a present value interest factor annuity table and a present value interest factor table could have been used to calculate the PV of debt.

Capitalizing operating lease payments requires that the cost of capital incorporates the effects of this source of financing and that operating income must be adjusted to reflect lease expenses, as discussed earlier in this chapter. Finally, to calculate the value of the firm's equity, both debt and the capitalized value of operating leases must be subtracted from the estimated enterprise value of the firm (FCFF).

Determining the Cash Impact of Deferred Taxes

A firm that actually pays $40,000 in income taxes based on its tax accounting statements but would have paid $60,000 in taxes on the income reported on its financial statements must show $20,000 in deferred income tax liabilities on its balance sheet. Deferred tax liabilities measure income taxes saved in the current year. Such differences between when the tax provision is recorded and when taxes are actually paid represent temporary timing differences. The impact of timing differences can be incorporated into present value calculations by including the future impact of all factors affecting a firm's effective tax rate in projections of the individual components of cash flow (see Copeland, Koller, and Murrin, 2005). Alternatively, the analyst could make assumptions about how the firm's effective tax rate will change and value current and future deferred tax liabilities separately from the calculation of the present value of the projected cash flows. As such, the impact on free cash flow of a change in deferred taxes can be approximated by the difference between a firm's marginal and effective tax rate multiplied by the firm's operating income before interest and taxes.

The author recommends calculating the impact of deferred taxes separately, since deferred tax liabilities can arise from many different sources such as uncollectible accounts receivable, warranties, options expensing, pensions, leases, net operating losses, depreciable assets, inventories, installment receivables, and intangible drilling and development costs (see Stickney, Brown, and Wahlen, 2007). Which factors contribute the most to changes in deferred tax liabilities depends on the type of business. For example, the impact of timing differences due to depreciation is likely to be greater for manufacturing than for service or high-tech firms. Companies actually paying more in taxes than shown as an expense on their income statements show an asset item called a deferred tax asset on their balance sheets as a measure of the future tax savings the firm will realize.

The greatest challenge with deferred tax liabilities is determining when they are likely to come due. Such a liability is likely only when the firm's growth rate slows. The choice of tax rate in estimating future after-tax operating income has different implications under alternative scenarios. The first scenario assumes after-tax operating income is calculated using the firm's current effective tax rate indefinitely, implicitly assuming that the firm's deferred tax liabilities will never have to be repaid. In the second scenario, the analyst estimates after-tax operating income using the firm's marginal rate indefinitely, which implies that the firm cannot defer taxes beyond the current period. In the final scenario, the analyst assumes the effective tax rate is applicable for a specific number of years (for sake of discussion assume 5 years) before reverting to the firm's marginal tax rate. The use of the effective tax rate for 5 years will increase the deferred tax liability to the firm during that period, as long as the effective rate is below the marginal rate. The deferred tax liability at the end of the fifth year can be estimated by adding to the current cumulated deferred tax liability the incremental liability for each of the next 5 years. This incremental liability is the sum of projected EBIT times the difference between the marginal and effective tax rates. Assuming tax payments on the deferred tax liability at the end of the fifth year will be spread equally over the following 10 years, the present value of the tax payments during that 10-year period is then estimated and discounted back to the current period.

Adjusting Firm Value for Nonequity Claims

Once we have estimated the market value of a firm's debt and other obligations such as deferred tax liabilities, the firm's common equity value can be estimated by deducting the market value of the firm's non-common equity claims from the enterprise value of the firm (see Exhibit 7-9). Non-common equity claims could include the market value of the firm's debt and preferred stock, as well as the present value of expected liabilities from lawsuits, of unfunded pension and health care obligations, and of deferred tax liabilities.

Exhibit 7-9
Estimating Common Equity Value by Deducting the Market Value of Debt
and Other Nonequity Claims from the Enterprise Value

Operating income, depreciation, working capital, and capital spending are expected to grow 10% annually during the next 5 years and 5% thereafter. The book value of the firm's debt is $300 million, with annual interest expense of $25 million and term to maturity of 4 years. The debt is a conventional "interest only" note with a repayment of principal at maturity. The firm's annual preferred dividend expense is $20 million. The prevailing market yield on preferred stock issued by similar firms is 11%. The firm does not have any operating leases; and pension and health care obligations are fully funded. The firm's current cost of debt is 10%. The firm's weighted average cost of capital is 12%. Because of tax deferrals, the firm's current effective tax rate of 25% is expected to remain at that level for the next 5 years. The firm's current deferred tax liability is $300 million. The projected deferred tax liability at the end of the fifth year is expected to be paid off in 10 equal amounts during the following decade. The firm's marginal tax rate is 40% and will be applied to the calculation of the terminal value. What is the value of the firm to common equity investors?

Financial Data

	Current Year	Year 1	Year 2	Year 3	Year 4	Year 5
EBIT	$200.0	$220.0	$242.0	$266.2	$292.8	$322.1
EBIT(1 − t)	$150.0	$165.0	$181.5	$199.7	$219.6	$241.6
Depreciation (Straight line)	$8.0	$8.8	$9.7	$10.7	$11.7	$12.9
Δ Net Working Capital	$30.0	$33.0	$36.3	$39.9	$43.9	$48.3
Gross Capital Spending	$40.0	$44.0	$48.4	$53.2	$58.6	$64.4
Free Cash Flow to the Firm	$88.0	$96.8	$106.5	$117.3	$128.8	$141.8
Present Value		$86.40	$84.9	$83.5	$81.85	$80.46
Terminal Value[1]	$795.48					
Total Firm Value	$1,212.59					

Solution:

$$PV_D \text{ (Debt)}^2 = \$25 \times \frac{[1 - (1/(1.10)^4)]}{.10} + \frac{\$300}{1.10^4}$$

$$= \$25(3.17) + \$300(.683)$$

$$= \$79.25 + \$204.90$$

$$= \$284.15$$

$$PV_{PFD} \text{ (Preferred Stock)}^3 = \$20/.11 = \$181.82$$

$$\text{Deferred Tax Liability by End of Year 5} = \$300 + (\$220 + \$242 + \$266.2 + \$292.8$$

$$+ \$322.1)(.40 - .25)$$

$$= \$501.47$$

$$PV_{DEF} \text{ (Deferred Taxes)} = \left\{ (\$501.47/10) \times \frac{[(1 - (1/(1.12)^{10}))]}{.12} \right\} \Big/ (1.12)^5$$

$$= (\$50.15 \times 5.65)/1.76$$

$$= \$160.99$$

$$P_{0,FCFE} = \$1,212.59 - \$284.15 - \$181.82 - \$160.99$$

$$= \$585.63$$

---

[1] The terminal value reflects the recalculation of the fifth year after tax operating income using the marginal tax rate of 40% and applying the constant growth model.

[2] The present value of debt is calculated using the PV of an annuity for 4 years and a 10% interest rate plus the PV of the principal repayment at the end of 4 years. Alternatively, rather than using the actual formulas, a present value interest factor annuity table and a present value interest factor table could have been used to calculate the PV of debt. The firm's current cost of debt of 10% is higher than the implied interest rate of 8% ($25/$300) on the loan currently on the firm's books. This suggests that the market rate of interest has increased since the firm borrowed the $300 million "interest only" note.

[3] The market value of preferred stock (PV_{PFD}) is equal to the preferred dividend divided by the cost of preferred stock.

Valuing Nonoperating Assets

Net operating cash flow is generated from operating assets liabilities. The cost of capital measures the cost of financing these assets. The value of such assets is calculated by discounting projected net operating cash flows to the present. However, other assets, which are not directly used in operating the firm, also may provide substantial value. Examples of such nonoperating assets include cash in excess of normal operating requirements, investments in other firms, and unused or underutilized assets. The value of such assets should be added to the value of the discounted cash flows from operating assets to determine the total value of the firm.

Cash and Marketable Securities

Cash and short-term marketable securities, held in excess of the target firm's minimum operating cash balance, represent value that should be added to the present value of operating assets to determine the value of the firm. If a firm has large cash balances in excess of those required to satisfy operating requirements at the beginning of the forecast period, the valuation approach outlined in this chapter, which focuses on cash flow generated from operating assets, assumes implicitly that it is treated as a one-time cash payout to the target firm's shareholders. Otherwise, the excess cash should be added to the present value of the firm's operating cash flows. On an ongoing basis, excess cash flows have already been taken into account in the valuation of cash flows from operating assets. Projected excess cash flows are assumed implicitly to be paid out to shareholders either as dividends or share repurchases. Note that it is the estimate of the firm's minimum cash balance that should be used in calculating net working capital in determining free cash flow from operations.

What constitutes the minimum cash balance will depend on the firm's cash conversion cycle. This cycle reflects the firm's tendency to build inventory, sell products on credit, and later collect accounts receivable. The delay between the investment of cash in the production of goods and the eventual receipt of cash inherent in this process reflects the amount of cash tied up in working capital. The length of time cash is committed to working capital can be estimated as the sum of the firm's inventory conversion period plus the receivables collection period less the payables deferral period.

The inventory conversion period is the average length of time in days required to produce and sell finished goods. The receivables collection period is the average length of time in days required to collect receivables. The payables deferral period is the average length of time in days between the purchase of and payment for materials and labor. To finance this investment in working capital, a firm must maintain a minimum cash balance equal to the average number of days its cash is tied up in working capital times the average dollar value of sales per day. The inventory conversion and receivables collection periods are calculated by dividing the dollar value of inventory and receivables by average sales per day. The payments deferral period is estimated by dividing the dollar value of payables by the firm's average cost of sales per day. See Exhibit 7-10 for an illustration of how to estimate minimum and excess cash balances.

Exhibit 7-10
Estimating Minimum and Excess Cash Balances

Prototype Incorporated's current inventory, accounts receivable, and accounts payables are valued at $14,000,000, $6,500,000, $6,000,000, respectively. Projected sales and cost of sales for the coming year total $100,000,000 and $75,000,000, respectively. Moreover, the value of the firm's current cash and short-term marketable securities is $21,433,000. What minimum cash balance should the firm maintain? What is the firm's current excess cash balance?

$$\frac{\$14,000,000}{\$100,000,000/365} + \frac{\$6,500,000}{\$100,000,000/365} - \frac{\$6,000,000}{75,000,000/365} =$$

$$51.1 \text{ days} + 23.7 \text{ days} - 29.2 \text{ days} = 45.6 \text{ days}$$

Minimum Cash Balance $= 45.6 \text{ days} \times \$100,000,000/365 = \$12,493,151$
Excess Cash Balances $= \$21,433,000 - \$12,493,151 = \$8,939,849$

While excess cash balances should be added to the present value of operating assets, any cash deficiency should be subtracted from the value of operating assets to determine the value of the firm. This reduction in the value will reflect the need for the acquirer to invest additional working capital to make up any deficiency.

Investments in Other Firms

Many target firms will have investments in other firms. These investments generally have value and need to be included in any valuation of the target's nonoperating assets. Such investments for financial reporting purposes may be classified as minority passive investments, minority active investments, or majority investments. These investments need to be valued individually and added to the present value of the firm's operating assets to determine the total value of the firm. Table 7-3 describes their accounting treatment and valuation methodology.

Unutilized and Undervalued Assets

Real estate on the books of the target firm at historical cost may have an actual market value substantially in excess of the value stated on the balance sheet. In other cases, a firm may have more assets on hand to satisfy future obligations than it currently might need. An illustration of such an asset would be an overfunded pension fund. Examples of intangible assets include such patents, copyrights, licenses, and trade names. Intangible assets, so-called intellectual property, are becoming increasingly important for high-tech and service firms. Intangible assets may represent significant sources of value on a target firm's balance sheet. However, they tend to be difficult to value. A study by Chan, Lakonishok, and Sougiannis (1999) provides evidence that the value of intangible spending such as R&D expenditures is indeed factored into a firm's current share price. Despite this evidence, it is doubtful that intellectual property rights such as patents, which a firm may hold but not currently use, contribute anything to the firm's current share price. In the absence of a predictable cash-flow stream, their value may be estimated using the Black–Scholes' Model or the cost of developing comparable inventions or technologies. These alternative valuation methods are discussed in Chapter 8.

Patents

How patents are valued depends on whether they have current applications, are linked to existing products or services, or can be grouped and treated as a single patent portfolio. Many firms have patents for which no current application within the firm has yet been identified. However, the patent may have value to an external party. Before closing, the buyer and seller may negotiate a value for a patent that has not yet been licensed to a third party based on the cash flows that can reasonably be expected to be generated over its future life. In cases where the patent has been licensed to third parties, the valuation is based on the expected future royalties that are to be received from licensing the patent over its remaining life.

When a patent is linked to a specific product, it is normally valued based on the "avoided cost" method. This method uses after-tax market-based royalty rates paid on comparable patents multiplied by the projected future stream of revenue from the products

TABLE 7-3 Investments in Other Firms

Ownership of Firm	Accounting Treatment	Valuation Methodology
Minority, Passive Investments (Investment <20% of other firm)	• Assets held to maturity are carried at book value with interest/dividends shown on income statement • Investments available for sale are carried at market value with unrealized gains/losses included as equity and not as income • Trading investments are shown at market value with unrealized gains/losses shown on the income statement	For investments recorded on investing firm's balance sheet at book value: • Value firm in which investment held • Multiply the firm's value by the proportionate share held by the investing firm to determine the investment's value • Add the investment's value to the value of the investing firm's nonoperating assets • For investments recorded at market value, add to the investing firm's nonoperating assets
Minority, Active Investments—Equity Method (Investment is between 20 and 50% of the other firm's value)	• Initial acquisition value is adjusted for proportional share of subsequent profits/losses • Market value estimated on liquidation and gain/loss reported on income statement	• Value the firms in which the investments are held • Estimate the investing firm's proportionate share • Add the resulting estimated value to the investing firm's nonoperating assets
Majority Investments (Investment >50% of other firm's value)	• Requires consolidation of both firms' balance sheets[1] • Shares held by other investors are shown as a minority interest on the liability side of the balance sheet	• If the parent owns 100% of the subsidiary, value the two on a consolidated basis[2] • If the parent owns less than 100%, value the parent and subsidiary on a consolidated basis and subtract the market value of minority interest shown as a liability on the parent's balance sheet[3]

Notes:
[1] A firm may be required to consolidate both firms' balance sheets even if it owns less than 50%, if its ownership position gives it effective control of the other firm.
[2] If the subsidiary is in a different industry from the parent, a weighted average cost of capital reflecting the different costs of capital for the two businesses should be used to discount cash flows generated by the consolidated businesses.
[3] If a subsidiary is valued at $500 million and the parent owns 75% of the subsidiary, the value of the subsidiary to the parent is $375 million (i.e., $500 million − .25 × $500 million to reflect the value owned by minority shareholders).

whose production depends on the patent discounted to its present value at the cost of capital.

Products and services often depend on a number of patents. This makes it exceedingly difficult to determine the amount of the cash flow generated by the sale of the products or services to be allocated to each patent. In this case, the patents are grouped together as a single portfolio and valued as a group using a single royalty rate applied to a declining percentage of the company's future revenue. The declining percentage of revenue reflects the likely diminishing value of the patents with the passage of time. This cash-flow stream is then discounted to its present value.

Trademarks and Service Marks

A trademark is the right to use a name associated with a company, product, or concept. A service mark is the right to use an image associated with a company, product, or concept. Trademarks and service marks have recognition value. Examples include Bayer Aspirin or Kellogg's Corn Flakes. For these firms and others like them, name recognition reflects the firm's longevity, cumulative advertising expenditures, the overall effectiveness of their marketing programs, and the consistency of perceived product quality. The cost-avoidance approach, the PV of projected license fees, or the use of recent transactions can be helpful in estimating a trademark's value.

The underlying assumption in applying the cost-avoidance approach to the valuation of trademarks and service marks is that cumulative advertising and promotion campaigns build brand recognition. The initial outlays for promotional campaigns are the largest and tend to decline as a percentage of sales over time as the brand becomes more recognizable. Consequently, the valuation of a trademark associated with a specific product or business involves multiplying projected revenues by a declining percentage to reflect the reduced level of spending, as a percentage of sales, which is required to maintain brand recognition. These projected expenditures then are adjusted for taxes (because marketing expenses are tax deductible) and discounted to the present at the acquiring firm's cost of capital.

Companies may license the right to use a trademark or service mark. The acquiring company may apply the license rate required to obtain the rights to comparable trademarks and service marks to a percentage of the cash flows that reasonably can be expected to be generated by selling the products or services under the licensed trademark or service mark. The resulting cash flows then are discounted to the present using the acquiring company's cost of capital. Alternatively, a value may be determined by examining recent outright purchases of comparable trademarks or, in the case of the Internet, Web addresses or domain names. See Fernandez (2002) for an excellent discussion of alternative ways to value brands, service marks, and trade names.

Overfunded Pension Plans

Defined benefit pension plans require firms to accumulate an amount of financial assets to enable them to satisfy estimated future employee pension payments. During periods of rising stock markets such as during the 1990s, firms with defined benefit pension plans routinely accumulated assets in excess of the amount required to meet expected obligations. As owners of the firm, shareholders have the legal right to these excess assets. In practice, if such funds are liquidated and paid out to shareholders, the firm will have to pay taxes on the pretax value of these excess assets. Therefore, the after-tax value of such funds may be added to the present value of projected operating cash flows.

Adjusting the Target Firm's Equity Value for Nonoperating Assets, Debt, and Other Obligations

In general, the value of a firm's equity is the value of the firm's operating cash flows plus the terminal or residual value less the market value of the firm's long-term debt. This assumes that the cash-flow impact of all nonoperating assets and liabilities, assumed by the acquiring firm, is reflected in the target's projected operating cash flows. Under ideal conditions, the actual price paid by the acquirer for the target firm's equity would fully reflect these considerations. However, this is often not the case because the actual price paid reflects the relative bargaining strength of the acquiring and target firms, which may involve the acquirer receiving valuable nonoperating assets or assuming significant off–balance sheet liabilities not fully reflected in the purchase price.

The value of the firm's equity may be understated or overstated if the estimated value provided by discounting operating cash flows is not adjusted for the existence of nonoperating assets and liabilities assumed by the acquirer. It is also important to include miscellaneous nonoperating cash outflows and inflows (if applicable) experienced on or about the closing date of the transaction in adjusting the firm's equity. These outflows include such items as investment banking, legal, and consulting fees. Cash inflows at closing could result from the sale of target assets to a third party negotiated prior to closing but not consummated until the closing date. Note that factors such as severance expenses and synergy-related items should already have been included in the valuation of operating cash flows. Exhibit 7-11 shows how firm value is adjusted for these factors to provide a more accurate estimate of the equity value of the firm.

Exhibit 7-11

Adjusting Firm Value

A target firm (which sells washing machines) initially is estimated to have a present value (PV) of annual cash flows for the next 5 years of $20 million and a terminal value of $34 million. The target firm has 2 million common shares outstanding, and the current market value of its long-term debt (LTD) and preferred stock are $12 million and $1 million, respectively. The present value of current and future deferred tax liabilities is $4 million. The acquirer is willing to assume these obligations. During due diligence, it is determined that the firm currently has excess operating cash balances of $2 million, unused patents that could be used by the acquiring firm with a PV of $3 million, and unused commercial property with an estimated market value of $3 million. Because the current commercial real estate market is depressed, it is expected to take 18–24 months to dispose of the property. Consequently, the PV of the surplus property is estimated to be $2.5 million.

It also is discovered that a product line consisting of several different models of washing machines had been discontinued the year before because of quality problems. Potential warranty claims are estimated to have a PV of $2 million. Furthermore, potential litigation with several customers could result in judgments against the target firm in the range of $5 million to $10 million over the next 4 years. The PV of these judgments is $7 million. Note that the cash-flow impact of pending warranty claims and potential litigation expenses were not included in the projection of the target firm's future cash flows. Investment banking and other closing-related cash outlays total $8 million. Calculate the adjusted equity value of the target firm as well as the equity value per share.

Impact of Operating and Nonoperating Assets and Liabilities	($ Millions)
PV of Cash Flow from Operations—Next 5 Years	20.0
PV of Terminal Value	34.0
Total PV (From Operating Cash Flows)	54.0
Plus Nonoperating Assets	
Excess Operating Cash & Short-Term Marketable Securities	2.0
PV of Surplus Commercial Property	2.5
PV of Unused Process Patents (Valued as a Call Option)	3.0
Total Nonoperating Assets	7.5
Less Miscellaneous Nonoperating Cash Outlays	8.0
Total Value of the Firm (before Nonoperating Liabilities)	53.5
Less Nonoperating and Non-LTD Liabilities (not included in operating) cash flows)	
PV of Warranty Claims	2.0
PV of Judgments	7.0
Total Nonoperating Liabilities	9.0
Less Long-Term Debt (including operating leases in present value terms)	12.0
Less: Preferred Stock	1.0
Less: PV of Deferred Tax Liabilities	4.0
Adjusted Equity Value	27.5
Adjusted Equity Value Per Share	$13.75

Things to Remember

The CAPM is used widely to estimate the cost of equity. The pretax cost of debt for nonrated firms can best be approximated by comparison with similar firms, whose debt is rated by the major credit-rating agencies or by looking at interest rates on debt currently on the firm's books. Weights for the firm's cost of capital should be calculated using market rather than book values and reflect the acquiring firm's target capital structure.

FCFF, free cash flow to the firm or enterprise cash flow, reflects cash from operating and investing activities. FCFE, free cash flow to equity investors or equity cash flow, includes cash from operating, investing, and financing activities. The present value of FCFF often is referred to as the enterprise value of the firm. Valuation based on FCFE commonly is called the equity method or equity value. Equity value also can be calculated by deducting the market value of the target firm's long-term debt (including operating leases expressed in present value terms) from the enterprise value.

Discounted cash-flow valuation is highly sensitive to the choice of the discount rate as well as the magnitude and timing of future cash flows. In the constant growth model, free cash flow to the firm is expected to grow at a constant rate. In the variable growth model, cash flow exhibits both a high and a stable growth period. Total PV in this case represents the sum of the discounted value of the cash flows over both periods.

The target firm's equity value should be adjusted for the value of nonoperating assets and liabilities not on the balance sheet. This value also is called the adjusted equity value. Thus, the equity value of the target firm is ultimately the sum of the firm's operating cash flows, terminal value, and nonoperating assets less the current market value of long-term debt and nonoperating liabilities not fully reflected on the balance sheet.

Chapter Discussion Questions

7-1. What is the significance of the weighted average cost of capital? How is it calculated? Do the weights reflect the firm's actual or target debt to total capital ratio? Why?

7-2. What does a firm's β measure? What is the difference between an unlevered and levered β? Why is this distinction significant?

7-3. Under what circumstances is it important to adjust the capital asset pricing model for firm size? Why?

7-4. What are the primary differences between FCFE and FCFF?

7-5. Explain the conditions under which it makes most sense to use the zero growth and constant growth DCF models? Be specific.

7-6. Which DCF valuation methods require the estimation of a terminal value? Why?

7-7. Do small changes in the assumptions pertaining to the estimation of the terminal value have a significant impact on the calculation of the total value of the target firm? If so, why?

7-8. How would you estimate the equity value of a firm if you knew its enterprise value and the present value of all nonoperating assets, nonoperating liabilities, and long-term debt?

7-9. Why is it important to distinguish between operating and nonoperating assets and liabilities when valuing a firm? Be specific.

7-10. Explain how you would value a patent under the following situations: a patent without any current application, a patent linked to an existing product, and a patent portfolio.

Answers to these Chapter Discussion Questions are available in the Online Instructor's Manual for instructors using this book.

Chapter Practice Problems and Answers

7-11. ABC Incorporated shares are currently trading for $32 per share. The firm has 1.13 billion shares outstanding. In addition, the market value of the firm's outstanding debt is $2 billion. The 10-year Treasury bond rate is 6.25%. ABC has an outstanding credit record and has earned a AAA rating from the major credit-rating agencies. The current interest rate on AAA corporate bonds is 6.45%. The historical risk premium over the risk-free rate of return is 5.5 percentage points. The firm's beta is estimated to be 1.1 and its marginal tax rate, including federal, state, and local taxes, is 40%.

a. What is the cost of equity?
b. What is the after-tax cost of debt?
c. What is the weighted average cost of capital?

Answers:

a. 12.3%
b. 3.9%
c. 11.9%

7-12. HiFlyer Corporation does not currently have any debt. Its tax rate is .4 and its unlevered beta is estimated by examining comparable companies to be 2.0. The 10-year bond rate is 6.25%, and the historical risk premium over the risk-free rate is 5.5%. Next year, HiFlyer expects to borrow up to 75% of its equity value to fund future growth.

a. Calculate the firm's current cost of equity.
b. Estimate the firm's cost of equity after it increases its leverage to 75% of equity.

Answers:

a. 17.25%
b. 22.2%

7-13. Abbreviated financial statements are given for Fletcher Corporation in Table 7-4.

TABLE 7-4

	2001	2002
Revenues	$600.0	$690.0
Operating expenses	520.0	600.0
Depreciation	16.0	18.0
Earnings before interest and taxes	64.0	72.0
Less interest expense	5.0	5.0
Less taxes	23.6	26.8
Equals: net income	35.4	40.2
Addendum:		
Year-end working capital	150	200
Principal repayment	25.0	25.0
Capital expenditures	20	10

Year-end working capital in 2000 was $160 million and the firm's marginal tax rate is 40% in both 2001 and 2002. Estimate the following for 2001 and 2002:

a. Free cash flow to equity.
b. Free cash flow to the firm.

Answers:

a. $16.4 million in 2001 and –$26.8 million in 2002
b. $44.4 million in 2001 and $1.2 million in 2002

7-14. No Growth Incorporated had operating income before interest and taxes in 2002 of $220 million. The firm was expected to generate this level of operating income indefinitely. The firm had depreciation expense of $10 million that same year. Capital spending totaled $20 million during 2002. At the end of 2001 and 2002, working capital totaled $70 million and $80 million, respectively. The firm's combined marginal state, local, and federal tax rate was 40%, and its debt outstanding had a market value of $1.2 billion. The 10-year Treasury bond rate is 5%, and the borrowing rate for companies exhibiting levels of creditworthiness similar to No Growth is 7%. The historical risk premium for stocks over the risk-free rate of return is 5.5%. No Growth's beta was estimated to be 1.0. The firm had 2,500,000 common shares outstanding at the end of 2002. No Growth's target debt to total capital ratio is 30%.

a. Estimate free cash flow to the firm in 2002.
b. Estimate the firm's weighted average cost of capital.
c. Estimate the enterprise value of the firm (i.e., includes the value of equity and debt) at the end of 2002, assuming that it will generate the value of free cash flow estimated in (a) indefinitely.
d. Estimate the value of the equity of the firm at the end of 2002.
e. Estimate the value per share at the end of 2002.

Answers:

a. $112 million
b. 8.61%
c. $1,300.8 million
d. $100.8 million
e. $40.33

7-15. Carlisle Enterprises, a specialty pharmaceutical manufacturer, has been losing market share for 3 years since several key patents have expired. Free cash flow to the firm is expected to decline rapidly as more competitive generic drugs enter the market. Projected cash flows for the next 5 years are $8.5 million, $7.0 million, $5.0 million, $2.0 million, and $.5 million. Cash flow after the fifth year is expected to be negligible. The firm's board has decided to sell the firm to a larger pharmaceutical company interested in using Carlisle's product offering to fill gaps in its own product offering until it can develop similar drugs. Carlisle's weighted average cost of capital is 15%. What purchase price must Carlisle obtain to earn its weighted average cost of capital?

Answer: $17.4 million

7-16. Ergo Unlimited's current year's free cash flow to equity is $10 million. It is projected to grow at 20% per year for the next 5 years. It is expected to grow at a more modest 5% beyond the fifth year. The firm estimates that its cost of equity is 12% during the next 5 years and then will drop to 10% beyond the fifth year as the business matures. Estimate the firm's current market value.

Answer: $358.3 million

7-17. In the year before going public, a firm has revenues of $20 million and net income after taxes of $2 million. The firm has no debt, and revenue is expected to grow at 20% annually for the next 5 years and 5% annually thereafter. Net profit margins are expected to remain constant throughout. Annual capital expenditures equal depreciation, and the change in working capital requirements is minimal. The average beta of a publicly traded company in this industry is 1.50 and the average debt/equity ratio is 20%. The firm is managed very conservatively and does not intend to borrow through the foreseeable future. The Treasury bond rate is 6%, and the tax rate is 40%. The normal spread between the return on stocks and the risk-free rate of return is believed to be 5.5%. Reflecting the slower growth rate in the sixth year and beyond, the discount rate is expected to decline by 3 percentage points. Estimate the value of the firm's equity.

Answer: $63.41 million

7-18. The following information is available for two different common stocks: Company A and Company B. (See Table 7-5.)

TABLE 7-5

	Company A	Company B
Free cash flow per share at the end of year 1	$1.00	$5.00
Growth rate in cash flow per share	8%	4%
Beta	1.3	.8
Risk-free return	7%	7%
Expected return on all stocks	13.5%	13.5%

a. Estimate the cost of equity for each firm.
b. Assume that the companies' growth rates will continue at the same rate indefinitely. Estimate the per share value of each company's common stock.

Answers:

a. Company A = 15.45%; Company B = 12.2%
b. Company A = $13.42; Company B = $61

7-19. You have been asked to estimate the beta of a high-tech firm that has three divisions with the following characteristics (see Table 7-6).

TABLE 7-6

Division	Beta	Market Value ($ Million)
Personal computers	1.6	100
Software	2.00	150
Computer mainframes	1.2	250

a. What is the beta of the equity of the firm?
b. If the risk-free return is 5% and the spread between the return on all stocks is 5.5%, estimate the cost of equity for the software division.
c. What is the cost of equity for the entire firm?
d. Free cash flow to equity investors in the current year (FCFE) for the entire firm is $7.4 million and for the software division is $3.1 million. If the total firm and the software division are expected to grow at the same 8% rate into the foreseeable future, estimate the market value of the firm and of the software division.

Answer:

a. 1.52
b. 16%
c. 13.4%
d. PV (total firm) = $147.96; PV (software division) = $41.88

7-20. Financial Corporation wants to acquire Great Western Inc. Financial has estimated the enterprise value of Great Western at $104 million. The market value of Great Western's long-term debt is $15 million, and cash balances in excess of the firm's normal working capital requirements are $3 million. Financial estimates the present value of certain licenses that Great Western is not currently using to be $4 million. Great Western is the defendant in several outstanding lawsuits. Financial Corporation's legal department estimates the potential future cost of this litigation to be $3 million, with an estimated present value of $2.5 million. Great Western has 2 million common shares outstanding. What is the adjusted equity value of Great Western per common share?

Answer: $46.75/share

Answers to these Practice Problems are available in the Online Instructor's Manual for instructors using this book.

Chapter Business Case

Case Study 7-1
The Hunt for Elusive Synergy—@ Home Acquires Excite

Background Information
@Home Network announced its merger with Excite Inc. in January 1999 for $6.7 billion. Prior to the announcement, Excite's market value was about $3.5 billion. The new company combines the search engine capabilities of one of the best known brands (at that time) on the Internet, Excite, with @Home's agreements with 21 cable companies worldwide. @Home gains access to the nearly 17 million households that are regular users of Excite. At the time, this transaction constituted the largest merger of Internet companies ever. As of July 1999, Excite Home displayed a P/E ratio in excess of 260 based on the consensus estimates for the year 2000 of $.21 per share. The firm's market value was $18.8 billion, 270 times sales. Investors had great expectations for the future performance of the combined firms, despite their lackluster profit performance since their inception. Founded in 1995, @Home provided interactive services to home and business users over its proprietary network, telephone company circuits, and through the cable companies' infrastructure. Subscribers paid $39.95 per month for the service.

Assumptions
- Excite is properly valued immediately prior to announcement of the transaction.
- Annual customer service costs equal $50 per customer.
- Annual customer revenue in the form of @Home access charges and ancillary services equals $500 per customer. This assumes that declining access charges in this highly competitive environment will be offset by increases in revenue from the sale of ancillary services.
- None of the current Excite user households are current @Home customers.
- New @Home customers acquired through Excite remain @Home customers in perpetuity.
- @Home converts immediately 2% or 340,000 of the current 17 million Excite user households.

- @Home's cost of capital is 20% during the growth period and drops to 10% during the slower, sustainable growth period; its combined federal and state tax rate is 40%.
- Capital spending equals depreciation; current assets equal current liabilities.
- FCFF from synergy increases by 15% annually for the next 10 years and 5% thereafter. Its cost of capital after the high-growth period drops to 10%.
- The maximum purchase price @Home should pay for Excite equals Excite's current market price plus the synergy that results from the merger of the two businesses.

Case Study Discussion Questions

1. Use discounted cash-flow methods (DCF) to determine if @Home overpaid for Excite.
2. What other assumptions might you consider in addition to those identified in the case study?
3. What are the limitations of the discounted cash-flow method employed in this case?

Answers to these Case Study Discussion Questions are available in the Online Instructors Manual for instructors using this book.

Chapter Business Case

Case Study 7-2
Creating a Global Luxury Hotel Chain

Fairmont Hotels & Resorts Inc. ("Fairmont") announced on January 30, 2006, that it had agreed to be acquired by Kingdom Hotels ("Kingdom") and Colony Capital ("Colony") in an all-cash transaction valued at $45 per share. The transaction is valued at $3.9 billion, including assumed debt. The purchase price represents a 28% premium over Fairmont's closing price on November 4, 2005, the last day of trading when Kingdom and Colony expressed interest in Fairmont. The combination of Fairmont and Kingdom will create a luxury global hotel chain with 120 hotels in 24 countries. Discounted cash-flow analyses, including estimated synergies and terminal value, value the firm at $43.10 per share. The net asset value of Fairmont's real estate is believed to be $46.70 per share.

Case Study Discussion Questions

1. Is it reasonable to assume that the acquirer could actually be getting the operation for "free," since the value of the real estate per share is worth more than the purchase price per share? Explain your answer.
2. Assume the acquirer divests all of Fairmont's hotels and real estate properties but continues to manage the hotels and properties under long-term management contracts. How would you estimate the net present value of the acquisition of Fairmont to the acquirer? Explain your answer.

Answers to these Case Study Discussion Questions are available in the Online Instructors Manual for instructors using this book.

Appendix A

A Primer on Forecasting Business Performance

There are two common approaches to forecasting: qualitative and quantitative. Qualitative forecasting methods are especially important when historical data is not available. These methods include the Delphi and market share approaches. The Delphi method involves solicitation of expert opinion. The market share method entails making an estimate of the current size of the total market and its future growth rate. The analyst must then assume the firm's future market share and how long it is likely to take the firm to achieve that penetration. Consequently, a firm's sales for a given year can be projected by multiplying the assumed market share by the projected size of the market in that year.

The focus in this Appendix will be on using quantitative methods analyzing historical time series to determine causal relationships between variables and using this information to project financial statements for target and acquiring companies. Other topics such as alternative regression models, model specification, the purpose of various types of test statistics, and the limitations of regression analysis are also addressed. Finally, the concepts discussed in this Appendix are illustrated using a Microsoft Excel-based application of multivariate regression analysis to predict a firm's annual sales growth. For a more rigorous and in-depth treatment of this subject matter, including cross-sectional analyses, see Hanke and Wichern (2005), Marks and Samuelson (2003), and Berenson, Levine, and Stephan (1999).

The Art of Forecasting

Forecasting is about projecting future trends in a key variable. For purposes of business valuation, key determinants of future valuation cash flows (i.e., those used in discounted cash flow analysis) include unit sales, costs, and selling prices. To project these factors, it is necessary to determine the key drivers behind their growth. For example, increases in auto sales may be a result of increasing consumer personal disposable income, while costs may be affected by changes in wage rates and other input expenses. Future selling prices may reflect an increase or decrease in intraindustry price competition. The drivers vary by the type of industry and business.

In general, the annual forecast period should be long enough so that the analyst is comfortable projecting growth to the sustainable growth period. For very high growth or cyclical companies, the analyst may need forecast periods of 10 years or more to reach a period reflecting sustainable growth for the firm. Whether the analyst should use 3, 5, 10 or more years of annual projections before assuming a sustainable growth period depends largely on how much confidence the analyst has in longer-term forecasts. The perceived credibility of any forecast depends on the reasonableness of the underlying assumptions. Ultimately, what forecasting is all about is translating the underlying assumptions into the numbers they imply. Some of the most critical forecast assumptions relate to the analyst's opinion about the firm's future growth rate in sales and profit relative to the industry's overall growth rate and how long it can be sustained.

General Guidelines for Sales and Profit Forecasting

Without significant competitive advantage, empirical studies show sales and profit growth rates are likely to revert to the long-term industry average. This reversion to the mean will also cause returns on total assets and equity to move to the industry average, as long as asset turnover (i.e., sales/assets) and financial leverage ratios (e.g., debt/total capital) do not change. Asset turnover rates are unlikely to change significantly in the absence of technological change resulting in production or process improvement. Moreover, target financial ratios seldom change reflecting the long-term nature of management decision making.

Time Series Analysis (Seasonal, Irregular, Cyclical, and Secular)

Time series models identify patterns in a single variable over time. Time series patterns can be broken down into four major categories: trend, business cycles, seasonal variation, and irregular or random fluctuations. A trend or secular movement is a steady movement in an economic variable over time. Superimposed on such trends are periodic business cycles or periods of accelerating or decelerating/declining growth in the economy. Seasonal variation refers to shorter cycles that depend on the time of the year, the season, or other conditions. For example, tourism, tax preparation services, ice cream, and clothing sales are affected by seasonal factors. Irregular movements are due to random or unpredictable factors such as droughts, strikes, wars, and spikes in commodity prices.

Understanding historical trends are generally the most useful for long-term forecasting. If the analyst is confident that the causal relationship between variables historically is likely to continue into the future, the analyst may simply extrapolate this trend growth rate from the base or initial year of the forecast. Growth rates can be readily calculated based on the historical experience of the firm or industry. The average annual growth rate, g, for a time series extending from time, t_1, to t_n can be calculated by solving the following equation:

$$g = (t_n/t_1)^{1/n} - 1 \qquad (7\text{-}19)$$

Care should be taken to discard aberrant data points resulting from infrequent or nonrecurring events such as labor shortages or droughts. Such data points distort the growth rate. Aberrant data points will be apparent by plotting the data. The length of the historical time period used in the analysis should be long enough to encompass one full business cycle (i.e., recession and recovery). Otherwise, the extrapolation may be distorted if the starting or ending point for calculating the average annual growth rate occurs when the economy is growing at above or below its trend rate of growth.

Analysts are often confronted with less than a full year's worth of data for the base year of the forecast period. For example, the fourth quarter for public companies is often not reported until April or May of the following year. Consequently, the analyst must estimate the full year based on three-quarters of data. Assuming little seasonality in the data, if we have data on the first three-quarters of the year, full year sales (S) can be estimated as $(S_1 + S_2 + S_3)/.75$, where $(S_1 + S_2 + S_3)$ represents the dollar value of sales during the first three-quarters. Suppose sales in the fourth quarter have historically accounted for 40% of annual sales, full year sales can be estimated as $(S_1 + S_2 + S_3)/.6$. This relationship can be generalized as follows:

$$S = \sum_{i=1}^{n-1} S_i/(1 - S_n) \qquad (7\text{-}20)$$

where S_i represents the dollar value of sales in the *i*th period of the year and n is equal to 1 to 3 periods for quarterly data and 1 to 11 for monthly data.

Alternative Time Series Regression Models Regression analysis is a statistical technique that estimates the mathematical or causal relationship between a dependent and independent variables. In analyzing mergers and acquisitions, regression analysis may be used to forecast sales and costs that provide the basis for projecting cash flow used in discounted cash-flow valuation. The basic assumption in time series regression analysis is that the factors that have influenced patterns of activity in the past will continue to do so in about the same way in the future. If the analyst feels comfortable with this assumption, she should then plot the data and observe its tendencies over time. Plotting the data enables the analyst to determine whether there is a long-term upward or downward trend. Linear regression involves the relationship between a dependent variable (Y) and a single independent variable (X). Multiple regression models use several explanatory or independent variables $(X_1, X_2, X_3, \ldots X_n)$ to predict the value of the dependent variable.

Simple Linear Regression Model A simple linear regression model may be expressed as follows:

$$Y_i = a_0 + b_1 X_i + \varepsilon_i \tag{7-21}$$

where a_0 = Y intercept for the data sample
b_1 = slope for the data sample
ε_i = random error in Y for observation i

Note that a_0 and b_1 in Equation 7-21 are estimates derived from a data sample taken from the total data population of the true values of the intercept, β_0, and the regression coefficient, β_1. The regression line which best "fits" the data, is that which minimizes the sum of the squared deviations between the values given by the line and the actual data points. Squaring the deviations prevents negative deviations from offsetting positive ones. Furthermore, the larger deviations have a greater influence, because they are squared. In this model, the slope of the line represents the expected change in Y per unit change in X. The Y intercept a_0 represents the average value of Y when X equals 0. ε_i represents the random error in Y for each observation, i, that occurs. ε_i represents the difference between the actual value of Y and $\hat{Y}$, the value estimated by the Equation $Y_i = a_0 + b_1 X_i$.

Quadratic Regression A linear time trend is not the only equation that can be used to fit the past data. The quadratic form can be expressed as follows:

$$Y_i = a_0 + b_1 X_1 + b_2 X_2^2 + \varepsilon_i \tag{7-22}$$

where a positive value of b_2 implies an increasing rate of growth in Y_i over time. In contrast, if b_2 is negative, Y_i tends to grow more slowly over time. The quadratic equation includes the linear equation as a special case when $b_2 = 0$.

Exponential Smoothing Another commonly estimated specification is the exponential form

$$Y_i = br^t \tag{7-23}$$

where coefficients b and r are to be estimated. Note that the coefficient r is raised to the power t. If r is greater than 1, Y_i grows proportionately more with the passage of time. For example, if r equals 1.06, Y_i grows by 6% annually. Alternatively, if r is less than one, Y_i decreases proportionately. If r equals .92, Y_i falls by 8% annually.

Test Statistics

Simple linear regression analysis (see Equation 7-20) focuses on finding the straight line that fits the data best. The best fit is defined as that straight line for which the differences between the actual and estimated values of Y_i are minimized. Total variation in estimated Y, $\hat{Y}$, about its average value can be decomposed into two components: explained and unexplained or residual variance. Explained variation is that portion of total variation in Y that can be explained or accounted for by variation or changes in independent variables in the equation. That portion of total variance that cannot be explained by changes in the independent variables is called unexplained variance.

A number of statistical indicators exist to assist in the determination of which model best fits the historical data. These indicators are called "goodness of fit" statistics. Other statistics help to determine the overall statistical significance of each independent variable (i.e., t-statistics), all independent variables as a group (i.e., F-statistics), and all independent variables plus the intercept (i.e., P-statistics). Statistical significance implies that there is an identifiable and measurable relationship between the dependent and independent variables that is not simply due to chance or coincidence. Statistical significance may be measured at the 5% level. Statistical significance at this level or lower allows the analyst to reject the "null hypothesis" that the estimated intercept, a_0, and regression coefficients, b_i, are different from zero. T-statistics can be used to construct "confidence intervals." Within such intervals, the analyst can be relatively confident that the true value of the intercept and regression coefficients lie within a specific range and that the estimated values of the intercept and regression coefficients lie at the midpoint of that range. See Table 7-7 for a summary of commonly used test statistics.

TABLE 7-7   Common Regression Test Statistics

Statistic	Description
Goodness of Fit	
R value	Degree of correlation between the dependent and independent variable. R = 1 indicates perfect correlation. R values fall between −1 (negative or inverse correlation) and +1 (positive or direct correlation).
Multiple R	Degree of correlation between the dependent and all of the independent variables.
R^2	Measures the percentage of variation in the dependent variable that is explained by the independent variables (i.e., explained variation in Y/total variation in Y).
Adjusted R^2	Removes spurious correlation that can result from adding more independent variables to the equation.
Analysis of variance (ANOVA)	
SS (sum of squares)	The sum of squared differences between each observed Y value and the average value of Y.
Standard error of estimate	Measures the variability of the actual values of Y around the predicted values, for given values of X_i.
Standard deviation	Square root of the variance of a_0 or b_i.

TABLE 7-7   Continued

Statistic	Description
Statistical Significance	
t-statistic[1]	A measure of the likelihood that there is a causal relationship between Y and X. In general, for t values greater than 2.0, the analyst can be 95% certain that the estimated values of a_0 or b_i are different from zero.
Confidence interval	Interval within which the true value of b, β, lies within a range of $\pm 2.5\%$ of the estimated value b. This interval may be constructed as the estimated value of $b \pm t_{.025} S_\beta$, where $t_{.025}$ is the value from a standard t-table and S_β is the standard deviation of b. A confidence level of 95% is approximately ± 2 standard deviations from the estimate.
P value (i.e., the probability value)	P represents the level at which we can reject the null hypothesis that $a_0 = 0$ and $b_i = 0$. P values of .05 or .01 are typically viewed as rejections of the null hypothesis. At these levels $(1 - P)$ is the level of statistical significance of the Y intercept and the independent variable(s) and suggests a strong rejection of the null hypothesis.
F-test[1]	A test of whether the independent variables as a group explain a statistically significant portion of the variation in Y. It is estimated as the ratio of the explained to the unexplained variance. Therefore, the larger the value the more statistically significant the set of independent variables. In general, for 2 to 5 independent variables and 10 to 20 observations, F values >4.5 are statistically significant.

Note:
  [1] T- and F-statistics are found in most statistics textbooks. See Berenson *et al.* (1999) or Hanke and Wichern (2005).

Model Specification

A model is an approximation of the perceived relationship between dependent and independent variables. Model specification refers to the direction of causation (i.e., which is the dependent variable), the initial identification of the possible variables whose variation is likely to explain changes in the dependent variable, and the form of the variables (e.g., linear or nonlinear). See Exhibit 7-12 for a generic specification of hypothetical models for forecasting sales, cost of sales, product/service selling prices, and profit margins.

Exhibit 7-12
Examples of Model Specification

Unit Sales (S) Forecasting Model: $S = f\{(-P_{own}/P_{sub}), +INC, -i, +W, +POP, +Tastes, X_i\}$

where P_{own} = product/service's own price
  P_{sub} = price of substitute products or services
  INC = consumer personal disposable income (After-tax cash flow if the firm is selling to businesses)
  i = interest rates (i.e., cost of borrowing)

W   = household wealth (Corporate net worth if the firm is selling to businesses)

POP   = population (Number of potential business customers if the firm is selling to businesses)

Tastes   = consumer tastes or personal preferences

Xi   = other variables specific to the firm (e.g., patent protection for pharmaceutical companies which limits the number of competitors)

Cost of Sales (COS) Forecasting Model: COS = f(+S, +W, −Prod, +PUR, +i)

where   W = wages, salaries, commissions, bonuses, and benefits
Prod = some measure of productivity (e.g., output/hour)
PUR = purchased materials

Selling Price (SP) Forecasting Model: SP = f(+S, +P$_{sub}$, +COS)

Profit Margin (PM) Forecasting Model: PM = f(+S, +SP, –COS)

Note: The positive or negative sign associated with each variable represent the hypothesized direction of correlation between the dependent and independent variable.

Table 7-8 provides a typical display of the results of applying ordinary least squares regression and the associated test statistics using Microsoft Excel's Data Analysis Toolpak. The steps for utilizing Toolpak are as follows:

1. From the menu bar, select Tools>Data Analysis>Regression
2. Set input Y-range: E5:E24
3. Set input X-range: C5:D24
4. Click boxes for labels and confidence level (95%)
5. Set output range: B29
6. Click OK

The model specified in Table 7-8 relates annual sales for a hypothetical firm to U.S. gross domestic output (GDP) annually from 1986 to 2005. The analyst hypothesizes that the relationship between sales and GDP can be best represented by a quadratic equation. Consequently, sales are regressed against GDP and the square of GDP.

The adjusted R^2 (B36) indicates that the model fits the historical data well, suggesting a strong positive relationship between the firm's sales and GDP. T (F47:F49), F (G42), and P (G47) statistics indicate that the independent variables and the intercept are statistically significant at the 95% confidence level. The positive sign of the coefficient of GDP^2 implies that the firm's sales have been increasing faster than the annual growth in GDP. The standard error of estimate of the dependent variable sales, S (B37), is $30,152. At a 95% confidence level, this implies that the actual sales figure will lie within a range of approximately plus or minus two standard errors (i.e., ±2 × $30,152 = $60,304) of the estimated sales figure. This error is less than 1% of sales.

TABLE 7-8 Regression Analysis of Sales as a Function of GDP and GDP Squared[1]

A	B	C	D	E	F	G	H
1			Historical Data				
2		GDP	GDP^2	Sales			
3			(Millions $)				
4							
5	1986	$4,462.80	$19,916,583.84	$1,090,000.00			
6	1987	$4,739.50	$22,462,860.25	$1,177,200.00			
7	1988	$5,103.80	$26,048,774.44	$1,259,604.00			
8	1989	$5,484.40	$30,078,643.36	$1,341,478.00			
9	1990	$5,803.10	$33,675,969.61	$1,442,089.00			
10	1991	$5,995.90	$35,950,816.81	$1,528,614.00			
11	1992	$6,337.70	$40,166,441.29	$1,617,274.00			
12	1993	$6,657.40	$44,320,974.76	$1,706,224.00			
13	1994	$7,072.20	$50,016,012.84	$1,812,010.00			
14	1995	$7,397.90	$54,728,924.41	$1,929,791.00			
15	1996	$7,816.90	$61,103,925.61	$2,045,578.00			
16	1997	$8,304.30	$68,961,398.49	$2,178,541.00			
17	1998	$8,747.00	$76,510,009.00	$2,320,146.00			
18	1999	$9,268.40	$85,903,238.56	$2,482,556.00			
19	2000	$9,817.00	$96,373,489.00	$2,681,160.00			
20	2001	$10,128.00	$102,576,384.00	$2,882,248.00			
21	2002	$10,487.00	$109,977,169.00	$3,026,360.00			
22	2003	$11,004.00	$121,088,016.00	$3,223,073.00			
23	2004	$11,735.00	$137,710,225.00	$3,480,919.00			
24	2005	$12,497.10	$156,177,508.41	$3,759,393.00			
			Forecast Data				
25	2006	$13,123.25	$172,219,690.56	**$4,063,930.1**			
26	2007	$13,910.00	$193,488,100.00	**$4,418,591.7**			
27	2008	$14,814.55	$219,470,891.70	**$4,843,978.7**			

continued

TABLE 7-8   continued

A	B	C	D	E	F	G	H
28	2009	$15,703.43	$246,597,713.76	**$5,280,358.9**			
29	2010	$16,724.15	$279,697,193.22	**$5,803,915.5**			
30							
31		SUMMARY OUTPUT					
32							
33		*Regression Statistics*					
34		Multiple R	0.999371432				
35		R Square	0.998743259				
36		Adjusted R Square	0.998595407				
37		Standard Error	30151.62941				
38		Observations	20				
39							
40		ANOVA					
41			*df*	*SS*	*MS*	*F*	*Significance F*
42		Regression	2	1.22823E+13	6.14114E+12	6755.027095	2.20591E−25
43		Residual	17	1545052851	909120755.9		
44		Total	19	1.22977E+13			
45							
46		*Coefficients*	*Standard Error*	*t-Stat*	*P Value*	*Lower 95%*	*Upper 95%*
47		Intercept	250727.6436	86168.96351	2.90972101	0.009759367	68927.02369	432528.2635
48		GDP	139.4060357	22.00066224	6.336447247	7.4456E−06	92.98869617	185.8233751
49		GDP^2	0.011518672	0.001316248	8.75114043	1.05337E−07	0.008741632	0.014295713
50							

51   [1] Adapted/updated from Abrams, 2000, Table 2-5, p. 43.

Using the intercept (B47) and coefficients (B48:B49), the estimated regression equation is as follows:

$$S = 250727.64 + 139.41GDP + .01GDP^2$$

Based on the forecast assumptions for GDP and GDP^2 in C25:D29, the analyst is able to obtain the firm's projected sales through 2010 (see D25:D29). Using the confidence interval estimated previously, the true value of sales for 2006 (i.e., the first forecast year) lies within the following range:

$$\$4,003,626.1 < \$4,063,930.1 < \$4,124,234.1$$

Limitations to Regression Analysis

Insufficient data often results in an increase in forecast error, as the limited data is inadequate to capture the true causal relationship between the variables. Moreover, factors affecting changes in the dependent variable historically often change during the forecast period. Such factors include the emergence of new products and competitors, increasing costs due to rising raw material prices, increased government regulation, or unionization of the firm's labor force. Finally, a forecast using a regression equation may result in erroneous projections because the assumptions underlying the future values of the independent variables are incorrect.

References

Abrams, Jay B., *Quantitative Business Valuation: A Mathematical Approach for Today's Professionals*, McGraw-Hill, New York, 2001.

Annema, Andre, and Marc H. Goedhart, "Betas: Back to Normal," *McKinsey Quarterly*, November 8, 2006.

Arzac, Enrique R., *Valuation for Mergers, Buyouts, and Restructuring*, Wiley & Sons, Somerset, NJ, 2005, pp. 121–140.

Berenson, Mark L., David M. Levine, and David Stephan, *Statistics for Managers*, 2nd Ed., Prentice-Hall, Upper Saddle River, NJ, 1999.

Bernard, Vic, Paul Healy, and Krishna G. Palepu, *Business Analysis & Valuation*, 2nd Ed., Southwestern College Publishing Company, Cincinnati, OH, 2000.

Burrus, Amy, and Mike McNamee, "Evaluating the Rating Agencies," *BusinessWeek*, April 8, 2002, pp. 39–40.

Chan, Louis K. C., Josef Lakonishok, and Theodore Sougiannis, "Investing in High R&D Stocks," *BusinessWeek*, October 11, 1999, p. 28.

Cheng, C. S., Chao-Shin Liu, and Thomas F. Schaefer, "Earnings Permanence and the Incremental Information Content of Cash Flow from Operations," *Journal of Accounting Research*, Spring 1996, pp. 173–181.

Claus, James, and Jacob Thomas, "Equity Premia as Low as Three Percent? Empirical Evidence from Analysts' Earnings Forecasts for Domestic and International Stock Markets," *Journal of Finance*, Vol. 56, October 2001, pp. 1629–1666.

Copeland, Tom, Tim Koller, and Jack Murrin, *Valuation: Measuring, and Managing the Value of Companies*, 4th Ed., Wiley & Sons, New York, 2005.

Damodaran, Aswath, *Investment Valuation: Tools and Techniques for Determining the Value of Any Asset*, 2nd Ed., John Wiley & Sons, New York, 2002, pp. 351–379.

Damodaran, Aswath, *The Dark Side of Valuation: Valuing Old Tech, New Tech, and New Economy Companies*, Prentice-Hall, New York, 2001.

Dechow, Patricia M., "Accounting Earnings and Cash Flows as Measures of Firm Performance: The Role of Accounting Accruals," *Journal of Accounting and Economics*, 1994, pp. 3–42.

Easton, Peter, Gary Taylor, Pervin Shroff, and Theodore Sougiannis, "Using Forecasts of Earnings to Simultaneously Estimate Growth and the Rate of Return on Equity Investment," *Journal of Accounting Research*, Vol. 40, June 2001, pp. 657–676.

Escherich, R., "Selected Results from Our Survey of U.S. Valuation Techniques," *Global Mergers & Acquisition Review*, J.P. Morgan, New York and London, January 1998, p. 31.

Fama, Eugene F., and Kenneth R. French, "The Cross-Section of Expected Stock Returns," *Journal of Finance*, Vol. 47, 1992, pp. 427–465.

Fama, Eugene F., and Kenneth R. French, "Common Risk Factors in the Returns on Stocks and Bonds," *Journal of Financial Economics*, Vol. 33, 1993, pp. 3–56.

Fama, Eugene F., and Kenneth R. French, "The Value Premium and the CAPM," *Journal of Finance*, October 2006.

Fernandez, Pablo, *Valuation Methods and Shareholder Value Creation*, Academic Press, New York, 2002, pp. 559–586.

Gitman, Lawrence J., *Principles of Managerial Finance*, 9th Ed., Addison-Wesley, New York, 2000.

Hanke, John E., and Dean W. Wichern, *Business Forecasting*, 8th Ed., Prentice-Hall, Upper Saddle River, NJ, 2005.

Ibbotson Associates, "Stock, Bonds, Bills, and Inflation," *Valuation Edition Yearbook*, Ibbotson Associates Inc., Chicago IL, 2002.

Lasher, William R., *Practical Financial Management*, 4th Ed., Southwestern College Publishing, Cincinnati, OH, 2005.

Levy, George, *Computational Finance: Numerical Methods for Pricing Financial Instruments*, Elsevier: Butterworth-Heinemann, New York, 2004.

Marks, Stephen G., and William F. Samuelson, *Managerial Economics*, 4th Edition, Wiley & Sons, New York, 2003.

Moyer, R. Charles, James R. McGuigan, and William J. Kretlow, *Contemporary Financial Management*, 7th Ed., Southwestern College Publishing, Cincinnati, OH, 1998.

Pastor, L., and R. F. Stambaugh, "The Equity Premium and Structural Breaks," *Journal of Finance*, Vol. 56, 2001, pp. 1207–1239.

Sloan, Richard G., "Do Stock Prices Fully Reflect Information in Accruals and Cash Flows about Future Earnings," *Accounting Review*, July 1996, pp. 289–315.

Stickney, Clyde P., Paul R. Brown, and James M. Wahlen, *Financial Reporting, Financial Statement Analysis, and Valuation: A Strategic Perspective*, Thompson South-Western Publishing: Houston, TX, 2007, pp. 580–583.

CHAPTER ◆ 8

Applying Relative, Asset-Oriented, and Real Option Valuation Methods to Mergers and Acquisitions

You earn a living by what you get, but you build a life by what you give.

—Winston Churchill

Inside M&A: A CBS "Decision Tree"

In 1999, CBS, a large U.S. television network, believed that the growth prospects for one of its major operating units appeared to be limited. The operating unit, Infinity Broadcasting Network, managed a series of radio stations. The CBS board faced a range of possible options. These included spinning off the unit to their shareholders, selling a portion of the subsidiary's stock to the public, or simply postponing the decision to a later date when Infinity's growth prospects would be clearer. Later that year, CBS issued a portion of the unit's stock to the public, using the proceeds to finance what they thought were more attractive options. It soon became apparent to the board that realizing synergy with the unit that was now partially owned by the public was going to be difficult. Consequently, CBS decided to repurchase the stake they had sold to the public in 2000 (Scherer and Scannell, *The Wall Street Journal*, 2000).

The decision tree on the following page illustrates the range of options available to the board. Each branch of the tree represents an alternative strategy. The decision tree framework is helpful in depicting the significant flexibility senior management often has in developing a business strategy. The challenge is to accurately value each option.

Chapter Overview

Chapter 7 discussed in detail how DCF analysis is applied to M&A valuation. This chapter will address alternative methods of valuation. These methods include relative valuation (i.e., market-based), asset-oriented methods, real options analysis (i.e., contingent

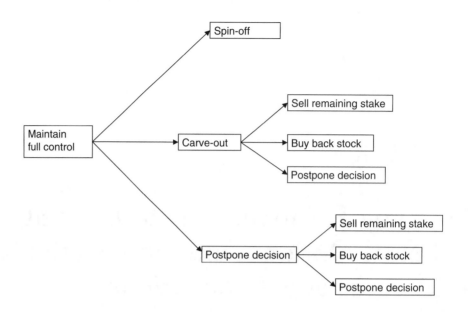

claims), and replacement cost. Relative valuation methods include comparable company, comparable transactions, comparable industry techniques, and value driver-based valuation. Asset-oriented methods include tangible book value and liquidation/breakup value techniques.

This chapter discusses in detail how to look at M&A valuation in the context of real options. This involves identifying preclosing and postclosing strategic and tactical alternatives and associated risks available to M&A participants. Real options valuation is illustrated both in the context of a decision tree framework and as call and put options, when the assets underlying the option exhibit the characteristics of financial options. A weighted average valuation approach, which attempts to incorporate the analyst's relative confidence in the various valuation methods, is also discussed. The chapter concludes with a summary of the strengths and weaknesses of the alternative valuation methods (including discounted cash flow). A review of this chapter is available on the CD-ROM accompanying this book.

Applying Relative Valuation (Market-Based) Methods

Relative valuation methods assume a firm's market value can be approximated by a value indicator for comparable companies, comparable transactions, or comparable industry averages. Value indicators could include the firm's earnings, operating cash flow, EBITDA (i.e., earnings before interest and taxes, depreciation, and amortization), sales, or book value. This approach is often described as market-based, as it reflects the amounts investors are willing to pay for each dollar of earnings, cash flow, sales, or book value. As such, it reflects theoretically the collective wisdom of investors in the marketplace. Because of the requirement for positive current or near-term earnings or cash flow, this approach is meaningful only for companies with a positive, stable earnings or cash-flow stream.

If comparable companies are available, the market value of a target firm T (MV_T) can be estimated by solving the following equation:

$$MV_T = (MV_C/VI_C) \times VI_T, \qquad (8\text{-}1)$$

where MV_C = market value of the comparable company C
VI_C = value indicator for comparable company C
VI_T = value indicator for firm T
(MV_C/I_C) = market value multiple for the comparable company

For example, if the P/E ratio for the comparable firm is equal to 10 (MV_C/VI_C) and the after-tax earnings of the target firm is \$2 million (VI_T), the market value of the target firm is \$20 million (MV_T). Relative value methods are popular for three reasons. First, such methods are relatively simple to calculate and require far fewer assumptions than discounted cash-flow techniques. Second, relative valuation is far easier to explain than DCF methods. Finally, the use of market-based techniques is more likely to reflect current market demand and supply conditions. Equation 8-1 can be used to estimate the value of the target firm in all of the relative valuation and asset-oriented methods discussed in this chapter.

Comparable Companies Method

Applying the comparable companies approach requires that the analyst identify companies that are substantially similar to the target firm (see Exhibit 8-1). This approach is used widely in so-called "fairness opinions," which investment bankers frequently are asked to give before a request for shareholder approval of an acquisition (see Case Study 8-3). Because it frequently is viewed as more objective than alternative approaches, the comparable companies' method also enjoys widespread use in legal cases.

Generally speaking, a comparable firm is one whose profitability, potential growth rate in earnings or cash flows, and perceived risk is similar to the firm to be valued. Note that by defining the method in such broad terms it is possible to utilize firms in other industries. As such, a computer hardware manufacturer can be compared to a telecommunications firm, as long as they are comparable in terms of profitability, growth, and risk. Consequently, if the firm to be valued has a 15% return on equity (i.e., profitability), expected earnings or cash-flow growth rates of 10% annually (i.e., growth), and a beta of 1.3 or debt-to-equity ratio of one (i.e., risk), the analyst must find a firm with similar characteristics either in the same industry or another industry. In practice, analysts look for comparable firms in the same industry and that are similar in terms of such things as markets served, product offering, degree of leverage, and size. The assumption implicit in looking for companies in the same industry is that such firms are substantially similar in terms of profitability, growth potential, and risk.

Even when companies appear to be substantially similar, there are likely to be significant differences in these data at any one moment in time. These differences may result from investor overreaction to one-time events. The impact of such events abates with the passage of time. Consequently, comparisons made at different times can provide distinctly different results. By taking an average of multiples over 6 months or 1 year, these differences may be minimized.

Exhibit 8-1

Valuing a Target Company Using Comparable Companies

An analyst selects two companies that are believed to be quite similar to the target company that she wishes to value. Using the formula specified in Equation 8-1, three value indicators are selected for the valuation of the target company. These include revenue, earnings before interest, taxes, depreciation, and amortization (EBITDA), and net income. The market value for each comparable company is given in row (1). The dollar value of each value indicator is given in rows (2)–(4). Market value multiples are given in rows (5)–(7). These multiples are calculated by dividing market value by the dollar value of each value indicator. Note that the market value to net income is equivalent to the price-to-earnings ratio. Estimated values of the target firm are obtained by multiplying column (3) by column (4). A single value of the target is determined by averaging the estimates in column (5).

Value Indicator	Comparable Company 1 Col. 1	Comparable Company 2 Col. 2	Comparable Company Average Col. 3	Target Company Projections ($Millions– VI_T) Col. 4	Estimated Value of Target ($Millions– MV_T) Col. 5
(1) Market Value	$120	$80	$100		
Value Indicators (VI_T—$Millions)					
(2) Revenue	$100	$57	$78.5		
(3) EBITDA	$ 10	$ 7	$ 8.5		
(4) Net Income	$ 7	$ 4	$ 5.5		
Market Value Multiples (MV_C/VI_C)					
(5) Revenue	1.2	1.4	1.3	$150	$195
(6) EBITDA	12	11.4	11.7	$ 23	$269.1
(7) Net Income	17.1	20	18.6	$ 15	$279
Average Estimated Value of Target					$247.7

Comparable Transactions Method

The comparable transactions approach is conceptually similar to the comparable companies approach. Multiples used to estimate the value of the target are based on purchase prices of comparable companies that recently were acquired. Price (i.e., market value) to earnings, sales, cash flow, EBITDA, and book value ratios are calculated using the purchase price for the recent transaction. Earnings, sales, cash flow, EBITDA, and book value for the target subsequently are multiplied by these ratios to obtain an estimate of the market value of the target company. This estimated value of the target firm obtained by using recent comparable transactions already reflects a purchase price premium, unlike the comparable companies approach to valuation. The obvious limitation to the comparable transactions method is the difficulty in finding truly comparable, recent transactions. Note that comparable recent transactions can be found in other industries as long as they are similar to the target firm in terms of profitability, expected earnings and cash flow growth, and perceived risk. Exhibit 8-1 illustrates how the recent transaction valuation method may be applied simply by replacing the data in the columns headed "Comparable Company" with data for "Recent Comparable Transactions."

Same or Comparable Industry Method

Using this approach, the target company's net income, revenue, cash flow, EBITDA, and book value are multiplied by the ratio of the market value of shareholders' equity to net income, revenue, cash flow, EBITDA, and book value for the average company in the target firm's industry or for a comparable industry (see Exhibit 8-2). Such information can be obtained from Standard & Poor's, Value Line, Moody's, Dun & Bradstreet, and Wall Street analysts. The primary advantage of this technique is the ease of use. Disadvantages include the presumption that industry multiples are actually comparable and that analysts' projections are unbiased. The use of the industry average may overlook the fact that companies, even in the same industry, can have drastically different expected growth rates, returns on invested capital, and debt-to-total capital ratios.

Exhibit 8-2

Valuing a Target Company Using the Same or Comparable Industries Method

A firm's earnings per share for the coming year are estimated to be $3.00 by an industry analyst. The industry in which the firm competes has an average price to earnings ratio of 20. Estimate the firm's price per share (see Equation 8-1).

$$MV_T = (MV_{IND}/VI_{IND}) \times VI_T$$

$$= 20 \times \$3$$

$$= \$60/share$$

where MV_T = market value per share of the target company

MV_{IND}/VI_{IND} = market value per share of the average firm in the industry divided by a value indicator for that average firm in the industry (e.g., industry average price to earnings ratio)

VI_T = value indicator for the target firm (e.g., estimated earnings per share)

Enterprise Value to EBITDA Method

In recent years, analysts have increasingly used the relationship between enterprise value to earnings before interest and taxes, depreciation, and amortization to value firms. Note that enterprise value can be defined either in terms of the asset or liability side of the balance sheet. (See Exhibit 8-3.) Recall that in Chapter 7, enterprise value was discussed

---

Exhibit 8-3
Defining Enterprise Value from Either Side of the Balance Sheet

---

Excess Cash (C)	Current Liabilities (CL)
Current Assets, Excluding Excess	Long-Term Debt (LTD)
Cash (CA)	Other Long-Term Liabilities (OLTL)
Long-Term Assets (LTA)	Shareholders Equity, Including
	Common & Preferred Equity (SE)

Enterprise Value $= C + CA - CL + LTA = SE$ (Common & Preferred Equity)
$+ LTD + OLTL$

---

from the perspective of the asset side or "left-hand side" of the balance sheet as the present value of free-cash flow to the firm (i.e., cash flows generated from operating assets and liabilities available for lenders and common and preferred shareholders). Thus defined, enterprise value was adjusted for the value of nonoperating assets and liabilities to estimate the value of common equity. In this chapter, enterprise value is viewed from the perspective of the liability or "right-hand side" of the balance sheet.

The enterprise value to EBITDA multiple relates the total market value of the firm from the perspective of the liability side of the balance sheet (i.e., long-term debt plus preferred and common equity), excluding cash, to EBITDA. In practice, other long-term liabilities often are ignored and "excess cash" is assumed to be equal to cash and short-term marketable securities on the balance sheet. In constructing the enterprise value, the market value of the firm's common equity value (MV_{FCFE}) is added to the market value of the firm's long-term debt (MV_D) and the market value of preferred stock (MV_{PF}). Cash and short-term marketable securities are deducted from the enterprise value of the firm because interest income from such cash is not counted in the calculation of EBITDA. Consequently, the inclusion of cash would overstate the enterprise value to EBITDA multiple, since the asset cash is included in the calculation of the enterprise value. The enterprise value (EV) to EBITDA method is commonly expressed as follows:

$$EV/EBITDA = (MV_{FCFE} + MV_D + MV_{PF} - Cash)/EBITDA \qquad (8-2)$$

The enterprise value to EBITDA method is useful because more firms are likely to have negative earnings than negative EBITDA. Consequently, relative valuation methods are more often applicable when EBITDA is used as the value indicator. Furthermore, net or operating income can be significantly affected by the way the firm chooses to calculate depreciation (e.g., straight-line versus accelerated). Such problems do not arise if the analyst uses a value indicator such as EBITDA that is estimated before deducting depreciation and amortization expense. Finally, the multiple can be compared more readily among firms exhibiting different levels of leverage than for other measures of earnings, since the numerator represents the total value of the firm and the denominator measures earnings before interest. See Exhibit 8-4 for an illustration of how to apply the enterprise value to EBITDA method.

Exhibit 8-4
Valuing a Target Company Using the Enterprise Value to EBITDA Method

Acquirer Inc. is considering two potential target firms. The market value of Firm A's common equity is $1,500 million and Firm B's is $1,200 million. The current market value of Firm A and Firm B's debt is $150 million and $50 million, respectively. Firm A has preferred stock whose market value is $25 million. Both firms show cash and short-term marketable securities on their balance sheets of $20 million. Firm A's and B's current income statements are summarized as follows:

	Firm A	Firm B
	($Millions)	
Revenue	600.00	500.00
Cost of Sales (Incl. S,G&A)	460.00	375.00
Depreciation Expense	100.00	90.00
Interest Expense	12.00	18.00
Taxes	11.20	6.80
Net Income	16.80	10.20

Which firm has the higher enterprise value to EBITDA ratio? (Hint: Use Equation 8-2.)

Answer: Firm A:
Firm A: ($1,500 + $150 + $25 − $20) / ($600 − $460) = 11.82
Firm B: ($1,200 + $50 − $20) / ($500 − $375) = 9.84

Adjusting Relative Valuation Methods for Firm Growth Rates

Assume Firm A and Firm B are direct competitors and have price-to-earnings ratios of 20 and 15, respectively. Which is the cheaper firm? It is not possible to answer this question without knowing how fast the earnings of the two firms are growing. The higher P/E ratio for Firm A may be justified if its earnings are expected to grow significantly faster than Firm B's future earnings.

For this reason, relative valuation methods may be adjusted for differences in growth rates among firms. The most common adjustment is the PEG ratio, commonly calculated by dividing the firm's price-to-earning ratio by the expected growth rate in earnings. This relative valuation method is both simple to compute and provides a convenient mechanism for comparing firms with different growth rates. The comparison of a firm's P/E ratio to its projected earnings is helpful in identifying stocks of firms that are under or overvalued. Conceptually, firms with P/E ratios less than their projected growth rates may be considered undervalued; while those with P/E ratios greater than their projected growth rates may be viewed as overvalued. It is critical for the analyst to remember that growth rates by themselves do not increase multiples such as a firm's price-to-earnings ratio, unless coupled with improving financial returns. Investors are willing to pay more for each dollar of future earnings only if they expect to earn a higher future rate of return. Investors may be willing to pay considerably more for a stock whose PEG ratio is greater than one if they believe the increase in earnings will result in future financial returns that significantly exceed the firm's cost of equity.

Empirical evidence suggests that forecasts of earnings and other value indicators are better predictors of firm value than value indicators based on historical data (Liu, Nissim, and Thomas, 2002; Moonchul and Ritter, 1999). Moreover, the PEG ratio can be helpful in evaluating the potential market values of a number of different firms in the same industry in selecting which may be the most attractive acquisition target.

While the PEG ratio uses P/E ratios, other value indicators may be used. This method may be generalized as follows:

$$\frac{(MV_T/VI_T)}{VI_{TGR}} = A \quad \text{and}$$

$$MV_T = A \times VI_{TGR} \times VI_T \tag{8-3}$$

where A = PEG ratio [i.e., market price to value indicator ratio (MV_T/VI_T) relative to the growth rate of the value indicator (VI_{TGR}), which could include the growth in net income, cash flow, EBITDA, revenue, etc.]

VI_{TGR} = projected growth rate of the value indicator. Because this method uses an equity multiple (e.g., price per share/net income per share), consistency suggests that the growth rate in the value indicator should be expressed on a per share basis. Therefore, if the value indicator is net income per share, the growth in the value indicator should be the growth rate for net income per share and not net income.

Equation 8-3 gives an estimate of the implied market value per share for a target firm based on its PEG ratio. As such, PEG ratios are useful for comparing firms whose expected future growth rates are positive and different to determine which is likely to have the higher firm value. For firms whose projected growth rates are zero or negative, this method implies zero firm value for firms that are not growing and a negative value for those whose projected growth rates are negative. The practical implications for such firms is that those that are not growing are not likely to increase in market value, while those exhibiting negative growth are apt to experience declining firm values. Exhibit 8-5 illustrates how to apply the "PEG" ratio.

Exhibit 8-5

Applying the PEG Ratio

An analyst at a firm conducting a search for potential acquisition targets is given the following information on Firm A and Firm B, two potential acquisition candidates. Firm A's and Firm B's current price-to-earnings ratios are 12.5 and 14, respectively. Firm A's earnings per share is $2.00, while Firm B's is $2.10 per share. The analyst also projects earnings per share to grow at a 10% rate annually for Firm A and 8% for Firm B. Which acquisition candidate would appear to be more attractive based on its PEG ratio? (Hint: see Equation 8-3.)

Answer: Firm B

Firm A:

$$\text{PEG Ratio} = 12.5/10 = 1.25$$

$$\text{Implied Share Price} = 1.25 \times 10 \times \$2 = \$25$$

Firm B:

$$\text{PEG Ratio} = 14/8 = 1.75$$

$$\text{Implied Share Price} = 1.75 \times 8 \times \$2.10 = \$29.40$$

Value Driver-Based Valuation

In the absence of earnings, other factors that drive the creation of value for a firm may be used for valuation purposes. Such factors commonly are used to value start-up companies and initial public offerings, which often have little or no earnings performance records. Measures of profitability and cash flow are simply manifestations of value indicators. These indicators are dependent on factors both external and internal to the firm. Value drivers exist for each major function within the firm including sales, marketing, and distribution; customer service; operations and manufacturing; and purchasing.

There are both micro value drivers and macro value drivers. Micro value drivers are those that directly influence specific functions within the firm. Micro value drivers for sales, marketing, and distribution could include product quality measures such as part defects per 100,000 units sold, on-time delivery, the number of multiyear subscribers, and the ratio of product price to some measure of perceived quality. Customer service drivers could include average waiting time on the telephone, the number of billing errors as a percent of total invoices, and the time required to correct such errors. Operational value drivers include average collection period, inventory turnover, and the number of units produced per manufacturing employee hour. Purchasing value drivers include average payment period, on-time vendor delivery, and the quality of purchased materials and services. Macro value drivers are more encompassing than micro value drivers by affecting all aspects of the firm. Examples of macro value drivers include market share, overall customer satisfaction measured by survey results, total asset turns (i.e., sales to total assets), revenue per employee, and "same store sales" in retailing.

Using value drivers to value businesses is straightforward. First, the analyst needs to determine the key determinants of value (i.e., the value drivers for the target firm). Second, the market value for comparable companies is divided by the value driver selected for the target to calculate the dollars of market value per unit of value driver. Third, multiply this figure by the same indicator or value driver for the target company. For example, assume that the primary macro value driver or determinant of a firm's market value in a particular industry is market share. How investors value market share can be estimated by dividing the market leader's market value by its market share. If the market leader has a market value and market share of $300 million and 30%, respectively, the market is valuing each percentage point of market share at $10 million (i.e., $300 million/30). If the target company in the same industry has a 20% market share, an estimate of the market value of the target company is $200 million (20 points of market share times $10 million).

Similarly, the market value of comparable companies could be divided by other known value drivers. Examples include the number of visitors or page views per month for an Internet content provider, the number of subscribers to a magazine, and the number of households with TVs in a specific geographic area for a cable TV company. Using this method, AT&T's acquisitions of the cable companies TCI and Media One in the late 1990s would appear to be a "bargain." AT&T spent an average of $5,000 per household (the price paid for each company divided by the number of customer households acquired) in purchasing these companies' customers. In contrast, Deutsche Telekom and Mannesmann spent $6,000 and $7,000 per customer, respectively, in buying mobile phone companies One 2 One and Orange Plc (BusinessWeek, 2000).

The major advantage of this approach is its simplicity. Its major disadvantage is the implied assumption that a single value driver or factor is representative of the total value of the business. The bankruptcy of many dot-com firms between 2000 and 2002 illustrates how this valuation technique can be misused. Many of these firms had never shown any earnings, yet they exhibited huge market valuations. Investors often justified these valuations by using page views and subscribers of supposedly comparable firms to value any firm associated with the Internet. These proved to be poor indicators of the firm's ability to generate future earnings or cash flow.

Despite the well-documented dangers of overpaying for firms, recent transactions involving Internet start-ups MySpace and YouTube suggest that what some might term "field of dreams" valuations pop up all too often. Amidst the euphoria of the moment, acquirers often overlook the risks associated with firms lacking meaningful revenues or profits and well-defined business models and base their valuations solely on the target firm's perceived potential. Case Study 8-1 illustrates how a value driver approach to valuation could have been used by Google to estimate the potential value of YouTube by collecting publicly available data for a comparable business. Note the importance of clearly identifying key assumptions underlying the valuation. The credibility of the valuation is ultimately dependent on the credibility of the assumptions.

Case Study 8-1
Google Buys YouTube: Brilliant or Misguided?

How much would you pay for a business without any significant revenues let alone profits? Ask Google. They purchased video-sharing Web site, YouTube, on October 9, 2006, for $1.65 billion in stock. At that time, the business had been in existence only 14 months and consisted of 65 employees. However, what it lacked in size it made up in global recognition and a rapidly escalating number of site visitors. This transaction followed a little more than 1 year after News Corp. paid $580 million for Intermix Media, the owner of MySpace, then the fifth most viewed Internet domain in the United States. MySpace.com users access the site for dating, making friends, professional networking, and sharing interests. With a larger percentage of advertising dollars moving from traditional outlets to the online venue, News Corp. and Google, like most media firms, are attempting to further increase their Internet exposure.

Under pressure to continue to fuel its own meteoric 77% annual revenue growth rate, Google moved aggressively to acquire YouTube in an attempt to assume center stage in the rapidly growing online video market. With no debt, $9 billion in cash, and a net profit margin of about 25%, Google is in remarkable financial health for a firm growing so rapidly. The acquisition is by far the most expensive acquisition by Google in its relatively short 8-year history. In 2005, Google spent $130.5 million in acquiring 15 small firms. Google seems to be placing a big bet that YouTube will become a huge marketing hub as its increasing number of viewers attracts advertisers interested in moving from television to the Internet.

Started in February 2005 in the garage of one of the founders, YouTube displays more than 100 million videos daily and has an estimated 72 million visitors from around the world each month, of which 34 million are unique. Unique visitors are those whose IP addresses are counted only once no matter how many times they visit a Web site during a given period. As part of Google, YouTube will retain its name and its current headquarters in San Bruno, California. In addition to receiving funding from Google, YouTube will be able to tap into Google's substantial technological and advertising expertise. Although YouTube does not currently run advertising within the videos shown on its sites, it has plans to do so in order to tap potentially lucrative advertising revenues.

While most videos on YouTube are homemade, the site also features material that is protected by copyrights. This has spurred some observers to predict that the firm will be buried in an avalanche of copyright infringement lawsuits filed by media companies and artists in a manner similar to Napster, a music file-sharing site. In an effort to ward off a similar fate, YouTube has announced new partnerships with Universal Music Group, CBS Corp., Sony BMG Music Entertainment, Warner Music Group Inc., and other important content providers. To insulate itself from potential lawsuits and associated legal fees and possible penalties for copyright violations, Google withheld 12.5% of the purchase price (457,000 shares valued at $224 million as of 11/14/2006) for 1 year in an escrow account.

To determine if Google is likely to earn its cost of equity on its investment in YouTube, we have to establish a base year free cash flow estimate for YouTube. This may be done by examining the performance of a similar but more mature Web site such as about.com. Acquired by the *New York Times* in February 2005 for $410 million, about.com is a Web site offering consumer information and advice and is believed to be one of the biggest and most profitable Web sites on the Internet, with estimated 2006 revenues of almost $100 million. With a monthly average number of unique visitors worldwide of 42.6 million, about.com's revenue per unique visitor is estimated to be about $.15, based on monthly revenues of $6.4 million. (Aboutmediakit, September 17, 2006, http://beanadvertiser.about.com/archive/news091606.html.)

If we assume that these numbers can be duplicated by YouTube within the first full year of ownership by Google, YouTube could potentially achieve monthly revenue of $5.1 million (i.e., $.15 per unique visitor × 34 million unique YouTube visitors) by the end of year. Assuming net profit margins comparable to Google's 25%, YouTube could generate about $1.28 million in after-tax profits on those sales. If that monthly level of sales and profits could be sustained for the full year, YouTube could achieve annual sales in the second year of $61.2 million (i.e., $5.1 × 12) and profit of $15.4 million ($1.28 × 12). Assuming optimistically that capital spending and depreciation grow at the same rate and that the annual change in working capital is minimal, YouTube's free cash flow would equal after-tax profits.

Recall that a firm earns its cost of equity on an investment whenever the net present value of the investment is zero. Assuming a risk-free rate of return of 5.5%, a beta of .82 (per Yahoo Finance), and an equity premium of 5.5%, Google's cost of equity would be 10%. For Google to earn its cost of equity on its investment in YouTube, YouTube would have to generate future cash flows whose present value would be at least $1.65 billion (i.e., equal to its purchase price). To achieve this result, YouTube's free cash flow to equity would have to grow at a compound annual average growth rate of 225% for the next 15 years, and then 5% per year thereafter. Note the present value of the cash flows during the initial 15-year period would be $605 million and the present value of the terminal period cash flows would be $1,005 million. Using a higher revenue per unique visitor assumption would result in a slower required annual growth rate in cash flows to earn the 10% cost of equity. However, a higher discount rate might be appropriate to reflect YouTube's higher investment risk. Using a higher discount rate would require revenue growth to be even faster to achieve an NPV equal to zero.

Google could easily have paid cash, assuming that the YouTube owners would prefer cash to Google stock. Perhaps Google saw its stock as overvalued and decided to use it now to minimize the number of new shares that it would have had to issue to acquire YouTube or perhaps YouTube shareholders simply viewed Google stock as more attractive than cash. Whatever the reason, Google appears to be placing a bet on the future that rests on highly optimistic growth assumptions to justify the purchase price.

The events of early 2007 suggest that these growth assumptions may, indeed, turn out to be wildly optimistic. In February, Viacom filed a $1 billion lawsuit against YouTube for failure to pay "reasonable" licensing fees for the use of copyrighted material. In late March, NBC Universal and News Corp. announced plans to create an online Web site to distribute professionally produced movies and TV content free to Internet users. The site will be funded by advertising.

Case Study Discussion Questions

1. What alternative valuation methods could Google have used to justify the purchase price it paid for YouTube? Discuss the advantages and disadvantages of each.
2. The purchase price paid for YouTube represented more than 1% of Google's then market value. If you were a Google shareholder at that time, how might you have evaluated the wisdom of the acquisition?
3. To what extent might the use of stock by Google have influenced the amount they were willing to pay for YouTube? How might the use of "overvalued" shares impact future appreciation of the stock?
4. What is the appropriate cost of equity for discounting future cash flows? Should it be Google's or YouTube's? Explain your answer.
5. What are the critical valuation assumptions implicit in the valuation method discussed in this case study? Be specific.

Answers to these Case Study Discussion Questions are available in the Online Instructors' Manual for instructors using this book.

Applying Asset-Oriented Methods

Tangible Book Value or Equity per Share Method

Book value is a much-maligned value indicator, because book asset values rarely reflect actual market values (Exhibit 8-6). They may over- or understate market value. For example, the value of land frequently is understated on the balance sheet, whereas inventory often is overstated if it is old or obsolete. The applicability of this approach varies by industry. Although book values generally do not mirror actual market values for manufacturing companies, they may be more accurate for distribution companies, whose assets are largely composed of inventory, and which exhibit high inventory turnover rates. Examples of such companies include pharmaceutical distributor Bergen Brunswick and personal computer distributor Ingram Micro. Book value is also widely used for valuing financial services companies, where tangible book value is primarily cash or liquid assets. Tangible book value is book value less goodwill.

Exhibit 8-6
Valuing Companies Using Book Value

Target Company has total assets (TA) of $15 million, of which goodwill (GW) accounts for $2 million. Total liabilities (TL) are $9 million. Total shares outstanding (S) are 2 million. Its tangible book value per share (BVS) is estimated as follows:

$$BVS = (TA - TL - GW)/S = (\$15 - \$9 - \$2)/2 = \$2$$

The tangible book value per share for the average firm in the industry is $5. Estimate the implied market value per share of Target Company using BVS as a value indicator (see Equation 8-1)

$$MV_T = (MV_{IND}/VI_{IND}) \times VI_T$$

$$= \$5 \times \$2$$

$$= \$10$$

where MV_T = market value per share of Target Company
MV_{IND}/VI_{IND} = market value per share of the average firm in the industry divided by the value indicator for the industry (i.e., industry average tangible book value per share)
VI_T = value indicator of Target Company (i.e., tangible book value per share)

Liquidation or Breakup Value

The terms liquidation and breakup value often are used interchangeably. However, there are subtle distinctions. **Liquidation** or **breakup value** is the projected price of the firm's assets sold separately less its liabilities and expenses incurred in liquidating or breaking up the firm. Liquidation may be involuntary as a result of bankruptcy or voluntary if a firm is viewed by its owners as worth more in liquidation than as a going concern. The **going concern value** of a company may be defined as the firm's value in excess of the sum of the value of its parts. The breakup value of the firm is synonymous with its voluntary liquidation value. Liquidation and breakup strategies will be explored further in Chapter 15.

During the late 1970s and throughout most of the 1980s, highly diversified companies routinely were valued by investors in terms of their value if broken up and sold as discrete operations as well as their going concern value as a consolidated operation. Companies lacking real synergy among their operating units or sitting on highly appreciated assets often were viewed as more valuable when broken up or liquidated. In early 2007, the Blackstone Group, a major private equity investor, acquired Equity Office Properties Trust (EOP) for $36 billion. While EOP had been slowly selling properties in less desirable markets, Blackstone intends to move much more aggressively to sell off the properties held by the real estate investment trust. (See Case Study 13-7 for more details.)

In practice, the calculation of liquidation value, voluntary or as a consequence of bankruptcy, requires a concerted effort by appraisers, who are intimately familiar with the operations to be liquidated. In some instances, the expenses incurred in terms of legal, appraisal, and consulting fees may constitute a large percentage of the dollar proceeds from the sale of the firm's assets. Guidelines do exist for the probable liquidation value of various types of assets. However, they will differ dramatically from one industry to another. They also depend on the condition of the economy and on whether the assets must be liquidated in a hurry to satisfy creditors.

Analysts may estimate the liquidation value of a target company to determine the minimum value of the company in the worst-case scenario of business failure and eventual liquidation. It is particularly appropriate for financially distressed firms. Analysts often make a simplifying assumption that the assets can be sold in an orderly fashion, which is defined as a reasonable amount of time to solicit bids from qualified buyers. "Orderly fashion" often is defined as 9–12 months. Under these circumstances, high-quality receivables typically can be sold for 80–90% of book value. Inventories might realize 80–90% of book value depending on the condition and the degree of obsolescence. The value of inventory may also vary depending on whether it consists of finished, intermediate, or raw materials. More rapid liquidation might reduce the value of inventories to 60–65% of book value. The liquidation value of equipment will vary widely depending on the age and condition.

Inventories need to be reviewed in terms of obsolescence, receivables in terms of the ease with which they may be collected, equipment in terms of age and effectiveness, and real estate in terms of current market value. Equipment such as lathes and computers with a zero book value may have a significant economic value (i.e., useful life). Land can be a hidden source of value, because it frequently is undervalued on GAAP balance sheets. Prepaid assets such as insurance premiums sometimes can be liquidated with a portion of the premium recovered. The liquidation value will be reduced dramatically if the assets have to be liquidated in "fire-sale" conditions under which assets are sold to the first rather than the highest bidder (Exhibit 8-7).

Exhibit 8-7
Calculating Liquidation Value

Titanic Corporation has declared bankruptcy and the trustee has been asked by the firm's creditors to estimate its liquidation value assuming orderly sale conditions. Note that this example does not take into account legal fees, taxes, management fees, and contractually required employee severance expenses. In certain cases, these expenses can comprise a substantial percentage of the proceeds from liquidation.

Balance Sheet Item	Book Value ($)	Orderly Sale Value ($)
Cash	100	100
Receivables	500	450
Inventory	800	720
Equipment (After Depreciation)	200	60
Land	200	300
Total Assets	1,800	1,630
Total Liabilities	1,600	1,600
Shareholders' Equity	200	30

Exhibit 8-8 illustrates a hypothetical estimation of the breakup value of a firm consisting of multiple operating units. The implicit assumption is that the interdependencies among the four operating units are limited such that they can be sold separately without a significant degradation of the value of any individual unit.

Exhibit 8-8
Calculating Breakup Value

Sea Bass Inc. consists of four operating units. The value of operating synergies among the units is believed to be minimal. All but $10 million in debt can be allocated to each of the four units. Such debt is associated with financing the needs of the corporate overhead structure. Legal, consulting, and investment banking fees, as well as severance expenses associated with terminating corporate overhead personnel, amount to $10 million. What is the breakup value of Sea Bass Inc.?

Operating Unit	Estimated Equity Value ($ Millions)
Unit 1	100
Unit 2	125
Unit 3	50
Unit 4	75
Total Equity Value	350
Less any unallocated liabilities held at the corporate level, corporate overhead expense, and costs associated with the breakup.	20
Total Breakup Value	330

Replacement Cost Method

The replacement cost approach estimates what it would cost to replace the target firm's assets at current market prices using professional appraisers less the present value of the firm's liabilities. The difference provides an estimate of the market value of equity. This approach does not take into account the going concern value of the company, which reflects how effectively the assets are being used in combination (i.e., synergies) to generate profits and cash flow. Valuing the assets separately in terms of what it would cost to replace them may seriously understate the firm's true going concern value. This approach may also be inappropriate if the firm has a significant amount of intangible assets on its books due to the difficulty in valuing such assets.

Valuing the Firm Using the Weighted Average (Expected Value) Method

This approach involves calculating the expected value (EXPV) or weighted average of a range of potential outcomes. Weights reflect the analyst's relative confidence in the various methodologies employed to value a business. Note that the value of the weights must sum to one. Assuming an analyst is equally confident in the accuracy of both methods, the expected value of a target firm valued at $12 million using discounted cash flow and $15 million using the comparable companies' method can be written as follows:

$$EXPV = .5 \times \$12 + .5 \times \$15 = \$13.5\,million$$

Note that neither valuation method in this example includes a purchase price premium.

Adjusting Valuation Estimates for Purchase Price Premiums

As explained in Chapter 1, the purchase premium reflects both the perceived value of obtaining a controlling interest in the target and the value of expected synergies (e.g., cost savings) resulting from combining the two firms. When using the weighted average or expected value valuation method, it is important to remember that unless adjusted to reflect a premium, the individual valuation methods discussed in Chapters 7 and 8 will not reflect the amount over market value that must be paid to gain a controlling interest in the target firm or to induce even a minority of shareholders to sell. The exception is the recent transactions method that already reflects a purchase price premium. The premium generally will be determined as a result of the negotiation process and should reflect premiums paid on recent acquisitions of similar firms. See Table 8-6 in Case Study 8-3 for an illustration of how investment bank Lazard Freres determined an appropriate premium for SunGard. How such premiums may be estimated in the absence of recent comparable transactions is discussed in more detail in Chapter 9.

Adjustments to estimated market values should be made with care. For example, the analyst should be careful not to mechanically add an acquisition premium to the target firm's estimated value based on the comparable companies' method if there is evidence that the market values of "comparable firms" already reflect the effects of acquisition activity elsewhere in the industry. For example, rival firms' share prices will rise in response to the announced acquisition of a competitor, regardless of whether the proposed acquisition is ultimately successful or unsuccessful (Song and Walkling, 2000). Akhigbe, Borde, and Whyte (2000) find that the increase in rivals' share prices may be even greater if the acquisition attempt is unsuccessful, because investors believe that the bidder will attempt to acquire other firms in the same industry. There is evidence the effects of merger activity in one country is also built into merger premiums in other countries in regions that are becoming more integrated such as the European Union (Bley and Medura, 2003).

If the expected value reflects a mix of methods, including the recent transactions' method that already reflects a purchase price premium, the analyst could add the same percentage premium to each valuation method whose estimate does not contain a premium before calculating the expected value of the alternative estimates. In practice, valuations of multiples based on recent comparable transactions frequently are given the greatest weight, followed by discounted cash-flow calculations. (See Exhibit 8-9.)

Exhibit 8-9
Weighted Average Valuation of Alternative Methodologies

An analyst has estimated the value of a company using multiple valuation methodologies. The discounted cash-flow value is $220 million, the comparable transactions value is $234 million, the P/E-based value is $224 million, and the firm's breakup value is $200 million. The analyst has greater confidence in certain methodologies than others. Estimate the weighted average value of the firm using all valuation methodologies and the weights or relative importance the analyst gives to each methodology.

Estimated Value ($Millions)	Relative Weight (As Determined by Analyst)	Weighted Average ($Millions)
220	.30	66.0
234	.40	93.6
224	.20	44.8
200	.10	20.0
	1.00	224.4

Analyzing Mergers and Acquisitions in Terms of Real Options

An option is the exclusive right, but not the obligation, to buy, sell, or use property for a specific period of time in exchange for a predetermined amount of money. Options traded on financial exchanges, such as puts and calls, are called financial options. Options, that involve real assets, such as licenses, copyrights, trademarks, and patents, are called real options. Other examples of real options include the right to buy land, commercial property, and equipment.

Real options refer to management's ability to adopt and later revise corporate investment decisions. Since flexibility can greatly change the value of a project, it should be considered in capital budgeting methodology. If we view a merger or acquisition as a single project, real options should be considered as an integral part of M&A valuation. Traditional DCF techniques fail to account for management's ability to react to new information and to make decisions that affect the outcome of a project. However, real options can be costly to obtain (e.g., the right to extend a lease or purchase property), complex to value, and dependent on highly problematic assumptions. They should not be considered unless they are clearly identifiable, unless management has the time and resources to exploit the option, and unless they would add significantly to the value of the underlying investment decision. For a highly intuitive discussion of real options, see Boer (2002) and Cromwell and Hodges (1998); for a more rigorous discussion of applying real options, see Damodaran (2002, pp. 772–815).

Identifying Real Options Embedded in M&A Decisions

Investment decisions, including M&As, often contain certain "embedded options" such as the ability to accelerate growth by adding to the initial investment (i.e., expand), to delay the timing of the initial investment (i.e., delay), or to walk away from the project (i.e., abandon). Frequently, the existence of the real option will increase the value of the expected NPV. For example, the NPV of an acquisition of a manufacturer operating at full capacity may have a lower value than if the NPV is adjusted for a decision made at a later date to expand capacity. If the additional capacity is fully utilized, the resulting higher level of future cash flows may increase the acquisition's NPV. In this instance, the value of the real option to expand is the difference between the NPV with and without expansion. An option to abandon an investment (i.e., divest or liquidate) will often increase the NPV because of its effect on reducing risk. By exiting the business, the acquirer may be able to recover a portion of its original investment and truncate projected negative cash flows associated with the acquisition. Similarly, an acquirer may be able to increase the expected NPV by delaying the decision to acquire 100% of the target firm until the acquirer can be more certain about projected cash flows.

Preclosing Options and Associated Risks

Expand, delay, and abandon options exist in the period prior to closing an acquisition. An example of an option to delay closing occurs when a potential acquirer chooses to purchase a "toehold" position in the target firm to obtain leverage by acquiring voting shares in the target firm. The suitor is required to prenotify the target firm and publicly file its intentions with the SEC if its share of the target firm's outstanding stock reaches 5%. At this point the acquirer may choose to delay adding to its position or to move aggressively through a tender offer to achieve a controlling interest in the target firm. The latter option is an example of an option to expand its position. There is an opportunity cost associated with each choice. If the suitor fails to expand its position, additional bidders made aware of its intentions may bid up the target firm's share price to a level considered prohibitive by the initial potential acquirer. Consequently, the initial acquirer may choose to abandon the entire effort. If the acquirer moves aggressively, it may lose the potential for reaching agreement with the target firm's board and management on friendly terms. The costs associated with a hostile takeover attempt include a potentially higher purchase price and the possible loss of key employees, customers, and suppliers during a more tumultuous integration of the target into the acquiring firm.

Other examples of delay options include an acquiring firm choosing to delay a merger until certain issues confronting the target are resolved, such as outstanding litigation or receiving regulatory approval (e.g., FDA approval for a new drug). The suitor may simply choose not to bid at that time and run the risk of losing the target firm to another acquirer or to negotiate an exclusive call option to buy the target at a predetermined price within a specified time period.

Postclosing Options and Associated Risks

Following closing, the acquirer also has the opportunity to expand, delay, or abandon new investment in the target firm. Acquiring firms generally have some degree of control over the timing of their investment decisions. For example, the acquiring firm's management may choose to make the level of investment in the target firm following closing contingent upon the performance of actual cash flows compared to projected cash flows. If actual performance exceeds expectations, the acquirer may choose to accelerate its level of investment. In contrast, if performance is disappointing, the acquirer may opt to delay investment or even to abandon the target firm either through divestiture or liquidation.

Valuing Real Options for Mergers and Acquisitions

Three ways to value real options are discussed in this book. The first is to use discounted cash flow, relative valuation, or asset-oriented methods and to ignore alternative real options by assuming that their value is essentially zero. The second is to value the real options in the context of a decision tree analysis. A decision tree is an expanded timeline that branches into alternative paths whenever an event can have multiple outcomes (see Lasher, 2005, pp. 428–433). The points at which the tree branches are called nodes. The decision tree is most useful whenever the investment decision is subject to a relatively small number of probable outcomes and the investment decision can be made in clearly defined stages. The section entitled "Inside M&A: A CBS Decision Tree" at the beginning of this chapter illustrates how a decision tree analysis may be used to assess alternative corporate restructuring options. The third method involves the valuation of the real option, assuming that the underlying asset has the characteristics of financial options such as calls or puts. Valuing real options in this manner is often referred to as contingent claim valuation. A **contingent claim** is a claim that pays off only under certain contingencies. For example, the value of the underlying asset must exceed a predetermined value for a call option to pay off or be less than a predetermined value for a put option to pay off.

Several methods are employed for valuing financial options. The standard method for valuing a financial option is the Black–Scholes model. This is an example of a "closed-form" model in which the underlying assumptions do not vary over time. A more flexible, albeit often more complex, valuation method is a lattice-based option valuation technique such as the binomial valuation model. The binomial option pricing model is based on the notion that the value of the underlying asset in any time period can change in one of two directions (i.e., either up or down), thereby creating a lattice of alternative asset pricing points. Because the lattice model, unlike the Black–Scholes model, values the asset (e.g., stock price) underlying the option at various points in time, such important economic assumptions as volatility and the risk-free rate of return can be assumed to vary over time. While the binomial model allows for changing key assumptions over time, it often requires a large number of inputs, in terms of expected future prices at each node or pricing point. While the binomial options model offers greater flexibility in terms of allowing assumptions to vary over time, the Black–Scholes model offers greater simplicity. For this reason, the valuation of real options expressed as call or put options will be valued in this book using the Black–Scholes method. For a recent discussion of alternative real option valuation methods, see Hitchner (2006), Whaley (2006), and Shreve (2005).

Valuing Real Options Using a Decision Tree Framework

Exhibit 8-9 illustrates how the presence of real options may affect the NPV associated with an acquisition in which management has identified two cash-flow scenarios (i.e., those associated with a successful acquisition and those with an unsuccessful one). Each pair of cash-flow scenarios is associated with what are believed to be the range of reasonable options associated with acquiring the target firm. These include the option to immediately acquire, delay, or to abandon the acquisition. Each outcome is shown as a "branch" on a tree. Each branch shows the cash flows and probabilities associated with each cash-flow scenario displayed as a timeline. The probability of realizing the "successful" cash-flow projections is assumed to be 60% and the "unsuccessful" one is 40%. The expected enterprise cash flow of the target firm is the sum of the projected cash flows of both the "successful" and "unsuccessful" scenarios multiplied by the estimated probability associated with each scenario. The target firm is assumed to have been acquired for $300 million, and the NPV is estimated using a 15% discount rate. The terminal value is calculated using the constant growth method with an assumed terminal period growth rate of 5%. With an NPV of –$7 million, the immediate investment option suggests that the acquisition should not be undertaken. However, the analyst should evaluate alternative options to determine if they represent attractive investment strategies.

By recognizing that the target firm could be sold or liquidated, the expected NPV based on the projected enterprise cash flows is $92 million, suggesting that the acquisition should be undertaken. This assumes that the target firm is sold or liquidated at the end of the third year following its acquisition for $152 million. Note that the cash flow in year 3 is $150 million, reflecting the difference between $152 million and the –$2 million in operating cash flow during the third year. The expected NPV with the option to delay is estimated at $34 million. Note that the investment is made after a 1-year delay only if the potential acquirer feels confident that competitive market conditions will support the projected "successful" scenario cash flows. Consequently, the "unsuccessful" scenario's cash flows are zero.

Figure 8-1 summarizes the results provided in Exhibit 8-10 in a decision tree framework. Of the three options analyzed, valuing the target including the value of the cash flows associated with the option to abandon would appear to be the most attractive investment strategy based on NPV. The values of the abandon and delay options are estimated as the difference between each of their NPVs and the NPV for the "immediate investment/acquisition" case.

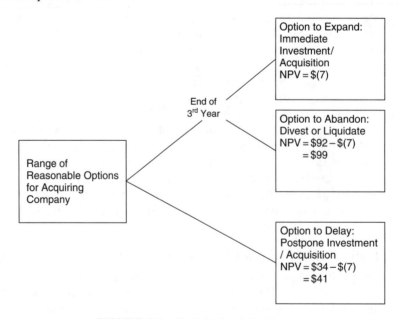

FIGURE 8-1   Real Options' decision tree

Exhibit 8-10
The Impact of Real Options on Valuing Mergers and Acquisitions

	Year 0	Year 1	Year 2	Year 3	Year 4	Year 5	Year 6	Year 7	Year 8	Year 9
First Branch: Option for Immediate Investment/Acquisition										
Enterprise Cash Flows		Projected Target Firm Cash Flows								
Successful Case	−300	30	35	40	45	50	55	60	65	
Unsuccessful Case	−300	−5	−5	−5	−5	−5	−5	−5	−5	
Weighted Cash Flows										
Successful Case (60%)	0	18	21	24	27	30	33	36	39	
Unsuccessful Case (40%)	0	−2	−2	−2	−2	−2	−2	−2	−2	
Expected Enterprise Cash Flow	−300	16	19	22	25	28	31	34	37	
Expected NPV Yr. 1–8 @ 15%										−166
Expected Terminal Value @ 13%; sustainable growth rate = 5%										159
Expected Total NPV										−7
Second Branch: Option to Abandon (Divest or Liquidate)										
Enterprise Cash Flows		Projected Target Firm Cash Flows								
Successful Case	−300	30	35	40	45	50	55	60	65	
Unsuccessful Case	−300	−5	−5	−5	−5	−5	−5	−5	−5	
Weighted Cash Flows										
Successful Case (60%)	0	18	21	24	27	30	33	36	39	
Unsuccessful Case (40%)	0	−2	−2	150	0	0	0	0	0	
Expected Enterprise Cash Flow	−300	16	19	174	27	30	33	36	39	
Expected NPV Yr. 1–6 @15%										−75
Expected Terminal Value @ 13%; sustainable growth rate = 5%										167
Expected Total NPV										92

	Year 0	Year 1	Year 2	Year 3	Year 4	Year 5	Year 6	Year 7	Year 8	Year 9
Third Branch: Option to Delay Investment/Acquisition										
Enterprise Cash Flows		Projected Target Firm Cash Flows								
Successful Case	0	−300	35	40	45	50	55	60	65	70
Unsuccessful Case	0	−300	0	0	0	0	0	0	0	0
Weighted Cash Flows										
Successful Case (60%)	0	0	21	24	27	30	33	36	9	42
Unsuccessful Case (40%)	0	0	0	0	0	0	0	0	0	0
Expected Enterprise Cash Flow	0	−300	21	24	27	30	33	36	39	42
Expected NPV @ 15%										−146
Expected Terminal Value @ 13%; sustainable growth rate = 5%										180
Expected Total NPV										34

Note: The NPV for the delay option is discounted at the end of year 1, while the other options are discounted from year 0 (i.e., the present).

Valuing Real Options Using the Black–Scholes Model

Options to assets whose cash flows have large variances and which have a long time before they expire are typically more valuable than those with smaller variances and less time remaining. The greater variance and time to expiration increases the chance that the factors affecting cash flows will change a project from one with a negative NPV to one with a positive NPV. If we know the values of five variables, we can use the Black–Scholes' model to establish a theoretical price for an option. The limitations of the Black–Scholes' model are the difficulty in estimating key assumptions (particularly risk), its assumptions that interest rates and risk are constant, that it can be exercised only on the expiration date, and that taxes and transactions costs are minimal. Modified versions of the Black–Scholes' Model are discussed in Arzac (2005, pp. 121–140). The basic Black–Scholes' formula for valuing a call option is given as follows:

$$C = SN(d_1) - Ee^{-Rt}N(d_2) \tag{8-4}$$

where C = theoretical call option value

$$d_1 = \frac{\ln(S/E) + [R + (1/2)\sigma^2]t}{\sigma\sqrt{t}}$$

$$d_2 = d_1 - \sigma\sqrt{t}$$

S = stock price or underlying asset price

E = exercise or strike price

R = risk-free interest rate corresponding to the life of the option

σ^2 = variance of the stock's or underlying asset's return

t = time to expiration of the option

$N(d_1)$ and $N(d_2)$ = cumulative normal probability values of d_1 and d_2

Risk can be estimated based on past experience with similar projects by calculating the average percentage difference between projected and actual cash flows for these projects. Alternatively, probabilities or risks can be assigned to optimistic, pessimistic, and most likely scenarios. The average of the probabilities in the three cases can be used to estimate the risk factor. The term Ee^{-Rt} is the present value of the exercise price when continuous discounting is used. The terms $N(d_1)$ and $N(d_2)$, which involve the cumulative probability function, are the terms that take risk into account. These two values are Z-scores from the normal probability function, and they can be found in cumulative distribution function tables for the standard normal random variable.

The net present value (NPV) of an investment can be adjusted for the value of the real option estimated as a call or put option as follows:

$$\text{Total NPV} = \text{Present Value} - \text{Investment} + \text{Option Value} \qquad (8\text{-}5)$$

Option to Expand To value a firm with an option to expand, the analyst must define the potential value of the option. For example, suppose a firm has an opportunity to enter a new market. The analyst must project cash flows that accrue to the firm if it enters the market. The cost of entering the market becomes the option's exercise price and the present value of the expected cash flows resulting from entering the market becomes the value of the firm or underlying asset. The present value is likely to be less than the initial entry costs or the firm would already have entered the market. The variance of the firm's value may be estimated by simulating different cash-flow growth rates and calculating deviations of the present values of the cash flows associated with the different scenarios from the average of the scenarios. Alternatively, variance of the firm's value can be estimated by using the variances of the market values of publicly traded firms that currently participate in that market. The option's life is the length of time during which the firm expects to achieve a competitive advantage by entering the market now. Exhibit 8-11 illustrates how to value an option to expand.

Exhibit 8-11

Valuing an Option to Expand Using the Black–Sholes' Model

AJAX Inc. is negotiating to acquire Comet Inc. to broaden its product offering. Based on its projections of Comet's cash flows as a standalone business, AJAX cannot justify paying more than $150 million for Comet. However, Comet is insisting on a price of $160 million. Following additional due diligence, AJAX believes that, by applying its technology, Comet's product growth rate could be accelerated significantly. By buying Comet, AJAX is buying an option to expand in a market in which it is not participating currently (by retooling Comet's manufacturing operations). The cost of retooling Comet's manufacturing operations to fully utilize AJAX's technology requires an initial investment of $100 million. The present value of the expected cash flows from making this investment today is $80 million. Consequently, based on this information, paying the higher purchase cannot be justified by making the investment in retooling now.

However, if Comet (employing AJAX's new technology) could be first to market with the new product offering, it could achieve a dominant market share. While the new product would be expensive to produce in small quantities, the cost of production is expected to fall as larger volumes are sold, making Comet the low-cost manufacturer. Moreover, because of patent protection, AJAX believes that it is unlikely that competitors will be able to develop a superior technology for at least 10 years. An analysis of similar investments in the past suggests the variance of the projected cash flows is 20%. The option is expected to expire in 10 years, reflecting the time remaining on AJAX's patent. The current 10-year Treasury bond rate (corresponding to the expected term of the option) is 6%. Is the value of the option to expand, expressed as a call option, sufficient to justify paying Comet's asking price of $160 million (see Equation 8-4)?

Solution:

Value of the asset (PV of cash flows from retooling Comet's operations) = $80 million
Exercise price (PV of the cost of retooling Comet's operations)   = $100 million
Variance of the cash flows   = .20
Time to expiration   = 10 years
Risk-free interest rate   = .06

$$d_1 = \frac{\ln(\$80/\$100) + [.06 + (1/2).2]10}{\sqrt{.2}\sqrt{10}} = \frac{-.2231 + 1.600}{.4472 \times 3.1623} = \frac{1.3769}{1.4142} = .9736$$

$$d_2 = .9736 - 1.4142 = -.4406$$

$$C = \$80(.8340) - \$100(2.7183)^{-.06 \times 10}(.3300) = \$66.72 - \$60.13 = \$6.59$$
(value of the call option)

The net present value of the investment in retooling Comet's operations including the value of the call option is $(13.41) million (i.e., $80 − $100 + $6.59). Therefore, it does not make sense for AJAX to exercise its option to retool Comet's operations, and AJAX cannot justify paying Comet its $160 million asking price.

Note: Z-values for d_1 and d_2 were obtained from a Cumulative Standardized Normal Distribution N(d) table in Levine, Berenson, and Stephan, 1999, pp. E6–E7.

Option to Delay   The underlying asset is the project to which the firm has exclusive rights. The current value is the present value of expected cash flows from undertaking the project now. The variance of cash flows from similar past projects or acquisitions can be used to estimate the variance for the project under consideration. Alternatively, the analyst could give probabilities to alternative market growth scenarios and then calculate the average variances of the present values computed for each scenario. A firm exercises an option to delay when it decides to postpone investing in a project. The option's exercise price is the cost of making the initial investment.

The option to delay expires whenever the exclusive rights to the project ends. Since the option eventually expires, excess profits associated with having the option will disappear as other competitors emerge to exploit the opportunity. This opportunity cost associated with delaying implementation of an investment is similar to an adjustment made to the Black–Scholes' model for stocks that pay dividends. The payment of a dividend is equivalent to reducing the value of the stock since such funds are not reinvested in the firm to support future growth. Consequently, for a project whose expected cash flows are spread evenly throughout the option period, each year the project is delayed the firm will lose 1 year of profits that it could have earned. Therefore the annual cost of delay is 1/n, where n is the time period for which the option is valid. If cash flows are not spread evenly, the cost of delay may be estimated as the projected cash flow for the next period as a percent of the current present value (see Exhibit 8-12). Equation 8-4 may be modified to reflect these considerations.

$$C = SN(d_1)e^{-DYt} - Ee^{-Rt}N(d_2) \qquad (8\text{-}6)$$

where $d_1 = \dfrac{\ln(S/E) + [R - DY + (1/2)\sigma^2]t}{\sigma\sqrt{t}}$

$d_2 = d_1 - \sigma\sqrt{t}$

DY = dividend yield or opportunity cost

Exhibit 8-12

Valuing an Option to Delay Using the Black–Scholes' Model

Aztec Corp. has an opportunity to acquire Pharmaceuticals Unlimited which has a new cancer-fighting drug recently approved by the Federal Drug Administration. While current market studies indicate that the new drug's market acceptance will be slow due to competing drugs, it is believed that the drug will have meteoric growth potential in the long term as new applications are identified. The R&D and commercialization costs associated with exploiting new applications are expected to require an up-front investment of $60 million. However, Aztec can delay making this investment until it is more confident of the new drug's actual growth potential.

It is believed that Pharmaceuticals Unlimited's research and development efforts give it a 5-year time period before competitors will have similar drugs on the market to exploit these new applications. However, if the higher growth for the new drug and its related applications do not materialize, Aztec estimates the NPV for Pharmaceuticals Unlimited to be $(30). That is, if the new cancer-fighting drug does not realize its potential, it makes no sense for Aztec to acquire Pharmaceuticals Unlimited. Cash flows from previous drug introductions have exhibited a variance equal to 50% of the present value of the cash flows. Simulating alternative growth scenarios for this new drug provides an expected value of $40 million. The 5-year Treasury bond rate (corresponding to the expected term of the option) is 6%. Despite the negative NPV associated with the acquisition, does the existence of the option to delay, valued as a call option, justify Aztec acquiring Pharmaceuticals Unlimited? (See Equation 8-6.)

Solution:

Value of the asset (PV of projected cash flows for the new drug) = $40 million
Exercise price (initial investment required to fully the new drug) = $60 million
Variance of the cash flows   = .5
Time to expiration (t)   = 5 years

Risk-free interest rate   = .06
Dividend yield or opportunity cost (cost of delay = 1/5)   = .2

$$d_1 = \frac{\ln(\$40/\$60) + [.06 - .2 + (1/2).5]5}{\sqrt{.5}\sqrt{5}} = \frac{-.4055 + .5500}{.7071 \times 2.2361} = \frac{.1445}{1.5811} = .0914$$

$$d_2 = .0914 - 1.5811 = -1.4897$$

$$C = \$40(.5359)2.7183^{-2\times5} - \$60(.0681)(2.7183)^{-.06\times5} = \$40 \times (.5359) \times .3679$$
$$- \$60 \times (.0681) \times .7408 = 7.89 - 3.03 = \$4.86 \text{ million (value of the call option)}$$

The modest $4.86 million value of the call option is insufficient to offset the negative NPV of $30 million associated with the acquisition. Consequently, Aztec should not acquire Pharmaceuticals Unlimited.

Note: Z-values for d_1 and d_2 were obtained from a Cumulative Standardized Normal Distribution N(d) table in Levine, Berenson, and Stephan, 1999, pp. E6–E7.

Option to Abandon   For a project with a remaining life of n years, the value of continuing the project should be compared to its value in liquidation (i.e., abandonment). The project should be continued if its value exceeds the liquidation value. Otherwise, the project should be abandoned.

The option to abandon is equivalent to a put option (i.e., the right to sell an asset for a predetermined price at or before a stipulated time). The Black–Scholes formula for valuing a call option (see Equation 8-4) can be rewritten to value a put option (P) as follows:

$$P = S\{1 - N(d_2)\}e^{-Rt} - E\{1 - N(d_1)\}e^{-DYt} \tag{8-7}$$

where P = theoretical put option value

$$d_1 = \frac{\ln(S/E) + [R - DY + (1/2)\sigma^2]t}{\sigma\sqrt{t}}$$

$$d_2 = d_1 - \sigma\sqrt{t}$$

Exhibit 8-13 illustrates how the abandonment or put option can be applied.

Exhibit 8-13

Valuing an Option to Abandon Using the Black–Scholes' Model

BETA Inc. has agreed to acquire a 30% ownership stake in Bernard Mining for $225 million to help finance the development of new mining operations. The mines are expected to have an economically useful life of 35 years. BETA estimates that the present value of its share of the cash flows would be $210 million, resulting in a negative NPV of $15 million (i.e., $210 million – $225 million). To induce BETA to make the investment, Bernard Mining has given BETA a put option enabling it to sell its share (i.e., abandon its investment) to

Bernard at any point during the next 5 years for $175 million. The put option limits the downside risk to BETA.

In evaluating the terms of the deal, BETA needs to value the put option, whose present value will vary depending upon when it is exercised. BETA estimates the average variance in the present values of future cash flows over a number of scenarios to be 20%. Since the value of the mines will diminish over time as the reserves are depleted, the present value of the investment will diminish over time because there will be fewer years of cash flows remaining. The dividend yield or opportunity cost is estimated to be 1/number of years of profitable reserves remaining. The risk-free rate of return is 4%. Is the value of the put option sufficient to justify making the investment despite the negative net present value of the investment without the inclusion of the option value (see Equation 8-7)?

Solution:

Present or expected value of BETA's 30% share of Bernard SA = $210 million
Exercise price of put option   = $175 million
Time to expiration of put option   = 5
Variance   = 20 percent
Dividend yield (1/35)   = .029

$$d_1 = \frac{\ln(\$210/\$175) + (.04 - .029 + (1/2).2)5}{\sqrt{.2} \times \sqrt{5}} = \frac{.1823 + .5550}{.4472 \times 2.2361} = \frac{.7373}{1.0} = .7373$$

$$d_2 = .7373 - 1.000 = -.2627$$

$$P = \$210 \times (1 - .6026) \times 2.7183^{-.04 \times 5} - \$175 \times (1 - .7673) \times 2.7183^{-.029 \times 5}$$

$$= \$210 \times .3974 \times .8187 - \$175 \times .2327 \times .8650$$

$$= \$33.10$$

The value of the put option represents the additional value created by reducing risk associated with the investment. This additional value justifies the investment, as the sum of the NPV of $(15) million and the put option of $33.10 million gives a total NPV of $18.10 million.

Note: Z-scores for d_1 and d_2 were obtained from a cumulative Standardized Normal Distribution N(d) table in Levine, Berenson, and Stephan, 1999, pp. E6–E7.

Comparing Alternative Approaches to Valuation

Table 8-1 summarizes commonly used methods to value firms. These methods include the discounted cash-flow (DCF) approach discussed in detail in Chapter 7, as well as the relative, asset-oriented, replacement cost, and contingent claims methods discussed in this chapter. These methods provide estimates of the economic value of a company (i.e., the firm's ability to generate future earnings and cash flow), which do not need to be adjusted if the intent is to acquire a small portion of the company. However, if the intention is to obtain a controlling interest in the firm, a control premium must be added to the estimated economic value of the firm to determine the purchase price. The exception would be the comparable recent transactions method, which already contains a premium. The contingent claims approach recognizes that additional value can be created if management has a viable option to expand, delay, or abandon an investment.

TABLE 8-1   Comparison of Alternative Valuation Methods

	Strengths	Weaknesses
Income or Discounted Cash-Flow Method (DCF)		
Discounted Cash Flow	• Considers differences in the magnitude/timing of cash flows and is forward looking • Adjusts for risk • Requires a clear statement of valuation assumptions	• Requires forecasting of cash flows for each period, a terminal value, and discount or capitalization rate(s), using limited or unreliable data • Highly sensitive to the accuracy of cash-flow and discount rate estimates • Terminal value may constitute a disproportionate share of the total value • Requires significant adjustment for highly cyclical firms or those likely to fail • Requires adjustment for nonoperating assets not generating cash flows
Relative Value (Market-Based) Methods		
Comparable Companies	• Utilizes market-based price-to-earnings, sales, or book value for substantially similar companies	• Truly comparable public companies rarely exist • Often reflects accounting-based historical data • May be distorted because of current market psychology
Comparable Transactions	• Uses the most accurate market-based valuation at a point in time • Valuations do not need to be adjusted to reflect control premiums	• May be few in number or not current • Limited availability of specific transaction-related data
Same or Comparable Industry	• Provides additional valuation option for comparative purposes when recent transactions or comparable firms do not exist	• Assumes industry average valuation multiples are applicable to a specific company • Industry information often nonexistent
Replacement Cost Approach (appraised asset values)	• Applicable whenever the DCF or relative valuation approaches are unsuitable because of limited information	• May be of limited use when a large share of the firm's assets are intangible or if the target firm is highly profitable • Ignores synergy created by operating the assets as a going concern

TABLE 8-1   continued

	Strengths	Weaknesses
Asset-Oriented Methods		
Tangible Book Value	• Useful for financial services and distribution companies where assets tend to be highly liquid	• Book value may not equate to market value • Limited availability of required data
Breakup Value	• May unlock value in operating subsidiaries whose actual value cannot be determined easily by analysts outside the company	• Assumes that individual businesses can be sold quickly without any material loss of value • Available markets often highly illiquid
Liquidation Value	• Provides estimate of minimum value of a firm • Primarily used for financially distressed firms	• Frequently assumes that an "orderly" liquidation is possible • Available markets often highly illiquid
Contingent Claims		
Real Options	• Augments DCF by reflecting such management choices to expand, delay, or abandon projects • Enables valuation of assets not currently producing cash flow	• Key assumptions often very difficult to quantify, especially volatility • Project delays may incur significant opportunity costs • Options often not independent; therefore, selecting one option may foreclose other options • Often requires complex modeling

Things to Remember

Relative valuation and asset-oriented techniques offer a variety of alternatives to discounted cash-flow estimates. The comparable companies approach entails the multiplication of certain value indicators for the target such as earnings by the appropriate valuation multiple for comparable companies. Similarly, the comparable transactions method involves the multiplication of the target's earnings by the same valuation multiple for recent, similar transactions. The comparable industry approach applies industry average multiples to earnings, cash flow, book value, or sales. Asset-oriented methods, such as tangible book value, are very useful for valuing financial services companies and distribution companies. Liquidation or breakup value is the projected price of the firm's assets sold separately less its liabilities and associated expenses. Of these methods, only the comparable recent transactions approach includes the value of the purchase price or control premium.

Since no single valuation approach ensures accuracy, analysts often choose to use a weighted average of several valuation methods to increase their level of confidence in the final estimate. This approach relies on an averaging process to achieve potentially more reliable estimates. It also allows the analyst to interject their own preferences for certain methods over others.

Real options, also called strategic management options, refer to management's ability to revise corporate investment decisions after they have been made. Traditional DCF techniques do not recognize management's ability to react to new information. Since real options can be costly, complex, and dependent on questionable assumptions, they should not be considered unless they are clearly identifiable, realizable, and significantly add to the value of the underlying investment.

Chapter Discussion Questions

8-1. Does the application of the comparable companies' valuation method require the addition of an acquisition premium? Why?/Why not?

8-2. Which is generally considered more accurate, the comparable companies' or recent transactions' method? Why?

8-3. What are key assumptions implicit in using the comparable company valuation method? The recent comparable transactions method?

8-4. Explain the primary differences between the income (discounted cash flow), market-based, and asset-oriented valuation methods?

8-5. Under what circumstances might it be more appropriate to use relative valuation methods rather than the DCF approach? Be specific.

8-6. PEG ratios allow for the adjustment of relative valuation methods for the expected growth of the firm. How might this be helpful in selecting potential acquisition targets? Be specific.

8-7. How is the liquidation value of the firm calculated? Why is the assumption of orderly liquidation important?

8-8. What are real options and how are they applied in valuing acquisitions?

8-9. Give examples of pre- and postclosing real options. Be specific.

8-10. Conventional DCF analysis does not incorporate the effects of real options into the valuation of an asset. How might an analyst incorporate the potential impact of real options into conventional DCF valuation methods?

Answers to these Chapter Discussion Questions are available in the Online Instructor's Manual for instructors using this book.

Chapter Practice Problems and Answers

8-11. BigCo's Chief Financial Officer is trying to determine a fair value for PrivCo, a nonpublicly traded firm that BigCo is considering acquiring. Several of PrivCo's competitors, Ion International and Zenon, are publicly traded. Ion and Zenon have P/E ratios of 20 and 15, respectively. Moreover, Ion's and Zenon's shares are trading at a multiple of earnings before interest, taxes, depreciation, and amortization (EBITDA) of 10 and 8, respectively. BigCo estimates that next year PrivCo will achieve net income and EBITDA of $4 million and $8 million, respectively. To gain a controlling interest in the firm, BigCo expects to have to pay at least a 30% premium to the firm's market value. What should BigCo expect to pay for PrivCo?

a. Based on P/E ratios?
b. Based on EBITDA?

Answers:

a. $91 million
b. $93.6 million

8-12. LAFCO Industries believes that its two primary product lines, automotive and commercial aircraft valves, are becoming obsolete rapidly. Its free cash flow is diminishing quickly as it loses market share to new firms entering its industry. LAFCO has $200 million in debt outstanding. Senior management expects the automotive and commercial aircraft valve product lines to generate $25 million and $15 million, respectively, in earnings before interest, taxes, depreciation, and amortization next year. The operating liabilities associated with these two product lines are minimal. Senior management also believes that they will not be able to upgrade these product lines because of declining cash flow and excessive current leverage. A competitor to its automotive valve business last year sold for 10 times EBITDA. Moreover, a company that is similar to its commercial aircraft valve product line sold last month for 12 times EBITDA. Estimate LAFCO's breakup value before taxes.

Answer: $230 million

8-13. Siebel Incorporated, a nonpublicly traded company, has 2002 earnings before interest and taxes (EBIT) of $33.3 million, which is expected to grow at 5% annually into the foreseeable future. The firm's combined federal, state, and local tax rate is 40%; capital spending will equal the firm's rate of depreciation; and the annual change in working capital is expected to be minimal. The firm's beta is estimated to be 2.0, the 10-year Treasury bond is 5%, and the historical risk premium of stocks over the risk-free rate is 5.5%. Rand Technology, a direct competitor of Siebel's, recently was sold at a purchase price of 11 times 2002 EBIT, which included a 20% premium. Siebel's equity owners would like to determine what it might be worth if they were to attempt to sell the firm in the near future. They have chosen to value the firm using the discounted cash-flow and comparable recent transactions methods. They believe that either method would provide an equally valid estimate of the firm's value.

a. What is the value of Siebel using the DCF method?
b. What is the value using the comparable recent transactions method?
c. What would be the value of the firm if we combine the results of both methods?

Answers:

a. $228.9 million
b. $220 million
c. $224.5 million

8-14. Titanic Corporation has reached agreement with its creditors to voluntarily liquidate its assets and to use the proceeds to pay off as much of its liabilities as possible. The firm anticipates that it will be able to sell off its assets in an orderly fashion, realizing as much as 70% of the book value of its receivables, 40% of its inventory, and 25% of its net fixed assets (excluding land). However, the firm believes that the land on which it is located can be sold for 120% of book value. The firm has legal and professional expenses associated with the liquidation process of $2.9 million. The firm has only common stock outstanding. Estimate the amount of cash that would remain for the firm's common shareholders once all assets have been liquidated.

Balance Sheet Item	Book Value of Assets	Liquidation Value
Cash	$10	
Accounts receivable	$20	
Inventory	$15	
Net fixed assets excluding land	$8	
Land	$6	
Total assets	$59	
Total liabilities	$35	
Shareholders' equity	$24	

Answer: $1.3 million

8-15. Financial Corporation wants to acquire Great Western Inc. Financial has estimated the enterprise value of Great Western at $104 million. The market value of Great Western's long-term debt is $15 million, and cash balances in excess of the firm's normal working capital requirements are $3 million. Financial estimates the present value of certain licenses that Great Western is not currently using to be $4 million. Great Western is the defendant in several outstanding lawsuits. Financial Corporation's legal department estimates the potential future cost of this litigation to be $3 million, with an estimated present value of $2.5 million. Great Western has 2 million common shares outstanding. What is the adjusted equity value of Great Western per common share?

Answer: $46.75/share

8-16. Delhi Automotive Inc. is the leading supplier of specialty fasteners for passenger cars in the U.S. market, with an estimated 25% share of this $5 billion market. Delhi's rapid growth in recent years has been fueled by high levels of reinvestment in the firm. While this has resulted in the firm having "state of the art" plants, it has also resulted in the firm showing limited profitability and positive cash flow. Delhi is privately owned and has announced that it is going to undertake an initial public offering in the near future. Investors know that economies of scale are important in this high fixed cost industry and understand that market share is an important determinant of future profitability. Thornton Auto Inc., a publicly traded firm and the leader in this market, has an estimated market share of 38% and an $800 million market value. How should investors value the Delhi IPO? Show your work.

Answer: $526.3 million

8-17. Photon Inc. is considering acquiring one of its competitors. Photon's management wants to buy a firm it believes is most undervalued. The firm's three major competitors, Ajax, Babo, and Comet, have current market values of $600 million, $830 million, and $750 million, respectively. The free cash flow to equity cash flow (FCFE) ratios for Ajax, Babo, and Comet are 4, 6, and 5, respectively. Ajax's FCFE is expected to grow at 12% annually, while Babo's and Comet's FCFE are projected to grow by 14 and 16% per year, respectively. Ajax, Babo, and Comet's projected FCFE for next year are $14, $9, and $8 million, respectively. Estimate the market value of each of the three potential acquisition targets based on the information provided? Which firm is the most undervalued? Which firm is the most overvalued? Show your work.

Answer: Ajax is most undervalued and Comet is most overvalued.

$$MV_{AJAX} = \$672 \text{ million}$$
$$MV_{BABO} = \$756 \text{ million}$$
$$MV_{COMET} = \$640 \text{ million}$$

8-18. Acquirer Incorporated's management believes that the most reliable way to value a potential target firm is by averaging multiple valuation methods, since all methods have their shortcomings. Consequently, Acquirer's Chief Financial Officer estimates that the value of Target Inc. could range, before an acquisition premium is added, from a high of $650 million using discounted cash flow analysis to a low of $500 million using the comparable companies' relative valuation method. A valuation based on a recent comparable transaction is $672 million. The CFO anticipates that Target Inc.'s management and shareholders would be willing to sell for a 20% acquisition premium. The CEO asks the CFO to provide a single estimate of the value of Target Inc. based on the three estimates. In calculating a weighted average of the three estimates, she gives a value of .5 to the recent transactions method, 3 to the DCF estimate, and .2 to the comparable companies' estimate. What is the weighted average estimate she gives to the CEO? Show your work.

Answer: $690 million

8-19. An investor group has the opportunity to purchase a firm whose primary asset is ownership of the exclusive rights to develop a parcel of undeveloped land sometime during the next 5 years. Without considering the value of the option to develop the property, the investor group believes the net present value of the firm is $(10) million. However, to convert the property to commercial use (i.e., exercise the option), the investors will have to invest $60 million immediately in infrastructure improvements. The primary uncertainty associated with the property is how rapidly the surrounding area will grow. Based on their experience with similar properties, the investors estimated that the variance of the projected cash flows represents 5% of the NPV, which is $55 million, of developing the property. Assume the risk-free rate of return is 4%. What is the value of the call option the investor group would obtain by buying the firm? Is it sufficient to justify the acquisition of the firm? Show your work.

Answer: The value of the option is $13.54 million. The investor group should buy the firm since the value of the option more than offsets the $(10) million NPV of the firm if the call option were not exercised.

8-20 Acquirer Company's management believes that there is a 60% chance that Target Company's free cash flow to the firm will grow at 20% per year during the next 5 years from this year's level of $5 million. Sustainable growth beyond the fifth year is estimated at 4% per year. However, they also believe that there is a 40% chance that cash flow will grow at half that annual rate during the next 5 years and then at a 4% rate thereafter. The discount rate is estimated to be 15% during the high-growth period and 12% during the sustainable growth period. What is the expected value of Target Company?

Answer: $94.93 million

Answers to these Chapter Practice Problems are available in the Online Instructor's Manual for instructors using this book.

Chapter Business Case

Case Study 8-2
Merrill Lynch and BlackRock Agree to Swap Assets

During the 1990s, many financial services companies began offering mutual funds to their current customers who were pouring money into the then booming stock market. Hoping to become financial supermarkets offering an array of financial services to their customers, these firms offered mutual funds under their own brand name. The proliferation of mutual funds made it more difficult to be noticed by potential customers and required the firms to boost substantially advertising expenditures at a time when increased competition was reducing mutual fund management fees. In addition, potential customers were concerned that brokers would promote their own firm's mutual funds to boost profits.

This trend reversed in recent years as banks, brokerage houses, and insurance companies are exiting the mutual fund management business. Merrill Lynch agreed on February 15, 2006, to swap its mutual funds business for an approximate 49% stake in money-manager, BlackRock Inc. The mutual fund or retail accounts represented a new customer group for BlackRock, founded in 1987, which had previously managed primarily institutional accounts.

At $453 billion in 2005, BlackRock's assets under management had grown four times faster than Merrill's $544 billion mutual fund assets. During 2005, BlackRock's net income increased to $270 million, or 63% over the prior year, as compared to Merrill's 27% growth in net income in its mutual fund business to $397 million. BlackRock and Merrill stock traded at 30 and 19 times estimated 2006 earnings.

Merrill assets and net income represented 55% and 60% of the combined BlackRock and Merrill assets and net income, respectively. Under the terms of the transaction, BlackRock will issue 65 million new common shares to Merrill. Based on BlackRock's February 14, 2005, closing price, the deal is valued at $9.8 billion. The common stock gave Merrill 49% of the outstanding BlackRock voting stock. PNC Financial and employees/public shareholders owned 34% and 17%, respectively. Merrill's ability to influence board decisions is limited since it has only two of 17 seats on the BlackRock board of directors. Certain "significant matters" require a 70% vote of all board members and 100% of the nine independent members, which include the two Merrill representatives. Merrill (along with PNC) must also vote its shares as recommended by the BlackRock board.

Case Study Discussion Questions

1. Merrill owns less than half of the combined firms, although it contributed more than one-half of the combined firms' assets and net income. Discuss how you might use DCF and relative valuation methods to determine Merrill's proportionate ownership in the combined firms.
2. Why do you believe Merrill was willing to limit its influence in the combined firms?
3. What method of accounting would Merrill use to show its investment in BlackRock?

Answers to these Case Study Discussion Questions are available in the Online Instructors Manual for instructors using this book.

Chapter Business Case

Case Study 8-3
Valuation Methods Employed in Investment Banking Fairness Opinion Letters

Background

A fairness opinion letter is a written third-party certification of the appropriateness of the price of a proposed transaction such as a merger, acquisition, leveraged buyout, or tender offer. A typical fairness opinion provides a range of what is believed to be fair values, with a presumption that the actual deal price should fall within this range. The data used in this case study are found in SunGard's Schedule 14A Proxy Statement submitted to the SEC in May 2005.

On March 27, 2005, the investment banking behemoth Lazard Freres (Lazard) submitted a letter to the board of directors of SunGard Corporation pertaining to the fairness of a $10.9 billion bid to take the firm private made by an investor group. Lazard employed a variety of valuation methods to evaluate the offer price. These included the comparable company approach, the recent transactions method, discounted cash-flow analysis, and an analysis of recent transaction premiums. The analyses were applied to each of the firm's major businesses: software services and recovery availability services. The software services' business provides software systems and support for application and transaction processing to financial services firms, universities, and government agencies. The recovery availability services business provides businesses and government agencies with backup and recovery support in the event their data processing systems are disrupted.

Comparable Company Analysis

Using publicly available information, Lazard reviewed the market values and trading multiples of the selected publicly held companies for each business segment. Multiples were based on stock prices as of March 24, 2005, and specific company financial data on publicly available research analysts' estimates for 2005. In the case of SunGard's software business, Lazard reviewed the market values and trading multiples of four publicly traded financial services companies and three publicly traded securities trading companies. In the case of SunGard's recovery availability services business, Lazard reviewed the market values and trading multiples of the six selected publicly traded business continuity services (i.e., recoverability services firms) companies. These firms were believed to be representative of these segments of SunGard's operations.

Lazard calculated enterprise values for these comparable companies as equity value plus debt, preferred stock, and all out-of-the-money convertibles (i.e., convertible debt whose conversion price exceeded the merger offer price), less cash and cash equivalents (i.e., short-term liquid securities). Estimated enterprise value multiples of earnings before interest, taxes, depreciation and amortization (i.e., EBITDA) were created for 2005 by dividing enterprise values by publicly available estimates of EBITDA for each comparable company. Similarly, price-to-earnings ratios were created by dividing equity values per share by earnings per share for each comparable company for calendar 2005. See Tables 8-2 and 8-3.

Based on this analysis, Lazard determined an enterprise value estimated 2005 EBITDA multiple range for SunGard's recovery availability services business of $5.5\times$ to $7.0\times$. Lazard also determined a 2005 estimated P/E range for this segment of $14.0\times$ to $16.0\times$. Multiplying SunGard's projected EBITDA and earnings per share for 2005 by these ranges, Lazard

TABLE 8-2   Enterprise Value Multiples for Comparable Recovery Availability Companies

	Enterprise Value as a Multiple of EBITDA	Price-to-Earnings Multiple (P/E)
	2005E[1]	2005E
High	9.0×	38.1×
Mean	6.7×	18.2×
Median	6.5×	15.3×
Low	3.8×	12.6×

Note:

[1] E = estimate.

TABLE 8-3   Enterprise Value Multiples for Comparable Software Companies

	Enterprise Value as a Multiple of EBITDA	Price-to-Earnings Multiple (P/E)
High	13.8×	21.5×
Mean	9.7×	18.8×
Median	9.0×	18.1×
Low	7.3×	16.9×

calculated an enterprise value range for SunGard's recovery availability services business of approximately $3.1 billion to $3.7 billion. Financial projections for SunGard were provided by SunGard's management.

Based on the results in Table 8-3, Lazard determined an enterprise value to estimated 2005 EBITDA multiple range for SunGard's software business of 7.5× to 9.5×. Lazard also determined a 2005 estimated P/E range for SunGard's software business of 17.0× to 19.0×. Multiplying SunGard's projected EBITDA and earnings per share for 2005 by these ranges, Lazard calculated an enterprise value range for SunGard's software business of approximately $4.3 billion to $5.2 billion.

Lazard then summed the enterprise value ranges for SunGard's software business and recovery availability services business to calculate a consolidated enterprise value range for SunGard of approximately $7.4 billion to $8.9 billion. Using this consolidated enterprise value range and assuming net debt (i.e., total debt less cash and cash equivalents on the balance sheet) of $273 million, Lazard calculated an implied price per share range for SunGard common stock of $24.20 to $29.00 by dividing the enterprise value less net debt by the SunGard shares outstanding.

Recent Transactions Method

For the recovery availability services business, Lazard reviewed 10 merger and acquisition transactions since October 2001 for companies in the information technology outsourcing business. To the extent publicly available, Lazard reviewed the transaction enterprise values of the recent transactions as a multiple of the last 12 months' EBITDA for the period ending on the recent transaction announcement date. See Table 8-4.

TABLE 8-4   Enterprise Value as a Multiple of Last 12 Months' EBITDA for Recovery Availability Business

High	10.8×
Mean	7.37×
Median	6.4×
Low	5.4×

Based on Table 8-4, Lazard determined an EBITDA multiple range of 6.5× to 7.5× and multiplied this range by the last 12 months' EBITDA for SunGard's recovery availability business to calculate an implied enterprise value range of approximately $3.4 billion to $4.0 billion.

Lazard reviewed 21 merger and acquisition transactions since February 2003 with a value greater than approximately $100 million for companies in the software business. To the extent publicly available, Lazard examined the transaction enterprise values of the recent transactions as a multiple of EBITDA for the last 12 months prior to the public announcement of the relevant recent transaction. See Table 8-5.

TABLE 8-5   Entrerprise Value as a Multiple of
Last 12 Months' EBITDA for the Software Business

High	11.6×
Mean	9.8×
Median	9.9×
Low	6.8×

Based on the information contained in Table 8-5, Lazard determined an EBITDA multiple range of 9.0× to 11.0× and multiplied this range by the last 12-month EBITDA for SunGard's software business to calculate an implied enterprise value range for this business segment of approximately $5.0 billion to $6.1 billion.

Lazard then summed the enterprise value ranges for SunGard's software business and recovery availability services business to calculate a consolidated enterprise value range for SunGard of approximately $8.4 billion to $10.1 billion. Using this consolidated enterprise value range and assuming net debt of $273 million, Lazard calculated the value per share of SunGard common stock of $27.60 to $32.70 by dividing the estimated consolidated enterprise value less net debt by common shares outstanding.

Discounted Cash-Flow Analysis
Using projections provided by SunGard's management, Lazard performed an analysis of the present value, as of March 31, 2005, of the free cash flows that SunGard could generate annually from calendar year 2005 through calendar year 2009. Lazard analyzed separately the cash flows for SunGard's software business and recovery availability services business.

For SunGard's software business, in calculating the terminal value, Lazard assumed perpetual growth rates (i.e., constant growth model) of 3.5 to 4.5% for the projected free cash flows for the periods subsequent to 2009. The projected annual cash flows through 2009 and beyond were then discounted to present value using discount rates ranging from 10.0 to 12.0%. Based on this analysis, Lazard calculated an implied enterprise value range for the software business of approximately $5.6 billion to $7.4 billion.

For SunGard's recovery availability services business, in calculating the terminal value Lazard assumed perpetual growth rates of 2.0 to 3.0% for the projected free cash flows for periods subsequent to 2009. The projected cash flows were then discounted to present value using discount rates ranging from 10.0 to 12.0%. Lazard then calculated an implied enterprise value range for SunGard's recovery availability business of approximately $2.6 billion to $3.3 billion.

Lazard then aggregated the enterprise value ranges for SunGard's two business segments to calculate a consolidated enterprise value range for SunGard of approximately $8.2 billion to $10.7 billion. Using this consolidated enterprise value range and assuming net debt of

$273 million, Lazard calculated an implied price per share range for SunGard common stock of $26.70 to $34.60.

Premiums Paid Analysis

Lazard performed a premiums paid analysis based upon the premiums paid in 73 recent transactions (not involving "mergers of equals" transactions) that were announced from January 2004 through March 2005 and involved transaction values in excess of $1 billion. In conducting its analysis, Lazard analyzed the premiums paid for recent transactions over $1 billion and those over $5 billion, since premiums paid may vary with the size of the transaction.

The analysis was based on the 1-day, 1-week, and 4-week implied premiums for the transactions examined. The implied premiums were calculated by comparing the offer price for the target firm on the announcement date with the per share price of the target firm 1 day, 1 week, and 4 weeks prior to the announcement of the transaction. The results of these calculations are given in Table 8-6.

TABLE 8-6   Premiums Paid Analysis

	Greater Than $1 Billion[1]			Greater Than $5 Billion		
	1 Day	1 Week	1 Month	1 Day	1 Week	1 Month
High	69.8%	67.8%	80.2%	33.4%	38.3%	44.0%
Mean	23.8%	26.6%	27.0%	15.3%	23.1%	26.2%
Median	21.3%	24.0%	25.7%	13.0%	25.4%	23.7%
Low	(9.5)%[2]	(8.0)%	(19.6)%	0.0%	(1.2)%	5.4%

Notes:

[1] The larger premiums paid for smaller transaction may reflect their potentially higher growth potential.

[2] Negative premiums may be a result of target firms whose expected financial performance had been deteriorating during the month prior to the announcement date.

Based on this analysis, Lazard determined an applicable premium range of 20 to 30% for SunGard and applied this range to SunGard's share price of $24.95 on March 18, 2005. Using this information, Lazard calculated an implied price per share range for SunGard common stock of $29.94 (i.e., $1.2 \times \$24.95$) to $32.44 ($1.3 \times \$24.95$).

Summary and Conclusions

Table 8-7 summarizes the estimated valuation ranges based on the alternative valuation methods employed by Lazard Freres. Note that the $36 per offer price compares favorably to the estimated average valuation range, representing a premium of 12% (i.e., $36/$27.11) to 33% (i.e., $36/$32.19). Consequently, Lazard Freres viewed the investor group's offer price for SunGard as fair.

TABLE 8-7   Valuation Range Summary

Valuation Method	Valuation Range ($/Common Share)	(Max. Valuation less Min. Valuation)/ Min. Valuation
Comparable Companies	24.20–29.00	19.8%
Recent Transactions	27.60–32.70	18.5%
Discounted Cash Flow	26.70–34.60	29.6%
Premiums Paid	29.94–32.44	8.4%
Average	27.11–32.19	18.7%

Case Study Discussion Questions

1. Discuss the strengths and weaknesses of each valuation method employed by these investment banks in constructing estimates of SunGard's value for the fairness opinion letter. Be specific.
2. Why do you believe that the percentage difference between the maximum and minimum valuation estimates varies so much from one valuation method to another?
3. Of the alternative valuation methods employed, which do you believe is likely to be the most reliable and why? (See Table 8-1.)

Answers to these Case Study Discussion Questions are available in the Online Instructors Manual for instructors using this book.

References

Aboutmediakit, September 17, 2006, http://beanadvertiser.about.com/archive/news 091606.html.

Akhigbe, Aigbe, Stephen F. Borde, and Anne Marie Whyte, "The Source of Gains to Targets and Their Industry Rivals: Evidence Based on Terminated Merger Proposals," *Financial Management,* Vol. 29, Winter 2000, pp. 101–118.

Arzac, Enrique R., *Valuation for Mergers, Buyouts, and Restructuring*, Wiley & Sons, Somerset, NJ, 2005, pp. 121–140.

Bley, Jorg, and Jeff Madura, "Intra-Industry and Inter-Country Effects of European Mergers," *Journal of Economics and Finance*, Vol. 27, Issue 3, Fall 2003, pp. 373–392.

Boer, Peter E., *The Real Options Solution: Finding Total Value in a High Risk World*, Wiley & Sons, New York, 2002.

Cromwell, Nancy O., and Charles W. Hodges, "Teaching Real Options in Corporate Finance Classes," *Journal of Financial Education*, Vol. 24, Spring 1998, pp. 33–48.

Damodaran, Aswath, *Corporate Finance: Theory and Practice,* Wiley & Sons, New York, 1997, pp. 160–193.

Damodaran, Aswath, *The Dark Side of Valuation: Valuing Old Tech, New Tech, and New Economy Companies*, Prentice-Hall, New York, 2001.

Damodaran, Aswath, *Investment Valuation: Tools and Techniques for Determining the Value of Any Asset*, Wiley & Sons, New York, 2002, pp. 162–163.

Hitchner, James R., *Financial Valuation: Applications and Models*, 2nd Ed., Wiley & Sons, Somerset, NJ, 2006.

Lasher, William R., *Practical Financial Management,* 4th Ed., Southwestern College Publishing, Cincinnati, OH, 2005.

Liu, Jing, Doron Nissim, and Jacob K. Thomas, "Equity Valuation Using Multiples," *Journal of Accounting Research*, Vol. 40, Number 1, March 2002, pp. 135–172.

Moonchul, Kim, and Jay R. Ritter, "Valuing IPOs," *Journal of Financial Economics*, Vol. 53, September 1999, pp. 409–437.

Scherer, Paul M., and Kara Scannell, "Deals and Deal Makers," *The Wall Street Journal*, 2000, p. 17.

Shreve, Steven, *Stochastic Calculus for Finance: The Binomial Asset Pricing Model*, Springer Publishing, 2005.

Song, M. H., and R. A. Walkling, "Abnormal Returns to Rivals of Acquisition Targets: A Test of the Acquisition Probability Hypothesis," *Journal of Financial Economics*, Vol. 55, 2000, pp. 143–171.

Whaley, Robert E., *Derivatives, Markets, Valuation, and Risk Management*, Wiley & Sons, Somerset, NJ, 2006.

CHAPTER • 9

Applying Financial Modeling Techniques to Value and Structure Mergers and Acquisitions

Great moments come from great opportunities.

—Herb Brooks

Inside M&A: Using Financial Models to Negotiate Deals

It was crunch time. Both parties to the negotiation were in heated discussions to resolve several key sticking points. The seller was insisting on a higher price for certain assets that the buyer simply could not justify paying. Nonetheless, the buyer was a seasoned veteran and realized that as long as both parties were motivated a deal was still possible. To bridge the gap between what the seller demanded and what the buyer was willing to pay, the buyer would have to be creative to meet the seller's needs. However, the proposed changes to the terms of the transaction clearly would have implications for the combined companies' taxes, leverage, compliance with loan covenants, and earnings per share.

The buyer turned to a financial model he had constructed of the combined firms to assess the impact of various changes in the terms of the transaction. After changing certain assumptions that had been used to generate the initial offer, the buyer was able to estimate the potential risk to the combined companies if the buyer made the changes demanded by the seller. The model's results were pleasantly surprising to the buyer. The impact of the changes on variables the buyer considered critical was much less than had been imagined. Armed with this information, the buyer returned to the negotiating table optimistic that an agreement could be reached.

Chapter Overview

Financial modeling refers to the application of spreadsheet software to define simple arithmetic relationships among variables within the firm's income, balance sheet, and cash-flow statements and to define the interrelationships among the various financial statements. The primary objective in applying financial modeling techniques is to create a computer-based model, which facilitates the acquirer's understanding of the affect of changes in certain operating variables on the firm's overall performance and valuation (Benninga, 2000). Once in place, these models can be used to simulate alternative plausible valuation scenarios to determine which one enables the acquirer to achieve its financial objectives without violating identifiable and measurable constraints. Financial objectives could include earnings per share (EPS) for publicly traded firms, return on total capital for privately held firms, or return on equity for leveraged buyout firms. Typical constraints include Wall Street analysts' expectations for the firm's EPS, the acquirer's leverage compared with other firms in the same industry, and loan covenants limiting how the firm uses its available cash flow and currently unencumbered assets as collateral for new borrowing. Another important constraint is the risk tolerance of the acquiring company's management, which could be measured by the acquirer's target debt-to-equity ratio.

The models can be used to answer several different sets of questions. The first set pertains to valuation. How much is the target company worth without the effects of synergy? What is the value of expected synergy? What is the maximum price that the acquiring company should pay for the target? The second set of questions pertains to financing. Can the maximum price be financed? What combination of potential sources of funds, both internally generated and external sources, provides the lowest cost of funds for the acquirer, subject to known constraints? The final set of questions pertains to deal structuring. What is the impact on the acquirer's financial performance if the deal is structured as a taxable rather than a nontaxable transaction? What is the impact on financial performance and valuation if the acquirer is willing to assume certain target company liabilities? Deal structuring considerations are discussed in more detail in Chapters 11 and 12.

The purpose of this chapter is to provide a process for building a financial model in the context of a merger or acquisition. The procedure allows the analyst to determine the minimum and maximum prices for a target firm and the initial offer price. The chapter contains numerous examples of how these techniques may be applied. Finally, simple formulae for calculating share-exchange ratios and assessing the impact on post-merger EPS are provided. The Microsoft Excel spreadsheets and formulae for the models described in this chapter are available in a file folder entitled "M&A Valuation and Structuring Model Templates" on the CD-ROM accompanying this book. This highly sophisticated model may be customized by the reader to meet the requirements of their own situation. The model methodology developed in this chapter also may be applied to operating subsidiaries and product lines of larger organization as well as joint ventures and partnerships. A review of this chapter is available on the CD-ROM accompanying this book. For advanced discussions on financial modeling, see Sengupta (2004) and Mun (2006).

Limitations of Financial Data

The output of models is only as good as the accuracy and timeliness of the numbers that are used to create them and the quality of the assumptions used in making projections. Consequently, analysts must understand on what basis numbers are collected and reported. Consistency and adherence to uniform standards become exceedingly important. However, imaginative accounting tricks threaten to undermine an analyst's ability to properly understand a firm's underlying dynamics. Recent examples of inordinate accounting abuses include WorldCom, Tyco, Enron, Sunbeam, Waste Management, and Cendant.

Generally Accepted Accounting Principles (GAAP) and International Accounting Standards (IAS)

U.S. public companies prepare their financial statements in accordance with GAAP. GAAP financial statements are those prepared in agreement with guidelines established by the Financial Accounting Standards Board (FASB). GAAP is a rules-based system, giving explicit instructions for every situation that the FASB has anticipated. In contrast, International Accounting Standards is a principles-based system, with more generalized standards to follow. The European Union will require all publicly traded companies within its membership to adopt IAS by 2007. The more than 400 foreign firms also listed on U.S. exchanges will have to continue to display their books in accordance with GAAP as well. GAAP and IAS currently exhibit significant differences. However, these differences are expected to narrow in the coming years.

Few would argue that GAAP ensures that all transactions are accurately recorded. Nonetheless, the scrupulous application of GAAP does ensure consistency in comparing one firm's financial performance to another. It is customary for definitive agreements of purchase and sale to require that a target company represent that its financial books are kept in accordance with GAAP. Consequently, the acquiring company at least understands how the financial numbers were assembled. During due diligence, the acquirer can look for discrepancies between the target's reported numbers and GAAP practices. Such discrepancies are often indications of potential problems.

Pro Forma Accounting

In recent years, there has been a trend toward using *pro forma financial statements*, which present financial statements in a way that purports to more accurately describe a firm's current or projected performance. Because there are no accepted standards for pro forma accounting, pro forma statements may deviate substantially from standard GAAP statements. Pro forma statements frequently are used to show what an acquirer's and target's combined financial performance would look like if they were merged. When one company acquires another, year-over-year earnings comparisons for the acquiring firm make little sense. Consequently, the acquirer simply adds the target's revenues and profits to its own and then calculates quarterly and annual changes in financial performance.

Although public companies still are required to file their financial statements with the Securities and Exchange Commission in accordance with GAAP, companies increasingly are using pro forma statements to portray their financial performance in what they argue is a more realistic (and usually more favorable) manner. Companies maintain that such statements provide investors with a better view of a company's core performance than reporting that strictly adheres to GAAP. Although pro forma statements do provide useful insight into how a proposed combination of businesses might look, such liberal accounting techniques easily can be abused so as to hide a company's poor performance. Exhibit 9-1 suggests some ways in which an analyst can tell if a firm is engaging in inappropriate accounting practices. For a more detailed discussion of these issues, see Sherman and Young (2001).

Exhibit 9-1
Accounting Discrepancy Red Flags

1. The source of the revenue is questionable. Beware of revenue generated by selling to an affiliated party, by selling something to a customer in exchange for something other than cash, or the receipt of investment income or cash received from a lender.
2. Income is inflated by nonrecurring gains. Gains on the sale of assets may be inflated by an artificially low book value of the assets sold.
3. Deferred revenue shows an unusually large increase. Deferred revenue increases as a firm collects money from customers in advance of delivering its products. It is reduced as the products are delivered. A jump in this balance sheet item could mean the firm is having trouble delivering its products.
4. Reserves for bad debt are declining as a percentage of revenue. This implies the firm may be boosting revenue by not reserving enough to cover probable losses from customer accounts that cannot be collected.
5. Growth in accounts receivable exceeds substantially the increase in revenue or inventory. This may mean that a firm is having difficulty in selling its products (i.e., inventories are accumulating) or that it is having difficulty collecting what it is owed.
6. The growth in net income is significantly different from the growth in cash from operations. Because it is more difficult to "manage" cash flow (i.e., a measure of cash coming in or flowing out) than net income, which is distorted easily because of improper revenue recognition, this could indicate that net income is being deliberately distorted. Potential distortion may be particularly evident if the analyst adjusts end-of-period cash balances by deducting cash received from financing activities and adding back cash used for investment purposes. Consequently, changes in the adjusted cash balances should reflect changes in reported net income.
7. An increasing gap between a firm's income reported on its financial statements and its tax income. While it is legitimate for a firm to follow different accounting practices for financial reporting and tax purposes, the relationship between book and tax accounting is likely to remain constant over time, unless there are changes in tax rules or accounting standards.
8. Unexpected large asset write-offs. This may reflect management inertia in incorporating changing business circumstances into its accounting estimates.
9. Extensive use of related party transactions. Such transactions may not be subject to the same discipline and high standards of integrity as unrelated party transactions.
10. Changes in auditing firms that are not well justified. The firm may be seeking a firm that will accept its aggressive accounting positions.

Model-Building Process

This process involves four discrete steps. First, value the acquiring and target firms as standalone businesses. A *standalone business* is one whose financial statements reflect all the costs of running the business and all of the revenues generated by the business.

Second, value the consolidated acquirer and target firms including the effects of synergy. The appropriate discount rate for the combined firms is generally the target's cost of capital unless the two firms have similar risk profiles and are based in the same country. It is particularly important to use the target's cost of capital if the acquirer is merging with a higher risk business resulting in an increase in the acquirer's cost of capital. Third, determine the initial offer price for the target firm. Fourth, determine the acquirer's ability to finance the purchase using an appropriate financial structure (Figure 9-1).

Step 1 Value Acquirer & Target as Standalone Firms	Step 2 Value Acquirer & Target Firms Including Synergy	Step 3 Determine Initial Offer Price for Target Firm	Step 4 Determine Combined Firms' Ability to Finance Transaction
1. Understand specific firm and industry competitive dynamics (see chapter 4: Figure 4-3)	1. Estimate a. Sources and destroyers of value and b. Implementation costs incurred to realize synergy	1. Estimate minimum & maximum purchase price range	1. Estimate impact of alternative financing structures
2. Normalize 3–5 years of historical financial data (i.e., add or subtract non-recurring losses/ expenses or gains to smooth data)	2. Consolidate the acquirer and target standalone values including the effects of synergy	2. Determine amount of synergy willing to share with target shareholders	2. Select financing structure that a. Meets acquirer's required financial returns b. Meets target's primary needs c. Does not raise cost of debt or violate loan covenants d. Minimizes EPS dilution and short-term reduction in financial returns
3. Project normalized cash flow based on expected market growth and competitive industry dynamics; calculate standalone values of acquirer & target firms	3. Estimate value of net synergy (i.e., consolidated firms including synergy less standalone values of acquirer and target)	3. Determine appropriate composition of offer price (i.e., cash, stock, or some combination)	
◄────── Key assumptions made for each step should be clearly stated. ──────►			

FIGURE 9-1 The mergers and acquisition model-building process

The appropriate financial structure (debt-to-equity ratio) is that which satisfies certain predetermined criteria. The appropriate financial structure can be determined from a range of different scenarios created by making small changes in selected value drivers. Value drivers are factors such as product volume, selling price, and cost of sales that have a significant impact on the value of the firm whenever they are altered (see Chapter 7).

Step 1: Value Acquirer (PV_A) and Target Firm (PV_T) as Standalone Businesses

The following discussion applies to both the acquiring and target firms. The analyst should apply as many valuation methods as data availability and common sense will allow. The estimates resulting from the various methods then can be averaged to arrive at a single valuation estimate using the weighted average valuation method (see Chapter 8).

Understand Specific Firm and Industry Competitive Dynamics

The accuracy of any valuation is heavily dependent on understanding the historical competitive dynamics of the industry, the historical performance of the company within the industry, and the reliability of the data used in the valuation. Competitive dynamics simply refer to the factors within the industry that determine industry profitability and cash flow (see the modified porter or 5 force framework discussed in Chapter 4). A careful examination of historical information can provide insights into key relationships among various operating variables and represents the first step in the process for modeling both the acquirer and the target companies. Examples of relevant historical relationships include seasonal or cyclical movements in the data, the relationship between fixed and variable expenses, and the impact on revenue of changes in product prices and unit sales. If these relationships can reasonably be expected to continue through the forecast period, they can be used to project the earnings and cash flows used in the valuation process.

Normalizing Historical Data

To ensure that these historical relationships can be accurately defined, it is necessary to cleanse the data of anomalies, nonrecurring changes, and questionable accounting practices. For example, cash flow may be adjusted by adding back unusually large increases in reserves or by deducting large decreases in reserves from free cash flow to the firm. Similar adjustments can be made for significant nonrecurring gains or losses on the sale of assets or for nonrecurring expenses such as those associated with the settlement of a lawsuit or warranty claim. Monthly revenue may be aggregated into quarterly or even annual data to minimize period-to-period distortions in earnings or cash flow resulting from inappropriate accounting practices. While public companies are only required to provide financial data for the current and 2 prior years, it is highly desirable to use data spanning at least one business cycle (i.e., about 5 to 7 years).

Common-size financial statements are among the most frequently used tools to uncover data irregularities. These statements may be constructed by calculating the percentage each line item of the income statement, balance sheet, and cash-flow statement is of annual sales for each quarter or year for which historical data are available. Common-size financial statements are useful for comparing businesses of different sizes in the same industry at a specific moment in time. Such analyses are called cross-sectional comparisons. By expressing the target's line-item data as a percentage of sales, it is possible to compare the target company with other companies' line-item data expressed in terms of sales to highlight significant differences. For example, a cross-sectional comparison may indicate that the ratio of capital spending to sales for the target firm is much less than for other firms in the industry. This discrepancy may simply reflect "catch-up" spending under way at the target's competitors, or it may suggest a more troubling development in which the target is deferring necessary plant and equipment spending. To determine which is true, it is necessary to calculate common-size financial statements for the target firm and its primary competitors over a number of consecutive periods. This type of analysis is called a multiperiod comparison. Comparing companies in this manner will help to confirm whether the target simply has completed a large portion of capital spending that others in the industry are undertaking currently or whether the target is woefully behind in making necessary expenditures.

Even if it is not possible to collect sufficient data to undertake cross-sectional and multiperiod comparisons of both the target firm and its direct competitors, constructing common-size statements for the target firm only will provide useful insights. Abnormally large increases or decreases in these ratios from one quarter or year to the next highlight the need for further examination to explain why these fluctuations occurred. If it is determined that they are likely to be one-time events, these fluctuations may be eliminated by averaging the data immediately preceding and following the period in which these anomalies occurred. The anomalous data then are replaced by the data created through this averaging process. Alternatively, anomalous data can be completely excluded from the analysis. In general, nonrecurring events affecting more than 10% of the net income or cash flow for a specific period should be discarded from the data to allow for a clearer picture of trends and relationships in the firm's historical financial data. Alternatively, such data irregularities can be "smoothed" by averaging the data over several time periods.

Financial ratio analysis is the calculation of performance ratios from data in a company's financial statements to identify the firm's financial strengths and weaknesses. Such analysis helps in identifying potential problem areas that may require further examination during due diligence. Because ratios adjust for the size of the firm, they enable the analyst to compare a firm's ratios with industry averages. Appendix A to this chapter lists commonly used formulas for financial ratios, how they are expressed, and how they should be interpreted. The analyst need not describe all the ratios listed; instead, only those that appear to have an impact on the firm's performance need be analyzed. These ratios should be compared with industry averages to discover if the company is out of line with others in the industry. A successful competitor's performance ratios may be used if industry average data is not available. Industry average data commonly is found in such publications as *Almanac of Business and Industrial Financial Ratios* (Prentice-Hall), *Annual Statement Studies* (Robert Morris Associates), *Dun's Review* (Dun & Bradstreet), *Industry Norms and Key Business Ratios* (Dun & Bradstreet), and *Value Line Investment Survey for Company and Industry Ratios*.

Project Normalized Cash Flow

Normalized cash flows should be projected for at least 5 years and possibly more until they turn positive or the growth rate slows to what is believed to be a sustainable pace. Projections should reflect the best available information about product demand growth, future pricing, technological changes, new competitors, new product and service offerings from current competitors, potential supply disruptions, raw material and labor cost increases, and possible new product or service substitutes. Projections also should include the revenue and costs associated with known new product introductions and capital expenditures, as well as additional expenses, required to maintain or expand operations by the acquiring and target firms during the forecast period.

A simple model to project cash flow involves the projection of revenue and the various components of cash flow as a percent of projected revenue. For example, cost of sales, depreciation, gross capital spending, and the change in working capital are projected as a percent of projected revenue. What percentage is applied to projected revenue for these components of free cash flow to the firm may be determined by calculating their historical ratio to revenue. In this simple model, revenue drives cash-flow growth. Therefore, special attention must be given to projecting revenue by forecasting unit growth and selling prices, the product of which provides estimated revenue. As suggested in Chapters 4 and 7, the product life cycle concept may be used to project unit growth and prices.

Revenue projections are commonly based on trend extrapolation, which entails extending present trends into the future using historical growth rates or multiple regression techniques. Another common forecasting method is to use scenario analysis. Cash flows under multiple scenarios are projected with each differing in terms of key variables (e.g., growth in gross domestic product, industry sales growth, fluctuations in exchange rates) or issues (e.g., competitive new product introductions, new technologies, and new regulations).

Step 2: Value Acquirer and Target Firms Including Synergy

Synergy generally is considered to consist only of those factors or sources of value adding to the economic value (i.e., ability to generate future cash flows) of the combined firms. However, factors that destroy value also should be considered in the estimation of the economic value of the combined firms. *Net synergy* (NS) is the difference between estimated sources of value and destroyers of value. The present value of net synergy can be estimated in either of two ways. The common approach is to subtract the sum of the present values of the acquirer and target firms on a standalone basis from the present value of the consolidated acquirer and target firms including the estimated effects of synergy. Alternatively, the present value of net synergy can be estimated by calculating present value of the difference between the cash flows from sources and destroyers of value. The first approach is illustrated in detail in this chapter. This approach has the advantage of enabling the analyst to create an interactive model to simulate alternative scenarios including different financing and deal-structuring assumptions. The alternative approach is described in the Case Study 9-2, "Ford Acquires Volvo's Passenger Car Operations."

Sources of Value

Look for quantifiable sources of value and destroyers of value while conducting due diligence. The most common include the potential for cost savings resulting from shared overhead, duplicate facilities, and overlapping distribution channels. Potential sources of value also include assets not recorded on the balance sheet at fair value and off–balance sheet items. Common examples include land, "obsolete" inventory and equipment, patents, licenses, and copyrights. Underutilized borrowing capacity also can make an acquisition target more attractive. The addition of the acquired company's assets, low level of indebtedness, and strong cash flow from operations could enable the buyer to increase substantially the borrowing levels of the combined companies. The incremental borrowing capacity can be estimated by comparing the combined firms' current debt-to-total capital ratio with the industry average. For example, assume Firm A's acquisition of Firm B results in a reduction in the combined firms' debt-to-total capital ratio to .25 (e.g., debt represents $250 million of the new firm's total capital of $1 billion). If the same ratio for the industry is .5, the new firm may be able to increase its borrowing by $250 million to raise its debt-to-total capital ratio to the industry average. Such incremental borrowing often is used to finance a portion of the purchase price paid for the target firm.

Other sources of value could include access to intellectual property (i.e., patents, trade names, and rights to royalty streams), new technologies and processes, and to new customer groups. Gaining access to new customers is often given as a justification for mergers and acquisitions. Kmart Holding Corp.'s acquisition of Sears, Roebuck and Co. in 2004 was in part motivated by the opportunity to sell merchandise with strong brand equity, which had been sold exclusively at Kmart (e.g., Joe Boxer), to a whole new clientele in Sears stores.

Income tax loss carry forwards and carry backs and tax credits also may represent an important source of value for an acquirer seeking to reduce its tax liability. Loss carry forwards and carry backs represent a firm's losses that may be used to reduce future taxable income or to recover some portion of previous taxes paid by the firm. Tax credits may be particularly valuable since they can be deducted directly from a firm's current tax liability. See Chapter 12 for a more detailed discussion of tax-related issues.

Destroyers of Value

Factors that can destroy value include poor product quality, wage and benefit levels above comparable industry levels, poor productivity, and high employee turnover. A lack of customer contracts or poorly written contracts often results in customer disputes about the terms and conditions of a contract and what amounts actually are owed. Verbal agreements made with customers by the seller's sales representatives also may become obligations for the buyer. These are particularly onerous, because commissioned sales forces frequently make agreements that are not profitable for their employer. Nonexistent or poorly written contracts are commonplace among large as well as small companies.

Environmental issues, product liabilities, unresolved lawsuits, and other current or pending liabilities are also major potential destroyers of value for the buyer. These also serve as ticking time bombs because the actual liability may not be apparent for years following the acquisition. Moreover, the magnitude of the liability actually may force a company into bankruptcy. In the 1980s, a major producer of asbestos, Johns Manville Corporation, was forced into bankruptcy because of the discovery that certain types of asbestos, which had been used for decades for insulating buildings, could be toxic. When China's Lenovo Group acquired IBM's PC business in 2005, it disclosed that high warranty costs attributable to a single problem component contributed significantly to the IBM PC business net losses in 2002 and 2003 of $171 million and $258 million, respectively.

Implementation Costs Often Overlooked

In calculating net synergy, it is important to include the costs associated with recruiting and training, realizing cost savings, achieving productivity improvements, and exploiting revenue opportunities. No matter how much care is taken to minimize employee attrition following closing, some employees will be lost. Often these are the most skilled. Once a merger or acquisition is announced, target company employees start to circulate their resumes. The best employees start to receive job solicitations from competitors or executive search firms. Consequently, the costs associated with replacing employees who leave following closing can escalate sharply. Not only will the firm incur recruitment costs; the firm also will incur the cost of training the new hires. Moreover, the new hires are not likely to reach the productivity levels of those they are replacing for some time.

Cost savings are likely to be greatest when firms with similar operations are consolidated and redundant or overlapping positions are eliminated. Many analysts take great pain to estimate savings in terms of wages, salaries, benefits, and associated overhead, such as support staff and travel expense, without accurately accounting for severance expenses associated with layoffs. How a company treats its employees during layoffs will have a significant impact on the morale of those that remain. Furthermore, if it is widely perceived that a firm treats laid off employees fairly, it will be able to recruit new employees more easily in the future. Consequently, severance packages should be as equitable as possible.

Realizing productivity improvements frequently will require additional spending in new structures and equipment, retraining employees that remain with the combined companies, or redesigning work flow. Such spending may be sizable. Similarly, exploiting revenue-raising opportunities may require substantial training of the sales force of the combined firms in selling each firm's products or services and additional advertising expenditures to inform current or potential customers of what has taken place.

Step 3: Determine Magnitude and Composition of Initial Offer Price for Target Firm

Factors Affecting Offer Price and Composition

In practice, many factors affect the amount and form of payment of the purchase price. Which are most important depends largely on the circumstances surrounding the transaction. In some cases, these factors can be quantified (e.g., synergy), whereas others are largely subjective (e.g., the degree of acquirer shareholder and management risk aversion). Table 9-1 identifies many of the factors that impact the magnitude and composition of the purchase price. The remainder of this section of this chapter will address how some of these factors can be incorporated into the model-building process.

Estimating Minimum and Maximum Offer Price Range (Stock and Asset Purchases)

For transactions in which there is potential synergy between the acquirer and target firms, the initial offer price for the target firm lies between the minimum and maximum offer prices. In a purchase of stock transaction, the minimum offer price may be defined as the

TABLE 9-1 Determinants of Magnitude and Composition of Initial Offer Price

	Magnitude	Composition
Acquirer's Perspective	• Estimated net synergy • Willingness to share net synergy with target shareholders • Relative attractiveness of alternative investment opportunities • Number of potential bidders • Effectiveness of target's defenses • Public disclosure requirements (May result in preemptive bid) • Degree of management's risk aversion	• Current borrowing capacity • After-tax cost of debt versus cost of equity • Size and duration of potential EPS dilution (Reduces attractiveness of share exchange) • Size of transaction (May make borrowing impractical) • Desire for risk sharing (May result in contingent or deferred payments)
Target's Perspective	• Number of potential bidders • Perception of bidder as friendly or hostile • Effectiveness of defenses • Size of potential tax liability (May require increase in purchase price) • Standalone valuation • Availability of recent comparable transactions • Relative attractiveness of alternative investment opportunities	• Perceived attractiveness of acquirer stock • Shareholder preference for cash versus stock • Size of potential tax liability (May make share exchange most attractive option) • Perceived upside potential of target (May result in contingent payout)

target's standalone or present value (PV_T) or its current market value (MV_T) (i.e., the target's current stock price times its shares outstanding). The maximum price is the sum of the minimum price plus the present value of net synergy (PV_{NS}). Note that the maximum price may be overstated if the current market value of the target firm reflects investor expectations of an impending takeover. As such, the current market value may already reflect some portion of future synergies. Consequently, simply adding the present value of net synergy to the current market value of the target firm can result in double counting some portion of future synergy. The initial offer price (PV_{IOP}) is the sum of both the minimum purchase price and some percentage between 0 and 1 of the PV of net synergy (Exhibit 9-2).

The standalone value is applicable for privately held firms. In an efficient market in which both the buyer and seller have access to the same information, the standalone value would be the price the rational seller expects to receive. In practice, markets for small, privately owned businesses are often inefficient. Either the buyer or seller may not have access to all relevant information about the economic value of the target firm, perhaps due to the absence of recent comparable transactions. Consequently, the buyer may attempt to purchase the target firm at a discount from what it believes is the actual economic or fair market value.

Exhibit 9-2
Determining the Initial Offer Price (PV_{IOP})—Purchase of Stock

a. $PV_{MIN} = PV_T$ or MV_T, whichever is greater. MV_T is the target firm's current share price times the number of shares outstanding

b. $PV_{MAX} = PV_{MIN} + PV_{NS}$, where $PV_{NS} = PV$ (sources of value) – PV (destroyers of value)

c. $PV_{IOP} = PV_{MIN} + \alpha PV_{NS}$, where $0 \leq \alpha \leq 1$

d. Offer price range for the target firm = $(PV_T$ or $MV_T) < PV_{IOP} < (PV_T$ or $MV_T) + PV_{NS}$

In an asset purchase, the target's equity would have to be adjusted to reflect the fair market value of the target assets and liabilities that are to be excluded from the transaction. The adjustment would be similar to those made in Exhibit 7-11 entitled "Adjusting Firm Value" in Chapter 7. Exhibit 9-3 illustrates the target firm's balance sheet with the assets and liabilities categorized as those assets (INA) and liabilities (INL) included and those assets (EXA) and liabilities (EXL) excluded from the transaction. Included assets and liabilities are those to be purchased (assets) or assumed (liabilities) by the buyer and excluded assets and liabilities are those retained by the seller. Adjusted target firm equity equals the difference between total assets (TA) and excluded assets and total liabilities (TL) and excluded liabilities. As such, the present value of adjusted equity (PV_{ADJEQ}) is the PV of the cash flows generated by included net assets (i.e., INA – INL). As indicated in Exhibit 9-3, the initial offer price in an asset purchase would equal the PV of adjusted target equity plus some portion of anticipated net synergy. The buyer is willing to pay the seller some portion of the strategic value to the buyer of the included net assets.

Exhibit 9-3
Determining the Initial Offer Price (PV_{IOP})—Purchase of Assets

Included Assets (INA)	Included Liabilities (INL)
Excluded Assets (EXA)	Excluded Liabilities (EXL)
Total Assets (TA)	Total Liabilities (TL)
	Shareholders' Equity (SE)

$ADJEQ = (TA - EXA) - (TL - EXL) = INA - INL$ (included net assets)

a. PV_{MIN} = Liquidation value of adjusted equity[1]

b. $PV_{MAX} = PV_{MIN} + PV_{NS}$, where $PV_{NS} = PV$ (sources of value) – PV (destroyers of value)

c. $PV_{IOP} = PV_{MIN} + \alpha PV_{NS}$, where $0 \leq \alpha \leq 1$

d. Offer price range for the target firm = $PV_{MIN} < PV_{IOP} < PV_{MIN} + PV_{NS}$

---

[1] A rational seller would not sell assets at less than their liquidation value.

Determining Distribution of Synergy between Acquirer and Target

In determining the initial offer price, the acquiring company must decide how much of anticipated synergy it is willing to share with the target firm's shareholders. It is logical that the offer price should fall between the minimum and maximum prices for three reasons. First, it is unlikely that the target company can be purchased at the minimum price, because the acquiring company normally will have to pay a premium to the current market value to induce target shareholders to transfer control to another firm. In an asset purchase, the rational seller would not sell at a price below the liquidation value of the net assets being acquired, as this represents what the seller could obtain by liquidating rather than selling the assets and using a portion of the proceeds to pay off liabilities that would have been assumed by the buyer. Second, at the maximum end of the range, the acquiring company would be ceding all of the net synergy value created by the combination of the two companies to the target company's shareholders. Third, it is prudent to pay significantly less than the maximum price, because the amount of synergy actually realized often tends to be less than the amount anticipated.

The acquirer's initial offer generally will be at the lowest point in the range between the minimum and maximum prices consistent with the acquirer's perception of what constitutes an acceptable price to the target firm. If the target's financial performance is remarkable, the target firm will command a high premium and the final purchase price will be close to the maximum price. Moreover, the acquirer may make a bid close to the maximum price to preempt other potential acquirers from having sufficient time to submit competing offers. However, in practice, hubris on the part of the acquirer's management or an auction environment may push the final negotiated purchase price to or even above the maximum economic value of the firm.

Adjusting Projections for Revenue-Related and Cost-Savings-Related Synergy

Broadly speaking, there are two general categories of synergy: revenue-related and cost-savings-related synergy. Revenue-related synergy arises from sales and marketing opportunities that can be realized as a result of combining of the target and acquiring firms. Similarly, cost-savings-related synergy refers to the opportunities for the elimination of duplicate operations, processes, and personnel, as well as productivity improvements, resulting from combining firms.

Revenue-Related Synergy   The customer base for the target and acquiring firms can be segmented into four categories: (1) those served only by the target, (2) those served only by the acquirer, (3) those served by both firms, and (4) those served by neither firm (Exhibit 9-4). The first two segments may represent revenue enhancement opportunities by enabling the target or the acquirer to sell its current products into the other's current customer base. The third segment could represent a net increase or decrease in revenue for the new firm. Incremental revenue may result from new products that could be offered only as a result of exploiting the capabilities of the target and acquiring firms in combination. However, revenue may be lost as some customers choose to have more than one source of supply. The last segment represents prospective customers who neither firm has been able to capture with its existing product offering but who may become customers for products that can be offered only as a result of combining the capabilities of the acquiring and target firms. The analysis is made simpler by focusing on the largest customers, because it often is true that 80% of a company's revenues come from about 20% of its customers.

Exhibit 9-4
Combined Firm Customer Base Segmentation Analysis

Segment: Customers served by	Segment: Represents potential
Target only	New customers for acquirer products
Acquirer only	New customers for target products
Both firms	Net gain or loss equal to
	−Gain from sale of new firm's products less
	−Loss from existing customers seeking to diversify suppliers
Neither firm	Prospective customers for new firm's combined product offering

Cost-Savings-Related Synergies   The cost of sales for the combined firms may be adjusted for cost savings resulting from such factors as the elimination of redundant jobs and bulk purchases of raw materials. Direct labor refers to those employees directly involved in the production of goods and services. Indirect labor refers to supervisory overhead. A distinction needs to be made because of likely differences in average compensation for direct and indirect labor. Sales, general, and administrative expenses (S,G,&A) may be reduced by the elimination of overlapping jobs and the closure of unneeded sales offices (see Table 9-2).

TABLE 9-2   Adjusting Cost of Sales and S,G,&A Due to Head Count Reduction and Purchasing Economies

	Year 1		Year 2	
	Head Count Reduction		Head Count Reduction	
	Staff Reduction	Dollar Savings	Staff Reduction	Dollar Savings
Cost of Sales				
Direct Labor[1]	65	4,057,143	129	8,845,714
Indirect Labor[2]	24	2,228,571	59	5,478,571
Total	89	6,285,714	188	14,324,285
Purchased materials[3]		3,160,000		3,360,000
S,G,&A				
Direct Sales[4]	10	1,071,421	25	2,678,571
Sales Administration[5]	5	285,714	10	571,429
Total	15	1,357,135	30	3,250,000
Lease Buyouts		765,000		382,197

Notes:
[1] Average direct annual salary of $48,000. Benefits equal 30% of annual salary.
[2] Averge indirect annual salary of $65,000. Benefits equal 30% of annual salary.
[3] Volume discount of 5% on total dollar value of purchased materials. Purchased materials equal to 40% of cost of sales. Therefore, the dollar value of purchased materials savings increases each year.
[4] Average direct sales annual salary of $75,000. Benefits equal 30% of annual salary.
[5] Average sales administration salary of $40,000. Benefits equal 30% of annual salary.

TABLE 9-3   Adjusting Cost of Sales (COS) for Productivity Improvements

	($ Millions)				
	Year 1	Year 2	Year 3	Year 4	Year 5
Net Revenue	1000.00	1040.00	1081.60	1124.86	1169.86
Cost of Sales[1]	800.00	832.00	865.28	899.89	935.89
Training Expense	25.00				
Cost Savings		16.64	17.31	18.00	18.72
Adjusted Cost of Sales[2]	825.00	815.36	847.97	881.89	917.17
Gross Profit	175.00	224.64	233.63	242.97	252.69
Gross Profit Margin (%)	17.5	21.6	21.6	21.6	21.6

Assumptions:
Postmerger labor costs without productivity improvement:
  One worker produces 10 widgets per hour
  Each worker is paid $20 per hour (including benefits)
  Nonlabor costs (e.g., materials, depreciation, etc.) = $2 per widget
  Hourly labor cost per widget = $20/10 = $2
  Total COS per widget[1] = labor cost + nonlabor cost = $2 + $2 = $4
Postmerger labor costs with productivity improvement:
  Hourly productivity per worker increases by 20% due to improved worker training resulting in each worker producing
    12 widgets per hours (10 × 1.2)
  Training expense in the first year totals $25,000,000
  3/4 of savings from productivity gain shared with labor to minimize turnover. (Actual amount shared depends on relative
    bargaining power of labor and management)
  Hourly labor cost per widget = $20/1.2 = $1.67
  Labor savings per widget due to productivity improvement = $2.00 − $1.67 = $.33
  Portion of savings shared with labor = .75 × $.33 = $.25 (Hourly wage rate increases to $20.25 from $20.00.)
  Total COS per widget[2] = labor + nonlabor costs = ($1.67 + $.25) + $2 = $3.92
  Total COS per widget reduced by 2 percentage points [i.e., 1 − ($3.92/$4.00)]
  Cost savings = .02 × cost of sales in year 2; year 3; etc.

Table 9-3 illustrates how to adjust the combined firm's income statement for productivity improvements. Such improvements may result from the application of the "best practices" of either the acquirer or target firm to the combined firms. Note that the gross profit margin of the combined firms, as well as the wage rate, increases due to the improvement in productivity. Gross margin increases from 20% (i.e., what it would have been in Year 1 if the $25 million training expense would not have been incurred) to 21.6% reflecting the productivity gain. Similarly, the average hourly wage rate increases by 1.3% to $20.25 from $20.00.

To realize the savings shown in Tables 9-2 and 9-3, the combined firms will experience certain one-time expenses such as severance associated with layoffs, the cost of buying out leases for sales offices that are to be closed, and the cost of retraining the workforce to employ "best practices." Severance expenses are often equal to several months of salary, including benefits, for each employee that is terminated. Other one-time expenses could include the cost of facility, equipment, technology, and process upgrades. The cost of sales and S,G,&A expenses including synergy then are used to calculate operating income (EBIT), which results in a higher free cash-flow number as a result of the effects of anticipated synergy (see Table 9-4). Note that operating earnings, including synergy, in Table 9-4 are calculated from the line items in bold type.

Determining the Appropriate Composition of the Offer Price

The purchase price offered to the target company could consist of the acquirer's stock, debt, cash, or some combination of all three. The actual composition of the purchase price

TABLE 9-4   Adjusting the Combined Acquirer and Target Company Projections for the Estimated Value of Synergy

	Forecast Period				
	Year 1	Year 2	Year 3	Year 4	Year 5
	($ Millions)				
Revenue[1]	198	210	222	236	250
Revenue-Related Synergy:					
—Target Customers	4	6	8	12	12
—Acquirer Customers	2	4	6	10	10
—Both Firms	(4)	0	3	4	8
—Neither Firm	0	0	2	2	6
Total	2	10	19	28	36
Revenue (Including Synergy)	**200**	**220**	**241**	**264**	**286**
Cost of Sales	158	168	178	189	200
Cost of sales-related synergy					
—Direct labor	4	8	8	8	8
—Indirect labor	2	5	5	5	5
—Purchased materials	3	3	4	4	4
Total	9	16	17	17	17
Cost of sales (Including Synergy)	**149**	**152**	**161**	**172**	**183**
S,G,&A Expenses	20	21	22	24	25
S,G,&A-Related Synergy	2	3	3	3	3
S,G,&A Expenses (Including Synergy)	**18**	**18**	**19**	**21**	**22**
Implementation Expenses	**3**	**4**			
Operating Earnings (EBIT) (Including Synergy)	**30**	**46**	**61**	**71**	**81**
Addendum:					
Cost of Sales/Revenue (%)	80	80	80	80	80
Cost of Sales (Including Net Synergy)/Revenue (Including Synergy) (%)	75	69	67	65	64
S,G,&A/Revenue (%)	10	10	10	10	10
S,G,&A (Including Synergy)/Revenue (Including Synergy) (%)	9	8	7	8	8

Note:
[1] Revenue of the combined firms before the effects of synergy is projected to grow at an annual rate of 6% during the forecast period.

depends on what is acceptable to the target and acquiring companies and what the financial structure of the combined companies can support. Consequently, the acquirer needs to determine the appropriate financing or capital structure of the combined companies, including debt, common equity, and preferred equity. In this chapter, the initial offer price is the market value or economic value (i.e., present value of the target firm defined as a standalone business) plus some portion of projected net synergy. In Chapter 5, the offer or purchase price was defined in a different context as total consideration, total purchase price or enterprise value, and net purchase price. These definitions were provided with the implicit assumption that the acquiring company had determined the economic value of the firm on a standalone basis and the value of net synergy. Economic value is determined before any consideration is given to how the transaction will be financed.

Step 4: Determine Combined Firms' Ability to Finance the Transaction

Estimating Impact of Alternative Financing Structures

The consolidated target and acquiring firms' financial statements, adjusted to reflect the net effects of synergy, are run through a series of scenarios to determine the impact on such variables as earnings, leverage, covenants, and borrowing costs. For example, each scenario could represent different amounts of leverage as measured by the firm's debt-to-equity ratio.

Selecting Appropriate Capital or Financing Structure

In theory, the optimal capital or financing structure is the one which maximizes the firm's share price. Capital or financing structure often refers to the ratio of a firm's debt-to-equity or to total capital (i.e., debt-plus-equity) ratio. To the extent to which higher levels of debt increase the firm's expected financial returns above the cost of capital, higher debt levels increase the firm's share price. This occurs when the borrowed funds are reinvested at above the firm's cost of capital. However, higher debt levels also increase the firm's cost of equity by raising its levered beta and, as such, work to lower the firm's share price. However, since many factors affect share price, it is difficult to determine the exact capital structure that maximizes the firm's share price.

In practice, financial managers attempt to forecast how changes in debt will affect those ratios that impact a firm's credit rating. Such factors include the interest coverage ratio, debt-to-equity ratio, times interest earned ratio, current ratio, etc. They subsequently discuss their projected pro forma financial statements with lenders and bond-rating agencies, who may make adjustments to the firm's projected financial statements. The lenders and rating agencies then compare the firm's credit ratios with those of other firms in the same industry to assess the likelihood that the borrower will be able to repay the borrowed funds (with interest) on schedule. For transactions in which the required purchase price is small relative to the value of the combined businesses, it is usual for the acquirer to borrow 100% of the purchase price, as this is normally the lowest cost source of funds.

For purposes of model building, the appropriate financing structure can be estimated by selecting that structure which satisfies certain predetermined selection criteria. These selection criteria should be determined as part of the process of developing the acquisition plan (see Chapter 4). For a public company, the appropriate capital structure could be that scenario whose debt-to-equity ratio results in the highest net present value for cash flows generated by the combined businesses, the least near-term EPS dilution, no violation of loan covenants, and no significant increase in borrowing costs. Excluding EPS considerations, private companies could determine the appropriate capital structure in the same manner. In effect, the acquirer should select the financing structure that enables the following criteria to be satisfied:

1. The acquirer is able to achieve its financial return objectives for the combined companies.
2. The primary needs of the target firm's shareholders are met.
3. There is no significant increase in the cost of debt or violation of loan covenants.
4. For public companies, EPS dilution, if any, is minimized and reductions in reported financial returns are temporary.

For publicly traded companies, financial return objectives often are couched in terms readily understood by investors, such as earnings per share. Acquiring companies must be able to convince investors that any EPS dilution is temporary and that the long-term EPS growth of the combined companies will exceed what the acquirer could have achieved without the acquisition. Financial returns for both public and private companies also may be described as the firm's estimated cost of capital or in terms of the return on total capital, assets, or equity. Moreover, the combined companies' cash flow must be sufficient to meet any incremental interest and principal repayments resulting from borrowing undertaken to finance all or some portion of the purchase price without violating existing loan covenants or deviating from debt service ratios typical for the industry. If loan covenants are violated, lenders may require the combined companies to take immediate remedial action or be declared in technical default and forced to repay the outstanding loans promptly. Moreover, if the combined firms' interest coverage or debt-to-equity ratios deviate significantly from what is considered appropriate for similar firms in the same industry, borrowing costs may escalate sharply.

The Importance of Stating Assumptions

The credibility of any valuation ultimately depends on the validity of its underlying assumptions. Valuation-related assumptions tend to fall into five major categories: (1) market, (2) income statement, (3) balance sheet, (4) synergy, and (5) valuation. Note that implicit assumptions about cash flow already are included in assumptions made about the income statement and changes in the balance sheet, which together drive changes in cash flow. *Market assumptions* are generally those that relate to the growth rate of unit volume and product price per unit. *Income statement assumptions* include the projected growth in revenue, the implied market share (i.e., the firm's projected revenue as a percent of projected industry revenue), and the growth in the major components of cost in relation to sales. *Balance sheet assumptions* may include the growth in the primary components of working capital and fixed assets in relation to the projected growth in sales. *Synergy assumptions* relate to the amount and timing associated with each type of anticipated synergy, including cost savings from workforce reductions, productivity improvements as a result of the introduction of new technologies or processes, and revenue growth as a result of increased market penetration or cross-selling opportunities. Finally, examples of important *valuation assumptions* include the acquiring firm's target debt-to-equity ratio used in calculating the cost of capital, the discount rates used during the forecast and stable growth periods, and the growth assumptions used in determining the terminal value.

Adjusting the Target's Offer Price for the Effects of Options and Convertible Securities

When the target firm has outstanding management stock options and convertible securities, it is necessary to adjust the offer price to reflect the extent to which options and convertible securities will be exchanged for new common shares. If the acquirer is intent on buying all of the target's outstanding shares, these new shares also will have to be purchased. Convertible securities commonly include preferred stock and debentures. Information on the number of options outstanding and their associated exercise prices, as well as convertible securities, will generally be available in the footnotes to the financial statements of the target firm. Note that "out-of-the-money" options (i.e., those whose exercise or conversion price exceeds the firm's current share price) often are exercisable if the firm faces a change of control. With respect to convertible securities, it is reasonable to assume that such securities will be converted to common equity if the conversion price is less than the current common share price. Such securities are said to be "in-the-money." Exhibit 9-5 illustrates how the offer price could be adjusted to reflect the conversion of outstanding options and convertible securities to new common equity.

Exhibit 9-5

Adjusting Offer Price for Options and Convertible Securities

Offer Price = (Total Shares Outstanding × Offer Price per Share) – Option Proceeds[1]

Key Assumptions

1. Total Shares Outstanding = Issued Shares + Shares from "In-the-Money" Options + Shares from "In-the-Money" Convertible Securities
2. Target's outstanding common stock (excluding "in-the-money" options and convertible securities) = 2,000,000
3. In-the money options outstanding = 150,000 @ exercise price equal to $15
4. Convertible securities = $10,000,000 (Face value for each security = $1,000; conversion price = $20; implied conversion ratio = 50)
5. Offer price per share = $25

$$\textit{Therefore, Total Shares Outstanding} = 2,000,000 + 150,000 + (\$10,000,000/\$1,000) \times 50$$
$$= 2,000,000 + 150,000 + 500,000$$
$$= 2,650,000$$
$$\text{Adjusted Offer Price} = 2,650,000 \times \$25 - 150,000 \times \$15$$
$$= \$66,250,000 - \$2,250,000$$
$$= \$64,000,000.$$

[1] Cash proceeds received from option holders choosing to exercise their options. This is assumed to be 100% of "in-the-money" options.

Factors Affecting Postmerger Share Price

Determining the appropriate P/E ratio to apply to the combined firms' postmerger EPS is an important assumption in estimating the postmerger share price. The analyst needs to anticipate how investors will react to the merger announcement. Frequently, the price of both the acquirer's and the target's stock will adjust immediately following the announcement of a pending acquisition. The target's current stock price will increase by somewhat less than the announced purchase price as arbitrageurs buy the target's stock in anticipation of a completed transaction. The difference between what they pay and the announced purchase price is their potential profit. The current stock price of the acquiring company may decline, reflecting a potential dilution of its EPS or a growth in EPS of the combined companies that is somewhat slower than the growth rate investors had anticipated for the acquiring company without the acquisition. For these reasons, immediately following the acquisition announcement, investors may place a somewhat lower price-to-earnings (P/E) ratio on the acquiring company's EPS and later on the combined companies' EPS than had prevailed for the acquiring company before the announcement of the acquisition.

Share-Exchange Ratios

For public companies, the exchange of the acquirer's shares for the target's shares requires the calculation of the appropriate exchange ratio. The share-exchange ratio (SER) can be negotiated as a fixed number of shares of the acquirer's stock to be exchanged for each share of the target's stock. Alternatively, SER can be defined in terms of the dollar value of the negotiated offer price per share of target stock (P_{TO}) to the dollar value of the acquirer's share price (P_A). The SER is calculated by the following equation:

$$SER = P_{TO}/P_A$$

The SER, defined in this manner, can be less than, equal to, or greater than one, depending on the value of the acquirer's shares relative to the offer price on the date set during the negotiation for valuing the transaction. Exhibit 9-6 illustrates how the SER is calculated.

Exhibit 9-6

Calculating Share-Exchange Ratios (SERs)

The price offered and accepted by the target company is $40 per share, and the acquiring company's share price is $60. What is the SER?

$$SER = \$40/\$60 = .6667$$

Implication   To complete the merger, the acquiring company will give .6667 shares of its own stock for each share of the target company.

Estimating Postmerger Earnings Per Share

The critical "go, no go" decision variable for senior management of many publicly traded acquiring companies often is the impact of the acquisition on EPS following the acquisition. This measure is perhaps the simplest summary measure available of the economic impact of an acquisition or merger on the acquirer's share price. Moreover, as noted in Chapter 7, earnings per share are more closely correlated with share price than is cash flow for periods of less than 5 years. As such, EPS is among the most widely followed indicators by market analysts and investors. Earnings dilution, although temporary, can cause a dramatic loss of market value for the acquiring company.

As illustrated in Exhibit 9-7, the calculation of postmerger EPS reflects the EPS of the combined companies, the price of the acquirer's stock, the price of the target's stock, and the number of shares of acquirer and target stock outstanding (Moyer, McGuigan, and Kretlow, 1998).

$$\text{Postmerger EPS} = \frac{E_{T+A}}{N_A + [N_T \times (P_{TO}/P_A)]}$$

E_{T+A} = the sum of the current earnings of the target and acquiring companies plus any earnings increase because of synergy

N_A = the acquiring company's outstanding shares

P_{TO} = price offered for the target company

N_T = number of target company's outstanding shares

P_A = current price of the acquiring company's stock

Exhibit 9-7
Calculating Postmerger Earnings per Share (EPS)

The acquiring company's share price is $40 and the price offered to the target, including an appropriate premium, is $20. The combined earnings of the two companies, including estimated synergies, are $1,000,000. If the acquiring company has 200,000 shares outstanding and the target company has 100,000 shares outstanding, what is the postmerger EPS for the combined companies?

$$\text{Postmerger EPS} = \frac{\$1,000,000}{200,000 + [100,000 \times (\$20/\$40)]}$$

$$= \frac{\$1,000,000}{250,000}$$

$$= \$4.00$$

Estimating Postmerger Share Price

The share price of the combined firms following an acquisition reflects both the anticipated EPS for the combined firms and the P/E ratio investors are willing to pay for the anticipated per-share earnings. Exhibit 9-8 provides an example of how this process works for a share-for-share exchange, for an all-cash purchase, and for a transaction whose purchase price includes a combination of stock and cash. The exhibit illustrates how the postmerger share price may be determined by multiplying the postmerger EPS by an appropriate P/E ratio. For simplicity, the prevailing postmerger P/E is assumed to be the acquiring firm's premerger P/E.

Exhibit 9-8
Calculating the Postmerger Share Price

Share-for-Share Exchange   The acquiring company is considering the acquisition of Target Company in a share-for-share transaction in which Target Company would receive $84.30 for each share of its common stock. The acquiring company does not expect any change in its P/E multiple after the merger and chooses to value the target company conservatively by assuming no earnings growth due to synergy. We have the following data on the companies:

	Acquiring Company	Target Company
Earnings available for common stock	$281,500	$62,500
Number of shares of common outstanding	112,000	18,750
Market price per share	$56.25	$62.50

1. Exchange ratio = Price per share offered for Target Company/Market price per share for the Acquiring Company
   = $84.30/$56.25
   = 1.5 (i.e., Acquiring Company issues 1.5 shares of stock for each share of Target Company's stock)
2. New shares issued by Acquiring Company = 18,750 (shares of Target Company) × 1.5 (exchange ratio) = 28,125
3. Total shares outstanding of the combined companies = 112,000 + 28,125
   = 140,125
4. Postmerger EPS of the combined companies = ($281,500 + $62,500)/140,125
   = $344,000/140,125
   = $2.46
5. Premerger EPS of Acquiring Company = $281,500/112,000 = $2.51
6. Premerger P/E = Premerger price per share/premerger earnings per share
   = $56.25/$2.51
   = 22.4
7. Postmerger share price = Postmerger EPS × Premerger P/E
   = $2.46 × 22.4
   = $55.10 (as compared with $56.25 premerger)
8. Postmerger equity ownership distribution:

$$\text{Target Company} = 28,125/140,125 = \quad 20.1\%$$

$$\text{Acquiring Company} = 100 - 20.1 = \frac{79.9}{100.0\%}$$

Implications   The acquisition results in a $1.15 reduction in the share price of the acquiring company as a result of a $.05 decline in the EPS of the combined companies. (Recall that the acquiring company assumed no gains in earnings of the combined companies due to synergy.) Whether the acquisition is a poor decision depends on what happens to the earnings of the combined companies over time. If the combined companies' earnings grow more rapidly than Acquiring Company's earnings would have in the absence of the acquisition, the acquisition may contribute to the market value of Acquiring Company.

All-Cash Purchase   Instead of a share-for-share exchange, Target Company agrees to an all-cash purchase of 100% of its outstanding stock for $84.30 for each of its 18,750 shares of common stock outstanding. When the transaction is closed, the 18,750 shares of Target Company's stock are retired. The acquiring company believes that investors will apply its premerger P/E to determine the postmerger share price. Moreover, the acquiring company finances the purchase price by using cash balances on hand in excess of its normal cash requirements.

1. Postmerger EPS of the combined companies = ($281,500 + $62,500)/112,000
$$= \$3.07$$
2. Postmerger share price = Postmerger EPS × Premerger P/E
$$= \$3.07 \times 22.4$$
$$= \$68.77 \text{ (as compared with \$56.25 premerger)}$$

Implications   The all-cash acquisition results in a $12.52 increase in the share price of the combined companies. This is a result of a $.56 improvement in the EPS of the combined companies as compared with the $2.51 premerger EPS of the acquiring company. In practice, the improvement in EPS would not have been as dramatic if the earnings of the combined companies had been reduced by accrued interest on the excess cash balances of the acquirer or by interest expense if the acquirer had chosen to finance the transaction using debt.

Combination Cash and Stock   If the offer price for the target firm consists of one share of acquirer stock valued at $56.25 (given in the problem) and $28.05 in cash ($84.30 offer price − $56.25), calculate the postmerger earnings per share and share price.

1. Postmerger EPS = ($281,500 + $62,500)/(112,000 + 18,750) = $2.63
2. Postmerger share price = 22.4 × $2.63 = $58.91

Implications   The combination cash and stock offer increases the share price of the combined firms by somewhat more than the all-stock offer, which actually results in some destruction of value but far less than the increase in shareholder value provided by the all-cash offer. Moreover, as with the all-cash offer, the combined firms' EPS must be adjusted to reflect the loss of interest earnings on any excess cash balances used by the acquirer to buy the target firm or interest expense if the acquirer borrowed to pay the cash portion of the purchase price.

Key Merger and Acquisition Model Formulas

Each component of cash flow used to value the acquiring and target firms individually (Step 1) and the consolidated acquirer and target firms including the effects of synergy (Step 2) is estimated by projecting the appropriate line items of the firm's income statement and balance sheet. Often many of the financial statement line items are forecast by calculating each item as a percentage of sales based on the last 3–5 years of historical information and then applying these historical percentages to projections of sales. This method is intuitively appealing because sales are normally the principal determinant of changes in cash flow over long time periods. This method also is simple to apply. Of course, the implicit assumptions are that all financial statement line items projected in this manner grow at the same rate as sales over time and that the historical relationship between these line items and sales will continue to apply to the forecast period. All financial statement line items need not or conceptually should not be expressed as a function of sales. These include such line items as depreciation and amortization expense, interest income and expense, and borrowing. Exhibit 9-9 lists the key formulas used to create the M&A model outlined in Steps 1–4 and illustrated in Case Study 9-1.

Exhibit 9-9

Key Financial Modeling Relationships

Projected financial data may be based on historical relationships observed in the normalized data.

1. Net sales equal net sales in the prior year × (1 + g), where g is the expected sales growth rate.
2. Variable component of cost of sales and S,G,&A determined as a percentage of sales.
3. Depreciation and amortization determined as a percentage of gross fixed assets (GFA).
4. Gross profit equals net revenue less variable component of cost of sales, depreciation and amortization, lease expense, and other expenses allocated to production activities.
5. Operating profit (EBIT) equals gross profit less S,G,&A.
6. Interest income equals the interest rate × cash and marketable securities.
7. Interest expense equals cost of borrowed funds × year-end debt outstanding.
8. Before-tax profit equals EBIT plus interest income less interest expense.
9. Tax liability equals before tax profits × marginal tax rate (federal, state, and local = .4)
10. Net profits equal before-tax profits less tax liability.
11. Other current assets (e.g., receivables, inventories, and prepaid assets) determined as a percentage of sales.
12. Cash and marketable securities equals cash needed for operations and short-term (nonoperating) investments.
13. Accumulated depreciation and amortization equals current depreciation and amortization plus accumulated depreciation and amortization in the prior year.
14. Net fixed assets (NFA) equal GFA less accumulated depreciation and amortization.
15. Total assets = Cash and marketable securities plus other current assets plus NFA.
16. Current liabilities determined as a percentage of net sales.

---

17. Long-term debt (LTD) equals existing debt plus new debt.[1]
18. Retained earnings equal net income after tax plus retained earnings in the prior year.
19. Shareholders' equity equals common stock (including earned surplus) plus retained earnings.
20. Total liabilities and shareholders' equity equal current liabilities plus LTD plus shareholders' equity.
21. Working capital equals current assets (excluding excess cash balances) less current liabilities. See Exhibit 7-10 in Chapter 7 for an illustration of how to estimate minimum and excess cash balances.[2]
22. Change in working capital equals working capital in the current year less working capital in the prior year.
23. Capital spending equals the actual change in gross fixed assets whenever the current year's sales growth exceeds some predetermined number; otherwise, it equals depreciation and amortization expense.[3]
24. Free cash flow (to the firm) equals EBIT $\times$ $(1 - t)$ plus depreciation and amortization less capital expenditures less the change in working capital.

Note: In solving the model using Microsoft Excel, the analyst should make sure the iteration command is turned on. The use of Excel's iteration capability will accommodate the "circularity or circular references" inherent in many financial models. For example, the change in cash and marketable securities impacts interest income, which affects net income and in turn the change in cash and marketable securities. Iteration is the recalculation of the worksheet until certain conditions are reached. Excel will recalculate the model the maximum number of times specified or until the results between the calculations change by less than the amount specified in the maximum change box. To turn on the iteration command, on the menu bar click on Tools>>>Options>>>Calculation. Select iteration and specify the maximum number of iterations and amount of maximum change.

---

[1] Existing debt on the firm's balance sheet consists of debt existing at the end of the year preceding the first annual forecast year. This debt declines throughout the annual forecast period by the amount of the yearly principal repayment. The terms (i.e., interest rate and maturity) of each type of loan and annual repayment schedule may be found in the footnotes associated with the firm's financial statements shown in the 10K. The annual interest expense associated with total debt outstanding is estimated by multiplying the weighted average interest on the outstanding debt times the amount of debt outstanding at the beginning of the year (i.e., beginning balance). The weights used to calculate the weighted average interest rate are determined by calculating each type of debt outstanding as a percent of total debt outstanding.

[2] Once determined, minimum cash balances may be projected by assuming they increase in direct proportion to the increase in sales.

[3] If sales grow at less than some predetermined rate, capital spending equals depreciation and amortization expenses, a proxy for the required level of maintenance spending. If sales growth exceeds that predetermined rate, the firm must add to its capacity. Therefore, capital spending equals the change in gross fixed assets, which reflects both spending for additional capacity and maintenance spending.

Merger and Acquisition Model Balance Sheet Adjustment Mechanisms

Projecting each line item of the balance sheet as a percent of sales does not ensure that the projected balance sheet will balance. Financial analysts commonly "plug" into financial models an adjustment equal to the difference between assets and liabilities plus shareholders' equity. While this may make sense for 1-year budget forecasting, it becomes very cumbersome in multiyear projections. Moreover, it becomes very time consuming to run multiple scenarios based on different sets of assumptions. By forcing the model to automatically balance, these problems can be eliminated. While practical, this automatic adjustment mechanism rests on the simplistic notion that a firm will borrow if cash flow is negative and add to cash balances if cash flow is positive. This assumption ignores other options available to the firm such as using excess cash flow to reduce outstanding debt.

The balance sheet adjustment methodology illustrated in Exhibit 9-10 requires that the analyst separate current assets into operating and nonoperating assets. Operating assets include minimum operating cash balances and other operating assets (e.g., receivables, inventories, and assets such as prepaid items). Current nonoperating assets are investments (i.e., cash generated in excess of minimum operating balances invested in short-term marketable securities). The firm issues new debt whenever outflows exceed cash inflows. Investments increase whenever cash outflows are less than cash inflows. For example, if net fixed assets (i.e., NFA) was the only balance sheet item that grew from one period to the next, new debt issued (i.e., ND) would increase by an amount equal to the increase in net fixed assets. In contrast, if current liabilities were the only balance sheet entry to rise from one period to the next, nonoperating investments (i.e., I) would increase by an amount equal to the increase in current liabilities. In either example, the balance sheet will automatically balance.

Exhibit 9-10
Model Balance Sheet Adjustment Mechanism

Assets	Liabilities
Current Operating Assets	Current Liabilities (CL)
Cash Needed for Operations (C)	
Other Current Assets (OCA)	Other Liabilities (OL)
Total Current Operating Assets (TCOA)	
Short-Term (Nonoperating) Investments (I)	Long-Term Debt (LTD)
	Existing Debt (ED)
	New Debt (ND)
Net Fixed Assets (NFA)	
Other Assets (OA)	
Total Assets (TA)	Total Liabilities (TL)
	Shareholders' Equity (SE)

Cash Outflows Exceed Cash Inflows:

- If $(TA - I) > (TL - ND) + SE$, the firm must borrow.

Cash Outflows are Less Than Cash Inflows:

- If $(TA - I) < (TL - ND) + SE$, the firm's nonoperating investments increases.

Cash Outflows Equal Cash Inflows:

- If $(TA - I) = (TL - ND) + SE$, there is no change in borrowing or nonoperating investments.

Case Study 9-1

Determining the Initial Offer Price: Alanco Technologies Inc. (Alanco) Acquires StarTrak Systems (StarTrak)

Background

In mid-2006, Alanco acquired all of the outstanding stock of STS, a provider of Global Positioning Satellite (GPS) tracking and wireless subscription data services to the transportation industry. StarTrak competes in the refrigerated segment of the transport industry and provides the dominant share of all wireless tracking, monitoring, and control services to this market segment. The firm's products increase efficiency and reduce logistical costs through the wireless monitoring and control of crucial data, including GPS location, cargo temperatures, and fuel levels. StarTrak has grown rapidly and currently has a substantial order backlog. Management projects escalating cash flows during the next 5 years.

StarTrak's GPS tracking, wireless information services technology, and large commercial market opportunity complement Alanco's own TSI PRISM Radio Frequency identification tracking business. The acquisition would further establish Alanco's leadership role in developing new markets for wireless tracking and management of people and assets. Alanco developed the TSI PRISM system to provide tracking services for the corrections industry. It tracks the location and movement of inmates and officers, resulting in prison operating cost reductions and enhanced officer security and facility security.

Alanco's management understood that a successful acquisition would be one that would create more shareholder value at an acceptable level of risk than if the firm retained its current "go it alone" strategy. Consequently, Alanco valued their own business on a standalone basis, StarTrak's business as a standalone unit, and then combined the two and included the effects of potential synergy. The difference between the combined valuation with synergy and the sum of the two businesses valued as standalone operations provided an estimate of the potential incremental value that could be created from the acquisition of StarTrak. Alanco's management also understood the importance of not paying too much for StarTrak, while offering enough to make the target's management take the bid seriously. Thus, the challenge was to determine the initial StarTrak offer price.

Analysis

Tables 9-5 to 9-8 provide pro forma financial output from an M&A model used to determine the initial StarTrak offer price. Each table corresponds to one step in the four-step process outlined in this chapter. The total value created by combining Alanco and StarTrak is summarized in Table 9-9.

- Table 9-5: Based on management's best estimate of future competitive dynamics and the firm's internal resources, Alanco devised a business plan that suggested that, if Alanco continued its current strategy, Alanco would be worth about $97 million. Reflecting limited data provided by StarTrak's management and publicly available information, Alanco normalized StarTrak's historical financial statements by eliminating nonrecurring gains, losses, or expenses. This provided Alanco with a better understanding of StarTrak's sustainable financial performance. Future performance was determined by adjusting the firm's past performance to reflect what Alanco's management thought was possible. Despite its significantly smaller size in terms of revenue, StarTrak's market value was estimated to be about $103 million—about $6 million more than Alanco's standalone market value.

- Table 9-6: By consolidating the two firms and estimating potential synergy, Alanco believed that together they could achieve about $118 million in additional shareholder value. This incremental value was to result from sustainable revenue increases of as much as $15 million annually as a result of improved product quality, a broader product offering, and cross-selling activities, as well as cost savings resulting from economies of scale and scope and the elimination of duplicate jobs.
- Table 9-7: After an extensive review of the data, Alanco's management proposed to StarTrak's CEO the acquisition of 100% of the firm's outstanding 3 million shares for $50.20 per share—a 46% premium over the current StarTrak share price. The initial offer consisted of 1.14 Alanco shares plus $12.55 in cash for each StarTrak share. If accepted, StarTrak shareholders would own about 77% of the stock of the combined firms.
- Table 9-8: It appeared that the combined firms would be able to finance the transaction without violating covenants on existing debt. Despite $40 million in additional borrowing to finance the transaction, the key credit ratios for the combined firms remained attractive relative to industry averages. This may enable the new firm to borrow additional funds to exploit selected future strategic opportunities as they arise. Finally, the after-tax return on total capital for the combined firms exceeded by 2010 what Alanco could have achieved on a standalone basis.
- Table 9-9: The estimated equity value for the combined firms is $251.7 million. This reflects the enterprise or total present value of the new firm, including synergy, adjusted for long-term debt and excess cash balances. The estimated posttransaction price per share is $56.95—$23.95 above Alanco's pretransaction share price.

Note: While the transaction is real, the data are hypothetical and are used to illustrate the application of the modeling process discussed in this chapter. The actual Excel spreadsheets used to create the financial statements for this case study are available on the CD-ROM accompanying this book in a worksheet designated "M&A Valuation and Structuring Model."

TABLE 9-5 "Step 1" Acquiring Company—Alanco

Forecast Assumptions (2006–2010)	2006	2007	2008	2009	2010
Net Sales Growth Rate	1.25	1.20	1.15	1.15	1.15
Cost of Sales (Variable)/Sales (%)	0.65	0.65	0.65	0.65	0.65
Dep. & Amort./Gross Fixed Assets (%)	0.1	0.1	0.1	0.1	0.1
Selling Expense/Sales (%)	0.09	0.09	0.09	0.09	0.09
General & Admin. Expense/Sales (%)	0.07	0.07	0.07	0.07	0.07
Interest on Cash/Marketable Securities	0.04	0.04	0.04	0.04	0.04
Interest Rate on Debt (%)	0.1	0.1	0.1	0.1	0.1
Marginal Tax Rate	0.4	0.4	0.4	0.4	0.4
Other Assets/Sales (%)	0.3	0.3	0.3	0.3	0.3
Gross Fixed Assets/Sales (%)	0.4	0.4	0.4	0.4	0.4
Minimum Cash Balances/Sales (%)	0.12	0.12	0.12	0.12	0.12
Current Liabilities/Sales (%)	0.1	0.1	0.1	0.1	0.1
Common Shares Outstanding (Mil.)	1	1	1	1	1

TABLE 9-5   continued

Forecast Assumptions (2006–2010)	2006	2007	2008	2009	2010
Discount Rate (2006–2010) (%)	0.15				
Discount Rate (Terminal Period) (%)	0.10				
Sustainable Cash-Flow Growth Rate	1.06				
Sustainable Cash-Flow Rate as %	0.06				
Market Value of Long-Term Debt ($ Mil.)[1]	23.8				

	Alanco Standalone Income, Balance Sheet, and Cash-Flow Statements									
	Historical Financials					Projected Financials				
Valuation Analysis	2001	2002	2003	2004	2005	2006	2007	2008	2009	2010
Income Statement ($ Mil.)										
Net Sales	27.4	31.5	41.0	53.3	66.6	83.2	99.8	114.8	132.0	151.9
Less: Cost of Sales										
Variable	17.8	20.5	26.6	34.6	43.3	54.1	64.9	74.6	85.8	98.7
Depreciation & Amortization	1.1	1.3	1.6	2.1	2.7	3.3	4.0	4.6	5.3	6.1
Lease Expense	0.4	0.4	0.6	0.7	0.8	1.0	1.2	1.2	1.3	1.3
Total Cost of Sales	19.3	22.1	28.9	37.4	46.7	58.4	70.1	80.4	92.4	106.1
Gross Profit	8.1	9.4	12.1	15.8	19.8	24.8	29.8	34.4	39.6	45.8
Less: Sales, General, & Admin. Expense (S,G,&A)										
Selling Expense	2.5	2.8	3.7	4.8	6.0	7.5	9.0	10.3	11.9	13.7
General & Admin. Expense	1.9	2.2	2.9	3.7	4.7	5.8	7.0	8.0	9.2	10.6
Total S,G,&A	4.4	5.0	6.6	8.5	10.7	13.3	16.0	18.4	21.1	24.3
Operating Profits (EBIT)	3.7	4.3	5.5	7.3	9.2	11.5	13.8	16.0	18.5	21.5
Plus: Interest Income	0.2	0.2	0.2	0.3	0.4	0.4	0.5	0.6	0.6	0.7
Less: Interest Expense	1.5	1.5	1.8	2.1	2.4	2.7	2.8	2.6	2.3	1.9
Net Profits before Taxes	2.4	3.0	4.0	5.5	7.2	9.2	11.4	14.0	16.9	20.3
Less: Taxes	0.9	1.2	1.6	2.2	2.9	3.7	4.6	5.6	6.7	8.1
Net Profits after Taxes	1.4	1.8	2.4	3.3	4.3	5.5	6.9	8.4	10.1	12.2
Earnings per Share ($/Share)	1.4	1.8	2.4	3.3	4.3	5.5	6.9	8.4	10.1	12.2
Balance Sheet (12/31)										
Current Assets										
Cash & Marketable Securities[2]	3.3	3.8	4.9	6.4	8.0	10.0	12.0	13.8	15.8	18.2
Other Current Assets	8.2	9.5	12.3	16.0	20.0	25.0	30.0	34.4	39.6	45.6
Total Current Assets	11.5	13.2	17.2	22.4	28.0	34.9	41.9	48.2	55.5	63.8
Gross Fixed Assets	11.0	12.6	16.4	21.3	26.6	33.3	39.9	45.9	52.8	60.7
Less: Accumulated Deprec. & Amort.	0.6	1.9	3.5	5.6	8.3	11.6	15.6	20.2	25.5	31.6
Net Fixed Assets	10.4	10.7	12.9	15.7	18.3	21.7	24.3	25.7	27.3	29.2
Total Assets	21.9	24.0	30.1	38.0	46.3	56.6	66.3	73.9	82.8	93.0
Current Liabilities	2.7	3.2	4.1	5.3	6.7	8.3	10.0	11.5	13.2	15.2
Long-Term Debt[3]	15.1	15.0	17.8	21.2	23.8	26.9	28.1	25.9	22.9	18.9
Common Stock[4]	2.0	2.0	2.0	2.0	2.0	2.0	2.0	2.0	2.0	2.0
Retained Earnings	2.0	3.8	6.2	9.5	13.8	19.3	26.2	34.6	44.7	56.9
Total Shareholders' Equity	4.0	5.8	8.2	11.5	15.8	21.3	28.2	36.6	46.7	58.9
Total Liabilities + Shareholders' Equity	21.9	24.0	30.1	38.0	46.3	56.6	66.3	73.9	82.8	93.0

continued

TABLE 9-5   continued

Valuation Analysis	Alanco Standalone Income, Balance Sheet, and Cash Flow Statements									
	Historical Financials					Projected Financials				
	2001	2002	2003	2004	2005	2006	2007	2008	2009	2010
Free Cash Flow ($ Millions)										
EBIT $(1-t)$	2.2	2.6	3.3	4.4	5.5	6.9	8.3	9.6	11.1	12.9
Plus: Depreciation & Amortization	1.1	1.3	1.6	2.1	2.7	3.3	4.0	4.6	5.3	6.1
Less: Capital Expenditures[5]	1.2	1.3	3.8	4.9	5.3	6.7	4.0	4.6	5.3	6.1
Less: Change in Working Capital	0.4	1.3	3.0	3.9	4.3	5.3	5.3	4.8	5.5	6.3
Equals: Free Cash Flow[6]	1.7	1.3	−1.8	−2.3	−1.4	−1.8	2.9	4.8	5.6	6.5
PV (2006–2010) @ 15%	10.3									
PV of Terminal Value @ 10%	86.3									
Total PV (Market Value of the Firm)	96.6									
Plus: Excess Cash Balances	0.0									
Less: Mkt. Value of Long-Term Debt	23.8									
Equity Value ($ Millions)	72.8									
Equity Value per Share ($/Share)	72.8									

Notes:
[1] PV of Alanco's debt $= C \times \text{PVIFA}_{i,n} + P \times \text{PVIF}_{i,n}$, where C is the average coupon rate in dollars on Alanco's debt at an interest rate, i, for the average remaining maturity on the debt, n. P is the principal in dollars. PVIFA is the present value interest factor for an annuity and PVIF is the present value interest factor for a single value.
[2] Cash & marketable securities = long-term debt + current liabilities + shareholders' equity − other current assets − net fixed assets.
[3] See Exhibit 9-10.
[4] Common stock includes both stock issued at par plus additional paid in capital (i.e., premium paid to the firm over par or stated value of the stock).
[5] Capital spending is undertaken to maintain existing and to provide additional capacity. Additions to capacity come at periodic intervals related to the level of utilization of existing production facilities. Consequently, capital spending equals the actual change in gross fixed assets (GFA) only if the current year's percentage change in sales exceeds 20% (a measure of facility utilization); otherwise, capital spending equals depreciation.
[6] Free cash flow equals after-tax EBIT + depreciation & amortization − capital expenditures − the change in working capital.

TABLE 9-5   continued

"Step 1" Target Company—StarTrak					
Forecast Assumptions (2006–2010)	2006	2007	2008	2009	2010
Net Sales Growth Rate	1.4	1.35	1.3	1.3	1.2
Cost of Sales (Variable)/Sales (%)	0.60	0.60	0.60	0.60	0.60
Dep. & Amort./Gross Fixed Assets (%)	0.1	0.1	0.1	0.1	0.1
Selling Expense/Sales (%)	0.08	0.08	0.08	0.08	0.08
General & Admin. Expense/Sales (%)	0.06	0.06	0.06	0.06	0.06
Interest on Cash/Marketable Sec.	0.04	0.04	0.04	0.04	0.04
Interest Rate on Debt (%)	0.1	0.1	0.1	0.1	0.1
Marginal Tax Rate	0.4	0.4	0.4	0.4	0.4
Other Assets/Sales (%)	0.3	0.3	0.3	0.3	0.3
Gross Fixed Assets/Sales (%)	0.35	0.35	0.35	0.35	0.35
Minimum Cash Balances/Sales (%)	0.12	0.12	0.12	0.12	0.12
Current Liabilities/Sales (%)	0.1	0.1	0.1	0.1	0.1
Common Shares Outstanding (Millions)	3	3	3	3	3

TABLE 9-5   continued

"Step 1" Target Company—StarTrak					
Forecast Assumptions (2006–2010)	2006	2007	2008	2009	2010
Discount Rate (2006–2010) (%)	0.15				
Discount Rate (Terminal Period) (%)	0.1				
Sustainable Cash-Flow Growth Rate	1.06				
Sustainable Cash-Flow Rate as %	0.06				
Market Value of Long-Term Debt ($ Mil.)[1]	3.1				

	StarTrak Income, Balance Sheet, and Cash-Flow Statements									
	Historical Financials					Projected Financials				
Valuation Analysis	2001	2002	2003	2004	2005	2006	2007	2008	2009	2010
Income Statement ($ Mil.)										
Net Sales	10.4	12.0	16.1	21.8	28.3	39.7	53.6	69.6	90.5	108.6
Less: Cost of Sales										
Variable	6.2	7.2	9.7	13.1	17.0	23.8	32.1	41.8	54.3	65.2
Depreciation & Amortization	0.4	0.4	0.6	0.8	1.0	1.4	1.9	2.4	3.2	3.8
Lease Expense	0.4	0.4	0.6	0.7	0.8	1.0	1.2	1.2	1.3	1.3
Total Cost of Sales	7.0	8.0	10.9	14.5	18.8	26.2	35.2	45.4	58.8	70.3
Gross Profit	3.4	4.0	5.3	7.3	9.5	13.5	18.3	24.2	31.7	38.3
Less: Sales, General, & Admin. Expenses (S,G,&A)										
Selling Expense	0.8	1.0	1.3	1.7	2.3	3.2	4.3	5.6	7.2	8.7
General & Admin. Expense	0.6	0.7	1.0	1.3	1.7	2.4	3.2	4.2	5.4	6.5
Total S,G,&A	1.5	1.7	2.3	3.1	4.0	5.6	7.5	9.7	12.7	15.2
Operating Profits (EBIT)	1.9	2.3	3.0	4.2	5.6	7.9	10.8	14.5	19.1	23.1
Plus: Interest Income	0.1	0.1	0.1	0.1	0.2	0.2	0.3	0.3	0.4	0.6
Less: Interest Expense	0.3	0.2	0.2	0.3	0.3	0.5	0.6	0.6	0.5	0.0
Net Profits before Taxes	1.7	2.2	2.9	4.0	5.4	7.6	10.5	14.2	19.0	23.7
Less: Taxes	0.7	0.9	1.2	1.6	2.2	3.1	4.2	5.7	7.6	9.5
Net Profits after Taxes	1.0	1.3	1.7	2.4	3.3	4.6	6.3	8.5	11.4	14.2
Earnings per Share ($/Share)	0.3	0.4	0.6	0.8	1.1	1.5	2.1	2.8	3.8	4.7
Balance Sheet (12/31)										
Current Assets										
Cash & Marketable Securities[2]	1.2	1.4	1.9	2.6	3.4	4.8	6.4	8.4	10.9	13.8
Other Current Assets	3.1	3.6	4.8	6.5	8.5	11.9	16.1	20.9	27.2	32.6
Total Current Assets	4.4	5.0	6.8	9.2	11.9	16.7	22.5	29.2	38.0	46.4
Gross Fixed Assets	3.6	4.2	5.7	7.6	9.9	13.9	18.7	24.4	31.7	38.0
Less: Accumulated Depreciation & Amortization	0.4	0.8	1.4	2.1	3.1	4.5	6.4	8.8	12.0	15.8
Net Fixed Assets	3.2	3.4	4.3	5.5	6.8	9.4	12.3	15.5	19.7	22.2
Total Assets	7.6	8.4	11.0	14.6	18.7	26.0	34.8	44.8	57.7	68.6
Current Liabilities	1.0	1.2	1.6	2.2	2.8	4.0	5.4	7.0	9.1	10.9
Long-Term Debt[3]	2.6	1.9	2.4	3.0	3.1	4.7	5.9	5.7	5.1	0.0
Common Stock[4]	2.0	2.0	2.0	2.0	2.0	2.0	2.0	2.0	2.0	2.0
Retained Earnings	2.0	3.3	5.0	7.5	10.7	15.3	21.6	30.2	41.6	55.8
Shareholders' Equity	4.0	5.3	7.0	9.5	12.7	17.3	23.6	32.2	43.6	57.8
Total Liabilities + Shareholders' Equity	7.6	8.4	11.0	14.6	18.7	26.0	34.8	44.8	57.7	68.6

continued

TABLE 9-5   continued

Valuation Analysis	StarTrak Income, Balance Sheet, and Cash-Flow Statements									
	Historical Financials					Projected Financials				
	2001	2002	2003	2004	2005	2006	2007	2008	2009	2010
Free Cash Flow ($ Millions)										
EBIT (1 – t)	1.2	1.4	1.8	2.5	3.3	4.8	6.5	8.7	11.4	13.9
Plus: Depreciation & Amortization	0.4	0.4	0.6	0.8	1.0	1.4	1.9	2.4	3.2	3.8
Less: Capital Expenditures[5]	1.2	0.4	1.5	2.0	1.0	4.0	4.9	2.4	3.2	3.8
Less: Change in Working Capital	0.4	0.5	1.3	1.8	2.1	3.6	4.4	5.1	6.7	6.6
Equals: Free Cash Flow[6]	−0.1	0.9	−0.4	−0.5	1.3	−1.5	−0.9	3.5	4.8	7.3
PV (2006–2010) @ 15%					6.7					
PV of Terminal Value @ 10%					96.0					
Total PV (Market Value of the Firm)					102.7					
Plus: Excess Cash Balances					0.0					
Less: Mkt. Value of Long-Term Debt					3.1					
Equity Value ($ Millions)					99.6					
Equity Value per Share ($/Share)					33.2					

Notes:
[1] PV of StarTrak's debt = $C \times PVIFA_{i,n} + P \times PVIF_{i,n}$, where C is the average coupon rate in dollars on StarTrak's debt at an interest rate, i, for the average remaining maturity on the debt, n. P is the principal in dollars. PVIFA is the present value interest factor for an annuity and PVIF is the present value interest factor for a single value.
[2] Cash & marketable securities = long-term debt + current liabilities + shareholders' equity – other current assets – net fixed assets.
[3] See Exhibit 9-10.
[4] Common stock includes both stock issued at par plus additional paid-in capital (i.e., premium paid to the firm over par or stated value of the stock).
[5] Capital spending equals the actual change in gross fixed assets if the percentage change in sales is greater than 30%; otherwise, capital spending is equal to depreciation and amortization.
[6] Free cash flow equals after-tax EBIT + depreciation & amortization – capital expenditures – the change in working capital. For purposes of calculating the working capital component of free cash flows used for valuation, current assets may be defined as minimum cash balances needed to meet working capital requirements (i.e., the minimum fraction of net sales that must be maintained in cash) plus other current assets.

TABLE 9-6   "Step 2" Acquirer/Target Consolidation

Forecast Assumptions (2006–2010)	2006	2007	2008	2009	2010
Sales-Related Synergy ($ Millions)	2	10	15	15	15
Variable COS/Sales (%)	0.63	0.63	0.63	0.63	0.63
Selling Expense/Sales (%)	0.085	0.08	0.08	0.08	0.08
General & Admin./Sales (%)	0.055	0.05	0.05	0.05	0.05
Integration Expenses	−5	−3			
Discount Rate (2006–2010)	0.15				
Discount Rate (Terminal Period)	0.1				
Sustainable Cash-Flow Growth Rate	1.065				
Sustainable Cash-Flow Rate as %	0.065				
Market Value of Long-Term Debt	26.9				

TABLE 9-6   continued

Valuation Analysis	Consolidated Alonco and StarTrak Income, Balance Sheet, and Cash-Flow Statements Including Synergy									
	Historical Financials					Projected Financials				
	2001	2002	2003	2004	2005	2006	2007	2008	2009	2010
Income Statement ($ Millions)										
Net Sales	37.8	43.5	57.1	75.0	94.9	122.9	153.4	184.4	222.6	260.5
Sales-Related Synergy[1]						2.0	10.0	15.0	15.0	15.0
Total Net Sales	37.8	43.5	57.1	75.0	94.9	124.9	163.4	199.4	237.6	275.5
Less: Cost of Sales										
Variable[2]	24.1	27.7	36.3	47.7	60.3	78.7	102.9	125.7	149.7	173.5
Depreciation & Amortization Expense	1.5	1.7	2.2	2.9	3.7	4.7	5.9	7.0	8.4	9.9
Lease Expense	0.8	0.8	1.2	1.4	1.6	2.0	2.4	2.4	2.6	2.6
Total Cost of Sales	26.3	30.1	39.7	52.0	65.5	85.4	111.2	135.1	160.7	186.0
Gross Profit	11.5	13.3	17.4	23.1	29.4	39.5	52.2	64.4	76.8	89.4
Less: Sales, General & Admin. Expense (S,G,&A)										
Selling Expense	3.3	3.8	5.0	6.5	8.3	10.6	13.1	16.0	19.0	22.0
General & Admin. Expense	2.5	2.9	3.8	5.0	6.4	6.9	8.2	10.0	11.9	13.8
Total S,G,&A[3]	5.8	6.7	8.8	11.6	14.6	17.5	21.2	25.9	30.9	35.8
Integration Expenses[4]						−5.0	−3.0	0.0	0.0	0.0
Operating Profits (EBIT)	5.7	6.6	8.6	11.5	14.8	17.0	27.9	38.4	46.0	53.6
Plus: Interest Income	0.2	0.3	0.3	0.5	0.6	0.6	0.7	0.9	1.1	1.3
Less: Interest Expense	1.8	1.7	2.0	2.4	2.7	3.2	3.4	3.2	2.8	1.9
Net Profits before Taxes	4.1	5.2	6.9	9.5	12.6	14.4	25.3	36.2	44.2	53.0
Less: Taxes	1.6	2.1	2.8	3.8	5.1	5.8	10.1	14.5	17.7	21.2
Net Profits after Taxes[5]	2.5	3.1	4.1	5.7	7.6	8.7	15.2	21.7	26.5	31.8
Balance Sheet (12/31)										
Current Assets										
Cash & Marketable Securities	4.5	5.2	6.9	9.0	11.4	14.7	18.4	22.1	26.7	32.1
Other Current Assets	11.3	13.0	17.1	22.5	28.5	36.9	46.0	55.3	66.8	78.1
Total Current Assets	15.9	18.3	24.0	31.5	39.9	51.6	64.4	77.5	93.5	110.2
Gross Fixed Assets	14.6	16.8	22.0	28.9	36.5	47.2	58.7	70.3	84.5	98.8
Less: Accumulated Depreciation	1.0	2.7	4.9	7.8	11.4	16.1	22.0	29.0	37.5	47.4
Net Fixed Assets	13.6	14.1	17.2	21.2	25.1	31.0	36.7	41.3	47.0	51.4
Total Assets	29.5	32.4	41.1	52.7	65.0	82.6	101.1	118.7	140.5	161.6
Current Liabilities	3.8	4.3	5.7	7.5	9.5	12.3	15.3	18.4	22.3	26.0
Long-Term Debt	17.7	16.9	20.2	24.2	26.9	31.7	33.9	31.5	28.0	18.9
Common Stock	4.0	4.0	4.0	4.0	4.0	4.0	4.0	4.0	4.0	4.0
Retained Earnings	4.0	7.1	11.3	17.0	24.5	34.6	47.8	64.8	86.3	112.7
Shareholders' Equity	8.0	11.1	15.3	21.0	28.5	38.6	51.8	68.8	90.3	116.7
Total Liabilities + Shareholders' Equity	29.5	32.4	41.1	52.7	65.0	82.6	101.1	118.7	140.5	161.6

continued

TABLE 9-6   continued

| Valuation Analysis | Consolidated Alanco and StarTrak Income, Balance Sheet, and Cash-Flow Statements Including Synergy | | | | | | | | | |
| | Historical Financials | | | | | Projected Financials | | | | |
	2001	2002	2003	2004	2005	2006	2007	2008	2009	2010
Free Cash Flow ($ Millions)										
EBIT $(1-t)$	3.4	4.0	5.1	6.9	8.9	10.2	16.8	23.1	27.6	32.2
Plus: Depreciation & Amortization	1.5	1.7	2.2	2.9	3.7	4.7	5.9	7.0	8.4	9.9
Less: Capital Expenditures	2.4	1.7	5.2	6.9	6.3	10.6	8.9	7.0	8.4	9.9
Less: Change in Working Capital	0.8	1.8	4.4	5.7	6.4	9.0	9.8	9.9	12.2	12.9
Equals: Free Cash Flow to the Firm	1.7	2.2	−2.3	−2.8	−0.2	−4.7	4.0	13.1	15.4	19.2
PV (2006–2010) @ 15%					26.0					
PV of Terminal Value @ 10% (8)					291.2					
Total PV (Market Value of the Firm)					317.2					
Plus: Excess Cash Balances					0.0					
Less: Mkt. Value of Long-Term Debt					26.9					
Equity Value ($ Millions)					290.2					
Equity Value Per Share ($/Share)					77.3					

Notes:
[1] Revenue increases as a result of improved product quality, a broader product offering, and cross-selling to each firm's customers.
[2] Production cost-related savings are realized as a result of economies of scale (i.e., better utilization of existing facilities) and scope (i.e., existing operations are used to produce a broader product offering) and the elimination of duplicate jobs.
[3] Selling expenses and administrative overhead savings result from the elimination of duplicate jobs.
[4] Integration expenses include severance, training, marketing, and advertising expenses, as well as production, process, and technology upgrades.
[5] EPS is not shown because the consolidated valuation does not consider how the acquisition will be financed. The use of stock to finance a portion of the offer price would affect the estimation of the EPS of the combined companies by affecting the number of shares outstanding.

TABLE 9-7   "Step 3" Offer Price Determination

Forecast Assumptions					
Acquirer (Alanco) Share Price[1]	$33.00				
Target (StarTrak) Share Price[2]	$34.50				
% Synergy Shared with Target[3]	0.4				
Target Firm Shares Outstanding (Mil)	3				
Acquirer Shares Outstanding (Mil)	1				
Cash Portion of Offer Price (%)[4]	0.25				

Financing Metrics	Standalone Value		Consolidated Alanco & StarTrak		Value of Synergy
	Alanco	StarTrak	Without Synergy	With	PV_{NS}
	(1)	(2)	(3)	Synergy	(4) − (3)
			(1) + (2)	(4)	
			$ Millions		
Valuations (See PV in Tables 9-3 and 9-4)	72.8	99.6	172.4	290.2	117.9
Minimum Offer Price (PV_{MIN}) ($ Mil)	103.5				

TABLE 9-7   continued

| Financing Metrics | Standalone Value | | Consolidated Alanco & StarTrak | | Value of Synergy |
	Alanco (1)	StarTrak (2)	Without Synergy (3) (1) + (2)	With Synergy (4)	PV_{NS} (4) − (3)
			$ Millions		
Maximum Offer Price (PV_{MAX}) ($ Mil)	221.4				
Initial Offer Price ($ Mil)	150.6				
Initial Offer Price per Share ($)	50.2				
Purchase Price Premium per Share	0.46				
Cash per Share ($)[5]	12.55				
Share-Exchange Ratio[6]	1.14				
New Shares Issued by Alanco	3.42				
Total Shares Outstanding (Alanco/StarTrak)	4.42				
Ownership Distribution in New Firm					
Alanco Shareholders (%)	0.23				
StarTrak Shareholders (%)	0.77				
Offer Price Composition	1.14 shares of Alanco stock + $12.55 for each share of Star Trak stock outstanding.				
Offer Price Incl. Assumed StarTrak Debt[7]	153.8				

Notes:
[1] Alanco share price at the close of business the day before the offer is presented to StarTrak's management. Note that Alanco's market value estimated by Alanco's management is substantially higher than that implied by its current share price, reflecting their greater optimism than investors.
[2] StarTrak share price at the close of business the day before the offer is received from StarTrak's management.
[3] This fraction represents the share of net synergy Alanco's management is willing to share initially with StarTrak shareholders.
[4] Alanco's management desired to limit the amount of borrowing associated with the transaction to 25% of the purchased price.
[5] Cash portion of the offer price equals .25 × $50.20.
[6] ($50.20 − .25 × $50.20)/$33.00 = ($50.20 − $12.55)/$33.00 = 1.14 Alanco shares for each StarTrak share. Note that $12.55 is the cash portion of the purchase price Alanco's management is willing to pay StarTrak shareholders.
[7] Alanco's management is willing to assume StarTrak's long-term debt outstanding of $3.1 million at the end of 2000.

TABLE 9-8   "Step 4" Financing Feasibility Analysis

Forecast Assumptions (2006–2010)	
New Transaction-Related Borrowing:	
Principal ($ Millions)[1]	40
Interest (%)	0.11
Loan Covenants on Existing Debt	
Debt/Total Capital	< 1.0
Fixed Payment Coverage Ratio	> 1.0
Current Assets/Current Liabilities	> 2.0
New Alanco Shares Issued (Millions)	3.42

continued

TABLE 9-8   continued

	Consolidated Alanco and StarTrak Financial Statements Including Synergy & Financing Effects					
	Projected Financials					Forecast Comments
Financial Reporting	2006	2007	2008	2009	2010	Data from Tables 9-5 and 9-6 unless otherwise noted.
Income Statement ($ Millions)						
Net Sales	124.9	163.4	199.4	237.6	275.5	
Less: Cost of Sales	85.4	111.2	135.1	160.7	186.0	
Gross Profit	39.5	52.2	64.4	76.8	89.4	
Less: Sales, General & Admin. Expense	17.5	21.2	25.9	30.9	35.8	
Integration Expenses	−5.0	−3.0	0.0	0.0	0.0	
Operating Profits (EBIT)	17.0	27.9	38.4	46.0	53.6	
Plus: Interest Income	0.6	0.7	0.9	1.1	1.3	
Less: Interest Expense	7.6	7.7	7.3	6.8	5.7	Includes interest on current and transaction related debt.
Net Profits before Taxes	10.0	21.0	32.1	40.3	49.3	
Less: Taxes	4.0	8.4	12.8	16.1	19.7	
Net Profits after Taxes	6.0	12.6	19.2	24.2	29.6	
Earnings per Share ($/Share)	1.4	2.9	4.3	5.5	6.7	Includes 1 million existing and 3.42 million newly issued Alanco shares
Balance Sheet (12/31)						
Current Assets						
Cash & Marketable Securities	53.5	55.9	58.1	61.0	64.6	
Other Current Assets	36.9	46.0	55.3	66.8	78.1	
Total Current Assets	90.4	101.9	113.4	127.8	142.7	
Gross Fixed Assets	47.2	58.7	70.3	84.5	98.8	
Less: Accumulated Depreciation	16.1	22.0	29.0	37.5	47.4	
Net Fixed Assets	31.0	36.7	41.3	47.0	51.4	
Total Assets	121.4	138.6	154.7	174.8	194.1	
Current Liabilities	12.3	15.3	18.4	22.3	26.0	
Long-Term Debt	38.8	37.6	36.1	34.5	32.8	
Existing Debt	31.7	33.9	31.5	28.0	18.9	
Transaction-Related Debt	38.8	37.5	36.0	34.3	32.5	$40 million, 15-year loan at 11% per annum
Total Long-Term Debt	70.5	71.4	67.5	62.3	51.4	
Common Stock	4.0	4.0	4.0	4.0	4.0	
Retained Earnings	34.6	47.8	64.8	86.3	112.7	
Shareholders' Equity	38.6	51.8	68.8	90.3	116.7	
Total Liabilities + Shareholders' Equity	121.4	138.6	154.7	174.8	194.1	
Addendum:						
Lease Payments	2.0	2.4	2.4	2.6	2.6	
Principal Repayments	5.6	5.6	5.6	5.6	5.6	[1]$40 million, 15-year loan at 11% per annum
Financial Scenario Selection Criteria						
After-Tax Return on Capital-Combined Firms (%)	9.7	13.7	16.7	17.7	20.7	[Net Income + (Interest and Lease Expense) × (1 − .4)]/ (Shareholders' Equity + Long-Term Debt + PV of Operating Leases)

TABLE 9-8 continued

Financial Reporting	Consolidated Alanco and StarTrak Financial Statements Including Synergy & Financing Effects					
	Projected Financials					Forecast Comments
	2006	2007	2008	2009	2010	Data from Tables 9-5 and 9-6 unless otherwise noted.
After-Tax Return on Capital-Alanco (%)	12.6	14.4	15.1	15.6	16.2	Same
Key Combined Firm Credit Ratios & Performance Measures						
Debt to Total Capital	0.65	0.58	0.50	0.41	0.31	Total Long-Term Debt/(Total Long-Term Debt + Equity)
Fixed-Payment Coverage Ratio	1.01	1.56	2.15	2.60	3.20	(EBIT + Lease Payments)/(Interest Expense + Lease Payment + Principal Repayment $\times [1/(1-.40)]$)
Current Assets/Current Liabilities	7.36	6.64	6.15	5.74	5.48	
Return on Equity	15.5	24.3	27.9	26.8	25.4	
Key Industry Average Credit Ratios & Performance Measures						
Debt to Total Capital	.72					
Fixed-Payment Coverage Ratio	.92					
Current Assets/Current Liabilities	3.15					
Return on Equity	16.4					

Notes:

[1] The $40 million in new debt borrowed to finance the cash portion of the purchase price is equal to $12.55 (i.e., the cash portion of the offer price per share) times 3 million StarTrak shares outstanding plus $2.35 million to cover anticipated acquisition-related investment banking, legal, and consulting fees.

[2] Level payment loan

Year	2006	2007	2008	2009	2005	2010	2011	2012	2013	2014	2015	2016	2017	2018	2019
Annual Payment[3]	5.6	5.6	5.6	5.6	5.6	5.6	5.6	5.6	5.6	5.6	5.6	5.6	5.6	5.6	5.6
Interest[4]	4.4	4.3	4.1	4.0	3.8	3.6	3.4	3.1	2.8	2.5	2.5	1.8	1.4	0.9	0.4
Principal[5]	1.2	1.3	1.5	1.6	1.8	2.0	2.2	2.5	2.8	3.1	3.4	3.8	4.2	4.7	5.2
Ending Balance[6]	38.8	37.5	36.0	34.3	32.5	30.5	28.2	25.7	23.0	19.9	16.5	12.7	8.5	3.8	−1.4

[3] Equal annual payments including principal and interest are calculated by solving $PVA = PMT - PVIAF_{11,15}$ (i.e., future value interest factor for 11% and 15 years) for PMT.

[4] Loan balance times annual interest rate.

[5] Annual payment less interest payment.

[6] Beginning loan balance less principal payment.

TABLE 9-9 Equity Value of the Combined Companies (Alanco/StarTrak)

	($ Millions)	Comments
Enterprise Value of the Combined Companies	317.20	Total PV of free cash flow to the firm from Table 9-6.
Less: Transaction-Related Debt	40.00	Alanco's incremental borrowing to finance the cash portion of the purchase price from Table 9-8.

continued

TABLE 9-9   continued

	($ Millions)	Comments
Alanco's Pretransaction Debt	23.80	Alanco's long-term debt at closing from Table 9-5 at year-end 2005.
StarTrak's Pretransaction Debt	3.10	StarTrak's long-term debt at closing from Table 9-5 at year-end 2005.
Total Debt of the Combined Companies	66.90	
Plus: Excess Cash Balances	1.40	• Minimum desired operating cash balances for the combined companies are estimated to be 8% of 2005 net sales. This is less than the 12% held previously by each firm as a result of the presumed increase in operating efficiencies of the combined firms. • Excess cash balances equal total cash and marketable securities of $11.4 million at the end of 2005 from Table 9-6 less .08 times net sales of $124.9 million in 2001 from Table 9-8.
Equals: Equity Value of the Combined Firms	251.70	
Estimated Combined Company Price per Share Following Acquisition ($/Share)	56.95	$251.7/4.42 (total shares outstanding of the combined firms from Table 9-7). Note that this share price compares quite favorably with the pretransaction share price of $33 for Alanco.

Alternative Applications of Merger and Acquisition Financial Models

When the Acquirer or Target Is Part of a Larger Legal Entity

The acquirer or target may be a wholly owned subsidiary, operating division, business segment, or product line of a parent corporation. When this is the case, they should be treated as standalone businesses (i.e., one whose financial statements reflect all the costs of running the business and all of the revenues generated by the business). This is the methodology suggested for "Step 1" in the modeling process outlined in this chapter (see Figure 9-1).

Wholly owned subsidiaries differ from operating divisions, business segments, and product lines in that they are units whose stock is entirely owned by the parent firm. Operating divisions, business segments, or product lines may or may not have detailed income, balance sheet, and cash-flow statements for financial reporting purposes. The parent's management may simply collect data they deem sufficient for tracking the unit's performance. For example, such operations may be viewed as "cost centers," responsible for controlling their own costs. Consequently, detailed costs may be reported, with little detail for assets and liabilities associated with the operation. This is especially true for product lines, which often share resources (e.g., manufacturing plants, shipping facilities, and accounting and human resource departments) with other product lines and businesses. The solution is to allocate a portion of the cost associated with each resource shared by the business to the business' income statement and to estimate the percentage of each asset and liability associated with the business to create a balance sheet.

Adjusting Revenue and Costs

As an operating unit within a larger company, administrative costs such as legal, tax, audit, benefits, and treasury may be heavily subsidized or even provided without charge to the subsidiary. Alternatively, these services may be charged to the subsidiary as part of an allocation equal to a specific percentage of the subsidiary's sales or cost of sales. If these expenses are accounted for as part of an allocation methodology, they may substantially overstate the actual cost of purchasing these services from outside parties. Such allocations are often ways for the parent to account for expenses incurred at the level of the corporate headquarters but that have little to do with the actual operation of the subsidiary. Such activities may include the expense associated with maintaining the corporation's headquarters building and airplanes.

If the cost of administrative support services is provided for free or is heavily subsidized by the parent, the subsidiary's reported profits should be reduced by the actual cost of providing these services. If the cost of such services is measured by using some largely arbitrary allocation methodology, the subsidiary's reported profits may be increased by the difference between the allocated expense and the actual cost of providing the services.

When the target is an operating unit of another firm, it is common for its reported revenue to reflect sales to other operating units of the parent firm. Unless the parent firm contractually commits as part of the divestiture process to continue to buy from the divested operation, such revenue may evaporate as the parent firm satisfies its requirements from other suppliers. Moreover, intercompany revenue may be overstated, because the prices paid for the target's output reflect artificially high internal transfer prices (i.e., the price products are sold by one business to another in the same corporation) rather than market prices. The parent firm may not be willing to continue to pay the inflated transfer prices following the divestiture.

If the unit, whose financials have been adjusted, is viewed by the parent firm as the acquirer, use its financials (not the parent's) as the acquirer in the computer model. Then proceed with Steps 1–4 of the model-building process described earlier in this chapter. You may wish to eliminate the earnings per share lines in the model. Similar adjustments are made for targets that are part of larger organizations.

Joint Ventures and Business Alliances

For alliances and joint ventures, the process is very much the same. The businesses or assets contributed by the partners to a JV should be valued on a standalone basis. For consistency with the model presented in this chapter, one of the partners may be viewed as the acquirer and the other as the target. Their financials are adjusted so that they are viewed on a standalone basis. Steps 1 and 2 enable the determination of the combined value of the JV and Step 4 incorporates the financing requirements for the combined operations. Step 3 is superfluous, as actual ownership of the partnership or JV depends on the agreed upon (by the partners) relative value of the assets or businesses contributed by each partner and the extent to which these assets and businesses contribute to creating synergy.

Things to Remember

Financial modeling in the context of M&As facilitates the process of valuation, deal structuring, and selecting the appropriate financial structure. The methodology developed in this chapter also may be applied to operating subsidiaries and product lines of larger organization as well as joint ventures and partnerships. The process outlined in this chapter entails a four-step procedure.

1. Value the acquirer and target firms as standalone businesses. All costs and revenues associated with each business should be included in the valuation. Understand industry and company competitive dynamics. This requires normalizing the components of historical valuation cash flow. Data aberrations should be omitted. Common-size financial statements applied at a point in time, over a number of periods, and compared with other companies in the same industry, provide insights into how to properly value the target firm. This normalized information can be used to understand both industry and company competitive dynamics. Multiple valuation methods should be used and the results should be averaged to increase confidence in the accuracy of the estimated value.

2. Value the combined financial statements of the acquirer and target companies including the effects of anticipated synergy. Ensure that all costs that are likely to be incurred in realizing synergy are included in the calculation of net synergy. All key assumptions should be stated clearly to provide credibility for the valuation and to inject a high degree of discipline into the valuation process.

3. Determine the initial offer price for the target firm. For stock purchases, define the minimum and maximum offer price range where the potential for synergy exists as follows: $(PV_T$ or $MV_T) < P_{IOP} < (PV_T$ or $MV_T + PV_{NS})$, where PV_T and MV_T are the economic value of the target as a standalone company and the market value of the target, respectively. PV_{NS} is the present value of net synergy, and P_{IOP} is the initial offer price for the target. For asset purchases, the minimum price is the liquidation value of acquired net assets.

4. Determine the combined companies' ability to finance the transaction. The appropriate capital structure of the combined businesses is that which enables the acquirer to meet or exceed its required financial returns, satisfies the seller's price expectations, does not significantly raise borrowing costs, and does not violate any significant financial constraints. Examples of financial constraints include loan covenants and prevailing industry average debt service ratios.

Chapter Discussion Questions

9-1. Why are financial modeling techniques used in analyzing M&As?

9-2. Give examples of the limitations of financial data used in the valuation process.

9-3. Why is it important to analyze historical data on the target company as part of the valuation process?

9-4. Explain the process of normalizing historical data and why it should be done before the valuation process is undertaken.

9-5. What are common-size financial statements, and how are they used to analyze a target firm?

9-6. Why should a target company be valued as a standalone business? Give examples of the types of adjustments that might have to be made if the target is part of a larger company.

9-7. Define the minimum and maximum purchase price range for a target company.

9-8. What are the differences between the final negotiated price, total consideration, total purchase price, and net purchase price?

9-9. Can the offer price ever exceed the maximum purchase price? If yes, why? If no, why not?

9-10. Why is it important to clearly state assumptions underlying a valuation?

Answers to these Chapter Discussion Questions are available in the Online Instructor's Manual for instructors using this book.

Chapter Practice Problems and Answers

9-11. Acquiring Company is considering the acquisition of Target Company in a share-for-share transaction in which Target Company would receive $50.00 for each share of its common stock. The Acquiring Company does not expect any change in its P/E multiple after the merger.

	Acquiring Co.	Target Co.
Earnings available for common stock	$150,000	$30,000
Number of shares of common stock outstanding	60,000	20,000
Market price per share	$60.00	$40.00

Using the information provided above on these two firms and showing your work, calculate the following:

a. Purchase price premium:
   Answer: 25%

b. Share-exchange ratio:
   Answer: .8333

c. New shares issued by Acquiring Company:
   Answer: 16,666

d. Total shares outstanding of the combined companies:
   Answer: 76,666

e. Postmerger EPS of the combined companies:
   Answer: $2.35

f. Premerger EPS of Acquiring Company:
   Answer: $2.50

g. Postmerger share price:
   Answer: $56.40 (as compared with $60.00 premerger)

9-12. Acquiring Company is considering buying Target Company. Target Company is a small biotechnology firm that develops products that are licensed to the major pharmaceutical firms. Development costs are expected to generate negative cash flows during the first 2 years of the forecast period of $(10) and $(5) million, respectively. Licensing fees are expected to generate positive cash flows during years 3 through 5 of the forecast period of $5 million, $10 million, and $15 million, respectively. Because of the emergence of competitive products, cash flow is expected to grow at a modest 5% annually after the fifth year. The discount rate for the first 5 years is estimated to be 20% and then to drop to 10% beyond the fifth year. Also, the present value of the estimated synergy by combining Acquiring and Target companies is $30 million. Calculate the minimum and maximum purchase prices for Target Company. Show your work.

Answer: Minimum price: $128.5 million
Maximum price: $158.5 million

Answers to these Chapter Practice Problems are available in the Online Instructor's Manual for instructors using this book.

Chapter Business Case

Case Study 9-2
Ford Acquires Volvo's Passenger Car Operations

This case illustrates how the dynamically changing worldwide automotive market is spurring a move toward consolidation among automotive manufacturers. The Volvo financials used in the valuation are for illustration only—they include revenue and costs for all of the firm's product lines. For purposes of exposition, we shall assume that Ford's acquisition strategy with respect to Volvo was to acquire all of Volvo's operations and later to divest all but the passenger car and possibly the truck operations. Note that synergy in this business case is determined by valuing projected cash flows generated by combining the Ford and Volvo businesses rather than by subtracting the standalone values for the Ford and Volvo passenger car operations from their combined value including the effects of synergy. This was done because of the difficulty in obtaining sufficient data on the Ford passenger car operations.

Background
By the late 1990s, excess global automotive production capacity totaled 20 million vehicles, and three-fourths of the auto manufacturers worldwide were losing money. Consumers continued to demand more technological innovations, while expecting to pay lower prices. Continuing mandates from regulators for new, cleaner engines and more safety measures added to manufacturing costs. With the cost of designing a new car estimated at $1.5 billion to $3 billion, companies were finding mergers and joint ventures an attractive means to distribute risk and maintain market share in this highly competitive environment.

By acquiring Volvo, Ford hoped to expand its 10% worldwide market share with a broader line of near-luxury Volvo sedans and station wagons as well as to strengthen its presence in Europe. Ford saw Volvo as a means of improving its product weaknesses, expanding distribution channels, entering new markets, reducing development and vehicle production costs, and capturing premiums from niche markets. Volvo Cars is now part of Ford's Premier Automotive Group, which also includes Aston Martin, Jaguar, and Lincoln. Between 1987 and 1998, Volvo posted operating profits amounting to 3.7% of sales. Excluding the passenger car group, operating margins would have been 5.3%. To stay competitive, Volvo would have to introduce a variety of new passenger cars over the next decade. Volvo viewed the capital expenditures required to develop new cars as overwhelming for a company its size.

Historical and Projected Data

The initial review of Volvo's historical data suggests that cash flow is highly volatile. However, by removing nonrecurring events, it is apparent that Volvo's cash flow is steadily trending downward from its high in 1997. Table 9-10 displays a common-sized, normalized income statement, balance sheet, and cash-flow statement for Volvo, including both the historical period from 1993 through 1999 and a forecast period from 2000 through 2004. Although Volvo has managed to stabilize its cost of goods sold as a percentage of net sales, operating expenses as a percentage of net revenue have escalated in recent years. Operating margins have been declining since 1996. To regain market share in the passenger car market, Volvo would have to increase substantially its capital outlays. The primary reason valuation cash flow turns negative by 2004 is the sharp increase in capital outlays during the forecast period. Ford's acquisition of Volvo will enable volume discounts from vendors, reduced development costs as a result of platform sharing, access to wider distribution networks, and increased penetration in selected market niches because of the Volvo brand name. Savings from synergies are phased in slowly over time, and they will not be fully realized until 2004. There is no attempt to quantify the increased cash flow that might result from increased market penetration.

Determining the Initial Offer Price

Volvo's estimated value on a standalone basis is $15 billion. The present value of anticipated synergy is $1.1 billion, suggesting that the purchase price for Volvo should lie within a range of $15 billion to about $16 billion. Although potential synergies appear to be substantial, savings due to synergies will be phased in gradually between 2000 and 2004. The absence of other current bidders for the entire company and Volvo's urgent need to fund future capital expenditures in the passenger car business enabled Ford to set the initial offer price at the lower end of the range. Thus, the initial offer price could be conservatively set at about $15.25 billion, reflecting only about one-fourth of the total potential synergy resulting from combining the two businesses. Other valuation methodologies tended to confirm this purchase price estimate. The market value of Volvo was $11.9 billion on January 29, 1999. To gain a controlling interest, Ford had to pay a premium to the market value on January 29, 1999. Applying the 26% premium Ford paid for Jaguar, the estimated purchase price including the premium is $15 billion, or $34 per share. This compares to $34.50 per share estimated by dividing the initial offer price of $15.25 billion by Volvo's total common shares outstanding of 442 million.

Determining the Appropriate Financing Structure

Ford had $23 billion in cash and marketable securities on hand at the end of 1998 (Naughton, 1999). This amount of cash is well in excess of its normal cash operating requirements. The opportunity cost associated with this excess cash is equal to Ford's cost of capital, which is estimated to be 11.5%—about three times the prevailing interest on short-term marketable securities at that time. By reinvesting some portion of these excess balances to acquire Volvo, Ford would be adding to shareholder value, because the expected return, including the effects of synergy, exceeds the cost of capital. Moreover, by using this excess cash, Ford also is making itself less attractive as a potential acquisition target. The acquisition is expected to increase Ford's EPS. The loss of interest earnings on the excess cash balances would be more than offset by the addition of Volvo's pretax earnings.

TABLE 9-10 Volvo Common-Size Normalized Income Statement, Balance Sheet, and Cash-Flow Statement (Percentage of Net Sales)

	1993	1994	1995	1996	1997	1998	1999	2000	2001	2002	2003	2004
						Income Statement						
Net Sales	1.000	1.000	1.000	1.000	1.000	1.000	1.000	1.000	1.000	1.000	1.000	1.000
Cost of Goods Sold	.772	.738	.749	.777	.757	.757	.757	.757	.757	.757	.757	.757
Operation Expense	.167	.101	.120	.077	.119	.133	.132	.131	.129	.128	.127	.126
Depreciation	.034	.033	.033	.034	.029	.038	.038	.039	.040	.040	.041	.042
EBIT	.027	.128	.098	.112	.088	.073	.073	.074	.074	.074	.075	.075
Interest on Debt	.050	.023	.022	.021	.015	.023	.023	.022	.021	.021	.020	.020
Earnings Before Taxes	.024	.017	.076	.091	.072	.049	.051	.052	.053	.054	.055	.056
Income Taxes	.004	.018	.022	.012	.015	.014	.014	.015	.015	.015	.015	.016
Net Income	.028	.087	.054	.079	.057	.035	.036	.037	.038	.039	.040	.040
						Balance Sheet						
Current Assets	.632	.503	.444	.524	.497	.500	.500	.500	.500	.500	.500	.500
Current Liabilities	.596	.400	.283	.298	.304	.350	.350	.350	.350	.350	.350	.350
Working Capital	.036	.103	.161	.226	.192	.150	.150	.150	.150	.150	.150	.150
Total Assets	1.21	.889	.809	.905	.889	.906	.880	.858	.839	.822	.808	.795
Long-Term Debt	.371	.211	.227	.236	.256	.234	.215	.196	.180	.165	.151	.307
Equity	.244	.278	.299	.371	.329	.321	.316	.312	.309	.308	.307	.307
					Selected Valuation Cash-Flow Items							
EBIT $(1-t)$	.022	.150	.126	.126	.105	.093	.094	.094	.095	.095	.096	.096
Capital Expenditures	.031	.027	.033	.053	.054	.061	.069	.078	.088	.099	.112	.126
Δ Working Capital	.025	.077	.068	.049	.000	.017	.020	.020	.020	.020	.020	.020
Free Cash Flow to the Firm (FCFF)	.047	.079	.053	.059	.088	.087	.044	.036	.027	.017	.005	(.008)

Epilogue

Seven months after the megamerger between Chrysler and Daimler-Benz in 1998, Ford Motor Company announced that it was acquiring only Volvo's passenger car operations. Ford acquired Volvo's passenger car operations on March 29, 1999, for $6.45 billion. At $16,000 per production unit, Ford's offer price was considered generous when compared with the $13,400 per vehicle that Daimler-Benz AG paid for Chrysler Corporation in 1998. The sale of the passenger car business allows Volvo to concentrate fully on its truck, bus, construction equipment, marine engine, and aerospace equipment businesses. (Note that the standalone value of Volvo in the case was estimated to be $15 billion. This included Volvo's trucking operations.)

Case Study Discussion Questions

1. What is the purpose of the common-size financial statements developed for Volvo (see Table 9-10)? What insights does this table provide about the historical trend in Volvo's historical performance? Based on past performance, how realistic do you think the projections are for 2000–2004?
2. Ford anticipates substantial synergies from acquiring Volvo. What are these potential synergies? As a consultant hired to value Volvo, what additional information would you need to estimate the value of potential synergies from each of these areas?
3. How was the initial offer price determined according to this case study? Do you find the logic underlying the initial offer price compelling? Explain your answer.
4. What was the composition of the purchase price? Why was this composition selected according to this case study?

Answers to these Case Study Discussion Questions are available in the Online Instructor's Manual for instructors using this book.

Appendix A

Commonly Used Financial Ratios

Financial Ratio (How Measured)	Formula	Interpretation
Liquidity Ratios:		
Current Ratio (Decimal)	Current Assets/Current Liabilities	Indicator of firm's ability to pay its short-term liabilities
Quick (Acid-Test) Ratio (Decimal)	$\dfrac{\text{Current Assets} - \text{Inventory}}{\text{Current Liabilities}}$	Measures firm's ability to pay off short-term liabilities from current assets excluding inventories
Profitability Ratios:		
Net Profit Margin (%)	Net Profits after Taxes/Net Sales	Indicates after-tax profits produced by each dollar of sales
Gross Profit Margin (%)	$\dfrac{\text{Net Sales} - \text{Cost of Sales}}{\text{Net Sales}}$	Margin available to cover expenses other than the cost of sales while still providing a profit

Financial Ratio (How Measured)	Formula	Interpretation
Return on Investment (%)	$$\frac{\text{Net Profit After Taxes}}{\text{Total Assets}}$$	Indicates return on the firm's total assets; it shows how efficiently the firm is using its assets regardless of how they are financed
Return on Equity (%)	$$\frac{\text{Net Profit after Taxes/}}{\text{Shareholders' Equity}}$$	Measures return on book value of shareholders' total investment in the firm
Earnings per Share (Dollars per Share)	$$\frac{\text{Net Profit after Taxes} - \text{Preferred Dividends}}{\text{Average Number of Common Shares}}$$	Measures after-tax earnings produced for each share of common stock outstanding
Activity Ratios:		
Inventory Turnover (Decimal)	Net Sales/Inventory	Indicates number of times average inventory is sold during a particular time period
Days in Inventory (Days)	Inventory/Cost of Goods Sold/365	Indicates number of days of inventory a firm has on hand at a particular time
Asset Turnover (Decimal)	Net Sales/Total Assets	Measures firm's utilization of its assets and net sales generated by each dollar of assets
Average Collection Period (Days)	Accounts Receivable/Annual Sales/365	Average number of days a firm must wait to receive payment after a sale is made
Accounts Payable (Days)	Accounts Payable/Annual Purchases/365	Indicates average length of time in days the firm takes to pay its suppliers
Leverage Ratios:		
Debt-to-Equity Ratio (%)	Total Debt/Shareholders' Equity	Measures funds provided by creditors versus those provided by shareholders
Long-Term Debt to Total Capital (%)	$$\frac{\text{Long-Term Debt}}{\text{Shareholders Equity} + \text{Long-Term Debt}}$$	Measures share of total financing received from long-term creditors
Times Interest Earned (Decimal)	$$\frac{\text{Earnings before Taxes} + \text{Internet Expense}}{\text{Internet Expense}}$$	Measures firm's capacity to pay its interest expense
Fixed Charge Coverage Ratio (Decimal)	$$\frac{\text{Profit before Taxes} + \text{Internet Expense}}{[\text{Profit before Taxes} + \text{Internet Expense} \text{ Principal Repayment} \times (1/(1\text{-Tax Rate}))]}$$	Indicates firm's ability to repay all fixed obligations

References

Benninga, Simon, *Financial Modeling*, MIT Press: Cambridge, MA, 2000.

Henry, David, "The Numbers Game," *BusinessWeek*, May 14, 2001, pp. 100–103.

Kelleher, James B., "The Numbers Racket," *Orange County Register*, Your Money Section, p. 1.

Moyer, Charles R., James R. McGuigan, and William J. Kretlo*w, Contemporary Financial Management*, South Western College Publishing, Cincinnati, OH, 1998, pp. 810–811.

Mun, Jonathan, *Modeling Risk: Applying Monte Carlo Simulation, Real Option Analysis, Forecasting, and Optimization*, Wiley & Sons, Somerset, NJ, 2006.

Naughton, Keith, "The Global Six," *BusinessWeek*, January 25, 1999, pp. 68–72.

Sengupta, Chandan, *Financial Modeling Using Excel and VBA*, Wiley & Sons, New York, 2004.

Sherman, David H., and S. David Young, "Tread Lightly Through These Accounting Minefields," *Harvard Business Review*, July–August, 2001, pp. 129–137.

Welch, David, and Daniel Howes, "Ford Buyout Will Save Volvo, Shareholders Told," *Detroit News*, February 24, 1999.

CHAPTER ◆ 10

Analysis and Valuation of Privately Held Companies

If the facts do not conform to the theory, they must be disposed of.

—Maier's Law

Inside M&A: When Things Just Do Not Seem Right

Things just did not seem to add up. Alan had led due diligence teams for his firm before. He was well aware that the reliability of the financial data provided by the 30-year-old family-owned microfiche company, Imaging Services, was not consistent with generally accepted accounting standards and that some of the firm's practices would have to change if the company were acquired. Although impressed with some of the family members on the payroll, he was not yet convinced that they were all contributing as much as they could to the overall operation of the firm. The "handshake agreements" the owners had with several large customers reflected the informal practices of many small companies. The absence of detailed travel expense accounts also was troubling.

Despite these observations, a restatement of the firm's historical profitability to eliminate certain anomalies indicated that the firm clearly had been consistently profitable for the last 5 years. Moreover, the firm's cash flow had shown a strong upward trend during this period. A survey of customers indicated substantial satisfaction with product quality and turnaround time—factors that were highly valued by the firm's clientele. Because of these considerations, customers were willing to pay a premium to have their paper records converted to microfilm by Imaging Services.

Alan was puzzled by the relatively small expense entry recorded for disposal of silver nitrate, a highly toxic chemical that is used in the conversion of paper to microfilm. The owners assured him that such chemicals had been disposed of properly and that they had negotiated favorable terms with a local waste disposal company. Alan decided to cross-check this explanation by interviewing several employees, who had been with the firm for a number of years and who were not family members or shareholders. During these interviews, Alan learned that chemicals often were dumped down the drain rather than into barrels that were to be emptied by the local waste disposal company. The drain emptied into a grassy area behind the building. An environmental consultant was hired to evaluate the toxicity of the property and confirmed Alan's worst fears. It would cost at least $500,000 to make the property compliant with both state and federal environmental standards.

Alan confronted the owners with an ultimatum. Accept a reduction in the purchase price or he would recommend that his firm not complete the acquisition. The owners relented. Imaging Services was acquired but at a much lower price.

Chapter Overview

If you own an interest in a privately held business, you cannot simply look in *The Wall Street Journal* or the local newspaper to see what your investment is worth. This is the situation with the vast majority of the nation's businesses. The absence of an easy and accurate method of valuing your investment can create significant financial burdens for both investors and business owners. Investors and business owners may need a valuation as part of a merger or acquisition, for settling an estate, or because employees wish to exercise their stock options. Employee stock ownership plans (ESOPs) also may require periodic valuations. In other instances, shareholder disputes, court cases, divorce, or the payment of gift or estate taxes may necessitate a valuation of the business.

In addition to the absence of a public market, there are other significant differences between publicly traded versus privately held companies. The availability and reliability of data for public companies tends to be much greater than for small private firms. Moreover, in large publicly traded corporations and large privately held companies, managers are often well versed in contemporary management practices, accounting, and financial valuation techniques. This is frequently not the case for small privately owned businesses. Finally, managers in large public companies are less likely to have the same level of emotional attachment to the business that frequently is found in family-owned businesses.

A *private corporation* is a firm whose securities are not registered with state or federal authorities. Consequently, they are prohibited from being traded in the public securities markets. Buying a private firm is, in some ways, easier than buying a public firm, because there are generally fewer shareholders. However, the lack of publicly available information and the lack of public markets in which to value their securities constitute formidable challenges. Most acquisitions of private firms are friendly takeovers. However, in some instances, a takeover may occur despite opposition from certain shareholders. To circumvent such opposition, the acquirer seeks the cooperation of the majority shareholders, directors, and management, because only they have access to the information necessary to properly value the business.

The intent of this chapter is to discuss how the analyst deals with these problems. Issues concerning making initial contact and negotiating with the owners of privately held businesses were addressed in Chapter 5. Consequently, this chapter will focus on the challenges of valuing private or closely held businesses. Following a brief discussion of the characteristics of privately held businesses, this chapter discusses in detail the hazards of dealing with both limited and often unreliable data associated with privately held firms. The chapter then focuses on how to properly adjust questionable data as well as how to select the appropriate valuation methodology and discount or capitalization rate. The chapter also includes a discussion of how corporate shells and leveraged ESOPs are used to acquire privately owned companies. A review of this chapter is available on the CD-ROM accompanying this book.

Demographics of Privately Owned Businesses

More than 99% of all businesses in the United States are small. They contribute about 75% of net new jobs added to the U.S. economy annually. Furthermore, such businesses employ about one-half of the U.S. nongovernment-related workforce and account for about 41% of nongovernment sales (see U.S. Small Business Administration, 2003).

Privately owned businesses are often referred to as "closely held" since they are usually characterized by a small group of shareholders controlling operating and managerial policies of the firm. These firms differ from publicly held firms in that ownership in public firms is widely dispersed and administration is done by professional managers. Most closely held firms are family-owned businesses. All closely held firms are not small, as families control the operating policies at many large, publicly traded companies. In many of these firms, family influence is exercised by family members holding senior management positions, seats on the board of directors, and through holding supervoting stock (i.e., stock with multiple voting rights). The latter factor enables control even though the family's shareholdings are less than 50%. Examples of large, publicly traded family businesses include Wal-Mart, Ford Motor, American International Group, Motorola, Loew's, Betchel Group, and Anheuser-Busch. Each of these firms has annual revenues of more than $16 billion.

Key Characteristics

The number of firms in the United States in 2002 totaled 23.3 million. Of these, about 5.7 million are firms with employee payrolls (i.e., employer firms), with the number of employees per firm averaging about 20. Of the approximately three-fourths without a payroll, most are self-employed persons operating unincorporated businesses, and they may or may not be the owner's primary source of income. Since such firms account for only 3% of the nation's private sector sales, they are often excluded from reported aggregate business statistics. However, since 1997, their numbers have been growing faster than firms with employees. The M&A market for employer firms tends to be concentrated among smaller firms, as firms in the United States with 99 or fewer employees account for 98% of all firms with employees (see Table 10-1).

TABLE 10-1   Average Number of Paid Employees per Firm

Employment Size of Enterprise	Number of Firms	Number of Paid Employees	Average per Firm
All Firms	23,343,821	112,400,654	4.8
Nonemployer Firms	17,646,062	Not Applicable	Not Applicable
Employer Firms	5,697,759	112,400,654	19.7
Less than 99 Employees	5,578,211	40,457,440	7.25
100 to 499	82,334	15,908,852	193.2
500–999	25,171	5,734,715	227.8
1000–2499	4,995	7,670,687	1,535.6
Greater than 2500	7,048	42,628,960	6,048.4

Source: 2002 *Economic Census* and *Statistics of U.S. Businesses*, United States Census Bureau.

Women-owned businesses in 2002 totaled 5.4 million, of which 15.6% had employees. Of the 3.4 million minority-owned businesses 20.2% had paid employees. Manufacturing, with 16.5 million employees, led all industries with the most small-business employees. Retail trade and health care were close behind with paid employment of 14.8 and 14.1 million, respectively.

Family-Owned Firms

Family-owned businesses account for about 89% of all businesses in the United States (Astrachan and Shanker, 2003). In such businesses, the family has effective control over the strategic direction of the business. Moreover, the business contributes significantly to the family's income, wealth, and identity. While confronted with the same business challenges as all firms, family-owned firms are often beleaguered by more severe internal issues than publicly traded firms. These issues include management succession, lack of corporate governance, informal management structure, less skilled lower level management, and a preference for ownership over growth.

Firms that are family owned but not managed by family members are often well managed, as family shareholders with large equity stakes carefully monitor those charged with managing the business (Bennedsen, Nielsen, Perez-Gonzalez, and Wolfenson, 2006; Perez-Gonzalez, 2006; Villalonga and Amit, 2006). However, management by the children of the founders typically adversely affects firm value (Claessens, Djankov, Fan, and Lang, 2002; Morck and Yeung, 2000). This may result from the limited pool of family members available for taking control of the business.

Succession is one of the most difficult challenges to resolve, with family-owned firms viewing succession as the transfer of ownership more than as a transfer of management. Problems arise from inadequate preparation of the younger generation of family members and the limited pool of potential successors who might not even have the talent or the interest to take over. For many such firms, the founder has always made key decisions and other family members often do not have the opportunity to develop business acumen. In such firms, mid-level management expertise often resides among nonfamily members, who often leave due to perceived inequity in pay scales with family members and limited promotion opportunities. While some firms display an ability to overcome the challenges of succession, others look to sell the business (see Case Study 10-1). With a large number of "baby boomers" nearing retirement, investors are confronted with a growing array of opportunities among family-owned firms.

Case Study 10-1
Deb Ltd. Seeks an Exit Strategy

In late 2004, Barclay's Private Equity acquired slightly more than one-half the equity in Deb Ltd. (Deb) valued at about $250 million. The private equity arm of Britain's Barclay's bank outbid other suitors in an auction to acquire a controlling interest in the firm. PriceWaterhouseCooper had been hired by the Williamson family, the primary stockholder in the firm, to find a buyer.

The sale solved a dilemma for Nick Williamson, the firm's CEO and son of the founder, who had invented the firm's flagship product, Swarfega. The company had been founded some 60 years earlier based on a single product, a car-cleaning agent. Since then, the Swarfega brand name had grown into a widely known brand associated with a broad array of cleaning products.

In 1990, the elder Williamson wanted to retire and his son Nick, along with business partner Roy Tillead, bought the business from his father. Since then, the business has continued to grow, and product development has accelerated. The company developed special Swarfega-dispensing cartridges that have applications in hospitals, clinics, and other medical faculties.

After 13 years of sustained growth, Williamson realized that some difficult decisions had to be made. He knew he would not be around forever, and he did not have a natural successor to take over the company. He no longer believed the firm could be managed successfully by the same management team. It was now time to think seriously about succession planning. So in early 2004, he began to seek a buyer for the business. He preferably wanted somebody who could bring in new talents, ideas, and up-to-date management techniques to continue the firm's growth.

The terms of the agreement called for Williamson and Tillead to work with a new senior management team until Barclay's decided to take the firm public. This was expected some time during the 5- to 7-year period following the sale. At that point, Williamson would sell the remainder of his family's stock in the business (Goodman, 2005).

Case Study Discussion Questions

1. Succession-planning issues are often a reason for family-owned businesses to sell. Why do you believe it may have been easier for Nick than his father to sell the business to a nonfamily member?
2. What other alternatives could Nick have pursued? Discuss the advantages and disadvantages of each.
3. What do you believe might be some of the unique challenges in valuing a family-owned business? Be specific.

Governance Issues in Privately Held/Family-Owned Firms

The approach taken to promote good governance in the Sarbanes–Oxley Act of 2002 (see Chapter 2) and under the market model of corporate governance (see Chapter 3) is to identify and apply "best practices." The focus on "best practices" has led to the development of generalized laundry lists, rather than specific actions leading to measurable results (Robinson, 2002). Moreover, what works for publicly traded companies may not be readily applicable to privately held or family-owed firms.

The market model relies on a large dispersed class of investors in which ownership and corporate control are largely separate. Moreover, the market model overlooks the fact that family-owned firms often have different interests, time horizons, and strategies from investors in publicly owned firms. In many countries, family-owned firms have been successful because of their shared interests and because investors place a higher value on the long-term health of the business rather than on short-term performance (de Visscher, Aronoff, and Ward, 1995; Habershon and Williams, 1999). Consequently, the control model of corporate governance discussed in Chapter 3 may be more applicable where ownership tends to be concentrated and the right to control the business is not fully separate from ownership.

Astrachan, Keys, Lane, and McMillan (2003) concluded that the control model (or some variation) is more applicable to family-owned firms than the market model. The authors argue that director independence is less important for family-owned firms, since outside directors can often be swayed by various forms of compensation. A board consisting of owners focused on the long-term growth of the business for future generations of the family may be far more committed to the firm than outsiders. While the owners are ultimately responsible for strategic direction, the board must ensure that strategy formulated by management is consistent with the owners' desires. However, a family-owned firm's board faces the sometimes daunting challenge of achieving the proper balance between monitoring and collaboration to minimize the emotionalism and overlapping roles that often characterize such firms.

Challenges of Valuing Privately Held Companies

Because of the need to satisfy both the demands of stockholders and regulatory agencies, public companies need to balance the desire to minimize taxes with the goal of achieving quarterly earnings levels consistent with investor expectations. Failure to do so frequently results in an immediate loss in the firm's market value. The presence of such regulatory agencies as the Securities and Exchange Commission (SEC) limits the ability of public companies to manipulate financial information. In contrast, private companies have much more opportunity to do so, particularly when they are not widely followed by investment analysts or subject to ongoing regulation and periodic review. The anonymity of many privately held firms, the potential for manipulation of information, problems specific to small firms, and the tendency of owners of private firms to manage in a way to minimize tax liabilities creates a number of significant valuation issues. These issues are addressed in the next sections of this chapter.

Lack of Externally Generated Information

There is generally a lack of analyses of private firms generated by sources outside of the company. There is little incentive for outside analysts to cover these firms because of the absence of a public market for their securities. Consequently, there are few forecasts of their performance other than those provided by the firm's management. Press coverage is usually quite limited, and what is available is again often based on information provided by the firm's management. Even highly regarded companies purporting to offer demographic and financial information on small privately held firms use largely superficial and infrequent telephone interviews with the management of such firms as their primary source of such information.

Lack of Internal Controls and Inadequate Reporting Systems

Private companies are generally not subject to the same level of rigorous controls and reporting systems as are public companies. Public companies are required to prepare audited financial statements for their annual reports. The SEC enforces the accuracy of these statements under the authority provided by the Securities and Exchange Act of 1934.

The use of audits is much more rigorous and thorough than other types of reports known as accounting reviews and compilations. Although accounting reviews are acceptable for quarterly 10Q reports, compilation reports are not acceptable for either 10Ks or 10Qs. The *audit* consists of a professional examination and verification of a company's accounting documents and supporting data for the purpose of rendering an opinion as to their fairness, consistency, and conformity with generally accepted accounting principles.

Although reporting systems in small firms are generally poor or nonexistent, the lack of formal controls, such as systems to monitor how money is spent and an approval process to ensure that funds are spent appropriately, invites fraud and misuse of company resources. Documentation is another formidable problem. Intellectual property is a substantial portion of the value of many private firms. Examples of such property include system software, chemical formulae, and recipes. Often only one or two individuals within the firm know how to reproduce these valuable intangible assets. The lack of documentation can destroy a firm if such an individual leaves or dies. Moreover, customer lists and the terms and conditions associated with key customer relationships also may be largely undocumented, creating the basis for customer disputes on a change in ownership. Furthermore, as is explained in the next section of this chapter, both revenue and costs may be manipulated to minimize the firm's tax liabilities or to make the business more attractive for sale.

Firm-Specific Problems

There are also a number of factors that may be unique to the private firm that make valuation difficult. The company may lack product, industry, and geographic diversification. There may be insufficient management talent to allow the firm to develop new products for its current markets or to expand into new markets. The company may be highly sensitive to fluctuations in demand because of significant fixed expenses. Its small size may limit its influence with regulators and unions. The company's size also may limit its ability to gain access to efficient distribution channels and leverage with suppliers and customers. Finally, the company may have an excellent product but very little brand recognition. Such considerations normally tend to reduce the standalone value of the business because of the uncertainty associated with efforts to forecast future cash flows. However, these considerations also present an opportunity for a shrewd buyer to realize synergy by merging with firms having complementary strengths.

Common Forms of Manipulating Reported Income

Misstating Revenue

Revenue may be over- or understated depending on the owner's objectives. If the intent is tax minimization, businesses operating on a cash basis may opt to report less revenue because of the difficulty outside parties have in tracking transactions. Private business owners intending to sell a business may be inclined to inflate revenue if the firm is to be sold. Common examples include manufacturers, which rely on others to distribute their products. These manufacturers can inflate revenue in the current accounting period by booking as revenue products shipped to resellers without adequately adjusting for probable returns. Membership or subscription businesses, such as health clubs and magazine publishers, may inflate revenue by booking the full value of multiyear contracts in the current period rather than prorating the payment received at the beginning of the contract period over the life of the contract. Such booking activity results in a significant boost to current profitability because not all of the costs associated with multiyear contracts, such as customer service, are incurred in the period in which the full amount of revenue is booked.

If the buyer believes that revenue has been overstated in a specific accounting period by the seller, the buyer can reconstruct revenue by examining usage levels, in the same accounting period, of the key inputs (e.g., labor and materials) required to produce the product or service. Although not necessarily precise, examining activity or usage levels does tend to highlight discrepancies that might exist in the data provided by the seller. Case Study 10-2 illustrates how this might be done.

Case Study 10-2
Due Diligence Uncovers Misstated Revenue

The owner of a custom brass doorknob manufacturer states that 1 million doorknobs of a certain specification were produced during the last calendar year. During due diligence, the potential buyer learns that one skilled worker can produce 100 brass doorknobs in 1 hour. He also learns that there was no overtime last year and that hourly workers were paid for a standard 2080 hours (52 weeks per year times 40 hours per week) each during the year and accrued 2 weeks of paid vacation and holiday time. In addition, he discovers that, because there was no reduction in finished goods inventories during the year, all products reported sold during the year must have been produced during that same year.

The prospective buyer reasons that one worker could produce in 1 year, assuming an average of 2 weeks of vacation time, 200,000 doorknobs (100 doorknobs per hour × 2000 hours). Because there were only four skilled workers employed during the year, annual production of this particular specification could not have exceeded 800,000 doorknobs. Therefore, the sales figures reported by the owner appear to be overstated by as much as 200,000 units. The owner needs to explain what appears to be a logical discrepancy between the reported number and the theoretically determined number of doorknobs produced.

Case Study Discussion Questions

1. How might the seller have rebutted the buyer's claims?
2. What alternative means could the potential acquirer have employed to evaluate the apparent discrepancy? Be specific.

Manipulation of Operating Expenses

Owners of private businesses attempting to minimize taxes may overstate their contribution to the firm by giving themselves or family members unusually high salaries, bonuses, and benefits. Because the vast majority of all businesses are family owned, this is a widespread practice. The most common distortion of costs comes in the form of higher than normal salary and benefits provided to family members and key employees. Other examples of cost manipulation include extraordinary expenses that are really other forms of compensation for the owner, his family, and key employees, which may include the rent on the owner's summer home or hunting lodge and salaries for the pilot and captain for the owner's airplane and yacht. Current or potential customers sometimes are allowed to use these assets. Owners frequently argue that these expenses are necessary to maintain customer relationships or to close large contracts and are therefore legitimate business expenses. One way to determine if these are appropriate business expenses is to ascertain how often these assets are used for the purpose the owner claims they were intended. Other areas that commonly are abused include travel and entertainment, personal insurance, and excessive payments to vendors supplying services to the firm. Due diligence frequently will uncover situations in which the owner or a family member is either an investor in or an owner of the vendor supplying the products or services.

Alternatively, if the business owner's objective is to maximize the selling price of the business, salaries, benefits, and other operating costs may be understated significantly. An examination of the historical trend in the firm's reported profitability may reveal that the firm's profits are being manipulated. For example, a sudden improvement in operating profits in the year in which the business is being offered for sale may suggest that expenses had been overstated, revenues understated, or both during the historical period. The onus of explaining this spike in profitability should be put on the business owner.

Adjusting the Income Statement

The purpose of adjusting the income statement is to provide an accurate estimate of the current year's net or pretax income, earnings before interest and taxes (EBIT), or earnings before interest, taxes, depreciation, and amortization expense (EBITDA). The various measures of income should reflect accurately all costs actually incurred in generating the level of revenue adjusted for doubtful accounts the firm booked in the current period. They also should reflect other expenditures (e.g., training and advertising) that must be incurred in the current period to sustain the anticipated growth in revenue.

The importance of establishing accurate current or base year data is evident when we consider how businesses—particularly small, closely held businesses—are often valued. If the current year's profit data are incorrect, future projections of the dollar value will be inaccurate, even if the projected growth rate is accurate. Furthermore, valuations based on relative valuation methods such as price-to-earnings ratios will be biased to the extent estimates of the target's current income are biased.

EBITDA has become an increasingly popular measure of value for privately held firms. The use of this measure facilitates the comparison of firms because it eliminates the potential distortion in earnings performance due to differences in depreciation methods and financial leverage among firms. Furthermore, this indicator is often more readily applicable in relative valuation methods than other measures of profitability because firms are more likely to display positive EBITDA than EBIT or net income figures. Despite its convenience, the analyst needs to be mindful that EBITDA is only one component of cash flow and ignores the impact on cash flow of changes in net working capital, investments, and financing activities. See Chapter 8 for a more detailed discussion of the use of EBITDA in relative valuation methods.

Making Informed Adjustments

Although finding reliable current information on privately held firms is generally challenging, some information is available, albeit often fragmentary and inconsistent. The first step for the analyst is to search the Internet for references to the target firm. This

TABLE 10-2   Information Sources on Private Firms

Source/Web Address	Content
Research Firms: Washington Researchers/www.washington researchers.com Fuld & Company/www.fuld.com	Provide listing of sources such as local government officials, local chambers of commerce, state government regulatory bodies, credit reporting agencies, and local citizen groups.
Databases: Dun & Bradstreet/smallbusiness.dnb.com	Information on firms' payments histories and limited financial data.
Hoover/www.hoovers.com	Data on 40,000 international and domestic firms, IPOs, not-for profits, trade associations, and small businesses and limited data on 12 million other companies
Integra/www.integrainfo.com	Provides industry benchmarking data
Standard & Poor's Net Advantage/ www.netadvantage.standardpoor.com	Financial data and management and directors' bibliographies on 85,000 firms
InfoUSA/www.infousa.com	Industry benchmarking and company specific data
Forbes/www.forbes.com/list	Provides list of top privately held firms annually
Inc/www.inc.com/inc500	Provides list of 500 of fastest growing firms annually

search should unearth a number of sources of information on the target firm. Table 10-2 provides a partial list of Web sites containing information on private firms.

Owner/Officer's Salaries

Before drawing any conclusions, the analyst should determine the actual work performed by all key employees and the compensation generally received for performing the same or a similar job in the same industry. Comparative salary information can be obtained by employing the services of a compensation consultant familiar with the industry or simply by scanning "employee wanted" advertisements in the industry trade press and magazines and the "help wanted" pages of the local newspaper. Such an effort should be part of any comprehensive due diligence activity. Case Study 10-3 illustrates how the failure to complete this type of analysis can lead to a substantial disruption to the business following a change in ownership.

Case Study 10-3

Loss of Key Employee Causes Carpet Padding Manufacturer's Profits to Go Flat

A manufacturer of carpet padding in southern California had devised a unique chemical process for converting such materials as discarded bedding and rags to high-quality commercial carpet padding. Over a period of 10 years, the firm established itself as the regional leader in this niche market. With annual sales in excess of $10 million, the firm consistently earned pretax profits of 18–20% of sales.

The owner and founder of the company had been trained as a chemist and developed the formula for decomposing the necessary raw materials purchased from local junkyards into a mixture to produce the foam padding. In addition, the owner routinely calibrated all of the company's manufacturing equipment to ensure that the machines ran at peak efficiency, without any deterioration in product quality. Over the years, the owner also had developed relationships with a network of local junk dealers to acquire the necessary raw materials. The owner's reputation for honesty and the firm's ability to produce consistently high-quality products ensured very little customer turnover. The owner was also solely responsible for acquiring several large accounts, which consistently contributed about 30% of annual revenue.

When the firm was sold, the owner's salary and benefits of $200,000 per year were believed to be excessive by the buyer. Efforts to reduce his total compensation caused him to retire. The new owner soon was forced to hire several people to replace the former owner, who had been performing the role of chemist, maintenance engineer, and purchasing agent. These were functions that did not appear on any organization chart when the buyer performed due diligence. Consequently, the buyer did not increase the budget for salaries and benefits to provide personnel to perform these crucial functions. This tended to overstate profits and inflated the purchase price paid by the buyer.

Ultimately, replacing the owner required hiring a chemist, a machinist, a purchasing agent, and a salesperson at an annual cost in salary and benefits of more than $300,000. Despite the additional personnel, the new owner also found it necessary to hire the former owner under a consulting contract valued at $25,000 per year. To add insult to injury, because of the change in ownership the firm lost several large customers who had had a long-standing relationship with the former owner. These customers accounted for $2 million in annual sales.

Case Study Discussion Questions

1. Explain how the buyer's inadequate due diligence contributed to its postclosing problems.
2. How could the buyer have retained the firm's president? Give several examples.

Benefits

Depending on the industry, benefits can range from 14–40% of an employee's base salary. Certain employee benefits, such as Social Security and Medicare taxes, are mandated by law and, therefore, are an uncontrollable cost of doing business. Other types of benefits may be more controllable. These include items such as pension contributions and life insurance coverage, which are calculated as a percentage of base salary. Consequently, efforts by the buyer to trim salaries, which appear to be excessive, also will reduce these types of benefits. Efforts to reduce such benefits also may contribute to higher overall operating costs in the short run. Operating costs may increase as a result of higher employee turnover and the need to retrain replacements, as well as the potential negative impact on the productivity of those that remain.

Travel and Entertainment

Travel and entertainment (T&E) expenditures tend to be one of the first cost categories cut when a potential buyer attempts to value a target company. The initial reaction is almost always that actual spending in this area is far in excess of what it needs to be. However, what may look excessive to one relatively unfamiliar with the industry may in fact be necessary for retaining current customers and acquiring new customers. Establishing, building, and maintaining relationships is particularly important for personal and business services companies, such as consulting and law firms. Account management may require consultative selling at the customer's site. A complex product like software may require on-site training. Indiscriminant reduction in the T&E budget could lead to a loss of customers following a change in ownership.

Auto Expenses and Personal Life Insurance

Before assuming auto expenses and life insurance are excessive, ask if they represent a key component of the overall compensation required to attract and retain key employees. This can be determined by comparing total compensation paid to employees of the target firm with compensation packages offered to employees in similar positions in the same industry. A similar review should be undertaken with respect to the composition of benefits packages. Depending on the demographics and special needs of the target firm's workforce, an acquirer may choose to alter the composition of the benefits package by substituting other types of benefits for those eliminated or reduced. By carefully substituting benefits that meet the specific needs of the workforce, such as on-site day-care services, the acquirer may be able to provide an overall benefits package that better satisfies the needs of the employees. Alternatively, the acquirer may find that administrative costs associated with reimbursable benefits such as car expenses may be reduced by simply offering a standard car allowance or by increasing the employees' salaries to compensate for anticipated car-related expenses.

Family Members

Similar questions need to be asked about family members on the payroll. Frequently, they do perform real services and tend to be highly motivated because of their close affinity with the business. If the business has been in existence for many years, the loss of key family members who have built relationships with customers over the years may result in a subsequent loss of key accounts. Moreover, family members may be those who possess proprietary knowledge necessary for the ongoing operation of the business.

Rent or Lease Payments in Excess of Fair Market Value

Check who owns the buildings housing the business or equipment used by the business. This is a frequent method used by the owner to transfer company funds to the owner in excess of their stated salary and benefits. However, rents may not be too high if the building is a "special-purpose" structure retrofitted to serve the specific needs of the tenant.

Professional Services Fees

Professional services could include legal, accounting, personnel, and actuarial services. This is an area that is frequently subject to abuse. Once again, check to see if there is any nonbusiness relationship between the business owner and the firm providing the service. Always consider any special circumstances that may justify unusually high fees. An industry that is subject to continuing regulation and review may incur what appear to be abnormally high legal and accounting expenses when compared with firms in other industries.

Depreciation Expense

Accelerated depreciation methodologies may make sense for tax purposes, but they may seriously understate current earnings. For financial reporting purposes, it may be appropriate to convert depreciation schedules from accelerated to straight-line depreciation if this results in a better matching of when expenses actually are incurred and revenue actually is received.

Reserves

Current reserves may be inadequate to reflect future events. An increase in reserves lowers taxable income, whereas a decrease in reserves raises taxable income. Collection problems may be uncovered following an analysis of accounts receivable. It may be necessary to add to reserves for doubtful accounts. Similarly, the target firm may not have adequately reserved for future obligations to employees under existing pension and health care plans. Reserves also may have to be increased to reflect known environmental and litigation exposures.

Accounting for Inventory

During periods of inflation, businesses frequently use the last-in, first-out (LIFO) method to account for inventories. This approach results in an increase in the cost of sales that reflects the most recent and presumably highest cost inventory; therefore, it reduces gross profit and taxable income. During periods of inflation, the use of LIFO also tends to lower the value of inventory on the balance sheet, because the items in inventory are valued at the lower cost of production associated with earlier time periods.

In contrast, the use of first-in, first-out (FIFO) accounting for inventory assumes that inventory is sold in the chronological order in which it was purchased. During periods of inflation, the FIFO method produces a higher ending inventory, a lower cost of goods sold, and higher gross profit. Although it may make sense for tax purposes to use LIFO, the buyer's objective for valuation purposes should be to obtain as realistic an estimate of actual earnings as possible in the current period. FIFO accounting would appear to be most logical for products that are perishable or subject to rapid obsolescence and, therefore, are most likely to be sold in chronological order. In an environment in which inflation is expected to remain high for an extended time period, LIFO accounting may make more sense.

Areas Commonly Understated

Projected increases in sales normally require more aggressive marketing efforts, more effective customer service support, and enhanced employee training. Nonetheless, it is common to see the ratio of annual advertising and training expenses to annual sales decline during the period of highest projected growth in forecasts developed by either the buyer or the seller. The seller has an incentive to hold costs down during the forecast period to provide the most sanguine outlook possible. The buyer simply may be overly optimistic about how much more effectively the business can be managed as a result of a change in ownership. Other areas that are commonly understated in projections but that can never really be escaped include the expense associated with environmental cleanup, employee safety, and pending litigation. Even in an asset purchase, the buyer still may be liable for certain types of risks such as environmental problems, pension obligations, and back taxes. From a legal standpoint, both the buyer and the seller often are held responsible for these types of obligations.

Areas Commonly Overlooked

Understandably, buyers find the valuation of tangible assets easier than intangible assets. Unfortunately, in many cases the value in the business is more in its intangible than tangible assets. The best examples include the high valuations placed on many Internet-related and biotechnology companies. The target's intangible assets may include customer lists, intellectual property, licenses, distributorship agreements, leases, regulatory approvals (e.g., U.S. Food and Drug Administration approval of a new drug), and employment contracts. An aggressive seller often attempts to "showcase" these items in an attempt to increase the buyer's perceived valuation of the firm. Valuing intangibles is often highly subjective. The prudent buyer should pay a professional appraiser with specific subject matter expertise to evaluate these items.

Table 10-3 illustrates how a target firm's financial reporting statements could be restated to reflect what the buyer believes to be a more accurate characterization of revenue and costs. Note that the cost of sales is divided into direct and indirect expenses. Direct cost of sales relates to costs incurred directly in the production process. Indirect costs are those incurred as a result of the various functions (senior management, sales, accounting, etc.) required to support the production process. The actual historical costs are displayed above the "adjustments" line. Some adjustments represent add backs to profit whereas others reduce profit. The adjusted EBITDA numbers at the bottom of the table represent what the buyer believes to be the most realistic estimate of the profitability of the business. Finally, by displaying the data historically, the buyer can see trends that may be useful in projecting the firm's profitability.

Specific adjustments require further explanation. The buyer believes that, because of the nature of the business, inventories are more accurately valued on a FIFO rather than LIFO basis. This change in inventory cost accounting results in a sizeable boost to the firm's profitability. Furthermore, due diligence revealed that the firm was overstaffed and that it could be adequately operated by eliminating the full-time position held by the former owner (including fees received as a member of the firm's board of directors) and a number of part-time positions held by the owner's family members. Note that although some cost items are reduced, others are increased. The implications for other cost categories of cost reductions in one area must be determined. For example, office space is reduced thereby lowering rental expense as a result of the elimination of out-of-state sales offices. However, the sales and marketing-related portion of the travel and entertainment budget is increased to accommodate the increased travel that will be necessary to service out-of-state customer accounts due to the closure of the regional offices. Furthermore, it is likely that advertising expense will have to be increased to promote the firm's products in those regions. The new buyer also believes that the firm's historical training budget has been woefully inadequate to sustain the growth of the business and more than doubles spending in this category.

TABLE 10-3   Adjusting the Target Firm's Financial Statements

	2003	2004	2005	2006	2007
	($ Thousands)				
Revenue	8000.0	8400.0	8820.0	9261.0	9724.1
Less: Direct Cost of Sales (COS), excluding depreciation & amortization	5440.0	5712.0	5997.6	6297.5	6612.4
Equals: Gross Profit	2560.0	2688.0	2822.4	2963.5	3111.7
Less: Indirect Cost of Sales					
Salaries & Benefits	1200.0	1260.0	1323.0	1389.2	1458.6
Rent	320.0	336.0	352.8	370.4	389.0
Insurance	160.0	168.0	176.4	185.2	194.5
Advertising	80.0	84.0	88.2	92.6	97.2
Travel & Entertainment	240.0	252.0	264.6	277.8	291.7
Director Fees	50.0	50.0	50.0	50.0	50.0
Training	10.0	10.0	10.0	10.0	10.0
All Other Indirect Expenses	240.0	252.0	264.6	277.8	291.7
Equals: EBITDA	260.0	276.0	292.8	310.4	329.0
Explanation of Adjustments	Add Backs/(Deductions)				
LIFO Direct COS is higher than FIFO cost; adjustment converts to FIFO costs	200.0	210.0	220.5	231.5	243.1
Eliminate part-time family members' salaries and benefits	150.0	157.5	165.4	173.6	182.3
Eliminate owner's salary, benefits, and director fees	125.0	131.3	137.8	144.7	151.9
Increase targeted advertising to sustain regional brand recognition	(50.0)	(52.5)	(55.1)	(57.9)	(60.8)
Increase T&E expense to support out-of-state customer accounts	(75.0)	(78.8)	(82.7)	(86.8)	(91.2)
Reduce office space (rent) by closing regional sales offices	120.0	126.0	132.3	138.9	145.9
Increase training budget	(25.0)	(26.3)	(27.6)	(28.9)	(30.4)
Adjusted EBITDA	705.0	743.3	783.4	825.6	869.9

Applying Valuation Methodologies to Private Companies

Defining Value

The most common generic definition of value used by valuation professionals is fair market value. Hypothetically, *fair market value* is the cash or cash-equivalent price that a willing buyer would propose and a willing seller would accept for a business if both parties have access to all relevant information. Furthermore, fair market value assumes that neither the seller nor the buyer is under any obligation to buy or sell. As described in Chapters 7 and 8, the income or market valuation approaches often are used to determine fair market value.

It is easier to obtain the fair market value for a public company because of the existence of public markets in which stock in the company is actively traded. The concept may be applied to privately held firms if similar publicly traded companies exist. However, because finding substantially similar companies is rare, valuation professionals have developed a related concept called fair value. *Fair value* is applied when no strong market exists for a business or it is not possible to identify the value of substantially similar firms. Fair value is by necessity more subjective, because it represents the dollar value of a business based on an appraisal of the tangible and intangible assets of the business.

Hiring Valuation Professionals

The usefulness of valuation methodologies depends on the competence and experience of the analyst conducting the valuation. Thus, the two most important elements in selecting a valuation professional are experience and demonstrated ability in the industry in which the firm to be valued competes. In selecting valuation professionals, it is important to understand what the various certifications obtained by valuation professionals really mean. The American Society of Appraisers (ASA) is one of the nation's oldest and most respected appraisal societies, and it generally is considered to be the leading accrediting body of business valuation professionals. The major business valuation firms require that their appraisers obtain an ASA certification. The requirements for the ASA's Accredited Senior Member certification include a minimum of 5 years of full-time business valuation experience and passing four courses in financial analysis and valuation techniques. Other certificates that are available include the Certified Business Appraiser, Certified Valuation Analyst, and Accredited in Business Valuation (ABV). Of these, only the ABV requires the candidate to have performed at least 10 valuations.

Selecting the Appropriate Valuation Methodology

Valuing private or closely held businesses involves three important steps. The first step involves the adjustment of data so that they accurately reflect the true profitability and cash flow of the firm. This was discussed at length previously in this chapter. The second and third steps entail the determination of the appropriate methodology for valuing the firm and the selection of the proper discount or capitalization rate. For a detailed discussion of the advantages and disadvantages of the various valuation methodologies, see Chapters 7 and 8. The adjustments that should be made to these methodologies when applied to privately owned businesses are summarized in the following sections.

The terms discount rate and capitalization rate often are used interchangeably. Whenever the growth rate of a firm's cash flows is projected to vary over time, the term *discount rate* generally refers to the factor used to convert the projected cash flows to present values. In contrast, if the cash flows of the firm are not expected to grow or are expected to grow at a constant rate indefinitely, the discount rate used by practitioners often is referred to as the *capitalization rate*.

As noted in Chapters 7 and 8, appraisers, brokers, and investment bankers generally classify valuation methodologies into four distinct approaches: income (discounted cash flow), relative or market-based, replacement cost, and asset-oriented. Although the strengths noted for each valuation technique apply when valuing private firms, the weaknesses tend to be most pronounced when applied to the valuation of private or closely held companies due to data limitations.

Income or Discounted Cash-Flow Approach

This method requires projected cash flows for a specific number of periods plus a terminal value to be discounted to the present using an appropriate discount rate. The method is heavily dependent on the particular definition of income or cash flow, the timing of those cash flows, and the selection of an appropriate discount rate. The conversion of a future income stream into a present value also is referred to as the capitalization process. Present values are sometimes referred to as capitalized values.

Capitalization rates are commonly converted to multiples by dividing one by the discount rate or the discount rate less the anticipated constant growth rate in cash flows. These *capitalization multiples* can be multiplied by the current period's cash flow (i.e., if applying the perpetuity valuation method) or the subsequent period's anticipated cash flow (i.e., if applying the constant growth valuation method) to estimate the market value of a firm. For example, if the discount rate is assumed to be 8% and the current level of a firm's cash flow is $1.5 million, which is expected to remain at that level in perpetuity, the implied valuation is $18.75 million [i.e., $(1/.08) \times \$1.5$]. Alternatively, if the current level of cash flow is expected to grow at 4% annually in perpetuity, the implied valuation is $39.0 million [i.e., $(1/(.08 - .04)) \times \$1.5 \times 1.04$].

Several alternative definitions of income or cash flow can be used in either the discounting or capitalization process. These include free cash flow to equity holders or to the firm; earnings before interest and taxes (EBIT); earnings before interest, taxes, depreciation amortization (EBITDA); earnings before taxes (EBT); and earnings after taxes (EAT or NI). The discount rate must be adjusted to reflect these different definitions before applying the discounting process. Capitalized values and capitalization rates often are used in valuing small businesses because of their inherent simplicity. Many small business owners lack sophistication in financial matters. Consequently, a valuation concept, which is easy to calculate, understand, and communicate to the parties involved, may significantly facilitate completion of the transaction. Finally, there is little empirical evidence that more complex valuation methods result in more accurate valuation estimates.

Relative Value or Market-Based Approach

The relative value or market-based approach is used widely in valuing private firms by business brokers or appraisers to establish a purchase price. The Internal Revenue Service (IRS) and the U.S. tax courts have encouraged the use of market-based valuation techniques. Therefore, in valuing private companies, it is always important to keep in mind what factors the IRS thinks are relevant to the process, because the IRS may contest any sale requiring the payment of estate, capital gains, or unearned income taxes. The IRS's positions on specific tax issues can be determined by reviewing revenue rulings. A *revenue ruling* is an official interpretation by the IRS of the Internal Revenue Code, related statutes, tax treaties, and regulations. These rulings represent the IRS's position on how the law is applied to a specific set of circumstances and are published in the Internal Revenue Bulletin to assist taxpayers, IRS personnel, and other concerned parties in interpreting the Internal Revenue Code.

Issued in 1959, Revenue Ruling 59–60 describes the general factors that the IRS and tax courts consider relevant in valuing private businesses. These factors include general economic conditions, the specific conditions in the industry, the type of business, historical trends in the industry, the firm's performance, and the firm's book value. In addition, the IRS and tax courts consider the ability of the company to generate earnings and pay dividends, the amount of intangibles such as goodwill, recent sales of stock, and the stock prices of companies engaged in the "same or similar" line of business. Tax courts historically have supported the use of the comparable company method of valuing private businesses.

Replacement Cost Approach

The replacement cost approach states that the assets of a business are worth what it would cost to replace them. The approach is most applicable to businesses that have substantial amounts of tangible assets for which the actual cost to replace them can be determined easily. In the case of a business whose primary assets consist of intellectual property, it may be difficult to determine the actual cost of replacing the firm's intangible assets using this method. The accuracy of this approach is heavily dependent on the skill and specific industry knowledge of the appraisers employed to conduct the analyses. Moreover, the replacement cost approach ignores the value created in excess of the cost of replacing each asset by operating the assets as a going concern. For example, an assembly line may consist of a number of different machines, each performing a specific task in the production of certain products. The value of the total production coming off the assembly line over the useful lives of the individual machines is likely to far exceed the sum of the costs to replace each machine. Consequently, the business should be valued as a going concern rather than the sum of cost to replace its individual assets.

The replacement cost approach sometimes is used to value intangible assets by examining the amount of historical investment associated with the asset. For example, the cumulative historical advertising spending targeted at developing a particular product brand or image may be a reasonable proxy for the intangible value of the brand name or image. However, because consumer tastes tend to change over time, applying historical experience to the future may be highly misleading.

Asset-Oriented Approach

Like the replacement cost approach, the accuracy of asset-oriented approaches depends on the overall proficiency of the appraiser hired to establish value and the availability of adequate information. Book value is an accounting concept and is generally not considered a good measure of market value, because book values generally reflect historical rather than current market values. However, as noted in Chapter 8, tangible book value (i.e., book value less intangible assets) may be a good proxy for the current market value for both financial services and product distribution companies. Breakup value is an estimate of what the value of a business would be if each of its primary assets were sold independently. This approach may not be practical if there are few public markets for the firm's assets. Liquidation value is a reflection of the firm under duress. A firm in liquidation normally must sell its assets within a specific time period. Consequently, the cash value of the assets realized is likely to be much less than their actual replacement value or value if the firm were to continue as a viable operation. Liquidation value is thus a reasonable proxy for the minimum value of the firm.

Developing Discount (Capitalization) Rates

The discount or capitalization rate can be derived from the capital asset pricing model (CAPM), cost of capital, accounting-based returns, price-to-earnings (P/E) ratio, or the buildup method. These five methods are explored below.

Capital Asset Pricing Model

The CAPM method provides an estimate of the acquiring firm's cost of equity, which may be used as the discount or capitalization rate when no debt is involved in the transaction. Like public firms, private firms are subject to nondiversifiable risk such as changes in interest rates, inflation, war, and terrorism. However, to estimate the firm's β, it is necessary to have sufficient historical data. Private firms and divisions of companies are not publicly traded and therefore do not have past stock price information. The common solution is to estimate the firm's β based on comparable publicly listed firms. Even if the firm's β can be estimated, the cost of equity may have to be adjusted to reflect risk specific to the target when it is applied to valuing a private or closely held company. For a detailed discussion of how to estimate betas for private firms, see Damodaran (2002).

The Nature of Specific Business Risk   The CAPM may understate significantly the specific business risk associated with acquiring a privately held firm, because it may not adequately reflect the risk associated with such firms. As noted earlier, private or closely held firms are often subject to risks not normally found with public firms. These include inconsistent or improperly stated financial information resulting in inaccurate financial statements, inadequate controls increasing the possibility of fraudulent activities, and potential "hidden" liabilities, such as noncompliance with Occupational Safety and Health Administration and Environmental Protection Agency regulations. Private or closely held firms also may lack management depth or be subject to significant commercial risk because of reliance on a few customers or suppliers or a narrow product offering. Consequently, it is appropriate to adjust the CAPM for the additional risks associated with private or closely held firms.

Recall from Chapter 7 that risk premiums for public companies are determined by examining the historical premiums earned by stocks over some measure of risk-free returns, such as 10-year Treasury bonds. This same logic may be applied to calculating specific business risk premiums for small private firms. The specific business risk premium can be measured by the difference between the junk bond and risk-free rate or the return on comparable small stocks and the risk-free rate. Other adjustments for the risks associated with firm size are given by Ibbotson Associates in Table 7-1 found in Chapter 7. Note that comparable small companies are more likely to be found on the NASDAQ, OTC, or regional stock exchanges than on the New York Stock Exchange (NYSE). For example, consider an acquiring firm that is attempting to value a small software company. If the risk-free return is 6%, the historical return on all stocks minus the risk-free return is 5.5%, the firm's β is one, and the historical return on OTC software stocks minus the risk-free return is 10%, the cost of equity (k_e) can be calculated as follows:

$$k_e = \text{Risk-Free Return} + \text{Market Risk or Equity Premium}$$
$$+ \text{Specific Business Risk Premium}$$
$$= 6\% + 5.5\% + 10\% = 21.5\%$$

Note that the rationale for this adjustment is similar to that discussed in Chapter 7 in adjusting the CAPM for firm size (i.e., small firms are generally less liquid and subject to higher default risk than larger firms).

Cost of Capital

In the presence of debt, the cost of capital method should be used to estimate the discount or capitalization rate. This method involves the calculation of a weighted average of the cost of equity and the after-tax cost of debt. The weights reflect the market value of the acquirer's target debt-to-equity ratio. Private firms seldom can access public debt markets and are therefore usually not rated by the credit-rating agencies. Most debt is bank debt and the interest expense on loans on the firm's books that is more than a year old may not reflect what it actually would cost the firm to borrow currently. The common solution is to assume that private firms can borrow at the same rate as comparable publicly listed firms or to estimate an appropriate bond rating for the company based on financial ratios and use the interest rate that public firms with similar ratings would pay. Such information is easily found in major financial newspapers such as *The Wall Street Journal* and *Investors' Business Daily*. See Chapter 7 for more detail.

Calculating the cost of capital requires the use of the market rather than the book value of debt-to-total capital ratios. Private firms generally will provide such ratios only in book terms. A common solution is to assume that the private firms will eventually adopt the industry average debt-to-total capital ratio expressed in market value terms. Therefore, the weights used in calculating the weighted average cost of capital would be the industry average debt-to-total capital ratio and equity-to-total capital ratio. Unlike the estimation of the cost of equity for small, privately held firms, it is unnecessary to adjust the cost of debt for specific business risk, since such risk should already be reflected in the interest rate.

Accounting-Based Returns

The return on equity (ROE) and the return on investment (ROI) sometimes are used as capitalization rates. ROE is the return to equity owners in the business. ROI measures the return on total capital, which includes both the debt and equity of the business. Although after-tax income normally is used to calculate these returns, pretax income should be used for private firms because of the unreliability of after-tax income for such companies (see Exhibit 10-1).

Exhibit 10-1
Accounting-Based Capitalization Rates

Doors Unlimited, Inc., has pretax earnings of $1 million, debt of $5 million, and equity of $15 million.

$$ROE = \$1/\$15 = 6.7\%$$

$$ROI = \$1/\$20 = 5.0\%$$

The capitalized value of the business using ROE is $1/.067 = $14.93 million.
The capitalized value of the business using ROI is $1/.05 = $20 million.

Price-to-Earnings Ratio

The capitalization or discount rate also can be measured by calculating the reciprocal of the P/E ratio (i.e., E/P). The P/E ratio used for this purpose can be for the current, the most recent, or a projected year. The P/E used for valuing a private firm should be selected from among the P/Es of comparable public companies adjusted to reflect risks specific to the target firm. Such adjustments are included in the so-called buildup method.

The Buildup Method

The buildup method is simply another name for multifactor models sometimes used in place of the simple CAPM model (see Chapter 7). The buildup method attempts to compensate for some of the shortcomings associated with applying CAPM or accounting-based returns to evaluating private or closely held businesses. The *buildup method* involves the adjustment of the underlying discount or capitalization rate to reflect risks associated with such businesses. The resulting capitalization rate can be expressed as free cash flow available for equity investors in the first year of the forecast period ($FCFE_1$) as a percent of the market value (P) of the privately held firm (i.e., $FCFE_1/P$). $FCFE_1$ represents the cash available for payment of dividends and for share repurchases.

$$P = \frac{FCFE_0(1+g)}{(coe - g)}$$

$$coe - g = \frac{FCFE_1}{P}$$

$$[R_f + \beta(R_m - R_f) + (R_j - R_f) + R_{ji}] - g = \frac{FCFE_1}{P}$$

If $g = 0$, $FCFE_1/P$ = Capitalization rate derived from the zero growth model

If $g > 0$, $FCFE_1/P$ = Capitalization rate derived from the constant growth model

where, R_f = the risk-free rate of return

R_m = the return on all stocks

R_j = the return on the jth stock

$(R_m - R_f)$ = the market or equity risk premium

$(R_j - R_f)$ = the specific business risk premium

R_{ji} = the liquidity or marketability risk (due to lack of a liquid market) of the jth stock

β = the β associated with the jth stock

g = the projected constant growth rate of $FCFE_0$ in perpetuity

The risk associated with an illiquid market for the specific stock (R_{ji}) often is referred to as *marketability* or *liquidity* risk. Liquidity is the ease with which investors can sell their stock without a serious loss of value of their investment. An investor in a small company may find it difficult to quickly sell his or her shares because of limited interest in the company. As such, the investor may find it necessary to sell their shares at a significant discount from what they paid for the shares. R_f is free of default risk and is usually taken to be the rate on U.S. Treasury bills, notes, or bonds depending upon the investor's anticipated holding period for the investment. The market or equity risk premium, $R_m - R_f$, the difference between the return on stocks and the risk-free rate, has historically averaged about 5.5%. (See Chapter 7.) The β for a private firm may be estimated by using the β for a comparable publicly traded firm or by using an industry-average β. The solution to the case study at the end of this chapter provides an example of how to estimate the β for a private firm if comparable publicly traded firms are available. In the absence of such firms, analysts may use the buildup methodology by assuming a β of 1.

The specific business risk premium, $R_j - R_f$, as measured by the difference between the return on small company stocks (i.e., Over-The-Counter stocks) and the risk-free rate, has been averaging about 9% since 1960. $R_j - R_f$ also can be measured using the difference between junk bond yields and the risk-free rate of return. Information on junk bonds and small stocks may be found in the financial press such as in *The Wall Street Journal* or *Investor's Business Daily*. Historical data are available through Ibbotson Associates (www.ibbotson.com). Note that this is similar to adjusting CAPM for firm size as discussed in Chapter 7.

Exhibit 10-2 summarizes the calculation of both the discount and capitalization rates using the buildup method. The risk-free return is assumed to be 6%, and the long-term rate of growth in earnings based on historical information is estimated at 4.5%. For purposes of illustration, R_{ji}, the marketability or illiquidity risk premium, is assumed to be 33%. The marketability risk premium is the amount required by investors to compensate for their potential loss if forced to sell their investment in an illiquid market. How this premium may be estimated is discussed next.

Exhibit 10-2
Calculating Capitalization Rates Using the Buildup Method

Risk-Free Rate (R_f)	6.0
+ Market Risk Premium Required to Invest in Stocks $(R_m - R_f)$[1]	5.5
+ Specific Business Risk Premium $(R_j - R_f)$	9.0
+ Marketability Risk Premium (R_{ji})	33.0
= *Discount/Capitalization Rate* (zero earnings growth model)	53.5
− Long-Term Earnings Growth Rate	4.5
= *Discount/Capitalization Rate* (constant earnings growth model)	49.0

[1] The β in this example is assumed to be one because, in this illustration, it is assumed that there are no publicly traded comparable firms.

Estimating Marketability/Liquidity Risk

We may account for marketability or liquidity risk in either one of two ways. It may be incorporated into the discount or capitalization rate as a marketability risk premium as in the buildup method illustrated in Exhibit 10-2. This discount rate then may be used to convert projected cash flows for the firm to a present value or to calculate a capitalization multiple (e.g., 1/discount rate if the cash flows are not expected to grow). The multiple could then be used to estimate the present value of the firm by multiplying it by the firm's current cash flow. Alternatively, marketability or liquidity risk may be expressed as a *marketability* or *liquidity discount* in the offer price for the target firm by reducing the value of the target firm estimated by examining the market values of comparable publicly traded firms to reflect the potential loss of value when sold due to the illiquidity of the market for similar assets.

When family-owned businesses are sold, it is common for appraisers to follow the guidelines suggested in Revenue Ruling 59–60 and to use the comparable companies' method to estimate the value of the subject firm. Valuation professionals frequently use P/E multiples and other indicators of value associated with publicly traded companies. The stock of such companies usually trades in more liquid markets than closely held companies. Consequently, estimates of the value of closely held companies based on the comparable companies' approach are likely to be overstated, because they do not reflect the lower marketability of closely held shares.

Numerous studies have been done to estimate the magnitude of the marketability or liquidity discount. These include analyses of restricted stock, initial public offerings (IPOs), and option pricing. The bulk of the studies suggest that estimates of the value of closely held firms based on publicly traded firms' multiples should be discounted by 33 to 50% (See Institutional Investor Study Report, 1971; Emory, 1985; Gelman, 1972; Koplin, Sarin, and Shapiro, 2000; Maher, 1976; Silber, 1991.) For example, if a private firm's value is estimated to be $20 million based on P/E ratios for comparable publicly traded firms, the potential buyer may reduce this estimate by 33 to 50% to $10 million (i.e., $20 × (1 − .5)) or $13.4 million (i.e., $20 million × (1 − .33)) to reflect the potential illiquidity of the target.

In a more recent study, Officer (2007) estimates the liquidity risk to be somewhat smaller, finding that sales of privately owned firms and subsidiaries of other firms sell at discounts of 15 to 30% below comparable publicly traded firms. He argues that this discount is the price paid by such firms for the liquidity provided by the acquiring firm.

Given the wide variability of estimates, it should be evident that such discounts must be applied to the value of the target estimated by using comparable firm multiples with great care. The implication is that there is no such thing as a standard marketability discount. Despite the subjective nature of these adjustments, some analysts argue that additional adjustments are required to reflect the size of the investor position or equity interest in the privately held firm (Pratt, 1998; Pratt, Reilly, and Scheweihs, 1995). These authors argue that investors interested in buying only a minority position should further discount the value of the firm based on comparable P/Es to reflect the disadvantages of holding a less than controlling interest. This additional discount is called a *minority discount*.

Intuitively, the size of the minority discount should vary with the size of the ownership position in the private firm. An investor holding a controlling interest in a company is better able to affect change in the company than is a minority shareholder. Control can include the ability to select management, determine compensation, set policy and change the course of the business, acquire and liquidate assets, award contracts, make acquisitions, sell or recapitalize the company, and register the company's stock for a public offering. Control also involves the ability to declare and pay dividends, change the articles of incorporation or bylaws, or block any of the aforementioned actions. Therefore, it may be argued that the size of the discount applied to value the investment of a shareholder with a minority interest should be higher than that for a controlling interest shareholder. The key question is how much higher.

A discount in the range of 33–50% may be appropriate for many transactions, with the size of the discount varying with the size of the equity interest being valued. For example, suppose a closely held firm is valued at \$5 million by applying P/E ratios for publicly traded firms to the firm's after-tax earnings. Assume that the marketability or liquidity discount could be approximately 33%, while the minority discount including the liquidity discount is about 50%. To adjust for the presumed marketability or liquidity risk of the target firm, investors discount the amount they are willing to offer to purchase 100% of the firm's equity by 33% to \$3.35 million (i.e., \$5 × .67). An investor desiring to purchase a minority interest of 20% equity in the firm may want to discount the offer price further and only be willing to pay \$500,000 for that ownership position. This reflects a larger discount of 50% to reflect both marketability and minority discounts (i.e., \$5 million × .2 × .5). While these adjustments may be useful in establishing initial offer prices, the actual purchase price will, of course, reflect the relative bargaining power of the buyer and seller.

Reverse Mergers

Many small businesses fail each year. In a number of cases, all that remains is a business with no significant assets or operations. Such companies are referred to as *shell corporations*. Shell corporations can be used as part of a deliberate business strategy in which a corporate legal structure is formed in anticipation of future financing, a merger, joint venture, spin-off, or some other infusion of operating assets. This may be accomplished in a transaction called a *reverse merger* in which the acquirer forms a new shell subsidiary, which is merged into the target in a statutory merger. The target is the surviving entity that must hold the assets and liabilities of both the target and shell subsidiary. See Chapter 11 for more on reverse mergers.

The Value of Corporate Shells

Is there any value in shells resulting from corporate failure or bankruptcy? The answer may seem surprising, but it is a resounding yes. Merging with an existing corporate shell of a publicly traded company may be a reasonable alternative for a firm wanting to go public that is unable to provide the 2 years of audited financial statements required by the SEC or unwilling to incur the costs of going public. Thus, merging with a shell corporation may represent an effective alternative to an IPO for a small firm.

Are Reverse Mergers Cheaper Than IPOs?

Direct issuance costs associated with going public include the underwriter spread and administrative and regulatory costs. The *underwriter spread* represents the difference between the price the underwriter receives for selling a firm's securities to the public and the amount it pays to the firm. The underwriter spread can range from less than 1% of gross proceeds for a high-quality company to more than 8% for lower quality companies. Administrative and regulatory fees consist of legal and accounting fees, taxes, and the cost of SEC registration. For offerings less than \$10 million in size, total direct issuance costs may exceed 10% of gross proceeds. For equity issues between \$20 million and \$50 million in size, these costs average less than 5% of gross proceeds and less than 3% for those issues larger than \$200 million (Hansen, 1986). Reverse mergers typically cost between $50,000 and $100,000, about one-quarter of the expense of an IPO and can be completed in about 60 days or one-third of the time to complete a typical IPO (Sweeney, 2005).

Despite these advantages, reverse takeovers may take as long as IPOs and are sometimes more complex. The acquiring company must still perform due diligence on the target and communicate information on the shell corporation to the exchange on which its stock will be traded and prepare a prospectus. Public exchanges often require the same level of information for companies going through reverse mergers as those undertaking IPOs. The principal concern is that the shell company may contain unseen liabilities such as unpaid bills, which in some instances can make the reverse merger far more costly than an IPO.

Financing Reverse Mergers

Private investment in public entities (PIPEs) is a commonly used method of financing reverse mergers. In such transactions, a public company sells equity at a discount to private investors, often hedge funds. As the issuer, it is up to the company to register its shares with the SEC within 120 days. Once approved by the SEC, the stock may be traded on public exchanges. PIPEs often are used in conjunction with a reverse merger to provide companies with not just an alternative way to go public but also with financing once they are listed on the public exchange. For example, assume a private company creates a shell corporation that is subsequently merged into a public company through a reverse merger. As the surviving entity, the public company raises funds through a privately placed equity issue (i.e., PIPE financing) to fund future investments.

PIPEs offer the advantage of being able to be completed more quickly, cheaply, and confidentially than a public stock offering, which requires registration up front and a more elaborate investor "road show" to sell the securities to public investors. In theory, the confidentiality inherent in the private placement aspect of PIPEs prevents short-sellers (i.e., speculators selling currently publicly traded borrowed shares of the company in the hope they can be repurchased at a lower price in the future) from pushing down the price of new public stock offerings of small companies. However, the SEC has filed lawsuits charging hedge fund investors in PIPEs with illegally trading on inside information about an impending financing. These investors have been accused of shorting the public firm's shares in advance of the new equity issue and replacing the borrowed shares with the shares they receive from the PIPE equity issue. In many PIPE transactions, the number of shares PIPE investors receive is tied to the value of the stock in order to preserve the value of the PIPE equity issue to investors. Therefore, as the price of the stock declines due to short-selling, PIPE investors receive more shares.

As private placements, PIPEs are most suitable for raising small amounts of financing, typically in the $5 million to $10 million range. Firms seeking hundreds of millions of dollars are more likely to be successful in going directly to the public financial markets in a public stock offering. Case Study 10-4 illustrates the reverse merger process.

Case Study 10-4
Panda Ethanol Goes Public in a Shell Corporation

In early 2006, Panda Ethanol (Panda), owner of ethanol plants in West Texas, decided to explore the possibility of taking its ethanol production business public to take advantage of the high valuations placed on ethanol-related companies in the public market at that time. The firm was confronted with the choice of taking the company public through an initial public offering or combining with a publicly traded shell corporation through a reverse merger. The reverse merger involves the acquirer's assets and liabilities being merged with the target firm (a public company), with the target surviving. Thus, the acquirer moves from being a privately owned to a public company.

After enlisting the services of a local investment banker, Grove Street Investors, Panda chose to "go public" through a reverse merger. This process entailed finding a shell corporation with relatively few shareholders who were interested in selling their stock. The investment banker identified Cirracor Inc., a publicly traded firm headquartered in Oceanside, California, as a potential merger partner. Cirracor was formed on October 12, 2001, to provide Web site development services and was traded on the over-the-counter bulletin board market (i.e., a market for very low priced stocks). The Web site business was not profitable, and the company had only 10 shareholders. As of June 30, 2006, Cirracor listed $4,856 in assets and a negative shareholders' equity of ($259,976). The continued financial viability of the firm was clearly problematic. Given the poor financial condition of Cirracor, the firm's shareholders were interested in either selling their shares for cash or owning even a relatively small portion of a financially viable company to recover their initial investments in Cirracor.

Grove Street formed a limited liability company called Grove Panda. Grove Panda bought 2.5 million Cirracor common shares, or 71% of the company, for $20,000. Grove subsequently purchased another 225,000 shares for $425,000 to boost its overall stake in the company to about 78%.

The merger proposal provided for one share of Cirracor common to be exchanged for each share of Panda Ethanol common outstanding and for Cirracor shareholders to own 4% of the newly issued and outstanding common stock of the surviving company. Panda Ethanol shareholders would own the remaining 96%. At the end of 2005, Panda had 13.8 million shares outstanding. On June 7, 2006, the merger agreement was amended to permit Panda Ethanol to issue 15 million new shares through a private placement to raise $90,000,000. This brought the total Panda shares outstanding to 28.8 million. Cirracor common shares outstanding at that time totaled 3.5 million. However, to achieve the agreed upon ownership distribution, the number of Cirracor shares outstanding had to be reduced. This would be accomplished by an approximate 3-for-1 reverse stock split immediately prior to the completion of the reverse merger (i.e., each Cirracor common share would be converted into .340885 shares of Cirracor common stock). As a consequence of the merger, the previous shareholders of Panda Ethanol were issued 28.8 million new shares of Cirracor common stock. The combined firm now has 30 million outstanding, with the Cirracor shareholders owning 1.2 million shares. The following table illustrates the effect of the reverse stock split.

	Shares Outstanding (Millions)	Ownership Distribution (%)	Shares Outstanding (Millions)	Ownership Distribution (%)
	(Before Reverse Split)		(After Reverse Split)	
Panda Ethanol	28.8	89.2	28.8	96
Cirracor Inc.	3.5	10.8	1.2	4

A special Cirracor shareholders' meeting was required by Nevada law (i.e., the state in which Cirracor was incorporated) in view of the substantial number of new shares that were to be issued as a result of the merger. The proxy statement filed with the Securities and Exchange Commission and distributed to Cirracor shareholders indicated that Grove Panda, a 78% owner of Cirracor common, had already indicated that it would vote its shares for the merger and the reverse stock split. Since Cirracor's articles of incorporation required only a simple majority to approve such matters, it was evident to all that approval was imminent.

On November 7, 2006, Panda completed its merger with Cirracor Inc. As a result of the merger, all shares of Panda Ethanol common stock (other than Panda Ethanol shareholders who had executed their dissenters' rights under Delaware law) would cease to have any rights as a shareholder, except the right to receive one share of Cirracor common per share of Panda Ethanol common. Panda Ethanol shareholders choosing to exercise their right to dissent would receive a cash payment for the fair value of their stock on the day immediately before closing. Cirracor shareholders had similar dissenting rights under Nevada law. While Cirracor is the surviving corporation, Panda is viewed for accounting purposes as the acquirer. Accordingly, the financial statements shown for the surviving corporation are those of Panda Ethanol.

Case Study Discussion Questions

1. Discuss the pros and cons of a reverse merger versus an initial public offering for taking a company public.
2. Why did Panda Ethanol undertake a private equity placement totaling $90 million shortly before implementing the reverse merger?
3. How was the Panda Grove investment holdings used to influence the outcome of the proposed merger?

Exploiting Intangible Value

Shell corporations also may be attractive for investors interested in capitalizing on the intangible value associated with the existing corporate shell. This could include name recognition; licenses, patents, and other forms of intellectual properties; and underutilized assets such as warehouse space and fully depreciated equipment with some economic life remaining. Case Study 10-5 illustrates one such instance.

Case Study 10-5
The Corporate Shell Game

ShellCo, a company widely known for providing security, cleaning, and office plant maintenance services to businesses, sold substantially all of its operating assets for cash at a significant gain for its shareholders. With few earnings-generating assets remaining, the company was essentially a corporate shell. Its primary assets following the sale include its reputation, a small office building that it owns free and clear of any liens, office furniture and equipment, several trucks, and all the state and local licenses necessary to do business in its municipality. The firm's monthly payments on a long-term lease negotiated some years earlier on prime commercial warehouse space are two-thirds of the currently prevailing lease terms for comparable space. The company name is widely recognized in the local business community and is synonymous with quality and reliability. The company has excess cash balances of $50,000.

The firm's dilemma is that without sufficient revenue it will have to liquidate its operations and force existing stockholders to incur additional tax liabilities. As an alternative to liquidation, the firm hired a local business broker to solicit other companies that may have an interest in the corporate shell. The business broker is charged with the responsibility of finding potential buyers who see value in the firm's name and reputation, valuable lease terms, office building, trucks, furniture and fixtures, and licenses and regulatory approvals. The broker understands that, in any likely transaction, the excess cash would be distributed to current shareholders and would therefore have no value to potential acquirers. The broker develops a list of local firms in the same or similar business as the shell corporation. The list includes other commercial security, cleaning, pest control, food, custodial, and temporary employment services that might be interested in growing their existing businesses or expanding their service offering to their current customers or ShellCo's former customers.

The broker is optimistic that a suitable buyer can be found. The current ShellCo stockholders are very interested in minimizing tax liabilities and dispensing with the risk of liquidation, which would involve the sale of the building; subleasing of the leased commercial office space; and disposal of office furniture and other miscellaneous assets. Potential buyers will be interested in the opportunity to utilize ShellCo's brand name in the local community and to dispense with the expense and aggravation of obtaining licenses and other regulatory approvals. They also will like the favorable lease terms and the office building. The broker begins to make initial contacts of the potential interested parties with these factors woven into a compelling sales pitch.

Case Study Discussion Questions

1. How would you "position" this business if you were the business broker hired to sell this business? Consider its key attributes.
2. What other types of firms not listed in the case study might be potential buyers?

Using Leveraged Employee Stock Ownership Plans to Buy Private Companies

An ESOP is a means whereby a corporation can make tax-deductible contributions of cash or stock into a trust. The assets are allocated to employees and are not taxed until withdrawn by employees. ESOPs generally must invest at least 50% of their assets in employer stock. There are three types of ESOPs recognized by the 1974 Employee Retirement Income Security Act: (1) leveraged (ESOP borrows to purchase qualified employer securities), (2) leverageable (ESOP is authorized but not required to borrow), and (3) nonleveraged (ESOP may not borrow funds). As noted in Chapter 1, ESOPs offer substantial tax advantages to sponsoring firms, lenders, and participating employees.

Employees commonly use leveraged ESOPs to buy out owners of private companies, who have most of their net worth in the firm. The firm establishes an ESOP. The owner sells at least 30% of his stock to the ESOP, which pays for the stock with borrowed funds. The owner may invest the proceeds and defer taxes if the investment is made within 12 months of the sale of the stock to the ESOP, the ESOP owns at least 30% of the firm, and neither the owner nor his family participates in the ESOP. The firm makes tax-deductible contributions to the ESOP in an amount sufficient to repay interest and principal. Shares held by the ESOP are distributed to employees as the loan is repaid. As the outstanding loan balance is reduced, the shares are allocated to employees who eventually own the firm.

Analyzing Private Shareholder Returns

In contrast to the mountain of empirical studies of the impact of M&A activity on public company shareholders, there are very few rigorous studies of privately held companies because of the limited availability of data. Chang (1998), in a study of the returns to public company shareholders when they acquire privately held firms, found an average positive 2.6% abnormal return for shareholders of bidding firms for stock offers but not for cash transactions. The finding of positive abnormal returns earned by buyers using stock to acquire private companies is in sharp contrast with the negative abnormal returns earned by U.S. bidders using stock to acquire publicly traded companies (see Chapter 1). Chang (1998) notes that ownership of privately held companies tends to be highly concentrated, such that an exchange of stock tends to create a few very large stockholders. Close monitoring of management and the acquired firm's performance may contribute to abnormal positive returns experienced by firms bidding for private firms. This finding is consistent with the positive announcement returns for acquirers of about the same magnitude in Canadian and European studies where ownership is often highly concentrated as opposed to the highly dispersed ownership of publicly traded firms in the United States (Ben-Amar and Andre, 2006; Bigelli and Mengoli, 2004; Boehmer, 2000; Dumontier and Pecherot, 2001). Ownership concentration and the accompanying active monitoring of incumbent management may explain the difference in announcement date returns for acquirers of public companies in the United States and foreign acquirers of non-U.S. firms.

This conclusion also is consistent with studies of returns to companies that issue stock and convertible debt in private placements (Fields and Mais, 1991; Hertzel and Smith, 1993; Wruck, 1989). It generally is argued that in private placements large shareholders are effective monitors of managerial performance, thereby enhancing the prospects of the acquired firm (Demsetz and Lehn, 1996). Ang and Kohers (2001) also found positive excess returns to bidder shareholders and for private firm shareholders regardless of the form of payment.

In a more recent study, Fuller, Netter, and Stegemoller (2002) also found that acquirers earn excess returns of as much as 2.1% when buying private firms or 2.6% for subsidiaries of public companies. They attribute the abnormal returns to the tendency of acquirers to pay less for non-publicly traded companies due to the relative difficulty in buying private firms or subsidiaries of public companies. In both cases, shares are not publicly traded and access to information is limited. Moreover, there may be fewer bidders for non-publicly traded companies. Consequently, these targets may be acquired at a discount from their actual economic value. As a consequence of this discount, bidder shareholders are able to realize a larger share of the anticipated synergies.

Other factors that may contribute to these positive abnormal returns include the introduction of more professional management into the privately held firms and tax considerations. Public companies may introduce more professional management systems into the target firms thereby enhancing the target's value. The acquirer's use of stock rather than cash may also induce the seller to accept a lower price since it allows the seller to defer taxes on any gains until they decide to sell their shares (see Chapter 11). Poulsen and Stegemoller (2002) found that the favorable tax consequences of a share-for-share exchange were an important factor in privately held firms selling to public companies for more than one-third of sellers surveyed.

Things to Remember

Privately owned (closely held) businesses are often characterized by a small group of shareholders controlling the firm's operating and management policies. Private firms differ from public firms, which are generally run by professional managers. Moreover, ownership in public firms is usually widely distributed and stock is traded on large public exchanges. While most private firms are family-owned businesses, they are not necessarily small, as families control many large, publicly traded companies.

Valuing private companies tends to be more challenging than efforts to value public companies. The current value of a private company can be very difficult to obtain because of the absence of published price information that is readily available for publicly traded companies. The absence of internal controls in many private firms means that fraud or waste may go largely undetected. Private firms often face problems that may be unique to their size and market position. These include inadequate management talent; lack of sophistication; limited access to capital; and a limited ability to influence customers, suppliers, unions, and regulators.

Owners considering the sale of their firms may overstate revenue by inadequately adjusting for product returns. Costs also may be understated if owners are desirous of selling the business. However, in examining the historical performance of privately owned firms, there is a greater likelihood that profits will be understated to minimize tax liabilities by failing to report revenue fully and by inflating operating expenses. Notwithstanding this tendency to overstate costs, there are areas that frequently are understated. These include employee training, advertising, safety, and environmental cleanup. Although many small businesses have few hard assets, they may have substantial intangible value in terms of customer lists, intellectual property, licenses and regulatory approvals, distributor agreements, franchises, supply contracts, leases, and employment contracts. In view of these considerations, it is crucial to restate the firm's financial statements to determine the current period's actual profitability. Once this has been achieved, comparisons with similar publicly traded firms or projections of cash flow to determine value will be more meaningful.

The discount rate for valuing private firms may be estimated using the CAPM, cost of capital, accounting returns, P/E ratio, and the buildup method. The latter equals the sum of the risk-free rate, the premium required to induce investors to invest in equities, the premium required to induce investment in a specific stock, and the marketability discount. Empirical evidence suggests that marketability discounts generally lie in a range of 33–50%, although factors specific to the firm could result in discounts outside of this range. The size of the adjustment should reflect the degree of control the equity interest has in the firm. The value of a controlling interest should be discounted less than that of a minority interest.

In contrast to studies involving acquisitions of U.S. publicly traded firms, which on average show zero to negative abnormal announcement date returns to acquirers, buyers of private firms in the United States often realize significant abnormal positive returns, particularly in share-for-share transactions. This result may be due to the concentration of ownership in private firms and the resulting aggressive monitoring of management, unlike publicly traded firms where ownership is often widely dispersed. When ownership is dispersed, the impact of incompetent management is spread over many shareholders rather than shouldered by a few. This finding is also supported by many studies of mergers in Canada, Germany, Italy, and in France, where ownership tends to be more heavily concentrated than in the United States.

Chapter Discussion Questions

10-1. Why is it more difficult to value privately held companies than publicly traded firms?
10-2. What factors should be considered in adjusting target company data?
10-3. What is the capitalization rate, and how does it relate to the discount rate?
10-4. What are the common ways of estimating the capitalization rate?
10-5. What is the marketability discount, and what are common ways of estimating this discount?
10-6. Give examples of private company costs that might be understated, and explain why.
10-7. How can an analyst determine if the target firm's costs and revenues are understated or overstated?
10-8. What is the difference between the concept of fair market value and fair value?
10-9. What is the importance of Revenue Ruling 59–60?
10-10. Why might shell corporations have value?

Answers to these Chapter Discussion Questions are available in the Online Instructor's Manual for instructors using this book.

Chapter Business Case

Case Study 10-6
Valuing a Privately Held Company

Background

BigCo is interested in acquiring PrivCo, whose owner desires to retire. The firm is 100% owned by the current owner. PrivCo has revenues of $10 million and an EBIT of $2 million in the preceding year. The market value of the firm's debt is $5 million; the book value of equity is $4 million. For publicly traded firms in the same industry, the average debt-to-equity ratio is .4 (based on the market value of debt and equity), and the marginal tax rate is 40%. Typically, the ratio of the market value of equity to book value for these firms is 2. The average β of publicly traded firms that are in the same business is 2.00. Capital expenditures and depreciation amounted to $0.3 million and $0.2 million in the prior year. Both items are expected to grow at the same rate as revenues for the next 5 years. Capital expenditures and depreciation are expected to be equal beyond 5 years (i.e., capital spending will be internally funded). As a result of excellent working capital management practices, the change in working capital is expected to be essentially zero throughout the forecast period and beyond. The revenues of this firm are expected to grow 15% annually for the next 5 years and 5% per year thereafter. Net income is expected to increase 15% a year for the next 5 years and 5% thereafter. The 10-year U.S. Treasury bond rate is 6%. The pretax cost of debt for a similar nonrated firm is 10%. No adjustment is made in the calculation of the cost of equity for a marketability discount. Estimate the shareholder value of the firm.

An answer to this Case is provided in the Online Instructor's Manual available for instructors using this book.

Chapter Business Case

Case Study 10-7
Pacific Wardrobe Acquires SurferDude Apparel by a Skillful Structuring of the Acquisition Plan

Pacific Wardrobe (Pacific) is a privately owned California corporation that has annual sales of $20 million and pretax profits of $2 million. Its target market is the surfwear/sportswear segment of the apparel industry. The surfwear/sportswear market consists of two segments: cutting-edge and casual brands. The first segment includes high-margin apparel sold at higher-end retail establishments. The second segment consists of brands that sell for lower prices at retail stores such as Sears, Target, and J.C. Penney. Pacific operates primarily as a U.S. importer/distributor of mainly casual sportswear for young men and boys between 10–21 years of age. Pacific's strategic business objectives are to triple sales and pretax profits during the next 5 years. Pacific intends to achieve these objectives by moving away from the casual sportswear market segment and more into the high-growth, high-profit cutting-edge surfer segment. Because of the rapid rate at which trends change in the apparel industry, Pacific's management believes that it can take advantage of current trends only through a well-conceived acquisition strategy.

Pacific's Operations and Competitive Environment
Pacific imports all of its apparel from factories in Hong Kong, Taiwan, Nepal, and Indonesia. Its customers consist of major chains and specialty stores. Most customers are lower-end retail stores. Customers include J.C. Penney, Sears, Stein Mart, Kids "R" Us, and Target. No one customer accounts for more than 20% of Pacific's total revenue. The customers in the lower-end market are extremely cost sensitive. Customers consist of those in the 10–21-years age range who want to wear cutting-edge surf and sport styles but who are not willing or able to pay high prices. Pacific offers an alternative to the expensive cutting-edge styles.

Pacific has found a niche in the young men's and teenage boy's sportswear market. The firm offers similar styles as the top brand names in the surf and sport industry, such as Mossimo, Red Sand, Stussy, Quick Silver, and Gotcha, but at a lower price point. Pacific indirectly competes with these top brand names by attempting to appeal to the same customer base. There are few companies that compete with Pacific at their level—low-cost production of "almost" cutting-edge styles.

Pacific's Strengths and Weaknesses
Pacific's core strengths lie in their strong vendor support in terms of quantity, quality, service, delivery, and price/cost. Pacific's production is also scaleable and has the potential

to produce at high volumes to meet peak demand periods. Additionally, Pacific also has strong financial support from local banks and a strong management team, with an excellent track record in successfully acquiring and integrating small acquisitions. Pacific also has a good reputation for high-quality products and customer service and on-time delivery. Finally, Pacific has a low cost of goods sold when compared with the competition. Pacific's major weakness is that it does not possess any cutting-edge/trendy labels. Furthermore, their management team lacks the ability to develop trendy brands.

Acquisition Plan

Pacific's management objectives are to grow sales, improve profit margins, and increase its brand life cycle by acquiring a cutting-edge surfwear retailer with a trendy brand image. Pacific intends to improve its operating margins by increasing its sales of trendy clothes under the newly acquired brand name, while obtaining these clothes from its own low-cost production sources.

Pacific would prefer to use its stock to complete an acquisition, because it is currently short of cash and wishes to use its borrowing capacity to fund future working capital requirements. Pacific's target debt-to-equity ratio is 3 to 1. The firm desires a friendly takeover of an existing surfwear company to facilitate integration and avoid a potential "bidding war." The target will be evaluated on the basis of profitability, target markets, distribution channels, geographic markets, existing inventory, market brand recognition, price range, and overall "fit" with Pacific. Pacific will locate this surfwear company by analyzing the surfwear industry; reviewing industry literature; and making discrete inquiries relative to the availability of various firms to board members, law firms, and accounting firms. Pacific would prefer an asset purchase because of the potentially favorable impact on cash flow and because it is concerned about unknown liabilities that might be assumed if it acquired the stock.

Pacific's screening criteria for identifying potential acquisition candidates include the following:

1. Industry: Garment industry targeting young men, teens, and boys
2. Product: Cutting-edge, trendy surfwear product line
3. Size: Revenue ranging from $5 million to $10 million
4. Profit: Minimum of breakeven on operating earnings for fiscal year 1999
5. Management: Company with management expertise in brand and image building
6. Leverage: Maximum debt-to-equity ratio of 3 to 1

After a review of 14 companies, Pacific's management determined that SurferDude best satisfied their criteria. SurferDude is a widely recognized brand in the surfer sports apparel line; it is marginally profitable, with sales of $7 million and a debt-to-equity ratio of 3 to 1. SurferDude's current lackluster profitability reflects a significant advertising campaign undertaken during the last several years. Based on financial information provided by SurferDude, industry averages, and comparable companies, the estimated purchase price ranges from $1.5 million to $15 million. The maximum price reflects the full impact of anticipated synergy. The price range was estimated using several valuation methods.

Valuation

On a standalone basis, sales for both Pacific and SurferDude are projected to increase at a compound annual average rate of 20% during the next 5 years. SurferDude's sales growth assumes that its advertising expenditures in 1998 and 1999 have created a significant brand image, thus increasing future sales and gross profit margins. Pacific's sales growth rate reflects the recent licensing of several new apparel product lines. Consolidated sales of the combined companies are expected to grow at an annual growth rate of 25% as a result of the sales and distribution synergies created between the two companies.

The discount factor was derived using different methods, such as the buildup method or the CAPM. Because this was a private company, the buildup method was utilized and then supported by the CAPM. At 12%, the specific business risk premium is assumed to be somewhat higher than the 9% historical average difference between the return on small stocks and the risk-free return as a result of the capricious nature of the highly style-conscious surfware industry. The marketability discount is assumed to be a relatively modest 20% because Pacific is acquiring a controlling interest in SurferDude. After growing at a compound annual average growth rate of 25% during the next 5 years, the sustainable long-term growth rate in SurferDude's standalone revenue is assumed to be 8%.

The buildup calculation included the following factors:

Risk-Free Rate:	6.00%
Market Risk Premium to Invest in Stocks:	5.50%
Specific Business Risk Premium:	12.00%
Marketability Risk Premium:	20.00%
Discount Rate:	43.50%
Less: Long-Term Growth Rate:	8.00%
Capitalization Rate:	35.50%

The CAPM method supported the buildup method. One comparable company, Apparel Tech, had a β estimated by Yahoo.Marketguide.com to be 4.74, which results in a k_e of 32.07 for this comparable company. The weighted average cost of capital using a target debt-to-equity ratio of 3 to 1 for the combined companies is estimated to be 26%.

The standalone values of SurferDude and Pacific assume that fixed expenses will decrease as a percentage of sales as a result of economies of scale. Pacific will outsource production through its parent's overseas facilities, thus significantly reducing the cost of goods sold. SurferDude's administrative expenses are expected to decrease from 25% of sales to 18% because only senior managers and the design staff will be retained. The sustainable growth rate for the terminal period for both the standalone and the consolidated models is a relatively modest 6%. Pacific believes this growth rate is reasonable considering the growth potential throughout the world. Although Pacific and SurferDude's current market concentration resides largely in the United States, it is forecasted that the combined companies will develop a global presence, with a particular emphasis in developing markets. The value of the combined companies including synergies equals $15 million.

Developing an Initial Offer Price

Using price-to-cash flow multiples to develop an initial offer price, the target was valued on a standalone basis and a multiple of 4.51 for a comparable publicly held company called Stage II Apparel Corp. The standalone valuation, excluding synergies, of SurferDude ranges from $621,000 to $2,263,000.

Negotiating Strategy

Pacific expects to initially offer $2.25 million and close at $3.0 million. Pacific's management believes that SurferDude can be purchased at a modest price when compared with anticipated synergy, because an all-stock transaction would give SurferDude's management ownership of between 25 and 30% of the combined companies.

Integration

A transition team consisting of two Pacific and two SurferDude managers will be given full responsibility for consolidating the businesses following closing. A senior Pacific manager will direct the integration team. Once an agreement of purchase and sale has been signed, the team's initial responsibilities will be to first contact and inform employees and customers of SurferDude that operations will continue as normal until the close of the transaction. As an inducement to remain through closing, Pacific intends to offer severance packages for those SurferDude employees who will be terminated following the consolidation of the two businesses.

Source: Adapted from Contino, Maria, Domenic Costa, Larui Deyhimy, and Jenny Hu, Loyola, Marymount University, MBAF 624, Los Angeles, CA, Fall 1999.

Case Study Discussion Questions

1. What were the key assumptions implicit in Pacific Wardrobe's acquisition plan, with respect to the market, valuation, and integration effort? Comment on the realism of these assumptions.
2. Discuss some of the challenges that Pacific Wardrobe is likely to experience during due diligence.
3. Identify alternative deal structures Pacific Wardrobe might have employed in order to complete the transaction. Discuss why these might have been superior or inferior to the one actually chosen.

Answers to these Case Study Discussion Questions are available in the Online Instructor's Manual for instructors using this book.

References

Ang, James, and Ninon Kohers, "The Takeover Market for Privately Held Companies: The U.S. Experience," *Cambridge Journal of Economics*, Vol. 25, 2001, pp. 723–748.

Astrachan, J. H., and M. C. Shanker, "Family Businesses Contributions to the U.S. Economy: A Closer Look," *Family Business Review*, Vol. 15, 2003, pp. 211–219.

Astrachan, J., A. Keys, S. Lane, and K. McMillan, "Loyola Guidelines for Family Business Boards of Directors," Loyola University of Chicago, Family Business Center, 2003.

Ben-Amar, Walid, and Paul Andre, "Separation of Ownership from Control and Acquiring Firm Performance: The Case of Family Ownership in Canada," *Journal of Business Finance and Accounting*, Vol. 33, April/May 2006, pp. 517–543.

Bennedsen, M., K. Nielsen, F. Perez-Gonzalez, and D. Wolfenson, "Inside the Family Firm: The Role of Families in Succession Decisions and Performance," Working Paper, New York University, New York, 2006.

Bigelli, M., and S. Mengoli, "Sub-Optimal Acquisition Decision under a Majority Share-holder System," *Journal of Management and Governance*, Vol. 8, 2004, pp. 373–403.

Boehmer, E. "Business Groups, Bank Control, and Large Shareholders: An Analysis of German Takeovers," *Journal of Financial Intermediation*, Vol. 9, 2000, pp. 117–148.

Chang, Saeyoung, "Takeovers of Privately Held Targets, Methods of Payment, and Bidder Returns," *Journal of Finance,* Vol. 53, June 1998.

Claessens, S., S. Djankov, J. Fan, and I. H. P. Lang, "Disentangling the Incentive and Entrenchment Effects of Large Shareholders," *Journal of Finance*, Vol. 57, 2002, pp. 2741–2771.

Damodaran, Aswath, *Investment Valuation: Tools and Techniques for Determining the Value of Any Asset*, 2nd Ed., 2002, pp. 664–666.

Demsetz, Harold, and Kenneth Lehn, "The Structure of Corporate Ownership: Causes and Consequences," *Journal of Political Economy,* Vol. 93, 1996, pp. 1155–1177.

De Visscher, F. M., C. E. Aronoff, and J. L. Ward, "Financing Transitions: Managing Capital and Liquidity in the Family Business," Business Owner Resources, Marietta, GA, 1995.

Dumontier, P., and B. Pecherot, "Determinants of Returns to Acquiring Firms around Ten-der Offer Announcement Dates: The French Evidence," ESA Universite de Grenoble, Working Paper, 2001.

Emory, John D., "The Value of Marketability as Illustrated in Initial Public Offerings of Common Stock," *Business Valuation News,* September 1985, pp. 21–24.

Fields, L. Paige, and Eric L. Mais, "The Valuation Effects of Private Placements of Convertible Debt," *Journal of Finance,* Vol. 46, 1991, pp. 1925–1932.

Fuller, Kathleen, Jeffry Netter, and Mike Stegemoller, "What Do Returns to Acquiring Firms Tell Us? Evidence from Firms that Make Many Acquisitions," *Journal of Finance*, August 2002, pp. 1763–1793.

Gelman, Martin, "An Economist-Financial Analyst's Approach to Valuing Stock of a Closely Held Company," *Journal of Taxation*, June 1972, pp. 46–53.

Goodman, Matthew, "The Role of Private Equity Firms," *SME Magazine*, 2005, http://sme.atalink.co.uk/articles/150.

Habbershon, T. G., and M. L. Williams, "A Resource-Based Framework for Assessing the Strategic Advantages of Family Firms," *Family Business Review*, Vol. 12, 1999, pp. 1–26.

Hansen, Robert, "Evaluating the Costs of a New Equity Issue," *Midland Corporate Finance Journal,* Spring 1986, pp. 42–55.

Hertzel, Michael, and Richard L. Smith, "Market Discounts and Shareholder Gains for Placing Equity Privately," *Journal of Finance,* Vol. 48, 1993, pp. 459–485.

Institutional Investor Study Report, Securities and Exchange Commission, Washington, DC: U.S. Government Printing Office, Document No. 93-64, March 10, 1971.

Kaplan, Steven N., and Richard S. Ruback, "The Valuation of Cash Flow Forecasts," *Journal of Finance,* Vol. 50, September 1995, pp. 1059–1094.

Koplin, J., A. Sarin, and A. C. Shapiro, "The Private Equity Discount," *Journal of Applied Corporate Finance*, Vol. 12, 2000, pp. 94–101.

Maher, J. Michael, "Discounts for Lack of Marketability for Closely Held Business Interests," *Taxes*, 54 (9), September 1976, pp. 562–571.

Morck, R., and B. Yeung, "Inherited Wealth, Corporate Control, and Economic Growth: The Canadian Experience," in R. Morck, ed., concentrated *Corporate Ownership*, National Bureau of Economic Research, 2000, pp. 319–369.

Officer, Micah S., "The Price of Corporate Liquidity: Acquisition Discounts for Unlisted Targets," *Journal of Financial Economics*, 2007.

Perez-Gonzalez, F., "Inherited Control and Firm Performance," *American Economic Review*, 2006.

Poulsen, Annette, and Michael Stegemoller, "Transitions from Private to Public Ownership" Working Paper, University of Georgia, Athens, GA, 2002.

Pratt, Shannon, *Cost of Capital: Estimation and Applications,* Wiley & Sons, New York, 1998.

Pratt, Shannon P., Robert F. Reilly (Contributor), and Robert P. Scheweihs (Contributor), *Valuing a Business: The Analysis and Appraisal of Closely Held Companies,* 3rd Ed., Irwin Professional Publishers, Toronto, October 1995.

Robinson, A., "Is Corporate Governance The Solution or the Problem?," *Corporate Board*, Vol. 23, 2002, pp. 12–16.

Silber, W. L., "Discounts on Restricted Stocks: The Impact of Illiquidity on Stock Prices," *Financial Analysts Journal*, Vol. 47, 1991, pp. 60–64.

Sweeney, Paul, "GAP," *Financial Executives Magazine*, September 2005, pp. 33–40.

United States Small Business Administration, "State Small Business Profile," Office of Advocacy, 2003.

Villalonga, B., and R. Amit, "How Do Family Ownership, Control, and Management Affect Firm Value," *Journal of Financial Economics*, Vol. 80, May 2006, pp. 385–417.

Wruck, Karen H., "Equity Ownership Concentration and Firm Value: Evidence from Private Equity Financing," *Journal of Financial Economics*, Vol. 23, 1989, pp. 3–28.

PART • IV

Deal Structuring and Financing Strategies

CHAPTER • 11

Structuring the Deal

Payment and Legal Considerations

If you can't convince them, confuse them.

—Harry S. Truman

Inside M&A: News Corp.'s Power Play in Satellite Broadcasting Seems to Confuse Investors

The share prices of Rupert Murdoch's News Corp., Fox Entertainment Group Inc., and Hughes Electronics Corp. (a subsidiary of General Motors Corporation) tumbled immediately following the announcement that News Corp. had reached an agreement to take a controlling interest in Hughes on April 10, 2003. Investors may have been reacting unfavorably to the complex financial structure of News Corp.'s proposed deal and perhaps to parallels that could be drawn to the ill-fated AOL Time Warner merger in 2000.

Hughes Electronics is a world leader in providing digital television entertainment, broadband satellite networks and services (DirecTV), and global video and data broadcasting. News Corp. is a diversified international media and entertainment company. News Corp.'s Chairman, Rupert Murdoch, had pursued control of Hughes, the parent company of DirecTV, for several years. News Corp.'s bid, valued at about $6.6 billion, to acquire control of Hughes Electronics Corp. and its DirecTV unit gives News Corp. a U.S. presence to augment its satellite TV operations in Britain and Asia. By transferring News Corp.'s stake in Hughes to Fox, in which it owns an 81% interest, Fox gained control over 11 million subscribers. It gives Fox more leverage for its cable networks when negotiating rights fees with cable operators that compete with DirecTV.

General Motors was motivated to sell its investment in Hughes because of its need for cash. GM and Hughes had first agreed to a deal with rival satellite broadcaster EchoStar Communications Inc. However, the deal was blocked by antitrust regulators. Subsequent discussions between GM/Hughes with SBC Communications and Liberty Media proved unproductive. GM's desire to quickly pull cash out of Hughes made News Corp.'s offer the most attractive.

News Corp. financed its purchase of a 34.1% stake in Hughes (i.e., GM's 20% ownership and 14.1% from public shareholders) by paying $3.1 billion in cash to GM, plus 34.3 million in nonvoting American Depository Receipts (ADRs) in News Corp. shares. Hughes' public shareholders were paid with 122.2 million nonvoting ADRs in News Corp., an Australian corporation. (ADRs are shares of foreign companies trading on U.S. exchanges.) Each ADR is equivalent to four News Corp. shares. The resulting issue of 156.5 million shares would dilute News Corp. shareholders by about 13%. Immediately following closing, News Corp.'s ownership interest was transferred to Fox in exchange for a $4.5 billion promissory note from Fox and 74 million new Fox shares. This transfer saddled Fox with $4.5 billion in debt.

Now that News Corp. controls DirecTV through its 81% ownership in Fox, it must find a way to revitalize DirecTV. News Corp. will now have to compete against larger, better financed cable operations, as well as the nimble, low-cost EchoStar Communications Corp.'s Dish Network. As an indication of the extent to which Hughes has stumbled in recent years, News Corp. made a formal bid to acquire all of Hughes for about $25 billion in cash in 2001. News Corp.'s current investment stake implies a valuation of less than $20 billion for 100% ownership of Hughes (i.e., $6.6 billion/.341).

In early 2005, News Corp. announced plans to buy all shares of Fox that it did not currently own in a stock swap worth roughly $6 billion. The deal was undertaken to simplify News Corp.'s capital structure. By owning 100% of Fox's shares, control would be centralized in News Corp., enabling the firm to more easily make major business decisions. A simplified deal structure may have been the best strategy for News Corp. all along.

Chapter Overview

Once management has determined that an acquisition is the best way to implement the firm's business strategy, a target has been selected, the target's fit with the strategy is well understood, and the preliminary financial analysis is satisfactory, it is time to consider how to properly structure the transaction. In this chapter, the deal-structuring process is described in terms of six interdependent components. These include the acquisition vehicle, the postclosing organization, the form of payment, the legal form of the selling entity, the form of acquisition, and tax considerations.

This chapter will only briefly address the form of the acquisition vehicle, postclosing organization, and legal form of selling entity because these are discussed in some detail elsewhere in this book. The chapter also will address the interrelatedness of payment, legal, and tax forms by illustrating how decisions made in one area affect other aspects of the overall deal structure. The focus in this chapter is on the form of payment, form of acquisition, and alternative forms of legal structures in which ownership is conveyed. The implications of alternative tax structures for the deal-structuring process and how transactions are recorded for financial reporting purposes are discussed in detail in Chapter 12. A review of this chapter is available on the CD-ROM accompanying this book.

The Deal-Structuring Process

The **deal-structuring process** is fundamentally about satisfying as many of the primary objectives of the parties involved and determining how risk will be shared. Risk sharing refers to the extent to which the acquirer assumes all, some, or none of the liabilities, disclosed or otherwise, of the target. The appropriate deal structure is that which satisfies, subject to an acceptable level of risk, as many of the primary objectives of the parties involved as necessary to reach overall agreement. The process may be highly complex in large transactions involving multiple parties, approvals, forms of payment, and sources of financing. Decisions made in one area inevitably affect other areas of the overall deal structure. Containing risk associated with a complex deal is analogous to catching a water balloon. Squeezing one end of the balloon simply forces the contents to shift elsewhere.

Key Components

Figure 11-1 summarizes the deal-structuring process. The process begins with addressing a set of key questions, whose answers greatly influence the primary components of the entire structuring process. Answers to these questions help to define initial negotiating positions, potential risks, options for managing risk, levels of tolerance for risk, and conditions under which the buyer or seller will "walk away" from the negotiations.

The *acquisition vehicle* refers to the legal structure created to acquire the target company. The *postclosing organization* or structure is the organizational and legal framework used to manage the combined businesses following the consummation of the transaction. Commonly used structures for both the acquisition vehicle and postclosing organization include the corporate or divisional, holding company, joint venture (JV), partnership, limited liability company (LLC), and employee stock ownership plan (ESOP) structures.

For transactions in which the target shares are purchased using the acquirer's stock or cash, the acquirer often creates a wholly owned acquisition subsidiary to transfer ownership. The transfer of ownership is commonly accomplished through a triangular forward three-party merger or a triangular reverse three-party merger. The *forward triangular merger* involves the acquisition subsidiary being merged with the target and the acquiring subsidiary surviving. The *reverse triangular merger* entails the merger of the target with the acquiring subsidiary, with the target surviving. Because the surviving entity is owned entirely by the parent, the parent now indirectly owns the target's assets and liabilities. The advantages and disadvantages of the forward and reverse triangular mergers, along with other mechanisms for conveying ownership, are discussed in more detail later in this chapter.

Although the two structures are often the same before and after completion of the transaction, the postclosing organization may differ from the acquisition vehicle depending upon the acquirer's strategic objectives for the combined firms. An acquirer may choose a corporate or divisional structure to purchase the target firm and to rapidly integrate the acquired business to realize synergies. Alternatively, the acquirer may opt to undertake the transaction using a JV or partnership vehicle to share risk. Once the operation of the acquired entity is better understood, the acquirer may choose to buy out its partners and to operate within a corporate or divisional structure. Similarly, the acquirer may complete the transaction using a holding company legal structure. The acquirer may operate the acquired firm as a wholly owned subsidiary to preserve the attractive characteristics of its culture for an extended time period and later move to a more traditional corporate or divisional framework.

The *form of payment* or total consideration may consist of cash, common stock, debt, or a combination of all three types. The payment may be fixed at a moment in time, contingent on the future performance of the acquired unit, or payable over time. The form of payment influences the selection of the appropriate form of acquisition and postclosing

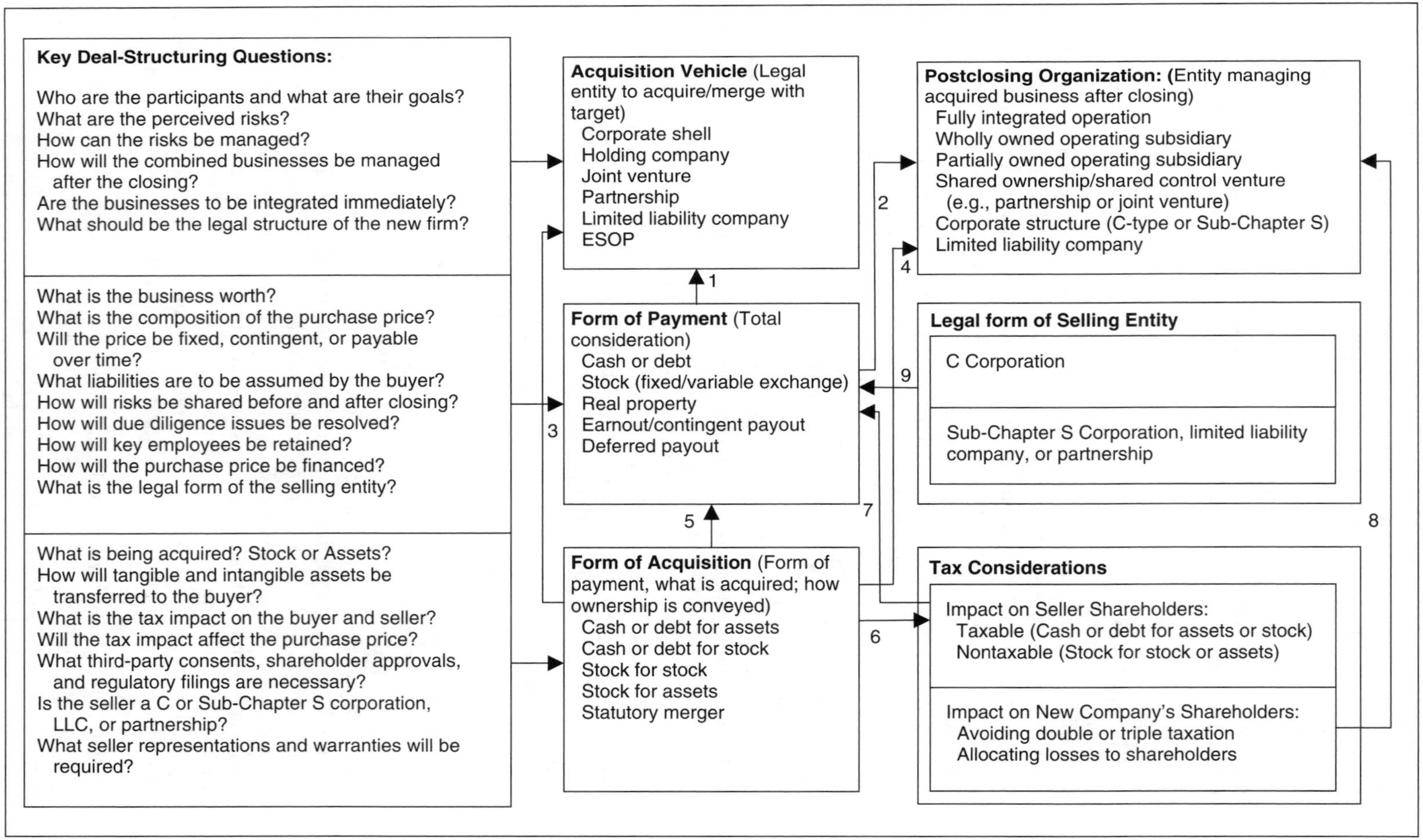

Key Deal-Structuring Questions:

Who are the participants and what are their goals?
What are the perceived risks?
How can the risks be managed?
How will the combined businesses be managed after the closing?
Are the businesses to be integrated immediately?
What should be the legal structure of the new firm?

What is the business worth?
What is the composition of the purchase price?
Will the price be fixed, contingent, or payable over time?
What liabilities are to be assumed by the buyer?
How will risks be shared before and after closing?
How will due diligence issues be resolved?
How will key employees be retained?
How will the purchase price be financed?
What is the legal form of the selling entity?

What is being acquired? Stock or Assets?
How will tangible and intangible assets be transferred to the buyer?
What is the tax impact on the buyer and seller?
Will the tax impact affect the purchase price?
What third-party consents, shareholder approvals, and regulatory filings are necessary?
Is the seller a C or Sub-Chapter S corporation, LLC, or partnership?
What seller representations and warranties will be required?

Acquisition Vehicle (Legal entity to acquire/merge with target)
Corporate shell
Holding company
Joint venture
Partnership
Limited liability company
ESOP

Form of Payment (Total consideration)
Cash or debt
Stock (fixed/variable exchange)
Real property
Earnout/contingent payout
Deferred payout

Form of Acquisition (Form of payment, what is acquired; how ownership is conveyed)
Cash or debt for assets
Cash or debt for stock
Stock for stock
Stock for assets
Statutory merger

Postclosing Organization: (Entity managing acquired business after closing)
Fully integrated operation
Wholly owned operating subsidiary
Partially owned operating subsidiary
Shared ownership/shared control venture (e.g., partnership or joint venture)
Corporate structure (C-type or Sub-Chapter S)
Limited liability company

Legal form of Selling Entity

C Corporation

Sub-Chapter S Corporation, limited liability company, or partnership

Tax Considerations

Impact on Seller Shareholders:
Taxable (Cash or debt for assets or stock)
Nontaxable (Stock for stock or assets)

Impact on New Company's Shareholders:
Avoiding double or triple taxation
Allocating losses to shareholders

1   2   3   4   5   6   7   8   9

FIGURE 11-1   Mergers and acquisitions deal-structuring process.

organization. The *form of acquisition* reflects what is being acquired (stock or assets) and, as such, tax considerations. *Tax considerations* entail tax structures and strategies that determine whether a transaction is taxable or nontaxable to the seller's shareholders and influence the choice of postclosing organization, which affects the potential for double taxation and the allocation of losses to owners. The form of acquisition also defines how the ownership of assets will be conveyed from the seller to the buyer, either by rule of law as in a merger or through transfer and assignment as in a purchase of assets. The *legal form of the selling entity* (i.e., whether it is a C or S chapter corporation, LLC, or partnership) also has tax implications. These considerations are explored in greater detail later in this chapter.

Common Linkages

For simplicity, many of the linkages or interactions that reflect how decisions made in one area affect other aspects of the deal are not shown in Figure 11-1. Common linkages or interactions among various components of the deal structure are illustrated through examples described next.

Form of Payment Influences Choice of Acquisition Vehicle and Postclosing Organization (Figure 11-1: Arrows 1–2)

If the buyer and seller agree on a price, the buyer may offer a purchase price that is contingent on the future performance of the target. The buyer may choose to acquire and to operate the acquired company as a wholly owned subsidiary within a holding company during the term of the "earnout." This facilitates monitoring the operation's performance during the earnout period and minimizes the potential for post-earnout litigation initiated by earnout participants.

Form of Acquisition (Figure 11-1: Arrows 3–6) Affects

- Choice of Acquisition Vehicle and Postclosing Organization: If the form of acquisition is a statutory merger, all known and unknown or contingent liabilities are transferred to the buyer. Under these circumstances, the buyer may choose to change the type of acquisition vehicle to one better able to protect the buyer from the liabilities of the target, such as a holding company arrangement. Acquisition vehicles and postclosing organizations that facilitate a sharing of potential risk or of the purchase price include JV or partnership arrangements.
- Form, Timing, and Amount of Payment: The assumption of all seller liabilities through a merger also may induce the buyer to change the form of payment by deferring some portion of the purchase price to decrease the present value of the cost of the transaction. The buyer also may attempt to negotiate a lower overall purchase price.
- Tax Considerations: The transaction may be tax free to the seller if the acquirer uses its stock to acquire substantially all of the seller's assets or stock in a stock-for-stock or stock-for-assets purchase.

Tax Considerations (Figure 11-1: Arrows 7–8) Affect

- Amount, Timing, and Composition of the Purchase Price: If the transaction is taxable to the target's shareholders, it is likely that the purchase price will be increased to

TABLE 11-1   Summary of Common Linkages within the Deal Structuring Process

Component of Deal Structuring Process	Influences Choice of
Form of Payment	Acquisition vehicle
	Postclosing organization
Form of Acquisition	Acquisition vehicle
	Postclosing organization
	Form, amount, and timing of payment
	Tax structure (taxable or nontaxable)
Tax Considerations	Form, amount, and timing of payment
	Postclosing organization
Legal Form of Selling Entity	Tax structure (taxable or nontaxable)

compensate the target's shareholders for their tax liability. The increase in the purchase price may affect the form of payment. The acquirer may maintain the present value of the total cost of the acquisition by deferring some portion of the purchase price by altering the terms to include more debt or installment payments.

• Selection of the Postclosing Organization: The decision as to what constitutes the appropriate organizational structure of the combined businesses is affected by several tax-related factors: the desire to minimize taxes and to pass through losses to owners. The S corporation, LLC, and the partnership eliminate double taxation problems. Moreover, current operating losses, loss carry forwards or carry backs, or tax credits generated by the combined businesses can be passed through to the owners if the postclosing organization is a partnership or an LLC.

Legal Form of Selling Entity Affects Form of Payment (Figure 11-1: Arrow 9)

Because of the potential for deferring shareholder tax liabilities, target firms that qualify as C corporations often prefer to exchange their stock or assets for acquirer shares. In contrast, owners of S corporations, LLCs, and partnerships are largely indifferent as to whether the transaction is taxable or nontaxable, because 100% of the proceeds of the sale are taxed at the shareholders ordinary tax rate. Table 11-1 provides a summary of these common linkages.

Form of Acquisition Vehicle

The acquisition vehicle is the legal entity used to acquire the target and generally continues to own and operate the acquired company after closing. Which form of legal entity is used has markedly different risk and tax implications for the acquirer. The various forms of potential acquisition vehicles and their specific advantages and disadvantages are discussed in considerable detail in Chapter 14. They include the corporate/divisional structure, LLCs, JV corporations, holding companies, general and limited liability partnerships (LLPs), and ESOPs.

The corporate structure or some variation is the most commonly used acquisition vehicle. In such an arrangement, the acquired company generally is integrated into an existing operating division or product line within the corporation. Used as an acquisition vehicle, the JV corporation or partnership offers a lower level of risk than a direct acquisition of the target firm by one of the JV corporate owners or individual partners. By acquiring the target firm through the JV, the corporate investor limits the potential liability to the extent of their investment in the JV corporation. For small, privately owned firms, an ESOP structure may be a convenient vehicle for transferring the owner's interest in the business to the employees (see Chapter 10). Non-U.S. buyers intending to make additional acquisitions may prefer a holding company structure. The advantages of this structure over a corporate merger for both foreign and domestic firms are the ability to control other companies by only owning a small portion of the company's voting stock and to gain this control without getting shareholder approval.

Postclosing Organization

What form the postclosing structure takes depends largely on the objectives of the acquiring company. These objectives could include the following: (1) facilitating post-closing integration, (2) minimizing risk to owners from the target's known and unknown liabilities, (3) minimizing taxes, and (4) passing through losses to shelter the owners' tax liabilities.

If the acquirer is interested in integrating the target business immediately following closing, the corporate or divisional structure may be most desirable, because the acquirer is most likely to be able to gain the greatest control by using this structure. In other structures, such as JVs and partnerships, decision making may be slower or more contentious as a result of dispersed ownership. Decision making is more likely to depend on close cooperation and consensus building, which may slow efforts to rapidly integrate the acquired company (see Chapter 6).

In contrast, a holding company structure in which the acquired company is managed as a wholly owned subsidiary may be preferable when an earnout is involved, the target is a foreign firm, or the acquirer is a financial investor. In an earnout agreement, the acquired firm must be operated largely independently from other operations of the acquiring firm to minimize the potential for lawsuits. If the acquired firm fails to achieve the goals required to receive the earnout payment, the acquirer may be sued for allegedly taking actions that prevented the acquired firm from reaching the necessary goals. When the target is a foreign firm, it is often appropriate to operate it separately from the rest of the acquirer's operations because of the potential disruption from significant cultural differences. Prevailing laws in the foreign country may also affect the form of the organization. Finally, a financial buyer may use a holding company structure because they have no interest in operating the target firm for any length of time.

A partnership or JV structure may be appropriate if the risk associated with the target firm is believed to be high. Consequently, partners or JV owners can limit their financial exposure to the amount they have invested in the partnership or JV. The acquired firm also may benefit from being owned by a partnership or JV because of the expertise that may be provided by the different partners or owners. The availability of such expertise actually may reduce the overall risk of managing the business. Finally, a partnership or LLC may be most appropriate for eliminating double taxation and passing through current operating losses, tax credits, and loss carry forwards and carry backs to the owners. Cerberus Capital Management's conversion of its purchase of General Motors Acceptance Corporation (GMAC) from General Motors in 2006 from a C corporation to a limited liability company at closing reflects the desire to eliminate double taxation of income while continuing to limit shareholder liability.

Legal Form of Selling Entity

Whether the seller will care about the form of the transaction (i.e., whether stock or assets are sold) may depend on whether the seller is an S, limited liability company, partnership, or a C corporation (i.e., corporations for which an election to be subject to subchapter S of the Internal Revenue Code has not been made). As noted previously, C corporations are subject to double taxation, whereas owners of S corporations, partnerships, and LLCs are not (see Exhibit 11-1).

Exhibit 11-1

How Legal Form of Seller Affects Form of Payment

Assume a business owner starting with an initial investment of $100,000 sells her business for $1,000,000. Different legal structures have different tax impacts.

1. After-tax proceeds of a stock sale: $(\$1,000,000 - \$100,000) \times (1 - .15) = \$765,000$. The S corporation shareholder or limited liability company member holding shares for more than 1 year pays a maximum capital gains tax equal to 15% of the gain on the sale.[1]
2. After-tax proceeds from an asset sale: $(\$1,000,000 - \$100,000) \times (1 - .4) \times (1 - .15) = \$900,000 \times .51 = \$459,000$. A C corporation typically pays tax equal to 40% (i.e., 35% federal and 5% state and local) and the shareholder pays a maximum capital gains tax equal to 15%, resulting in double taxation of the gain on sale.

Implications:

1. C corporation shareholders generally prefer acquirer stock for their stock or assets to avoid double taxation.
2. S corporation and LLC owners often are indifferent to an assets sale or stock sale because 100% of the corporation's income passes through the corporation untaxed to the owners who are subject to their own personal tax rates. The S corporation shareholder or LLC member still may prefer a share-for-share exchange if they are interested in deferring their tax liability, or they are attracted by the long-term growth potential of the acquirer's stock.

[1] This is the current capital gains tax as of the date of publishing of this text.

Form of Payment or Total Consideration

Determining the proper form of payment can be a complicated exercise. Each form of payment can have significantly different implications for the parties involved in the transaction. Of total transactions between 1980 and 2004, on average, cash accounted for 42%, stock for 33%, and cash–stock combinations for 25% of total transactions (*Mergerstat Review*, 2005).

Cash

The use of cash is the simplest and most commonly used means of payment for acquiring shares or assets. Although cash payments generally will result in an immediate tax liability for the target company's shareholders, there is no ambiguity about the value of the transaction as long as no portion of the payment is deferred. Whether cash is the predominant form of payment will depend on a variety of factors. These include the acquirer's current leverage, potential near-term earnings per share dilution, the seller's preference for cash or acquirer stock, and the extent to which the acquirer wishes to maintain control.

A highly leveraged acquirer may be unable to raise sufficient funds at an affordable rate of interest to make a cash purchase practical. Issuing new shares may result in significant erosion of the combined firm's earnings per share immediately following closing, which may prove to be unacceptable to investors. The seller's preference for stock or cash will reflect their potential capital gains and the attractiveness of the acquirer's shares. Finally, a bidder may choose to use cash rather than to issue voting shares if the voting control of its dominant shareholder is threatened as a result of the issuance of voting stock to acquire the target firm (Faccio and Masulis, 2005). The preference for using cash appears to be much higher in Western European countries where ownership tends to be more heavily concentrated in publicly traded firms than in the United States. In Europe, 63% of publicly traded firms have a single shareholder who directly or indirectly controls 20% or more of the voting shares; in the United States, the figure is 28% (Faccio and Lang, 2002).

Noncash Forms of Payment

The use of common equity may involve certain tax advantages for the parties involved. This is especially true for the selling company. However, the use of shares is much more complicated than cash, because it requires compliance with the prevailing security laws (see Chapter 2). Moreover, the acquirer's share price may suffer if investors believe that the newly issued shares will result in a long-term dilution in earnings per share (EPS) (i.e., a reduction in an individual shareholder's claim on future earnings and the net assets that produce those earnings). The use of convertible preferred stock or debt can be attractive to both buyers and sellers. Convertible preferred stock provides some downside protection to sellers in the form of continuing dividends, while providing upside potential if the acquirer's common stock price increases above the conversion point. Acquirers often find convertible debt attractive because of the tax deductibility of interest payments. The major disadvantage in using securities of any type is that the seller may find them unattractive. Debt instruments may be unacceptable because of the perceived high risk of default associated with the issuer. When offered common equity, shareholders of the selling company may feel the growth prospects of the acquirer's stock may be limited or that the historical volatility of the stock makes it unacceptably risky. Finally, debt or equity securities may be illiquid because of the small size of the resale market for these types of securities.

Other forms of payment include real property, rights to intellectual property, royalties, earnouts, and contingent payments. Real property consists of such things as a parcel of real estate. So-called "like-kind" exchanges or swaps may have favorable tax consequences (see Chapter 12). Real property exchanges are most common in commercial real estate transactions. Granting the seller access to valuable licenses or franchises limits the use of cash or securities at the time of closing; however, it does raise the possibility that the seller could become a future competitor. The use of debt or other types of deferred payments reduces the overall present value of the purchase price to the buyer by shifting some portion of the purchase price into the future.

Using a Combination of Cash and Stock

Bidders may use a combination of cash and noncash forms of payment as part of their bidding strategies to broaden the appeal to target shareholders. Payment options may include all cash, all stock, and a combination of cash and stock. The cash option appeals to those shareholders who either place a high value on liquidity or do not view acquirer stock as attractive. The all-stock option is attractive to target shareholders who may be interested in deferring their tax liabilities in a share-for-share exchange. Finally, the combination of cash and stock should appeal to those who value cash but who also want to participate in any appreciation in the acquirer's stock.

The bidding strategy of offering target firm shareholders multiple payment options increases the likelihood that more target firm shareholders will participate in a tender offer. Such bidding strategies are common in "auction" environments or when the bidder is unable to borrow the amount necessary to support an all-cash offer or unwilling to absorb the potential earnings per share dilution in an all-stock offer. However, the multiple option bidding strategy introduces a certain level of uncertainty in determining the amount of cash the acquirer will have to ultimately pay out to target firm shareholders, since the number choosing the all-cash or cash-and-stock option is not known prior to the completion of the tender offer. Acquirers resolve this issue by including a "proration clause" in tender offers and merger agreements, which allows them to fix the total amount of cash they will ultimately have to pay out at the time the tender offer is initiated. How this is done is illustrated in Case Study 11-4 at the end of this chapter.

Closing the Gap on Price

Balance sheet adjustments, earnouts, rights to intellectual property, licensing fees, and consulting agreements commonly are used to consummate the deal, when buyers and sellers cannot reach agreement on purchase price.

Balance Sheet Adjustments

Balance sheet adjustments most often are used in purchases of assets when the elapsed time between the agreement on price and the actual closing date is lengthy. This may be a result of the need to obtain regulatory or shareholder approvals or a result of ongoing due diligence. During this period, balance sheet items, particularly those related to working capital may change significantly.

As indicated in Table 11-2, to protect the buyer or seller, the buyer reduces the total purchase price by an amount equal to the decrease in net working capital or shareholders' equity of the target and increases the purchase price by any increase in these measures during this period. Buyers and sellers generally view purchase price adjustments as a form of insurance against any erosion or accretion in assets, such as receivables or inventories.

TABLE 11-2   Balance Sheet Adjustments ($ Millions)

	Purchase Price		Purchase Price Reduction	Purchase Price Increase
	At Time of Negotiation	At Closing		
If Working Capital Equals	110	100	10	
If Working Capital Equals	110	125		15

Such adjustments protect the buyer from receiving a lower dollar value of assets than originally believed or the seller from transferring to the buyer more assets than expected. The actual payments are made between the buyer and seller after a comprehensive audit of the target's balance sheet by an independent auditor is completed some time after closing.

Earnouts

An *earnout* agreement is a financial contract whereby a portion of the purchase price of a company is to be paid in the future contingent on the realization of a previously agreed upon future earnings level or some other performance measure. The terms of the earnout are stipulated in the agreement of purchase and sale. Earnouts frequently are used whenever the buyer and seller cannot agree on the probable performance of the seller's business over some future period. Earnout agreements may also be used to retain and motivate key target firm managers. The earnout normally requires that the acquired business be operated as a wholly owned subsidiary of the acquiring company under the management of the former owners or key executives of the business. Both the buyer and seller are well advised to keep the calculation of such goals and resulting payments as simple as possible because disputes frequently arise as a result of the difficulty in measuring actual performance to the goals.

Earnouts may take many forms. Some earnouts are payable only if a certain performance threshold is achieved; others depend on average performance over a number of periods. Still other arrangements may involve periodic payments depending upon the achievement of interim performance measures rather than a single, lump-sum payment at the end of the earnout period. Moreover, the value of the earnout is often capped. In some cases, the seller may have the option to repurchase his company at some predetermined percentage of the original purchase price in case the buyer is unable to pay the earnout at maturity.

Exhibit 11-2 illustrates how an earnout formula could be constructed reflecting the considerations outlined in the preceding paragraph. The purchase price consists of two components. At closing, the seller receives a lump-sum payment of $100 million. The seller and the buyer agree to a baseline projection for a 3-year period and that the seller will receive a fixed multiple of the average annual performance of the acquired business in excess of the baseline projection. Thus, the earnout provides an incentive for the seller to operate the business as effectively as possible. Normally, the baseline projection is what the buyer used to value the seller's business. Shareholder value for the buyer is created whenever the acquired business's actual performance exceeds the baseline projection and the multiple applied by investors at the end of the 3-year period exceeds the multiple used to calculate the earnout payment. This assumes that the baseline projection

---

Exhibit 11-2

Hypothetical Earnout as Part of the Purchase Price

Purchase Price:

1. Lump sum payment at closing: The seller receives $100 million.
2. Earnout payment: The seller receives four times the excess of the actual average annual net operating cash flow over the baseline projection at the end of 3 years not to exceed $35 million.

Base Year (First Full Year of Ownership)	Year 1	Year 2	Year 3
Baseline Projection (Net Cash Flow)	$10	$12	$15
Actual Performance (Net Cash Flow)	$15	$20	$25

Earnout at the end of 3 years:[1]

$$\frac{(\$15 - \$10) + (\$20 - \$12) + (\$25 - \$15)}{3} \times 4 = \$30.67$$

Potential increase in shareholder value:[2]

$$\frac{\{(\$15 - \$10) + (\$20 - \$12) + (\$25 - \$15) \times 10\}}{3} - \$30.67 = \$46$$

[1] The cash-flow multiple of four applied to the earnout is a result of negotiation before closing.
[2] The cash-flow multiple of 10 applied to the potential increase in shareholder value for the buyer is the multiple the buyer anticipates that investors would apply to a 3-year average of actual operating cash flow at the end of the 3-year period.

---

accurately values the business and that the buyer does not overpay. By multiplying the anticipated multiple investors will pay for operating cash flow at the end of the 3-year period by projected cash flow, it is possible to estimate the potential increase in shareholder value.

Earnouts tend to shift risk from the acquirer to the seller in that a higher price is paid only when the seller or acquired firm has met or exceeded certain performance criteria. However, earnouts also may create some perverse results during implementation. Management motivation may be lost if the acquired firm does not perform well enough to achieve any payout under the earnout formula or if the acquired firm substantially exceeds the performance targets, effectively guaranteeing the maximum payout under the plan. Moreover, the management of the acquired firm may have an incentive to take actions not in the best interests of the acquirer. For example, management may cut back on certain expenses such as advertising and training to improve the operation's current cash-flow performance. In addition, management may make only those investments that improve short-term profits at the expense of investments that may generate immediate losses but favorably affect profits in the long term. As the end of the earnout period approaches, management may postpone any investments at all to maximize their bonus under the earnout plan.

Earnouts, also known as contingent payouts, accounted for roughly 2.5% of total transactions in the 1990s. Kohers and Ang (2000) and Datar, Frankel, and Wolfson (2001) found that earnouts are more commonly used when the targets are small, private firms or subsidiaries of larger firms rather than for large, publicly traded firms. Contingent payout contracts are more easily written and enforced when there are relatively few shareholders. Earnouts tend to be most common in high-tech and service industries, when the acquirer and target firms are in different industries, when the target firm has a significant number of assets not recorded on the balance sheet, when access to seller information is limited, and when little integration will be attempted.

The Kohers and Ang (2000) study also showed that earnouts, if fully realized, on average account for 45% of the total purchase price paid for private firms and 33% for subsidiary acquisitions. Moreover, target firm shareholders tend to realize about 62% of the potential earnout amount. Interestingly, in transactions involving earnouts, acquirers earn abnormal returns of 5.39% around the announcement date, in contrast to transactions not involving contingent payments in which abnormal returns to acquirers tend to be zero or negative. The authors argue that the positive abnormal returns to acquiring company shareholders are a result of investor perception that with an earnout the buyer is less likely to overpay and more likely to retain key target firm talent.

Earnouts may also be based on share of equity ownership when the business is sold. For example, assume an entrepreneur believes her business is worth $20 million without additional investment and the private equity investor estimates the business to be worth only $15 million without additional investment. If the entrepreneur wants $5 million in equity investment, the entrepreneur perceives the market value including the equity infusion to be $25 million (i.e., $20 million standalone plus $5 million in equity). From the viewpoint of the entrepreneur, the implied ownership distribution is 80/20, with the entrepreneur receiving 80% (i.e., $20/$25) and the equity investor receiving 20% (i.e., $5/$25).

However, the equity investor sees the value of the business including the equity investment to be only $20 million (i.e., $15 million standalone plus $5 million equity investment). The implied ownership is 75/25, with the entrepreneur receiving only 75% ownership (i.e., $15/$20) and the equity investor 25% ownership (i.e., $5/$20). The ownership gap of 5 percentage points can be closed by the entrepreneur and equity investor agreeing to the 80/20 distribution if certain cash-flow or profit targets can be reached prior to exiting the business sufficient to justify the $25 million net present value (see Exhibit 11-3).

Rights, Royalties, and Fees

Other forms of payment that can be used to close the gap between what the buyer is willing to offer and what the seller expects include such things as the rights to intellectual property, royalties from licenses, and fee-based consulting or employment agreements. Having the right to use a proprietary process or technology for free or at a below the prevailing market rate may be of interest to the former owners who are considering pursuing business opportunities in which the process or technology would be useful. Note

---

Exhibit 11-3
Earnouts Based on Ownership Distribution

Distribution of ownership equity if average annual free cash flow is less than $5 million in years 3–5:[1]

Entrepreneur:	75%
Private Investor:	25%
Total:	100%

Distribution of ownership equity if average annual free cash flow is greater than $5 million in years 3–5:

Entrepreneur:	80%
Private Investor:	20%
Total:	100%

[1] A 3-year average cash-flow figure is used to measure performance to ensure that the actual performance is sustainable as opposed to an aberration.

---

that such an arrangement, if priced at below market rates or if free to the seller, would represent taxable income to the seller. Obviously, such arrangements should be coupled with reasonable agreements not to compete in the same industry as their former firm. Contracts may be extended to both the former owners and their family members. By spreading the payment of consulting fees or salary over a number of years, the seller may be able to reduce the income tax liability that might have resulted from receiving a larger lump-sum purchase price.

Using Collar Arrangements to Preserve Shareholder Value

A *share-exchange ratio* is the number of shares of acquirer stock offered for each share of target stock (see Chapter 9). A *fixed or constant share-exchange ratio* is one in which the number of acquirer shares exchanged for each target share is unchanged between the signing of the agreement of purchase and sale and closing. Most stock mergers have a fixed share-exchange ratio. However, collar arrangements have become more common in recent years, with about 20% of stock mergers employing some form of collar as part of the bid structure. *Collar agreements* provide for certain changes in the exchange ratio contingent on the level of the acquirer's share price around the effective date of the merger. This date is often defined as the average acquirer share price during a 10- to 20-day period just prior to the closing date.

A *fixed exchange collar agreement* may involve a fixed exchange ratio as long as the acquirer's share price remains within a narrow range, calculated as of the effective date of merger. For example, the acquirer and target may agree that the target would receive .5 shares of acquirer stock for each share of target stock, as long as the acquirer's share price remains between $20 and $24 per share during a 10-day period just prior to closing. This implies a collar around the bid price of $10 (i.e., .5 × $20) to $12 (i.e., .5 × $24) per target share. The collar arrangement may further stipulate that if the acquirer price falls below $20 per share the target shareholder would receive $10 per share; if the acquirer share price exceeds $24 per share, the target shareholder would receive $12 per share. Therefore, the acquirer and target shareholders can be assured that the actual bid or offer price will be between $10 and $12 per target share.

A *fixed payment collar agreement* guarantees that the target firm shareholder receives a certain dollar value in terms of acquirer stock as long as the acquirer's stock remains within a narrow range, and a fixed exchange ratio if the acquirer's average stock price is outside the bounds around the effective date of the merger. For example, the acquirer and target may agree that target shareholders would receive $40 per share, as long as the acquirer's share price remains within a range of $30 to $34 per share. This would be achieved by adjusting the number of acquirer shares exchanged for each target share (i.e., the number of acquirer shares exchanged for each target share increases if the acquirer share price declines toward the lower end of the range and decreases if the acquirer share price increases). If the acquirer share price increases above $34 per share, target shareholders would receive 1.1765 shares of acquirer stock (i.e., $40/$34); if the acquirer share price drops below $30 per share, target shareholders would receive 1.333 shares of acquirer stock (i.e., $40/$30) for each target share they own.

Both the acquirer and target boards of directors have a fiduciary responsibility to demand that the merger terms be renegotiated if the value of the offer made by the bidder changes materially relative to the value of the target's stock or if there has been any other material change in the target's operations. Merger contracts routinely contain "material adverse effects clauses," which provide a basis for a buyer to withdraw from or renegotiate the contract. For example, in 2006, Johnson and Johnson (J&J) demanded that Guidant Corporation, a leading heart pacemaker manufacturer, accept a lower purchase price than that agreed to in their merger agreement. J&J was reacting to news of government recalls of Guidant pacemakers and federal investigations that could materially damage the value of the firm.

Renegotiation can be expensive for either party due to the commitment of management time and the cost of legal and investment banking advice. Collar agreements protect the acquiring firm from "overpaying" in the event that its share price is higher or the target firm's share price is lower on the effective date of the merger than it was on the day agreement was reached on merger terms. Similarly, the target shareholders are protected from receiving less than the originally agreed to purchase price if the acquirer's stock declines in value by the effective date of the merger. If the acquirer's share price has historically been highly volatile, the target may demand a collar to preserve the agreed upon share price. Similarly, the acquirer may demand a collar if the target's share price has shown great variation in the past in order to minimize the potential for overpaying if the target's share price declines significantly relative to the acquirer's share price. Officer (2005) concludes in an evaluation of 1127 stock mergers between 1991 and 1999, of which approximately one-fifth had collar arrangements, that collars are more likely to be used the greater the volatility of the acquirer share price compared to the target share price. He further concluded that the use of collars reduces substantially the likelihood that merger terms would have to be renegotiated. How collars may be used to reduce risk to both the acquirer's and the target's shareholders is illustrated in Northrop Grumman's bid for TRW (Case Study 11-1).

Case Study 11-1

Northrop Grumman Makes a Bid for TRW: How Collar Arrangements Affect Shareholder Value

On March 5, 2002, Northrop Grumman initiated a tender offer for 100% of TRW's common shares by offering to exchange $47.00 in market value of Northrop Grumman common stock for each share of TRW common stock. The tender offer would expire at the end of the month. Northrop implicitly was offering to exchange .4352 (i.e., $47/$108) of its own common shares (based on its March 5 share price of $108.00) for each share of TRW stock. However, the actual share-exchange ratio would be based on the average Northrop share price during the last 5 business days of the month. The $47 offer price is assured within a narrow range to TRW shareholders by placing a collar of plus 5% ($113.40) or minus 5% ($102.60) around the $108 Northrop share price on the tender offer announcement date. The range of share-exchange ratios implied by this collar is as follows:

$$.4581(\text{i.e., } \$47/\$102.60) < .4352(\text{i.e., } \$47/\$108) < .4145(\$47/\$113.40)$$

The .4581 and .4145 share-exchange ratios represent the maximum and minimum fraction of a share of Northrop stock that would be offered for each TRW share during this tender offer period. The collar gave TRW shareholders some comfort that they would receive $47 per share and enabled Northrop to determine the number of new shares it would have to issue within a narrow range to acquire TRW and the resulting impact on EPS of the combined firms.

An increase in Northrop's share price to $117.40 on April 10, 2002, enabled Northrop to increase its offer price to $53 per share of TRW stock outstanding on April 15, 2002, without issuing more than the maximum number of shares they were willing to issue in their March 5 offer. This could be accomplished because the maximum share-exchange ratio of .4581 would not be exceeded as long as the share price of Northrop stock remained above $115.75 per share (i.e., .4581 × $115.75 = $53).

In an effort to boost its share price, TRW repeatedly rejected Northrop's offers as too low and countered with its own restructuring plan. This plan would split the firm into separate defense and automotive parts companies while selling off the aeronautical systems operation. TRW also moved aggressively to solicit bids from other potential suitors. TRW contended that its own restructuring plan was worth as much as $60 per share to its shareholders. In June, TRW reached agreement with Goodrich Corporation to sell the aeronautical systems unit for $1.5 billion.

Northrop Grumman and TRW finally reached an agreement on July 1, 2002. Under the terms of the agreement, Northrop would acquire all of TRW's outstanding common stock for $60 per share in a deal valued at approximately $7.8 billion. Northrop also agreed to assume approximately $4 billion of TRW's debt. Moreover, Northrop withdrew its original tender offer. The actual share-exchange ratio would be determined by dividing the $60 offer price by the average of the reported prices per share of Northrop common stock on the five consecutive trading days prior to the closing date. Under a revised collar arrangement, the exchange ratio would not be less than .4348 or more than .5357 of Northrop's shares.

Case Study Discussion Questions

1. What type of collar arrangement did Northrop use (i.e., fixed exchange rate or fixed payment)? Explain your answer.
2. What would have been the implications for TRW shareholders had a fixed exchange ratio without a collar been used? Explain your answer.
3. How did the collar arrangement facilitate the completion of the transaction? Explain your answer.

Table 11-3 summarizes the various forms of payment in terms of their advantages and disadvantages. Note the wide range of options available to satisfy the various needs of the parties to the transaction.

TABLE 11-3 Form of Payment Risk Evaluation

Form of Payment	Advantages	Disadvantages
Cash (Including highly marketable securities)	*Buyer*: Simplicity.	*Buyer*: Must rely solely on protections afforded in contract to recover claims.
	Seller: Ensures payment if acquirer's creditworthiness questionable.	*Seller*: Creates immediate tax liability.
Stock —Common —Preferred —Convertible Preferred	*Buyer*: High P/E relative to seller's P/E may increase value of combined businesses.	*Buyer*: Adds complexity; potential EPS dilution.
	Seller: Defers taxes and provides potential price increase. Retains interest in the business.	*Seller*: Potential decrease in purchase price if the value of equity received declines. May delay closing because of registration requirements.
Debt —Secured —Unsecured —Convertible	*Buyer*: Interest expense tax deductible. *Seller*: Defers tax liability on principal.	*Buyer*: Adds complexity and increases leverage. *Seller*: Risk of default.
Performance-Related Earnouts	*Buyer*: Shifts some portion of risk to seller. *Seller*: Potential for higher purchase price.	*Buyer*: May limit integration of businesses. *Seller*: Increases uncertainty of sales price.
Purchase Price Adjustments	*Buyer*: Protection from eroding values of working capital before closing. *Seller*: Protection from increasing values of working capital before closing.	*Buyer*: Audit expense. Buyer and seller often share audit costs. *Seller*: Audit expense. (Note that buyers and sellers often split the audit expense.)

continued

TABLE 11-3   continued

Form of Payment	Advantages	Disadvantages
Real Property —Real Estate —Plant and Equipment —Business or Product Line	*Buyer*: Minimizes use of cash.	*Buyer*: Opportunity cost.
	Seller: May minimize tax liability.	*Seller*: Real property may be illiquid.
Rights to Intellectual Property —License —Franchise	*Buyer*: Minimizes cash use.	*Buyer*: Potential for setting up new competitor.
	Seller: Gains access to valuable rights and spreads taxable income over time.	*Seller*: Illiquid; income taxed at ordinary rates.
Royalties from —Licenses —Franchises	*Buyer*: Minimizes cash use.	*Buyer*: Opportunity cost.
	Seller: Spreads taxable income over time.	*Seller*: Income taxed at ordinary rates.
Fee-Based —Consulting Contract —Employment Agreement	*Buyer*: Uses seller's expertise and removes seller as potential competitor for a limited time.	*Buyer*: May involve demotivated employees.
	Seller: Augments purchase price and allows seller to stay with the business.	*Seller*: Limits ability to compete in same line of business. Income taxed at ordinary rates.

Form of Acquisition

The form of acquisition describes the mechanism for conveying or transferring ownership of assets or stock and associated liabilities from the target to the acquiring firm. The most commonly used methods include the following: asset purchases for cash or acquirer stock, stock purchases for cash or acquirer stock, and statutory mergers using cash or acquirer stock as the form of payment. For excellent discussions of commonly used methods of conveying ownership, see Bainbridge (2003), Hunt (2003), Lajoux and Nesvold (2004), Oesterle (2005), Sherman (2006), Aspatore (2006), and Ginsburg and Levin (2006).

Asset purchases involve the acquiring company buying all or a portion of the target company's assets and assuming all, some, or none of the target's liabilities in exchange for cash or assets. *Stock purchases* involve the exchange of the target's stock for either cash, debt, or the stock of the acquiring company. A *statutory merger* involves the combination of the acquiring and target firms, in which one firm ceases to exist. The assets and liabilities of the corporation that ceases to exist are merged into the surviving firm as a "matter of law." The statutes of the state in which the combined businesses will be incorporated govern such transactions. State statutes typically address considerations such as the percentage of the total voting stock that is required for approval of the transaction, who is entitled to vote, how the votes are counted, and the rights of the dissenting voters. In a statutory merger, dissenting shareholders are required to sell their shares, although they may have the right to be paid the appraised value of their shares under some state statutes. ***Stock-for-stock*** or ***stock-for-assets*** transactions represent alternatives to a merger.

An important advantage of an asset purchase over a purchase of stock is that no minority shareholders remain. Without a merger, shareholders cannot be forced to sell their shares. The acquirer may choose to operate the target firm as a subsidiary, in which some target shareholders, albeit a minority, could remain. Consequently, the buyer's subsidiary must submit annual reports to these shareholders, hold shareholder meetings, and elect a board of directors by allowing shareholder votes, while being exposed to potentially dissident shareholders. Table 11-4 highlights the primary advantages and disadvantages of these alternative forms of acquisition. Each alternative form of acquisition will be discussed in more detail during the remainder of this chapter.

TABLE 11-4 Advantages and Disadvantages of Alternative Forms of Acquisition

Alternative Forms	Advantages	Disadvantages
Cash Purchase of Assets	*Buyer:* • Allows targeted purchase of assets • Asset write-up • May renegotiate union and benefits agreements • May avoid need for shareholder approval • No minority shareholders	*Buyer:* • Lose NOLs[1] and tax credits • Lose rights to intellectual property • May require consents to assignment of contracts • Exposed to liabilities transferring with assets (e.g., warranty claims) • Subject to taxes on any gains resulting in asset write-up • Subject to lengthy documentation of assets in contract
	Seller: • Maintains corporate existence and ownership of assets not acquired • Retains NOLs and tax credits	*Seller:* • Potential double taxation if shell liquidated • Subject to state transfer taxes • Necessity of disposing of unwanted residual assets
Cash Purchase of Stock	*Buyer:* • Assets/liabilities transfer automatically • May avoid need to get consents to assignment for contracts • Less documentation • NOLs and tax credits pass to buyer • No state transfer taxes • May insulate from target liabilities if kept as subsidiary • No shareholder approval if funded by cash or debt • Enables circumvention of target's board in hostile tender offer	*Buyer:* • Responsible for known and unknown liabilities • No asset write-up unless 338 election taken by buyer[2] • Union and employee benefit agreements do not terminate • Potential for minority shareholders[3]

continued

TABLE 11-4   continued

Alternative Forms	Advantages	Disadvantages
	Seller: • Liabilities generally pass to the buyer • May receive favorable tax treatment if acquirer stock received in payment	*Seller*: • Loss of NOLs and tax credits • Favorable tax treatment lost if buyer adopts 338 election
Statutory Merger	*Buyer*: • Flexible form of payment (stock, cash, or debt) • Assets and liabilities transfer automatically, without lengthy documentation • No state transfer taxes • No minority shareholders as shareholders required to tender shares (minority freeze-out) • May avoid shareholder approval	*Buyer*: • May have to pay dissenting shareholders' appraised value of stock • May be time consuming because of the need for target shareholder and board approvals, which may delay closing
	Seller: • Favorable tax treatment if purchase price primarily in acquirer stock • Allows for continuing interest in combined companies • Flexible form of payment	*Seller*: • May be time consuming • Target firm often does not survive • May not qualify for favorable tax status
Stock-for-Stock Transaction	*Buyer*: • May operate target company as a subsidiary • See purchase of stock above *Seller*: See purchase of stock above	*Buyer*: • May postpone realization of synergies • See purchase of stock above *Seller*: See purchase of stock above
Stock-for-Assets Transaction	*Buyer*: • See purchase of assets above *Seller*: See purchase of assets above	*Buyer*: • May dilute buyer's ownership position • See purchase of assets above *Seller*: See purchase of assets above
Staged Transactions	Provides greater strategic flexibility	May postpone realization of synergies

Notes:
[1] Net operating loss carry forwards or carry backs.
[2] In Section 338 of the U.S. tax code, the acquirer in a purchase of 80% or more of the stock of the target may elect to treat the acquisition as if it were an acquisition of the target's assets.
[3] Minority shareholders in a subsidiary may be eliminated by a so-called "back-end" merger following the initial purchase of target stock. As a result of the merger, minority shareholders are required to abide by the majority vote of all shareholders and sell their shares to the acquirer. If the acquirer owns more than 90% of the target's shares, it may be able to use a short-form merger, which does not require any shareholder vote.

Purchase of Assets

In an asset purchase, a buyer acquires all rights a seller has to an asset for cash, stock, or some combination. Ownership is transferred whenever the seller provides the buyer with documents that demonstrate that title has been transferred. Such documents include a bill of sale and a deed. Asset purchases are governed by the Uniform Commercial Code (UCC), a portion of which includes the bulk sales law. The bulk sales law focuses on inventory transfer to the buyer and requires that, if inventory ownership is transferred, notice of the transfer must be sent to creditors of the seller 10 days before the transfer takes place. Because such inventory may have been used for collateral, the notice must indicate whether the seller's obligation to the creditors will be satisfied before transferring title to the inventory.

In a *cash-for-assets* acquisition, the acquirer pays cash for the seller's assets and may choose to accept some or all of the seller's liabilities. Seller shareholders must vote to approve the transaction, whenever the seller's board votes to sell all or "substantially all" of the firm's assets. What constitutes "substantially all" does not necessarily mean that most of the firm's assets have been sold; rather, it could mean that the assets sold, while comprising a relatively small percentage of the firm's total assets, are critical to the ongoing operation of the business. Hence, any sale of assets that does not leave the firm with "significant continuing business activity" may force the firm to liquidate. Significant business activity remains following the sale of assets if the selling firm retains at least 25% of total pretransaction operating assets and 25% of pretransaction income or revenue. Unless required by the firm's bylaws, the buyer's shareholders do not vote to approve the transaction.

After receiving the cash from the buyer, the selling firm may reinvest all the cash in its operations, reinvest some and pay a dividend to shareholders with the remaining cash, or pay it out in a single liquidating distribution. The selling firm's shares are extinguished if shareholders approve the liquidation of the firm. After paying for any liabilities not assumed by the buyer, the assets remaining with the seller and the cash received from the acquiring firm are transferred to the seller's shareholders in a liquidating distribution.

In a *stock-for-assets* transaction, once approved by the seller's board and shareholders, the seller's shareholders receive buyer stock in exchange for the seller's assets and liabilities. In a second stage, the seller dissolves the corporation, following shareholder ratification of such a move, leaving its shareholders with buyer stock. Consequently, the shareholders of the two firms have effectively pooled their ownership interests in the buyer's corporation, which holds the combined assets and liabilities of both firms. Many states and public stock exchanges give acquiring firm shareholders the right to vote to approve a stock-for-assets transaction if the new shares issued by the buyer exceed more than 20% of the firm's total shares outstanding before the transaction.

Advantages: Buyer's Perspective

Buyers can be selective as to which assets of the target will be purchased. The buyer is generally not responsible for the seller's liabilities, unless specifically assumed under the contract. However, the buyer can be held responsible for certain liabilities such as environmental claims, property taxes, and in some states, substantial pension liabilities and product liability claims. To protect against such risks, buyers usually insist on seller *indemnification* (i.e., the seller is held responsible for payment of damages resulting from such claims). Of course, such indemnification is worthwhile only as long as the seller remains solvent. (Note that in most agreements of purchase and sale buyers and sellers agree to indemnify each other from claims for which they are directly responsible. Liability under such arrangements usually is subject to specific dollar limits and is in force only for a specific time period.)

Acquired assets may be revalued to market value on the closing date under the purchase method of accounting. (Purchase accounting is a form of financial reporting of business combinations that is discussed in detail in Chapter 12.) This increase or **step-up** in the tax basis of the acquired assets to fair market value provides for higher depreciation and amortization expense deductions for tax purposes. Such expense deductions are said to shelter (i.e., protect) pretax income from taxation. Buyers are generally free of any undisclosed or contingent liabilities. The asset purchase normally results in the termination of union agreements, thereby providing an opportunity to renegotiate agreements viewed as too restrictive. Benefit plans may be maintained or terminated at the discretion of the acquirer. While termination of certain contracts and benefit plans is possible in a purchase of assets, buyers may be reluctant to do so because of the potential undermining of employee morale and productivity.

Advantages: Seller's Perspective

Sellers are able to maintain their corporate existence and hence ownership of tangible assets not acquired by the buyer and of intangible assets such as licenses, franchises, and patents. The seller retains the right to use the corporate identity in subsequent marketing programs, unless ceded to the buyer as part of the transaction. The seller also retains the right to use all tax credits and accumulated net operating losses, which can be used to shelter future income from taxes. Such tax considerations remain with the holders of the target firm's stock.

Disadvantages: Buyer's Perspective

The buyer loses the seller's net operating losses and tax credits. Rights to assets such as licenses, franchises, and patents cannot be transferred to buyers. Such rights are viewed as belonging to the owners of the business (i.e., target stockholders). These rights sometimes can be difficult to transfer because of the need to obtain consent from the agency (e.g., U.S. Patent Office) issuing the rights. The buyer must seek the consent of customers and vendors to transfer existing contracts to the buyer. The transaction is more complex and costly, because acquired assets must be listed on appendices to the definitive agreement and the sale of and titles to each asset transferred must be recorded and state title **transfer taxes** must be paid. Such taxes must be paid whenever titles to assets are transferred. Moreover, a lender's consent may be required if the assets to be sold are being used as collateral for loans.

Disadvantages: Seller's Perspective

Taxes also may be a problem because the seller may be subject to double taxation. If the tax basis in the assets or stock is low, the seller may experience a sizable gain on the sale. In addition, if the corporation subsequently is liquidated, the seller may be responsible for the recapture of taxes deferred as a result of the use of accelerated rather than straight-line depreciation. If the number of assets transferred is large, the amount of state transfer taxes may become onerous. Whether the seller or the buyer actually pays the transfer taxes or they are shared is negotiable.

Purchase of Stock

In *cash-for-stock* or *stock-for-stock* transactions, the buyer purchases the seller's stock directly from the seller's shareholders. This is in marked contrast to a statutory merger in which the boards of directors of the firms involved must first ratify the proposal before submitting it to their shareholders for approval. Consequently, a purchase of stock is the approach most often taken in hostile takeovers. If the buyer is unable to convince all of the seller's shareholders to tender their shares, then a minority of seller shareholders remains outstanding. The target firm would then be viewed not as a wholly owned but rather as a partially owned subsidiary of the buyer or acquiring company. No seller shareholder approval is required in such transactions as the seller's shareholders are expressing approval by tendering their shares. As required by most major stock exchanges, acquiring company shareholders have the right to approve a stock-for-stock transaction if the amount of new acquirer shares issued exceeds 20% of the firm's total outstanding shares before the transaction takes place.

Advantages: Buyer's Perspective

All assets are transferred with the target's stock, resulting in less need for documentation to complete the transaction. State asset transfer taxes may be avoided with a purchase of shares. Net operating losses and tax credits pass to the buyer with the purchase of stock. The right of the buyer to use the target's name, licenses, franchises, patents, and permits also is preserved. Furthermore, the purchase of the seller's stock provides for the continuity of contracts and corporate identity. This obviates the need to renegotiate contracts and enables the acquirer to utilize the brand recognition that may be associated with the name of the target firm. However, some customer and vendor contracts, as well as permits, may stipulate that the buyer must obtain their consent before the contract is transferred. While the acquirer's board normally approves any major acquisition, approval by shareholders is not required if the purchase is financed primarily with cash or debt. If stock that has not yet been authorized is used, shareholder approval is likely to be required. Neither the target's board nor shareholders need to approve a sale of stock; however, shareholders may simply refuse to sell their stock.

Advantages: Seller's Perspective

The seller is able to defer paying taxes. If stock is received from the acquiring company, taxes are paid by the target's shareholders only when the stock is sold. The applicable tax is the more favorable capital gains rate, as opposed to the ordinary tax rate. All obligations, disclosed or otherwise, transfer to the buyer. This advantage for the seller usually is attenuated by the insistence by the buyer that the seller indemnify the buyer from damages resulting from any undisclosed liability. However, as previously noted, indemnification clauses in contracts generally are in force for only a limited time period. Finally, the seller is not left with the problem of disposing of assets that the seller does not wish to retain but that were not purchased by the acquiring company.

Disadvantages: Buyer's Perspective

The buyer is liable for all unknown, undisclosed, or contingent liabilities. The seller's tax basis is carried over to the buyer at historical cost, unless the seller consents to take certain tax code elections. These elections potentially can create a tax liability for the seller. Therefore, they are used infrequently. Consequently, there is no step-up in the cost basis of assets and no tax shelter is created. Dissenting shareholders have the right to have their shares appraised, with the option of being paid the appraised value of their shares or remaining as minority shareholders. The purchase of stock does not terminate existing union agreements or employee benefit plans.

The existence of minority shareholders creates significant administrative costs and practical concerns. Significant additional expenses are incurred as the parent must submit annual reports, hold annual shareholder meetings, and allow such shareholders to elect a board through a formal election process. Furthermore, implementing strategic business moves may be inhibited. In an effort to sell its MTU Friedrichshafen diesel engine assembly operations in 2006, DaimlerChrysler announced the purchase of minority shareholders' interests whose holdings comprised less than 10% of firm's outstanding stock. Prior to the buyout, DaimlerChrysler had been unable to reach agreement with enough shareholders to enable it to sell the business.

Disadvantages: Seller's Perspective

The seller cannot pick and choose the assets to be retained and loses all net operating losses and tax credits.

Mergers

Unlike purchases of target stock, mergers require approval of the acquirer's board and the target's board of directors and the subsequent submission of the proposal to the shareholders of both firms. Unless otherwise required by a firm's bylaws, a simple majority of all the outstanding voting shares must ratify the proposal. The merger agreement must then be filed with the state in which the merger is to be consummated. There are several exceptions under which no vote is required by the acquirer's (i.e., surviving firm) shareholders. The first exception involves a transaction that is not considered material in that the acquirer issues new shares to the target's shareholders in an amount that comprises less than 20% of the acquirer's voting shares outstanding before the transaction. This is sometimes referred to as the "small-scale" merger exception. The second exception under which a vote is not required in a statutory merger occurs when a subsidiary is being merged into the parent and the parent owns a substantial majority (over 90% in some states) of the subsidiary's stock before the transaction. Such a merger in which the subsidiary is merged into the parent firm (often called a short-form or parent-sub exception) requires only the approval of the parent's board. These mergers are sometimes called upstream mergers. When the parent is merged into the subsidiary in a downstream merger, the shareholders of the parent firm are allowed to vote.

The purchase price in a merger can consist of cash, stock, or debt, giving the acquiring company more latitude in how it will pay for the purchase of the target's stock. If the seller receives acquirer shares in exchange for their shares (with the seller's shares subsequently canceled), the merger is a *stock-for-stock statutory* or *stock swap merger*. If the shareholders of the selling firm receive cash or some form of nonvoting investment (e.g., debt, or nonvoting preferred or common stock) for their shares, the merger is referred to as a *cash-out* or *cash statutory merger*. Mergers are generally not suitable for hostile transactions, because they require the approval of the target's board.

Advantages

The primary advantage of a merger is that the transfer of assets and the exchange of stock between the acquirer and the target happen automatically by "rule of law." (Rule of law refers to the accumulation of applicable federal and state laws and legal precedents resulting from numerous court cases establishing when and how ownership is transferred.) When a majority (i.e., 51%) of target shareholders has approved the merger, all shareholders are required to sell their shares, even if they did not support the transaction. This avoids a situation in which a minority of shareholders holds up the completion of a proposed transaction. Such shareholders are said to have been "frozen-out" of their position. As with the purchase of stock, dissenting shareholders have the right to have their shares appraised according to the statutes of many states and to be paid the appraised value rather than what is being offered by the acquiring firm. Transfer taxes are not paid because there are no asset transfer documents. Contracts, licenses, patents, and permits automatically transfer, unless they require "consent to assignment." This means that the buyer convinces all parties to the contracts to agree to consign them to the new owner. This transfer can be accomplished by merging a subsidiary set up by the buyer with the target. The subsidiary can be merged with the parent immediately following closing.

Disadvantages

Mergers of public corporations can be costly and time consuming because of the need to obtain shareholder approval and to comply with proxy regulations (see Chapter 2). The resulting delay can open the door to other bidders, create an auction environment, and boost the purchase price.

Staged Transactions

An acquiring firm may choose to complete a takeover of another firm in stages spread over an extended period of time. Staged transactions may be used to structure an earnout, to enable the target to complete the development of a technology or process, to await regulatory approval, to eliminate the need to obtain shareholder approval, and to minimize cultural conflicts with the target.

As part of an earnout agreement, the acquirer may agree to allow the target to operate as a wholly owned but largely autonomous unit until the earnout period expires. This suggests that there will be little attempt to integrate facilities, overhead operations, and distribution systems during the earnout period.

The value of the target may be greatly dependent on the target developing a key technology or production process, receiving approval from a regulatory authority such as the Federal Communications Commission (FCC), or signing a multiyear customer or vendor contract. The target's ability to realize these objectives may be enhanced if it is aligned with a larger company or receives a cash infusion to fund the required research. A potential acquirer may assume a minority investment in the target with an option to acquire the company at a later date.

If the long-term value of the acquirer's stock offered to the target is dependent on the acquirer receiving approval from a regulatory agency, developing a new technology, or landing a key contract, the target may be well advised to wait. The two parties may enter into a letter of intent, with the option to exit the agreement without any liability to either party if certain key events are not realized within a stipulated time.

Eliminating the need for a shareholder vote may be accomplished through a triangular merger in which the acquiring firm uses a relatively small percentage of its voting stock (usually less than 20%) to purchase the target firm. The use of less than 20% avoids the need for acquiring shareholders to approve the transaction, as required by many stock exchanges. State merger statutes generally do not require the acquirer's shareholders to vote upon a merger between the acquirer's subsidiary and a target firm. Therefore, the acquiring company may create a special merger subsidiary. The subsidiary subsequently is funded by the consideration to be used in the merger and the subsidiary and the target company merge. Because the acquirer is the sole shareholder in the operating subsidiary, the only approval required may be the board of directors of the subsidiary. This board may be essentially the same as that of the parent or acquiring company. However, acquirer shareholders still may be required by the firm's bylaws to vote to authorize the creation of new shares of stock to be offered in the transaction.

Companies that acquire a foreign firm may choose to initially manage the acquired company as a subsidiary because of substantial cultural differences. Daimler-Benz managed Chrysler Corporation as a wholly owned subsidiary, even maintaining separately traded stocks, before merging the two corporations more than 1 year after closing.

Case Study 11-2 illustrates a staged transaction in which Phelps Dodge attempted to acquire two other metals companies by acquiring all of the outstanding stock of Inco. The strategy was to in one grand gesture make Phelps Dodge the world's second largest metals mining company, behind Australia's BHP Billiton. This three-way transaction is reminiscent of U.S.-based Andarko's acquisition of Western Gas Resources and Kerr-McGee for $21 billion in June 2006 (see Chapter 1).

Case Study 11-2
Phelps Dodge Attempts to Buy Two at the Same Time

Buoyed by high metals prices, many major mining companies were experiencing huge increases in their cash reserves. Expectations of continued high prices sparked an M&A boom among Canadian mining companies late in 2005. These companies were seeking to rapidly increase revenue and improve profitability through savings generated by consolidating the industry.

In October 2005, Inco Ltd. had made a bid to buy Falconbridge Ltd. However, in early May 2006, another Canadian mining company, Teck Cominco Ltd., offered to buy Inco. By mid-May, Swiss mining company, Xstrata, initiated a bidding war with Inco for Falconbridge. Finally, Phelps Dodge (Phelps) entered the fray with a complex plan involving three companies.

In what was heralded by some as a bold strategic move, Phelps proposed to acquire Canadian mining companies Inco and Falconbridge in a three-way transaction valued at $47.9 billion. The new company would be named Phelps Dodge Inco Company and would be the world's largest producer of nickel and the second largest producer of copper and molybdenum, a mineral used to strengthen steel.

The transaction was to be completed in two stages. The first stage called for Inco to complete its acquisition of Falconbridge by offering a combination of Inco shares and cash. Regulators in North America had already approved the deal. In the second stage, Inco shareholders would receive a combination of cash and Phelp's stock for their shares, once

Falconbridge shares were converted to Inco shares. Inco shareholders were to receive a healthy premium for their shares. Phelps was betting that the premium could be easily recovered by realizing huge cost savings in combining the operations of the three businesses. Phelps' bid for Inco was not contingent on Inco successfully acquiring Falconbridge. When the deal was completed, Phelps anticipated buying back $5 billion worth of its shares. Financing the transaction (including the share buyback) would require that Phelps borrow more than $27 billion. The complex three-way deal is illustrated next, with the dollar figures in parentheses indicating the market value of each company.

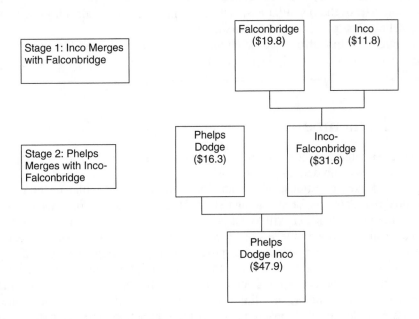

As many deals do, this one looked good on paper but was very difficult to execute. In late July, Inco lost to Xstrata in its effort to acquire Falconbridge. Phelps' share price continued to drop as investors recognized that the loss of Falconbridge significantly reduced the value of anticipated cost savings that would have been realized by combining the three firms. Without Falconbridge, expected annual cost savings fell from $900 million to $350 million.

The skies darkened further for Phelps Dodge in mid-August, when Inco's board entered into talks with Brazil's Companhia Vale do Rio Doce (CVRD), which offered to buy Inco for $17.6 billion in cash. Simultaneously, Inco's board urged shareholders to support the earlier agreement it had made with Phelps Dodge to avoid triggering penalties in the agreement and recommended the rejection of a third competing bid from Teck Cominco.

Amid concerns among its own shareholders about dilution and lack of support among Inco shareholders for its offer, Phelps Dodge withdrew its bid to buy Inco in early September 2006. Phelps Dodge stated publicly that they would focus on increasing its own copper production from the firm's current mines. The firm's share price rose as the firm's shareholders celebrated the demise of the deal. The firm's institutional shareholders had long been critical of what they believed was an excessive offer price that would dilute owners' equity and saddle Phelps Dodge with excessive amounts of debt. Phelps is entitled to receive a break-up fee from Inco of $125 million and potentially another $350 if Inco is acquired anytime during the following year.

Within a little more than two months of Phelps' aborted takeover attempt, the hunter was itself acquired. In late November of 2006, Freeport-McMoran Copper & Gold Inc. announced that it had reached agreement to acquire Phelps for $25.9 billion.

Case Study Discussion Questions

1. Given the complexity of the three-way transaction, what factors may have motivated Phelps Dodge's management to adopt this strategy? Be specific.
2. What are the primary risks associated with a three-way transaction? Be specific.
3. With the loss of the potential cost savings from integrating Falconbridge, why do you believe Phelps continued to pursue Inco?
4. How might Phelps' effort to execute this complex three-way transaction have contributed to its eventually being acquired?

Things to Remember

The deal-structuring process addresses satisfying as many of the primary objectives of the parties involved and determines how risk will be shared. The process begins with addressing a set of key questions, whose answers help to define initial negotiating positions, potential risks, options for managing risk, levels of tolerance for risk, and conditions under which the buyer or seller will "walk away" from the negotiations. The deal-structuring process can be defined in terms of six major components. These components include the form of the acquisition vehicle, the postclosing organization, the form of payment, the form of acquisition, the legal form of the selling entity, and tax considerations.

The form of the acquisition vehicle refers to the legal structure used to acquire the target. The postclosing organization is the legal framework used to manage the combined businesses following the consummation of the transaction. The postclosing organization may differ from the acquisition vehicle depending on the acquirer's strategic objectives for the combined firms. The form of payment or total consideration may consist of cash, common stock, debt, or some combination of all three. The form of acquisition refers to what is being acquired: stock or assets. The form of acquisition affects the form of payment, tax considerations, as well as the choice of acquisition vehicle and postclosing organization. Tax considerations also are affected by the legal structure of the selling entity.

Chapter Discussion Questions

11-1. Describe the deal-structuring process.
11-2. Provide two examples of how decisions made in one area of the deal-structuring process are likely to affect other areas.
11-3. What are the reasons acquirers may choose a particular form of acquisition vehicle?
11-4. Describe techniques used to "close the gap" when buyers and sellers cannot agree on price.
11-5. Why do bidders sometimes offer target firm shareholders multiple payments options (e.g., cash and stock)?
11-6. What are the advantages and disadvantages of a purchase of assets from the perspective of the buyer and seller?
11-7. What are the advantages and disadvantages of a purchase of stock from the perspective of the buyer and seller?

11-8. What are the advantages and disadvantages of a statutory merger?

11-9. What are the reasons some acquirers choose to undertake a staged or multistep takeover?

11-10. What forms of acquisition represent common alternatives to a merger? Under what circumstances might these alternative structures be employed?

Answers to these Chapter Discussion Questions are available in the Online Instructor's Manual for instructors using this book.

Chapter Business Case

Case Study 11-3

Vivendi Universal and GE Combine Entertainment Assets to Form NBC Universal

Ending a 4-month-long auction process, Vivendi Universal SA agreed on October 5, 2003, to sell its Vivendi Universal Entertainment (VUE) businesses, consisting of film and television assets, to General Electric Corporation's wholly owned NBC subsidiary. Vivendi received a combination of GE stock and stock in the combined company valued at approximately $14 billion. Vivendi would combine the Universal Pictures movie studio, its television production group, three cable networks, and the Universal theme parks with NBC. The new company would have annual revenues of $13 billion based on 2003 pro forma statements.

This transaction was among many made by Vivendi in its effort to restore the firm's financial viability. Having started as a highly profitable distributor of bottled water, the French company undertook a diversification spree in the 1990s, which pushed the firm into many unrelated enterprises and left it highly in debt. With its stock plummeting, Vivendi had been under considerable pressure to reduce its leverage and to refocus its investments.

Applying a multiple of 14 times estimated 2003 EBITDA of $3 billion, the combined company has an estimated value of approximately $42 billion. This multiple is well within the range of comparable transactions and is consistent with the share price multiples of television media companies at that time. Of the $3 billion in 2003 EBITDA, GE will provide $2 billion and Vivendi $1 billion. This values GE's assets at $28 billion and Vivendi's at $14 billion. This implies that GE's assets contribute two-thirds and Vivendi's one-third of the total market value of the combined company.

NBC Universal's total assets of $42 billion consist of VUE's assets valued at $14 billion and NBC's at $28 billion. Vivendi is to receive an infusion of liquidity at closing consisting of $3.8 billion in cash by selling its right to receive $4 billion in GE stock during the next 2 years and the transfer of $1.6 billion in debt carried by VUE's businesses to the combined company.

Note that by exercising its right to sell the stock immediately, Vivendi receives only 95% of the $4 billion fair market value of the stock or $3.8 billion. Vivendi would retain an ongoing approximate 20% ownership in the new company valued at $8.4 billion after having received $5.4 billion in liquidity at closing. GE would have 80% ownership in the new company in exchange for providing $5.4 billion in liquidity (i.e., $3.8 billion in cash and assuming $1.6 billion in debt). Vivendi has the option to sell its 20% ownership interest in the future beginning in 2006 at fair market value. GE would have the first right (i.e., the first right of refusal) to acquire the Vivendi position.

The combined operations of VUE and NBC expect to achieve incremental revenues of at least $100 million annually and cost reductions of $400 million annually. GE anticipates that its 80% ownership position in the combined company would be accretive for GE shareholders beginning in the second full year of operation. The impact in the first year is expected to be neutral.

Case Study Discussion Questions

1. From a legal standpoint, identify the acquirer and the target firms.
2. What is the form of acquisition? Why might this form have been agreed to by the parties involved in the transaction.
3. What is the form of acquisition vehicle and the postclosing organization? Why do you think the legal entities you have identified were selected?
4. What is the form of payment or total consideration? Why do you believe the parties to this transaction agreed to this form of payment?
5. Based on a total valuation of $42 billion, Vivendi's assets contributed one-third and GE's two-thirds of the total value of NBC Universal. However, after the closing, Vivendi would only own a 20% equity position in the combined business. Why?

Answers to these Case Study Discussion Questions are available in the Online Instructor's Manual for instructors using this book.

Chapter Business Case

Case Study 11-4
Using Form of Payment as a Takeover Strategy: Chevron's Acquisition of Unocal

Background
Unocal ceased to exist as an independent company on August 11, 2005, and its shares were delisted from the New York Stock Exchange. The new firm is known as Chevron. In a highly politicized transaction, Chevron battled Chinese oil producer, CNOOC, for almost 4 months for ownership of Unocal. A cash and stock bid by Chevron, the nation's second largest oil producer, made in April valued at $61 per share was accepted by the Unocal board when it appeared that CNOOC would not counterbid. However, CNOOC soon followed with an all-cash bid of $67 per share. Chevron amended the merger agreement with a new cash and stock bid valued at $63 per share in late July. Despite the significant difference in the value of the two bids, the Unocal board recommended to its shareholders that they accept the amended Chevron bid in view of the growing doubt that U.S. regulatory authorities would approve a takeover by CNOOC.

Winning Approval by Appealing to the Varied Interests of Target Shareholders
In its strategy to win Unocal shareholder approval, Chevron offered Unocal shareholders three options for each of their shares: (1) $69 in cash, (2) 1.03 Chevron shares, or (3) .618 Chevron shares plus $27.60 in cash. Unocal shareholders not electing any specific option would receive the third option. Moreover, the all-cash and all-stock offers were subject to proration in order to preserve an overall per share mix of .618 of a share of Chevron common stock and $27.60 in cash for all of the 272 million outstanding shares of Unocal common stock. This mix of cash and stock provided a "blended" value of about $63 per share of

Unocal common stock on the day that Unocal and Chevron entered into the amendment to the merger agreement on July 22, 2005. The "blended" rate was calculated by multiplying .618 by the value of Chevron stock on July 22 of $57.28 plus $27.60 in cash. This resulted in a targeted purchase price that was about 56% Chevron stock and 44% cash.

This mix of cash and stock implied that Chevron would pay approximately $7.5 billion (i.e., $27.60 × 272 million Unocal shares outstanding) in cash and issue approximately 168 million shares of Chevron common stock (i.e., .618 × 272 million of Unocal shares) valued at $57.28 per share as of July 22, 2005. The implied value of the merger on that date was $17.1 billion (i.e., $27.60 × 272 million Unocal common shares outstanding plus $57.28 × 168 million Chevron common shares). An increase in Chevron's share price to $63.15 on August 10, 2005, the day of the Unocal shareholders' meeting, boosted the value of the deal to $18.1 billion.

Option (1) was intended to appeal to those Unocal shareholders who were attracted to CNOOC's all-cash offer of $67 per share. Option (2) was designed for those shareholders interested in a tax-free exchange. Finally, it was anticipated that option (3) would attract those Unocal shareholders who were interested in cash but also wished to enjoy any appreciation in the stock of the combined companies.

Adjusting Unocal Investor Elections

The agreement of purchase and sale between Chevron and Unocal contained a "proration clause." This clause enabled Chevron to limit the amount of total cash it would pay out under those options involving cash that it had offered to Unocal shareholders and to maintain the "blended" rate of $63 it would pay for each share of Unocal stock. Approximately 242 million Unocal shareholders elected to receive all cash for their shares, 22.1 million opted for the all-stock alternative, and 10.1 million elected the cash and stock combination. No election was made for approximately .3 million shares. Based on these results, the amount of cash needed to satisfy the number of shareholders electing the all-cash option far exceeded the amount that Chevron was willing to pay. Consequently, as permitted in the merger agreement, the all-cash offer was prorated resulting in the Unocal shareholders who had elected the all-cash option receiving a combination of cash and stock rather than $69 per share. The mix of cash and stock was calculated as shown in Table 11.5.

TABLE 11-5 Prorating All-Cash Elections

---

1. Determine the available cash election amount (ACEA): Aggregate cash amount minus the amount of cash to be paid to Unocal shareholders selecting the combination of cash and stock (i.e., Option 3).

    ACEA = $27.60 × 272 million (Unocal shares outstanding) − 10.1 million
            (shares electing cash and stock option) × $27.60
        = $7.5 − $.3
        = $7.2 billion

2. Determine the elected cash amount (ECA): Amount equal to $69 multiplied by the number of shares of Unocal common stock electing the all-cash option.

    ECA = $69 × 242 million = 4$16.7 billion

3. Determine the cash proration factor (CPF): ACEA/ECA

    CPF = $7.2/$16.7 = .4311

continued

TABLE 11-5   continued

4. Determine the stock and cash mix (SCM): Sum of the prorated cash (PCMC) and stock (PSMC) merger considerations exchanged for each share of Unocal common stock.

   PCMC = $69 × .4311 = $29.74

5. Determine the prorated stock merger consideration (PSMC): 1.03 multiplied by 1 – CPF.

   PSMC = 1.03 × (1 − .4311) = .5860

6. Determine the stock and cash mix (SCM): Sum of the prorated cash (PCMC) and stock (PSMC) merger considerations exchanged for each share of Unocal common stock.

   SCM = $29.74 + .5860 of a Chevron share

TABLE 11-6   Prorating All-Stock Elections

1. Determine the available cash election amount (ACEA): Same as Step 1 above.

   ACEA = $7.2 billion

2. Determine the elected cash amount (ECA): Amount equal to $69 multiplied by the number of shares of Unocal common stock electing the all-cash option.

   ECA = $69 × 22.1 million = $1.5 billion

3. Determine the excess cash amount (EXCA): Difference between ACEA and ECA.

   EXCA = $7.2 − $1.5 = $5.7

4. Determine the prorated cash merger consideration (PCMC): EXCA divided by number of Unocal shares elected the all-stock option.

   PCMC = $5.7/242 million = $23.55

5. Determine the stock proration factor (SPF): $69 minus the prorated cash merger consideration divided by $69.

   SPF = ($69 − $23.55)/$69 = .$45.45/$69 = .6587

6. Determine the prorated stock price consideration (PSPC): The number of shares of Chevron stock equal to 1.03 multiplied by the stock proration factor.

   PSPC = 1.03 × .6587 = .6785

7. Determine the stock and cash mix (SCM): Each Unocal share to be exchanged in an all-stock election is converted into the right to receive the prorated cash merger consideration and the prorated stock merger consideration.

   SCM = $23.55 + .6785 of a Chevron share for each Unocal share

---

If too many Unocal shareholders had elected to receive Chevron stock, those making the all-stock election would not have received 1.03 shares of Chevron stock for each share of Unocal stock. Rather, they would have received a mix of stock and cash to help preserve the approximate 56% stock and 44% cash composition of the purchase price desired by Chevron. For purposes of illustration, assume the number of Unocal shares to be exchanged for the all-cash and all-stock options are 22.1 and 242 million, respectively. This is the reverse of what actually happened. The mix of stock and cash would have been prorated as shown in Table 11.6.

Conclusions

It is typical of large transactions in which the target has a large, diverse shareholder base that acquiring firms offer target shareholders a "menu" of alternative forms of payment. The objective is to enhance the likelihood of success by appealing to a broader group of shareholders. To the unsophisticated target shareholder, the array of options may prove appealing. However, it is likely that those electing all-cash or all-stock purchases are likely to be disappointed due to probable proration clauses in merger contracts. Such clauses enable the acquirer to maintain an overall mix of cash and stock in completing the transaction. This enables the acquirer to limit the amount of cash they must borrow or the number of new shares they must issue to levels they find acceptable.

Case Study Discussion Questions

1. What was the form of payment employed by both bidders for Unocal? In your judgment, why were they different? Be specific.
2. How did Chevron use the form of payment as a potential takeover strategy?
3. Is the "proration clause" found in most merger agreements in which target shareholders are given several ways in which they can choose to be paid for their shares in the best interests of the target shareholders? In the best interests of the acquirer? Explain your answer.

Answers to these Case Study Discussion Questions are available in the Online Instructor's Manual for instructors using this book.

References

Aspatore Staff, *M&A Negotiations: Leading Lawyers on Negotiating Deals: Structuring Contracts and Resolving Merger and Acquisition Disputes*, Aspatore Books, Bostin, MA, 2006.

Bainbridge, Stephen M., *Mergers and Acquisitions*, Foundation Press, Abilene, Texas, 2003.

Faccio, Mara, and Larry H. P. Lang, "The Ultimate Ownership of Western European Corporations," *Journal of Financial Economics*, Vol. 65, 2002, pp. 365–395.

Faccio, Mara, and Ronald Masulis, "The Choice of Payment Method in European Mergers and Acquisitions," *Journal of Finance*, Vol. 60, 2005, pp. 1345–1388.

Ginsburg, Martin D., and Jack S. Levin, *Mergers, Acquisitions, and Buyouts*, Aspen Publishers, New York, 2006.

Hunt, Peter, *Structuring Mergers and Acquisitions: A Guide to Creating Shareholder Value*, Aspen Publishers, New York, 2003.

Kohers, Ninon, and James Ang, "Earnouts in Mergers: Agreeing to Disagree and Agreeing to Stay," *The Journal of Finance*, Vol. 73, July 2000, pp. 445–476.

Lajoux, Alexandra Reed, and H. Peter Nesvold, *The Art of M&A Structuring: Techniques for Mitigating Financial, Tax, and Legal Risk*, McGraw-Hill, New York, 2004.

Mergerstat Global Mergers and Acquisitions Information, *Mergerstat Review*, Santa Monica: California, 2005.

Oesterle, Dale A., *Mergers and Acquisitions Law*, 3rd Ed., West Publishing, Saint Paul, MN, 2005.

Officer, Micah S., "Collars and Renegotiation in Mergers and Acquisitions," *Journal of Finance*, Vol. 59, 2004, pp. 2719–2743.

Sherman, Andrew J., *Mergers and Acquisitions from A to Z*, 2nd Ed., AMACOM, New York, 2006.

Srikant, Datar, Richard Frankel, and Mark Wolfson, "Earnouts: The Effects of Adverse Selection and Agency Costs on Acquisition Techniques," *Journal of Law, Economics, and Organization*, Vol. 17, April 2001, pp. 201–238.

CHAPTER ♦ 12

Structuring the Deal

Tax and Accounting Considerations

One person of integrity can make a difference, a difference of life and death.

—Elie Wiesel

Inside M&A: Meeting the Needs of the Parties Involved

It was apparent that the fast-paced, highly informal, and entrepreneurial environment of HiTech Corporation would not readily blend with the more structured and reserved environment of BigCo, Inc. Nonetheless, BigCo's senior management knew that they needed access to certain patents owned by HiTech to become more cost competitive in the firm's primary markets. Concerned about creating competitors, HiTech chose not to license its technologies to others. Consequently, BigCo felt compelled to gain complete control of these patents and any further updates to this technology by acquiring HiTech.

As Chief Executive Officer (CEO) of BigCo, Kristen Bailey and her staff studied the demographic profile of HiTech shareholders and employees. As a publicly traded company, considerable information was available through Securities and Exchange Commission (SEC) filings, newspaper articles, and presentations made by HiTech's senior managers at trade association meetings. She understood that almost one-half of the stock was held by the firm's founders, about one-fourth by employees whose average age was about 30, and the remainder by unaffiliated investors and institutions. At last year's stockholders' meeting, HiTech's management, while responding to questions from attendees, indicated that remaining independent would better serve the shareholders' interests at this stage of the firm's development. After all, the firm was less than 10 years old, and management believed they were on the verge of a technological breakthrough whose full commercial value could not yet be determined. Management did acknowledge that once the technology had been developed, they might consider being acquired or partnering with another firm that had excess manufacturing capacity and effective distribution channels that HiTech currently lacked.

Kristen believed that, once BigCo's bid for HiTech became public knowledge, BigCo's competitors were likely to make offers for HiTech. To preempt its competitors, Kristen

477

reasoned that BigCo's initial offer would have to be structured to meet as many of the primary needs of HiTech's shareholders, managers, and employees as possible. By satisfying the firm's board and management's concerns, BigCo was more likely to gain their support in obtaining approval by HiTech's shareholders. Moreover, by meeting the needs of managers and employees, BigCo was more likely to minimize employee attrition once the transaction was completed.

Kristen recommended to her board of directors that BigCo acquire the stock of HiTech to ensure that it would own the rights to the firm's existing and future intellectual property. If need be, a back-end merger could be implemented at a later date to eliminate minority shareholders. She suggested that BigCo's stock be used as the primary form of payment. By combining BigCo's state-of-the-art manufacturing facilities, which were only 65% utilized, and highly effective sales force with HiTech's technology, she believed that HiTech's shareholders and senior managers could be persuaded that the combined companies would be able to grow more rapidly than if HiTech remained independent. Furthermore, by accepting stock, HiTech shareholders could defer the payment of capital gains taxes. This would be highly attractive to the founders, whose average cost basis in the stock was very low. Furthermore, in view of the relative youthfulness of the workforce, HiTech employees might jump at the chance to own an interest in the combined companies. Finally, BigCo would assure HiTech managers that HiTech would be operated as a wholly owned subsidiary, at least for a time, with minimal interference in its daily operations from BigCo's management.

Kristen received approval to proceed. Contact was made through a BigCo board member who had served on an industry trade association board with HiTech's CEO. HiTech's CEO said that he was flattered by the proposal and would like to confer with his board before making a formal response. Kristen waited impatiently for the drama to unfold.

Chapter Overview

In Chapter 11, the deal-structuring process was described in terms of the acquisition vehicle, the postclosing organization, the form of payment, the legal form of the selling entity, the form of acquisition, and tax considerations. The author stressed how changes made in one area of the process could impact significantly other areas of the overall deal structure.

While Chapter 11 discussed in detail the first five components of the process, this chapter will focus on the implications of tax considerations for the deal-structuring process. As noted previously, tax considerations can affect the amount, timing, and composition of the purchase price. If a transaction is taxable, target shareholders typically will demand a higher purchase price to offset the anticipated tax liability. The increase in the purchase price may cause the acquirer to defer some portion of the purchase price by altering the terms to include more debt or installment payments to maintain the same purchase price in present value terms. Moreover, the decision as to the appropriate organizational structure of the combined businesses is affected by such factors as the desire to minimize taxes and to pass through losses to owners. The S corporation, LLC, and the partnership eliminate double taxation problems. Current operating losses, loss carry forwards or carry backs, or tax credits generated by the combined businesses can be passed through to the owners if the postclosing organization is a partnership or an LLC.

In addition, this chapter will address how transactions are recorded for financial reporting purposes. Since the elimination of pooling of interests as an alternative to purchase accounting in 2001, acquirers, whose stock is publicly traded, are increasingly vulnerable to massive write-offs of goodwill, often resulting from excessive prices paid for target companies. This ever-present threat may exert some discipline into the negotiating process, affecting both the amount and timing of offer prices.

The chapter business cases provide illustrations of the role of the deal-structuring process in recent successful (Boston Scientific–Guidant) and unsuccessful (JDS Uniphase–SDL) megamergers. A review of this chapter is available on the CD-ROM accompanying this book.

Tax Considerations

Taxes are an important consideration in almost any transaction. However, taxes are seldom the primary motivation for an acquisition. The fundamental economics of the transaction always should be the deciding factor. Tax benefits accruing to the buyer should simply reinforce a purchase decision. From the viewpoint of the seller or target company shareholder, transactions may be tax free or entirely or partially taxable. The sale of stock, rather than assets, is generally preferable to the target firm shareholders to avoid double taxation, if the target firm is structured as a C corporation. Various taxable and tax-free structures, including both statutory mergers (two-party transactions) and triangular mergers (three-party transactions), are summarized in Table 12-1. The structure of transactions that create an immediate tax liability for the target's shareholders is discussed next, followed by those structures that enable such taxes to be deferred to a later date. For a detailed discussion of the application of the tax code to M&As, see PricewaterhouseCoopers (2006); CCH Tax Law Editors (2005); Hurter, Petersen, and Thompson (2005); Ginsburg and Levin (2004); Tillinghast (1998).

Taxable Transactions Are Those Immediately Taxable to Target Shareholders

A transaction generally will be considered taxable to the seller or target firm's shareholder if it involves the purchase of the target's stock or assets for substantially all cash, notes, or some other nonequity consideration. In this type of transaction, the term cash often is synonymous with the use of notes or other nonequity consideration as part of or as the entire purchase price. Using the term cash to represent all forms of nonequity

TABLE 12-1   Alternative Taxable and Nontaxable Structures

Taxable Transactions:	Nontaxable Transactions:
Immediately Taxable to Target Shareholders	Tax Deferred to Target Shareholders
1. Purchase of assets with cash	1. Type A reorganization (statutory stock merger or consolidation)
2. Purchase of stock with cash	
3. Statutory cash merger or consolidation	2. Type B reorganization (stock for stock)
4. Triangular statutory cash mergers	3. Type C reorganization (stock for assets)
a. Forward	4. Triangular statutory stock mergers
b. Reverse	a. Forward
	b. Reverse

payment, such transactions may take the form of a cash purchase of target assets, a cash purchase of target stock, a statutory cash merger or consolidation, or a triangular statutory cash merger. In a triangular cash merger, the target firm may either be merged into an acquirer's operating or shell acquisition subsidiary with the subsidiary surviving (i.e., a forward triangular cash merger) or the acquirer's subsidiary is merged into the target firm with the target surviving (i.e., a reverse triangular cash merger).

The major advantages of using a triangular structure are limitations of the voting rights of acquiring shareholders and that the acquirer gains control of the target through a subsidiary without being directly responsible for the target's known and unknown liabilities. Recall that the acquiring firm is not required to get shareholder approval if the stock used to purchase the target represents less than 20% of the firm's total shares outstanding. However, this advantage may be nullified if the stock is newly issued and if the firm's bylaws require such approval. Hostile transactions frequently start as cash tender offers (i.e., taxable transactions); however, they may later be structured as tax free if the target's board is willing to support the proposed takeover.

The sale of a capital asset held for more than 1 year creates a long-term capital gain and is, for sellers other than C corporations, taxed at a much lower rate. If the taxable gain occurs from a capital asset held for less than 1 year, it is as short-term capital gain, which is generally taxed like ordinary income. C corporations are subject to identical federal income tax rates on their ordinary and capital gain income, so whether the capital gain is short- or long-term is irrelevant from the standpoint of taxes. It is generally very important and most often required that the buyer and seller agree on the allocation of the sales price among the assets being sold, since the allocation will determine the potential tax liability that would be incurred by the seller but that could be passed on to the buyer through the terms of the sales contract.

Taxable Purchase of Target Assets with Cash

If a transaction involves a cash purchase of target assets, the target company's tax cost or basis in the acquired stock or assets is increased or "stepped up" to their fair market value (FMV), which is equal to the purchase price paid by the acquirer. The resulting additional depreciation and amortization in future years reduces the present value of the tax liability of the combined companies. The target firm realizes an immediate gain or loss on assets sold equal to the difference between the FMV of the asset and the asset's adjusted tax basis (i.e., book value adjusted for depreciation).

The target's shareholders could be taxed twice, once when the firm pays taxes on any gains and a second time when the proceeds from the sale are paid to the shareholders either as a dividend or distribution following liquidation of the corporation. A liquidation of the target firm may occur if a buyer acquires enough of the assets of the target causing it to cease operations. To compensate the target company shareholders for any tax liability they may incur, the buyer usually will have to increase the purchase price (Ayers, Lefanowicz, and Robinson, 2003). Buyers are willing to do this only if the present value of the tax savings resulting from the step-up of the target's assets is greater than the increase in the purchase price required to compensate the target's shareholders for the increase in their tax liability.

There is little empirical evidence that the tax shelter resulting from the ability of the acquiring firm to increase the value of acquired assets to their FMV is a highly important motivating factor for a takeover (Auerbach and Reishus, 1988, pp. 69–88). However, taxable transactions have become somewhat more attractive to acquiring firms since 1993, when a change in legislation allowed acquirers to amortize intangible assets qualifying under Section 197 of the Internal Revenue Service Code. Such assets include goodwill, going concern value, assembled workforce, books and records, customer lists, licenses, permits, franchises, and trademarks. A "197" intangible must be amortized over 15 years for tax purposes. Moreover, the current tax code allows operating losses (including those resulting from the write-down of impaired goodwill) to be used to recover taxes paid in the preceding 2 years and to reduce future tax liabilities up to 20 years. The treatment of net operating loss carry backs and carry forwards is discussed in more detail later in this chapter in a section entitled "Net Operating Losses (NOLs)."

Taxable Purchase of Target Stock with Cash

Taxable transactions often involve the purchase of the target's voting stock, because the purchase of assets automatically will trigger a taxable gain for the target if the FMV of the acquired assets exceeds the target firm's tax basis in the assets. All stockholders are affected equally in a taxable purchase of assets, because the target firm is paying the taxes. In contrast, in a taxable stock purchase, double taxation does not occur as the transaction takes place between the acquirer and the target firm's shareholders. Therefore, the target firm does not pay any taxes on the transaction. The effect of the tax liability will vary depending on the individual shareholder's tax basis.

The target firm does not restate (i.e., revalue) its assets and liabilities for tax purposes to reflect the amount that the acquirer paid for the shares of common stock. Rather, the tax basis (i.e., their value on the target's financial statements) of assets and liabilities of the target before the acquisition carries over to the acquirer after the acquisition. This represents a potential problem for the buyer in a purchase of stock, since the buyer loses the additional tax savings that would result from acquiring assets and writing them up to fair market value. The loss of the resulting deductions of depreciation and amortization means the government will fund less of the buyer's purchase price through future tax savings. Consequently, the buyer may want to reduce what it is willing to pay to the seller.

Section 338 Election

The acquirer and target firms can jointly elect Section 338 of the Internal Revenue Code and thereby record assets and liabilities at their fair market value for tax purposes. According to Section 338 of the U.S. tax code, a purchaser of 80% or more of the stock of the target may elect to treat the acquisition as if it were an acquisition of the target's assets for tax purposes. This enables the acquiring corporation to avoid having to transfer assets and obtain consents to assignment of all contracts (as would be required in a direct purchase of assets), while still benefiting from the write-up of assets. By not being viewed as a transfer of assets, asset transfer, sales, and use taxes may be avoided. However, the 338 election generates an immediate tax liability for the target firm, which is viewed by the IRS as an "old" corporation selling its assets to a "new" corporation. Consequently, the target must recognize and pay taxes on any gains of the sale of assets. To compensate for the immediate tax liability, the target firm may demand a higher selling price.

Triangular Cash-Out Mergers

The IRS generally views forward triangular cash mergers as a purchase of target assets followed by a liquidation of the target for which target shareholders will recognize a taxable gain or loss as if they had sold their shares. Having in effect sold its operating assets, the target firm is frequently liquidated. Because the target firm ceases to exist, its tax attributes in the form of any tax loss carry forwards or carry backs or investment tax credits do not carry over to the acquirer. However, its assets and liabilities do transfer as it is a merger. Taxes are paid by the target firm on any gain on the sale of its assets and again by shareholders who receive a liquidating dividend. With the merger, no minority shareholders remain as all shareholders are required to accept the terms of the merger, although dissident shareholders may have appraisal rights for the stock they are required to sell. See Figure 12-1.

In contrast, the IRS treats the reverse triangular cash merger as a purchase of target shares, with the target firm, including its assets, liabilities, and tax attributes, surviving. Consequently, the cash is only taxed once when the target firm shareholders pay taxes on any gain on the sale of their stock. However, if the acquirer and target agree to invoke a 338 election (i.e., treating a stock purchase as a purchase of assets), the target will have to pay taxes on any gains on assets written up to their fair market value. As a result of the 338 election, the IRS treats the purchase of target shares as a taxable purchase of assets which can be stepped up to fair market value. See Figure 12-2. Table 12-2 summarizes the key characteristics of taxable transaction structures.

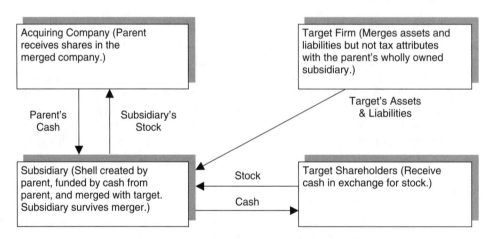

FIGURE 12-1   Forward triangular cash merger.

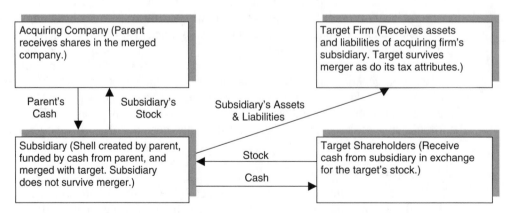

FIGURE 12-2   Reverse triangular cash merger.

TABLE 12-2 Key Characteristics of Alternative Taxable (to Target Shareholders) Transaction Structures

Transaction Structure	Form of Payment	Acquirer Retains Tax Attributes of Target	Target Survives?	Parent Exposure to Target Liabilities	Shareholder Vote Required?		Minority Freeze Out?	Automatic Transfer of Contracts?[1]
					Acquirer	Target		
Purchase of Stock	Mostly cash, debt, or other non-equity payment	Yes, but no asset step-up without 338 election[2]	Yes	High	No[4]	No, but shareholder may not sell shares	No	Yes
Purchase of Assets	Mostly cash, debt, other non-equity payment	No, but can step-up assets	Perhaps[3]	Low, except for assumed liabilities	No[4]	Yes, if sale of assets is substantial	No minority created	No
Statutory Merger or Consolidation	Mostly cash, debt, or other non-equity payment	Yes	No	High	No[4]	Yes	Yes[5]	Yes
Forward Triangular Cash Merger (Treated as an asset purchase by IRS as target generally liquidated)	Mostly cash, debt, or other non-equity payment	No	No	Low—limited by subsidiary	No[4]	Yes	Yes	No
Reverse Triangular Cash Merger (Treated as a stock purchase by IRS)	Mostly cash, debt, or other non-equity payment	Yes	Yes	Low—limited by subsidiary	No[4]	Yes	Yes	Yes

Notes:
[1] Contracts, leases, licenses, and rights to intellectual property automatically transfer unless contracts stipulate consent to assignment required.
[2] An acquirer may treat a stock purchase as an asset purchase if it and the target agree to invoke a Section 338 (of the Tax Code) election. However, the tax on any gain from writing up the acquired assets to FMV is likely to be paid by the buyer.
[3] The target may choose to liquidate if the sale of assets is substantial; to distribute the proceeds to its shareholders; or to continue as a shell.
[4] May be required by public stock exchanges or by legal counsel if deemed material to the acquiring firm or if the parent needs to authorize new stock. In practice, most big mergers require shareholders approval.
[5] Target shareholders must accept terms due to merger, although in some states dissident shareholders have appraisal rights for their shares.

Tax-Free Transactions Defer Tax to Target Firm Shareholders

As a general rule, a transaction is tax-free if the form of payment is primarily acquirer's stock. Transactions may be partially taxable if the target shareholders receive some nonequity consideration, such as cash or debt, in addition to the acquirer's stock. This nonequity consideration or **boot** is taxable if paid as a dividend to all shareholders, and it is taxed as ordinary income.

Acquirers and targets planning to enter into a tax-free transaction will frequently seek to get an **advance ruling** from the IRS to determine its tax-free status. This is a binding formal ruling from the IRS. However, the certainty of the formal letter may diminish if any of the key assumptions underlying the transaction change prior to closing. Moreover, the process of requesting and receiving a letter may take 5 or 6 months. Alternatively, acquirers may rely on the opinion of trusted legal counsel.

If the transaction is tax free, the acquiring company is able to transfer or carry over the target's tax basis to its own financial statements. In the tax-free transaction, there is no increase or step-up in assets to FMV. A tax-free reorganization envisions the acquisition of all or substantially all of a target company's assets or shares. Consequently, the tax-free structure is generally not suitable for the acquisition of a division within a corporation.

Continuity of Interests and Continuity of Business Enterprise Requirements

Under the law, tax-free transactions contemplate substantial continuing involvement of the target company's shareholders. To demonstrate continuity of interests (COI), target shareholders must continue to own a substantial part of the value of the combined target and acquiring firms. To demonstrate continuity of business enterprise (COBE), the acquiring corporation must either continue the acquired firm's "historic business enterprise" or use a significant portion of the target's "historic business assets" in a business. This continued involvement is intended to demonstrate a long-term or strategic commitment on the part of the acquiring company to the target. Nontaxable or tax-free transactions usually involve mergers, with the acquirer's stock exchanged for the target's stock or assets. Nontaxable transactions also are called **tax-free reorganizations**. The purpose of the continuity of interests' requirement is to prevent transactions that more closely resemble a sale from qualifying as a tax-free reorganization.

Avoiding the Loss of Tax-Free Status

Tax-free reorganizations generally require that all or substantially all of the target company's assets or shares be acquired. The divestiture of a significant portion of the acquired company immediately following closing could jeopardize the tax-free status of the transaction. Such an action would run counter to the Internal Revenue Service's (IRS) notion that the acquirer is making a long-term strategic commitment to the entire business for the transaction to be tax free. The loss of tax-free status can be avoided by spinning off the unwanted business to the target's shareholders in a tax-free exchange. The target then is merged into a subsidiary of the acquirer in a tax-free statutory merger. Tax-free reorganizations also require that substantially all of the consideration received by the target's shareholders be paid in common or preferred stock. However, if the preferred stock is redeemable or has a dividend that is indexed to interest rates, the IRS could view it as debt and disallow the tax-free status.

Alternative Tax-Free Reorganizations

The eight principal forms of tax-free reorganizations are described in Section 368 of the Internal Revenue Code. Three are excluded from our discussion. These include Type D, transfers between related corporations; Type E, the restructuring of a firm's capital structure; and Type F, a reorganization in which the firm's name or location is changed. What follows is a discussion of the Type A reorganization involving statutory mergers and consolidations, the Type B reorganization involving a stock-for-stock purchase, the Type C reorganization entailing a stock-for-assets purchase, and the forward and reverse triangular subsidiary mergers in which the acquiring company creates a shell subsidiary as an intermediary to complete the transaction.

Type A and B are the most common tax-free reorganizations for mergers in which a combination of stock, cash, or debt is used to acquire the target's stock or assets. Forward and reverse triangular mergers are used primarily when the acquirer stock is the predominate form of payment used to purchase the target's stock or assets. Since the IRS requires that target shareholders continue to hold a substantial equity interest in the acquiring company, the tax code defines what constitutes a substantial equity interest. The definition varies with the type of tax-free reorganization used. Reorganizations under the tax code may be wholly (all stock) or partially tax free (stock and other nonequity consideration). Triangular mergers are commonly used for tax-free transactions.

Type A reorganizations are statutory mergers or consolidations governed by state law. To qualify for a Type A reorganization, the transaction must be either a merger or a consolidation. There are no limitations on the type of consideration involved. Target company shareholders may receive cash, voting or nonvoting common or preferred stock, notes, or real property. Moreover, target shareholders do not have to be treated equally in that some may receive all stock, others all cash, and others a combination of the two. The acquirer may choose not to purchase all of the target's assets. At least 40% of the purchase price must be acquiring company stock to ensure that the IRS's continuity of interests' requirement is satisfied.

For target company shareholders receiving acquiring company shares, no taxable gain or loss is recognized at the time of the transaction, and the basis in the target shares carries over to the shares received from the acquiring company. Any taxable gain is deferred until the acquiring firm's shares are sold.

Type A reorganizations are used widely as a result of their great flexibility. Because there is no requirement to utilize voting stock, acquiring firms enjoy more options. By issuing nonvoting stock, the acquiring corporation may acquire control over the target without diluting control over the combined or newly created company. Moreover, there is no maximum amount of cash that may be used in the purchase price, and the limitations articulated by both the IRS and the courts allow significantly more cash than Types B or C reorganizations. Flexibility with respect to the amount of cash being used may be the most important consideration, because it enables the acquirer to better satisfy the disparate requirements of the target's shareholders. Some will want cash, and some will want stock. The acquirer must be careful that not too large a proportion of the purchase price be composed of cash, because this might not meet the IRS's requirement for continuity of interests of the target shareholders and disqualify the transaction as a Type A reorganization.

In a ***Type B stock-for-stock reorganization***, the acquirer, using its voting common stock, must purchase an amount of voting stock that comprises at least 80% of the voting power of all voting stock outstanding (recall that some voting shares may have multiple voting rights). In addition, the acquirer must purchase at least 80% of each class of nonvoting shares. Any cash or debt will disqualify the transaction as a Type B reorganization. However, cash may be used to purchase fractional shares. Type B reorganizations are used as an alternative to a merger or consolidation. Following the merger, the target may be liquidated into the acquiring company or maintained as an independent operating subsidiary. The transaction also may be phased over a certain period. The target's stock may be purchased over 12 months or less as part of a formal acquisition plan. Only stock may be used to acquire the target, although the acquirer may have used cash to purchase some portion of the target's stock in the past as long as it was not part of the acquisition plan. Type B reorganizations may be appropriate if the acquiring company wishes to conserve cash or its borrowing capacity. Since shares are being acquired directly from shareholders, there is no need for a target shareholder vote. Finally, contracts, licenses, etc., transfer with the stock, thereby obviating the need to receive consent to assignment, unless specified in the contract.

A ***Type C stock-for-assets reorganization*** requires that at least 80% of the FMV of the target's assets, as well as the assumption of certain specified liabilities, are acquired solely in exchange for acquirer voting stock. Since the cash portion of the purchase price must be reduced by assumed liabilities (which are viewed by the IRS as equivalent to cash), cash may be used to purchase the remainder of the stock only if the assumed liabilities amount to less than 20% of the FMV of the acquired assets. Since assumed liabilities frequently exceed 20% of the FMV of the acquired assets, the form of payment as a practical matter is generally 100% stock.

As part of the plan of reorganization, the target subsequent to closing dissolves and distributes the acquirer's stock to the target's shareholders for the now-canceled target stock. The Type C reorganization is used when it is essential for the acquirer not to assume any undisclosed liabilities. It is technically more difficult than a merger because all of the acquired assets must be conveyed. In a merger, all assets (and liabilities) pass by rule of law. The requirement to use only voting stock is also a major deterrent to the use of this type of reorganization. While a purchase of assets will allow the acquirer to step up the basis of the acquired assets, asset purchases will result in the target recognizing a taxable gain if the purchase price exceeds the firm's tax basis in the assets. If the target is liquidated to enable the firm to pay the sale proceeds to its shareholders, target shareholders will then have to pay taxes of such payouts. The potential for double taxation will generally make the purchase of stock more attractive than an asset purchase. In contrast to a stock-for-stock reorganization in which the target remains a wholly owned subsidiary of the buyer, the stock-for-assets reorganization will result in the assessment of sales, use, and other transfer taxes.

A ***forward triangular merger*** is the most commonly used form of reorganization for tax-free asset acquisitions in which the form of payment is acquirer stock. It involves three parties: the acquiring firm, the target firm, and a shell subsidiary of the acquiring firm (Figure 12-3). As with the forward triangular cash merger described earlier, the parent funds the shell corporation by buying stock issued by the shell with its own stock. All of the target's stock is acquired by the subsidiary with the stock of the parent, and the target's stock is canceled, with the acquirer subsidiary surviving. The target company's assets and liabilities are merged into the acquirer's subsidiary in a statutory merger. The parent's stock may be voting or nonvoting, and the acquirer must purchase substantially all of the target's assets and liabilities. Substantially all is defined as 90% of the fair

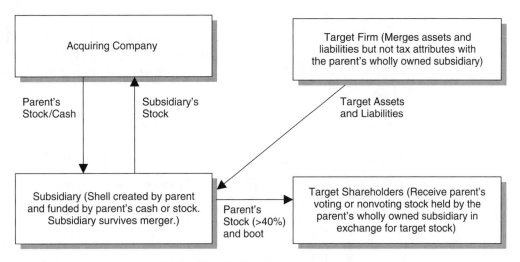

FIGURE 12-3   Forward triangular stock merger.

market value of the target's net assets (i.e., assets minus liabilities). According to new rules announced by the IRS in 2006, the substantially all requirement may not apply if a so-called "disregarded unit" such as a limited liability company is used as the acquiring subsidiary and the target firm (structured as a C corporation) ceases to exist. As such, no limitations would be placed on the amount of target net assets that would have to be acquired in order to qualify as a tax-free reorganization. This is explained in more detail later in this chapter.

Asset sales by the target firm just prior to the transaction may threaten the tax-free status of the deal. Moreover, tax-free deals are disallowed within 2 years of a spin-off. The IRS imposes these limitations to preclude sellers from engaging in restructuring activities that make them more attractive to potential acquirers which might be willing to consummate a tax-free deal if the size of the target firm were smaller. At least 40% of the purchase price must consist of acquirer stock, with the remainder consisting of boot tailored to meet the needs of the target's shareholders. The transaction qualifies as a Type A tax-free reorganization. The parent indirectly owns all of the target's assets and liabilities, because it owns all of the subsidiary's voting stock.

The advantages of the forward triangular merger may include the avoidance of approval by the parent firm's shareholders. However, public exchanges on which the parent firm's stock trades still may require parent shareholder approval if the amount of the parent stock used to acquire the target exceeds some predetermined percentage of parent voting shares outstanding. Other advantages include the possible insulation of the parent from the target's liabilities, which remain in the subsidiary, and the avoidance of asset recording fees and transfer taxes, because the target's assets go directly to the parent's wholly owned subsidiary.

The *reverse triangular merger* most commonly is used to effect tax-free stock acquisitions in which the form of payment is predominately the acquirer's voting stock (Figure 12-4). The acquirer forms a new shell subsidiary, which is merged into the target in a statutory merger. The target is the surviving entity and must hold substantially all of the assets and liabilities of both the target and shell subsidiary. Substantially all is generally defined as at least 90% of the FMV of net assets. The target firm's shares are canceled. The target shareholders receive the acquirer's or parent's shares. The parent

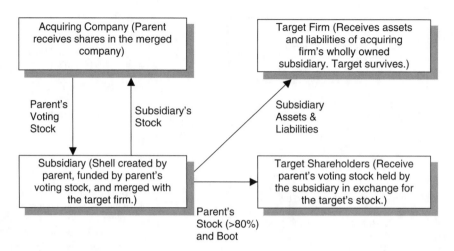

FIGURE 12-4   Reverse triangular stock merger.

corporation, which owned all of the subsidiary stock, now owns all of the new target stock and indirectly all of the target's assets and liabilities. To qualify as a tax-free transaction, at least 80% of the total consideration paid to the target must be in the form of the acquirer's parent voting stock. This stock may be common or preferred equity. Like the forward triangular merger, a reverse triangular merger precludes asset sales or spin-offs just prior to the completion of the transaction. This transaction qualifies as a Type A tax-free reorganization. Note that, unlike a forward triangular merger, the substantially all requirement cannot be circumvented by merging an LLC created by a parent corporation with a target C Corporation and exchanging parent stock for target stock.

Although the reverse triangular merger is similar to a Type A reorganization in which the acquiring company purchases the target's stock in exchange for its stock, it permits the acquirer to use up to 20% cash. The reverse merger also may avoid the need for parent company shareholder approval. Because the target firm remains in existence, the target can retain any nonassignable franchise, lease, or other valuable contract rights. Also, the target's liabilities are isolated in a subsidiary of the acquirer. Moreover, by avoiding the dissolution of the target firm, the acquirer avoids the possible acceleration of loans outstanding. Finally, insurance, banking, and public utility regulators may require the target to remain in existence in exchange for their granting regulatory approval. See Table 12-3 for a summary of the key characteristics of alternative tax-free deal structures and Case Study 12-1 for an illustration of the various facets of deal structuring in a transaction in which Israel's Teva Pharmaceuticals merges with U.S.-based Ivax Corporation.

Expanding the Role of Mergers in Tax-Free Reorganizations

In late 2006, the IRS finalized regulations under Treasury Regulation Section 1.368-2 defining the term statutory merger or consolidation for purposes of using tax-free reorganizations. The new regulations offer more flexibility to businesses in using the statutory merger or consolidation with respect to transactions involving so-called "disregarded entities." Such entities include separate limited liability companies, a corporation that is a qualified real estate investment trust subsidiary, and a corporation that is a qualified subchapter S subsidiary, as well as transactions completed under the laws of foreign jurisdictions. The new rules apply to transactions taking place on or after January 22, 2006.

TABLE 12-3 Key Characteristics of Alternative Tax-Free (to Target Shareholders) Transaction Structures[1]

Transaction Structure (Type of Reorganization)	Form of Payment	Limitation[2]	Acquirer Retains Target Tax Attributes	Target Survives?	Parent Exposure to Target Liabilities	Shareholder Vote Required? Acquirer	Shareholder Vote Required? Target	Minority Freeze-Out?	Automatic Transfer of Contracts?[3]
Statutory Merger or Consolidation (Type A Reorganization)	At least 40% parent voting or non-voting stock	No limitations on target net assets purchased	Yes, but no asset step-up	No	High, unless merged into subsidiary[4]	No[6,7]	Yes	Yes	Yes
Forward Triangular Stock Merger (Type A Reorganization)	At least 40% parent voting or nonvoting stock	Must purchase as least 90% of FMV of net assets unless LLC acquiring subsidiary	Yes, but no asset step-up	No	Low, limited by subsidiary	No[6,7]	Yes	Yes	No
Reverse Triangular Stock Merger (Type A Reorganization)	At least 80% parent voting stock (common/preferred)	Must purchase at least 90% of FMV of net assets	Yes, but no asset step-up	Yes	Low, limited by subsidiary	No[6,7]	Yes	Yes	Target retains non-assignable contracts, etc.

continued

TABLE 12-3   continued

| Transaction Structure (Type of Reorganization) | Form of Payment | Limitation[2] | Acquirer Retains Target Tax Attributes | Target Survives? | Parent Exposure to Target Liabilities | Shareholder Vote Required? | | Minority Freeze-Out? | Automatic Transfer of Contracts?[3] |
						Acquirer	Target		
Purchase of Stock—Without a Merger (Type B Reorganization)	100% parent voting stock (common/ preferred)	Must purchase at least 80% of voting power and of nonvoting shares	Yes, but no asset step-up	Yes	Low, limited by subsidiary	No[6]	No, as shares bought directly from shareholders	No	Yes
Purchase of Assets (Type C Reorganization)	100% voting stock[8]	Must purchase at least 80% FMV of net assets	No and no asset step-up	No	Low,[5] except for assumed liabilities	No[6]	Yes, if sale of assets substantial	No minority created	No

Notes:

[1] Target shareholders are taxed at ordinary rates on any "boot" received (i.e., anything other than acquiring company stock).

[2] Asset sales or spin-offs 2 years prior (may reflect effort to reduce size of purchase) or subsequent to (violates continuity requirement) closing may invalidate tax-free status. Forward triangular mergers do not require any limitations on purchase of target net assets if a so-called "disregarded unit" such as an LLC is used as the acquiring entity and the target is a C corporation which ceases to exist as a result of the transaction.

[3] Contracts, leases, licenses, and rights to intellectual property automatically transfer with the stock unless contracts stipulate consent to assignment required. Moreover, target retains any non-assignable franchise, lease or other contract right, as long as target is the surviving entity as in a reverse triangular merger.

[4] Acquirer may be insulated from a target's liabilities as long as it is held in a subsidiary except for liabilities such as unpaid taxes, unfunded pension obligations, and environmental liabilities.

[5] The parent is responsible for those liabilities conveying with the assets such as warranty claims.

[6] May be required by public stock exchanges or by legal counsel if deemed material to the acquiring firm or if the parent needs to authorize new stock.

[7] Mergers are generally ill-suited for hostile transactions, because they require approval of both the target's board and shareholders.

[8] While cash may be used to pay for up to 20% of the FMV of net assets, it must be offset by assumed liabilities, making the purchase price usually 100% stock.

Case Study 12-1
Teva Pharmaceuticals Acquires Ivax Corp.

Teva Pharmaceutical Industries (Teva), the number one source of generic drugs in the United States, announced on July 25, 2005, that it would acquire Ivax Corp (Ivax) for about $7.4 billion to become the world's largest manufacturer of generic drugs. For Teva, based in Israel, and Ivax, headquartered in Miami, the merger eliminated a large competitor and created a distribution chain that spans 50 countries. The two firms will have combined annual revenues exceeding $7 billion.

Under the terms of the merger agreement, Ivax shareholders could elect to receive for each of their shares either of the following: (1) .8471 of American Depository Receipts (ADRs) representing Teva shares or (2) $26 in cash. This represents a 14.5% premium over Ivax's closing share price of $22.88 on the day of the announcement. ADRs represent the receipt given to U.S. investors for the shares of a foreign-based corporation held in the vault of a U.S. bank. Holders of ADRs are entitled to all dividends paid and capital gains associated with the stock. Ivax shareholders have the opportunity to receive a significant portion of the total consideration (i.e., purchase price) in cash, thereby receiving immediate liquidity and the remainder in Teva ADRs. By receiving Teva ADRs, Ivax shareholders will be able to participate in any future appreciation of Teva stock.

As a result of the merger, each previously outstanding share of Ivax common stock was canceled. Each canceled share represented the right to receive, at the election of the Ivax shareholders made at least 2 business days prior to the closing of the merger, either of these two payments options. The actual proportions of stock and cash received would depend on the proration clause in the merger agreement. This clause describes the method of allocating the payment of cash and stock to Ivax shareholders. The aggregate amount of cash to be paid by Teva and new Teva shares issued would be adjusted according to the terms of the merger agreement so that 50% of Ivax common stock would be converted into cash. The remaining 50% of Ivax common stock would be converted into Teva shares according to the share-exchange ratio of .8471 Teva ADRs per Ivax share. See Case Study 11-4 in Chapter 11 for a detailed description of how the proration clause used in the merger agreement between Chevron and Unocal was constructed.

The merger agreement also provided for the acquisition of Ivax by Teva through a merger of Merger Sub, a newly formed and wholly owned subsidiary of Teva, with and into Ivax. As the surviving corporation, Ivax would be a wholly owned subsidiary of Teva. After the merger, Ivax shareholders will own 15% of the combined companies. The cash portion of the purchase price will be financed by Teva out of cash on hand and through its current lines of credit.

The merger involving the exchange of Teva ADRs for Ivax shares will be considered as tax-free under U.S. law. The possibility of a decrease in the value of Teva's ADRs between the date of execution of the merger agreement and the completion of the merger would lessen the value of the fixed number of Teva ADRs that comprise the stock portion of the total consideration. The merger agreement did not provide Ivax shareholders with any collar mechanism that would adjust the exchange ratio to compensate Ivax shareholders for the potential loss of value.

Case Study Discussion Questions

1. What are the legal forms of the acquisition vehicle and postclosing organization used in this transaction? In your judgment, why might these have been selected?
2. What type of merger structure [i.e., statutory cash or stock merger; triangular (forward or reverse) cash or stock merger] did Teva employ in this transaction? In your opinion, why was this structure chosen? (Hint: Consider such factors as the impact of taxes, potential liabilities, the value of the Ivax brand name, consents to assignment of contracts, etc.)
3. Why do you believe that Teva wanted to ensure that the proportion of Ivax shares converted to Teva stock would be limited to 50% and the remainder of the purchase price would be paid in cash? (Hint: Consider the impact of the form of payment on the merger structure and tax status, the potential impact of additional leverage on Teva's borrowing capacity, etc.)
4. Why is the merger considered nontaxable under U.S. law?

Under the new regulations, only the continuity of interests and the continuity of business enterprise tests and not the more restrictive substantially all requirement must be satisfied. Previously, two-party statutory Type A mergers offered greater flexibility than three-party transactions since they did not place any restriction on the amount of target net assets that could be acquired and allowed the use of nonvoting stock. In contrast, Type A triangular mergers generally require the purchase of at least 90% of the fair market value of the net assets of the target firm.

It is now possible for a merger of a corporation into a single-member (i.e., parent firm) limited liability company established by the parent corporation in a triangular merger to qualify as a two-party Type A merger. However, the target firm must be a C corporation that ceases to exist after the transaction is completed. As a two-party Type A statutory merger, there is no limitation on the amount of target net assets the buyer must acquire. Because three parties are involved in the forward triangular merger, the target firm can be operated as a subsidiary thereby insulating the parent from its liabilities. Furthermore, no vote of parent firm shareholders is required because the parent firm is the sole owner of the subsidiary unless the increase in shares issued to complete the transaction exceeds 20% of total parent shares outstanding. All of this can be accomplished without endangering the tax-free status of the transaction.

For years, the IRS had contended that a foreign corporation could not participate in a Type A tax-free reorganization because the term statutory merger referred only to a merger completed under the laws of the United States, a state, or the District or Colombia. With the advent of the new regulations, the merger of a foreign corporation into another foreign corporation (or the creation of a new corporation in a consolidation) in accordance with the host country's laws will qualify as a Type A reorganization. As such, the exchange would be tax free for any U.S. shareholders in the target firm receiving acquirer shares or shares in the new company formed as a result of the consolidation. The new regulations make it easier to qualify foreign acquisitions, both unrelated party transactions and internal restructurings and reorganizations, as Type A tax-free reorganizations. Therefore, if a U.S. firm buys a foreign firm having U.S. shareholders, the transaction can be structured so that the purchase is free of U.S. taxes to the U.S. shareholders.

Tax-Free Transactions Arising from 1031 "Like-Kind" Exchanges

The prospect of being able to defer taxable gains indefinitely is often associated with 1031 exchanges of real estate property. The potential benefits are significant, with capital gains taxes currently at 15% at the federal level and between 10 and 15% at the state level. Furthermore, depreciation recapture taxes (i.e., applied to the difference between accelerated and straight-line depreciation) also may be postponed with applicable federal income tax rates as high as 35% and some state income tax rates approaching 10%.

The concept involves selling one property and buying another subject to certain restrictions and time limitations. 1031 exchanges are relevant to M&As in that they represent a means of using "like-kind" assets to finance all or a portion of the purchase price of the target firm, while deferring the payment of taxes.

A section of the U.S. tax code known as 1031 allows investors to make a "like-kind" exchange of investment properties. A wide variety of investment properties can be swapped for others such as an apartment complex for land or an oil and gas property for a commercial strip mall. Investors can continue exchanging existing properties for new properties of equal or greater value, while deferring any tax consequences.

By postponing the tax payments, investors have more money to reinvest in new properties. For example, assume a property was purchased 10 years ago for $5 million and it is now worth $15 million. If the property were sold without any subsequent purchase of a substantially similar property within the required time period, the federal capital gains tax bill would be $1.5 million [i.e., ($15 − $5) × .15]. This ignores the potential for state taxes or depreciation recapture taxes, which could be owed if the owner took deductions for depreciation. However, by entering into a 1031 exchange, the owner could use the entire $15 million from the sale of the property as a down payment on a more expensive property. If the investor acquires a property of a lesser value, taxes are owed on the difference.

To qualify for a 1031 exchange, the property must be an investment property or one that is used in a trade or business (e.g., a warehouse, store, or commercial office building). Delayed exchanges are the most common means of implementing this type of a tax strategy. When a property is sold, a replacement property must be identified within 45 days of the closing. The deal for the replacement property must be closed within 180 days. An independent party known as a "qualified intermediary" must hold the proceeds of the sale until the next property is purchased. The intermediary cannot be a party directly involved in the transaction such as your real estate broker, lawyer, or accountant. Moreover, if the taxpayer were to take control of the proceeds of the sale, it would invalidate the "like-kind" exchange. Qualified intermediaries can be found by contacting the Federation of Exchange Accommodators (www.1031.org).

In a tax-free asset swap, News Corp. reached agreement in early 2007 to buy Liberty Media's 19% or $11 billion stake in the media giant in exchange for News Corp.'s 38.6% stake in satellite TV firm DirecTV Group, $550 million in cash, and three sports TV channels. While the two investments were approximately equal in price, Liberty's management believed that DirecTV's stock was inflated by speculation about the impending deal. The cash and media assets were added to ensure that Liberty Media is exchanging its stake in News Corp. for "like-kind" assets of an equivalent or higher value to qualify as a tax-free exchange. By structuring the deal in this manner, the transaction is viewed as an asset swap rather than a sale of assets, resulting in Liberty Media being able to save billions of dollars in taxes that would have been owed due to its low basis in its investment in News Corp. If the assets had been divested the two companies would have had to pay an estimated $4.5 billion in taxes due to likely gains on the sale of these assets (Angwin and Drucker, September 16, 2006).

Other Tax Considerations Affecting Corporate Restructuring Activities

Many areas of the tax code affect corporate restructuring activities. Treatment of net operating losses, corporate capital gains taxes, the alternative corporate minimum tax, the treatment of greenmail for tax purposes, and Morris Trust transactions are discussed in the next section of this chapter.

Net Operating Losses (NOLs)

Net operating loss carry backs and carry forwards are provisions in the tax laws allowing firms to use NOLs generated in the past to carry those losses back 2 years (to obtain a tax refund if those years were profitable) and forward 20 years to offset future taxable income. The Tax Reform Act of 1986 introduced an annual limit on the use of net operating loss (NOL) carry forwards. The limit takes effect if there is a greater than 50% change in ownership in a corporation generating cumulative losses during the 3 years preceding the change in ownership. Such corporations are referred to as loss corporations. The maximum amount of the NOL that can be used annually to offset earnings is limited to the value of the "loss corporation" on the date of the acquisition multiplied by the long-term tax-exempt bond rate. Furthermore, "loss corporations" cannot use a net operating loss carry forward unless they remain viable and in essentially the same business for at least 2 years following the closing of the acquisition.

Despite the limitations imposed by the tax code, NOLs may still represent a potentially significant source of value to acquirers that should be considered during the process of valuing an acquisition target. Lucent Technologies had accumulated numerous losses since the bursting of the Internet bubble in 2000. By acquiring Lucent in 2006, Alcatel obtained $3.5 billion in net operating losses that could be used to shelter future income for many years (Drucker and Silver, April 26, 2006). Exhibit 12-1 illustrates how the analyst might value NOLs on the books of a target corporation.

Exhibit 12-1
Valuing Net Operating Losses

Acquiring Company is contemplating buying Target Company, which has a tax loss carry forward of $8,000,000. Acquiring Company has a 40% marginal tax rate. Assume the tax loss carry forward is within the limits of the Tax Reform Act of 1986 and that the firm's cost of capital is 15%. The following information is given for the two firms:

Years Remaining in Loss Carry Forward	Amount ($000)	Years After Acquisition	Earnings Before Tax ($000)
1	2,000	1	1,800
2	2,000	2	2,000
3	800	3	1,000
4	1,200	4	1,000
5	800	5	2,000
Total	6,800	Total	7,800

Calculate Acquiring Company's tax payments without the acquisition.

Years	Tax Benefit
1	720
2	800
3	400
4	400
5	800

Calculate Acquiring Company's tax payment for each year with the proposed acquisition.

Years	Earnings Before Taxes ($000)	Tax Loss ($000)	Amount Carried Forward ($000)	Use of Tax Loss ($000)	Taxable Income ($000)	Tax Payment ($000)
1	1,800	2,000		1,800	0	0
2	2,000	2,000	200	2,000	0	0
3	1,000	800	0	1,000	0	0
4	1,000	1,200	200	1,000	0	0
5	2,000	800	0	1,000	1,000	400

What is the most the Acquiring Company should pay for the Target Company if its only value is its tax loss?

Answer: The Acquiring Company should not pay more than the present value of the net tax benefit: $720,000, $800,000, $400,000, $400,000, and $400,000. The present value of the cumulative tax benefits discounted at a 15% cost of capital is $1,921,580.

Notes:
1. Tax benefits are equal to earnings before tax times the 40% marginal tax rate of the Acquiring Company. Therefore, the tax benefit in year 1 is $1,800,000 × .4 = $720,000.
2. The net tax benefit in the fifth year is equal to the $800,000 tax benefit less the $400,000 in tax payments required in the fifth year.

Although NOLs represent a potential source of value, their use must be monitored carefully to realize the full value resulting from the potential for deferring income taxes. An acquirer must be highly confident that an expected future pretax income stream will be realized. Without the future income, the NOLs will expire worthless. Because the acquirer can never be certain that future income will be sufficient to fully realize the value of the NOLs, loss carry forwards alone rarely justify an acquisition. Studies show that it is easy to overstate the value of loss carry forwards because of the potential for them to expire before they can be fully used. Empirical analyses indicate that the actual tax savings realized from loss carry forwards tend to be about one-half of their expected value (Auerbach and Poterba, 1987).

Corporate Capital Gains Taxes

Since both short-term and long-term corporate capital gains are taxed as ordinary income and are subject to a maximum federal corporate tax rate of 35%, acquirers often adopt alternative legal structures having more favorable tax attributes in making acquisitions. These include master limited partnerships (MLPs), subchapter S corporations, and limited liability companies (LLCs). Profits distributed directly to MLP partners, subchapter S corporation shareholders, and LLC members are taxed at their personal tax rates. See Chapter 14 for a more detailed discussion of taxation concerning these types of so-called "pass-through" organizations.

Alternative Corporate Minimum Tax

Under certain circumstances in which corporate taxes have been significantly reduced, corporations may be subject to an alternative minimum tax with a flat rate of 20%. The introduction of the alternative minimum tax has proven to be particularly burdensome for leveraged buyouts. LBOs are by intent highly leveraged and have little if any taxable income because of their high annual interest expense. Consequently, the imposition of the alternative minimum tax reduced the potential returns to equity investors that could be achieved as a result of highly leveraged transactions. See Chapter 13 for a more detailed discussion of LBOs.

Greenmail Payments

Greenmail refers to payments made to "corporate raiders" to buy back positions they had taken in target companies (see Chapter 3). Greenmail was made more expensive by changes in the tax code, which sharply reduced the amount of such payments that could be deducted from before tax profits.

Morris Trust Transactions

So-called Morris Trust transactions tax code rules restrict how certain types of corporate deals can be structured to avoid taxes. Assume Firm A sells an operating unit to Firm B and makes a profit on the transaction on which it would owe taxes. To avoid the payment of taxes, Firm A spins off the operating unit as a dividend to its shareholders. The operating unit, still owned by Firm A's shareholders, is subsequently merged with Firm B. This causes shareholders in Firm A to become shareholders in Firm B. By spinning off the operating unit, Firm A was able to avoid the payment of corporate taxes on taxable gains and Firm A's shareholders were able to defer the payment of personal taxes on any gains until they sold their stock in Firm B.

To make such transactions less attractive, the tax code was amended in 1997 to require that taxes would not have to be paid only if no cash changed hands and if Firm A's shareholders end up as majority owners in Firm B. Without the maintenance of "continuity of ownership" in the operating unit, the IRS views this type of transaction as a sale having taken place. The practical effect of the requirement that Firm A maintain majority ownership is that merger partners such as Firm B in these types of transactions must be significantly smaller than Firm A. This reduces significantly the number of potential deal candidates.

The tax code was changed in 1997 in response to deals that were done on a tax-free basis that appeared to be sales in disguise. In some instances, parent companies would borrow money through a subsidiary and keep the money, while leaving responsibility for repaying the debt with the subsidiary. The subsidiary was then spun off to its shareholders. Later, the former subsidiary would be merged with another company. The cash was effectively transferred from the merger partner to the former parent company tax free, even if the parent would have earned a profit on the transaction if it had sold the business outright. (Note that if a corporation borrows funds, retains the funds, but later transfers responsibility for repayment to another entity, the funds are viewed as taxable income to the original borrower by the IRS.)

The change in the law has had a material impact on the way M&A business is conducted. For example, in 2005, Alltel announced it was getting rid of its local telephone business. Although Alltel had been in talks with phone companies, their size made the prospects of tax-free transaction more complicated. In the end, Alltel sold the business to a far smaller firm, Valor Communications Group Inc., to meet the requirements of the tax code.

Financial Reporting of Business Combinations

Historically, the two principal forms of accounting for financial reporting purposes for M&As were the pooling of interests and purchase accounting. A *pooling of interests* was defined as the representation of two formerly independent shareholder groups as a single group. Under a pooling of interests, the assets and liabilities of both companies were added together. Any transaction that could not qualify as a pooling of interests had to be accounted for using the purchase method.

In *purchase accounting*, the acquiring firm records the target at the actual purchase price. Acquisitions are viewed as conceptually similar to buying a single asset such as a piece of equipment. Acquired assets and assumed liabilities are revalued to their fair market value on the date of acquisition and recorded on the books of the acquiring company. When the buyer prepares consolidated statements, it allocates the purchase price to the fair value of the assets excluding liabilities acquired in the acquisition. The purchase price is first allocated to tangible and then to intangible assets. Any remaining excess of the purchase price over the target firm's net asset value (i.e., the fair market value of total identifiable acquired assets less assumed liabilities) is allocated to *goodwill*.

Effective December 15, 2001, new accounting rules promulgated by the Financial Accounting Standards Board Statements 141 and 142, an independent organization funded entirely by the private sector, changed the guidelines covering business combinations.

All M&As had to be accounted for using the purchase method. For an excellent discussion of financial reporting and statements analysis, see Stickney, Brown, and Wahlen (2007) and Gale and Morris (2006).

Impact of Purchase Accounting on Financial Statements

Goodwill no longer has to be amortized over its projected life, but it must be written off if it is deemed to have been impaired. Impairment reviews are to be taken annually or whenever the firm has experienced an event that materially affects the value of its assets. Such events could include the loss of key customer contracts, patent protection expiration, or the failure to achieve anticipated cost-saving synergies. FASB Statement 142 specifies that a long-term asset is *impaired* if its fair value falls below its book or carrying value. If this is the case, the firm is required to report a loss equal to the difference between the asset's fair value and its carrying value. The write-down of assets associated with an acquisition constitutes a public admission by the firm's management of having substantially overpaid for the acquired assets.

Since the new accounting rules requiring the use of purchase accounting for recording business combinations, auditors have increasingly required that factors underlying goodwill be tied to specific intangible assets such as customer lists, brand names, or assembled workforce. These intangible assets must be capitalized and shown on the balance sheet. Consequently, if the cash flows from a customer list have not materialized, the asset value of the customer list must be written off. Consequently, the creation of goodwill as a "catchall" estimate of the intangible value created by combining two businesses is less common today. Whenever possible, acquiring companies will strive to fully allocate the purchase price of acquired net assets so as to avoid the creation of goodwill.

Balance Sheet Considerations

For financial reporting purposes, the purchase price (PP) paid for the target company consists of the fair market value of total identifiable acquired tangible and intangible assets (FMV_{TA}), total acquired liabilities (FMV_{TL}), and goodwill (FMV_{GW}). The difference between FMV_{TA} and FMV_{TL} is called *net asset value*.

These relationships can be summarized as follows:

1. Allocation (distribution) of purchase price: $PP = FMV_{TA} - FMV_{TL} + FMV_{GW}$
2. Calculation of goodwill: $FMV_{GW} = PP - FMV_{TA} + FMV_{TL} = PP - (FMV_{TA} - FMV_{TL})$

Consequently, if an acquirer pays $26 million for a firm and the fair market value of the acquired tangible assets, intangible assets, and liabilities are $16, $8, and $6 million, respectively, goodwill is equal to $8 million (i.e., $26 - $16 - $8 + $6). From (2), it should be noted that as net asset value increases, FMV_{GW} decreases. Also note that from (2) the calculation of goodwill can result in either a positive (i.e., PP > net asset value), or negative (i.e., PP < net asset value). Negative goodwill arises if the acquired assets are purchased at a discount to their FMV. The specific methodology for valuing each major balance sheet category is discussed in Exhibit 12-2.

Exhibit 12-2

Valuation Methodology for Purchase Accounting

1. Cash and accounts receivable, reduced for bad debt and returns, are valued at their values on the books of the target before the acquisition.
2. Marketable securities are valued at their realizable value after any transaction costs.
3. Inventories are broken down into finished goods and raw materials. Finished goods are valued at their liquidation value; raw material inventories are valued at their current replacement cost. Last-in, first-out inventory reserves maintained by the target before the acquisition are eliminated.
4. Property, plant, and equipment are valued at FMV.
5. Accounts payable and accrued expenses are valued at the levels stated on the target's books before the acquisition.
6. Notes payable and long-term debt are valued at their net present value of the future cash payments discounted at the current market rate of interest for similar securities.
7. Pension fund obligations are booked at the excess or deficiency of the present value of the projected benefit obligations over the present value of pension fund assets. This may result in an asset or liability being recorded by the consolidated firms.
8. All other liabilities are recorded at their net present value of future cash payments.
9. Intangible assets are booked at their appraised values.
10. Goodwill is the difference between the acquisition purchase price less the fair market value of the target's net asset value. Positive goodwill is recorded as an asset, whereas negative goodwill is allocated to all long-lived acquired assets other than marketable securities.

Many assets, such as intangibles, are not specifically identified on the firm's balance sheet. In the United States, companies expense the cost of investing in intangibles in the year in which the investment is made. The rationale for immediately expensing such assets is the difficulty in determining whether a particular expenditure results in a future benefit (i.e., an asset) or not (i.e., an expense). For example, the value of the Coca-Cola brand name clearly has value extending over many years, but there is no estimate of this value on the firm's balance sheet.

Firms capitalize (i.e., value and display as assets on the balance sheet) the costs of acquiring intangible assets from others. The value of such assets can be ascertained from similar transactions made elsewhere. The acquirer must consider the future benefits of the intangible asset to be at least equal to the price paid. Specifically, identifiable assets must have a finite life. Firms must amortize the value of the asset over this estimated life span. Firms must periodically test the value of intangible assets that are amortized for impairment following a procedure similar to that used for goodwill. The test compares the "carrying value" (i.e., value as shown on the firm's financial statements) to the fair value of the intangible asset and requires recognition of an impairment loss whenever the carrying value exceeds the fair value.

The test for intangibles not requiring amortization (e.g., goodwill) is different from that of tangibles. The test for assets requiring amortization necessitates the comparison of the undiscounted cash flows of the asset to the assets carrying value. Intangibles not requiring amortization have an indefinite life and thus no defined period over which to project cash flows. Therefore, determining the fair value of goodwill is often difficult. It entails estimating the fair value of the reporting unit that resulted from a previously acquired firm to which the acquirer allocated a portion of the purchase price to goodwill. Generally, the reporting unit does not have shares trading on a public exchange. Firms often employ comparable industry measures to value the reporting unit.

Intangible assets can be classified into three categories: operational intangibles, production or product intangibles, and marketing intangibles (Table 12-4). Operational intangibles have been defined as the ability of a business to continue to function and generate income without interruption because of a change in ownership. Production or product intangibles are values placed on the accumulated intellectual capital resulting from the production and product design experience of the combined entity. Marketing intangibles are those factors that help a firm to sell a product or service. For tax and financial reporting purposes, goodwill is a residual item equal to the difference between the purchase price for the target company and net asset value, including operational, production, and marketing intangible assets. In most cases, intangible assets, like tangible assets, have separately determinable values with limited useful lives. In certain cases, the useful lives are defined by the legal protection afforded by the agency issuing the protection, such as the U.S. Patent Office. In contrast, the useful life of such intangible assets as customer lists is more difficult to define. The concepts and methodologies discussed in Chapters 7 and 8 may be applied to different types of intangible assets.

Exhibit 12-3 illustrates the balance sheet impacts of purchase accounting on the acquirer's balance sheet and the effects of impairment subsequent to closing. Assume that Acquirer Inc. purchases Target Inc. on December 31, 2006, for $500 million. The purchase price is allocated to all of the reporting unit's identifiable assets and liabilities, with any remaining excess considered as the fair value of goodwill. The fair value of the "reporting unit" (i.e., Target Inc.) is determined annually to ensure that its fair value exceeds its carrying value. As of December 31, 2007, it is determined that the fair value of Target Inc. has fallen below its carrying value due largely to the loss of a number of key customers.

TABLE 12-4   Intangible Asset Categories

Intangible Asset Categories	Examples
Operating Intangibles	Assembled and trained workforce
	Operating and administrative systems
	Corporate culture
Production or Product Intangibles	Patents
	Technological know-how
	Production standards
	Copyrights
	Software
	Favorable leases and licenses
Marketing Intangibles	Customer lists and relationships
	Price lists and pricing strategies
	Marketing strategies, studies, and concepts
	Advertising and promotional materials
	Trademarks and service marks
	Trade names
	Covenants not to compete
	Franchises

Exhibit 12-3
Balance Sheet Impacts of Purchase Accounting

Target Inc. 12/31/2006, Purchase Price Paid		$500,000,000
Fair Values of Target Inc.'s Net Assets @ 12/31/2006		
Current Assets	$40,000,000	
Plant and Equipment	200,000,000	
Customer List	180,000,000	
Copyrights	120,000,000	
Current Liabilities	(35,000,000)	
Long-Term Debt	(100,000,000)	
Value Assigned to Identifiable Net Assets		$405,000,000
Value Assigned to Goodwill		$ 95,000,000
Carrying Value as of 12/31/2006		$500,000,000
Fair Values of Target Inc.'s Net Assets @ 12/31/2007		$400,000,000
Current Assets	$30,000,000	
Plant and Equipment	175,000,000	
Customer List	100,000,000	
Copyrights	120,000,000	
Current Liabilities	(25,000,000)	
Long-Term Debt	(90,000,000)	
Value Assigned to Identifiable Net Assets		$310,000,000
Value Assigned to Goodwill		$ 90,000,000
Carrying Value After Impairment @12/31/2007		$400,000,000
Impairment Loss		$100,000,000

Income Statement and Cash-Flow Considerations

For financial reporting purposes, an upward valuation of tangible and intangible assets, other than goodwill, raises depreciation and amortization expenses, which lowers operating and net income. For tax purposes, goodwill created after July 1993 may be amortized up to 15 years and is tax deductible. Goodwill booked before July 1993 is not tax deductible. Cash flow benefits from the tax deductibility of additional depreciation and amortization expenses that are written off over the useful lives of the assets. This assumes that the acquirer paid more than the target's net asset value. If the purchase price paid is less than the target's net asset value, the acquirer records a one-time gain equal to the difference on its income statement. If the carrying value of the net asset value subsequently falls below its fair market value, the acquirer records a one-time loss equal to the difference.

International Accounting Standards

Ideally, financial reporting would be the same across the globe but that has not yet occurred. The discussion of financial reporting for business combinations is focused on the application of Generally Accepted Accounting Principles (GAAP) of the Financial Accounting Standards Board (FASB) in the United States. Many of the same challenges are addressed in the application of International Financial Reporting Standards of the International Accounting Standards Board (IASB). When comparing financial information for companies operating in multiple countries, it is important to achieve comparability of the reporting methods and accounting principles employed by the acquisition and merger targets.

The overarching objective of the IASB is the convergence of accounting standards worldwide and the establishment of global standards, sometimes referred to as "global GAAP." The IASB issues International Financial Reporting Standards (IFRS) and as of 2005 firms across the European Union must conform to IFRS directives. FASB and IASB have pledged that they will work diligently to ensure that GAAP and IFRS will be compatible as soon as practicable.

Non-U.S. firms that have debt or equity securities trading in the United States must either file a form 10K using GAAP or file a Form 20-F report with the U.S. Securities and Exchange Commission. The Form 20-F report must include a reconciliation of shareholders' equity and net income as reported in the firm's local country with GAAP in the United States. Such information enables the translation of the financial statements of a non-U.S. firm to achieve comparable accounting principles in the United States.

Things to Remember

Taxes are an important, but rarely an overarching, consideration in most M&A transactions. The deciding factor in any transaction should be whether it makes good business sense. Tax benefits simply provide an additional reason for doing the deal.

Transactions may be either partly or entirely taxable to the target firm's shareholders or tax free. A transaction generally will be considered taxable to the seller if the buyer uses mostly cash, notes, or some nonequity consideration to purchase the target's stock or assets. Conversely, the transaction is generally considered tax free, if mostly acquirer stock is used to purchase the stock or assets of the target firm. Tax-free transactions are also called tax-free reorganizations.

Tax considerations and strategies are likely to have an important impact on how a deal is structured by affecting the amount, timing, and composition of the price offered to a target firm. Moreover, tax factors are likely to affect how the combined firms are organized following closing, as the tax ramifications of a corporate structure are quite different from those of a limited liability company or partnership.

For financial reporting purposes, all M&As must be recorded using the purchase method of accounting. Under the purchase method of accounting, the excess of the purchase price over the target's net asset value is treated as goodwill on the combined firm's balance sheet. If the fair value of the target's net assets later falls below its carrying value, the acquirer must record a loss equal to the difference. The threat of this possibility may introduce additional discipline for public acquirers when negotiating with target company boards and management, since such an event would be a public admission that management had overpaid for past acquisitions.

Chapter Discussion Questions

12-1. When does the IRS consider a transaction to be nontaxable to the target firm's shareholders? What is the justification for the IRS' position?

12-2. What are the advantages and disadvantages of a tax-free transaction for the buyer? Be specific.

12-3. Under what circumstances can the assets of the acquired firm be increased to fair market value when the transaction is deemed a taxable purchase of stock?

12-4. When does it make sense for a buyer to use a Type A tax-free reorganization?

12-5. When does it make sense for a buyer to use a Type B tax-free reorganization?

12-6. What are net operating loss carry forwards and carry backs? Why might they add value to an acquisition?

12-7. Explain how tax considerations affect the deal-structuring process?

12-8. How does the purchase method of accounting affect the income statement, balance sheet, and cash-flow statements of the combined companies?

12-9. What is goodwill and how is it created?

12-10. Under what circumstances might an asset become impaired? How might this event affect the way in which acquirers bid for target firms?

Answers to these Chapter Discussion Questions are available in the Online Instructor's Manual for instructors using this book.

Chapter Business Case

Case Study 12-2
Boston Scientific Overcomes Johnson and Johnson to Acquire Guidant: A Lesson in Bidding Strategies

Background

Johnson and Johnson (J&J), the behemoth American pharmaceutical company, announced an agreement in December 2004 to acquire Guidant for $76 per share in a combination of cash and stock. Guidant is a leading manufacturer of implantable heart defibrillators and other products used in angioplasty procedures. The market for such defibrillators has been growing at 20% annually. J&J desired to reenergize its slowing growth rate by diversifying into the more rapidly growing medical stent market.

Soon after the agreement was signed, Guidant's defibrillators became embroiled in a regulatory scandal over failure to inform doctors about rare malfunctions. Guidant suffered a serious erosion of market share when it recalled five models of its defibrillators. Part of the risk in completing the takeover of Guidant is the potential jeopardy the company faces from federal investigations and civil lawsuits.

The apparent erosion in the value of Guidant prompted J&J to renegotiate the deal under a material adverse change clause common in most M&A agreements. Such clauses are predicated on a continuation of the target business without any significant changes that degrade value between the signing of the agreement and the actual closing. J&J was able to get Guidant to accept a lower price of $63 a share in mid-November. However, this new agreement was not without risk.

An Auction Emerges

The renegotiated agreement gave Boston Scientific an opportunity to intervene with a more attractive informal offer on December 5, 2005, of $72 per share. The offer price consisted of 50% stock and 50% cash. Boston Scientific, a leading supplier of heart stents, saw the proposed acquisition as a vital step in the company's strategy of diversifying into the high-growth implantable defibrillator market. Heart stents prop open arteries leading to the heart potentially preventing heart attacks; implantable defibrillators regulate heartbeats through a series of electrical impulses. The bid pitted Boston Scientific against its major competitor in the drug-coated stent market. The two firms have been embroiled in litigation over stent technology.

Despite the more favorable offer, Guidant board's decided to reject Boston Scientific's offer in favor of an upwardly revised offer of $71 per share made by J&J on January 11, 2005. The board continued to support J&J's lower bid, despite the furor it caused among big Guidant shareholders. With a market capitalization nine times the size of Boston Scientific, the Guidant board continued to be enamored with J&J's size and industry position relative to Boston Scientific. The board argued that a J&J combination would result in much more rapid growth than merging with the much smaller Boston Scientific.

Boston Scientific's Bidding Strategy

Boston Scientific realized that they would only be able to acquire Guidant if it made an offer that Guidant could not refuse without risking major shareholder lawsuits. Boston Scientific reasoned that if J&J hoped to match an improved bid that it would have to be at least $77, slightly higher than the $76 J&J had offered in its initial agreement with Guidant in December 2004. With its greater borrowing capacity, Boston Scientific knew that J&J also had the option of converting its combination stock and cash bid to an all-cash offer. Such an offer could be made a few dollars lower than Boston Scientific's bid since Guidant investors might view such an offer more favorably than one consisting of both stock and cash whose value could fluctuate between the signing of the agreement and the actual closing. This was indeed a possibility since the J&J offer did not include a collar arrangement.

Boston Scientific decided to boost the new bid to $80 per share, which it believed would deter any further bidding from J&J. J&J had been saying publicly that Guidant was already "fully valued." Boston Scientific reasoned that J&J had created a public relations nightmare for itself. If J&J raised its bid, it would upset J&J shareholders and make it look like an undisciplined buyer. According to the agreement it had with Guidant, J&J had 5 days to respond to the sweetened Boston Scientific bid. J&J refused to up its offer saying that such an action would not be in the best interests of its shareholders. Table 12-5 summarizes the key events timeline.

TABLE 12-5   Boston Scientific and Johnson and Johnson Bidding Chronolgy

Date	Comments
December 15, 2004	J&J reaches agreement to buy Guidant for $25.4 billion in stock and cash
November 15, 2005	Value of J&J deal is revised downward to $21.5 billion
December 5, 2005	Boston Scientific offers $25 billion
January 11, 2006	Guidant accepts a J&J counter offer valued at $23.2 billion
January 17, 2006	Boston Scientific submits a new bid valued at $27 billion
January 25, 2006	Guidant accepts the Boston Scientific bid when J&J fails to improve its offer

Abbot Labs Helps Seal the Deal

A side deal with Abbot Labs made the lofty Boston Scientific offer possible. The firm entered into an agreement with Abbott Laboratories in which Boston Scientific would divest Guidant's stent business, while retaining the rights to Guidant's stent technology. In return, Boston Scientific received $6.4 billion in cash on the closing date, consisting of $4.1 billion for the divested assets, a loan of $900 million, and Abbot's purchase of $1.4 billion of Boston Scientific stock. The additional cash helped fund the purchase price. This deal also helped Boston Scientific gain regulatory approval by enabling Abbot Labs to become a competitor in the stent business. Merrill Lynch and Bank of America are each lending $7 billion to fund a portion of the purchase price and to provide the combined firms with additional working capital.

Boston Scientific's Investors Express Nervousness

To complete the transaction, Boston Scientific paid $27 billion consisting of cash and stock to Guidant shareholders and another $800 million as a break-up fee to J&J. In addition, the firm is burdened with $14.9 billion in new debt. Within days of Boston Scientific's winning bid, the firm received a warning from the U.S. Food and Drug Administration to delay the introduction of new products until the firm's safety procedures improve. In the longer term, whether the deal earns Boston Scientific shareholders an appropriate return on their investments depends largely on the continued rapid growth in the defibrillator market and the outcome of civil suits surrounding the recall of Guidant products.

Between December 2004, the date of Guidant's original agreement with J&J, and January 25, 2006, the date of its agreement with Boston Scientific, Guidant's stock rose by 16% reflecting the bidding process. During the same period, J&J's dropped by a modest 3%, while Boston Scientific's shares plummeted by 32%, as investors fretted over the earnings outlook for the firm.

Epilogue

As a result of product recalls and safety warnings on more than 50,000 Guidant cardiac devices, the firm's sales and profits have plummeted. Between the announcement date of its purchase of Guidant in December 2005 and year-end 2006, Boston Scientific has lost more than $18 billion in shareholder value. The operations acquired in the Guidant transactions are not profitable and no recovery is anticipated until product quality problems are resolved. By year-end 2006 Boston Scientific's shares had dropped to the high teens, reflecting the enormous dilution of the firm's earnings per share. In acquiring Guidant, Boston Scientific increased its total shares outstanding by more than 80% and assumed responsibility for $6.5 billion in debt, without any proportionate increase in earnings. To add insult to injury, in late September 2006, Johnson and Johnson sued Boston Scientific, Guidant, and Abbott for $5.5 billion arguing that they had violated terms of J&J's deal with Guidant.

Case Study Discussion Questions

1. What might J&J have done differently to avoid igniting a bidding war?
2. What evidence is given that J&J may not have taken Boston Scientific as a serious bidder?
3. Explain how differing assumptions about market growth, potential synergies, and the size of the potential liability related to product recalls affected the bidding?

Answers to these Case Study Discussion Questions are available in the Online Instructor's Manual for instructors using this book.

Chapter Business Case

Case Study 12-3
JDS Uniphase–SDL Merger Results in Huge Write-Off

What started out as the biggest technology merger in history up to that point saw its value plummet in line with the declining stock market, a weakening economy, and concerns about the cash-flow impact of actions the acquirer would have to take to gain regulatory approval. The $41 billion megamerger, proposed on July 10, 2000, consisted of JDS Uniphase (JDSU) offering 3.8 shares of its stock for each share of SDL's outstanding stock. This constituted an approximate 43% premium over the price of SDL's stock on the announcement date. The challenge facing JDSU was to get Department of Justice (DoJ) approval of a merger that some feared would result in a supplier (i.e., JDS Uniphase–SDL) that could exercise enormous pricing power over the entire range of products from raw components to packaged products purchased by equipment manufacturers. The resulting regulatory review lengthened the period between the signing of the merger agreement between the two companies and the actual closing to more than 7 months. The risk to SDL shareholders of the lengthening of the time between the determination of value and the actual receipt of the JDSU shares at closing was that the JDSU shares could decline in price during this period.

Given the size of the premium, JDSU's management was unwilling to protect SDL's shareholders from this possibility by providing a "collar" within which the exchange ratio could fluctuate. The absence of a collar proved particularly devastating to SDL shareholders, which continued to hold JDSU stock well beyond the closing date. The deal that had been originally valued at $41 billion when first announced more than 7 months earlier had fallen to $13.5 billion on the day of closing.

The Participants
JDSU manufactures and distributes fiber-optic components and modules to telecommunication and cable systems providers worldwide. The company is the dominant supplier in

its market for fiber-optic components. In 1999, the firm focused on making only certain subsystems needed in fiber-optic networks, but a flurry of acquisitions has enabled the company to offer complementary products. JDSU's strategy is to package entire systems into a single integrated unit. This would reduce the number of vendors that fiber-optic network firms must deal with when purchasing systems that produce the light that is transmitted over fiber. SDL's products, including pump lasers, support the transmission of data, voice, video, and Internet information over fiber-optic networks by expanding their fiber-optic communications networks much more quickly and efficiently than would be possible using conventional electronic and optical technologies. SDL had approximately 1700 employees and reported sales of $72 million for the quarter ending March 31, 2000.

As of July 10, 2000, JDSU had a market value of $74 billion with 958 million shares outstanding. Annual 2000 revenues amounted to $1.43 billion. The firm had $800 million in cash and virtually no long-term debt. Including one-time merger-related charges, the firm recorded a loss of $905 million. With its price-to-earnings (excluding merger-related charges) ratio at a meteoric 440, the firm sought to use stock to acquire SDL, a strategy that it had used successfully in 11 previous acquisitions. JDSU believed that a merger with SDL would provide two major benefits. First, it would add a line of lasers to the JDSU product offering that strengthened signals beamed across fiber-optic networks. Second, it would bolster JDSU's capacity to package multiple components into a single product line.

Regulators expressed concern that the combined entities could control the market for a specific type of pump laser used in a wide range of optical equipment. SDL is one of the largest suppliers of this type of laser, and JDS is one of the largest suppliers of the chips used to build them. Other manufacturers of pump lasers, such as Nortel Networks, Lucent Technologies, and Corning, complained to regulators that they would have to buy some of the chips necessary to manufacture pump lasers from a supplier (i.e., JDSU), which in combination with SDL, also would be a competitor.

As required by the Hart–Scott–Rodino (HSR) Antitrust Improvements Act of 1976, JDSU had filed with the DoJ seeking regulatory approval. On August 24, the firm received a request for additional information from the DoJ, which extended the HSR waiting period. On February 6, JDSU agreed as part of a consent decree to sell a Swiss subsidiary, which manufactures pump laser chips, to Nortel Networks Corporation, a JDSU customer, to satisfy DoJ concerns about the proposed merger. The divestiture of this operation set up an alternative supplier of such chips, thereby alleviating concerns expressed by other manufacturers of pump lasers that they would have to buy such components from a competitor.

The Deal Structure

On July 9, 2000, the boards of both JDSU and SDL unanimously approved an agreement to merge SDL with a newly formed, wholly owned subsidiary of JDS Uniphase, K2 Acquisition, Inc. K2 Acquisition, Inc. was created by JDSU as the *acquisition vehicle* to complete the merger. In a *reverse triangular merger*, K2 Acquisition Inc. was merged into SDL, with SDL as the surviving entity. The *postclosing organization* consisted of SDL as a wholly owned subsidiary of JDS Uniphase. The *form of payment* consisted of exchanging JDSU common stock for SDL common shares. The *share-exchange ratio* was 3.8 shares of JDSU stock for each SDL common share outstanding. Instead of a fraction of a share, each SDL stockholder received cash, without interest, equal to dollar value of the fractional share at the average of the closing prices for a share of JDSU common stock for the 5 trading days before the completion of the merger.

Under the rules of the NASDAQ National Market, on which JDSU's shares are traded, JDSU is required to seek stockholder approval for any issuance of common stock to acquire another firm. This requirement is triggered if the amount issued exceeds 20% of its issued and outstanding shares of common stock and of its voting power. In connection with the merger, both SDL and JDSU received fairness opinions from advisors employed by the firms.

The merger agreement specified that the merger could be consummated when all of the conditions stipulated in the agreement were either satisfied or waived by the parties to the agreement. Both JDSU and SDL were subject to certain closing conditions. Such conditions were specified in the September 7, 2000, S4 filing with the SEC by JDSU, which is required whenever a firm intends to issue securities to the public. The consummation of the merger was to be subject to approval by the shareholders of both companies, the approval of the regulatory authorities as specified under the HSR, and any other foreign antitrust law that applied. For both parties, representations and warranties (statements believed to be factual) must have been found to be accurate and both parties must have complied with all of the agreements and covenants (promises) in all material ways.

The Aftermath of Overpaying

Despite dramatic cost-cutting efforts, the company reported a loss of $7.9 billion for the quarter ending June 31, 2001, and $50.6 billion for the 12 months ending June 31, 2001. This compares to the projected pro forma loss reported in the September 9, 2000, S4 filing of $12.1 billion. The actual loss was the largest annual loss ever reported by a U.S. firm up to that time. The fiscal year 2000 loss included a reduction in the value of goodwill carried on the balance sheet of $38.7 billion to reflect the declining market value of net assets acquired during a series of previous transactions. Most of this reduction was related to goodwill arising from the merger of JDS FITEL and Uniphase and the subsequent acquisitions of SDL, E-TEK, and OCLI.

The stock continued to tumble in line with the declining fortunes of the telecommunications industry such that it was trading as low as $7.5 per share by mid-2001, about 6% of its value the day the merger with SDL was announced. Thus, the JDS Uniphase–SDL merger was marked by two firsts—the largest purchase price paid for a pure technology company and the largest write-off (at that time) in history. Both of these infamous "firsts" occurred within 12 months.

Case Study Discussion Questions

1. What is goodwill? How is it estimated? Why did JDS Uniphase write down the value of its goodwill in 2001? Why did this reflect a series of poor management decisions with respect to mergers completed between 1999 and early 2001?
2. How might the use of stock, as an acquisition "currency," have contributed to the sustained decline in JDS Uniphase's stock through mid-2001? In your judgment what is the likely impact of the glut of JDS Uniphase shares in the market on the future appreciation of the firm's share price? Explain your answer.
3. What are the primary differences between a forward and a reverse triangular merger? Why might JDS Uniphase have chosen to merge its K2 Acquisition Inc. subsidiary with SDL in a reverse triangular merger? Explain your answer.
4. Discuss various methodologies you might use to value assets acquired from SDL such as existing technologies, "core" technologies, trademarks and trade names, assembled workforce, and deferred compensation?
5. Why do boards of directors of both acquiring and target companies often obtain so-called "fairness opinions" from outside investment advisors or accounting firms?

What valuation methodologies might be used in constructing these opinions? Should stockholders have confidence in such opinions? Why or why not?

Answers to these Case Study Discussion Questions are available in the Online Instructor's Manual for instructors using this book.

References

Angwin, Julia, and Jesse Drucker, "How News Corp. and Liberty Media Can Save $4.5 Billion," *The Wall Street Journal*, September 16, 2006, p. A3.

Auerbach, Alan J., and James Poterba, "Tax Loss Carry Forwards and Corporate Tax Incentives," in Martin Feldstein, ed., *The Effect of Taxation on Capital Accumulation*, University of Chicago Press, Chicago, 1987.

Auerbach, Alan J., and David Reishus, "Taxes and the Merger Decision," in John C. Coffee, Jr., Louis Lowenstein, and Susan Rose Ackerman, eds., *Knights, Raiders, and Targets*, Oxford University Press, New York, 1988, pp. 69–88.

Ayers, Benjamin C., Craig E. Lefanowicz, and John R. Robinson, "Shareholder Taxes in Acquisition Premiums: The Effect of Capital Gains Taxation," *Journal of Finance*, Vol. 58, Issue 6, December 2003, pp. 2783–2801.

CCH Tax Law Editors, *U.S. Master Tax Code*, Commerce Clearinghouse, Chicago, IL, 2005.

Drucker, Jesse, and Sara Silver, "Alcatel Stands to Reap Tax Benefits on Merger," *The Wall Street Journal*, April 26, 2006, p. C3.

Gale, William J., and Joseph M. Morris, *Mergers and Acquisition: Business Strategy for Accountants*, 2nd Ed., Cumulative Supplement, Wiley & Sons, Somerset, NJ, 2006.

Ginsburg, Martin D., and Jack S. Levin, *Mergers, Acquisitions and Buyouts: A Transactional Analysis of Governing Tax, Legal, and Accounting Considerations*, Aspen Publishers, New York, 2004.

Hurter, William H., Jeffrey R. Petersen, and Kenton E. Thompson, *Merger, Acquisitions, and 1031 Tax Exchanges*, Lorman Education Services, New York, 2005.

PricewaterhouseCoopers, *Mergers and Acquisitions: A Global Tax Guide*, Wiley & Sons, Somerset, NJ, 2006.

Stickney, Clyde P., Paul R. Brown, and James M. Wahlen, *Financial Reporting, Financial Statement Analysis, and Valuation*, 6th Ed., Southwestern, Thomson, GA, 2007.

Tillinghast, David R. "Tax Aspects of Inbound Merger and Acquisition and Joint Venture Transactions," in David J. Ben Daniel and Arthur H. Rosenbloom, eds., *International M&A, Joint Ventures, and Beyond: Doing the Deal*, Wiley & Sons, New York, 1998, pp. 151–164.

CHAPTER • 13

Financing Transactions

Private Equity, Hedge Funds, and Leveraged Buyout Structures and Valuation

A billion dollars isn't what it used to be.

—Nelson Bunker Hunt

Inside M&A: Cox Enterprises Offers to Take Cox Communications Private

In an effort to take the firm private, Cox Enterprises announced on August 3, 2004, a proposal to buy the remaining 38% of Cox Communications' shares that they did not currently own for $32 per share. The deal was valued at $7.9 billion and represented a 16% premium to Cox Communication's share price at that time. Cox Communications would become a subsidiary of Cox Enterprises and would continue to operate as an autonomous business. In response to the proposal, the Cox Communications Board of Directors formed a special committee of independent directors to consider the proposal. Citigroup Global Markets and Lehman Brothers Inc. committed $10 billion to the deal. Cox Enterprises would use $7.9 billion for the tender offer, with the remaining $2.1 billion used for refinancing existing debt and to satisfy working capital requirements.

Cable service firms have faced intensified competitive pressures from satellite service providers DirecTV Group and EchoStar communications. Moreover, telephone companies continue to attack cable's high-speed Internet service by cutting prices on high-speed Internet service over phone lines. Cable firms have responded by offering a broader range of advanced services like video-on-demand and phone service. Since 2000, the cable industry has invested more than $80 billion to upgrade their systems to provide such services, causing profitability to deteriorate and frustrating investors. In response, cable company stock prices have fallen. Cox Enterprises stated that the increasingly competitive cable industry environment makes investment in the cable industry best done through a private company structure.

511

Chapter Overview

The corporate takeover market (as described in Chapter 3) has been undergoing a dramatic change in recent years. Driving much of this change is the emergence of private equity and hedge funds, awash in low-cost financing, in pursuit of higher financial returns. Of the $1.56 billion and $3.78 billion of M&As in 2006 in the United States and worldwide, respectively, private equity and hedge funds accounted for 25% of the total in the United States and 27% globally. This compares to 10% of the total value of U.S. M&As and 6% of transactions worldwide in 2005, according to Thompson Financial. In 2006, such private equity and hedge funds raised $156 billion in new capital, bringing the total dollar value of monies to invest to more than $400 billion (Kirkland, 2007). Assuming an average debt-to-equity ratio of 5-to-1, this represents about $2 trillion dollars that could be used to make acquisitions. Much of this new money is being and will be used to finance highly leveraged transactions, commonly referred to as leveraged buyouts.

In a *leveraged buyout* (LBO), borrowed funds are used to pay for most of the purchase price. LBOs can be of an entire company or divisions of a company. Typically, the tangible assets of the firm to be acquired are used as collateral for the loans. The most highly liquid assets often are used as collateral for obtaining bank financing. Such assets commonly include receivables and inventory. The firm's fixed assets commonly are used to secure a portion of long-term senior financing. Subordinated debt, either unrated or low-rated debt, is used to raise the balance of the purchase price. This debt often is referred to as *junk bond* financing. When a public company is subject to an LBO, it is said to be *going private*, because the equity of the firm has been purchased by a small group of investors and is no longer publicly traded. Buyers of the firm targeted to become a leveraged buyout often consist of managers from the firm that is being acquired. The LBO that is initiated by the target firm's incumbent management is called a *management buyout* (MBO).

In recent years, private equity and hedge funds have exhibited increasing similarities. Both raise money from institutions such as pension funds and insurance companies and from wealthy individuals. Both use borrowed funds aggressively in their investment strategies. Private equity funds tend to make longer-term investments by taking companies private, often waiting years before realizing significant financial returns. Hedge funds tend to engage in more short-term trading. However, as noted in Chapter 1, more and more their investment strategies are converging. Some private equity and hedge funds raise funds in public markets. Hedge funds are increasingly willing to provide longer-term loans in financing leveraged buyouts. In 2006, 19 equity and hedge funds sold shares on foreign exchanges, raising $12.4 billion. On February 10, 2007, Fortress Investment Group LLC, which manages $30 billion, became the first private equity and hedge fund manager to sell shares on the U.S. equity markets (Zuckerman, Sender, and Patterson, February 10, 2007).

This chapter begins with a discussion of the evolution of LBOs in the context of the risks associated with alternative financing options from asset-based or secured lending to pure cash-flow-based lending. Subsequent sections discuss typical LBO structures, the risks associated with poorly constructed deals, how to take a company private, how to develop viable exit strategies, and the increasing role of private equity and hedge funds in highly leveraged transactions. The term "buyout firm" will be used throughout the chapter to include the variety of investor groups, such as private equity investors and hedge funds, which commonly engage in LBO transactions. Empirical studies of pre- and postbuyout returns to shareholders also are reviewed. The chapter concludes with a discussion of how to analyze and value LBO transactions and an example illustrating the methodology. A detailed Microsoft Excel-based LBO valuation and structuring model is available on the CD-ROM that accompanies this book. The model reflects the sophistication used by the professionals and may be customized by the reader to meet the unique characteristics of their situation. A review of this chapter is available on the CD-ROM accompanying this book.

The Emergence of the Financial Buyer

Investors in LBOs frequently are referred to as *financial buyers*, because they are primarily focused on relatively short- to intermediate-term financial returns. Financial buyers tend to concentrate on actions that enhance the target firm's ability to generate cash to satisfy their substantial debt service requirements. The existence of substantial leverage made the potential returns to equity much more attractive than less leveraged transactions (see Table 13-1).

Characteristics of LBOs in the Early 1980s

The number of LBO transactions in the United States remained relatively modest until the 1980s. In the early 1980s, debt was normally 4 to 5 times equity (Lehn and Poulsen, 1988). This implied typical debt-to-total capital ratios of 80 to 83% (i.e., if debt is 4 or 5 times equity, debt divided by debt plus equity is 4/5 and 5/6, respectively). Debt was likely to be amortized over a 5- to 7-year period and certainly no more than 10 years. The LBO firm generally was taken public or sold to a corporate buyer whenever the tax benefits provided by the leverage started to diminish. Existing corporate management was encouraged to participate as equity owners. The skill of the financial buyer during this period was largely in constructing a capital structure that would allow for the highest possible leverage while still enabling the firm to meet debt service requirements (i.e., interest and principal repayments) through improvements in operating performance. Secured debt

TABLE 13-1   Impact of Leverage on Return to Shareholders[1]

	All-Cash Purchase	50% Cash/ 50% Debt	20% Cash/ 80% Debt
Purchase Price	$100	$100	$100
Equity (Cash Investment)	$100	$ 50	$ 20
Borrowings	0	$ 50	$ 80
Earnings before Interest and Taxes	$ 20	$ 20	$ 20
Interest @ 10%	0	$ 5	$ 8
Income before Taxes	$ 20	$ 15	$ 12
Less Income Taxes @ 40%	$ 8	$ 6	$ 4.8
Net Income	$ 12	$ 9	$ 7.2
After-Tax Return on Equity	12%	18%	36%

Note:
[1] Unless otherwise noted, all numbers are in millions of dollars.

often comprised about 60% of the total purchase price with unsecured debt or junk financing accounting for about 20–25%. The remainder of the purchase price consisted of preferred and common equity (Roden and Lewellen, 1995).

LBOs in the Mid-to-Late 1980s

LBOs in the mid-to-late 1980s had many of the same characteristics of earlier LBOs, with two notable differences. First, debt was serviced from both operating cash flow and asset sales. Changes in the tax laws reduced the popularity of divesting assets to reduce leverage, because asset sales immediately on the closing of the transaction are no longer deemed tax free. Previously, it was possible to buy stock in a company and sell the assets, and any gain on asset sales was offset by an equivalent reduction in the value of the stock. This was made illegal as a result of the Tax Reform Act of 1986. The second half of the 1980s saw the emergence of the nontraditional sources of LBO financing from LBO funds and private equity investor partnerships. They provided both secured and unsecured financing. Their sources of funding came from large institutional investors such as life insurance companies and pension funds. These institutional investors also would lend directly to the LBO.

By the late 1980s, LBOs were viewed with greater skepticism than ever before by both government officials and the public. They were sometimes vilified as a means of enriching a few at the expense of many. Moreover, MBO proposals in particular were receiving increasing scrutiny from investors. The concern was that the interests of the senior managers who would receive equity in the MBO once completed were at odds with those of other investors (i.e., the so-called agency problem). Increasingly, the boards of firms targeted for MBOs would exclude senior managers directly involved in the takeover proposal from board meetings. Board committees consisting only of independent board members were established to invite other bidders. The hope was that all shareholders would receive a better deal in an auction environment.

While empirical evidence supports the view that LBOs improved overall efficiency of the target firms during the first half of the 1980s, the potential to improve operating efficiency was largely offset by the enormous amounts of debt taken on by target firms during the second half of the decade. Approximately one-third of the LBOs completed after 1985 defaulted on their debt (Holmstrom and Kaplan, 2001).

LBOs in the 1990s

From a peak of $66 billion, about one-fifth of total merger and acquisition (M&A) transactions in 1989, the total dollar volume of LBO transactions plummeted to $7 billion in 1991, about 5% of total transactions in that year. During the 5 years ending in 1999, LBOs averaged about 4% of the total dollar volume of M&As. The dollar value of LBOs tends to be small, averaging $40 million to $50 million, with many falling in the $4 million to $5 million range.

Lingering memories of the excesses of LBO financing, the resulting bankruptcies in the late 1980s, and a serious reduction of suitable candidates for such transactions precluded any significant resurgence of highly leveraged transactions during the decade of the 1990s. Reflecting the powerful equity markets of the period, the primary exit strategy during this decade was through stock offerings to the public. Debt-to-equity ratios were typically more conservative than during the 1980s. Deals often were structured so that debt repayment was not required until 10 years after the transaction was structured. This tended to reduce pressure on near-term earnings performance. The LBO firm's strategy was to enable the target firm to establish a period of escalating reported earnings to make it more attractive whenever it was ultimately taken public. Moreover, LBO firms often purchased a firm to use as a platform to undertake other leveraged buyouts in the same industry. The acquired firms then would be merged and taken public at a later date. Firms created through a series of acquisitions in the same industry are often referred to as "roll-ups."

A common technique used during the 1990s was to wait for favorable periods in the stock market to sell a portion of the LBO's equity to the public. The proceeds of the issue would be used to repay debt, thereby reducing the LBO's financial risk. Once the LBO's shares had traded for a few months, additional or secondary stock offerings often were made as the initial investors liquidated some portion of their equity positions. Whenever the firm had paid off a sufficient portion of its debt, a search was initiated for a strategic buyer willing to pay a premium to the LBO's investors to gain a controlling interest. In addition, LBO investors have become much more actively involved in managing target firms in recent years than they have in the past. Companies such as Clayton, Dubilier & Rice (CD&R) have tended to focus on targeting firms it viewed as having only marginally effective management. CD&R then would bring new management with considerable previous experience and establish compensation systems that tightly linked management's total compensation to the target's financial performance.

LBOs in the New Millennium

Probably the most remarkable developments in recent years are the explosion in the average size of and frequency of highly leveraged transactions, as well as their increasing risk. Seven of the 10 largest buyouts of all time were announced in 2006. Such deals are being driven by a world awash in savings, resulting in cheap financing and excess capacity in many industries encouraging consolidation among competitors. Deals in excess of $10 billion are becoming commonplace. In the 1980s and through most of the 1990s, a billion dollar deal was considered big. RJR Reynolds going private in 1988 was the biggest on record at $25 billion ($31 billion including assumed debt). This was narrowly eclipsed in 2006 when hospital chain operator, HCA, announced a leveraged buyout totaling $33 billion including debt. As a sign of the times, the HCA transaction was eclipsed in terms of size just 3 months later when private equity investor, the Blackstone Group, announced on November 21, 2006, that it had reached an agreement to acquire Equity Office Property Trust for $36 billion including assumed debt. Closing was scheduled for early 2007. On February 26, 2007, Texas-based electric utility TXU Corp. announced a new record setting LBO transaction valued at $45 billion, including assumed debt of $13.2 billion. The TXU transaction was notable not only for its size but also for the preconsultation that took place between the private equity buyers and environmental groups to gain support for approval by regulatory agencies.

In the largest management buyout in U.S. history at that time, Kinder Morgan Inc. management proposed to take the oil and gas pipeline firm private in 2006 in a transaction that valued the firm's outstanding equity at $13.5 billion. Under the proposal, Chief Executive Richard Kinder and other senior executives would contribute shares valued at $2.8 billion to the newly private company. An additional $4.5 billion would come from private equity investors including Goldman Sachs Capital partners, American International

Group Inc., and the Carlyle Group. Including assumed debt, the transaction is valued at about $22 billion. The transaction also was notable for the ethical issues that it raised (See Case Study 13-1).

Case Study 13-1
Kinder Morgan Buyout Raises Ethical Questions

SEC proxy filings following the announcement of the management buyout at the time revealed potentially questionable behavior by top management of Kinder Morgan Inc. The filings revealed that they waited 2 months before informing the firm's board of their desire to take the company private. The delay is particularly troublesome since it is the board that has the overarching fiduciary responsibility to protect shareholders interests. It is customary for boards governing firms whose managements were interested in buying out public share-holders to create a committee within the board consisting of independent board members (i.e., nonmanagement) to solicit other bids. While the Kinder Morgan board did eventually create such a committee, the board's lack of awareness of the pending management proposal gave management an important lead over potential bidders in structuring their proposal. The delay in telling the board also precluded the board from overseeing the process, which is generally considered the proper role of the board in such matters. By being involved early on in the process, a board has more time to negotiate terms more favorable to shareholders. The transaction also raises questions about the potential conflicts of interest of investment bankers who are hired to advise management and the board on the "fairness" of the offer price but who also are potential investors in the buyout.

Kinder Morgan's management hired Goldman Sachs in February 2006 to explore "strategic" options for the firm to enhance shareholder value. The leveraged buyout option was proposed by Goldman Sachs on March 7 and was later followed by their proposal to become the primary investor in the LBO on April 5, according to the proxy materials. Subsequently, the management buyout group hired a number of law firms and other investment banks as advisors and discussed the proposed buyout with credit-rating firms to assess how much debt the firm could support without experiencing a significant downgrade of its credit rating.

On May 13, 2006, the full board was finally made aware of the proposal. The board immediately demanded that a standstill agreement that had been signed by Richard Kinder, CEO and leader of the buyout group, not to talk to any alternative bidders for a period of 90 days be terminated. While investment banks and buyout groups often propose such an agreement to ensure that they can perform adequate due diligence, this extended period is not necessarily in the interests of the firm's shareholders because it puts alternative suitors coming in later at a distinct disadvantage. Later bidders simply will not have sufficient time to make an adequate assessment of the true value of the target and to structure their own proposals. In this way, the standstill agreement could discourage alternative bids for the business.

The special committee of the board set up to negotiate with the management buyout group was ultimately able to secure a $107.50 per share price for the firm, significantly higher than the initial offer. The discussions were rumored to have been very contentious due to the board's annoyance with the delay in informing them (Berman and Sender, 2006). The deal between the management group and the board was hammered out in about 2 weeks.

In contrast to the Kinder Morgan deal, a management group within HCA, a large U.S. hospital operator, took less than 1 month to inform its board of their interest in an LBO. The special committee of the board took 3 months to negotiate a deal with the firm's buyout group.

There is some evidence that the Sarbanes–Oxley Act of 2002 has also been a factor in some firms going private in recent years as a result of the onerous reporting requirements of the bill. This has been a particular burden to smaller firms. Some studies estimate that the cost of being a public firm was more than $14 million in 2004, almost twice the cost incurred in the prior year (Engel, Hayes, and Xang, 2004; Hartman, 2005; Kamar, Karaca-Mandic, and Talley, 2006). Reflecting concern over the burden on small firms, Sarbanes–Oxley requirements were relaxed for firms with market values of less than $75 million as of December 15, 2007.

The explosion of LBO activity has been accompanied by a substantial rise in risk. More than one-half of the loans in so-called highly leveraged transactions carry S&P's single B rating. According to S&P, a single B rated firm has a more than 13% chance of defaulting on their loans within 3 years. The average debt burden of companies owned by LBO private equity firms has climbed to about 8 times EBITDA. This compares to 4 times EBITDA for the average transaction during the 2000–2002 period (Sender, June 13, 2006). Moreover, buyout firms are actively pursuing targets that would have once been considered too risky because of their relatively unpredictable cyclical cash flows. For example, a private equity group, led by the Blackstone Group, announced that it had reached an agreement in late 2006 to acquire Freescale Semiconductor for $17.6 billion, for the largest ever LBO in the technology sector.

The growth in LBO activity is not simply a U.S. phenomenon. Western Europe has seen a veritable explosion in private equity investors taking companies private, reflecting ongoing liberalization in the European Union as well as cheap financing and industry consolidation. In the United Kingdom, LBOs accounted for half of the total M&A activity (as measured by value) in 2005 (Wright, Renneboog, Simons, and Scholes, 2006). In 2006, a large European telephone company, TDC AS of Denmark, agreed to be acquired for $12 billion ($15.6 billion including assumed debt) by a group of private equity investors. This LBO transaction is the largest ever in Europe. Globally, buyouts, valued at about $700 billion, reached almost 2700 in 2006.

While some private equity partnerships were taking firms private, others were "cashing out." For example, the Blackstone Group and two other firms paid themselves $450 million in dividends in early 2004 only 2 months after they had acquired water-treatment firm Ondeo Nalco for $4.2 billion. Seven months after having acquired Hertz Corp. from Ford, CD&R, along with Merrill Lynch Global Private Equity (MLGPE), announced plans in July 2006 for an initial public offering. About the same time, CD&R and MLGPE had Hertz borrow $1 billion to pay a special dividend, enabling them to recover nearly one-half of the $2.3 billion in cash they had invested in acquiring Hertz.

To finance the increased average size of targets taken private in 2006, buyout firms started to bid for target firms as groups of investors. The increased tendency of buyout firms to invest as a group is often referred to as "clubbing." The HCA, SunGard, and Kinder Morgan transactions all involved at least four private equity investor funds. While mitigating risk, banding together to buy large LBO targets has also made buyout firms vulnerable to accusations of colluding in an effort to limit prices offered for target firms.

Alternative Financing Options

Once a prospective target has been identified, the buyer has a number of financing options. For the risk-adverse acquirer, the ideal mechanism might be to finance the transaction out of cash held by the target in excess of normal working capital requirements. Such situations are usually very difficult to find. Venture capital or so-called angel investors also may be available to fund the transaction. However, this may represent very expensive financing, because the buyer may have to give up as much as 70% of the ownership of the acquired company. Use of the buyer's stock may be an appropriate way to minimize the initial cash outlay, but such an option is rarely available in an MBO or a buyout by privately held companies. The seller may be willing to accept debt issued by the buyer if an up-front cash payment is not important. This may be highly disadvantageous to the buyer if the seller places substantial restrictions on how the business may be managed. The use of a public issue of long-term debt to finance the transaction may minimize the initial cash outlay, but it is also subject to restrictions placed on how the business may be operated by the investors buying the issue. Moreover, public issues are expensive in terms of administrative, marketing, and regulatory reporting costs. For these reasons, asset-based lending has emerged as an attractive alternative to the use of cash, stock, or public debt issues if the target has sufficient tangible assets to serve as collateral. Exhibit 13-1 summarizes the key elements venture capitalists, private equity investors, angel investors, and others look for in determining which investments are most attractive.

Exhibit 13-1

What Equity Investors Look for in Deciding Which Businesses to Finance

Private equity investors, hedge funds, venture capitalists, and angel investors review literally thousands of business plans annually before making decisions. For the firm seeking equity capital, it is crucial that they know what such investors typically look for before making the decision to invest.

1. Sound Management: Investors want to see a complete management team, with sufficient experience to demonstrate competence.
2. Focus: Investors prefer to see a management team that is reasonably focused on a single or relatively few products that will lead to more "follow-on" products to ensure long-term growth.
3. Practical Technology or Product: Management must be able to demonstrate that people will be willing to pay for what they are selling.

4. Market Analysis: The potential market should be big enough to result in an acceptable financial return to investors, yet small enough to be definable.

5. Competition: While having a few competitors may help educate the market, few investors are willing to invest in a business with well-established competitors.

6. Assumptions-Based Projections: The projections need to show that a tremendous return is possible when based on realistic assumptions. The assumptions underlying the projections should be clearly defined. LBO firms often seek financial returns on their equity investments in the 20 to 40% range (Baker and Smith, 1998).

7. Vision: The management team must have a long-term view.

8. Risk Estimate: Potential risks should be clearly identified, with contingency plans in place to mitigate risks should they arise.

9. Exit Strategy Offering Appropriate Returns: A variety of ways for investors to cash out of the business should be provided, ranging from IPOs, recapitalization (i.e., a second round of borrowing to pay out a special dividend to investors once the debt acquired to finance the purchase has been reduced significantly), or sale to a strategic investor or private equity firm.

10. Referrals: A referral from a knowledgeable person in the investment community directs the entrepreneur to the right potential investors and indicates that the firm has passed an initial screening.

Source: Adapted from Shuttleworth (2004).

Asset-Based or Secured Lending

Under asset-based lending, the borrower pledges certain assets as collateral. Asset-based lenders look at the borrower's assets as their primary protection against the borrower's failure to repay. Such loans are often short term (i.e., less than 1 year in maturity) and secured by assets that can be liquidated easily, such as accounts receivable and inventory. Borrowers often seek *revolving lines of credit* that they draw upon on a daily basis to run their business. Under a revolving credit arrangement, the bank agrees to make loans up to a specified maximum for a specified period, usually a year or more. As the borrower repays a portion of the loan, an amount equal to the repayment can be borrowed again under the terms of the agreement. In addition to interest on the notes, the bank charges a fee for the commitment to hold the funds available. For a fee, the borrower may choose to convert the revolving credit line into a term loan. A *term loan* usually has a maturity of 2 to 10 years and is usually secured by the asset that is being financed, such as new capital equipment.

Acquiring firms generally prefer to borrow funds on an unsecured basis because the added administrative costs involved in pledging assets as security significantly raise the total cost of borrowing. Secured borrowing also can be onerous because the security agreements can severely limit a company's future borrowing. However, in many instances, borrowers may have little choice but to obtain secured lending for at least a portion of the purchase price. Asset-based lenders generally require personal guarantees from the buyer, in which the buyer is pledging such personal assets as their principal residence. This is especially true in small transactions if the buyer does not have a demonstrated track record in buying and operating businesses.

Loan Documentation

The lending process entails the negotiation of a loan agreement, security agreement, and promissory note. The *loan agreement* stipulates the terms and conditions under which the lender will loan the firm funds. The *security agreement* specifies which of the borrower's assets will be pledged to secure the loan. The *promissory note* commits the borrower to repay the loan, even if the assets when liquidated do not fully cover the unpaid balance. These agreements contain certain security provisions and protective covenants limiting what the borrower may do as long as the loan is outstanding. The security agreement is filed at a state regulatory office in the state where the collateral is located. Future lenders can check with this office to see which assets a firm has pledged and which are free to be used as future collateral. The filing of this security agreement legally establishes the lender's security interest in the collateral. If the borrower defaults on the loan or otherwise fails to honor the terms of the agreement, the lender can seize and sell the collateral to recover the value of the loan. The process of determining which of a firm's assets are free from liens is made easier today by commercial credit-reporting repositories such as Dun & Bradstreet, Experian, Equifax, and Transunion.

Pledging Receivables and Inventory

Depending on the extent to which they are collectable, lenders may lend as much as to 80–90% of the book value of the receivables. Asset-based lenders generally are willing to lend against only those receivables that are due within 90 days; that are more than 90 days past due are those that are likely to be difficult to collect.

Inventories are also commonly used to provide collateral for LBO transactions. As is true of receivables, inventories are often highly liquid. Inventory consists of raw material, work-in-process, and finished goods. Lenders normally consider only raw material and finished goods inventories as suitable collateral. The amount that a lender will advance against the book value of inventory depends on its ease of identification, liquidity, and marketability. In general, lenders will loan between 50 and 80% of the value of inventory, lending less if the inventory is viewed as perishable, subject to rapid obsolescence, or as having relatively few potential buyers.

Pledging Equipment and Real Estate to Support Term Loans

Borrowers often prefer term loans because they can be structured in such a way that the term of the loan corresponds with the economic life of the item being financed. Durable equipment and real estate often are used to secure loans. Lenders are frequently willing to lend up to 80% of the appraised value of equipment and 50% of the value of land. Term loans sometimes are used in LBO transactions to reduce the overall cost of borrowing. Because term loans are negotiated privately between the borrower and the lender, they are much less expensive than the costs associated with floating a public debt or stock issue.

Security Provisions and Protective Covenants

Security provisions and protective covenants in loan documents are intended to ensure that the interest and principal of outstanding loans will be repaid in a timely fashion. The number and complexity of security provisions depends on the size of the firm. Loans to small firms tend to be secured more often than term loans to large firms.

Security Provisions

Typical security features include the assignment of payments due under a specific contract to the lender, an assignment of a portion of the receivables or inventories, and a pledge of marketable securities held by the borrower. Other features could include a mortgage on property, plant, and equipment held by the borrower and the assignment of the cash surrender value of a life insurance policy held by the borrower on key executives.

Covenants

An *affirmative covenant* is a portion of a loan agreement that specifies the actions the borrowing firm agrees to take during the term of the loan. These typically include furnishing periodic financial statements to the lender, carrying sufficient insurance to cover insurable business risks, and maintaining a minimum amount of net working capital. A *negative covenant* restricts the actions of the borrower. They include limiting the amount of dividends that can be paid, the level of salaries and bonuses that may be given to the borrower's employees, and the total amount of indebtedness that can be assumed by the borrower. The borrower also may be required to obtain the lender's approval before certain assets can be sold or businesses acquired.

Default Provisions

All loan agreements have default provisions permitting the lender to collect the loan immediately under certain conditions. These conditions might include the borrower failing to pay interest, principal, or both in accordance with the terms of the loan agreement; the borrower materially misrepresenting information on the firm's financial statements; and the borrower failing to observe any of the affirmative or negative covenants. Loan agreements also commonly have *cross-default provisions* allowing a lender to collect its loan immediately if the borrower is in default on a loan to another lender.

Cash-Flow or Unsecured Lenders

Cash-flow lenders view the borrower's future cash-flow generation capability as the primary means of recovering a loan and the borrower's assets as a secondary source of funds in the event of default by the borrower.

Loans from such lenders often are unsecured. Unsecured debt often is referred to as *mezzanine financing*. Such debt lies between senior debt and the equity layers. It includes senior subordinated debt, subordinated debt, bridge financing, and LBO partnership financing. It frequently consists of high-yield junk bonds, which may also include zero coupon deferred interest debentures (i.e., bonds whose interest is not paid until maturity) used to increase the postacquisition cash flow of the acquired entity. In liquidation, it lies between the secured or asset-based debt and preferred and common equity. Unsecured financing often consists of several layers of debt, each subordinate in liquidation to the next most senior issue.

Bridge financing consists of unsecured loans provided by investment banks to provide short-term "bridge" financing pending the placement of subordinated debt (i.e., long-term or "permanent" financing). Bridge financing is usually expected to be replaced 6 to 9 months after the closing date of the LBO transaction.

Types of Long-Term Financing

Long-term debt generally is classified according to whether it is secured or not. **Secured debt** issues usually are called mortgage bonds or equipment trust certificates. Issues not secured by specific assets are called **debentures**. Because debentures are unsecured, their quality depends on the general creditworthiness of the issuing company. The attractiveness of long-term debt is its relatively low after-tax cost as a result of the tax deductibility of interest. In addition, leverage can help improve earnings per share and returns on equity. However, too much debt can increase the risk of default on loan repayments and bankruptcy.

Senior and Junior Debt

Long-term debt issues also are classified by whether they are senior or junior in liquidation. Senior debt has a higher priority claim to a firm's earnings and assets than junior debt. Unsecured debt also may be classified according to whether it is subordinated to other types of debt. In general, subordinated debentures are junior to other types of debt, including bank loans, and even may be junior to all of a firm's other debt. The extent to which a debt issue is junior to other debt depends on the restrictions placed on the company by the purchasers of the issue in an agreement called an indenture.

Indentures

An **indenture** is a contract between the firm that issues the long-term debt securities and the lenders. The indenture details the nature of the issue, specifies the way in which the principal must be repaid, and specifies affirmative and negative covenants applicable to the long-term debt issue. Typical covenants include maintaining a minimum interest coverage ratio, a minimum level of working capital, a maximum amount of dividends that the firm can pay, and restrictions on equipment leasing and issuing additional debt (Emery and Finnerty, 1992).

Seller Financing

A sometimes-overlooked source of financing is to have the seller agree to carry a promissory note for some portion of the purchase price. This may be especially important when the buyer is unable to finance the bulk of the purchase price and is unwilling or unable to put in more equity capital. Seller financing may be used as a means of "closing the gap" on the purchase price. Such financing generally is unsecured. If the business being purchased is part of a larger parent company, the borrower may be able to obtain certain concessions from the parent. For example, the parent may be willing to continue to provide certain products and services to the business at cost to increase the likelihood that the business is successful and that its note will be repaid in a timely fashion.

Bond Ratings

Debt issues are rated by various rating agencies according to their relative degree of risk. These agencies include Moody's Investors Services and Standard & Poor's (S&P) Corporation. Factors considered by these agencies when assessing risk include a firm's earnings stability, interest coverage ratios, the relative amount of debt in the firm's capital structure, the degree of subordination of the issue being rated, and the firm's past performance in meeting its debt service requirements. Each rating agency has a scale for identifying the risk of an issue. For Moody's, the ratings are Aaa, Aa, A, Baa, Ba, B, Caa, Ca, and C, with Aaa the lowest and C the highest risk category. AAA denotes the lowest risk category for S&P. This rating is followed by AA, A, BBB, BB, B, CCC, CC, C, and D.

Junk Bonds

Junk bonds are high-yield bonds either rated by the credit-rating agencies as below investment grade or not rated at all. Noninvestment grade bonds usually are rated Ba or lower by Moody's or BB or lower by S&P. When originally issued, junk bonds frequently yield more than 4 percentage points above the yields on U.S. Treasury debt of comparable maturity. Junk bond financing exploded in the 1980s. Although junk bonds were a popular source of financing for takeovers, about three-fourths of the total proceeds of junk bonds issued between 1980 and 1986 were used to finance the capital requirements of high-growth corporations (Yago, 1991). The remainder was used to finance corporate takeovers. This source of LBO financing dried up as a result of a series of defaults of overleveraged firms in the late 1980s, coupled with alleged insider trading and fraud at such companies as Drexel Burnham, the primary market maker for junk bonds. The collapse of several large savings and loans, which had been major investors in junk bonds, and the onslaught of the 1990–1991 recessions compounded these problems.

The rapid growth of the junk bond market coincided with a growing deterioration in the quality of such issues. Wigmore (1994) found that the quality of the junk bonds issued during the 1980s deteriorated in terms of such measures as interest coverage ratios (i.e., earnings before interest and taxes/interest expense), debt/net tangible book value, and cash flow as a percentage of debt. Cumulative default rates for junk bonds issued in the late 1970s reached as high as 34% by 1986 (Asquith, Mullins, and Wolff, 1989). Despite these high default rates, some portion of the face value of the junk bond issues often was recovered because firms formerly in default emerged from bankruptcy. Altman and Kishore (1996) found that recovery rates for senior secured debt averaged about 58% of the original principal. Taking recovery rates into consideration, they found the actual realized spread between junk bonds and 10-year U.S. Treasury securities was actually about 2 percentage points between 1978 and 1994 rather than more than 4 percentage points when they were issued originally.

Leveraged Loans and Collateralized Loan Obligations

In the United States, almost $500 billion in high-yield or leveraged loans were issued in 2006 compared to about $127 billion in junk bonds (Koons, January 13, 2007). In the European Union, the leveraged loan market also surpassed the junk bond market in size in 2006. *Leveraged loans* include second mortgages, which typically have a floating rate and give lenders a lower level of security than first mortgages. Nonetheless, such loans are often less costly than junk bonds because they often provide a higher level of security than unsecured junk bonds. Some analysts include other forms of debt instruments in this market such as mezzanine or senior unsecured debt, discussed earlier in this chapter, and *payment-in-kind notes*, for which interest is paid in the form of more debt. Globally, the syndicated loan market (which includes leveraged loans, senior unsecured debt, and payment-in-kind notes) is growing more rapidly than public markets for debt and equity. Syndicated loans are those typically issued through a consortium of institutions including hedge funds, pension funds, and insurance companies to individual borrowers. Since such lending usually avoids the public debt markets, it often is referred to as the "private debt market."

Similar to mortgage backed securities, **collateralized loan obligations** (CLOs) represent loans (including leveraged, senior unsecured debt, and payment-in-kind notes) that are packaged into pools from which different securities are created to sell to investors. While the loans are typically unrated or have received a low credit rating, the securities that are created from such pools are of investment grade. This is due to the dispersion of risk among a broadly diversified loan portfolio and as a result of the creation of different rankings or tranches of securities, each of which represents a different level of risk. Investors in the highest ranking tranche have first claim on interest and principal payments made on the loans in the portfolio, with those in lower ranked tranches paid only after those in higher tranches have been compensated. Reflecting their willingness to shoulder additional risk, those at the bottom of the ranking also earn the highest returns, reaching 13 to 14% (more than 2½ times the return on U.S. Treasury securities of comparable maturities) at the end of 2006. Investors in the lowest tranches often include insurance companies and hedge funds.

CLOs are making capital cheaper for companies by lowering the risk for lenders as such high-risk loans can be packaged with other loans, thereby achieving some degree of diversification, and more readily sold than individual loans. Therefore, banks can generate fee income for originating the loans and use the proceeds from their sale to make additional loans. By carving up the loan pool into different risk categories, CLOs have been able to attract both domestic and foreign insurance companies, pension funds, and other investors seeking to invest in securities exhibiting different levels of risk. For borrowers, bank loans often are preferable to bonds because loans often can be repaid whenever the borrower chooses rather than according to the fixed maturity schedule of the bond. This gives LBO investors greater flexibility in deciding when to exit their investment.

Other Sources of Funds

Unlike debt and preferred stock, which are fixed income securities, common stock is a variable income security. Common stockholders participate in the firm's future earnings, receiving a larger dividend if earnings increase. Like common stock, preferred stock is part of shareholders' equity. Although preferred stockholders receive dividends instead of interest payments, it is considered a fixed income security. Dividends on preferred stock are generally constant over time, like interest payments on debt. However, the firm is generally not obligated to pay dividends at a specific point in time. Unpaid dividends may cumulate for eventual payment by the issuer if the preferred stock is a special cumulative issue. In liquidation, bondholders are paid first, then preferred stockholders; common stockholders are paid last. Preferred stock often is issued in LBO transactions, because it provides investors a fixed income security, which has a claim that is senior to common stock in the event of liquidation. In order to conserve cash, LBOs frequently issue paid-in-kind (PIK) preferred stock, where the dividend obligation can be satisfied by issuing additional par amounts of the preferred security. Table 13-2 summarizes the key characteristics of an LBO's capital structure.

TABLE 13-2 Leveraged Buyout Capital Structure

Type of Security	Backed by	Debt — Lenders Loan Up to	Lending Source
Secured Debt —Short-Term (<1 Year) Debt	—Liens generally on receivables and inventories	—50–80% depending on quality	—Banks and finance companies
—Intermediate Term (1–10 Years) Debt	—Liens on land and equipment	—Up to 80% of appraised value of equipment and 50% of real estate	—Life insurance companies, private equity investors, pension and hedge funds
Unsecured or Mezzanine Debt (Subordinated and Junior Subordinated Debt, Including Seller Financing) —First Layer —Second Layer —Etc. Bridge Financing Payment-in-Kind	Cash generating capabilities of the borrower	Face value of securities	Life insurance companies, pension funds, private equity, and hedge funds.
Equity			
Preferred Stock —Payment-in-Kind	Cash generating capabilities of the borrower		Life insurance companies, pension funds, hedge funds, and private equity investors
Common Stock	Cash generating capabilities of the borrower		Life insurance, pension, private equity, hedge, and venture capital funds

Managing Risk through Credit-Default Swaps

A credit-default swap is an insurance contract that is tied to or derived from an underlying asset such as a corporate bond. Such arrangements are called financial derivatives. A buyer of the swap pays an annual fee for such a derivative. If the bond issuer defaults, the losses will be paid by the seller of the contract. The cost of such contracts rises as the likelihood of default of the underlying debt increases. The domestic and foreign credit-default markets have grown to more than $17 trillion in recent years as such contracts have been written on trillions of dollars of debt (Scannell, Ng, and MacDonald, August 31, 2006). Credit-default swaps do not trade on major exchanges but rather "over the counter," tending to be negotiated privately over the telephone.

Credit-default swap derivatives were created by banks and others to manage their risks by shifting the risk associated with default from the buyer of the debt to those willing to accept that risk for a fee. Consequently, the market has grown rapidly as it efficiently distributes risk between investors who are largely risk adverse to those wiling to accept more risk. Credit-default swaps have become increasingly popular among hedge funds that are active in either directly financing highly leveraged transactions or in earning fees for accepting some portion of the risk from banks and other institutions providing permanent financing for such deals. Hedge funds are estimated to account for as much as 56% of the trading in these derivatives (Fisher, October 16, 2006). See Case Study 13-2 for a description of what buyout firms look for in an LBO target and how such firms and their lenders attempt to manage LBO risk.

Case Study 13-2
Private Equity Firms Acquire Yellow Pages Business

Qwest Communications agreed to sell its yellow pages business, QwestDex, to a consortium led by the Carlyle Group and Welsh, Carson, Anderson and Stowe for $7.1 billion. In a two-stage transaction, Qwest sold the eastern half of the yellow pages business for $2.75 billion in late 2002. This portion of the business included directories in Colorado, Iowa, Minnesota, Nebraska, New Mexico, South Dakota, and North Dakota. The remainder of the business, Arizona, Idaho, Montana, Oregon, Utah, Washington, and Wyoming, was sold for $4.35 billion in late 2003. Caryle and Welsh Carson each put in $775 million in equity (about 21% of the total purchase price).

Qwest was in a precarious financial position at the time of the negotiation. The telecom was trying to avoid bankruptcy and needed the first-stage financing to meet impending debt repayments due in late 2002. Qwest is a local phone company in 14 western states and one of the nation's largest long-distance carriers. It had amassed $26.5 billion in debt following a series of acquisitions during the 1990s.

The Carlyle Group has invested globally, mainly in defense and aerospace businesses, but it has also invested in companies in real estate, health care, bottling, and information technology. Welsh Carson focuses primarily on the communications and health care industries. While the yellow pages business is quite different from their normal areas of investment, both firms were attracted by its steady cash flow. Such cash flow could be used to trim debt over time and generate a solid return. The business' existing management team will continue to run the operation under the new ownership. Financing for the deal will come from JP Morgan Chase, Bank of America, Lehman Brothers, Wachovia Securities, and Deutsche Bank. The investment groups agreed to a two-stage transaction to facilitate borrowing the large amounts required and to reduce the amount of equity each buyout firm had to invest. By staging the purchase, the lenders could see how well the operations acquired during the first stage could manage their debt load.

The new company will be the exclusive directory publisher for Qwest yellow page needs at the local level and will provide all of Qwest's publishing requirements under a 50-year contract. Under the arrangement, Qwest will continue to provide certain services to its former yellow pages unit, such as billing and information technology, under a variety of commercial services and transitional services agreements (Qwest, 2002).

Case Study Discussion Questions

1. Why was QwestDex considered an attractive LBO candidate? Do you think it has significant growth potential? Explain the following statement: "A business with high-growth potential may not be a good candidate for an LBO."
2. Why did the buyout firms want a 50-year contract in order to be the exclusive provider of publishing services to Qwest Communications?
3. Why would the buyout firms want Qwest to continue to provide such services as billing and information technology support? How might such services be priced?
4. Why would it take five very large financial institutions to finance the transactions?
5. Why was the equity contribution of the buyout firms as a percentage of the total capital requirements so much higher than amounts contributed during the 1980s?

Answers to this case are provided in the Online Instructor's Manual for instructors using this book.

Common Forms of Leveraged Buyout Deal Structures

As noted previously, LBOs are either asset- or cash-flow based. As a result of the epidemic of bankruptcies of overleveraged cash-flow-based LBOs in the late 1980s, the most common form of LBO today is the asset-based LBO. This type of LBO can be accomplished in two ways: (1) the sale of assets by the target to the acquiring company or (2) a merger of the target into the acquiring company (direct merger) or a wholly owned subsidiary of the acquiring company (subsidiary merger) (see Chapter 11).

Lender Commitment Letters

The typical transaction begins with a term sheet or a letter of intent between the seller and buyer, stipulating such basic items as price, terms of sale, assumption of liabilities, and closing deadlines. The acquirer often is asked for a **commitment letter** from a lender, which commits the lender to providing financing for the transaction. Closing is conditioned on the acquirer's ability to obtain financing. The commitment letter allows the lender to have access to the target company's records for credit evaluation and to conduct asset appraisals. It outlines the maximum loan amounts, interest charges, repayment schedule, and ratio of advances to assets pledged (i.e., collateral). The commitment letter is conditioned on the lender having performed adequate due diligence and the execution of an agreement of purchase and sale between the buyer and seller.

Direct Merger

If the LBO is structured as a direct merger in which the seller receives cash for stock, the lender will make the loan to the buyer once the appropriate security agreements are in place and the target's stock has been pledged against the loan. The target then is merged into the acquiring company, which is the surviving corporation. Payment of the loan proceeds is made directly to the seller in accordance with a letter of direction drafted by the buyer. For closely held corporations, the lender may make the loan directly to the selling corporation, which then transfers the proceeds as a dividend to its stockholders, or to the buyer, who has responsibility for paying the selling corporation's stockholders.

Subsidiary Merger

LBOs may be consummated by establishing a new subsidiary that merges with the target. This may be done to avoid any negative impact that the new company might have on existing customer or creditor relationships. If some portion of the parent's assets are to be used as collateral to support the ability of its operating subsidiary to fund the transaction, both the parent and the subsidiary may be viewed as having a security interest in the debt. As such, they may be held jointly and severally liable for the debt. To avoid this situation, the parent may make a capital contribution to the subsidiary rather than provide collateral or a loan guarantee.

Legal Pitfalls of Improperly Structured LBOs

Fraudulent conveyance laws take effect whenever a company goes into bankruptcy following a highly leveraged transaction. Under the law, the new company created by the LBO must be strong enough financially to meet its obligations to current and future creditors. If the new company is found by the court to have been inadequately capitalized to remain viable, the lender could be stripped of its secured position in the assets of the company or its claims on the assets could be made subordinate to those of the general or unsecured creditors. Consequently, lenders, sellers, directors, or their agents, including auditors and investment bankers, may be required to compensate the general creditors. Fraudulent conveyance laws are intended to preclude shareholders, secured creditors, and others from benefiting at the expense of unsecured creditors.

Lender Due Diligence

The lender can be expected to make a careful evaluation of the quality of the assets to be used as collateral. Receivables will be analyzed to determine the proportion beyond normal collection terms. An assessment of the likelihood that the receivables realistically can be converted to cash also will be made. A physical inspection of the inventory and inventory records will be made to establish both the quantitative and qualitative values of the inventory. Obsolete and unmarketable goods will be written down in value. Fixed assets will be appraised at their realistic "quick-sale" values by professional appraisers. Values also should be placed on off–balance sheet assets such as patents, trademarks, licenses, franchises, copyrights, and blueprints.

Critical Success Factors

Factors critical to the success of a leveraged buyout include knowing what to buy, not overpaying, and the ability to improve operating performance.

Knowing What to Buy

Firms that represent good candidates for an LBO are those that have substantial tangible assets, unused borrowing capacity, predictable positive operating cash flow, and assets that are not critical to the continuing operation of the business (Carow and Roden, 1998). Competent and highly motivated management is always crucial to the eventual success of the LBO. Finally, firms in certain types of industries or which are part of larger firms often represent attractive opportunities.

Unused Borrowing Capacity, Tax Shelter, and Redundant Assets

A number of factors enhance borrowing capacity. These include cash balances on the books of the target company in excess of working capital requirements, a low debt-to-total capital ratio (as compared to the industry average), and a demonstrated ability to generate consistent earnings and cash-flow growth. Firms with undervalued assets may use such assets as collateral for loans from asset-based lenders. Such assets also provide a significant tax shelter, because they may be revalued and depreciated or amortized over their allowable tax lives. In addition, operating assets, such as subsidiaries that are not germane to the target's core business and that can be sold quickly for cash, can be divested to accelerate the payoff of either the highest cost debt or the debt with the most restrictive covenants.

Management Competence and Motivation

Although the quality of management is always an important factor in the eventual success of a merger or acquisition, it tends to be critical to LBOs. Although management competence is a necessary condition for success, it does not ensure that the firm's performance will meet investor expectations. Management must be highly motivated by the prospect of abnormally large returns in a relatively short time. Consequently, management of the firm to be taken private is normally given an opportunity to own a significant portion of the equity of the firm.

Attractive Industries

Typical targets are in mature industries such as manufacturing, retailing, textiles, food processing, apparel, and soft drinks. Such industries usually are characterized by large tangible book values; modest growth prospects; relatively stable cash flow; and limited research and development (R&D), new product, or technology requirements. Such industries are generally not dependent on technologies and production processes that are subject to rapid change. Empirical studies have shown that industries that have high free cash flows and limited growth opportunities are good candidates for LBOs (Opler and Titman, 1993; Phan, 1995). However, in recent years, the availability of low cost financing has caused private equity investors to take private firms in such non-traditional industries as healthcare, services, and technology.

Large Company Operating Divisions

The best candidates for management buyouts often are underperforming divisions of larger companies in which the division is no longer considered critical to the parent firm's overarching strategy. Frequently, such divisions are saddled with excessive administrative overhead, often required by the parent, and expenses are allocated to the division by the parent for services such as legal, auditing, and treasury functions that could be purchased less expensively from sources outside the parent firm.

Not Overpaying

Although overpaying for any acquisition, highly leveraged or otherwise, almost always impairs the ability of the acquiring firm to achieve expected financial returns, it can be disastrous for LBOs. Failure to meet debt service obligations in a timely fashion often requires that the LBO firm renegotiate the terms of the loan agreements with the lenders. In exchange for deferring debt repayments or for reducing interest payments, lenders will demand concessions in the form of increased equity ownership in the LBO firm. The issuance of additional shares to accommodate the lenders' demands for increased ownership dilutes the ownership position of the initial investors. If the parties to the transaction cannot reach a compromise, the firm may be forced to file for bankruptcy, often wiping out the value of the initial investors' investment.

Highly leveraged firms also are subject to aggressive tactics from major competitors. Such competitors understand that taking on large amounts of debt will raise the breakeven point for the firm. If the amount borrowed is made even more excessive as a result of having paid more than the economic value of the target firm, the competitors may opt to gain market share by cutting product prices. The ability of the LBO firm to match such price cuts is limited because of the need to maintain enough cash flow to meet required interest and principal repayments.

Improving Operating Performance

Financial buyers succeed through improving operational performance. The discipline imposed by the need to satisfy debt service requirements focuses management's attention on maximizing operating cash flows. Standard tactics include attempting to negotiate employee wage and benefit concessions in exchange for a profit sharing or stock ownership plan. Outsourcing services once provided by the parent often result in significant savings. Other cost-cutting tactics include moving the corporate headquarters to a less expensive location, aggressively pruning marginally profitable customer accounts, and eliminating such perks as corporate aircraft.

Often operating performance can be improved simply by paying more attention to short-term considerations rather than focusing on more involved long-term strategies. This switch in emphasis may result in less money being spent on R&D, new product development, and new technologies. This behavior does not necessarily imply that the LBO firm is mortgaging its future. It may mean that the discipline imposed by debt may compel managers to more clearly prioritize investment opportunities and to concentrate their available resources on those with the shortest payback period. Holthausen and Larker (1996) found that LBOs after being taken public tended to increase capital expenditures and working capital while they were outperforming their industry competitors. Even as the proportion of debt in highly leveraged transactions has tended to drop during the last decade, there is no reason to believe that LBO managers will be any less motivated than in the glory days of the 1980s. As board members, buyout specialists such as LBO funds tend to take a much more active role in monitoring management performance. Empirical studies show that LBOs whose board members actively monitor and motivate management tend to perform better than those whose investors are largely passive.

While most LBOs are predicated on improving operating performance through a combination of aggressive cost cutting and revenue growth, HCA has laid out a somewhat unconventional approach in its effort to take the firm private. See Case Study 13-3.

Case Study 13-3
HCA's LBO Represents a High-Risk Bet on Growth

Founded in 1968, HCA profoundly impacted the U.S. health care system. Before HCA, most hospitals were run as local charitable organizations. HCA decided that a national hospital chain could use its purchasing muscle and modern management methods to generate cost savings through economies of scale while providing consistent quality. HCA first went private in 1989 in a buyout valued at $5 billion. Primarily through very aggressive cost cutting, the firm was able to rapidly boost cash flow, reduce indebtedness, and to again go public in 1992. On July 24, 2006, management again announced that it would be taking the firm private in a deal valued at $33 billion including the assumption of $11.7 billion in existing debt.

The approximate $21.3 billion purchase price for HCA stock will be financed by a combination of $12.8 billion in senior secured term loans of varying maturities and an estimated $8.5 billion in cash provided by Bain Capital, Merrill Lynch Global Private Equity, and Kohlberg Kravis Roberts & Company. HCA will also take out a $4 billion revolving credit line to satisfy immediate working capital requirements.

Unlike HCA's first effort, the firm has publicly announced a strategy of improving performance through growth rather than through cost cutting. HCA's network of 182 hospitals and 94 surgery centers is expected to benefit from an aging U.S. population and the resulting increase in health care spending. The deal also seems to be partly contingent on the government assuming a larger share of health care costs in the future. Finally, with many nonprofit hospitals faltering financially, HCA may be able to acquire them inexpensively.

While the longer-term trends in the health care industry are unmistakable, shorter-term developments appear troublesome. These include sluggish hospital admissions, an increasing number of uninsured patients, and higher bad debt expenses. Moreover, with Medicare and Medicaid increasingly financially insolvent, it is unclear if future increases in government health care spending will be sufficient to enable HCA investors to achieve their expected financial returns. With the highest operating profit margins in the industry, it is uncertain if HCA's cash flows could be significantly improved by cost cutting, if the revenue growth assumptions fail to materialize. HCA's management and equity investors have put themselves in a position in which they seem to have relatively little influence over the factors that directly impact the firm's future cash flows.

Case Study Discussion Questions

1. What are the key assumptions underlying the HCA proposal? Are they reasonable? Why?/Why not?
2. What future options does HCA's management have if these key assumptions turn out to be overly optimistic? Be specific.
3. What factors limit downside risk for HCA investors? Be specific.

Developing an Exit Strategy

Investors are able to realize their return only after they have been able to "cash out" of the business. Common exit strategies include a sale to a strategic buyer, an initial public offering, a leveraged recapitalization, or a sale to another buyout firm (Rickertsen, 2001). Selling to a strategic buyer usually results in the best price as the buyer may be able to generate significant synergies by combining the firm with its existing business. An IPO is often less attractive due to the massive amount of public disclosure required, the substantial commitment of management time, the difficulty in timing the market, and the potential for incorrectly valuing the IPO.

In the absence of a strategic buyer or an IPO opportunity, the original investors can cash out while management remains in charge of the business through a leveraged recapitalization. Once the firm has paid down its original debt level, the firm may borrow additional monies to repurchase stock from other shareholders, leaving the firm with a more conventional capital structure. Finally, if the original buyout firm's investment fund is coming to an end, the firm may be able to sell the LBO to another buyout firm that is looking for new investment opportunities. This option is best used when the LBO's management is still enthusiastic about growing the firm rather than cashing out. Consequently, the LBO may be attractive to another buyout firm. In late 2005, Oaktree Capital sold its investment in Maidenform Brands Inc., a maker of intimate apparel, to Ares Management, which is funding the deal through an initial public offering.

The exit strategy must be worked out in advance and explained to investors and managers alike if a buyout firm expects to be able to raise sufficient equity capital to avoid excessively levering the target firm. While it would seem logical to plan to exit the business when the business was healthy and the purchase price multiples for such businesses were the highest, the ability to actually time the exit is highly problematic. The exact exit date is determined largely by the opportunities that unfold. Case Study 13-4 illustrates a common exit strategy and how the challenges of potentially incompatible LBO investor expectations can threaten failure. Moreover, the case illustrates how employing "creative" techniques can satisfy seller concerns and how nimble decision making can steal victory from the jaws of defeat.

Case Study 13-4
Sony Buys MGM

Sony's long-term vision has been to create synergy between its consumer electronics products and music, movies, and games. Sony, which bought Columbia Pictures in 1989 for $3.4 billion, had wanted to control Metro-Goldwyn-Mayer's film library for years, but it did not want to pay the estimated $5 billion it would take to acquire it. On September 14, 2004, a consortium, consisting of Sony Corp. of America, Providence Equity Partners, Texas Pacific Group, and DLJ Merchant Banking Partners, agreed to acquire MGM for $4.85 billion, consisting of $2.85 billion in cash and the assumption of $2 billion in debt. The cash portion of the purchase price consisted of about $1.8 billion in debt and $1 billion in equity capital. Of the equity capital, Providence contributed $450 million, Sony and Texas Pacific Group $300 million, and DLJ Merchant Banking $250 million.

The combination of Sony and MGM created the world's largest film library of about 7600 titles, with MGM contributing about 54% of the combined libraries. Sony controlled MGM and Comcast distributed the films over cable TV. Sony shut down MGM's film-making operations and moved all operations to Sony. Kirk Kerkorian, who held a 74% stake in MGM, made $2 billion because of the transaction. The private equity partners could cash out within 3 to 5 years, with the consortium undertaking an initial public offering or sale to a strategic investor. Major risks included the ability of the consortium partners to maintain harmonious relations and the problematic growth potential of the DVD market.

Sony and MGM negotiations proved to be highly contentious for almost 5 months when media giant Time Warner Inc. emerged to attempt to satisfy Kerkorian's $5 billion asking price. The offer was made in stock on the assumption that Kerkorian would want a tax-free transaction. MGM's negotiations with Time Warner stalled around the actual value of Time Warner stock, with Kerkorian leery about Time Warner's future growth potential. Time Warner changed its bid in late August to an all cash offer, albeit somewhat lower than the Sony consortium bid, but it was more certain. Sony still did not have all of its financing in place. Time Warner had a "handshake agreement" with MGM by Labor Day for $11 per share, about $.25 less than Sony's.

The Sony consortium huddled throughout the Labor Day weekend to put in place the financing for a bid of $12 per share. What often takes months to work out in most leveraged buyouts was hammered out in 3 days of marathon sessions at law firm Davis Polk & Wardwell. In addition to getting final agreement on financing arrangements including loan guarantees from JP Morgan Chase & Company, Sony was able to reach agreement with Comcast to feature MGM movies in new cable and video-on-demand TV channels. This distribution mechanism meant additional revenue for Sony, making it possible to increase the bid to $12 per share. Sony also offered to make a $150 nonrefundable cash payment to MGM. As a testament to the adage that timing is everything, the revised Sony bid was faxed to MGM just before the beginning of a board meeting to approve the Time Warner offer.

Epilogue

About 2 years after closing the transaction, MGM's board voted unanimously to oust Sony Pictures Entertainment as its domestic distributor after it failed to meet previously agreed upon performance goals. While it remains a 20% investor in MGM, Sony has lost control of the film library, the very asset it has sought in engineering the takeover in mid-2004. Sony lost control to News Corp.'s 20th Century Fox studios and had to give up the potential to earn as much as $50 million annually in future fees. This episode highlights the dangers for minority investors of aligning with investors whose investment holding periods differ from their own.

Case Study Discussion Questions

1. Do you believe that MGM is an attractive LBO candidate? Why? Why not?
2. In what way do you believe that Sony's objectives might differ from those of the private equity investors making up the remainder of the consortium? How might such differences affect the management of MGM? Identify possible short-term and long-term effects.
3. How did Time Warner's entry into the bidding affect the pace of the negotiations and the relative bargaining power of MGM, Time Warner, and the Sony consortium?
4. What do you believe were the major factors persuading the MGM board to accept the revised Sony bid? In your judgment, do these factors make sense? Explain your answer.

Answers to these Case Study Discussion Questions are available in the online instructor's manual available to instructors using this book.

Impact on Shareholder Returns of Leveraged Buyouts

Prebuyout Returns to Target Shareholders

The studies cited in Table 13-3 show that the premium paid by LBOs and MBOs to target company shareholders consistently exceed 40% in nondivisional buyouts. The distinction made in these studies of highly leveraged transactions between MBOs and LBOs is that in the MBO management is providing a portion of the equity. These empirical studies also include so-called **reverse LBOs** (RLBOs). These are public companies that are taken private and later are taken public again through an IPO. The second effort to take the firm public is called a **secondary public offering**.

As noted previously, **divisional buyouts** represent opportunities for improved operating efficiency as the division is removed from the bureaucracy of the parent. Although this may be a source of gain for the acquirer, it does not seem to be true for the shareholders of the parent firm divesting the division. The parent firm's shareholders seem to receive only miniscule returns. The small size of these returns often may reflect the division's relatively small share of the parent corporation's total market value. Alternatively, the parent's management may forego the auction process in favor of the division's management. In either case, the parent corporation's share price is unlikely to materially benefit from the divestiture. The fact that parent shareholders experience any gain at all may suggest that the parent's resources are redeployed to higher return investments.

TABLE 13-3   Returns to Shareholders (Prebuyout Returns)

Empirical Study[1]	
Nondivisional Buyouts	Premium Paid to Target Shareholders
DeAngelo, DeAngelo, and Rice (1984)	56% (1973–1983)[2]
(Sample size = 72 MBOs)	76% (when there are 3 or more bids)
Lowenstein (1985)	48% (1979–1984)
(Sample size = 28 MBOs)	
Lehn and Poulsen (1988)	41% (1980–1984)
(Sample size = 92 LBOs)	
Divisional Buyouts	Return to Parent Corporation Shareholders
Hite and Vetsuypens (1989)	.55% (1983–1987)
(Sample = 151 MBOs)	
Muscarella and Vetsuypens (1990)	1.98% (1983–1988)
(Sample size = 45 MBOs)	

Notes:
[1] MBO, management buyout; LBO, leveraged buyout.
[2] The years in parentheses represent the time period in which the study took place.

Factors Determining Prebuyout Target Shareholder Returns

Table 13-4 summarizes the empirical research, which attempts to identify the factors that explain sizable gains in share price that accrue to prebuyout target shareholders. Although a number of factors are at work, the sizeable returns to prebuyout shareholders as noted in Table 13-1 seem to reflect anticipated improvements in operating efficiency due to management incentives and large tax benefits.

TABLE 13-4   Factors Contributing to Pre-LBO Buyout Returns to Target Shareholders

Factor	Theory	Evidence[1]
Management Incentives		
Equity Ownership Kaplan (1991) (Sample size = 76 MBOs)	Management will improve performance when their ownership stake increases.	Management ownership increased for MBOs between 1980 and 1986 from 8.3% before the buyout to 29% after the buyout.
Incentive (Profit Sharing) Plans Muscarella and Vetsuypens (1990) (Sample size = 72 reverse LBOs)	Stock option and share appreciation plans motivate management to take cost-cutting actions that might otherwise have been unacceptable.	96% of LBOs had at least one and 75% had two incentive plans in place during the 1983–1988 period. Moreover, the change in shareholder gain is positively correlated with the fraction of shares owned by LBO's officers.
Improved Operating Performance Holthausen and Larker (1996) (Sample size = 90 reverse LBOs)	Equity ownership and incentive plans motivate management to initiate aggressive cost-reduction plans and to change marketing strategies.	For the 1983–1988 period, sales were up by 9.4% in real terms and operating profits were up by 45.4% between the LBO announcement date and the secondary initial public offering. Firm performance also was highly correlated with the amount of ownership by officers and directors
Kaplan (1989b)		Operating income in LBO firms increased more than in other firms in the same industry during 2 years following the LBO.

continued

TABLE 13-4   continued

Factor	Theory	Evidence[1]
Tax Shelter Benefits		
Kaplan (1989a)	An LBO can be tax free for as long as 5–7 years.	Median value of tax shelter contributed 30% of the premium.
Lehn and Poulsen (1988)		Premium paid to pre-LBO shareholders positively correlated with pre-LBO tax liability/equity.
Wealth Transfer Effects		
Lehn and Poulsen (1988)	Premiums represent a transfer of wealth from bondholders to common stockholders.	Found no evidence that bondholders and preferred stockholders lose value when an LBO is announced.
Travlos and Cornett (1993)		Found small losses associated with the LBO announcement.
Billet, King, and Mauer (2004) Sample size = 3073 LBOs		Found no evidence of wealth transfer between bondholders and stockholders
Investor Group Has Better Information Than Public Shareholders on MBO Target		
Kaplan (1988) and Smith (1990)	Investor group believes target worth more than shareholders believe it is.	Found no evidence to support this theory.
Improved Efficiency in Decision Making		
Travlos and Cornett (1993)	Private firms are less bureaucratic and do not incur reporting and servicing costs associated with public shareholders.	Shareholder-related expenses are not an important factor; difficult to substantiate more efficient decision making.

Note:
[1] MBO, managed buyout; LBO, leveraged buyout.

Anticipated Improvement in Efficiency and Tax Benefits

The most often cited sources of these returns are from tax benefits and from expected post-LBO improvements in efficiency as a result of management incentives and the discipline imposed by the need to repay debt, which motivate aggressive cost cutting. Michael Jensen (1986) argues that managers cannot be trusted to invest free cash flows in a manner that is necessarily in the best interests of the stockholders. Debt imposes a discipline that forces them to stay focused on maximizing operating cash flows. Tax benefits are largely predictable and are built into the premium offered for the public shares of the target firm as a result of the negotiation process (Kaplan, 1989b; Newbould, Chatfield, and Anderson, 1992). Successful MBOs are associated with improved operating performance, while firms undertaking MBOs that were not completed showed no subsequent improvement in operating performance (Ofek, 1994).

Wealth Transfer Effects

The evidence supporting wealth transfer effects is mixed for most LBO transactions. The exception may be for very large LBOs such as RJR Nabisco, where largely anecdotal evidence seems to suggest that a significant transfer of wealth may have taken place between the firm's pre-LBO debt holders and shareholders.

Superior Knowledge

It sometimes is argued that LBO investors have knowledge of a business that is superior to that held by the firm's public shareholders. Such knowledge is sometimes referred to as *asymmetric information* in that it is not equally available to both investors and public shareholders. Therefore, the LBO investors are motivated to pay such high premiums because they understand better how to achieve cost savings and productivity improvements.

More Efficient Decision Making

There is also little empirical evidence to support the notion that decision making is more efficient. Nonetheless, the intuitive appeal of the simplified decision-making process of a private company is compelling when contrasted with a public company with multiple constituents directly or indirectly affecting decision making. Examples of such constituents include a board of directors with outside directors, public shareholders, government regulatory agencies, and Wall Street analysts.

Factors Determining Postbuyout Returns

Table 13-5 summarizes the studies on returns to shareholders following a leveraged buyout. A number of empirical studies suggest that investors in LBOs have earned abnormal profits on their initial investments. The presumption in these studies seems to be that the full effect of increased operating efficiency following a leveraged buyout is not fully reflected in the pre-LBO premium. These studies may be subject to *selection or survivor bias* in that only LBOs that are successful in significantly improving their operating performance are able to undertake a secondary public offering. Mian and Rosenfeld (1993) noted that in many instances the abnormal returns earned by postbuyout shareholders were the result of the LBO being acquired by another firm in the 3 years immediately following the LBO announcement.

Using a larger sample and longer time period than earlier studies, Cao and Lerner (2006) found that reverse LBOs showed a much larger 3-year cumulative return (except for those "flipped" within 1 year of acquisition) than earlier studies. The authors suggest that new owners choosing to retain their investment longer have more time to put the proper controls and reporting/monitoring systems in place for firms to survive the rigor of being a public company. In contrast, unless in place when acquired, firms resold within a year simply do not have the time to adequately prepare for participating in public

TABLE 13-5   Postbuyout Returns to LBO Shareholders[1]

Empirical Study	Impact on Postbuyout Performance
Muscarella and Vetsuypens (1990) (Sample Size = 45 MBOs from 1983 to 1987)	Of 41 firms going public, median annual return was 36.6% in 3 years following buyout.
Kaplan (1991) (Sample size = 21 MBOs from 1979 to 1986)	Median annualized return was 26% higher than the gain on the S&P 500 during the 3-year postbuyout period.
Mian and Rosenfeld (1993) (Sample Size = 85 reverse LBOs from 1983 to 1989)	Of the 33 LBOs that were acquired by another firm during the 3 years following the LBO, cumulative abnormal returns exceeded 21%. Of those not acquired, cumulative abnormal returns were zero.
Holthausen and Larker (1996) (Sample Size = 90 reverse LBOs from 1983 to 1988)	Firms outperformed their industries over the 4 years following the secondary IPO.
Cao and Lerner (2006) (Sample Size = 496 reverse LBOs from 1980 to 2002)	RLBOs consistently outperform other IPOs and the overall stock market, exhibiting a cumulative 3-year return of 43.8%. In contrast, "quick flips" (i.e., buyout firm sells its investment within a year of acquisition) underperformed the S&P 500 by a cumulative 5 percentage points during the following 3-year period.

Note:
[1] MBO, managed buyout; LBO, leveraged buyout.

markets. However, the results may be seriously biased, because IPOs generally would not be undertaken for poorly performing LBOs. These laggards may have either gone into bankruptcy or have been sold to strategic buyers.

Analyzing Leveraged Buyouts

An LBO can be evaluated from the perspective of common equity investors only or from the perspective of all investors, including preferred stockholders and debt holders/lenders. Conventional capital budgeting procedures may be used to evaluate the LBO. The transaction makes sense from the viewpoint of all investors in the transaction if the present value (PV) of the cash flows to the firm (PV_{FCFF}) or enterprise value, discounted at the weighted average cost of capital, equals or exceeds the total investment consisting of debt, common equity, and preferred equity ($I_{D+E+PFD}$) required to buy the outstanding shares of the target company.

$$PV_{FCFF} - I_{D+E+PFD} \geq 0 \qquad (13\text{-}1)$$

If this is true, the target firm can earn its cost of capital and return sufficient cash flow to all parties to the transaction, enabling them to meet or exceed their minimum required returns.

However, it is possible for a leveraged buyout to make sense to common equity investors but not to other investors such as pre-LBO debt holders and preferred stockholders. The market value of the debt and preferred stock on the books of the target firm before the announcement of the LBO reflects two factors. First, the firm must be able to repay in a timely fashion both principal and interest. Second, the firm must be able to continue to make required dividend payments on preferred equity. The future ability to meet these obligations often is measured by comparing such ratios for the target firm as debt-to-equity and interest coverage with those of comparable firms. Once the LBO has been consummated, the firm's perceived ability to meet these obligations often will deteriorate because the firm takes on a substantial amount of new debt. The firm's pre-LBO debt and preferred stock may be revalued in the open market by investors to reflect this higher perceived risk, resulting in a significant reduction in the market value of both debt and preferred equity owned by pre-LBO investors. Although there is little empirical evidence to show that this is typical of LBOs, this revaluation may characterize large LBOs such as RJR Nabisco in 1989, HCA in 2006, and TXU Corp. in 2007.

What follows is a discussion of two methods for valuing leveraged buyouts. The variable risk method attempts to adjust future cash flows for changes in the cost of capital as the firm reduces its outstanding debt. The second method, adjusted present value, sums the value of the firm without debt plus the value of future tax savings resulting from the tax deductibility of interest.

Valuing LBOs: The Variable Risk Method (VR)

As long as the debt-to-equity ratio is expected to be constant, applying conventional capital budgeting techniques that discount future cash flows with a constant weighted average cost of capital is appropriate. However, the extremely high leverage associated with leveraged buyouts significantly increases the riskiness of the cash flows available to equity investors as a result of the increase in fixed interest and principal repayments that must be made to lenders. Consequently, the cost of equity should be adjusted for the increased leverage of the firm. However, since the debt is to be paid off over time, the cost of equity will decrease over time. Therefore, in valuing a leveraged buyout, the analyst must project free cash flows, but instead of discounting the cash flows at a constant discount rate, the discount rate must decline with the firm's declining debt to equity ratio. To determine if the deal makes sense, the analyst compares the estimated value of the firm with the purchase price of the firm.

What follows is a five-step procedure that allows for the discount rate to vary with changes in leverage in order to determine if a leveraged buyout opportunity makes sense.

Project Annual Cash Flows (Step 1)

Step 1 involves projecting free cash flow to equity (FCFE). FCFE measures the cash flow available for common equity investors after all other financing obligations have been satisfied. These cash flows should be projected annually until the LBO has achieved its target debt-to-equity ratio. Because the LBO investors wish to recover their investment and required return by either selling to a strategic buyer or engaging in a secondary public offering, they must make two calculations to determine the appropriate target debt-to-equity ratio. The first is to determine at what level of debt relative to equity the firm will have to resume paying taxes. The point at which this occurs depends on the firm's debt repayment schedule and projected pretax income. The second calculation is highly subjective and involves estimating the amount of leverage that may be acceptable to strategic buyers or investors in a secondary public offering at some point in the future. Thus, the target debt-to-equity ratio is that level of outstanding debt relative to equity at which the firm resumes paying taxes and which appears to be acceptable to strategic buyers or investors in a secondary public offering.

Project Debt-to-Equity Ratios (Step 2)

The decline in debt-to-equity ratios depends on known debt repayment schedules and the projected growth in the market value of shareholders' equity. The market value of common equity can be assumed to grow in line with the projected percentage growth in net income available to common shareholders.

Calculate Terminal Value (Step 3)

Calculate the terminal value of equity (TVE) and of the firm in year t.

$$\text{Terminal value of equity (TVE)} = FCFE_{t+1}/(k_e - g) \tag{13-2}$$

The cost of equity, k_e, and g represent the cost of equity and the cash-flow growth rate that can be sustained during the stable growth or terminal period. TVE represents the present value of equity of the dollar proceeds available to the firm at time t. These proceeds are commonly generated by selling equity to the public or to a strategic buyer.

Adjust the Discount Rate to Reflect Changing Risk (Step 4)

The high leverage associated with a leveraged buyout increases the risk of the cash flows available for equity investors by increasing debt service requirements. As the LBO's extremely high initial debt level is reduced, the firm's cost of equity needs to be adjusted to reflect the decline in risk, as measured by the firm's levered beta (β_{FL}). This adjustment may be estimated starting with the firm's levered β in period 1 (β_{FL1}) as follows:

$$\beta_{FL1} = \beta_{IUL1}[1 + (D/E)_{F1}(1 - t_F)] \tag{13-3}$$

where β_{IUL1} is industry unlevered β in period 1; $(D/E)_{F1}$ and t_F are the firm's debt-to-equity ratio and marginal tax rate, respectively; and $\beta_{IUL1} = \beta_{IL1}/[1 + (D/E)_{I1}(1 - t_I)]$, where β_{IL1}, $(D/E)_{I1}$, and t_I are the industry's levered β, debt-to-equity ratio, and tax rate, respectively. The firm's β in each successive period should be recalculated using the firm's projected debt-to-equity ratio for that period. The firm's cost of equity (k_{eF}) must be recalculated each period using that period's estimated β determined by Equation 13-3.

Because the firm's cost of equity changes over time, the firm's cumulative cost of equity is used to discount projected cash flows. Recall that the future value of $1 ($FV_{\$1}$) in 2 years invested at a 5% return in the first year and 8% in the second year is $1 \times [(1 + .05)(1 + .08)] = \$1.13$; the present value of $1 received in 2 years earning the same rates of return ($PV_{\$1}$) is $1/[(1 + .05)(1 + .08)] = \$.88$. This reflects the fact that each period's cash flows generate a different rate of return. The cumulative cost of equity is represented as follows:

$$PV_1 = FCFE_1/(1 + COE_1)$$

$$PV_2 = FCFE_2/[(1 + COE_1)(1 + COE_2)]$$

$$\vdots$$

$$PV_n = FCFE_n/[(1 + COE_1)(1 + COE_2) \dots (1 + COE_{n-1})(1 + COE_n)] \tag{13-4}$$

Determine If Deal Makes Sense (Step 5)

Making sense of the deal requires calculating the PV of FCFE discounted by the cumulative cost of equity generalized by Equation 13-4 in Step 4, including the terminal value estimated by Equation 13-2 in Step 3. Compare this result to the value of the equity invested in the firm including transaction-related fees. The deal makes sense to common equity investors if the PV of FCFE exceeds the value of the equity investment in the deal. The deal makes sense to lenders and noncommon equity investors if the PV of FCFF exceeds the total cost of the deal (see Equation 13-1). See Table 13-11 for an illustration of how to calculate the value of an LBO using the variable risk method.

Valuing LBOs: Adjusted Present Value Method (APV)

Some analysts suggest that the problem of a variable discount rate can be avoided by separating the value of a firm's operations into two components: (1) the firm's value as if it were debt free and (2) the value of interest tax savings. The total value of the firm is the present value of the firm's free cash flows to equity investors plus the present value of future tax savings discounted at the firm's unlevered cost of equity. Brigham and Ehrhardt (2005, p. 597) argue that the unlevered cost of equity is the appropriate discount rate rather than the cost of debt or a risk-free rate, because tax savings are subject to risk since the firm may default on its debt or may be unable to utilize the tax savings due to continuing operating losses.

The justification for the APV method rests on the theoretical notion that the value of a firm should not be affected by the way in which it is financed (Brealey and Meyers, 1996). This notion assumes investors have access to perfect information, the firm is not growing and no new borrowing is required, and there are no taxes and transaction costs, and implicitly that the firm is free of default risk. Under these assumptions, the earning power and risk associated with the firm's assets determine the value of the firm. For the APV model to be applicable in highly leveraged transactions, the analyst needs to introduce the costs of bankruptcy. Consequently, the present value of a highly leveraged transaction (PV_{HL}) would reflect its present value without leverage (PV_{UL}), plus the present value of tax savings (i.e., interest expense i times the firm's marginal tax rate t) or tax shield (Pv_{ti}) resulting from leverage, and the present value of costs associated with financial distress. The latter factor reflects the increased burden of debt repayment due to increased leveraged and expected bankruptcy (PV_{BK}).

$$PV_{HL} = PV_{UL} + PV_{ti} - PV_{BK} \qquad (13-5)$$

Unfortunately, the costs associated with possible bankruptcy and financial distress cannot be easily measured and are often ignored by analysts using the APV method.

Theoretically, the same estimate of the firm's equity value can be obtained by deducting the market value of debt from the enterprise value of the firm if the analyst is able to estimate the firm's true cost of equity and debt. The key considerations are the choice of discount rate and the assumption that the discount rate is unaffected by changes in the firm's leverage. For an excellent discussion of alternative valuation methods for highly leveraged firms, see Ruback (2002) and Arzac (2005). Molina (2005) discusses alternative ways of estimating the probability of financial distress by examining firms' credit ratings. The following steps for applying the APV method illustrate its relative simplicity.

Project Annual Cash Flows and Interest Tax Savings (Step 1)

For the period during which the debt-to-total capital ratio (i.e., the firm's capital structure) is changing, the analyst should project free cash flows to equity and the interest tax savings. During the firm's terminal period, the debt-to-total capital structure is assumed to be stable and the free cash flows are projected to grow at a constant rate.

Value Target Excluding Tax Savings (Step 2)

Estimate the unlevered cost of equity (COE) for discounting cash flows during the period in which the capital structure is changing and the weighted average cost of capital (WACC) for discounting during the terminal period. The WACC is estimated using the COE and after-tax cost of debt and the proportions of debt and equity that make up the firm's capital structure in the final year of the period during which the capital structure is changing.

Estimate Present Value of Tax Savings (Step 3)

Project the annual tax savings resulting from the tax deductibility of interest. Discount projected tax savings at the firm's unlevered cost of equity, since it reflects a higher level of risk than either the WACC or after-tax cost of debt. Tax savings are subject to risk comparable to the firm's cash flows in that a highly leveraged firm may default and the tax savings go unused.

Calculate Total Value of Firm (Step 4)

To determine the total value of the firm, add the present value of the firm's cash flows to equity, interest tax savings, and terminal value discounted at the firm's unlevered cost of equity. Note that the terminal value is calculated using WACC but that it is discounted to the present using the unlevered COE. This is done because it represents the present value of cash flows in the final year of the period in which the firm's capital structure is changing.

Determine If the Deal Makes Sense (Step 5)

This requires that the sum of the present values of the firm's cash flows during the period of a changing debt-to-total capital ratio and the terminal period, as well as tax savings, must be greater than or equal to zero. See Table 13-12 for an illustration of how to calculate the value of an LBO using the adjusted present value method.

Comparing Variable Risk and Adjusted Present Value Methods

Although the proposition that the value of the firm should be independent of the way in which it is financed may make sense for a firm whose debt-to-capital ratio is relatively stable and is similar to the industry's, it strains credulity when it is applied to highly leveraged transactions. In these situations, the LBO's leverage may be three or four times the industry's average leverage, thereby dramatically increasing the potential for bankruptcy. Intuitively, the APV method is likely to overestimate the value of the firm unless the resulting estimated value is adjusted for both the likelihood of and costs associated with bankruptcy (see Equation 13-5). Without such an adjustment, the APV method implies that the value of the firm could be increased by continuously taking on more debt. Thus, the primary drawback to the APV method is the implication that the firm should optimally use 100% debt financing to take maximum advantage of the tax shield created by the tax deductibility of interest (Booth, 2002).

The primary advantage of the APV method is its relative computational simplicity. Although somewhat more complex, the variable risk method attempts to adjust for the changing level of risk over time as the LBO reduces its leverage over time. Thus, the VR method takes into account what is actually happening in practice. For more information on valuing LBOs, see Damadoran (1997). Table 13-6 summarizes the process steps as well as the strengths and weaknesses of the variable risk and adjusted present value methods.

TABLE 13-6   Comparative LBO Valuation Methodologies

Process Steps	Variable Risk Method	Adjusted Present Value Method
Step 1	Project annual cash flows, including all financing considerations and tax savings until anticipate exiting the business	Project annual cash flows to equity investors and interest tax savings
Step 2	Project annual debt-to-equity ratios	Value target without tax savings, including terminal value
Step 3	Calculate terminal value in year	Estimate PV of tax savings
Step 4	Adjust discount rate to reflect declining cost of equity as debt is repaid	Add PV of firm without debt including terminal period and PV of tax savings
Step 5	Determine if NPV of projected cash flows ≥ 0	Determine if NPV of projected cash flows ≥ 0
Advantages	• Adjusts discount rate to reflect diminishing risk	• Simplicity
Disadvantages	• Calculations more tedious than alternative methods	• Ignores effects of leverage on discount rate as debt repaid • Ignores potential for bankruptcy of excessively leveraged firms • Unclear whether true discount rate is cost of debt, unlevered COE, or somewhere between the two

Applying LBO Valuation Models

The process of valuing highly leveraged transactions using an LBO valuation model is illustrated in Case Study 13-5. Please see the Excel-based LBO valuation and analysis model on the CD-ROM enclosed with this book to see the underlying formulae used to generate the spreadsheets displayed in this Case Study.

Case Study 13-5

Pacific Investors Acquires California Kool in a Leveraged Buyout

Pacific Investors (PI) is a small private equity limited partnership with $3 billion under management. The objective of their fund is to give investors at least a 30% annual average return on their investment by judiciously investing these funds in highly leveraged transactions. PI has been able to realize such returns over the last decade because of their focus on investing in industries that have slow but predictable growth in cash flow, modest capital investment requirements, and relatively low levels of research and development spending. In the past, PI has made several lucrative investments in the contract packaging industry, which provides packaging for beverage companies that produce various types of noncarbonated and carbonated beverages. Because of its commitments to its investors, PI likes to liquidate its investments within 4–6 years of the initial investment through a secondary public offering or sale to a strategic investor.

Following its past success in the industry, PI currently is negotiating with California Kool (CK), a privately owned contract beverage packaging company with the technology required to package many different types of noncarbonated drinks. CK's 2003 revenue and net income are $190.4 million and $5.9 million, respectively. With a reputation for effective management, CK is a medium-sized contract packaging company that owns its own plant and equipment and has a history of continually increasing cash flow. The company also has significant unused excess capacity, suggesting that production levels can be increased without substantial new capital spending.

The owners of CK are demanding a purchase price of $70 million. This is denoted on the balance sheet (see Table 13-9) as a negative entry in Additional Paid in Capital. This price represents a multiple of 11.8 times 2003's net income, almost twice the multiple for comparable publicly traded companies. Despite the "rich" multiple, PI believes that it can finance the transaction through an equity investment of $25 million and $47 million in debt. The equity investment consists of $3 million in common stock, with PI and CK each contributing $1.5 million. Debt consists of a $12 million revolving loan to meet immediate working capital requirements, $20 million in senior bank debt secured by CK's fixed assets, and $15 million in a subordinated loan from a pension fund. The total cost of acquiring CK is $72 million, $70 million paid to the owners of CK and $2 million in legal and accounting fees.

As indicated on Table 13-9, the change in total liabilities plus shareholders' equity (i.e., total sources of funds or cash inflows) must equal the change in total assets (i.e., total uses of funds or cash outflows). Therefore, as shown in the "Adjustments" column, total liabilities increase by $47 million in total borrowings and shareholders' equity declines by $45 million (i.e., $25 million in preferred and common equity provided by investors less $70 million paid to CK owners). The excess of sources over uses of $2 million is used to finance legal and accounting fees incurred in closing the transaction. Consequently, total assets increase by $2 million and total liabilities plus shareholders' equity increase by $2 million between the pre- and postclosing balance sheets as shown in the adjustments column.[1]

Revenue for CK is projected to grow at 4.5% annually through the foreseeable future. Operating expenses and sales, general, and administrative expenses as a percent of sales are expected to decline during the first 3 years of operation due to aggressive cost cutting and the introduction of new management and engineering processes. Similarly, improved working capital management results in significant declines in working capital as a percent of sales during the first year of operation. Gross fixed assets as percent of sales is held constant at its 2003 level during the forecast period reflecting reinvestment requirements to support the projected increase in net revenue. Equity cash flow adjusted to include cash generated in excess of normal operating requirements (i.e., denoted by the change in investments available for sale) is expected to reach $8.5 million annually by 2010. Using the variable risk valuation (VR) method, the cost of equity declines in line with the reduction in the firm's β as the debt is repaid from 26% in 2004 to 16.5% in 2010. In contrast, the adjusted present value (APV) method employs a constant unlevered COE of 17%.

The deal would appear to make sense from the standpoint of PI, since, projected average annual internal rates of return (IRRs) for investors exceed PI's minimum desired 30% rate of return in all scenarios considered between 2007 and 2009 (see Table 13-7). This is the period during which investors would like to "cash out." The rates of return scenarios are calculated assuming the business can be sold at different multiples of adjusted equity cash flow in the year in which the business is assumed to be sold. Consequently, IRRs are calculated using the cash outflow (initial equity investment in the business) in the first year offset by any positive equity cash flow from operations generated in the first year, equity cash flows for each subsequent year, and the sum of equity cash flow in the year in which the business in sold or taken public plus the estimated sale value (e.g., 8 times equity cash flow) in that year. Adjusted equity cash flow includes free cash flow generated from operations and the increase in "investments available for sale." Such investments represent cash generated in excess of normal operating requirements; and, as such, this cash is available to LBO investors.

The actual point at which CK will either be taken public, sold to a strategic investor, or sold to another LBO fund will depend on stock market conditions, CK's leverage relative to similar firms in the industry, and cash-flow performance as compared to plan. Discounted cash flow analysis also suggests that PI should do the deal since the total present value of adjusted equity cash flow of $57.2 million using the VR method is more than twice the magnitude of the initial equity investment. At $61.1 million, the APV method results in an approximate 7% higher estimate of total present value. See Tables 13-8, 13-9, and 13-10 for the income, balance sheet, and cash-flow statements, respectively, associated with this transaction. Tables 13-11 and 13-12 illustrate the calculation of present value of the transaction based on the variable risk and the adjusted present value methods, respectively. Note the actual Excel spreadsheets and formulas used to create these financial tables are available on the CD-ROM accompanying this book in a work sheet designated "LBO Valuation and Structuring Model."

---

[1] Δ Total Assets $= \Delta$ Total Liabilities $+ \Delta$ Shareholders' Equity

$2 million $= $47 million $- $45 million $= $2 million

TABLE 13-7 California Kool Model Output Summary

Sources (Cash Inflows) and Uses (Cash Outflows) of Funds

Sources of Funds	Amount ($)	Interest Rate (%)	Uses of Funds	Amount ($)
Cash from Balance Sheet	$0.0	0.0%	Cash to Owners	$70.0
New Revolving Loan	$12.0	9.0%	Seller's Equity	$0.0
New Senior Debt	$20.0	9.0%	Seller's Note	$0.0
New Subordinated Debt	$15.0	12.0%	Excess Cash	$0.0
New Preferred Stock (PIK)	$22.0	12.0%	Paid to Owners	$70.0
New Common Stock	$3.0	0.0%	Debt Repayment	$0.0
			Buyer Expenses	$2.0
Total Sources	$72.0		Total Uses	$72.0

Pro Forma Capital Structure

Form of Debt and Equity	Market Value	% of Total Capital
Revolving Loan	$12.0	16.7%
Senior Debt	$20.0	27.8%
Subordinated Debt	$15.0	20.8%
Total Debt	$47.0	65.3%
Preferred Equity	$22.0	30.6%
Common Equity	$3.0	4.2%
Total Equity	$25.0	34.7%
Total Capital	$72.0	

Equity Investment

	Ownership Distribution ($)			% Distribution		Fully Diluted Ownership Distribution				
	Common	Preferred	Total	Common	Preferred	Warrants	Common	Pre-Option Ownership	Perform. Options	Fully Dil. Ownership
Equity Investor	1.5	22.0	23.5	50.0%	100.0%	0.0%	50.0%	50.0%	0.0%	50.0%
Management	1.5	0.0	1.5	50.0%	0.0%	0.0%	50.0%	50.0%	0.0%	50.0%
Total Equity Investment	$3.0	$22.0	$25.0	100.0%	100.0%	0.0%	100.0%	100.0%	0.0%	100.0%

TABLE 13-7 continued

Internal Rates of Return	Total Investor Return (%)			Equity Investor Investment Gain ($)			Management Investment Gain ($)		
	2007	2008	2009	2007	2008	2009	2007	2008	2009
Multiple of Adjusted Equity Cash Flow[1]									
8 × Terminal Yr. CF	0.42	0.35	0.33	$66.6	$78.9	$96.0	$4.3	$5.0	$6.1
9 × Terminal Yr. CF	0.46	0.39	0.35	$73.8	$86.6	$104.5	$4.7	$5.5	$6.7
10 × Terminal Yr. CF	0.51	0.42	0.37	$81.0	$94.2	$113.0	$5.2	$6.0	$7.2

Financial Projections and Analysis	2001	2002	2003	2004	2005	2006	2007	2008	2009	2010
Net Sales	$177.6	$183.5	$190.4	$197.1	$205.0	$214.2	$223.8	$233.9	$244.4	$255.4
Annual Growth Rate	4.2%	3.3%	3.8%	3.5%	4.0%	4.5%	4.5%	4.5%	4.5%	4.5%
EBIT as % of Net Revenue	5.5%	1.3%	5.1%	8.5%	9.5%	10.2%	11.2%	11.4%	11.4%	11.4%
Adjusted Enterprise Cash Flow[2]	$4.2	$0.2	$0.1	$9.5	$9.6	$10.8	$13.0	$13.4	$14.2	$14.9
Adjusted Equity Cash Flow	$4.2	$0.2	$0.1	$0.3	$0.2	$1.8	$7.4	$7.7	$8.1	$8.5
Total Debt Outstanding	0	0	$47.0	$39.5	$31.5	$23.8	$19.2	$14.3	$8.8	$2.7
Total Debt/Adjusted Enterprise Cash Flow	0.0	0.0	NA	4.1	3.3	2.2	1.5	1.1	0.6	0.2
EBIT/Interest Expense	0	0	0	3.6	4.9	6.6	10.1	13.3	18.6	30.9
PV of Adjusted Equity Cash Flow @ 26%	$57.2									
PV of 2004–2010 Adj. Equity CF/Terminal Val.	28.1%									

Note:
[1] Net Income + Depreciation & Amortization − Gross Capital Spending − Chg. in Working Capital − Principal Repayments − Change Investments Available for Sale (i.e., increases in such investments are a negative cash flow entry, but represent cash in excess of normal operating needs.)
[2] EBIT(1 − t) + Depreciation & Amortization − Gross Capital Spending − Chg. in Working Capital − Chg. in Investments Available for Sale

547

TABLE 13-8 California Kool Income Statement and Forecast Assumptions

Income Statement Assumptions	Historical Period			Projections: Twelve Months Ending December 31,						
	2001	2002	2003	2004	2005	2006	2007	2008	2009	2010
Net Sales Growth (%)	0.042	0.033	0.038	0.035	0.040	0.045	0.045	0.045	0.045	0.045
Cost of Sales as % of Sales	0.805	0.814	0.780	0.765	0.758	0.755	0.750	0.750	0.750	0.750
SG&A as % of Sales	0.133	0.144	0.142	0.135	0.130	0.125	0.120	0.120	0.120	0.120
Effective Tax Rate (%)	0.400	0.400	0.400	0.400	0.400	0.400	0.400	0.400	0.400	0.400
Income Statement:										
Net Sales	$177.6	$183.5	$190.4	$197.1	$205.0	$214.2	$223.8	$233.9	$244.4	$255.4
Cost of Sales	143.0	149.3	148.5	150.8	155.4	161.7	167.9	175.4	183.3	191.6
Gross Profit	34.6	34.1	41.9	46.3	49.6	52.5	56.0	58.5	61.1	63.9
Depreciation	1.3	5.4	5.1	2.4	2.9	3.4	3.5	3.7	3.8	4.0
Amortization of Financing Fees				0.5	0.5	0.5	0.5			
Total Depreciation & Amortization	1.3	5.4	5.1	2.9	3.4	3.9	4.0	3.7	3.8	4.0
SG&A	23.6	26.4	27.0	26.6	26.6	26.8	26.9	28.1	29.3	30.7
Management Fee				0.1	0.1	0.1	0.1	0.1	0.1	0.1
Operating Income (EBIT)	9.7	2.3	9.7	16.7	19.5	21.7	25.0	26.6	27.8	29.1
(Interest Income)	0.1	0.1	0.1	0.0	0.1	0.1	0.1	0.1	0.1	0.1
New Revolver Interest Expense				1.0	0.7	0.4	0.0	0.0	0.0	0.0
New Senior Debt Interest Expense				1.8	1.6	1.4	1.2	0.9	0.6	0.3
Subordinated Debt Interest Expense				1.8	1.7	1.5	1.3	1.1	0.9	0.6
Total Interest Expense	0	0	0	4.6	4.0	3.3	2.5	2.0	1.5	0.9
Earnings before Taxes	9.8	2.4	9.8	12.1	15.6	18.5	22.6	24.7	26.4	28.3
Taxes @40%	3.9	0.9	3.9	4.8	6.2	7.4	9.0	9.9	10.6	11.3
Net Income	$5.9	$1.4	$5.9	$7.3	$9.4	$11.1	$13.6	$14.8	$15.9	$17.0
PIK Preferred Dividend				2.6	3.0	3.3	3.7	4.2	4.7	5.2
Net Income to Common	$5.9	$1.4	$5.9	$4.6	$6.4	$7.8	$9.9	$10.7	$11.2	$11.7

TABLE 13-9 California Kool Balance Sheet and Forecast Assumptions

	Historical Period			Adjustments	Closing	Projections: Twelve Months Ended December,						
	2001	2002	2003		2003	2004	2005	2006	2007	2008	2009	2010
Balance Sheet Assumptions:												
Cash & Marketable Securities (%Sales)	0.02	0.02	0.02	0.0	0.02	0.02	0.02	0.02	0.02	0.02	0.02	0.02
Accounts Receivable (%Sales)	0.161	0.158	0.167	0.0	0.167	0.155	0.155	0.155	0.155	0.155	0.155	0.155
Other Current Assets (%Sales)	0.054	0.057	0.063	0.0	0.063	0.055	0.055	0.055	0.055	0.055	0.055	0.055
Gross Prop., Plant & Equip. (%Sales)	0.473	0.5	0.52	0.0	0.52	0.52	0.52	0.52	0.52	0.52	0.52	0.52
Accumulated Depreciation (%G E)	0.7	0.7	0.7	0.0	0.7	0.7	0.7	0.7	0.7	0.7	0.7	0.7
Accounts Payable (%Sales)	0.08	0.083	0.084	0.0	0.084	0.078	0.078	0.078	0.078	0.078	0.078	0.078
Other Current Liabilities (%Sales)	0.074	0.079	0.076	0.0	0.076	0.07	0.07	0.07	0.07	0.07	0.07	0.07
Assets					($ Millions)							
Current Assets												
Cash and Marketable Securities	3.6	3.7	3.8	0.0	3.8	4.1	4.3	4.5	4.7	4.9	5.1	5.1
Accounts Receivable	28.6	29.0	31.8	0.0	31.8	30.6	31.8	33.2	34.7	36.3	37.9	39.6
Other Current Assets	9.6	10.5	12.0	0.0	12.0	10.8	11.3	11.8	12.3	12.9	13.4	14.0
Total Current Assets	41.7	43.1	47.6	0.0	47.6	45.5	47.3	49.5	51.7	54.0	56.4	58.8
Investments Available for Sale	0.0			0.0	0.0	0.0	0.0	0.0	0.0	0.0	0.0	0.0
Gross Property, Plant & Equipment	84.0	91.7	99.0	0.0	99.0	102.5	106.6	111.4	116.4	121.6	127.1	132.8
Less: Accumulated Depreciation	58.8	64.2	69.3	0.0	69.3	71.7	74.6	78.0	81.5	85.1	89.0	93.0

549

TABLE 13-9 continued

	Historical Period			Adjustments	Closing	Projections: Twelve Months Ended December,						
	2001	2002	2003		2003	2004	2005	2006	2007	2008	2009	2010
					($ Millions)							
Net Property, Plant & Equipment	25.2	27.5	29.7	0.0	29.7	30.7	32.0	33.4	34.9	36.5	38.1	39.8
Transaction Fees and Expenses	0.0	0.0	0.0	2.0	2.0	1.5	1.0	0.5	0.0	0.0	0.0	0.0
Purchase price in excess of book value					0.0	0.0	0.0	0.0	0.0	0.0	0.0	0.0
Total Assets	66.9	70.6	77.3	2.0	79.3	77.7	80.3	83.4	95.5	106.8	118.8	131.3
Liabilities & Shareholders' Equity												
Current Liabilities:												
Accounts Payable	14.2	15.2	16.0	0.0	16.0	15.4	16.0	16.7	17.5	18.2	19.1	19.9
Other Current Liabilitiles	13.1	14.5	14.5	0.0	14.5	13.8	14.3	15.0	15.7	16.4	17.1	17.9
Total Current Liabilities	27.4	29.7	30.5	0.0	30.5	29.2	30.3	31.7	33.1	34.6	36.2	37.8
Long-Term Debt:												
Revolving Loan				12.0	12.0	7.9	3.7	0.0	0.0	0.0	0.0	0.0
Senior Debt				20.0	20.0	17.8	15.5	12.9	10.1	7.0	3.7	0.0
Subordinated Debt				15.0	15.0	13.8	12.4	10.9	9.2	7.2	5.1	2.7
Total Long-Term Debt	0.0	0.0	0.0		47.0	39.5	31.5	23.8	19.2	14.3	8.8	2.7
Shareholders' Equity												
Preferred Stock (PIK)				22.0	22.0	24.6	27.6	30.9	34.6	38.8	43.4	48.6
Common Stock				3.0	3.0	3.0	3.0	3.0	3.0	3.0	3.0	3.0
Additional Paid in Capital				(70.0)	(70.0)	(70.0)	(70.0)	(70.0)	(70.0)	(70.0)	(70.0)	(70.0)
Retained Earnings	39.5	40.9	46.8	0.0	46.8	51.4	57.8	65.7	75.5	86.2	97.4	109.1
Total Shareholders' Equity	39.5	40.9	46.8		1.8	9.1	18.4	29.6	43.1	58.0	73.8	90.8
Total Liabilities & Shareholders' Equity	66.9	70.6	77.3	2.0	79.3	77.7	80.3	85.0	95.5	106.8	118.8	131.3

TABLE 13-10 California Kool Cash Flow Statement and Analysis

	Historical Data			Projections: Twelve Months Ended December 31,						
	2001	2002	2003	2004	2005	2006	2007	2008	2009	2010
				GAAP Cash Flow ($ Millions)						
Cash Flow from Operating Activities:										
Net Income Available to Common Equity	5.9	1.4	5.9	4.6	6.4	7.8	9.9	10.7	11.2	11.7
Adjustments to Reconcile Net Income to Net Cash Flow										
Depreciation	1.3	5.4	5.1	2.4	2.9	3.4	3.5	3.7	3.8	4.0
Amortization of Financing Fees	0.0	0.0	0.0	0.5	0.5	0.5	0.5	0.0	0.0	0.0
PIK Preferred Dividends	0.0	0.0	0.0	2.6	3.0	3.3	3.7	4.2	4.7	5.2
Net Change in Working Capital	0.0	1.1	(3.6)	1.1	(0.5)	(0.6)	(0.6)	(0.6)	(0.7)	(0.7)
Net Cash Flow from Operations	7.2	5.7	14.6	11.3	12.2	14.4	17.0	17.9	19.0	20.3
Cash Flow from Investing Activities:										
(Increase) Decrease in Investments Available for Sale				0.0	0.0	0.0	(8.9)	(7.4)	(7.9)	(8.5)
(Increase) Decrease in Gross Property, Plant & Equipment				(3.5)	(4.1)	(4.8)	(5.0)	(5.2)	(5.5)	(5.7)
Net Cash Used in Investments	0.0	0.0	0.0	(3.5)	(4.1)	(4.8)	(13.9)	(12.7)	(13.3)	(14.2)
Cash Flows from Financing Activities:										
Net Debt (Repayment) or Issuance	0.0	0.0	0.0	(7.5)	(8.0)	(7.8)	(4.5)	(5.0)	(5.5)	(6.1)
Net Cash (Used in) Provided by Financing Activities	0.0	0.0	0.0	(7.5)	(8.0)	(7.8)	(4.5)	(5.0)	(5.5)	(6.1)
Net Increase (Decrease) in Cash & Marketable Securities				0.3	0.2	1.8	(1.5)	0.2	0.2	0.0
Beginning Balances—Cash & Marketable Securities				3.8	4.1	4.3	6.1	4.7	4.9	5.1
Ending Balances—Cash & Marketable Securities				4.1	4.3	6.1	4.7	4.9	5.1	5.1

continued

TABLE 13-10 continued

	Historical Data			Projections: Twelve Months Ended December 31,						
	2001	2002	2003	2004	2005	2006	2007	2008	2009	2010
	Valuation Cash Flow ($ Millions)									
Net Income to Available to Common Equity	5.9	1.4	5.9	4.6	6.4	7.8	9.9	10.7	11.2	11.7
After-Tax Net Interest Expense (Income)	0	0	0	1.7	1.4	1.2	1.0	0.8	0.6	0.4
Depreciation	1.3	5.4	5.1	2.4	2.9	3.4	3.5	3.7	3.8	4.0
Amortization of Financing Fees	0	0	0	0.5	0.5	0.5	0.5	0	0	0
PIK Preferred Dividend	0	0	0	2.6	3.0	3.3	3.7	4.2	4.7	5.2
Net Cash Flow Before Working Capital	7.2	6.8	11.0	11.9	14.2	16.1	18.6	19.3	20.3	21.3
Net Change in Working Capital	0.0	1.1	(3.6)	1.1	(0.5)	(0.6)	(0.6)	(0.6)	(0.7)	(0.7)
Net Cash Flow Before Gross Property, Plant & Equip. Spending	7.2	7.9	7.4	13.0	13.7	15.6	18.0	18.7	19.6	20.7
(Increase) Decrease in Invest Available for Sale				0.0	0.0	0.0	(8.9)	(7.4)	(7.9)	(8.5)
(Increase) Decrease in Gross Property, Plant & Equipment	(3.0)	(7.7)	(7.3)	(3.5)	(4.1)	(4.8)	(5.0)	(5.2)	(5.5)	(5.7)
Enterprise Cash Flow	4.2	0.2	0.1	9.5	9.6	10.8	4.1	6.0	6.3	6.5
After-Tax Net Interest Expense (Income)	0.0	0.0	0.0	1.7	1.4	1.2	1.0	0.8	0.6	0.4
Net Debt (Repayments) or Issuance	0.0	0.0	0.0	(7.5)	(8.0)	(7.8)	(4.5)	(5.0)	(5.5)	(6.0)
Equity Cash Flow	4.2	0.2	0.1	0.3	0.2	1.8	(1.5)	0.2	0.2	0.0
Dividends on Common Stock	0.0	0.0	0.0	0.0	0.0	0.0	0.0	0.0	0.0	0.0
Net Stock (Repurchase) or Issuance	0.0	0.0	0.0	0.0	0.0	0.0	0.0	0.0	0.0	0.0
Net Increase (Decrease) in Cash Balance	4.2	0.2	0.1	0.3	0.2	1.8	(1.5)	0.2	0.2	0.0
Beginning Balances—Cash & Marketable Securities		3.6	3.8	3.9	4.2	4.4	6.2	4.8	5.0	5.2
Ending Balances—Cash & Marketable Securities	3.6	3.8	3.9	4.2	4.4	6.2	4.8	5.0	5.2	5.2
Adjusted Equity Cash Flow	4.2	0.2	0.1	0.3	0.2	1.8	7.4	7.7	8.1	8.5

TABLE 13-11 Present Value of California Kool Adjusted Equity Cash Flow Using the Variable Risk (VR) Method

Assumptions	2003	2004	2005	2006	2007	2008	2009	2010
Market Value of Preferred Equity ($ Millions)	22	24.6	27.6	30.9	34.6	38.8	43.4	48.6
Market Value of Common Equity ($ Millions)	3	2.3	3.3	4.0	5.0	5.4	5.7	6.0
Equity[1] ($ Millions)	25	27.0	30.9	34.9	39.6	44.2	49.1	54.6
Debt ($ Millions)	47	39.5	31.5	23.8	19.2	14.3	8.8	2.7
Comparable Firm:								
Price/Earnings Ratio	6							
Levered Beta (β)	2.4							
Debt/Equity Ratio	.3							
Unlevered Beta[2]	2.0							
Marginal Tax Rate	.4							
10-yr. Treasury Bond Rate	.05							
Risk Premium on Stocks (%)	.055							
Terminal Period Growth Rate (%)	.045							
Terminal Period Cost of Equity (%)	.10							

continued

TABLE 13-11   continued

Year	Debt/ Equity	Leveraged Beta[3]	Cost of Equity	Cumulative Discount Factor[4]	Adjusted Equity Cash Flow	PV of Adjusted Equity Cash Flow[5]
2004	1.5	3.8	.260	$1/(1.26) = .7937$	.3	.3
2005	1.0	3.3	.230	$1/[(1.26)(1.23)] = .6452$	.2	.1
2006	.7	2.9	.208	$1/[(1.26)(1.23)(1.208)] = .5341$	1.8	1.0
2007	.5	2.6	.194	$1/[(1.26)(1.23)(1.208)(1.194)] = .4474$	7.4	3.3
2008	.3	2.4	.184	$1/[(1.26)(1.23)(1.208)$ $(1.194)(1.184)] = .3778$	7.7	2.9
2009	.2	2.3	.174	$1/[(1.26)(1.23)(1.208)$ $(1.194)(1.184)(1.174)] = .3218$	8.1	2.6
2010	.0	2.1	.165	$1/[(1.26)(1.23)(1.208)(1.194)$ $(1.184)(1.174)(1.165)] = .2762$	8.5	2.4
PV (2004–2010)						12.5
Terminal Value						44.7
Total PV						57.2

Notes:
[1] Market value of common equity is assumed to grow by the rate of growth in income available to common; preferred equity is assumed to equal to its book value; and debt outstanding reflects the projected repayment schedule.
[2] Comparable firm unlevered $\beta_u = \beta_l/[1 + (D/E)(1-t)]$.
[3] Firm's levered beta $\beta_l = \beta_u[1 + (D/E)(1-t)]$.
[4] Because of the changing D/E ratio, the discount factor is expressed in multiplicative form to reflect the differing cash-flow streams generated by investments made at each level of the D/E ratio.
[5] PV of adjusted equity cash flow equals the cumulative discount factor times the adjusted equity cash flow.

554

TABLE 13-12   Present Value of California Kool Adjusted Equity Cash Flows Using the Adjusted Present Value (APV) Method

	2004	2005	2006	2007	2008	2009	2010
Assumptions:							
Marginal Tax Rate	0.4						
Comparable Company Unlevered Beta	2						
10-Year Treasury Bond Rate	0.05						
Risk Premium on Stocks	0.055						
Terminal Period Growth Rate	0.045						
2004–2020 Unlevered Cost of Equity[1]	0.17						
Terminal Period WACC[2]	0.12						
Adjusted Equity Cash Flow	0.3	0.2	1.8	7.4	7.7	8.1	8.5
Plus: Tax Shield[3]	1.8	1.6	1.3	1.0	0.8	0.6	0.4
Plus: Terminal Value[4]							123.8
Equals: Total Cash Flow	2.2	1.8	3.2	8.4	8.5	8.7	132.7
PV of 2004–2010 cash flows							$61.07

Notes:
[1] $COE = .06 + 2.0(.055)$.
[2] $WACC = COE \times W1 + Pref \times W2 + i \times (1 - .t) \times W3$, where COE = unlevered cost of equity; Pref = yield on preferred stock; i = interest rate on outstanding debt; W1 = common equity's share of total terminal year capital; W2 = preferred stock's share of total terminal year capital; W3 = debt's share of total terminal year capital; and t = marginal tax rate.
[3] Tax shield is the product of total interest expense times the marginal tax rate.
[4] The terminal value is calculated using the constant growth method estimated based on total 2010 cash flow, terminal period WACC, and terminal period sustainable period cash-flow growth rate.

Things to Remember

The motivation in structuring an LBO is to finance the transaction with as much debt as possible. Much of the debt will be secured with the assets of the target firm. Often, the proceeds from the sale of assets are used to pay off debt as quickly as possible. Success in structuring a leveraged buyout is a result of knowing what to buy, not overpaying, and being able to substantially improve operating performance. Good LBO candidates are those that have substantial tangible assets, unused borrowing capacity, predictable positive operating cash flow, and assets that are not critical to the continuing operation of the business. Although overpaying for any acquisition, highly leveraged or otherwise, almost always impairs the ability of the acquiring firm to achieve expected financial returns, it can be disastrous for highly leveraged transactions.

Successful LBOs rely heavily on management incentives to improve operating performance and the discipline imposed by the demands of satisfying interest and principal repayments. The premium paid to target company shareholders by LBO and MBO investors often exceed 40%, substantially more than premiums paid to the target shareholders in less leveraged transactions. The most often cited sources of these LBO premiums paid to target shareholders are from improvements in efficiency and tax benefits. Tax benefits are largely predictable; and, as such, they are often built into the premium offered for the public shares of the target firm as a result of the negotiation process. Post-LBO abnormal returns average between 30 and 40% during the 3 years following the announcement of the LBO. The primary reasons for these gains seem to be improvements in operating efficiency whose value was not captured in the premium paid to pre-LBO stockholders and the potential for the LBO firm to be acquired.

The high leverage associated with the LBO increases the risk of the cash flows available for equity investors by increasing debt service requirements. As the LBO's extremely high initial debt level is reduced, the firm's cost of equity needs to be adjusted to reflect the decline in risk. This implies a changing cost of equity over time. Excessive leverage and the resultant higher level of fixed expenses makes LBOs vulnerable to business cycle fluctuations and aggressive competitor actions, which LBOs often cannot counteract.

Chapter Discussion Questions

13.1 What potential conflicts arise between management and shareholders in an MBO? How can these conflicts be minimized?

13-2. Describe how and why LBO strategies have changed since the early 1980s.

13-3. What are the primary ways in which an LBO is financed?

13-4. How do loan and security covenants affect the way in which an LBO is managed? Note the differences between positive and negative covenants.

13-5. What are the primary factors that explain the magnitude of the premium paid to pre-LBO shareholders?

13-6. What are the primary uses of junk bond financing?

13-7. Describe a typical LBO's preferred capital structure in the 1980s and 1990s, and compare it to what you think the structure would look like today.

13-8. Describe some of the legal problems that can arise from an improperly structured LBO.

13-9. Is it possible for an LBO to make sense to equity investors but not to other investors in the deal? If so, why? If not, why not?

13-10. How does the risk of an LBO change over time? How can the impact of changing risk be incorporated into the valuation of the LBO?

Answers to these Chapter Discussion Questions are available in the Online Instructor's Manual for instructors using this book.

Chapter Business Case

Case Study 13-6
Financing LBOs—The SunGard Transaction

In a move reminiscent of the blockbuster buyouts of the late 1980s, seven private investment firms acquired 100% of the outstanding stock of SunGard Data Systems Inc. (SunGard) in the third quarter of 2005. SunGard is a financial software firm known for providing application and transaction software services and creating backup data systems in the event of disaster. The company's software manages 70% of the transactions made on the Nasdaq stock market, but its biggest business is creating backup data systems in case a client's main systems are damaged or disabled by a natural disaster, blackout, or terrorist attack. Its large client base for disaster recovery and backup systems provides a substantial and predictable cash flow.

With their cash hoards accumulating at an unprecedented rate, there was little that buyout firms could do but to invest in larger firms. Consequently, the average size of LBO transactions grew significantly during 2005. However, hundreds of analysts and thousands of investors follow public companies and finding a true bargain amidst all this scrutiny is demanding in markets where many investors have access to the same information.

SunGard's new owners include Silver Lake Partners, Bain Capital LLC, The Blackstone Group L.P., Goldman Sachs Capital Partners, Kohlberg Kravis Roberts & Co., Providence Equity Partners Inc., and Texas Pacific Group. Buyout firms in 2005 tended to band together to spread the risk of a deal this size and to reduce the likelihood of a bidding war. Indeed, with SunGard, there was only one bidder, the investor group consisting of these seven firms.

The downside to investors in these buyout firms is that the firms inevitably post similar rates of return on their investments. As long as the returns are attractive, pension funds and universities that invest in buyout funds managed by these firms have not objected as long as they have outpaced the return on the broader stock market. Among the major disadvantages to buyout firms of banding together is that it limits their ability to achieve financial returns, which exceed those of other buyout firms. Investor groups also increase the likelihood that disagreements will arise as to the timing of the exit strategy. Buyout firms also may be charged with anticompetitive practices if collaboration reduces the likelihood of auctions for target businesses.

The software side of SunGard is believed to have significant growth potential, while the disaster-recovery side provides a large stable cash flow. SunGard's senior management team and its business plan will remain largely unchanged after the sale. Unlike many LBOs, the deal was announced as being all about growth of the financial services software side of the business. This is in marked contrast to many LBOs whose success is predicated on breakups or asset sales, lessening service, or cutting costs.

The deal is structured as a merger, since SunGard would be merged into a shell corporation created by the investor group for acquiring SunGard. Going private, allows SunGard to invest heavily in software without being punished by investors, since such investments are expensed and reduce reported earnings per share. Going private also allows the firm to eliminate the burdensome reporting requirements of being a public company.

The buyout represented potentially a significant source of fee income for the investor group. In addition to the 2% management fees buyout firms collect from investors in the funds they manage, they receive substantial fee income from each investment they make on behalf of their funds. For example, the buyout firms receive a 1% deal completion fee, which is more than $100 million in the SunGard transaction. Buyout firms also receive fees paid for by the target firm that is "going private" for arranging financing. Moreover, there are also fees for conducting due diligence and for monitoring the ongoing performance of the firm taken private. Finally, when the buyout firms exit their investments in the target firm via a secondary IPO or sale to a strategic buyer, they receive 20% (i.e., so-called carry fee) of any profits.

Under the terms of the agreement, SunGard shareholders received $36 per share, a 14% premium over the SunGard closing price as of the announcement date of March 28, 2005, and 40% more than when the news first leaked about the deal a week earlier. From the SunGard shareholders' perspective, the deal is valued at $11.4 billion dollars consisting of $10.9 billion for outstanding shares and "in-the-money" options (i.e., options whose exercise price is less than the firm's market price per share) plus $500 million in debt on the balance sheet.

The seven equity investors provided $3.5 billion in capital with the remainder of the purchase price financed by commitments from a lending consortium consisting of Citigroup, JP Morgan Chase & Co., and Deutsche Bank. The purpose of the loans is to finance the merger, repay or refinance SunGard's existing debt, provide ongoing working capital, and pay fees and expenses incurred in connection with the merger. The total funds necessary to complete the merger and related fees and expenses is approximately $11.3 billion, consisting of approximately $10.9 billion to pay SunGard's stockholders and approximately $400.7 million to pay fees and expenses related to the merger and the financing arrangements. Note that the fees that are to be financed comprise almost 4% of the purchase price. Ongoing working capital needs and capital expenditures required obtaining commitments from lenders well in excess of $11.3 billion.

The merger financing consists of several tiers of debt and "credit facilities." Credit facilities are arrangements for extending credit. The senior secured debt and senior subordinated debt are intended to provide "permanent" or long-term financing. The senior secured debt contained common affirmative and negative covenants. These include restrictions on new borrowing, investments, sales of assets, mergers and consolidations, prepayments of subordinated indebtedness, capital expenditures, liens and dividends and other distributions, as well as a minimum interest coverage ratio (i.e., operating income before interest and taxes/interest expense) and a maximum total leverage ratio (i.e., debt/total capital).

If the offering of notes is not completed on or prior to the closing of the merger, the banks providing the financing have committed to provide up to $3 billion in loans under a senior subordinated bridge credit facility. The bridge loans are intended as a form of temporary financing to satisfy immediate cash requirements until permanent financing can be arranged. If the bridge loans are not paid in full on or before the first anniversary of the merger, the lenders may require the borrower to exchange the loans for notes that must be sold to the public, with the lenders repaid from the proceeds. The maturity of any bridge loans that are not exchanged for notes will be automatically extended to the 10th anniversary of the closing of the merger. Payment-in-kind notes represent another form of temporary financing in which interest payments take the form of additional debt issued by the company.

A special purpose SunGard subsidiary will purchase receivables from SunGard, with the purchases financed through the sale of the receivables to the lending consortium. The lenders subsequently finance the purchase of the receivables by issuing commercial paper, which is repaid as the receivables are collected. The special purpose subsidiary is not shown on the SunGard balance sheet. Based on the value of receivables at closing, the subsidiary could provide up to $500 million. The obligation of the lending consortium to buy the receivables will expire on the sixth anniversary of the closing of the merger. The receivables facility will provide funding at the same rate as the senior notes. The receivables credit facility fees will include a usage fee equal to 1.50% per annum of the amount funded and a commitment fee of 0.50% on the unused portion of the total bank commitments.

Table 13-3 illustrates SunGard's postmerger pro forma capital structure. Note that the pro forma capital structure is portrayed as if SunGard uses 100% of bank lending commitments. Also, note that individual LBO investors may invest monies from more than one fund they manage. This may be due to the perceived attractiveness of the opportunity or the limited availability of money in any single fund.

TABLE 13-13   SunGard Capital Structure

Premerger Existing SunGard Debt Outstanding	$ Millions
Senior Notes (3.75% due in 2009)	250,000,000
Senior Notes (4.785% due in 2014)	250,000,000
Total Existing Debt Outstanding	500,000,000
Debt Portion of Merger Financing:	
Senior Secured Notes (not to exceed $5 billion)	5,000,000,000
$1 billion revolving credit facility with a 6-year term	
$4 billion term loan maturing in 7½ years	
Senior Subordinated Notes (not to exceed $3 billion)	3,000,000,000
Payment-in-Kind Senior Notes (not to exceed $.5 billion)	500,000,000
Receivables Credit Facility (not to exceed $.5 billion)	500,000,000
Total Merger Financing (as if fully utilized)	9,000,000,000
Equity Portion of Merger Financing	
Equity Investor	Commitment ($ Millions)
Silver Lake Partners II, L.P.[1]	540,000,000
Bain Capital Fund VIII, L.P.	540,000,000
Blackstone Capital Partners IV, L.P.	270,000,000
Blackstone Communications Partners I, L.P.	270,000,000
GS Capital Partners 2000, L.P.	250,000,000
GS Capital Partners V, L.P.	250,000,000
KKR Millennium Fund, L.P.	540,000,000
Providence Equity Partners V, L.P.	300,000,000
TPG Partners IV, L.P.	540,000,000
Total	3,500,000,000
Total Debt and Equity	13,000,000,000

Note:

[1] The roman numeral II refers to the fund providing the equity capital managed by the partnership.

Case Study Discussion Questions

1. SunGard is a software company with relatively few tangible assets. Yet, the ratio of debt to equity is almost 2.6 to 1. Why do you think lenders would be willing to engage in such a highly leveraged transaction for a firm of this type?
2. Under what circumstances would SunGard refinance after the merger of the $500 million in senior debt existing before the merger? Be specific.
3. In what ways is this transaction similar to and different from those common in the 1980s? Be specific.
4. Why are payment-in-kind securities (e.g., debt or preferred stock) particularly well suited for financing LBOs? Under what circumstances might they be most attractive to lenders or investors?
5. Explain how the way in which the LBO is financed affects the way it is operated and the timing of when equity investors choose to exit the business. Be specific.

Answers to these Case Study Discussion Questions are available in the Online Instructor's Manual for instructors using this book.

Chapter Business Case

Case Study 13-7
Blackstone's Buyout of Equity Office Properties Sets New Record among Private Equity Deals

Reflecting the wave of capital flooding into commercial real estate and the growing power of private equity investors, the Blackstone Group (Blackstone) succeeded in acquiring Equity Office Properties (EOP) following a bidding war with Vornado Realty Trust (Vornado). On February 8, 2007, Blackstone Group closed the purchase of EOP for $39 billion, consisting of about $23 billion in cash and $16 billion in assumed debt. (Note that the value of this transaction, a record at the time, was exceeded by TXU Corp.'s $45 billion LBO barely 2 weeks later.)

EOP was established in 1976 by Sam Zell, a veteran property investor known for his ability to acquire distressed properties. EOP's commercial real estate portfolio consisted of 590 buildings and 105 million square feet of office space. Blackstone, one of the nation's largest private equity buyout firms, entered the commercial real estate market for the first time in 2005. In contrast, Vornado, a publicly traded real estate investment trust, had a long-standing reputation for savvy investing in the commercial real estate market.

EOP signed a definitive agreement to be acquired by Blackstone for $48.50 per share in cash in November 2006, subject to approval by EOP's shareholders. Reflecting the view that EOP's breakup value exceeded $48.50 per share, Vornado bid $52 per share, 60% in cash and the remainder in Vornado stock. Blackstone countered with a bid of $54 per share, if EOP would raise the break-up fee (i.e., the amount it would pay to Blackstone, if EOP accepted an alternative bid) to $500 million from $200 million. Ostensibly designed to compensate Blackstone for expenses incurred in its takeover attempt, the break-up fee also raised the cost of acquiring EOP by another bidder, which as the new owner would actually pay the fee.

Within a week, Vornado responded with a bid valued at $56 per share. While higher, EOP continued to favor Blackstone's offer since the value of the offer was less certain than Blackstone's bid. It could take as long as 3 to 4 months for Vornado to get shareholder approval. The risks are that the value of Vornado's stock could decline and that shareholders could nix the deal. Moreover, the Vornado proposal was submitted to the EOP board in the form of a 2-page letter rather than as a definitive agreement that would have allowed EOP to hammer out a final agreement more rapidly.

Throughout this auction process, Blackstone exercised its right (negotiated in its definitive agreement with EOP) to prevent Vornado from obtaining proprietary data about EOP and from having direct conversations with EOP management. This put Vornado at a significant disadvantage, since they would lack the necessary information to value properly EOP's commercial property portfolio. Reluctant to raise its offer price, Vornado agreed to increase the cash portion of the purchase price and to pay shareholders the cash more quickly than had been envisioned in its initial offer. The next day, Blackstone increased their bid to $55.25 and eventually to $55.50 at Zell's behest in exchange for an increase in the break-up fee to $720 million. Vornado's failure to counter gave Blackstone the win.

Blackstone had a huge incentive to close the deal. In doing so, the firm will receive an acquisition fee valued at about .5% or $195 million no matter how well the investment fares long term. Similarly, advisers such as Goldman Sachs and the law firm Simpson Thacker &

Bartlett will also earn million in fees. Of the estimated $23 billion in cash required to buy out EOP shareholders, Blackstone is investing a modest $3.75 billion of its own money.

To fund the transaction, Blackstone was intent on selling rapidly many of the EOP properties immediately following closing. EOP barred Blackstone initially from entering into negotiations to sell EOP properties until they reached an agreement in mid-November. However, as soon as Vornado Realty Trust's competing bid emerged, EOP gave Blackstone permission to aggressively market EOP properties to potential buyers. This gave Blackstone a significant competitive edge in the subsequent auction for EOP, since they had a better idea than Vornado how much they could agree to pay for EOP and how it could be financed. Shortly after closing, Blackstone announced that it had reached agreement to sell a $7 billion portfolio of EOP's New York office buildings to Macklowe Properties, a private real estate group, and an additional EOP portfolio valued at $6.5 billion to Beacon Capital Partners.

Private equity firms have significant advantages over publicly traded companies in auctions as they do not have to hold shareholder votes and often are more experienced in adding substantial debt to finance such transactions. On the news that Blackstone had won, Vornado's stock jumped by 5.8% and EOP's fell by 1% to just below Blackstone's final offer price.

Case Study Discussion Questions

1. Describe Blackstone's negotiating strategy with EOP in its effort to counter Vornado's bids. Be specific.
2. What could Vornado have done to assuage EOP's concerns about the certainty of the value of the stock portion of its offer?
3. Explain the reaction of EOP's and Vornado's share prices to the news that Blackstone was the winning bidder. What does the movement in Vornado's share price tell you about the likelihood that the firm's shareholders would have approved the takeover of EOP?

Answers to these Case Study Discussion Questions are available in the Online Instructor's Manual for instructors using this book.

References

Altman, Edward I., and Vellore M. Kishore, "Almost Everything You Wanted to Know about Recoveries on Defaulted Bonds," *Financial Analysts Journal*, November/December 1996, pp. 57–64.

Arzac, Enrique R., *Valuation for Mergers, Buyouts, and Restructuring*, Wiley & Sons, Somerset, NJ, 2005, pp. 89–105.

Asquith, Paul, David Mullins, and Eric Wolff, "Original Issue High Yield Bonds: Aging Analysis of Defaults, Exchanges and Calls," *Journal of Finance*, Vol. 44, September 1989, pp. 923–952.

Baker, G., and G. Smith, *The New Financial Capitalists*, Cambridge University Press, Cambridge, 1998.

Berman, Dennis K., and Henny Sender, "Backstory of Kinder LBO Underscores Web of Ethical Issues Such Deals Face," *The Wall Street Journal*, September 30, 2006, p. A6.

Billet, Matthew T., Tao-Hsien Dolly King, and Daivd C. Mauer, "Bondholder Wealth Effects on Mergers and Acquisitions: New Evidence from the 1980s and 1990s," *Journal of Finance*, 2004, p. 23.

Booth, Laurence, "Finding Value Where None Exists: Pitfalls in Using Adjusted Present Value," *Journal of Applied Corporate Finance*, Vol. 15, Spring 2002, pp. 1–15.

Borden, Arthur M., *Going Private*, Law Journal Seminar Press, New York, 1987, pp. 1–6

Brealey, Richard A., and Stewart C. Meyers, *Principles of Corporate Finance*, 5th Ed., McGraw-Hill, New York, 1996, pp. 525–541.

Brigham, Eugene F., and Michael C. Ehrhardt, *Financial Management: Theory and Practice*, Thomson-Southwestern Publishing, Atlanta, GA, 2005.

Cao, Jerry, and Josh Lerner, "The Success of Reverse Leveraged Buyouts," *Working Knowledge for Business Leaders*, Harvard Business School, Cambridge, MA, October 11, 2006.

Carow, Kenneth A., and Dianne M. Roden, "Determinants of the Stock Price Reaction to Leveraged Buyouts," *Journal of Economics and Finance,* Vol. 22, Spring 1998, pp. 37–47.

Copeland, Tom, Tim Koller, and Jack Murrin, *Valuation: Measuring and Managing the Value of Companies*, 3rd Ed., Wiley & Sons, New York, 2000, pp. 477–483.

Cotter, James F., and Sarah W. Peck, "The Structure of Debt and Active Equity Investors: The Case of the Buyout Specialist," *Journal of Finance*, Vol. 59, January 1, 2001.

Damadoran, Aswath, *Corporate Finance: Theory and Practice*, Wiley & Sons, New York, 1997, pp. 502–537.

Damadoran, Aswath, *Investment Valuation: Tools and Techniques for Determining the Value of Any Asset*, Wiley & Sons, New York, 2002, p. 13.

DeAngelo, Harry, Linda DeAngelo, and Edward Rice, "Going Private: Minority Freeze-outs and Stockholder Wealth," *Journal of Law and Economics*, Vol. 27, October 1984, pp. 367–401.

Emery, Douglas R., and John D. Finnerty, "A Review of Recent Research Concerning Corporate Debt Provisions," *Financial Markets, Institutions, and Instruments*, Vol. 1, December 1992, pp. 23–39.

Engel, Ellen, Rachel Hayes, and Xue Xang, "The Sarbanes–Oxley Act and Firms' Going Private Decisions," Working Paper, University of Chicago, Chicago, 2004.

Fisher, Daniel, "A Dangerous Game," *Forbes Magazine*, October 16, 2006, pp. 40–43.

Greenwald, J., "Where's the Limit?," *Time*, December 5, 1988, pp. 66–70.

Hartman, Thomas E., "The Costs of Being Public in the Era of Sarbanes-Oxley," *Foley & Lardner LLP Annual Survey*, June 16, 2005.

Hite, G. L., and M. R. Vetsuypens, "Management Buyouts of Divisions and Shareholder Wealth," *Journal of Finance*, Vol. 44, 1989, pp. 953–970.

Holmstrom, Bengt, and Steven N. Kaplan, "Corporate Governance and Merger Activity in the United States: Making Sense of the 1980s and 1990s," *Journal of Economic Perspectives*, Vol. 13, Spring 2001, pp. 121–144.

Holthausen, Robert W., and David F. Larker, "The Financial Performance of Reverse Leveraged Buyouts," *Journal of Financial Economics*, Vol. 42, 1996, pp. 293–332.

Jensen, Michael C., "Agency Costs of Free Cash Flow, Corporate Finance, and Takeovers," *American Economic Association Papers and Proceedings*, May 1986, pp. 323–329.

Kamar, Ehud, Pinar Karaca-Mandic, and Eric Talley, "Going-Private Decisions and the Sarbanes-Oxley Act of 2002: A Cross-Country Analysis," University of Southern California Law School Working Paper, Los angeles, CA, 2006.

Kaplan, Steven, "Management Buyouts: Efficiency Gains or Value Transfers," *University of Chicago Working Paper*, 244, October 1988.

Kaplan, Steven, "The Effects of Management Buyouts on Operating Performance and Value," *Journal of Financial Economics*, Vol. 24, 1989a, pp. 217–254.

Kaplan, Steven, "Management Buyouts: Efficiency Gains or Value Transfers," *Journal of Finance*, Vol. 3, July 1989b, pp. 611–632.

Kaplan, Steven, "The Staying Power of Leveraged Buyouts," *Journal of Financial Economics*, Vol. 29, October 1991, pp. 287–314.

Kirkland, Rik, "Private Money," *Fortune*, March 7, 2007.

Koons Cynthia, "Junk Bond Holders Losing Their Status," *The Wall Street Journal*, January 13, 2007, p. B4.

Lehn, Ken, and Annette Poulsen, "Leveraged Buyouts: Wealth Created or Wealth Redistributed?" in M. Weidenbaum and K. Chilton, eds., *Public Policy Towards Corporate Takeovers*, Transaction Publishers, New Brunswick, NJ, 1988.

Lowenstein, Louis, "Management Buyouts," *Columbia Law Review*, 85, 1985, pp. 730–784.

Lowenstein, Louis, *What's Wrong with Wall Street?* Addison-Wesley, Reading, MA, 1987, p. 184.

Mian, Shehzad, and James Rosenfeld, "Takeover Activity and the Long-Run Performance of Reverse Leveraged Buyouts," *Financial Management*, Vol. 22, Winter 1993, pp. 46–57.

Molina, Carlos A., "Are Firms Unleveraged? An Examination of the Effect of Leverage on Default Probabilities," *Journal of Finance*, Vol. 60, 2006, pp. 1427–1459.

Morrow, D. J., "Why the IRS Might Love Those LBOs," *Fortune*, December 5, 1988, pp. 145–146.

Muscarella, C. J., and M. R. Vetsuypens, "Efficiency and Organizational Structure: A Study of Reverse LBOs," *Journal of Finance*, Vol. 45, December 1990, pp. 1389–1413.

Nelson, Brett, "The LBO Method," *Forbes*, Vol. 173, Issue 13, June 21, 2004, pp. 187–190.

Newbould, Gerald D., Robert E. Chatfield, and Ronald F. Anderson, "Leveraged Buyouts and Tax Incentives, *Financial Management*, Vol. 21, 1992, pp. 1621–1637.

Ofek, Eli, "Efficiency Gains in Unsuccessful Management Buyouts," *Journal of Finance*, Vol. 49, June 1994, pp. 627–654.

Opler, Tim, and Sheridan Titman, "The Determinants of Leveraged Buyout Activity: Free Cash Flow vs. Financial Distress Costs," *Journal of Finance*, Vol. 48, December 1993, pp. 1985–2000.

Phan, P. H., "Organizational Restructuring and Economic Performance in Leveraged Buyouts: An Ex Post Study," *Academy of Management Journal*, Vol. 38, pp. 704–739.

Qwest, "Qwest Communications Sells QwestDex," News Releases, August 20, 2002, www.qwest.com.

Rickertsen, Rick, *Buyout: The Insider's Guide to Buying Your Own Company*, AMACOM, New York, 2001, pp. 222–232.

Roden, Dianne M., and Wilbur G. Lewellen, "Corporate Capital Structure Decisions: Evidence from Leveraged Buyouts," *Financial Management*, Vol. 24, Summer 1995, pp. 76–87.

Ruback, Richard S., "Capital Cash Flows: A Simple Approach to Valuing Risky Cash Flows," *Financial Management*, Summer 2002, pp. 85–103.

Scannell, Kara, Serena Ng, and Alistair MacDonald, "Can Anyone Police Swaps," *The Wall Street Journal*, August 31, 2006, pp. C1–C2.

Sender, Henne, "High Risk Debt Still Has Allure for Buyout Deals," *The Wall Street Journal*, June 13, 2006, p. C2.

Shuttleworth, Richard, "Twelve Keys to Venture Capital, Tech Coast Angels, 2004," http://techcoastangels.com.

Smith, Abbie, "Corporate Ownership Structure and Performance: The Case of Management Buy-Outs," *Journal of Financial Economics*, Vol. 27, September 1990, pp. 143–164.

Travlos, N. G., and M. N. Cornett, "Going Private Buyouts and Determinants of Shareholders' Returns," *Journal of Accounting, Auditing and Finance*, Vol. 8, 1993, pp. 1–25.

Wasserstein, Bruce, *Big Deal: The Battle for Control of America's Leading Corporations*, Warner Books, New York, 1998, pp. 113–116.

Wigmore, Barry, "The Decline in Credit Quality of Junk Bond Issues, 1980–1988," in Patrick A. Gaughan, ed., *Readings in Mergers and Acquisitions*, Basil Blackwell, Cambridge, 1994, pp. 171–184.

Wright, Mike, Luc Renneboog, Tomas Simons, and Louise Scholes, "Leveraged Buyouts in the U.K. and Continental Europe: Retrospect and Prospect," *Journal of Applied Corporate Finance*, Vol. 18, 2006, pp. 38–55.

Yago, Glenn, *Junk Bonds: How High Yield Securities Restructured Corporate America*, Oxford University Press, New York, 1991.

Zuckerman, Gregory, Henny Sender, and Scott Patterson, "Hedge Fund Crowd Sees More Green as Fortress Its Jackpot with IPO," *The Wall Street Journal*, February 10, 2007, p. A1.

PART • V

Alternative Business and Restructuring Strategies

CHAPTER • 14

Joint Ventures, Partnerships, Strategic Alliances, and Licensing

Humility is not thinking less of yourself. It is thinking less about yourself.

—Rick Warren

Inside M&A: Getting Wired: Wal-Mart–America Online and Other Internet Marketing Alliances

During the second half of 1999, the number of marketing alliances between major retailers and Internet companies exploded. Wal-Mart Stores, the world's biggest retailer, and Circuit City, a large consumer electronics retailer, announced partnerships with America Online (AOL). Best Buy, the largest U.S. consumer electronics chain, partnered with Microsoft, which previously had joined with Tandy Corporation's RadioShack stores. Signaling its own strategy of bringing its service to anyone, anywhere, AOL announced in 2000 partnerships with Sprint PCS and Nokia to help move AOL's service from the desktop to phones, pagers, organizers, and even TVs.

Wal-Mart and AOL

Wal-Mart and AOL have agreed to create a low-cost Web service for consumers who lack access and to promote each other's services. Wal-Mart customers will get software that allows them to set up the service through AOL's CompuServe service. The retailer also will distribute AOL's software with a link to Wal-Mart's Web site, Wal-Mart.com. The Internet access service will be geared to Wal-Mart customers in smaller towns that currently do not have local numbers to dial for online connections. Wal-Mart wants to funnel as many customers as possible to its revamped Web site, which contains a pharmacy, a photo center, and travel services in addition to general merchandise. The alliance gives AOL access to the 90–100 million people who shop at Wal-Mart weekly.

Microsoft, Best Buy, and RadioShack

Through its alliance with Best Buy, Microsoft is selling its products—including Microsoft Network (MSN) Internet access services and handheld devices such as digital telephones, handheld organizers, and WebTV that connect to the Web—through kiosks in Best Buy's 354 stores nationwide. In exchange, Microsoft has invested $200 million in Best Buy. Microsoft has a similar arrangement with Tandy Company's RadioShack stores in which it agreed to invest $100 million in Tandy's online sales site in exchange for in-store displays promoting Microsoft products and services. Both Best Buy and RadioShack are major advertisers on MSN and share in the monthly revenue from some of the Microsoft Internet access services they sell through their stores. Best Buy has issued 4 million new shares of common stock to Microsoft in exchange for its investment, giving Microsoft approximately a 2% ownership position in Best Buy.

Circuit City and America Online

AOL and Circuit City entered a strategic alliance to provide in-store promotion of AOL products and services to Circuit City shoppers nationwide, to make AOL Circuit City's preferred Internet online service, and to feature Circuit City as an anchor tenant in AOL's shopping mall. Under the agreement, AOL products and services are displayed prominently in dedicated retail space in Circuit City's 615 stores across the nation. Access to the Internet is available via AOL through dial-up service and developing broadband technologies, including digital subscriber line and satellite, as well as wireless interactive devices. Circuit City is promoting AOL and its in-store offerings in its print and television advertising programs and in other promotional and marketing campaigns. As an anchor tenant on AOL's shopping mall, Circuit City will have access to AOL's subscriber base.

Chapter Overview

For many years, joint ventures (JVs) and alliances have been commonplace in high-tech industries; many segments of manufacturing; the oil exploration, mining, and chemical industries; media and entertainment; financial services; among pharmaceutical and biotechnology firms; and in real estate. They have taken the form of licensing, distribution, comarketing, research and development agreements, and equity investments.

The term *business alliance* will be used throughout this chapter to include joint ventures, partnerships, strategic alliances, equity partnerships, licensing agreements, and franchise alliances. What all of these arrangements have in common is that they generally involve sharing the risk, reward, and control among all participants.

The primary theme of this chapter is that well-constructed business alliances often represent viable alternatives to mergers and acquisitions (M&As) and that they always should be considered as one of the many options for achieving strategic business objectives. The principal differences in the various types of business alliances were discussed in some detail in Chapter 1; as such, they only are summarized in Table 14-1. This chapter discusses the wide variety of motives for business alliances and the factors that are common to most successful alliances. Also addressed are advantages and disadvantages of alternative legal structures, important deal-structuring issues, and empirical studies that purport to measure the contribution of business alliances to creating shareholder wealth. A review of this chapter is available on the CD-ROM accompanying this book.

TABLE 14-1 Key Differences among Business Alliances

Type	Key Characteristics
Joint Ventures (JV)	• Independent legal entity involving 2 or more parties • May be organized as a corporation, partnership, or other legal/business organization selected by the parties • Ownership, responsibilities, risks, and rewards allocated to parties • Each party retains corporate identity and autonomy • Created by parties contributing assets for a specific purpose and for a limited duration
Strategic Alliances (e.g., technology transfer, R&D sharing, cross-marketing)	• Do not involve the formation of separate legal entities • May be precursor to JV, partnership, or acquisition • Generally not passive but involve cross-training, coordinated product development, and long-term contracts based on performance metrics such as product quality rather than price
Equity Partnerships	• Have all the characteristics of an alliance • Involve making minority investment in other party (e.g., 5–10%) • Minority investor may have an option to buy a larger stake in other party
Licensing —Product —Process —Merchandise and Trademark	• Patent, trademark, or copyright licensed in exchange for royalty or fee • Generally no sharing of risk or reward • Generally stipulates what is being sold, how and where it can be used, and for how long • Payments usually consist of an initial fee and royalties based on a percentage of future license sales
Franchising Alliances	• Network of alliances in which partners linked by licensing agreements (e.g., fast-food chains, hardware stores) • Often grant exclusive rights to sell or distribute goods or services in specific geographic areas or markets • Licensees may be required to purchase goods and services from other firms in the alliance
Network Alliances	• Interconnecting alliances among companies crossing international and industrial boundaries • May involve companies collaborating in one market while competing in others (e.g., computers, airlines, cellular telephones) • Most often formed to access skills from different but converging industries
Exclusive Agreements	• Usually involve rights for manufacturing or marketing specific products or services • Each party benefits from the specific skills or assets the other party brings to the relationship

Motivations for Business Alliances

Business alliances are generally not created as a result of one company making a passive investment in another. Money alone rarely provides the basis for a successful long-term business alliance. A partner often can obtain funding from a variety of sources but may be able to obtain access to a set of skills or nonfinancial resources only from a specific source. The motivation for an alliance can include risk sharing, gaining access to new markets, globalization, cost reduction, a desire to acquire (or exit) a business, or the favorable regulatory treatment they often receive as compared with M&As.

Risk Sharing

Risk is the potential for losing, or at least not gaining, value. Risk often is perceived to be greater the more money, management time, or other resources a company has committed to an endeavor and the less certain the outcome. To mitigate perceived risk, companies often enter into alliances to gain access to know-how and scarce resources or to reduce the amount of resources they would have to commit if they were to do it on their own. For example, in late 2004, General Motors and DaimlerChrysler (at that time the world's largest and fifth largest auto manufacturers) agreed to jointly develop hybrid gasoline–electric engines for cars and light trucks. Neither corporation felt comfortable in assuming the full cost and risk associated with developing this new automotive technology. Moreover, each company would be willing to contribute the results of their own internal R&D efforts to the joint development of a technology to be shared by the two companies.

Sharing Proprietary Knowledge

Developing new technologies can be extremely expensive. Given the pace at which technology changes, the risk is high that a competitor will be able to develop a superior technology before a firm can bring its own new technology to market. Consequently, high-tech companies with expertise in a specific technology segment often combine their efforts with another company or companies with complementary know-how to reduce the risk of failing to develop the "right" technology. Moreover, by having multiple contacts throughout an industry, it is unlikely that a firm will overlook new innovations or best practices. For example, TiVo, a small manufacturer of set-top boxes that provide interactive TV service, raised $32 million in 1999 through a series of private debt placements with CBS, NBC, Disney/ABC, Hughes's Direct TV satellite service, and Comcast (a leading cable TV service). By lending to TiVo, these companies would be able to obtain access to the latest technologies that may someday be necessary to remain competitive in their respective markets.

In 1983, Rockwell, Sperry, Boeing, Control Data, Honeywell, Digital Equipment, Kodak, Harris, Lockheed, 3M, Martin Marietta, Motorola, NCR, National Semiconductor, and RCA formed Micro-Electronics Computer Corporation (MCC). MCC was formed to share the cost of developing semiconductor, computer, and software technology that could not otherwise be developed cost effectively by these companies. In 1988, Sematech was founded as a research alliance consisting of IBM, National Semiconductor, Advanced Micro Devices, and other major companies. In the late 1980s, Union Carbide and AlliedSignal combined their skills to launch UOP, a joint venture that develops process technology for the oil-refining and petrochemical industries. Since its inception, it has become the world's largest process-licensing organization, with annual revenues exceeding $800 million.

The Microsoft and Intel relationship is one of the better known technology partnerships; it is also one of the more confusing. The two cooperate to enhance the "Wintel" world, which combines Windows operating systems with Intel microchips. Although the partnership is viewed as highly successful, there have been disagreements. For example,

Intel wants more competition and lower prices on software bundled with personal computers to reduce the pricing pressure on PC components such as microchips as PC prices decline. Microsoft has been very slow to reduce the price of its Windows operating system software, presumably to maintain profit margins.

Sharing Management Skills and Resources

Firms often lack the management skills and resources to solve complex tasks and projects. These deficiencies can be remedied by aligning with other firms, which possess the requisite skills and proprietary knowledge. Building contractors and real estate developers have collaborated for years by pooling their resources to construct, market, and manage large, complex commercial projects. Similarly, the contribution of Dow Chemical personnel to a JV with Cordis, a small pacemaker manufacturer, enabled the JV to keep pace with accelerating production.

The huge research and development (R&D) requirements, the relatively low success rate, near-term patent expiration of profitable drugs, and the high cost of marketing new drugs have resulted in a dramatic escalation of the use of partnerships in the pharmaceutical industry. Reflecting the bureaucratic inertia often found in megacorporations, large pharmaceutical firms also actively seek partnerships with smaller, more nimble and innovative firms as a way of revitalizing their new drug pipelines. Such relationships are also commonplace among biotechnology firms. Lerner, Shane, and Tsai (2003) found that small biotechnology firms are in fact likely to fund their R&D through JVs with large corporations, with the larger partner receiving the controlling interest.

In mid-2006, Nokia, a Finnish firm specializing in wireless communications, and Siemens, a German company with a strong position in fixed line telecommunications, agreed to pool their networking equipment divisions in a joint venture. The new firm, called Nokia Siemens Networks, is based in Finland and is the third largest telecom equipment maker in the world. By pooling their technical and manufacturing resources, the partners believe they can develop integrated products for the major telecommunications companies competing to sell a combination of fixed line, broadband Internet, wireless, and television.

Sharing Substantial Capital Outlays

As the U.S. cellular phone market became saturated, wireless carriers fought tenaciously to increase market share in a maturing market. Increased price competition and the exorbitant costs of creating and supporting national networks contributed to consolidation in the industry. Regional and foreign carriers were encouraged to join forces to achieve the scale necessary to support these burdensome costs. Vodafone and Verizon Communications joined forces in 1999 to form Verizon Wireless. SBC and Bell Atlantic formed the Cingular Wireless partnership, which acquired AT&T Wireless in early 2004.

Securing Sources of Supply

The chemical industry is highly vulnerable to swings in energy costs and other raw materials. Chemical companies such as Dow, Hercules, and Olin, have used JVs to build new plants throughout the world. When shortages of raw materials threaten future production, these firms commonly form JVs to secure future sources of supply. Similarly, CNOOC, the large Chinese oil concern, has been busily trying to invest in oil and natural gas assets in highly diverse geographic areas to obtain reliable sources of supply.

CNOOC's efforts have ranged from outright acquisition (e.g., the attempted takeover of Unocal in the United States), to long-term contracts (e.g., Canadian tar sands), to joint ventures in various locations in Africa (e.g., Sudan and Kenya).

Cost Reduction

In the 1980s and 1990s, retailers and financial services firms outsourced such back-office activities as information and application processing to such firms as IBM and EDS. Others have outsourced payroll processing and benefits management to such firms as ADP. More recently, firms have entered so-called logistics alliances. Such alliances cover both transportation and warehousing services and utilize a single provider for these services.

In January 2001, the U.S. Postal Service (USPS) and Federal Express (FedEx) announced an agreement in which FedEx will haul the USPS' Express Mail and Priority Mail as well as some first class mail. FedEx will provide guaranteed space at a cost of $6.3 billion over 7 years. Moreover, FedEx will pay the USPS at least $126 million to place its collection boxes at post offices. The USPS is expected to save more than $1 billion by phasing out its Indianapolis hub and by allowing a number of leases to expire. In turn, FedEx is guaranteed a specific volume of mail and will have access to a large number of package drop-off points at USPS offices (Schmid, 2001).

Companies also may choose to combine their manufacturing operations in a single facility with the capacity to meet the production requirements of all parties involved. By building a large facility, the firms jointly can benefit from lower production costs resulting from spreading fixed costs over larger volumes of production. This type of arrangement is commonplace within the newspaper industry in major cities in which there are several newspapers engaged in "head-to-head" competition. Similar cost benefits may be realized if one party closes its production facility and satisfies its production requirements by buying at preferred prices from another party with substantial unused capacity.

Other examples of competitors combining operating units to achieve economies of scale include Sony and Ericsson combining their mobile-handset units to compete with Nokia and Motorola in the late 1990s, as well as Hitachi and Mitsubishi forming an $8 billion a year semiconductor joint venture in 2000. In 2005, Canon and Toshiba created a new manufacturing operation to satisfy their requirements for SED displays for TVs by investing a combined $1.8 billion in a JV.

Gaining Access to New Markets

Gaining access to new customers is often a highly expensive proposition involving substantial initial marketing costs such as advertising, promotion, warehousing, and distribution expenses. The cost may be prohibitive unless alternative distribution channels providing access to the targeted markets can be found. For example, despite concerns about the viability of many Chinese banks awash in bad loans, Bank of America, the second largest bank in the United States, paid $2.5 billion in 2005 for a 9% stake in China Construction Bank to gain access to what could be potentially a large and lucrative market. Despite competing in various markets, Google was able to inexpensively gain access to eBay's non-U.S. customers. In an alliance with eBay in late 2006, eBay granted Google the exclusive right to display text advertisements on eBay's auction Web sites outside the United States, with eBay sharing in the revenue generated by the advertisements. Earlier that same year, Yahoo signed a similar agreement with eBay for sites within the United States.

Using Another Firm's Distribution Channel

A company may enter into an alliance to sell its products through another firm's direct sales force, telemarketing operation, retail outlets, or Internet site. The alliance may involve the payment of a percentage of revenue generated in this manner to the firm whose distribution channel is being used. Alternatively, firms may enter into a "cross-marketing" relationship in which they agree to sell the other firm's products through their own distribution channels. The profitability of these additional sales can be significant, because neither firm has to add substantially to its overhead expense or to its investment in building or expanding its distribution channels.

The Convergence of "Bricks and Clicks"

Although marketing alliances have been commonplace for years, we now are seeing a convergence of conventional brick-and-mortar retail operations and cyberspace distribution channels. Companies are using their recognizable consumer brands and complementary sales and distribution channels to comarket products and services. More than 80% of U.S. consumers were online by the end of 2006. Retailers and Internet companies now are trying to gain access to consumers who are not currently online. In recent years, a slew of partnerships were announced between major retail outlets and Internet players for this purpose.

Globalization

The dizzying pace of international competition has increased the demand for alliances and JVs to enable companies to enter markets in which they lack production or distribution channels or in which laws prohibit 100% foreign ownership of a business. Moreover, a major foreign competitor might turn out to be an excellent partner in fighting domestic competition. Alternatively, a domestic competitor could become a partner in combating a foreign competitor.

The automotive industry uses alliances to provide additional production capacity, distribution outlets, technology development, and parts supply. Many companies, such as General Motors and Ford, take minority equity positions in other companies within the industry to gain access to foreign markets. By aligning with Lenovo Group as a strategic partner, IBM has an opportunity to enlarge dramatically its market share in China (see Case Study 14-1).

Case Study 14-1
IBM Partners with China's Lenovo Group

IBM was able to satisfy two objectives in selling its ailing PC business to China's Lenovo Group for $1.75 billion in cash, stock, and assumed liabilities in late 2004. First, the firm is able to eliminate the business' ongoing operating losses from its books. Second, IBM could sharply enhance its position in information technology in China, which is rapidly emerging as one of the world's largest information technology markets.

Under the terms of the transaction, Lenovo will relocate its world headquarters from Beijing to Armonk, New York, near IBM's headquarters. Lenovo will be managed by senior

IBM executives. IBM owns an 18.9% stake in the new company, which will sell PCs under the IBM brand name. IBM gets to continue selling PCs, which helps it sell other products and services to corporations as packages. IBM hopes to exploit Lenovo's influence in China to sell additional information technology products. As China's number one PC maker, Lenovo has a 27% overall market share and strong positions in both the government and education markets. The firm's presence in these markets is expected to strengthen, because the Chinese government owns 46% of the new company. Lenovo hopes to benefit by obtaining a global PC operation and to expand its sales under the widely recognized and respected IBM brand.

The challenges of implementing the new business are daunting. Enormous geographic and cultural differences will make communication difficult. While former IBM employees will be among the product designers, some corporate customers may not trust Lenovo to deliver the quality and innovation they have come to expect from IBM.

Case Study Discussion Questions

1. Which party (i.e., IBM or Lenovo) to this transaction do you think will benefit the most? Explain your answer.
2. What other challenges to making this relationship work would you anticipate? Be specific.
3. What challenges might arise for IBM due to the Chinese government's ownership of such a large part of Lenovo? Be specific.

A Prelude to Acquisition or Exit

Rather than acquire a company, a firm may choose to make a minority investment in another company. In exchange for the investment, the investing firm may receive board representation, preferred access to specific proprietary technology, and an option to purchase a controlling interest in the company. The investing firm is able to assess the quality of management, cultural compatibility, and the viability of the other firm's technology without having to acquire a controlling interest in the firm.

Case Study 14-2 illustrates how a JV may be used to acquire selected assets of another company. In an *acquisition JV*, one company purchases a controlling interest in an existing subsidiary of another company. The former wholly owned subsidiary subsequently is managed as a JV corporation.

Case Study 14-2
Bridgestone Acquires Firestone's Tire Assets

Bridgestone Tire, a Japanese company, lacking a source of retail distribution in the United States, approached its competitor, Firestone, to create a JV whose formation involved two stages. In the first stage, Firestone, which consisted of a tire manufacturing and distribution division and a diversified rubber products division, agreed to transfer its tire manufacturing operations into a subsidiary. This subsidiary was owned and operated by Firestone's worldwide tire business. In the second stage, Firestone sold three-fourths of its equity in the tire subsidiary to Bridgestone, making the subsidiary a JV corporation. Firestone received

$1.25 billion in cash, $750 million from Bridgestone, and $500 million from the JV. Firestone also retained 100% ownership in the diversified products division and 25% of the tire JV corporation. For its investment, Bridgestone acquired a 75% ownership interest in a worldwide tire manufacturing and distribution system.

Case Study Discussion Questions

1. What other options for entering the United States could Bridgestone have considered?
2. Why do you believe Bridgestone chose to invest in Firestone rather than pursue another option?

Favorable Regulatory Treatment

As noted in Chapter 2, the Department of Justice (DoJ) has looked on JVs far more favorably than mergers or acquisitions. Mergers result in a reduction in the number of firms. In contrast, JVs increase the number of firms because the parents continue to operate while another firm is created. Project-oriented JVs often are viewed favorably by regulators. Regulatory authorities tend to encourage collaborative research, particularly when the research is shared among all the parties to the JV.

Critical Success Factors for Business Alliances

Research suggests that the success of a JV or alliance is dependent on a specific set of identifiable factors (Child and Faulkner, 1998; Kantor, 2002; Lynch, 1990; Lynch, 1993). These factors most often include the following: synergy; cooperation; clarity of purpose, roles, and responsibilities; accountability; a "win–win" situation; compatible time frames and financial expectations for the partners; and support from top management.

Synergy

Successful alliances are usually characterized by partners who have attributes that either complement existing strengths or offset significant weaknesses. Examples include economies of scale and scope, access to new products, distribution channels, and proprietary know-how. As with any merger or acquisition, the perceived synergy should be measurable to the extent possible. Interestingly, successful alliances are often those in which the partners contribute a skill or resource in addition to or other than money. Such alliances often make good economic sense and, as such, will be able to get financing.

Cooperation

All parties involved must be willing to cooperate at all times. A lack of cooperation contributes to poor communication and reduces the likelihood that the objectives of the JV or alliance will be realized. Not surprisingly, companies with similar philosophies, goals, rewards, operating practices, and ethics are more likely to be able to cooperate over the long run.

Clarity of Purpose, Roles, and Responsibilities

The purpose of the business alliance must be evident to all involved. A purpose that is widely understood drives timetables, division of responsibility, commitments to milestones, and measurable results. Internal conflict and lethargic decision making will inevitably result from poorly defined roles and responsibilities of those participating in the alliance.

Accountability

Successful alliances hold managers accountable for their actions. Once roles and responsibilities have been clearly defined and communicated, measurable goals to be achieved in identifiable time frames should be established for all managers. Such goals should be directly tied to the key objectives for the alliance. Incentives should be in place to reward good performance with respect to goals and those failing to perform should be held accountable.

Win–Win Situation

All parties to an alliance must believe they are benefiting from the activity for it to be successful. Johnson and Johnson's (J&J) alliance with Merck & Company in the marketing of Pepcid AC is a classic win–win situation. Merck contributed its prescription drug Pepcid AC to the alliance so that J&J could market it as an over-the-counter drug. With Merck as the developer of the upset stomach remedy and J&J as marketer, the product became the market share leader in this drug category. In contrast, the attempt by DaimlerChrysler, Ford, and GM to form an online auction network for parts, named Covisint, in early 2000 failed in part because the partners did not feel they were benefiting equally. Cooperation disintegrated when the automakers and suppliers believed that they would lose competitive information. At the end of 2003, Covisint sold its online auction service to FreeMarkets.com and redirected its efforts toward providing data communication and process integration among suppliers and automakers.

Compatible Time Frames and Financial Expectations

The length of time an alliance agreement remains in force depends on the partners' objectives, the availability of resources needed to achieve these objectives, and the accuracy of the assumptions on which the alliance's business plans are based. Incompatible time frames are a recipe for disaster. The management of a small Internet business may want to "cash out" within the next 12–18 months, whereas a larger firm may wish to gain market share over a number of years.

Support from the Top

Top management of the parents of a business alliance must involve themselves aggressively and publicly. Such support should be unambiguous and consistent. Tepid support or worse, indifference, will filter down to lower level managers and prove to be highly demotivating. Middle-level managers will tend to focus their time and effort on those activities that tend to maximize their compensation and likelihood of promotions. These activities may divert time and attention from the business alliance.

Alternative Legal Forms of Business Alliances

As is true of M&As, determining the legal form of a business alliance should follow the creation of a coherent business strategy. The choice of legal structure should be made only when the parties to the business alliance are comfortable with the venture's objectives, potential synergy, and preliminary financial analysis of projected returns and risk. Business alliances may assume a variety of different legal structures. These include the following: corporate, partnership, franchise, equity partnership, or written contract. Technically, a "handshake" agreement is also an option. However, given the inordinate risk associated with the lack of a written agreement, those seeking to create a business alliance are encouraged to avoid this type of arrangement. However, in some cultures, this type of informal agreement may be most appropriate. Efforts to insist on a detailed written agreement or contractual relationship may be viewed as offensive. The five basic legal structures, excluding the handshake agreement, are discussed in detail in the following section. Each has its own implications with respect to taxation, control by the owners, ability to trade ownership positions, limitations on liability, duration, and raising capital. The relative merits of each legal form are summarized in Table 14-2.

Corporate Structures

A corporation is a legal entity created under state law in the United States with an unending life and limited financial liability for its owners. Corporate legal structures include a generalized corporate form (also called C-type corporation) and the subchapter S (S-type) corporation. The S-type corporation contains certain tax advantages intended to facilitate the formation of small businesses, which are perceived to be major contributors to job growth. For an excellent discussion of the corporation, see Truitt (2006).

C-Type Corporations

A JV corporation normally involves a standalone business. The corporation's income will be taxed at the prevailing corporate tax rates. Corporations, other than S-type corporations, are subject to "double" taxation. Taxes are paid by the corporation when profits are earned and again by the shareholders when the corporation issues dividends. Moreover, setting up a corporate legal structure may be more time consuming and costly than other legal forms because of legal expenses incurred in drafting a corporate charter and bylaws. Although the corporate legal structure does have adverse tax consequences and may be more costly to establish, it does offer a number of important advantages over other legal forms. The four primary characteristics of a C-corporate structure include managerial

TABLE 14-2   Alternative Legal Forms Applicable to Business Alliances

Legal Form	Advantages	Disadvantages
Corporate Structures:		
—C Corporation	Continuity of ownership	Double taxation
	Limited liability	Inability to pass losses on to
	Provides operational autonomy	shareholders
	Provides for flexible financing	Relatively high set-up costs
	Facilitates tax-free merger	including charter and bylaws
—Sub-Chapter S	Avoids double taxation	Maximum of 75 shareholders
	Limited liability	Excludes corporate shareholders
		Must distribute all earnings
		Allows only one class of stock
		Lacks continuity of C
		corporate structure
		Difficult to raise large sums of
		money
Limited Liability	Limited liability	Owners also must be active
Company (LLC)	Owners can be managers without	participants in the firm
	losing limited liability	Lacks continuity of a corporate
	Avoids double taxation	structure
	Allows an unlimited number of	State laws governing LLC
	members or owners	formation differ making it
	Allows corporate shareholders	difficult for LLCs doing
	Can own more than 80% of another	business in multiple
	company	states
	Allows flexibility in allocating	Member shares often illiquid
	investment, profits, losses, and	because consent of members
	operational responsibilities	required to transfer ownership
	among members	
	Life set by owners	
	Can sell shares to "members"	
	without SEC registration	
	Allows foreign corporations as	
	investors	
Partnership Structures:		
—General Partnerships	Avoids double taxation	Partners have unlimited liability
	Allows flexibility in allocating	Lacks continuity of corporate
	investment, profits, losses, and	structure
	operational responsibilities	Partnership interests illiquid
	Life set by general partner	Partners jointly and severally
		liable
		Each partner has authority to bind
		the partnership to contracts
—Limited Liability	Limits partner liability (except for	Partnership interests illiquid
Partnerships	general partner)	Partnership dissolved if a partner
	Avoids double taxation	leaves
	State laws consistent (covered under	Private partnerships limited to 35
	the Uniform Limited	partners
	Partnership Act)	

TABLE 14-2 continued

Legal Form	Advantages	Disadvantages
Franchise Alliances	Allows repeated application of a successful business model	Success depends on quality of franchise sponsor support
	Minimizes start-up expenses	Royalty payments (3–7% of revenue)
	Facilitates communication of common brand and marketing strategy	
Equity Partnerships	Facilitates close working relationship	Limited tactical and strategic control
	Potential prelude to merger	
	May preempt competition	
Written Contracts	Easy start-up	Limited control
	Potential prelude to merger	Lacks close coordination
		Potential for limited commitment

autonomy, continuity of ownership or life, ease of transferring ownership and raising money, and limited liability. These characteristics are discussed next.

Managerial autonomy most often is used when the JV is large or complex enough to require a separate or centralized professional management organization. The corporate structure works best when the JV requires a certain amount of operational autonomy to be effective. The parent companies would continue to set strategy, but the JV's management would manage the day-to-day operations.

Unlike other legal forms, the corporate structure has an indefinite life as it does not have to be dissolved as a result of the death of the owners or if one of the owners wishes to liquidate their ownership position. A corporate legal structure may be warranted if the JV's goals are long term and if the parties choose to contribute cash directly to the JV. In return for the cash contribution, the JV partners receive stock in the new company. If the initial strategic reasons for the JV change and the JV no longer benefits one of the partners, the stock in the JV can be sold. Alternatively, the partner/shareholder can withdraw from active participation in the JV corporation, but it can remain a passive shareholder in anticipation of potential future appreciation of the stock. In addition, the corporate structure facilitates a tax-free merger in which the stock of the acquiring firm can be exchanged for the stock or assets of another firm. In practice, the transferability of ownership interests is strictly limited by the stipulations of a shareholder agreement created when the corporation is formed.

Under a corporate structure ownership can be easily transferred, which facilitates raising money. A corporate structure also may be justified if the JV is expected to have substantial future financing requirements. A corporate structure provides a broader array of financing options than other legal forms. These include the ability to sell interests in the form of shares and the issuance of corporate debentures and mortgage bonds. The ability to sell new shares enables the corporation to raise funds to expand while still retaining control if less than 51% of the corporation's shares are sold.

Under the corporate structure, the parent's liability is limited to the extent of its investment in the corporation. Consequently, an individual stockholder cannot be held responsible for the debts of the corporation or of other shareholders. Creditors cannot take the personal assets of the owners. However, an owner of a corporation can be held personally liable if he directly injures someone or personally guarantees a bank loan or a business debt on which the corporation defaults. Other exceptions to personal liability include the failure to deposit taxes withheld from employees' wages or the commission of intentional fraud that causes harm to the corporation or to someone else. Finally, an owner may be liable if she treats the corporation as an extension of her personal affairs by failing to adequately capitalize the corporation, hold regular directors and shareholders meetings, or to keep business records and transactions separate from the owners.

Subchapter S Corporations

A firm having 75 or fewer shareholders may qualify as an S-type corporation and may elect to be taxed as if it were a partnership and thus avoid double taxation. The major disadvantages to an S-type corporation are the exclusion of any corporate shareholders, the requirement to issue only one class of stock, the necessity of distributing all earnings to the shareholders each year, and that no more than 25% of the corporation's gross income may be derived from passive income. To be treated as an S corporation, all shareholders must simply sign and file IRS Form 2553. C corporations may convert to sub-chapter S corporations to eliminate double taxation of income; asset sales within 10 years of the conversion from a C to an S corporation are subject to capital gains taxes. However, after 10 years, such gains are tax free. In 2007, turnaround specialist, Sam Zell, after taking the Tribune corporation private, converted the firm to an S corporation to take advantage of the favorable tax treatment. Because the limited liability company offers its owners the significant advantage of greater flexibility in allocating profits and losses and because the LLC is not subject to the many restrictions of the S corporation, the overall popularity of the S corporation has declined.

Limited Liability Company

LLCs were first recognized for tax purposes in 1988 and are now available in all 50 states. While creating an LLC is more difficult than creating a partnership, managing one is significantly easier than running a corporation. Like a corporation, the LLC limits the liability of all its owners (called members) to the extent of their investment. Like a limited partnership, the LLC passes through all the profits and losses of the entity to its owners without itself being taxed.

To obtain this favorable tax status, the IRS generally requires that the LLC adopt an organization agreement that eliminates the characteristics of a C corporation: management autonomy, continuity of ownership or life, and free transferability of shares. Management autonomy is limited by expressly placing decisions about major issues pertaining to the management of the LLC (e.g., mergers or asset sales) in the hands of all its members. LLC organization agreements require that they be dissolved in case of the death or retirement or resignation of any member, thereby eliminating continuity of ownership for life. Free transferability is limited by making a transfer of ownership subject to the approval of all members.

Unlike S-type corporations, LLCs can own more than 80% of another corporation and have an unlimited number of shareholders or members. Also, corporations as well as non-U.S. residents can own LLC shares. Equity capital is obtained through offerings to owners or members. Capital is sometimes referred to as interests rather than shares since the latter denotes something, which may be freely traded. The LLC can sell shares or interests to members without completing the costly and time-consuming process of registering them with the Securities and Exchange Commission (SEC), which is required for corporations that sell their securities to the public. However, LLC shares are not traded on public exchanges. This arrangement works well for corporate JVs or projects developed through a subsidiary or affiliate. The parent corporation can separate a JV's risk from its other businesses while getting favorable tax treatment and greater flexibility in the allocation of revenues and losses among owners. Finally, LLCs can incorporate before an initial public offering tax free. This is necessary as they must register such issues with the SEC. The life of the LLC is determined by the owners and is generally set for a fixed number of years in contrast to the typical unlimited life for a corporation.

While a limited liability company must have members or owners, its management structure may be determined in whatever manner the members desire. Members may manage the LLC directly or provide for the election of a manager, officer, or board to conduct LLC's activities. Members hold final authority in the LLC, having the right to approve extraordinary actions such as mergers or asset sales. Member approval may be granted through meetings, written consents, and conference calls. Managers may represent the LLC in dealings with third parties.

The LLC's drawbacks are evident if one owner decides to leave. All other owners must formally agree to continue the firm. Also, all of the LLC's owners must take active roles in managing the firm. LLC interests are often illiquid as transfer of ownership is subject to the approval of other members. LLCs must be set for a limited time, typically 30 years. Each state has different laws about LLC formation and governance, so an LLC that does business in several states might not meet the requirements in every state. LLCs are formed when two or more "persons" (i.e., individuals, LLPs, corporations, etc.) agree to file Articles of Organization with the secretary of state's office. The most common types of firms to form LLCs are family-owned businesses, professional services firms such as lawyers, and companies with foreign investors.

Partnership Structures

Partnership structures frequently are used as an alternative to a corporation. Partnership structures include general partnerships and limited partnerships. While the owners of a partnership are not legally required to have a partnership agreement, it usually makes sense to have one. The partnership agreement spells out how business decisions are to be made and how profits and losses will be shared.

General Partnerships

Under the general partnership legal structure, investment, profits, losses, and operational responsibilities are allocated to the partners. The arrangement has no effect on the autonomy of the partners. Because profits and losses are allocated to the partners, the partnership is not subject to tax. The partnership structure also offers substantial flexibility in how the profits and losses are allocated to the partners. Typically, a corporate partner will form a special-purpose subsidiary to hold its interest. This not only limits liability but also may facilitate disposition of the JV interest in the future. The partnership structure is preferable to the other options when the business alliance is expected to have short (3–5 years') duration and if high levels of commitment and management interaction are necessary for short time periods.

The primary disadvantage of the general partnership is that all the partners have unlimited liability and may have to cover the debts of less financially sound partners. Each partner is said to be jointly and severally liable for the partnership's debts. For example, if one of the partners negotiates a contract resulting in a substantial loss, each partner must pay for a portion of the loss, based on a previously determined agreement on the distribution of profits and losses. Because each partner has unlimited liability for all the debts of the firm, creditors of the partnership may claim assets from one or more of the partners if the remaining partners are unable to cover their share of the loss. Another disadvantage includes the ability of any partner to bind the entire business to a contract or other business deal. Consequently, if one partner purchases inventory at a price that the partnership cannot afford, the partnership is still obligated to pay.

Partnerships also lack continuity in that they must be dissolved if a partner dies or withdraws, unless a new partnership agreement can be drafted. To avoid this possibility, a partnership agreement should include a buy–sell condition or right of first refusal allowing the partners to buy out a departing partner's interest so the business can continue. Finally, partnership interests may also be difficult to sell because of the lack of a public market, thus making the partnership difficult to liquidate or to transfer partnership interests.

Forming a partnership generally requires applying for a local business license or tax registration certificate. If the business name does not contain all of the partners' last names, the partnership must register a fictitious or assumed business name in the county in which it is established. The body of law governing partnerships is the Uniform Partnership Act (UPA). In cases where the partnership agreement is silent, the UPA provides the precedence in general partnership law.

Limited Partnerships

A limited liability partnership is one in which one or more of the partners can be designated as having limited liability as long as at least one partner has unlimited liability. It is governed by state law and, unless the partnership strictly conforms to state restrictions, will be regarded as a general partnership. Limited partners usually cannot lose more than their capital contribution. Those who are responsible for the day-to-day operations of the partnership's activities, whose individual acts are binding on the other partners, and who are personally liable for the partnership's total liabilities are called ***general partners***. Those who contribute only money and who are not involved in management decisions are called ***limited partners***. Usually limited partners receive income, capital gains, and tax benefits, whereas the general partner collects fees and a percentage of the capital gain and income.

Typical limited partnerships are in real estate, oil and gas, and equipment leasing, but they also are used to finance movies, R&D, and other projects. Public limited partnerships are sold through brokerage firms, financial planners, and other registered securities representatives. Public partnerships may have an unlimited number of investors and their partnership plans must be filed with the SEC. Private limited partnerships are constructed with fewer than 35 limited partners who each invest more than $20,000. Their plans do not have to be filed with the SEC.

The sources of equity capital for limited partnerships are the funds supplied by the general and limited partners. The total amount of equity funds needed by the limited partnerships is typically committed when the partnership is formed. Therefore, ventures that are expected to grow are not usually set up as limited partnerships. LLPs are very popular for accountants, physicians, attorneys, and consultants. With the exception of Louisiana, every state has adopted either the Uniform Limited Partnership Act (ULPA) or the Revised Uniform Limited Partnership Act (RULPA).

Franchise Alliance

Franchises typically involve a franchisee making an initial investment to purchase a license, plus additional capital investment for real estate, machinery, and working capital. For this initial investment, the franchisor provides training, site-selection assistance, and economies of scale in purchasing. Royalty payments for the license typically run 3–7% of annual franchisee revenue. Franchise success rates exceed 80% over a 5-year period as compared with some types of start-ups, which have success rates of less than 10% after 5 years (Lynch, 1990, p. 253). The franchise alliance is preferred when a given business format can be replicated many times. Moreover, franchise alliances are also appropriate when there needs to be a common, recognizable identity presented to customers of each of the alliance partners and when close operational coordination is required. In addition, a franchise alliance may be desirable when a common marketing program needs to be coordinated and implemented by a single partner. Multistate franchises must be careful to be in full compliance with the franchise laws of the states in which they have franchisees. Such laws often differ considerably from one state to the next.

The franchisor and franchisee operate as separate entities, usually as corporations or LLCs. There are four basic types of franchises: distributor (auto dealerships), processing (bottling plants), chain (restaurants), and area franchises (a geographic region is licensed to new franchisee to subfranchise to others). Franchisors are required to comply with the Federal Trade Commission's Franchise Rule, which requires franchisors to make a presale disclosure nationwide to prospective franchisees. Registration of franchises falls under state law modeled on the Uniform Franchise Offering Circular, which requires franchisors to make specific presale disclosures to prospective franchisees, including their balance sheets, income statements for the preceding 3 years, terms and conditions of the franchise agreement, territory restrictions, etc.

Equity Partnership

An equity partnership involves a company's purchase of stock (resulting in a less than controlling interest) in another company or a two-way exchange of stock by the two companies. It often is referred to as a partnership because of the equity ownership exchanged. Equity partnerships commonly are used in purchaser–supplier relationships, technology development, marketing alliances, and in situations in which a larger firm makes an investment in a smaller firm to ensure its continued financial viability. In exchange for an equity investment, a firm normally receives a seat on the board of directors and possibly an option to buy a controlling interest in the company. The equity partnership may be preferred when there is a need to have a long-term or close strategic relationship, to preempt a competitor from making an alliance or acquisition, or as a prelude to an acquisition or merger.

Written Contract

The written contract is the simplest form of legal structure. This form is used most often with strategic alliances because it maintains an "arm's-length" or independent relationship between the parties to the contract. The contract normally stipulates such things as how the revenue is divided, the responsibilities of each party, the duration of the alliance, and confidentiality requirements. No separate business entity is established for legal or tax purposes. The written contract most often is used when the business alliance is expected to last less than 3 years, when frequent close coordination is not required, when capital investments are made independently by each party to the agreement, and when the parties have had little previous contact.

Strategic and Operational Plans

Planning should precede deal-structuring activities. Too often, the parties to a proposed alliance get bogged down early in the process in such details as legal structure, control, ownership, and other deal-structuring issues. They do not spend sufficient energy in determining if the proposal makes good strategic and operational sense in terms of the participants' financial and nonfinancial objectives. Before any deal-structuring issues are addressed, the prospective parties must agree on the basic strategic direction and purpose of the alliance as defined in the alliances' strategic plan, as well as the financial and nonfinancial goals established in the operations plan.

The strategic plan identifies the primary purpose or mission of the business alliance; communicates specific quantifiable targets such as financial returns or market share and milestones; and analyzes the business alliance's strengths and weaknesses and opportunities and threats relative to the competition. The purpose of a business alliance could take various forms as diverse as R&D, cross-selling the partners' products, or jointly developing an oil field. The roles and responsibilities of each partner in conducting the day-to day operations of the business alliance are stipulated in an operations plan. Teams representing all parties to the alliance should be involved from the outset of the discussions in developing both a strategic and operations plan for the venture. The operations plan should reflect the specific needs of the proposed business alliance. The operations plan should be written by those responsible for implementing the plan. The operations plan is typically a 1-year plan that outlines for managers what is to be accomplished, when it is to be accomplished, and what resources are required. The operations plan also is referred to as the annual operating budget. The short-term objectives of the operations plan must be consistent with the more long-term objectives of the strategic plan. Chapter 4 describes tools and methods for developing strategic and operational business plans.

Note that some deal-structuring decisions, such as the legal form, may affect the financial analysis because of the tax implications for the cash flow of the business alliance and how it is funded. Nonetheless, the decision to proceed with forming the alliance should never be justified based on tax benefits alone but rather on the strategic value of the alliance to the participants.

Resolving Business Alliance Deal-Structuring Issues

Generally speaking, the purpose of deal structuring in a business alliance is to allocate fairly risks, rewards, resource requirements, and responsibilities among participants. The formation of a successful alliance requires that a series of issues be resolved before signing an alliance agreement. Table 14-3 summarizes the key issues and related questions that need to be addressed as part of the business alliance deal-structuring process. This section discusses how these issues most often are resolved. For an excellent discussion of deal structuring in this context, see Ebin (1998), Freeman and Stephens (1994), Fusaro (1995), and Lorange and Roos (1992).

TABLE 14-3 Business Alliance Deal-Structuring Issues

Issue	Key Questions
Scope	What products are included and what are excluded? Who receives rights to distribute, manufacture, acquire, or license technology or purchase future products or technology?
Duration	How long is the alliance expected to exist?
Legal Form	What is the appropriate legal structure—standalone entity or contractual?
Governance	How are the interests of the parents to be protected? Who is responsible for specific accomplishments?
Control	How are strategic decisions to be addressed? How are day-to-day operational decisions to be handled?
Resource Contributions and Ownership Determination	Who contributes what and in what form? Cash? Assets? Guarantees/loans? Technology including patents, trademarks, copyrights, and proprietary knowledge? How are contributions to be valued? How is ownership determined?
Financing Ongoing Capital Requirements	What happens if additional cash is needed?
Distribution	How are profits and losses allocated? How are dividends determined?
Performance Criteria	How is performance to plan measured and monitored?
Dispute Resolution	How are disagreements resolved?
Revision	How will the agreement be modified?
Termination	What are the guidelines for termination? Who owns the assets on termination? What are the rights of the parties to continue the alliance activities after termination?
Transfer of Interests	How are ownership interests to be transferred? What are the restrictions on the transfer of interests? How will new alliance participants be handled? Will there be rights of first refusal, drag-along, tag-along, or put provisions?
Tax	Who receives tax benefits?
Management/Organization	How is the alliance to be managed?
Confidential Information	How is confidential information handled? How are employees and customers of the parent firms protected?
Regulatory Restrictions and Notifications	What licenses are required? What regulations need to be satisfied? What agencies need to be notified?

Scope

A basic question in setting up a business alliance involves which products specifically are included and excluded from the business alliance. This question deals with defining the scope of the business alliance. Scope outlines how broadly the alliance will be applied in pursuing its purpose. For example, an alliance whose purpose is to commercialize products developed by the partners could be broadly or narrowly defined in specifying what products or services are to be offered, to whom, in what geographic areas, and for what time period. Failure to define scope adequately can lead to situations in which the alliance may be competing with the products or services offered by the parent firms. Furthermore, alliances are not static. Products developed for one purpose may prove to have other applications in the future. With respect to both current and future products, the alliance agreement should identify who receives rights to market or distribute products, manufacture products, acquire or license technology, or purchase products from the venture.

In certain types of alliances, intellectual property may play a very important role. It is common for a share in the intangible benefits of the alliance, such as rights to new developments of intellectual property, to be more important to an alliance participant than its share of the alliance's profits. What started out as a symbiotic marketing relationship between two pharmaceutical powerhouses, Johnson and Johnson and Amgen, deteriorated into a highly contentious feud (Case Study 14-3). The failure to properly define which parties would have the rights to sell certain drugs for certain applications and to sell future drugs that may have been developed as a result of the alliance laid the groundwork for a lengthy legal battle between these two corporations.

Case Study 14-3
Johnson and Johnson Sues Amgen

In 1999, Johnson and Johnson (J&J) sued Amgen over their 14-year alliance to sell a blood-enhancing treatment called erythropoietin. The disagreement began when unforeseen competitive changes in the marketplace and mistrust between the partners began to strain the relationship. The relationship had begun in the mid-1980s with J&J helping to commercialize Amgen's blood-enhancing treatment, but the partners ended up squabbling over sales rights and a spin-off drug.

J&J booked most of the sales of its version of the $3.7 billion medicine by selling it for chemotherapy and other broader uses, whereas Amgen was left with the relatively smaller dialysis market. Moreover, the companies could not agree on future products for the JV. Amgen won the right in arbitration to sell a chemically similar medicine that can be taken weekly rather than daily. Arbitrators ruled that the new formulation was different enough to fall outside the licensing pact between Amgen and J&J.

Case Study Discussion Questions

1. What could these companies have done before forming the alliance to have mitigated the problems that arose after the alliance was formed? Why do you believe they may have avoided addressing these issues at the outset?
2. What types of mechanisms could be used other than litigation to resolve such differences once they arise?

Duration

The participants need to agree on how long the business alliance is to remain in force. Participant expectations must be compatible. The management of a large corporation may view the alliance as critical to its long-term strategy; in contrast, the management of a small, start-up operation may be interested in "cashing out" as soon as possible. The expected longevity of the alliance is also an important determinant in the choice of a legal form. For example, the corporate structure more readily provides for a continuous life than a partnership structure because of its greater ease of transferring ownership interests. There is conflicting evidence on how long most business alliances actually last. Mercer Management Consulting in ongoing research concludes that most JVs last only about 3 years (Lajoux, 1998), whereas Booz-Allen and Hamilton (1993) reported an average life span of 7 years. The critical point is that most business alliances have a finite life corresponding to the time required to achieve the original strategic objectives when the alliance was first established.

Legal Form

The legal entity chosen for your business is a critical decision because of the significant legal and business consequences that result from choosing an inappropriate legal structure for your circumstances. Most businesses that are growth oriented or intend to eventually go public through an IPO generally become a C corporation due to its financing flexibility, unlimited life, continuity of ownership, and ability to combine on a tax-free basis with other firms. With certain exceptions concerning frequency, firms may convert from one legal structure to a C corporation before going public. The nature of the business will greatly influence the legal form you choose. See Table 14-4.

Governance

In the context of a business alliance, governance may be defined broadly as an oversight function providing for efficient, informed communication between two or more parent companies. The primary responsibilities of this oversight function are to protect the interests of the corporate parents, approve changes to strategy and annual operating

TABLE 14-4   Key Factors Affecting Choice of Legal Entity

Determining Factors: Businesses with	Should Select
High liability risks	C corporation, LLP, or LLC
Large capital/financing requirements	C corporation
Desired continuity of existence	C corporation
Desire for managerial autonomy	C corporation
Desire for growth through M&A	C corporation
Owners who are also active participants	LLCs
Foreign corporate investors	LLCs
Desire to allocate investments, profits, losses, and operating responsibilities among owners	LLCs and LLPs
Project focus/expected limited existence	LLPs
Owners who want to remain inactive	LLPs and C corporations
Large marketing expenses	Franchise
Strategies that are easily replicated	Franchise
Close coordination among participants not required	Written "arm's-length" agreement
Low risk/low capital requirements	Sole proprietorship or partnership

plans, allocate resources needed to make the alliance succeed, and arbitrate conflicts among lower levels of management. Historically, governance of business alliances has followed either a quasi-corporate or quasi-project approach. For example, the oil industry traditionally has managed alliances by establishing a board of directors to provide oversight of managers and to protect the interests of nonoperating owners. In contrast, in the pharmaceutical and automotive industries where nonequity alliances are common, firms treat governance like project management by creating a steering committee that allows all participants to comment on issues confronting the alliance.

As companies pursue alliances with different goals, duration, resource contributions, and potentially greater contributions to shareholder value, the traditional governance models will have to be modified. Alliances are becoming a key underpinning of a firm's overall business strategy. For highly complex alliances, governance may have to be implemented through multiple boards of directors, steering committees, operating committees, alliance managers, and project committees. For example, the General Electric and Honeywell industrial controls JV recognized that the interaction required to manage the JV was too extensive to be managed by a single board. Consequently, an operating committee and several project committees were established to address issues involving specialized expertise (Kalmbach and Roussel, 1999).

Resource Contributions and Ownership Determination

As part of the negotiation process, the participants must agree on a fair value for all tangible and intangible assets contributed to the business alliance. The valuation of partner contributions is important in that it often provides the basis for determining ownership shares in the business alliance. The shares of the corporation or the interests in the partnership will be distributed among the owners in accordance with the value contributed by each participant. The partner with the largest risk, the largest contributor of cash, or the person who contributes critical tangible or intangible assets generally is given the greatest equity share of a JV.

It is relatively easy to value tangible or "hard" contributions such as cash, promissory cash commitments, contingent commitments, stock of existing corporations, and assets and liabilities associated with an ongoing business in terms of actual dollars or their present values. A party contributing "hard" assets, such as a production facility, may want the contribution valued in terms of the value of increased production rather than its replacement cost or lease value. The contribution of a fully operational, modern facility to a venture interested in being first to market with a particular product may provide far greater value than if the venture attempted to build a new facility because of the delay inherent in the normal "break-in" period associated with new operations.

In contrast, intangible or "soft" or "in-kind" contributions such as skills, knowledge, services, patents, licenses, brand names, and technology are often much more difficult to value. Partners providing such services may be compensated by having the business alliance pay a market-based royalty or fee for such services. If the royalties or fees paid by the alliance are below standard market prices for comparable services, the difference between the market price and what the alliance actually is paying may become taxable income to the alliance. Alternatively, contributors of intellectual property may be compensated by receiving rights to future patents or technologies developed by the alliance. Participants in the business alliance contributing brand identities, which facilitate the alliance's entry into a particular market, may require assurances that they can purchase a certain amount of the product or service, at a guaranteed price, for a specific time period.

Financing Ongoing Capital Requirements

The business alliance may finance future capital requirements that cannot be financed out of operating cash flow by calling on the participants to make a capital contribution, issuing additional equity or partnership interests, or borrowing. Cingular's 2004 purchase of AT&T Wireless in an all cash offer totaling $41 billion (the largest all cash purchase on record) resulted in SBC and Bell Atlantic (co-owners of the Cingular JV) contributing 60 and 40% of the purchase price, respectively, to the joint venture to fund the acquisition. Their percentage equity contributions reflected their ownership shares of the joint venture.

If it is decided that the alliance should be able to borrow, the participants must agree on an appropriate financial structure for the enterprise. Financial structure refers to the amount of equity that will be contributed to the business alliance and how much debt it will carry. The financial structure will differ with the type of legal structure selected for the business alliance. Alliances established through a written contract obviate the need for such a financing decision, because each party to the contract will finance their own financial commitments to the alliance. Because of their more predictable cash flows, project-based JVs, particularly those that create a separate corporation, sometimes sell equity directly to the public or though a private placement. Banks and insurance companies also may be a source of funding.

Owner or Partner Financing

The equity owners or partners may agree to make contributions of capital in addition to their initial investments in the enterprise. The contributions usually are made in direct proportion to their equity or partnership interests. If one party chooses not to make a capital contribution, the ownership interests of all the parties are adjusted to reflect the changes in their cumulative capital contributions. This adjustment results in an increase in the ownership interests of those making the contribution and a reduction in the interests of those not making contributions.

Equity Financing

JVs formed as a corporation may issue different classes of either common or preferred stock. JVs established as partnerships raise capital through the issuance of limited partnership units to investors, with the sponsoring firms becoming general partners. An LLC structure may be necessary when one of the owners is a foreign investor. When a larger company aligns with a smaller company, it may make a small equity investment in the smaller firm to ensure it remains solvent or to benefit from potential equity appreciation. Such investments often include an option to purchase the remainder of the shares, or at least a controlling interest, at a predetermined price if the smaller firm or the JV satisfies certain financial targets. In some instances, the general partner of a partnership may be required, as part of the original agreement, to invest specific amounts of capital in the venture at regular intervals or when certain milestones are reached. These requirements normally are stipulated in the original articles of partnership.

Debt Financing

Non-project-related alliances or alliances without financial track records often will find it very difficult to borrow. Banks and insurance companies generally require loan guarantees from the participating owners. Such guarantees give lenders recourse to the participating owners in the event the alliance fails to repay its debt. The amount that the alliance ultimately can borrow is likely to be based more on the financial viability of the owners than on the venture's cash flows. ***Nonrecourse financing*** (i.e., loans granted to the venture without partner guarantees) usually is reserved for ventures that already have demonstrated that they are viable businesses.

Control

Control is distinguishable from ownership by the use of agreements among investors or voting rights or by issuing different classes of shares. Control issues should be negotiated with an eye to differentiating between day-to-day management and major strategic decisions. The most successful JVs are those in which one party is responsible for most routine management decisions, with the other parties participating in decision making only when the issue is fundamental to the success of the business alliance. The business alliance agreement must define what issues are to be considered fundamental to the alliance and address how they are to be resolved, either by majority votes or by veto rights given to one or more of the parties. Whichever owner is responsible for the results of the alliance will want operational control. Operational control should be placed with the owner most able to manage the JV. In some cases, the partner with operational control could be a minority owner.

If the owner having the largest equity share does not also have operational control, the owner is likely to insist on being involved in the operations of the business alliance by having a seat on the board of directors or steering committee. The owner also may insist on having veto rights over issues it views as fundamental to the success of the alliance. These issues often include changes in the alliance's purpose and scope, overall strategy, capital expenditures over a certain amount of money, key management promotions, salary increases applying to the general employee population, the amount and timing of dividend payments, buyout conditions, and acquisitions or divestitures. In LLCs and LLPs, one owner may be given responsibility for managing tax issues related to the alliance. This owner is usually the one most able to utilize any losses incurred by the alliance. Case Study 14-4 illustrates common control issues when one firm makes a minority investment in another.

Case Study 14-4
Conoco Phillips Buys a Stake in Russian Oil Giant Lukoil

In late 2004, Conoco Phillips (Conoco) announced the purchase of 7.6% of Lukoil's (a largely government-owned Russian oil and gas company) stock for $2.36 billion during a government auction of Lukoil's stock. The deal gives Conoco access to Russia's huge, but largely undeveloped, oil and natural gas reserves. Conoco intends to boost its investment to 10% by year-end and to 20% within 2 to 3 years. To help ensure that Conoco's interests are protected, even though it has only a minority position, Conoco will have one seat on Lukoil's board and Lukoil changed its corporate charter to require unanimous board approval for the most important decisions such as payment of dividends and major new investments. Conoco will gain one additional seat once its ownership share climbs to 20%. Conoco has also agreed to pay $370 million to Lukoil for a 30% stake in a joint venture to develop reserves in northern Russia. The two firms will split operational responsibilities equally. Conoco's stock fell more than 1% immediately following the announcement.

Case Study Discussion Questions

1. Describe the operational and managerial challenges facing the two partners.
2. Do you believe that Conoco gained an effective say in Lukoil's operations following its investment? Explain your answer.
3. Why do you believe Conoco's stock fell immediately following the announcement?

Distribution Issues

Distribution issues relate to dividend policies and how profits and losses are allocated among the owners. The dividend policy determines the cash return each partner should receive. How the cash flows of the venture will be divided generally depends on the initial equity contribution of each partner, ongoing equity contributions, and noncash contributions in the form of technical and managerial resources. Allocation of profits and losses normally follows directly from the allocation of shares or partnership interests. When the profits flow from intellectual property rights contributed by one of the parties, royalties or payments for expertise may be used to compensate the party contributing the property rights. When profits are attributable to distribution or marketing efforts of a partner, fees and commission can be used to compensate the partners. Similarly, rental payments can be used to allocate profits attributable to specific equipment or facilities contributed by a partner.

Performance Criteria

The lack of adequate performance measurement criteria can result in significant disputes among the partners and eventually contribute to the termination of the venture. In early 2000, the Carlyle Group took a 20% stake in French paper products manufacturer Otor for $54 million. The shareholder agreement included provisions for Carlyle to assume majority control of the business should Otor fail to meet certain profitability targets. Two years later, incumbent management, who remained with the firm after the investment, resisted Carlyle's efforts to take control after claiming that the targets had not been met. After more than 3 years in the French court system, Carlyle finally received ownership of 80% of the firm.

Performance criteria should be both measurable and simple enough to be understood and used by the partners and by managers at all levels. Vague or overly complex criteria provide opportunities for future disputes over their interpretation. Performance criteria should be spelled out clearly in the business alliance agreement. Nonfinancial performance measures should be linked to financial return drivers. For example, factors such as market share, consistent product quality, and customer service may be critical to success in the marketplace. Improvements in the venture's performance against these critical success factors ultimately should result in increasing financial returns to the partners.

The balanced scorecard technique may be applied to measuring alliance performance by having the partners agree on a small number (i.e., 5–10) of relevant indicators. The number of indicators should be limited. This enables alliance managers to more easily track performance to plan. The indicators should include financial and nonfinancial, short- and long-term, and internal and customer-focused measures. Examples of performance indicators include return on investment, operating cash flow, profit margins, asset turnover, market share, on-time delivery, and customer satisfaction survey results. Many alliances fail to adequately measure costs, because they fail to estimate the actual cost of coordinating owner activities and the value of senior managers time. Alliance benefits may be understated if the revenue generated for the owners by products sold in conjunction with those sold by the alliance are not taken into account. Alliances also generate intangible benefits such as opportunities for learning, and access to new technologies and markets.

Managers will ignore performance indicators if their compensation is not linked to their actual performance against these measures. The top alliance managers should be evaluated against the full list of balanced scorecard performance measures. The performance of lower level managers should be evaluated only against those measures over which they have some degree of control.

Dispute Resolution

No matter how well the participants draft the venture agreement, disputes between parties to the agreement will arise. There are several ways to resolve such disputes. One is a *choice of law provision* in the alliance agreement indicating which state's or country's laws will have jurisdiction in settling disputes. This provision should be drafted with an understanding of the likely outcome of litigation in any of the participants' home countries or states and the attitude of these countries' or states' courts in enforcing choice of law provisions in the JV agreements.

In international JVs, the choice of common law or civil law countries for settling disputes can have profoundly different outcomes. Common laws countries, found typically in North America and Western Europe, rely on case law (i.e., resolutions of prior disputes) for guidance in resolving current disputes. In contrast, civil law countries located primarily in Asia do not rely on case law but allow magistrates to apply their interpretation of existing statutes to resolve current disputes. Consequently, the outcome of certain types of disputes may be less predictable in civil rather than common law countries, which rely heavily on historical precedents.

Another important clause is the definition of what constitutes a deadlock or impasse when a disagreement arises. This clause should include a clear statement of what events trigger various types of dispute-resolution procedures. Care should be taken not to define the events triggering dispute-resolution procedures so narrowly that minor disagreements are subject to the dispute mechanism. Finally, an *arbitration clause* usually is used to address major disagreements. Such a clause should define the type of dispute subject to arbitration and how the arbitrator will be selected.

Revision

No matter how well conceived the business alliance was at the time of formation, changing circumstances and partner objectives may prompt a need to revise the objectives of the business alliance. If one of the parties to the agreement wishes to withdraw, the participants should have agreed in advance how the withdrawing party's ownership interest would be divided among the remaining parties. Moreover, a product or technology may be developed that was not foreseen when the alliance first was conceived. The alliance agreement should indicate that the rights to manufacture and distribute the product or technology might be purchased by a specific alliance participant. If revisions cannot be made to meet the needs of the partners, it may be necessary to terminate the enterprise. The events triggering dissolution usually are spelled out in the ***deadlock clause***.

Termination

In general, business alliances are not intended to become permanent arrangements. A business alliance may be terminated as a result of the completion of a project, successful operations resulting in merger of the partners, diverging strategic objectives of the partners, and failure of the alliance to achieve stated objectives. Termination provisions in the alliance agreement should include buyout clauses enabling one party to purchase another's ownership interests, prices of the buyout, and how assets and liabilities are to be divided if the venture fails or the partners elect to dissolve the operation. What will happen to key personnel and who owns tangible and intangible property such as trade secrets and patents also should be considered in the termination provisions. In some instances, a JV may convert to a simple licensing arrangement. Consequently, the partner may disengage from the JV without losing all benefits by purchasing rights to the product or technology.

Transfer of Interests

JV and alliance agreements often limit how and to whom parties to the agreements can transfer their interests. This is justified by noting that each party entered the agreement with the understanding of who their partners would be. In agreements that permit transfers under certain conditions, the partners or the JV itself may have ***rights of first refusal*** (i.e., the party wishing to leave the JV first must offer their interests to other participants in the JV). Usually, the agreement will permit the parties to transfer their interests to corporate affiliates without restrictions.

Parties to the agreement may have the right to "put" or sell their interests to the venture, and the venture may have a call option or right to purchase such interests. There also may be "tag-along" and "drag-along" provisions, which have the effect of a third-party purchaser acquiring not only the interest of the JV party whose interest it seeks to acquire but also the interests of other parties as well. A ***drag-along*** provision specifically *requires* a party not otherwise interested in selling its ownership interest to the third party to do so. A ***tag-along*** provision gives a party to the alliance, who was not originally targeted by the third party, the *option* to join the targeted party in conveying its interest to the third party.

Buyout clauses in alliances that give one party an option to sell their share of the partnership to the other at a fixed price can backfire. Examples abound. AOL Time

Warner had to pay a German media firm $6.75 billion for its half of AOL Europe, four times its estimated value at the time. The best alliance agreements avoid clauses such as fixed or minimum buyout prices, short payment periods, and strict payment options, such as cash only, to avoid giving substantial leverage to one party over the other. In early 2005, General Motors and Fiat agreed to dissolve their 5-year partnership after GM agreed to pay Fiat $2 billion in cash to avoid having to exercise a put option to buy the financially weak Fiat Auto.

Taxes

Each of the different types of business alliance legal structures has different tax implications. Although tax considerations should never drive the transaction, failure to explore their different implications can have painful financial consequences for all parties involved. As is true for a merger, the primary tax concerns of the JV partners will be to avoid the recognition of taxable gains on the formation of the venture and to minimize taxes on the distribution of its earnings.

In addition to the double taxation of dividends discussed earlier, the corporate structure may have other adverse tax consequences. If the partner's owns less than 80% of the alliance, its share of the alliance's results cannot be included in its consolidated income tax return. This has two effects. First, when earnings are distributed, they will be subject to an intercorporate dividend tax, which can be 7% if the partner's ownership interest in the venture is 20% or more. Second, losses of the business alliance cannot be used to offset other income earned by the participant (Tillinghast, 1998, pp. 163–164). For tax purposes, the preferred alternative to a corporate legal structure is to use a "pass-through" legal structure such as a limited liability company or partnership.

Because the profits and losses are allocated directly to the partners, the partnership does not have to pay taxes. Each partner in the JV will report its share of the enterprise's income or loss in its own consolidated return, and no intercorporate dividend tax will be imposed. In addition, the partnership can be structured in such a way that some partners can receive a larger share of the profits, whereas others receive a larger share of the losses. This flexibility in tax planning is an important factor stimulating the use of partnerships and LLCs. These entities can allocate to each JV partner a portion of a particular class of revenue, income, gain, loss, or expense. These "special allocations" can be made in the documents governing the creation of the partnership or limited liability company. Thus, partners or members (i.e., LLCs) need not share the results of the venture on a pro rata basis. The business alliance itself does not incur any tax because no separate legal entity has been created. Any profits earned or losses incurred by parties to the alliance are taxed at their own effective tax rates.

When one of the partners contributes technology, patent rights, or other property to the JV, the contribution may be structured so that the partner receives equity in exchange for the contribution. Otherwise, it will be viewed by the IRS as an attempt to avoid making cash contributions and will be treated as taxable income to the JV.

If a new corporation has been created, expenses related to the start-up (e.g., advertising, training, and equipment/facility lease payments) are capitalized as deferred expenses and amortized over a 5-year period rather than expensed in the first year. However, once the venture is actively engaged in business, these types of expenses generally can be treated as operating expenses and deducted for tax purposes.

Services provided to the JV, such as accounting, auditing, legal, human resource, and treasury services are not viewed by the IRS as being "at risk" if the JV fails. The JV should pay prevailing market fees for such services. Services provided to the JV in return for equity may be seen as taxable to the JV by the IRS if such services are not truly "at risk."

Management and Organizational Issues

Before a business alliance agreement is signed, the partners must decide what type of organizational structure will provide the most effective management and leadership.

Steering or Joint Management Committee

Control of business alliances most often is accomplished through a steering committee. The steering committee is the ultimate authority for ensuring that the venture stays focused on the strategic objectives agreed to by the partners. To maintain good communication, coordination, and teamwork, the committee should meet at least monthly. The committee should provide operations managers with sufficient autonomy so they can take responsibility for their actions and be rewarded for their initiative.

Methods of Dividing Ownership and Control

The first method of control is the *majority–minority framework*, which relies on identifying a clearly dominant partner. A dominant partner is defined as having at least a 51% ownership stake in the enterprise. In this scenario, the equity, control, and distribution of rewards reflect the majority–minority relationship. This type of structure tends to promote the ability to make rapid mid-course corrections and clearly defines who is in charge. This framework is most appropriate for high-risk ventures where quick decisions often are required. The major disadvantage of this approach is that the minority partner may feel powerless and become passive or alienated.

The second method of control is the *equal division of power framework*, which usually means that equity is split 50/50. This assumes that the initial contribution, distribution, decision making, and control are split equally. This approach helps keep the partners actively engaged in the management of the venture. This is best suited for partners sharing a strong common vision for the venture and possessing similar corporate cultures. However, this approach can lead to deadlocks and to the eventual dissolution of the alliance, in the absence of mutual respect, good problem-solving skills, and patience by the partners.

Under the *"majority rules" framework*, the equity distribution may involve three partners. Two of the partners have large equal shares, whereas the third partner may have less than 10%. The minority partner is used to break deadlocks. This approach enables the primary partners to remain actively engaged in the enterprise without stalemating the decision-making process.

In the *multiple party framework*, no partner has control. Instead, control resides with the management of the venture. Consequently, decision making can be nimble and made by those that best understand the issues. This framework is well suited for international ventures, where a country's laws may prohibit a foreign firm from having a controlling interest in a domestic firm. In this instance, it is commonplace for a domestic company to own the majority of the equity but for the operational control of the venture to reside with the foreign partner. In addition to a proportional split of the dividends paid, the foreign company may receive additional payments in the form of management fees and bonuses (Armstrong and Hagel, 1997).

Confidential Information

Parties to a business alliance will have access to a substantial amount of confidential information, including proprietary know-how, customers, and employees. The alliance agreement should specify how such information should be treated. Confidential information should never be released without the consent of all parties involved. Moreover, the alliance agreement also should contain clauses preventing the various partners from soliciting the other's employees for purposes of employment or from soliciting the other partner's customers.

Regulatory Restrictions and Notifications

From an antitrust perspective, the DoJ has historically looked on business alliances far more favorably than mergers or acquisitions. Nonetheless, JVs may be subject to Hart–Scott–Rodino filing requirements, because the parties to the JV are viewed as acquirers and the JV itself is viewed as a target. For JVs between competitors to be acceptable to regulators, competitors should be able to do something together that they could not do alone.

In general, competitors can be relatively confident that a partnership will be acceptable to regulators if in combination they do not control more than 20% of the market. Project-oriented ventures are looked at most favorably. Collaborative research is encouraged, particularly when the research is shared among all the parties to the alliance. However, regulators will move aggressively to investigate any perceived restraint of competition between partners, such as price fixing and market allocation, or any effort to deprive competitors from accessing a much-needed resource. Alliances among competitors are likely to spark a review by the regulators, because they have the potential to result in price fixing and dividing up the market. See Chapter 2 for a more detailed discussion of regulations covering business combinations. Case Study 14-5 illustrates many of the previously discussed deal-structuring issues.

Case Study 14-5
Pixar and Disney Part Company

The announcement on February 5, 2004, of the end of the wildly successful partnership between Walt Disney Company ("Disney") and Pixar Animation Studios ("Pixar") rocked the investment and entertainment world. While the partnership continued until the end of 2005, the split-up underscores the nature of the rifts that can develop in business alliances of all types. The dissolution of the partnership ends a relationship in existence since 1995 in which Disney produced and distributed the highly popular films created by Pixar. Under the terms of the original partnership agreement, the two firms cofinanced each film and split the profits evenly. Moreover, Disney received 12.5% of film revenues for distributing the films. Negotiations to renew the partnership after 2005 foundered on Pixar's desire to get a greater share of the partnership's profits. Disney CEO, Michael Eisner, refused to accept a significant reduction in distribution fees and film royalties; while Steve Jobs, Pixar's CEO, criticized Disney's creative capabilities and noted that marketing alone will not make a poor film successful.

After 10 months of talks between Disney and Pixar, Disney rejected a deal that would have required it to earn substantially less from future Pixar releases. Disney also would have had to relinquish potentially lucrative copyrights to existing films such as *Toy Story* and *Finding Nemo*. Disney shares immediately fell by almost 2% on the news of the announcement, while Pixar's shares skyrocketed almost 4% by the end of the day. Pixar contributed more than 50% of Disney Studio's operating profits, and Disney Studios accounted for about one-fourth of Disney's total operating profits. While Disney now faces Pixar as a competitor, it retains the rights to make video and theatrical sequels and TV shows to the movies covered by the current partnership agreement. However, while Disney does retain the right to make sequels to Pixar films, it does not own the underlying technology and must re-create the millions of lines of computer code for each character.

The key challenge for Disney will be to fill the creative vacuum left by the loss of Pixar writers and animators. Disney is particularly vulnerable in that it has severely cut back its own feature animation department and has stumbled in recent years with a variety of box office duds (e.g., *Treasure Planet*). Reflecting concern that Disney would not be able to compete with Pixar, bond-rating service, Fitch Ratings, suggested a possible downgrade of Disney debt. Pixar announced that it was seeking another production studio. Immediately following this announcement, Sony and others approached Pixar with proposals to collaborate in making animated films.

Epilogue

In early 2006, Pixar agreed to be acquired by Disney. See Case Study 4-4 in Chapter 4 for a detailed discussion of this transaction.

Case Study Discussion Questions

1. In your opinion, what were the motivations for forming the Disney–Pixar partnership in 1995? Which partner do you believe had the greatest leverage in these negotiations? Explain your answer.
2. What happened since 1995 that might have contributed to the breakup? (Hint: Consider partner objectives, personalities of Steve Jobs and Michael Eisner, perceived relative contribution, and Disney's in-house capabilities.)
3. How does the dissolution of the partnership leave Disney vulnerable? What could Disney have done to protect itself from these vulnerabilities in the original negotiations? (Hint: Consider scope of the agreement, management and control, dispute resolution mechanisms, valuation of tangible and intangible assets, ownership of partnership assets following dissolution, and performance criteria.)
4. What does the reaction of the stock market and credit-rating agencies tell you about how investors value the contribution of the two partners to the partnership? Do you think investors may have overreacted? Explain your answer.

Answers to these Case Study Discussion Questions are available in the Online Instructor's Manual for this book.

Empirical Findings

Abnormal Returns

There is empirical evidence that JVs and strategic alliances create value for their participants. (See Table 14-5.) Abnormal returns (i.e., those in excess of what would have been predicted by the capital asset pricing model) average about 1.5% around the announcement date. Participants in horizontal relationships (i.e., those involving partners in the same industry) tend to share equally in the wealth creation. However, for vertical JVs, suppliers experienced a greater portion of the wealth created (Johnson and Houston, 2000). Moreover, the increase in wealth was much greater for horizontal alliances involving the transfer of technical knowledge than for nontechnical alliances (Chan, Kensinger, Keown, and Martin, 1997; Das, Sen, and Sengupta, 1998). Finally, as is true for M&As, firms with greater alliance experience enjoy a greater likelihood of success and greater wealth creation than those that have little experience (Kale, Dyer, and Singh, 2002).

The Growing Role of Business Alliances

The average large company, which may have had no alliances in 1990, now has more than 30 (Kalmbach and Roussel, 1999). During the last decade, the number of reported alliances has been increasing at about 30% per year. Robinson (2002) reported that the number of merger transactions per year between 1985 through 1989 averaged 2599 as compared to 726 per year for alliances. Between 1990 and 1995, the average annual rate at which alliances were formed accelerated to 4196 versus 2616 for M&A transactions. The sharp acceleration in alliance formation in part reflected a loosening of antitrust regulatory policies that extended the encouragement of alliances for R&D activities to joint production operations.

Despite rapid growth, there is evidence that most companies have yet to develop the skill to implement alliances successfully. The Kalmbach and Roussel (1999) study

TABLE 14-5   Abnormal Returns to Alliance Participants around Announcement Dates

McConnell and Nantell (1985): 136 JVs from 1972 to 1979	2.15%
Woolridge and Snow (1990): 767 JVs from 1972 to 1987	2.45%
Koh and Venkatraman (1991): 239 technology firms in JVs from 1972 to 1986	.87%
Chan, Kensinger, Keown, and Martin (1997): 345 strategic alliances from 1983 to 1992	.64% for both horizontal and non-horizontal alliances 3.54% for horizontal alliances involving technical knowledge transfer
Das, Sen, and Sengupta (1998): 119 strategic alliances from 1987 to 1991	1% (for technology transfer alliances)
Johnson and Houston (2000): 191 JVs from 1991 to 1995	1.67%
Kale, Dyer, and Singh (2002): 1572 strategic alllliances from 1988 to 1997	1.35% (for firms with significant alliance experience); otherwise .18%

indicates that 61% of the alliances are viewed as either disappointments or outright failures. This figure substantiates earlier findings by Robert Spekman of the Darden Graduate School of Business Administration that 60% of all ventures fail to meet expectations (Ellis, 1996). Klein (2004) reports that 55% of alliances fall apart within 3 years of their formation. These studies do not make allowances for different levels of experience in forming and managing alliances among the firms in their samples. As is true for M&As, cumulative experience is an important factor in increasing the likelihood that an alliance will meet expectations. According to a Booz-Allen survey of 700 alliances (Booz-Allen and Hamilton, 1993), financial returns on investment are directly related to a company's experience in forming and managing business alliances. Companies with one or two alliances in place tended to earn a 10% average return on investment as compared with 15% for those with three to five, 17% for those with six to eight, and 20% for those with nine or more.

Things to Remember

Business alliances may represent attractive alternatives to M&As. The motivations for business alliances can include risk sharing, gaining access to new markets, accelerating the introduction of new products, technology sharing, globalization, a desire to acquire (or exit) a business, and the perception that they are often more acceptable to regulators than are acquisitions or mergers.

Business alliances may assume a variety of different legal structures. These include the following: corporate, limited liability company, partnership, franchise, equity partnership, and written contract. Corporate legal structures include a generalized C-type and S-type structure. Although the corporate structure is subject to double taxation, it does provide for centralized management, continuity of ownership, ease of raising capital, and limited liability. Limited liability companies and partnerships frequently are used as an alternative to the corporate structure because of their greater flexibility in allocating gains and losses and their more favorable tax treatment. The written contract is the simplest legal structure and most often is used in strategic alliances.

Deal structuring in the context of a business alliance concerns the fair allocation of risks, rewards, resource requirements, and responsibilities among participants. Key issues that must be resolved include the alliance's scope, duration, legal form, governance, and control mechanism. The valuation of resource contributions ultimately determines ownership interests. How profits and losses will be distributed and how performance will be measured also must be determined. Alliance agreements also must be flexible enough to be revised when necessary and contain mechanisms for breaking deadlocks, transferring ownership interests, and dealing with the potential for termination.

Empirical studies suggest that business alliances contribute to shareholder value and that they are likely to become increasingly popular in the future. Studies suggest that alliances formed by partners in the same industry are more likely to create value than those that are not. Partners in such horizontal alliances are more likely to share equally in the benefits than are parties to vertical alliances between a customer and a supplier. In such arrangements, studies suggest that suppliers tend to experience a disproportionate amount of the benefit. Finally, the greatest value creation seems to occur for horizontal alliances that result in a technology or knowledge transfer among the parties to the alliance. Nonetheless, their success rate in terms of meeting participants' expectations does not seem to be materially different from that of M&As.

Chapter Discussion Questions

14-1. Under what circumstances does a business alliance represent an attractive alternative to a merger or acquisition?

14-2. Compare and contrast a corporate and partnership legal structure.

14-3. What are the primary motives for creating a business alliance? How do they differ from the motives for a merger or acquisition?

14-4. What factors are critical to the success of a business alliance?

14-5. Why is a handshake agreement a potentially dangerous form of business alliance? Are there any circumstances under which such an agreement may be appropriate?

14-6. What is a limited liability company? What are its advantages and disadvantages?

14-7. Why is defining the scope of a business alliance important?

14-8. Discuss ways of valuing tangible and intangible contributions to a JV.

14-9. What are the advantages and disadvantages of the various organizational structures that could be used to manage a business alliance?

14-10. What are the common reasons for the termination of a business alliance?

Answers to these Chapter Discussion Questions are available in the Online Instructor's Manual for instructors using this book.

Chapter Business Case

Case Study 14-6
Coca-Cola and Procter & Gamble's Aborted Effort to Create a Global Joint Venture Company

Background
Coca-Cola (Coke), arguably the world's best known brand, manufactures and distributes Coca-Cola as well as 230 other products in 200 countries through the world's largest distribution system. Procter & Gamble (P&G) sells 300 brands to nearly 5 billion consumers in 140 countries and holds more food patents than the three largest U.S. food companies combined. Moreover, P&G has a substantial number of new food and beverage products under development. Both firms have been competing in the health and wellness segment of the food market for years. P&G spends about 5% of its annual sales, about $1.9 billion, on R&D and holds more than 27,000 patents. The firm employs about 6000 scientists, including about 1200 people with Ph.D.s.

Both firms have extensive distribution systems. P&G uses a centralized selling and warehouse distribution system for servicing high-volume outlets such as grocery store chains. With a warehouse distribution system, the retailer is responsible for in-store presentations of the brands, including shelving, display, and merchandising. The primary disadvantage of this type of distribution system is that it does not reach many smaller outlets cost effectively, resulting in many lost opportunities. In contrast, Coke uses three distinct systems. Direct store delivery consists of a network of independently operated bottlers, which bottle and deliver the product directly to the outlet. The bottler also is responsible for in-store merchandising. Coke's warehouse distribution is similar to P&G's and is used primarily to distribute

Minute Maid products. Coke also sells beverage concentrates to distributors and food service outlets.

On February 21, 2001, Coca-Cola and Procter & Gamble announced, amid great fanfare, plans to create a standalone joint venture corporation focused on developing and marketing new juice and juice-based beverages as well as snacks on a global basis. The new company expected to benefit from Coca-Cola's worldwide distribution, merchandising, and customer marketing skills and P&G's R&D capabilities and wide range of popular brands. The new company would focus on the health and wellness segment of the food market. Less than 9 months later, Coke and P&G released a one-sentence joint statement on September 21, 2001, that they could achieve better returns for their respective shareholders if they pursued this opportunity independently. Although it is unclear what may have derailed what initially had seemed to the potential partners like such a good idea, it is instructive to examine the initial rationale for the proposed joint effort.

The New Company
Each parent would own 50% of the new company. Because of the businesses each partner was to contribute to the JV, the firm would have annual sales of $4 billion. The new firm would be an LLC, having its own board of directors consisting of two directors each from Coke and P&G. Moreover, the new firm would have its own management and dedicated staff providing administrative and R&D services. Coke was contributing a number of well-known brands including Minute Maid, Hi-C, Five Alive, Cappy, Kapo, Sonfil, and Qoo; P&G contributed Pringles, Sunny Delight, and Punica beverages. The new company would have had 15 manufacturing facilities and about 6000 employees.

Although the new firm was to have access to all distribution systems of the parents, it would have been free to choose the best route to market for each product. Although Minute Maid was to continue to use Coke's distribution channels, it also was to take advantage of existing refrigerated distribution systems built for Sunny Delight. Pringles was to use a variety of distribution systems, including the existing warehouse system. The Pringles brand was expected to take full advantage of Coke's global distribution and merchandising capabilities. Minute Maid was to gain access to new outlets through Coke's fountain and direct store distribution system.

Key Synergies
The new company's sales were expected to grow from $4 billion during the first 12 months of operation to more than $5 billion within 2 years. The combination of increasing revenue and cost savings was expected to contribute about $200 million in pretax earnings annually by 2005. Specifically, Pringles' revenue growth as a result of enhanced distribution was expected to contribute about $120 million of this projected improvement in pretax earnings. The importance of improved distribution is illustrated by noting that Coke has access to 16 million outlets globally. In the United States alone, that represents a 10-fold increase for Pringles, from its current 150,000 points of outlet. Similarly, improved merchandising and distribution of Sunny Delight was expected to contribute an additional $30 million in pretax income. The remaining $50 million in pretax earnings was to come from lower manufacturing, distribution, and administrative expenses and through discounts received on bulk purchases of foodstuffs and ingredients. P&G and Coke were hoping to stimulate innovation by combining global brands and distribution with talent from both firms in what

was hoped would be a highly entrepreneurial corporate culture. The parents also hoped that the standalone firm would be able to achieve focus and economies of scale that could not have been achieved by either firm separately.

Financial Impact on the Partners

The results of the LLC were not to be consolidated with those of the parents but rather shown using the equity method of accounting. Under this method of accounting, each parent's proportionate share of earnings (or losses) are shown on their income statement, and their equity interest in the LLC is displayed on their balance sheets. The new company was expected to be nondilutive of the earnings of the parents during its first full year of operations and contribute to earnings per share in subsequent years. The incremental earnings were expected to improve the market value of the parents by at least $1.5–2.0 billion.

Some observers suggested that P&G would stand to benefit the most from the JV. It would have gained substantially by obtaining access to the growing vending machine market. Historically, P&G's penetration in this market has been miniscule. It may have been this perceived disproportionate benefit accruing to P&G that may have contributed to the eventual demise of the joint venture effort. Coke may have sought additional benefits from the JV that P&G was simply not willing to cede. Once again, we see that no matter how attractive the concept may seem to be on the surface, the devil is indeed in the details when it comes to making it happen.

Case Study Discussion Questions

1. In your opinion, what were the motivating factors for the Coke and P&G business alliance?
2. Why do you think the parents selected a limited liability corporate structure for the new company? What are the advantages and disadvantages of this structure over alternative legal structures?
3. The parents estimate that the new company will add at least $1.5–2.0 billion to their market values. How do you think this estimated incremental value was determined?
4. Why do you think the parents opted to form a 50/50 distribution of ownership? What are some possible challenges of operating the new company with this type of an ownership arrangement? What can the parents do to overcome these challenges?
5. Do you think it is likely that the new company will become highly entrepreneurial and innovative? Why or why not? What can the parents do to stimulate the development of this type of an environment within the new company?
6. What factors may have contributed to the decision to discontinue efforts to implement the joint venture? Consider control, scope, financial, and resource contribution issues.

Answers to these Case Study Discussion Questions are available in the Online Instructor's Manual for instructors using this book.

Chapter Business Case

Case Study 14-7
Strains Threaten Verizon and Vodafone Joint Venture

Vodafone Group, the U.K-based cell phone behemoth wanted to expand geographic coverage in the United States. In 2000, they teamed up with Verizon Communications to form Verizon Wireless. The profitable business had annual revenues of $20 billion and a coast-to-coast network serving more U.S. customers than any other carrier. However, Vodafone's global ambitions and its buyout option threatened to put the venture at risk of breaking up.

Vodafone executives expressed frustration by the company's lack of control in the United States, because it owns just 45% of the venture. Vodafone, seeking to establish its own brand name, has been unable to get its name attached to a single product of the joint venture. Moreover, it has been unable to persuade the venture to use a technology compatible with that used by Vodafone in most of the 28 other countries in which it does business. This issue has proven to be particularly irksome since part of the Vodafone strategy is that its European, Asian, and Middle Eastern customers would be able to travel to the United States and use their cell phones on Vodafone's network in the United States. Vodafone also complains that Verizon Wireless has been slow to push next-generation wireless services such as photo and text messaging. Verizon Wireless also receives three times as many customer complaints as the average of Vodafone European units. Vodafone is reduced to being a passive financial investor in the operation. The two partners are also at odds in their strategies for owning wireless assets. Verizon Communications increasingly uses the venture to support its declining landline telephone business, by bundling wireless at a discount with other services. Vodafone considers landlines as having no future for its strategy.

The cloud hanging over Verizon Wireless is the put that Vodafone received as part of its initial investment, which gives it the right to sell its interests to Verizon at certain points through 2006. Vodafone can demand that Verizon pay it $10 billion in return for its stake. Mindful of the put, the partners have discussed friendlier ways to alter their relationship. For example, Vodafone could swap part of its stake in the venture for Verizon Communications' interest in Italian wireless operation Omnitel. Anything that reduced Vodafone's interest in Verizon Wireless below 20% would free Vodafone from a noncompete clause that precludes the firm from opening up its own operation in the United States.

Case Study Discussion Questions

1. What did Verizon Communications and Vodafone expect to get out of the business alliance?
2. To what extent are the problems plaguing the venture today a reflection of failure to communicate during the negotiations to form the joint venture? What should they have done differently?
3. Give examples of how the partners' objectives differ.
4. How could Verizon Communications have protected itself from the leverage Vodafone's put option provides? Explain your answer.

Answers to these Case Study Discussion Questions are available in the Online Instructor's Manual for instructors using this book.

References

Armstrong, Arthur, and John Hagel, *Net Gain: Expanding Markets through Virtual Communities,* Harvard Business School Press, Cambridge, MA, 1997.

Booz-Allen and Hamilton, *A Practical Guide to Alliances: Leapfrogging the Learning Curve,* Los Angeles, 1993.

Chan, Su Han, John W. Kensinger, Arthur J. Keown, and John D. Martin, "Do Strategic Alliances Create Value?," *Journal of Financial Economics,* Vol. 46, November 1997, pp. 199–221.

Child, John, and David Faulkner, *Strategies of Cooperation: Managerial Alliances, Networks, and Joint Ventures*, Oxford University Press, Oxford, 1998.

Das, Somnath, Pradyot K. Sen, and Sanjit Sengupta, "Impact of Strategic Alliances on Firm Valuation," *Academy of Management Journal,* Vol. 41, February 1998, pp. 27–41.

Ebin, Robert F., "Legal Aspects of International Joint Ventures and Strategic Alliances," in David J. Ben Daniel and Arthur H. Rosenbloom, eds., *International M&A, Joint Ventures and Beyond: Doing the Deal,* Wiley & Sons, New York, 1998, pp. 315–360.

Ellis, Caroline, "Briefings from the Editors," *Harvard Business Review,* Vol. 74, July/August 1996, p. 8.

Freeman, Louis S., and Thomas M. Stephens, "Advantages, Key Issues, and Tax Strategies in the Use of Partnerships by Corporate Joint Ventures," *Tax Strategies for Corporate Acquisitions, Dispositions, Spin-Offs, Joint Ventures and Other Strategic Alliances, Financings, Reorganizations, and Restructurings,* Practicing Law Institute, New York, 1994.

Fusaro, Robert F. X., "Issues to Consider in Drafting Joint Venture Agreements," *Drafting Corporate Agreements,* Practicing Law Institute, New York, 1995.

Hyde, Justin, "GM, Ford, DaimlerChrysler Join Online Ordering Forces," CNNfn, February 22, 2000.

Johnson, Shane A., and Mark B. Houston, "A Re-examination of the Motives and Gains in Joint Ventures," *Journal of Financial and Quantitative Analysis*, Vol. 35, March 2000.

Kale, Prashant, Jeffrey H. Dyer, and Harbir Singh, "Alliance Capability, Stock Market Response, and Long-Term Alliance Success: The Role of the Alliance Function," *Strategic Management Journal*, Vol. 23, August 2002, pp. 747–767.

Kalmbach, Charles, Jr., and Charles Roussel, "Dispelling the Myths of Alliances," Andersen Consulting, 1999, www.accenture.com/xd/xd.asp?it=enWeb&xd=ideas/outlook/special99/over_special_intro.xml.

Kantor, Rosabeth Moss, "Collaborative Advantage: The Art of Alliances," *Harvard Business Review on Strategic Alliances*, Harvard Business School Press, Cambridge, MA, 2002.

Klein, Karen E., "Urge to Merge? Take Care to Beware," *BusinessWeek,* July 1, 2004, p. 68.

Koh, Jeongsuk, and N. Venkatraman, "Joint Venture Formations and Stock Market Reactions: An Assessment in the Information Technology Sector," *The Academy of Management Journal*, Vol. 34, December 1991, pp. 869–892.

Lajoux, Alexandra Reed, *The Art of M&A Integration,* McGraw-Hill, New York, 1998, p. 41, note 7.

Lerner, J., H. Shane, and A. Tsai, "Do Equity Financing Cycles Matter?," *Journal of Financial Economics,* Vol. 67, 2003, pp. 411–446.

Lorange, Peter, and Johan Roos, *Strategic Alliances: Formation, Implementation, and Evolution,* Oxford: Blackwell, 1992.

Lynch, Robert Porter, *The Practical Guide to Joint Ventures and Corporate Alliances,* Wiley & Sons, New York, 1990.

Lynch, Robert Porter, *Business Alliance Guide: The Hidden Competitive Weapon,* Wiley & Sons, New York, 1993.

McConnell, John J., and Timothy J. Nantell, "Corporate Combinations and Common Stock Returns: The Case of Joint Ventures," *Journal of Finance,* Vol. 40, June 1985, pp. 519–536.

Robinson, David T., "Strategic Alliances and the Boundaries of the Firm," Working Paper, Columbia University, New York, May 1, 2002.

Schmid, Randolph E., "Post Office, FedEx Become Partners," *Orange County Register,* January 11, 2001, Business Section, p. 2.

Tillinghast, David R., "Tax Aspects of Inbound Merger and Acquisitions and Joint Venture Transactions," in David J. Ben Daniel and Arthur H. Rosenbloom, eds., *International M&A, Joint Ventures and Beyond: Doing the Deal,* Wiley & Sons, New York, 1998, pp. 151–180.

Truitt, Wesley B., *The Corporation,* Greenwood Press, New York, 2006.

Vodafone AirTouch, "Listing Particulars Relating to the Issue of Ordinary Shares in Vodafone AirTouch Plc in Connection with the Offer for Mannesmann AG," Filing with the Registrar of Companies in England and Wales, October 7, 1999, pp. 363–369.

Woolridge, J. Randall, and Charles C. Snow, "Stock Decisions," *Strategic Management Journal,* Vol. 11, June 1990, pp. 353–363.

CHAPTER • 15

Alternative Exit and Restructuring Strategies

Divestitures, Spin-Offs, Carve-Outs, Split-Ups, Split-Offs, Bankruptcy, and Liquidation

Experience is the name everyone gives to their mistakes.

—Oscar Wilde

Inside M&A: Financial Services Firms Streamline Their Operations

During 2005 and 2006, a wave of big financial services firms announced their intentions to spin-off operations that did not seem to fit strategically with their core business. In addition to realigning their strategies, the parent firms noted the favorable tax consequences of a spin-off, the potential improvement in the parent's financial returns, the elimination of conflicts with customers, and the removal of what for some had become a management distraction.

American Express announced plans in early 2005 to jettison its financial advisory business through a tax-free spin-off to its shareholders. The firm also noted that it would incur significant restructuring-related expenses just before the spin-off. Such one-time write-offs by the parent are sometimes necessary to "clean-up" the balance sheet of the unit to be spun off and to unburden the newly formed company's earnings performance. American Express anticipates substantial improvement in future financial returns on assets as it will be eliminating more than $410 billion in assets from its balance sheet that had been generating relatively meager earnings.

Investment bank Morgan Stanley announced in mid-2005 its intent to spin off its Discover Credit Card operation. While Discover Card generated about one-fifth of the firm's pretax profits, Morgan Stanley has been unable to realize significant synergies with its other operations. The firm announced that a spin-off restructure was undertaken rather than an outright divestiture because it was more "tax-efficient." The firm noted that, if properly structured, its shareholders would not have to pay income taxes on any gains they might realize until they decided to sell their Discover Card stock. Furthermore, by spinning off the unit, Morgan Stanley would not have to pay any tax on gains that might have been realized if it had sold the business outright. The move was also viewed as an attempt by senior Morgan Stanley management to mute shareholder criticism of the company's lackluster stock performance due to what many viewed had been the firm's excessive diversification.

Similarly, JP Morgan Chase announced plans in 2006 to spin off its $13 billion private equity fund, JP Morgan Partners. As an independent entity, the partners in the fund will have ownership stakes typical of most private equity firms The bank will invest up to $1 billion in a new fund JP Morgan Partners plans to open as a successor to the current Global Fund. Because the bank's ownership position will be less than 25%, it will be classified as a passive partner. The expectation is that by jettisoning this operation the bank will be able to reduce earnings volatility and decrease competition between the bank and large customers when making investments.

Chapter Overview

Many corporations, particularly large, highly diversified organizations, are reviewing constantly ways in which they can enhance shareholder value by changing the composition of their assets, liabilities, equity, and operations. These activities generally are referred to as restructuring strategies. Restructuring may embody both growth and exit strategies. Growth strategies have been discussed elsewhere in this book. The focus in this chapter is on those strategic options that allow the firm to maximize shareholder value by redeploying assets through contraction and downsizing of the parent corporation. Divestitures, spin-offs, equity carve-outs, split-ups, split-offs, and bust-ups are commonly used strategies to exit businesses and to redeploy corporate assets by returning cash or noncash assets through a special dividend to shareholders. The intent of this chapter is to discuss why parent corporations may choose to exit certain businesses, why one strategy may be selected over other options, and how such actions affect shareholder value. This chapter also addresses how firms deal with business failure through voluntary or involuntary restructuring and reorganization and, in some instances, liquidation. A review of this chapter is available on the CD-ROM accompanying this book.

Motives for Exiting Businesses

The motives for exiting businesses are both numerous and diverse. They include increasing corporate focus, a desire to exit underperforming businesses, a lack of fit, regulatory concerns, and tax considerations. Other motives include a need to raise funds, reduce risk, move away from the core business, discard unwanted businesses from prior acquisitions, and to avoid conflicts with customers. Although there is empirical evidence to demonstrate that changing corporate strategies or focus are common reasons for firms to exit businesses, the extent to which the other motives are commonplace is less clear.

Increasing Corporate Focus

Managing highly diverse and complex portfolios of businesses is both time consuming and distracting. This is particularly true when the businesses are in largely unrelated industries. There is a limited understanding by senior management of the nuances of each business and of what constitutes worthwhile opportunities for the parent to fund adequately. A unit may be a small portion of a parent company's sales and may not be receiving sufficient time or attention from management at the corporate level. Often, senior management may not completely understand the opportunities facing such a business, resulting in limited funding of potentially attractive opportunities. A business that is rich in high-growth opportunities may be an excellent candidate for divestiture to a strategic buyer with significant cash resources and limited growth opportunities.

Empirical Evidence

A substantial body of evidence indicates that reducing a firm's complexity (i.e., increasing its focus) can improve substantially financial returns to shareholders. The difficulty in managing diverse portfolios of businesses in many different industries and the difficulty in accurately valuing these portfolios contributed to the "deconglomeration" movement of the 1970s and 1980s. Of the acquisitions made between 1970 and 1982 by companies in industries unrelated to the acquirer's primary industry focus, 60% were divested by 1989 (Petty, Keown, Scott, and Martin, 1993). John and Ofek (1995) found that abnormal returns earned by the shareholders of a firm divesting a business result largely from improved management of the assets that remain after the divestiture is completed. They attributed these returns to increased focus and the ability of management to understand fewer lines of business. As evidence of the challenges of understanding businesses in diverse industries, they also found that 75% of divested units were unrelated to the selling company. Reducing a firm's complexity also has been related to improving shareholder returns in a number of more recent studies (Ball, 1997; Burkhart, Gromb, and Panunzi, 1997; Dittmer and Shivdasani, 2003; Krishnaswami and Subramaniam, 1999; Maksimovic and Phillips, 2001; Rajan, Servaes, and Zingales, 2000; Scharfstein and Stein, 2000).

Examples of Achieving Greater Focus

In the late 1980s, TRW divested many of its low-tech businesses to shift into high-tech segments of the information systems and services, space and defense, and automotive parts industries. Although ultimately acquired by Northrop Grumman, TRW presented its shareholders in 2002 with an alternative option to enhance shareholder value in which TRW would spin off its automotive business to shareholders and divest another business, using the proceeds to accelerate the repayment of debt. In 1987, Allegis Corporation reversed its previous strategy of providing a broader range of travel services by selling its hotel and car rental businesses to become UAL Corporation and to concentrate on operating United Airlines. In the late 1990s, General Motors (GM) spun off its Hughes Electronics and Delphi Automotive Parts operations to focus on its passenger car and light truck businesses. In 1999, Allegheny Teledyne spun off its software and engineering systems, communication and electronics, and aircraft engine businesses to focus on its specialty metals businesses. In 2005, Agilent announced that it had reached agreement to sell its semiconductor unit and its stake in a lighting technology company for $3.6 billion in order to focus on its core measurement products business. Similarly, Sara Lee announced in early 2006 that it would divest or spin off businesses accounting for as much as 40% of its current revenue to focus on its food and beverage business.

Underperforming Businesses

Parent firms often exit businesses that consistently fail to meet or exceed the parent's hurdle rate requirements. These hurdle rates frequently consist of the parent's cost of capital adjusted for any special risks associated with the business or the industry in which it competes. Baxter International Inc. announced in late 1999 its intention to spin off its underperforming cardiovascular business, creating a new company specializing in treatments for heart disease. In 2004, IBM announced the sale of its ailing PC business to China's Lenovo Group. In May 2007, General Electric announced the sale of its plastics operations for $11.6 billion to Saudi Basic Industries Corporation as part of the firm's strategy to sell slower growing businesses and to move into faster growing businesses such as healthcare and water processing.

Regulatory Concerns

A firm with substantial market share purchasing a direct competitor may create concerns about violations of antitrust laws. Regulatory agencies still may approve the merger if the acquiring firm is willing to divest certain operations that, in combination with similar units in the acquiring company, are deemed to be anticompetitive. As a result of an antitrust suit filed by the Department of Justice (DoJ), the government and AT&T reached an agreement effective January 1, 1984, to break up AT&T's 22 operating companies into seven regional Bell operating companies (RBOCs). The RBOCs became responsible for local telephone service, and AT&T kept responsibility for long-distance service and certain telecommunications equipment manufacturing operations. See Case Study 2-1 (Chapter 2) for a more detailed discussion of how the Justice Department required AlliedSignal and Honeywell to divest overlapping businesses before approving their merger in 1999.

Lack of Fit

Individual businesses may be undervalued because investors believe that there are insufficient benefits from synergy to offset the overhead expenses associated with being part of a holding company. This may have been a factor in AT&T's choice to implement a split-up of its business in the mid-1990s into three separate entities, each with its own stock traded on the public exchanges. In late 1999, a failed attempt to redirect the business into more lucrative telecommunications industry segments such as broadband and wireless caused AT&T to again undertake a strategy to spin off or divest some portions of the firm. See Case Study 15-8.

Companies may divest units after they have had time to learn more about the business. Raytheon sold its D.C. Heath textbook publishing company to Houghton Mifflin Company in 1995. Although large on a standalone basis, D.C. Heath did not fit with the other three much larger core Raytheon businesses, which included defense electronics, engineering, and avionics. Similarly, TRW's decision to sell its commercial and consumer information services businesses in 1997 came after years of trying to find a significant fit with its space and defense businesses.

Tax Considerations

Restructuring actions may provide tax benefits that cannot be realized without undertaking a restructuring of the business. Marriott Corporation contributed its hotel real estate operations to a Real Estate Investment Trust (REIT) in 1989 through a spin-off. Because REITs do not have to pay taxes on income that is distributed to shareholders, Marriott was able to enhance shareholder value by eliminating the double taxation of income. The income from these properties had been taxed as rental income to the parent and again when distributed to shareholders.

Raising Funds/Worth More to Others

Parent firms may choose to fund new initiatives or acquisitions or reduce leverage through the sale or partial sale of units that are no longer considered strategic or are underperforming corporate expectations. Such sales also may result from the need to improve near-term cash flow. Examples include Andarko's announcement in late 2006 to sell its Canadian gas properties to Canadian Natural Resources for $4.1 billion to help finance its purchase of two smaller competitors earlier in the year (see "Inside M&A" in Chapter 1). Another example is Chrysler's sale of its highly profitable tank division to avoid bankruptcy in the early 1980s. Similarly, Navistar, formerly International Harvester, sold its profitable Solar Turbines operation to Caterpillar Tractor to reduce its indebtedness. Others may view a firm's operating units as much more valuable than the parent and be willing to pay a "premium" price for such businesses.

Risk Reduction

A firm may reduce its perceived risk associated with a particular unit by selling a portion of the business to the public. For example, American Express viewed Shearson Lehman as much riskier than its credit card business. Although the firm believed that there were opportunities to sell its credit cards to Shearson Lehman customers, it decided to reduce its exposure to the cyclical securities business by selling a portion of the unit in 1987. In addition, major tobacco companies have been under pressure for years to divest or spin off their food businesses because of the litigation risk associated with their tobacco subsidiaries. RJR Nabisco bowed to such pressure in 1998 with the spin-off of Nabisco Foods. For similar reasons, Altria spun off its Kraft food operations in 2007. Parent firms may attempt to dump debt or other liabilities by assigning them to a subsidiary and later exiting those businesses. In early 2002, Citigroup sold 21% of its Travelers Property Casualty unit in a $3.9 billion initial public offering (IPO), announcing that the remainder would be sold off at a later date. The parent's motivation for this exit strategy could have been to distance itself from the potential costs of asbestos-related claims by Travelers' policyholders. Similarly, Goodrich passed on its asbestos liabilities to EnPro Industries, its diversified industrial products subsidiary, which it spun off in mid-2002.

Moving Away from the Core Business

Management may not believe that investment opportunities in their current core business are attractive. They may believe that their firm's core skills or competencies in manufacturing or distribution can be used to pursue growth opportunities in other industries. Consequently, current core business assets may be sold to fund these diversification opportunities. Case Study 15-1 illustrates one of the most dramatic redirections of a corporation's business strategy in U.S. history.

Case Study 15-1
**Hughes Corporation Moves from the Defense Industry into
the Entertainment Industry**

Once California's largest manufacturing employer, Hughes Corporation built spacecraft, the world's first working laser, communications satellites, radar systems, and military weapons systems. By the late 1990s, the one-time defense industry behemoth advertised itself as the world's largest digital entertainment and communications company. This transformation culminated in the firm being acquired in 2004 by News Corp., a global media empire.

To accomplish this transformation, Hughes divested its communications satellite businesses and even its auto electronics operation. The corporate overhaul created a firm focused on direct-to-home satellite broadcasting with its DirecTV service offering. DirecTV's introduction to nearly 12 million U.S. homes was a technology made possible by U.S. military spending during the early 1980s. Although military spending had fueled much of Hughes' growth during the decade of the 1980s, it was becoming increasingly clear by 1988 that the level of defense spending of the Reagan years was coming to a close with the winding down of the Cold War.

For the next several years, Hughes attempted to find profitable niches in the rapidly consolidating U.S. defense contracting industry. Hughes acquired General Dynamics' missile business and made about 15 smaller acquisitions. Eventually, Hughes' parent firm, General Motors, lost enthusiasm for additional investment in defense-related businesses. The decision was made that if Hughes could not participate in the shrinking defense industry, then there was no reason to retain any interests in the industry at all. In November 1995, Hughes initiated discussions with Raytheon, and 2 years later, it sold its aerospace and defense business to Raytheon for $9.8 billion and merged Delco with GM's Delphi automotive systems. What remained was the firm's telecommunications division. Hughes had transformed itself from a $16 billion defense contractor to a svelte $4 billion telecommunications business.

Hughes' telecommunications unit was its smallest operation but, with DirecTV, its fastest growing. The transformation was to exact a huge cultural toll on Hughes' employees, most of whom had spent their careers dealing with the U.S. Department of Defense. Hughes moved to hire aggressively people from the cable and broadcast businesses. By the late 1990s, former Hughes' employees comprised only 15–20% of DirecTV's total employees.

Restructuring continued through the end of the 1990s. In 2000, Hughes sold its satellite manufacturing operations to Boeing for $3.75 billion. This eliminated the last component of the old Hughes and cut its workforce in half. In December 2000, Hughes paid about $180 million for Telocity, a firm that provides digital subscriber line service through phone lines. This acquisition allowed Hughes to provide high-speed Internet connections through its existing satellite service, mainly in more remote rural areas, as well as phone lines targeted at city dwellers. Hughes now could market the same combination of high-speed Internet services and video offered by cable providers, Hughes' primary competitor.

In late 2000, GM put Hughes up for sale, expressing confidence that there would be a flood of lucrative offers. However, the faltering economy and stock market resulted in GM receiving only one serious bid, from media tycoon Rupert Murdoch of News Corp. in February 2001. However, internal discord within Hughes and GM over the possible buyer of Hughes Electronics caused GM to backpedal and seek alternative bidders. In late October 2001, GM agreed to sell its Hughes Electronics subsidiary and its DirecTV home satellite network to EchoStar Communication for $25.8 billion. However, this transaction was disallowed by regulators concerned about the antitrust implications of the deal. In early 2004, News Corp., General Motors, and Hughes reached a definitive agreement in which News Corp. acquired GM's 19.9% stake in Hughes and an additional 14.1% of Hughes from public shareholders and GM's pension and other benefit plans. News Corp. paid about $14 per share, making the deal worth about $6.6 billion for 34.1% of Hughes. The implied value of 100% of Hughes is $19.4 billion.

Case Study Discussion Questions

1. How did changes in Hughes' external environment contribute to its dramatic 20-year restructuring effort? Cite specific influences in answering this question.
2. What risks did Hughes face in moving completely away from its core defense business and into a high-tech commercial business? In your judgment, did Hughes move too quickly or too slowly? Explain your answer.
3. Why did Hughes move so aggressively to hire employees from the cable TV and broadcast industry?

Discarding Unwanted Businesses from Prior Acquisitions

Acquiring companies often find themselves with certain assets and operations of the acquired company that do not fit their primary strategy. These redundant assets may be divested to raise funds to help pay for the acquisition and to enable management to focus on integrating the remaining businesses into the parent without the distraction of having to manage nonstrategic assets. In 2002, Northrop Grumman Corporation announced that it would acquire TRW. Northrop stated that it would retain TRW's space and defense businesses and divest its automotive operations, which were not germane to Northrop's core defense business. Nestle acquired Adams, Pfizer's chewing gum and confectionery business, in early 2003 for $4.6 billion. Pfizer viewed Adams as a noncore business it had acquired as part of its $84 billion acquisitions of Warner-Lambert in 2000. In mid-2007, Daimler announced it was divesting its Chrysler operations to private equity firm, Cerberus, in exchange for Cerberus' willingness to pay off $18 billion in future retirement and healthcare liabilities. Daimler had acquired Chrysler in 1998 for $36 billion.

Avoiding Conflicts with Customers

For years, many of the RBOCs spun off by AT&T in 1984 have been interested in competing in the long-distance market, which would put them in direct competition with their former parent. Similarly, AT&T sought to penetrate the regional telephone markets by gaining access to millions of households by acquiring cable TV companies. In preparation for the implementation of these plans, AT&T announced in 1995 that it would split up the company into three publicly traded global companies. The three companies included Communications Services (long-distance services), Communications Systems (later renamed Lucent Technologies, a provider of network switches and transmission equipment), and Global Information Solutions (later renamed NCR, a provider of systems integration services). The primary reason for the split up was to avoid conflicts between AT&T's former equipment manufacturer and its main customers, the RBOCs.

Divestitures

A *divestiture* is the sale of a portion of a firm to an outside party generally resulting in a cash infusion to the parent. A firm may choose to sell an undervalued operation that it determined to be nonstrategic or unrelated to the core business and to use the proceeds of the sale to fund investments in potentially higher return opportunities. Alternatively, the firm may choose to divest the undervalued business and return the cash to shareholders either through a liquidating dividend or share repurchase. Between 1970 and 2006, divestitures averaged about 40% of total M&A transactions (Thomson Financial). The number of divestitures surged in the early-to-mid 1970s, in the early 1990s, and again in the early 2000s, following the merger boom periods of the late 1960s, the 1980s, and the second half of the 1990s.

Many corporations review their business portfolio periodically to determine which operations continue to fit their core strategies. As part of this review, the parent will conduct a financial analysis to determine if the business is worth more to shareholders if it is sold and the proceeds either returned to the shareholders or reinvested in opportunities offering higher returns. Weighing the future of its plastics business with other perceived opportunities, General Electric announced in late 2006 that it was selling its silicone and quartz business for $3.4 billion to private equity firm Apollo Management. GE's portfolio of companies has been undergoing change since the current CEO, Jeffrey Immelt, took control in September 2001. Since then, GE has completed transactions valued at more than $100 billion in buying and selling various operating units.

To Sell or Not to Sell

An analysis undertaken to determine if a business should be sold involves a multistep process. These steps include determining the after-tax cash flows generated by the unit, an appropriate discount rate reflecting the risk of the business, the after-tax market value of the business, and the after-tax value of the business to the parent. The decision to sell or to retain the business depends on a comparison of the after-tax value of the business to the parent with the after-tax proceeds from the sale of the business. These steps are outlined below.

Step 1: Calculating After-Tax Cash Flows

To decide if a business is worth more to the shareholder if sold, the parent must first estimate the after-tax cash flows of the business viewed on a standalone basis (i.e., as if it were operated as an independent operating unit). This requires adjusting the cash flows for intercompany sales and the cost of services (e.g., legal, treasury, and audit) provided by the parent. Intercompany sales refer to operating unit revenue generated by selling products or services to another unit owned by the same parent. For example, in a vertically integrated business, such as a steel manufacturer that obtains both iron ore and coal from its operating subsidiaries, the majority of the revenue generated by the iron ore and coal operations often comes from sales to the parent company's steelmaking operations. The parent may value this revenue for financial reporting purposes using product transfer prices, which may reflect current market prices or some formula such as a predetermined markup over the cost of production. If the transfer prices do not reflect actual market prices, intercompany revenue may be artificially high or low, depending on whether the transfer prices are higher or lower than actual market prices. Intercompany revenues associated with the operating unit should be restated to reflect actual market prices. Services provided by the parent to the business may be subsidized (i.e., provided at below actual cost) or at a markup over actual cost. To reflect these factors, operating profits should be reduced by the amount of any subsidies and increased by any markup over what the business would have to pay if it purchased comparable services from sources outside of the parent firm.

Step 2: Estimating the Discount Rate

Once the after-tax standalone cash flows have been determined, a discount rate should be estimated that reflects the risk characteristics of the industry in which the business competes. The cost of capital of other firms in the same industry is often a good proxy for the discount rate of the business being analyzed.

Step 3: Estimating the After-Tax Market Value of the Business

The discount rate then is used to estimate the present or market value of the projected after-tax cash flows of the business as if it were a standalone business. The valuation is based on cash flows that have been adjusted for intercompany revenues not on the books at market prices and services provided to the operating unit by the parent firm at something other than actual cost.

Step 4: Estimating the Value of the Business to the Parent

The after-tax equity value (EV) of the business as part of the parent is estimated by subtracting the market value of the business's liabilities (L) from its after-tax market value (MV) as a standalone operation. This relationship can be expressed as follows:

$$EV = MV - L$$

EV is a measure of the after-tax market value of shareholder equity of the business, where the shareholder is the parent firm.

Step 5: Deciding to Sell

The decision to sell or retain the business is made by comparing EV with the after-tax sale value (SV) of the business. Assuming other considerations do not outweigh any after-tax gain on the sale of the business, the decision to sell or retain can be summarized as follows:

If SV > EV, divest.
If SV < EV, retain.

Although the sale value may exceed the equity value of the business, the parent may choose to retain the business for strategic reasons. For example, the parent may believe that the business' products (e.g., ties) may facilitate the sale of other products the firm offers (e.g., custom shirts). The firm may lose money on the sale of ties but make enough money on the sale of custom shirts to earn a profit on the combined sales of the two products. In another instance, one subsidiary of a diversified parent may provide highly complex components critical to the assembly of finished products produced by other subsidiaries of the parent firm. Under these circumstances, the parent may choose to incur a small loss on the production of components to ensure the continued high quality of its highly profitable finished products.

Timing of the Sale

Obviously, the best time to sell a business is when the owner does not need to sell to raise new capital or to repay creditors or when the demand for the business to be divested is greatest. The decision to sell also should reflect the broader financial environment. Selling when business confidence is high, stock prices are rising, and interest rates are low is likely to fetch a higher price for the unit. If the business to be sold is highly cyclical, the sale should be timed to coincide with the firm's peak year earnings. Businesses also can be timed to sell when they are considered most popular. In 1980, the oil exploration business was booming; by 1983, it was in the doldrums. It recovered again by the mid-1990s. What's hot today can be a fizzle tomorrow. A similar story could be told about many of the high-flying Internet-related companies of the late 1990s.

The Selling Process

The selling process may be reactive or proactive (see Figure 15-1). Reactive sales occur when the parent is unexpectedly approached by a buyer either for the entire firm or for a portion of the firm such as a product line or subsidiary. If the bid is sufficiently attractive, the parent firm may choose to reach a negotiated settlement with the bidder without investigating other options. This may occur if the parent is concerned about potential degradation of its business, or that of a subsidiary, if its interest in selling becomes public knowledge.

In contrast, proactive sales may be characterized as public or private solicitations. In a **public solicitation**, a firm can announce publicly that it is putting itself, a subsidiary, or a product line up for sale. In this instance, potential buyers contact the seller. This is a way to relatively easily identify interested parties. Unfortunately, this approach can also attract unqualified bidders (i.e., those lacking the financial resources necessary to complete the deal). In a **private solicitation**, the parent firm may hire an investment banker or undertake on its own to identify potential buyers to be contacted. Once a list

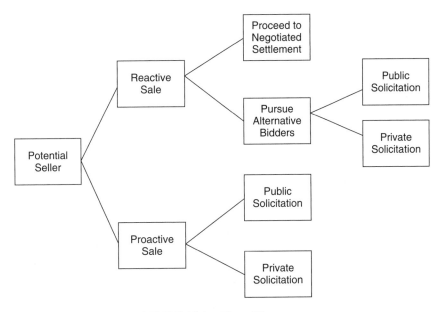

FIGURE 15-1   The selling process

of what are believed to be qualified buyers has been compiled, contact is made. (See the discussion of the screening and contacting process in Chapter 5 for more detail.)

In either a public or private solicitation, interested parties are asked to sign confidentiality agreements before they are given access to proprietary information. In a private solicitation, they may also be asked to sign a standstill agreement requiring them not to make an unsolicited bid. Parties willing to sign these agreements are then asked to submit preliminary, nonbinding "indications of interest" (i.e., a single number or a bid expressed as a range).

Those parties submitting preliminary bids are then ranked by the selling company in terms of the size of the bid, form of payment (i.e., composition), the ability of the bidder to finance the transaction, form of acquisition (i.e., whether bidder proposes to buy stock or assets), and ease of doing the deal. The latter factor involves an assessment of the difficulty in obtaining regulatory approval, if required, and of the integrity of the bidder. A small number of those submitting preliminary bids are then asked to submit a best and final offer (BAFO). Such offers must be binding on the bidder. At this point, the seller may choose to initiate an auction among the most attractive bids or go directly into negotiating a purchase agreement with a single party.

Tax and Accounting Considerations for Divestitures

The divesting firm is required to recognize a gain or loss for financial reporting purposes equal to the difference between the fair value of the consideration received for the divested operation and its book value. However, if the transaction is an exchange of similar assets or an equivalent interest in similar productive assets, the company should not recognize a gain or loss other than a loss resulting from the impairment of value. If the divested division or subsidiary is a discontinued segment, the parent firm must estimate the gain or loss from the divestiture on the date that management approves a formal plan to dispose of the division or subsidiary. For tax purposes, the gain or loss is the difference between the proceeds and the parent's tax (i.e., cost) basis in the stock or assets. Net gains (i.e., capital gains in excess of losses) are taxed at the same rate as other business income.

Spin-Offs and Split-Ups

A *spin-off* is a transaction in which a parent creates a new legal subsidiary and distributes shares it owns in the subsidiary to its current shareholders as a stock dividend. The shares are distributed in direct proportion to the shareholders' current holdings of the parent's stock. Consequently, the proportional ownership of shares in the new legal subsidiary is the same as the stockholders' proportional ownership of shares in the parent firm. The new entity has its own management and operates independently from the parent company (see Case Study 15-2). Unlike the divestiture or equity carve-out (explained later in this chapter), the spin-off does not result in an infusion of cash to the parent company. The average size of spin-offs is 20% of the parent's original market value (Shipper and Smith, 1983). Some of the more notable spin-offs include the spin-off of Medco by Merck; Allstate by Sears; Payless by May Department Stores; Dean Witter/Discover by Sears; CBS by Westinghouse; and Pizza Hut, KFC, and Taco Bell by PepsiCo. A *split-up* involves creating a series of spin-offs by issuing a new class of stock for each of the parent's operating subsidiaries, paying current shareholders a dividend of each new class of stock, and then dissolving the remaining corporate shell.

Motives for Spin-Offs

In addition to the motives for exiting businesses discussed earlier, spin-offs provide a means of rewarding shareholders with a nontaxable dividend (if properly structured). Parent firms with a low tax basis in a business may choose to spin off the unit as a tax-free distribution to shareholders rather than sell the business and incur a substantial tax liability. In addition, the unit, now independent of the parent, has its own stock to use for possible acquisitions. Finally, the managers of the business that is to be spun off have a greater incentive to improve the unit's performance if they own stock in the unit. There is evidence that managers and directors of the public subsidiaries buy substantial amounts of stock in their business immediately following spin-offs (Allen, 2001). This behavior may be explained by insiders having substantially better information than other investors regarding the operations and financial performance of the unit.

Tax and Accounting Considerations for Spin-Offs

If properly structured, spin-offs or split-ups are generally not taxable to shareholders. According to the Internal Revenue Service (IRS) Code Section 355, a spin-off must satisfy five conditions for it to be considered tax free to the parent firm's shareholders. These are as follows:

1. *Control*: The parent firm must have a controlling interest in the subsidiary before it is spun off. Control is defined as the parent owning at least 80% of the voting stock in the subsidiary and 80% of each class of nonvoting stock.

2. *Active Business*: After the spin-off, both the parent and the subsidiary must remain in the same line of business in which each was involved for at least 5 years before the spin-off.
3. *Prohibition against Tax Avoidance*: The spin-off cannot have been used as a means of avoiding dividend taxation by converting ordinary income into capital gains.
4. *Continuity of Interest*: The parent's shareholders must maintain significant ownership in both the parent and the subsidiary following the transactions.
5. *Business Purpose*: The transaction must have a significant business purpose separate from tax savings.

For financial reporting purposes, the parent firm should account for the spin-off of a subsidiary's stock to its shareholders at book value with no gain or loss recognized, other than any reduction in value due to impairment. The reason for this treatment is that the ownership interests are essentially the same before and after the spin-off.

Spin-Offs That Will Not Go Away

Parent firms thinking about engaging in spin-offs must recognize the potential long-term implications of their actions. Parent firms need to ensure that units to be spun off are able to achieve long-term viability or the parent may be forced to shoulder future liabilities under "fraudulent conveyance" laws (i.e., regulations governing the jettisoning of businesses to shareholders simply to rid the parent of liabilities). General Motors and Ford in an effort to shore up their automotive parts manufacturing units agreed to take responsibility for certain salary and benefit, as well as administrative, costs after the units had been spun off. Moreover, both had long-term supply arrangements with the units. GM has been subsidizing Delphi by paying $2 billion above market annually for the parts it buys from the former division. The results of these post-spin-off relationships and obligations have been financially disastrous for GM and Ford.

After having been spun off by General Motors Corporation in 1999, auto parts manufacturer, Delphi Corporation, sought bankruptcy protection from its creditors in late 2005. Visteon Corporation, spun off by Ford Motor Corporation in 2000, dumped 24 money-losing plants on Ford in October 2005, as part of its second bailout in 2 years.

While the two parts manufacturers remain GM's and Ford's largest suppliers, there are other reasons why the automakers are still on the hook for liabilities of these former operating units. Except for their stock, they never completely severed all ties to make them independent companies. Visteon remained tied to Ford for payroll and benefits processing, information technology support, and accounting services and paid Ford for these services. If the parts maker fails, Ford is contractually obligated to assume responsibility for the retirement benefits of Visteon's union workers. Similarly, GM is to pay benefits to Delphi's retirees if it fails.

Given their excessive labor costs when they were spun off, these parts companies seemed destined to fail in an increasingly competitive environment. In other words, Delphi and Visteon were not spun off as viable independent companies. To avoid the potential return of these parts makers to their former parents, GM and Ford are struggling to prop up their former subsidiaries. Consequently, GM will provide $3 to $4 billion to Delphi to fund retiree medical plans. In taking back Visteon factories and their 17,000 workers, Ford is liable for about $1 billion. Moreover, Ford may have to continue paying part of the wages of union workers in order to sell the plants to other suppliers. Ford expects to incur operating losses on the plants taken back from Visteon until they can be sold or shutdown. In early 2007, Ford announced that it had reached agreement to sell 2 of the 24 plants that had been returned by Visteon in late 2005.

The lessons to be learned from the Delphi and Visteon debacles are that parent firms should be prepared to make a clean break with the unit to be spun off. Total independence from the parent gives the unit's management the flexibility to build the business. The parent should resist the temptation to load debt on the unit, which would simply limit the ability of the unit to compete. The parent should diligently avoid conflicts of interest with the unit. If the spin-off is a supplier, it should be treated like every other supplier. Finally, management of the spin-off should be generous with incentives by distributing company stock widely so employees will act like owners and accept tougher performance standards.

Case Study 15-2
Anatomy of a Spin-Off

On October 18, 2006, Verizon Communication's board of directors declared a dividend to the firm's shareholders consisting of shares in a company comprising the firm's domestic print and Internet yellow pages directories publishing operations (Idearc Inc.). The dividend consisted of one share of Idearc stock for every 20 shares of Verizon common stock. Idearc shares were valued at $34.47 per share. On the dividend payment date, Verizon shares were valued at $36.42 per share. The 1-to-20 ratio constituted a 4.73% yield [i.e., $34.47/($36.42 \times 20)$], approximately equal to Verizon's then current cash dividend yield.

Because of the spin-off, Verizon will contribute to Idearc all of its ownership interest in Idearc Information Services and other assets, liabilities, businesses, and employees currently employed in these operations. In exchange for the contribution, Idearc will issue to Verizon shares of Idearc common stock to be distributed to Verizon shareholders. In addition, Idearc will issue senior unsecured notes to Verizon in an amount approximately equal to the debt Verizon incurred in financing Idearc's operations historically. Idearc will also transfer $2.5 billion in excess cash to Verizon. The parent owns such cash balances, since they were generated while Idearc was part of the parent.

Verizon announced that the spin-off would enable the parent and Idearc to focus on their core businesses, which may facilitate expansion and growth of each firm. The spin-off will also allow each company to determine their own capital structure, to enable Idearc to pursue an acquisition strategy using its own stock, and to permit Idearc to enhance the effectiveness of equity-based compensation programs offered to its employees. Because of the spin-off, Idearc will become an independent public company, although Idearc will continue to have a number of significant commercial arrangements with Verizon. Moreover, no vote of Verizon shareholders is required to approve the spin-off, since it constitutes the payment of a dividend permissible by the board of directors according to the bylaws of the firm. Finally, Verizon shareholders have no appraisal rights in connection with the spin-off.

Case Study Discussion Questions

1. How do you believe the Idearc shares were valued for purposes of the spin-off? Be specific.
2. Do you believe that it is fair for Idearc to repay a portion of debt incurred by Verizon relating to Idearc's operations even though Verizon included Idearc's

earnings in its consolidated income statement? Is the transfer of excess cash to the
parent fair? Explain your answer.

3. Do you believe shareholders should have the right to approve a spin-off? Explain
your answer?

Equity Carve-Outs

Equity carve-outs are often difficult to define. They are most appropriately viewed as
hybrid or intermediate transactions. They are hybrid transactions in that they are similar
to spin-offs. Both result in the subsidiary's stock being traded separately from the parent's
stock. They are also like divestitures and IPOs as they provide a cash infusion to the
parent. However, unlike the spin-off or divestiture, the parent generally retains control
of the subsidiary in a carve-out transaction. A potentially significant drawback to the
carve-out is the creation of minority shareholders. General Motors 2006's sale of a 51%
stake in its profitable GMAC finance unit to private investor group Cerberus for $14
billion is a recent example of an equity carve-out. In this transaction, GM retained the
right (i.e., a call option) to buy back GMAC during the 10-year period following the
close of the transaction.

In addition to the motives for exiting businesses outlined above, equity carve-outs
provide an opportunity to raise funds for reinvestment in the subsidiary or for paying a
dividend to the parent firm. Moreover, the carve-out or IPO provides an opportunity to
value the business by selling stock in a public stock exchange.

There are two basic forms of an equity carve-out: the initial public offering and the
subsidiary equity carve-out. These are discussed in the following section.

Initial Public Offerings

An *initial public offering* (*IPO*) is the first offering to the public of common stock of
a formerly privately held firm. The sale of the stock provides an infusion of cash to the
parent. The cash may be retained by the parent or returned to shareholders. United Parcel
Service's IPO of a small share of its stock in 1999 is an example of an IPO (see Case
Study 15-3).

Case Study 15-3
United Parcel Service Goes Public in an Equity IPO

On November 10, 1999, United Parcel Service (UPS) raised $5.47 billion by selling 109.4
million shares of Class B common stock at an offering price of $50 per share in the biggest
IPO by any U.S. firm in history. The share price exploded to $67.38 at the end of the
first day of trading. The IPO represented 9% of the firm's stock and established the firm's
total market value at $81.9 billion [i.e., ($67.38 × 109.4/.09)]. With 1998 revenue of $24.8
billion, UPS transports more than 3 billion parcels and documents annually. The company
provides services in more than 200 countries.

By issuing only a portion of its Class B stock to the public, UPS was interested in ensuring that control would remain in the hands of current management. The cash proceeds of the stock issue were used to buy back about 9% of the Class A voting stock held by employees and by heirs to the founding Casey family, thereby keeping the total number of shares outstanding constant. The Class B shares have one vote each, whereas the Class A shares have 10 votes. In addition, the issuance of Class B stock provides a currency for making acquisitions. UPS had attempted unsuccessfully to acquire certain firms that had indicated a strong desire for UPS shares rather than cash.

The beneficiaries of the sale include UPS employees from top management to workers on the loading docks. In a growing trend in U.S. companies to generate greater employee loyalty and productivity, UPS offered all 330,000 employees worldwide an opportunity to buy shares in this highly profitable company at prices as low as $20 per share. Before UPS, the largest IPOs included Conoco in October 1998 at $4.40 billion, Goldman Sachs in May 1999 at $3.66 billion, Charter Communications in November 1999 at $3.23 billion, and Lucent Technologies in April 1996 at $3 billion.

Case Study Discussion Questions

1. Describe the motivation for UPS to undertake this type of transaction.
2. In what way might an IPO make the parent company vulnerable to a takeover attempt?

Subsidiary Equity Carve-Outs

The *subsidiary carve-out* is a transaction in which the parent creates a wholly owned independent legal subsidiary, with stock and a management team that is different from the parent's, and issues a portion of the subsidiary's stock to the public. Alternatively, a portion of the stock of an existing subsidiary could be sold to the public for the first time. Usually only a minority share of the parent's ownership in the subsidiary is issued to the public (Schipper and Smith, 1986). Although the parent retains control, the shareholder base of the subsidiary may be different than that of the parent as a result of the public sale of equity. The cash raised may be retained in the subsidiary or transferred to the parent as a dividend, as a stock repurchase, or as an intercompany loan. The return of any portion of the proceeds to the shareholder is taxable to the shareholder. An example of a subsidiary carve-out is the sale to the public by Phillip Morris in June 2001 of 15% of its wholly owned Kraft subsidiary. While the firm was able to raise $8.68 billion, Phillip Morris' voting power over Kraft was only reduced to 97.7% because Kraft had a dual-class share structure (i.e., different classes of stock had different numbers of votes) in which only low-voting shares were issued in the public stock offering.

Equity Carve-Outs as Staged Transactions

Equity may be sold to the public in several stages. A partial sale of equity either in a wholly owned subsidiary (a subsidiary equity carve-out) or in the consolidated business (an IPO) may be designed to raise capital and to establish a market price for the stock. In the United States, many parents initially offer 20% or less of a subsidiary's stock to the public to continue to be able to consolidate the subsidiary's operations. This enables the parent to avoid incurring capital gains taxes that it might have to pay by selling more than that amount, raise some cash, and place a value on the stock. Later, once a market has been established for the stock, the remainder of the subsidiary's stock may be issued to the public. Alternatively, the parent may choose to spin off its remaining shares in the subsidiary to the parent's shareholders as a dividend. Few carve-outs remain under the parent's control in the long term. In a study of more than 200 carve-outs, only 8% of the firms held more than 50% of the equity of their carve-outs after 5 years; 31% of the parents held less than 25% of the equity, and 39% of the carve-outs have been acquired or merged with third parties (Annema, Fallon, and Goedhart, 2002).

Hewlett-Packard's (HP) staged spin-off of its Agilent Technologies subsidiary is an example of a staged transaction. It began with an equity carve-out of a minority position in its wholly owned Agilent subsidiary in late 1999. The spin-off was completed in 2000 (see Case Study 15-4).

Case Study 15-4
Hewlett-Packard Spins Out Its Agilent Unit in a Staged Transaction

Hewlett-Packard (HP) announced the spin-off of its Agilent Technologies unit to focus on its main business of computers and printers, where sales had been lagging behind such competitors as Sun Microsystems. Agilent makes test, measurement, and monitoring instruments; semiconductors; and optical components. It also supplies patient-monitoring and ultrasound-imaging equipment to the health care industry. HP retained an 85% stake in the company. The cash raised through the 15% equity carve-out was paid to HP as a dividend from the subsidiary to the parent. Hewlett-Packard provided Agilent with $983 million in start-up funding. HP retained a controlling interest until mid-2000, when it spun off the rest of its shares in Agilent to HP shareholders as a tax-free transaction.

Case Study Discussion Questions

1. Discuss the reasons why HP may have chosen a staged transaction rather than an outright divestiture of the business.
2. Discuss the conditions under which this spin-off would constitute a tax-free transaction.

Tracking, Targeted, and Letter Stocks

Tracking or *targeted stocks* are separate classes of common stock of the parent corporation. The parent firm divides its operations into two or more operating units and assigns a common stock to each operation. Tracking stock is a class of common stock that links the shareholders' return to the operating performance of a particular business segment or unit (i.e., the targeted business unit). Tracking stock represents an ownership interest in the company as a whole, rather than a direct ownership interest in the targeted business segment or unit. The concept was introduced in 1984 when General Motors issued a class of stock identified as E stock, often referred to as letter stock at that time, to buy Electronic Data Systems (EDS). In 1985, GM issued another class of stock called

H stock when it acquired Hughes Corporation. In 1991, U.S. Steel Company created a USX-Marathon stock for its oil business and a USX stock for its steel operations. The next year, USX created a third tracking stock when it sold shares of the USX-Delhi group in an IPO. For voting purposes, each of the three tracking stocks is considered common stock of the parent.

The Motivation for Tracking Stocks

The purpose in creating tracking stock is to enable the financial markets to value the different operations within a corporation based on their own performance. Such stocks represent **pure plays** in that they give investors an opportunity to invest in a single operating unit of a diversified parent firm. Tracking or targeted stocks provide the parent company with an alternative means of raising capital for a specific operation by selling a portion of the stock to the public and an alternative "currency" for making acquisitions. In addition, stock-based incentive programs to attract and retain key managers can be implemented for each operation with its own tracking stock. Although tracking stocks may not be created initially for the purpose of exiting a business, they make such a move easier for the parent at a later date. Following a restructure of its Hughes Electronics subsidiary, GM spun off and subsequently merged its defense electronics unit with Raytheon Corporation in 1997. Dividends paid on the tracking stocks for both USX and GM are based on the performance of each individual operation (see Case Study 15-5).

Case Study 15-5

USX Bows to Shareholder Pressure to Split Up the Company

As one of the first firms to issue tracking stocks in the mid-1980s, USX relented to ongoing shareholder pressure to divide the firm into two pieces. After experiencing a sharp "boom–bust" cycle throughout the 1970s, U.S. Steel had acquired Marathon Oil, a profitable oil and gas company, in 1982 in what was at the time the second largest merger in U.S. history. Marathon had shown steady growth in sales and earnings throughout the 1970s. USX Corp. was formed in 1986 as the holding company for both U.S. Steel and Marathon Oil. In 1991, USX issued its tracking stocks to create "pure plays" in its primary businesses—steel and oil—and to utilize USX's steel losses, which could be used to reduce Marathon's taxable income. Marathon shareholders have long complained that Marathon's stock was selling at a discount to its peers because of its association with USX. The campaign to split Marathon from U.S. Steel began in earnest in early 2000.

On April 25, 2001, USX announced its intention to split U.S. Steel and Marathon Oil into two separately traded companies. The breakup gave holders of Marathon Oil stock an opportunity to participate in the ongoing consolidation within the global oil and gas industry. Holders of USX–U.S. Steel Group common stock (target stock) would become holders of newly formed Pittsburgh-based United States Steel Corporation, a return to the original name of the firm formed in 1901. Under the reorganization plan, U.S. Steel and Marathon would retain the same assets and liabilities already associated with each business. However, Marathon would assume $900 million in debt from U.S. Steel, leaving the steelmaker with $1.3 billion of debt. This assumption of debt by Marathon was an attempt to make U.S. Steel, which continued to lose money until 2004, able to stand on its own financially.

The investor community expressed mixed reactions, believing that Marathon would be likely to benefit from a possible takeover attempt, whereas U.S. Steel would not fare as well. Despite the initial investor pessimism, investors in both Marathon and U.S. Steel saw their shares appreciate significantly in the years immediately following the breakup.

Case Study Discussion Questions

1. Why do you believe U.S. Steel may have decided to acquire Marathon Oil? Did this combination make economic sense? Explain your answer.
2. Why do you think USX issued separate tracking stocks for its oil and steel businesses?
3. Why do you believe USX shareholders were not content to continue to hold tracking stocks in Marathon Oil and U.S. Steel?
4. In your judgment, did the breakup of USX into Marathon Oil and United States Steel Corporation make sense? Why or why not?
5. What other alternatives could USX have pursued to increase shareholder value? Why do you believe they pursued the breakup strategy rather than some of the alternatives?

Answers to these Case Study Discussion Questions are available in the Online Instructor's Manual for instructors using this book.

Tax and Accounting Considerations for Tracking Stocks

For financial reporting purposes, a distribution of tracking stock splits the parent firm's equity structure into separate classes of stock without a legal split-up of the firm. Tracking stocks may be issued as dividends to the parent's current shareholders. Unlike the case with spin-offs, the IRS currently does not require the business for which the tracking stock is created to be at least 5 years old and that the parent retains a controlling interest in the business for the stock to be exempt from capital gains taxes. Unlike a spin-off or carve-out, the parent retains complete ownership of the business. Each tracking stock is considered as common stock for the consolidated parent company and not of the subsidiary. In general, a proportionate distribution by a company to its shareholders in the company's stock is tax free to shareholders.

Problems with Tracking Stocks

Tracking stocks may create internal operating conflicts among the parent's business units. Such conflicts arise in determining how the parent's overhead expenses will be allocated to the business units and what price one business unit is paid for selling products to other business units. In addition to creating internal problems, tracking stocks can stimulate shareholder lawsuits. Although the unit for which a tracking stock has been created may be largely autonomous, the potential for conflict of interest is substantial because the parent's board and the target stock's board are the same. The parent's board approves overall operating unit and capital budgets. Decisions made in support of one operating unit may appear to be unfair to those holding a tracking stock in another unit. Thus, tracking stocks can pit classes of shareholders against one another and lead to lawsuits.

When GM sold part of its Hughes unit and all of EDS, holders of H shares sued the GM board of directors, complaining that they were underpaid. Although shareholders may be less concerned with potential conflicts of interest when they first receive tracking stocks, the potential for antagonism among different classes of stockholders often grows with time.

Tracking stocks may be penalized if the parent's management continues to operate them conservatively. With a spin-off, the firm has a separate board of directors that can introduce a more aggressive management style than the parent may have been willing to tolerate. In addition, tracking stocks may not have voting rights. Finally, the chances of a hostile takeover of a firm with a tracking stock are virtually zero, because the firm is controlled by the parent. Hence, there is no takeover premium built into the stock price. Reflecting investor disenchantment with tracking stocks, Billett and Vijh (2004) have found average excess returns to shareholders of 13.9% around the date of the announcement that target stock structures would be removed in 11 instances between 1984 and 1999.

Split-Offs

A *split-off* is a variation of a spin-off in which some parent company shareholders (e.g., those holding a specific class of stock) receive shares in a subsidiary in return for surrendering their parent company shares. For example, in 2001, AT&T spun off its 86%-owned wireless operations to investors holding tracking shares in the subsidiary. This was accomplished by giving common shares in the wireless subsidiary to those holding tracking shares in exchange for their tracking shares. In 2004, Viacom spun off its movie rental chain by exchanging shares in its 81%-owned Blockbuster Inc. subsidiary for Viacom common shares.

Split-offs are best suited for disposing of a less than 100% investment stake in a subsidiary. The purpose of the split-off is to reduce the pressure on the spun-off firm's share price, because shareholders who exchange their stock are less likely to sell the new stock. Presumably, those shareholders willing to make the exchange believe the stock in the subsidiary has greater appreciation potential than does the parent's stock. The exchange also increases the earnings per share of the firm initiating the split-off by reducing the number of its shares outstanding. In a complex transaction, General Motors and Hughes Electronics reached a definitive agreement in which News Corp. would acquire GM's 19.9% stake in Hughes and an additional 14.1% of Hughes from public shareholders. The GM split-off of Hughes was a critical part of the transaction (see Case Study 15-6).

Case Study 15-6
General Motors Splits Off Hughes Electronics

On December 22, 2003, GM and Hughes announced that they had successfully completed the split-off of Hughes from GM and the acquisition by News Corporation of 34% of the outstanding common stock of Hughes. GM split off Hughes by distributing its holdings of Hughes common stock to the holders of GM Class H common stock (a tracking stock) in exchange for the shares they own. As a result of this transaction, Hughes became a separate and independent company.

The Hughes split-off was accomplished in two related steps: the payment of the Hughes special dividend and the Hughes split-off share exchange. The first step involved a special dividend by Hughes to GM of a $275 million special cash dividend. The special cash dividend was to provide additional liquidity to GM. It was intended to compensate GM for the increased value to GM Class H Hughes tracking stockholders that resulted from the exchange of tracking stock for Hughes common. The presumption was that the Hughes stock would have greater appreciation potential than would the tracking stock. The second step involved the distribution, on a one-share-for-one-share basis, of shares of Hughes common stock to the holders of GM Class H common stock in exchange for all of the GM Class H common stock outstanding. The distributed shares represent approximately 80.2% of the outstanding equity in Hughes. All of the formerly outstanding shares of GM Class H common stock were canceled. Both steps were conducted simultaneously.

Case Study Discussion Questions

1. How does a split-off differ from a spin-off? (Hint: Do existing shareholders of the parent have to give up their shares in the parent in a spin-off?)
2. How does a split-off differ from an equity carve-out?

Answers to these Case Study Discussion Questions are available in the Online Instructors Manual for instructors using this book.

Voluntary Liquidations (Bust-Ups)

Involuntary liquidations, normally associated with bankruptcy, are discussed later in this chapter and occur when creditors and the bankruptcy court concur that they will realize more value through liquidation than by reorganizing the firm. *Voluntary liquidations* reflect the judgment that the sale of individual parts of the firm could realize greater value than the value created by a continuation of the combined corporation. This may occur when management views the firm's growth prospects as limited. This option generally is pursued only after other restructure actions have failed to provide a significant improvement in the firm's overall market value.

In 2005, Cendant, a leisure and real estate conglomerate, announced it would split into four separate businesses in an attempt to revive its stock. The new entities will include real estate, travel, hospitality (hotels), and car rental. Each will be spun off into a separate publicly traded company. Current Cendant shareholders will receive shares in each and will continue to receive dividends. Cendant's decision came 6 months after Viacom announced plans to separate CBS and its cable television operations into two companies. In 2006, conglomerate Tyco International announced the separation of the company into three independent units as the best approach to achieve their full potential. Tyco shareholders will receive shares in Tyco Healthcare, Tyco Electronics, and Tyco Fire and Security. Tyco plans on allocating the firm's debt among the three entities.

In general, a merger has the advantage over the voluntary bust-up of deferring the recognition of a gain by the stockholders of the selling company until they eventually sell the stock. In liquidation, the selling shareholders must recognize the gain immediately. Unused tax credits and losses belonging to either of the merged firms are carried over in a nontaxable merger but are lost in liquidation.

TABLE 15-1   Key Characteristics of Alternative Exit/Restructuring Strategies

Characteristics	Divestitures	Equity Carve-Outs/IPOs	Spin-Offs	Split-Ups	Split-Offs	Voluntary Liquidation (Bust-Ups)	Tracking Stocks
Cash Infusion to Parent	Yes	Yes	No	No	No	No	Yes
Change in Equity Ownership	Yes	Yes	No	Sometimes[1]	Yes	Yes	Sometimes
Parent Ceases to Exist	No	No	No	Yes	No	Yes	No
New Legal Entity Created	Sometimes	Yes[2]	Yes	Yes	No	No	No
New Shares Issued	Sometimes	Yes	Yes	Yes	No	No	Yes
Parent Remains in Control	No	Generally	No	No	No	No	Yes
Taxable to Shareholders	Yes[3]	Yes[3]	No[4]	No[4]	No[4]	Yes	No[5]

Notes:
[1] Parent firm shareholders may exchange their shares for one or more of the spin-offs shares resulting in a different distribution of ownership.
[2] Applies to subsidiary carve-outs only.
[3] The proceeds are taxable if returned to shareholders as a dividend or tax deferred if used to repurchase the parent's stock.
[4] The transaction is generally not taxable if properly structured.
[5] Only dividend payments and shareholder gains on the sale of stock are taxable.

Comparing Alternative Exit Restructuring Strategies

Table 15-1 summarizes the primary characteristics of each of the restructuring strategies discussed thus far in this chapter. Note that divestitures and carve-outs provide cash to the parent, whereas spin-offs, split-ups, and bust-ups do not. Equity ownership does not change in spin-offs, but it may change in split-ups as parent company shareholders may exchange their shares or shares in one or more of the spin-offs. The parent remains in existence in all restructuring strategies except split-ups and bust-ups. A new legal entity generally is created with each restructuring strategy, except for voluntary liquidations. With the exception of the carve-out, the parent generally loses control of the division involved in the restructuring strategy. Only spin-offs and split-ups are generally not taxable to shareholders.

Choosing among Divestiture, Carve-Out, and Spin-Off Restructuring Strategies

The reasons for selecting a divestiture, carve-out, or spin-off strategy are inherently different. Parent firms that engage in divestitures are often highly diversified in largely unrelated businesses and have a desire to achieve greater focus or to raise cash. Parent firms that use carve-out strategies usually operate businesses in somewhat related industries exhibiting some degree of synergy and desire to raise cash. Consequently, the parent firm may pursue a carve-out rather than a divestiture or spin-off strategy to retain perceived synergy. There is empirical evidence that the timing of the carve-out is influenced by when management sees its subsidiary's assets as overvalued (Powers, 2003). Firms engaging in spin-offs are often highly diversified but less so than those prone to pursue divestiture strategies and have little need to raise cash (John and Ofek, 1995; Kaplan and Weisbach, 1992). Table 15-2 identifies characteristics of parent firm operating units that often are subject to certain types of restructuring activities.

The decision to exit a business is essentially a two-stage process. The first stage involves the firm deciding to exit a line of business or product line for one or more of the reasons described earlier in this chapter in the section entitled "Motives for Exiting Businesses." The second stage entails selecting the appropriate exit strategy. Divestitures, carve-outs, and spin-offs are the most commonly used restructuring strategy when a parent corporation is considering partially or entirely exiting a business. The decision as to which of these three strategies to use is often heavily influenced by the parent firm's need for cash, the degree of synergy between the business to be divested or spun off and the parent's other operating units, and the potential selling price of the division (Powers, 2001). However, these factors are not independent. Parent firms needing cash are more likely to divest or engage in an equity carve-out for operations exhibiting high selling prices relative to their synergy value. Parent firms not needing cash are more likely to spin off units exhibiting low selling prices and synergy with the parent. Parent firms with moderate cash needs are likely to engage in equity carve-outs when the unit's selling price is low relative to perceived synergy. Table 15-3 illustrates this two-stage procedure.

On the surface, it may seem that a divestiture or carve-out generally would be preferable to a spin-off if the after-tax proceeds from the sale of all or a portion of the operating unit exceed their after-tax equity value to the firm. Unlike a spin-off, a divestiture or

TABLE 15-2 Characteristics of Parent Company Operating Units That Undergo Divestiture, Carve-Out, or Spin-Off

Exit/Restructuring Strategy	Characteristics
Divestitures	• Usually unrelated to other businesses owned by parent • Operating performance generally worse than the parent's consolidated performance • Slightly underperform their peers in year before announcement date • Generally sell at a lower price than carve-outs measured by market value to book assets
Carve-Outs	• Generally more profitable and faster growing than spun off or divested businesses • Operating performance often exceeds parent's • Usually operate in industries characterized by high market to book values • Generally outperform peers in year before announcement date
Spin-Offs	• Generally faster growing and more profitable than divested businesses • Most often operate in industries related to other industries in which the parent operates • Operating performance worse than parent's • Slightly underperform peers in year before announcement date

Sources: Ravenscroft and Scherer (1991), Cho and Cohen (1997), Hand and Skantz (1997), Kang and Shivdasani (1997), and Powers (2001).

TABLE 15-3 Divestitures, Carve-Outs, and Spin-Offs: Selecting the Appropriate Restructuring Strategy

Stage One Considerations (Primary Motive for Restructuring)	Stage Two Considerations		Appropriate Restructuring Strategy	Restructuring Strategy More Likely If Parent
	Need for Cash	Value of Business/Degree of Synergy		
		High Price/High Synergy	Carve-Out	Can retain synergy
		Low Price/High Synergy	Carve-Out	Can retain synergy
	Needs Cash ——→	High Price/Low Synergy	Divestiture	Can shield taxable gains[1]
		Low Price/Low Synergy	Divestiture	
Change Strategy/Increase Focus ——→		High Price/High Synergy	Carve-Out	Can retain synergy
		Low Price/High Synergy	Carve-Out	Can retain synergy
	Little Need for Cash ——→	High Price/Low Synergy	Spin-Off	Cannot shield potential gains
		Low Price/Low Synergy	Spin-Off	
Underperforming Businesses ——→	Needs Cash ————		Divestiture	Can shield taxable gains
	Little Need for Cash ——→		Spin-Off	

Motive	Condition	Divestiture/Spin-Off	Outcome
Regulatory Concerns			Carve-out not an option
	Needs Cash	Divestiture	Can shield taxable gains
Lack of Fit	Little Need for Cash	Spin-Off	Cannot shield potential gains
Tax Considerations		Spin-Off	Can shield taxable gains
Raising Funds/Worth More to Others		Divestiture	
Risk Reduction		Carve-Out	
Moving Away from Core Business		Divestiture/Carve-out	Can shield taxable gains
Discarding Unwanted Businesses from Prior Acquisitions		Divestiture	Can shield taxable gains
Avoiding Customer Conflicts	Need Cash	Divestiture	Can shield taxable gains
	Little Need for Cash	Spin-Off	Cannot shield taxable gains

Note:

[1] Parent can shield any taxable gains on the sale by offsetting such gains with losses incurred elsewhere in the consolidated firm.

carve-out generates a cash infusion to the firm, which either can be reinvested or paid to shareholders as a dividend or share buyback. In fact, a spin-off may create greater shareholder wealth for several reasons.

First, a spin-off is tax free to the shareholders if it is properly structured. In contrast, the cash proceeds from an outright sale may be taxable to the parent to the extent a gain is realized. Moreover, management must be able to reinvest the after-tax proceeds in a project that has a reasonable likelihood of returning the firm's cost of capital. If management chooses to return the cash proceeds to shareholders as a dividend or through a stock repurchase, the shareholders also must pay taxes on the dividend or on any gain realized through the share repurchase. Second, a spin-off enables the shareholder to decide when to sell their shares. Third, a spin-off may be less traumatic than a divestiture for an operating unit. The divestiture process can degrade value if it is lengthy. Employees leave, worker productivity generally suffers, and customers may not renew contracts until the new owner is known.

Returns to Shareholders

Preannouncement Abnormal Returns

Empirical studies indicate that the alternative exit/restructure strategies discussed in this chapter generally provide positive abnormal returns to the shareholders of the company implementing the strategy. However, the size of the abnormal returns varies widely among the alternative strategies (see Table 15-4). In general, the magnitude of the abnormal returns is positively related to the size of the division subject to divestiture, spin-off, or

TABLE 15-4   Returns to Shareholders of Firms Undertaking Restructuring Actions

Restructuring Action	Average Preannouncement Abnormal Returns
Divestitures	1.8%
Spin-Offs	3.7%
Tracking Stocks	3.0%
Equity Carve-Outs	4.7%
Voluntary Bust-Ups	17.3%

Study	Preannouncement Abnormal Returns by Study[1]
Divestitures:	
Alexander, Benson, and Kampmeyer (1984): 53 from 1964 to 1973	.17%
Linn and Rozeff (1984): 77 from 1977 to 1982	1.45%
Jain (1985): 1107 from 1976 to 1978	.70%
Klein (1986): 202 from 1970 to 1979	1.12%
	When percentage of equity sold is <10%: None
	> 10 < 50%: 2.53%
	> 50%: 8.09%

TABLE 15-4 continued

Study	Preannouncement Abnormal Returns by Study[1]
	2.0% for firms distributing proceeds to shareholders; (.5)% for those reinvesting proceeds
Lang, Poulsen, and Stulz (1995): 93 from 1984 to 1989	.8%
Allen (2000): 48 from 1982 to 1991	2.6%
Mulherin and Boone (2000): 139 from 1990 to 1998	2.6%
Dittmar and Shivdasani (2002): 188 from 1983 to 1994	1.2% for firms using proceeds to reduce debt
	.7% for firms using proceeds to repurchase stock or pay dividends
Bates (2005): 372 from 1990 to 1998	1.9% for seller receiving cash
Slovin, Sushka, and Polonchek (2005): 327 from 1983 to 2000	3.2% for seller receiving equity

Spin-Offs:

Hite and Owers (1983): 56 from 1963 to 1979	3.8%
Miles and Rosenfeld (1983): 62 from 1963 to 1981	2.33%
Michaely and Shaw (1995): 91 master limited partnerships from 1981 to 1989	4.5%
Loh, Bezjak, and Toms (1995): 59 from 1982 to 1987	1.5%
JP Morgan (1995): 77 since beginning of 1995	5%
	6% if spin-off > 10% of parent's equity
	4% if spin-off < 10% of parent's equity
Vroom and van Frederikslust (1999): 210 worldwide spin-offs from 1990 to 1998	2.6%
Mulherin and Boone (2000): 106 from 1990 to 1998	4.51%
Davis and Leblond (2002): 93 from 1980 to 1999	2.92%
Veld and Veld-Merkoulova (2002): 200 from 1987 to 2000	2.66%
Maxwell and Rao (2003): 80 from 1976 to 1997	3.60%

Tracking Stocks:

Logue, Seward, and Walsh (1996): 9 from 1991 to 1995	2.9%
D'Souza and Jacob (2000)	3.6%
Elder and Westra (2000): 35 from 1984 to 1999	3.1%
Haushalter and Mikkelson (2001): 31 from 1994 to 1996	3.0%
Chemmanur and Paeglis (2001): 19 from 1984 to 1998	3.1%
Billet and Vijh (2004): 29 from 1984 to 1999	2.2%

continued

TABLE 15-4   continued

Study	Preannouncement Abnormal Returns by Study[1]
Equity Carve-Outs/IPOs:	
Schipper and Smith (1986): 81 from 1965 to 1983	1.7%
Michaely and Shaw (1995): 91 limited partnerships from 1981 to 1989	4%
Allen and McConnell (1998): 188 from 1978 to 1993	6.63% when proceeds used to pay off debt; zero otherwise
Vijh (1999): 628 from 1981 to 1995	6.2%
Mulherin and Boone (2000): 125 from 1990 to 1998	2.3%
Prezas, Tarimcilar, and Vasduevan (2000): 237 from 1985 to 1996	5.8%
Hulburt, Miles, and Wollridge (2002): 245 from 1981 to 1994	2.1%
Hogan and Olson (2004): 458 from 1990 to 1998	8.8%
Voluntary Liquidations:	
Skantz and Marchesini (1987): 37 from 1970 to 1978	21.4%[2]
Hite, Owers, and Rogers (1987): 49 from 1966 to 1975	13.6%[2]
Kim and Schatzberg (1987): 73 from 1963 to 1981	14%
Erwin and McConnell (1997): 61 from 1970 to 1991	20%

Notes:
[1] Abnormal returns measured from 1–3 days before and including announcement date of restructure action.
[2] Abnormal returns measured during the month of the announced restructure action.

carve-out relative to the size of the parent (JP Morgan, 1995; Klein, 1986). Moreover, abnormal returns tend to be larger for divestitures and carve-outs if the parent has announced that it will use the proceeds from a divestiture or carve-out to repay debt or pay dividends (Allen and McConnell, 1998; Bates, 2005; Byers, Lee, and Opler, 1996; Lang, Poulsen, and Stulz, 1995). Finally, abnormal returns tend to be larger for restructuring activities that tend to focus the firm (Daley, Mehrotra, and Sivakumar, 1997; Desai and Jain, 1999; John and Ofek, 1995; Veld and Veld-Merkoulova, 2004).

The exceptional abnormal returns for voluntary bust-ups may reflect investors' concurrence with management that continued operation of the firm is likely to erode shareholder value. Liquidation of the firm results in the firm's assets being redeployed by the firm's shareholders to potentially higher alternative financial returns. Firms that tend to liquidate voluntarily often have low market-to-book ratios, cash balances well in excess of their operating needs, low debt-to-equity levels, and high equity ownership by senior managers. Such firms often liquidate after takeover attempts (Fleming and Moon, 1995).

Form of Payment Affects Abnormal Seller Restructuring Returns

Studies by Klein (1986), Hite, Owers, and Rogers (1987), and Lang, Poulsen, and Stulz (1995) suggest that sellers realize small, but statistically significant excess returns, while buyers do not. Slovin, Sushka, and Polonchek (2005) investigate the extent to which the form of payment affects excess returns. The authors find that abnormal returns to sellers are much smaller when the seller receives cash rather than buyer equity.

These results challenge the widely held and well-documented view that the issuance or the use of equity typically results in a reduction of the value of the firm issuing the equity (see Chapter 1). This is especially true where one corporation is merged with another or one takes a controlling interest in another. However, this may not be the case when a buyer uses equity to acquire an operating unit or subsidiary from another firm.

Asset for buyer equity sales generate excess returns of about 10% for buyers and 3% for sellers. The higher returns for buyers may reflect information communicated to the seller not generally known by the investing public about the synergy between the divested asset and the buyer's operations and the overall future earnings potential of the buyer's business. In contrast, excess returns to sellers receiving cash average about 3% for sellers and about zero for buyers.

Post-Spin-Off Returns to Shareholders

Empirical studies show that shares in carve-outs and spin-offs tend to significantly outperform the Standard & Poor's (S&P) 500 during the 2 years following the announcement (see Table 15-5). In contrast, tracking stocks tend to underperform the gains in the S&P 500.

Carve-outs and spin-offs may tend to outperform the broader stock market indices because their share prices reflect speculation that they will be acquired rather than any improvement in the operating performance of the units once they have been spun off from the parent. One-third of spin-offs are acquired within 3 years after the unit is spun off by the parent. Once those spin-offs that have been acquired have been removed from the sample, the remaining spin-offs do not perform better than their peers (Cusatis, Miles, and Woolridge, 1993). McConnell, Ozbilgin, and Wahal (2001) conclude that many historical studies showing superior post-spin-off returns are indeed heavily biased by the inclusion of one or two firms in the sample whose excess returns are the result of their having been acquired. Spin-offs simply may create value by providing an efficient method of transferring corporate assets to acquiring companies.

In a study of 232 spin-offs and equity carve-outs during the 1990s, Booz-Allen & Hamilton found that only 26% of the units outperformed the broader stock market indices during the 2 years following their separation from the parent (Scherreik, 2002). Smaller spin-offs (i.e., those with a market cap of less than $200 million) tend to outperform larger ones (i.e., those with a market cap greater than $200 million) (JP Morgan, 1999). This

TABLE 15-5   Returns to Postrestructuring Shareholders

Study	Average Annual Returns (2–3 Years Following Announcement)
Spin-Offs	6–11% above the S&P 500[1]
Carve-Outs	3–10% above the S&P 500[2]
Tracking Stocks	2–12% less than the S&P 500[3]

Notes:
[1] Oppenheimer & Company (1981), Cusatis, Miles, and Woolridge (1993), JP Morgan (1999), McKinsey & Company (1999), Allen (2001).
[2] JP Morgan (1999), McKinsey & Company (1999), Prezas, Tarimcilar, and Vasudevan (2000).
[3] McKinsey & Company (1999), Vijh (1999), Billett (2000), Billett and Vijh (2004).

may be a result of a tendency of investors relatively unfamiliar with the business that is spun off by the parent to undervalue the spin-off. Carve-outs that are largely independent of the parent (i.e., in which the parent tended to own less than 50% of the equity) tended to significantly outperform the S&P 500 (Annema, Fallon, and Goedhart, 2002).

Spin-Offs Transfer Wealth from Bondholders to Stockholders

There is evidence that spin-offs transfer wealth from bondholders to stockholders for several reasons. First, the assets that are spun off to the parent's shareholders reduce the assets available for liquidation in the event of business failure. Therefore, investors may view the firm's existing debt as more risky. (Note that assets that are actually pledged as collateral to current debt may not be spun off without violating loan covenants.) Second, the loss of the cash flow generated by the spin-off may result in less total parent cash flow to cover interest and principal repayments on the parent's current debt. Maxwell and Rao (2003) in a sample of 80 spin-offs between 1976 and 1997 noted that bondholders on average suffer a negative abnormal return of .8% in the month of the spin-off announcement. Stockholders experience an increase of about 3.6% during the same period.

Business Failure

According to Dun & Bradstreet (1997), the leading causes of business failure in order of priority include recession, excessive operating expenses and leverage, and management inexperience. When a firm is unable to pay its liabilities as they come due, it is said to be *technically insolvent. Legal insolvency* occurs when a firm's liabilities exceed the fair market value of its assets. U.S. courts treat both technical insolvency and legal insolvency as a financial failure of the firm. *Bankruptcy* is a federal legal proceeding designed to protect the technically or legally insolvent firm from lawsuits by its creditors until a decision can be made to shut down or to continue to operate the firm. A firm is not considered to be bankrupt or in bankruptcy until it or its creditors file a petition for reorganization or liquidation with the federal bankruptcy courts.

Voluntary Settlements with Creditors Outside of Bankruptcy

An insolvent firm may reach an agreement with its creditors to restructure its obligations out of court to avoid the costs of bankruptcy proceedings. The voluntary settlement process usually is initiated by the debtor firm, because it generally offers the best chance for the current owners to recover a portion of their investments either by continuing to operate the firm or through a planned liquidation of the firm. This process normally involves the debtor firm requesting a meeting with its creditors. At this meeting, a committee of creditors is selected to analyze the debtor firm's financial position and to recommend an appropriate course of action. The committee can recommend either that the firm continue or that it be liquidated.

Increasingly, distressed companies are choosing to restructure outside of bankruptcy court (Lovely, February 7, 2007). Smaller firms are inclined to use out-of-court settlements because of the excessive expenses associated with reorganizing in bankruptcy courts. More mid-sized companies moving into international markets also contribute to the growth in out-of-court restructurings. Such firms may not be able to restructure through U.S. bankruptcy courts if the ruling is not recognized overseas. Large companies often have a difficult time achieving out-of-court settlements because they usually have hundreds of creditors.

Voluntary Settlement Resulting in Continued Operation

Plans to restructure the debtor firm developed cooperatively with creditors commonly are called **workouts**. Because of the firm's weak financial position, the creditors must be willing to restructure the insolvent firm's debts to enable it to sustain its operations. **Debt restructuring** involves concessions by creditors that will lower an insolvent firm's payments so that it may remain in business. Restructuring normally is accomplished in three ways: an extension, a composition, or a debt-for-equity swap.

An **extension** occurs when creditors agree to lengthen the period during which the debtor firm can repay its debt. Creditors often agree to temporarily suspend both interest and principal repayments. A **composition** is an agreement in which creditors agree to settle for less than the full amount they are owed. A **debt-for-equity swap** occurs when creditors surrender a portion of their claims on the firm in exchange for an ownership position in the firm. If the reduced debt service payments enable the firm to prosper, the value of the stock may in the long run far exceed the amount of debt the creditors were willing to forgive. In 2004, Revlon reached agreement with Fidelity Management & Research Company and MacAndrews & Forbes to exchange $155 million and $775 million, respectively, in debt for common stock.

Exhibit 15-1 illustrates a debt restructure or composition of a bankrupt company that will enable the firm to continue operation by converting debt to equity. Although the firm, Survivor Incorporated, has positive earnings before interest and taxes, it is not enough to meet its interest payments. When principal payments are considered, cash flow becomes significantly negative. Therefore, it is technically insolvent. As a result of the restructuring of the firm's debt, Survivor Incorporated is able to continue to operate. However, the firm's lenders now have a controlling interest in the firm. Note the same type of restructuring could take place either voluntarily outside the courts or as a result of reorganizing under the protection of the bankruptcy court. The latter scenario will be discussed later in this chapter.

Exhibit 15-1
Survivor Inc. Restructures Its Debt

Survivor Inc. currently has 400,000 shares of common equity outstanding at a par value of $10 per share. The current rate of interest on its debt is 8% and the debt is amortized over 20 years. The combined federal, state, and local tax rate is 40%. The firm's cash flow and capital position are shown below.

Income and Cash Flow		Total Capital	
Earnings before Interest & Taxes	$500,000	Debt	$10,000,000
Interest	800,000	Equity	4,000,000
Earnings before Taxes	(300,000)	Total	$14,000,000
Taxes	120,000		
Earnings after Taxes	(180,000)	Debt/Total Capital	71.4%
Depreciation	400,000		
Principal Repayment	(500,000)		
Cash Flow	(280,000)		

Assume bondholders are willing to convert $5,000,000 of debt to equity at the current par value of $10 per share. This necessitates that Survivor Inc. issues 500,000 new shares. These actions result in positive cash flow, a substantial reduction in the firm's debt-to-total capital ratio, and a transfer of control to the bondholders. The former stockholders now own only 44.4% (4,000,000/9,000,000) of the company.

Income and Cash Flow		Total Capital	
Earnings before Interest & Taxes	$500,000	Debt	$5,000,000
Interest	400,000	Equity	9,000,000
Earnings before Taxes	100,000	Total	$14,000,000
Taxes	40,000		
Earnings after Taxes	60,000	Debt/Total Capital	35.7%
Depreciation	400,000		
Principal Repayment	(250,000)		
Cash Flow	$210,000		

Voluntary Settlement Resulting in Liquidation

If the creditors conclude that the insolvent firm's situation cannot be resolved, liquidation may be the only acceptable course of action. Liquidation can be conducted outside the court in a private liquidation or through the U.S. bankruptcy court. If the insolvent firm is willing to accept liquidation and all creditors agree, legal proceedings are not necessary. Creditors normally prefer private liquidations to avoid lengthy and costly litigation. Through a process called an *assignment*, a committee representing creditors grants the power to liquidate the firm's assets to a third party called an *assignee or trustee*. The responsibility of the assignee is to sell the assets as quickly as possible while obtaining the best possible price. Once the assets have been sold, the assignee distributes the proceeds to the creditors and to the firm's owners if any monies remain.

Reorganization and Liquidation in Bankruptcy

In the absence of a voluntary settlement out of court, the debtor firm may seek protection from its creditors by initiating bankruptcy or may be forced into bankruptcy by its creditors. When the debtor firm files the petition with the bankruptcy court, the bankruptcy is said to be *voluntary*. When creditors do the filing, the action is said to be *involuntary bankruptcy*. Once either a voluntary or involuntary petition is filed, the debtor firm is protected from any further legal action related to its debts until the bankruptcy proceedings are completed. The filing of a petition allows the debtor firm to stop all principal and interest payments owed to creditors, while preventing secured creditors from taking possession of their collateral.

Bankruptcy Laws and Procedures

Under the 1978 Bankruptcy Reform Act, the conditions under which companies could file were broadened such that a firm could declare bankruptcy without having to wait until it was virtually insolvent. The intent of making the bankruptcy code less rigid was to increase the likelihood that creditors and owners would reach agreement on plans to reorganize rather than liquidate insolvent firms. Although most companies that file for bankruptcy do so as a result of their deteriorating financial position, companies increasingly are seeking bankruptcy protection to avoid litigation and hostile takeovers.

In the mid-1980s, Johns Manville Corporation used bankruptcy to negotiate a reduction in huge liability awards granted in the wake of asbestos-related lawsuits. Similarly, Texaco used the threat of bankruptcy in the early 1990s as a negotiating ploy to reduce the amount of court-ordered payments to Occidental Petroleum resulting from the court's determination that Texaco had improperly intervened in a pending merger transaction. To protect them from litigation, Washington Construction Group required Morrison Knudsen Corporation to file for bankruptcy as a closing condition in the agreement of purchase and sale in 2000. Saddled with crushing pension and other retiree benefit obligations, 33 steel companies have sought the protection of the bankruptcy court to either reorganize or liquidate their businesses. In 2001, LTV sold its plants while in bankruptcy to W.L. Ross and Company, which restarted the plants in 2002 in a new company named the International Steel Group (ISI). By simply buying assets, ISI does not have the obligation to pay the pension, health care, or insurance liabilities, which remained with LTV. More recently, a bankruptcy judge in late 2004 approved a settlement enabling two subsidiaries of the energy giant, Halliburton, to emerge from bankruptcy. Under the settlement, Halliburton agreed to establish a $4.2 billion trust fund to pay potential future asbestos claims. Delphi, the ailing auto parts manufacturer used its bankrupt status to threaten to abrogate union contracts to gain substantial wage and benefit concessions from its employees.

Chapters 7 and 11 of the U.S. Bankruptcy Code

The two key chapters in the Bankruptcy Reform Act are Chapters 7 and 11. *Chapter 7* deals with liquidation and provides for a court-appointed interim trustee with broad powers and discretion to operate the debtor firm in such a way to prevent further deterioration in the overall financial position of the firm and the removal of assets by owners before liquidation. **Chapter 11** deals with reorganization, which provides for the debtor to remain in possession, unless the court rules otherwise, of the business and in control of its operations. The debtor and creditors are permitted considerable flexibility in working together. This enables them to negotiate debt repayment schedules, the restructuring of debt, and the granting of loans by the creditors to the debtor. If a workable plan cannot be formulated, the firm will be liquidated in accordance with the procedures outlined in Chapter 7.

United Airlines (UAL) emerged from bankruptcy in February 2006 after 38 months in Chapter 11, the longest time period under court protection in U.S. bankruptcy history. UAL used the time to radically restructure the company and to trim $7 billion in annual costs, including two rounds of employee pay cuts and the elimination of 25,000 jobs. The firm also transferred successfully its defined benefit pension plans to the U.S Pension Benefit Guaranty Corporation and further reduced its cost structure by shedding more than 100 planes from its fleet, cutting some U.S. flights, and expanding internationally.

Bris, Welch, and Zhu (2006) argue that Chapter 7 liquidations appear to be as costly in terms of legal expenses and related fees, as well as the time required to complete the proceedings, as Chapter 11 reorganization. However, Chapter 11 reorganization does allow creditors to recover relatively more of what they are owed than under liquidation. In liquidation, bankruptcy professionals, including attorneys, accountants, and trustees, end up with the majority of the proceeds generated by selling the assets of the failing firm.

Filing for Chapter 11 Reorganization

Figure 15-2 summarizes the process for filing for reorganization under Chapter 11. The process begins by filing in a federal bankruptcy court. In the case of an involuntary petition, a hearing must be held to determine whether the firm is insolvent. If the firm is found to be insolvent, the court enters an **order for relief**, which initiates the bankruptcy proceedings. On the filing of a reorganization petition, the filing firm becomes the **debtor in possession** of all the assets. The debtor firm's managers are able to continue to make operating decisions, and they have the exclusive right to propose a reorganization plan during the 120 days after filing for Chapter 11 bankruptcy. The court often grants extensions if requested by management. However, changes in U.S. bankruptcy laws that took effect on October 17, 2005, require corporations operating under Chapter 11 protection to make decisions faster and to pay back a larger percentage of their debt. Congress decided to limit the leeway bankruptcy judges have to determine the duration of cases and allow exceptions. A firm filing for Chapter 11 will have at

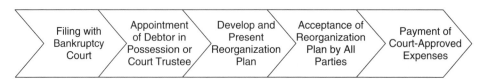

FIGURE 15-2   Procedures for reorganizing in bankruptcy.

most 18 months, including extensions granted by bankruptcy judges, to submit a restructuring plan. After this period has elapsed or if management's plan is rejected, creditors have the right to submit their own plans. The new laws may force more companies to liquidate rather than to work out their financial problems. Creditors may request that the court appoint a trustee instead of the debtor to manage the firm during the reorganization period.

Federal bankruptcy courts evaluate reorganization plans in terms of their fairness and feasibility. Fairness means that the creditor claims are to be satisfied in accordance with the order of priorities listed in the bankruptcy laws. Feasibility refers to whether the assumptions underlying the plan are realistic. When the court approves a reorganization plan, creditors and owners are grouped according to the similarity of claims. In the case of creditors, the plan must be approved by holders of at least two-thirds of the dollar value of the claims as well as a simple majority of the creditors in each group. In the case of owners, two-thirds of those in each group (e.g., common and preferred shareholders) must approve the plan. Once approved by all groups, the plan takes effect. Finally, the debtor is responsible for paying the expenses approved by the court of all parties whose services contributed to the approval or disapproval of the plan.

Such expenses may be minimized if the failing firm initiates a **_prepackaged bankruptcy_** in which it negotiates with creditors well in advance of filing for a Chapter 11 bankruptcy. Because there is general approval of the plan before the filing, the formal Chapter 11 reorganization that follows generally averages only a few months and results in substantially lower legal and administrative expenses (Altman, 1993; Betker, 1995; Tashjian, Lease, and McConnell, 1996). More than one-fifth of major bankruptcy cases between 2001 and 2005 were prepackaged deals (Lovely, February 7, 2007).

Chapter 7 Liquidation

If the bankruptcy court determines that reorganization is infeasible, the failing firm may be forced to liquidate. A trustee is appointed by the court to handle the administrative aspects of the liquidation. The trustee is given the responsibility to liquidate the firm's assets, keep records, examine creditors' claims, disburse the proceeds, and submit a final report on the liquidation. The priority in which the claims are paid is stipulated in Chapter 7 of the Bankruptcy Reform Act, which must be followed by the trustee when the firm is liquidated. All secured creditors are paid when the firm's assets that were pledged as collateral are liquidated. If the proceeds of the sale of these assets are inadequate to satisfy all of the secured creditors' claims, they become unsecured or general creditors for the amount that was not recovered. If the proceeds of the sale of pledged assets exceed secured creditors' claims, the excess proceeds are used to pay general creditors.

Exhibit 15-2 illustrates how a legally bankrupt company could be liquidated. The bankruptcy court, owners, and creditors could not agree on an appropriate reorganization plan for DOA Inc. Consequently, the court has ordered that the firm be liquidated in accordance with Chapter 7. Note that this illustration would differ from a private or voluntary out-of-court liquidation in two important respects. First, the expenses associated with conducting the liquidation would be lower, because the liquidation would not involve extended legal proceedings. Second, the distribution of proceeds could reflect a prioritization of claims negotiated between the creditors and the owners that differs from that set forth in Chapter 7 of the Bankruptcy Reform Act.

Exhibit 15-2

Liquidation of DOA, Inc. under Chapter 7

DOA has the following balance sheet. The only liability that is not shown on the balance sheet is the cost of the bankruptcy proceedings, which are treated as expenses and are not capitalized.

Balance Sheet			
Assets		Liabilities	
Cash	$ 35,000	Accounts Payable	$ 750,000
Accounts Receivable	2,300,000	Bank Notes Payable	3,000,000
Inventories	2,100,000	Accrued Salaries	720,000
Total Current Assets	$4,435,000	Unpaid Benefits	140,000
Land	1,500,000	Unsecured Customer Deposits	300,000
Net Plant & Equipment	2,000,000	Taxes Payable	400,000
Total Fixed Assets	$3,500,000	Total Current Liabilities	$5,310,000
Total Assets	$7,935,000	First Mortgage	2,500,000
		Unsecured Debt	200,000
		Total Long Term Debt	$2,700,000
		Preferred Stock	50,000
		Common Stock	100,000
		Paid in Surplus	500,000
		Retained Earnings	(725,000)
		Total Stockholders' Equity	$ (75,000)
		Total Shareholders' Equity &	$7,935,000
		Total Liabilities	

The sale of DOA's assets generates $5.4 million in cash. The distribution of the proceeds results in the following situation. Note that the proceeds are distributed in accordance with the priorities stipulated in the current commercial bankruptcy law and that the cost of administering the bankruptcy totals 18% of the proceeds from liquidation.

Distribution of Liquidation Proceeds	
Proceeds from Liquidation	$5,400,000
Expenses of Administering Bankruptcy	972,000
Salaries Owed Employees	720,000
Unpaid Employee Benefits	140,000
Unsecured Customer Deposits	300,000
Taxes	400,000
Funds Available for Creditors	$2,868,000
First Mortgage (From sale of fixed assets)	1,500,000
Funds Available for Unsecured Creditors	$1,368,000

Once all prior claims have been satisfied, the remaining proceeds are distributed to the unsecured creditors. The pro rata settlement percentage of 27.64% is calculated by dividing funds available for unsecured creditors by the amount of unsecured creditor claims (i.e., $1,368/$4,950). The shareholders receive nothing because not all unsecured creditor claims have been satisfied.

Pro Rata Distribution of Funds among Unsecured Creditors		
Unsecured Creditor Claims	Amount	Settlement at 27.64%
Unpaid Balance from First Mortgage	$1,000,000	$ 276,400
Accounts Payable	750,000	207,300
Notes Payable	3,000,000	829,200
Unsecured Debt	200,000	55,280
Total	$4,950,000	$1,368,000

Strategic Options for Failing Firms

A failing firm's strategic options are to merge with another firm, reach an out-of-court voluntary settlement with creditors, or file for Chapter 11 bankruptcy. The firm may voluntarily liquidate as part of an out-of-court settlement or be forced to liquidate under Chapter 7 of the bankruptcy code. The implications of each option are summarized in Table 15-6. The choice of which option to pursue is critically dependent on which provides the greatest present value for creditors and shareholders. To evaluate these options, the firm's management needs to estimate the going concern, selling price, and liquidation values of the firm.

TABLE 15-6   Alternative Strategies for Failing Firms

Assumptions	Options: Failing Firm	Outcome: Failing Firm
Selling Price > Going Concern or Liquidation Value	1. Is acquired by or 2. Merges with another firm	1. Continues as subsidiary of acquirer 2. Merged into acquirer and ceases to exist
Going Concern Value > Sale or Liquidation Value	1. Reaches out-of-court settlement with creditors 2. Seeks bankruptcy protection under Chapter 11	1. Continues with debt for equity swap, extension, and composition 2. Continues in reorganization
Liquidation Value > Sale or Going Concern Value	1. Reaches out-of-court settlement with creditors 2. Liquidates under Chapter 7	1. Ceases to exist; assignee liquidates assets and distributes proceeds to creditors on a pro rata basis 2. Ceases to exist; trustee supervises liquidation and distributes proceeds according to statutory priorities

Merging with Another Firm

If the failing firm's management estimates that the sale price of the firm is greater than the going concern or liquidation values, management should seek to be acquired by or to merge with another firm. If a strategic buyer can be found, management must convince the firm's creditors that they will be more likely to receive what they are owed and that shareholders are more likely to preserve share value if the firm is acquired rather than liquidated or allowed to remain independent. International Steel Group's acquisition of LTV Steel's assets in 2002 and bankrupt Bethlehem Steel in early 2003, along with U.S. Steel's purchase of bankrupt National Steel shortly thereafter, are examples of such transactions. In 2005, Time Warner Inc. and Comcast Corp. reached an agreement to buy bankrupt cable operator Adelphia Communications Corp. for nearly $18 billion. Time Warner and Comcast will pay Adelphia bondholders and other creditors in cash and warrants for stock in a new company formed by combining Timer Warner's cable business and Adelphia.

In a study of 38 takeovers of distressed firms from 1981 to 1988, Clark and Ofek (1994) found that bidders tend to overpay for these types of firms. Although this strategy may benefit the failing firm's shareholders, such takeovers do not seem to benefit the acquirer's shareholders. Clark and Ofek also found that, in most cases, the acquiring firms fail to successfully restructure the acquired firms.

Reaching an Out-of-Court Voluntary Settlement with Creditors

Alternatively, the going concern value of the firm may exceed the sale or liquidation values. Management must be able to demonstrate to creditors that a restructured or downsized firm will be able to repay its debts if creditors are willing to accept less, extend the maturity of the debt, or exchange debt for equity. If management cannot reach agreement with the firm's creditors, it may seek protection under Chapter 11.

A voluntary settlement may be difficult to achieve because the debtor often needs the approval of all of its creditors. Known as the *holdout problem*, smaller creditors sometimes have an incentive to attempt to hold up the agreement unless they receive special treatment. Consensus may be accomplished by paying all small creditors 100% of what they are owed and the larger creditors an agreed-on percentage. A preference on the part of certain institutions for debt rather than equity and inadequate access by creditors to the necessary information to enable them to value properly the equity they are being offered in a debt-for-equity swap also limit the use of voluntary agreements. Because of these factors, there is some evidence that firms that attempt to restructure outside of Chapter 11 bankruptcy have more difficulty in reducing their indebtedness than those that negotiate with creditors while under the protection of Chapter 11 (Gilson, 1997).

Voluntary and Involuntary Liquidations

The failing firm's management, shareholders, and creditors may agree that the firm is worth more in liquidation than in sale or as a continuing operation. As noted earlier in this chapter, studies show that voluntary liquidations often result in significant returns to the shareholders of the failing firm. If management cannot reach agreement with its creditors on a private liquidation, the firm may seek a Chapter 7 liquidation.

Returns to Firms Emerging from Bankruptcy

When firms emerge from bankruptcy, they often cancel the old stock and issue new common stock. Empirical studies show that firms emerging from bankruptcy often show very attractive returns to holders of the new stock immediately following the announcement that the firm is emerging from bankruptcy (Alderson and Betker, 1996; Eberhart, Altman, and Aggarwal, 1999). Despite these results, long-term performance often deteriorates. Hotchkiss (1995) found that 40% of the firms studied continued to experience operating losses in the 3 years after emerging from Chapter 11. Almost one-third subsequently file for bankruptcy again or have to again restructure their debt. After 5 years, about one-quarter of all firms that reorganize are liquidated, merge, or refile for bankruptcy (France, 2002).

Things to Remember

Divestitures, spin-offs, equity carve-outs, split-ups, and voluntary bust-ups are commonly used exit strategies to redeploy assets by returning cash or noncash assets through a special dividend to shareholders. The motives for firms undertaking these strategies include a changing corporate strategy or a desire to exit underperforming businesses. Tax and regulatory considerations, a desire to reduce risk, abandoning the core business, discarding unwanted businesses from prior acquisitions, and avoiding conflicts with customers are also factors causing firms to restructure.

A divestiture is the sale of a portion of the firm to an outside party generally resulting in a cash infusion to the parent. Equity carve-outs tend to fall into two categories. The first type, the IPO, involves a transaction in which a privately held firm offers a portion of the stock of the consolidated entity to the general public. The second category, the subsidiary equity carve-out, involves a parent selling a portion of the stock in a newly created, wholly owned subsidiary to the public. As is true with subsidiary equity carve-outs, spin-offs entail the creation of a new legal entity. However, there is no cash infusion to the parent as these new shares are distributed, as a stock dividend, to the parent's current shareholders. In a split-up, the entire company is broken up into a series of spin-offs, with the parent ceasing to exist. Tracking stock transactions are those in which a parent divides its operations into two or more operating units and assigns a common stock to each operation. The tracking stock is owned by the parent and not by the subsidiary. Voluntary liquidations or bust-ups reflect the judgment that the sale of individual parts of the firm could realize greater value than by continuing the combined corporation. A split-off is a variation of a spin-off in which some parent company shareholders receive shares in a subsidiary in return for exchanging their parent company shares.

A failing firm's strategic options are to merge with another firm, reach an out-of-court settlement with creditors, or file for Chapter 11 bankruptcy. The firm may liquidate voluntarily as part of an out-of-court settlement or may be forced by its creditors to liquidate. The choice of which option to pursue depends on which provides the greatest present value for creditors and shareholders. A failing firm or its creditors may file a bankruptcy petition. Once filed, the bankruptcy procedures normally involve a reorganization, debt restructuring, or liquidation. A reorganization in bankruptcy is a business plan, which, if acceptable to the court, creditors, and shareholders, allows the failing firm to continue to operate. Before the firm is able to emerge from bankruptcy, the firm's debt usually is restructured with creditors granting concessions that will lower an insolvent firm's payments. Finally, liquidation involves closing the firm, selling its assets, and distributing the proceeds to its creditors and owners.

Chapter Discussion Questions

15-1. How do tax and regulatory considerations influence the decision to exit a business?

15-2. How would you decide when to sell a business?

15-3. What are the major differences between a spin-off and an equity carve-out?

15-4. Under what conditions is a spin-off tax free to shareholders?

15-5. Why would a firm decide to voluntarily split up?

15-6. What are the advantages and disadvantages of tracking stocks to investors and to the firm?

15-7. What factors contribute to the high positive abnormal returns to shareholders before the announcement of a voluntary bust-up?

15-8. What are the primary factors contributing to business failure?

15-9. Why would creditors make concessions to a failing firm?

15-10. What are the primary options available to a failing firm? What criteria might the firm use to select a particular option?

Answers to these Chapter Discussion Questions are available in the Online Instructor's Manual for instructors using this book.

Chapter Business Case

Case Study 15-7
The Enron Shuffle—A Scandal to Remember

What started in the mid-1980s as essentially a staid "old economy" business became the poster child in the late 1990s for companies wanting to remake themselves into "new economy" powerhouses. Unfortunately, what may have started with the best of intentions emerged as one of the biggest business scandals in U.S. history. Enron was created in 1985 as a result of a merger between Houston Natural Gas and Internorth Natural Gas. In 1989, Enron started trading natural gas commodities and eventually became the world's largest buyer and seller of natural gas. In the early 1990s, Enron became the nation's premier electricity marketer and pioneered the development of trading in such commodities as weather derivatives, bandwidth, pulp, paper, and plastics. Enron invested billions in its broadband unit and water and wastewater system management unit and in hard assets overseas. In 2000, Enron reported $101 billion in revenue and a market capitalization of $63 billion.

The Virtual Company
Enron was essentially a company whose trading and risk management business strategy was built on assets largely owned by others. The complex financial maneuvering and off–balance sheet partnerships that former CEO Jeffrey K. Skilling and Chief Financial Officer Andrew S. Fastow implemented were intended to remove everything from telecommunications fiber to water companies from the firm's balance sheet and into partnerships. What

---

distinguished Enron's partnerships from those commonly used to share risks were their lack of independence from Enron and the use of Enron's stock as collateral to leverage the partnerships. If Enron's stock fell in value, the firm was obligated to issue more shares to the partnership to restore the value of the collateral underlying the debt or to immediately repay the debt. Lenders in effect had direct recourse to Enron stock if at any time the partnerships could not repay their loans in full. Rather than limiting risk, Enron was assuming total risk by guaranteeing the loans with its stock.

Enron also engaged in transactions that inflated its earnings, such as selling time on its broadband system to a partnership at inflated prices at a time when the demand for broadband was plummeting. Enron then recorded a substantial profit on such transactions. The partnerships agreed to such transactions, because Enron management seems to have exerted disproportionate influence in some instances over partnership decisions although its ownership interests were very small, often less than 3%. Curiously, Enron's outside auditor, Arthur Andersen, may have had a dual role in these partnerships, collecting fees for helping to set them up and for auditing them.

Time to Pay the Piper
At the time the firm filed for bankruptcy on December 2, 2001, it had $13.1 billion in debt on the books of the parent company and another $18.1 billion on the balance sheets of affiliated companies/partnerships. In addition to the partnerships created by Enron, a number of bad investments both in the United States and abroad contributed to the firm's malaise. Meanwhile, Enron's core energy distribution business was deteriorating. Enron was attempting to gain share in a maturing market by paring selling prices. Margins also suffered from poor cost containment.

Dynegy Corp. agreed to buy Enron for $10 billion on November 2, 2001. On November 8, Enron announced that its net income would have to be restated back to 1997, resulting in a $586 million reduction in reported profits. On November 15, Chair Kenneth Lay admitted that the firm had made billions of dollars in bad investments. Four days later Enron said it would have to repay a $690 million note by mid-December and that it might have to take an additional $700 million pretax charge. At the end of the month, Dynegy withdrew its offer and Enron's credit rating was reduced to junk bond status. Enron was responsible for another $3.9 billion owed by its partnerships. Enron had less than $2 billion in cash on hand.

The end came quickly as investors and customers completely lost faith in the energy behemoth as a result of its secrecy and complex financial maneuvers, forcing the firm into bankruptcy in early December. Enron's stock, which had reached a high of $90 per share on August 17, 2001, was trading at less than $1 by December 5, 2001.

In addition to its angry creditors, Enron faced class-action lawsuits by shareholders and employees, whose pensions were invested heavily in Enron stock. Enron also faced intense scrutiny from Congressional committees and the U.S. Department of Justice. By the end of 2001, shareholders had lost more than $63 billion from its previous 52-week high, bondholders lost $2.6 billion in the face value of their debt, and banks appeared to be at risk on at least $15 billion of credit they had extended to Enron. In addition, potential losses on uncollateralized derivative contracts totaled $4 billion. Such contracts involved Enron commitments to buy various types of commodities at some point in the future.

Questions remain as to why Wall Street analysts, Arthur Andersen, federal or state regulatory authorities, the credit-rating agencies, and the firm's board of directors did not sound the alarm sooner. It is surprising that the audit committee of the Enron board seems to have somehow been unaware of the firm's highly questionable financial maneuvers. Inquiries following the bankruptcy declaration seem to suggest that the audit committee followed all of the rules stipulated by federal regulators and stock exchanges regarding director pay, independence, disclosure, and financial expertise. Enron seems to have collapsed in part because such rules did not do what they were supposed to do. For example, paying directors with stock may have aligned their interests with shareholders, but it is also possible to have been a disincentive to aggressively question senior management about their financial dealings.

The Lessons of Enron

Enron may be the best recent example of a complete breakdown in corporate governance, a system intended to protect shareholders. Inside Enron, the board of directors, management, and the audit function failed to do the job. Similarly, the firm's outside auditors, regulators, credit-rating agencies, and Wall Street analysts also failed to alert investors. What seems to be apparent is that if the auditors fail to identify incompetence or fraud, the system of safeguards is likely to breakdown. The cost of failure to those charged with protecting the shareholders, including outside auditors, analysts, credit-rating agencies, and regulators, was simply not high enough to ensure adequate scrutiny.

What may have transpired is that company managers simply undertook aggressive interpretations of accounting principles and then challenged auditors to demonstrate that such practices were not in accordance with GAAP accounting rules (Weil, 2002). This type of practice has been going on since the early 1980s and may account for the proliferation of specific accounting rules applicable only to certain transactions to insulate both the firm engaging in the transaction and the auditor reviewing the transaction from subsequent litigation. In one sense, the Enron debacle represents a failure of the free market system and its current shareholder protection mechanisms in that it took so long for the dramatic Enron shell game to be revealed to the public. However, this incident highlights the remarkable resilience of the free market system. The free market system worked quite effectively in its rapid imposition of discipline in bringing down the Enron house of cards, without any noticeable disruption in energy distribution nationwide.

Epilogue

Due to the complexity of dealing with so many different types of creditors, Enron filed its plan with the federal bankruptcy court to reorganize one and half years after seeking bankruptcy protection on December 2, 2001. The resulting reorganization has been one of the most costly and complex on record, with total legal and consulting fees exceeding $500 million by the end of 2003. More than 350 classes of creditors, including banks, bondholders, and other energy companies that traded with Enron said they were owed about $67 billion.

Under the reorganization plan, unsecured creditors received an estimated 14 cents for each dollar of claims against Enron Corp., while those with claims against Enron North America received an estimated 18.3 cents on the dollar. The money came in cash payments and in stock in two holding companies, CrossCountry containing the firm's North American pipeline assets and Prisma Energy International containing the firm's South American operations. While Enron shareholders did not receive anything under the reorganization, some investors may receive additional payouts in the future based on a series of lawsuits against banks and professional firms that assisted Enron with its web of complex financial arrangements.

After losing its auditing license in 2004, Arthur Andersen, formerly among the largest auditing firms in the world, has ceased operation. In 2006, Andrew Fastow, former Enron Chief Financial Officer and Lea Fastow plead guilty to several charges of conspiracy to commit fraud. Andrew Fastow received a sentence of 10 years in prison without the possibility of parole. His wife received a much shorter sentence. Also in 2006, Enron Chair Kenneth Lay died while awaiting sentencing, and Enron President, Jeffery Skilling, received a sentence of 24 years in prison.

Case Study Discussion Questions

1. In your judgment, what were the major factors contributing to the demise of Enron? Of these factors, which were the most important?
2. In what way was the Enron debacle a breakdown in corporate governance (oversight)? Explain your answer.
3. How were the Enron partnerships used to hide debt and inflate the firm's earnings? Should partnership structures be limited in the future? If so, how?
4. What should (or can) be done to reduce the likelihood of this type of situation arising in the future? Assess the impact of your proposals on the willingness of corporate managers to take risks. Be specific.

Answers to these Case Study Discussion Questions are available in the Online Instructor's Manual available for instructors using this book.

Chapter Business Case

Case Study 15-8
AT&T—A Poster Child for Restructuring Gone Awry

Between 1984 and 2000, AT&T underwent four major restructuring programs. These included the government-mandated breakup in 1984, the 1996 effort to eliminate customer conflicts, the 1998 plan to become a broadband powerhouse, and the most recent restructuring program announced in 2000 to correct past mistakes. It is difficult to identify another major corporation that has undergone as much sustained trauma as AT&T.

The 1984 Restructure: Changed the Organization but Not the Culture
The genesis of Ma Bell's problems may have begun with the consent decree signed with the Department of Justice in 1984, which resulted in the spin-off of its local telephone operations to its shareholders. AT&T retained its long-distance and telecommunications equipment manufacturing operations. Although the breadth of the firm's product offering was changed dramatically, little else seems to have changed. The firm remained highly bureaucratic, risk averse, and inward looking. However, substantial market share in the lucrative long-distance market continued to generate huge cash flow for the company, thereby enabling the company to be slow to react to the changing competitive dynamics of the marketplace.

The 1996 Restructure: Lack of a Coherent Strategy
Cash accumulated from the long-distance business was spent on a variety of ill-conceived strategies such as the firm's foray into the personal computer business. After years of unsuccessfully attempting to redefine the company's strategy, AT&T once again resorted to a major restructure of the firm. In 1996, AT&T spun off Lucent Technologies (its

telecommunications equipment business) and NCR (a computer services business) to share-holders to facilitate Lucent equipment sales to former AT&T operations and to eliminate the noncore NCR computer business. However, this had little impact on the AT&T share price.

The 1998 Restructure: Vision Exceeds Ability to Execute

In its third major restructure since 1984, AT&T CEO Michael Armstrong passionately unveiled in June of 1998 a daring strategy to remake AT&T from what were a struggling long-distance telephone company into a broadband Internet access and local phone services company. To accomplish this end, he outlined his intentions to acquire cable companies MediaOne Group and Telecommunications Inc. for $58 billion and $48 billion, respectively. The plan was to use cable TV networks to deliver the first fully integrated package of broadband Internet access and local phone service via the cable TV network.

AT&T Could Not Handle Its Early Success

During the next several years, Armstrong seemed to be up to the task, cutting sales, general, and administrative expense's share of revenue from 28 to 20%, giving AT&T a cost structure comparable to its competitors. He attempted to change the bureaucratic culture to one able to effectively compete in the deregulated environment of the post-1996 Telecommunications Act by issuing stock options to all employees, tying compensation to performance, and reducing layers of managers. He used AT&T's stock to buy the cable companies before the decline in AT&T's long-distance business pushed the stock into a free fall. He also transformed AT&T Wireless from a collection of local businesses into a national business.

Notwithstanding these achievements, AT&T experienced major missteps. Employee turnover became a big problem, especially among senior managers. Armstrong also bought Telecommunications and MediaOne when valuations for cable television assets were near their peak. He paid about $106 billion in 2000, when they were worth about $80 billion. His failure to cut enough deals with other cable operators (e.g., Time Warner) to sell AT&T's local phone service meant that AT&T could market its services only in regional markets rather than on a national basis. In addition, AT&T moved large corporate customers to its Concert joint venture with British Telecom, alienating many AT&T salespeople, who subsequently quit. As a result, customer service deteriorated rapidly and major customers defected. Finally, Armstrong seriously underestimated the pace of erosion in AT&T's long-distance revenue base.

AT&T May Have Become Overwhelmed by the Rate of Change

What happened? Perhaps AT&T fell victim to the same problems many other acquisitive companies have. AT&T is a company capable of great vision but seemingly incapable of great execution. Effective execution involves buying or building assets at a reasonable cost. Its substantial overpayment for its cable acquisitions meant that it would be unable to earn the returns required by investors in what they would consider a reasonable time period. Moreover, Armstrong's efforts to shift from the firm's historical business by buying into the cable TV business through acquisition has saddled the firm with $62 billion in debt.

AT&T tried to do too much too quickly. New initiatives such as high-speed Internet access and local telephone services over cable television networks were too small to pick up the slack. Much time and energy seems to have gone into planning and acquiring what were viewed as key building blocks to the strategy. However, there appears to have been insufficient focus and realism in terms of the time and resources required to make all the pieces of the strategy fit together. Some parts of the overall strategy were at odds with other parts. For example, AT&T undercut its core long-distance wired telephone business by offers of free long-distance wireless to attract new subscribers. Despite aggressive efforts to change the culture, AT&T continued to suffer from a culture that evolved in the years before 1996 during which the industry was heavily regulated. That atmosphere bred a culture based on consensus building, ponderously slow decision making, and a low tolerance for risk. Consequently, the AT&T culture was unprepared for the fiercely competitive deregulated environment of the late 1990s (Truitt, 2001).

Furthermore, AT&T created individual tracking stocks for AT&T Wireless and for Liberty Media. The intention of the tracking stocks was to link the unit's stock to its individual performance, create a currency for the unit to make acquisitions, and to provide a new means of motivating the unit's management by giving them stock in their own operation. Unlike a spin-off, AT&T's board continued to exert direct control over these units. In an IPO in April 2000, AT&T sold 14% of AT&T's Wireless stock to the public to raise funds and to focus investor attention on the true value of the Wireless operations.

Investors Lose Patience

Although all of these actions created a sense that grandiose change was imminent, investor patience was wearing thin. Profitability foundered. The market share loss in its long-distance business accelerated. Although cash flow remained strong, it was clear that a cash machine so dependent on the deteriorating long-distance telephone business soon could grind to a halt. Investors' loss of faith was manifested in the sharp decline in AT&T stock that occurred in 2000.

The 2000 Restructure: Correcting the Mistakes of the Past

Pushed by investor impatience and a growing realization that achieving AT&T's vision would be more time and resource consuming than originally believed, Armstrong announced on October 25, 2000, the breakup of the business for the fourth time. The plan involved the creation of four new independent companies including AT&T Wireless, AT&T Consumer, AT&T Broadband, and Liberty Media.

By breaking the company into specific segments, AT&T believed that individual units could operate more efficiently and aggressively. AT&T's consumer long-distance business would be able to enter the digital subscriber line (DSL) market. DSL is a broadband technology based on the telephone wires that connect individual homes with the telephone network. AT&T's cable operations could continue to sell their own fast Internet connections and compete directly against AT&T's long-distance telephone business. Moreover, the four individual businesses would create "pure-play" investor opportunities. Specifically, AT&T proposed spinning off in early 2001 AT&T Wireless to shareholders in exchange for Wireless tracking stock, and issuing tracking stocks to the public in late 2001 for AT&T Consumer operations, including long-distance and Worldnet Internet service and AT&T Broadband (cable) operations. The tracking shares would at a later date be converted to regular AT&T common shares as if issued by AT&T Broadband, making it an independent entity. AT&T would retain AT&T Business Services (i.e., AT&T Lab and Telecommunications Network) with the surviving AT&T entity. Investor reaction was swift and negative. Investors were not swayed by the proposal because the stock dropped 13% in 1 day. Moreover, it ended 2000 at $17^1/_2$, down 66% from the beginning of the year.

The More Things Change the More They Stay the Same
On July 10, 2001, AT&T Wireless Services became an independent company, in accordance with plans announced during the 2000 restructure program. AT&T Wireless became a separate company when AT&T converted the tracking shares of the mobile-phone business into common stock. AT&T Wireless shares have fallen 44% since AT&T first sold the tracking stock in April 2000. On August 10, 2001, AT&T spun off Liberty Media.

After extended discussions, AT&T agreed on December 21, 2001, to merge its broadband unit with Comcast to create the largest cable television and high-speed Internet service company in the United States. Without the future growth engine offered by Broadband and Wireless, AT&T's remaining long-distance businesses and business services operations had limited growth prospects. After a decade of tumultuous change, AT&T was back where it was at the beginning of the 1990s. At about $15 billion in late 2004, AT&T's market capitalization was about one-sixth of that of such major competitors as Verizon and SBC. SBC Communications (a former local AT&T operating company) acquired AT&T on November 18, 2005, in a $16 billion deal and promptly renamed the combined firms AT&T.

Case Study Discussion Questions

1. What were the primary factors contributing to AT&T's numerous restructuring efforts since 1984? How did they differ? How were they similar?
2. Why do you believe that AT&T chose to spin off its wireless operations rather than to divest the unit? What might you have done differently?
3. Was AT&T proactive or reactive in initiating its 2000 restructuring program? Explain your answer.
4. Do you believe that AT&T overpaid for many of its largest acquisitions made during the 1990s? How might this have contributed to its subsequent restructuring efforts?
5. To what extent were AT&T's ineffectual restructuring efforts a function of factors beyond management's control and to what extent were they due to poor implementation? Be specific.
6. What challenges did AT&T face in trying to split up the company in 2000? What might you have done differently to overcome these obstacles?

Answers to these Case Study Discussion Questions are available in the Online Instructor's Manual for instructors using this book.

References

Alderson, Michael J., and Brian L. Betker, "Assessing Post-Bankruptcy Performance: An Analysis of Reorganized Firms' Cash Flows," Working Paper, Saint Louis University, Saint Louis, MO, 1996.

Alexander, Gordon J., George Benson, and Joan M. Kampmeyer, "Investigating the Valuation Effects Announcements on Valuing Corporate Sell-Offs," *Journal of Finance*, Vol. 39, June 1984, pp. 503–517.

Allen, Jeffrey, "Private Information and Spin-off Performance," *The Journal of Business*, Vol. 74, April 2001, pp. 281–306.

Allen, Jeffrey, and John J. McConnell, "Equity Carve Outs and Managerial Discretion," *Journal of Finance*, Vol. 53, February 1998, pp. 163–186.

Allen, Phillips, "Corporate Equity Ownership, Strategic Alliances, and Product Market Relationships," *Journal of Finance*, Vol. 55, 2000, pp. 2791–2816.

Altman, E. I., *Corporate Financial Distress and Bankruptcy*, 2nd Ed., Wiley & Sons, New York, 1993.

Annema, Andre, William C. Fallon, and Marc H. Goedhart, "When Carve-Outs Make Sense," *The McKinsey Quarterly*, 2, 2002.

Ball, M., "How a Spin-Off Could Lift Your Share Value," *Corporate Finance*, May 1997, pp. 23–29.

Bates, Thomas, W., "Asset Sales, Investment Opportunities, and the Use of Proceeds," *Journal of Finance*, February 2005.

Betker, B., "An Empirical Examination of Prepackaged Bankruptcy," *Financial Management*, Spring 1995, pp. 3–18.

Billett, Matthew T., "Long-Term Returns from Tracking Stocks," *Social Science Research Network*, Working Paper Series, June 27, 2000.

Billett, Matthew T., and Anand M. Vijh, "The Wealth Effects of Tracking Stock Restructurings," *Journal of Financial Research*, Vol. 27, Winter 2004, pp. 559–583.

Bris, Arturo, Avo Welch, and Ning Zhu, "The Costs of Bankruptcy: Chapter 7 Liquidation versus Chapter 11 Reorganization," *Journal of Finance*, Vol. 61, 2006, pp. 1253–1303.

Burkhart, Mike, Denis Gromb, and Fausto Panunzi, "Larger Shareholders, Monitoring and the Value of the Firm," *Quarterly Journal of Economics*, 1997, pp. 693–728.

Byers, Steven S., D. Scott Lee, and Tim C. Opler, "Equity Carve-Outs and Management Change," Idaho State University Working Paper, Pocatello, ID, 1996.

Chemung, T., and I. Paeglis, "Why Issue Tracking Stock," Working Paper, 2000, available by email from chemmanu@bc.edu.

Cho, Myeong-Hyeon, and Mark A. Cohen, "The Economic Causes and Consequences of Corporate Divestiture," *Managerial and Decision Economics*, 18, August 1997, pp. 367–374.

Clark, Kent, and Eli Ofek, "Mergers as a Means of Restructuring Distressed Firms: An Empirical Investigation," *Journal of Financial and Quantitative Analysis*, 29, December 1994, pp. 541–565.

Cusatis, Patrick J., James A. Miles, and J. Randall Woolridge, "Restructuring Through Spin-Offs," *Journal of Financial Economics*, Vol. 33, 1993, pp. 293–311.

Daley, Lane, Vikas Mehrotra, and Ranjini Sivakumar, "Corporate Focus and Value Creation, Evidence from Spin-Offs," *Journal of Financial Economics*, Vol. 45, 1997, pp. 257–281.

Davis, A., and M. Leblond, "A Spin-Off Analysis: Evidence from New and Old Economies," Working Paper, Queen's University, 2002, available by email from adavis@business.queensu.ca.

Desai, Hermang, and Prem Jain, "Firm Performance and Focus: Long-Run Stock Market Performance Following Spin-Offs," *Journal of Financial Economics*, Vol. 54, 1999, pp. 75–101.

Dittmar, Amy, and Anil Shivdasani, "Divestitures and Divisional Investment Policies," *Journal of Finance*, Vol. 58, December 2003, pp. 2711–2744.

D'Souza, John Jacob, "Why Firms Issue Targeted Stock," *Journal of Financial Economics*, Volume 56, June 2000, pp. 459–483.

Dun & Bradstreet Corporation, New York, *Business Failure Record*, 1997.

Eberhart, Allan C., Edward I. Altman, and Reena Aggarwal, "The Equity Performance of Firms Emerging from Bankruptcy," *Journal of Finance*, Vol. 54, October 1999, pp. 1855–1868.

Elder, J., and P. Westra, "The Reaction of Security Prices to Tracking Stock Announcements," *Journal of Economics and Finance*, Vol. 24, 2000, pp. 36–55.

Erwin, Gayle R., and John J. McConnell, "To Live or Die? An Empirical Analysis of Piecemeal Voluntary Liquidations," *Journal of Corporate Finance*, Vol. 3, December 1997, pp. 325–354.

Fleming, Michael J., and John J. Moon, "Preserving Firm Value through Exit: The Case of Voluntary Liquidations," Federal Reserve Bank of New York, *Staff Reports*, 8, December 1995.

France, Michael, "Bankruptcy Reform Won't Help Telecom," *BusinessWeek,* October 21, 2002, p. 40.

Gilson, Stuart, "Transactions Costs and Capital Structure Choice: Evidence from Financially Distressed Firms," *Journal of Finance*, Vol. 52, March 1997, pp. 161–196.

Hand, John R., and Terrance R. Skantz, "Market Timing Through Equity Carve-Outs," University of North Carolina Working Paper, Raleigh, NC, 1997.

Haushalter, D., and W. Mikkelson, "An Investigation of the Gains from Specialized Equity: Tracking Stocks and Minority Carve-Outs," Working Paper, University of Oregon, Eugene, OR, 2001.

Hite, Gailen, and James E. Owers, "Security Price Reactions around Corporate Spin-Off Announcements," *Journal of Financial Economics*, Vol. 12, 1983, pp. 409–436.

Hite, Gailen, James Owers, and Ronald Rogers, "The Market for Inter-Firm Asset Sales: Partial Sell-Offs and Total Liquidations," *Journal of Financial Economics*, Vol. 18, June 1987, pp. 229–252.

Hogan, Karen M., and Gerard T. Olson, "The Pricing of Equity Carve-Outs During the 1990s," *Journal of Financial Research*, Vol. 27, Winter 2004, pp. 521–537.

Hotchkiss, Edith S., "The Post-Emergence Performance of Firms Emerging from Chapter 11," *Journal of Finance*, Vol. 50, 1995, pp. 3–21.

Hulburt, Heather M., James A. Miles, and J. Randall Wollridge, "Value Creation from Equity Carve-Outs," *Financial Management*, Vol. 31, Spring 2002, pp. 83–100.

Jain, Prem C., "The Effects of Voluntary Sell-Off Announcements on Shareholder Wealth," *Journal of Finance*, Vol. 40, March 1985, pp. 209–224.

John, Kose, and Eli Ofek, "Asset Sales and Increase in Focus," *Journal of Financial Economics*, Vol. 37, January 1995, pp. 105–126.

JP Morgan, "Monitoring Spin-Off Performance," *Morgan Markets*, New York, June 6, 1995.

JP Morgan, "Monitoring Spin-Off Performances," *Morgan Markets*, New York, August 20, 1999.

Kang, Jun-Koo, and Anil Shivdasani, "Corporate Restructuring During Performance Declines in Japan," *Journal of Financial Economics*, Vol. 46, October 1997, pp. 29–65.

Kaplan, Steven N., and Michael S. Weisbach, "The Success of Acquisitions: Evidence from Divestitures," *Journal of Finance*, Vol. 47, March 1992, pp. 107–138.

Kim, E. Han, and Hohn Schatzberg, "Voluntary Corporate Liquidations," *Journal of Financial Economics*, 19(2), December 1987, pp. 311–328.

Klein, A., "The Timing and Substance of Divestiture Announcements: Individual, Simultaneous and Cumulative Effects," *Journal of Finance*, Vol. 41, 1986, pp. 685–697.

Krishnaswami, Sudha, and Venkat Subramaniam, "Information Asymmetry, Valuation and the Corporate Spin-off Decision," *Journal of Financial Economics*, Vol. 53, July 1999, pp. 73–112.

Lang, Larry, Annette Poulsen, and Rene Stulz, "Asset Sales, Firm Performance, and the Agency Costs of Managerial Discretion," *Journal of Financial Economics*, Vol. 37, January 1995, pp. 3–37.

Linn, Scott C., and Michael S. Rozeff, "The Corporate Sell-Off," *Midland Corporate Finance Journal*, Vol. 2, Summer 1984, pp. 17–26.

Logue, Dennis E., James K. Seward, and James W. Walsh, "Rearranging Residual Claims: A Case for Targeted Stock," *Financial Management*, Vol. 25, Spring 1996, pp. 43–61.

Loh, Charmen, Jennifer Russell Bezjak, and Harrison Toms, "Voluntary Corporate Divestitures as an Anti-Takeover Mechanism," *The Financial Review*, Vol. 30, February 1995, pp. 21–24.

Lovely, Erika, "How Troubled Firms Skip Bankruptcy Court," *The Wall Street Journal*, February 7, 2007, p. C2.

Maksimovic, Vojislav, and Gordon M. Phillips, "The Market for Corporate Assets: Who Engages in Mergers and Assets Sales and Are There Efficiency Gains?," *Journal of Finance*, December 2001, p. 27.

Maxwell, William F., and Ramesh P. Rao, "Do Spin-Offs Expropriate Wealth from Bondholders?," *The Journal of Finance*, Vol. 58, Issue 5, October 2003, pp. 2087–2108.

McConnell, John J., Mehmet Ozbilgin, and Sunil Wahal, "Spin-Offs: Ex Ante," *The Journal of Business*, Vol. 74, April 2001, pp. 245–280.

McKinsey & Co., "Spin-Offs May Overshadow Other Investments," *BusinessWeek*, December 13, 1999, pp. 196–197.

Michaely, Roni, and Wayne H. Shaw, "The Choice of Going Public: Spin-Offs vs. Carve-Outs," *Financial Management*, Vol. 24, Autumn 1995, pp. 15–21.

Miles, James, and James Rosenfeld, "An Empirical Analysis of the Effects of Spin-Off Announcements on Shareholder Wealth," *Journal of Finance*, Vol. 38, December 1983, pp. 15–28.

Mulherin, J. Harold, and Audra L. Boone, "Comparing Acquisitions and Divestitures," *Social Science Research Network*, Working Paper Series, April 19, 2000, p. 38.

Oppenheimer & Company, "The Sum of the Parts," New York, January 14, 1981.

Petty, J. William, Arthur J. Keown, David F. Scott, Jr., and John D. Martin, *Basic Financial Management*, 6th Ed., Prentice-Hall, Englewood Cliffs, NJ, 1993, p. 798.

Powers, Eric A., "Spinoffs, Selloffs, and Equity Carveouts: An Analysis of Divestiture Method Choice," *Social Science Research Network*, Working Paper Series, January 2001, pp. 2–4.

Powers, Eric A., "Deciphering the Motives for Equity Carve-Outs," *The Journal of Financial Research*, Vol. 26, No. 1, Spring 2003, pp. 31–50.

Prezas, A., M. Tarimicilar, and G. Vasudevan, "The Pricing of Equity Carve-Outs," *Financial Review*, Vol. 35, 2000, pp. 123–138.

Rajan, Raghuram, Henri Servaes, and Luigi Zingales, "The Cost of Diversity: The Diversification Discount and Inefficient Investment," *Journal of Finance*, Vol. 55, 2000, pp. 35–38.

Ravenscroft, D. J., and F. M. Scherer, "Divisional Sell-Off: A Hazard Function Analysis," *Managerial and Decision Economics*, Vol. 12, 1991, pp. 429–438.

Scharfstein, David, and Jeremy Stein, "The Dark Side of Internal Capital Markets: Divisional Rent-Seeking and Inefficient Investment," *Journal of Finance*, LV(6), 2000, pp. 128–145.

Scherreik, Susan, "Gems Among the Trash," *BusinessWeek*, April 15, 2002, pp. 112–113.

Schipper, Katherine, and Abbie Smith, "Effects of Re-Contracting on Shareholder Wealth," *Journal of Financial Economics*, Vol. 12, 1983, pp. 437–467.

Schipper, Katherine, and Abbie Smith, "A Comparison of Equity Carve-Outs and Equity Offerings: Share Price Effects and Corporate Restructuring," *Journal of Financial Economics*, Vol. 15, 1986, pp. 153–186.

Skantz, Terrance, and Roberto Marchesini, "The Effect of Voluntary Corporate Liquidation on Shareholder Wealth," *Journal of Financial Research*, Vol. 10, Spring 1987, pp. 65–75.

Slovin, Myron B., Marie E. Sushka, and John A. Polonchek, "Methods of Payment in Asset Sales: Contracting with Equity Versus Cash," *Journal of Finance*, Vol. 60, October 2005, pp. 2385–2407.

Solomon, Deborah, "AT&T Prepares Its Cable-Access Program," *The Wall Street Journal*, June 6, 2001, p. C1.

Tashjian, Elizabeth, Ronald Lease, and John J. McConnell, "Prepacks: An Empirical Analysis of Prepackaged Bankruptcies," *Journal of Financial Economics*, Vol. 40, January 1996, pp. 135–162.

Truitt, Wesley B., *Business Planning: A Comprehensive Framework and Process*, Greenwood Publishing, Westport, CT, October 30, 2001, p. 183.

U.S. Small Business Administration, "Financial Difficulties of Small Businesses and Reasons for Their Failure," Office of Advocacy, RS 188, March 1999.

Veld, C., and Y. Veld-Merkoulova, "Do Spin-Offs Really Create Value?," *Journal of Banking and Finance*, Vol. 28, December 2004, pp. 1111–1135.

Vijh, Anand M., "Long-Term Returns from Equity Carveouts," *Journal of Financial Economics*, Vol. 51, 1999, pp. 273–308.

Vroom, Harald Janssens de, and Ruud van Frederikslust, "Shareholder Wealth Effects of Corporate Spinoffs: The Worldwide Experience 1990–1998," *SSRN Working Paper Series*, August 9, 1999.

Weil, Roman L., "Fundamental Causes of the Accounting Debacle at Enron: Show Me Where It Says I Can't," Testimony before the U.S. House of Representatives Committee on Energy and Commerce, February 6, 2002.

CHAPTER 16

Cross-Border Mergers and Acquisitions

Analysis and Valuation

> *Courage is not the absence of fear. It is doing the thing you fear the most.*
>
> —Rick Warren

Inside M&A: Arcelor Outbids ThyssenKrupp for Canada's Dofasco Steelmaking Operations

Arcelor Steel of Luxembourg, the world's second largest steelmaker, was eager to make an acquisition. Having been outbid by Mittal, the world's leading steel firm, in its efforts to buy Turkey's state-owned Erdemir and Ukraine's Kryvorizhstal, Guy Dolle, Arcelor's CEO, seemed determined not to let that happen again.

Arcelor and Dofasco had been in talks for more than 4 months before Arcelor decided to initiate a tender offer on November 23, 2005, valued at $3.8 billion in cash. Dofasco, Canada's largest steel manufacturer, owned vast coal and iron ore reserves, possessed a nonunion workforce, and sold much of its steel to Honda assembly plants in the United States. The merger would enable Arcelor, whose revenues were primarily concentrated in Europe, to diversify into the United States. Contrary to their European operations, Arcelor found the flexibility offered by Dofasco's nonunion labor force highly attractive. Moreover, by increasing its share of global steel production, Arcelor's management reasoned that they would be able to exert additional pricing leverage with both customers and suppliers.

Serving the role of "white knight," Germany's ThyssenKrupp, the sixth largest steel firm in the world, offered to acquire Dofasco 1 week later for $4.1 billion in cash. Dofasco's board accepted the bid, which included a $187 million break-up fee should another firm acquire Dofasco. Immediately following the announcement, Dofasco's shares rose above ThyssenKrupp's offer price as investors anticipated further bids. Investors soundly criticized Dofasco's board for not opening up the bidding to an auction. In its defense, the board expressed concern about stretching out the process in an auction over several weeks.

In late December 2005, Arcelor topped the ThyssenKrupp bid by offering $4.2 billion. Not to be outdone, ThyssenKrupp matched the Arcelor offer on January 4, 2006. The Dofasco board reaffirmed its preference for the ThyssenKrupp bid, due to the break-up fee and ThyssenKrupp's willingness (unlike Arcelor) to allow Dofasco to continue to operate under its own name and management.

In a bold attempt to put Dofasco out of reach of the already highly leveraged ThyssenKrupp, Arcelor raised its bid to $4.8 billion on January 16, 2006. This bid represented an approximate 80% premium over Dofasco's closing share price on the day Arcelor announced its original tender offer. The Arcelor bid was contingent on Dofasco withdrawing its support for the ThyssenKrupp bid. Under its previous agreement with Dofasco, ThyssenKrupp had 1 week to respond to other bidders. On January 24, ThyssenKrupp said it would not raise its bid.

Events in the dynamically changing global steel market were not to end here. The Arcelor board and management barely had time to savor their successful takeover of Dofasco before Mittal initiated a hostile takeover of Arcelor. Ironically, Mittal succeeded in acquiring its archrival, Arcelor, just 6 months later in a bid to achieve further industry consolidation. See Chapter 3 (Case Study 3-1) for a discussion of the Mittal–Arcelor transaction.

Chapter Overview

There are as many motives as there are strategies for international expansion. This chapter addresses common motives for international expansion, as well as the advantages and disadvantages of a variety of international market entry strategies. However, the focus in this chapter is on mergers and acquisitions (M&A) as a market entry or expansion mode, because cross-border M&As comprise on average one-fourth of total global transactions and more than one-half of direct foreign investment annually (Chen and Findlay, 2002; Kang and Johansson, 2001; Letto-Gillies, Meschi, and Simonetti, 2001). Furthermore, this chapter concentrates on the challenges of M&A deal structures, valuation, and execution in for both developed and emerging countries. Finally, the chapter summarizes empirical studies investigating the actual benefits to both target and acquiring company shareholders. A review of this chapter is available on the CD-ROM accompanying this book.

Throughout the chapter, the term *local country* will refer to the target's country of residence, while *home country* will refer to the acquirer's country of residence. *Developed countries* are those having significant and sustainable per capita economic growth, globally integrated capital markets, a well-defined legal system, transparent financial statements, currency convertibility, and a stable government. According to the World Bank, *emerging countries* have a growth rate in per capita gross domestic product that is significantly below that of developed countries. Note that while many emerging countries show annual GDP growth well in excess of that of developed countries, their per capita GDP growth rate, generally considered a better measure of economic well-being, is usually much lower. Moreover, emerging countries frequently lack many of the other characteristics normally associated with developed nations.

Table 16-1 provides examples of developed and emerging economies as defined by Morgan Stanley Capital International (MSCI). Other organizations such as the

TABLE 16-1 Examples of Developed and Emerging Economies

Developed Economies		Emerging Economies	
Australia	Japan	Argentina	Mexico
Austria	Netherlands	Brazil	Morocco
Belgium	New Zealand	China	Pakistan
Canada	Norway	Columbia	Peru
Denmark	Portugal	Czech Republic	Philippines
Finland	Singapore	Egypt	Poland
France	Spain	Hungary	Russia
Germany	Sweden	India	South Africa
Greece	Switzerland	Indonesia	Sri Lanka
Hong Kong	United Kingdom	Israel	Taiwan
Ireland	United States	Jordan	Thailand
Italy		Korea	Turkey
		Malaysia	Venezuela

Source: Morgan Stanley Capital International (www.msci.com).

Organization for Economic Cooperation and Development (OECD) and the United Nations (UN) include a somewhat different mix of countries. Despite definitional differences, Brazil, Russia, India, and China make everyone's list of emerging nations. These four countries (often grouped together under the acronym BRIC) constitute about four-fifths of the total GDP of emerging countries (see *The Economist*, September 16, 2006).

While both developed and emerging country economies have become increasingly interdependent in recent years, there also is substantial evidence that regional and individual country capital markets have become increasingly integrated. Reflecting the emergence of a global capital market, correlation among individual countries' capital markets on average has increased (Bekaert and Harvey, 2002). For example, in 2005, foreigners held 12% of U.S. stocks, 25% of U.S. corporate bonds, and 44% of U.S. Treasury securities, as compared to 4%, 1%, and 20%, respectively, in 1975 (Farrell, Key, and Shavers, 2006). Reflecting this integration, correlation between the performance of U.S. and European stocks has increased from less than 30% in the 1970s to 90% currently (Blackman, February 5, 2006). While the correlation tends to be high on average over long periods of time such as 10-year periods, the correlation can decline significantly over 2–3 year periods.

Globally integrated capital markets provide foreigners with unfettered access to local capital markets and local residents to foreign capital markets. Factors contributing to the integration of global capital markets include the reduction in trade barriers, removal of capital controls, the harmonization of tax laws (which reduce the impact of different tax rates on trade and investment), floating exchange rates, and the free convertibility of currencies. Improving accounting standards and shareholder protections (i.e., corporate governance) also encourage cross-border capital flows. Transaction costs associated with foreign investment portfolios have also fallen because of advances in information technology and competition. Consequently, multinational corporations can more easily raise funds in both domestic and foreign capital markets. This increase in competition among lenders and investors has resulted in a reduction in the cost of capital for such firms.

Unlike globally integrated capital markets, **segmented capital markets** exhibit different bond and equity prices in different geographic areas for identical assets in terms of risk and maturity. Arbitrage should drive the prices in different markets to be the same, as investors sell those assets that are overvalued to buy those that are undervalued. Segmentation arises when investors are unable to move capital from one market to another due to capital controls or simply because they prefer to invest in their local markets. Investors in segmented markets will bear a higher level of risk by holding a disproportionately large share of their investments in their local market as opposed to the level of risk if they invested in a globally diversified portfolio. Reflecting this higher level of risk, investors and lenders in such markets require a higher rate of return to make local market investments than if investing in a globally diversified portfolio of stocks. Therefore, the cost of capital for firms in segmented markets, without easy access to global markets, often is higher than the global cost of capital.

Despite the increasing correlation of cash flows and share prices among firms in developed countries, there is evidence that capital markets in these countries may be segmented to the extent that local factors are more important in determining the cash flows, access to capital, and share prices of small firms than of large firms (Eun, Huang, and Lai, 2007). Consequently, the share price of a major French retailer like Carrefour may trade very much like the giant U.S. retailer Wal-Mart. However, the stock of a small French retail discount chain, more impacted by factors in its local market segment, may trade differently from either Carrefour or Wal-Mart and exhibit a much higher cost of capital.

Motives for International Expansion

Reasons firms expand internationally include the desire to achieve geographic diversification, accelerate growth, consolidate industries, utilize natural resources and lower labor costs elsewhere, and to leverage intangible assets. Other motives include minimizing tax liabilities, avoiding entry barriers, fluctuating exchange rates, and following customers into foreign markets.

Geographic and Industrial Diversification

Firms may diversify by investing in different industries in the same country, the same industries in different countries, or different industries in different countries. Firms investing in industries or countries whose economic cycles are not highly correlated may lower the overall volatility in their consolidated earnings and cash flows. By increasing earnings and cash flow predictability, such firms may reduce their cost of capital. Numerous studies show that diversified international firms often exhibit a lower cost of capital than firms whose investments are not well diversified (Chan, Karolyi, and Stulz, 1992; Stulz, 1995a, 1995b and Stulz and Wasserfallen, 1995).

Accelerating Growth

Foreign markets represent an opportunity for domestic firms to grow. U.S. firms have historically invested in potentially higher growth foreign markets. Similarly, the United

States represents a large, growing, and politically stable market. Consequently, foreign firms have increased their exports to and direct investment (including M&As) in the United States.

Facing increasingly saturated home markets, many European telecommunications companies such as Vodafone and Spain's Telefonica have set their sights on emerging markets to fuel future expansion. The number of cell phone subscribers in Europe has been increasing at a tepid 6–8% pace as compared to 34% in the Middle East and 55% per annum in Africa (Bryan-Low, December 10, 2005).

Industry Consolidation

Excess capacity in many industries often drives M&A activity as firms strive to achieve greater economies of scale and scope, as well as pricing power with customers and suppliers. The highly active consolidation in recent years in the metals industries (e.g., steel, nickel, and copper) represents an excellent example of this global trend. Global consolidation has also been common in such industries as financial services, media, oil and gas, telecommunications, and pharmaceuticals.

Once industries become more concentrated, smaller competitors often are compelled to merge, thereby accelerating the pace of consolidation. In late 2006, mid-size European drug makers Merck KFaA agreed to buy Swiss biotechnology company Serono SA for $11 billion, and Germany's Alana AF said it would sell its pharmaceutical business to Danish drug manufacturer Nycomed for $5 billion. Smaller drug companies have found it difficult to compete with behemoths Pfizer Inc. and GlaxoSmithKline PLC, which have much larger research budgets and sales forces. Midsize firms also are more likely to be reliant on a few drugs for the bulk of their revenue, which makes them highly vulnerable to generic copies of their drugs.

Utilization of Lower Raw Material and Labor Costs

Emerging markets may be particularly attractive since they often represent low labor costs, access to inexpensive raw materials, and low levels of regulation (Dunning, 1988). Thus, shifting production overseas represents an opportunity to reduce significantly operating expenses and to become more competitive in global markets.

Leveraging Intangible Assets

Firms with significant expertise, brands, patents, copyrights, and proprietary technologies seek to grow by exploiting these advantages in emerging markets. Foreign buyers may seek to acquire firms with intellectual property so that they can employ such assets in their own domestic markets (Eun, Kolodny, and Scherage, 1996; Morck and Yeung, 1991). Caves (1982) demonstrated that firms with a reputation for superior products in their home markets might find that they can successfully apply this reputation in foreign markets (e.g., Coke, Pepsi, and McDonalds). Ferreira and Tallman (2005) argue that firms seeking to leverage their capabilities are likely to acquire controlling interests in foreign firms. However, as Wal-Mart has discovered sometimes even a widely recognized brand name is insufficient to overcome the challenges of foreign markets (see Case Study 16-1).

Case Study 16-1
Wal-Mart Stumbles in Its Global Expansion Strategy

2006 marked the most significant retrenchment for Wal-Mart since it undertook its international expansion in the early 1990s in an effort to rejuvenate sales growth. Wal-Mart, the world's largest retailer, admitted defeat in its long-standing effort to penetrate successfully the German retail market. On July 30, the behemoth announced that it was selling its operations in Germany to German retailer Metro AG. Wal-Mart had been trying to make its German stores profitable for 8 years. Wal-Mart announced a pretax loss on the sale of $1 billion. Wal-Mart had previously announced in May that it would sell its 16 stores in South Korea.

Wal-Mart had apparently underestimated the ferocity of German competitors, the frugality of German shoppers, and the extent to which regulations, cultural differences, and labor unions would impede its ability to apply in Germany what had worked so well for it in the United States. German discount retailers offer very low prices, and German shoppers have shown they can be very demanding. Germany's shoppers are accustomed to buying based primarily on price. They are willing to split their shopping activities among various retailers, which blunt the effectiveness of the "superstores" offering one location for all the shoppers needs. Employees filed a lawsuit against the retailer's policy against romantic relationships between employees and supervisors. Accustomed to putting their own groceries in shopping bags, German shoppers were alienated by clerks who bagged groceries. Moreover, German regulations have limited Wal-Mart's ability to offer extended and weekend hours, as well as to sell merchandise below cost in an effort to lure consumers with so-called "loss leaders." Strong unions also limited the firm's ability to contain operating costs.

Wal-Mart also experienced a loss of seasoned executives when it acquired several German retailers. The two retailers were headquartered in different cities. Following the mergers, Wal-Mart consolidated the two headquarters in one city, prompting many executives to leave rather than relocate. Perhaps reflecting this "brain drain," Wal-Mart's German operations had four presidents in 8 years.

Wal-Mart has not been alone in finding the German discount market challenging. Nestle SA and Unilever are among the large multinational retailers that have had to change the way they do business in Germany. France's Carrefour SA, Wal-Mart's largest competitor worldwide, has diligently avoided Germany.

With the withdrawal from the German and South Korean markets, Wal-Mart is currently operating in 11 countries. This compares to Carrefour of France (29 countries), and Metro of Germany (30 countries), the second and third largest global retailers, respectively. Wal-Mart's international ambitions are now centered in Asia and Latin America, with India and China the firm's most promising growth markets. However, Wal-Mart can expect to experience similar growth challenges in these countries. For example, India does not permit foreign firms to establish stores unless they sell only one brand. In late 2006, Wal-Mart agreed with China's state-run union to set up unions at its 60 stores in that country. Moreover, China is limiting the size of large-scale retail outlets, which is likely to limit Wal-Mart's plans to introduce the superstore concept.

Case Study Discussion Questions

1. Wal-Mart's missteps in Germany may represent an example of the limitations of introducing what works in one market (i.e., so-called best practices) in another.

To what extent do you believe that Wal-Mart's failure represented a strategic error? To what extent did the firm's lack of success represent an implementation error?

2. Based on this experience, do you believe Wal-Mart should limit its international expansion? Explain your answer.

3. In your judgment, what criteria should Wal-Mart employ in selecting other foreign markets to enter? Be specific.

Minimizing Tax Liabilities

Firms in high tax countries may shift production and reported profits by building or acquiring operations in countries with more favorable tax laws. Evidence supporting the notion that such strategies are commonly used is mixed. Servaes and Zenner (1994) found a positive correlation between cross-border mergers and differences in tax laws. However, Manzon, Sharp, and Travlos (1994) and Dewenter (1995) found little correlation.

Avoiding Entry Barriers

Quotas and tariffs on imports imposed by governments to protect domestic industries often encourage foreign direct investment. Foreign firms may acquire existing facilities or start new operations in the country imposing the quotas and tariffs to circumvent such measures.

Fluctuating Exchange Rates

Changes in currency values can have a significant impact on where and when foreign direct investments are made. Appreciating foreign currencies relative to the dollar reduce the overall cost of investing in the United States. The impact of exchange rates on cross-border transactions has been substantiated in a number of studies (Feliciano and Lipsey, 2002; Harris and Ravenscraft, 1991; Vasconcellos and Kish, 1998; Vasconcellos, Madura, and Kish, 1990).

Following Customers

Often suppliers are encouraged to invest abroad in order to better satisfy the immediate needs of their customers. For example, auto parts suppliers worldwide have set up operations next to large auto manufacturing companies in China. Parts suppliers were able to reduce costs and to make parts available as needed by the auto companies.

Common International Market Entry Strategies

The method of market entry chosen by a firm reflects the firm's risk tolerance, perceived risk, competitive conditions, and the firm's overall resources. Figure 16-1 summarizes the conditions motivating the selection of one entry strategy versus another.

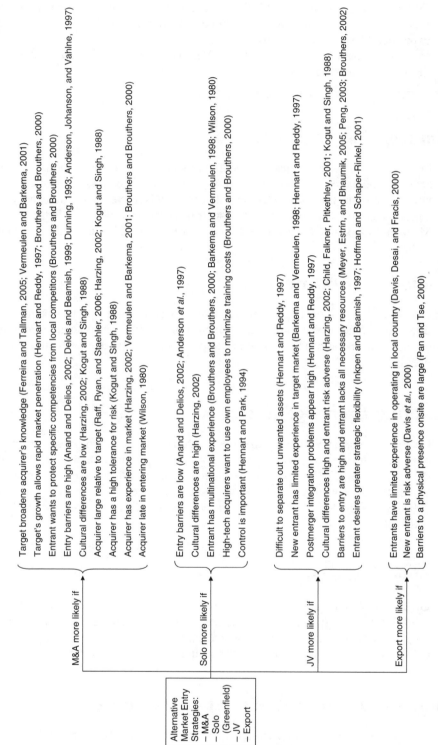

Alternative Market Entry Strategies:
- M&A
- Solo (Greenfield)
- JV
- Export

M&A more likely if
- Target broadens acquirer's knowledge (Ferreira and Tallman, 2005; Vermeulen and Barkema, 2001)
- Target's growth allows rapid market penetration (Hennart and Reddy, 1997; Brouthers and Brouthers, 2000)
- Entrant wants to protect specific competencies from local competitors (Brouthers and Brouthers, 2000)
- Entry barriers are high (Anand and Delios, 2002; Delois and Beamish, 1999; Dunning, 1993; Anderson, Johanson, and Vahlne, 1997)
- Cultural differences are low (Harzing, 2002; Kogut and Singh, 1988)
- Acquirer large relative to target (Raff, Ryan, and Staehler, 2006; Harzing, 2002; Kogut and Singh, 1988)
- Acquirer has a high tolerance for risk (Kogut and Singh, 1988)
- Acquirer has experience in market (Harzing, 2002; Vermeulen and Barkema, 2001; Brouthers and Brouthers, 2000)
- Acquirer late in entering market (Wilson, 1980)

Solo more likely if
- Entry barriers are low (Anand and Delios, 2002; Anderson et al., 1997)
- Cultural differences are high (Harzing, 2002)
- Entrant has multinational experience (Brouthers and Brouthers, 2000; Barkema and Vermeulen, 1998; Wilson, 1980)
- High-tech acquirers want to use own employees to minimize training costs (Brouthers and Brouthers, 2000)
- Control is important (Hennart and Park, 1994)

JV more likely if
- Difficult to separate out unwanted assets (Hennart and Reddy, 1997)
- New entrant has limited experience in target market (Barkema and Vermeulen, 1998; Hennart and Reddy, 1997)
- Postmerger integration problems appear high (Hennart and Reddy, 1997)
- Cultural differences high and entrant risk adverse (Harzing, 2002; Child, Falkner, Pitkethley, 2001; Kogut and Singh, 1988)
- Barriers to entry are high and entrant lacks all necessary resources (Meyer, Estrin, and Bhaumik, 2005; Peng, 2003; Brouthers, 2002)
- Entrant desires greater strategic flexibility (Inkpen and Beamish, 1997; Hoffman and Schaper-Rinkel, 2001)

Export more likely if
- Entrants have limited experience in operating in local country (Davis, Desai, and Fracis, 2000)
- New entrant is risk adverse (Davis et al., 2000)
- Barriers to a physical presence onsite are large (Pan and Tse, 2000)

FIGURE 16-1   Alternative Market Entry Strategies

Mergers and Acquisitions as an Entry Strategy

M&As can provide quick access to a new market; however, they are subject to many of the same problems associated with domestic M&As. They are often very expensive, complex to negotiate, subject to myriad regulatory requirements, and beset by intractable cultural issues.

Greenfield or Solo Ventures as an Entry Strategy

Start-ups enable firms to control technology, marketing, and product distribution. Studies show that firms with significant intangible assets (e.g., proprietary know-how) are frequently able to earn above average returns, which can be leveraged in a greenfield or start-up venture (Brouthers and Brouthers, 2000). However, the firm's total investment is at risk, and the need to hire local residents ensures that the firm will face the challenges associated with managing a culturally diverse employee base.

Alliances and Joint Ventures as an Entry Strategy

Alliances allow firms to share the risks and costs of international expansion, develop new capabilities, and gain access to important resources (Zahra and Elhagrasey, 1994). Most strategic alliances are with a local firm that understands the competitive conditions, legal and social norms, and cultural standards of the country. Local firms may be interested in alliances to gain access to the technology, brand recognition, and innovative products of the foreign firm. Despite these benefits, many alliances fail due to conflict between partners (see Chapter 14). Alliances are also difficult to manage. Pan and T. Chi (1999) show that alliances tend to produce higher financial returns if the partners have an equity interest.

In contrast to earlier studies showing increasing use of alliances and joint ventures, Desai, Foley, and Hines (2002) showed a decline between 1982 and 1997 in the number of JVs. Factors contributing to this decline included lower coordination costs between domestic and foreign operations due to easier communication, reduced transportation costs, and integration of world financial markets. During the sample period minority owned affiliates declined from 17.9 to 10.6%, while wholly owned affiliates increased from 72.3 to 80.4%.

Alliances are often a precursor to acquisition. Wal-Mart's successful entry into Mexico started with a joint venture in 1991 with Grupo Cifra, Mexico's largest retail chain, culminating in the acquisition of the Mexican retailer in 1997. Grupo Cifra brought name recognition, while Wal-Mart contributed expertise in merchandising, distribution, warehousing, logistics, and data management.

Exporting as an Entry Strategy

Exporting does not require the expense of establishing local operations. However, exporters must establish some means of marketing and distributing their products at the local level. The disadvantages of exporting include high transportation costs, exchange rate fluctuations, and possible tariffs placed on imports into the local country. Moreover, the exporter has limited control over the marketing and distribution of its products in the local market.

Licensing as an Entry Strategy

Licensing allows a firm to purchase the right to manufacture and sell another firm's products within a specific country or set of countries. The licensor is normally paid a royalty on each unit sold. The licensee takes the risks and makes the investments in facilities for manufacturing, marketing, and distribution of goods and services. Consequently, licensing is possibly the least costly form of international expansion. Therefore, licensing is an increasingly popular entry mode for smaller firms with insufficient capital and limited brand recognition (Hitt and Ireland, 2000). Disadvantages include the lack of control over the manufacture and marketing of the firm's products in other countries. The risk may be high if the firm's brand or trademark is put in jeopardy. Furthermore, licensing often is the least profitable entry strategy, because the profits must be shared between the licensor and licensee. Finally, the licensee may learn the technology and sell a similar competitive product after the license expires.

Planning and Implementing Cross-Border Transactions in Developed Countries

The following discussion consists of two sections: (1) foreign acquisitions of U.S. businesses and (2) U.S. and non-U.S acquisitions of foreign businesses. Each section discusses acquisition vehicles, forms of payment, forms of acquisition, postclosing organizations, ownership transfer mechanisms, and tax strategies. Buyer due diligence, postmerger integration, and financing issues common to all cross-border transactions are also considered. Case Study 16-2 illustrates the inevitable increase in complexity of cross-border transactions compared to purely domestic transactions.

Case Study 16-2

Cadbury Buys Adams in a Sweet Deal

Cadbury Schweppes Plc. is a confectionary and beverage company headquartered in London, England. Cadbury Schweppes (Cadbury) acquired Adams Inc., a chewing gum and cough drop manufacturer, from Pfizer Corporation in 2003 for $4.2 billion. The acquisition enables Cadbury to gain access to new markets, especially in Latin America. The purchase also catapulted Cadbury to the top spot in the global confectionary market. Adams' major brands are in the fastest growing segments of the global market and complement Cadbury's existing chocolate business.

Cadbury bought 100% of the business of the Adams Division of Pfizer. The decision whether to transfer assets or stock depended on which gave Cadbury and Pfizer optimum tax advantages. The transaction was complicated by the significant interdependencies between the parent and division. Many employees had positions with both the parent and the operating unit. In addition, the parent supplied numerous support services for its subsidiary. While this is normal in the purchase of a unit of a larger company, this purchase was made more difficult by the fact that Adams operated in 40 different countries representing 40 different legal jurisdictions.

Cadbury and Pfizer representatives agreed on a single asset and stock sale and purchase agreement (i.e., the master agreement), which transferred the relevant U.S. assets and stock in

Adams' subsidiaries to Cadbury. The master agreement contained certain overarching terms including closing conditions, representations and warranties, covenants, and indemnification clauses that applied to all legal jurisdictions. However, the master agreement required Pfizer or Adams to enter into separate local "implementation" agreements. This was done to complete the transfer of either Adams' assets in non-U.S. jurisdictions or shares in non-U.S. Adams' subsidiaries to local Cadbury subsidiaries depending upon which provided the most favorable tax advantages and where necessary to accommodate differences in local legal conditions. The parties entered into more than 20 such agreements to transfer asset and stock ownership. All the agreements used the master agreement as a template. The various contracts were written in English and were governed by New York law, the state in which Pfizer is headquartered. Exceptions were made where there was a requirement that the law governing the contract be that of the local country.

A team of 5 Cadbury in-house lawyers and 40 outside attorneys conducted the legal review. Cadbury staff carried out separate environmental due diligence exercises because Adams had long-standing assets in the form of plant and machinery in each of 22 factories in 18 countries. Cadbury filed with antitrust regulators in a number of European and non-European countries, including Germany, the Czech Republic, Turkey, Greece, Italy, Portugal, Spain, the United Kingdom, South Africa, and Brazil. The requirements varied in each jurisdiction. It was necessary to obtain regulatory clearance before closing in countries where prenotification was required. The master agreement was conditional on antitrust regulatory approval in the United States, Canada, and Mexico, Adams' largest geographic markets.

Cadbury expects that the acquisition will provide tax benefits contributing $450 million in incremental cash flow over 15 years. The tax benefits result from Adams' significant intangible assets, such as intellectual property. Such assets are tax deductible in some countries in which the combined firms operate.

Cadbury wanted all 12,900 Adam's employees across 40 countries to transfer to it with the business. However, because not all of them were fully dedicated Adams' employees (i.e., some had both Adams and Pfizer functions), it was necessary to determine on a site-by-site basis which employees should remain with Pfizer and which should transfer to Cadbury. Partly due to the global complexity of the deal, the preclosing and closing meetings lasted 3 full days and nights. The closing checklist was 129 pages long (Birkett, 2003).

Case Study Discussion Questions

1. Discuss how cross-border transactions complicate the negotiation of the agreement of purchase and sale and due diligence. Be specific.
2. How does the complexity described in your answer to the first question add to the potential risk of the transaction? Be specific.
3. What conditions would you, as a buyer, suggest be included in the agreement of purchase and sale that might minimize the potential risk mentioned in your answer to the second question? Be specific.

Acquisitions of U.S. Businesses by Foreign Firms

Acquisition Vehicle

Non-U.S. firms often use partnerships, limited liability companies, or C corporations to acquire the shares or assets of U.S. targets.

A C corporation is the typical acquisition vehicle used by foreign buyers of U.S. businesses due to its flexibility. C corporations are relatively easy to organize quickly, since all states permit such structures and no prior governmental approval is required. There is no limitation on non-U.S. persons or entities acting as shareholders in U.S. corporations, except for certain regulated industries. The C corporation also allows for limited liability (i.e., limited to the extent of the shareholder's investment) and management autonomy (i.e., operational independence of management from the parent). Moreover, this structure provides for continuity of ownership (i.e., does not require dissolution due to the death of a shareholder) and permits unrestricted transfer of ownership shares (i.e., equity owners can freely trade shares).

A limited liability company (LLC) also limits investor liability and avoids double taxation. Unlike a partnership, LLCs allow owners to participate as managers without losing their limited liability protection. An LLC is also attractive for joint ventures in which the target is to be owned by two or more unrelated parties, corporations, or nonresident investors. While not traded on public stock exchanges, LLC shares can be sold freely to members. This facilitates the parent firm operating the acquired firm as a subsidiary or JV. Management autonomy is limited as major decisions are subject to the vote of membership; continuity is limited by the need for dissolution in the event of death, retirement, or resignation of a member; and transfer of ownership is subject to the approval of all members.

Partnerships may be either a general partnership, with unlimited liability for all partners, or a limited partnership, with limited liability for the limited partners and unlimited liability for the general partner. The limited partners cannot participate in the operation of the partnership. Corporations may be partners in either type of partnership. Partnerships also avoid double taxation. A partnership may also have advantages for investors from certain countries (e.g., Germany) where income earned from a U.S. partnership is not subject to taxation.

Holding company structures are commonly used acquisition vehicles, since they may have only one shareholder (i.e., the foreign parent). Such structures allow the parent to offset gains from one subsidiary with losses generated by another, serve as a platform for future acquisitions, and provide the parent with additional legal protection in the event of lawsuits.

Form of Payment

Target shareholders most often receive cash rather than shares in cross-border transactions (Ceneboyan, Papaioannou, and Travlos, 1991). Shares and other securities require registration with the Securities and Exchange Commission and compliance with all local securities (including state) laws. Target shareholders are interested in receiving acquirer shares only if there is a significant public market for the shares. Shares or securities do not require filing a registration statement with the SEC as long as they are not redistributed in the United States.

Form of Acquisition

While a foreign buyer may acquire shares or assets directly, share acquisitions are generally the simplest form of acquisition. Share acquisitions result in all assets and liabilities of the target firm on or off the balance sheet transferred to the acquirer by "rule of law." In certain cases, the seller may choose to retain selected assets or liabilities. Asset purchases result in the transference of all or some of the assets of the target firm to the acquirer (see Chapter 11).

Postmerger Organization

A highly centralized organization may be appropriate to realize synergies (e.g., anticipated cost savings) rapidly in order to recover the premium paid for the target (see Chapter 6). The centralized organization could later give way to a decentralized organization in which local management receives substantially greater responsibility in decision making.

It is often unwise to force significantly different cultures to work together. This is especially true immediately following closing. For example, Chrysler and Daimler-Benz maintained dual headquarters, dual stock listings, and dual chairpersons immediately following closing, before Daimler assumed direct control several years later. It is also rarely useful to centralize postmerger sales management in a company with diverse markets, high marketing costs, and or local production. In these instances, local management is much more likely to be sensitive to local marketplace changes than management in the parent country.

The location of incorporation needs to be determined early in the negotiations. Will the combined firms be in the jurisdiction of the target or acquirer or a third location? When selecting a place of incorporation, management must consider the prevailing corporation law, taxes, and the sophistication of its judiciary.

Tax Strategies

There are three basic deal-structuring strategies for determining whether the transaction is tax free or taxable. The first deal-structure strategy is the *tax-free reorganization or merger*, in which target shareholders receive acquirer stock in exchange for substantially all of the target's assets or shares. The target firm merges with a U.S. subsidiary of the foreign acquirer in a statutory merger under state laws. To qualify as a U.S. corporation for tax purposes, the foreign firm must own at least 80% of the stock of the domestic subsidiary. As such, the transaction can qualify as a Type A tax-free reorganization. Shareholders of the target company receive stock of the foreign acquirer in exchange for their stock in the target firm. The stock of the foreign acquirer may be voting or nonvoting. The U.S. subsidiary must acquire substantially all of the assets of the target company. The most commonly used form of tax-free share acquisition is the *reverse triangular merger*. The foreign acquirer forms a new shell U.S. subsidiary, which merges with the target in a statutory merger, with the target surviving.

The second form of deal structure is the *taxable purchase*, which involves the acquisition by one company of the shares or assets of another usually in exchange for cash or debt. Such a transaction is called taxable, because the target firm's shareholders recognize a taxable gain or loss on the exchange. The *forward triangular cash merger* is the most common form of *taxable transaction*. The target company merges with a U.S. subsidiary of the foreign acquirer with shareholders of the target firm receiving acquirer shares as well as cash, although cash is the predominate form of payment. This structure is useful when the foreign acquirer is willing to issue some shares and some target company shareholders want shares, while others want cash.

Hybrid transactions represent a third form of transaction. This type of structure affords the U.S. target corporation and its shareholders tax-free treatment, while avoiding the issuance of shares of the foreign acquirer. In general, a hybrid transaction may be taxable to some target shareholders and tax free to others. To structure hybrid transactions, some target company shareholders may exchange their common shares for a nonvoting preferred stock, while the foreign acquirer or its U.S. subsidiary buys the remaining common stock for cash. This transaction is tax free to target company shareholders taking preferred stock and taxable to those selling their shares for cash.

Note that tax laws and their application differ significantly across countries. Consequently, it is critical to utilize advisors familiar with the specific conditions pertaining to your transaction. For an excellent discussion of the different tax laws in various countries, see PricewaterhouseCoopers (2006).

Acquisitions of Non-U.S. Businesses by U.S. or Non-U.S. Acquirers

Acquiring businesses outside the U.S. involves additional obstacles atypical of domestic acquisitions. These include investment and exchange control approvals, tax clearances, clearances under local competition laws, and unusual due diligence problems. Other problems involve the necessity of agreeing on an allocation of the purchase price among assets located in various jurisdictions and compliance with local law relating to the documentation necessary to complete the transaction.

Acquisition Vehicle

The rules governing such entities will be crucial, since the buyer must often organize a local company to hold acquired shares or assets. In common law countries (e.g., United Kingdom, Canada, Australia, India, Pakistan, Hong Kong, Singapore, and other former British colonies), the acquisition vehicle will be a corporation-like structure. In civil law countries (which include Western Europe, South America, Japan, and Korea), the acquisition will generally be in the form of a share company or limited liability company. Civil law also is known as codified law, continental law, or the Napoleonic Code.

Islamic law, sometimes called Muslim law, is practiced in some Middle Eastern Muslim countries and in some countries in Southeast Asia (e.g., Indonesia and Malaysia). The Koran is the basis for such law. Since many of these countries were once part of the colonial empires of various European states, the type of law actually practiced is a mixture of civil and Muslim law. Muslim countries having certain characteristics of English common law include Egypt, Jordan, and Malaysia, which were once under the control of Britain.

In countries practicing civil law, every type of business entity is considered a company. All companies must register with the government. In the European Union, there is not overarching law or EU directive requiring a specific corporate form. Rather, corporate law is the responsibility of each member nation.

Corporations in United Kingdom and other Commonwealth countries are similar to those in the United States. In many civil law countries, smaller enterprises often use a limited liability company. A share company is used for larger enterprises, particularly those with public shareholders. The rules applicable to limited liability companies tend to be flexible and are particularly useful for wholly owned subsidiaries. In contrast, share companies are subject to numerous restrictions and applicable securities laws. However, their shares trade freely on public exchanges.

Share companies tend to be more heavily regulated than U.S. corporations. Share companies must register with the commercial registrar in the location of its principal place of business. It may take considerable time to organize a share company having large operations in many foreign jurisdictions. There may be bureaucratic delays from several weeks to several months between the filing of the appropriate documents and the organization of the company. Most civil law countries require that there be more than one shareholder. Usually there is no limitation on foreigners acting as shareholders. The directors in many share companies function as both officers and directors as they do in a U.S. corporation. Many countries require that either a majority or at least some specific number of directors be citizens of the country.

Limited liability companies outside the United States are generally more flexible (i.e., subject to fewer restrictions) than share companies. LLCs have interests or quotas rather than shares, since a share denotes something that is traded freely on an exchange. An LLC will typically be required to have more than one quota holder. Quotas may be issued for cash or real property. In general, either domestic or foreign corporations or individuals may be quota holders in an LLC. For an excellent discussion of alternative corporate structures in common and civil law countries, see Truitt (2006).

Form of Payment

Payment in transactions involving non-U.S. firms is most likely to be cash. Acquirer shares often are less attractive to potential targets because of the absence of a liquid market for resale or because the acquirer is not widely recognized by the target firm's shareholders.

Form of Acquisition

As in the United States, share acquisitions are often the simplest mechanism for conveying ownership. All assets and liabilities remain with the target; as such, they transfer to the buyer when the target's shares are purchased. Since assets remain with the target, few transfer documents are required and transfer taxes may be limited or avoided. This is particularly important in countries where transfer taxes (i.e., those paid whenever asset ownership transfers) are onerous. In share acquisitions, licenses, permits, and franchises, contracts and leases transfer to the buyer, without the need to get approvals from licensors, permit holders, etc. However, third-party approval may still be required if a change of ownership clause is stipulated in the contract. The major disadvantage of a share purchase is that all of the target's known and unknown liabilities transfer to the buyer. When the target is in a foreign country, full disclosure of liabilities is often limited. With tax avoidance and fraud common in many countries, the buyer may find that some assets will transfer encumbered by tax liens.

Asset sales are used if a single line of business is being sold. Asset transactions also allow the seller to retain some of the liabilities. However, in many foreign countries the sale of substantially all of the assets of a business is made more complicated than in the United States. For example, in some European countries, the sale of a business means that its employees automatically become the acquirer's employees. As in the United States, asset purchases are more complex than share purchases, since each asset requires separate transfer documents, third-party consents to assignment may be required, and transfer taxes may be substantial.

Mergers are not legal in all countries, often due to the requirement that minority shareholders must assent to the will of the majority vote. Where they are permissible, the primary advantage is the automatic transfer of assets (both known and unknown at closing) from seller to buyer. This greatly facilitates the transfer of valuable permits and contracts.

Postclosing Organization

Some acquired companies operate as self-sufficient, standalone businesses. In contrast, others may be completely integrated with the acquirer's existing business and lose all or part of their prior corporate identity. For those targets operating as standalone operations, the parent firm may encounter considerable difficulty in monitoring the financial position and performance of the acquired firm at a distance.

Tax Strategies

International transactions tend to be highly challenging, as they typically involve multiple tax and legal jurisdictions (see Case Study 16-2). If the acquisition is structured as an asset purchase because the target is only a division of a foreign company or because the seller agrees to sell assets, the U.S. buyer of the assets must decide whether to acquire them directly or to use a new or existing foreign company to do so. The choice will affect future U.S. and non-U.S. tax consequences.

Buyer Due Diligence

As in the United States, any representations and warranties in an acquisition agreement are intended to cause the seller to disclose significant information. However, because of local custom, they are often less extensive than in the United States. Hence, the buyer should independently verify as much as possible about the target. The legal protections afforded by representations and warranties are never a substitute for the buyer performing on-site due diligence. For an excellent in-depth discussion of how to conduct a cross-border due diligence, see Rosenbloom (2002).

Employment and Labor Law

Employees receive far greater legal protection in many developed foreign countries than they do in the United States. Consequently, explicit covenants, representations, and warranties on these matters need to be included in the agreement of purchase and sale. Some European countries give employees a role in conducting the business. As such, they may have substantial input into the negotiations. Even for asset purchases, the buyer may be required to assume all obligations under collective bargaining agreements. Since employees automatically transfer with the change of ownership, the buyer will inherit all related liabilities, especially when employees retire or are terminated. If the buyer fails to employ target employees on terms no less favorable than those offered by the seller, the employees are viewed as terminated. This triggers the payment of substantial severance benefits. In Western European countries, government agencies manage pensions. Consequently, there are no labor-related benefits to transfer or liabilities for the buyer to assume.

Environmental and Product Liability Laws

Environmental regulation is stricter outside of the United States. In share purchases, permits and licenses will transfer with the target. In the case of an asset purchase, as in the United States, such permits and licenses may not be assignable and new permits and licenses must be obtained before closing. Product liability claims currently are less frequent and judgments are smaller outside the United States.

Financial Statements

Accounting practices vary widely from country to country. The seller should be required to confirm that their financial statements have been prepared in accordance with generally accepted accounting principles. Although the statements may have been audited, they are generally less reliable than audited statements prepared by accountants familiar with the target and with the full cooperation of the target's management.

Material Assets

Regulations pertaining to intellectual property vary substantially from one country to another. In many countries, registration of a trademark is critical in protecting the acquirer's rights. Without registration, all rights to enforce a trademark against third-party infringements may be lost. In most countries, unless specifically restricted, registrations are assignable.

Other Regulatory Considerations

Government approvals are commonly required for foreign investment, exchange control, and antitrust matters, as well as tax clearances, fillings, or payments. Failure to obtain the required governmental approvals may void the acquisition. While the failure to gain certain approvals may not affect the validity of the acquisition, it may prevent the buyer from repatriating earnings. The buyer could also lose tax benefits. In most cases, the acquisition agreement should make the closing subject to obtaining all necessary local government approvals.

Financing Considerations

Debt is most often used to finance cross-border transactions. The proceeds of the debt financing may be used either to purchase the target's outstanding shares for cash or to repurchase acquirer shares issued to target shareholders. Sources of financing exist in capital markets in the acquirer's home, the target's local country, or in some third country. Domestic capital sources available to cross-border acquirers include banks willing to provide bridge financing and lines of credit, bond markets, and equity markets. Increasingly, credit-default swaps are used to defray the risk of default of debt issued to finance many types of cross-border investments including M&As. Such swaps enable the lender to be protected from the risk of default for some future period by paying an annual fee to the seller of the insurance contract. For a more detailed discussion of credit-default swaps, see Chapter 13.

Debt Markets

Eurobonds represent a common form of financing for cross-border transactions. Eurobonds are debt instruments expressed in terms of U.S. dollars or other currencies and sold to investors outside the country in whose currency they are denominated. A typical Eurobond transaction could be a dollar-denominated bond issued by a French firm through an underwriting group. The underwriting group could be composed of the overseas affiliate of a New York investment bank, a German commercial bank, and a consortium of London banks.

Bonds issued by foreign firms and governments in local markets have existed for many years. Such bonds are issued in another country's domestic bond market, denominated in its currency, and are subject to that country's regulations. Bonds of a non-U.S. issuer registered with the SEC for sale in the U.S. public bond markets are called "Yankee" bonds. Similarly, a U.S. company issuing a bond in Japan would be issuing a "Samurai" bond.

Equity Markets

The American Depository Receipt (ADR) market evolved as a means of enabling foreign firms to raise funds in the U.S. equity markets. ADRs represent the receipt for the shares of a foreign-based corporation held in a U.S. bank. The ADR entitles the holder to all dividends and capital gains. American depositary shares (ADS) are shares issued under a deposit agreement representing the underlying common share, which trades in the issuer's market. The terms ADS and ADR often are used interchangeably.

Euroequity markets are equivalent to the Eurobond market. The Euroequity market reflects equity issues by a foreign firm tapping a larger investor base than the firm's home equity market. The foreign firm may also be trying to avoid its domestic market regulations and expenses.

Often the target's shareholders are reluctant to accept an acquirer's shares if the buyer is not well known in the target's home market. Target shareholders may be able to sell the shares only at a discount in their home market. In this instance, the buyer may have to issue shares in its home market or possibly to the international equities market and use the proceeds to acquire the target for cash. Alternatively, the acquirer may issue shares in the target's market if by doing so it creates a resale market for target shareholders. The buyer could also offer target shareholders the opportunity to sell the shares in the buyer's home market through an investment banker.

Postmerger Integration

Language barriers, different customs, working conditions, work ethics, and legal structures create a new set of challenges in integrating cross-border transactions. If corporate and national cultures are extremely different, integration may be inappropriate. However, recent studies suggest that acquisitions involving firms from countries with very dissimilar cultures perform better in the long run than those between firms from countries with similar cultures (Chakrabarti, Jayaraman, and Mukherjee, 2005; Langford and Brown, 2004; and Morosini, Shane, and Singh, 1998). These studies distinguish between national culture and corporate culture. Diversity arising from highly different national cultures may help the combined acquirer and target firms to compete more effectively in the global marketplace. However, differences in corporate cultures that impair cooperation offset such synergy. The salutary effects of diverse national cultures often tend to outweigh the undermining effects of diverse corporate cultures.

In choosing how to manage an acquisition in a new country, a manager with an in-depth knowledge of the acquirer's priorities, decision-making processes, and operations is appropriate, especially when the acquirer expects to make very large new investments. However, when the acquirer already has existing operations within the country, a manager with substantial industry experience in the country is generally preferable because of their cultural sensitivity and knowledge of local customers, laws, and regulations.

Planning and Implementing Cross-Border Transactions in Emerging Countries

Entering emerging economies poses a host of new challenges not generally encountered in developed countries. These challenges may include a range of political and economic risks.

Political and Economic Risks

It is difficult to differentiate between political and economic risks, since they are often highly interrelated. Examples of political and economic risk include excessive local government regulation, confiscatory tax policies, restrictions on cash remittances, currency inconvertibility, restrictive employment policies, outright expropriation of assets of foreign firms, civil war or local insurgencies, and corruption. Another, sometimes overlooked, challenge is the failure of the legal system in an emerging country to honor contracts (Khanna, Palepu, and, Sinha, 2005).

Many of these risks will result in gyrating exchange rates, which heighten the level of risk associated with direct investment in an emerging country. Unanticipated changes in exchange rates can substantially influence the competitiveness of products produced in the local market for export to the global marketplace. Furthermore, changes in exchange rates will alter the value of assets invested in the local country and earnings repatriated from the local operations to the parent corporation in the home country.

Sources of Information for Assessing Political and Economic Risk

Information sources include consultants in the local country, joint venture partners, a local counsel, or appropriate government agency such as the U.S. Department of State. Other sources of information include the major credit-rating agencies such as Standard & Poor's, Moody's, and Fitch IBCA. Trade magazines such as *Euromoney* and *Institutional Investor* provide overall country risk ratings updated semiannually. The Economic Intelligence Unit (EIU) also provides numerical risk scores for individual countries. The International Country Risk Guide (ICRG), published by the Political Risk Services Group, offers overall numerical risk scores for individual countries as well as separate scores for political, financial, and economic risks. While such publications provide a means of ranking countries in terms of risk, they provide little insight in measuring the magnitude of the risk.

Using Insurance to Manage Risk

The decision to buy political risk insurance depends on the size of the investment and the perceived level of political and economic risk. Parties will have a variety of sources from which to choose. For instance, the export credit agency in a variety of countries such as Export Import Bank (United States), SACE (Italy), and Hermes (Germany), may offer coverage for companies based within their jurisdictions. The Overseas Private Investment Corporation (OPIC) is available to firms based in the United States, while the World Bank's Multilateral Investment Guarantee Agency (MIGA) is available to all firms. These governmental and quasi-governmental insurers are the only substantial providers of war/political violence coverage.

Using Options and Contract Language to Manage Risk

In theory, a thorough due diligence of the target firm should uncover the majority of significant risks for the acquirer. However, in emerging countries where financial statements may be haphazard and gaining access to the information necessary to adequately assess risk is limited, it may be impossible to perform an adequate due diligence. Under these circumstances, acquirers may protect themselves by including a put option in the agreement of purchase and sale. Such an option would enable the buyer to require the seller to repurchase shares from the buyer at a predetermined price under certain circumstances. Alternatively, the agreement could include a clause requiring a purchase price adjustment. For example, in late 2005, the Royal Bank of Scotland purchased shares in the Bank of China. If subsequent to closing, there were material restatements to the Bank of China's financial statements, the purchase price would be adjusted in the Royal Bank's favor.

Valuing Cross-Border Transactions

The methodology for valuing cross-border transactions using discounted cash-flow analysis is similar to that employed when both the acquiring and target firms are within the same country. The basic differences between within-country and cross-border valuation methods is that the latter involves converting cash flows from one currency into another and adjusting the discount rate for risks not generally found when the acquirer and target firms are within the same country.

Converting Foreign Target Cash Flows into Acquirer Domestic Cash Flows

Cash flows of the target firm can be expressed in its own currency including expected inflation (i.e., in nominal terms), its own currency without inflation (i.e., real terms), or the acquirer's currency. Real cash-flow valuation adjusts all cash flows for inflation and uses real discount rates. Normally, M&A practitioners utilize nominal cash flows except when inflation rates are high. Under these circumstances, real cash flows are preferable. Real cash flows are determined by dividing the nominal cash flows by the country's gross domestic product (GDP) deflator or some other broad measure of inflation. Future real cash flows are estimated by dividing future nominal cash flows by the current GDP deflator increased by the expected rate of inflation. Real discount rates are determined by subtracting the expected rate of inflation from nominal discount rates. Nominal or real cash flows should give the same net present values if the expected rate of inflation used to convert future cash flows to real terms is the same inflation rate used to estimate the real discount rate.

Inflation in the target country may affect the various components of the target firm's cash flows differently. For example, how the inventory component of working capital is impacted by inflation will reflect in part how sensitive certain raw materials, etc., are to inflation and how such inventory is recorded (i.e., LIFO or FIFO basis). Moreover, straight-line depreciation may not adequately account for the true replacement cost of equipment in an inflationary environment. Since conversions of the various components of cash flow from local to home country currency may result in unnecessary distortions, it is advisable to project the target's cash flows in terms of its own currency and then convert the cash flows into the acquirer's currency. This requires estimating future exchange rates between the target (local) and acquirer's (home) currency.

Interest rates and expected inflation in one country compared to another country affect exchange rates between the two countries. The current rate at which one currency can be exchanged for another is called the spot exchange rate. Consequently, the translation to the acquirer's currency can be achieved by using future spot exchange rates estimated either from relative interest rates (interest rate parity theory) in each country or by the relative rates of expected inflation (purchasing power parity theory). For a detailed discussion of the interest rate parity and purchasing power parity theories, see Shapiro (2005).

When Target Firms Are in Developed (Globally Integrated) Capital Market Countries

For developed countries, such as Western Europe, the interest rate parity theory provides a useful framework for estimating forward currency exchange rates (i.e., future spot exchange rates). To illustrate this process, consider a U.S. acquirer's valuation of a firm in the European Union (EU), with projected cash flows expressed in terms of euros. The target's cash flows can be converted into dollars by using a forecast of future dollar to euro spot rates. The *interest rate parity theory* relates forward or future spot exchange rates to differences in interest rates between two countries adjusted by the spot rate. Therefore, the dollar to euro exchange rate $(\$/€)_n$ (i.e., the future or forward exchange rate), n periods into the future, would be expected to appreciate (depreciate) according to the following relationship:

$$(\$/€)_n = \{(1 + R_{\$n})^n / (1 + R_{€n})^n\} \times (\$/€)_0 \qquad (16\text{-}1)$$

Similarly, the euro to dollar exchange rate $(€/\$)_n$, n periods into the future, would be expected to appreciate (depreciate) according to the following relationship:

$$(€/\$)_n = \{(1 + R_{€n})^n / (1 + R_{\$n})^n\} \times (€/\$)_0 \qquad (16\text{-}2)$$

Note that $(\$/€)_0$ and $(€/\$)_0$ represent the spot rate for the dollar to euro and euro to dollar exchange rates, respectively; $R_{\$n}$ and $R_{€n}$ represent the interest rate in the United States and in the EU, respectively. Equations 16-1 and 16-2 imply that if U.S. interest rates rise relative to those in the EU, investors will buy dollars with euros at the current spot rate and sell dollars for euros in the forward or futures market to offset the risk of exchange rate changes n periods into the future. By doing so, investors avoid the potential loss of the value of their investment expressed in terms of dollars when they wish to convert their dollar holdings back into euros. In this way, the equality in these two equations is maintained. Exhibit 16-1 illustrates how to convert a target company's nominal free cash flows to the firm (FCFF) expressed in euros (i.e., the local country or target's currency) into those expressed in dollars (i.e., home country or acquirer's currency).

Exhibit 16-1
Converting Euro-Denominated into Dollar-Denominated Free Cash Flows
Using Interest Rate Parity Theory

	2008	2009	2010
Target's Euro-Denominated FCFF Cash Flows (Millions)	€124.5	€130.7	€136.0
Target Country's Interest Rate (%)	4.50	4.70	5.30
U.S. Interest Rate (%)	4.25	4.35	4.55
Current Spot Rate ($/€) = 1.2044			
Projected Spot Rate ($/€)	1.2015	1.1964	1.1788
Target's Dollar-Denominated FCFF Cash Flows (Millions)	$149.59	$156.37	$160.32

Note: Calculating the projected spot rate using Equation 16-1:

$$(\$/\text{€})_{2008} = \{(1.0425)/(1.0450)\} \times 1.2044 = 1.2015$$
$$(\$/\text{€})_{2009} = \{(1.0435)^2/(1.0470)^2\} \times 1.2044 = 1.1964$$
$$(\$/\text{€})_{2010} = \{(1.0455)^3/(1.0530)^3\} \times 1.2044 = 1.1788$$

When Target Firms Are in Emerging (Segmented) Capital Market Countries

Cash flows are converted as before using the interest rate parity theory or by using the purchasing power parity theory. The latter is used if there is not sufficient information about interest rates in the emerging market. The *purchasing power parity theory* states that one currency will appreciate (depreciate) with respect to another currency according to the expected relative rates of inflation between the two countries. To illustrate, the dollar to Mexican peso exchange rate $(\$/\text{Peso})_n$ and the Mexican peso/dollar exchange $(\text{Peso}/\$)_n$ rate n periods from now (i.e., future exchange rates) would be expected to change according to the following relationships:

$$(\$/\text{Peso})_n = [(1 + P_{us})^n/(1 + P_{mex})^n] \times (\$/\text{Peso})_0 \qquad (16\text{-}3)$$

and

$$(\text{Peso}/\$)_n = [(1 + P_{mex})^n/(1 + P_{us})^n] \times (\text{Peso}/\$)_0 \qquad (16\text{-}4)$$

where P_{us} and P_{mex} are the expected inflation rates in the U.S. and Mexico, respectively, and $(\$/\text{Peso})_0$ and $(\text{Peso}/\$)_0$ are the dollar to peso and peso to dollar spot exchange rates, respectively. If future U.S. inflation is expected to rise faster than the Mexican inflation rate, the forward dollar to peso exchange rate (i.e., future spot rates shown by Equation 16-3) will depreciate, as U.S. citizens sell dollars for pesos to buy relatively cheaper Mexican products. See Exhibit 16-2 for an illustration of how this might work in practice.

Exhibit 16-2

**Converting Peso-Denominated into Dollar Denominated Free Cash Flows
to the Firm Using Purchasing Power Parity Theory**

	2008	2009	2010
Target's Peso-Denominated FCFF Cash Flows (Millions of Pesos)	$1,050.5	$1,124.7	$1,202.7
Current Mexican Expected Inflation Rate = 6%			
Current U.S. Expected Inflation Rate = 4%			
Current Spot Rate ($/Peso) = .0877			
Projected Spot Rate ($/Peso)	.0860	.0844	.0828
Target's Dollar-Denominated FCFF Cash Flows (Millions of $)	$90.34	$94.92	$99.58

Note: Calculating the projected spot rate using Equation 16-3:

$$(\$/Peso)_{2008} = \{(1.04)/(1.06)\} \times .0877 = .0860$$

$$(\$/Peso)_{2009} = \{(1.04)^2/(1.06)^2\} \times .0877 = .0844$$

$$(\$/Peso)_{2010} = \{(1.04)^3/(1.06)^3\} \times .0877 = .0828$$

Selecting the Correct Marginal Tax Rate

Since corporate tax rates vary widely among countries, determining whether the acquirer's or the target's marginal tax rate should be used in calculating cash flows and the weighted average cost of capital is challenging in cross-border transactions. In general, the correct marginal tax rate should be that prevailing in the country in which the cash flows are generated. If the acquirer's country makes foreign income exempt from further taxation once taxed in the foreign country, the correct tax rate would be the marginal tax rate in the foreign country because that is where taxes are actually paid. Consequently, taxes paid on earnings in the foreign country would satisfy the acquirer's total taxes owed on income earned from this investment. Alternatively, the correct tax rate should be the acquirer's country rate, if it is higher than the target's country rate and if taxes paid in a foreign country are deductible from the taxes owed by the acquirer in its home country. The acquirer must still pay taxes owed in the country in which it resides in excess of any credits received for foreign taxes paid.

Estimating Cost of Capital in Cross-Border Transactions

While almost three-fourths of U.S. corporate Chief Financial Officers surveyed use the capital asset pricing model to calculate the cost of equity, there is considerable disagreement in how to calculate the cost of equity in cross-border transactions (Graham and Harvey, 2001). To the extent a consensus exists, the basic capital asset pricing model or a multifactor model (CAPM plus a factor to adjust for the size of the firm, etc.) should be used in developed countries with liquid capital markets. For emerging countries, the estimation of the cost of equity is more complex. Harvey (2005) documents 12 different approaches to estimating the international cost of equity. Each method endeavors to incorporate adjustments to the discount rate to account for potential capital market segmentation and specific country risks. Still other approaches attempt to incorporate the risk of investing in emerging countries not by adjusting the discount rate but by adjusting projected cash flows. In either case, the adjustments often appear arbitrary.

Developed economies seem to exhibit little differences in the cost of equity due to the relatively high integration of their capital markets in the global capital market. Thus, adjusting the cost of equity for specific country risk does not seem to make any significant difference (Bodnar, Dumas, and Marston, 2003; Koedijk and Van Dijk, 2000; Koedijk, Kool, Schotman, and Van Kijk, 2002; Mishra and O'Brien, 2001). However, for emerging market countries with segmented capital markets, political instability, limited liquidity, currency fluctuations, and currency inconvertibility seem to make adjusting the target firm's cost of equity for these factors, to the extent practical, desirable.

Bodnar *et al.* (2003) argue that, in addition to the risk-free rate of return, the firm's cost of equity (k_e) should be adjusted for such factors as the risk arising from variation in returns on a global stock market, country-specific stock market risk, and industry-specific risk. Other factors include exchange rate, political, and liquidity risk. Unfortunately, the substantial amount of information needed to estimate the adjustments required in such extensive multifactor models usually makes this approach impractical.

The following discussion incorporates the basic elements of valuing cross-border transactions, distinguishing between the different adjustments made when investing in developed and emerging countries. Nonetheless, the reader must keep in mind that that considerable debate continues in this area. See Harvey (2005) for an excellent discussion of the issues.

Estimating the Cost of Equity in Developed (Globally Integrated) Countries

The following discussion is very similar to the capital asset pricing model formulation (CAPM) outlined in Chapter 7, except for the use of either national or globally diversified stock market indices in estimating β and calculating the equity market risk premium.

Basic Capital Asset Pricing Model The basic CAPM suggests that, for a large capitalization company, the cost of equity includes both a risk-free rate of return and an equity risk premium (see Chapter 7). Total risk consists of both a diversifiable (i.e., business-specific risk) and a nondiversifiable component (i.e., risk affecting all firms). Investors are compensated only for assuming nondiversifiable risk, as all other risk can be diversified away.

Adjusting CAPM for Risk (Developed Countries) The equity premium, reflecting the difference between the return on a well-diversified portfolio and the risk-free return, is the incremental return required to induce investors to buy stocks. The use of a well-diversified portfolio eliminates risk specific to a business or so-called diversifiable risk. The firm's β is a measure of nondiversifiable risk. In a world in which capital markets are fully integrated, equity investors hold globally diversified portfolios. When measured in the same currency, the equity premium is the same for all investors, because each security's β is estimated by regressing its historical financial returns, or that of a comparable firm, against the historical returns on a globally diversified equity index.

Alternatively, an analyst could use a well-diversified country index that is highly correlated with the global index. In the United States, an example of a well-diversified portfolio is the Standard & Poor's 500 stock index (S&P 500); in the global capital markets, the Morgan Stanley Capital International World Index (MSCI) is commonly used as a proxy for a well-diversified global equity portfolio. Thus, the equity premium may be estimated on a well-diversified portfolio of U.S. equities, another developed country's equity portfolio, or on a global equity portfolio.

Adjusting CAPM for Firm Size   As noted in Chapter 7, studies show that the capital asset pricing model should be adjusted for the size of the firm. The size factor serves as a proxy for factors such as smaller firms being subject to higher default risk and generally being less liquid than large capitalization firms (Berk, 1995). See Chapter 7 (Table 7-1) for estimates of the amount of the adjustment to the cost of equity to correct for firm size, as measured by market value.

Estimating the Risk-Free Rate of Return (Developed and Emerging Countries)   For developed countries, the risk-free rate is the local country's government bond rate, whenever the projected cash flows for the target firm are expressed in local currency. Conversely, the risk-free rate is the U.S. Treasury bond rate if projected cash flows are in terms of dollars. For emerging economies, data limitations often preclude using the local country's government bond rate as the risk-free rate. If the target firm's cash flows are in terms of local currency, the U.S. Treasury bond rate often is used to estimate the risk-free rate. To create a local nominal interest rate, the Treasury bond rate should be adjusted for the difference in the anticipated inflation rates in the two countries. See Equation 16-6 to determine how to make this adjustment.

Global CAPM Formulation (Developed Countries)   In globally integrated markets, it makes little difference whether the β is calculated by regressing the target firm's (or a similar firm's) historical returns against the returns for a broadly defined global index, U.S. equity market index, or a broadly defined equity index in the target's country. When using a global equity index, the resulting CAPM often is called the ***global or international capital asset pricing model***. If the risk associated with the target firm is similar to that faced by the acquirer, the acquirer's cost of equity may be used to discount the target's cash flows.

The global capital asset pricing model for the target firm may be expressed as follows:

$$k_{e,dev} = R_f + \beta_{devfirm,global} \ (R_m - R_f) + FSP \qquad (16\text{-}5)$$

where

$k_{e,dev}$ = required return on equity for a firm operating in a developed country

R_f = local country's risk-free financial rate of return if cash flows are measured in the local country's currency or U.S. Treasury bond rate if in dollars.

$(R_m - R_f)$ = difference between the expected return on the global market portfolio (i.e., MSCI), U.S. equity index (S&P 500), or a broadly defined index in the target's local country and R_f. This difference is the equity premium, which should be approximately the same when expressed in the same currency for countries with globally integrated capital markets.

$\beta_{devfirm,global}$ = measure of nondiversifiable risk with respect to a globally diversified equity portfolio or a well-diversified country portfolio highly correlated with the global index. Alternatively, $\beta_{devfirm,global}$ may be estimated indirectly as illustrated in Equation 16-7.

FSP = firm size premium reflecting the additional return smaller firms must earn relative to larger firms to attract investors.

Note the similarity of the global capital asset pricing model (Equation 16-5) with the capital asset pricing model adjusted for firm size discussed in Chapter 7 (see Equation 7-2).

Applying the Fisher Effect The so-called Fisher Effect states that nominal interest rates can be expressed as the sum of the real interest rate (i.e., interest rates excluding inflation) and the anticipated rate of inflation. The Fisher Effect can be shown for the United States and Mexico as follows:

$$(1+i_{us}) = (1+r_{us})(1+P_{us}) \quad \text{and} \quad (1+r_{us}) = (1+i_{us})/(1+P_{us})$$

$$(1+i_{mex}) = (1+r_{mex})(1+P_{mex}) \quad \text{and} \quad (1+r_{mex}) = (1+i_{mex})/(1+P_{mex})$$

If real interest rates are constant among all countries, nominal interest rates between countries will vary only by the difference in the anticipated inflation rates. Therefore,

$$(1+i_{us})/(1+P_{us}) = (1+i_{mex})/(1+P_{mex}) \tag{16-6}$$

where

i_{us} and i_{mex} = nominal interest rates in the United States and Mexico, respectively
r_{us} and r_{mex} = real interest rates in the United States and Mexico, respectively
P_{us} and P_{mex} = anticipated inflation rates in the United States and Mexico, respectively

If the analyst knows the Mexican interest rate and the anticipated inflation rates in Mexico and the United States, solving Equation 16-6 provides an estimate of the U.S. interest rate [i.e., $i_{us} = (1+i_{mex}) \times ((1+P_{us})/(1+P_{mex})) - 1$]. Exhibit 16-3 illustrates how the cost of equity may be estimated in one currency and converted easily to another using Equation 16-6. Although the historical equity premium in the United States is used in calculating the cost of equity, the historical U.K. or MSCI premium also could have been employed.

Exhibit 16-3

Calculating the Target Firm's Cost of Equity in Both Home and Local Currency

Acquirer, a U.S. multinational firm, is interested in purchasing Target, a small U.K.-based competitor, with a market value of 550 million pounds or about $1 billion. The current risk-free rate of return for U.K. 10-year government bonds is 4.2%. The anticipated inflation rates in the United States and the United Kingdom are 3 and 4%, respectively. The estimated size premium for a small capitalization firm is 1.2% (see Chapter 7: Table 7-1). The historical equity risk premium in the United States is 5.5%.[1] Acquirer estimates Target's β to be .8, by regressing Target's historical financial returns against the S&P 500. What is the cost of equity ($k_{e,uk}$) that should be used to discount Target's projected cash flows when they are expressed in terms of British pounds (i.e., local currency)? What is the cost of equity ($k_{e,us}$) that should be used to discount Target's projected cash flows when they are expressed in terms of U.S. dollars (i.e., home currency)?[2]

$k_{e,uk}$ (see Equation 16-5) = .042 + .8 × (.055) + .012 = .098 = 9.80%

$k_{e,us}$ (see Equation 16-6) = (1 + .098) × [(1 + .03)/(1 + .04)] − 1 = .0875 = 8.75%

---

[1] The U.S. equity premium or the U.K. equity premium could have been used since equity markets in either country are highly correlated.

[2] The real rate of return is the same in the United Kingdom (r_{uk}) and the United States (r_{us}). r_{uk} = 9.8% − 4.0% = 5.8%, and r_{us} = 8.8% − 3.0% = 5.8%.

Estimating the Cost of Equity in Emerging (Segmented) Capital Market Countries

If individual country's capital markets are segmented, the global capital asset pricing model must be adjusted to reflect the tendency of investors in individual countries to hold local country rather than globally diversified equity portfolios. Consequently, equity premiums differ among countries reflecting the nondiversifiable risk associated with each country's equity market index.

Adjusting CAPM for Risk (Emerging Countries) An analyst can determine if a country's equity market is likely to be segmented from the global equity market if the β derived by regressing returns in the foreign market with returns on the global equity market is significantly different from one. This implies that the local country's equity premium differs from the global equity premium, reflecting the local country's nondiversifiable risk.

Nondiversifiable risk for a firm operating primarily in its emerging country's home market, whose capital market is segmented, is measured mainly with respect to the country's equity market index ($\beta_{emfirm,country}$) and to a lesser extent with respect a globally diversified equity portfolio ($\beta_{country,global}$). The emerging country firm's global β ($\beta_{emfirm,global}$) can be adjusted to reflect the relationship with the global capital market as follows:

$$\beta_{emfirm,global} = \beta_{emfirm,country} \times \beta_{country,global} \qquad (16\text{-}7)$$

$\beta_{emfirm,country}$ is estimated by regressing historical returns for the local firm against returns for the country's equity index. In the absence of sufficient historical information, $\beta_{emfirm,country}$ may be estimated by using the β for a similar local firm or a similar foreign firm. $\beta_{country,global}$ can be estimated by regressing the financial returns for the local country index (or for the index in a similar country) against the historical financial returns for a global index.

Alternatively, a more direct approach would be to regress the local firm's historical returns against the financial returns for a globally diversified portfolio of stocks to estimate $\beta_{emfirm,global}$. Furthermore, the β between a similar local or foreign firm and the global index could be used for this purpose. However, the regression of the local firm's historical financial returns against the global index may not work for many local firms whose business is not dependent on exports and is not highly correlated with the global economy.

Due to absence of historical data in many emerging economies, the equity risk premium often is estimated using the "prospective method" implied in the constant-growth valuation model. As noted in Chapter 7 (Equation 7-17), this formulation provides an estimate of the present value of dividends growing at a constant rate in perpetuity. Recall that this method requires that the dividends paid in the current period (d_0) are grown at a constant rate of growth (g) such that d_1 equals $d_0(1 + g)$.

Assuming the stock market values stocks correctly and we know the present value of a broadly defined index in the target firm's country ($P_{country}$) or in a similar country, dividends paid annually on this index in the next period (d_1), and the expected dividend growth (g), we can estimate the expected return ($R_{country}$) on the stock index as follows:

$$P_{country} = d_1/(R_{country} - g) \quad \text{and} \quad R_{country} = (d_1/P_{country}) + g \qquad (16\text{-}8)$$

From Equation 16-8, the equity risk premium for the local country's equity market is $R_{country} - R_f$, where R_f is the local country's risk-free rate of return. Exhibit 16-4 illustrates how to calculate the cost of equity for a firm in an emerging country in the absence of perceived significant country or political risk not captured in the β or equity risk premium. Note that the local country's risk-free rate of return is estimated using the U.S. Treasury bond rate adjusted for the expected inflation in the local country relative to the United States. This converts the U.S. Treasury bond rate into a local country nominal interest rate.

Exhibit 16-4
Calculating the Target Firm's Cost of Equity for Firms in Emerging Countries

Assume next year's dividend yield on an emerging country's stock market is 5% and that earnings for the companies in the stock market index are expected to grow by 6% annually in the foreseeable future. The country's global β ($\beta_{country,global}$) is 1.1. The U.S Treasury bond rate is 4%, and the expected inflation rate in the emerging country is 4% compared to 3% in the United states. Estimate the country's risk-free rate (R_f), the return on a diversified portfolio of equities in the emerging country ($R_{country}$), and the country's equity risk premium ($R_{country} - R_f$). What is the cost of equity for a local firm ($k_{e,em}$), whose country β ($\beta_{emfirm,country}$) is 1.3, in the local currency?

Solution:

$$R_f = [(1+.04) \times ((1+.04)/(1+.03)) - 1] = .0501 = 5.01\%$$

$$R_{country} \text{ (see Equation 16-8)} = 5.00 + 6.00 = 11.00\%$$

$$(R_{country} - R_f) = 11.00 - 5.01 = 5.99\%$$

$$\beta_{emfirm,global} \text{ (see Equation 16-7)} = 1.3 \times 1.1 = 1.43$$

$$k_{e,em} = 5.01 + 1.43(5.99) = 13.58\%$$

Adjusting CAPM for Country or Political Risk Recall that a country's equity premium reflects systematic risk (i.e., factors affecting all firms). However, the country's equity premium may not capture all the events that could jeopardize a firm's ability to operate. For example, political instability could result in a government that assumes an antiforeign business stance resulting in potential nationalization, limits on repatriation of earnings, capital controls, or the levying of confiscatory or discriminatory taxes. Such factors could increase significantly the firm's likelihood of default. Unless the analyst includes the risk of default by the firm in projecting a local firm's cash flows, the expected cash-flow stream will be overstated to the extent that it does not reflect the costs of financial distress (e.g., higher borrowing costs). If the U.S. Treasury bond rate is used as the risk-free rate in calculating CAPM, adding a country risk premium to the basic CAPM estimate is appropriate. The country risk premium (CRP) often is measured as the difference between the yield on the country's sovereign or government bonds and the U.S. Treasury bond rate of the same maturity. The difference or "spread" is the additional risk premium that investors demand for holding the emerging country's debt rather than U.S. Treasury bonds.

Note a country risk premium should not be added to the cost of equity if the risk-free rate is the country's sovereign or government bond rate, since the effects of specific country or political risk would already be reflected. Consequently, adding a country risk premium would double count the effects of country or political risk.

Standard & Poor's (www.standardardandpoors.com), Moody's Investors Service (www.moodys.com), and Fitch IBCA (www.fitchibca.com) provide sovereign bond spreads. In practice, the sovereign bond spread is computed from a bond with the same maturity as the U.S. benchmark Treasury bond used to compute the risk-free rate for the calculation of the cost of equity. The U.S. benchmark rate usually is the 10-year Treasury bond rate.

Global CAPM Formulation (Emerging Countries) To estimate the cost of equity for a firm in an emerging economy ($k_{e,em}$), Equation 16-5 can be modified for specific country risk as follows:

$$k_{e,em} = R_f + \beta_{emfirm,global} \ (R_{country} - R_f) + FSP + CRP \tag{16-9}$$

where

R_f = local risk-free rate or the U.S. Treasury bond rate converted to a local nominal rate if cash flows are in the local currency (see Equation 16-6); if cash flows are in dollars, the U.S. Treasury bond rate.

$(R_{country} - R_f)$ = difference between expected return on a well-diversified equity index in the local country or in a similar country and the risk-free rate.

$\beta_{emfirm,global}$ = emerging country firm's global β (see Equation 16-7)

FSP = firm size premium reflecting the additional return smaller firms must earn relative to larger firms to attract investors

CRP = specific country risk premium expressed as difference between the local country's (or a similar country's) government bond rate and the U.S. Treasury bond rate of the same maturity. Add to the CAPM estimate only if the U.S. Treasury bond rate is employed as a proxy for the local country's risk-free rate.

Estimating the Local Firm's Cost of Debt in Emerging Markets

The cost of debt for an emerging market firm (i_{emfirm}) should be adjusted for default risk due to events related to the country and those specific to the firm. When a local corporate bond rate is not available, the cost of debt for a specific local firm may be estimated by using an interest rate in the home country (i_{home}) that reflects a level of creditworthiness comparable to the firm in the emerging country. The country risk premium (CRP) is added to the appropriate home country interest rate to reflect the impact of such factors as political instability on i_{emfirm}. Therefore, the cost of debt can be expressed as follows:

$$i_{emfirm} = i_{home} + CRP \tag{16-10}$$

Most firms in emerging markets are not rated. Therefore, to determine which home country interest rate to select, it is necessary to assign a credit rating to the local firm. This "synthetic" credit rating may be obtained by comparing financial ratios for the target firm to those used by U.S. rating agencies. The estimate of the unrated firm's credit rating may be obtained by comparing interest coverage ratios used by Standard & Poor's to the firm's interest coverage ratio to determine how S&P would rate the firm. See Exhibit 16-5 for an illustration of how to calculate the cost of emerging market debt.

Exhibit 16-5
Estimating the Cost of Debt in Emerging Market Countries

Assume a firm in an emerging market has annual operating income before interest and taxes of $550 million and annual interest expense of $18 million. This implies an interest coverage ratio of 30.6 (i.e., $550/$18). For Standard & Poors, this corresponds to an AAA rating. The current interest rate on U.S. triple A rated bonds is 6.0%. Assume further that the country's government bond rate is 10.3% and that the U.S. Treasury bond rate is 5%. Assume the firm's marginal tax rate is .4. What is the firm's cost of debt before and after tax?

Solution:

$$\text{Cost of debt before taxes (see Equation 16-10)} = 6.0 + (10.3 - 5.0) = 11.3\%$$

$$\text{After-tax cost of debt} = 11.3 \times (1 - .4) = 6.78\%$$

Exhibit 16-6 illustrates the calculation of WACC in cross-border transactions. Note the adjustments made to the estimate of the cost of equity for firm size and country risk. Note also the adjustment made to the local borrowing cost for country risk. The risk-free rate of return is the U.S. Treasury bond rate converted to a local nominal rate of interest.

Exhibit 16-6
Estimating the Weighted Average Cost of Capital (WACC)
in Cross-Border Transactions

Acquirer Inc., a U.S.-based corporation, wants to purchase Target Inc. Acquirer's management believes that the country in which Target is located is segmented from global capital markets, because the β estimated by regressing the financial returns on the country's stock market with those of a global index is significantly different from one.

Assumptions: The current U.S. Treasury bond rate (R_{us}) is 5%. The expected inflation rate in the target's country is 6% annually as compared to 3% in the United States. The country's risk premium (CRP) provided by Standard & Poor's is estimated to be 2.0%. Based on Target's interest coverage ratio, its credit rating is estimated to be AA. The current interest rate on AA rated U.S. corporate bonds is 6.25%. Acquirer Inc. receives a tax credit for taxes paid in a foreign country. Since its marginal tax rate is higher than the target's, Acquirer's marginal tax rate of .4 is used in calculating WACC. Acquirer's pretax cost of debt is 6%. The firm's total capitalization consists only of common equity and debt. Acquirer's projected debt-to-total capital ratio is .3.

Target's β and the country β are estimated to be 1.3 and .7, respectively. The equity premium is estimated to be 6% based on the spread between the prospective return on the country's equity index and the estimated risk-free rate of return. In view of its relatively small $1 billion market capitalization, Target's size premium (FSP) is estimated at 1.2% (see Chapter 7: Table 7-1). What is the appropriate weighted average cost of capital Acquirer should use to discount target's projected annual cash flows expressed in its own local currency?

Solution:

$$k_{e,em} \text{ (see Equation 16-9)} = ((1+.05) \times ((1+.06)/(1+.03)) - 1)$$
$$\times 100^1 + 1.3 \times .7(6.0) + 1.2 + 2.0 = 16.72\%$$

$$i_{local} \text{ (see Equation 16-10)} = 6.25 + 2.0 = 8.25\%$$

$$wacc_{em} \text{ (see Equation 7-4)} = 16.72 \times .(1-.3) + 8.25 \times (1-.4) \times .3 = 13.19\%$$

[1] Note that the expression $((1+.05) \times ((1+.06)/(1+.03)) - 1) \times 100$ represents the conversion of the U.S. Treasury bond rate to a local nominal rate of interest using Equation 16-6. Also note that $1.3 \times .7$ results in the estimation of target's global β, as indicated in Equation 16-7.

Table 16-2 summarizes methods commonly used for valuing cross-border transactions involving firms in developed and emerging countries. The WACC calculation assumes the firm uses only common equity and debt financing. Note that the country risk premium is added to both the cost of equity and the after-tax cost of debt in calculating the WACC for a target firm in an emerging country, if the U.S. Treasury bond rate (or home country government bond rate) is used as the risk-free rate of return. The analyst should avoid adding the country risk premium to the cost of equity if the risk-free rate used to estimate the cost of equity is the local country's government bond rate. References to home and local countries in Table 16-2 refer to the acquirer's and the target's countries, respectively.

Evaluating Risk Using Scenario Planning

Many emerging countries have few publicly traded firms and even fewer M& A transactions to serve as guides in valuing companies. Furthermore, with countries such as China and India growing at or near double-digit rates, the future may be too dynamic to rely on discounted cash flows. Projecting cash flows beyond 3 years may seem like pure guesswork.

As an alternative to making seemingly arbitrary adjustments to the target firm's cost of capital, the acquirer may incorporate risk into the valuation by considering alternative economic scenarios for the emerging country. The variables that would define these alternative scenarios could include GDP growth, inflation rates, interest rates, and foreign exchange rates. Each of these variables can be used to project cash flows using regression analysis. The scenarios may also be built on alternative industry or political conditions. For example, a best case scenario can be based on projected cash flows assuming the emerging market's economy grows at a moderate real growth rate of 2% per annum for the next 5 years. Alternative scenarios could assume a 1- to 2-year recession. A third scenario could assume a dramatic devaluation of the country's currency. The NPVs are weighted by subjectively determined probabilities. The actual valuation of the target firm reflects the expected value of the three scenarios. Note that if a scenario approach is used to incorporate risk in the valuation, there is no need to modify the discount rate for perceived political and economic risk in the local country. See Chapter 8 (Exhibit 8-10) for a more detailed discussion and illustration of scenario planning in the context of a decision tree framework.

TABLE 16-2   Common Methodologies for Valuing Cross-Border Transactions

Developed Countries (Integrated Capital Markets)	Emerging Countries (Segmented Capital Markets)
Step 1: Project and Convert Cash Flows	Step 1: Project and Convert Cash Flows
a. Project target's cash flows in local currency.	a. Project target's cash flows in local currency.
b. Convert local cash flows into acquirer's home currency employing forward exchange rates projected using interest rate parity theory.	b. Convert local cash flows into acquirer's home currency using forward exchange rates. Project exchange rates using purchasing power parity theory, if little reliable data on interest rates available.
Step 2. Adjust Discount Rates	Step 2. Adjust Discount Rates
$k_{e,dev} = R_f + \beta_{devfirm,global}{}^1 (R_m - R_f) + FSP$ $i = \text{cost of debt}^3$ $wacc = k_e \times W_e + i(1-t) \times W_d$	$k_{e,em} = R_f + \beta_{emfirm,global}{}^1 (R_{country} - R_f)^2$ $\qquad + FSP + CRP$ $i_{local} = i_{home} + CRP$ $wacc = k_e \times W_e + i_{local} (1-t) \times W_d$
a. R_f is the long-term government bond rate in the home country	a. R_f is long-term government bond rate in the local country or the U.S. Treasury bond rate converted to a local nominal rate if cash flows in local currency; if cash flows in dollars, the U.S. Treasury bond rate. Note if local risk-free rate used, do not add CRP.
b. $\beta_{devfirm,global}$ is nondiversifiable risk associated with a well-diversified global, U.S., or local country equity index.	
c. R_m is the return on a well-diversified U.S., local, or global equity index	b. $\beta_{emfirm,global}$ is nondiversifiable risk associated with target's local country β and local country's global β.
d. FSP is the firm size premium	
e. t is the appropriate marginal tax rate	c. $R_{country}$ is the return on a diversified local equity index or a similar country's index
f. W_e is the acquirer's target equity to total capital ratio and W_d is $1 - W_e$	d. CRP is the country risk premium
	e. $i_{home} = $ Home country cost of debt
	f. $i_{local} = $ Local country cost of debt

Notes:

[1] β may be estimated directly for firms, whose business is heavily dependent on exports, operating in either developing or emerging countries, by directly regressing the firm's historical financial returns against returns on a well-diversified global equity index. For firms operating primarily in their home markets, β may be estimated indirectly by using Equation 16-7.

[2] $(R_{country} - R_f)$ also could be the equity premium for well-diversified U.S. or global equity indices if the degree of local segmentation is believed to be small.

[3] For developed countries, either the home or local country cost of debt may be used. There is no need to add a country risk premium, as would be the case in estimating a local emerging country's cost of debt.

While building risk into the projected cash flows is equivalent to adjusting the discount rate in applying the discounted cash-flow method, it also appears to be subject to making arbitrary or highly subjective adjustments. What are the appropriate scenarios to be simulated? How many of the scenarios are needed to incorporate adequately risk into the projections? What is the likelihood of each scenario occurring? The primary advantage of adopting a scenario approach is that it forces the analyst to evaluate a wider range of possible outcomes. The major disadvantage is the substantial additional effort required.

Empirical Studies of Financial Returns to International Diversification

International Diversification May Contribute to Higher Financial Returns

Empirical studies suggest that international diversification may increase financial returns by reducing risk, if economies are relatively uncorrelated (Delios and Beamish, 1999; Madura and Whyte, 1990; Tang and Tikoo, 1999). Higher financial returns from international diversification may also be attributable to potential economies of scale and scope, geographic location advantages associated with being nearer customers, increasing the size of the firm's served market, and learning new technologies (Caves, 1982; Zahra, Ireland, and Hitt, 2000). Controversy continues as to whether returns are higher for multinational companies that diversify across countries or across industries spanning political boundaries. In either case, the importance of selecting an appropriate country remains very important. Diermeier and Solnik (2001) provide evidence that supports diversifying across industries. Isakov and Sonney (2002) find evidence of the importance of country choice.

Foreign Buyers of U.S. Firms Tend to Pay Higher Premiums Than U.S. Buyers Pay

Foreign bidders have historically paid higher premiums to acquire U.S. firms than have domestic acquirers of U.S. firms. Harris and Ravenscraft (1991) showed that between 1970 and 1987, foreign acquirers paid an average of 10 percentage points in higher premiums than did U.S. acquirers. The higher premiums often resulted from more favorable foreign currency exchange rates, contributing to lower overall purchase prices when expressed in terms of foreign currency. Between 1990 and 2005, the premium paid by foreign buyers of U.S. firms over those paid by U.S. acquirers has narrowed to about 4 percentage points on average (*Mergerstat Review*, 2005). The continued higher premiums paid by foreign buyers may reflect their efforts to preempt U.S. buyers, U.S. target firm shareholders lack of familiarity with foreign acquirers, and concern that the transaction will not be consummated due to political (e.g., Unocal and CNOOC) and economic considerations (i.e., lack of financial resources).

Returns for Cross-Border Transactions Consistent with Domestic Results

Event studies analyze returns on or about the announcement of a merger or acquisition. Abnormal returns are those that are either more or less than would have been predicted given the competitive conditions and risk characteristics of the industry(ies) in which the buyer and seller competes. Shareholders of target firms in cross-border transactions receive substantial abnormal returns. Such returns for shareholders of U.S. targets of foreign buyers range from about 23% (Kuipers, Miller, and Patel, 2003) to about 40% (Eun *et al.*, 1996; Harris and Ravenscraft, 1991; Servaes and Zenner, 1994; Seth, Song, and Pettit, 2000).

Abnormal returns to shareholders of U.S. and non-U.S. buyers of foreign firms are about zero to slightly negative (Biswas *et al.*, 1997; Cakici and Tandon, 1996; Eckbo and Thorburn, 2000; Kuipers *et al.*, 2003; Markides and Oyon, 1998; Seth *et al.*, 2000). Moeller and Schlingemann (2002) in a sample of 4430 transactions between 1985 and 1995 compared returns in cross-border transactions to domestic deals and found that U.S. acquirers realize stock returns for cross-border transactions as much as 1% lower than for U.S. deals. The authors argue that increasing global integration, while providing new investment opportunities for multinational businesses, is increasing the level of competition for attractive foreign targets and reducing the gains from diversification into formerly segmented markets. Chatterjee and Aw (2004) for the U.K. and Thorburn (2004) for Canadian targets acquired by U.S. firms also found that bidders buying foreign targets underperform those acquiring domestic firms. In contrast, Chari, Ouimet, and Tesar (2004) found that acquirer returns increase on average by 1.65 to 3.1% when the targets are in emerging markets. This improvement is attributable to the achievement of control (e.g., enabling the protection of intellectual property), the elimination of minority shareholders, and the encouragement of investment in the target by the parent.

Good Corporate Governance Supports Cross-Border M&A Activity

Higher firm valuations are often found in countries with better shareholder protections (La Porta, Lopez-De-Silanes, and Shleifer, 2002; Lemmons and Lins, 2003; Peng, Lee, and Lang, 2005). Leuz, Lins, and Warnock (2004) found that inflows of foreign investment are highest in countries that enforce laws requiring firms to disclose information and to provide good shareholder protections. This finding underscores the importance of countries' having legal systems that actively enforce contracts and prevailing securities laws. Rossi and Volpin (2004) also found that M&A activity is substantially larger in countries with better accounting standards and shareholder safeguards. Moreover, the authors found that targets in cross-border deals are typically from countries with poorer investor protection than in the acquirer's country. The transference of corporate governance practices through cross-border mergers may improve shareholder safeguards and in turn the value of the target firm (Bris and Cabolis, 2004). Target firms in weaker corporate governance countries relative to the acquirer often adopt the better practices because of a change in the country of incorporation of the firm.

Things to Remember

The motives for international corporate expansion include a desire to accelerate growth, achieve geographic diversification, consolidate industries, and to take advantage of natural resources and lower labor costs available elsewhere. Other motives include applying a firm's widely recognized brand name or unique intellectual property in new markets, minimizing tax liabilities, following customers into foreign markets, as well as avoiding such entry barriers as tariffs and import barriers. Alternative strategies for entering foreign markets include exporting, licensing, alliances/joint ventures, solo ventures or greenfield operations (i.e., establishing new wholly owned subsidiaries), and mergers and acquisitions.

The methodology for valuing cross-border transactions is quite similar to that employed when both the acquiring and target firms are within the same country. The methodology involves projecting the target firm's cash flows and converting these future cash flows to current or present values using an appropriate discount rate. The basic differences between within-country and cross-border valuation methods is that the latter involves converting cash flows from one currency into another and adjusting the discount rate for risks not generally found when the acquirer and target firms are within the same country. An important issue in calculating the cost of equity for cross-border transactions is the degree of integration of global capital markets. If markets are integrated, a global β and a global equity premium are appropriate. However, in segmented markets, a local β and a local equity premium should be used.

Chapter Discussion Questions

16-1. Find a recent example of a cross-border merger or acquisition in the business section of a newspaper. Discuss the motives for the transaction. What challenges would the acquirer experience in managing/integrating the target firm? Be specific.

16-2. Classify the countries of the acquirer and target in a recent cross-border merger or acquisition as developed or emerging. Identify the criteria you use to classify the countries. How might your classification of the target firm's country affect the way you analyze the target firm?

16-3. Describe the circumstances under which a firm may find a merger or acquisition a more favorable market entry strategy than a joint venture with a firm in the local country.

16-4. Discuss some of the options commonly used to finance international transactions. If you were the Chief Financial Officer of the acquiring firm, what factors would you consider in determining how to finance a transaction?

16-5. Compare and contrast laws that might affect acquisitions by a foreign firm in the United States. In the European Union.

16-6. Discuss the circumstances under which a non-U.S. buyer may choose a U.S. corporate structure as its acquisition vehicle. A limited liability company? A partnership?

16-7. What factors influence the selection of which tax rate to use (i.e., the target's or the acquirer's) in calculating the weighted average cost of capital in cross-border transactions?

16-8. Discuss adjustments commonly made in estimating the cost of debt in emerging countries.

16-9. Find an example of a recent cross-border transaction in the business section of a newspaper. Discuss the challenges an analyst might face in valuing the target firm.

16-10. Discuss the various types of adjustments for risk that might be made to the global CAPM before valuing a target firm in an emerging country. Be specific.

Answers to these Chapter Discussion Questions are found in the Online Instructor's Manual for instructors using this book

Chapter Business Case

Case Study 16-3
Political Risk of Cross-Border Transactions: CNOOC's Aborted Attempt to Acquire Unocal

Background

In what may be the most politicized takeover battle in U.S. history, Unocal announced on August 11, 2005, that its shareholders overwhelmingly approved the proposed buyout by Chevron. The combined companies will produce the equivalent of 2.8 million barrels of oil per day and the acquisition will increase Chevron's reserves by about 15%. With both companies owning assets in similar regions, it is easier to cut duplicate costs. The deal also makes Chevron the top international oil company in the fast-growing Southeast Asia market. Unocal is much smaller than Chevron. As a pure exploration and production company, Unocal has operations in nine countries. Chevron operates gas stations, drilling rigs, and refineries in 180 countries.

The Transaction Timeline

Sensing an opportunity, Chevron moved ahead with merger talks and made an all-stock $16 billion offer for Unocal in late February 2005. Unocal rebuffed the offer as inadequate and sought bids from China's CNOOC and Italy's ENI SPA. While CNOOC offered $17 billion in cash, ENI was willing to offer only $16 billion. Chevron subsequently raised its all-stock offer to $16.5 billion, in line with the board's maximum authorization. Hours before final bids were due, CNOOC informed Unocal it was not going to make any further bids. Believing that the bidding process was over, Unocal and Chevron signed a merger agreement on April 4, 2005. The merger agreement was endorsed by Unocal's board and cleared all regulatory hurdles. Despite its earlier reluctance, CNOOC boosted its original bid to $18.5 billion in late June to counter the Chevron offer. About three-fourths of CNOOC's all-cash offer was financed through below market rate loans provided by its primary shareholder, the Chinese government. On July 22, Chevron upped its offer to $17.7 billion, of which about 60% was in stock and 40% in cash. By the time Unocal shareholders actually approved the deal, the appreciation in Chevron's stock boosted the value of the deal to more than $18.1 billion.

The Political Firestorm

CNOOC's all-cash offer of $67 per share in June sparked instant opposition from members of Congress, who demanded a lengthy review by President George Bush and introduced legislation to place even more hurdles in CNOOC's way. Hoping to allay fears, CNOOC offered to sell Unocal's U.S. assets and promised to retain all of Unocal's workers, something Chevron was not prone to do. CNOOC also argued that its bid was purely commercial and not connected in any way with the Chinese government. U.S. lawmakers expressed concern that Unocal's oil drilling technology might have military applications and that CNOOC's ownership structure (i.e., 70% owned by the Chinese government) would enable the firm to secure low-cost financing that was unavailable to Chevron. The final blow to CNOOC's bid was an amendment to an energy bill passed in July requiring the Departments of Energy, Defense, and Homeland Security to spend 4 months studying the proposed takeover before granting federal approval.

China's Reaction

Perhaps somewhat naively, the Chinese government viewed the low-cost loans as a way to "recycle" a portion of the huge accumulation of dollars they were experiencing. While the Chinese remained largely silent through the political maelstrom, CNOOC's management appeared to be greatly surprised and embarrassed by the public criticism in the United States about the proposed takeover of a major U.S. company. Up to that point, the only other major U.S. firm acquired by a Chinese firm was the 2004 acquisition of IBM's personal computer business by Lenovo, the largest PC manufacturer in China. While the short-term effects of the controversy appear benign, the long-term implications are less clear. It remains to be seen how well international business and politics can coexist between the world's major economic and military superpower and China, an emerging economic and military superpower in its own right.

Conclusions

Cross-border transactions often require considerable political risk. In emerging countries, this is viewed as the potential for expropriation of property or disruption of commerce due to a breakdown in civil order. However, as CNOOC's aborted effort to takeover Unocal illustrates, foreign firms have to be highly sensitive to political and cultural issues in any host country, developed or otherwise.

Case Study Discussion Questions

1. Should CNOOC have been permitted to buy Unocal? Why? Why not?
2. How might the Chinese have been able to persuade U.S. regulatory authorities to approve the transaction?
3. The U.S. and European firms are making substantial investments (including M&As) in China. How should the Chinese government react to this rebuff?

Answers to these Case Study Discussion Questions are available in the Online Instructor's Manual for instructors using this book.

Chapter Business Case

Case Study 16-4
Vodafone AirTouch Acquires Mannesmann in a Record-Setting Deal

On February 4, 2000, Vodafone AirTouch Plc., the world's largest wireless communications company, agreed to buy Mannesmann AG in a $180.0 billion stock swap. At that time, the deal was the largest transaction in M&A history. The value of this transaction exceeded the value of the AOL Time Warner merger at closing by an astonishing $74 billion. Including $17.8 billion in assumed debt, the total value of the transaction soared to $198 billion. After a protracted and heated contest with Mannesmann's management as well as German labor unions and politicians, the deal finally closed on March 30, 2000. In this battle of titans, Klaus Esser, CEO of Mannesmann, the German cellular phone giant, managed to squeeze nearly twice as much money as first proposed out of Vodafone, the British cellular phone powerhouse. This transaction illustrates the intricacies of international transactions in countries in which hostile takeovers are viewed negatively and antitakeover laws generally favor target companies. (See Chapter 3 for a more detailed discussion of antitakeover laws.)

Vodafone AirTouch Corporate Profile

Vodafone AirTouch, itself the product of a $60 billion acquisition of U.S.-based AirTouch Communications in early 1999, is focused on becoming the global leader in wireless communication. Although it believes the growth opportunities are much greater in wireless than in wired communication systems, Vodafone AirTouch has pursued a strategy in which customers in certain market segments are offered a package of integrated wireless and wired services. Vodafone AirTouch is widely recognized for its technological innovation and for pioneering creative new products and services. Vodafone has been a global leader in terms of geographic coverage since 1986 in terms of the number of customers, with more than 12 million at the end of 2000. Vodafone AirTouch's operations cover the vast majority of the European continent, as well as potentially high-growth areas such as Eastern Europe, Africa, and the Middle East. Vodafone AirTouch's geographic coverage received an enormous boost in the United States by entering into the joint venture with Bell Atlantic. Vodafone AirTouch has a 45% interest in the joint venture. The JV has 23 million customers (including 3.5 million paging customers). Covering about 80% of the U.S. population, the joint venture offers cellular service in 49 of the top 50 U.S. markets and is the largest wireless operator in the United States. (See Chapter 12 for a more detailed discussion of this JV.)

Mannesmann's Corporate Profile

Mannesmann is an international corporation headquartered in Germany and focused on the telecommunications, engineering, and automotive markets. Mannesmann transformed itself during the 1990s from a manufacturer of steel pipes, auto components, and materials-handling equipment into Europe's biggest mobile-phone operator. Rapid growth in its telecom activities has accounted for much of the growth in the value of the company in recent years.

Strategic Rationale for the Merger

With Mannesmann, Vodafone AirTouch intends to consolidate its position in Europe and then to undertake a global brand strategy. In Europe, Vodafone and Mannesmann will have controlling stakes in 10 European markets, giving the new company the most extensive European coverage of any wireless carrier. Vodafone AirTouch will benefit from the additional coverage provided by Mannesmann in Europe, whereas Mannesmann's operations will benefit from Vodafone AirTouch's excellent U.S. geographic coverage. The merger will create a superior platform for the development of mobile data and Internet services.

Mannesmann's "Just Say No" Strategy

What supposedly started on friendly terms soon turned into a bitter battle, involving a personal duel between Chris Gent, Vodafone's CEO, and Klaus Esser, Mannesmann's CEO. In November 1999, Vodafone AirTouch had announced for the first time its intention to make a takeover bid for Mannesmann. Mannesmann's board rebuked the overture as inadequate noting its more favorable strategic position. After the Mannesmann management had refused a second, more attractive bid, Vodafone AirTouch went directly to the Mannesmann shareholders with a tender offer. A central theme in Vodafone AirTouch's appeal to Mannesmann shareholders was what it described as the extravagant cost of Mannesmann's independent strategy. Relations between Chris Gent and Klaus Esser turned highly contentious.

The decision to undertake a hostile takeover was highly risky. Numerous obstacles stood in the way of foreign acquirers of German companies.

Culture Clash

Hostile takeovers of German firms by foreign firms are rare. It is even rarer when it turns out to be one of the nation's largest corporations. Vodafone AirTouch's initial offer immediately was decried as a job killer. The German tabloids painted a picture of a pending bloodbath for Mannesmann and its 130,000 employees if the merger took place. Vodafone AirTouch had said that it was only interested in Mannesmann's successful telecommunications operations and that it was intending to sell off the companies' engineering and automotive businesses, which employ about 80% of Mannesmann's total workforce. The prospect of what was perceived to be a less caring foreign firm doing the same thing led to appeals from numerous political factions for government protection against the takeover.

German law at the time also stood as a barrier to an unfriendly takeover. German corporate law required that 75% of outstanding shares be tendered before control is transferred. In addition, the law allows individual shareholders to block deals with court challenges that can drag on for years. In a country where hostile takeovers are rare, public opinion was squarely behind management.

To defuse the opposition from German labor unions and the German government, Chris Gent said that the deal would not result in any job cuts and the rights of the employees and trade unions would be fully preserved. Moreover, Vodafone would accept fully the Mannesmann corporate culture including the principle of codetermination through employee representation on the Mannesmann supervisory board. Because of these reassurances, the unions decided to support the merger.

The Offer Mannesmann Could Not Refuse

When it became clear that Vodafone's attempt at a hostile takeover might succeed, the Mannesmann management changed its strategy and agreed to negotiate the terms for a friendly takeover. The final agreement is based on an improved offer for Mannesmann shareholders to exchange their shares in the ratio of 58.96 Vodafone AirTouch shares for one Mannesmann share, an improvement over the previous offer of 53.7 to 1. Furthermore, the agreement defined terms for the integration of the two companies. For example, Dusseldorf was retained as one of two European headquarters with responsibility for Mannesmann's existing continental European mobile and fixed-line telephone business. Moreover, with the exception of Esser, all of Mannesmann's top managers would remain in place.

Epilogue

Undoubtedly, the Mannesmann shareholders could celebrate their sweet victory. Throughout the hostile takeover battle, Vodafone AirTouch had said that it was reluctant to offer Mannesmann shareholders more than 50% of the new company; in sharp contrast, Mannesmann had said all along that it would not accept a takeover that gives its shareholders a minority interest in the new company. Esser managed to get Mannesmann shareholders almost 50% ownership in the new firm, despite Mannesmann contributing only about 35% of the operating earnings of the new company.

Vodafone, currently the world's largest (by revenue) cell phone service provider, has experienced continuing share price erosion amidst intensifying product price erosion from competition in Western European markets and new technologies such as Internet calling which are slowing revenue growth and shrinking profit margins. Shares in Vodafone have underperformed the U.K. market by 40% since the firm acquired Mannesmann. In 2006, the company recorded an impairment charge of $49 billion. This charge reflected the lower current value of the Mannesmann assets acquired by Vodafone in 2000, effectively making it official that the firm has substantially overpaid for Mannesmann.

While hostile bids were relatively rare at the time of the Vodafone–Mannesmann transaction, they have become increasingly more common in recent years. Since 2002, Europe has seen more hostile or unsolicited deals than in the United States. In part, Europe is simply catching up to the United States after many years in which there were virtually no hostile bids. For years, national governments and regulators in Europe had been able to deter easily cross-border deals that they felt could threaten national interests, even though European Union rules are supposed to allow a free and fair market within its jurisdiction. However, the rise of big global rivals, as well as a rising tide of activist investors, is making companies more assertive.

Case Study Discussion Questions

1. Who do you think negotiated the best deal for their shareholders, Chris Gent or Klaus Esser? Explain your answer in terms of short- and long-term impacts.
2. Both firms were pursuing a similar strategy of expanding their geographic reach. Does this strategy make sense? Why or why not? What are the risks associated with this strategy?
3. Do you think the use of all stock, rather than cash or a combination of cash and stock, to acquire Mannesmann helped or hurt Vodafone AirTouch's shareholders? Explain your answer.
4. Do you think that Vodafone AirTouch conceded too much to the labor unions and Mannesmann's management to get the deal done? Explain your answer.
5. What problems do you think Vodafone AirTouch might experience if they attempt to introduce what they view as "best operating practices" to the Mannesmann culture? How might these challenges be overcome? Be specific.

Answers to these Case Study Discussion Questions are available in the Online Instructor's Manual for instructors using this book.

References

Anand, J., and A. Delios, "Absolute and Relative Resources as Determinants of International Acquisitions," *Journal of Strategic Management*, Vol. 23, 2002, pp. 119–134.

Anderson, U., Johanson, J., and J. E. Vahlne, "Organic Acquisitions in the International Process of the Business Firm," *Management International Review*, Vol. 37, 1997, pp. 67–84.

Barkema, H. G., and F. Vermeulen, "International Expansion through Start-Up or Acquisition: A Learning Perspective," *Journal of the Academy of Management*, 1998, pp. 7–26.

Bekaert, G., and C. R. Harvey, "Research in Emerging Markets Finance: Looking to the Future," Presentation to the Conference on Valuation in Emerging Markets at University of Virginia, Charlottesville, VA, May 28–30, 2002, p. 3.

Berk, J. B., "A Critique of Size Related Anomalies," *The Review of Financial Studies*, Vol. 8, 1995, pp. 275–286.

Birkett, Kirsten, "Sweets to the Sweet: Cadbury Schweppes Buys Adams," Shearman & Sterling, crossborder.practicallaw.com/3-102-3481?jurisFilter=&tab=5, May 27, 2003.

Blackman, Andrew, "Your U.S. Fund May Be Scurrying Abroad," *The Wall Street Journal*, February 5, 2006, p. C2.

Bodnar, G., B. Dumas, and R. Marston, "Cross-border Valuations: The International Cost of Capital," INSEAD Working Paper, Fontainebleau, France, 2003.

Bris, Arturo, and Christos Cabolis, "Adopting Better Corporate Governance: Evidence from Cross-border Mergers," Yale Working Paper, New Haven, CT, January 2004.

Brouthers, K. D., "Institutional, Cultural, and Transaction Cost Influences on Entry Mode Choice and Performance," *Journal of International Business Studies*, Vol. 33, 2002, pp. 203–221.

Brouthers, K. D., and L. E. Brouthers, "Acquisition, Greenfield Start-up: Institutional, Cultural, and Transaction Cost Influences," *Strategic Management Journal*, Vol. 21, 2000, pp. 89–97.

Bryan-Low, Cassell, "European Telecoms Vie for Emerging Markets," *The Wall Street Journal*, December 10, 2005, p. B2.

Cakici, N. G., and K. Tandon, "Foreign Acquisitions in the U.S.: Effects on Shareholder Wealth of Foreign Acquiring Firms," *Journal of Banking and Finance*, Vol. 20, 1996, pp. 307–329.

Caves, R. E., *Multinational Enterprise and Economic Analysis*, Cambridge University Press, Cambridge, MA, 1982.

Ceneboyan, A. S., G. J. Papaioannou, and N. Travlos, "Foreign Takeover Activity in the U.S. and Wealth Effects for Target Firm Shareholders," *Financial Management*, Vol. 31, 1991, pp. 58–68.

Chakrabarti, Rajesh, N. Jayaraman, and S. Mukherjee, "Mars-Venus Marriages: Culture and Cross-Border M&A," Working Paper, Georgia Institute of Technology, Atlanta, GA, March 2005.

Chan, K. C., G. A. Karolyi, and R. M. Stulz, "Global Financial Markets and the Risk Premium of U.S. Equity," *Journal of Financial Economics*, Vol. 32, 1992, pp. 137–167.

Chari, Anusha, Paige Ouiment, and Linda Tesar, "Cross-border Mergers and Acquisitions in Emerging Markets: The Stock Market Valuation of Corporate Control," University of Michigan Working Paper, Ann Arbor, MI, March 2004.

Chatterjee, R. A., and M. S. B. Aw, "The Performance of UK: Firms Acquiring Large Cross-Border and Domestic Takeover Targets, *Applied Financial Economics*, Vol. 14, 2004, pp. 337–349.

Chen, C., and C. Findlay, "A Review of Cross-border Mergers and Acquisitions in APEC," The Australian National University, Canberra, 2002.

Child, J., D. Falkner, and R. Pitkethley, *The Management of International Acquisitions*, Oxford University Press, Oxford, 2001.

Davis, P. S., Desai, A. B., and J. D. Fracis, "Mode of International Entry: An Isomorphian Perspective," *Journal of International Business Studies*, Vol. 31, 2000, pp. 239–258.

Delios, A., and P. W. Beamish, "Ownership Strategy of Japanese Firms: Transactional and Institutional Influence," *Strategic Management Journal*, Vol. 20, 1999, pp. 915–933.

Delios, A., and P. W. Beamish, "Geographic Scope, Product Diversification, and the Corporate Performance of Japanese Firms," *Strategic Management Journal*, Vol. 20, 1999, pp. 711–727.

Desai, Mehir, A., C. Frity Foley, and James R. Hines, "The Costs of Shared Ownership: Evidence from International Joint Ventures," Harvard Business School Working Paper, No. 03-017, July 2002.

Dewenter, K. L., "Does the Market React Differently to Domestic and Foreign Takeover Announcements? Evidence from the U.S. Chemical and Retail Industries," *Journal of Financial Economics*, Vol. 37, 1995, pp. 421–441.

Diermeier, J., and B. Solnik, "Global Pricing of Equity," *Financial Analysts Journal*, Vol. 57, 2001, pp. 17–47.

Dunning, J., *Multinational Enterprises and the Global Economy*, Addison-Wesley, Reading, MA, 1993.

Dunning, J. H., "The Eclectic Paradigm of International Production: A Restatement and Some Possible Extensions," *Journal of International Business Studies*, 1988, pp. 1–31.

Eckbo, E., and K. S. Thorburn, "Gains to Bidder Firms Revisited: Domestic and Foreign Acquisitions in Canada," *Journal of Financial and Quantitative Analysis*, Vol. 35, March 2000, pp. 1–25.

Eun, C. S., R. Kolodny, and C. Scherage, "Cross-Boarder Acquisition and Shareholder Wealth: Tests of the Synergy and Internationalization Hypotheses," *Journal of Banking and Finance*, Vol. 20, 1996, pp. 1559–1582.

Eun, Cheol S., Wei Huang, and Sandy Lai, "International Diversification with Large and Small Cap Stocks," *Journal of Financial and Quantitative Analysis*, 2007.

Farrell, Diana, Aneta Marcheva Key, and Tim Shavers, "Mapping the Global Capital Markets," *McKinsey Quarterly*, December 2, 2006.

Feliciano, Z., and R. E. Lipsey, "Foreign Entry Into U.S. Manufacturing by Takeovers and the Creation of New Firms," Working Paper 9122, National Bureau of Economic Research, 2002.

Ferreira, Manuel P., and Stephen B. Tallman, "Building and Leveraging Knowledge Capabilities Through Cross-Border Acquisitions," Presentation to the Academy of Management Meeting, Cambridge, MA, 2005.

Graham, John R., and Campbell R. Harvey, "The Theory and Practice of Corporate Finance: Evidence from the Field," *Journal of Financial Economics*, Vol. 60, 2001, pp. 187–243.

Harris, R. S., and David Ravenscraft, "The Role of Acquisitions in Foreign Direct Investment: Evidence from the U.S. Stock Market," *Journal of Finance*, Vol. 46, 1991, pp. 825–844.

Harvey, Campbell R., "Twelve Ways to Calculate the International Cost of Capital," Duke University and National Bureau of Economic Research Working Paper, Durham, NC, October 14, 2005.

Harzing, A. W., "Acquisitions versus Greenfield Investments: International Strategy and Management of Entry Modes," *Strategic Management Journal*, Vol. 23, 2002, pp. 211–227.

Hennart, J. F., and Y. R. Park, "Location, Governance, and Strategic Determinants of Japanese Manufacturing Investment in the United States," *Journal of Strategic Management*, Vol. 15, 1993, pp. 419–436.

Hennart, J. F., and S. Reddy, "The Choice between Mergers, Acquisitions, and Joint Ventures: The Case of Japanese Investors in the United States," *Strategic Management Journal*, Vol. 18, 1997, pp. 1–12.

Hitt, M. A., and R. D. Ireland, "The Intersection of Entrepreneurship and Strategic Management Research," in D. Sexton and H. Landstrom, Eds., *The Blackwell Handbook of Entrepreneurship*, Blackwell Oxford, 2000.

Hitt, M. A., R. E. Hoskisson, and H. Kim, "International Diversification: Effects on Innovation and Firm Performance in Product Diversified Firms," *Academy of Management Journal*, Vol. 40, 1999, pp. 767–798.

Hoffman, W. H., and W. Schaper-Rinkel, "Acquire or Ally?—A Strategic Framework for Deciding Between Acquisition and Cooperation," *Management International Review*, Vol. 41, 2001, pp. 131–159.

Inkpen, A. C., and P. W. Beamish, "Knowledge, Bargaining Power, and the Instability of International Joint Ventures," *The Academy of Management Review*, Vol. 22, 1997, pp. 177–202.

Isakov, D., and F. Sonney, "Are Parishioners Right? On the relative importance of Industrial Factors in International Stock Returns," Working Paper, HEC-University of Geneva, 2002.

Kang, N. H., and S. Johansson, "Cross-border Mergers and Acquisitions: Their Role in Industrial Globalization," STI Working Papers 2000/1, Paris: OECD, 2001.

Khanna, T., K. Palepu, and J. Sinha, "Strategies That Fit Emerging Markets," *Harvard Business Review*, Vol. 83, 2005.

Koedijk, K., and M. Van Dijk, "The Cost of Capital of Cross-Listed Firms," Erasmus University, Working Paper, Rotterdam, 2000.

Koedijk, K., C. Kool, P. Schotman, and M. Van Kijk, "The Cost of Capital in International Markets: Local or Global," Centre for Economic Policy Research, Working Paper, London, UK, 2002.

Kogut, B., and H. Singh, "The Effect of National Culture on the Choice of Entry Mode," *Journal of International Business Studies*, Vol. 19, 1988, pp. 411–432.

Kuipers, D., D. Mieer, and A. Patel, "The Legal Environment and Corporate Valuation: Evidence from Cross-border Mergers," Texas Tech Working Paper, Lubbock, TX, January 2003.

Langford, R., and C. Brown, "Making M&A Pay: Lessons from the World's Most Successful Acquirers," Strategy and Leadership, Vol. 32, 2004, pp. 5–14.

La Porta, R., F. Lopez-De-Silanes, and A. Shleifer, "Investor Protection and Corporate Valuation," *Journal of Finance*, Vol. 57, 2002, pp. 147–170.

Lemmons, M. L., and K. V. Lins, "Ownership Structure, Corporate Governance, and Firm Value: Evidence from the East Asian Financial Crisis," *Journal of Finance*, Vol. 58, 2003, pp. 1147–1170.

Letto-Gilles, G., M. Meschi, and R. Simonetti, "Cross-border Mergers and Acquisitions: Patterns in the EU and Effects," South Bank University, London, 2001.

Leuz, Christian, Karl V. Lins, and Francis E. Warnock, "Do Foreigners Invest Less in Poorly Governed Firms," University of Virginia, ECGI-Finance Working Paper No. 43, Charlottesville, VA, 2004.

Lins, Karl V., "Equity Ownership and Firm Value in Emerging Markets," *Journal of Financial and Quantitative Analysis*, Vol. 38, 2004, pp. 159–184.

Madura, J., and A. Whyte, "Diversification Benefits of Direct Foreign Investment," *Management International Review*, Vol. 30, 1990, pp. 73–85.

Manzon, K. G. K., D. J. Sharp, and N. Travlos, "An Empirical Study of the Consequences of U.S. Tax Rules for International Acquisitions by U.S. Firms," *Journal of Finance*, Vol. 49, 1994, pp. 1893–1904.

Markides, C., and D. Oyon, "International Acquisitions: Do They Create Value for Shareholders?" *European Management Journal*, Vol. 16, 1998, pp. 125–135.

Meyer, Klaus E., Saul Estrin, and Samon Bhaumik, "Institutions and Business Strategies in Emerging Economies: A Study of Entry Mode Choice," Working Paper, London Business School, November 3, 2005.

Mishra, D., and T. O'Brien, "A Comparison of Cost of Equity Estimates of Local and Global CAPMs," *Financial Review*, Vol. 36, 2001, pp. 27–48.

Moeller, S. B., and F. P. Schlingemann, "Are Cross-border Acquisitions Different from Domestic Acquisitions?" Evidence on Stock and Operating Performance for U.S. Acquirers," University of Pittsburgh Working Paper, Pittsburgh, PA, 2002.

Morck, R., and B. Yeung, "Why Investors Value Multinationality," *Journal of Business*, Vol. 64, 1991, pp. 165–188.

Morosoni, P., S. Shane, and H. Singh, "National Cultural Distance and Cross-Border Acquisition Performance," *Journal of International Business Studies*, Vol. 29, 1998, pp. 137–156.

Pan, Y., and D. K. Tse, "The Hierarchical Model of Market Entry Modes," *Journal of International Business Studies*, Vol. 31, 2000, pp. 535–554.

Pan, Y., and P. S. K. Chi, "Financial Performance and Survival of Multinational Corporations in China," *Strategic Management Journal*, Vol. 20, 1999, pp. 359–374.

Park, S. H., and G. R. Ungson, "The Effect of National Culture, Organizational Complementarity, and Economic Motivation on Joint Venture Dissolution," *Academy of Management Journal*, Vol. 40, 1997, pp. 279–307.

Pay, Y., S. Li, and K. K. Tse, "The Impact of Order and Mode of Market Entry on Profitability and Market Share," *Journal of International Business Studies*, Vol. 30, 1999, pp. 81–104.

Peng, M. W., "Institutional Transitions and Strategic Choices," *Academy of Management Review*, Vol. 28, 2003, pp. 275–296.

Peng, M. W., S. H. Lee, and D. Y. L. Lang, "What Determines the Scope of the Firm Over Time? A Focus on Institutional Relatedness," *Academy of Management Review*, Vol. 30, 2005, pp. 622–633.

PricewaterhouseCoopers, *Mergers and Acquisitions: A Global Tax Guide*, Wiley and Sons, New York, 2006.

Raff, Horst, Michael Ryan, and Frank Staehler, "Asset Ownership and Foreign-Market Entry," CESifo Working Paper No. 1676, Category 7: Trade Policy, February 2006.

Rosenbloom, Arthur H., ed. *Due Diligence for Global Deal Making: The Definitive Guide to Cross-border Mergers and Acquisitions, Joint Ventures, Financings, and Strategic Alliances*, 1st Ed., Bloomberg Press, New York, 2002.

Rossi, Stefano, and Paolo F. Volpin, "Cross-Country Determinants of Mergers and Acquisitions," ECGI-Finance Working Paper No. 25/2003, AFA 2004 San Diego Meetings, September 2004.

Servaes, H., and M. Zenner, "Taxes and the Returns to Foreign Acquisitions in the U.S.," *Financial Management*, Vol. 23, 1994, pp. 42–56.

Seth, A. K., P. Song, and R. Pettit, "Synergy, Managerialism or Hubris? An Empirical Examination of Motives for Foreign Acquisitions of U.S. Firms," *Journal of International Business Studies*, 2000.

Shapiro, Alan C., *Foundations of Multinational Financial Management*, 5th Ed., Wiley & Sons, New York, 2005.

Stulz, R. M., "Globalization of the Capital Markets and the Cost of Capital: The Case of Nestle," *Journal of Applied Corporate Finance*, Vol. 8, 1995a, pp. 30–38.

Stulz, R. M., "The Cost of Capital in Internationally Integrated Markets: The Case of Nestle," *European Financial Management*, Vol. 1, March 1995b, pp. 11–22.

Stulz, R. M., and W. Wasserfallen, "Foreign Equity Invest Restrictions, Capital Flight, and Shareholder Wealth Maximization: Theory and Evidence," *The Review of Financial Studies*, Vol. 8, Winter 1995, pp. 1019–1057.

Tang, C. Y., and S. Tikoo, "Operational Flexibility and Market Valuation of Earnings," *Strategic Management Journal*, Vol. 20, 1999, pp. 749–761.

The Economist, "A Survey of the World Economy," September 16, 2006, p. 12.

Truitt, Wesley B., *The Corporation*, Greenwood Press: Westport, CT, 2006, pp. 139–159.

Vasconcellos, G. M., and R. J. Kish, "Cross-border Mergers and Acquisitions: The European-U.S. Experience," *Journal of Multinational Financial Management*, Vol. 8, 1998, pp. 173–189.

Vasconcellos, G. M., J. Madura, and R. J. Kish, "An Empirical Investigation of Factors Affecting Cross-border Acquisitions: U.S. Versus Non-U.S. Experience," *Global Finance Journal*, Vol. 1, 1990, pp. 173–189.

Vermeulen, F., and H. G. Barkema, "Learning through Acquisitions," *Journal of the Academy of Management*, Vol. 44, 2001, pp. 457–476.

Wilson, B. D., "The Propensity of Multinational Companies to Expand Through Acquisitions," *Journal of International Business Studies*, Vol. 11, 1980, pp. 59–64.

Zahra, S., and G. Elhagrasey, "Strategic Management of International Joint Ventures," *European Management Journal*, Vol. 12, March 1994, pp. 83–93.

Zahra, S. A., R. D. Ireland, and M. A. Hitt, "International Expansion by New Venture Firms: International, Mode of Market Entry, Technological Learning and Performance," *Academy of Management Journal*, 2000, pp. 244–257.

Glossary

Abnormal return   The return to shareholders due to nonrecurring events that differs from what would have been predicted by the market. It is the return due to an event such as a merger or acquisition.

Acquirer   A firm that attempts to acquire a controlling interest in another company.

Acquisition   The purchase by one company of a controlling ownership interest in another firm, a legal subsidiary of another firm, or selected assets of another firm.

Acquisition vehicle   The legal structure used to acquire another company.

Advance notice provision   Requires announcement of shareholders proposals well in advance of the actual vote.

Advance ruling   An IRS ruling sought by acquirers and targets planning to enter into a tax-free transaction. A favorable ruling is often a condition of closing.

Affirmative covenant   A portion of a loan agreement that specifies the actions the borrowing firm agrees to take during the term of the loan.

Agency problems   The conflict of interest between a firm's incumbent managers and shareholders.

Antigreenmail amendments   Amendments to corporate charters restricting the firm's ability to repurchase shares from specific shareholders at a premium.

Antitakeover amendments   Amendments to corporate charters designed to slow or make more expensive efforts to take control of the firm.

Antitrust laws   Federal laws prohibiting individual corporations from assuming too much market power.

Appraisal rights   Rights to seek "fair value" for their shares in court given to target company shareholders who choose not to tender shares in the first or second tier of a tender offer.

Arbitrageurs ("arbs")   In the context of M&As, arbs are speculators who attempt to profit from the difference between the bid price and the target firm's current share price.

Arbitration clause   Wording in a contract defining the type of dispute subject to arbitration and how the arbitrator will be selected.

Articles of incorporation   A document filed with a state government by the founders of a corporation.

Asset-based lending   A type of lending in which the decision to grant a loan is based largely on the quality of the assets collateralizing the loan.

Asset impairment   An asset is said to be impaired according to FASB Statement 142 if its fair value falls below its book or carrying value.

Asset purchases   Transactions in which the acquirer buys all or a portion of the target company's assets and assumes all, some, or none of the target's liabilities.

Assignment   The process through which a committee representing creditors grants the power to liquidate a firm's assets to a third party called an assignee or trustee.

Asymmetric information   Information about a firm that is not equally available to both managers and shareholders.

Auction   Multiple bidders competing for the same target firm.

Audit   An activity consisting of a professional examination and verification of a company's accounting documents and supporting data for the purpose of rendering an opinion as to their fairness, consistency, and conformity with generally accepted accounting principles.

Back-end merger   The merger following either a single- or two-tier tender offer consisting of either a long form or short form merger, with the latter not requiring a target firm shareholder vote.

Back-end plans   A takeover defense in which shareholders receive a dividend of rights, which give them the option of exchanging the rights for cash or senior debt securities at a specific price set by the target's board.

Back-end value   The amount paid in the second stage to those shareholders not participating in the first stage of a two-tier tender offer.

Balance sheet assumptions   Relate to growth in major balance sheet components.

Bankruptcy   A federal legal proceeding designed to protect the technically or legally insolvent firm from lawsuits by its creditors until a decision can be made to shut down or to continue to operate the firm.

Bear hug   A takeover tactic involving the mailing of a letter containing an acquisition proposal to the board of directors of a target company without prior warning and demanding a rapid decision.

Beta (β)   A measure of nondiversifiable risk or the extent to which a firm's (or asset's) return changes because of a change in the market's return.

Bidder   See acquirer.

Blank check preferred stock   Preferred stock that has been authorized but not yet issued.

Boot   The nonequity portion of the purchase price.

Break-up fee   A fee that would be paid to the potential acquirer if the target firm decides to accept an alternative bid. Also called a termination fee.

Bridge financing   Temporary unsecured short-term loans provided by investment banks to pay all or a portion of the purchase price and to meet immediate working capital requirements until permanent or long-term financing is found.

Buildup method   A method of adjusting a firm's discount rate to reflect risks associated with such businesses.

Business alliance   A generic term referring to all forms of business combinations other than mergers and acquisitions.

Business combination provisions State laws forbidding the sale of a target firm's assets for a specific period of time following closing in an attempt to discourage highly leveraged transactions.

Business judgment rule A code of conduct for directors requiring them to act in a manner that could reasonably be seen as being in the best interests of the shareholders. It is a presumption that the courts will not interfere with, or second-guess, business decisions made by directors.

Business-level strategies Strategies pertaining to a specific operating unit or product line within a firm.

Business–market attractiveness matrix A way of comparing the attractiveness of markets with a firm's capabilities.

Business plan A comprehensive analysis of all aspects of a business resulting in a vision for the firm and a strategy for achieving that vision.

Business strategy That portion of a business plan detailing the way the firm intends to achieve its vision.

Buyback See share repurchase plans.

Buyout Change in controlling interest in a corporation.

Capital asset pricing model (CAPM) A framework for measuring the relationship between expected risk and return.

Capital budgeting process A process of allocating available investment funds by prioritizing projects based on projected rates of return.

Capitalization multiple The multiple estimated by dividing one by the estimated discount or capitalization rate which can be used to estimate the value of a business by multiplying it by an indicator of value such as free cash flow.

Capitalization rate The discount rate used by practitioners if the cash flows of the firm are not expected to grow or are expected to grow at a constant rate indefinitely.

Cash cows Businesses generating cash in excess of their reinvestment requirements.

Cash-out provisions State statutes requiring a bidder, whose purchases of stock exceed a stipulated amount, to buy the remainder of the target stock on the same terms granted to those shareholders whose stock was purchased at an earlier date.

Cash-out statutory merger A merger in which the shareholders of the selling firm receive cash or some form on nonvoting investment (e.g., debt, or nonvoting preferred or common stock) for their shares.

Certificate of incorporation A document received from the state once the articles of incorporation have been approved.

Chapter 7 The portion of the U.S. Bankruptcy Code dealing with liquidation of a firm that cannot be reorganized while under the protection of the bankruptcy court.

Chapter 11 That portion of the U.S. Bankruptcy Code dealing with reorganization, which provides for the debtor to remain in possession, unless the court rules otherwise, of the business and in control of its operations.

Chewable poison pill   A poison pill which becomes void in the face of a fully financed offer at a substantial premium to the target firm's current share price.

Choice of law provision   A contract provision in an M&A or alliance agreement indicating which state's or country's laws that will have jurisdiction in settling disputes.

Classified board   An antitakeover defense involving the separation of a firm's board into several classes, only one of which is up for election at any one point in time. Also called a staggered board.

Closing   The phase of the acquisition process in which ownership is transferred from the target to the acquiring firm in exchange for some agreed-upon consideration following the receipt of all necessary shareholder, regulatory, and third-party approvals.

Closing conditions   Stipulations that must be satisfied before closing can take place.

Coinsurance   The combination of firms whose cash flows are relatively uncorrelated.

Collar agreement   An arrangement providing for certain changes in the share-exchange ratio contingent on the level of the acquirer's share price around the effective date of the merger.

Collateralized loan obligations   Loans that are packaged into pools from which different securities are created to sell to investors.

Commitment letter   A document obligating a lender to provide financing.

Common size financial statements   Calculated by taking each line item as a percentage of revenue.

Composition   An agreement in which creditors consent to settling for less than the full amount they are owed.

Concentration   The percentage of an industry's total sales accounted for by a specific number of firms.

Confidentiality agreement   A mutually binding accord defining how information exchanged among the parties may be used and the circumstances under which the discussions may be made public. Also known as a nondisclosure agreement.

Conglomerate discount   The share prices of conglomerates often trade at a discount from focused firms or from their value if they were broken up and sold in pieces.

Conglomerate mergers   Transactions in which the acquiring company purchases firms in largely unrelated industries.

Consent solicitation   A process enabling dissident shareholders in certain states to obtain shareholder support for their proposals by simply obtaining their written consent.

Consolidation   A business combination involving two or more companies joining to form a new company, in which none of the combining firms survive.

Constant growth model   A valuation method that assumes that cash flow will grow at a constant rate.

Contingent claims   A claim that pays off only under certain contingencies.

Contingent payments   Payments to the seller that depend on the achievement of certain revenue, profit, or cash-flow targets.

Contingency plans   Actions that are undertaken if the firm's current business strategy appears not to be working.

Control premium   The excess over the target's current share price the acquirer is willing to pay to gain a controlling interest. A pure control premium would be one in which the anticipated synergies are small, and the perceived value of the purchase is in gaining control of the target.

Core competencies   Bundles of skills that can be applied to extend a firm's product offering in new areas.

Corporate bylaws   Rules governing the internal management of the corporation, which are determined by the corporation's founders.

Corporate charters   A state license defining the powers of the firm and the rights and responsibilities of its shareholders, board of directors, and managers. The charter consists of articles of incorporation and a certificate of incorporation.

Corporate culture   The common set of values, traditions, and beliefs that influence behavior of a firm's employees.

Corporate governance   The systems and controls in place to protect the rights of corporate stakeholders.

Corporate-level strategies   Strategies cutting across business unit organizational lines, which entail such decisions as financing the growth of certain businesses, operating others to generate cash, divesting some units, or pursuing diversification.

Corporate restructuring   Actions taken to expand or contract a firm's basic operations or fundamentally change its asset or financial structure.

Corporate vision   A statement intended to describe the corporation's purpose for existing and where the corporation hopes to go.

Cost leadership   A strategy designed to make a firm the cost leader in its market by constructing efficient production facilities, by tightly controlling overhead expense, and by eliminating marginally profitable customer accounts.

Covenants   Promises made by the borrower that certain acts will be performed and others will be avoided.

Cram down   A legal reorganization occurring whenever one or more classes of creditors or shareholders approve, even though others may not.

Cross-default provisions   Clauses in loan agreements allowing a lender to collect its loan immediately if the borrower is in default on a loan to another lender.

Crown jewels lockup   An arrangement in which the initial bidder obtains an option to buy important strategic assets of the target, if the target chooses to sell to another party.

Cumulative voting rights   In an election for a board of directors, each shareholder is entitled to as many votes as shall equal the number of shares the shareholder owns multiplied by the number of directors to be elected. Furthermore, the shareholder may cast all of these votes for a single candidate or for any two or more of them.

Data room   The seller limits the acquirer's due diligence team to management presentations and selected data made available in a single room.

Dead hand poison pill   A poison pill security containing special features, which prevent the board of directors from taking action to redeem or rescind the pill unless the directors were the same directors who adopted the pill.

Deadlock clause   The portion of a contract that specifies the events triggering a dissolution of the joint venture or partnership.

Deal breakers   Issues that a party to the negotiation cannot concede without making the deal unacceptable.

Deal-structuring process   The process focused on satisfying as many of the primary objectives of the parties involved and determining how risk will be shared.

Debentures   Debt issued that is secured primarily by the cash flow of the issuer.

Debt-for-equity swap   Creditors surrender a portion of their claims on the firm in exchange for an ownership position in the firm.

Debtor in possession   On the filing of a reorganization petition, the firm's current management remains in place to conduct the ongoing affairs of the firm.

Defensive acquisition   One made to reduce a firm's cash position or borrowing capacity.

Deferred purchase price payments   Involves the placement of some portion of the purchase price in escrow until certain contractual conditions have been realized.

Definitive agreement of purchase and sale   The legal document indicating all of the rights and obligations of the parties both before and after closing.

Destroyers of value   Factors that can reduce the future cash flow of the combined companies.

Developed country   Those having significant and sustainable per capita economic growth, globally integrated capital markets, a well-defined legal system, transparent financial statements, currency convertibility, and a stable government.

Differentiation   A strategy in which the product or service offered is perceived to be slightly different by customers from other product or service offerings in the marketplace.

Discounted cash flow   The conversion of future to current cash flows by applying an appropriate discount rate.

Discount rate   The opportunity cost associated with investment in the firm used to convert the projected cash flows to present values.

Discretionary assets   Undervalued or redundant assets not required to run the acquired business.

Dissident shareholders   Those that disagree with a firm's incumbent management and attempt to change policies by initiating proxy contests to gain representation on the board of directors.

Diversifiable risk   Risk that is specific to an individual firm such as strikes and lawsuits.

Diversification   A strategy of buying firms outside of the company's primary line of business.

Divestiture   The sale of all or substantially all of a company or product line to another party for cash or securities.

Divisional organization   An organizational structure in which groups of products are combined into independent divisions or "strategic business units."

Dogs   Businesses with low growth and market share.

Drag-along   A contract provision common to joint venture or partnership agreements specifically requiring a party not otherwise interested in selling its ownership interest to a third party to do so.

Dual-class recapitalization   A takeover defense in which a firm issues multiple classes of stock in which one class has voting rights that are 10 to 100 times those of another class. Such stock is also called supervoting stock.

Due diligence   The process by which the acquirer seeks to determine the accuracy of the target's financial statements, evaluate the firm's operations, validate valuation assumptions, determine fatal flaws, and identify sources and destroyers of value.

Earnouts   Payments to the seller based on the acquired business achieving certain profit or revenue targets.

Economic value   Present value of a firm's projected cash flows.

Economies of scale   The spreading of fixed costs over increasing production levels.

Economies of scope   The use of a specific set of skills or an asset currently used to produce a specific product to produce related products.

Effective control   Control achieved when one firm has purchased another firm's voting stock, it is not likely to be temporary, there are no legal restrictions on control such as from a bankruptcy court, and there are no powerful minority shareholders.

Emerging country   A country whose sustainable growth rate in per capita gross domestic product is below that realized by developed countries. Such countries generally lack many of the characteristics of developed countries.

Employee stock ownership plan (ESOP)   A trust fund or plan that invests in the securities of the firm sponsoring the plan on behalf of the firm's employees. Such plans are generally employee-defined contribution retirement plans.

Enterprise cash flow   Cash available to shareholders and lenders after all operating obligations of the firm have been satisfied.

Enterprise value   Viewed from the liability side of the balance sheet, it is the sum of the market or present value of a firm's common equity plus preferred stock and long-term debt. For simplicity, other long-term liabilities are often excluded from the calculation. From the perspective of the asset side of the balance sheet, it is equal to cash plus the market value of current operating and nonoperating assets less current liabilities plus long-term assets.

Equity carve-out   A transaction in which the parent firm issues a portion of its stock or that of a subsidiary to the public.

Equity cash flow   Cash available to common shareholders after all operating obligations of the firm have been satisfied.

Equity premium   The rate of return in excess of the risk-free rate that investors require to invest in equities.

Escape clause   A feature common to poison pills enabling the board of the issuing company to redeem the pill through a nominal payment to the shareholders.

Excess returns   See abnormal returns.

Exchange offer   A tender offer involving a share-for-share exchange.

Exit strategy   A strategy enabling investors to realize their required returns by undertaking an initial public offering or selling to a strategic buyer.

Expense investments   Expenditures made that are not capitalized on the balance sheet such as application software development, database construction, research and development, training, and advertising to build brand recognition.

Experience curve   Postulates that as the cumulative historical volume of a firm's output increases cost per unit of output decreases.

Extension   Creditors agree to lengthen the period during which the debtor firm can repay its debt and in some cases to temporarily suspend both interest and principal repayments.

External analysis   The development of an in-depth understanding of the business' customers and their needs, underlying market dynamics or factors determining profitability, and emerging trends that affect customer needs and market dynamics.

Fair market value   The cash or cash-equivalent price that a willing buyer would propose and a willing seller would accept for a business if both parties have access to all relevant information.

Fairness opinion letter   A written and signed third-party assertion certifying the appropriateness of the price of a proposed deal involving a tender offer, merger, asset sale, or leveraged buyout.

Fair price provisions   A takeover defense requiring that all target shareholders of a successful tender offer receive the same price as those tendering their shares.

Fair value   An estimate of the value of an asset when no strong market exists for a business or it is not possible to identify the value of substantially similar firms.

Financial buyer   Acquirers who focus on relating short-to-intermediate financial returns.

Financial ratio analysis   Calculation of performance ratios from data in a company's financial statements.

Financial restructuring   Describes actions by the firm to change its total debt and equity structure.

Financial risk   The buyer's willingness and ability to leverage a transaction as well as the willingness of shareholders to accept near-term earnings per share dilution.

Financial synergy   The reduction in the cost of capital as a result of more stable cash flows, financial economies of scale, or a better matching of investment opportunities with available funds.

First-generation poison pill   Involves issuing preferred stock, which had to be registered with the SEC, in the form of a dividend to shareholders convertible into the common stock but only after the takeover was completed.

Fixed exchange collar agreement   A fixed exchange ratio as long as the acquirer's share price remains within a narrow range, calculated as of the effective date of merger.

Fixed or constant share-exchange ratio   An exchange ratio in which the number of acquirer shares exchanged for each target share is unchanged between the signing of the agreement of purchase and sale and closing.

Fixed payment exchange collar agreement   A guarantee that the target firm's shareholders receive a certain dollar value in terms of acquirer stock as long as the acquirer's stock remains within a narrow range.

Flip-in poison pill   A shareholders' rights plan in which the shareholders of the target firm can acquire stock in the target firm at a substantial discount.

Flip-over poison pill   A shareholders' rights plan in which target firm shareholders may convert such rights to acquire stock of the surviving company at a substantial discount.

Float   The amount of stock that can be most easily purchased by the acquirer.

Focus strategy   A strategy in which firms tend to concentrate their efforts by selling a few products or services to a single market and compete primarily on the basis of understanding their customers' needs better than the competition.

For cause provisions   Specify the conditions for removing a member of the board of directors.

Form of acquisition   Reflects what is being acquired (i.e., stock or assets).

Form of payment   May consist of cash, common stock, debt, or some combination. Some portion of the payment may be deferred or dependent on the future performance of the acquired entity.

Forward triangular merger   The acquisition subsidiary being merged with the target and the acquiring subsidiary surviving.

Franchise   A privilege given to a dealer by a manufacturer or franchise service organization to sell the franchises product as service in a given area.

Fraudulent conveyance   Laws governing the rights of shareholders if the new company created following an acquisition or LBO is inadequately capitalized to remain viable. In bankruptcy, the lender could be stripped of its secured position in the assets of the company or its claims on the assets could be made subordinate to those of the unsecured creditors.

Free cash flow   The difference between cash inflows and cash outflows, which may be positive, negative, or zero.

Freeze-in   A situation in which the remaining shareholders are dependent on the decisions made by the majority shareholders, if the acquirer does not decide to acquire 100% of the target's stock. Also referred to as a freeze-out or squeeze-out.

Friendly takeover   The target's board and management are receptive to the idea and recommend shareholder approval.

Functional organization   Employees are assigned to specific groups or departments such as accounting, engineering, marketing, sales, distribution, customer service, manufacturing, or maintenance.

Functional strategies   Describe in detail how each major function (e.g., manufacturing, marketing, and human resources) within the firm will support the business strategy.

Generally Accepted Accounting Principles (GAAP)   Accounting guidelines established by the Financial Accounting Standards Board (FASB).

General partner   Individual responsible for the daily operations of limited partnerships.

Global capital asset pricing model   A version of the capital asset pricing model in which a global equity index is used in calculating the equity risk premium.

Globally integrated capital markets   Capital markets providing foreigners with unfettered access to local capital markets and local residents to foreign capital markets.

Going concern value   The value of a company defined as the firm's value in excess of the sum of the value of its parts.

Going private   The purchase of the publicly traded shares of a firm by a group of investors.

Golden parachutes   Employee severance arrangements, which are triggered whenever a change in control takes place.

Goodwill   The excess of the purchase price over the target firm's net asset value.

Go-Shop provision   A provision allowing a seller to continue to solicit other bidders for a specific time period after an agreement has been signed but before closing. However, if the seller accepts another bid, it must pay a break-up fee to the bidder with whom they had a signed agreement.

Greenmail   The practice of a firm buying back its shares at a premium from an investor threatening a takeover.

Growth strategy   A business strategy which concentrtes on growing a firm's revenue, profit, and cash flow.

Hedge fund   Private investment limited partnerships (for U.S. investors) or an offshore investment corporation (for non-U.S. or tax exempt investors) in which the general partner has made a substantial personal investment. Hedge fund bylaws generally allow the fund to engage in a wide variety of investing activities.

Herfindahl–Hirschman Index   A measure of industry concentration used by the Federal Trade Commission as one criterion in determining when to approve mergers and acquisitions.

Highly leveraged transactions   Those involving a substantial amount of debt relative to the amount of equity invested.

High-yield debt   See junk bond financing.

Holding company   A legal entity often having a controlling interest in one or more companies.

Hold-out problem   Tendency for smaller creditors during reorganization to hold up the agreement among creditors unless they receive special treatment.

Home country   The acquirer's country of residence.

Horizontal merger   A combination of two firms within the same industry.

Hostile takeover Occurs when the initial bid was unsolicited, the target was not seeking a merger at the time of the approach, the approach was contested by the target's management, and control changed hands.

Hostile tender offer A tender offer that is unwanted by the target's board.

Hubris An explanation for takeovers that attributes a tendency to overpay to excessive optimism about the value of a deal's potential synergy or excessive confidence in management's ability to manage the acquisition.

Impaired asset Defined by FASB as a long-term asset whose fair value falls below its book or carrying value.

Implementation strategy The way in which the firm chooses to execute the business strategy.

Income statement assumptions Relate to projected growth in revenue, the implied market share, and the major components of cost.

Incentive systems Bonus, profit-sharing, or other performance-based payments made to motivate both acquirer and target company employees to work to implement the business strategy for the combined firms.

Indemnification A common contractual clause requiring the seller to indemnify or absolve the buyer of liability in the event of misrepresentations or breaches of warranties or covenants. Similarly, the buyer usually agrees to indemnify the seller.

Indenture A contract between the firm that issues the long-term debt securities and the lenders.

Industry A collection of markets.

Initial offer price A price that lies between the estimated minimum and maximum offer prices for a target firm.

Initial public offering (IPO) The first offering to the public of common stock of a formerly privately held firm.

In play A firm is believed by investors to be vulnerable to or willing to undergo a takeover due to a bid or rumors of a bid.

Insider trading Involves individuals buying or selling securities based on knowledge not available to the general public.

Interest rate parity theory A theory that relates forward or future spot exchange rates to differences in interest rates between two countries adjusted by the spot rate.

Internal analysis The determination of the firm's strengths and weaknesses as compared to its competitors.

Investment bankers Advisors who offer strategic and tactical advice and acquisition opportunities; screen potential buyers and sellers; make initial contact with a seller or buyer; and provide negotiation support, valuation, and deal-structuring advice.

Involuntary bankruptcy A situation in which creditors force a debtor firm into bankruptcy.

Joint venture   A cooperative business relationship formed by 2 or more separate entities to achieve common strategic objectives.

Junk bond financing   Subordinated debt, either unrated or noninvestment grade. Also called high-yield debt.

Legal form of the selling entity   Refers to whether the seller is a C or Subchapter S Corporation, a limited liability company, or a partnership. These considerations can influence both the tax structure of the deal and form of payment.

Legal insolvency   Occurs when a firm's liabilities exceed the fair market value of its assets.

Lehman formula   Investment banking fee structure in which fees equal 5% of the 1st million, 4% of the 2nd, 3% of the 3rd, 2% of the 4th, and 1% of the remainder.

Letter of intent   A preliminary agreement between two companies intending to merge that stipulates major areas of agreement between the parties, as well as their rights and limitations.

Leveraged buyout   Transactions involving the purchase of a company financed primarily by debt.

Leveraged loans   Second mortgages, payment-in-kind notes, and senior unsecured debt, which typically give lenders a lower level of security.

Leveraged recapitalization   A situation in which a firm assumes substantial amounts of new debt, often used to either buy back stock, finance a dividend to shareholders, or to make itself less attractive to a potential bidder.

License   Granting to others rights to use specific proprietary assets.

Limited partnerships   Partners contributing money to a partnership who are not involved in management decisions and whose liability is limited to the extent of their investment.

Liquidation   The value of a firm's assets sold separately less its liabilities and expenses incurred in breaking up the firm.

Liquidating dividend   A final dividend paid by a firm to its shareholders after paying off outstanding creditor obligations.

Liquidity discount   The discount or reduction in the offer price for the target firm made by discounting the value of the target firm estimated by examining the market values of comparable publicly traded firms to reflect the potential loss in value when sold due to the illiquidity of the market for similar types of investments. The liquidity discount also is referred to as a marketability discount.

Liquidity risk   See marketability risk.

Loan agreement   Stipulates the terms and conditions under which the lender will loan the firm funds.

Local country   The target firm's country of residence.

Long form merger   Mergers requiring shareholder approval.

Management buyout   A leveraged buyout in which managers of the firm to be taken private are also equity investors in the transaction.

Management entrenchment theory   A theory that managers use a variety of takeover defenses to ensure their longevity with the firm.

Management integration team   Consists of senior managers from the two merged organizations and is charged with delivering on sales and operating synergies identified during the preclosing due diligence.

Management preferences   The boundaries or limits that senior managers of the acquiring firm place on the acquisition process.

Managerialism theory   A theory espousing that managers acquire companies to increase the acquirer's size and their own remuneration.

Markets   Collections of customers, whether individual consumers or other firms, exhibiting common characteristics and needs.

Market assumptions   Relate to growth rate of unit volume and product price per unit.

Marketability discount   The discount or reduction in the offer price for the target firm made by discounting the value of the target firm estimated by examining the market values of comparable publicly traded firms to reflect the potential loss of value when sold due to the illiquidity of the market for similar assets. The marketability discount also is referred to as a liquidity discount.

Marketability risk   The risk associated with an illiquid market for the specific stock. Also called liquidity risk.

Market-based valuation methods   Techniques that assume a firm's market value can be approximated by an indicator of value for comparable companies, comparable transactions, or comparable industry averages. Also referred to as relative valuation methods.

Market power hypothesis   A theory that firms merge to gain greater control over pricing.

Market segmentation   A process involving identifying customers with common characteristics and needs.

Maximum offer price   The sum of the minimum price plus the present value of net synergy.

Merger   A combination of two or more firms in which all but one legally cease to exist.

Merger/acquisition plan   A specific type of implementation strategy that describes in detail the motivation for the acquisition and how and when it will be achieved.

Merger arbitrage   An investment strategy that attempts to profit from the spread between a target firm's current share price and a pending takeover bid.

Merger of equals   A merger framework usually applied whenever the merger participants are comparable in size, competitive position, profitability, and market capitalization.

Mezzanine financing   Capital that in liquidation has a repayment priority between senior debt and common stock.

Minimum offer price   The target's standalone or present value or its current market value.

Minority discount   The amount by which investors seeking to acquire a less than controlling interest should reduce the purchase price of a firm.

Minority investment   A less than controlling interest in another firm.

Monitoring systems   Implemented to track the actual performance of the combined firms against the business plan.

Negative covenants   Restrictions found in loan agreements on the actions of the borrower.

Net asset value   The difference between the fair market value of total identifiable acquired assets and the value of acquired liabilities.

Net debt   Includes the market value of debt assumed by the acquirer less cash and marketable securities on the books of the target firm.

Net operating loss carry forward/carry backs   Provisions in the tax laws allowing firms to use accumulated net tax losses to offset income earned over a specified number of future years or to recover taxes paid during a limited number of prior years.

Net purchase price   The total purchase price plus other assumed liabilities less the proceeds from the sale of discretionary or redundant target assets.

Net synergy   The difference between estimated sources of value and destroyers of value.

Nondiversifiable risk   Risk that is generated by factors that affect all firms such as inflation and war.

Nonrecourse financing   Loans granted to a venture without partner guarantees.

Normal financial returns   The rate of return that would have been expected by assessing normal risk and return factors in the absence of the occurrence of any specific events such as an M&A.

No-shop agreement   Prohibits the takeover target from seeking other bids or making public information that is not currently readily available while in discussions with a potential acquirer.

One-tier offer   A bidder announces the same offer to all target shareholders.

Open market share repurchase   The act of a corporation buying its shares in the open market at the prevailing price as any other investor, as opposed to a tender offer for shares or a repurchase resulting from negotiation such as with an unwanted investor.

Operating risk   Relates to the ability of the buyer to manage the acquired company.

Operating synergy   Consists of both economies of scale and scope.

Operational restructuring   Refers to the outright or partial sale of companies or product lines or to downsizing by closing unprofitable or nonstrategic facilities.

Opportunity cost   A foregone opportunity.

Option   The exclusive right, but not the obligation, to buy, sell, or utilize property for a specific period of time in exchange for an agreed upon sum of money.

Order for relief   A court order initiating bankruptcy proceedings if it is determined that a firm is insolvent.

Overpayment risk   The dilution of EPS or a reduction in the earnings growth rate resulting from paying significantly more than the economic value of the acquired company.

Pac-Man defense   A rarely used defense in which the target makes a hostile tender offer for the bidder.

Payment-in-kind (PIK) securities   Equity or debt that pays dividends or interest in the form of additional equity or debt.

Permanent financing   Financing usually consisting of long-term unsecured debt.

Poison pills   A new class of securities issued as a dividend by a company to its shareholders, giving shareholders rights to acquire more shares at a discount. These securities have no value unless an investor acquires a specific percentage of the target firm's voting stock.

Poison puts   A takeover defense in which the target issues bonds containing put options exercisable into cash or more debt if and only if an unfriendly takeover occurs.

Pooling of interests   A form of accounting for financial reporting purposes in which two formerly independent shareholder groups are combined as a single group. As of December 2001, all business combinations must be reported using the purchase method of accounting.

Portfolio balance theory   Reflects the movement of a firm's products through their life cycle.

Portfolio companies   Companies in which the hedge or private equity fund has made investments.

Postclosing organization   The organizational and legal framework used to manage the combined businesses following the completion of the transaction.

Prepackaged bankruptcies   A situation in which the failing firm starts negotiating with its creditors well in advance of filing for a Chapter 11 bankruptcy in order to reach agreement on major issues before formally filing for bankruptcy.

Private corporation   A firm whose securities are not registered with state or federal authorities.

Private placements   The sale of securities to institutional investors, such as pension funds and insurance companies, for investment rather than for resale. Such securities do not have to be registered with the SEC.

Private solicitation   A firm hires an investment banker or undertakes on its own to identify potential buyers to be contacted as potential buyers for the entire firm or a portion of the firm.

Product intangible   Values placed on the accumulated intellectual capital resulting from the production and product design experience of the combined acquiring and target firms.

Product life cycle   Characterizes a products evolution in 4 stages: embryonic, growth, maturity, and decline.

Product or service organization   Organizations in which functional specialists are grouped by product line or service offering.

Pro forma financial statements   A form of accounting that presents financial statements in a way that purports to more accurately describe a firm's current or projected performance.

Promissory note   A legal document committing the borrower to repay a loan, even if the assets when liquidated do not fully cover the unpaid balance.

Proxy contest   An attempt by dissident shareholders to obtain representation on the board of directors or to change a firm's bylaws. Also called proxy battle.

Proxy statement   Information required by the SEC to be sent to shareholders before they authorize a proxy to vote their shares.

Public solicitation   A firm announces publicly that it is putting itself, a subsidiary, or a product line up for sale.

Purchase accounting   A form of accounting for financial reporting purposes in which the acquired assets and assumed liabilities are revalued to their fair market value on the date of acquisition and recorded on the books of the acquiring company.

Purchase premium   The excess of the offer price over the target's current share price, which reflects both the value of expected synergies and the amount necessary to obtain control.

Purchasing power parity theory   A theory stating that one currency will appreciate (depreciate) with respect to another currency according to the expected relative rates of inflation between the two countries.

Pure play   A firm whose products or services focus on a single industry or market.

Q-ratio   The ratio of the market value of a firm to the cost of replacing its assets.

Real options   Refer to management's ability to adopt and later revise corporate investment decisions.

Reincorporation   The act of firm changing its state of incorporation to one in which the laws are more favorable for implementing takeover defenses.

Retention bonuses   Incentives granted to key employees of the target firm, if they remain with the combined companies for a specific period following completion of the transaction.

Revenue ruling   An official interpretation by the IRS of the Internal Revenue Code, related statutes, tax treaties, and regulations.

Reverse LBOs   Public companies that are taken private and later are taken public again. The second effort to take the firm public is called a secondary public offering.

Reverse merger   A merger in which the acquirer forms a new shell subsidiary, which is merged into the target in a statutory merger.

Reverse triangular merger   The merger of the target with a subsidiary of the acquiring firm, with the target surviving.

Revolving credit line   A credit line allowing borrowers to borrow on a daily basis to run their business. Under a revolving credit arrangement, the bank agrees to make loans up to a specified maximum for a specified period, usually a year or more.

Right of first refusal A contract clause requiring that a party wishing to leave a joint venture or partnership to first offer their interests to other participants in the JV or partnership.

Risk The degree of uncertainty associated with the outcome of an investment.

Risk-free rate of return The return on a security with an exceedingly low probability of default, such as U.S. Treasury securities, and minimal reinvestment risk.

Risk premium The additional rate of return in excess of the risk-free rate that investors require to purchase a firm's equity. Also called the equity premium.

Road show To arrange both bridge and permanent financing, the buyer often develops elaborate presentations to convince potential lenders and investors of their attractiveness as a borrower or as an investment.

Second generation poison pill Also known as a flip-over pill, it includes a rights plan which can be exercised if 100% of the firm's stock has been acquired.

Secondary public offerings A stock offering by a private company that had previously been a public company.

Secured debt Debt backed by the borrower's assets.

Security agreement A legal document stipulating which of the borrower's assets will be pledged to secure the loan.

Segmented capital markets Capital markets exhibiting different bond and equity prices in different geographic areas for identical assets in terms of risk and maturity.

Self-tender offer A tender offer used when a firm seeks to repurchase its stock from its shareholders.

Share control provisions State statutes requiring that a bidder obtain prior approval from stockholders holding large blocks of target stock once the bidder's purchases of stock exceed some threshold level.

Share-exchange ratio The number of shares of the acquirer's stock to be exchanged for each share of the target's stock.

Shareholder interest's theory The presumption that management resistance to proposed takeovers is a good bargaining strategy to increase the purchase price for the benefit of the target firm shareholders.

Share repurchase plans Stock purchases undertaken by a firm to reduce the number of shares that could be purchased by the potential acquirer or by those such as arbitrageurs who will sell to the highest bidder. Also called a stock buyback.

Shark repellants Specific types of takeover defenses that can be adopted by amending either a corporate charter or its bylaws.

Shell corporation One that is incorporated but has no significant assets or operations.

Short form merger A merger not requiring the approval of the parent's shareholders if the parent's ownership in the acquiring subsidiary exceeds the minimum threshold set by the state in which the firm is incorporated.

Sources of value Factors increasing the cash flow of the combined companies.

Spin-off   A transaction in which a parent creates a new legal subsidiary and distributes shares it owns in the subsidiary to its current shareholders as a stock dividend.

Split-off   A variation of a spin-off in which some parent company shareholders receive shares in a subsidiary in return for relinquishing their parent company shares.

Split-up   A transaction creating a new class of stock for each of the parent's operating subsidiaries, paying current shareholders a dividend of each new class of stock, and then dissolving the remaining corporate shell.

Staggered board election   A takeover defense involving the division of the firm's directors into a number of different classes, with no two classes up for reelection at the same time. Also called a classified board.

Stakeholders   Groups having interests in a firm such as customers, shareholders, employees, suppliers, regulators, and communities.

Standalone business   One whose financial statements reflect all the costs of running the business and all of the revenues generated by the business.

Standstill agreement   A contractual arrangement in which the acquirer agrees not to make any further investments in the target's stock for a stipulated period.

Stars   A firm's products which show high growth relative to the industry.

State blue sky laws   Statutes intended to protect individuals from investing in fraudulent security offerings by requiring significant disclosure of information.

Statutory consolidation   Involves two or more firms joining to form a new company.

Statutory merger   The combination of the acquiring and target firms, in which one firm ceases to exist, in accordance with the statutes of the state in which the combined businesses will be incorporated.

Stock-for-stock statutory merger   A merger in which the seller receives acquirer shares in exchange for their shares (with the seller shares subsequently canceled). Also called a stock swap merger.

Stock lockup   An option granted to the bidder to buy the target firm's stock at the first bidder's initial offer that is triggered whenever a competing bid (usually higher) is accepted by the target firm.

Stock purchases   The exchange of the target's stock for either cash, debt, or the stock of the acquiring company.

Strategic alliance   An informal cooperative arrangement such as an agreement to co-develop a technology, product, or process.

Strategic buyer   An acquirer primarily interested in increasing shareholder value by realizing long-term synergies.

Strategic realignment   A theory suggesting that firms use takeovers as a means of rapidly adjusting to changes in their external environment such as deregulation and technological innovation.

Subsidiary carve-out   A transaction in which the parent creates a wholly owned independent legal subsidiary, with stock and a management team that is different from the parent's, and issues a portion of the subsidiary's stock to the public.

Subsidiary merger   A transaction in which the target becomes a subsidiary of the parent.

Success factors   Those strengths or competencies necessary to compete successfully in the firm's chosen market.

Supermajority rules   A takeover defense requiring a higher level of approval for amending the charter or for certain types of transactions such as a merger or acquisition.

Supervoting Stock   A class of voting stock having voting rights many times those of other classes of stock.

SWOT analysis   The external and internal analyses undertaken to determine a business' strengths, weaknesses, opportunities, and threats.

Syndicate   An arrangement in which a group of investment banks agrees to purchase a new issue of securities from the acquiring company for sale to the investing public.

Synergy   The notion that the value of the combined enterprises will exceed the sum of their individual values.

Synergy assumptions   Relate to the amount and timing of expected synergy.

Tag-along   A provision in a partnership agreement that enables a partner to sell to a third party that had only been interested in buying another partner's ownership interest.

Takeover defenses   Protective devices put in place by a firm to frustrate, slow down, or raise the cost of a takeover.

Takeovers   Generic terms referring to a change in the controlling ownership interest of a corporation.

Target company   The firm that is being solicited by the acquiring company.

Taxable transaction   Transactions in which the form of payment is primarily something other than acquiring company stock.

Tax considerations   Structures and strategies determining whether a transaction is taxable or non-taxable to the seller's shareholders.

Tax-free reorganization   Nontaxable transactions usually involving mergers, with the form of payment primarily acquirer's stock exchanged for the target's stock or assets.

Tax-free transactions   Transactions in which the form of payment is primarily acquiring company stock. Also called tax-free reorganizations.

Tax shield   The reduction in the firm's tax liability due to the tax deductibility of interest.

Technically insolvent   A situation in which a firm is unable to pay its liabilities as they come due.

Tender offer   The offer to buy shares in another firm, usually for cash, securities, or both.

Tender offer statement   Schedule on which an acquirer must disclose its intentions and business plans with respect to the target.

Terminal value   The discounted value of the cash flows generated during the stable growth period. Also called the sustainable, horizon, or continuing growth value.

Term loan   A loan usually having a maturity of 2 to 10 years and is usually secured by the asset that is being financed, such as new capital equipment.

Term sheet   A document outlining the primary areas of agreement between the buyer and the seller, which is often used as the basis for a more detailed letter of intent.

Third generation poison pill   Also known as a flip-in pill, the rights can be exercised with a less than 100% change in ownerships.

Toehold strategy   A variation of the two-tier tender offer in which the buyer purchases a minority position in the target firm in the open market and subsequently initiates a tender offer to gain a controlling interest. After control has been achieved, the buyer offers a lower purchase price for any remaining shares.

Total capitalization   The sum of a firm's debt and all forms of equity.

Total consideration   A commonly used term in legal documents to reflect the different types of remuneration received by target company shareholders.

Total purchase price   Consists of the total consideration plus the market value of the target firm's debt assumed by the acquiring company. Also referred to as enterprise value.

Tracking stocks   Separate classes of common stock of the parent corporation whose dividend payouts depend on the financial performance of a specific subsidiary. Also called target or letter stocks.

Transfer taxes   State taxes paid whenever titles to assets are transferred as in an asset purchase.

Trigger points   Events initiating a change in strategy.

Two-tiered offer   A tender offer in which target shareholders receive an offer for a specific number of shares. Immediately following this offer, the bidder announces its intentions to purchase the remaining shares at a lower price or using something other than cash.

Type A reorganization   A tax-free merger or consolidation in which target shareholders receive cash, voting/non-voting common or preferred stock, or debt for their shares at least 40% of purchase price must be in acquirer stock.

Type B stock for stock reorganization   A tax-free transaction in which the acquirer uses its voting common stock to purchase at least 80% of the voting power of the target's outstanding voting stock and at least 80% of each class of non-voting shares. Used as an alternative to a merger.

Type C stock for assets reorganization   A tax-free transaction in which acquirer voting stock is used to purchase at least 80% of the fair market value of the target's net assets.

Underwriter spread   The difference between the price the underwriter receives for selling a firm's securities to the public and the amount it pays to the firm.

Valuation   Assumptions relate to acquirer's target debt-to-equity ratio, discount rates, and growth assumptions.

Valuation cash flows   Restated GAAP cash flows used for valuing a firm or a firm's assets.

Variable-growth valuation model   A valuation method which assumes that a firm's cash flows will experience periods of high growth followed by a period of slower, more sustainable growth.

Vertical merger   One in which companies that do not own operations in each major segment of the value chain choose to backward integrate by acquiring a supplier or to forward integrate by acquiring a distributor.

Voluntary bankruptcy   A situation in which the debtor firm files for bankruptcy.

Voluntary liquidation   Management concludes that the sale of the firm in parts could realize greater value than the value created by a continuation of the combined corporation.

Weighted average cost of capital   A broader measure than the cost of equity that represents the return that a firm must earn to induce investors to buy its stock and bonds.

White knight   A potential acquirer that is viewed more favorably by a target firm's management and board than the initial bidder.

Winner's curse   The tendency of the auction winners to show remorse believing that they may have paid too much.

Workouts   Plans to restructure the debtor firm developed cooperatively with creditors.

Zero-growth valuation model   A valuation model that assumes that free cash flow is constant in perpetuity.

Index

Page numbers followed by "f" denote figures; those followed by "t" denote tables

725